Keep on the Sunny Side.

At Days Inns our promise is as sure as the sun.

A sunny, warm welcome. A fresh Daybreak® Breakfast.*

More rewards more often with TripRewards®,

the world's largest hotel rewards program.** At Days Inns,

it's not just about the change we put in your pocket.

It's about the change we make in your journey.

**AAA Members: Save up to 10%†
at more than 50 AAA approved
Days Inn® hotels in AZ & NM.**

For specific locations and reservations, call
1-800-432-9755 or
daysinn.com

The Best Value Under The Sun™

Find Hotels As Easy As 1-2-3-4-5!

For reliable hotel stays matched to your needs, every time, use AAA's valuable two-part rating system:

- First, rest assured that *every* hotel designated **AAA Approved** upholds qualities important to members – cleanliness, service, and value.

- Focus your selection using the descriptive one-to-five **AAA Diamond Ratings** assigned exclusively to Approved properties to help you match your expectations.

Find AAA Approved and Diamond rated properties in the TourBook®, in print and on aaa.com. Look for the AAA logo on signage and billboards.

Read about **AAA Lodging Diamond Rating** requirements on page 20-21

Show Your Card
Approved Lodging

Arizona &
New Mexico

Published by AAA Publishing
1000 AAA Drive
Heathrow, FL 32746-5063
Copyright AAA 2005

Hospital information
© 2005 HealthForum, LLC

The publisher is not responsible for changes that occur after publication. TourBook® guides are published for the exclusive use of AAA members. Not for sale.

Advertising Rate and Circulation Information: (407) 444-8280

Printed in the USA by Quebecor World, Buffalo, NY

Photo Credit: (Cover & Title Page) Organ Pipe Cactus National Monument, AZ / © David Muench Corbis

 Printed on recyclable paper.
Please recycle whenever possible.

 Mixed Sources
Product group from well-managed forests and other controlled sources
www.fsc.org Cert no. SW-COC-1610
© 1996 Forest Stewardship Council
FSC

Stock #4602

Arizona &
New Mexico

New Mexico

Featured Information

A reflection of how you travel today.

How you take a vacation hasn't changed—your travel money choices have.

Today there are many ways to take your vacation money with you, and the prepaid AAA Visa TravelMoney® card is the most secure, convenient way to carry your funds. Simply preload your card with your travel funds before you leave, and you are ready to use your card for payment at any Visa® debit merchant or withdraw local currency at any Visa® Interlink/PLUS ATM around the world. Vacation with the Visa TravelMoney card—it is safer than cash.

The AAA Visa TravelMoney Card:

- Accepted at millions of Visa® debit merchants and hundreds of thousands of Visa® Interlink/PLUS ATMs worldwide
- More secure because it is not linked to your other cards or accounts
- Reloadable to help you track spending
- Includes Purchase Security, Zero Liability, and Emergency Assistance

AAA Visa TravelMoney card, safer than cash.

*Terms and conditions apply, see detailed terms and conditions provided with your card fulfillment kit. Information correct at time of printing, subject to change.

 Visit Participating AAA offices
Click aaa.com/travelmoney
Call 866-339-3378

Other Travel Money products include:

 Foreign Currency

 Travelers Cheques

For hotel reservations and vacation planning, get right to the point on *aaa.com*. Reserve AAA Approved and Diamond rated hotels at the lowest online prices. Plus, enjoy these additional tools and benefits:

Online TourBook® – Find thousands of AAA Approved and Diamond rated hotels and restaurants, plus thousands of things to see and do.

Internet TripTik® – Get complete trip routings with hotel reservations, sightseeing stops, member discount locations, and more.

AAA Drive Trips* – Enjoy nearly 100 flexible, preplanned driving itineraries for popular destinations.

Vacation Getaways – Get exclusive benefits on flights, tours, cruises, and Disney vacation packages from AAA's Preferred Travel Partners.

AAA Map Gallery* – Print your own AAA maps for top destinations.

Hertz Rental – Save up to 20% on car rental.

Show Your Card & Save® – Search for exclusive member savings at 150,000 locations worldwide.

AAA Travel Money – Get no-fee travelers cheques, foreign currency, and prepaid cards.

Books – Save 5% on AAA travel, childrens, specialty, and automotive publications at aaa.com/barnesandnoble.

AAA Credit Card – Get up to 5% gas rebate.

AAA Approved Auto Repair – Find reliable service locations at home and away.

Plan your next trip on *aaa.com* — the only travel Web site backed by thousands of highly trained travel professionals at more than 1,000 AAA/CAA offices!

aaa.com
Plan to go.

*Products and services available through participating AAA and CAA clubs.

Attractions, lodgings and restaurants are listed on the basis of merit alone after careful evaluation and approval by one of AAA/CAA's full-time, professionally trained Tourism Editors. Evaluations are unannounced to ensure that we see an establishment just as you would see it.

An establishment's decision to advertise in the TourBook guide has no bearing on its evaluation or rating. Advertising for services or products does not imply AAA endorsement.

All information in this guide was reviewed for accuracy before publication. However, since changes inevitably occur between annual editions, we suggest you work with your AAA travel professional or check on aaa.com to confirm prices and schedules.

How the TourBook Guide is Organized

The TourBook guide is organized into three distinct sections.

The **Points of Interest** section helps you plan daily activities and sightseeing excursions and provides details about the city or attraction you are visiting.

The **Lodgings and Restaurants** section helps you select AAA Approved accommodations and dining facilities meeting your specific needs and expectations.

The **Reference** section provides indexes for locating information within this guide and items to aid the trip planning process.

Locating the Attractions, Lodgings and Restaurants

Attractions, lodgings and restaurants are listed under the city in which they physically are located - or in some cases under the nearest recognized city. Most listings are alphabetically organized by state, province, region or island, then by city and establishment name.

A color is assigned to each state or province so that you can match the color bars at the top of the page to switch from the **Points of Interest** section to the **Lodgings and Restaurants** section.

Spotting maps help you physically locate points of interest, lodgings and restaurants in the major destinations.

The Comprehensive City Index located in the **Reference** section contains an A-to-Z list of cities.

Destination Cities and Destination Areas

Destination cities, established based on government models and local expertise, include metropolitan areas plus nearby vicinity cities. **Destination areas** are regions with broad tourist appeal; several cities will comprise the area.

If a city falls within a destination's vicinity, the city name will appear at its alphabetical location in the book, and a cross reference will give you the exact page on which listings for that city begin.

An orientation map appears at the beginning of each destination section to orient you to that destination.

Understanding the Points of Interest Listing

GEM Designation

A ⬦GEM indicates the attraction has been rated a AAA GEM, a "must see" point of interest that offers a *Great Experience for Members®*. These attractions have been judged to be of exceptional interest and quality by AAA Tourism Editors.

A GEM listing page with a brief description of individual GEM attractions follows the Orientation map near the beginning of each state or province Points of Interest section. Cross-references guide the reader to the attraction's listing page.

Discount Savings

The SAVE icon denotes those attractions offering AAA/CAA, AAA MasterCard, AAA VISA or international Show Your Card & Save discount cardholders a discount off the attraction's standard admission. Present your card at the attraction's admission desk.

A list of participating points of interest appears in the Reference section of this guide.

Shopping establishments preceded by a SAVE icon also provide to AAA/CAA members a discount and/or gift with purchase; present your card at the mall's customer service center to receive your benefit.

Exceptions

- Members should inquire in advance concerning the validity of the discount for special rates.
- The SAVE discount may not be used in conjunction with other discounts.
- Attractions that already provide a reduced senior or child rate may not honor the SAVE discount for those age groups.
- All offers are subject to change and may not apply during special events, particular days or seasons or for the entire validity period of the TourBook guide.

Shopping areas: Mast General Store, 630 W. Swain King St., operates out of a 1913 building, stocked Box with a variety of goods ware. A

RED OAK, is off I-95 exit 4A, just n. to Dogwoo restored 1812 house has eight 60-foot columns and Allow 1 hour minimum. Daily 9-5, Apr. 1-Labor D Labor Day-Nov. 30; by appointment rest of year. C 6-12, $5; ages 2-5, $4; family rate (two adults and two chil 5555 or (800) 555-5555.

RED OAK, is off I-95 exit 4A, just n. to Dogwood Dr., then 2 mi. e. to 610 Magno-lia St. The restored 1812 house has eight 60-foot columns and is furnished in period. Costumed guides demonstrate the 1812 lifestyle. Allow 1 hour minimum. Daily 9-5, Apr. 1-Labor Day; Thurs.-Sun. 9-5. Feb.-Mar. 31 and day after Labor Day-Nov. 30; by appointment rest of year. Closed holidays. Admission $8; over 65 and ages 6-12, $5; ages 2-5, $4; family rate (two adults and two children) $12. DS, MC, VI. ($10). Phone (828) 555-5555 or (800) 555-5555.

RECREATIONAL ACTIVITIES
White-water Rafting

- **River Adventures**, 1 mi. s. on SR 50. Write P.O. Box 1012, Gale, NC 35244. Trips daily May-Oct. Phone (828) 555-5555.

BREVARD (F-3) pop. 6,789, elev. 2,229'

The town is a popular summer resort at the en-trance to Pisgah National Forest (*see place listing p. 165*). Brevard is in an area known as the "Land of Waterfalls," sporting more than 250 named wa-terfalls such as Laughing Falls and Courthouse Falls. Brevard Music Center offers concerts nightly last weekend in June to mid-August.

Brevard i
por

RECREATIONAL ACTIVIT
White-water Rafting

- **River Adventures**, 1 mi. s. o Box 1012, Gale, NC 35244. Phone (828) 555-5555.

Directions

Unless otherwise specified, directions are given from the center of town, using the following highway designations:

I=interstate highway **US**=federal highway
SR=state route **CR**=county road
FM=farm to market **FR**=forest road
Mex.=Mexican highway **Hwy.**=Canadian or Caribbean highway

Prices and Dates of Operations

Admission prices are quoted without sales tax. Children under the lowest age specified are admitted free when accompanied by an adult. Days, months and age groups written with a hyphen are inclusive.

Prices pertaining to points of interest in the United States are quoted in U.S. dollars; points of interest in Canada are quoted in Canadian dollars; prices for points of interest in Mexico and the Caribbean are quoted as an approximate U.S. dollar equivalent.

Credit Cards Accepted

AX=American Express **JC**=Japan Credit Bureau
CB=Carte Blanche **MC**=MasterCard
DC=Diners Club **VI**=VISA
DS=Discover

Bulleted Listings

Casino gambling establishments are visited by AAA personnel to ensure safety; casinos within hotels are presented for member information regardless of whether the lodging is AAA Approved.

Recreational activities of a participatory nature (requiring physical exertion or special skills) are not inspected.

Wineries are inspected by AAA Tourism Editors to ensure they meet listing requirements and offer tours.

All are presented in an abbreviated bulleted format for informational purposes.

NE — BURLINGTON, NC   125

Chamber of Commerce: P.O.
on City, NC 28713; phone (828)
....

hen 2 mi. e. to 610 Magnolia St. The
shed in period. Costumed guided tours.
rs.-Sun. 9-5, Feb.-Mar. 31 and day after
lidays. Admission $8, over 65 and ages
2. DS, MC, VI. ($10). Phone (828) 555-

y. 19W. Write
y. 19W, Bryson City, NC 28713. Trips
y-Sept. Phone (828) 488-9366 or (800)

aft, 12 mi. s. on US 19W. Write 1104
W, Bryson City, NC 28713. Trips daily
pt. Phone (828) 488-3316 or (800)
8.

ter Ltd., 12 mi. s.w. on US 19/74W.
P.O. Box 309, Long Creek, SC 29658.
daily Apr.-Oct. Phone (828) 488-2384 or
451-9972. See color ads starting on p. 146.

NGTON (B-5) pop. 44,917, elev. 656'

ngton is a textile industry center with nu-
factory outlet shops that attract bargain
from nearby states. Clothing, leather goods,
blankets, sheets, carpets and furniture are
products.

centerpiece of 76-acre City Park, at South
Street and Overbrook Road, is a 1910 Dent-
nagerie Carousel. Known for their detail and
te carvings, only 14 such carousels still exist
wide. In addition to 26 horses, the hand-
d animals include a lion, tiger, giraffe and re-
r, four pigs, rabbits, ostriches and cats. Phone
sel operates seasonally and hours vary; Phone
222-5030.

ngton/Alamance County Convention and
eau: 610 S. Lexington Ave., P.O.
ngton, NC 27216-0519; phone
637-3804.

ington Manufacturer's
145, houses more

50. Write P.O.
daily May-Oct.

TATE HISTORIC
mi. s.w. on SR
e between Royal-
tia and an inexpe-
mers known as the
xes, corrupt officials
ohn Allen house, a log

Understanding the Lodging Listing

Official Appointment

(AAA) or (CAA) indicates our Official Appointment (OA) lodgings. These properties guarantee members the lowest public rate available at the time of booking for the dates of stay or a minimum 10% discount off the standard room rates published in TourBook guides. We highlight these properties with red and a [SAVE] icon to help you quickly identify them.

Diamond Rating

The number of diamonds informs you of the overall complexity of a lodging's amenities and service. Red indicates an Official Appointment lodging. An [fyi] in place of diamonds indicates the property has not been rated but is included as an "information only" service. A detailed description of each rating level appears on page 20.

Classification

All diamond rated lodgings are classified using three key elements: style of operation, overall concept and service level. See pages 22-23 for details on our classifications.

Online Reservations

This notation indicates AAA/CAA members can conveniently check room availability, validate room rates and make reservations for this property in a secure online environment at aaa.com.

Rates

Shown from left to right: dates the rates are effective; any meal plan included in the rates (see below); standard room rates for 1 person (1P) or 2 persons (2P); extra person charge (XP); and any applicable family plan indicator (see below).

Rates are provided to AAA by each lodging and represent the regular (rack) rate ranges for a standard room. Rates are rounded to the nearest dollar and do not include taxes. U.S., Mexican and Caribbean rates are in U.S. dollars; rates for Canadian lodgings are in Canadian dollars.

Meal Plan Indicators

AP = American Plan of three meals daily
BP = Breakfast Plan of full hot breakfast
CP = Continental Plan of pastry, juice and another beverage
ECP = Expanded Continental Plan, which offers a wider variety of breakfast items
MAP = Modified American Plan of two meals daily

See individual listing "Terms" for additional meal plans not included in the room rate.

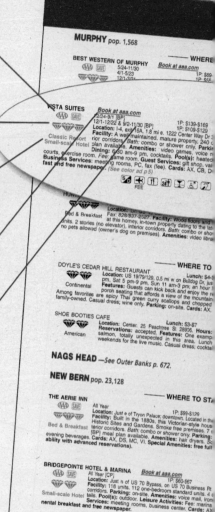

Family Plan Indicators

F = Children stay free
D = Discounts for children
F17 = Children 17 and under stay free
D17 = Discount for children 17 or under

The number displayed will reflect the property's age policy.

Credit Cards Accepted

AX=American Express
CB=Carte Blanche
DC=Diners Club
DS=Discover

JC=Japan Credit Bureau
MC=MasterCard
VI=VISA

Spotting Symbol

Black ovals with white numbers are used to locate, or "spot," lodgings on maps we provide for larger cities.

Service Availability

Unit types, amenities and room features preceded by the word "Some" indicate the item is available on a limited basis, potentially within only one unit.

Special Amenities

Some OA properties offer special amenities such as free continental breakfast; expanded continental breakfast or full breakfast; early check-in and late check-out; free room upgrade or preferred room; free local phone calls; or free daily newspaper. This does not imply that only these properties offer these amenities.

Icons

Lodging icons represent some of the member values, services and facilities offered.

Discounts

ASK May offer discount

SD Offers minimum 10% senior discount to members over 59

Member Services

⊕ Airport transportation

🐑 Pets allowed

🍴 Restaurant on premises

🍴+ Restaurant off premises (walking distance)

24 24-hour room service

Y Cocktail lounge

👶 Child care

Accessibility Features

♿M Accessible features

👂 Hearing-impaired equipment available

♿ Roll-in showers

In-Room Amenities

✗ Designated non-smoking rooms

VCR VCR

🎬 Movies

DATA PORT Data port/modem line

🧊 Refrigerator

📟 Microwave

☕ Coffee maker

AC̸ No air conditioning

TV̸ No TV

CTV̸ No cable TV

☎̸ No telephones

Leisure Activities

🎰 Full-service casino

🏊 Pool

💪 Health club on premises

💪 Health club off premises

✗ Recreational activities

Safety Features (see page 24)
(Mexico and Caribbean only)

S Sprinklers

D Smoke detectors

SOME UNITS printed above the icons indicates the amenity is available on a limited basis, potentially in only one unit. **FEE** appearing below an icon indicates that an extra charge applies.

Understanding the Restaurant Listing

Official Appointment

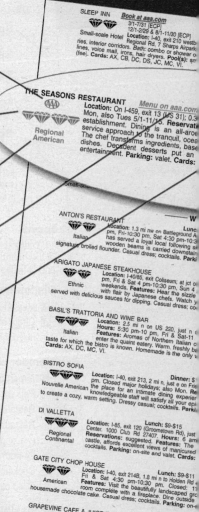

AAA or CAA indicates our Official Appointment (OA) restaurants. The OA program permits properties to display and advertise the AAA or CAA emblem. We highlight these properties in red to help you quickly identify them. The AAA or CAA Approved sign helps traveling members find restaurants that want member business.

Diamond Rating

The number of diamonds informs you of the overall complexity of food, presentation, service and ambience. Red indicates an Official Appointment restaurant. A detailed description of each diamond level appears on page 21.

Cuisine Type

The cuisine type helps you select a dining facility that caters to your individual taste. AAA currently recognizes more than 90 different cuisine types.

Menus

This notation indicates AAA/CAA members can conveniently view the restaurant's menu in a secure online environment at aaa.com.

Credit Cards Accepted

AX=American Express

CB=Carte Blanche

DC=Diners Club

DS=Discover

JC=Japan Credit Bureau

MC=MasterCard

VI=VISA

Prices

Rates shown represent the minimum and maximum entree cost per person. Exceptions may include one-of-a-kind or special market priced items. Rates are rounded to the nearest dollar and do not include taxes. U.S., Mexican and Caribbean rates are in U.S. dollars; rates for Canadian restaurants are in Canadian dollars.

Spotting Symbol

White ovals with black numbers serve as restaurant locators and are used to locate, or "spot," restaurants on maps we provide for larger cities.

Icons

Icons provide additional information about services and facilities.

- No air-conditioning
- Accessible features
- Cocktail lounge
- Designated smoking section available

Classifications

If applicable, a restaurant may be defined as:

Classic - renowned and/or landmark restaurant in business longer than 25 years, known for unique style and ambience.

Historic - properties must meet one of the following criteria:
- Listed on the U.S. National Register of Historic Places
- Designated a U.S. National Historic Landmark
- Located in a U.S. National Register Historic District

Separate criteria designate historic properties in Canada, Mexico and the Caribbean.

GREENSBORO, NC 625

599
579   2P: $64-$104   Phone: (236)931-1272
           2P: $54-$84   XP: $5   F18
d), just n; exit 210 eastbound, just e on Albert Pick Rd, then just n on
336/931-1496. **Facility:** 116 one-bedroom standard units. 7 sto-
-site. **Terms:** cancellation fee imposed. **Amenities:** dual phone
est Services: valet and coin laundry. Business Services: tax

SOME UNITS

Dinner: $16-$36   Phone: 336/555-5555   (5)
R 802. 1000 Ocean Blvd 30244. **Hours:** 6 pm-10 pm. Closed:
sted. **Features:** Guests are in for a treat at this top-notch
able experience—from the wait staff's casually elegant
g to the striking grounds views from the cozy dining area.
s seasonally and regionally available, into mouthwatering
mark on the meal. Dressy casual attire; cocktails;
, DS, MC, VI. **Classic**

DINE

Dinner: $8-$19   Phone: 336/273-1380
ndover Ave. 1628 Battleground Ave 27408. **Hours:** 11 am-10
major holidays; also 12/24 & Sun. **Features:** This eatery
stic Italian theme with black and white table cloths and
dining area. Famous for its lasagna, it also features a
ards: AX, MC, VI.

$18-$30
Patterson St. 1200 S Holden Rd 27407. **Hours:** 5 pm-10
losed: 11/25, 12/24, 12/25. **Reservations:** suggested:
k, chicken, shrimp and 12/25. g cooked right at your table and enjoy huge portions
g; on-site. **Cards:** AX, MC, VI.

9-$30
e; in Irving Park Plaza. 1720 Battleground Ave 27408.
ajor holidays; also Sun. **Reservations:** suggested.
the wood-burning oven and reach diners as they
ed in olive oil is one small example of the delicious
ual dress; cocktails; entertainment. **Parking:** on-site.

ust s. 616 Dolley Madison Rd 27410. **Hours:** 5 pm-10
uggested. **Features:** Elegant but not stuffy, this is a
French cuisine served by extremely helpful and
. The Bistro was a house that has been converted
ards: AX, DC, MC, VI.

r: $19-$30
Grandover Pkwy; in Grandover Resort & Conference
30 pm, Sun 6-11 am, 11:30-2:30 & 6-10 pm.
, which reflects the ambience of a European
the 18th hole of the east course. Casual dress;
DS, MC, VI.

her: $19-$30
06 S Holden Rd 27407. **Hours:** 11:30 am-10 pm,
2/25; also Sun. **Reservations:** suggested.
upscale bistro, which features a private dining
nd end your meal with the creamy, mile-high
, DC, DS, MC, VI.

ner: $4-$10
435B Dolley Madison Rd 27410. **Hours:** 11 am-8
n entrees, fresh fruits and vegetable juices;
dishes. Casual dress; beer only. **Parking:**

Lodging Rates Guaranteed

AAA/CAA members are guaranteed they will not be charged more than the maximum regular rate printed in the TourBook guide in each rate range for a standard room. Rates may vary within the range, depending on season and room type. Listed rates are based on last standard room availability. Obtain current AAA/CAA member rates and make reservations at aaa.com.

Discounts

Member discounts will apply to rates quoted within the rate range and are applicable at the time of booking. Special rates used in advertising, as well as special short-term promotional rates lower than the lowest listed rate in the range, are not subject to additional member discounts.

Exceptions

Rates for properties operating as concessionaires for the U.S. National Park Service are not guaranteed due to governing regulations. Rates in the Mexico TourBook are not guaranteed and may fluctuate based on the exchange rate of the peso.

Lodgings may temporarily increase room rates, not recognize discounts or modify pricing policies during special events. Examples of special events range from Mardi Gras and the Kentucky Derby (including pre-Derby events) to college football games, holidays, holiday periods and state fairs. Although some special events are listed in AAA/CAA TourBook guides and on aaa.com, it is always wise to check in advance with AAA travel professionals for specific dates.

Get the Room You Reserved

When making your reservation, identify yourself as a AAA or CAA member and request written confirmation to guarantee: type of room, rate, dates of stay, and cancellation and refund policies. At registration, show your membership card.

When you find your room is not as specified, and you have written confirmation of reservations for a certain type of accommodation, you should be given the option of choosing a different room or finding one elsewhere. Should you choose to go elsewhere and a refund is refused or resisted, submit the matter to AAA/CAA within 30 days, along with complete documentation, including your reasons for refusing the room and copies of your written confirmation and any receipts or canceled checks associated with this problem.

If you are charged more than the maximum rate listed in the TourBook guide for a standard

room, question the additional charge. If management refuses to adhere to the published rate, pay for the room and submit your receipt and membership number to AAA/CAA within 30 days. Include all pertinent information: dates of stay, rate paid, itemized paid receipts, number of persons in your party and the room number you occupied, and list any extra room equipment used. A refund of the amount paid in excess of the stated maximum will be made if our investigation indicates that unjustified charging occurred.

Deposit, Refund and Cancellation Policies

Most establishments give full deposit refunds if they have been notified at least 48 hours before the normal check-in time. Listing prose will note if more than 48 hours' notice is required for cancellation. Some properties may charge a cancellation or handling fee. When this applies, "cancellation fee imposed" will appear in the listing. If you cancel too late, you have little recourse if a refund is denied.

When an establishment requires full or partial payment in advance and your trip is cut short, a refund may not be given.

When canceling a reservation, phone the lodging immediately. Make a note of the date and time you called, the cancellation number if there is one, and the name of the person who handled the cancellation. If your AAA/CAA club made your reservation, allow them to make the cancellation for you as well, so you will have proof of cancellation.

Check-in and Check-out Times

Check-in and check-out times are shown in the lodging listings, under Terms, only if they are before 10 a.m. or after 3 p.m. respectively.

Members Save With Our Partners

These National Show Your Card & Save® partners provide the listed member benefits. Admission tickets that offer greater discounts may be available for purchase at the local AAA/CAA club. A maximum of six tickets is available at the discount price at the gate. Visit aaa.com to discover all of the great Show Your Card & Save® discounts in your area.

Attraction Partners

SeaWorld/Busch Gardens aaa.com/SeaWorld

- Save $5 at SeaWorld and Busch Gardens
- Save $3 at Sesame Place, Water Country USA and Adventure Island
- Save 10% on select aaa.com/BuschGardens
  up-close dining. Reservations are required; visit Guest Relations for details

Six Flags Theme Parks

- Save $4 on general admission at the gate
- Save $12 on general admission at the gate each Wednesday
- Save 10% on selected souvenirs and dining (check at main gate for details)

Universal Orlando aaa.com/Universal

- Save $4 on a 2-day/2-park pass or $5 on a 3-day/2-park pass at Universal Orlando's theme parks (savings apply to tickets purchased at the gate)
- Save 10% on select dining and souvenirs at both Universal Orlando theme parks and at select Universal CityWalk Orlando restaurants (excludes Emeril's)

Universal Studios Hollywood

- Save $3 on a 1-day aaa.com/Universal
  Universal Studios Hollywood pass (savings applies to tickets purchased at the gate)
- Save 10% on select dining and souvenirs at Universal Studios Hollywood and Universal CityWalk

Gray Line aaa.com/GrayLine

- Save 10% on sightseeing tours of 1 day or less

Restaurant Partners

Landry's Seafood House, The Crab House, Chart House, Muer Seafood Restaurants, Joe's Crab Shack

- Save 10% on food and non-alcoholic beverages at all restaurants
- Save 10% on merchandise at Joe's Crab Shack
- Savings applicable to AAA/CAA members and up to six people

Hard Rock Cafe

- Save 10% on food, beverage and merchandise at all U.S. and select Canadian and international locations
- Savings applicable to AAA/CAA members and up to six people

AAA Dining Network aaa.com/dining

Save an average of 10% or more at over 2,500 restaurants across the United States and Canada simply by showing your AAA membership card

Lodging Partners

SAVINGS. SELECTION. SATISFACTION.—When contacting one of these lodging partners, you will be given AAA's best rates for your dates of stay. Your valid membership card must be presented at check-in. Select the chain you want and have your membership card available when making a reservation and checking in. Let the property know if you are dissatisfied with any part of your stay. If the matter cannot be resolved, you are entitled to recompense (see page 17).

Offer good at time of publication; chains and offers may change without notice. Lodging partners offering discounts to AAA/CAA members may vary in Mexico and the Caribbean.

Visit Over 1,100 AAA Offices **Click** aaa.com **Call** 866-AAA-SAVE

C H O I C E   H O T E L S   I N T E R N A T I O N A L

Understanding the Diamond Ratings

AAA/CAA Tourism Editors have evaluated and rated each of the 55,000 lodging and restaurant establishments in the TourBook series to ensure quality travel information for our members. Listings are provided free of charge to AAA Approved establishments that have met AAA's 27 minimum requirements (for lodgings) concerning cleanliness, comfort and security - or - AAA's 12 minimum requirements (for restaurants) pertaining to cleanliness, food preparation and service.

Eligible applicants receive an unannounced evaluation by a AAA/CAA Tourism Editor that includes two distinct components:

- AAA Approval: The Tourism Editor first must determine whether the property meets the criteria required to be AAA Approved. Every establishment that meets these strict guidelines offers AAA members the assurance that, regardless of the diamond rating, it provides acceptable quality, cleanliness, service and value.
- AAA Diamond Rating: Once an establishment becomes AAA Approved, it is then assigned a rating of one to five diamonds, indicating the extensiveness of its facilities, amenities and services, from basic to moderate to luxury. These diamond ratings guide members in selecting establishments appropriately matched to their needs and expectations.

LODGINGS

1 Diamond

One diamond lodgings typically appeal to the budget-minded traveler. They provide essential, no-frills accommodations and basic comfort and hospitality.

2 Diamond

Two diamond lodgings appeal to family travelers seeking affordable yet more than the basic accommodations. Facilities, decor and amenities are modestly enhanced.

3 Diamond

Three diamond lodgings offer a distinguished style. Properties are

multi-faceted, with marked upgrades in physical attributes, amenities and guest comforts.

4 Diamond

Four diamond lodgings are refined and stylish. Physical attributes are upscale. The fundamental hallmarks at this level include an extensive array of amenities combined with a high degree of hospitality, service and attention to detail.

5 Diamond

Five diamond lodgings provide the ultimate in luxury and sophistication. Physical attributes are extraordinary in every manner. Service is meticulous, exceeding guest expectations and maintaining impeccable standards of excellence. Extensive personalized services and amenities provide first-class comfort.

fyi The lodging listings with **fyi** in place of diamonds are included as an *information only* service for members. The icon indicates that a property has not been rated for one or more of the following reasons: too new to rate, under construction, under major renovation, not evaluated, may not meet all AAA requirements.

A property not meeting all AAA requirements is included for either its member value or because it may be the only accommodation available in the area. Listing prose will give insight as to why the **fyi** designation was assigned.

4 Diamond

Four diamond restaurants provide a distinctive fine-dining experience that is typically expensive. Surroundings are highly refined with upscale enhancements throughout. Highly creative chefs use imaginative presentations to augment fresh, top-quality ingredients. A proficient service staff meets or exceeds guest expectations. A wine steward may offer menu-specific knowledge to guide selection.

5 Diamond

Five diamond restaurants are luxurious and renowned for consistently providing a world-class experience. Highly acclaimed chefs offer artistic menu selections that are imaginative and unique, using only the finest ingredients available. A maitre d' leads an expert service staff in exceeding guest expectations, attending to every detail in an effortless and unobtrusive manner.

RESTAURANTS

1 Diamond

One diamond restaurants provide simple, familiar specialty food (such as burgers, chicken, pizza or tacos) at an economical price. Often self-service, basic surroundings complement a no-nonsense approach.

2 Diamond

Two diamond restaurants offer a familiar, family-oriented experience. Menu selection includes home-style foods and family favorites, often cooked to order, modestly enhanced and reasonably priced. Service is accommodating yet relaxed, a perfect complement to casual surroundings.

fyi The restaurants with [fyi] in place of diamonds are included as an *information only* service for members. These listings provide additional dining choices but have not yet been evaluated.

3 Diamond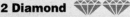

Three diamond restaurants convey an entry into fine dining and are often positioned as adult-oriented experiences. The atypical menu may feature the latest cooking trends and/or traditional cuisine. Expanded beverage offerings complement the menu. The ambiance is well coordinated, comfortable and enhanced by a professional service staff.

Understanding the Lodging Classifications

To ensure that your lodging needs and preferences are met, we recommend that you consider an establishment's classification when making your travel choices. While the quality and comfort at properties with the same diamond rating should be consistent (regardless of the classification), there are differences in typical decor/theme elements, range of facilities and service levels.

Large-scale Hotel

A multistory establishment with interior room entrances. A variety of guest unit styles is offered. Public areas are spacious and include a variety of

Hotel Royal Plaza, Lake Buena Vista, FL

facilities such as a restaurant, fitness center, spa, business center, shops or meeting rooms.

Small-scale Hotel

A multistory establishment typically with interior room entrances. A variety of guest unit styles is offered. Public areas are limited

Baymont Inn, Dallas Ft. Worth-Airport N, TX

in size and/or the variety of facilities available.

Motel

A 1- to 3-story establishment typically with exterior room entrances facilitating convenient access to parking. The

Best Western Deltona Inn, Deltona, FL

standard guest units have one bedroom with a bathroom and are typically similar in decor and design throughout. Public areas are limited in size and/or the variety of facilities available.

Country Inn

Similar in definition to a bed and breakfast but usually larger in scale, with spacious public areas offering a

Greenville Inn, Greenville, ME

dining facility that serves at least breakfast and dinner.

Bed & Breakfast

Small-scale properties emphasizing a high degree of personal touches that provide guests an "at home" feeling. Guest units tend to be individually

1884 Paxton House Inn, Thomasville, GA

decorated. Rooms may not include some modern amenities such as televisions and telephones, and may have a shared bathroom. Usually owner-operated with a common room or parlor separate from the innkeeper's living quarters, where guests and operators can interact during evening and breakfast hours. Evening office closures are normal. A continental or full, hot breakfast is served and is included in the room rate.

Condominium

Vacation-oriented or extended-stay, apartment-style accommodations that are routinely available for rent through a management company. Units vary in design and decor and often contain one or more bedrooms, a living room,

Sands of Kahana, Kahana, Maui, HI

full kitchen and an eating area. Studio-type models combine the sleeping and living areas into one room. Typically, basic cleaning supplies, kitchen utensils and complete bed and bath linens are supplied. The guest registration area may be located off-site.

Cabin/Cottage

Vacation-oriented, small-scale, freestanding houses or cabins. Units vary in design and decor and often contain one

Desert Rose Inn, Bluff, UT

or more bedrooms, a living room, kitchen, dining area and bathroom. Studio-type models combine the sleeping and living areas into one room. Typically, basic cleaning supplies, kitchen utensils, and complete bed and bath linens are supplied. The guest registration area may be located off-site.

Ranch

Typically a working ranch with an obvious rustic, Western theme. In general, equestrian-related activities are featured, but ranches may

C Lazy U Ranch, Granby, CO

include other animals and activities as well. A variety of guest unit styles is offered in a family-oriented atmosphere.

Vacation Home

Vacation-oriented or extended-stay, large-scale, freestanding houses that are routinely available for rent through a management company. Houses

ResortQuest, Hilton Head Island, SC

vary in design and decor and often contain two or more bedrooms, a living room, full kitchen, dining room and multiple bathrooms. Typically, basic cleaning supplies, kitchen utensils, and complete bed and bath linens are supplied. The guest registration area may be located off-site.

Lodging Subclassifications

The following are subclassifications that may appear along with the classifications listed previously to provide a more specific description of the lodging.

Casino

Extensive gaming facilities are available such as blackjack, craps, keno and slot machines. Note: This subclassification will not appear beneath its diamond rating in the listing. It will be indicated by a ⊛ icon and will be included in the row of icons immediately below the lodging listing.

Classic

Renowned and landmark properties, older than 50 years, well-known for their unique style and ambience.

Historic

These properties are typically over 75 years of age and exhibit many features of a historic nature with respect to architecture, design, furnishings, public record or acclaim. Properties must meet one of the following criteria:

- Maintained the integrity of the historical aspect
- Listed on the U.S. National Register of Historic Places
- Designated a U.S. National Historic Landmark
- Located in a U.S. National Register Historic District

Separate criteria designate historic properties in Canada, Mexico and the Caribbean.

Resort

Recreation-oriented, geared to vacation travelers seeking a specific destination experience. Travel packages, meal plans, themed entertainment, and social and recreational programs are typically available. Recreational facilities are extensive and may include spa treatments, golf, tennis, skiing, fishing, water sports, etc. Larger resorts may offer a variety of guest accommodations.

Guest Safety

Room Security

In order to be approved for listing in AAA/CAA TourBook guides for the United States and Canada, accommodations must have dead-bolt locks on all guest room entry doors and connecting room doors.

If the area outside the guest room door is not visible from inside the room through a window or door panel, viewports must be installed on all guest room entry doors. Bed and breakfast properties and country inns are not required to have viewports. Ground floor and easily accessible sliding doors must be equipped with some type of secondary security locks.

Tourism Editors view a percentage of rooms at each property since it is not feasible to evaluate every room in every lodging establishment. Therefore, AAA cannot guarantee that there are working locks on all doors and windows in all guest rooms.

Fire Safety

Because of the highly specialized skills needed to conduct professional fire safety inspections, AAA/CAA Tourism Editors cannot assess fire safety.

Properties must meet all federal, state and local fire codes. Each guest unit in all U.S. and Canadian lodging properties must be equipped with an operational, single-station smoke detector. A AAA/CAA Tourism Editor has evaluated a sampling of the rooms to verify this equipment is in place.

Mexico and the Caribbean

Requirements for some features, such as door locks and smoke detectors/sprinkler systems, differ in Mexico and the Caribbean. If a property met AAA's security requirements at the time of the evaluation, the phrase "Meets AAA guest room security requirements" appears in the listing.

Service Animals

The Americans With Disabilities Act (ADA) prohibits U.S. businesses that serve the public from discriminating against persons with disabilities. Some businesses have mistakenly denied access to persons who use service animals. Businesses must permit entry to guests and their service animals, as well as allow service animals to accompany guests to all public areas of a property.

A property is permitted to ask whether the animal is a service animal or a pet, and whether the guest has a disability. The property may not, however, ask questions about the nature of the disability, the service provided by the animal or require proof of a disability or certification that the animal is a service animal. These regulations may not apply in Canada, Mexico or the Caribbean.

No fees or deposits, even those normally charged for pets, may be charged for service animals. Service animals fulfill a critical need for their owners—they are not pets.

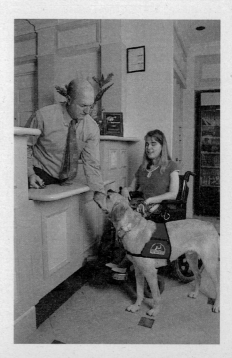

Savings for all Seasons

Hertz rents Fords and other fine cars. ® REG. U.S. PAT. OFF. © HERTZ SYSTEM INC., 1999-2006/99

No matter the season, Hertz offers AAA members exclusive discounts and benefits.

Operating in 150 countries at over 7,400 locations, Hertz makes traveling more convenient and efficient wherever and whenever you go. Hertz offers AAA members discounts up to 20% on car rentals worldwide.

To receive your exclusive AAA member discounts and benefits, mention your AAA membership card at time of reservation and present it at time of rental. **In addition**, to receive a free one car class upgrade on daily, weekly or weekend rental in the United States and Canada, mention PC# 969194, and in Puerto Rico mention PC# 969183 at the time of reservation. Offer available through 12/15/06.

For reservations and program details, call your AAA Travel office or the Hertz/AAA Desk at **1-800-654-3080**.

Arizona

The Grandest of Them All

The Grand Canyon is one of America's premier natural sites

Oases in the Desert

Plush resorts, spas and dude ranches offer Southwestern hospitality

Monuments, Parks and Historic Sites

Arizona's Native American heritage is preserved throughout the state

Reliving the Old West

Shootouts at the O.K. Corral help keep the image of the Old West alive in Tombstone

Images of the Past and Present

Mesas, deserts, cliff dwellings, mountains, pueblos—what was, still is

Organ Pipe Cactus National Monument © Ray Manley SuperStock

the past lives in the present

Bell Rock, Coconino National Forest / © Bob and Suzanne Clemenz

Take a minute. Close your eyes and think about Arizona. What do you see? Chances are the images that first come to mind are those of the Old West—cowboys, Indians, deserts, cacti—stuff straight out of TV Westerns. You half expect Wyatt Earp or Cochise to emerge from behind a wagon train.

Cowboys still do exist here, but they are more likely to be found assisting city slickers at modern guest ranches than lassoing cattle on a trail drive.

Native Americans, the first Arizonans, though a small percentage of today's population, are a major influence in everyday life. Reminders of their heritage are evident in national monuments, tribal parks and historic sites that preserve

their ancient dwellings, customs and crafts.

As for the deserts, well, the sand and the intricate rock formations are still there, but their expanse is now broken by major metropolitan areas such as Phoenix and Tucson and golf courses that seem strangely out of place. And rare species of cactus, such as the organ pipe and saguaro, are protected in their own preserves.

Wagon trains no longer cross Arizona's plains. Adventure now comes courtesy of four-wheel-drive vehicles and weekend hikes in the state's hills and mountains. Mr. Earp and Cochise would be amazed.

"Did the government build it?"

More than one flabbergasted visitor has asked this upon first seeing Arizona's Grand Canyon. Although it may sound preposterous, it's a question you're sure to find less naive after gazing at these myriad erosion-carved columns, arches and windows—a virtual city-scape of landforms that would make a Man-hattanite feel at home.

Thank You, Father Time

No doubt politicians would love to claim responsibility for the Grand Canyon, but only Father Time can take credit for this natural wonder. Over millions of years geologic up-heaval forced a former sea bottom into the sky, allowing wind and water to work their rock-sculpting magic. The result is a spectacle so awesome that at least 5 million people from all over the world visit every year and walk away struggling for words to describe it.

Theodore Roosevelt remarked that it was "the one great sight which every American should see." And while Uncle Sam can't take credit for building the canyon, he does protect it for future generations as part of the national park system.

Like most visitors, you'll probably want to begin your canyon experience at the South Rim, site of the park's visitor center. This area boasts many of the best vantage points from which to gape at the canyon in all its multi-hued glory. What's more, the tall pine trees here hide the great chasm from view until you are almost at its edge. Abruptly confronting this breathtaking scene as you emerge from the forest is an experience you won't want to miss.

Visit during the early morning or late after-noon when colors dance along canyon walls in the rapidly changing sunlight. And if a storm comes your way, don't despair: Shad-ows of drifting rain clouds can create striking patterns of darkness as they move across the canyon's depths.

But even after visiting the Grand Canyon, don't think you've seen it all. An equally spectacular play of color and light awaits you at Monument Valley Navajo Tribal Park. Visi-tors are less likely to suspect the govern-ment's hand in constructing these weathered monoliths, but you just might feel like you're walking through a Hollywood set, and with

---

Franciscan friar Marcos de Niza searches unsuccessfully for the fabled Seven Cities of Cíbola throughout the Southwest.
1539

The Gadsden Purchase brings the rest of the area that is currently Arizona and New Mexico under U.S. control.
1853

Phoenix is chosen as the territorial capital.
1889

Arizona enters the Union as the 48th state.
1912

©Gibson Stock Photography

1848
Following the Mexican War the Treaty of Guadalupe-Hidalgo cedes the Territory of New Mexico, which includes part of Arizona, to the expanding United States.

©Ray Manley/SuperStock

Arizona Historical Timeline

1911
The completion of the Roosevelt Dam on the Salt River delivers much-needed water to the area.

good reason: This valley has served as backdrop for numerous classic Westerns and countless car commercials. Ask someone to imagine "the West" and they'll likely describe the immense, rose-tinted buttes and mesas of this picturesque land.

Grand Canyon visitors frequently overlook another Arizona jewel—the red rock territory around Sedona. Though not as large as the big gorge to the north, Sedona's Oak Creek Canyon has its own collection of buttes, spires and sheer rock walls that shimmer with shades of beige, ocher, salmon and scarlet. And if you get too hot, you can go with Oak Creek's flow at Slide Rock State Park, where a waterslide—natural, not man-made—splashes from pool to pool.

And it's not just Arizona's rocky terrain that evokes comparisons to unnatural objects; the Canyon State's plant life does so as well. Cactuses at Organ Pipe Cactus National Monument appear as if they could produce music, and the saguaros dotting Saguaro National Park resemble a crowd of captured bank robbers, arms raised in a perpetual gesture of surrender.

"Married to the Ground"

Arizona's inhabitants also have blurred the line between natural and artificial. Ancient cliff dwellings at Montezuma Castle, Canyon de Chelly and Navajo national monuments blend with their surroundings so well, they seem to have sprouted from the precipices they are perched upon.

Centuries after these towns in the sky were abandoned, architect Frank Lloyd Wright designed buildings according to his belief that they should harmoniously coexist with their surroundings. Taliesin West, Wright's former home and studio in Scottsdale, illustrates how a modern house can be integrated into its environment, not unlike Arizona's venerable cliff dwellings.

Wright once summed up his design philosophy by saying his buildings were "married to the ground." It's easy to see why he chose Arizona as his studio's setting. Here the terrain seems a willing companion to man's handiwork: mesas rise from the desert like skyscrapers and pinnacles soar like church spires. Although these "buildings" took billions of years to construct, you'll have to admit they were worth waiting for.

In Miranda vs. Arizona, the U.S. Supreme Court decides that police must inform arrested persons of their rights, including the right to remain silent, before they are questioned.

1966

Arizonan Sandra Day O'Connor is appointed as the first woman member of the U.S. Supreme Court.

1981

U.S. Supreme Court

The 4-year-old Arizona Diamondbacks defeat the New York Yankees in the World Series.

2001

©Gibson Stock Photography

1974

Work begins on the Central Arizona Project to bring Colorado River water to dry parts of the state.

Biosphere 2

1991

Eight scientists begin living in the glass-enclosed biomes of Biosphere 2 near Oracle to provide information about the sustainability of Earth's ecosystems.

Recreation

Canyons. Mountains. Forests. Lakes. The extensive Colorado River. Arizona, derived from the Native American word meaning "little spring," is a veritable fountain of fun for outdoor types.

Hopefully you packed your putter. With more than 225 **golf** courses to choose from, people drive from all over the country to chip and putt. But watch out for hazards—Mesa, Phoenix, northern Scottsdale and Tucson are chock-full of challenging fairways.

Simply Gorges!

Then there's *the* Canyon, the grandest of them all. Peer off the edge while **hiking** along the South Rim Trail—the view from the top will simply knock your socks off.

If you're more adventurous, a whole new world awaits below the rim—numerous corridor trails beginning at the South Rim provide access to the depths of the gorge. Begin with the Bright Angel Trail—established in the 1890s as the canyon's first hiking path, it's a day hike that remains one of the best for beginners. The South Kaibab and North Kaibab trails (departing from the popular South and sylvan North rims, respectively) also are good treks on foot or on hoof: **Mule rides** are available for 2-day jaunts. Advanced reservations are required before you saddle up.

Since it takes a full day to descend to the bottom, **camping** is a popular option on the canyon floor. Be sure to acquire a backcountry permit for overnight travel by contacting Trip Planner, Grand Canyon National Park, P.O. Box 129, Grand Canyon, AZ 86023; phone (928) 638-7888.

Rafting trips on the Colorado River, which weaves through the canyon, can be arranged at Page, Lees Ferry or in Grand Canyon National Park. Trips range from 3 days to 3 weeks. For a bird's-eye view, try a **helicopter** or **airplane tour** across the gaping chasm; trips depart from the Grand Canyon National Park Airport south of Tusayan. To capture that Old West spirit of adventure, ride a train from Williams to the Grand Canyon.

Ah, Agua. . .

Despite Arizona's arid landscape, there are plenty of places to find refreshment. Water buffs will want to dip their toes, jet skis, sailboards and speedboats into the waves on Lake Powell in Glen Canyon National Recreation Area and lakes Mead and Mojave in Lake Mead National Recreation Area.

Water-skiers and **swimmers** play on—and in—these lakes, where views of the surrounding colorful cliffs are astounding. Or you might choose to soak in the view from the deck of a houseboat. Canoes and sailboats often drift on Lake Havasu, and inner tubes float lazily along the Colorado River as it flows through Yuma.

Take to the air in a giant hot air balloon, where you'll become part of a striking panorama as you ascend over Oak Creek Canyon in Sedona's spectacular Red Rock area. Experience this reddish region while hanging onto the roll bar of a **jeep;** you can pilot yourself or ride along with a guide. At Monument Valley on the Navajo Indian Reservation, Navajo guides relate tribal legends while ushering passengers on **four-wheel-drive tours** amid the stark, fantastic rock formations.

If **fishing** is your sport, head for the Black River in the White Mountains area, where you can hook all sorts of trout—native Apache, brook, brown, cutthroat and rainbow are a few varieties—as well as bass, crappie, arctic grayling, northern pike and catfish. For information about **hunting** trophy elk or other game, phone the Arizona Game and Fish Department.

When it gets chilly, **skiing** at the Arizona Snowbowl, just north of Flagstaff in the Coconino National Forest, is the cool thing to do. In summer, ski runs are converted to trails for hiking and **mountain biking.** Other places to catch a chairlift are Sunrise Park, in central Arizona's White Mountains; Mount Lemmon, north of Tucson; and Williams Ski Area in Williams. North Rim Nordic Center near the North Rim of the Grand Canyon has **cross-country skiing** trails.

Recreational Activities

Throughout the TourBook, you may notice a Recreational Activities heading with bulleted listings of recreation-oriented establishments listed underneath. Similar operations also may be mentioned in Destination City recreation sections. Since normal AAA inspection criteria cannot be applied, these establishments are presented only for information. Age, height and weight restrictions may apply. Reservations often are recommended and sometimes are required. Addresses and/or phone numbers are provided so visitors can contact the attraction for additional information.

Fast Facts

POPULATION: 5,130,632.

AREA: 113,909 square miles; ranks 6th.

CAPITAL: Phoenix.

HIGHEST POINT: 12,643 ft., Humphreys Peak.

LOWEST POINT: 70 ft., Colorado River.

TIME ZONE(S): Mountain. DST on Navajo Reservation only.

MINIMUM AGE FOR UNRESTRICTED DRIVER'S LICENSE: 16.

MINIMUM AGE FOR GAMBLING: 21.

SEAT BELT/CHILD RESTRAINT LAWS: Seat belts required for driver and front-seat passengers 16 and over. Children ages 5-15 are required to wear a seat belt; child restraints required for under 5.

HELMETS FOR MOTORCYCLISTS: Required for riders under 18.

RADAR   DETECTORS: Permitted.

FIREARMS LAWS: Vary by state and/or county. Contact the Law Library of Arizona, 1700 W. Washington St., 3rd Floor, Phoenix, AZ 85007; phone (602) 542-5297.

HOLIDAYS: Jan. 1; Martin Luther King Jr. Day, Jan. (3rd Mon.); Presidents Day, Feb. (3rd Mon.); Memorial Day, May (last Mon.); July 4; Labor Day, Sept. (1st Mon.); Columbus Day, Oct. (2nd Mon.); Veterans Day, Nov. 11; Thanksgiving, Nov. (4th Thurs.); Christmas.

TAXES: Arizona's statewide sales tax is 5.6 percent, with local options to impose additional increments on goods and services, including lodgings.

DAYLIGHT-SAVING TIME: The Navajo Reservation is the only area in the state to observe daylight-saving time.

INDIAN RESERVATIONS: Indian reservations are regarded as sovereign nations, making and enforcing laws regarding their land. The following rules are the most relevant to visitors to the reservations: alcoholic beverages are prohibited (including transportation and use); leaving established roadways and hiking cross-country is prohibited unless permission is obtained from the local tribal office; seat belts must be worn by motorists; helmets must be worn by motorcyclists.

INFORMATION CENTERS: State welcome centers that provide details about state attractions, accommodations, historic sites, parks and events are in Lupton off I-4 westbound exit 359, and in Phoenix at 1110 W. Washington St., Suite 155.

FURTHER INFORMATION FOR VISITORS:

> Arizona Office of Tourism
> 1110 W. Washington St.,
>   Suite 155
> Phoenix, AZ 85007
> (602) 364-3700

RECREATION INFORMATION:

STATE PARKS:
  Arizona State Parks Board
    1300 W. Washington
    Phoenix, AZ 85007
    (602) 542-4174

  Public Lands:
    Arizona Public Lands
      Information Center

1 N. Central Ave.
Phoenix, AZ 85004
(602) 417-9300

FISHING AND HUNTING REGULATIONS:

Game and Fish Department
2222 W. Greenway Rd.
Phoenix, AZ 85023
(602) 942-3000

NATIONAL FOREST INFORMATION:

Southwestern Region
Public Affairs Office
333 Broadway S.E.
Albuquerque, NM 87102
(505) 842-3292
(877) 444-6777 (reservations)

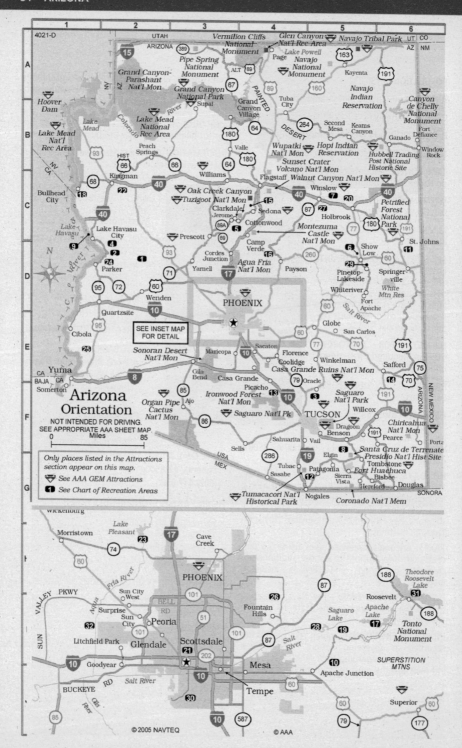

4021-D

Arizona Orientation

NOT INTENDED FOR DRIVING.
SEE APPROPRIATE AAA SHEET MAP.

0   Miles   85

Only places listed in the Attractions
section appear on this map.

▽ See AAA GEM Attractions
❶ See Chart of Recreation Areas

SEE INSET MAP
FOR DETAIL

© 2005 NAVTEQ   © AAA

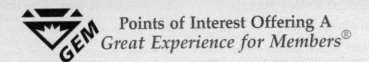

Points of Interest Offering A *Great Experience for Members*®

Benson (F-5)

KARTCHNER CAVERNS STATE PARK—An important cave discovery affords visitors a look at rare formations, including one of the world's largest soda straws. See p. 41.

Canyon de Chelly National Monument (B-6)

CANYON DE CHELLY NATIONAL MONUMENT—Ruins from a succession of Native American villages provide insights into the cultures of the tribes that lived in the caves and at the base of these red sandstone cliffs from 2500 B.C. to the present-day Navajo residents. See p. 43.

Casa Grande Ruins National Monument (E-4)

CASA GRANDE RUINS NATIONAL MONUMENT—The remains of the four-story "big house" built by the Hohokam about 1350 leave no clue to its purpose or the reason for the tribe's sudden disappearance a century later. See p. 44.

Chiricahua National Monument (F-6)

CHIRICAHUA NATIONAL MONUMENT—This homeland of Cochise and the Chiricahua Apaches is accented with precariously balanced boulders, spires and fantastic rock formations. See p. 44.

Dragoon (F-5)

AMERIND FOUNDATION MUSEUM— True to its name, a contraction of American and Indian, the museum is the repository of a  world-class collection of Native American artifacts spanning 10,000 years. See p. 48.

Ganado (B-6)

HUBBELL TRADING POST NATIONAL HISTORIC SITE—This trading post in the Navajo Nation was purchased in 1878 by John L. Hubbell and is still open for business, dealing in crafts such as rugs, baskets and jewelry made by the Hopi, Navajo and Zuni tribes; the family home overflows with Western art and Native American crafts. See p. 51.

Glen Canyon National Recreation Area (A-4)

GLEN CANYON NATIONAL RECREATION AREA—Shared with Utah, man-made Lake Powell is the main attraction of this 1.25-million-acre recreation area along the Colorado River; boating, fishing, water skiing, hiking and camping are a few of the activities to be enjoyed here. See p. 52.

Grand Canyon National Park (A-3)

GRAND CANYON NATIONAL PARK—They just don't come any grander than this immense, awe-inspiring chasm; spectacular vistas and overlooks along the canyon's rim are accessible by automobile and on foot. See p. 53.

TUSAYAN RUIN AND MUSEUM—Remains of a pueblo built by the Anasazi about 1185 provide a glimpse of what life was like at their agrarian village. See p. 57.

Lake Mead National Recreation Area (B-1)

HOOVER DAM—The Discovery Tour reveals what makes Hoover Dam a modern engineering marvel. See p. 63.

LAKE MEAD NATIONAL RECREATION AREA—A year-round recreation mecca, Lake Mead beckons boaters, fishermen, hikers and water skiers as well as those simply in search of scenic drives. See p. 63.

Montezuma Castle National Monument (C-4)

MONTEZUMA CASTLE NATIONAL MONUMENT—This five-story Sinagua Indian cliff dwelling, built during the 12th and 13th centuries, was originally reached only by ladders; too fragile for visitors, the ruins can be seen from a self-guiding trail. See p. 64.

Monument Valley Navajo Tribal Park (A-5)

MONUMENT VALLEY NAVAJO TRIBAL PARK—Self-guiding tours of this park, which is entirely within the Navajo Indian Reservation, provide insights into tribal culture; tours on horseback or in four-wheel-drive vehicles also are available. See p. 64.

Navajo National Monument (A-4)

NAVAJO NATIONAL MONUMENT—Reservations are needed for ranger-led tours to two remarkably preserved 13th-century Anasazi cliff dwellings, both reachable by strenuous hikes during summer months only; a visitor center compensates with a videotape and displays of prehistoric pottery and other artifacts. See p. 65.

Organ Pipe Cactus National Monument (F-2)

ORGAN PIPE CACTUS NATIONAL MONUMENT—The national monument preserves the habitat and inhabitants of this section of the Sonoran Desert, in particular its namesake, an immense cactus found only in this area. See p. 67.

Petrified Forest National Park (C-6)

PAINTED DESERT—Stained multiple hues over the ages by various minerals, the badlands of the Painted Desert seem to change colors as shadows progressively move across the hills. See p. 71.

PETRIFIED FOREST NATIONAL PARK—Horizontal fragments of petrified logs and fossils of long-departed dinosaurs and plants dot the multicolored, rugged landscape along a 28-mile drive through the park. See p. 70.

Phoenix (D-3)

ARIZONA CAPITOL MUSEUM—The old state capitol building, completed in 1900, now houses a museum dedicated to Arizona's history; restored offices contain memorabilia, documents and artifacts. See p. 73.

DESERT BOTANICAL GARDEN—Specializing in plants indigenous to desert areas, the garden is a must-see for those interested in cacti and other flora common to arid climates. See p. 80.

HALL OF FLAME MUSEUM OF FIREFIGHTING—Anything and everything relating to firefighting can be found in this museum's collections, including horse-drawn pumpers, hook-and-ladder wagons, helmets, uniforms and badges. See p. 78.

HEARD MUSEUM—There is no better place to learn about Native American art, culture and heritage than the Heard Museum; innovative displays of baskets, ceramics, jewelry and kachina dolls are enhanced by examples of typical lodgings and audiovisual presentations. See p. 79.

Prescott (C-3)

SHARLOT HALL MUSEUM—Pioneer artifacts and documents collected by author and territorial historian Sharlot M. Hall are displayed in the old governor's mansion she helped restore; an amphitheater, other period buildings and extensive gardens are part of the complex. See p. 93.

Saguaro National Park (F-5)

SAGUARO NATIONAL PARK—Separated into two divisions east and west of Tucson, the park protects the saguaro cactus and its Sonoran Desert environment; scenic drives and trails lead to stands of these giant, many-armed plants. See p. 117.

Sedona (C-4)

OAK CREEK CANYON—The 16-mile-long narrow canyon, which can be explored along a scenic stretch of SR 89A, is noted for the outcroppings of juniper, cypress and pine on its multicolored cliffs and for the trout-filled creek that flows through it. See p. 100.

Supai (B-3)

HAVASU CANYON—On the Havasupai Reservation, the canyon floor and sparkling waterfalls are remote and reachable only by a precipitous 8-mile trip by foot, horseback or helicopter and an arduous return climb. See p. 103.

Superior (J-6)

BOYCE THOMPSON ARBORETUM STATE PARK—This garden in the desert is home to plants and trees native to arid regions around the world; scenic walkways meander through the park. See p. 103.

Tombstone (G-5)

TOMBSTONE—"The town too tough to die" is alive and well; the O.K. Corral, Boothill Graveyard, the *Tombstone Epitaph* building, saloons, the 1882 courthouse and dance halls attest to this old mining boomtown's Wild West atmosphere. See p. 103.

Tucson (F-5)

ARIZONA-SONORA DESERT MUSEUM—A hybrid combination of zoo and garden, the animals and plants that thrive here in natural settings are all natives of Arizona's Sonoran Desert region. See p. 110.

ARIZONA STATE MUSEUM—On the campus of the University of Arizona, the museum is known for its collections of prehistoric Hohokam and Mogollon artifacts and for its exhibits about Native American tribes of the Southwest, both historic and contemporary. See p. 111.

MISSION SAN XAVIER DEL BAC—Founded by Jesuits in the 1600s, the present Spanish mission-style structure was built 1783-97 by the Franciscans; this "White Dove of the Desert" continues to serve its Tohono O'odham parishioners. See p. 112.

TUCSON MOUNTAIN PARK—Come to this park in the Tucson Mountains not only to hike and to ride horses, but also to see one of the Southwest's largest saguaro forests. See p. 113.

Tumacácori National Historical Park (G-4)

TUMACÁCORI NATIONAL HISTORICAL PARK—The ruins of the never-completed Mission San Jose de Tumacácori, begun by the Franciscans, date to the early 1800s; the adobe church is partially restored. See p. 119.

Tuzigoot National Monument (C-3)

TUZIGOOT NATIONAL MONUMENT—The site preserves the ruins of a Sinagua Indian pueblo occupied approximately 1000-1425; a visitor center contains artifacts uncovered from its 110 rooms. See p. 119.

Walnut Canyon National Monument (C-4)

WALNUT CANYON NATIONAL MONUMENT—Filled with centuries-old ruins, artifacts and petroglyphs, this archeological site boasts more than 300 pre-Columbian dwellings scattered along the rim and within wall niches of a 400-foot-deep gorge. See p. 119.

Williams (C-3)

GRAND CANYON RAILWAY—Vintage railroad cars take riders on a Western discovery journey to a majestic destination—the Grand Canyon. See p. 122.

Winslow (C-5)

METEOR CRATER—Formed 50,000 years ago when a meteorite crashed into Earth, the crater is nearly 1 mile across; Apollo astronauts were trained here. See p. 122.

Wupatki National Monument (B-4)

WUPATKI NATIONAL MONUMENT—Well-preserved ruins of hundreds of pueblos and cliff dwellings allow a look into the agricultural lifestyles of the Native Americans who lived here more than 700 years ago. See p. 123.

RECREATION AREAS

	MAP LOCATION	CAMPING	PICNICKING	HIKING TRAILS	BOATING	BOAT RAMP	BOAT RENTAL	FISHING	SWIMMING	PETS ON LEASH	BICYCLE TRAILS	NATURE PROGS.	VISITOR CENTER	LODGE/CABINS	FOOD SERVICE
NATIONAL PARKS (See place listings)															
Grand Canyon (A-3) 1,218,376 acres.		•	•	•		•				•		•	•	•	•
Petrified Forest (C-6) 93,533 acres.			•	•						•			•		•
Saguaro (F-4) 91,000 acres.		•	•	•						•	•	•	•		
NATIONAL FORESTS (See place listings)															
Apache-Sitgreaves 2,008,308 acres. East-central Arizona. Horse rental.		•	•	•	•	•	•	•		•	•	•	•		•
Coconino 1,821,495 acres. Northern Arizona.		•	•	•	•	•	•	•	•	•		•		•	•
Coronado 1,780,196 acres. Southeastern Arizona.		•	•	•	•	•	•	•		•	•	•	•		•
Kaibab 1,556,432 acres. North-central Arizona.		•	•	•	•		•	•		•		•	•	•	•

RECREATION AREAS

	MAP LOCATION	CAMPING	PICNICKING	HIKING TRAILS	BOATING	BOAT RAMP	BOAT RENTAL	FISHING	SWIMMING	PETS ON LEASH	BICYCLE TRAILS	NATURE PROGS.	VISITOR CENTER	LODGE/CABINS	FOOD SERVICE
Prescott 1,238,154 acres. Central Arizona. Electric boat motors only. Horse rental.		•	•	•	•	•	•	•	•		•				•
Tonto 2,900,000 acres. Central Arizona.		•	•	•	•	•	•	•	•	•	•		•	•	•
NATIONAL RECREATION AREAS *(See place listings)*															
Glen Canyon (A-4) North-central Arizona.		•	•	•	•	•	•	•	•	•		•	•	•	•
Lake Mead (B-1) Northwest Arizona. Scuba diving.		•	•	•	•	•	•	•	•	•		•	•	•	•
STATE															
Alamo Lake (D-2) 5,642 acres 38 mi. n. of US 60 via a paved road. *(See Wenden p. 119)*	❶	•	•		•	•		•		•			•		•
Buckskin Mountain State Park & River Island Unit (D-2) 1,677 acres 11 mi. n. off SR 95. *(See Parker p. 68)*	❷	•	•	•	•	•		•	•	•			•		•
Catalina (F-5) 5,511 acres 9 mi. n. off SR 77. *(See Tucson p. 111)*	❸	•	•	•						•	•	•	•		
Cattail Cove (D-2) 5,520 acres off SR 95. *(See Lake Havasu City p. 62)*	❹	•	•	•	•	•	•	•	•	•			•		•
Dead Horse Ranch (C-3) 866 acres off 10th St. *(See Cottonwood p. 47)*	❺	•	•	•		•		•		•		•	•		
Fool Hollow Lake Recreation Area (D-5) 850 acres 2 mi. n. of US 60 off SR 260, then e. on Old Linden Rd. to 32nd Ave. *(See Show Low p. 102)*	❻	•	•	•	•	•		•		•			•		
Homolovi Ruins (C-5) 4,000 acres 3 mi. e. on I-40 to exit 257, then 1 mi. n. on SR 87. *(See Winslow p. 122)*	❼	•	•	•						•		•	•		
Kartchner Caverns (F-5) 550 acres 9 mi. s. of I-10 exit 302 off SR 90. Cave system. *(See Benson p. 41)*	❽	•	•							•			•		
Lake Havasu (D-1) 6,200 acres n. of London Bridge off London Bridge Rd. *(See Lake Havasu City p. 62)*	❾	•	•	•	•	•	•		•	•	•		•		
Lost Dutchman (I-5) 320 acres 5 mi. n.e. off SR 88. *(See Apache Junction p. 85)*	❿	•	•	•						•	•	•	•		
Lyman Lake (D-6) 1,180 acres 11 mi. s. off US 191. *(See St. Johns p. 95)*	⓫	•	•	•	•	•	•	•	•	•			•		•
Patagonia Lake (G-5) 640 acres 7 mi. s.w. on SR 82, then 5 mi. w. following signs. *(See Patagonia p. 69)*	⓬	•	•	•	•	•	•	•	•	•			•		•
Picacho Peak (F-4) 3,600 acres .5 mi. s. off I-10. *(See Picacho p. 92)*	⓭	•	•	•						•			•		
Roper Lake (E-6) 319 acres 1 mi. s. off US 191. *(See Safford p. 95)*	⓮	•	•	•		•		•	•	•			•		
Slide Rock (C-4) 43 acres 7 mi. n. off SR 89A within Oak Creek Canyon. *(See Sedona p. 101)*	⓯		•	•				•	•	•			•		•
Tonto Natural Bridge (D-4) 160 acres 3 mi. n.w. off SR 87. *(See Payson p. 70)*	⓰		•	•						•	•		•		•
OTHER															
Apache Lake (I-5) 2,656 acres 30 mi. n.e. on SR 88. *(See Apache Junction p. 84)*	⓱	•	•		•	•	•	•	•	•				•	•
Bullhead (C-1) 20 acres .25 mi. s. of Bullhead City. No tent camping.	⓲		•		•	•		•	•	•					
Canyon Lake (I-5) 950 acres 16 mi. n.e. on SR 88. *(See Apache Junction p. 84)*	⓳	•	•		•	•	•	•	•	•					•
Cholla Lake (C-5) 360 acres 2 mi. e. of Joseph City on I-40. Water skiing.	⓴	•	•		•	•		•		•					
Encanto (I-3) 66 acres at 2605 N. 15th Ave. Golf (nine and 18 holes). *(See Phoenix p. 78)*	㉑		•		•		•		•	•	•				
Hualapai Mountain (C-2) 2,200 acres 12 mi. s.e. of Kingman.	㉒	•	•	•				•		•			•	•	
Lake Pleasant (H-2) 24,500 acres 29 mi. e. on SR 74, then 2 mi. n. off Castle Hot Springs Rd. *(See Morristown p. 64)*	㉓	•	•	•	•	•		•		•			•		•
La Paz County (D-2) 165 acres 8 mi. n. of Parker via SR 95.	㉔	•	•	•	•	•		•	•	•			•		•
Martinez Lake (E-1) 600 acres 25 mi. n. of Yuma. Water skiing.	㉕	•	•		•	•		•	•	•				•	•
McDowell Mountain (H-4) 20,941 acres 15 mi. n.e. of Scottsdale.	㉖	•	•	•											

RECREATION AREAS	MAP LOCATION	CAMPING	PICNICKING	HIKING TRAILS	BOATING	BOAT RAMP	BOAT RENTAL	FISHING	SWIMMING	PETS ON LEASH	BICYCLE TRAILS	NATURE PROGS.	VISITOR CENTER	LODGE/CABINS	FOOD SERVICE
McHood (C-5) 160 acres 5 mi. s.e. of Winslow off SR 99.	27		•		•	•		•	•	•					
Saguaro Lake (I-5) 1,280 acres 25 mi. n.e. of Mesa via US 60 and Bush Hwy. *(See Mesa p. 87)*	28		•		•	•	•	•	•	•				•	•
Show Low Lake (D-5) 100 acres 5.5 mi. s.e. of Show Low via SR 260.	29	•	•	•	•			•	•	•					
South Mountain (J-3) 16,500 acres 8 mi. s. on S. Central Ave. Horse rental, playground. *(See Phoenix p. 81)*	30		•	•						•	•		•		
Theodore Roosevelt Lake (H-6) 17,315 acres 29 mi. n.w. of Globe via SR 88. *(See Roosevelt p. 94)*	31	•	•	•	•	•	•	•	•	•				•	•
White Tank Mountain (I-1) 26,337 acres 8 mi. s. of Surprise via SR 303, then 4 mi. w. on Olive Ave. *(See Surprise p. 89)*	32	•	•	•						•					

Arizona Temperature Averages
Maximum / Minimum
From the records of the National Weather Service

	JAN	FEB	MAR	APR	MAY	JUNE	JULY	AUG	SEPT	OCT	NOV	DEC
Douglas	65/30	72/34	71/39	84/46	87/52	95/59	95/69	92/64	89/62	85/50	76/35	67/30
Flagstaff	41/14	44/17	48/20	57/27	67/33	76/40	81/50	78/49	74/41	63/31	51/22	43/16
Grand Canyon	41/17	45/20	51/24	59/30	69/37	81/45	83/52	80/51	75/45	64/34	53/26	44/17
Kingman	57/31	61/34	66/37	75/42	82/49	94/57	97/67	96/65	90/57	79/47	67/38	56/31
Phoenix	65/38	69/41	74/45	84/52	93/60	101/68	105/77	102/76	98/70	88/57	75/45	66/38
Prescott	51/23	53/26	60/31	69/38	77/45	87/54	91/61	88/59	84/53	74/42	61/30	53/25
Springerville	47/15	51/18	55/22	63/30	71/37	80/46	80/52	78/49	75/42	68/32	58/21	48/14
Tucson	63/38	67/40	71/44	81/50	90/57	98/66	98/74	95/72	93/67	84/56	72/49	65/39
Winslow	46/20	53/25	60/29	70/37	80/45	90/54	94/63	91/61	85/53	73/41	58/28	47/21
Yuma	68/43	73/46	78/50	86/57	93/64	101/71	106/81	104/81	100/74	90/62	76/50	68/44

Points of Interest

AGUA FRIA NATIONAL MONUMENT
(D-4)

North of Phoenix off I-17 exit 259 to Bloody Basin Road or off exit 256 to Badger Springs, Agua Fria National Monument embraces 71,100 acres including the Agua Fria River canyon between Black Canyon City and Cordes Junction.

The river canyon, at an elevation of 2,150 feet above sea level, and Perry and Black mesas are the primary formations; elevations in the northern hills reach 4,600 feet. The monument preserves more than 450 prehistoric sites. Petroglyphs, terraced landscapes and pueblo ruins suggest the area was heavily populated A.D. 1250-1450 by an agrarian society skilled at growing food and sustaining life in the desert.

Semidesert grasslands and a riparian forest support abundant wildlife, including mountain lions, javelinas and white-tailed deer.

Camping, hiking and picnicking are permitted. There are no developed recreation sites or trails. Four-wheel drive vehicles are recommended. For further information contact the Monument Manager, Phoenix Field Office, Bureau of Land Management, 21605 N. 7th Ave., Phoenix, AZ 85027; phone (623) 580-5500.

AJO (F-3) pop. 3,705, elev. 1,747'

The name Ajo comes either from the Tohono O'odham word for "paint" or the Spanish name for "garlic." Home to the first copper mine in the state, Ajo did not boom until ore-refining methods made the mining of low-grade ore profitable in the early 1900s.

In 1906 Col. John Greenway formed the New Cornelia Copper Co., which was eventually purchased by one of the nation's largest copper companies, Dodge Corp., in 1921. Visitors to the town can view the New Cornelia Open Pit Mine on Indian Village Road. Nearly 2 miles in diameter and 1,000 feet deep, the mine has a visitor center and observation area.

Organ Pipe Cactus National Monument (see place listing p. 67), 20 miles south of Ajo, preserves a portion of the Sonoran Desert; its inhabitants include the statuesque organ pipe cactus as well as such desert foliage as saguaro, paloverde and ocotillo.

As in much of the southwest, the Spanish and American Indian influence can be seen in Ajo's Spanish Colonial Revival town square surrounded by a park, mission churches and Southwestern-style buildings. The Ajo Historical Museum, 161 Mission St., is housed in a mission church built in the 1940s; phone (520) 387-7105. Other historic buildings include the 1919 Curley School and the Greenway Mansion on Indian Village Road. A historic building tour takes place the last week in March; phone (520) 387-7742.

Ajo District Chamber of Commerce: 400 Taladro St., Ajo, AZ 85321; phone (520) 387-7742.

CABEZA PRIETA NATIONAL WILDLIFE REFUGE is at 1611 N. Second Ave.; an entry permit must be obtained at the visitor center. Created in 1939 for the conservation and development of natural wildlife resources and to protect desert bighorn sheep, the 860,000-acre refuge protects such wildlife as kangaroo rats, pocket gophers, jackrabbits, lizards and endangered species such as the Sonoran pronghorn antelope, ferruginous pygmy-owl and lesser longnose bat.

Note: A four-wheel-drive vehicle is required on most of the refuge. Firearms and campfires are prohibited; check with the refuge for regulations. Mon.-Fri. 7:30-noon and 1-4:30. Donations. Phone (520) 387-6483.

APACHE JUNCTION—see Phoenix p. 84.

APACHE-SITGREAVES NATIONAL FORESTS

Elevations in the forests range from 3,500 ft. in the Upper Sonoran Desert to 11,300 ft. at Mount Baldy. Refer to AAA maps for additional elevation information.

Along the south rim of the Colorado Plateau in east-central Arizona, the Apache-Sitgreaves national forests comprise nearly 2.1 million acres. They are named, respectively, for the Apaches and for Lt. Lorenzo Sitgreaves, who in 1851 led the first military topographical mapping expeditions across Arizona. The forests include the Mount Baldy, Bear Wallow and Escudilla wilderness areas and the Blue Range Primitive Area.

Hunting is permitted in season. Numerous lakes and streams offer trout fishing. Boats with motors larger than 8 horsepower are prohibited; on some lakes only electric motors are permitted. Trails are available for varying interests, including horseback riding, mountain biking, and hiking as well as for off-road vehicles. Picnic facilities are available in summer. Winter activities include cross-country skiing, snowmobiling, snowshoeing and ice fishing.

Visitor centers are at Big Lake and on the Mogollon Rim near Heber. Visitor information also is available in summer from attendants at developed campgrounds in the forests and district ranger offices.

The Coronado Trail Scenic Byway (US 191), 127 miles long and ranging from 3,500 to 9,000 feet high, connects the cities of Clifton/Morenci to Springerville/Eagar. The present Coronado Trail (US 191) commemorates portions of the historic route followed by Francisco Vásquez de Coronado when he sought the fabled Seven Cities of Cíbola in 1540. The road traverses areas that remain much as they were more than 450 years ago.

From Clifton the road climbs a corkscrew grade up Rose Peak to an elevation of 8,550 feet. Near this point a Forest Service lookout tower affords a magnificent panorama. Continuing northward, the trail rises to an elevation of 9,200 feet at Blue Vista. The steep, narrow road is not recommended for vehicles pulling trailers more than 20 feet long.

From the rim northward the road is noted for its spectacular autumn coloring. The named portion of the trail ends at Springerville, where US 191 joins US 60.

The White Mountains Scenic Byway is a series of connecting roads that forms a loop through the White Mountains of the Apache-Sitgreaves national forests. The 123-mile loop includes parts of SRs 73, 260, 273 and 373.

For more information contact the Forest Supervisor's Office, Apache-Sitgreaves National Forests, 309 S. Mountain Ave., P.O. Box 640, Springerville, AZ 85938; phone (928) 333-4301. *See Recreation Chart and the AAA Southwestern CampBook.*

BENSON (F-5) pop. 4,711, elev. 3,581'

On the Southern Pacific Railroad route, Benson grew as a distribution center for copper and silver mined in the San Pedro Valley. When railroad transportation began to decline in the 1920s, the town welcomed a new breed of traveler, fledgling motorists out to discover the Southwest. Benson's mining, ranching and railroad history is recalled at the San Pedro Valley Arts and Historical Society Museum; phone (520) 586-3070.

Benson/San Pedro Valley Chamber of Commerce: 249 E. 4th St., Benson, AZ 85602; phone (520) 586-2842.

KARTCHNER CAVERNS STATE PARK, 9 mi. s. of I-10 exit 302 off SR 90, contains one of the world's few living wet caves open for viewing. The guided Rotunda/Throne Room Tour takes visitors through rooms that contain more than 30 types of colorful speleothems growing for more than 200,000 years out of the limestone beneath the Whetstone Mountains. The guided Big Room Tour features striking rock formations and giant boulders.

Discovered in 1974, the 7-acre cave system holds the world's second-longest soda straw formation: Kubla Khan, a 54-foot-high column. The skeleton of a Shasta ground sloth from the Pleistocene period is among the fossil finds.

Within the 550-acre park are a discovery center with exhibits and interactive displays, an interpretive nature path and 5 miles of hiking trails.

Cameras are not permitted in the cave. Picnicking and camping are permitted. Food is available. Allow

2 hours, 30 minutes minimum. Park open daily 7:30-6; closed Dec. 25. Guided 1-hour Rotunda/Throne Room tours are given daily every 15 minutes 8:40-4:40. Guided 1.5-hour Big Room tours are given daily every 30 minutes 8:15-4:15, Oct. 15-Apr. 15.

Admission $5 per private vehicle (up to two persons and $2 each additional person). Rotunda/Throne Room tour $18.95; ages 7-13, $9.95. Big Room tour $22.95; ages 7-13, $12.95. Under 7 are not permitted on Big Room tour. Rates may vary; phone ahead. Reservations are recommended. MC, VI. Phone (520) 586-4100 for information or (520) 586-2283 for tour reservations. *See Recreation Chart.*

BISBEE (G-6) pop. 6,090, elev. 5,300'

Bisbee became internationally renowned during the 1880s mining rush, with the discovery of the Copper Queen Lode. Bisbee mines, nestled in the foothills of the Mule Mountains in southeast Arizona, have produced more than $2 billion in copper, gold, lead, silver and zinc. By 1900 Bisbee was the largest cosmopolitan center between St. Louis and San Francisco. Besides operating several stock exchanges, the town was a major venue for rodeos, circus, vaudeville, theater and lectures.

By the early 1970s most of the mines had closed, and artists' studios replaced the miner's shacks. Bisbee is now home to numerous art galleries and studios and serves as an enclave for more than 100 resident artists and artisans as well as actors, dancers, writers, musicians and photographers. Events and cultural activities are held throughout the year; contact the chamber of commerce for further information.

Artifacts and period furnishings of early Bisbee are displayed at the Muheim Heritage House at 207 Youngblood Hill; phone (520) 432-7698. The house was completed in 1914 by a prominent local businessman. Another museum that preserves Bisbee's past through artifacts, clothing and memorabilia is the Bisbee Restoration Museum at 37 Main St.; phone (520) 432-5421.

Greater Bisbee Chamber of Commerce: 1 Main St., P.O. Box BA, Bisbee, AZ 85603; phone (520) 432-5421.

Shopping areas: The downtown section known as Old Bisbee has several specialty shops that sell antiques, assorted crafts, gifts, jewelry, turquoise and Western items.

BISBEE MINING AND HISTORICAL MUSEUM, 5 Copper Queen Plaza, jct. Main St. and Brewery Gulch, is in the building that served as the headquarters of the Copper Queen Consolidated Mining Company. An affiliate of the Smithsonian Institution, the museum examines local history and culture 1877-1917. The archival library contains photographs, manuscripts, documents and research books about state history and the copper mining era. Daily

10-4; closed Jan. 1 and Dec. 25. Admission $4; over 59, $3.50; under 17, $1. Phone (520) 432-7071.

QUEEN MINE, on SR 80 next to The Lavender Pit mine, offers 1.25-hour tours by mine car into an underground copper mine. The tours are conducted by former miners. **Note:** Sweaters or jackets are recommended. Tours depart daily at 9, 10:30, noon, 2 and 3:30; closed Thanksgiving and Dec. 25. Admission $12; ages 5-15, $5. Reservations are recommended. MC, VI. Phone (520) 432-2071.

SURFACE MINE AND HISTORIC DISTRICT VAN TOUR departs from the Queen Mine Tour Office on SR 80. The tour visits the town of Bisbee as well as an inactive $25 million open-pit copper mine from which 41 million tons of concentrated ore were mined. It is 1.25 miles long, nearly a mile wide and 950 feet deep and can be viewed from SR 80, which traverses a bench of the pit. An 11-mile, 1.25-hour van tour departs daily at 10:30, noon, 2 and 3:30; closed Thanksgiving and Dec. 25. Fare $7. Reservations are recommended. MC, VI. Phone (520) 432-2071.

Naco, Mexico

Approximately 11 miles south of Bisbee, Naco is a small border town in the state of Sonora. U.S. and Canadian visitors must carry proof of citizenship; a valid U.S. or Canadian passport is the most convenient, since it serves as a photo ID and facilitates many transactions such as cashing traveler's checks. The U.S., Canadian and Mexican governments also recognize a birth certificate (must be a certified copy from the government agency that issued it). A driver's license or baptismal certificate is *not* proof of citizenship.

The Mexican government charges a 195-peso (approximately $20 U.S.) tourist entry fee for each visitor entering Mexico for pleasure or business. The fee must be paid in order to have your tourist permit validated if you plan to remain anywhere in Mexico for more than 72 hours, or stay less than 72 hours and travel beyond the 12-mile (20-kilometer) border zone.

A government-issued tourist permit (actually a form) is available upon presentation of proof of citizenship from Mexican consulates in the United States and Canada or immigration offices at official points of entry. Before driving into Mexico check with a AAA office for information about documentation and insurance requirements. The border is open daily 24 hours. The Mexican Customs office is usually open daily 8-5; the U.S. Customs office is open daily 8:30-4:30.

BULLHEAD CITY (C-1)
pop. 33,769, elev. 540'

Established originally as a supply and support base for builders of the Davis Dam, which impounds Lake Mojave in the Lake Mead National Recreation Area, Bullhead City has evolved into a vacation community. Sailing, water-skiing and fishing are available on the Colorado River, Lake Mohave and Lake Mead National Recreation Area *(see place listing p. 63)*. The city's accommodations industry thrives on the thousands of visitors drawn to the casinos across the river in Laughlin, Nev. Two bridges connect the towns, and a free river ferry is available.

Bullhead Area Chamber of Commerce: 1251 SR 95, Bullhead City, AZ 86429; phone (928) 754-4121.

COLORADO RIVER MUSEUM is at 2201 SR 68. Exhibits feature Mojave Indian artifacts, a Native American village display, the first telephone switchboard used in Bullhead City, a replica of 1885 Fort Mojave, a gold mine replica, minerals and gemstones, steamboat models and an 1859 Steinway grand piano. Allow 30 minutes minimum. Tues.-Sun. 10-4, Sept.-June; closed Jan. 1, Easter, Thanksgiving and Dec. 25. Donations. Phone (928) 754-3399.

CAMP VERDE (D-4) pop. 9,451, elev. 3,160'

Camp Verde was founded as Camp Lincoln in 1866 by Arizona Volunteers to defend pioneers from Apache raids. The fort was renamed Fort Verde a few years later by the U.S. Army. As the area became more peaceful, residents turned their energies toward cattle raising and farming, the two major industries in the broad Verde Valley. Native American ruins and cliff dwellings may be seen at nearby Montezuma Castle National Monument *(see place listing p. 64)* and Montezuma Well.

Camp Verde Chamber of Commerce: 385 S. Main St., Camp Verde, AZ 86322; phone (928) 567-9294.

FORT VERDE STATE HISTORIC PARK is 3 mi. e. of I-17. In one of the four restored structures of the old fort are Native American, pioneer and military artifacts. Officers' quarters, bachelor's housing and the doctor's quarters are furnished in period. Allow 1 hour minimum. Daily 8-5; closed Dec. 25. Admission $2, under 14 free. Phone (928) 567-3275.

OUT OF AFRICA WILDLIFE PARK, from I-17 exit 287, 2.5 mi. w. on SR 260 to entrance at 260 Verde Valley Justice Center Rd., features a variety of wild creatures within their natural settings, including spotted and snow leopards; mountain lions; panthers; hyenas; Bengal and Siberian tigers; zebras and wildebeests. Visitors may ride a two-story safari vehicle through a 40-acre natural habitat on the Serengeti Safari, where they may feed giraffes and view lion prides.

Food is available. Allow 1 hour minimum. Park open Tues.-Sun. 9:30-5 (also Sat. 5-dusk), Memorial Day weekend-Labor Day; Tues.-Sun. 9:30-5, rest of year. Closed Thanksgiving and Dec. 25. Admission $12; over 64, $11; ages 3-12, $10. Serengeti Safari tour fare $12; over 64, $11; ages 3-12, $10. Combination ticket $22; over 64, $20; ages 3-12, $18. AX, DS, MC, VI. Phone (928) 567-2840. *See color ad p. 42.*

CASINOS

- **Cliff Castle Casino** is off I-17 exit 289 at 555 Middle Verde Rd. Daily 24 hours. Phone (800) 381-7568.

RECREATIONAL ACTIVITIES

White-water Rafting

- [SAVE] **AAM's Mild to Wild Rafting & Jeep Tours Inc.** departs from Super 8 Motel at 1550 SR 260. Write 53 Rio Vista Cir., Durango, CO 81301. Other activities are offered. Daily late Feb.-May 31. Phone (888) 567-7238.

[GEM] CANYON DE CHELLY NATIONAL MONUMENT (B-6)

In the Navajo Reservation 3 miles east of Chinle, Canyon de Chelly (d'-SHAY) National Monument is reached from Gallup or Shiprock, N.M., and Chambers, Holbrook, Winslow or Tuba City, Ariz. Five periods of Native American culture (Archaic, Basketmakers, early Pueblo, Hopi and Navajo), dating from 2500 B.C. to present, are represented within the 83,849-acre monument.

Archaic, Basketmakers and early Pueblo groups successively occupied the canyons until a reduction in population in A.D. 1350. During the 14th and 15th centuries the Hopis utilized the canyons. The Navajo arrived sometime in the 17th century and continue to live in the canyons, growing corn and peaches and herding livestock.

The 26-mile-long Canyon de Chelly is joined by the 25-mile-long Canyon del Muerto; red sandstone walls rise from 30 to 1,000 feet in a sheer, remarkably smooth ascent. Pictographs painted on the walls date from the earliest occupation to the Navajo era.

The principal area ruins are White House, Antelope House, Standing Cow and Mummy Cave. White House was first explored in 1848, and its architecture may indicate connections with Chaco Canyon. Antelope House is named for the large pictograph of running antelopes that appears there. Mummy Cave, in which some well-preserved human remains were discovered, has a three-story tower.

Authorized Navajo guides are available for canyon trips. The Thunderbird Lodge near the monument headquarters conducts trips into the canyon daily, depending on high water conditions, with six-wheel-drive vehicles. All-day tour (including lunch) $64.95. Half-day tour $39.95; under 12, $30.50; phone (928) 674-5841 or (800) 679-2473.

For individuals with their own four-wheel-drive vehicles, authorized guides are available at the visitor center for $15 per hour (3-hour minimum). Other regulations apply; *see Fast Facts.* Guided tours on horseback also are available.

Except for a self-guiding trail from White House Overlook to the White House Ruin, all visitors within the canyons *must* be accompanied by a park ranger or an authorized guide.

Scenic drives traverse both sides of the canyon, affording views of most major ruins from overlooks. Allow 2 hours for each drive if stopping at all of the overlooks. Food and gas are available. The visitor center is open daily 8-6, May-Sept.; 8-5, rest of year. Closed Dec. 25. The Navajo Reservation observes daylight-saving time, unlike the rest of the state; times listed reflect this when applicable. Monument admission free. For further information contact Canyon de Chelly National Monument, P.O. Box 588, Chinle, AZ 86503; phone (928) 674-5500, ext. 222.

CASA GRANDE (E-3)

pop. 25,224, elev. 1,387′

Casa Grande, founded in 1879, was named for the Hohokam Indian ruins *(see Casa Grande Ruins National Monument)* 20 miles northeast of town. The town, once dependent on agriculture and mining, is now a diversified community.

Casa Grande Chamber of Commerce: 575 N. Marshall, Casa Grande, AZ 85222; phone (520) 836-2125 or (800) 916-1515.

SAVE **CASA GRANDE VALLEY HISTORICAL SO-CIETY AND MUSEUM,** 110 W. Florence Blvd., has more than 3,000 items relating to life in the desert and regional history. Included are three period rooms, Native American artifacts, mining and agricultural exhibits, three antique fire engines, an antique doll house and a historical diorama. A barn and a restored 1935 one-room schoolhouse are on the grounds. Mon.-Sat. 1-5, Sept.-May; closed major holidays. Admission $3, under 18 free. Phone (520) 836-2223.

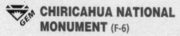

CASA GRANDE RUINS NATIONAL MONUMENT (E-4)

Off SR 87/287, Casa Grande Ruins National Monument lies within the city limits of Coolidge *(see place listing p. 45).* The Casa Grande (Big House) was built by prehistoric peoples called Hohokam prior to 1350 A.D. Partially ruined, the four-story structure is constructed of layers of caliche mud and represents the height of Hohokam architecture. Around the main building are the remains of a walled village. A viewing platform overlooking a prehistoric ball court is behind the picnic area.

The Hohokam lived in the area for many centuries prior to the construction of the Casa Grande. Some time around 1450 Casa Grande was abandoned for unknown reasons after the Hohokam had used it for only a century. The ruins were seen and named in 1694 by Father Eusebio Francisco Kino, a missionary who was led to the site by local Pima Indians.

The visitor center features a museum. Self-guiding tours and picnic facilities are available. Allow 1 hour minimum. Monument open daily 8-5; closed Dec. 25. Admission $3, under 17 free. For further information contact the Superintendent, Casa Grande Ruins National Monument, 1100 Ruins Dr., Coolidge, AZ 85228; phone (520) 723-3172.

CAVE CREEK — *see Phoenix p. 85.*

CHANDLER — *see Phoenix p. 85.*

CHIRICAHUA NATIONAL MONUMENT (F-6)

Approximately 70 miles northeast of Douglas via US 191 and SR 181 or 36 miles southeast of Willcox via SR 186 and SR 181, Chiricahua (cheer-ee-KAH-wah) National Monument, also called the "Wonderland of Rocks," is in the Chiricahua Mountains at an elevation ranging from 5,180 to 7,825 feet. Nine miles of the 21-mile county road that runs south from Bowie across Apache Pass to SR 186 are unpaved and rough in places. Unseasoned mountain drivers and cars pulling trailers should avoid the narrow, winding route from Portal; it is closed in winter.

The 11,985-acre area encompasses lands once controlled by the Chiricahua Apaches under Cochise, who led the Native Americans' resistance to the white man during the 1860s.

The Chiricahua Mountains rise above the surrounding grasslands, providing shady forests and glens that harbor Mexican chickadees, raccoonlike coatimundis, javelinas and a number of other wildlife species. Among the monument's outstanding features are gigantic, erosion-sculptured monoliths of volcanic rock.

Current research indicates that about 27 million years ago violent eruptions from the nearby Turkey Creek caldera took place, covering the area with white-hot ash. After the ash fused and cooled into an almost 2,000-foot layer of rock, the forces of erosion sculpted it into the odd array of shapes that can be seen.

Formations include the Totem Pole, 137 feet high and only a yard thick at its narrowest point; the Mushroom; and Big Balanced Rock, weighing 1,000 tons and resting on a base about 4 feet thick. In some places canyon walls rise as much as 1,000 feet. Many areas can be reached only on foot.

Among the first pioneers to settle in the area were Ja Hu Stafford and Neil and Emma Erickson. By the 1920s one of the Erickson daughters, Lillian, and her husband, Ed Riggs, had turned the homestead into a guest ranch, built trails into the rocks and were the driving force in the creation of Chiricahua National Monument. Today Faraway Ranch is preserved as a historic site with tours offered *(see attraction listing).*

Picnicking, camping and parking areas are available near the headquarters in Bonita Canyon. Reached from the visitor center by 6 miles of paved mountain road, 6,780-foot Massai Point offers an overlook and an exhibit building. Trails lead to all parts of the monument. Campfire programs are conducted at designated times every week April through May and September through October; contact the visitor center for a schedule of evening programs.

A visitor center containing exhibits and an audiovisual display is 2 miles inside the monument entrance. Vehicles longer than 29 feet are not permitted beyond the visitor center. A hiker's shuttle departs to the high country daily at 8:30. Visitor center daily 8-4:30; closed Dec. 25. Park entrance fee $5 per person, under 16 free. Shuttle free. Campers must register at the campground; a $12 per night fee is charged. Campgrounds will not accommodate travel trailers more than 29 feet long; most motor homes are acceptable.

For further information contact the Superintendent, Chiricahua National Monument, 13063 E. Bonita Canyon Rd., Willcox, AZ 85643; phone (520) 824-3560, ext. 302.

FARAWAY RANCH, 1.5 mi. w. of the monument visitor center, is the homestead of pioneers Neil and Emma Erickson. The home was built in 1888 and additions were made through 1917. By the 1920s the Ericksons' daughter Lillian and her husband had turned the homestead into a working cattle and guest ranch.

Allow 1 hour minimum. Homestead site accessible daily dawn-dusk. Guided tours of the home are given. Hours vary; phone ahead. Free. Phone (520) 824-3560, ext. 302.

CIBOLA (E-1) pop. 172, elev. 240'

CIBOLA NATIONAL WILDLIFE REFUGE is 17 mi. s. on Neighbors Blvd., across the Cibola Bridge, then 3.5 mi. s. to 66600 Cibola Lake Rd. Home to many wildlife species including more than 288 species of birds as well as desert tortoises, mule deer and bobcats, the refuge has a visitor center with interpretive displays. A 1-mile nature trail winds through three native habitats: cottonwood, mesquite and willow.

From an elevated observation deck, winter visitors can view flocks of geese, ducks and sandhill cranes on a 20-acre pond. Picnicking is permitted. Allow 30 minutes minimum. Daily 8-4:30, Nov.-Feb.; Mon.-Fri. 8-4:30, rest of year. Closed major holidays. Free. Phone (928) 857-3253.

CLARKDALE (C-3) pop. 3,422, elev. 3,545'

Clarkdale was named after its founder, William Andrews Clark, who purchased the United Verde Copper Co. in Jerome in 1888. In 1911, the mine's smelter was relocated and Clarkdale was created to house the company's 7,000 employees. Clark controlled every detail of the town's construction and incorporated modern details including a sewer system and hardwood flooring in every home.

The town's proximity to Tuzigoot National Monument *(see place listing p. 119)*, Prescott National Forest *(see place listing p. 94)* and Coconino National Forest allows for outdoor activities such as hiking and bird-watching.

Clarkdale Chamber of Commerce: 900 Main St., Clarkdale, AZ 86324; phone (928) 634-9438.

VERDE CANYON RAILROAD, 300 N. Broadway, offers a 4-hour scenic ride through the North Verde River Canyon and Sycamore Wilderness Area near Sedona. Visitors can see Sinagua Indian ruins and desert flora and fauna including bald eagles, blue herons and deer. Open-air viewing cars are available. Other trips are available.

Departures Wed.-Mon., early Feb.-May 31 and late Sept.-late Nov.; Wed.-Sun., early June to mid-Sept.; schedule varies rest of year. First-class fare $59.95 (all ages). Regular fare $39.95; over 64, $35.95; ages 2-12, $24.95. Reservations are required. AX, DS, MC, VI. Phone (928) 639-0010 or (800) 293-7245.

COCONINO NATIONAL FOREST

Elevations in the forest range from 2,600 ft. at Fossil Creek in the Verde Valley to 12,643 ft. at the San Francisco Peaks. Refer to AAA maps for additional elevation information.

Surrounding Flagstaff and Sedona, Coconino National Forest covers 1,821,495 acres. In the south the forest is cut by deep canyons; in the north the San Francisco Peaks attain the highest elevation in Arizona. These peaks, including Mount Humphreys,

the state's highest point, and Mount Agassiz, are some of the places in Arizona where alpine conditions exist. Many roads provide scenic drives.

Outstanding features include Oak Creek Canyon *(see Sedona p. 100)* and the Mogollon Rim, at an altitude of 7,600 feet. Among the recreational facilities within the forest is the Snowbowl winter sports area *(see Flagstaff p. 50)*. Lake Mary offers good fishing, boating, snowmobiling and waterfowl hunting. Limited camping facilities are available in the area Memorial Day-Labor Day; a $10-$18 per night fee is charged. Campfire restrictions may be in effect.

For additional information contact the Forest Supervisor, 1824 S. Thompson St., Flagstaff, AZ 86001; phone (928) 527-3600. *See Recreation Chart and the AAA Southwestern CampBook.*

COOLIDGE (E-4) pop. 7,786, elev. 1,430'

Coolidge is east of the entrance to Casa Grande Ruins National Monument *(see place listing p. 44)* and just west of Pinal Pioneer Parkway (SR 79), a scenic route south to Tucson.

(SAVE) **GOLDEN ERA TOY AND AUTO MUSEUM,** off SR 87 at 297 W. Central Ave., features a collection of antique toys, dolls and model trains as well as restored automobiles. Fri.-Sun. 11-5, Jan.-May. Admission $5; under 13, $2. Phone (480) 948-9570 or (520) 723-5044.

CORDES JUNCTION (D-3) elev. 2,825'

Cordes Junction is a good access point for trips into the Bradshaw Mountains, where there are several deserted mining camps and ghost towns. The mountains are popular with rockhounds. Some unpaved roads are very rough; check locally for road conditions.

CORNVILLE (C-4) pop. 3,335, elev. 3,304'

PAGE SPRINGS FISH HATCHERY is 5 mi. s. on Page Springs Rd. Rainbow trout are raised here for release into the Verde River and Oak Creek. A walking tour of the facility, a nature trail and a visitors center are available. Daily 7-3:30. Free. Phone (928) 634-4805.

CORONADO NATIONAL FOREST

Elevations in the forest range from 2,800 ft. in the Santa Catalina Mountains to 10,720 ft. in the Pinaleno Mountains. Refer to AAA maps for additional elevation information.

In southeastern Arizona and southwestern New Mexico, Coronado National Forest's 12 widely scattered sections cover 1,780,196 acres. Named for Spanish explorer Francisco Vásquez de Coronado, who journeyed through southern Arizona in 1540, the forest's varied plant and animal life reflects the area's extremes of elevation: Flat deserts of cactuses and paloverde give way to rugged, heavily forested mountains covered with oak, juniper, pine, fir and spruce, depending on the elevation.

Within the forest's boundaries are five fishing lakes. Mount Lemmon, northeast of Tucson, is one of the southernmost ski areas in the country. More than 1,100 miles of trails offer hiking opportunities.

Madera Canyon, nestled in the Santa Rita Mountains, is a popular bird-watching spot with more than 200 species, including hummingbirds, woodpeckers and swallows. Hiking trails, a nature trail, picnic areas and campgrounds complete the area.

Scenic drives include Swift Trail in the Pinaleno Mountains (Mount Graham), Ruby Road in the Tumacácori Mountains, Onion Saddle Road and Rucker Canyon Road in the Chiricahua Mountains and SRs 82 and 83. The winding 28-mile Sky Island Scenic Byway begins at Tanque Verde Road in the desert just outside the Tucson city limits and extends to the top of Mount Lemmon in the Santa Catalina Mountains. Pullouts provide opportunities to observe the contrasts of the lower and upper regions.

Legend has it that Cochise's grave is somewhere within the Cochise Stronghold Recreation Area in the Dragoon Mountains. A natural rock fortress, the stronghold is where the Chiricahua Apache leader hid from his enemies. Camping and picnicking are permitted, and interpretive trails are available.

Further information can be obtained at district offices in Douglas, Nogales, Safford, Sierra Vista and Tucson, or contact the Supervisor, Coronado National Forest, Federal Building, 300 W. Congress St., Tucson, AZ 85701; phone (520) 388-8300. *See Recreation Chart and the AAA Southwestern CampBook.*

WHIPPLE OBSERVATORY is atop Mount Hopkins in the Santa Rita Mountains. The visitor center is accessible from I-19 exit 56 (Canoa Rd.); from Canoa Rd. turn e. to Frontage Rd., 3 mi. s. to Elephant Head Rd., 1 mi. e. to Mount Hopkins Rd., then 7 mi. s.e. The observatory houses one of the world's largest multi-mirror telescopes for conducting interstellar investigations. A visitor center has exhibits about astronomy, astrophysics and natural science as well as scenic views. A 6-hour guided tour of the observatory is available by appointment; phone for more information.

Visitor center open Mon.-Fri. 8:30-4:30. Tour departs Mon., Wed. and Fri. at 9, Mar.-Nov. Closed holidays. Visitor center free. Observatory tour $7; ages 6-12, $2.50. Under 6 are not recommended. Reservations are required. DS, MC, VI. Phone (520) 670-5707.

CORONADO NATIONAL MEMORIAL (G-5)

Lying 22 miles south of Sierra Vista and 5 miles off SR 92, Coronado National Memorial was established to commemorate Francisco Vásquez de Coronado's exploration of the Southwest. The expedition, the first European venture across what is now the U.S.-Mexican border, began in February 1540 when the viceroy of Mexico sent young Coronado northward in search of gold from the fabled Seven Cities of Cíbola.

Coronado led an expedition of more than 1,400 soldiers and natives as well as 1,500 animals. Five months of hard travel brought the party not to the gold of the fabled cities but to the rock and adobe pueblos of the Zuni Indians near Zuni, N.M. After traveling as far east as central Kansas, the expedition gave up its search and retraced the route to Mexico in 1542.

Although they never found the city of gold, Coronado and his men found the Grand Canyon as well as the many Hopi, Zuni and other villages scattered along the Rio Grande and into northern New Mexico. Besides paying tribute to Coronado's journey, the memorial's 4,750 acres provide a natural habitat for a variety of plants and animals.

The park, at the southern end of the Huachuca Mountains, is mostly oak woodland sprinkled with yucca, cholla and beargrass, which bloom from April to August. The mountains and canyons harbor wildlife ranging from bobcats to golden eagles. A sweeping view of the area extends from Montezuma Pass, 3.5 miles west of the visitor center.

An alternative to driving to the pass is a 3-mile trail that begins near the visitor center. A half-mile hiking trail, with benches for resting and markers bearing quotations from Coronado's journals, extends from the pass to Coronado Peak. The visitor center has a 14-foot-long window wall for viewing wildlife. Picnic facilities are available dawn-dusk.

The visitor center is open daily 9-5; closed Thanksgiving and Dec. 25. Free. For further information write the Visitor Center, Coronado National Memorial, 4101 E. Montezuma Canyon Rd., Hereford, AZ 85615; phone (520) 366-5515.

CORONADO CAVE is accessible via a steep .75-mi. trail from the visitor center. The cave, which remains in its natural state with no lighting or guardrails, features two chambers connected by a narrow passageway. Several tunnels branch from the main cavern and require some crawling. Daily 9-5. **Note:** Visitors must obtain a free permit at the visitor center and be equipped with one flashlight per person. Comfortable walking shoes and water also are required.

CORONADO TRAIL—
see Apache-Sitgreaves National Forests p. 40.

COTTONWOOD (C-4) pop. 9,179, elev. 3,314'

One of two Arizona towns called Cottonwood, this Cottonwood is located in the center of the 1,500-square-mile Verde Valley, which contributed to its development as a commerce center for the area. In 1874 soldiers from nearby Camp Verde were quartered in town. Settlers eventually arrived and named the community for a nearby stand of 16 large cottonwood trees. Cottonwood is about 2 miles southeast of Tuzigoot National Monument (*see place listing p. 119*).

Cottonwood Chamber of Commerce: 1010 S. Main St., Cottonwood, AZ 86326; phone (928) 634-7593.

SAVE **BLAZIN' M RANCH** is 1 mi. n. on 10th St. to 1875 Mabery Ranch Rd., following signs. Cowboy-style entertainment and a chuckwagon supper are offered in a re-created Western town with a museum and farm animals. Miniature train rides around the ranch are available as well as pony rides, a shooting gallery and a Western-themed photography studio.

Allow 2 hours minimum. Performances are given Wed.-Sat. at 6:30 p.m., Feb.-July and Sept.-Dec. Gates open 90 minutes before performances. Admission $22.95; ages 4-12, $12.95. Reservations are recommended. AX, DS, MC, VI. Phone (928) 634-0334 or (800) 937-8643.

CLEMENCEAU HERITAGE MUSEUM is at 1 N. Willard St. The museum is housed in a former schoolhouse built 1923-24. Seven railroads that operated in the Verde Valley 1895-1953 are depicted in a working railroad diorama. The diorama also depicts farming and ranching. Exhibits on permanent display include a typical 1920s bedroom, kitchen and dining room as well as a schoolroom. Allow 30 minutes minimum. Fri.-Sun. 11-3, Wed. 9-noon. Donations. Phone (928) 634-2868.

DEAD HORSE RANCH STATE PARK, off 10th St., was named for a large horse skeleton found in the area by local children. Once the stomping grounds of Native Americans and Spanish conquistadors, the park now features Quetta Seed Pine Orchard, a stocked fishing pond, bird-watching, row boats, hiking trails and picnic areas overlooking the Verde River. Camping is available. Daily 8-5; ranger station closed Dec. 25. Admission $6 per private vehicle. Camping $12-$19 per private vehicle. Phone (928) 634-5283. *See Recreation Chart.*

RECREATIONAL ACTIVITIES

Hot Air Ballooning

- **Sky High Balloon Adventures** provides transportation to the departure point in Prescott National Forest. Write 105 Canyon Diablo Rd., Sedona, AZ 86351. Tours depart daily at dawn (weather permitting); closed Jan. 5-Feb. 5. Phone (928) 204-1395 or (800) 551-7597.

DOUGLAS (G-6) pop. 14,312, elev. 3,955'

Douglas, on the Mexican border, began as the site of annual roundups for surrounding ranches. The town was founded in 1901 by a copper-smelting company and is now a center for commerce, manufacturing, agriculture and tourism.

The Gadsden Hotel, 1046 G Ave., was built in 1906 and has a high-ceilinged lobby with a mural of Tiffany stained glass and a curving staircase. Of interest in the vicinity are many ghost towns and mining camps as well as shopping and sightseeing opportunities in nearby Agua Prieta, Mexico.

Douglas Visitors Center: 345 16th St., Douglas, AZ 85607; phone (520) 364-2478.

Self-guiding tours: Maps detailing self-guiding historical tours of Douglas are available at the visitors center.

SAN BERNARDINO RANCH NATIONAL HISTORIC LANDMARK (SLAUGHTER RANCH MUSEUM), 16 mi. e. on 15th St. (which turns into Geronimo Tr.), was the home of John Slaughter. The former Texas Ranger and sheriff of Cochise County developed the property he purchased in 1884 into a vast cattle ranch. Now restored, the opulent main house contains many original family photographs and furnishings. Also on the ranch are a car shed, granary, barn, icehouse and washhouse. Near the ranch is an early 1900s military outpost.

Note: Geronimo Trail is accessible only under dry conditions. Picnicking is permitted. Allow 2 hours minimum. Wed.-Sun. 10-3; closed Jan. 1, Thanksgiving and Dec. 25. Admission $5, under 14 free. Phone (520) 558-2474.

Agua Prieta, Mexico

Adjoining Douglas in the state of Sonora is Agua Prieta. U.S. and Canadian visitors must carry proof of citizenship; a valid U.S. or Canadian passport is the most convenient, since it serves as a photo ID and facilitates many transactions such as cashing traveler's checks. The U.S., Canadian and Mexican governments also recognize a birth certificate (must be a certified copy from the government agency that issued it). A driver's license or baptismal certificate is *not* proof of citizenship.

DID YOU KNOW

The only place where four states meet is at Four Corners—a monument marks the spot where Arizona, Colorado, New Mexico and Utah touch.

The Mexican government charges a 195-peso (approximately $20 U.S.) tourist entry fee for each visitor entering Mexico for pleasure or business. The fee must be paid in order to have your tourist permit validated if you plan to remain anywhere in Mexico for more than 72 hours, or stay less than 72 hours and travel beyond the 12-mile (20-kilometer) border zone.

A government-issued tourist permit (actually a form) is available upon presentation of proof of citizenship from Mexican consulates in the United States and Canada or immigration offices at official points of entry. Before driving into Mexico check with a AAA office for information about documentation and insurance requirements. Mexican and U.S. customs offices are open daily 24 hours.

DRAGOON (F-5) elev. 4,615′

AMERIND FOUNDATION MUSEUM, off Dragoon Rd. at 2100 N. Amerind Rd., is an extension of the Amerind (a contraction of American and Indian) Foundation's archeological research facility. Featured are artifacts, crafts, art and photographs documenting Native American cultures of the Southwest and Mexico. Items from Arctic and South American civilizations also are included.

An art gallery contains works with Western themes by such well-known artists as Carl Oscar Borg, William Leigh and Frederic Remington as well as a variety of paintings and furnishings dating from the 17th century. Picnicking is permitted. Allow 1 hour, 30 minutes minimum. Tues.-Sun. 10-4; closed major holidays. Admission $5; over 60, $4; ages 12-18, $3. Phone (520) 586-3666.

ELGIN (F-5) pop. 309, elev. 4,700′

WINERIES

• **Sonoita Vineyards**, 3 mi. s. on Elgin/Canelo Rd. Daily 10-4; closed major holidays. Phone (520) 455-5893.

FLAGSTAFF (C-4) pop. 52,894, elev. 6,905′

Flagstaff rests on the Colorado Plateau under the gaze of the San Francisco Peaks amid ponderosa pine forests, high deserts and lakes. Dusted with snow in winter and wildflowers in summer, the mountains provide a scenic backdrop for what was once a mere rest stop.

The town's name was established by locals in 1881. It is believed that it refers to a ponderosa pine tree that was stripped of its branches and used as a flagstaff by members of an exploration party during Fourth of July celebrations in 1876. The flagstaff, visible from afar, remained in place to serve as a landmark for wagon trains bound for California; transients knew that they would find a good place to camp when they spotted the flagstaff.

Shepherd Thomas F. McMillan, said to be the town's first permanent resident, deemed the land perfect for raising sheep when he arrived in 1876. Early industry revolved around timber, sheep and

cattle, but when the Atlantic and Pacific Railway Co. (now the Santa Fe) decided to merge with the Southern Pacific line, settlers again put out their welcome mats, providing water and supplies to the railroad crews. The railroad reached Flagstaff in 1882. The Flagstaff Railroad Depot, on SR 66 between S. San Francisco and S. Beaver streets, opened in 1926. Impressive with its Revival Tudor style, it now houses a visitor center.

Downtown Flagstaff, which grew up around the railroad depot, contains many historic buildings dating from the late 1800s to early 1900s. Plaques give insight to buildings' former functions.

The Northern Arizona Normal School, established in 1899, was renamed Northern Arizona University in 1966. The university contributes to Flagstaff's "college town" feel. NAU's north campus, which encompasses 140 acres, boasts numerous restored buildings constructed 1894-1935 of local sandstone. This area reputedly contains the largest number of restored sandstone buildings in the Southwest.

In the 1920s, Route 66 brought travelers through town; they stayed briefly yet contributed to the economy. Money from tourism helped Flagstaff become an incorporated city in 1928, and the route continues to attract visitors.

Another popular drive is the 54-mile scenic stretch of SR 89A that begins in Flagstaff, winds its way south through Oak Creek Canyon and ends in Jerome. (The steep, narrow road is not recommended for vehicles pulling trailers more than 40 feet long.)

The city remains a good home base for many day trips. Within the boundaries of Coconino County, the second largest in the country, visitors will find Grand Canyon National Park *(see place listing p. 53)*, Meteor Crater *(see Winslow p. 122)*, Oak Creek Canyon *(see Sedona p. 100)*, Sunset Crater Volcano National Monument *(see place listing p. 103)*, Walnut Canyon National Monument *(see place listing p. 119)* and Wupatki National Monument *(see place listing p. 123)*. The landscape varies from deep green woodlands to rugged, rocky escarpments and provides for nearly every recreational pursuit, from skiing and hiking to camping, hunting and fishing.

Flagstaff Convention & Visitors Bureau: 211 West Aspen Ave., Flagstaff, AZ 86001; phone (928) 779-7611 or (800) 217-2367. *See color ad on inside front cover.*

Self-guiding tours: A map outlining a walking tour of Flagstaff's historic downtown area is available at the Flagstaff Visitor Center in the historic train station on Route 66.

Shopping areas: Flagstaff Mall, 6 miles east at 4650 SR 89N, has more than 60 stores, including Dillard's, JCPenney and Sears. Flagstaff's downtown historic district also offers shopping opportunities.

THE ARBORETUM AT FLAGSTAFF, 3 mi. w. on SR 66, then 4 mi. s. to 4001 S. Woody Mountain Rd., highlights more than 2,500 regional plant species in natural settings and formal gardens. One of

Because the voyage of your dreams just happens to be theirs, too.

Trust AAA/CAA Travel to take you there.

On a *Disney Cruise Line* vacation, you'll find something enchanting for every member of the family—it's the kind of magic only Disney can create. And when you book through AAA/CAA Travel, you'll enjoy many special benefits! So call or stop by today.

Travel

www.aaa.com

Ships' Registry: The Bahamas
CST#1022229-50

the country's largest collection of mountain wild-flowers may be seen. A nature trail traverses meadows and a ponderosa pine forest. A guided behind-the-scenes tour is offered. Allow 2 hours minimum. Daily 9-5, Apr. 1-Dec. 15. Guided tour daily at 11 and 1. Admission $5; over 64, $3; ages 6-17, $2. Phone (928) 774-1442.

[SAVE] **LOWELL OBSERVATORY** is 1 mi. w. of downtown via Santa Fe Ave. to 1400 W. Mars Hill Rd., following signs. Founded in 1894 by Percival Lowell, discoveries made include Lowell's observations about the planet Mars, the basis for the theory of the expanding universe and the discovery of the ninth planet, Pluto, in 1930.

A guided tour begins with a multimedia presentation. Interactive exhibits are featured as well as the Pluto Walk, a model of the planets in sequential order. Open daily 9-5, Apr.-Oct.; noon-5, rest of year. Evening hours vary; phone ahead. Nightly viewings through the 24-inch Clark refracting telescope are available; phone for details. Admission $5; senior citizens and university students with ID $4; ages 5-17, $2. AX, MC, VI. Phone (928) 774-2096.

[SAVE] **MUSEUM OF NORTHERN ARIZONA** is 3 mi. n. to 3101 N. Fort Valley Rd. (US 180). The museum contains displays about artistic traditions, native cultures and natural science, including exhibits about anthropology, biology and geology. A reproduction of a kiva—a meeting place and ceremonial room—also is featured. Recreation programs and a Native American marketplace are offered in summer.

c Daily 9-5; closed Jan. 1, Thanksgiving and Dec. 25. Admission $5; over 55, $4; students with ID $3; Native Americans $2; ages 7-17, $2. Phone (928) 774-5213.

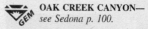 **OAK CREEK CANYON—**
see Sedona p. 100.

PIONEER MUSEUM is .3 mi. n. of jct. SR 66 and Humphreys St., then 1.2 mi. n.w. to 2340 N. Fort Valley Rd. The museum is in a former hospital built in 1908. Exhibits include farm machinery, pioneer memorabilia, medical equipment, toys, household items, a 1929 Baldwin articulated locomotive and a Santa Fe caboose. A 1910 barn houses a sheep wagon and a 1923 American La France fire truck.

A 1908 homesteader's cabin is on the premises. Allow 1 hour minimum. Mon.-Sat. 9-5; closed Jan. 1, Thanksgiving and Dec. 25. Admission $3; senior citizens and ages 12-18, $2. Phone (928) 774-6272.

RIORDAN MANSION STATE HISTORIC PARK is .5 mi. n. of jct. I-17 and I-40 (off Milton Rd.) at 409 W. Riordan Rd. Built in 1904, the 40-room mansion was home to prominent lumbermen Timothy and Michael Riordan and their families. The rustic exterior incorporates log-slab siding, volcanic stone arches and hand-split wood shingles. The lavish Arts and Crafts-style interior contains handcrafted and Stickley furniture, a Steinway piano, stained-glass windows and personal family items.

Picnicking is permitted. Allow 1 hour minimum. Grounds open daily 8:30-5, May-Oct.; 10:30-5, rest of year. Closed Dec. 25. Guided tours of the mansion are given daily on the hour, beginning 30 minutes after opening. Admission $6; ages 7-13, $2.50. Reservations are recommended for guided tours. Phone (928) 779-4395.

SCHULTZ PASS ROAD leads n. off US 180, then circles n.e. to join US 89. The dirt road is a scenic drive through Schultz Pass between the San Francisco Peaks and the Elden Mountains. A scenic portion of SR 89/89A extends from the I-40 junction in Flagstaff 54 miles southeast to Jerome. Check locally for road conditions.

RECREATIONAL ACTIVITIES
Skiing

• **Snowbowl,** in the San Francisco Peaks, is 7 mi. n. on Fort Valley Rd. (US 180), then 7 mi. n. on Snowbowl Rd. Write P.O. Box 40, Flagstaff, AZ 86002. Other activities are offered. Skiing is available daily 9-4, mid-Dec. to mid-Apr. (weather permitting). Phone (928) 779-1951.

FLORENCE (E-4) pop. 17,054, elev. 1,493′

One of Arizona's oldest towns and the seat of Pinal County, Florence was founded by Levi Ruggles in 1866. Many historic homes and buildings perpetuate its frontier atmosphere.

Scenic desert highways from Florence include Kelvin Highway, a county road running east to Kelvin, and the Pinal Pioneer Parkway, a part of SR 79 leading southeast to Oracle Junction. Markers along the parkway identify desert wildlife.

Greater Florence Chamber of Commerce and Visitor Center: 291 N. Bailey St., P.O. Box 929, Florence, AZ 85232; phone (520) 868-9433 or (800) 437-9433.

McFARLAND STATE HISTORIC PARK, Main St. and Ruggles Ave., features the first Pinal County courthouse. The 1878 building includes exhibits about the jail, courthouse and hospital once housed there. The World War II POW Camp exhibit portrays life at what was reportedly the largest POW camp in Arizona, housing more than 5,600 prisoners.

Photographs, movies, uniforms and German and Italian memorabilia from 1942 are on display. Allow 1 hour minimum. Thurs.-Mon. 8-5; closed Dec. 25. Admission $2, under 14 free. Phone (520) 868-5216.

PINAL COUNTY HISTORICAL MUSEUM, 715 S. Main St., displays Indian artifacts from the Southwest, blacksmith equipment, antique woodworking tools, cactus furniture, more than 100 varieties of barbed wire and documents relating to the county's history. Farm machinery, a restored and furnished homesteader's shack, an Arizona state prison exhibit, and a collection of Tom Mix memorabilia also are offered.

Allow 1 hour minimum. Tues.-Sat. 11-4, Sun. noon-4, Sept. 1-July 14; closed major holidays. Donations. Phone (520) 868-4382.

FORT APACHE (D-5)

FORT APACHE HISTORIC PARK, s. off SR 73, is a 288-acre site containing pre-Columbian and historic petroglyphs, the White Mountain Apache Cultural Center and Museum, a military cemetery and a re-created Apache village. More than 20 buildings dated 1870-1930 are featured and include officers' quarters, guardhouse, stables and magazine. Guided tours are available. Daily 8 a.m.-dusk. Admission $5, over 63 and students with ID $3, under 7 free. Phone (928) 338-4625.

White Mountain Apache Cultural Center and Museum is s. off SR 73 to Indian Rte. 46, then .5 mi. e. to 127 Scout Rd. A good starting point for a visit to Fort Apache Historic Park, the museum contains two permanent collections: The Fort Apache Legacy and Footprints of the Apache, about the Apache creation story. Cultural and historical relics such as clothing, weapons and dolls are on display. A video presentation about traditional Apache music is available. The museum features local artists' work.

Picnicking is permitted. Allow 1 hour minimum. Mon.-Sat. 8-5, May-Sept.; Mon.-Fri. 8-5, rest of year. Closed major holidays. Admission $5, over 63 and students with ID $3, under 7 free. AX, MC, VI. Phone (928) 338-4625, or (928) 338-4525 for recorded information.

FORT DEFIANCE (B-6)
pop. 4,061, elev. 6,862'

Fort Defiance lies at the mouth of Canyon Bonito, or Blue Canyon, in the Navajo Reservation. In some places sheer walls overhang the canyon floor. Established in 1851, Fort Defiance saw action in the Navajo wars that occurred during the 1860s. For many years it has been the headquarters of the Bureau of Indian Affairs, Fort Defiance Agency.

Navajos on the reservation maintain much of their traditional way of life. They engage in agriculture, stock raising, employment on the reservation and seasonal off-reservation work. Many still dwell in hogans, circular log and earth huts. Distinctive Navajo blankets, rugs and silver and turquoise jewelry are crafted.

FORT HUACHUCA (G-5)

In southeastern Arizona, Fort Huachuca (wa-CHOO-ka) was founded in 1877 to combat raids by Native Americans and outlaws. In 1954 the fort became the site of the Army Electronic Proving Ground. The 73,272-acre fort is headquarters of the U.S. Army Information Systems Command, the U.S. Army Intelligence Center and various other military organizations. The Old Post retains many of the original buildings constructed in the late 19th century.

FORT HUACHUCA MUSEUM is 3.6 mi. n.w. of Fort Huachuca's main gate in the Old Post area at Boyd and Grierson aves. Southwest history and the U.S. Army's activities in the area are depicted through exhibits in three buildings. Mon.-Fri. 9-4, Sat.-Sun. 1-4; closed Jan. 1, Thanksgiving and Dec. 25. Donations. Phone (520) 533-5736.

FOUNTAIN HILLS—*see Phoenix p. 85.*

FOUR CORNERS MONUMENT—
see Window Rock p. 122.

GANADO (B-6) pop. 1,505, elev. 6,386'

Ganado is one of the traditional meeting and trading centers of the Pueblo Colorado Valley. For centuries the valley has been a favored Native American gathering place, first for the Anasazi and now for the Navajo. When John Hubbell bought the original trading post, he christened it Ganado to honor his Navajo friend Ganado Mucho and to distinguish the community from Pueblo, Colo.

Visitors to the reservation should be aware of certain travel restrictions; *see Fast Facts.*

HUBBELL TRADING POST NATIONAL HISTORIC SITE, 1 mi. w. via SR 264, is the oldest continuously operated trading post in the Navajo Nation. In 1878 John L. Hubbell bought the trading post and established himself as a leading trader. Hubbell's collection of Western art and Native American crafts are displayed in his furnished house on the site.

The trading post and the Hubbell home depict the role of trading in the history of the Southwest and the life of a trader's family. The trading post conducts business much as it did when the Hubbell family ran it. Members of the Navajo, Hopi, Zuni and other tribes sell and trade such crafts as hand-woven rugs, jewelry, baskets and pottery. Ranger-led programs, guided house tours and weaving demonstrations are offered.

Allow 1 hour minimum. Daily 8-6, May-Sept.; 8-5, rest of year. Closed Jan. 1, Thanksgiving and Dec. 25. **Note:** In summer the reservation observes daylight-saving time, which is an hour later than outside the reservation. Donations. Hubbell home tour $2. Phone (928) 755-3475.

GILA BEND (E-3) pop. 1,980, elev. 735'

Gila Bend is the center for a prosperous stock-raising and farming region in the Gila River Valley. The first farms were established in 1699 by Jesuit missionary Father Eusebio Francisco Kino. Just west of town is the site of the infamous 1851 Oatman Massacre, where all but three children of a westward-bound family were killed by Apaches. Exhibits about area history are displayed in a museum at the information center.

Gila Bend Tourist Information Center and Chamber of Commerce: 644 W. Pima, P.O. Box A, Gila Bend, AZ 85337; phone (928) 683-2002.

GLEN CANYON NATIONAL RECREATION AREA (A-4)

Along the Colorado River from Grand Canyon National Park *(see place listing p. 53)* in far north-central Arizona to Canyonlands National Park in southeastern Utah, Glen Canyon National Recreation Area is home to one of the highest dams in the United States. Part of the Colorado River storage project, the Glen Canyon Dam generates hydroelectric power that is distributed to cities and industries throughout the West; the dam's main purpose is water storage.

Reaching out to hidden canyons, sandy coves and inlets, and winding through towering red cliffs, 186-mile-long Lake Powell presents an ever-changing array of scenery and such recreational opportunities as water skiing, boating and fishing. Amenities include campsites, marinas and boat rentals and tours. A copy of fishing regulations can be obtained at park ranger stations, the Carl Hayden Visitor Center, the Navajo Bridge Interpretive Center, the Bullfrog Visitor Center or at the administration offices in Page.

The Bullfrog Visitor Center, at the Bullfrog Marina in Utah, exhibits the natural and cultural history of Glen Canyon and includes a life-size slot canyon model. The Navajo Bridge Interpretive Center, on US 89A near Lees Ferry, features a historic pedestrian bridge over the Colorado River at Marble Canyon and outdoor exhibits highlighting the early river crossings.

Exhibits in the Carl Hayden Visitor Center, next to US 89, Glen Canyon Dam and Glen Canyon Bridge in Page, illustrate the construction of the dam and bridge and include a relief model of the canyon country. Guided tours of the dam are available throughout the year. The center is open daily 8-6, Memorial Day-Labor Day; 8-5, rest of year. Closed Jan. 1, Thanksgiving and Dec. 25. Free evening programs are given at Wahweap campground, 7 miles northwest of Page off US 89, Memorial Day-Labor Day; phone or stop by the visitor center for a list of scheduled performance days and times.

Arrangements for boat tours on Lake Powell can be made at Wahweap Lodge and Marina; facilities, including public launching ramps, boat rentals, camping and boat and automobile fuel, are provided at Wahweap and at three other marinas on the lake. A boat ramp providing access to 15 miles of the Colorado River below Glen Canyon Dam is available at Lees Ferry, 5 miles north of Marble Canyon.

Boat excursions, which last from 1 hour to all day, are available; phone (602) 278-8888 in Phoenix, or (800) 528-6154. One-day raft trips on the Colorado River below the dam can be arranged in Page. Half-day and full-day trips are available to Rainbow Bridge National Monument, Utah, which is about 50 miles from Wahweap. Trips on the San Juan River leave from Mexican Hat and Bluff, Utah.

Park admission is $10 per private vehicle, or $5 per individual on foot or bicycle (both valid for up to 7 days). An additional entrance fee is charged for each motorized vessel. For further information contact the Superintendent, Glen Canyon National Recreation Area, Box 1507, Page, AZ 86040; phone (928) 608-6404 or (928) 608-6200. *See Recreation Chart and the AAA Southwestern CampBook.*

GLENDALE — *see Phoenix p. 86.*

GLOBE (E-5) pop. 7,486, elev. 3,517'

Named for a globe-shaped piece of almost pure silver reputedly found nearby, Globe has a colorful history punctuated by mining discoveries. It began as a mining community in 1876. The town's first boom was silver; the second was copper, which is still mined in large quantities. Globe also serves as a trading center for the San Carlos Apache Reservation *(see San Carlos p. 95)* 4 miles east.

Salt River Canyon, traversed by US 60 about 45 miles northeast, is 1,500 to 2,000 feet deep. About 5 miles wide at the top, the vertical-walled canyon winds for many miles with sedimentary rock layers visible from the road. At the foot of the canyon is a state roadside park. Running westward from Globe, scenic US 60 traverses Devil's Canyon before reaching Superior *(see place listing p. 103).*

Globe is the eastern terminus of yet another scenic highway, the Apache Trail (SR 88). The road runs northwest to Roosevelt and Theodore Roosevelt Lake Recreation Area *(see Recreation Chart)* before turning southwest toward Apache Junction *(see attraction listing p. 84 for an advisory about driving this route).*

Greater Globe-Miami Chamber of Commerce: 1360 N. Broad St., Globe, AZ 85501; phone (928) 425-4495 or (800) 804-5623.

[SAVE] **BESH-BA-GOWAH ARCHAEOLOGICAL PARK**, 1.5 mi. s. via Jess Hayes Rd., is a 300-room pueblo inhabited 1225-1400 by Salado Indians. Several rooms are restored and furnished in period. Artifacts from the ruins are displayed in the museum, and an ethnobotanical garden illustrating how native plants were used by the Salado is featured. A videotape presentation also is available. Daily 9-5; closed Jan. 1, Thanksgiving and Dec. 25. Admission $3; over 64, $2; under 12 free with an adult. Phone (928) 425-0320.

COBRE VALLEY CENTER FOR THE ARTS, 101 N. Broad St., is housed in the 1906 Old Gila County Courthouse. The center presents sculptures, photography, paintings, ceramics, jewelry, quilts, hand weaving and other art forms created by local artists. A working stained-glass studio and glassblowing studio may be seen. The Copper City Community Players present live performance pieces in the center's theater; phone for schedule.

Allow 30 minutes minimum. Mon.-Fri. 10-5, Sat. 10-4, Sun. noon-4; closed major holidays. Donations. Phone (928) 425-0884.

DEVIL'S CANYON, w. on US 60, is noted for its sharp ridges, rock strata and cathedral-like tower formations that illustrate the enormous geological pressures exerted on the region. The mineral wealth of the area is credited mainly to these forces. The Queen Creek Gorge, Bridge and Tunnel are on the drive through the canyon.

THEODORE ROOSEVELT DAM AND LAKE— *see Roosevelt p. 94.*

RECREATIONAL ACTIVITIES
White-water Rafting

- [SAVE] **AAM's Mild to Wild Rafting & Jeep Tours Inc.** is 40 mi. n. off US 60/SR 77, following signs. Write 1111 Camino del Rio, Durango, CO 81301. Daily late Feb.-late May. Phone (888) 567-7238.

- **Arizona Rafting** is 45 mi. e. off US 60. Passenger pick-up is available in Phoenix. Write P.O. Box 1550, Buena Vista, CO 81211. Daily late Feb.-May. Phone (800) 231-7238.

GOLD CANYON (J-5) pop. 200, elev. 1,839′

RECREATIONAL ACTIVITIES
Horseback Riding

- **D-Spur Ranch** is e. on US 60 to Peralta Rd. (between Mileposts 204 and 205), 3 mi. n.e. to a dirt road, then 1 mi. e. to 15371 E. Ojo Rd. Write P.O. Box 4587, Apache Junction, AZ 85278. Daily year-round; closed Dec. 25. Phone (602) 810-7029 or (866) 913-7787.

GOODYEAR—*see Phoenix p. 86.*

◤GEM◢ GRAND CANYON NATIONAL PARK (A-3)

See map page 55.

> Elevations in the park range from 1,200 ft. in the lower part of the canyon to 9,000 ft. at the North Rim. Refer to AAA maps for additional elevation information.

In northwestern Arizona, the Grand Canyon of the Colorado River is one of the world's most outstanding spectacles. In form, glowing color and geological significance, it is unsurpassed. The canyon is 277 miles long and averages 10 miles in width from rim to rim; the canyon bottom is 5,700 feet below the North Rim, which averages about 1,200 feet higher than the South Rim.

The park's eastern border is bounded by lofty, multicolored walls; beyond lies the Painted Desert. The western portion of the canyon includes the broad Havasu Canyon, part of the Havasupai Reservation *(see Supai p. 103).* This small agricultural tribe was present before the first European explorers arrived in 1540. Some 250 tribal members still live in the canyon.

The region possesses five of the seven life zones ascribed to the Northern Hemisphere. The geological aspect of the Grand Canyon is of great scientific importance. At no other place in the world is such a vast view of time displayed so clearly. Each stratum of rock distinctly marks a period of the Earth's history from 2 billion to 250 million years ago.

The first recorded viewing of the canyon by a European was in 1540 when a member of Francisco Vásquez de Coronado's expedition in search of the Seven Golden Cities of Cíbola were guided by Native Americans to the great gorge. Centuries later Maj. John Wesley Powell led the first expedition to explore the length of the canyon. He and his party of nine boatmen left Green River, Wyo., in late May of 1869; on Aug. 30 six of them emerged into open country at the Virgin River on the western end of the canyon.

General Information and Activities

The South Rim is open all year; however, heavy snows close the North Rim roads from about late October until mid-May. For road conditions and weather information phone (928) 638-7888. During the summer travel season visitors may encounter slow traffic; an early start is suggested to avoid difficulties with parking.

During the winter snow accumulates in the pine and juniper forests along the South Rim, but trails into the canyon are usually open. Anyone attempting the trails should be in good physical condition. Trail conditions should be verified at the Backcountry Office or at park headquarters. Since nights are cool even in summer, visitors should bring warm clothing. However, be prepared for high summer temperatures at the bottom of the canyon.

The park presents a variety of scheduled activities and programs. All are outlined in detail in *The Guide,* a newsprint publication, and in a recorded message; phone (928) 638-7888. Schedules of these activities also are posted at various points throughout the park. Among the programs offered are campfire talks, ranger-led hikes, children's programs, and nature, history and geology walks.

Visitors planning to backpack anywhere in the park or camp below the canyon rim must obtain a permit from the Backcountry Information Center, P.O. Box 129, Grand Canyon, AZ 86023. Permits and back-country camping reservations are accepted by mail or in person. For information about backpacking below the rim phone (928) 638-7875, Mon.-Fri. 1-5, or write the park directly to request a "Backcountry Trip Planner."

Several campgrounds are near the rim and just outside the park's boundaries. Reservations for National Park Service-operated campgrounds on the North and South rims can be made up to 5 months in advance by phoning Spherix at (800) 365-2267; reservation requests by mail should be sent to National Park Reservations Service, P.O. Box 1600, Cumberland, MD 21501. *See Recreation Chart and the AAA Southwestern CampBook.*

At the South Rim shuttle service along Hermit Road is available from about mid-March through November; shuttles run year-round in Grand Canyon Village. Passenger vehicles are not permitted on Hermit Road during the summer months.

Shuttle bus transportation is available for a fee for rim-to-rim hikers and others who need transportation between the canyon's North and South rims from mid-May to mid-October. Reservations are required; phone Transcanyon Shuttle at (928) 638-2820 for information and reservations.

Sightseeing buses departing from Yavapai Lodge and Bright Angel Lodge offer the following tours: Hermit's Rest Tour ($16.75, 2 hours); Desert View Tour ($29, 4 hours); Sunrise and Sunset Tour ($12.75, 90 minutes). Children under 17 are free. Phone (928) 638-2631 or (888) 297-2757 for information.

For lodging information and reservations within the park, contact Grand Canyon National Park Lodges at (303) 297-2757 or (888) 297-2757.

Both helicopter and airplane tours of the canyon are available from the Grand Canyon National Park Airport in Tusayan, 5 miles south of the park headquarters. For information and reservations contact Air Grand Canyon, (928) 638-2686 or (800) 247-4726; SAVE Grand Canyon Airlines, (866) 235-9422; Maverick Airstar, (928) 638-2622 or (800) 962-3869; or Papillon Grand Canyon Helicopters *(see color ad p. 56),* (928) 638-2419 or (800) 541-4537.

Flight tours also are offered at many airports in other cities, including Page, Phoenix, Scottsdale and Williams.

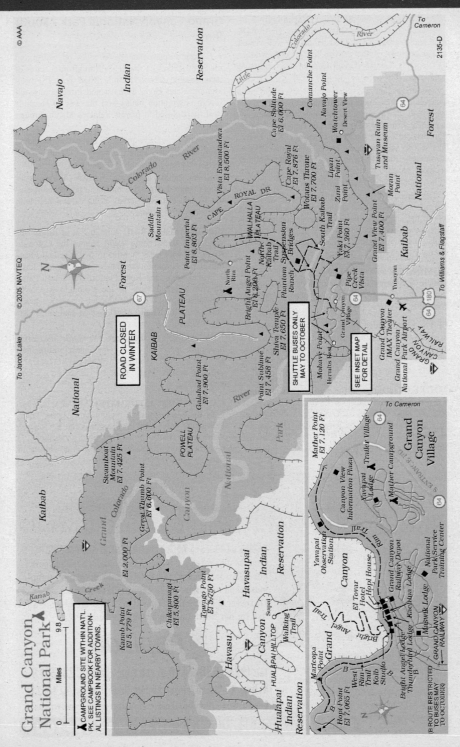

Grand Canyon
National Park

© AAA
© 2005 NAVTEQ
2135-D

ROAD CLOSED
IN WINTER

SHUTTLE BUSES ONLY
MAY TO OCTOBER

SEE INSET MAP
FOR DETAIL

CAMPGROUND SITE WITHIN NATL.
PK. SEE CAMPBOOK FOR ADDITION-
AL LISTINGS IN NEARBY TOWNS.

Grand Canyon Village

Another way to see the Grand Canyon is by tours conducted in four-wheel-drive vehicles. These back road sightseeing trips are led by guides well-versed in the ecology of the canyon, its history, wildlife and legends. Contact Grand Canyon Jeep Tours & Safaris at (928) 638-5337 or (800) 320-5337.

Pedestrians and bicyclists may view the Grand Canyon on the Grand Canyon Greenway, a paved trail with three segments on the South Rim. A 2-mile segment currently connects Yavapai Observation Station to Pipe Creek Vista on East Rim Drive. The second segment is 2.1 miles from Canyon View Information Plaza to Grand Canyon Village. Another segment runs from Canyon View Information Plaza to the Grand Canyon Railway Depot.

The Greenway is wheelchair-accessible, with an average width of 12 feet and rest areas every 30 feet where the slope approaches 5 percent. When completed, the Greenway will provide up to 45 miles of trails on the South Rim and 28 miles on the North Rim.

ADMISSION to the park area is $20 per private vehicle or $10 per individual on foot or by bicycle (both valid for up to 7 days). Admission includes both rims.

PETS are permitted in the park only if they are leashed, crated or otherwise physically restrained at all times. Pets are excluded entirely from backcountry areas and are not allowed below the rim; kennels are available.

ADDRESS inquiries to the Superintendent, Grand Canyon National Park, P.O. Box 129, Grand Canyon, AZ 86023; phone (928) 638-7888. Information also is available from the Grand Canyon Chamber of Commerce, P.O. Box 3007, Grand Canyon, AZ 86023; phone (928) 638-2901.

Grand Canyon National Park - South Rim

Covering approximately 35 miles on well-paved roads, the drives on the South Rim afford a series of incomparable views. Hermit Road passes Powell Memorial and Hopi, Mohave and Pima points—all superb observation points—on the way to Hermit's Rest; it is closed to private vehicles March through November.

Desert View Drive passes many points, including Yaki, Grandview, Moran and Lipan, on its way to Desert View, 25 miles from Grand Canyon Village.

Kolb Studio, in Grand Canyon Village near Bright Angel Lodge, was built as a photography studio in 1904; it now serves as an exhibit hall with changing art displays.

BRIGHT ANGEL TRAIL starts just w. of Bright Angel Lodge. Descending 4,460 feet to the Colorado River, the trail leads 9 miles to the river and Phantom Ranch. From Indian Garden a branch trail leads 1.5 miles across the Tonto Platform to Plateau Point, offering a grand view of the Colorado River. To view the depths from the rim, telescopes are available near the Bright Angel Lodge and at Desert View Watchtower.

Note: Hikers should check *The Guide,* the park's newsprint publication, for the latest information about the trail. Overnight hikers must obtain a camping permit. Water must be carried on all canyon trails.

CANYON VIEW INFORMATION PLAZA is 5 mi. n. of the South Entrance Station near Mather Point. Parking is not available; the plaza can be reached via a free shuttle bus from various locations in Grand Canyon Village. The plaza is at an altitude of

6,950 feet and features indoor displays, outdoor exhibits, an information center and views of the South Rim from an observation point. **Note:** Inquire at the center about local road conditions. Daily 8-6, Memorial Day-Labor Day; 8-5, day after Labor Day-day before Memorial Day. Ranger programs are presented; phone for schedule. Free. Phone (928) 638-7888.

 GRAND CANYON RAILWAY— *see Williams p. 122.*

 HAVASU CANYON—*see Supai p. 103.*

LIPAN POINT, at an elevation of 7,250 feet, offers a fine view of the river, Unkar delta and the San Francisco Peaks.

NATIONAL GEOGRAPHIC VISITOR CENTER GRAND CANYON & IMAX THEATER, 7 mi. s. of Grand Canyon Village on SR 64 in Tusayan, is equipped with a seven-story screen and a six-track sound system. The theater presents "Grand Canyon—The Hidden Secrets," a film that depicts the history and captures the beauty of this geologic formation. Food is available. The film is shown daily every hour on the half-hour 8:30-8:30, Mar.-Oct.; 10:30-6:30, rest of year. Admission $10; ages 6-12, $7. Phone (928) 638-2468.

PHANTOM RANCH, in Bright Angel Canyon, is reached by hiking *(see Bright Angel Trail)* or muleback trips *(see attraction listing).* The only lodging available below the rim, it provides dormitory accommodations, cabins and a dining room. Dormitories are available to hikers; cabin lodging is included with overnight mule trips. Reservations are required for lodging and meals and must be made well in advance, especially during summer and holidays. Phone (303) 297-2757 or (888) 297-2757.

RIM TRAIL extends nearly 12 mi. along the rim of the canyon from Hermits Rest to Desert View Dr. (near Yaki Point). Relatively flat, the paved 5-mile section from Maricopa Point to Pipe Creek Vista is better for children and casual hikers than the park's other more strenuous canyon trails. A portion extending from the visitor center is a self-guiding nature trail. Pamphlets about the biology and geology of the canyon can be obtained from boxes along the trail.

SOUTH KAIBAB TRAIL begins near Yaki Point, 3.5 mi. e. of Grand Canyon Village. This is a steep, 7-mile trail to a Colorado River suspension bridge. Hikers can descend the trail and return by following the Colorado River .5 mile to the Bright Angel Trail which leads to Grand Canyon Village. A good 3-mile round-trip day hike leads from the head of Kaibab Trail to Cedar Ridge, where beautiful views of the canyon may be seen.

Note: Visitors should not attempt to hike from the South Rim to the river and back in 1 day. The Kaibab Trail is strenuous and not recommended for hiking out of the canyon. The trip is recommended only for hardy individuals. Hikers should carry water (1 gallon per person per day), since none is available along the trail. The road to the trailhead is closed to private vehicles and may be reached by shuttle bus. Conducted hikes to Cedar Ridge are scheduled in summer.

SOUTH RIM MULEBACK TRIPS : One-day guided mule trips along the Bright Angel Trail to Plateau Point or overnight trips to Phantom Ranch in the bottom of the canyon can be arranged. Reservations must be made well in advance, particularly during summer and holidays. For reservations contact Xanterra Parks and Resorts, 14001 E. Iliff, Suite 600, Aurora, CO 80014.

Note: For safety purposes, riders must be fluent in English, over 4 feet 7 inches tall, and weigh less than 200 pounds when fully dressed (including equipment). The trips are strenuous and should be undertaken only by those in good physical condition; pregnant women are not permitted on the trips. Rates for 1-day and overnight trips vary; phone ahead. Phone (303) 297-2757 or (888) 297-2757.

 TUSAYAN RUIN AND MUSEUM is 22 mi. e. of Grand Canyon Village on a short spur leading off Desert View Dr. The museum traces the development of the Native American culture at the canyon. Exhibits include models of the ruin, displays about modern tribes and Anasazi artifacts such as pottery, twig figurines and rock drawings.

Tusayan Ruin is a U-shaped, prehistoric pueblo inhabited 1185-1225 by two generations of Anasazi; it contains about 15 rooms and about 30 people lived there. The Anasazi, also known as Ancestral Puebloans, are believed to be the ancestors of the Hopi.

An adjacent .2-mile paved trail leads to the pueblo. A self-guiding brochure is available at the trailhead. **Note:** Inclement weather may result in winter closures; phone ahead. Daily 9-5. Guided tours are given daily; phone for schedule. Free. Phone (928) 638-7888.

WATCHTOWER is 26 mi. e. of Grand Canyon Village at Desert View. Built in 1932, the 70-ft. tower built of stone and mortar is a re-creation of prehistoric towers found throughout the southwest. From the brink of the canyon wall, the tower commands views of the river, the canyon, the Painted Desert and Kaibab National Forest *(see place listing p. 61)*; telescopes extend the view far into the Navajo Reservation and to the Colorado River.

Also at Desert View are food concessions, a ranger station, general store, seasonal campground and gas station. Daily 8-dusk, Memorial Day-Labor Day; 9-dusk, day after Labor Day-day before Memorial Day. Free.

YAVAPAI OBSERVATION STATION, 1.5 mi. e. of Grand Canyon Village, offers exhibits and programs that explain the geologic history of the region. A panoramic view of the canyon is visible through the building's windows. **Note:** The station will close on Labor Day 2005 and is scheduled to reopen Memorial Day 2006. Daily 8-8, June-Aug.; 8-6 in May and Sept.; 8-5, rest of year. Free.

RECREATIONAL ACTIVITIES
Horseback Riding
White-water Rafting
- **Raft Trips** is on the Colorado River. Write River Subdistrict Office, Grand Canyon National Park, P.O. Box 129, Grand Canyon, AZ 86023, or Rivers & Oceans *(see color ad p. 57)*, A Travel Company, Inc., 12620 N. Copeland Ln., Flagstaff, AZ 86004. Trips operate Apr.-Oct. Phone (928) 526-4575 or (800) 473-4576.

Grand Canyon National Park - North Rim

Less visited than the South Rim, the North Rim is not as extensively developed. The views from the North and South rims differ considerably. Observers at Bright Angel Point on the North Rim can see the San Francisco Peaks, which are 80 miles south of the South Rim.

From Grand Canyon Village on the South Rim, it is 215 miles to Grand Canyon Lodge via SR 64 to Cameron, US 89 to its junction with US 89A, US

89A to Jacob Lake and scenic SR 67 to the North Rim Entrance Station. The 5-hour drive passes through the Navajo reservation, the Painted Desert and Kaibab National Forest.

A road runs 22 miles southeast from the Grand Canyon Lodge road to Point Imperial, Vista Encantada and Cape Royal. Point Imperial, at 8,803 feet, is the highest point on the canyon rim. These points all afford splendid views. Reservations for the North Rim Campground can be made by phoning Spherix at (800) 365-2267. *See Recreation Chart and the AAA Southwestern CampBook.*

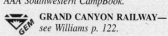

GRAND CANYON RAILWAY— *see Williams p. 122.*

MARBLE CANYON, at the n.e. end of the park, is traversed by US 89A via the Navajo Bridge, which is 616 feet long and 467 feet high. The Colorado River lies in a 500-foot-deep gorge that cuts across the level plain on which the highway sits. A herd of bison inhabits House Rock Valley, about 22 miles west on a rough dirt road off US 89A.

NORTH KAIBAB TRAIL starts at the head of Roaring Springs Canyon. This 14.2-mile trail descends 5,850 feet to the river and Phantom Ranch, following Bright Angel Creek. **Note:** Only experienced hikers in good physical condition should use the trail. Check *The Guide,* the park's newsprint publication, for the latest information about the trail. Overnight hikers must obtain a camping permit and make camping reservations.

NORTH RIM MULEBACK TRIPS : Both half- and 1-day muleback trips into the canyon are offered. Mule trips do not go to the Colorado River. A 1-hour trip of the North Rim also is available. For reservations contact Grand Canyon Trail Rides, Box 128, Tropic, UT 84776.

Note: For safety purposes, riders must be fluent in English and weigh less than 200 pounds when fully dressed (including equipment). For the 1-hour rim trip, riders must weigh less than 220 pounds when fully dressed. The trips are strenuous and should be undertaken only by those in good physical condition; pregnant women are not permitted on the trips. One-day trips depart trailhead daily at 7:30, half-day trips depart trailhead daily at 7:30 and 12:30, 1-hour rim trips depart daily on the hour at 9:30 and 1:30, mid-May to mid-Oct.

One-day trip $105; half-day trip $55; 1-hour rim trip $30. Under 12 are not permitted on 1-day trip; under 10 are not permitted on half-day trip; under 7 are not permitted on 1-hour rim trip. Phone (435) 679-8665.

RAFT TRIPS—*see South Rim p. 58.*

TUWEEP AREA is in the n.w. corner, via SR 389 and a 60-mile dirt road west of Fredonia; the road is impassable when wet.

The remote area embraces 40 miles of the Grand Canyon between Kanab Creek and the Pine Mountains. Toroweap Overlook offers exceptional views of the Grand Canyon's inner gorge and of lava flows. Here the canyon is 3,000 feet deep and averages less than a mile in width. Vulcan's Throne, a cinder cone, is on the Esplanade just west of Toroweap Overlook.

Note: Due to a lack of accommodations, the trip should not be attempted without adequate preparation and equipment. No water, gasoline or camping supplies are available. Limited camping is offered south of the Tuweep Ranger Station.

GRAND CANYON-PARASHANT NATIONAL MONUMENT (A-2)

In the northwestern corner of the state, Grand Canyon-Parashant National Monument comprises more than 1 million undeveloped acres bordered on the west by Nevada and on the south by Grand Canyon National Park *(see place listing p. 53).*

Exposed in the remote, unspoiled canyons and mesas are layers representing nearly 1.7 billion years of the earth's formation. Human occupation can be traced through such archeological finds as petroglyphs, pithouses and villages, with evidence pointing to habitation by hunter-gatherers as early as the Paleo-Indian and Archaic periods, and later by Puebloan and Southern Paiute cultures. Abandoned homesteads, ranches and mining camps are among the 19th- and 20th-century ruins preserved.

Wildlife is as diverse as the scenery. Two extreme ecological regions, the Mojave Desert and the Colorado Plateau, intersect within the boundaries of the monument, which is inhabited by bighorn sheep, coyotes, mule deer, turkeys and Kaibab squirrels as well as the endangered California condor.

Hiking, picnicking and primitive camping are permitted. There are no paved roads, services or developed recreation sites. Graded dirt roads are passable by two-wheel drive vehicles when dry but become impassable when wet. Use four-wheel drive vehicles with full-sized spare tires to travel alternative routes. Be prepared for adverse and isolated conditions. For maps and further information contact the Arizona Strip Field Office, Bureau of Land Management, 345 E. Riverside Dr., St. George, UT 84790; phone (435) 688-3246.

HAYDEN (E-5) pop. 892, elev. 2,062′

RAY MINE, off SR 177 at 27809 N. Mineral Creek, is an open-pit copper mine. An overlook is open daily 8:30-5:30. Phone (520) 356-2333.

HEREFORD (G-5) pop. 300, elev. 7,587′

THE NATURE CONSERVANCY'S RAMSEY CANYON PRESERVE is 5.9 mi. s. on SR 92 from jct. SR 90, then 3.5 mi. w. to 27 Ramsey Canyon Rd. The 380-acre preserve serves as a sanctuary for more than 400 species of plants; 170 species of birds, including painted redstarts and hummingbirds; many species of butterflies; and wildlife such as mountain lions and canyon tree frogs. A natural history and conservation interpretive center is available.

Tips for Motorists

Summer Temperatures

Summer temperatures can cause the air inside a closed vehicle to expand enough to shatter a windshield, so consider leaving a side window open a crack to allow air to escape.

Temperatures in a closed vehicle can exceed 160 degrees Fahrenheit, so never leave children or pets unattended.

© Kent Vineyard / Index Stock

Animal Crossings

When driving in areas of high elevation, be on the lookout for elk and deer that may either be on the road or dart into the path of your vehicle. Remember not to outdrive your headlights.

Note: Parking is limited to 23 spaces. Picnicking is not permitted. Pets are not permitted. Daily 8-5, Apr.-Oct.; 9-4, rest of year. Closed Jan. 1, Thanksgiving and Dec. 25. Guided 2-hour nature walks are offered Tues., Thurs. and Sat. at 9, Mar.-Oct. Admission $5, under 16 free. Admission is valid for 7 days. MC, VI. Phone (520) 378-2785.

HOLBROOK (C-5) pop. 4,917, elev. 5,080'

Holbrook was founded in 1881 when the Atlantic and Pacific Railroad reached this point. Once called the "town too tough for women and churches," the community was named for Henry R. Holbrook, chief engineer of the railroad project. The seat of Navajo County, Holbrook is close to Petrified Forest National Park *(see place listing p. 70)* and several reservations.

The Little Colorado River's sweeping turns traverse westward through town, and the terrain consists of flat plains, rugged hills and small buttes. Official U.S. mail is delivered to Scottsdale in late January when the Pony Express rides from Holbrook.

Holbrook Chamber of Commerce: 100 E. Arizona St., Holbrook, AZ 86025; phone (928) 524-6558 or (800) 524-2459. *See color ad.*

Self-guiding tours: A self-guiding tour including the Navajo County Courthouse/Museum is available. Brochures can be obtained at the chamber of commerce.

IRONWOOD FOREST NATIONAL MONUMENT (F-3)

Northwest of Tucson 25 miles via I-10 to Avra Valley Road, Ironwood Forest National Monument contains the highest density of ironwood trees in the Sonoran Desert. The diverse ironwood provides food and shelter for a variety of wildlife, including desert bighorn sheep, tortoises and hawks. Preserved within the monument are several petroglyphs, more than 200 prehistoric Hohokam sites, remnants of the Mission Santa Ana and significant archeological finds. For further information contact the Tucson Field Office, Bureau of Land Management, 12661

E. Broadway, Tucson, AZ 85748; phone (520) 258-7200.

JEROME (C-3) pop. 329, elev. 5,435'

In 1582 Spanish missionaries exploring the Verde Valley recorded that natives were using the copper mines near what is now Jerome. The missionaries' description of the mines was identical to the workings found in 1883 by the United Verde Co. Eugene Jerome of New York agreed to finance the mining project on condition the camp be named for him. In 1886 a smelter arrived by rail from Ash Fork and operations began in earnest.

Once a city with a population of 15,000, Jerome became a virtual ghost town when the United Verde Branch copper mines of the Phelps Dodge Corp. closed in 1953. Since then, shops, galleries, studios and museums have been established in the restored town. Some of the restored homes are open during the Home Tour in May.

A 54-mile scenic stretch of SR 89A begins in Flagstaff and winds its way south through Oak Creek Canyon *(see Sedona p. 100)* and ends in Jerome. The steep, narrow road is not recommended for vehicles pulling trailers more than 40 feet long. The nearby mountains are ideal for camping, fishing and hunting.

Jerome Chamber of Commerce: 310 Hull Ave., Box K, Jerome, AZ 86331; phone (928) 634-2900.

JEROME STATE HISTORIC PARK is off SR 89A. The park museum in the 1916 adobe brick Douglas Mansion traces the history of local mining and the family of James S. Douglas, developer of the rich United Verde Extension Mine in the early 1900s. A movie highlighting the history of Jerome is shown continuously. Picnicking is permitted. Allow 1 hour minimum. Park daily 8-5. Museum daily 8:30-5. Closed Dec. 25. Admission (including museum) $3, under 14 free. Phone (928) 634-5381.

[SAVE] **MINE MUSEUM,** 200 Main St., depicts Jerome's history through mine artifacts and equipment. Daily 9-4:30; closed Thanksgiving and Dec. 25. Admission $2; over 59, $1; under 12 free. Phone (928) 634-5477.

KAIBAB NATIONAL FOREST

Elevations in the forest range from
5,500 ft. in the southwest lowlands to
10,418 ft. at Kendrick Peak. Refer to AAA
maps for additional elevation
information.

Comprised of three districts north and south of
Grand Canyon National Park *(see place listing p.
53)*, Kaibab National Forest covers 1,556,432 acres.
The portion north of the canyon includes Grand
Canyon National Game Preserve, a thickly forested,
domed limestone plateau. The north Kaibab Plateau
is the only known home of the Kaibab squirrel, a
dark gray squirrel with a white tail and tufted ears.
The southernmost of the three districts contains volcanic cones and scattered forested peaks.

Big game animals can be seen in roadside meadows and throughout the forest. Fishing can be enjoyed at several lakes. Recreational opportunities
within the national forest include camping, hiking,
mountain biking, horseback riding and cross-country
skiing.

The Kaibab Plateau-North Rim Scenic Byway has
been described as the most beautiful 44 miles in the
United States. The scenic parkway begins at Jacob
Lake and winds through dense forests and alpine
meadows to culminate at the North Rim of the
Grand Canyon; the road is closed mid-October
through May. For further information contact the
Kaibab Plateau Visitor Center, US 89 and SR 67, Jacob Lake, AZ 86022, phone (928) 643-8167; or the
Williams and Forest Service Visitor Center, 200 W.
Railroad Ave., Williams, AZ 86046; phone (928)
635-4061 or (800) 863-0546. *See Recreation Chart
and the AAA Southwestern CampBook.*

KAYENTA (A-5) pop. 4,922, elev. 5,641′

Kayenta grew from a trading post that John Wetherill established in 1910. He first called it Oljeto,
but eventually changed the name to Kayenta after a
deep spring nearby. The area's uranium and coal deposits are important in the town's economy. Scenic
US 163, beginning at US 160, passes through Kayenta before running 22 miles north to the Utah border and the entrance to Monument Valley Navajo
Tribal Park *(see place listing p. 64)*.

Crawley's Monument Valley Tours offers back-
country trips into areas of the park. For further information about the tours and the area contact
Crawley's Monument Valley Tours, P.O. Box 187,
Kayenta, AZ 86033; phone (928) 697-3463.

KEAMS CANYON (B-5)
pop. 260, elev. 6,184′

Keams Canyon is within the Hopi Reservation
that occupies a large tract in the center of the vast
Navajo Reservation of northeastern Arizona. The
reservation is crossed by SR 264, which runs between US 491, 8 miles north of Gallup, N.M., and
US 160 at Tuba City. Noted for weaving, pottery
and jewelry, the Hopi also farm and raise livestock.

Information about Hopi ceremonies can be obtained
from the Hopi Indian Agency in Keams Canyon,
(928) 738-2222, or from the Hopi tribal headquarters in Kykotsmovi, (928) 734-2441.

Of particular interest are the villages of Old
Oraibi and Walpi on First Mesa. High on a narrow,
rocky mesa, Old Oraibi is possibly the oldest of the
present Hopi villages; it is thought to be one of the
oldest continuously inhabited cities in the country. A
trading post and schools are in each village, and the
main tribal headquarters is at nearby Kykotsmovi.
Walpi occupies the end of a high mesa, where ancestors of the present inhabitants began building
about 1680.

No photography, painting, recording or sketching
are permitted while on the Hopi Reservation. Primitive campgrounds are at Second Mesa, next to the
Hopi Cultural Center; phone (928) 734-2401.

KINGMAN (C-2) pop. 20,069, elev. 3,334′

The seat of Mohave County, Kingman was
founded in 1880 when the railroad was built through
the area.

Kingman's popularity is maintained as the main
stop on the longest existing stretch of Historic Route
66—the first completely paved transcontinental
highway in the country. Linking hundreds of towns
and cities between Chicago and Los Angeles, Route
66 formed the main street of towns along its route,
thus its nickname "Main Street of America." Today
travelers can traverse some 140 miles of historic
roadway beginning west of Ashfork, continuing
from Seligman through Peach Springs to Kingman
and through Oatman and Goldroad to Topock. For a
self-guiding driving tour brochure contact the Historic Route 66 Association, P.O. Box 66, Kingman,
AZ 86402; phone (928) 753-5001.

At the junction of I-40 and US 93, Kingman is an
access point to lakes Mead, Mohave and Havasu.
Ghost towns surround this former gold-mining community. One such town is Oatman, a business and
social center for surrounding mining camps during
the early 20th century. With many of its original
buildings still standing, Oatman draws both film-
makers and tourists. Visitors may even hand-feed
the burros that roam the town's streets. From Kingman, Oatman is reached by SR 66 (Old Route 66).

Hualapai Mountain Park, 12 miles southeast, is
named for the Native Americans who inhabited the
mountains until the 1870s. Mountain elevations
range from 5,000 to 8,500 feet. A variety of native
wildlife lives here, including deer, eagles, elk, foxes,
hawks, rabbits and squirrels. *See Recreation Chart.*

Kingman Powerhouse Visitor Center: 120 W.
Andy Devine Ave., Kingman, AZ 86401; phone
(928) 753-6106.

BONELLI HOUSE is e. off I-40 exit 48, then .2 mi.
n. to 430 E. Spring St. Built in 1915, Bonelli House
depicts the lifestyle of a prominent Arizona family
in the early 20th century. It is outfitted with original
furnishings and other period pieces similar to those
used by the Bonelli family.

Features include a Victorian-style cupola where the children acted as sentries for their father's arrival from work, and a large wall clock that was once the only clock in town. Allow 1 hour minimum. Mon.-Fri. 11-3; closed holidays. Donations. Phone (928) 753-3195.

HISTORIC ROUTE 66 MUSEUM is at 120 W. Andy Devine Ave. Dioramas, murals and photos depict the history of historic Route 66 from its early use by Native Americans and pioneers to the travelers of the 1950s. A short film is presented; a reading room and archive are available. Food is available. Allow 30 minutes minimum. Daily 9-6, Apr.-Sept.; 9-5, rest of year. Closed Thanksgiving and Dec. 25. Admission $4; over 55, $3; under 13 free. MC, VI. Phone (928) 753-9889.

MOHAVE MUSEUM OF HISTORY AND ARTS is off I-40 exit 48 .25 mi. s.e. to 400 W. Beale St. (US 93). Collections of turquoise, re-created Mohave and Hualapai dwellings and local artifacts and artwork depict the history of northwest Arizona. Other exhibits feature Andy Devine memorabilia, Lawrence Williams' portraits of presidents and first ladies and Mohave County ranching history. A re-created copper mine outfitted with original mining equipment depicts miners at work.

Mon.-Fri. 9-5, Sat. 1-5; closed major holidays. Admission $4; over 59, $3; under 12 free when accompanied by adult. Admission includes pass to Historic Route 66 Museum. Phone (928) 753-3195.

LAKE HAVASU CITY (C-2)
pop. 41,938, elev. 482'

Lake Havasu City takes its name from the lake by which it lies. Formed by the impoundment of Parker Dam in 1938, Lake Havasu is fed by the Colorado River. The 45-mile-long lake has a maximum width of 3 miles and supplies water to Arizona, Los Angeles and intermediate cities. Paved roads cross the lake at Topock on the north end and Parker Dam at the south end.

Originally an Army Air Corps landing strip and rest camp, the land was purchased by industrialist Robert P. McCulloch Sr. in 1963 and turned into a planned recreational and retirement community.

The town captured the world's attention in 1968 when McCulloch bought the London Bridge. Originally built in 1831 by architect John Rennie, the multi-arch bridge resided over the Thames River until 1968, when it began to sink into the river. Dismantled stone by stone, the bridge was brought over from London and reconstructed over a man-made inlet on the Colorado River.

Lake Havasu provides a setting for all types of water sports. The London Bridge is a center for boat tours of Lake Havasu and Topock Gorge. Operators offering a variety of excursions dock their boats under the celebrated span. London Bridge Watercraft Tours offers Colorado River adventures aboard personal watercraft as well as boat rentals; phone (928) 453-8883. Narrated cruises aboard various types of watercraft are offered through Blue Water Charters,

(928) 855-7171 or (888) 855-7171. Numerous companies rent canoes, houseboats, personal watercraft, outboards, pontoon boats and sailboats for use on the lake; consult a telephone directory for vendors.

Fishing is excellent, especially for striped and large-mouth bass, bluegill and crappie. Open stretches of water make Lake Havasu an ideal spot for national outboard, sailing, water skiing and personal watercraft championships.

Lake Havasu City Convention and Visitors Bureau: 314 London Bridge Rd., Lake Havasu City, AZ 86403; phone (928) 453-3444 or (800) 242-8278.

Shopping areas: Agave Retail Center, The English Village, Island Mall, London Bridge Shopping Center and Shambles Villages all provide shopping opportunities in the London Bridge area.

CATTAIL COVE STATE PARK, 15 mi. s. off SR 95, is named after the numerous cattails located in the park's cove. Water activities abound in the park. Hiking and camping also are available. Food is available. Daily 8-5. Admission $9 per private vehicle. Camping $19 per private vehicle. Phone (928) 855-1223. *See Recreation Chart.*

HAVASU NATIONAL WILDLIFE REFUGE consists of two areas: Topock Gorge, s. of jct. I-40 and the Colorado River, and Topock Marsh, n. of I-40 on the Arizona side of the river. Topock Gorge includes the 18,000-acre Havasu Wilderness Area. The 37,515-acre refuge is home to the southwestern willow flycatcher, the Yuma clapper rail, migratory birds, beavers and bighorn sheep. The refuge headquarters is in Needles, Calif.

Note: The gorge is accessible only by boat or on foot. Hunting and fishing (in season) are permitted, as are boating and camping in designated areas. Refuge open daily 24 hours; closed major holidays. Office open Mon.-Fri. 7:30-3. Free. Phone (760) 326-3853.

LAKE HAVASU STATE PARK, n. of London Bridge off SR 95 and London Bridge Rd., stretches along the river. Camping and hiking are available. Daily 8 a.m.-10 p.m. Day use fee $9 per private vehicle. Camping $14 per vehicle. Phone (928) 855-2784. *See Recreation Chart.*

LONDON BRIDGE, off US 95 along the Colorado River, once the famed span on the Thames River in London, now crosses a man-made channel of the Colorado River in the Arizona desert. The channel created an island that contains recreational facilities, including a golf course, marina and campground. Transported block by block from England and reassembled at this location in its original form, the bridge is a striking landmark in this community. Phone (928) 453-8883.

RECREATIONAL ACTIVITIES
Jeep Tours

- **Outback Off-Road Adventures Inc.** offers passenger pick-ups at area hotels. Write 440 London Bridge Rd., Lake Havasu City, AZ 86403. Tours depart daily; phone for schedule. Reservations are required. Phone (928) 680-6151.

▼ LAKE MEAD NATIONAL RECREATION AREA (B-1)

Extending about 140 miles along the Colorado River from Grand Canyon National Park to Bullhead City, Lake Mead National Recreation Area embraces 1.5 million acres in western Arizona and southern Nevada. Included are Lake Mohave and Lake Mead as well as an isolated pocket of land north of the lower portion of Grand Canyon National Park.

Three of America's four desert ecosystems—the Mojave, the Great Basin and the Sonoran deserts—meet in Lake Mead National Recreation Area. Therefore the area is home to numerous plants and animals, including bighorn sheep, mule deer, coyotes, foxes and bobcats as well as lizards and snakes. Such threatened and endangered species as the desert tortoise and peregrine falcon also live here.

Fishing is popular in both lakes all year; licenses are required. Largemouth bass, striped bass and catfish are the chief catches in Lake Mead, while rainbow trout and bass are plentiful in Lake Mohave. The recreation area can be enjoyed year-round and is a prime destination for swimming, boating and skiing.

Food is available. Area open daily 24 hours. Admission $5 per private vehicle, $3 per person arriving by other means. Passes are valid for up to 5 days. For further information contact the Superintendent, Lake Mead National Recreation Area, 601 Nevada Hwy., Boulder City, NV 89005; phone (702) 293-8990 or (702) 293-8907. *See the Recreation Chart and the AAA Southwestern CampBook.*

▼ HOOVER DAM,

on SR 93, stands 726 feet high and is one of the highest concrete dams ever constructed. Completed in 1935 for flood control and water storage, it impounds Lake Mead, one of the largest man-made lakes in the United States.

The self-guiding Discovery Tour of the Hoover Dam Visitor Center includes a 25-minute film about construction of the dam and a live theater presentation depicting how irrigation from the Colorado River turned desert into farmland. The power plant's eight generators may be explored via an elevator that descends 500 feet into Black Canyon. An exhibit gallery highlights the region's natural history and an overlook atop the visitor center provides scenic views. Talks are presented every 15 minutes at the overlook and other locations.

Visitor center daily 9-4:45; closed Thanksgiving and Dec. 25. Last admission is 30 minutes before closing. Overlook closes at 5:30. Admission $10; over 62 and military with ID $8; ages 7-16, $4. Parking $5. AX, MC, VI. Phone (702) 597-5970 or (866) 291-8687.

LAKE MEAD, 110 miles long and averaging 200 feet deep, has a 700-mile shoreline. There are six major recreational centers with marinas and launch facilities.

Films and exhibits about natural and cultural history are offered at the Alan Bible Visitor Center, 4 miles east of Boulder City at US 93 and Lakeshore Road, overlooking Lake Mead. A botanical and cactus garden surrounds the visitor center. Visitor center daily 8:30-4:30; closed Jan. 1, Thanksgiving and Dec. 25. Free. Parking $5. Phone (702) 293-8990. *See Recreation Chart and the AAA California & Nevada CampBook.*

SAVE *Lake Mead Cruises* depart from the Lake Mead Cruises Landing on Lakeshore Rd. (SR 166). Excursion cruises on a paddlewheeler include a narration about area history and the construction of Hoover Dam. Breakfast, dinner, dance and midday sightseeing cruises also are available. Ninety-minute round-trip excursion cruises depart daily at noon, 2 and 4. Fare $20; ages 2-11, $9. Reservations are recommended. AX, DS, MC, VI. Phone (702) 293-6180.

LAKE MOHAVE extends 67 mi. s. from Hoover Dam to Davis Dam. Launching ramps, trailer sites, refreshment concessions, boat rentals and overnight accommodations are available at Katherine Landing, about 35 miles west of Kingman, and at Cottonwood Cove, 14 miles east of Searchlight, Nev. Willow Beach, 28 miles east of Boulder City on US 93, offers a launch ramp and concession facilities. Information regarding recreational facilities is available at all three sites.

LAKE POWELL—
see Glen Canyon National Recreation Area p. 52.

LAKESIDE— *see Pinetop-Lakeside p. 92.*

LITCHFIELD PARK— *see Phoenix p. 86.*

MARICOPA (E-3) pop. 1,040, elev. 1,177′

Prevalent clear blue skies beckon fans of soaring to Maricopa. This area at the foot of the Sierra Estrella Mountains is noted for its thermal conditions. The Estrella Sailport, (520) 568-2318, is on SR 238W.

CASINOS

- **Harrah's Phoenix Ak-Chin Casino**, 1 mi. s. on SR 347 to 15406 Maricopa Rd. Daily 24 hours. Phone (800) 427-7247.

MAYER (D-3) pop. 1,408, elev. 4,402′

ARCOSANTI is off I-17 exit 262, then 2.5 mi. n.e. on a dirt road, following signs; the road may be rough due to weather conditions. The town is architect Paolo Soleri's prototype urban design based on his philosophy of arcology (architecture plus ecology). The town, which will occupy only 25 acres of a 4,000-acre preserve, will be a pedestrian-oriented city with a goal of reducing urban sprawl and its impact on the environment. The area is still in the midst of construction.

Visitor center daily 9-5. One-hour tours are conducted daily on the hour 10-4; closed Jan. 1, Thanksgiving and Dec. 25. Tour $8, under 12 free. Visitor center free. AX, DS, MC, VI. Phone (928) 632-7135.

MCNARY (D-6) pop. 349, elev. 7,309'

RECREATIONAL ACTIVITIES
Skiing

- **Sunrise Ski Area** is 15 mi. e. on SR 260, then 7 mi. s. on SR 273. Write P.O. Box 117, Greer, AZ 85927. Daily 9-4, Dec.-Apr. Hours may vary; phone ahead. Phone (928) 735-7669.

MESA—*see Phoenix p. 87.*

METEOR CRATER—
see Winslow p. 122.

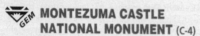
MONTEZUMA CASTLE NATIONAL MONUMENT (C-4)

Off I-17 exit 289 on Montezuma Castle Hwy., Montezuma Castle National Monument contains ruins of an early cliff dwelling. Built in the 12th and 13th centuries, it is among the best preserved dwellings of its type. The foundation is in a vertical cliff 46 feet above the talus slope. The five-story castle, believed to be inhabited by Sinagua Indians, contains 20 rooms and was once accessible only by ladders. Other ruins dot the cliffs and hilltops around Beaver Creek.

As a preservative measure, tours into Montezuma Castle are not allowed, but a self-guiding trail offers good views of the castle and displays a scale model of its interior. The visitor center contains artifacts found in the area. Picnicking is permitted in designated areas. Allow 1 hour minimum. Visitor center and monument open daily 8-6, Memorial Day-Labor Day; 8-5, rest of year. Admission $3, under 16 free. Phone (928) 567-3322.

MONTEZUMA WELL, about 11 mi. n.e., is a detached portion of the monument. The limestone sinkhole, 470 feet wide and 55 feet deep, is rimmed by pueblos and cliff dwellings. A source of water to the fields of ancient peoples, some of the ditches dug A.D. 1200-1300 are still visible. Picnic facilities and a self-guiding trail are available. Allow 1 hour minimum. Daily 8-6, Memorial Day-Labor Day; 8-5, rest of year. Free. Phone (928) 567-5276.

MONUMENT VALLEY NAVAJO TRIBAL PARK (A-5)

Reached via scenic US 163 from Kayenta and from Gouldings and Mexican Hat, Utah, Monument Valley Navajo Tribal Park is a colorful region covering several thousand square miles within the Navajo Indian Reservation. The park contains Mystery Valley, where isolated monoliths of red sandstone tower as much as 1,000 feet above the valley floor.

The visitor center, 4 miles southeast of US 163, provides information about self-guiding tours. Guided tours from the center are offered daily; camping and picnicking are permitted. Horseback and four-wheel-drive trips through Monument Valley can be arranged through agencies in Kayenta and in Utah at Bluff, Mexican Hat and Monument Valley. Overnight accommodations also are available in Gouldings, Kayenta and Mexican Hat; reservations are recommended.

Visitors should not photograph the Navajo people, their homes or their possessions without asking permission; a gratuity is usually requested. Other restrictions apply; *see Fast Facts.* For more information contact Monument Valley Navajo Tribal Park, P.O. Box 360289, Monument Valley, UT 84536.

The park and visitor center are open daily 6 a.m.-8 p.m., May-Sept.; 8-5, rest of year (weather permitting); Thanksgiving 8-noon. Closed Dec. 25. Last admission 30 minutes before closing. **Note:** Recreational vehicles longer than 25 feet are not permitted on self-guiding tour. Admission $5, under 10 free. Phone (435) 727-5870.

MORRISTOWN (H-1) pop. 400, elev. 1,971'

LAKE PLEASANT REGIONAL PARK, 12 mi. e. on SR 74, then 2 mi. n. off Castle Hot Springs Rd., encompasses more than 24,500 acres. A 10-lane boat

ramp and a visitor center are available at the main entrance, and a four-lane ramp is at the north entrance. Books, brochures and exhibits about the Central Arizona Project, Waddell Dam and the lake are offered at the visitor center.

Picnicking is permitted. Camping is available. Admission $5 per private vehicle (additional $2 per watercraft). Camping $10-$18 per private vehicle. Phone (928) 501-1710. *See Recreation Chart.*

Waddell Dam impounds Lake Pleasant. On the Agua Fria River the earthen dam completed in 1992 is 4,700 feet long and 300 feet high.

⬥ NAVAJO NATIONAL MONUMENT (A-4)

Reached via US 160 and a 9-mile paved road (SR 564), Navajo National Monument preserves some of the largest and most intact of Arizona's known cliff dwellings in perhaps the most awe-inspiring area in the Southwest. There are two areas that can be visited by ranger guided tours, each of which contains a remarkable 13th-century Pueblo ruin.

The monument lies within the Navajo Indian Reservation. Traveling off paved roads is not permitted. Most of the unmarked dirt-surfaced roads on the reservation are private driveways; private Navajo property is not open to visitors. Visitors should be aware of certain restrictions; *see Fast Facts.*

Free year-round camping and picnicking are permitted near the monument headquarters. The 41 campsites are available on a first-come first-served basis and are usually filled by dusk during the summer; vehicles must be no longer than 25 feet in length. Accommodations are available at Kayenta; reservations are recommended. Gas and grocery services are not available in the park; the nearest services are 9 miles south at the junction of SR 564 and US 160.

Note: In summer the Navajo Reservation observes daylight-saving time, which is an hour later than outside the reservation.

At an elevation of approximately 7,300 feet, the visitor center at the monument headquarters offers exhibits of ancestral Native American artifacts, a 20-minute videotape tour of the Betatakin ruins, a 25-minute videotape about the prehistoric culture and summer campfire programs. Check for fire restrictions at the campgrounds. Visitor center open daily 8-7, Memorial Day-Labor Day; 8-5, rest of year. Closed Jan. 1, Thanksgiving and Dec. 25. Free. Phone (928) 672-2700.

BETATAKIN AREA is 2.5 mi. from monument headquarters by way of a strenuous 5-mi. round-trip trail. This is the monument's most accessible area and is home to its headquarters. Rangers guide tours daily at 8:30 and 11:30 from Memorial Day through Labor Day (weather permitting). Hikers should arrive early to ensure a spot; this popular tour is limited to 25 people per day on a first-come, first-served basis. The cliff dwelling also can be viewed across the canyon from the end of the Sandal Trail year-round via a 1-mile round-trip self-guiding walk.

Note: Sturdy shoes and 2 quarts of water are recommended; the high altitude, heat and steep grade of the trail make good physical condition a requirement. Daily 8-5. For information and schedule updates phone (928) 672-2700.

KEET SEEL AREA is accessible by hiking a difficult 17-mi. round-trip trail. The area contains the largest and best-preserved cliff dwellings in the vicinity, which date 1250-1300. To protect these fragile ruins there is a daily limit of 20 people.

Note: This trip is not recommended for inexperienced hikers. Hikers are required to attend a trail briefing to receive a permit and are advised to bring sufficient bottled water. Primitive campgrounds are available for hikers. Trail open Memorial Day-Labor Day. Schedules for tours of the ruins vary. Free. Check with rangers at the visitor center for reservations; they can and should be made within 5 months of the date of the trip and be confirmed 1 week prior. Reservations are required. For reservations, information and schedule updates phone (928) 672-2700.

NAVAJOLAND (A-5)

Encompassing some 27,000 square miles, Navajoland includes parts of Arizona, Utah and New Mexico. Larger than the state of West Virginia, the sovereign nation is the largest Native American nation in the country.

From the stark monoliths of Monument Valley Navajo Tribal Park *(see place listing p. 64)* and the sheer walls of Canyon de Chelly National Monument *(see place listing p. 43)* to the ancient ruins of Navajo National Monument *(see place listing p. 65),* Navajoland is home to more than a dozen national monuments. The area also contains the Petrified Forest National Park *(see place listing p. 70),* 186-mile-long Lake Powell and various tribal parks and historic sites.

Heritage is important to the Navajo, and singing and dancing give the Navajo a chance to wear their traditional attire. Tribal dress includes knee-high moccasins, velvet vests, concho belts and silver and turquoise jewelry for both men and women. Powwows often are performed throughout the Navajo nation and visitors are invited to observe.

The Navajo, or Dineh, consider themselves an extension of Mother Earth and therefore treat nature with great respect. Not only rich in culture, the Navajo live in an area rich in minerals; oil, gas, coal and uranium lie beneath the arid desert. The discovery of oil in the 1920s prompted the Navajo to form their own tribal government to help handle the encroachment of mining companies.

Reorganized in 1991, the Navajo government consists of an elected president, vice president and 88 council delegates representing 110 local units of government. Council meetings take place four times a year in Window Rock *(see place listing p. 122);* visitors are welcome.

Tradition also can be seen in the Navajo's arts and crafts. Famous for their distinct style of rugs and blankets, the Navajo also are excellent silversmiths, sandpainters and basketweavers. Visitors to the area can purchase Navajo wares at various shops throughout the area.

The following places in Navajoland are listed separately under their individual names: Fort Defiance, Ganado, Kayenta, Keams Canyon, Page, Second Mesa, Tuba City and Window Rock. Visitors should be aware of certain restrictions while in Navajoland; *see Fast Facts.*

Navajo Tourism Department—Navajoland: P.O. Box 663, Window Rock, AZ 86515; phone (928) 871-7371.

NOGALES (G-5) pop. 20,878, elev. 3,865'

Nogales (noh-GAH-lehs) is rich in Spanish history; Franciscan missionary Fray Marcos de Niza entered Santa Cruz County as early as 1539.

Mexico's Pacific Highway, a four-lane divided highway, starts in Nogales and continues through Guadalajara, Mexico, with connecting roads to Mexico City. Nogales is a popular port of entry for U.S. travelers as well as for more than 75 percent of winter fruits and vegetables shipped throughout the United States and Canada. Retail and wholesale trade with Northern Mexico also is an important industry in the town.

Nogales-Santa Cruz Chamber of Commerce: 123 W. Kino Park Pl., Nogales, AZ 85621; phone (520) 287-3685.

WINERIES

- **Arizona Vineyards**, 3 mi. e. on SR 82. Daily 10-6; closed Dec. 25. Phone (520) 287-7972.

Nogales, Mexico

Nogales, Mexico, is just across the international border from Nogales, Ariz. U.S. and Canadian visitors must carry proof of citizenship; a valid U.S. or Canadian passport is the most convenient, since it serves as a photo ID and facilitates many transactions such as cashing traveler's checks. The U.S., Canadian and Mexican governments also recognize a birth certificate (must be a certified copy from the government agency that issued it). A driver's license or baptismal certificate is *not* proof of citizenship.

The Mexican government charges a 195-peso (approximately $20 U.S.) tourist entry fee for each visitor entering Mexico for pleasure or business. The

fee must be paid in order to have your tourist permit validated if you plan to remain anywhere in Mexico for more than 72 hours, or stay less than 72 hours and travel beyond the 12-mile (20-kilometer) border zone.

A government-issued tourist permit (actually a form) is available upon presentation of proof of citizenship from Mexican consulates in the United States and Canada or immigration offices at official points of entry. Before driving into Mexico check with a AAA office for information about documentation and insurance requirements. Mexican and U.S. Customs offices are open daily 24 hours.

With several good restaurants and an array of shops selling everything from cheap curios to high-quality handicrafts, Nogales is a popular day-trip destination. Since almost all of the tourist-oriented shopping is within easy walking distance of the border, it is easiest to park on the Arizona side and head into Mexico on foot. From the Nogales, Ariz., Chamber of Commerce, just off the intersection of Grand Avenue and US 82, it's about a 1.5-mile drive south to a series of guarded lots; the parking fee is $4. The turnstiles to Mexico are at the foot of the port of entry.

The shops and markets catering to tourists are concentrated near the border along Avenida Obregón. They offer pottery, baskets, leather goods, glassware, furniture, rugs, jewelry and more. Most business is conducted in English; bargaining is acceptable and even expected and American currency is preferred. The more exclusive establishments carry crafts and items from all over Mexico. When buying at stalls or from street vendors, always check for quality.

OAK CREEK CANYON—
see Sedona p. 100.

ORACLE— *see Tucson p. 117.*

ORAIBI— *see Keams Canyon p. 61.*

ORGAN PIPE CACTUS NATIONAL MONUMENT (F-2)

In southwestern Arizona, Organ Pipe Cactus National Monument preserves a diverse and relatively undisturbed sample of the Sonoran Desert of particular interest to desert aficionados. The organ pipe cactus thrives within the United States primarily in this 516-square-mile preserve. The spectacular saguaro cactuses, along with the paloverde, ironwood and ocotillo, also contribute to the desert landscape.

The monument contains a graded dirt park road: the 21-mile Ajo Mountain Drive. The scenic drive begins near the visitor center, and conditions are generally good for car travel. The drive is closed occasionally because of adverse weather conditions or construction; phone ahead. No trailers or recreational vehicles over 25 feet are permitted on this park road.

Cactus

An indelible symbol of the Great American Desert, the cactus embodies the evolutionary theory of survival of the fittest. Withering to most other plant life, the desert brings out the best in cactuses. Their brilliantly colored blossoms all but vanquish any image of the desert as a drab and barren place.

A type of succulent, cactuses can live for long periods without water. Their stems act as storage chambers for the precious rainwater absorbed by their shallow roots. The thorny spines that adorn most species are actually highly modified leaves, trimmed down to prevent transpiration. These spines also shield the plants

Digital Archives

from wildlife, especially non-native cattle that have all but wiped out smooth-textured varieties.

Sadly, the cactus' needles are no match for the threats posed by encroaching civilization. Research teams at the University of Arizona seek means to control decay caused by disease, worms and pollution. Greatly diminished populations of coyote and other predators have led to an overabundance of desert rodents, which feed on and nest in cactuses, often causing irreparable damage.

Because cactuses have become increasingly popular houseplants, poaching has become a serious problem. State laws now impose heavy fines on those who willfully damage or attempt to remove free-growing specimens. The federal government has set aside large portions of the Sonoran Desert as the Organ Pipe Cactus National Monument *(see place listing p. 67)* and Saguaro National Park *(see place listing p. 117).*

The visitor center, 17 miles south of the park entrance on scenic SR 85, is open daily 8-5; closed Memorial Day, July 4, Labor Day and Dec. 25. Exhibits interpret the flora, fauna and cultural history of the monument. A 15-minute introductory slide program is shown upon request. Self-guiding interpretive trails are near the visitor center and the campground area. The campground ($12 per night) and back-country primitive camping are available to those with permits, which are distributed at the visitor center.

Admission $8 per private vehicle. For further information contact the Superintendent, Organ Pipe Cactus National Monument, 10 Organ Pipe Dr., Ajo, AZ 85321; phone (520) 387-6849. *See the AAA Southwestern CampBook.*

PAGE (A-4) pop. 6,809, elev. 4,281'

Established to provide housing and facilities for workers on the Glen Canyon Dam project, Page was named for John Chatfield Page, the commissioner of reclamation who devoted many years to the development of the upper Colorado River. The town is a center for outfitters who provide trips into the Glen Canyon National Recreation Area *(see place listing p. 52).*

Scenic flights over Lake Powell and the surrounding Navajo country as well as to the Grand Canyon depart from the Page airport. Lake Powell boat trips and Glen Canyon raft trips can be arranged through the chamber of commerce.

Page-Lake Powell Chamber of Commerce: 608 Elm St., Suite C, P.O. Box 727, Page, AZ 86040; phone (928) 645-2741.

ANTELOPE CANYON NAVAJO TRIBAL PARK, 1 mi. e. on SR 98, comprises two slot canyons with graceful, swirling red sandstone canyon walls carved by wind and rain over thousands of years. Visitors are driven 3.5 miles to the canyons and must tour the canyons with a licensed guide. Access to Lower Antelope Canyon requires a climb down ladders bolted to the canyon walls. On the Upper Antelope Canyon tour visitors walk right into the canyon.

Allow 1 hour minimum. Daily 8-5. May-Oct. Park admission $6, under 8 free. Guided tour fees vary; phone ahead. Phone (928) 698-2808.

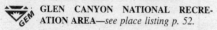 **GLEN CANYON NATIONAL RECREATION AREA**—*see place listing p. 52.*

JOHN WESLEY POWELL MUSEUM AND VISITOR INFORMATION CENTER, Lake Powell Blvd. and N. Navajo Dr., contains exhibits relating to area development, Native American culture, geology, paleontology, the Colorado River and John Wesley Powell, the river's first modern scientist-explorer. The museum staff can book Lake Powell, Colorado River and scenic air tours.

Nearby slot canyons may be viewed by guided tours only; tickets are available at the museum. Mon.-Fri. 9-5, mid-Feb. to mid-Dec.; closed

Thanksgiving. Admission $5; over 61, $3; ages 5-12, $1. Phone (928) 645-9496 or (888) 597-6873 to confirm hours or make bus reservations.

NAVAJO VILLAGE is at 1253 Coppermine Rd. Guests experience the Navajo culture and lifestyle in a traditional village. Navajo artisans such as silversmiths, rug weavers, potters and basket weavers may be seen. The 4-hour Grand Tour includes an indepth cultural presentation, dinner, Native American dances and campfire stories. The 2-hour Mini Tour includes a brief cultural presentation, dances and campfire stories; dinner is optional.

Food is available. Allow 2 hours minimum. Mon.-Sat. 9-4, Apr.-Oct. Grand Tour is offered at 4. Mini Tour is offered at 5 and 6. Grand Tour $49.95; ages 6-12, $34.95. Mini Tour with dinner $34.95; ages 6-12, $24.95. Mini Tour without dinner $29.95; ages 6-12, $19.95. MC, VI. Phone (928) 660-0304.

◥ GEM PAINTED DESERT—
see Petrified Forest National Park p. 71.

PARADISE VALLEY—*see Phoenix p. 88.*

PARKER (D-2) pop. 3,140, elev. 1,642'

Parker, founded in 1908, was named for Ely Parker, the first Native American commissioner for the U.S. government. The city originally was located south of its current location but was moved to accommodate the Santa Fe Railroad. Parker is a trade center for the surrounding Native American communities and a water recreation destination attracting nearly 1 million visitors each year.

The Parker Dam and Power Plant, 17 miles north on SR 95, is considered the world's deepest because 65 percent of its structural height is below the riverbed. Overlooks on top of the dam provide views of Lake Havasu and the Colorado River. Just north of town on SR 95 is La Paz County Park *(see Recreation Chart).*

Parker Area Chamber of Commerce: 1217 California Ave., Parker, AZ 85344; phone (928) 669-2174.

BILL WILLIAMS RIVER NATIONAL WILDLIFE REFUGE is off SR 95 (between Mileposts 160 and 161) at the delta of the Bill Williams River at its confluence with the Colorado River. A 9-mile corridor along the river encompasses desert riparian and upland habitat. Named after a trapper who explored the area in the 1800s, the 6,000-acre refuge preserves some of the last remaining riparian habitat in the Lower Colorado River Valley.

The refuge is home to beavers, bobcats, foxes, mule deer, bighorn sheep, raccoons and 342 species of birds. Fishing and limited hunting are permitted (in season). Camping is prohibited. Office open Mon.-Fri. 8-4. Free. Phone (928) 667-4144.

BUCKSKIN MOUNTAIN STATE PARK & RIVER ISLAND UNIT, 11 mi. n. off SR 95, is the state's "water playground" on the Colorado River. Activities include hiking, swimming, boating and fishing.

The island unit is 1 mile north of the park. Food is available. Daily 8 a.m.-10 p.m. Admission $8 per private vehicle. Camping $20-$23 per private vehicle. Phone (928) 667-3231. *See Recreation Chart.*

COLORADO RIVER INDIAN TRIBES MUSEUM AND LIBRARY is 2 mi. s. via SR 95 at 2nd Ave. and Mohave Rd. The museum houses the Beebee Brown Basket Collection, excavations from the restoration of the nearby ghost town of La Paz, and historical and modern material about local tribes. The adjacent library contains books, original manuscripts, records and tapes pertaining to various Native American cultures. Mon.-Fri. 8-noon and 1-5; closed holidays. Donations. Phone (928) 669-1335.

PATAGONIA (G-5) pop. 881, elev. 4,057′

PATAGONIA LAKE STATE PARK, 7 mi. s.w. on SR 82, then 4 mi. w. following signs, is home to southeastern Arizona's largest lake. Bird-watching is a popular activity. Pontoon boat tours are available early October through April.

Boating, fishing, camping and swimming are available. Food and gas are available. Daily 8 a.m.-10 p.m. (opens at 4 a.m. for fishing). Admission $8 per private vehicle (up to four passengers, plus $2 for each additional adult passenger) Sat.-Sun. and holidays, Memorial Day-Labor Day. Admission rest of year $7 per private vehicle. Camping $15-$22 per private vehicle. Phone (520) 287-6965, (520) 287-5545, or (520) 828-2791 for pontoon tour information. *See Recreation Chart.*

PATAGONIA-SONOITA CREEK PRESERVE, w. off SR 82 onto 4th St., then 1.7 mi. s. on Pennsylvania Ave., is home to many species of birds as well as mountain lions, bobcats, deer, javelinas, coyotes, turtles and rattlesnakes. The preserve also protects the cottonwood-willow riparian forest containing some of the largest and oldest Fremont cottonwood trees in the world. A self-guiding nature trail and a visitor center are available. Wed.-Sun. 7:30-4; closed Jan. 1, first 2 weeks in July, Thanksgiving and Dec. 25. Guided walks Sat. at 9. Admission $5; under 16 free. Phone (520) 394-2400.

PAYSON (D-4) pop. 13,620, elev. 4,887′

Known by such names as Green Valley, Long Valley, Big Valley and Union City, Payson was first settled by prospectors who came to the area seeking wealth. Payson's mines produced little, and cattle and lumber soon became the community's livelihood. With the help of Senator Payson of Chicago, the early residents helped establish a post office and named it and the town in his honor.

Surrounded by the lakes and dense woodlands of Tonto National Forest *(see place listing p. 104)* and the nearby Mogollon Rim, Payson has become a convenient getaway for visitors, with Phoenix only 90 minutes away.

Rim Country Regional Chamber of Commerce: 100 W. Main St., P.O. Box 1380, Payson, AZ 85547; phone (928) 474-4515 or (800) 672-9766.

Dust Storms

Dust storms can strike without warning and make driving conditions hazardous. Reddish-brown walls of dust can seriously limit a driver's view. Areas especially prone to storms include I-10 between Phoenix and Tucson and I-8 from Gila Bend to Casa Grande. Dust storm alert signs with changeable messages are posted along I-10 and I-8. During normal driving conditions the signs contain directional information. The message "Dust Storm Alert" appears, however, when dust activity is detected in the area.

Digital Archives

Storm warnings also are issued on radio stations KOY (550 AM), KTAR (620 AM) and KFYI (910 AM).

Dust storms usually last only a few minutes, but drivers should follow established procedures to reduce the possibility of accident or injury.

If a dense dust cloud is observed, do not enter the area. Pull off the roadway as far as possible, stop, turn any lights off and set the emergency brake. Make sure your foot does not rest on the brake pedal when you are stopped—other cars will follow your brake lights thinking that you are moving and an accident could ensue. If the car is engulfed on the roadway, do not stop on the pavement, but instead try to pull the car off the roadway as far as possible. If conditions prevent pulling off the roadway, proceed at a slow speed with the lights on, using the center line as a guide. Under no circumstances should a motorist stop on the roadway.

MUSEUM OF RIM COUNTRY ARCHAEOLOGY is .5 mi. w. from jct. SR 87 at 510 W. Main St. Exhibits pertain to archeology and its relationship to other sciences such as astronomy, botany and paleontology. Petroglyphs, pottery, ancient tools and a ceremonial room provide a glimpse into the culture of the Native Americans who lived in the Rim Country hundreds of years ago.

Allow 30 minutes minimum. Wed.-Sun. noon-4; closed Jan. 1, Thanksgiving and Dec. 25. Admission $2.50; over 54, $2; ages 12-17, $1.50. A combination ticket is available with the Rim Country Museum. AX, DS, MC, VI. Phone (928) 468-1128.

RIM COUNTRY MUSEUM, 1 mi. w. on Main St. from jct. SR 87, then just n. to 700 Green Valley Pkwy., is comprised of several historic structures. A replica of the turn-of-the-20th-century Herron Hotel contains exhibits about the ancient cultures that developed around the Mogollon Rim as well as a 1908 kitchen and blacksmith shop. Payson's original forest ranger's station and residence, built in 1907, depict the life of the forest ranger. Firefighting equipment and a fire truck also are featured.

Picnicking is permitted. Allow 30 minutes minimum. Wed.-Sun. noon-4; closed Jan. 1, Thanksgiving and Dec. 25. Admission $3; over 54, $2.50; ages 13-17, $2. A combination ticket is available with the Museum of Rim Country Archaeology. AX, DS, MC, VI. Phone (928) 474-3483.

TONTO NATURAL BRIDGE STATE PARK, 3 mi. n.w. off SR 87, is bordered by Tonto National Forest. The bridge, among the world's largest natural travertine structures, reaches a height of 183 feet; the opening beneath is 150 feet wide and 400 feet long. A historic lodge (not available for overnight stays) is furnished with antiques that were lowered into the canyon using ropes and mules.

Note: The trail from the top of the bridge into the canyon below is steep and difficult for many persons to negotiate. Pets are not permitted on canyon trails. Daily 8-7, Memorial Day-Labor Day; 8-6, Apr. 1-day before Memorial Day and day after Labor Day-Oct. 31; 9-5, rest of year. Closed Dec. 25. Last admission 1 hour before closing. Admission $3, children under 14 free with adult. Rates may vary; phone ahead. Phone (928) 476-4202. *See Recreation Chart.*

CASINOS

- **Mazatzal Casino**, .5 mi. s. on SR 87 (Beeline Hwy.) at Milepost 251. Daily 24 hours. Phone (928) 474-6044 or (800) 777-7529.

PEACH SPRINGS (B-2)
pop. 600, elev. 4,788′

Peach Springs is the trading center and headquarters for the Hualapai Indian Reservation, which covers nearly a million acres between the town and the Colorado River. The town also serves as the transportation corridor to the western parts of Grand

Canyon National Park *(see place listing p. 53).* Fishing is allowed on the river and at small ponds on the reservation. Primitive camping also is available.

GRAND CANYON CAVERNS, 12 mi. e. on SR 66, is reached by a 21-story elevator descent. The temperature is 56 degrees Fahrenheit throughout the year. Nearly a mile of lighted trails highlights colorful mineral formations. A tour by flashlight is offered. An abbreviated tour is available for the physically impaired. Food is available. Daily 9-6, Memorial Day-Labor Day; 9-5, rest of year. Closed Dec. 25. Admission $12.95; under 13, $9.95. Flashlight tour $14.95; under 12, $11.95. AX, DS, MC, VI. Phone (928) 422-3223.

PEARCE (F-6) elev. 4,400′

Pearce at the end of the 19th century was a booming mining town. Following the gold strike by John Pearce in 1894 people swarmed to the area, all but depopulating nearby Tombstone, whose mines were no longer productive. The Commonwealth Mine, Pearce's claim, maintained full operation until 1904, when an impeding water level and a cave-in reduced activities. It was worked sporadically until the late 1930s.

Pearce-Sunsites Chamber of Commerce: 133 Frontage Rd., P.O. Box 308, Pearce, AZ 85625; phone (520) 826-3535.

PEORIA — *see Phoenix p. 88.*

◆◆ PETRIFIED FOREST NATIONAL PARK (C-6)

Elevations in the park range from 5,300 ft. at the Puerco River to 6,235 ft. at Pilot Rock. Refer to AAA maps for additional elevation information.

East of Holbrook, Petrified Forest National Park contains an abundance of petrified logs. Most of the brilliantly colored trees in the 93,533-acre park are prone, and many are in fragments. Early dinosaurs and other reptiles once roamed the area, and numerous fossil bones and fossil plants have been discovered in the park.

About 225 million years ago trees clinging to eroding riverbanks fell into streams and were carried to this wet, swampy lowland. The trees were submerged in water and buried under volcanic ash sediments rich in silica; a replacement process began to take place. Silica replaced the wood until the logs were virtually turned to stone. Iron oxide and other minerals stained the silica to produce rainbow colors.

Later the region was uplifted, and erosion exposed part of the logs; many remain buried to a depth of 300 feet. There are five areas with heavy concentrations of petrified wood in the park: Blue Mesa, Jasper Forest, Crystal Forest, Rainbow Forest (comprising Long Logs and Giant Logs near US 180) and Black Forest. The first four are accessible by the park road. Black Forest, in a designated wilderness area, can be reached from the parking lot at

Kachina Point, down a switchback unimproved trail to the desert floor. The Rainbow Forest area contains the most colorful concentration of petrified wood.

General Information and Activities

The park is open daily 8-5; closed Dec. 25. Hours may be extended May-Sept. Phone to confirm schedule.

The 28-mile drive through the park offers breathtaking views from Pintado Point and Kachina Point. Other scenic overlooks include Nizhoni, Tawa, Tiponi and Whipple points.

Westbound motorists on I-40 should use the northern entrance to avoid backtracking. Visitors can view the Painted Desert *(see attraction listing)*, ancient pueblos and petroglyphs, petrified log deposits and the Rainbow Forest Museum *(see attraction listing)*. Motorists should exit on US 180 and continue west to Holbrook. Eastbound motorists can use the southern (Rainbow Forest) entrance off US 180, 19 miles from Holbrook, to see the same attractions in reverse order, then exit onto I-40 east. Allow 2 hours minimum.

Within the park it is unlawful to gather plants, sand, rocks or specimens of petrified wood of any size whatsoever; archeological material is likewise protected. Violations are punishable by heavy fines and imprisonment. Curio stores sell a variety of polished specimens collected from privately owned land outside the park.

There are no overnight accommodations in the park; backpack camping is allowed by permit only for hikers staying overnight in the Painted Desert wilderness area. Picnic sites are near the Rainbow Forest Museum and on the Painted Desert rim at Chinde Point. Gas, oil and food services are available next to the Painted Desert Visitor Center. *See Recreation Chart.*

ADMISSION to the park is $10 per private vehicle, $5 per person arriving by other means.

PETS are permitted in the park only if they are leashed, crated or otherwise physically restricted at all times. Pets are excluded entirely from back-country buildings and wilderness areas.

ADDRESS inquiries to the Superintendent, Petrified Forest National Park, P.O. Box 2217, Petrified Forest National Park, AZ 86028; phone (928) 524-6228.

Points of Interest

AGATE BRIDGE is a petrified log that spans a 40-foot-wide ravine; 111 feet of the concrete-supported log are exposed.

NEWSPAPER ROCK bears prehistoric petroglyphs that can be viewed through spotting scopes from an overlook. Access is via a short side road 1 mile south of Puerco Pueblo.

 PAINTED DESERT, partially contained in the northern part of the park, is an area of badlands that displays a variety of hues. Covered by a soft layer of earth, the desert's colorful erosion effects were created over the eons by mineralized water flows and mineral deposits. Overlooks with an especially scenic view include Chinde Point, Kachina Point, Pintado Point, Tawa Point and Tiponi Point. The Painted Desert Visitor Center, open during park hours, offers a 20-minute film every 30 minutes that explains how wood is petrified. Free. Phone (928) 524-6228.

PUERCO PUEBLO, s. of the Puerco River, is the remains of an ancient Indian pueblo. It was abandoned more than 6 centuries ago. Petroglyphs can be seen along a short trail; a spiral petroglyph is interpreted by a park ranger during summer solstice in June.

RAINBOW FOREST MUSEUM, near the s. entrance, contains polished petrified wood, fossil leaves, fossil casts and exhibits telling the story of the early dinosaurs and the petrified forest. Allow 30 minutes minimum. Daily 8-5; hours may be extended May-Sept. Free. Phone (928) 524-6822 or (928) 524-6823.

Phoenix

City Population: 1,321,045 Elevation: 1,092 ft.

Editor's Picks:

Arizona Capitol Museum........... *(see p. 73)*
Desert Botanical Garden .... *(see p. 80)*
Heard Museum...................... *(see p. 79)*

© Gibson Stock Photography

Bold and sophisticated, vigorous and vital, a medley of Mexican-American, Native American and American West cultures, home of the cowboy and the cosmopolitan, cultural and industrial center of the new Southwest—Phoenix generates the spirit of its heritage.

Scientific discoveries and tribal legends indicate that prehistoric Hohokam Indians mastered the Salt River Valley desert by building irrigation ditches, and then mysteriously disappeared about 1450. On the ancient Hohokam site John Smith established a hay camp in 1864 and contracted to supply forage to Camp McDowell, an Army outpost 30 miles away. During this time the name Phoenix was suggested, as a new city could be expected to rise from the remnants of the vanished civilization, just as the mythical phoenix rose from its own ashes.

By 1879 the village was the supply point for the north-central Arizona Territory, with its rich mining districts and hundreds of prospectors. Stagecoaches began to roll in; saloons and gambling palaces sprang up; soldiers, miners and cowboys frequented the town; and outlawry was rampant. The 1800s ended abruptly with two public hangings in an attempt to regain law and order in this raucous, rapidly growing frontier town.

In the 20th century four milestones marked Phoenix's rapid progress. In 1911 the Roosevelt Dam on the Salt River was completed, converting d¹esert into farmland and supplying power for industrial development. In 1926 population growth received its first great impetus when the Southern Pacific Railroad connected Phoenix with the East, enabling the less adventurous to journey west in relative comfort and safety.

The advent of air conditioning catalyzed industrial growth and brought even more people. Finally, water supplied by the Central Arizona Project's system of aqueducts spurred the tremendous growth that has made Phoenix the country's sixth largest city.

Phoenix is the thriving capital of Arizona. Countless suburbs, sprawling shopping centers and rambling ranch-style homes retain a Western look, while high-rise office buildings stand as gleaming symbols of Eastern influence. Spanish Colonial and Native American pueblo architecture add color and variety.

The city displays enthusiasm and pride in the many athletic and cultural activities it supports. The arts are pursued at excellent theaters, numerous museums, and lectures at colleges and universities. The Civic Plaza downtown houses a state-of-the-art convention center and a symphony hall. Greyhound races, horse races, golf tournaments and rodeos add to the city's entertainment scene.

Phoenix is an agricultural, industrial and service center. Cotton as well as dates, olives, citrus and other subtropical fruits and vegetables are grown in the area. The dry climate and natural beauty have attracted companies in the fields of electronics, high-tech research and development, communications and aerospace; tourism also is big business, with an increasing number of visitors enjoying the city's quality of life.

Getting There — *starting on p. 73*

Getting Around — *starting on p. 73*

What To See — *starting on p. 73*

What To Do — *starting on p. 78*

Where To Stay — *starting on p. 276*

Where To Dine — *starting on p. 284*

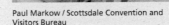
Paul Markow / Scottsdale Convention and
Visitors Bureau

Getting There

By Car

Major highways make Phoenix readily accessible from all directions. The main route from Flagstaff and other points north is I-17, while the main route from the south and southeast is I-10. US 60, coming from the east, joins I-10 just north of Baseline Road.

In Phoenix I-10 intersects I-17 at 20th Street and leads west to Los Angeles. West of Phoenix, SR 85 intersects with I-10 and continues south to Gila Bend; I-8 can then be followed to Yuma and San Diego.

Getting Around

Street System

The streets in Phoenix form an orderly grid. Numbered streets run north and south, intersected by named streets going east and west. The axis is formed by Washington Street, which divides the city north and south, and Central Avenue, which determines the east and west sections. All avenues run west of Central; all streets, east.

Unless otherwise posted the speed limit on most streets is 25 mph. A right turn on red after a complete stop is legal unless otherwise posted. During rush hours the center turn lanes of 7th Avenue and 7th Street are reverse traffic flow lanes: morning rush hour one way into the city and evening rush hour one way out of the city. Try to avoid rush hours, 7-9 a.m. and 4-6 p.m.

Parking

Parking is regulated by meters. During business hours and in the downtown area certain one-way streets have restricted parking hours. Rates at public lots start at $1.50 per hour.

What To See

ARIZONA MINING AND MINERAL MUSEUM, 1502 W. Washington St., displays more than 3,000 specimens, including industrial minerals, gemstones, copper and other ores found in Arizona, as well as a small collection of mining equipment. Mon.-Fri. 8-5, Sat. 11-4; closed state holidays. Admission $2, under 18 free. Phone (602) 255-3791 for the Department of Mines and Minerals.

ARIZONA CAPITOL MUSEUM is in the Arizona Capitol building at 1700 W. Washington St. The Capitol is built of tuff stone from Kirkland Junction and granite from the Salt River Mountains. Opened in 1900, the four-story building served as the territorial capitol until statehood came in 1912; it then became the state capitol.

The restored wings feature artifacts and documents of early Arizona; political memorabilia; the

Destination Phoenix

© Mark Gibson
Index Stock

Basking in sunshine more than 300 days a year, sprawling Phoenix is centered within the aptly named Valley of the Sun.

Although renowned for its warm, dry climate, Arizona's capital city offers much more than great weather. Phoenix, one of the 10 largest urban areas in America, abounds with museums, art galleries and theaters.

Phoenix Museum of History.
Exhibits reveal how Phoenix developed into a modern metropolis. (See listing page 79)

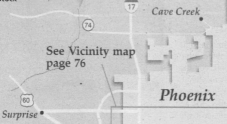

Desert Botanical Garden, Phoenix.
Meander through gardens containing desert plants from around the globe, including succulents, wildflowers, vegetables and herbs. (See listing page 80)

© SuperStock

Greater Phoenix CVB

Rosson House, Phoenix.
This 10-room Victorian home contains all the accoutrements of an upperclass Phoenix family circa 1895. (See listing page 80)

See Vicinity map
page 76

Cave Creek

Phoenix

Surprise

Sun City/
Sun City West
Peoria

Glendale

Litchfield
Park

Goodyear

See Downtown
map page 77

Tempe

Mesa

Fountain
Hills

Paradise Valley

Scottsdale

Apache
Junction

Phoenix Zoo.
More than 1,300 creatures from Africa and Arizona prowl through four natural environments. (See listing page 80)

Chandler

Places included in this AAA Destination City:

© Phoenix Zoo

The Informed Traveler

Sales Tax: Arizona's statewide sales tax is 5.6 percent; an additional 1.8 percent is added in Maricopa County. There is a hotel/motel tax of 10.35 percent. Rental cars incur a 13.8 percent tax, plus a 10 percent concession fee.

WHOM TO CALL

Emergency: 911

Police (non-emergency): (602) 262-6151

Time and Weather: (602) 265-5550

Hospitals: Banner Good Samaritan Medical Center, (602) 239-2000; St. Joseph's Hospital and Medical Center, (602) 406-3000.

WHERE TO LOOK

Newspapers

The city's daily newspaper is the *Arizona Republic,* published in the morning.

Radio

Phoenix radio station KTAR (620 AM) is an all-news/weather station; KJZZ (91.5 FM) is a member of National Public Radio.

Visitor Information

Greater Phoenix Convention and Visitors Bureau Downtown Visitor Information Center: 50 N. 2nd St., Phoenix, AZ 85004; phone (602) 254-6500 or (877) 225-5749.

Greater Phoenix Convention and Visitors Bureau Biltmore Fashion Park Visitor Information Center: 2404 E. Camelback Rd., Phoenix, AZ 85016; phone (602) 254-6500 or (877) 225-5749.

Both Greater Phoenix Convention and Visitors Bureau offices distribute the helpful *Greater Phoenix Explorer/Visitors Guide* and *Greater Phoenix Dining Guide.*

TRANSPORTATION

Air Travel

Sky Harbor International Airport, 4 miles southeast of downtown, is served by major airlines. SuperShuttle is a 24-hour shared-ride service; phone (602) 244-9000 in metro Phoenix, or (800) 258-3826 outside Arizona. Execu-Car also is available from SuperShuttle; phone (602) 232-4630 or (888) 473-9227.

Airport limousine service, independent of the hotels, costs $60-$150. Some companies that serve the airport and certain downtown hotels are Arizona Limousines, (602) 267-7097 or (800) 678-0033; Carey Limousine, (602) 996-1955 or (800) 336-4646; and Desert Rose Limousine Service, (623) 780-0159 or (800) 716-8660. Cab service to downtown averages 30 minutes and costs an average of $30.

Rental Cars

Several rental car companies serve the Phoenix metropolitan area. Located at the airport, Hertz, (602) 267-8822 or (800) 654-3080, offers discounts to AAA members. Check the telephone directory for additional listings.

Buses

Greyhound Lines Inc. has terminals at 2115 Buckeye Rd., (602) 389-4200, and 2647 W. Glendale Ave., (602) 246-4341, (800) 231-2222, or (800) 531-5332 (Spanish).

Taxis

Taxi companies serving the greater Phoenix area are Express Transportation, (480) 994-1616, and Yellow Cab, (602) 252-5071.

Public Transport

Phoenix Transit System buses serve Glendale, Mesa, Phoenix, Scottsdale and Tempe. Most routes operate 6 a.m.-6:30 p.m. The Bus Book, which outlines available routes, can be obtained at Phoenix metropolitan libraries.

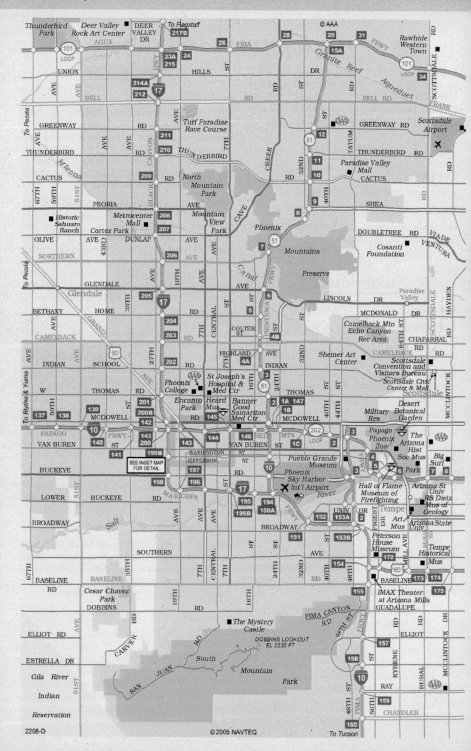

© 2005 NAVTEQ

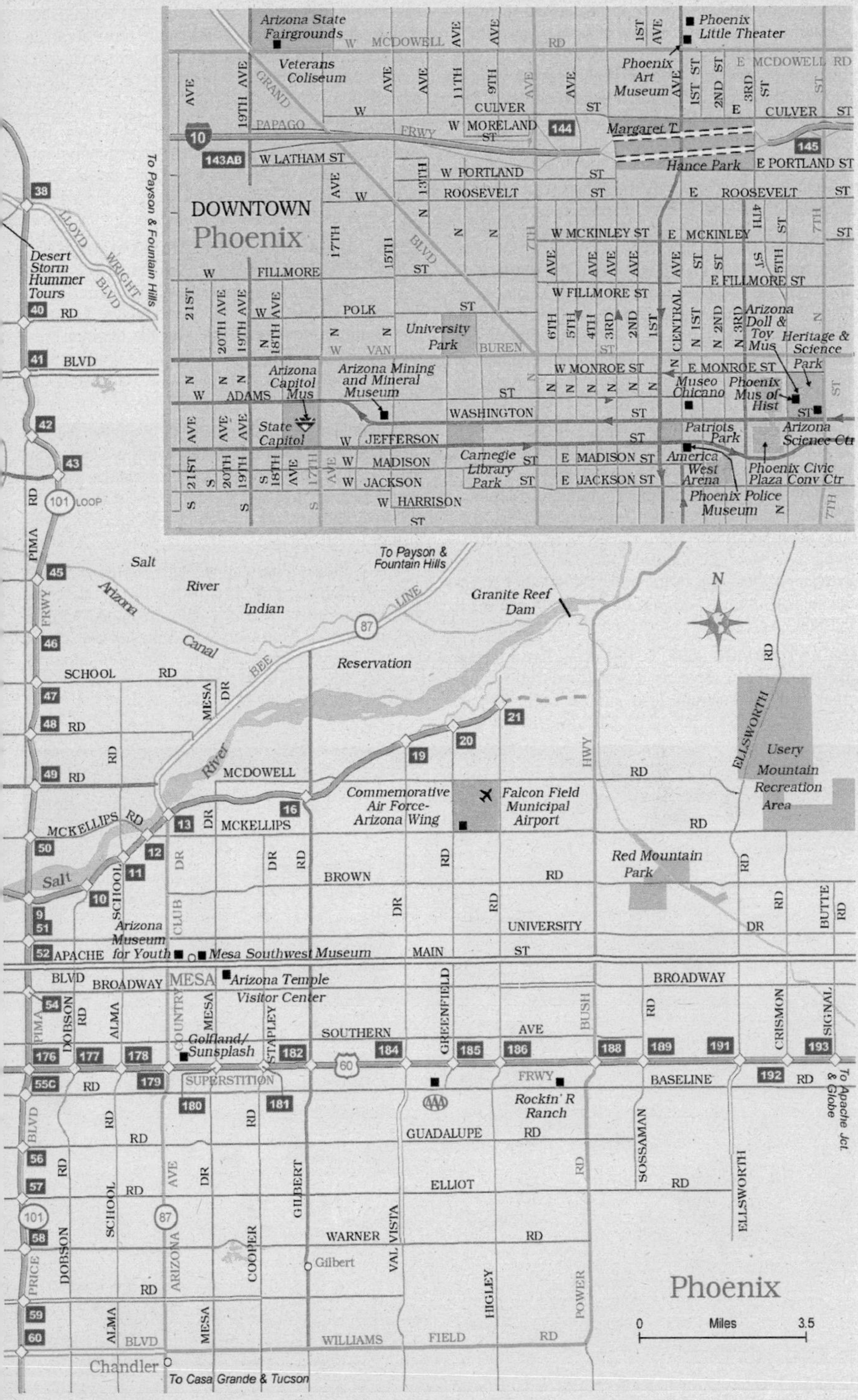

DOWNTOWN Phoenix

Arizona State Fairgrounds

Veterans Coliseum

Phoenix Little Theater

Phoenix Art Museum

W MCDOWELL AVE
E MCDOWELL RD

GRAND AVE
PAPAGO FRWY
W MORELAND ST
CULVER ST
E CULVER ST

W LATHAM ST
Margaret T. Hance Park
E PORTLAND ST

W PORTLAND ST
ROOSEVELT ST
E ROOSEVELT ST

W MCKINLEY ST
E MCKINLEY ST

FILLMORE
W FILLMORE ST
E FILLMORE ST

POLK ST
University Park
W VAN BUREN

Arizona Capitol Mus

Arizona Mining and Mineral Museum

W MONROE ST
E MONROE ST
Museo Chicano
Phoenix Mus of Hist

Heritage & Science Park

Arizona Doll & Toy Mus

ADAMS
WASHINGTON ST

State Capitol
W JEFFERSON ST
Patriots Park
Arizona Science Ctr

Carnegie Library Park
W MADISON — E MADISON ST
America West Arena
Phoenix Civic Plaza Conv Ctr

W JACKSON ST — E JACKSON ST
Phoenix Police Museum

W HARRISON ST

Desert Storm Hummer Tours
LLOYD WRIGHT BLVD
To Payson & Fountain Hills

Salt River
Arizona Canal
Indian Reservation
Granite Reef Dam
N

To Payson & Fountain Hills

SCHOOL RD
MESA DR
MCDOWELL

Commemorative Air Force-Arizona Wing
Falcon Field Municipal Airport
Usery Mountain Recreation Area
ELLSWORTH RD

MCKELLIPS RD
BROWN
Red Mountain Park

Salt River
SCHOOL
CLUB
UNIVERSITY
BUTTE

Arizona Museum for Youth
APACHE BLVD
Mesa Southwest Museum
MAIN ST

BROADWAY MESA
Arizona Temple Visitor Center
BROADWAY

Golfland/Sunsplash
STAPLEY
SOUTHERN
GREENFIELD
BUSH
CRISMON
SIGNAL

SUPERSTITION FRWY
BASELINE RD
To Apache Jct. & Globe

Rockn' R Ranch
GUADALUPE RD

ELLIOT

DOBSON
SCHOOL
ARIZONA
MESA
COOPER
GILBERT
VAL VISTA
HIGLEY
FIELD
POWER
ELLSWORTH
SOSSAMAN

WARNER RD
Gilbert

WILLIAMS FIELD RD

Chandler
To Casa Grande & Tucson

To Payson & Fountain Hills

Phoenix

0   Miles   3.5

offices of the governor, mine inspector and secretary of state; the House and Senate chambers; an exhibit about the USS *Arizona;* and a wax figure of the first governor of Arizona, George Hunt. How a bill becomes a law is explained in an exhibit called A Tale of Two Chambers. Behind the building is a 1974 structure containing executive branch offices. The legislative galleries adjoin the Capitol.

Mon.-Fri. 8-5; closed state holidays. Guided tours are given at 10 and 2. Free. Phone (602) 542-4675.

BIG SURF—*see Tempe p. 91.*

[SAVE] **DEER VALLEY ROCK ART CENTER,** I-17 exit Deer Valley Road W., then 2 mi. w. to 3711 W. Deer Valley Rd., is dedicated to the preservation and interpretation of more than 1,500 prehistoric petroglyphs. Most are on hillside boulders at the Hedgpeth Hills and can be viewed from the base.

Inside exhibits explain the history of petroglyphs. An introductory videotape runs continuously. A .25-mile trail leads to the main viewing area.

Allow 1 hour, 30 minutes minimum. Tues.-Sat. 9-5, Sun. noon-5, Oct.-Apr.; Tues.-Fri. 8-2, Sat. 8-5, Sun. noon-5, rest of year. Closed July 4, Thanksgiving and Dec. 25. Guided tours are available by reservation Oct.-Apr. Admission $5; senior citizens and students with ID $3; ages 6-12, $2. Phone (623) 582-8007.

ENCANTO PARK, 2605 N. 15th Ave., has a lagoon and islands that serve as a waterfowl refuge; unusual trees and shrubs also can be seen. Tennis,

basketball, racquetball and volleyball courts, boat rentals, a swimming pool and nature trails are available. A children's amusement park with a carousel, train rides and bumper boats is on one of the islands.

Daily 5:30 a.m.-11 p.m. Park admission free. Amusement park rides priced individually; one ticket $1, book of 20 tickets $13, all day under 54 inches tall $10, all day over 54 inches tall $6. Phone (602) 261-8994. *See Recreation Chart.*

[GEM] **HALL OF FLAME MUSEUM OF FIRE-FIGHTING,** 6101 E. Van Buren St., houses one of the largest collections of firefighting equipment dating from 1725. A 10-minute videotape presentation introduces visitors to the museum's exhibits, which include hand- and horse-drawn pumpers, hook-and-ladder wagons and vehicles dating 1800-1969.

A wildland firefighting gallery explains the history and techniques of fighting wildfires. Other displays include fire marks, helmets, badges, patches, an interactive fire safety exhibit and play area for children, and artwork depicting major events in the history of fire service.

The National Firefighting Hall of Heroes recognizes firefighters who died in the line of duty and were decorated for bravery. Allow 2 hours, 30 minutes minimum. Mon.-Sat. 9-5, Sun. noon-4; closed Jan. 1, Thanksgiving and Dec. 25. Admission $6; over 62, $5; ages 6-17, $4; ages 3-5, $1.50. AX, MC, VI. Phone (602) 275-3473.

Herberger Theater / © Andre Jenny / Alamy

HEARD MUSEUM, 2301 N. Central Ave., is a museum of native cultures and art. Among the exhibits in its 10 galleries are ethnological, historical and contemporary materials of Southwestern Native Americans; Native American basketry, jewelry and pottery; and kachina dolls.

Visitors are greeted with colorful images as they enter the exhibit area. The architecture, foods, culture and religious beliefs of 21 tribes from desert, uplands and the Colorado Plateau regions are examined. Interactive exhibits allow visitors to work on a bead loom and experience re-created geographic settings of Native Americans. Changing exhibits and audiovisual presentations also are featured.

Allow 1 hour minimum. Daily 9:30-5; closed Easter, Memorial Day, July 4, Labor Day, Thanksgiving and Dec. 25. Guided tours are given daily at noon, 1:30 and 3. Admission $10; over 64, $9; students with ID $5; ages 6-12, $3; Native Americans free. AX, DS, MC, VI. Phone (602) 252-8840 or (602) 252-8848.

HERITAGE AND SCIENCE PARK is on Monroe St. between 5th and 7th sts. The park includes Heritage Square, comprised of eight late 19th-century structures that were part of the original site of Phoenix; they contain exhibits, museums and restaurants. Other sites are the Arizona Science Center and the Phoenix Museum of History *(see attraction listings).* The modern Lath House Pavilion serves as a community meeting area, botanical garden and festival site. Buildings open Wed.-Sat. 10-4, Sun. noon-4; closed mid-Aug. through Labor Day. Phone (602) 262-5029.

Arizona Doll and Toy Museum, 7th and Monroe sts. at 602 E. Adams, exhibits antique dolls and toys from around the world. One exhibit is devoted to a late 19th-century schoolroom, featuring the dolls as students. Allow 30 minutes minimum. Tues.-Sat. 10-4, Sun. noon-4, day after Labor Day-July; closed major holidays. Admission $3; under 13, $1. Phone (602) 253-9337.

Arizona Science Center, 600 E. Washington St., offers some 350 changing interactive exhibits for all ages. Hands-on displays allow visitors to explore aerospace, geology, computers, weather, biology, psychology and physics in a fun environment. A giant screen theater and planetarium also are featured. Daily 10-5; closed Thanksgiving and Dec. 25. Admission $9; over 61 and ages 3-12, $7. Theater shows $7; over 61 and ages 3-12, $6. Planetarium show $5; over 61 and ages 3-12, $4. MC, VI. Phone (602) 716-2000.

Phoenix Museum of History is at 105 N. 5th St. Interactive exhibits include telegraphy, wagon loading for a cross-country trek and design of a Victorian mansion. Visitors can discover how time and place have influenced the development of Phoenix from a dusty desert town to a modern metropolis. Allow 1 hour, 30 minutes minimum. Tues.-Sat. 10-5; closed Jan. 1, July 4, Thanksgiving and Dec. 25. Admission $5; over 64 and military and

AAA and Motorsports

AAA, a pioneer in the development and growth of auto racing during the first half of the 20th century, has returned to the racetrack. Today the association is the "Official Auto Club" and "Official Roadside Assistance Provider" of 11 tracks owned and operated by the International Speedway Corporation (ISC), which hosts the NASCAR NEXTEL Cup Series and Indy Racing League (IRL) events.

As part of an agreement with ISC, AAA's widely recognized logo appears on track safety and recovery vehicles as well as on track signs, in racing programs and at other promotional venues. ISC, a leading promoter of motorsports activities in the United States, conducts more than 100 events annually. ISC/AAA facilities include California Speedway in Fontana, Calif.; Darlington Raceway in Darlington, S.C.; Daytona International Speedway in Daytona Beach, Fla.; Homestead-Miami Speedway in Homestead, Fla.; Kansas Speedway in Kansas City, Kan.; Martinsville Speedway in Martinsville, Va.; Michigan International Speedway in Cambridge Junction, Mich.; Phoenix International Raceway in Phoenix, Ariz.; Richmond International Raceway in Richmond, Va.; Talladega Superspeedway in Talladega, Ala.; and Watkins Glen International in Watkins Glen, N.Y.

© International Speedway Corporation

students with ID $3.50; ages 7-12, $2.50. MC, VI. Phone (602) 253-2734.

Rosson House, 7th and Monroe sts., was built in 1895 for Dr. Roland Lee Rosson, mayor of Phoenix 1895-96. The restored Victorian mansion, constructed in 6 months at a cost of $7,525, features lathe-worked posts on the veranda, pressed-tin ceilings, parquet floors, an elaborately carved staircase and period furnishings. Various events are presented throughout the year.

Guided tours are given Wed.-Sat. 10-3:30, Sun. noon-3:30, day after Labor Day to mid-Aug.; closed major holidays. Admission $4; over 62, $3; ages 6-12, $1. Phone (602) 262-5029.

MUSEO CHICANO (CHICANO MUSEUM), 147 E. Adams St., displays various artworks dedicated to the Chicano heritage. Changing exhibits, seminars and special events also are offered. Tues.-Sat. 10-4. Admission $2; over 54 and under 12, $1. AX, CB, DS, MC, VI. Phone (602) 257-5536.

THE MYSTERY CASTLE, near South Mountain Park, is s. on Central Ave. then e. to 800 E. Mineral Rd. Built 1930-45 by Boyce Luther Gulley as his dream castle for his daughter, the house is constructed of native stone. Allow 30 minutes minimum. Thurs.-Sun. 11-4, Oct.-June. Admission $5; ages 6-15, $2. Phone (602) 268-1581.

NORTH MOUNTAIN PARK, 9 mi. n. at 10600 N. 7th St., accesses more than 7,000 acres of the Phoenix Mountains Preserve. Nature trails traverse the park. Daily 5 a.m.-11 p.m. Free. Phone (602) 262-7901 or (602) 495-5868.

PAPAGO PARK, jct. Galvin Pkwy. and Van Buren St., covers 1,200 acres and features fishing lagoons, bicycle paths, nature trails, picnic areas and a golf course. Daily 6 a.m.-11 p.m. Free. Phone (602) 256-3220 or (602) 262-4599.

Desert Botanical Garden, 1201 N. Galvin Pkwy., covers more than 145 acres in Papago Park. The garden is devoted exclusively to arid land plants of the world. The paved Desert Discovery Trail leads visitors through the garden; other walkways include the Plants and People of the Sonoran Desert Trail, the Sonoran Desert Nature Trail, the Center for Desert Living Trail and the Harriet K. Maxwell Wildflower Trail. The majority of the garden's plants are succulents, such as cactuses, aloes and century plants. The height of the wildflower blooming season is March through May.

Summer evening programs are offered May through August; call for event schedule. Food is available. Allow 2 hours minimum. Daily 7 a.m.-8 p.m., May-Sept.; 8-8, rest of year. Admission $9; over 65, $8; students with ID $5; ages 3-12, $4. AX, DS, MC, VI. Phone (480) 941-1225.

Phoenix Zoo, off Galvin Pkwy. in Papago Park, exhibits more than 1,300 mammals, birds and reptiles. The 125-acre zoo features four trails and is home to Southwestern animals; African animals such as meerkats, lions and a warthog; rain forest creatures; and a spectacled bear.

Other features include Feel the Difference for the visually impaired, Baboon Kingdom, Harmony Farm, the Tropical Flights Rain Forest and a Safari Train.

Food and picnic facilities are available. Allow 2 hours minimum. Daily 9-5, Sept.-May; Mon.-Fri. 7-1, Sat.-Sun. 7-4, rest of year. Closed Dec. 25. Admission $14; over 60, $9; ages 3-12, $6. AX, DS, MC, VI. Phone (602) 273-1341.

PHOENIX ART MUSEUM, 1625 N. Central Ave., features more than 17,000 works of American, European, Asian, Latin American, Western American and contemporary art. The museum presents international exhibitions by renowned artists, and also contains an interactive Artworks Gallery for children, the Fashion Design collection and the Thorne Miniature Rooms of historic interiors.

Guided tours and food are available. Allow 1 hour minimum. Tues.-Sun. 10-5 (also Thurs. 5-9); closed major holidays. Admission $9; over 64 and students with ID $7; ages 6-17, $3; free to all Thurs. Phone (602) 257-1222.

PHOENIX INTERNATIONAL RACEWAY is w. off I-10 to exit 126 (Estrella Parkway), 5 mi. s. on Estrella Pkwy., then 1.5 mi. e. on Vineyard Rd., following signs. Opened in 1964 at the foot of the Estrella Mountains, the raceway took off in 1988 with the arrival of the NASCAR NEXTEL Cup Series.

The annual Fall NASCAR weekend and the Checker Auto Parts 500 NASCAR Winston Cup Series in November are the raceway's main draws. The facility has reserved seats for 65,000; opening in April 2006, the Bobby Allison Grandstand will add 14,000 seats. With hillside and infield seating on both sides of the 1-mile oval paved racetrack, the raceway can accommodate more than 100,000 fans.

Five major race weekends take place in Jan., Mar., Apr., Sept. and Nov. Phone (623) 772-2000 for track information, or (602) 252-2227, (866) 408-7223 or TDD (866) 472-8725 for tickets.

© International Speedway Corporation

AAA is the Official Auto Club of Phoenix International Raceway

PHOENIX POLICE MUSEUM is at 101 S. Central Ave., Suite 100. Exhibits include antique police cars, motorcycles, uniforms and badges. Highlights include 1880s and 1930s jail cells and a 1919 Ford Model A police car. A memorial room pays tribute to police officers killed in the line of duty. Allow 30 minutes minimum. Mon., Wed., Fri. 9-3; closed Martin Luther King Day, Memorial Day and day after Thanksgiving. Donations. Phone (602) 534-7278.

PIONEER LIVING HISTORY MUSEUM is off I-17 exit 225 to 3901 W. Pioneer Rd. More than 26 original and reconstructed buildings, spread over a wide area, replicate the territorial days of the Southwest 1863-1912. Costumed interpreters re-enact life in territorial Arizona. Themed special events change monthly.

Guided tours are available. Allow 2 hours minimum. Wed.-Sun. 9-5, Oct.-May; 8-3, rest of year. Closed Dec. 25. Admission $7; over 60, $6; ages 6-18, $5. MC, VI. Phone (623) 465-1052.

PUEBLO GRANDE MUSEUM, 4619 E. Washington St., contains a prehistoric Hohokam village ruin that includes a platform mound, ball court and irrigation canals. Outdoor exhibits include full-size replicas of Hohokam pit houses and adobe compound houses. Museum exhibits center on archeology and the life of the Hohokam. Changing exhibits and tours also are available. An Indian market is held in December.

Allow 1 hour minimum. Mon.-Sat. 9-4:45, Sun. 1-4:45; closed Memorial Day, July 4, Labor Day, Thanksgiving and Dec. 25. Admission $2; over 54, $1.50; ages 6-17, $1; free to all Sun. Phone (602) 495-0901 or (877) 706-4408.

SHEMER ART CENTER, 5005 E. Camelback Rd., is in the first house built in the Arcadia section of Phoenix; the house was completed in the early 1920s. The restored Santa Fe Mission-style building with adobe walls contains changing exhibits of fine art. A highlight is a Colonial mansion doll house. The landscaped grounds feature orchards and sculpture gardens. Mon.-Fri. 10-5 (also Tues. 5-9), Sat. 9-1; closed major holidays. Donations. Phone (602) 262-4727.

SOUTH MOUNTAIN PARK, 8 mi. s. on S. Central Ave., contains 16,500 acres of peaks, canyons and strange rock formations as well as native Arizona flora. There is a drive to the crest of South Mountain. The Environmental Education Center just inside the park entrance features displays about the park and offers visitor information. Dobbins Lookout affords an excellent view; phone ahead for hours, as road closing times vary. Daily 5 a.m.-10 p.m. Environmental Education Center Wed.-Sat. 9-3, Sun. 9-2. Free. Phone (602) 495-0222 or (602) 534-6324. *See Recreation Chart.*

WATERWORLD SAFARI, 4243 W. Pinnacle Peak Rd., features 20 acres of water slides and wave pools, including the Endless River Ride. Changing rooms and showers are on the premises; lockers and tubes can be rented. Food is available. Mon.-Thurs. 10-8, Fri.-Sat. 10-9, Sun. 11-7, Memorial Day-Labor Day. Admission $21; under 48 inches tall $17; over age 54, $11; under age 3, $1. AX, DS, MC, VI. Phone (623) 581-8446.

What To Do

Sightseeing

Bus, Four-wheel-drive and Van Tours

A tour is the best way to get an overall view of the city, and a variety are available. SAVE Gray Line Tours offers a wide range of sightseeing tours ranging from a 4-hour city tour to a 14-hour Grand Canyon trip; for details phone (602) 437-3484 or (800) 777-3484.

Several companies offer four-wheel-drive or van tours of the desert: Open Road Tours *(see color ad),* (602) 997-6474 or (800) 766-7117; Vaughan's Southwest Custom Tours, (602) 971-1381 or (800) 513-1381; and Wayward Wind Tours Inc., (602) 867-8162 or (800) 804-0480.

Plane Tours

Westwind Air Tour and Charter provides scenic tours of the Grand Canyon. For flight arrangements phone (480) 991-5557 or (888) 869-0866.

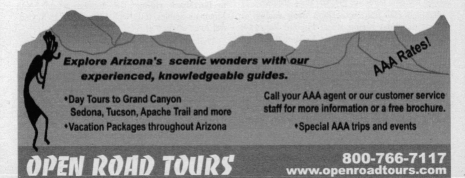

Sports and Recreation

·Phoenix's mild winters make it an all-year sports paradise. For spectators the winter months mean **horse racing** at Turf Paradise from October through early May; phone (602) 942-1101. **Dog racing** at Phoenix Greyhound Park takes place Thursday through Tuesday all year; phone (602) 273-7181.

Note: Policies vary concerning admittance of children to pari-mutuel betting facilities. Phone for information.

In spring **baseball** arrives as the Oakland Athletics begin their training at Phoenix Municipal Stadium, (602) 495-7239. Other teams with spring training sites in the Phoenix area include the Anaheim Angels at Tempe Diablo Stadium in Tempe, (480) 350-5205; Chicago Cubs at Ho Ho Kam Park in Mesa, (480) 964-4467; the Kansas City Royals and the Texas Rangers at Surprise Stadium in Surprise, (623) 594-5600; the San Diego Padres and the Seattle Mariners at Peoria Sports Complex in Peoria, (623) 878-4337; and the San Francisco Giants at Scottsdale Stadium in Scottsdale, (480) 312-2580. The Arizona Diamondbacks, 2001 World Series champions, play ball at the domed Bank One Ballpark in downtown Phoenix; phone (602) 514-8400.

The America West Arena, 201 E. Jefferson St., is the site of many of Phoenix's sporting events. It is the home court of the NBA Phoenix Suns **basketball** team November through April; phone (602) 379-7867. The WNBA's Phoenix Mercury take over the arena's court May through August; phone (602) 252-9622. April through August the arena also houses the Arizona Rattlers, Phoenix's professional **arena football** team; phone (602) 514-8383. September through April Glendale Arena, 9400 W. Maryland Ave., is the home of the Phoenix Coyotes, the city's National **Hockey** League team; phone (480) 563-7825.

Professional **football** is played in Tempe, where the NFL Arizona Cardinals take the field at Arizona State University's Sun Devil Stadium; phone (602) 379-0102 or (623) 266-5000. The Fiesta Bowl football classic at the stadium is a January highlight. **Note:** Cardinals Stadium, 9301 W. Maryland Ave., is scheduled to open August 2006 in Glendale and will be the new home for the Arizona Cardinals.

National Hot Rod Association **drag racing** as well as **dragboat racing** are at Firebird Raceway, about 8 miles south of Phoenix at Maricopa Road and I-10; phone (602) 268-0200. Indy cars, NASCAR **stock cars and trucks,** and Grand Am sports cars race at Phoenix International Raceway; phone (623) 463-5400 (see attraction listing).

Licensed drivers can experience race car driving at Bob Bondurant School of High Performance Driving, I-10 and Maricopa Road; phone (480) 403-7600.

A round of **golf** in a panorama of mountain peaks and blue skies entices not only Arizona residents but visitors too. Golfing is a year-round activity in Arizona. There are more than 325 golf courses in the state, both public and private, appealing to all levels of proficiency—Phoenix has nearly 120.

Phoenix courses include Club West, (480) 460-4400, 16400 S. 14th Ave.; Encanto, (602) 253-3963, at 2775 N. 15th Ave.; The Foothills, (480) 460-4653, at 2201 E. Clubhouse Dr.; Maryvale, (623) 846-4022, at 5902 W. Indian School Rd.; Papago, (602) 275-8428, in Papago Park at 5595 E. Moreland St.; Phantom Horse, (602) 431-6480, at .7777 S. Pointe Pkwy.; The Pointe Golf Club at Lookout Mountain, (602) 866-6356, at 11111 N. 7th St.; and Stonecreek, (602) 953-9110, at 4435 E. Paradise Village Pkwy. S.

Golf courses in nearby Mesa include: Dobson Ranch, (480) 644-2291, at 2155 S. Dobson Rd.; Red Mountain Ranch, (480) 985-0285, at 6425 E. Teton Cir.; and Superstition Springs, (480) 985-5555, at 6542 E. Baseline Rd.

Courses in Scottsdale include: Marriott's Camelback, (480) 596-7050, at 7847 N. Mockingbird Ln.; Marriott's Mountain Shadows Resort, (480) 905-8999, at 5641 E. Lincoln Dr.; McCormick Ranch, (480) 948-0260, at 7505 E. McCormick Pkwy.; Starfire at Scottsdale Country Club, (480) 948-6000, at 11500 N. Hayden Rd.; TPC Scottsdale, (480) 585-3600, at 17020 N. Hayden Rd.; and Troon North, (480) 585-5300, at 10320 E. Dynamite Blvd.

Other area courses include: Gold Canyon, (480) 982-9449, at 6100 S. Kings Ranch Rd. in Apache Junction; Ocotillo, (480) 917-6660, at 3751 S. Clubhouse Dr. in Chandler; The Legend at Arrowhead, (623) 561-0953, at 21027 N. 67th Ave. in Glendale; The Wigwam Resort, (623) 935-3811, at 300 E. Wigwam Blvd. in Litchfield Park; Hillcrest, (623) 584-1500, at 20002 N. Star Ridge Dr. in Sun City West; ASU-Karsten, (480) 921-8070, at 1125 E. Rio Salado Pkwy. in Tempe; and Ken McDonald, (480) 350-5250, at 800 E. Divot Dr. in Tempe.

Tennis courts open to the public are plentiful at several high schools and park areas, including Granada Park, 6505 N. 20th St., and Encanto Park, 15th Avenue and Encanto Drive. The Phoenix Tennis Center, (602) 249-3712, at 6330 N. 21st Ave., has 22 lighted courts and reasonable rates; reservations are accepted.

The valley's beautiful desert country lends itself to **horseback riding**. The Ponderosa and South Mountain Stables, (602) 268-1261, at 10215 S. Central Ave., offers trail rides.

Trails for **hiking** and **bicycling** are plentiful. A favorite hike is the 1-mile scenic trek to the summit of Piestewa Peak. Formerly known as Squaw Peak, the peak was renamed in honor of Lori Piestewa, an American servicewoman and Hopi who was killed in combat during Operation Iraqi Freedom in 2003.

The Phoenix Parks and Recreation Department, (602) 262-6861, operates a number of parks; some have municipal **swimming** pools. Saguaro Lake and Canyon Lake (see Recreation Chart) offer **water skiing, boating** and **fishing.** The Salt River is popular with **tubing** enthusiasts. Salt River Tubing and Recreation (see Mesa p. 88), (480) 984-3305, rents tubes and also provides shuttle-bus service along the Salt River.

For the **shooting** enthusiast, the Ben Avery Shooting Range, (623) 582-8313, 25 miles north of Phoenix off I-17 exit 223, offers pistol, rifle and archery ranges and trap and skeet fields.

The suburb of Tempe boasts inland **surfing** at Big Surf *(see Tempe p. 91)*, (480) 947-7873; **roller skating** at Surfside Skateland, (480) 968-9600, at 1625 E. Weber Dr.; and **ice skating** at the Oceanside Ice Arena, (480) 947-2470, at 1520 N. McClintock Dr.

Hot air balloon rides over the metropolitan area and the Sonora Desert are available through several companies. Balloon rides average 1 hour and are usually followed by a champagne brunch. Many companies operate October through May, but some offer flights year-round. Prices range from $145 to $225 per person. Companies include: [SAVE] A Aerozona Adventure, (480) 991-4260 or (888) 991-4260; Aerogelic Ballooning, (602) 595-9793 or (866) 359-8329; Hot Air Expeditions, (480) 502-6999 or (800) 831-7610; and Unicorn Balloon Co., (800) 755-0935. **Soaring** is available at Turf Soaring School, (602) 439-3621, at 8700 W. Carefree Hwy. in Peoria.

Shopping

Shopping in Phoenix can be diverse and exciting. Dolls, Native American handicrafts, jewelry, rugs, and Western fashions are only a few of the temptations. Shopping malls such as Metrocenter, 9617 N. Metro Pkwy. W., and Paradise Valley Mall, 4568 E. Cactus Rd., incorporate innovative architecture with a colorful array of shops.

Malls and centers include the Arizona Center, Van Buren between 3rd and 5th streets; Arrowhead Towne Center, 7700 W. Arrowhead Towne Center; Biltmore Fashion Park, 2502 E. Camelback Rd.; Desert Ridge Marketplace, Tatum Boulevard and SR 101 Pima Freeway; Desert Sky Mall, 7611 W. Thomas Rd.; and Town & Country Shopping Center, 2021 E. Camelback Rd. Anchor stores include Dillard's, JCPenney, Macy's, Robinsons-May, Saks Fifth Avenue (Biltmore Fashion Park only) and Sears.

For shoppers interested in a bargain, the Park 'n' Swap, 3801 E. Washington, offers garage sale-style shopping on 54 acres; Indoor Swapmart, 5115 N. 27th Ave., also offers bargains. Northwest of Phoenix is The Outlets at Anthem at 4250 W. Anthem Way.

There are many Native American handicraft stores that sell everything from jewelry to Navajo rugs. Among the best in Phoenix are the Heard Museum Shop, 2301 N. Central Ave., and Gilbert Ortega's, at several locations including 122 N. 2nd St. In Scottsdale Native American handicrafts are sold at Atkinson's Herman Indian Trading Post, 3957 N. Brown Ave.; Gilbert Ortega's, 7237 E. Main St.; and Grey Wolf, 7239 E. First Ave.

Theater and Concerts

Phoenix's rapid growth has been cultural as well as industrial. The following theaters present a mix of classic and contemporary drama: Herberger Theater, (602) 252-8497, 222 E. Monroe; Phoenix Theatre, (602) 254-2151, 100 E. McDowell Rd.; Stagebrush Theater, (480) 990-7405, 7020 E. 2nd St. in Scottsdale; and TheaterWorks, (623) 815-7930, at The Lakes Club, 10484 W. Thunderbird Blvd. in Sun City. Arizona's professional state theater group, the Arizona Theater Co., (602) 256-6995, performs at the Herberger Theater during its October to June season.

The historic Orpheum Theatre, 203 W. Adams St., was originally built for vaudeville acts and movies in 1929. Scheduled to be condemned, the city bought the theater and in 1997 reopened it as a 1,400-seat performing arts center. Free guided tours of the Spanish Baroque Revival building are available; phone (602) 534-5600.

For music and dance lovers, the Arizona Opera, Ballet Arizona and Phoenix Symphony offer performances throughout the year. The symphony performs in the striking Symphony Hall, Phoenix Civic Plaza, 225 E. Adams St.; phone (602) 262-7272.

Cabarets, special concerts, big-name entertainment, shows and lectures are presented at the Herberger Theater, (602) 252-8497, 222 E. Monroe; the SunDome Center for the Performing Arts, (623)

975-1900, 19403 N. R.H. Johnson Blvd. in Sun City West; and the Grady Gammage Auditorium, (480) 965-3434, on the campus of Arizona State University at Mill Avenue and Apache Boulevard in Tempe.

Other special performance areas include America West Arena, (602) 379-7800, 201 E. Jefferson St.; Arizona Veteran's Memorial Coliseum, (602) 252-6771, 1826 W. McDowell Rd.; Celebrity Theatre, (602) 267-1600, 440 N. 32nd St.; Cricket Pavilion, (602) 254-7200, 2121 N. 83rd Ave.; and the Dodge Theatre, (602) 379-2800, 400 W. Washington St. In Mesa are the Mesa Arts Center, (480) 644-6500; and the Mesa Amphitheater, (480) 644-2560, 263 N. Center St.

Special Events

New Year's in Tempe begins with the Fiesta Bowl and all its pregame activities; the Fiesta Bowl Parade ranks among the largest parades in the country. Also in January, Scottsdale hosts the Parada del Sol and the Phoenix Open Golf Tournament.

The month of February is highlighted by a popular event among equestrians, the All-Arabian Horse Show. February also is when the American Racing Hot Rod Association holds the Winternationals. In March, catch the LPGA Safeway Ping or the Indian Fair and Market, held at the Heard Museum. The Maricopa County Fair happens in April. The Cinco de Mayo Festival corresponds to other Mexican celebrations that occur in early May.

Various fall festivals take place in the Phoenix area from October into November. The Arizona State Fair and the Cowboy Artists of America Exhibition in October draw crowds. In November the Thunderbird Balloon Classic and Air Show is held at Westworld of Scottsdale, 16601 N. Pima Rd.; phone (480) 312-6810.

The Pueblo Grande Museum Auxiliary Indian Market is held the second weekend in December at the Steele Indian School Park, 300 E. Indian School Rd. The year's festivities conclude with *posadas*, Mexican neighborhood celebrations that take place during the 9 days preceding Christmas.

The Phoenix Vicinity

APACHE JUNCTION (I-5)
pop. 31,814, elev. 1,715′

As its name implies, Apache Junction—the western terminus of the Apache Trail—is at the junction of US 60 and SR 88. The surrounding desert, lakes and mountains make Apache Junction a natural recreation site. Hiking, horseback riding, picnicking, rockhounding and water sports facilities are available.

At the junction of Old West Highway and SR 88 stands a monument to the memory of Jacob Waltz, purported discoverer of the Lost Dutchman Gold Mine, which is said to be in the nearby Superstition Mountains.

For eight consecutive weekends from the first Saturday in February through the last Sunday in March, the Arizona Renaissance Festival is held 9 miles east on US 60. Beginning at 10 a.m. and ending at 6 p.m., activities during this re-creation of a 16th-century European village at play during a market fair include jousting tournaments, wandering musicians, theatrical events and demonstrations of period crafts. For more information phone (520) 463-2700.

Apache Junction Chamber of Commerce: 567 W. Apache Tr., P.O. Box 1747, Apache Junction, AZ 85217; phone (480) 982-3141 or (800) 252-3141.

APACHE LAKE, 30 mi. n.e. on SR 88, is part of the Salt River chain of lakes. A popular recreation area, it is surrounded by the Tonto National Forest *(see place listing p. 104).* To the south lies the Superstition Wilderness. *See Recreation Chart.*

APACHE TRAIL (SR 88) starts at Apache Junction and proceeds for 78 mi., climbing past the famed Superstition Mountains, passing through Fish Creek Canyon and skirting the southern edges of Apache, Saguaro, Canyon and Roosevelt lakes, ending at Globe. The trail was created in 1905 to transport supplies from Phoenix and Globe to the construction site of Roosevelt Dam. The road parallels the ancient route of the Apaches through the canyons of the Salt River.

Note: The 25-mile portion of Apache Trail between Tortilla Flat and Roosevelt is a narrow, winding gravel road. It is not recommended during rainy weather, for inexperienced drivers or for vehicles over 35 feet. West-to-east travel from Apache Junction to Globe will put you on the inside lane and grant all passengers the security of rock walls rather than the steep cliffs on the other side.

Fish Creek Canyon is approximately 25 mi. n.e. of Apache Junction. The canyon is noted for massive, vividly colored walls rising as much as 2,000 feet above the highway. Formed by Fish Creek, which runs from the center of the Superstition Mountains northwest towards the Salt River, the canyon floor is lush with saguaro cacti, trees, bushes, reeds and waterfalls.

CANYON LAKE, 16 mi. n.e. on SR 88, is one of a series of lakes on the Salt River. Impounded by the Mormon Flat Dam, Canyon Lake twists for 10 miles through a magnificent gorge to Horse Mesa Dam. *See Recreation Chart.*

SAVE **GOLDFIELD GHOST TOWN & MINE TOURS,** 5 mi. n.e. on SR 88, passing Milepost 200 to 4650 N. Mammoth Mine Rd., offers mine tours, gold panning, gunfights and specialty shops within view of the spectacular Superstition Mountains. A museum features a large exhibit of antique mining equipment. A scenic narrow-gauge railroad also encompasses the town.

Food is available. Daily 10-5, Nov.-May; Thurs.-Sun. 10-5, rest of year. Museum daily 10-5, Sept.-May; Tues.-Wed. and Fri.-Sun. 10-5, rest of year. Train ride daily 10-5, Sept.-May; Thurs.-Mon. 10-5, rest of year. Closed Dec. 25. Town free. Mine tour $6; over 55, $5; ages 6-12, $3. Train ride $5; over 55, $4; ages 6-12, $3. Phone (480) 983-0333.

Apache Trail Tours depart from Goldfield Ghost Town. Participants partake in 2- to 8-hour guided jeep tours of the Apache Trail, the Superstition Mountains and the Four Peaks. Gold-panning and hiking are available. Allow 2 hours minimum. Departures require a minimum of 4 people. Tours depart daily; phone for schedule. Closed Thanksgiving and Dec. 25. Fare $70-$165, under 13 varies; phone for rates. Reservations are recommended. AX, DS, MC, VI. Phone (480) 982-7661.

LOST DUTCHMAN STATE PARK, 5 mi. n.e. off SR 88 to 6109 N. Apache Tr., offers 320 acres of hiking trails, camping and picnicking areas. Special moonlight hikes are offered monthly and guided hikes and campfire programs are offered weekly November through April. Daily dawn-10 p.m. Office daily 8-5. Admission $5 per private vehicle. Camping $12 per private vehicle. Phone (480) 982-4485. *See Recreation Chart.*

SUPERSTITION MOUNTAINS, e. of town, were named for the many legends surrounding them. The fabled Lost Dutchman Gold Mine lies somewhere in these mountains. Whether the mine really exists is uncertain, but at least eight men were killed because of it and many others died searching for it. Monuments at Roosevelt Dam and Apache Junction commemorate Jacob Waltz, who allegedly discovered the mine.

CAVE CREEK (H-3) pop. 3,728, elev. 2,129′

Cave Creek was originally home to the Hohokam, who irrigated their fields with water from Cave Creek. In 1870 a road was built to link the newly formed town of Cave Creek to Fort McDowell on the Verde River. The late 1800s saw the establishment of numerous mining camps in the surrounding mountains, and permanent settlers who followed took to ranching and farming.

Recreational activities abound in Cave Creek with the Tonto National Forest *(see place listing p. 104)* as its neighbor. Six lakes in the forest offer numerous opportunities for swimming, fishing and boating.

Carefree-Cave Creek Chamber of Commerce: P.O. Box 734, Carefree, AZ 85377; phone (480) 488-3381.

CAVE CREEK MUSEUM is at 6140 E. Skyline Dr. Exhibits depict archeological sites as well as what life was like for area pioneers, miners and ranchers. The museum features artifacts attributed to Hohokam, Anasazi and Mogollon Indian cultures. A cabin from a tuberculosis sanitarium operating nearby in the 1920s is on the grounds as well as the first church in Cave Creek. Allow 30 minutes minimum. Wed.-Sun. 1-4:30, Oct.-May. Admission $3, senior citizens and students with ID $2, under 12 free. Phone (480) 488-2764.

CHANDLER (J-4) pop. 176,581

Chandler was founded by Dr. Alexander J. Chandler, a veterinary surgeon who bought 80 acres of land in the Salt River Valley in 1891 and created a series of canals. By 1900 his ranch covered 18,000 acres; in 1912, Chandler sold $50,000 worth of land to 300 speculators and the city was born. In the beginning, Chandler's chief industry was agriculture; alfalfa, cotton and grain were common crops. Today agriculture, while still in the picture, takes a back seat to manufacturing and electronics.

A return to the good old days of the West takes place at Rawhide Western Town & Steakhouse at Wild Horse Pass *(see attraction listing)* for 4 days in March during the US West National Festival of the West. Western music; a Western film festival; a cowboy trade show, featuring everything from horse gear to art to furniture; rodeo and shooting competitions; cowboy poetry; a mountain man encampment; a chuckwagon cook-off; special children's activities; and period costumes recall the glory days of early Western settlement.

RAWHIDE WESTERN TOWN & STEAKHOUSE AT WILD HORSE PASS, 5700 W. North Loop Rd., is a replica of an 1880s frontier town. Craftsmen sell their wares in antique buildings and shops. The family-style entertainment includes stunt and comedy shows, sundown cookouts and stagecoach and train rides.

Note: Rawhide Western Town will remain at its original location at 23023 Scottsdale Rd. in Scottsdale through October 31, 2005. It is scheduled to re-open in December 2005 at the Wild Horse Pass Development in the Gila River Indian Community in Chandler. Phone ahead for information. Food is available. Mon.-Thurs. 5-10, Fri.-Sun. 11-10, Oct.-May; daily 5-10, rest of year. Closed Dec. 25. Summer and holiday hours may vary; phone ahead.

Western town and parking free. Ride and show tickets $1 each, or 25 tickets for $20 (rides and shows require 2-5 tickets each). AX, CB, DC, DS, MC, VI. Phone (480) 502-5600.

FOUNTAIN HILLS (I-4)
pop. 20,235, elev. 1,600′

Fountain Hills is named for its rolling terrain and celebrated fountain. The community provides a number of recreation and vacation opportunities.

Fountain Hills Chamber of Commerce: P.O. Box 17598, Fountain Hills, AZ 85269; phone (480) 837-1654.

THE FOUNTAIN is off Saguaro Blvd. in Fountain Park. Within a 28-acre lake, the 560-foot-tall white jet of water shoots above the town for 15 minutes daily on the hour 10-9. Wind gusts over 12 miles per hour may prevent operation. The surrounding park is open daily dawn-11 p.m. Free. Phone (480) 816-5252.

GLENDALE (I-3) pop. 218,812, elev. 1,154'

Established in 1892, Glendale retains much of its turn-of-the-20th-century charm. A tree-lined town square, red brick sidewalks and gaslights form an appropriate setting for the abundance of antique shops around shady Murphy Park in the city's historic downtown.

In a more modern vein, Glendale also is home to Thunderbird, The American Graduate School of International Management and the jet fighter wing at Luke Air Force Base.

City of Glendale Tourism Division: 5800 W. Glenn Dr., Suite 140, Glendale, AZ 85301; phone (623) 930-4500 or (877) 800-2601.

Shopping areas: Known as the Antique Capital of Arizona, more than 90 antique stores, specialty shops and restaurants are concentrated around Glendale's town square, Murphy Park, at the intersection of Glendale and 58th avenues. Old Towne Glendale and the Historic Catlin Court Shops District specialize in oak furniture, dolls, jewelry, period clothing and Western memorabilia. Arrowhead Towne Center contains 150 stores, including Dillard's and Robinsons-May.

[SAVE] **HISTORIC SAHUARO RANCH** is 2.5 mi. n. of Glendale Ave. to 9802 N. 59th Ave.; or take I-10 exit 138, then go n. 7.6 mi. on N. 59th Ave. Seventeen acres of a model fruit farm developed by

William Henry Bartlett in 1885 feature seven original buildings, including an adobe house, a foreman's house, the main house and a fruit packing shed. A lavish rose garden planted in 1890, several citrus groves and free-roaming peacocks enhance the fenced grounds. Guided tours of the main house are available.

Allow 1 hour minimum. Wed.-Fri. 10-2, Sat. 10-4, Sun. noon-4; closed major holidays. Guided main house tours are available. Hours may vary; phone ahead. Grounds free. Admission is charged during events. House tour $3, under 13 free. Phone (623) 930-4200.

GOODYEAR (I-2) pop. 18,911, elev. 1,000'

In the early 1900s Goodyear Tire & Rubber Company obtained tracts of land in the Salt River Valley, with the intent of growing Egyptian cotton, a component in tire cords. The small farms established on this land evolved into company towns, including one named for its originator. Just 14 miles west of Phoenix, the town is now a suburban residential community.

Southwest Valley Chamber of Commerce: 289 N. Litchfield Rd., Goodyear, AZ 85338; phone (623) 932-2260.

ESTRELLA MOUNTAIN REGIONAL PARK, off I-10 Estrella Pkwy. S. exit, contains 19,840 acres of rugged desert terrain, riding trails and an 18-hole golf course. Equestrian and rodeo events are held throughout the year. Park open Sun.-Thurs. 6 a.m.-8 p.m., Fri.-Sat. 6 a.m.-10 p.m. Admission $5 per private vehicle, $1 on foot, horseback or bicycle. Phone (623) 932-3811.

LITCHFIELD PARK (I-2) pop. 3,810

WILDLIFE WORLD ZOO, 16501 W. Northern Ave., presents more than 320 rare and exotic species of

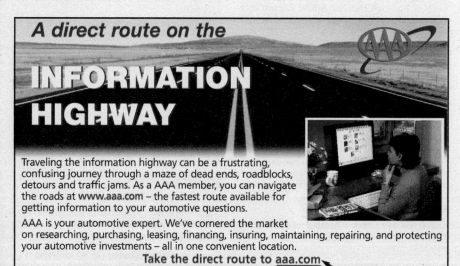

animals including camels, giraffes, jaguars, rhinoceroses, tigers and more than 40 species of tropical birds. Featured are lory parrot feeding, a safari train ride, a boat ride, a sky ride and wildlife encounter shows. The Tropics of the World exhibit is home to pythons, crocodiles and iguanas. Food is available. Daily 9-5. Admission $14.95; over 60 (Tues. only) $13.95; ages 3-12, $6.95. Sky ride $3. Phone (623) 935-9453.

MESA (I-4) pop. 396,375, elev. 1,234'

Mesa (Spanish for "tabletop") is in the center of the Salt River Valley on a plateau. The area has long been inhabited by Native Americans, including the Hohokam, or "the Departed Ones." The resourceful tribe realized the need for water for irrigation and dug some 125 miles of canals around 700 B.C. Some of these irrigation ditches are still in use and can be seen at the Park of the Canals and Mesa Grande Ruins.

In 1883 the founding Mormon community discovered the ancient canal system and used it to irrigate the thousands of fertile acres of farmland above the Salt River. Alfalfa, cotton, wheat and grapes were the major crops; citrus was introduced in 1897. Agriculture carried the town into the 20th century and now tourism plays a big role in Mesa's economy.

Recreational areas east and north of the city are easily accessible from Mesa. Rafting and other water sports on the Salt River are popular, as are varied activities available within the Apache, Canyon and Theodore Roosevelt Lake recreational areas (see Apache Junction p. 84) and Saguaro Lake (see Recreation Chart).

Mesa Convention and Visitors Bureau: 120 N. Center St., P.O. Box 5529, Mesa, AZ 85201-5529; phone (480) 827-4700 or (800) 283-6372.

Shopping areas: The largest shopping centers in the city are Fiesta Mall, US 60 and Alma School Road, which offers Dillard's, Macy's, Robinsons-May and Sears; and Superstition Springs Center, at US 60 and Superstition Springs Boulevard, which offers Dillard's, JCPenney, Mervyn's and Sears.

Bargain hunters can find discounted name-brand merchandise at VF Factory Outlet Mall, a half-mile south of US 60 at Power and Baseline roads. The Mesa Market Place and Swap Meet offers produce and new and used merchandise at its indoor facility at 10550 E. Baseline Rd.

SAVE **ARIZONA MUSEUM FOR YOUTH,** 35 N. Robson St., offers children the opportunity to view, create and explore various forms of art. Three new exhibitions are introduced each year, and workshops teach a variety of skills from printmaking to clay sculpturing. ArtVille, a permanent gallery, highlights art activities for children under age 4. Allow 1 hour minimum. Tues.-Sun. 9-5; closed major holidays. Main gallery closed periodically for exhibit installation; phone ahead. Admission $3.50, under 1 free. Phone (480) 644-2467.

ARIZONA TEMPLE VISITOR CENTER is at 525 E. Main St. The center presents dioramas and an audiovisual program that explains the purpose of the temple and the history of the Mormon religion; paintings and statues are featured. Free guided tours of the visitor center end in a religious question-and-answer session. A pageant is presented during the week before Easter, and a holiday lights display is featured late November through early January. Allow 1 hour minimum. Daily 9-9. Guided tours are given daily. Free. Phone (480) 964-7164.

SAVE **COMMEMORATIVE AIR FORCE—ARIZONA WING,** e. on SR 202 to jct. McKellips Rd. and Greenfield Rd. at 2017 N. Greenfield Rd. (adjoining Falcon Field), is dedicated to the preservation of World War II warplanes. Displays include such war artifacts as flight equipment and ration coupons. Of special interest is Sentimental Journey, a restored World War II B-17 bomber in flying condition. Allow 1 hour minimum. Daily 10-4; closed Thanksgiving and Dec. 25. Sentimental Journey is on display late fall-spring. Admission $7; ages 6-14, $3. AX, DS, MC, VI. Phone (480) 924-1940.

GOLFLAND/SUNSPLASH, 155 W. Hampton Ave., is a 12-acre miniature golf and water park complex featuring three miniature golf courses, 10 water slides including the Master Blaster and the Sidewinder, a wave pool, bumper boats, go-carts, a children's pool, a video arcade and a river for tubing.

Changing rooms, lockers and food are available. Sunsplash Mon.-Thurs. 10-8, Fri.-Sat. 10-9, Sun. 11-7, Memorial Day-Labor Day. Golfland Mon.-Thurs. 10-10, Fri.-Sat. 10 a.m.-midnight, Sun. noon-10, year-round. Admission $21; under 49 inches tall $17; over age 54, $11; under age 3, $1. Twilight admission (after 4) $17. Separate fees for golf, go-carts and bumper boats. AX, DS, MC, VI. Phone (480) 834-8319.

MESA HISTORICAL MUSEUM is .9 mi. e. on Main St., then 3 mi. n. on Horne St. to 2345 N. Horne St. Antique farm equipment, furniture, clothing and other artifacts are housed in the main building, formerly a schoolhouse built in 1913. The Phelps/Bowen/Morris Room showcases a turn-of-the-20th-century urban home. Replicas of Fort Utah and an 1882 adobe schoolhouse are featured.

Picnicking is permitted. Allow 30 minutes minimum. Mon.-Sat. 10-4, Sept.-May; 9-1, rest of year. Closed major holidays. Donations. Phone (480) 835-7358.

MESA SOUTHWEST MUSEUM, 53 N. Macdonald St., covers the history of Arizona from the days of the dinosaurs to the 20th century. Permanent and temporary exhibits focus on Arizona's prehistoric life, featuring animated dinosaurs, dinosaur skeletons and other fossil specimens. Archeology displays highlight the life of Arizona's ancient Hohokam people, while reminders of old Mesa's past include territorial jail cells and the Dutchman's Treasure Mine.

Allow 1 hour minimum. Tues.-Sat. 10-5, Sun. 1-5; closed major holidays. Admission $6; over 55 and students with ID $5; ages 3-12, $3. AX, DS, MC, VI. Phone (480) 644-2230.

SAVE **ROCKIN' R RANCH,** 6136 E. Baseline Rd., is a re-creation of a Western town where you can pan for gold. All-you-can-eat chuckwagon suppers are served cowboy style. A stage show has songs and humor of the Old West; a gunfight is staged after the show.

Meal preceding stage show begins at 6:30 Wed.-Sat., Dec.-Mar.; Thurs.-Sat., in Nov.; Fri.-Sat., Apr.-May and Sept. 26-Oct. 31; Sat., rest of year. Admission $25; over 64, $23; ages 3-12, $15. Reservations are required. AX, DC, MC, VI. Phone (480) 832-1539.

RECREATIONAL ACTIVITIES
Tubing
• **Salt River Tubing and Recreation** is 10 mi. s.e. of SR 87 on Bush Hwy., P.O. Box 6568, Mesa, AZ 85216. Daily 9-4, May-Oct. Phone (480) 984-3305.

PARADISE VALLEY (I-3)
pop. 13,664, elev. 1,340'

COSANTI FOUNDATION, 6433 E. Doubletree Ranch Rd., is the headquarters and workshop of architect-craftsman Paolo Soleri. Displays include sculptures, windbells and photographs of the models for the city of Arcosanti *(see Mayer p. 63),* Soleri's prototype urban design. Allow 1 hour minimum. Mon.-Sat. 9-5, Sun. 11-5; closed major holidays. Donations. Phone (480) 948-6145.

PEORIA (I-3) pop. 108,364, elev. 1,138'

CHALLENGER SPACE CENTER OF ARIZONA is 3.2 mi. n. on 91st Ave., 1 mi. e. on Lake Pleasant Blvd., then .3 mi. n. to 21170 N. 83rd Ave. An affiliate of the Smithsonian Institute, the center features permanent and temporary space exhibits as well as stargazing and planetarium programs. A highlight is the 2-hour simulated space mission, including launching and docking. The mission control room is based on the design of the Johnson Space Center; the spacecraft simulates a room on the International Space Station.

Allow 1 hour minimum. Mon.-Fri. 9-4, Sat. 10-4; closed Jan. 1, Memorial Day, Labor Day and Thanksgiving. Space mission departs Sat. at 10:30 and 1, year-round; Tues. and Thurs. at 1, early June-early Aug. Admission $6, senior citizens and students with ID $4, under 6 free. Space mission $17.50, senior citizens and students with ID $15. Third- and fourth-grade students must be with an adult on space mission. Under 7 are not recommended on space mission; reservations are required. AX, MC, VI. Phone (623) 322-2001.

SCOTTSDALE (I-3) pop. 202,705, elev. 1,259'

Scottsdale was named for Chaplain Winfield Scott, Civil War veteran and retired military man who purchased some farmland in 1888. Throughout his travels, Scott promoted the fertile land and encouraged settlement, and in 1896 there were enough children in the town to form School District #48.

Known for the rugged beauty of the surrounding Sonoran Desert and for more than 120 art galleries, Scottsdale also is home to craft shops, specialty stores, golf courses, resorts and torchlit swimming pools. The Indian Bend Wash Greenbelt along Hayden Road offers seven miles of trails for bicyclists and runners.

McCormick-Stillman Railroad Park, 7301 E. Indian Bend Rd., (480) 312-2312, offers 1-mile rides on a scale train. Several full-size railroad cars, two train depots, a 1907 locomotive, two Navajo hogans, playgrounds and an operating 1950s carousel are in the park. Picnic facilities are available.

Scottsdale Convention and Visitors Bureau: 4343 N. Scottsdale Rd., Suite 170, Scottsdale, AZ 85251; phone (480) 421-1004 or (800) 782-1117.

Self-guiding tours: Maps detailing self-guiding walking tours of Scottsdale's Old Town are available from the chamber of commerce.

Shopping areas: Borgata of Scottsdale, an elegant shopping and dining complex designed after San Gimignano (Town of Towers) in Italy, is .25 miles south of Lincoln Drive on Scottsdale Road. Many specialty and gift shops can be found along Fifth Avenue between Marshall Way and Main Street as well as in Old Town, where Western storefronts re-create an aura of the past.

Other shopping areas include Fashion Square at Scottsdale and Camelback roads. It has more than 165 stores and restaurants, including Dillard's, Neiman Marcus, Nordstrom and Robinsons-May, as well as such retailers as Banana Republic and Tiffany & Co.

SAVE **DESERT STORM HUMMER TOURS** picks up passengers at the Rock Bottom Grille, jct. Shea Blvd. and SR 101 at 8668 E. Shea Blvd. Visitors journey in an all-terrain Hummer driven by an experienced guide, exploring the vast Sonoran Desert and its desert views, bouldered canyons, abundant plant life and rock formations. The tour includes a 30-minute nature walk with a guided presentation about plant and animal life.

Allow 4 hours minimum. Departures daily at 8 and 1. Fare $100; ages 6-12, $75. Transportation to the departure point is available for a fee. Reservations are required. AX, DS, MC, VI. Phone (480) 922-0020 or (866) 374-8637.

HEARD MUSEUM NORTH is at 34505 N. Scottsdale Rd. Native American artwork from the Heard Museum's vast collection is shown here; exhibits change semiannually. The video Our Voices, Our Land presents Native Americans speaking about their culture. Allow 30 minutes minimum. Mon.-Sat. 9:30-5, Sat. noon-5; closed Jan. 1, Easter, Memorial Day, July 4, Labor Day, Thanksgiving and Dec. 25. Donations. Phone (480) 488-9817.

SCOTTSDALE CIVIC CENTER AND MALL, at Drinkwater Blvd. and 2nd St., includes a library, municipal buildings, a park, fountains, sculptures, a pond and landscaped lawns. Also on the mall is the Scottsdale Center for the Performing Arts, a forum for the visual and performing arts; changing exhibits are featured. Center for the Arts Mon.-Sat. 10-5, Sun. noon-5. Free. Phone (480) 994-2787.

Scottsdale Historical Museum, 7333 E. Civic Center Mall, is housed in a 1909 red brick grammar school furnished in period. A replica of a barbershop, complete with a barber chair and tools, and an old-fashioned kitchen are featured. Other exhibits include a display of town memorabilia and a replica of a 1900 schoolroom. Allow 30 minutes minimum. Wed.-Sat. 10-5, Sun. noon-4, Oct.-May; Wed.-Sat. 10-2, Sun. noon-4, in June and Sept. Donations. Phone (480) 945-4499.

SAVE **Scottsdale Museum of Contemporary Art,** 7380 E. 2nd St., features works by contemporary artists from Arizona and around the world. Displays focusing on modern architecture and design also are offered. Wed. noon-5, Thurs. 10-8, Fri.-Sat. 10-5, Sun. noon-5; closed major holidays. Admission $7, students with ID $5, under 16 free; free to all Thurs. Phone (480) 994-2787.

TALIESIN WEST, 114th St. (Frank Lloyd Wright Blvd.) and Cactus Rd., was the winter home and studio of architect Frank Lloyd Wright. On 550 acres of Sonoran Desert at the foothills of the McDowell Mountains, the complex of buildings is connected by walkways, gardens and terraces.

Tours include a 1-hour Panorama Tour, a 90-minute Insights Tour, a 3-hour Behind the Scenes Tour, and a 90-minute Desert Walk. Other tours also are available.

Allow 1 hour minimum. Panorama Tours depart daily 9:15-4:15, Nov.-Apr.; 9-11 a.m., rest of year. Insights Tours depart daily 9-4, Nov.-Apr.; 9:30-4, rest of year. Behind the Scenes Tours depart Mon., Thurs. and Sat. at 9:15 in May and Sept.-Oct.; Mon. and Sat. at 9:15, June-Aug., Mon. and Thurs. at 9:15, rest of year. Desert Walks depart daily at 11:15, Nov.-Apr. Hours may vary; phone ahead. Closed Jan. 1, Easter, Thanksgiving and Dec. 25.

Panorama Tour Nov.-Apr. $18; over 65 and students with ID $16; ages 4-12, $5. Fee rest of year $14; over 65 and students with ID $12; ages 4-12, $4.50. Insights Tour Nov.-Apr. $22.50; over 65 and students with ID $20; ages 4-12, $15. Fee rest of year $16.50; over 65, students with ID and ages 4-12, $14.50. Behind the Scenes Tour Nov.-Apr. $45; fee rest of year $25. Desert walk $20. Combination rates are available. Rates may vary; phone

ahead. Tours not recommended for children under 4. Reservations are recommended for some tours. AX, MC, VI. Phone (480) 860-2700, or (480) 860-8810 for recorded tour information.

SUN CITY/SUN CITY WEST (I-2)

pop. 64,653, elev. 1,140'

Twelve miles northwest of Phoenix but part of the metropolitan area of the capital city, Sun City is one of the largest and most popular retirement communities in the country. By 1978 it had reached its population goal of more than 40,000, with most residential property in use. Sun City West, 2.5 miles west via Grand Avenue, offers a similar array of golf courses, stores, restaurants, recreation areas and other services.

The Sundome presents concerts with nationally known entertainers. For a schedule of events contact the Sundome, 19403 R.H. Johnson Blvd., Sun City West, AZ 85375; phone (623) 975-1900 or (623) 544-8942.

Sun City Visitors Center: 16824 N. 99th Ave., Sun City, AZ 85351; phone (623) 977-5000 or (800) 437-8146.

SURPRISE (I-2) pop. 30,848, elev. 1,178'

In the Sonoran desert, Surprise was founded in 1937 by Homer C. Ludden, a state legislator who named the town after his hometown in Nebraska. Surprise Stadium is the spring training center for the Kansas City Royals and the Texas Rangers. Eight miles southwest is White Tank Mountain Regional Park *(see Recreation Chart)*, which offers 22 miles of trails for hiking, horseback riding and mountain biking; Hohokam petroglyphs may be seen.

Northwest Valley Chamber of Commerce: 12801 W. Bell Rd., Suite 14, Surprise, AZ 85374; phone (623) 583-0692.

WEST VALLEY ART MUSEUM is off SR 101, then 4 mi. w. on Bell Rd. to 17420 N. Avenue of the Arts (114th Ave.). The museum's collection includes an extensive permanent exhibit of ethnic dress from more than 60 countries with an emphasis on Africa, Asia and Latin America.

Also featured is 19th- and 20th-century American art, with a focus on the works of Henry Varnum Poor and George Resler, as well as 19th-century Japanese woodcut prints and cultural artifacts from Africa, Asia and South America. Food is available. Allow 30 minutes minimum. Tues.-Sun. 10-4; closed major holidays. Admission $7, students with ID $2, under 6 free. Phone (623) 972-0635.

TEMPE (I-3) pop. 158,625, elev. 1,159'

Founded as Hayden's Ferry in 1872, Tempe originally was named for Charles Trumbull Hayden, who owned a flour mill and operated a ferry across the Salt River; Hayden Flour Mill is purportedly the oldest continuously operating industry in the state. The town was renamed Tempe (Tem-PEE) in 1878 for the area's alleged resemblance to the Vale of Tempe in ancient Greece.

In 1886 the dusty cow town became the home of the Arizona Territorial Normal School, later to become Arizona State University *(see attraction listing)*. Education and farming contributed to continued growth.

One of the last major buildings designed by Frank Lloyd Wright, the Gammage Center for the Performing Arts, is on the campus of Arizona State University. Depending on the special events scheduled, free guided tours of the center depart from the box office on the half-hour Mon.-Fri. 1-4, Aug.-May.

Tempe kicks off Arizona's calendar of events on New Year's Day with the Fiesta Bowl Football Classic, one of the nation's largest college bowl games. The game is played at Arizona State University's Sun Devil Stadium, which also is the home stadium for the Arizona Cardinals professional football team.

Tempe Convention and Visitors Bureau: 51 W. Third St., Suite 105, Tempe, AZ 85281; phone (480) 894-8158 or (800) 283-6734. *See color ad.*

Shopping areas: Specialty shops are scattered throughout Old Town Tempe, the four-block segment of Mill Avenue between 3rd and 7th streets. Arizona Mills Mall, I-10 and Baseline Road, is one of the state's largest shopping and entertainment complexes.

THE ARIZONA HISTORICAL SOCIETY MUSEUM, in Papago Park at 1300 N. College Ave., portrays the history of the state through exhibits, hands-on displays and films. Visitors can view a 35-foot reconstructed section of the Roosevelt Dam, use a kiosk to learn about the development of the area, and visit a turn-of-the-20th-century saloon and general store. Changing exhibits, guided tours and a research library and archives are available.

Picnicking is permitted. Tues.-Sat. 10-4, Sun. noon-4; closed Jan. 1, July 4, Thanksgiving and Dec. 25. Admission $5, senior citizens and students with ID $4, under 12 free; free to all first Sat. of the month. Phone (480) 929-0292.

ARIZONA STATE UNIVERSITY is at University Dr. and Mill Ave. Located in the heart of Tempe, the university's main campus includes distinctive Gammage Auditorium, a concert hall designed by Frank Lloyd Wright that is one of his last completed nonresidential designs. The Arboretum at ASU encompasses the entire campus. Self-guiding walking tour brochures are available at the Information Center in the Memorial Union and the Visitors Center. Arboretum open daily dawn-dusk. Phone (480) 965-9011.

Arizona State University Art Museum, housed in the Nelson Fine Arts Center at 10th St. and Mill Ave., displays American and European prints from the 15th century through present-day and American paintings and sculptures from the 19th century to the present. The museum's primary focus is on contemporary art and works by Latino artists. A ceramic research center features more than 3,000 pieces. Changing exhibitions also are presented. Nelson Fine Arts Center open Tues.-Sat. 10-5 (also Tues. 5-9, Sept.-Apr.). Donations. Phone (480) 965-2787.

Arizona State University R.S. Dietz Museum of Geology is in the Physical Sciences Building, F Wing, near the intersection of University Dr. and McAllister St. Displays include a working seismograph; a six-story Foucault pendulum demonstrating the Earth's rotation; Columbian mammoth bones; and minerals, gemstones and fossils. Mon.-Fri. 9-noon. Museum closed during school holidays; phone ahead. Free. Phone (480) 965-7065.

BIG SURF, 1500 N. McClintock Rd., provides man-made waves in a wave pool and beaches. There also are 18 waterslides, several volleyball courts and three activity pools. Mon.-Sat. 10-6, Sun. 11-7, Memorial Day-Labor Day. Admission $21; under 48 inches tall $17; under age 3, $1. Reduced rates after 3 p.m. AX, DS, MC, VI. Phone (480) 947-2477.

IMAX THEATER AT ARIZONA MILLS, off I-10 Baseline Rd. exit at the mall, presents films that are based on both IMAX and IMAX 3D technology. IMAX 3D films require the use of 3D headsets. The lifelike images are projected on a screen that is six stories high. Both types of films are shown daily. Hours vary; phone ahead. Admission for IMAX 3D films $9.50; over 59, $8.50; under 13, $7.50. Double feature prices are available. AX, MC, VI. Phone (480) 897-4629.

PETERSEN HOUSE MUSEUM is at 1414 W. Southern Ave. on the corner of Southern Ave. and Priest Dr. Built in 1892 by Niels Petersen, a leading Tempe businessman, the two-story house is a classic example of Queen Anne Victorian architecture, featuring gables, bay windows, 12-foot ceilings, gold-leaf picture railings and hand-stenciled wallpaper borders.

Partially remodeled in 1930, the house also features exhibits from the Great Depression. Allow 1 hour minimum. Tues.-Thurs. and Sat. 10-2; closed major holidays. Donations. Phone (480) 350-5151.

TEMPE HISTORICAL MUSEUM, off US 60 exit 174 (Rural Rd.), then .4 mi. n. to 809 E. Southern Ave., tells the story of Tempe and the Salt River through exhibits about the prehistoric Hohokam tribe, founding father Charles Trumbull Hayden and Tempe's first settlers. A 40-foot interactive model of the Salt River demonstrates the history of water development in the desert; visitors can redirect water into canals and fields.

Two galleries feature temporary exhibits. Picnicking is permitted. Mon.-Thurs. and Sat. 10-5, Sun. 1-5; closed major holidays. Donations. Phone (480) 350-5100.

© Bill Bachmann / Index Stock

This ends listings for the Phoenix Vicinity.
The following page resumes the alphabetical listings of cities in Arizona.

PICACHO (F-4) elev. 1,607'

PICACHO PEAK STATE PARK, .5 mi. s. off I-10 exit 219, is the site of Arizona's westernmost Civil War battle. In 1862 a dozen Union soldiers defeated 17 Confederate cavalrymen. The park is home to the 1,500-foot peak that was used as a landmark for settlers traveling between New Mexico and California.

Today trails meander throughout the park and to the top of the peak. A Civil War re-enactment is held each spring. Camping, hiking and picnicking are permitted. Daily 8 a.m.-10 p.m. Admission $6 per private vehicle, $2 per person, day after Labor Day-day before Memorial Day. Admission rest of year $3 per private vehicle, $2 per person. Camping fees $12-$20, day after Labor Day-day before Memorial Day. Camping fees rest of year $10-$15. Phone (520) 466-3183. *See Recreation Chart.*

PINE (D-4) pop. 1,931

PINE-STRAWBERRY MUSEUM is on SR 87 between Hardscrabble Rd. and Randall Dr. The museum houses artifacts from prehistoric Native American cultures and the Spanish, Anglo and Mormon pioneers who first settled the area. Exhibits include World War II memorabilia, farming implements, furnishings and clothing from the late 1800s. Allow 1 hour minimum. Mon.-Sat. 10-4, Sun. 1-4, May 15-Oct. 15; Mon.-Sat. 10-2, rest of year. Closed Jan. 1, Thanksgiving and Dec. 25. Donations. Phone (928) 476-3547.

PINETOP (D-5) pop. 3,582, elev. 6,800'

CASINOS

- **Hon-Dah Resort Casino and Conference Center**, 3 mi. e. at jct. SRs 260 and 73. Daily 24 hours. Phone (928) 369-0299.

PINETOP-LAKESIDE (D-5)
pop. 3,582, elev. 6,960'

Lakeside originally was named Fairview in 1880 by Mormon pioneers. Pinetop, also founded by Mormons, began in 1878 with a sawmill and ranching on the open range of the White Mountains. Before tourism, logging and ranching were the mainstays of the area. The twin towns were incorporated in 1984 as a resort area.

Pinetop-Lakeside, on the edge of the White Mountain Apache Reservation, is 10 miles southeast of Show Low on SR 260 on the edge of Mogollon Rim. The elevation makes the area cool in summer for trout fishing, camping and other activities. Winter sports such as snowmobiling, skiing and ice fishing are popular in the Apache-Sitgreaves National Forests *(see place listing p. 40)* and on the reservation. Fishing also is permitted by fee on the reservation.

Pinetop-Lakeside Chamber of Commerce: 102-C W. White Mountain Blvd. in Lakeside, P.O. Box 4220, Pinetop, AZ 85935; phone (928) 367-4290 or (800) 573-4031.

PIPE SPRING NATIONAL MONUMENT (A-3)

Off SR 389 15 miles west of Fredonia, Pipe Spring National Monument preserves a life-sustaining water source that Paiute Indians called Mu-tum-wa-va, or Dripping Rock. In the early 1870s, Mormon pioneers discovered the springs and built a compound consisting of a sandstone fort and ranch house. Tours of the fort, named Winsor Castle, are offered. Pipe Spring also served as a way station for weary travelers. The visitor center offers exhibits about Kaibab Paiute and pioneer culture and history.

Allow 1 hour minimum. Daily 7-5, June-Sept.; 8-5, rest of year. Closed Jan. 1, Thanksgiving and Dec. 25. Tours of Winsor Castle are given daily on the half-hour. Admission $5, under 15 free. Phone (928) 643-7105.

PORTAL (F-6) elev. 4,773'

Portal received its name because it is at the entrance to Cave Creek Canyon. The town became a popular summer vacation spot for those seeking cool, high altitudes and such recreational pastimes as camping, fishing, hiking and hunting.

CAVE CREEK CANYON, s.w. via a paved road, displays brilliant colors and rugged towering cliffs of red rhyolite rising from the canyon floor. The Southwestern Research Station of the American Museum of Natural History in New York City is at the upper end of the canyon; its laboratories are closed to the public. Bird-watching, camping and hiking opportunities are available. Phone (520) 364-3468.

PRESCOTT (C-3) pop. 33,938, elev. 5,346'

The area around Prescott was first settled in 1864 by miners prospecting for gold. It was the presence of gold that prompted the cash-poor Union to designate Arizona as a territory in 1863. President Abraham Lincoln chose an area just north of Prescott as the first seat of government because the gold fields were nearby and because Southern sympathizers dominated Tucson. In 1867 the capitol was moved south to Tucson. However, Prescott briefly became capital again in 1877, a title it lost to Phoenix in 1889.

Named to honor historian William Hickling Prescott, the town was incorporated in 1883. Because of the surrounding pine forests, wooden structures rather than the typical adobe buildings were built. Fire devastated Prescott in 1900, but determined townsfolk rebuilt and developed a water system utilizing Del Rio Springs.

Surrounded by mountain ranges and nearly encircled by the Prescott National Forest, the town is now a resort community. Outdoor enthusiasts can indulge in camping, horseback riding, hiking, fishing, rockhounding and picnicking.

Yavapai Downs offers Thoroughbred and quarterhorse races Saturday through Tuesday, Memorial

Day weekend through Labor Day weekend; phone (928) 775-8000.

Note: Policies concerning admittance of children to pari-mutuel betting facilities vary. Phone for information.

Prescott Chamber of Commerce: 117 W. Goodwin St., Prescott, AZ 86303; phone (928) 445-2000 or (800) 266-7534. *See color ad.*

Self-guiding tours: A leaflet outlining a self-guiding walking tour of Prescott's Victorian-era neighborhoods can be obtained at the chamber of commerce.

Shopping areas: Dillard's, JCPenney and Sears anchor the Prescott Gateway Mall, 3250 Gateway Blvd. near SR 69 and Lee Boulevard. Whiskey Row/Courthouse Square, downtown off SR 89 and Cortez Street, offers antique, souvenir and clothes shopping opportunities as well as several eateries.

BUCKY O'NEILL MONUMENT, on Courthouse Plaza, was created by Solon H. Borglum. It pays tribute to the First U.S. Volunteer Cavalry (Roosevelt's Rough Riders) and Capt. William O'Neill, the first volunteer in the Spanish-American War and organizer of the Rough Riders.

GRANITE BASIN, just inside Prescott National Forest about 12 mi. n.w., is a 7-acre lake lying at the foot of Granite Mountain. A recreation area offers hiking, horse trails and facilities, camping and fishing. Parking $2. Phone (928) 443-8000.

GRANITE DELLS (Point of Rocks), 4 mi. n. on SR 89, is a summer playground on Watson Lake. Granite formations line the highway for 2 miles. Recreational vehicle camping is available. Camping $21 per recreational vehicle. Phone (928) 445-9018.

HERITAGE PARK ZOO, 6 mi. n. via SR 89, off Willow Creek Rd. in Heritage Park, presents exotic and native wild animals in their natural settings. Guided tours are available by appointment. Daily 9-5, May-Oct.; 10-4, rest of year. Admission $6; over 64, $5; ages 3-12, $3. Phone (928) 778-4242.

PHIPPEN ART MUSEUM, 6 mi. n.e. at 4701 SR 89N, displays a collection of works by prominent Western artists, together with contemporary artwork depicting the American West. Allow 30 minutes minimum. Tues.-Sat. 10-4, Sun. 1-4. Admission $5; over 60 and students with ID, $4; under 12 free. AX, DS, MC, VI. Phone (928) 778-1385.

SHARLOT HALL MUSEUM, downtown at 415 W. Gurley St., contains 3.5 acres of galleries and gardens. The museum features the Territorial Mansion, which had been restored by poet and historian Sharlot M. Hall. Hall filled the mansion with Arizona pioneer artifacts donated to her for use in the museum, which opened in 1928. Six historic buildings and several exhibits trace the heritage of the area.

Also on the grounds are an amphitheater that hosts plays during the summer; herb and rose gardens; and Fort Misery, the first cabin built in Prescott. The buildings were constructed 1864-1937. The Museum Center contains archives and a library for research.

Allow 1 hour minimum. Mon.-Sat. 10-5, Sun. noon-4, May-Sept.; Mon.-Sat. 10-4, rest of year. Closed Jan. 1, Thanksgiving and Dec. 25. Admission $5, under 19 free. Phone (928) 445-3122.

Governor's Mansion was completed in 1864 for John N. Goodwin, Arizona's first territorial governor. The mansion's furnishings and artifacts depict the period 1864-67. The exhibit Behind Whiskey Row tells the story of Prescott's second-class citizens, including its Chinese workers, during the late 1800s.

John C. Frémont House was built in 1875 and served as the home of the celebrated "Pathfinder" during his term as fifth territorial governor of Arizona. The furnishings and artifacts depict the period 1875-81.

William C. Bashford House, built in 1877, represents the late Victorian style. The home is furnished in period.

SMOKI MUSEUM, n. of Gurley St. at 147 N. Arizona St., is patterned after early Pueblo structures

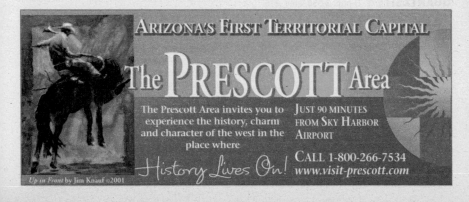

both in architecture and interior design. The museum contains artifacts and documents pertaining to Native American pre-history and history with emphasis on the Prescott region. Ceramics, baskets, beaded ornaments, clothing, jewelry and paintings are among the items displayed. Mon.-Sat. 10-4, Sun. 1-4. Hours may vary; phone ahead. Admission $4; over 55, $3; students with ID $2; under 11 free. Phone (928) 445-1230.

THUMB BUTTE, 4 mi. w., is a rugged outcropping of granite. Extensive views are offered from the summit, which can be reached on foot. Picnic facilities are available. Parking $2.

CASINOS

• **Bucky's Casino,** in the Prescott Resort at 1500 E. SR 69, just e. of jct. SR 89. Daily 24 hours. Phone (928) 776-5695.

PRESCOTT NATIONAL FOREST

Elevations in the forest range from 3,071 ft. in the Verde Valley to 7,971 ft. at Mount Union. Refer to AAA maps for additional elevation information.

Accessed via SR 89, SR 89A and SR 69 off I-17 in central Arizona, Prescott National Forest encompasses two long mountain ranges with varying elevations. In addition to its major access routes, other scenic but primitive roads not recommended for low-clearance vehicles penetrate the 1,238,154-acre forest. Check locally for road conditions.

Developed recreation areas are at Mingus Mountain and in Prescott Basin. Camping, picnicking, hiking and backpacking are popular recreational pursuits; many trails can be enjoyed year-round. Some popular day-use areas in Prescott have a $2 parking fee. Hunting is permitted in season with the appropriate state game license obtained from the Game and Fish Department; phone (928) 692-7700.

For further information contact Prescott National Forest, 344 S. Cortez St., Prescott, AZ 86303; phone (928) 443-8000 Mon.-Fri. 8-4:30. *See Recreation Chart and the AAA Southwestern CampBook.*

QUARTZSITE (E-2) pop. 3,354, elev. 876'

A settler named Charles Tyson built a fort on this site in 1856 for protection against Native Americans. Because of a good water supply it soon became a stagecoach stop on the Ehrenburg-to-Prescott route. As the stage lines vanished, Fort Tyson, or Tyson's Wells (as it became known), was abandoned. A small mining boom in 1897 revitalized the area, and the settlement revived as Quartzsite.

The winter population of this desert town swells to 1 million during January and February because of the gem and mineral shows in the area. The Pow Wow Rock and Mineral Show began the rockhound winter migration to town in 1965; now eight major shows entice gem enthusiasts, collectors and jewelers to Quartzsite to buy and sell. In an event that

has attained international scope, thousands of dealers offer raw and handcrafted merchandise throughout January and February.

Quartzsite Chamber of Commerce: 100 E. Main St., P.O. Box 85, Quartzsite, AZ 85346; phone (928) 927-5600.

HI JOLLY MEMORIAL, e. on I-10 in the old cemetery, honors Hadji Ali. Nicknamed Hi Jolly by soldiers and pioneers, the Arab came to Arizona in 1856 with an Army consignment of camels. The camels adapted well to their new environment but were never used successfully, partly because the sight of them caused horses, mules and cattle to stampede.

KOFA NATIONAL WILDLIFE REFUGE, encompassing the Kofa and Castle Dome mountains, preserves the habitat of the desert bighorn sheep.

Remote Palm Canyon is 18 miles south of Quartzsite on US 95, then 7 miles east on a maintained gravel road. It is one of the few places in Arizona where native palms grow. They can be seen from a point 200 yards away via a .5-mile hike up a moderately steep trail.

Note: The last 200 yards to the palms present a strenuous climb. Refuge roads are rough and are best navigated by four-wheel-drive and high-clearance vehicles. Firearms are prohibited in the refuge, except during special hunting seasons. Refuge and canyon accessible daily 24 hours. Free. Phone (928) 783-7861.

ROOSEVELT (H-6) elev. 2,215'

THEODORE ROOSEVELT DAM AND LAKE is reached via SR 188 or SR 88 (the Apache Trail), a dirt road. Modern Arizona's reclamation of the Salt River Valley began with the completion of the Roosevelt Dam in 1911. Unlike other dams, the Roosevelt was made with thousands of hand-hewn stones.

As the first major federal reclamation project, the dam provides water and power to one of the state's richest agricultural regions. Many recreational opportunities are available on the lake. For further information phone (928) 467-3200. *See Recreation Chart.*

SACATON (E-4) pop. 1,584, elev. 1,127'

Sacaton, first visited by Spanish missionaries in 1696, was even then an ancient Pima Indian settlement; currently the town is the headquarters for the Pima Reservation. American pioneers noted the abundance of very tall grass, from which they derived the town name.

GILA RIVER CULTURAL CENTER, next to I-10 exit 175 on Casa Blanca Rd., contains a park with reconstructed Indian homes from various tribes that depict more than 2,000 years of Native American life in the Gila River Basin. The communities represent the Akimel, Apache, Hohokam, Pee-Posh and

Tohono O'odham cultures. A museum and craft center adjoin the park. Food is available. Allow 1 hour minimum. Daily 8-5; closed major holidays. Donations. Phone (520) 315-3411.

SAFFORD (E-6) pop. 9,232, elev. 2,920'

The first American colony in the Gila Valley, Safford was founded in 1874 by farmers whose previous holdings had been washed away by the Gila River. From Safford the Swift Trail winds 36 miles to the top of 10,720-foot Mount Graham. En route the trail traverses five of the seven ecological zones in Western North America. Camping, hiking and picnicking are permitted. Gila Box Riparian National Conservation Area, 15 miles northeast, offers seasonal river floating opportunities.

The region south of Safford is known for its hot mineral water baths. Information about area spas is available from the chamber of commerce.

For seekers of fire agates and other semiprecious stones, there are two rockhound areas administered and maintained by the U.S. Bureau of Land Management. Black Hills Back Country Byway is a 21-mile scenic drive through the Black Hills. The drive is a graded dirt road with sharp turns and steep drops.

Round Mountain Rockhound Area, featuring chalcedony roses and fire agates, is 12 miles south of Duncan on US 70, west at Milepost 5.6, 7.1 miles to the BLM sign, then 2.5 miles south to the first collection area. A second collection area is 4.5 miles south using the left fork in the road. **Note:** The road is not maintained and is very rough. Because of the area's remote location, visitors should bring along plenty of water and gasoline. Phone ahead for road conditions. Information about these areas can be obtained by contacting the Bureau of Land Management, 711 S. 14th Ave., Safford, AZ 85546; phone (928) 348-4400.

Graham County Chamber of Commerce: 1111 Thatcher Blvd., Safford, AZ 85546; phone (928) 428-2511 or (888) 837-1841.

ROPER LAKE STATE PARK, 1 mi. s. off US 191, is at the base of Mount Graham. The park features a rock-lined pool filled with water from the natural mineral hot springs. Camping, hiking, swimming and picnicking are available. Daily 6 a.m.-10 p.m. Admission $3 per private vehicle. Camping $10 per private vehicle (additional $2 for hookups). Phone (928) 428-6760. *See Recreation Chart.*

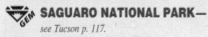 **SAGUARO NATIONAL PARK—**
see Tucson p. 117.

SAHUARITA—*see Tucson p. 118.*

ST. JOHNS (C-6) pop. 3,269, elev. 5,650'

APACHE COUNTY HISTORICAL SOCIETY MUSEUM, .25 mi. w. of jct. US 191 and SR 61 at 180 W. Cleveland St., displays pioneer artifacts, mammoth bones, Native American artifacts, miniature replicas of early St. Johns homes, and antique guns and slot machines. Allow 30 minutes minimum. Mon.-Fri. 9-5; other times by appointment. Closed holidays. Donations. Phone (928) 337-4737.

LYMAN LAKE STATE PARK, 11 mi. s. on US 180/191, offers acres of rolling grassland that provide a home to wildlife. A water ski course is set up on the lake during the summer months. A tour of Native American ruins and prehistoric rock art is available. Park daily 24 hours. Office daily 8-5. Tour is given Sat.-Sun. at 10, Memorial Day-Labor Day. Admission $5 per private vehicle. Camping $12-$19 per private vehicle. Tour $2. Phone (928) 337-4441. *See Recreation Chart.*

ST. MICHAELS (B-6) pop. 1,295

ST. MICHAELS HISTORICAL MUSEUM, 24 Mission Rd. off SR 264 in the St. Michaels Mission complex, features permanent displays chronicling the work of the Franciscan Friars on the Navajo Nation. Temporary exhibits include examples of Navajo life and culture. The museum is housed in the original mission building, restored to its 1898 appearance. Allow 30 minutes minimum. Daily 9-5, Memorial Day-Labor Day. Donations. Phone (928) 871-4171.

SAN CARLOS (E-5) pop. 3,716, elev. 2,432'

San Carlos, north of Coolidge Dam, is a trading center and headquarters for the San Carlos Indian Agency. The Apaches operate one of the largest cattle ranches in this area. The San Carlos Apache Reservation offers some of the best trophy-hunting and fishing in the state; permits are required. For permit information contact the San Carlos Recreation and Wildlife Department, P.O. Box 97, San Carlos, AZ 85550; phone (928) 475-2343.

Coolidge Dam, about 9 miles southeast on the Gila River, impounds the waters that irrigate the Casa Grande Valley. Construction of the dam was delayed until a solution satisfactory to the Apache Indians was found concerning the disturbance of tribal burial grounds. Once it was agreed that a concrete slab would cover the cemetery, construction resumed.

SANTA CRUZ DE TERRENATE PRESIDIO NATIONAL HISTORIC SITE (F-5)

Santa Cruz de Terrenate Presidio National Historic Site is 4 miles north of Tombstone on SR 80, 6 miles west on SR 82 to Fairbank, .75 miles west to Kellar Road, then 2 miles north in the San Pedro Riparian National Conservation Area. Established by the Spanish in 1776 on the banks of the San Pedro River, the presidio was built to protect the overland route east of Tucson. Because of the frequent Apache raids as well as the lack of proper supplies, Terrenate was abandoned less than 5 years after its establishment.

The site, once consisting of seven structures built around a central courtyard, contains signs showing what each of the structures originally looked like. Many of the adobe walls that surrounded the presidio are eroded and only a few remain. They were planned to be 15 feet tall, but were built to only 12 feet due to lack of funds. In addition, the bastion/gunpowder storehouse was never completed, and less than one-fourth of the planned barracks were never constructed because of insufficient funding.

The historic site is fragile, and visitors are instructed by signs to stay on the trails and not to touch the remaining structures. A 1.2-mile dirt trail leads from the parking lot to the presidio. Camping is permitted. Visitors should bring their own food and water as no facilities are available. Site admission free. Camping $2 per person per night. Phone (520) 439-6400.

SASABE (G-4) elev. 3,560'

BUENOS AIRES NATIONAL WILDLIFE REFUGE, 7 mi. n. on SR 286 at Milepost 8, is a 118,000-acre refuge established to preserve the endangered masked bobwhite quail and other grassland wildlife. It is home to more than 300 species of birds, including grayhawks, vermilion fly catchers and golden eagles. Other wildlife include coyotes, deer, foxes, javelinas, pronghorn antelope and bobcats. Trails are located on the eastern side near the town of Arivaca.

Allow 4 hours minimum. Refuge daily dawn-dusk. Visitor center daily 7:30-4, mid-Aug. to May; Mon.-Fri. 7:30-4, rest of year. Guided tours to Brown Canyon are offered every other Sat., Nov.-Apr. Refuge free. Guided tours $5; reservations are required. Phone (520) 823-4251, ext. 116.

SCOTTSDALE — *see Phoenix p. 88.*

SECOND MESA (B-5) pop. 814, elev. 5,680'

Second Mesa, near the junction of SRs 264 and 87, is within a Hopi Reservation that occupies a large tract in the center of the vast Navajo Reservation of northeastern Arizona.

HOPI CULTURAL CENTER MUSEUM, 5 mi. w. of SR 87 on SR 264, displays basketry, weaving, jewelry and other artifacts depicting the history of the Hopi. Kachina dolls, representations of divine ancestral spirits, also are featured. Allow 1 hour minimum. Mon.-Fri. 8-5, Sat.-Sun. 9-3. Admission $3; under 14, $1. Phone (928) 734-6650.

SEDONA (C-4) pop. 10,192, elev. 4,400'

Sedona is nestled between the massive, fire-hued rocks of Red Rock State Park and the lush gorges of Oak Creek Canyon *(see attraction listing p. 100).* The dusty, semi-arid topography is the base for giant, striped monoliths that take on shades from bright red to pale sand and seem to change color with each passing cloud or ray of sunshine. Since most of the rock is sedimentary, the portrait is constantly eroding and changing shape. Verdant Oak Creek Canyon, with juniper and cypress trees lining a clear stream, provides a sharp contrast.

So prominent are the buttes and pinnacles that locals have named them. Some of the more popular rock stars are Bell Rock, Cathedral Rock, Chimney Rock, Coffeepot Rock, Courthouse Butte and Snoopy Rock. Formations in the shape of a castle or merry-go-round also can be spotted. Conveniently, two nuns overlook a chapel. And close by, a submarine surfaces near a mushroom cap.

Sedona's rugged red rocks and canyons have even shared the screen with Hollywood movie stars. The area has served as a backdrop for dozens of Western movies. Some popular titles filmed here include "Angel and the Badman," "Broken Arrow," "Firecreek," "Midnight Run" and "The Quick and the Dead."

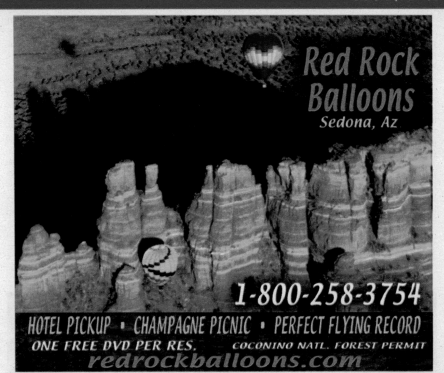

Mother Nature was kind to Sedona, blessing her with sharp light, bright blue skies, colorful terrain, picturesque sunsets and animated clouds. Inspired painters, sculptors and other creative souls flocked to Sedona and now call the area home. In 1965 the Cowboy Artists of America, a successful art organization, was founded in what is now Uptown; its goals remain to ensure authentic portrayal of Western scenes in art. An established art colony, Sedona boasts ubiquitous galleries and studios that display residents' artistic endeavors: Pottery, sculpture, paintings and jewelry embody a variety of styles, from Western and Southwestern to modern.

Tlaquepaque, on SR 179 just south of SR 89A (referred to locally as the "Y"), is a shopping village modeled after a small Mexican village. Notable for its architectural features alone, it houses a collection of galleries and restaurants as well as a chapel; musicians often perform in the courtyards.

Alongside artists live spiritualists, who embrace the energy set forth by such natural splendor. Sedona is purportedly home to several vortexes, specific fields that emit energy upward from the earth.

First channeled and defined by Page Bryant in 1980, a vortex is said to emanate three types of energy: electrical (masculine), magnetic (feminine) or electromagnetic (neutral). Found at various locations, these natural power fields are thought to energize and inspire.

Sedona is said to contain a curiously high number of vortexes and is one of the few places in the world that possesses all three types of energy. Countless businesses in Sedona specialize in new age medicine, and many offer vortex or spiritual tours. Visitors may find vortexes at Bell Rock, Cathedral Rock and Boynton Canyon. At Airport Mesa, the attraction is twofold: Guests may locate an electric force as well as a great spot from which to view a spectacular sunset.

The town received its name in 1902 from T. Carl Schnebly, one of the first settlers in the area. Schnebly wanted to establish a post office, yet both names he submitted to the postmaster general—Schnebly Station and Oak Creek Crossing—were deemed too long for a cancellation stamp. At the

suggestion of his brother, he suggested his wife's name, and it stuck.

The Schneblys weren't the first ones to reside in Sedona. Ancient cliff dwellings found in the area were constructed by the Southern Sinagua people (Spanish for "without water") around A.D. 1130-1300. Two of the largest cliff dwellings, Honanki and Palatki *(see attraction listings)*, still retain a number of pictographs in the shapes of animals, people and various designs.

Sedona is the starting point for hikes and scenic drives through the Red Rock area. From the vista point on the Mogollon Rim to Sedona, Oak Creek Canyon Drive (SR 89A) winds through the canyon, offering a continuous display of natural beauty, including the area's signature colored rock formations as well as sudden changes in vegetation. Oak Creek flows between 1,200-foot-tall canyon walls toward the red rocks of Sedona.

A Red Rock Pass is required for parking when visiting or hiking the many scenic areas in Sedona. Passes may be purchased at the Sedona Chamber of Commerce. A daily pass is $5; a weekly pass is $15. Passes are not valid in state parks or campgrounds.

Red Rock Country is just the spot for an exhilarating, hang-on-tight jeep adventure. Guided tours of the back country are offered by Sedona Red Rock Jeep Tours *(see color ad p. 98)*; phone (928) 282-6826 or (800) 848-7728.

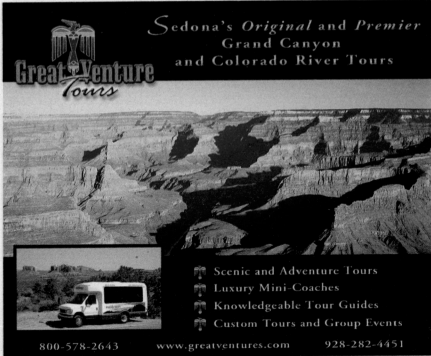

SAVE Great West Adventure Co. provides transportation and tours to the Grand Canyon as well as scenic tours of Sedona via 14-passenger buses; Colorado River rafting trips also are available. Phone (928) 204-5506 or (877) 367-2383.

Sedona-Oak Creek Canyon Chamber of Commerce: 331 Forest Rd., P.O. Box 478, Sedona, AZ 86336; phone (928) 282-7722 or (800) 288-7336.

Shopping areas: Art galleries and restaurants intermingle with specialty shops at Tlaquepaque, just south of Uptown on SR 179. Oakcreek Factory Outlets, 7 miles south on SR 179, offers more than 30 outlet stores. Other areas featuring galleries and shops are Hillside Sedona, Hozho Center and along SR 89A near the village of Oakcreek.

ADVENTURE COMPANY JEEP TOURS is at 336 SR 179, Suite F-103. Experienced guides take passengers on jeep excursions to Broken Arrow, Bear Wallow Canyon, the Red Rock Outback or Sedona vortexes. Guests also may rent and drive a jeep for 3 hours while a guide leads the way. Allow 1 hour minimum. Daily 9-dusk. Fare $30-$60; under 13, $15-$30. Jeep rental $250. AX, MC, VI. Phone (928) 204-1973 or (877) 281-6622.

ARIZONA HELICOPTER ADVENTURES, departing from the Sedona Airport, offers a variety of in-flight, narrated sightseeing tours of Sedona and environs, including the Native American ruins of Boynton Canyon and the area's scenic red rock formations. Daily 9-5; closed Dec. 25. Length of tours varies. Fare $58-$138. Reservations are recommended. AX, DS, MC, VI. Phone (928) 282-0904 or (800) 282-5141.

SAVE **ARIZONA SAFARI JEEP TOURS,** .3 mi. n. of jct. SRs 179 and 89A to 335 Jordan Rd., offers a variety of tours of Sedona, the Colorado Plateau and the Sonoran Desert. All tours include narration by educated guides with backgrounds in biology, geology and game and range management; hands-on animal demonstrations are featured. Allow 2 hours minimum. Daily dawn-dusk. Fares $54-$195; under 12, $41-$145. MC, VI. Phone (928) 282-3012.

CHAPEL OF THE HOLY CROSS, .8 mi. s. off SR 179 on Chapel Rd., stands on a small mountain that provides scenic views. The contemporary Catholic shrine is constructed on the area's noted red rock. Built in 1956, the chapel is situated between two large red sandstone peaks with a ramp leading to the entrance. A 90-foot cross dominates the structure. Allow 30 minutes minimum. Daily 9-5. Free. Phone (928) 282-4069.

SAVE **A DAY IN THE WEST JEEP TOURS** is at 252 N. SR 89A, .3 mi. n.e. from jct. SR 179. Comprehensive jeep tours of canyons, rock formations and trails are offered. Guides in old-fashioned cowboy garb dispense photography tips and provide information about local animals, geology, history

and vegetation. Cowboy cookouts and horseback rides also are offered.

Note: Comfortable walking shoes are recommended. Food is available. Inquire about weather policies. Allow 1 hour minimum. Tours daily 7:30-dusk. Fare $45-$145; ages 1-12, $35-$110. Under 18 months are not permitted. Reservations are recommended. AX, DS, MC, VI. Phone (928) 282-4320 or (800) 973-3662.

SAVE **GRAND CANYON GREAT VENTURE TOURS,** with pick-up from local hotels, offers a 3.5-hour narrated coach tour along the east and south rims of the Grand Canyon. Highlights include the Painted Desert, the Navajo Indian Reservation and an optional lunch at the 1916 Trading Post in Cameron (not included in fare). Daily 9:30-5:30. Fare $99; ages 3-15, $89. Reservations are required. AX, DS, MC, VI. Phone (928) 282-4451 or (800) 578-2643. *See color ad p. 99.*

HONANKI SOUTHERN SINAGUA CLIFF DWELLINGS, 10 mi. s.w. on SR 89A to Milepost 365, .5 mi. s. to FR 525, then 10.2 mi. n. via FR 525 (dirt road), is one of the largest ruins of Southern Sinagua cliff dwellings in the Red Rocks area; occupation is estimated A.D. 1130-1280. The earliest pictographs on the rock walls predate Sinagua habitation. **Note:** Phone the chamber of commerce for information about road conditions. Daily 10-5:30, Memorial Day-Labor Day; 9:30-3:30, rest of year. Closed Jan. 1, Thanksgiving and Dec. 25. Admission $5 (free with Red Rock Pass), under 17 free with adult. Phone (928) 282-4119.

GEM **OAK CREEK CANYON,** n. on SR 89A, is traversed by a scenic stretch of that road.

About 16 miles long and rarely more than 1 mile wide, the canyon is known for its spectacularly colored white, yellow and red cliffs dotted with pine, cypress and juniper. Rocky gorges, unusual rock formations and buttes add interest to the drive.

Oak Creek is noted for trout fishing; throughout the canyon are Forest Service camping and picnicking grounds. Area maps are available from the chambers of commerce in Flagstaff and Sedona.

PALATKI RUINS AND RED CLIFFS ROCK ART SITE is 10 mi. s. on SR 89A, then 8 mi. n. via FRs 525 and 795 (dirt roads), following signs. Pictographs dating from the Archaic period of Native American culture are preserved in rock alcoves. It is believed that nearby cliff dwellings were occupied A.D. 650-1300 by the Southern Sinagua people.

Note: Sites are reached via walking trails; comfortable shoes are recommended. Guided tours are available. Picnicking is permitted. Allow 1 hour, 30 minutes minimum. Daily 9:30-3:30; closed Jan. 1, Thanksgiving and Dec. 25. Admission $5 per vehicle (free with Red Rock Pass). Reservations are required. Phone (928) 282-4119; for reservations, phone (928) 282-3854.

PINK JEEP TOURS is at 204 N. SR 89A, .4 mi. n.e. from jct. SR 179. Passengers journey through the red-rock canyons, desert and forests of Sedona to 700-year-old Sinaguan cliff dwellings and Native American rock art sites. Well-trained guides share lore about local flora, fauna, geology and Native American history and legends. Other tours are available.

Allow 1 hour, 30 minutes minimum. Departures require a minimum of 2 people. Tours daily 7-dusk; closed Dec. 25. Fare $40-$125; under 13, $32-$115. Under 18 months are not permitted. Rates may vary; phone ahead. AX, DC, DS, MC, VI. Phone (928) 282-5000 or (800) 873-3662. *See color ad p. 98.*

[SAVE] **RED ROCK BI-PLANE TOURS AND SKY SAFARI,** 1 mi. w. of SR 179 on SR 89A, then s. to 1225 Airport Rd., offers guided bi-plane tours over Sedona. Passengers can view from the air ancient Native American dwellings not accessible by foot or vehicle. Departures require a minimum of two people. Daily 8-5. Fare $89-$459. AX, CB, DC, DS, MC, VI. Phone (928) 204-5939 or (888) 866-7433. *See color ad p. 97.*

RED ROCK STATE PARK, 3 mi. s. off SR 89A on Lower Red Rock Loop Rd., features 286 acres of a riparian ecosystem. Oak Creek runs through the park creating a diverse riparian habitat that abounds with plants and wildlife. Displays in the visitor center highlight the ecology and conservation of Oak Creek. Nature hikes, bird walks, theater presentations and other planned activities are offered; phone for schedule.

Park open daily 8-8, May-Aug.; 8-6, Apr. and Sept.; 8-5, rest of year. Visitor center open daily 9-6, May-Aug.; 9-5, rest of year. Admission $6 per private vehicle (up to four persons, plus $2 each additional person), $2 per pedestrian, under 14 free. Phone (928) 282-6907.

[SAVE] **REDSTONE TOURS,** with pick-up from local hotels, provides tours led by naturalist guides. The 2-hour Scenic Sedona tour takes guests to such sites as the Airport Vortex, Bell Rock and Tlaquepaque. The full-day Grand Canyon tour includes the South, East and West Rims; Painted Desert; Anasazi ruins and a Navajo Indian reservation; lunch is provided. A 7-hour Ruins and Volcanoes tour and Colorado River float trip also are available.

Allow 2 hours minimum. Tours daily 8-6. Reservations are required. Fare $24-$169. AX, MC, VI. Phone (928) 203-0396 or (866) 473-3786. *See color ad p. 99.*

SEDONA HERITAGE MUSEUM is off SR 89A, then .6 mi. n. to 735 N. Jordan Rd. The museum features a restored one-room cabin built in 1930; additional rooms were added 1937-46. One exhibit is dedicated to more than 80 movies made in Sedona (mainly Westerns) and another depicts the lifestyle of the cowboy. A 1940 apple grading machine and a 1942 fire truck are on display. Picnicking is permitted. Allow 1 hour minimum. Daily 11-3; closed major holidays. Admission $3, under 13 free. Phone (928) 282-7038.

[SAVE] **SEDONA SUPERVUE THEATER,** 7 mi. s. on SR 179 at Oak Creek Factory Outlets, presents a 34-minute giant-screen film journey through the Red Rock area. Other feature films are offered. Daily 10-7. Show times may vary; phone ahead. Admission $7.50; ages 3-11, $5; under 3 free with adult. MC, VI. Phone (928) 284-3214 or (928) 284-3813.

SEDONA TROLLEY is at 276 N. SR 89A in the Sedona Center. Drivers provide sightseeing narration of the Sedona area. Two 55-minute tours are available. Sedona Highlights covers the south side of Sedona, including a stop at the Chapel of the Holy Cross. Seven Canyons takes passengers out of town to Dry Creek Valley, Boynton Canyon and Long Canyons.

Allow 1 hour minimum. Sedona Highlights tour departs daily 10-4. Seven Canyons tour departs daily 9-5, Feb.-Oct; daily 9-3, rest of year. Closed Thanksgiving and Dec. 25. One tour $10; ages 3-12, $5. Two tours $18; ages 3-12, $9. AX, DS, MC, VI. Phone (928) 282-4211.

SLIDE ROCK STATE PARK is 7 mi. n. on SR 89A to 6871 N. SR 89A, within Oak Creek Canyon. Developed around a natural 70-foot waterslide, the park is the site of the historic Pendley homestead and an apple orchard. Activities include swimming and picnicking.

Note: Glass containers are not permitted. Food is available. Pets are not permitted. Daily 8-7, June-Sept.; 8-6, Apr.-May and in Oct.; 8-5, rest of year. Closed Dec. 25. Admission $10 per private vehicle (up to four passengers), $2 for each additional passenger over age 13, $2 per individual on foot or by bicycle. Phone (928) 282-3034. *See Recreation Chart.*

V-BAR-V RANCH PETROGLYPH SITE, 3 mi. e. off I-17 exit 298, following signs, contains 13 panels with more than 1,000 petroglyphs representing the Beaver Creek style of rock art. It is believed that the images of snakes, turtles, coyotes, stick-figured humans and palmlike trees were chiseled into the rock walls by the Sinagua people. Guided tours are available. Picnicking is permitted. Allow 1 hour minimum. Fri.-Mon. 9:30-3:30; closed Dec. 25. Admission $5 per vehicle (free with Red Rock Pass). Phone (928) 282-4119.

RECREATIONAL ACTIVITIES

Hot Air Ballooning

- **Northern Light Balloon Expeditions** provides transportation to the departure point. Write P.O. Box 1695, Sedona, AZ 86339. Tours depart daily at dawn (weather permitting). Phone (928) 282-2274 or (800) 230-6222. *See color ad p. 96.*

- **Red Rock Balloon Adventures** provides transportation to the departure point. Write 105 Canyon Diablo Rd., Sedona, AZ 86351. Tours depart daily at dawn (weather permitting). Phone (928) 284-0040 or (800) 258-3754. *See color ad p. 97.*

Jeep Tours (Self-driving)

- **Sedona Jeep Rentals** is at 235 Air Terminal Dr. at the Sedona Airport, Sedona, AZ 86336. Daily 8-5; closed Dec. 25. Phone (928) 282-2227 or (800) 879-5337.

SELLS (F-3) pop. 2,799, elev. 2,379′

Originally known as Indian Oasis, Sells was renamed in 1918 in honor of Indian commissioner Cato Sells. The dependable water supply made the area a popular stop for travelers, even in prehistoric times.

Sells is the headquarters of the Tohono O'odham Indian Reservation. In addition to this vast reservation west of Tucson, a smaller tract is south of Tucson at the site of Mission San Xavier del Bac *(see Tucson p. 112)*. Mainly farmers and ranchers, the Tohono O'odham are known for their handcrafted baskets and pottery.

KITT PEAK NATIONAL OBSERVATORY is 20 mi. e. on SR 86, then 12 mi. s. on SR 386, within the Tohono O'odham reservation in the Quinlan Mountains. The site contains 24 major research instruments, including the world's largest solar telescope and the Mayall 4-meter telescope.

The facility monitors solar, stellar and extragalactic activities. Exhibits, videotaped programs and a nightly stargazing program utilizing 16- and 20-inch telescopes are featured.

Picnic facilities are available. Travelers are advised to check on weather and road conditions. Open daily 9-4; closed Jan. 1, Thanksgiving and Dec. 25. Guided tours of the facility are offered at 10, 11:30 and 1:30. Night observation program begins at dusk, Sept. to mid-July. Guided tours $2; ages 6-12, $1. Admission for night observation program $39; over 54 and students and military with ID $36. Reservations are required for night observation program. Phone (520) 318-8726.

SHOW LOW (D-5) pop. 7,695, elev. 6,347′

Show Low took its name from the winning hand in a poker game between Native American scout Col. Croyden E. Cooley and his friend Marion Clark. The town's main street, Deuce of Clubs, was named after the winning card.

Situated on the edge of the Mogollon Rim, the town offers numerous recreational pursuits, including fishing, camping, hiking and horseback riding.

Show Low Chamber of Commerce: 81 E. Deuce of Clubs, Show Low, AZ 85901; phone (928) 537-2326 or (888) 746-9569.

FOOL HOLLOW LAKE RECREATION AREA, 2 mi. n. of US 60 off SR 260, then e. on Old Linden Rd. to park entrance, offers fishing and boating in a lake covering the old town site of Adair. Camping among the 100-foot-tall pine trees also is available. Park daily 6 a.m.-10 p.m. Office daily 8-5. Admission $6 per private vehicle. Camping $15-$20 per

private vehicle. Phone (928) 537-3680. *See Recreation Chart.*

SHOW LOW HISTORICAL SOCIETY MUSEUM is at 541 E. Deuce of Clubs. Turn-of-the-20th-century items are on display, including replicas of a kitchen and a jail, firefighting tools, Native American pottery and memorabilia from World Wars I and II. Tues.-Sat. 11-3, Mar.-Nov. Donations. Phone (928) 532-7115.

SIERRA VISTA (G-5)
pop. 37,775, elev. 4,600′

Sierra Vista has been built upon the historic past of Fort Huachuca *(see place listing p. 51)*, established in 1877. The fort is now the largest single employer in southern Arizona, and most of its personnel live in the area. The scenery makes Sierra Vista special: The city is nestled on the eastern slopes of the Huachuca Mountains and overlooks the San Pedro River Valley. Nature lovers are attracted to nearby Coronado National Memorial *(see place listing p. 46)*, San Pedro Riparian Conservation Area (24 miles west) and Ramsey Canyon Preserve.

Sierra Vista Convention and Visitor Bureau: 3020 E. Tacoma St., Sierra Vista, AZ 85635; phone (520) 417-6960 or (800) 288-3861.

FORT HUACHUCA MUSEUM— *see Fort Huachuca p. 51.*

SOMERTON (E-1) pop. 7,266, elev. 103′

CASINOS

- **Cocopah Casino,** jct. US 95 (Ave. B) and 15th St. at 15318 Ave. B. Daily 24 hours. Phone (928) 726-8066.

SONORAN DESERT NATIONAL MONUMENT (E-2)

South of Phoenix in south-central Arizona, Sonoran Desert National Monument comprises mountain ranges, wide valleys and several saguaro cactus forests on 486,000 acres. The functioning desert ecosystem is a habitat for an array of wildlife, including desert bighorn sheep, mule deer, bobcats, desert tortoises, raptors, owls and bats.

It is believed that ancestors of the O'odham, Quechan, Cocopah and other tribes occupied villages in the area, which contains archeological and historical sites. Remnants of historic trails used by Juan de Anza, the Mormons and the Overland Stage can be found along a well-worn 20-mile corridor. A high-clearance vehicle is required. For further information contact the Phoenix Field Office, Bureau of Land Management, 21605 N. 7th Ave., Phoenix, AZ 85027; phone (623) 580-5500.

SPRINGERVILLE (D-6)
pop. 1,972, elev. 6,862′

Springerville is in a cattle-ranching area of eastern Arizona. Created by shield volcanoes, the town is a gateway to the White Mountains, where visitors can enjoy outdoor activities year-round. In a wing of the Latter-day Saints Church on Apache Street is a collection of European artworks and furniture dating from the Renaissance to the early 20th century. The Renee Cushman Art collection is shown by appointment; phone (928) 333-4514.

Springerville-Eagar Regional Chamber of Commerce: 318 E. Main St., P.O. Box 31, Springerville, AZ 85938; phone (928) 333-2123.

SAVE **CASA MALPAIS PUEBLO,** 318 E. Main St., is a 15-acre restoration project of Mogollon and ancient pueblo ruins occupied 1250-1400. Pottery, food and baskets unearthed at the project are displayed at the visitor center. After watching an orientation film, visitors drive to the site for a guided walking tour.

Allow 1 hour, 30 minutes minimum. Center daily 8-4. Guided tours depart the visitor center at 9, 11 and 2. Fee $7, over 55 and students with ID $5, under 2 free. Phone (928) 333-5375.

SUN CITY/SUN CITY WEST—
see Phoenix p. 89.

SUNSET CRATER VOLCANO NATIONAL MONUMENT (B-4)

Lying approximately 12 miles north of Flagstaff via US 89, then 2 miles east on Sunset Crater-Wupatki Loop Road, the 1,000-foot-high cinder cone of Sunset Crater Volcano dominates the surrounding fields of cinders, lava flows and spatter cones. The bright-reddish hues of the decomposed, water-stained sulfuric rock at the summit are in stark contrast with the black basalt of the adjacent rocks. From a distance the mountain appears to be on fire. Dark at the base, the volcano also has shades of red, orange and yellow leading to the summit and takes on a rosy tint during the hour before sunset. In 1892 John Wesley Powell noted the phenomenon and purportedly gave the cone its name.

Sunset Crater Volcano first erupted A.D. 1064-65 and was active intermittently for nearly 200 years. A self-guiding trail leads over the Bonito lava flow; sturdy walking shoes are recommended. A paved road crosses the lava flow and connects the monument with Wupatki National Monument *(see place listing p. 123).* Picnicking is permitted.

Allow 30 minutes minimum. Visitor center daily 8-6, June-Aug.; 8-5, Jan.-May and Sept.-Nov.; 9-5, in Dec. Closed Dec. 25. Admission $5 per person (includes Wupatki National Monument), under 17 free. Phone (928) 526-0502.

SUPAI (B-3) elev. 3,195′

HAVASU CANYON is accessible from Hualapai Hilltop, which is reached from SR 66 via a turnoff 5 miles e. of Peach Springs. There are no services after the turnoff. Most of the 65-mile road from Peach Springs is in good condition.

Havasu Canyon is home to the village of Supai, which serves as the governmental center of the Havasupai Indian Reservation. Automobiles must be left at Hualapai Hilltop; the 8-mile journey to the canyon floor and Havasu Falls can be covered on horseback, helicopter or on foot down a precipitous trail.

Note: The trail is only recommended for experienced hikers in good physical condition. The return climb out of the canyon is very arduous. Summer temperatures should be taken into account when planning daytime trips. Hikers must carry at least one gallon of water. Camping is permitted; no open fires are allowed. Swimming is permitted. Horse rental is available. Office hours daily 5:30-5, Apr.-Oct.; 9-3, rest of year.

Entrance fee $25. Campground fee $10 per person. Helicopter fee $85 per person. Reservations for horses and campgrounds are required. MC, VI. Phone (928) 448-2141 or (928) 448-2237 for general information and reservations.

SUPERIOR (J-6) pop. 3,254, elev. 2,730′

Although it began as a silver-mining town, Superior owes its existence to its proximity to some of the deepest and richest copper lodes in the country. Near Superior is Apache Leap Cliff, where, according to legend, 75 Apache warriors leaped to their deaths rather than be captured by the cavalry. The town also is near the southern terminus of US 60 (Gila/Pinal Scenic Drive), which travels northward through Tonto National Forest, Salt River Canyon and the Fort Apache Indian Reservation.

Superior Chamber of Commerce: 230 Main St., P.O. Box 95, Superior, AZ 85273; phone (520) 689-0200.

BOYCE THOMPSON ARBORETUM STATE PARK, 3 mi. w. on US 60 at Milepost 223, has more than 300 acres of desert plants collected from all over the world; 50 acres are accessible for viewing. Founded in the 1920s by mining magnate Col. William Boyce Thompson, the arboretum has nature paths leading past towering trees, cacti, mountain cliffs, a streamside forest, a desert lake, hidden canyon and panoramic views.

Two miles of developed trails are available for hiking. An interpretive center has educational displays and two greenhouses housing cacti and succulents. Picnicking is available. Leashed pets are permitted. Allow 1 hour minimum. Daily 8-5; closed Dec. 25. Admission $7.50; ages 5-12, $3. Phone (520) 689-2811.

SURPRISE— *see Phoenix p. 89.*

TEMPE— *see Phoenix p. 90.*

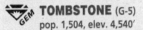 **TOMBSTONE** (G-5)
pop. 1,504, elev. 4,540′

"The Town Too Tough To Die," Tombstone was perhaps the most renowned of Arizona's old mining camps. When Ed Schieffelin came to Camp Huachuca with a party of soldiers and left the fort to prospect, his comrades told him that he would find his tombstone rather than silver. Thus, in 1877 Schieffelin named his first claim Tombstone, and rumors of rich strikes made a boomtown of the settlement that adopted this name.

Over the course of 7 years the mines produced millions of dollars in silver and gold before rising underground waters forced suspension of operations.

Days of lawlessness and violence in Tombstone climaxed with the infamous battle between Wyatt Earp and his brothers against the Clanton brothers, fought at the rear entrance to the O.K. Corral.

Many of Tombstone's historic buildings are within an area bounded by Fremont, 6th, Toughnut and 3rd streets. Among them are St. Paul's Episcopal Church, built in 1882; the Crystal Palace, one of the most luxurious saloons in the West; and the *Tombstone Epitaph* building, where the oldest continuously published paper in Arizona is still being printed. Western printing history exhibits in the front office are free to the public.

Tombstone Office of Tourism: P.O. Box 248, Tombstone, AZ 85638; phone (800) 457-3423.

BIRD CAGE THEATRE, 6th and Allen sts., was built in 1881 and remains virtually unchanged, with the original fixtures, furnishings and interior still intact. A combination theater, saloon and dance hall, the theater was known in its heyday as the bawdiest nightspot between Basin Street and the Barbary Coast. The refrain from the song "Only a Bird in a Gilded Cage" was inspired by this opera house saloon. Allow 1 hour minimum. Daily 8-6; closed Dec. 25. Admission $6; over 60, $5.50; ages 8-18, $5; family rate $17. Phone (520) 457-3421.

BOOTHILL GRAVEYARD, at the w. city limits off SR 80, contains 300 marked graves of early citizens as well as graves of some of the town's famous and infamous residents. This is reportedly the first cemetery to be called "Boot Hill." Allow 1 hour minimum. Daily 7:30-6. Donations. Phone (520) 457-9344.

HISTORAMA is next to the main entrance of the O.K. Corral. A 25-minute multimedia presentation narrated by actor Vincent Price offers a look at Tombstone's history. This is a good starting point for a tour of the town. Shows run every 30 minutes daily 9:30-4:30; closed half-day on Thanksgiving and Dec. 25. Admission $5.50, under 6 free. Combination ticket with O.K. Corral (includes gunfight reenactment) $7.50, under 6 free. Phone (520) 457-3456.

O.K. CORRAL, between 3rd and 4th sts. on Allen St., includes the site where the Earp-Clanton gunfight took place on Oct. 26, 1881. A re-enactment of the gunfight takes place daily at 2 p.m. Allow 30 minutes minimum. Daily 9-5. Combination ticket with Historama (includes gunfight reenactment) $7.50, under 6 free. Phone (520) 457-3456.

Camillus Fly Studio is between 3rd and 4th sts. on Fremont St., entered through the O.K. Corral. This is the re-created studio and boardinghouse of the pioneer photographer. Photographs of early Tombstone and its personalities are displayed. Allow 30 minutes minimum. Thurs.-Mon. 9-5. Admission included with O.K. Corral. Phone (520) 457-3456.

[SAVE] **ROSE TREE MUSEUM AND BOOKSTORE,** 116 S. 4th St. at the corner of 4th and Toughnut sts., features the world's largest rosebush, which now covers more than 8,000 square feet; the size of the bush is verified by "The Guinness Book of World Records" yearly. The white-blossomed shrub was planted as a cutting sent from Scotland about 1885. Rose slips may be purchased. Exhibits include antique furniture brought to Tombstone by covered wagon in 1880.

Allow 30 minutes minimum. Daily 9-5; closed Thanksgiving and Dec. 25. Admission $3, under 14 free when accompanied by adult. MC, VI. Phone (520) 457-3326.

SCHIEFFELIN HALL is at 4th and Fremont sts. Early Tombstone's theatrical and civic center, Schieffelin Hall is one of the largest adobe structures in the West. It is closed to the public.

TOMBSTONE COURTHOUSE STATE HISTORIC PARK, 219 E. Toughnut St., was built in 1882. The building contains displays pertaining to the history of Tombstone and Cochise County, using antiques and artifacts to present the lives of former citizens. Allow 1 hour minimum. Daily 8-5; closed Dec. 25. Admission day after Labor Day-day before Memorial Day $4, under 14 free. Admission rest of year $3, under 14 free. Phone (520) 457-3311.

TONTO NATIONAL FOREST

Elevations in the forest range from 1,300 ft. at Apache Junction to 7,900 ft. at the Mogollon Rim in the Payson District. Refer to AAA maps for additional elevation information.

Stretching some 90 miles south from the scenic Mogollon Rim to the city of Scottsdale, the Tonto National Forest encompasses 2.9 million acres of spectacular pine, brush and cactus country, making it one of the largest national forests. Elevations range from 1,300 feet to almost 7,900 feet in the northern pine country. Eight regions have been designated as wilderness areas; the entire forest offers more than 860 miles of trails for backpacking, hiking and horse travel.

Scenic roadways in the area include the Apache Trail (SR 88) *(see Apache Junction p. 84)*, Beeline Highway (SR 87) and Young Highway (SR 288). Some unpaved roads are very rough, so check locally for road conditions.

Six lakes offer recreational areas for boating, swimming and fishing; Saguaro, Bartlett, Canyon, Apache and Theodore Roosevelt lakes have marina facilities. Tubing is a popular pastime in the summer on the lower Salt River. Campgrounds, picnic sites and other recreational opportunities also are available throughout the forest. A map showing roads, recreation sites and tourist services can be obtained from the local Forest Service office for $6.

For further information contact the Forest Supervisor's Office, Tonto National Forest, 2324 E. McDowell Rd., Phoenix, AZ 85006; phone (602) 225-5200. *See Recreation Chart and the AAA Southwestern CampBook.*

TONTO NATIONAL MONUMENT (I-6)

East of Roosevelt Dam on SR 88/188, Tonto National Monument preserves the most accessible of south-central Arizona's prehistoric cliff dwellings. The remains of a two-story pueblo built in a natural cave are visible from the headquarters parking area. A .5-mile paved foot trail ascends 350 feet and leads to cliff dwellings that were occupied by the Salado culture in the 13th and 14th centuries. Summer temperatures are high; wear a hat and suitable shoes and carry sufficient water.

Ranger-conducted, 3-hour tours to the less accessible 40-room Upper Cliff Dwelling are available November through April. The tour is limited to 15 people per day; reservations are required. Write Tonto National Monument, HC 02, Box 4602, Roosevelt, AZ 85545 or phone (928) 467-2241 for reservations.

A visitor center and museum contain artifacts from the Salado culture, including examples of the pottery and woven textiles for which they are noted. Allow 1 hour, 30 minutes minimum. Park and visitor center open daily 8-5; closed Dec. 25. Trail to the Lower Cliff Dwelling closes 1 hour before park closing. Picnic area 8-4:45. Admission $3, under 17 free. Phone (928) 467-2241.

TUBA CITY (B-4) pop. 8,225, elev. 4,936′

Tuba City was named after Tuve, a Hopi leader. Natural springs attracted generations of Hopi, Navajo and Paiute Indians to the area. In 1875 the city was laid out and settled by Mormons, who used blocks of dressed stone from nearby prehistoric sites to build structures, some of which still stand.

The town lies on US 160, 10 miles east of US 89 within Arizona's northeastern Indian country, which encompasses the Navajo and Hopi Indian reservations. A variety of Native American crafts are produced, including baskets, pottery and silver products.

TUBAC (G-4) pop. 949, elev. 3,200′

Tubac, meaning "sinking water," was a Pima village when Jesuit Eusebio Francisco Kino visited the area in 1691. A presidio and mission were established in 1752 (the first military base in Arizona) shortly after the Pima revolted against Spanish encroachment. Between 1752 and 1856 some 500 people lived at Tubac, but in 1776 the presidio was moved to help fortify the strategically important Tucson. With the Gadsden Purchase in 1853, the town became a part of the United States.

The Mexican War, the California gold rush of 1849 and the raiding Apaches depopulated the town throughout much of the 19th century. However, in 1859 Arizona's first newspaper was printed by a local mining company who revived the town. By 1860 Tubac was the largest town in Arizona, but the Civil War left the town unprotected, and it was deserted once again. Once the Apaches ceded control of the area in the late 1800s, Tubac began to grow, but it never regained its earlier importance.

Modern Tubac is a small community of writers and artists located next to the old presidio; many of the shops and galleries in town sell the local art.

Tubac Chamber of Commerce: P.O. Box 1866, Tubac, AZ 85646; phone (520) 398-2704.

TUBAC PRESIDIO STATE HISTORIC PARK is off I-19. Arizona's first state park encompasses the Spanish military site that made Tubac Arizona's first European settlement in 1752. An underground exhibit reveals portions of the captain's house.

The visitor center and museum contain Native American, Spanish, Mexican and territorial artifacts, a restored 1885 schoolhouse and the press that printed Arizona's first newspaper in 1859. Allow 1 hour minimum. Daily 8-5; closed Dec. 25. A living-history program depicting life in Tubac 1752-76 is presented Sun. 1-4, Oct.-Mar. Admission $3; ages 7-13, $1. Phone (520) 398-2252.

Tucson

City Population: 486,699   Elevation: 2,389 ft.

Editor's Picks:

Sunshine, dry air, mountains and rich desert vegetation are Tucson's drawing cards. The city boasts an average of 3,800 hours of sunshine a year, placing it high on any list of health and winter resorts. More than just a vacation destination, Tucson also is a culturally active city. In addition to the visual arts, all areas of the performing arts—dance, opera, theater, music—are well represented.

The 321-acre University of Arizona is a major asset both culturally and economically—the needs of its 31,000 students create diverse jobs. Davis-Monthan Air Force Base, which contains a large aircraft storage facility, is another leading employer. Such large private companies as IBM, Garrett AiResearch and Hughes Aircraft have operations in Tucson.

Tucson is in a high desert valley, once the floor of an ancient inland sea. It is surrounded by four mountain ranges: the Santa Catalinas to the north, the Rincons to the east, the Santa Ritas to the south and the Tucsons to the west. These protective mountains and the Santa Cruz River attracted humans approximately 12,000 years ago. The Native American name for the ancient settlement was *stjukshon*. Pronounced like Tucson, it loosely translates into "spring at the foot of the black hill," a reference to the springs that once lined the banks of the Santa Cruz.

In 1700 Spanish Jesuit Eusebio Francisco Kino established the San Xavier Mission at the nearby village of Bac. Spanish ranchers and miners soon penetrated the valley, forcing the natives (particularly the Apaches) to protect their territory. After numerous Indian attacks, a garrison was built near the mission in Tubac *(see place listing p. 105)* and moved in 1776 to a new walled presidio in Tucson. The city's nickname "The Old Pueblo" refers to these walls.

When Mexico shook off Spanish rule in 1821, Tucson came under Mexican jurisdiction. The

© Gibson Stock Photography

American flag was first raised over Tucson in 1846 by the commander of the Mormon Battalion during the Mexican War. The wagon road the Mormons built to California became a major east-west corridor that was used by thousands of homesteaders and miners during the California gold rush. Disputes over right-of-way through this corridor prompted the Gadsden Purchase in 1853, which joined southern Arizona and Tucson with the rest of the Arizona Territory.

Overland stage service to San Diego from San Antonio began in 1857, and Tucson gained a certain notoriety as a stage stop. A stay in Tucson usually meant sleeping in the infamous Tucson bed, which the traveler made by lying on his stomach and covering himself with his back. Despite its no-frills reputation, the village remained a major outpost, offering protection against the Apaches and supplies for travelers.

The Civil War interrupted travel along this southern route to California. After the war Tucson continued as a supply and distribution point, first for the Army and then for miners. From 1867 through 1877 Tucson was the territorial capital. The "Old Pueblo" began to shed its outpost image with the arrival of the Southern Pacific Railroad in 1880 and the

---

founding of the University of Arizona in 1885. Tucson entered the 20th century as Arizona's largest city and remained so until 1920, when it was surpassed by Phoenix.

Tucson's Native American and Mexican roots are ever present. Mexican-Americans make up a substantial portion of the population. Spanish is widely spoken and Native American dialects are occasionally heard. Mexican restaurants abound, serving the neighboring country's distinctive cuisine. Architecturally, the city has a number of low, Pueblo-style buildings with adobe walls and flat, tiled roofs. Interiors are decorated with Navajo rugs and Pueblo pottery, and many festivals celebrate the cultures of the city's original inhabitants.

A multicultural city, Tucson's Jewish heritage is represented by the 1910 Stone Avenue Temple; one of Arizona's first synagogues, it features a mix of neoclassic, Romanesque and Moorish styles. Tours are offered highlighting the renovated temple's architecture and history; phone (520) 670-9073.

In the 1950s dude ranches were Tucson's main attractions. Now these guest ranches are complemented by elaborate resorts, and renovations have given the downtown business district a new look. La Placita Village incorporates fountains, territorial architecture and modern buildings in a contemporary blend; the adjoining Community Center has facilities for conventions, sports, theater and entertainment.

These complexes, connected by plazas, parks, walkways and bridges, and combined with a sprinkling of 19th-century houses, form an inviting and compact downtown area. While a Western atmosphere has been preserved, Tucson has emerged as a cosmopolitan city. The walls of "The Old Pueblo" have yielded to new structures that no longer defend but welcome.

La Fiesta de los Vaqueros / Gill Kenny / Metropolitan Tucson Convention and Visitors Bureau

Getting There

By Car

Tucson's major approach and through-route is I-10, the nation's southernmost transcontinental highway. Primarily an east-west route, it angles into the city from the southeast and the northwest. Northbound, I-10 intersects with I-19 in south Tucson and then continues along the west side of the city, providing access to the downtown area. Once I-10 leaves the city, it proceeds northwest to Phoenix, 120 miles away.

A major approach from the west is I-8, which originates in San Diego and joins with I-10 about midway between Phoenix and Tucson. Because both I-10 and I-8 traverse desert country, some of their sections are subject to dust storms, particularly in spring and early summer. Local radio stations broadcast advisories during these fluctuating weather conditions, and interstate signs with changeable messages warn motorists.

Destination Tucson

*T*he heritage of the Old West meets trendy Southwestern chic in this dynamic Sunbelt city, home to both Spanish colonial adobes and high-tech facilities.

*L*a Casa Cordova, Tucson's oldest house, testifies to the city's Spanish and Mexican background, while Old Tucson Studios dramatizes its history as a wild frontier outpost. On the flip side are the Biosphere 2 Center in Oracle and Kitt Peak National Observatory, both renowned, cutting-edge research institutions.

Gill Kenny / Metropolitan Tucson CVB

Kitt Peak National Observatory, Sells. Exhibits and films reveal the secrets of the heavens; a glimpse through a 16-inch telescope is sure to leave you starry-eyed. (See listing page 102)

Old Tucson Studios. Gunfights, musicals and movie stunts re-create life in the Old West. (See listing page 112)

David Jewell / Metropolitan Tucson CVB

© Pima Air and Space Museum

Pima Air and Space Museum With names such as King Cobra, Flying Fortress, and Skyraider, the aircraft on display will take your imagination on a sentimental journey. (See listing page 112)

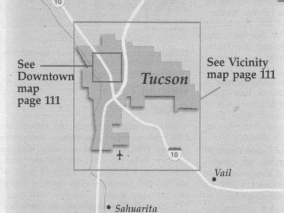

See Downtown map page 111

Tucson

See Vicinity map page 111

Vail

• Sahuarita

*P*laces included in this AAA Destination City:

© Tucson Botanical Gardens

Tucson Botanical Gardens. Stop and smell the wildflowers in one of the 16 themed gardens at this peaceful five-acre retreat. (See listing page 113.

The Informed Traveler

Sales Tax: Arizona's statewide sales tax is 5.6 percent; an additional 2 percent is levied in Tucson. The tax on a hotel room in Tucson is 9.5 percent, plus $1 per room per night; the tax is 7.5 percent elsewhere in Pima County. There is a rental car tax of 10 percent, plus a concession fee of 10 percent if the car is picked up at the airport; the tax is 12 percent if the car is picked up off airport property, but within the Tucson city limits. Pima County imposes a car rental fee of $3.50.

WHOM TO CALL

Emergency: 911

Police (non-emergency): (520) 791-4444

Hospitals: Carondelet St. Joseph's, (520) 296-3211; Carondelet St. Mary's, (520) 872-3000; Northwest Medical Center, (520) 742-9000; University Medical Center, (520) 694-0111.

WHERE TO LOOK

Newspapers

The two major newspapers are the *Arizona Daily Star*, published in the morning, and the *Tucson Citizen*, which is published in the afternoon. These papers are supplemented by local journals.

Radio

Tucson radio station KTUC (1400 AM) is an all-news/weather station; KUAT (90.5 FM and 1550 AM) is a member of National Public Radio. There are two Spanish-language radio stations.

Visitor Information

Metropolitan Tucson Convention & Visitors Bureau: 100 S. Church Ave., Tucson, AZ 85701; phone (520) 624-1817 or (800) 638-8350.

The bureau can provide a variety of information, including the *Official Visitors Guide to Metropolitan Tucson*. The bureau's visitor center is open Mon.-Fri. 8-5, Sat.-Sun. 9-4; closed major holidays.

TRANSPORTATION

Air Travel

Ten miles south of downtown, Tucson International Airport is served by many major passenger airlines. Short-term airport parking costs $1 per half-hour; long-term parking costs $8 for 24 hours.

The Arizona Stage Coach, (520) 889-1000, provides van service throughout the Tucson area; prices range from $5-$45. Sunset Limousine, (520) 573-9418 or (800) 266-8059, provides limousine service throughout the Tucson area; prices range $50-$200 per hour. Cab service to downtown averages 20 minutes and costs $17-$25.

Rental Cars

Hertz, (520) 573-5200 or (800) 654-3080, offers discounts to AAA members. Check the telephone directory for listings of other agencies.

Rail Service

The Amtrak Station, 400 E. Toole, accommodates Amtrak rail lines. For ticket and schedule information phone (520) 623-4442 or (800) 872-7245. Tickets may be purchased at 400 N. Second Ave.

Buses

The terminal for Greyhound Lines Inc. is at 2 S. Fourth Ave.; phone (520) 792-3475 or (800) 231-2222.

Taxis

There are many independent taxi companies in Tucson. Rates are not regulated by the city. One company that serves the area is Yellow Cab, (520) 624-6611.

Public Transport

Sun Tran operates buses throughout the metropolitan area. The fare is $1 to all points. Passes are available for senior citizens and the physically impaired. For schedule and route information phone (520) 792-9222.

A well-known route reaching Tucson from the north is SR 77. One of the area's oldest two-lane routes, it is especially scenic. South of Tucson, Bus. Rte. 19 parallels sections of I-19, which is the more recent link with the Mexican border at Nogales.

Getting Around

Street System

Tucson is laid out in a grid pattern. Numbered streets run east-west to the south of Speedway Boulevard, and numbered avenues run north-south to the west of Euclid Avenue. Address numbers start at the intersection of Broadway, the north-south divider, and Stone, the east-west divider. Unless otherwise posted the speed limit on most streets is 25 to 30 mph.

During rush hours the center turn lanes of Broadway, 22nd Street, Grant Road and Speedway Boulevard are reverse traffic flow lanes: morning rush hour one way into the city and evening rush hour one way out of the city. Rush-hour traffic, 7-9 a.m. and 4-6 p.m., should be avoided.

Parking

Metered parking is available on many downtown streets, but be sure to check signs and meters for restricted times and limits. There also are a number of commercial garages and lots. Rates are $2 per hour or $5 per day.

What To See

ARIZONA HISTORICAL SOCIETY/TUCSON MUSEUM, 949 E. 2nd St., houses a museum documenting Arizona's cultural history, a research library, an Arizona mining exhibit and changing exhibits. The society also administers the Fort Lowell Museum, the Sosa-Carrillo-Frémont House *(see attraction listings)* and the Downtown History Museum.

Allow 1 hour minimum. Open Mon.-Sat. 10-4; closed major holidays. Library open Mon.-Fri. 10-3, Sat. 10-1. Admission $5; over 59 and ages 12-18, $4. Phone (520) 628-5774.

Arizona Historical Society/Downtown History Museum is at 140 N. Stone Ave. Exhibits depict Tucson's history from its origins as a Spanish presidio in 1775 to the present, concentrating on contributions to the community by the police, the military, the fire department, educators and businesses. An exhibit describes the capture of the John Dillinger gang in the late 1930s. Allow 30 minutes minimum. Mon.-Fri. 10-4; closed major holidays. Admission $3; over 59 and ages 12-18, $2; free to all first Fri. of the month. Phone (520) 770-1473.

ARIZONA-SONORA DESERT MUSEUM, 14 mi. w. in Tucson Mountain Park at 2021 N. Kinney Rd., exhibits more than 300 live animal species, including mountain lions, prairie dogs, Gila monsters, hawks, bighorn sheep and hummingbirds in natural habitats. Almost 2 miles of paths lead visitors through landscapes containing

Mission San Xavier del Bac / Gill Kenny / Metropolitan Tucson Convention and Visitors Bureau

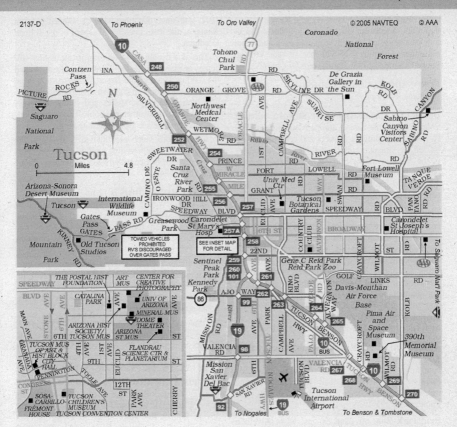

over 1,300 species of plants indigenous to the Sonoran Desert region; included are desert grasslands, cactus and desert gardens.

A pollination gardens complex shows interactions between insects, birds, bats and plants, and a fenceless enclosure allows javelinas to explore hillsides and take mud baths.

A simulated walk-through limestone cave features a collection of regional gems and minerals. A display about how the planet has evolved with explanations of erosion, volcanic and seismic activity and plate tectonics also is featured. Food is available. Allow 2 hours minimum. Daily 7:30-5, Mar.-Sept. (also Sat. 5-10, June-Aug.); 8:30-5, rest of year. Admission May-Oct. $9; ages 6-12, $2. Admission rest of year $12; ages 6-12, $4. MC, VI. Phone (520) 883-2702.

ARIZONA STATE MUSEUM is on the University of Arizona campus at Park Ave. and University Blvd. in Buildings 26 and 30. Reputedly the region's oldest and largest anthropology museum, it preserves material objects and interprets the history of Southwestern cultures, from prehistoric mammoth hunters to present-day Native

Americans and northern Mexico natives. A collection of Hohokam artifacts is considered the most comprehensive in existence.

The Paths of Life: American Indians of the Southwest exhibit highlights the origin, history and contemporary life of Apache, Hopi, Navajo, Tohono O'odham, Southern Paiute and other indigenous groups.

Southwest Native American pottery from the museum's 20,000-piece collection spanning 2,000 years is showcased. Other exhibits include hand-carved Mexican folk masks and a full-size replica of a 700-year-old cliff dwelling.

Allow 1 hour minimum. Museum open Mon.-Sat. 10-5, Sun. noon-5; closed major holidays. Library open Mon.-Fri. 9:30-4:30. Donations. Phone (520) 621-6302 or (520) 621-4695 for the library and archives.

BIOSPHERE 2 CENTER—*see Oracle p. 117.*

CATALINA STATE PARK, 9 mi. n. off SR 77 Milepost 81 to 11570 N. Oracle Rd., is home to 5,511 acres of desert plants. Situated at the base of the Santa Catalina Mountains, the park's activities include bird-watching, hiking, camping and horseback riding. Park open daily dawn-10 p.m. Ranger station daily 7-5. Admission $6 per private vehicle (up to four passengers), $1 for bicycles and each additional passenger. Camping $15-$20 per private vehicle. Phone (520) 628-5798. *See Recreation Chart.*

CORONADO NATIONAL FOREST—
see place listing p. 45.

DE GRAZIA GALLERY IN THE SUN is 1 mi. n. of Sunrise Rd. in the Santa Catalina Mountains at 6300 N. Swan Rd. Paintings, bronzes and ceramics by artist Ted De Grazia are displayed. Next to the gallery is the Mission in the Sun, an open-air chapel De Grazia built and decorated with frescoes. Daily 10-4; closed Easter, Thanksgiving and Dec. 25. Donations. Phone (520) 299-9191 or (800) 545-2185.

FORT LOWELL MUSEUM, Fort Lowell and Craycroft rds. in Fort Lowell Park, embraces the ruins of the old fort that played a major role in the Apache Indian wars. The building, a reconstruction of the commanding officer's quarters, contains exhibits relating to military life at Fort Lowell, with a room furnished in period. Military equipment and changing photography exhibits are displayed. Allow 1 hour minimum. Wed.-Sat. 10-4; closed holidays. Admission $3; over 60 and ages 12-18, $2; free to all first Sat. of the month. Phone (520) 885-3832.

GENE C. REID PARK, 22nd St. and Country Club Rd., is a 160-acre park offering picnic areas, tennis courts and Hi Corbett Field, where the Colorado Rockies professional baseball team holds spring training. Park open daily 6:30 a.m.-10:30 p.m. Free. Phone (520) 791-4873.

Reid Park Zoo, off 22nd St. just w. of Alvernon Rd. in Gene C. Reid Park, houses more than 550 animals representing 150 species, including bears, baboons, giraffes, zebras and ostriches. Each habitat and species is fully described. Allow 2 hours minimum. Daily 9-4; closed Dec. 25. Admission $5; over 61, $4; ages 2-14, $2. Phone (520) 791-3204.

INTERNATIONAL WILDLIFE MUSEUM is 5 mi. w. of I-10 on Speedway Blvd. to 4800 W. Gates Pass Rd. Tucson's interactive natural history museum contains dioramas depicting more than 400 species of mammals, insects, birds and prehistoric animals from around the world. Hands-on exhibits and interactive displays are found throughout the 38,000-square-foot museum.

A 98-seat theater offers hourly natural history films. Food is available. Mon.-Fri. 9-5, Sat.-Sun. 9-6; closed Thanksgiving and Dec. 25. Admission $7; over 61 and students with ID $5.50; ages 4-12, $2.50. AX, DC, MC, VI. Phone (520) 629-0100.

MISSION SAN XAVIER DEL BAC is 9 mi. s. off I-19 exit 92, on San Xavier Rd. in the Tohono O'odham Indian Reservation. Though founded by Jesuit Father Eusebio Francisco Kino before 1700, the present structure was built 1783-97 by the Franciscans. The missionaries were forced to leave San Xavier in 1828 but returned in

1911, and since that time have maintained old San Xavier as the main church and school of the Tohono O'odham.

This is the only Kino mission in the nation still active in preaching to the Tohono O'odham. Called the "White Dove of the Desert," the structure is an impressive example of Spanish mission architecture. The domes, carvings, arches and flying buttresses distinguish it from other missions. The interior murals and the altar are especially noteworthy.

A continuous video presentation is shown in the museum, and a self-guiding tour is available. Mission daily 8-5. Museum daily 8-4. Donations. Phone (520) 294-2624.

OLD TUCSON STUDIOS is 12 mi. w. via Speedway Blvd. or Ajo Way in Tucson Mountain Park; follow signs. Erected in 1939, this replica of 1860s Tucson was the location for the movies "Arizona" and "Tombstone." More than 350 films, TV episodes, series and commercials have been filmed here.

Highlights include stagecoach rides, live gunfights, stunt demonstrations, Western musical revues, the Town Hall and Film History Museum. Thirty-minute trail rides and concerts featuring national acts are offered.

Food is available. Sun.-Fri. 10-3, Sat. 10-4; closed Thanksgiving and Dec. 25. Admission Sat. $12.95; ages 4-11, $7.95. Admission Sun.-Fri. $9.95; ages 4-11, $6.95. Hours and prices may vary; phone ahead. AX, DS, MC, VI. Phone (520) 883-0100.

[SAVE] **PIMA AIR AND SPACE MUSEUM** is at 6000 E. Valencia Rd.; from I-10 eastbound take the Valencia Rd. exit, or from I-10 westbound take exit 267 to Wilmot Rd. More than 250 vintage aircraft are displayed including the DC-6 used by Presidents John F. Kennedy and Lyndon B. Johnson. Also featured are interactive exhibits designed to simulate a space mission.

One-hour bus tours of the Aircraft Maintenance and Regeneration Center (AMRC) on Davis-Monthan Air Force Base feature more than 4,400 U.S. military aircraft.

Note: A photo ID is required to enter the base, and visitors are not permitted to leave the bus. Food is available. Museum daily 9-5; closed Thanksgiving and Dec. 25. Last admission 1 hour before closing. DC-6 open for touring 9-3:30. Bus tour schedule varies; phone ahead. Museum Nov.-May $11.75; over 62 and military with ID $9.75; ages 7-12, $8. Museum rest of year $9.75; over 62 and military with ID $8.75; ages 7-12, $6. Bus tours $6; under 13, $3. AX, DS, MC, VI. Phone (520) 574-0462 for museum information or (520) 618-4806 for bus tour reservations.

390th Memorial Museum is at 6000 E. Valencia Rd. The museum honors the men of the 390th Bombardment Group, many of whom died while flying B-17 bombers in World War II. Exhibits include a B-17 (also known as the "Flying Fortress"), aircraft models, flight gear, guns, photos, a Quonset hut and other memorabilia. A 54-minute video presentation includes interviews with surviving members and actual film clips from the war.

Guided tours are available. Allow 30 minutes minimum. Daily 10-4:30; closed Thanksgiving and Dec. 25. Free with paid admission to Pima Air and Space Museum. MC, VI. Phone (520) 574-0287.

THE POSTAL HISTORY FOUNDATION, 920 N. First Ave., features stamps, postmarks and books tracing the history of the U.S. Postal Service and caters to serious philatelists and postal historians. Original equipment from the Naco post office as well as antique file cabinets and post office memorabilia are on display. An adjacent building houses a collection of Civil War memorabilia and documents. Guided tours are available. Allow 30 minutes minimum. Mon.-Fri. 8-3; closed holidays. Donations. Phone (520) 623-6652.

SABINO CANYON is 17 mi. e. via Tanque Verde Rd. and Sabino Canyon Rd. Part of the Coronado National Forest *(see place listing p. 45)*, this desert oasis in the Santa Catalina Mountains offers recreational activities including swimming, hiking, bird-watching and picnicking. Sabino Canyon Tours offers narrated excursions into the canyon aboard shuttle buses. A shuttle also transports hikers to the Bear Canyon trailhead.

Motor vehicles and pets are not allowed in the canyon. Allow 1 hour minimum. Visitor reception area open Mon.-Fri. 8-4:30, Sat.-Sun. 8:30-4:30. Tour hours vary; phone ahead. Visitor center and trails free. Tours $7.50; ages 3-12, $3. Shuttle $3; ages 3-12, $1. Parking $5. Phone (520) 749-8700, or (520) 749-2327 for tour information.

 SAGUARO NATIONAL PARK—
see place listing p. 117.

SENTINEL PEAK PARK, off Broadway w. of I-10 on Sentinel Peak Rd., contains the peak more popularly known as "A" Mountain because of the big "A" annually whitewashed on it by University of Arizona freshmen. It affords an excellent view of Tucson and surrounding mountains. At night the city's lights are particularly captivating from this vantage point. Mon.-Sat. 8-8, Sun. 8-6. Phone (520) 791-5909.

SOSA-CARRILLO-FRÉMONT HOUSE, 151 S. Granada Ave. in the Convention Center Complex, is a restored 1880 Mexican-American house said to be one of Tucson's oldest adobe buildings. Period furnishings, memorabilia of the Sosa, Carrillo and Frémont families, and changing exhibits are displayed.

Two-hour guided walking tours of the historic districts start with a house tour Thurs. and Sat. at 10, Nov.-Mar. Allow 30 minutes minimum. Wed.-Sat. 10-4; closed holidays. House admission $3; over 59 and students with ID $2; under 13 free. Walking tours $10. Reservations are recommended for the walking tours. Phone (520) 622-0956.

TITAN MISSILE MUSEUM—*see Sahuarita p. 118.*

TOHONO CHUL PARK is at 7366 N. Paseo del Norte. Tohono O'odham for "desert corner," Tohono Chul Park is a 49-acre desert preserve set amid a rapidly growing urban area. The park features nature trails, a Geology Wall, a Children's Garden, a greenhouse and changing art exhibits. Displays educate visitors about water conservation, arid lands and the traditions and cultures of the Southwest. Guided and self-guiding tours are available.

Food is available. Park open daily 8-5. Exhibit building open daily 9-5. Admission $5; over 61, $4; students with ID $3; ages 5-12, $2. Free to all first Tues. of the month. Phone (520) 742-6455.

TUCSON BOTANICAL GARDENS, 2150 N. Alvernon Way, covers 5 acres and features cactus, children's, herb, historical, iris, sensory, bird-watching, and xeriscape gardens as well as Native American crop gardens. Exhibits include useful tropical forest plants and a butterfly garden.

Guided tours are available. Daily 8:30-4:30; closed Jan. 1, July 4, Thanksgiving and Dec. 25. Admission $5; ages 6-12, $2.50. Phone (520) 326-9686.

TUCSON CHILDREN'S MUSEUM, 200 S. 6th Ave., encourages learning through hands-on exhibits and programs for ages 2-11 that include a bakery, emergency vehicles, a maze, Dinosaur Canyon and Ocean Discovery Center. Mon.-Sat. 10-5, Sun. noon-5, Memorial Day to mid-Aug.; Tues.-Sat. 10-5, Sun. noon-5, rest of year. Holiday hours may vary; phone ahead. Last admission 30 minutes before closing. Admission $5.50; over 60, $4.50; ages 2-16, $3.50. Phone (520) 792-9985.

TUCSON MOUNTAIN PARK, 8 mi. w. on Speedway Blvd. and Kinney Rd., encompasses approximately 17,000 acres of the Tucson Mountains and adjoining mesa land and embraces one of the largest areas of saguaro and natural desert growth in the Southwest. Camping is available at the Gilbert Ray Campground *(see the AAA Southwestern CampBook).* Trails for hiking and horseback riding are available. Picnicking is permitted. Park open daily 7-dusk. Park free. Camping $10-$20 per night, students with ID $3. For campground information phone (520) 877-6000 or (520) 883-4200.

TUCSON MUSEUM OF ART AND HISTORIC BLOCK is at 140 N. Main Ave. Collections include pre-Columbian, Spanish Colonial and Western American art. Changing exhibits of historical and contemporary art also are presented.

Four homes in the El Presidio Historic District are part of the museum and are open to the public: the Palice Pavilion, La Casa Cordova, the 1906 Corbett House and the John K. Goodman Pavilion of Western Art.

Museum open Tues.-Sat. 10-4, Sun. noon-4; closed major holidays. Walking tours of El Presidio Historic District are offered Oct.-Apr. Admission $8; over 59, $6; students with ID $3; under 13 free; free to all first Sun. of the month. Phone (520) 624-2333.

UNIVERSITY OF ARIZONA, bounded by Euclid Ave., E. Helen St., Campbell Ave. and E. 7th St., was founded in 1885 as the state's first institution of higher learning. Today the campus encompasses 353 acres and is one of the nation's top research universities. A 1.5-hour guided walking tour of the campus is available; tours depart from the Nugent Building. Walking tour Mon., Wed. and Fri. at 10 and 2, Tues. and Thurs. at 11 and 2, Sat. at 10, Sept.-May. Hours vary rest of year. Free. Phone (520) 621-3641.

Center for Creative Photography is at 1030 N. Olive Rd., n. of 2nd St. Metered public parking is available in the visitor section of the Park Avenue Garage, just n. of Speedway Blvd., with direct pedestrian access to the center's front door. The center houses more than 60,000 photographs representing the work of about 1,400 photographers, one of the most comprehensive collections in the world. Temporary exhibitions are on display.

The center's library contains more than 10,000 monographs, catalogs, books and periodicals. Videotaped interviews and lectures and the archives of major photographers are available for viewing. Building open daily 8-5. Library open Mon.-Fri. noon-4. Gallery Mon.-Fri. 9-5, Sat.-Sun. noon-5. Free. Reservations are recommended for the print-viewing room. Phone (520) 621-7968.

Dome Theater, in the planetarium on the first floor of the Flandrau Science Center, has elaborate projection and sound systems. The 1-hour programs are of a historical and educational nature. Tickets go on sale the day of the show. Planetarium admission $5.50; over 54, military with ID and ages 3-15, $4. Under 3 are not permitted. Admission may vary in summer; phone for rates. For schedule information phone (520) 621-7827.

Flandrau Science Center & Planetarium, 1601 E. University Blvd. at Cherry Ave., has interactive science exhibits about sound, light, optical illusions, magnetism and astronomy. Displays also highlight scientific research being conducted at the university as well as current scientific issues. The multimedia planetarium theater presents science, cultural, astronomy and laser light shows. In the public observatory a 16-inch telescope is available for night viewing (weather permitting).

Mon.-Sat. 9-5 (also Thurs.-Sat. 7-9 p.m.), Sun. 1-5; closed major holidays. Night viewing Wed.-Sat. 7-10 p.m. Exhibits (includes Mineral Museum) $3; ages 3-15, $2 (free with theater ticket). Theater tickets $4-$5.50. Telescope free. MC, VI. Phone (520) 621-7827.

Mineral Museum, on the lower level of the Flandrau Science Center, displays fine gems, meteorites and mineral specimens from around the world. The museum specializes in minerals from Arizona and Mexico. Visitors can use a microscope to see microsize specimens. Mon.-Sat. 9-5, Sun. 1-5; closed major holidays. Admission included with Flandrau

Science Center & Planetarium. Phone (520) 621-4227.

University of Arizona Museum of Art, s.e. corner of Park Ave. and Speedway Blvd. in the Fine Arts Complex, displays more than 50 European paintings from the Renaissance through the 17th century, including Fernando Gallego's "Retablo of the Ciudad Rodrigo" and works by Giovanni Piazzetta and Jacopo Pontormo.

Among the museum's 20th-century paintings and sculpture are works by Jacques Lipchitz, Pablo Picasso, Auguste Rodin and Andrew Wyeth. Changing exhibits also are featured. Allow 1 hour minimum. Tues.-Fri. 9-5, Sat.-Sun. noon-4; closed major holidays. Donations. Hourly rate parking is available. Phone (520) 621-7567.

CASINOS

- **Casino of the Sun**, I-19 Valencia exit, 4.5 mi. w., then .5 mi. s. to 7406 S. Camino de Oeste. Daily 24 hours. Phone (800) 344-9435.

- **Desert Diamond Casino**, I-19 Valencia exit, 1 mi. e., then 1 mi. s. to 7350 S. Old Nogales Hwy. Daily 24 hours. Phone (520) 294-7777.

What To Do

Sightseeing

Bus Tours

[SAVE] Gray Line Tours, (520) 622-8811, offers sightseeing tours to Tucson's major sites as well as trips to Nogales, Mexico, and the Grand Canyon. Overnight and multiple-day tours are available. Reservations are advised.

Plane Tours

Tucson Aeroservice Center, (520) 682-2999, provides air transportation to the Grand Canyon and offers helicopter sightseeing tours over the canyon.

Walking Tours

For those who prefer to explore the city and its environs on their own, the *Official Visitors Guide to Metropolitan Tucson*, distributed by the Metropolitan Tucson Convention and Visitors Bureau, 100 S. Church Ave., contains walking tour information; phone (520) 624-1817 or (800) 638-8350. The bureau is open Mon.-Fri. 8-5, Sat.-Sun. 9-4.

Guided group 2-hour walking tours of the downtown historic districts depart the Sosa-Carrillo-Frémont House *(see attraction listing p. 113)* Sat. at 10, Nov.-Mar.; phone (520) 622-0956.

Sports and Recreation

Tucson's city parks and Pima County parks offer facilities for almost any activity. A number of **swimming** pools and **tennis, racquetball** and **handball** courts are available as well as picnic areas, playgrounds, and **soccer** and ball fields. For information about facilities and reservations for their use contact the Pima County Parks and Recreation office at 3500 W. River Rd., (520) 877-6000, or Tucson Parks and Recreation at 900 S. Randolph, (520) 791-4873.

Tucson's climate is made to order for **golf** addicts. More than 40 courses are in the vicinity—everything from world-renowned resorts to public access courses. Some were designed by Robert Cupp, Tom Fazio, Arthur Hill, Robert Trent Jones, Jack Nicklaus and other noted architects.

Among the courses in Tucson are: Hilton Tucson El Conquistador Golf and Tennis Resort, Pusch Ridge Golf Course, (520) 544-1770 or (520) 544-1800, 10000 N. Oracle Rd. and 10555 N. La Cañada Dr.; Omni Tucson National, (520) 575-7540, 2727 W. Club Dr.; Randolph Municipal, (520) 791-4336, 600 S. Alvernon Way; Santa Rita, (520) 762-5620, 16461 S. Houghton Rd.; and Ventana Canyon, (520) 577-4061, 6200 N. Clubhouse Ln. Also in the area is Canoa Hills, (520) 648-1880, at 1401 W. Calle Urbano in Green Valley.

For those who prefer the more rugged outdoors, the Metropolitan Tucson Convention and Visitors Bureau's visitors guide contains a map and listings of the **camping** areas in Arizona; phone (520) 624-1817 or (800) 638-8350.

Hiking is probably the best way to discover the flora and fauna of this desert environment. Trails are abundant in Tucson Mountain Park. The Santa Catalina Mountains also are accessible and offer many areas of unspoiled beauty. Trails into the Catalinas can be found at the north end of Alvernon Way, the north end of Campbell Road, and at 1st Avenue and Magee Road. Hiking permits are required for these areas. Empty vehicles will be towed if a permit is not displayed.

Permits can be obtained from Pima County Parks and Recreation. Catalina State Park *(see attraction listing p. 111, the Recreation Chart and the AAA Southwestern CampBook)*, (520) 628-5798, has trails that can challenge the experienced hiker but not intimidate the novice; two longer trails begin at the end of the park's paved road. For more information about hiking phone the county's recreation office at (520) 877-6000.

Another great way to see the countryside is on a trail ride. Several stables offer half-day, full-day and overnight **horseback riding** trips into the mountains and desert. Check the telephone directory for listings. **Skiing** is available at Mount Lemmon Ski Valley, a scenic 30-mile drive northeast from Tucson. The southernmost ski area in the nation, Mount Lemmon offers both downhill and cross-country skiing. A sky ride on the ski lift is offered during the off season. For information about snow conditions phone (520) 576-1400.

For fans of the national pastime, several Major League **Baseball** teams are participants in the Cactus League. The National League's Arizona Diamondbacks and American League's Chicago White Sox conduct spring training at Tucson Electric Park, 2500 E. Ajo Way; phone (520) 434-1021. The Colorado Rockies practice at the US West Sports Complex at Hi Corbett Field, in Gene C. Reid Park off E. Broadway; for ticket information phone (520) 327-9467.

The AAA Pacific Coast League's Tucson Sidewinders, the Arizona Diamondbacks' farm team, also play their games at Tucson Electric Park from April through September.

The University of Arizona's Wildcats excite crowds during the **football** and **basketball** seasons. Home football games are played at Arizona Stadium, and basketball teams square off at McKale Memorial Center.

The Tucson Fireballs professional soccer team plays at Catalina High School throughout the summer. Soccer is played all year by two area leagues. Matches are held most Sundays at Jacobs, Reid and Udall parks.

Greyhound racing is available at Tucson Greyhound Park, (520) 884-7576, 2601 S. 3rd Ave. at 36th Street. The dogs race Tuesday through Sunday, year-round.

Note: Policies concerning admittance of children to pari-mutuel betting facilities vary. Phone for information.

Shopping

Tucson is filled with specialty shops containing Mexican and Native American handmade items.

Among the featured items are baskets, cactuses, feathered and furred kachina dolls, silver and gold jewelry, moccasins, Pueblo pottery, Navajo rugs and Western wear. A popular place to find such purchases is Old Town Artisans, 201 N. Court Ave.; phone (520) 623-6024 or (800) 782-8072.

Within a one-block adobe restoration area the works of more than 150 local artists are displayed, along with Native American and Latin folk art. The Mercado, Broadway and Wilmot, encompasses 20 shops with similar offerings as well as Oriental works.

For shopping with an old-time Western flavor, Trail Dust Town, 6541 E. Tanque Verde Rd., offers a variety of wares, including Western apparel, leather goods, antiques, fine arts and jewelry; phone (520) 296-4551.

Downtown Tucson's shopping district stretches along 4th Avenue between University and 9th streets, where everything from antiques to the latest fashions can be purchased. Lovers of flea markets will find varied goods at the Tanque Verde Swap Meet, Palo Verde Road just south of Ajo. The swap meet is open to visitors for bargaining Thurs.-Fri. 3-11 p.m. and Sat.-Sun. 7 a.m.-11 p.m.

University of Arizona fans will find an array of items bearing the school's name at Arizona Wildwear, 905 E. University Blvd. Souvenirs and T-shirts are popular items.

For one-stop shopping in air-conditioned comfort, Tucson offers four shopping malls: El Con Mall, near downtown at 3601 E. Broadway at Alvernon; Foothills Mall, 7401 N. La Cholla Blvd. at Ina Road; Park Place, east at 5870 E. Broadway at Wilmot; and Tucson Mall, 4500 N. Oracle Rd. The major department stores in these malls are Dillard's, Macy's and Robinsons-May.

Theater and Concerts

When it comes to theater, Tucson offers many choices. Top billing is given to the Arizona Theatre Company, 330 S. Scott Ave., (520) 622-2823, Arizona's professional state theater. This premier company performs six plays during its September through May season at the Temple of Music and Art. A forum for experimental theater is The Invisible Theatre, (520) 882-9721, 1400 N. 1st Ave., which stages six plays between September and June.

Entertainment for the entire family is available at the Gaslight Theatre, (520) 886-9428, 7010 E. Broadway, where melodramas encourage audience participation; reservations are required. The University of Arizona adds to Tucson's theater offerings. The school's resident company, (520) 621-1162, presents its offerings of musicals and serious drama in spring, summer and fall, while the UA Presents series brings national touring companies to Centennial Hall.

No bit players, Tucson's opera company plays a major part in the performing arts arena. Accompanied by a full orchestra in the Tucson Convention Center from October through April, members of the Arizona Opera, (520) 293-4336, present five operas.

Completing the cultural scene are the city's orchestras. The Tucson Symphony Orchestra, (520) 882-8585, plays both classical and pop music in the Tucson Convention Center September to May. Under the desert skies at the Reid Park Bandshell, the Tucson Pops Orchestra, (520) 722-5853, entertains audiences in the spring and fall. From September through May the University of Arizona's Centennial Hall resounds with sounds from Broadway shows to jazz to chamber music performed by guest artists and musicians.

Special Events

The Southern Arizona Square and Round Dance Festival begins the year's activities in January. In February the city boasts another superlative: the world's largest gem and mineral show. During the 14-day International Tucson Gem & Mineral Showcase, the Tucson Convention Center and area hotels are filled with hundreds of dealers selling to both wholesalers and the public; visitors should note that rooms are booked well in advance. Special museum exhibits also are featured.

If you like horses and cowboys, Tucson is the place to be in late February during La Fiesta de los Vaqueros, held at the rodeo grounds. This classic professional rodeo event begins with a "cowboy breakfast" and a 3-hour parade, with people afoot, on horseback and in every size and shape of horse-drawn vehicle. The fiesta ends 4 days later with the rodeo finals, in which some of the best riders and ropers on the circuit compete. In March the Randolph Golf Course is the site of the PING/Welch's LPGA Championship; the Tucson PGA Open is played in late February or early March at Omni Tucson National Resort and Spa.

The Yaqui Easter Lenten Ceremony combines old Yaqui traditions with Christian beliefs in a weeklong celebration. In March and again in December Tucson's 4th Avenue transforms into a street fair filled with artisans selling and demonstrating their crafts. Enhanced by music and an abundance of food and drink, these weekends attract visitors and residents alike. The Annual International Mariachi Conference comes to town in April. Mid-month brings the Pima County Fair.

Tucson's fall activities begin in late September and early October as Mount Lemmon Ski Valley plays host to Octoberfest. The Desert Thunder Pro Rodeo takes place the third weekend in October at the Tucson Rodeo Grounds. Luminaria Nights are held for 3 nights at the Tucson Botanical Gardens.

The Tucson Vicinity

ORACLE (E-5) pop. 3,563, elev. 4,513'

Oracle is named for the ship which carried the town's founder, Albert Weldon, to the United States in the late 1800s. A local miner, Weldon built a brush camp where the town now stands. Originally a copper mining town, Oracle's present-day economy is based on tourism, electronics and arts and crafts.

Located in the foothills of the Santa Catalina Mountains, 35 miles northeast of Tucson, Oracle's high altitude provides visitors a respite from the heat of the desert. Just 2 miles south off SR 77 on Mount Lemmon Road is Oracle State Park, which allows access to 7 miles of the Arizona Trail; hiking, mountain biking and horseback riding are permitted. Tours of the historic Kannally ranch house on site are available on weekends; phone (520) 896-2425.

San Manuel/Mammoth/Oracle Chamber of Commerce: P.O. Box 1886, Oracle, AZ 85623; phone (520) 385-9322.

BIOSPHERE 2 CENTER, 5 mi. n.e. of jct. SRs 79 and 77 to 32540 S. Biosphere Rd., is a glass and steel structure that encompasses 3 acres and five biomes: rain forest, ocean, savanna, desert and marsh.

The guided Under the Glass tour provides visitors a closer look at the interior of the facility, including its ocean, lung and technological systems. The tour begins with a film presentation at the visitor center and includes a .25-mile walking tour inside the Biosphere 2.

Comfortable walking shoes are recommended. Allow 2 hours minimum. Daily 9-4; closed Thanksgiving and Dec. 25. Tours are given daily; phone ahead for schedule. Admission $19.95; ages 6-12, $12.95. Reservations are recommended. AX, MC, VI. Phone (520) 838-6100.

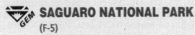 SAGUARO NATIONAL PARK
(F-5)

Elevations in the park range from 2,500 ft. on the desert floor along the loop roads to 8,666 ft. at Mica Mountain. Refer to AAA maps for additional elevation information.

Near Tucson, Saguaro National Park is divided into two districts: Rincon Mountain (Saguaro East) is about 15 miles east via Old Spanish Trail, and Tucson Mountain (Saguaro West) is 15 miles west via Speedway Boulevard. Both districts typify the Sonoran arboreal desert and contain stands of saguaro cactuses, known for their sometimes humanlike shapes.

The saguaro grows only in southern Arizona, in California along the Colorado River and in the northern Mexican state of Sonora. It can live more than 200 years, attaining heights of 30 to 40 feet; a few exceptional ones exceed 50 feet. Its blossom, the state flower, appears in May and June. Native Americans use its fruit for food and as a beverage base.

In addition to protecting the saguaro and other desert vegetation of the Sonoran Desert, the park's Saguaro West District has rock formations decorated with Native American petroglyphs and designs.

At the park headquarters in Saguaro East a visitor center contains plant and animal exhibits and offers nature programs in the winter; phone (520) 733-5153. The 8-mile Cactus Forest Drive begins at the visitor center parking lot. Picnic facilities are available. The 6-mile Bajada Loop Drive winds through Saguaro West. A visitor center has exhibits; phone (520) 733-5158.

Saguaro East is open daily 7 a.m.-dusk. Saguaro West is open 6 a.m.-dusk, Oct.-May; 7 a.m.-dusk, rest of year. Visitor centers open daily 9-5; closed Dec. 25. Admission to Saguaro East or Saguaro West is by 7-day or annual permit; 7-day permits cost $10 per private vehicle or $5 for persons arriving by other means. Backpack camping only; no drive-in camping permitted. Rates may vary; phone ahead. AX, DS, MC, VI. For additional information contact the Superintendent, Saguaro National Park, 3693 S. Old Spanish Tr., Tucson, AZ 85730-5601; phone (520) 733-5153. *See Recreation Chart.*

SAHUARITA (F-4) pop. 3,242, elev. 2,702'

ASARCO MINERAL DISCOVERY CENTER, off I-19 exit 80 to 1421 W. Pima Mine Rd., features hands-on exhibits about mining and minerals. A theater offers presentations about mining, mineral resources and reclamation. A 1-hour tour provides a look inside an operating open-pit copper mine. Allow 1 hour, 30 minutes minimum. Tues.-Sat. 9-5. Guided tours are given at 9:30, 11, 12:30, 2 and 3:30. Hours vary in summer; phone ahead. Center free. Mine tour $6; over 61, $5; ages 5-12, $4. AX, DS, MC, VI. Phone (520) 625-7513 or (520) 625-8233.

SAVE   **TITAN MISSILE MUSEUM,** .75 mi. w. of I-19 exit 69 off Duval Mine Rd., is a formerly active Intercontinental Ballistic Missile (ICBM) complex preserved as a museum. Of the 54 Titan II ICBM sites in the U.S. weapon system, all except the missile museum have been destroyed.

Note: The tour includes descending/ascending 55 steps and might be cumbersome for the physically challenged or those with a heart condition. Arrangements may be made for the use of an elevator for the physically challenged. Guided tours are available. Allow 1 hour minimum, Guided tours daily 9-4; closed Thanksgiving and Dec. 25. Tours are given every half-hour. Admission $8.50; over 62 and military with ID $7.50; ages 7-12, $5. AX, DS, MC, VI. Phone (520) 625-7736.

VAIL (F-5) pop. 2,484, elev. 3,225'

COLOSSAL CAVE MOUNTAIN PARK, off I-10 exit 279, then 7 mi. n. on Vail Rd. to 16721 E. Old Spanish Trail Rd., is a 2,200-acre park with what is considered by some to be the world's largest dry cavern. Only partially explored, the cave has chambers and lighted passageways. The park also includes a museum, butterfly garden and gemstone sluice as well as stagecoach rides and hiking and horse trails. Guided 45-minute cave tours are offered; extended tours are available.

Camping and picnicking are permitted. Mon.-Sat. 8-6, Sun. 8-7, mid-Mar. to mid-Sept.; Mon.-Sat. 9-5, Sun. 9-6, rest of year. Park $5 per private vehicle (up to six people, $1 extra per passenger). Cave $8.50; ages 6-12, $5. DS, MC, VI. Phone (520) 647-7275.

Arizona-Sonora Desert Museum / Gill Kenny / Metropolitan Tucson Convention and Visitors Bureau

This ends listings for the Tucson Vicinity.
The following page resumes the alphabetical listings of cities in Arizona.

TUMACÁCORI NATIONAL HISTORICAL PARK (G-4)

Approximately 19 miles north of Nogales off I-19 exit 29, Tumacácori National Historical Park preserves the abandoned Mission San Jose de Tumacácori. Once a Pima Indian village, Tumacácori was visited by Jesuit Eusebio Francisco Kino in 1691. In 1767 the Jesuits were expelled from Tumacácori by the King of Spain and replaced by Franciscans. The Franciscans began building the present massive adobe church about 1800, but it was never completed. Apache raids, neglect and a terrible winter contributed to its abandonment in 1848, yet afterward people continued to visit the site.

Anglo-Americans first visited the site in 1849, but Apache raids forced the settlers to leave. The area became a national monument in 1908. The 1990 addition of two Spanish mission sites, Guevavi and Calabazas, increased the total acreage to 47. Guevavi and Calabazas can presently be visited by reservation only on Wednesday, September through April. A historic museum distinguished by architectural features of the Sonora missions unfolds local history and describes mission life.

A self-guiding tour includes the church and cemetery, mortuary chapel, portions of the convent area, a patio garden and a visitor center/museum. Picnic facilities are available. Allow 1 hour minimum. Daily 8-5; closed Thanksgiving and Dec. 25. Admission $3, under 16 free. Phone (520) 398-2341.

TUZIGOOT NATIONAL MONUMENT (C-3)

About 2 miles northwest of Cottonwood via Main Street to Tuzigoot Road, Tuzigoot National Monument preserves the ruins of a pueblo that was occupied by the Sinagua Indians from about A.D. 1000 until it was abandoned in 1425. From more than 110 rooms archeologists have recovered stone and bone tools, textiles, pottery, shell beads and bracelets, which are displayed in the visitor center.

Allow 1 hour minimum. Daily 8-6, Memorial Day-Labor Day; 8-5, rest of year. Admission $3, under 17 free. Phone (928) 634-5564.

VAIL—see Tucson p. 118.

VALLE (B-3)

AIR MUSEUM PLANES OF FAME is at the Valle Airport near jct. SR 64 and US 180 at 755 Mustang Way. Covering aviation history from World War I through the supersonic jet age, the museum's collection includes Gen. Douglas MacArthur's personal transport plane *Bataan*, a Lockheed C-121A Constellation. Other aircraft include a 1944 Messerschmitt BF109G-10, a Grumman F-11F Tiger formerly used by the Navy's Blue Angels and many others. An air show is held in June.

Allow 1 hour minimum. Daily 9-6, May-Sept.; 9-5, rest of year. Closed Thanksgiving and Dec. 25.

Admission $5.95; ages 5-12, $1.95. Constellation tour $3. AX, DC, DS, MC, VI. Phone (928) 635-1000.

VERMILION CLIFFS NATIONAL MONUMENT (A-3)

Bounded on the east by Glen Canyon National Recreation Area, on the west by Kaibab National Forest, to the north by the Utah border and to the south by SR 89, remote Vermilion Cliffs National Monument contains 293,000 acres of unspoiled plateaus, canyons and cliffs. Elevations range from 3,100 to 7,100 feet.

Ancestral Puebloan villages can be found on the monument lands, which were traversed by Spanish explorers, Mormon missionaries and Mexican traders. Animal inhabitants include desert bighorn sheep, pronghorn antelopes and mountain lions. For further information contact the Arizona State Office, Bureau of Land Management; 345 E. Riverside Dr., St. George, UT 84790; phone (435) 688-3246.

WALNUT CANYON NATIONAL MONUMENT (C-4)

Off I-40 exit 204, 7.5 miles east of Flagstaff, Walnut Canyon National Monument preserves the remains of more than 300 pre-Columbian dwellings built on a series of ledges in the 400-foot-deep gorge. Inhabited by the Sinagua Indians about 1000-1200, these single-family dwellings are visible from the visitor center on the canyon rim.

The self-guiding Island Trail, which descends 185 feet over the course of a half mile, is an interesting but arduous paved path that leads past 25 of the cliff dwelling rooms. The Rim Trail, a pleasant .75-mile round trip, features two overlooks into the canyon as well as access to a small pueblo and pit house. Snow and ice might close both trails at times in winter and spring.

Interpretive programs are available from Memorial Day through Labor Day. A museum and picnic facilities are available; however, food is not available. Pets are not allowed on park trails, in buildings or tied to fixed objects.

Note: The Island Trail includes descending/ascending 240 steps and might be cumbersome for the physically challenged and those with heart conditions.

Allow 1 hour, 30 minutes minimum. Daily 8-6, June-Aug.; 8-5, rest of year. Closed Dec. 25. Last admittance to main trail is 1 hour before closing. Admission $5 per person, under 17 free. For further information contact the District Ranger, Walnut Canyon National Monument, Walnut Canyon Road #3, Flagstaff, AZ 86004; phone (928) 526-3367.

WALPI—see Keams Canyon p. 61.

WENDEN (D-2) pop. 556, elev. 1,869'

ALAMO LAKE STATE PARK, 38 mi. n. of US 60 via a paved road, offers views of the Buckskin and

Rawhide mountains from its site on the Bill Williams River. Activities include fishing, camping, boating and hiking. Daily 7-5. Admission $5 per private vehicle. Camping $10-$19 per private vehicle. Phone (928) 669-2088. *See Recreation Chart.*

WHITERIVER (D-5) pop. 5,220

Center of the Fort Apache Reservation fishing, camping and recreation area, Whiteriver also is the administrative headquarters of the 1,664,874-acre reservation. Four miles south is Fort Apache *(see place listing p. 51),* an active post during the Indian wars; it is now the site of the Theodore Roosevelt Indian School.

Seven miles west of town via a dirt road are the Kinishba Ruins, a partially restored Pueblo village inhabited 1050-1350; check locally to confirm road and weather conditions. Visitors are welcome at both the Alchesay National Fish Hatchery, (928) 338-4901, 8 miles north via SR 73, and the Williams Creek Hatchery, (928) 334-2346, 16 miles n. via SR 73 following signs.

WICKENBURG (G-1) pop. 5,082, elev. 2,071'

Nineteen miles southwest of Wickenburg is the Vulture Gold Mine, which yielded more than $20 million in gold during the hectic period following its discovery by Henry Wickenburg in 1863. Allegedly Wickenburg found the gold in one of the rocks he was hurling at his escaping mule.

The gold rush that ensued reached such proportions that by 1866 Wickenburg was the third largest city in Arizona and missed becoming the territorial capital by only two votes. Still standing in the center of town is the old mesquite jail tree to which lawmen chained their prisoners during the early boom years; no one wanted to take time from mining to build a proper jail.

The Hassayampa River, running through town, was called "the river which flows upside down" by Native Americans because its main flow is 20 feet below the surface. It is one of the last and greatest natural riparian areas in the state.

Wickenburg, known for its Old West atmosphere and many dude ranches, brings the past to life in February during Gold Rush Day and again in August, when the Desert Caballeros ride into the Bradshaw Mountains to spend several days under the stars; the whole town gathers to bid the horsemen farewell as they ride off into the mountains.

Wickenburg Chamber of Commerce: 216 N. Frontier St., Wickenburg, AZ 85390; phone (928) 684-5479 or (800) 942-5242.

[SAVE] **DESERT CABALLEROS WESTERN MUSEUM,** 21 N. Frontier St., contains dioramas depicting the town's history, a re-creation of an early Wickenburg street scene, ancient native artifacts and collections of gems and minerals. A gallery displays some 600 pieces of cowboy gear, including saddles, spurs and chaps, along with works by such noted Western artists as Frederic Remington and Charles Russell.

Allow 1 hour minimum. Mon.-Sat. 10-5, Sun. noon-4, Sept.-June; Tues.-Sat. 10-5, Sun. noon-4, rest of year. Closed Jan. 1, Easter, Thanksgiving and Dec. 25. Admission $6; over 59, $4.50; ages 6-16, $1. Phone (928) 684-2272.

ROBSON'S MINING WORLD is 24 mi. w. on US 60, 4 mi. n.e. on SR 71, then 1.5 mi. e. on a dirt road between Mileposts 89 and 90, following signs. This re-created mining town contains a museum with an extensive collection of antique mining equipment and a minerals exhibit. The complex of more than 30 buildings also includes a gold-panning sluice, replicas of old stores stocked with period goods, a newspaper office with original printing equipment and an early telephone system. Hiking trails lead to petroglyphs.

Guided tours are available. Picnicking is permitted. Food is available. Allow 30 minutes minimum. Mon.-Fri. 10-4, Sat.-Sun. 9-5, Oct. 1-May 1. Admission $5; over 55, $4.50; under 11 free. Phone (928) 685-2609.

WILLCOX (F-5) pop. 3,733, elev. 4,156'

Willcox grew from a small cow town into one of the country's major cattle-shipping centers. In days past the large cattle ranches in the surrounding hills and valleys were notorious as refuges for fugitive gunslingers, who often brought their business to town: Wyatt Earp's brother Warren was killed at Headquarters Saloon in 1900. Saloons and other buildings from the late 1800s can be seen in or near the historic district, bounded by Railroad and Haskell avenues and Maley and Stewart streets.

Rex Allen was born and raised in Willcox. Tributes to the cowboy actor include the Rex Allen Arizona Cowboy Museum *(see attraction listing)* on Railroad Avenue and a bronze statue in a park across from the museum. A bronze heart imbedded in the statue at Allen's request represents his enduring love for his hometown.

Cattle raising is still important, but added to the contemporary economic mix are ostrich farming and the cultivation of apples, peaches, pistachios, onions and tomatoes. At a variety of "U-pick" farms northwest via Fort Grant Road, visitors can pluck fresh produce straight from the orchards and fields July through October.

Birding is a popular diversion in Sulphur Springs Valley, a mecca for migrating waterfowl and shorebirds as well as wintering raptors. Sandhill cranes arrive in October and stay through February.

Southeast of town at Apache Pass is the isolated Old Fort Bowie National Historic Site. The fort was built in 1862 to guard the Butterfield Overland Trail and to protect pioneers from Apache raids and skirmishes with Native Americans led by Cochise and Geronimo. The site can only be reached by traveling the last 1.5 miles on foot. The high elevation and temperature extremes might make this hike unsuitable for some. Water is available at the fort, but hikers should bring their own canteen. Beware of flash floods, mountain lions and rattlesnakes. All historic items and natural features are strictly protected; metal detectors, digging tools, guns and hunting are prohibited.

Willcox Regional Visitor Center and Chamber of Commerce: 1500 N. Circle I Rd., Willcox, AZ 85643; phone (520) 384-2272 or (800) 200-2272.

Self-guiding tours: Brochures for a self-guiding walking tour of the historic district are available from the visitor center.

CHIRICAHUA REGIONAL MUSEUM is at 127 E. Maley St. History exhibits cover such topics as the railroad, Butterfield Stage Line, U.S. Cavalry, Apache Indians and development of farming, ranching and mining. The museum is housed in a turn-of-the-20th-century hardware store featuring original wooden floors and a pressed tin ceiling. Allow 30 minutes minimum. Mon.-Sat. 10-4; closed major holidays. Donations. Phone (520) 384-3971.

SAVE **REX ALLEN ARIZONA COWBOY MUSEUM AND COWBOY HALL OF FAME,** 150 N. Railroad Ave., honors the career of Western star Rex Allen, who was born in Willcox in 1920. Allen's life is depicted from his ranching and homesteading years through his radio, television and film career. Through photographs, storyboards, clothing and ranch implements the museum also highlights the pioneers and ranchers who shaped the West. Rex Allen Days take place the first weekend in October.

Daily 10-4; closed Jan. 1, Thanksgiving and Dec. 25. Admission $3 per couple, $2 per person, family rate $5. Phone (520) 384-4583 or (877) 234-4111.

WILLIAMS (C-3) pop. 2,842, elev. 6,752′

Williams was named after William (Bill) Shirley Williams, the early mountain man who guided trapping parties and expeditions through the wilderness.

Primarily a resort town, Williams marks the beginning of the major entrance route to Grand Canyon National Park *(see place listing p. 53)*. The town is at the base of Bill Williams Mountain, which boasts a ski area offering both downhill and cross-country skiing. Cross-country skiing also is popular in the surrounding Kaibab National Forest *(see place listing p. 61)*. Cataract, Kaibab Dog Trail and White Horse lakes offer camping, picnicking and fishing *(see the AAA Southwestern CampBook)*.

Williams and Forest Service Visitor Center: 200 West Railroad Ave., Williams, AZ 86046; phone (928) 635-4061 or (800) 863-0546.

SAVE **GRAND CANYON DEER FARM,** 6752 E. Deer Farm Rd. off I-40, has several varieties of deer and such other animals as peacocks, reindeer, llamas and antelope. Visitors are permitted to walk among the deer and feed them. Daily 8-7, June-Aug.; 9-6, Mar.-May and Sept.-Oct.; 10-5, rest of year. Closed Thanksgiving and Dec. 25. Admission $6.75; over 62, $5.75; ages 3-13, $3.95. AX, DS, MC, VI. Phone (928) 635-4073 or (800) 926-3337.

Petroglyphs and Pictographs

As forerunners of true writing, Native Americans used petroglyphs and pictographs as a way to communicate with each other as well as to record history. A petroglyph is a symbol that is scratched or carved into the veneer of a rock with another rock. Scientists believe that veneer is created by years of accumulated dirt slowly building—clay dust and minerals are cemented to the surface by bacteria living in the rocks. After the veneer is chipped away and a petroglyph is created, a new layer of veneer slowly begins to build over the carving. Over time, the petroglyphs

Digital Archives

darken as the veneer thickens. While petroglyphs are carved, pictographs are painted on the surface of a rock. Visitors to Arizona can view the historic and prehistoric symbols at various sites throughout the state.

GRAND CANYON RAILWAY, .5 mi. s. of I-40 exit 163 (Grand Canyon Blvd.), offers round-trip excursions through grassy plains and pine forests to the South Rim of the Grand Canyon aboard historic railroad cars pulled by turn-of-the-20th-century steam engines (Memorial Day weekend through September) or vintage diesel locomotives (rest of year). On-board strolling musicians, Western characters and refreshments are provided. Five classes of train service are available. For an additional fee, bus tours of the South Rim with lunch are available.

A Wild West show takes place daily at 9:30. A museum at the restored 1908 Williams Depot contains railroad, mining, ranching and logging artifacts and photographs. Constructed 1910, the Grand Canyon Depot, in the historic district at the South Rim, is the only working log depot in the country.

Train departs daily at 10 and returns at 5:45, with a 3.25-hour stopover at the canyon; closed Dec. 24-25. Schedule is subject to change; phone ahead. Round-trip coach fare $60; ages 11-16, $35; under 11, $25. One-way fare available; upgraded seats are available for an additional fee. Fare does not include admission to Grand Canyon National Park. Fares may vary; phone ahead. Reservations are recommended. AX, DS, MC, VI. Phone (800) 843-8724. *See color ad p. 54.*

WINDOW ROCK (B-6) pop. 3,059

Window Rock is the capital of the Navajo nation and seat of its tribal government. The elected tribal council meets in the council house at least four times a year. Window Rock also contains the U.S. government's Bureau of Indian Affairs, Navajo Area Office.

The headquarters of the Navajo Arts and Crafts Enterprises is just east of the junction of SR 264 and Navajo Route 12. The Navajo Nation Museum, several blocks east at SR 264 and Loop Road, contains items relating to the history and culture of the Navajo and to the prehistoric cultures of the Four Corners region. Phone (928) 871-7941.

Navajo Tourism Department—Window Rock: P.O. Box 663, Window Rock, AZ 86515; phone (928) 871-6436.

FOUR CORNERS MONUMENT, in Navajo Tribal Park e. on SR 264, n. on US 491, w. on US 64 to E. US 160, is the only place in the country where four states meet. The juncture of Arizona, Utah, Colorado and New Mexico is marked by a concrete monument bearing each state's seal. The Navajo and Ute sell their wares near the site. Daily 7 a.m.-8 p.m., May 1 to mid-Aug.; 8-5 rest of year. Closed Jan. 1, Thanksgiving and Dec. 25. Admission $3. Phone (928) 871-6647.

WINKELMAN (E-5) pop. 443, elev. 1,928′

A mining and agricultural center, Winkelman is near the 8.5-mile Aravaipa Canyon, a wilderness retreat that was once the headquarters of the Apache Indians. The canyon's abundant vegetation, nourished by the year-round flow of Aravaipa Creek, contrasts with the surrounding desert terrain. Off SR 77, then 13 miles east on a paved and gravel road, the canyon is within the 4,044-acre Aravaipa Canyon Primitive Area. Permits are required to enter the area; contact the Bureau of Land Management's District Office in Safford; phone (928) 348-4400. Visitation to the area is limited; reservations are required.

WINSLOW (C-5) pop. 9,520, elev. 4,856′

Winslow was named after Gen. Edward Francis Winslow, a president of the Atlantic and Pacific Railroad. This railroad center is an important shipping and trading site. A two-story mural and bronze statue at Standin' on the Corner Park in downtown Winslow illustrate the Eagles' song "Take It Easy" and its well-known reference to the town. The Apache-Sitgreaves National Forests *(see place listing p. 40)* lie south of town.

Winslow Chamber of Commerce: 101 E. Second St., Winslow, AZ 86047; phone (928) 289-2434.

HOMOLOVI RUINS STATE PARK, 3 mi. e. on I-40 to exit 257, then 1.5 mi. n. on SR 87, is 4,000 acres containing more than 300 archeological sites including large pueblo ruins and petroglyphs. Sunset Cemetery, all that remains of an 1876 Mormon settlement, also is on the site. The visitor center/museum provides interpretive information about the Anasazi as well as the park. It is illegal to damage or remove any pre-Columbian or historic site, artifact or rock art within the park.

Picnic facilities and campsites are available. Visitor center 8-5; closed Dec. 25. Park daily dawn-dusk. Admission $5 per private vehicle. Camping $12-$19 per private vehicle. Phone (928) 289-4106 for camping information. *See Recreation Chart.*

METEOR CRATER, 22 mi. w. on I-40, then 6 mi. s. off exit 233, was formed nearly 50,000 years ago by a meteorite; the crater is 550 feet deep, 2.4 miles in circumference and nearly 1 mile across.

The meteor, estimated to have been 150 feet across and weighing several hundred thousand tons, slammed into the rocky plain and left a crater that was originally 700 feet deep and over 4,000 feet across. Because the terrain of the crater is very similar to that of the moon, NASA once trained Apollo astronauts here.

The Learning Center at the visitor center features interactive displays, a large-screen theater, the Astronaut Wall of Fame, an Apollo Space Capsule and an overview of astronaut training at the crater.

Guided trail tours of the rim are offered. Food is available. Inquire about weather policies. Appropriate footwear is required. Allow 2 hours minimum. Daily 7-7, Memorial Day-Sept. 15; 8-5, rest of year. Closed Dec. 25. Guided trail tours depart daily 9:15-2:15 (weather permitting). Admission $12; over 59, $11; ages 6-17, $6. DS, MC, VI. Phone (928) 289-2362 or (800) 289-5898. *See color ad p. 64.*

WUPATKI NATIONAL MONUMENT (B-4)

Lying north of Flagstaff and reached via US 89, 35,253-acre Wupatki National Monument contains hundreds of ruins. With increased rainfall resulting from the late 11th-century eruption of Sunset Crater Volcano, south of the monument, farming became productive enough that at one time the region may have been one of the more densely populated sections of northern Arizona. The original inhabitants of Wupatki are believed to have been ancestors of the Hopi Indians.

The largest and one of the most impressive sites is Wupatki, or "Long-cut House," containing more than 100 rooms. Nearby are a ceremonial amphitheater, ball court and "blow hole." Other important ruins are the Citadel, Nalakihu, Lomaki and the three-story Wukoki, all reachable by short, self-guiding trails. Most of the ruins were inhabited from about 1100-1225. Picnicking is available.

Allow 1 hour minimum. Visitor center open daily 8-6, June-Aug.; 8-5, Sept.-Nov. and Mar.-May; 8-5, rest of year. Closed Dec. 25. Ruins open daily dawn-dusk. Admission $5 per person, under 17 free. Admission includes Sunset Crater Volcano National Monument *(see place listing p. 103).* Phone (928) 679-2365.

YARNELL (D-3) pop. 645, elev. 4,800′

Yarnell sprang up as a gold-mining town after a prospector named Harrison Yarnell struck gold on a nearby mountain peak in 1863. Some active mines still produce silver, gold and copper; however, the area's primary industries are cattle raising and tourism. Many vacationers visit Yarnell in the summer to escape the desert heat and to enjoy the many recreational pursuits the area offers.

Yarnell/Peeples Valley Chamber of Commerce: P.O. Box 275, Yarnell, AZ 85362; phone (928) 427-6582.

SHRINE OF ST. JOSEPH OF THE MOUNTAINS, .5 mi. w. off SR 89, is an open-air mountainside shrine with statues that depict scenes of The Last Supper, Garden of Gethsemane, The Way of the Cross and the Risen Christ. Information is available at the shrine or by writing P.O. Box 1027, Yarnell, AZ 85362. Open daily 24 hours. Donations.

YUMA (E-1) pop. 77,515, elev. 200′

Although he was not the first white man to visit the area, Father Eusebio Francisco Kino was the first to recognize the Yuma Crossing as the gateway to California. Yet Kino's discovery would not be used for almost a century until another priest, Father Francisco Garces, followed it in his own search for a land route to California.

In 1779 two missions were founded at the crossing by Father Garces, who, along with all the colonists, was later killed during the last major uprising of the Yuma Indians. With the destruction of the colony the crossing again faded from memory. Fifty years passed before it was rediscovered, this time by Kit Carson. It finally became a permanent settlement during the California gold rush.

Lutes Casino on Main Street, the oldest continuous pool hall and domino parlor in the state, began as a grocery store in 1901. Today visitors can play dominos and pool or just browse around the room filled with eclectic memorabilia.

Yuma is host to a number of outdoor events. The city becomes flooded with hunters when hunting season opens over Labor Day weekend. Golf is a popular pastime with 13 lush golf courses from which to choose.

Yuma Convention and Visitors Bureau: 377 S. Main St., Suite 102, Yuma, AZ 85364; phone (928) 783-0071 or (800) 293-0071.

Self-guiding tours: The Colorado River crossing in Yuma is the site of several historical and cultural buildings, most of which are open to the public. Brochures about self-guiding tours are available from the convention and visitors bureau.

Shopping areas: Yuma Palms Regional Center, 1463 S. Yuma Palms Pkwy., is anchored by Dillard's and JCPenney.

ARIZONA HISTORICAL SOCIETY/SANGUINETTI HOUSE MUSEUM AND GARDENS, 240 Madison Ave., was the home of pioneer merchant E.F. Sanguinetti. The house contains late 19th-century period rooms and exhibits about Yuma history. The surrounding gardens and aviaries are maintained as they were in the early 1900s. Tues.-Sat. 10-4; closed holidays. Admission $3; over 59 and ages 12-18, $2. Phone (928) 782-1841.

IMPERIAL NATIONAL WILDLIFE REFUGE encompasses 25,125 acres along the lower Colorado River. The Arizona section of the refuge is 40 mi. n. off US 95 via Martinez Lake Rd., following signs. The remainder of the refuge can be reached best by boat or four-wheel-drive vehicle. Canadian geese, ducks, egrets and eagles gather at the refuge. Hiking, hunting, fishing and boating are permitted in designated areas. Maps and public-use regulations are available upon request.

Daily dawn-dusk. Visitor center open Mon.-Fri. 7:30-4, Sat.-Sun. 9-4, Nov. 15-Mar. 31; Mon.-Fri. 7:30-4, rest of year. Closed federal holidays. Free. Phone (928) 783-3371.

KOFA NATIONAL WILDLIFE REFUGE— *see Quartzsite p. 94.*

YUMA CROSSING STATE HISTORIC PARK, I-8 4th Ave. exit to 201 N. 4th Ave., is on a 20-acre site on the s. side of the Colorado River. The park salutes 5 centuries of transportation across the Colorado River. From 1864 through 1883 the U.S. Army Quartermaster Depot stored and distributed supplies for military posts throughout the Southwest. Five restored buildings stand on the site that once comprised the depot. The depot office was built in 1872. Daily 9-5; closed Dec. 25. Admission $3, under 14 free. Phone (928) 329-0471.

YUMA TERRITORIAL PRISON STATE HISTORIC PARK is off I-8 exit 2 (Giss Pkwy.), on a bluff on the s. side of the Colorado River "meander" (where the river bends). Erected in 1876, the building was a prison until 1909. The adobe walls, which no longer stand, were 8 feet thick at the base and 5 feet thick at the top, and at full capacity confined 400 prisoners. Of interest are the cellblocks, the "dark cell" and a museum. Interpretive programs are offered. Open daily 8-5; closed Dec. 25. Admission $4, under 14 free. Phone (928) 783-4771.

New Mexico

Spectacular Carlsbad Caverns

Colorful limestone formations create a subterranean wonderland

Ancient Pueblos

Continuing native traditions and culture at centuries-old dwellings

Dawn of the Nuclear Age

White gypsum sands mark the birthplace of the first atomic weapon

The Wild West

Legendary outlaws once ravaged the old Southwest

The Santa Fe Trail

Wagon wheel ruts lead past dazzling mountain and desert scenery

Fort Union National Monument / New Mexico Department of Tourism

City of Rocks State Park, Deming / Mark Nohl / New Mexico Department of Tourism

New Mexico is a mosaic of azure skies, adobe architecture and red rock cliffs.

A coyote, silhouetted by a glorious desert sunset, sings a mysterious song. A roadrunner pauses near a cactus—then with a clatter of his bill, he races away.

It is enchanting scenes like these that inspired such artisans as author D.H. Lawrence and artist Georgia O'Keeffe.

But New Mexico's scenic grandeur reveals more than mere beauty. Its landscape tells the stories of ancient civilizations who carved dwellings from the rocks and cliffs, of desperados who gave rise to the term "Wild West," of cattle barons who tamed the southeast plains and traded along the Santa Fe Trail.

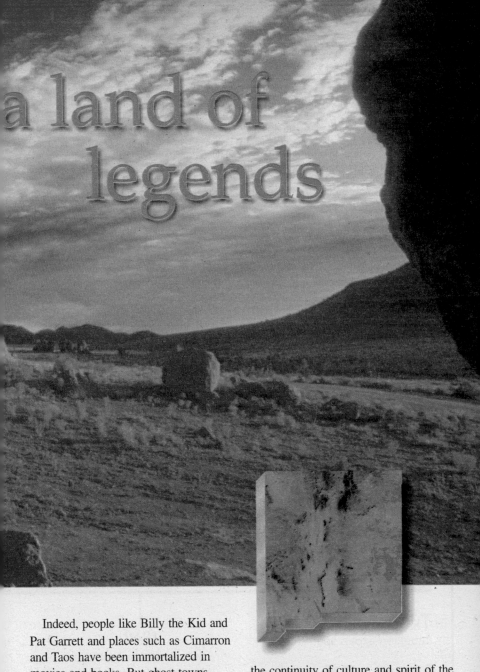

a land of legends

Indeed, people like Billy the Kid and Pat Garrett and places such as Cimarron and Taos have been immortalized in movies and books. But ghost towns, rugged mountains, gypsum sands and wild rivers stimulate the imagination as well.

Pueblos, built thousands of years ago and still functioning today, demonstrate the continuity of culture and spirit of the American Indians who dwell here.

The state is a saga of many chapters. Whether the story is that of prehistoric cliff-dwellers or the birthplace of the nuclear age, New Mexico is legendary.

"Beware: Hot Stuff" warns the label on a jar of spicy green chile salsa. Welcome to New Mexico, deemed the home of the world's finest chile peppers, where you can fire up your taste buds with more than 10 varieties—most in the "extra hot" category.

Ristras, colorful strings of sun-dried chile peppers, drape cafe entryways and residential doorways. They are said to ward off evil, welcome visitors and alert guests to the fiery delicacies served there. Start with chile con queso, and then move to chorizo (spicy pork sausage) or green chile stew. Locals know one thing about chile: It's the hottest ingredient in any dish, and that's putting it mildly.

Feeling Hot, Hot, Hot

But chile isn't the only thing that heats things up. The radiant symbol that has come to represent New Mexico (found on its license plate and flag) is the Zia Pueblo sign for sun. Four rays extend from the center, signifying directions, seasons, periods of the day and stages of life.

Under the glow of the sun, hundreds of rainbow-colored gentle giants fill the sky with hot air during balloon festivals held across the state. The selection is anything but ordinary at the Albuquerque International Balloon Fiesta: It's common to see such diverse shapes as a castle, parrot, spare tire, cola can, corncob, dragon and yes, even Dumbo, everyone's favorite flying elephant.

From the basket of a balloon you may catch a glimpse of centuries-old, flat-roofed houses and cliff dwellings, which remain quintessential elements of New Mexico. Constructed of adobe—sun-dried bricks of earth, sand, charcoal and grass—they blend into the landscape in color and cast. Sunny weather and lack of rainfall were fundamental in the establishment of adobe due to its ability to keep cool in summer and warm in winter. This mixture served as the primary building material for pueblos, communal settlements established by the Spanish in the 16th century.

Nineteen working pueblos remain at Taos and other locations in north-central New Mexico. Each retains an independent government, social order and religious practice as well as a distinct artistic flair. Artisans produce traditional art individual to their own pueblo: Turquoise jewelry, storyteller dolls, pottery, drums, carvings, Navajo rugs and

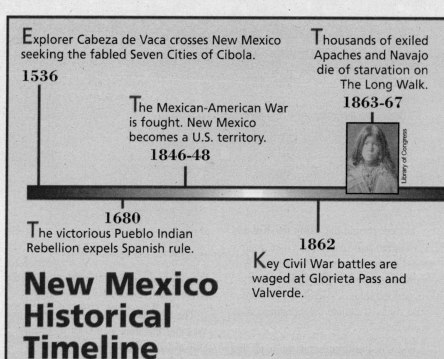

Explorer Cabeza de Vaca crosses New Mexico seeking the fabled Seven Cities of Cibola.
1536

The Mexican-American War is fought. New Mexico becomes a U.S. territory.
1846-48

Thousands of exiled Apaches and Navajo die of starvation on The Long Walk.
1863-67

Library of Congress

1680
The victorious Pueblo Indian Rebellion expels Spanish rule.

1862
Key Civil War battles are waged at Glorieta Pass and Valverde.

New Mexico Historical Timeline

weavings are coveted by visitors and collectors alike.

Some pueblos welcome guests to experience their heritage at annual festivals held in honor of the pueblo's patron saint. Corn, deer or buffalo dances are executed according to strict standards, culminating in a flamboyant display of colorful costumes.

While native traditions at the pueblos continue, only stark stone and adobe walls remain at the uninhabited Chaco Culture National Historical Park, and at Aztec Ruins and Bandelier national monuments. Explore what were once thriving Ancestral Puebloan communities; multistory cliff dwellings with remnants of hundreds of rooms, kivas (ceremonial meeting halls) and petroglyphs offer a warm welcome into the state's rich cultural past.

Sizzling Secrets

Southeastern New Mexico was a hotbed of controversy when, in 1947, a farmer discovered exotic metal debris on a sheep ranch. Some are convinced it was the wreckage of a flying saucer, while others believe it to be the result of tests performed by the U.S. Air Force.

The mysteries surrounding what was dubbed the "Roswell Incident" make the International UFO Museum & Research Center all the more intriguing. Here you can purchase your very own alien (stuffed, magnetic or featured on a rubber doormat). And don't pass up the annual Roswell UFO Encounter Festival: Here, aliens are the hot ticket.

Or you can learn more about another top secret scientific development—the Manhattan Project. Los Alamos was chosen as the hot spot for a weapons laboratory that developed and tested the atomic bomb during World War II. Visit the Bradbury Science Museum and peruse some 500 artifacts from the project.

If you can't stand the heat, pack a parka and head for the cool solace of Carlsbad Cavern. At 830 feet below the surface, its three-level Big Room begs exploration. Arguably one the biggest underground chambers in the world, it encompasses 14 acres—and at a chilly 56 F, it's definitely cool.

Spicy food, sunny skies, intriguing history, warmhearted residents and even hot springs—New Mexico knows how to put a spark in any itinerary.

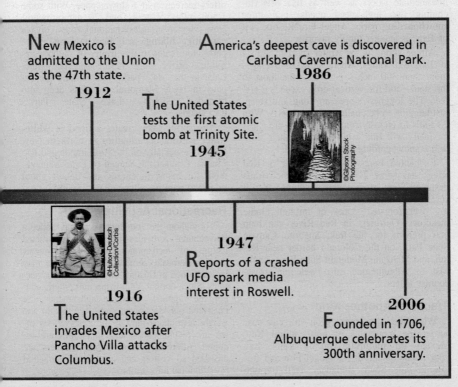

New Mexico is admitted to the Union as the 47th state.
1912

America's deepest cave is discovered in Carlsbad Caverns National Park.
1986

The United States tests the first atomic bomb at Trinity Site.
1945

©Gibson Stock Photography

©Hulton-Deutsch Collection/Corbis

1916
The United States invades Mexico after Pancho Villa attacks Columbus.

1947
Reports of a crashed UFO spark media interest in Roswell.

2006
Founded in 1706, Albuquerque celebrates its 300th anniversary.

Recreation

From snow-clad mountains and sandy desert lowlands to rusty looking canyons and verdant timbered forests, the New Mexico landscape is a tapestry of colors and shapes that can be enjoyed to the fullest in any season.

Drawing the Line

North-central New Mexico is the place to go for **snow skiing.** Sandia Peak Ski Area, just east of Albuquerque in the Cibola National Forest, packs a variety of trails, bowls and catwalks into a wedge of mountain. A 100-passenger aerial tramway ascends the western slope of the mountain to the 10,378-foot summit, but the ski runs from this height are recommended only for experienced skiers; a novice ski area on the eastern slope can be accessed by private vehicle.

The Sangre de Cristo Mountain Range supports a cluster of ski resorts open mid-December to mid-March. Santa Fe Ski Area, north of Santa Fe off US 285, attracts families and first-timers to its groomed slopes for downhill skiing; this resort's Chipmunk Corner teaches children to swish safely on powder. With 52 runs for beginning and intermediate skiers as well as five lifts (including two high-speed quads) and three **snowboarding** parks, Angel Fire Resort, east of Taos, is another family favorite.

Alpine skiing is the winter sport of choice at Taos Ski Valley, where snowfall averages more than 300 inches per year—the most in the state—and the vertical drop exceeds 2,600 feet. The toughest slopes are long and steep, just begging to be challenged by experts. With 72 trails to choose from, skiers who are "less inclined" will find a hill to match their skill. Sorry, snowboarding is not permitted.

Enchanted Forest, 3.5 miles east of Red River, has some 21 miles of groomed trails designed for cross-country skiing. You'll surely catch a glimpse of wildlife while striding over forested slopes or through alpine meadows. Outfitters in Red River can help you prepare for the trek. Sugarite Canyon State Park, on the Colorado border near Raton, and Manzano Mountain State Park, southeast of Albuquerque, also welcome cross-country skiers.

Tracks of Another Kind

When the snow melts, you still can soar across the mountains of north-central New Mexico—on **mountain biking** trails. Lay your treads on the dirt at Angel Fire and follow 23-mile South Boundary Trail through

Carson National Forest to Taos. The scenery is spectacular, but you'll have to be in shape to see it; this daylong trip starts with a 4-mile climb and tops out at 10,800 feet.

Trails in southern New Mexico are as varied as the terrain. Fresnal Canyon Loop traverses the Sacramento Mountains foothills, just northeast of Alamogordo, passing through villages as well as cherry and apple orchards. Riding time depends on how many glasses of cider you stop to sample. Race the jack rabbits on a 4.5-mile loop around Tortugas Mountain, 1 mile southeast of Las Cruces. The riding surface in this desertlike comes in three textures: rocky, sandy and smooth.

Bicycling on paved surfaces can be a family event at Chaco Culture National Historical Park, in the northwest. An easy 8-mile circle tour begins at the visitor center and offers stops at several archeological ruins that you can tour at your leisure. The king of the road-rides may well be a 70-mile round-trip excursion via state and forest roads from Carlsbad to Sitting Bull Falls, in Lincoln National Forest; a rest beside the waterfall will rejuvenate you for the return trip.

The Gila National Forest, in the southwest, offers recreation at a slower pace. With some 1,500 miles of trails and 20 campgrounds, New Mexico's largest national forest invites **camping, hiking** and **backpacking.** State parks, too, cater to this trinity of outdoor activities. Strike camp beside Elephant Butte Lake in that state park; walk among the aspens in Hyde Memorial; or press deep into primitive Morphy Lake State Park's backwoods.

The spring thaw creates a flood of **whitewater rafting** opportunities in northern New Mexico, especially on the Rio Grande and Rio Chama. Contact the Bureau of Land Management for maps, brochures and details about rules and permits; phone (505) 758-8851.

Recreational Activities

Throughout the TourBook, you may notice a Recreational Activities heading with bulleted listings of recreation-oriented establishments listed underneath. Similar operations also may be mentioned in Destination City recreation sections. Since normal AAA inspection criteria cannot be applied, these establishments are presented only for information. Age, height and weight restrictions may apply. Reservations often are recommended and sometimes are required. Addresses and/or phone numbers are provided so visitors can contact the attraction for additional information.

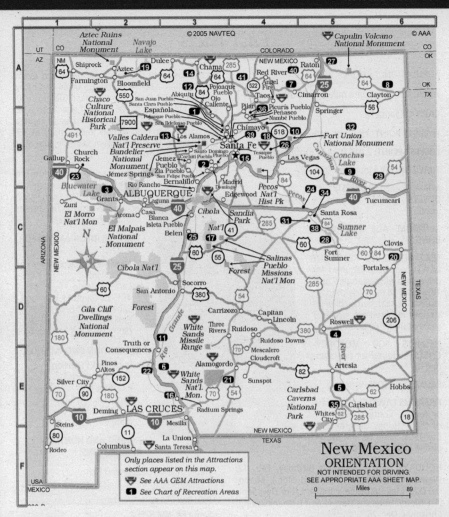

© 2005 NAVTEQ

© AAA

New Mexico
ORIENTATION
NOT INTENDED FOR DRIVING.
SEE APPROPRIATE AAA SHEET MAP.

0   Miles   89

Only places listed in the Attractions
section appear on this map.

See AAA GEM Attractions

See Chart of Recreation Areas

Fast Facts

POPULATION: 1,819,046.

AREA: 121,666 square miles; ranks 5th.

CAPITAL: Santa Fe.

HIGHEST POINT: 13,161 ft., Wheeler Peak.

LOWEST POINT: 2,817 ft., Red Bluff Reservoir.

TIME ZONE(S): Mountain. DST.

MINIMUM AGE FOR UNRESTRICTED DRIVER'S LICENSE: 16 years, 6 months.

MINIMUM AGE FOR GAMBLING: 21

SEAT BELT/CHILD RESTRAINT LAWS: Seat belts required for driver and all passengers over 18; ages 7-18 must use child restraints or seat belts; child restraints required for under 7 years or under 60 pounds.

HELMETS FOR MOTORCYCLISTS: Required for riders under 18.

RADAR DETECTORS: Permitted.

FIREARMS LAWS: Vary by state or county. Contact the Office of the Attorney General, P.O. Box 1508, Santa Fe, NM 87504; phone (505) 827-6000.

HOLIDAYS: Jan. 1; Lincoln's Birthday, Feb. 12; Washington's Birthday, Feb. (3rd Mon.); Memorial Day, May (last Mon.); July 4; Labor Day, Sept. (1st Mon.); Veterans Day, Nov. 11; Thanksgiving; Christmas, Dec. 25.

TAXES: New Mexico's statewide sales tax is 5 percent, with local option for additional increments of up to 2.2 percent.

ROAD CONDITIONS: The State Department of Transportation provides current information about road closures and conditions; phone (800) 432-4269.

INFORMATION CENTERS: State welcome centers that provide maps, weather information, brochures and information about attractions, accommodations, historic sites, parks and events are at I-10W near Anthony; US 64/84 at Chama; I-40 exit 22 at Gallup; I-40W near Glenrio; I-10E exit 20 at Lordsburg; I-25 exit 451 near Raton; I-25 mile marker 268, 17 miles south of Santa Fe, near the Santo Domingo Indian Reservation; at 491 Old Santa Fe Tr. in downtown Santa Fe; and at US 60/70/84 near Texico.

SPECIAL NOTE: Plague bacilli, a condition promoted by fleas, is endemic to New Mexico. Pet owners are advised to provide flea protection for their animals.

FURTHER INFORMATION FOR VISITORS:

New Mexico Department of Tourism
Lamy Building
491 Old Santa Fe Tr.
Santa Fe, NM 87501
(505) 827-7400
(800) 733-6396

RECREATION INFORMATION:

State Parks Division
1220 St. Francis Dr.
P.O. Box 1147
Santa Fe, NM 87504
(505) 476-3355
(888) 667-2757

FISHING AND HUNTING REGULATIONS:

Department of Game and Fish
1 Wildlife Way
P.O. Box 25112
Santa Fe, NM 87504
(505) 476-8000
(800) 862-9310

NATIONAL FOREST INFORMATION:

Southwestern Region
333 Broadway S.E.
Albuquerque, NM 87102
(505) 842-3292
(877) 444-6777
or TTY (877) 833-6777 (reservations)

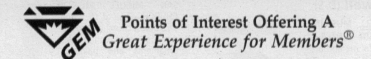

Points of Interest Offering A
Great Experience for Members®

Alamogordo (E-4)

NEW MEXICO MUSEUM OF SPACE HISTORY—This large complex includes Stapp Air and Space Park, Astronaut Memorial Garden and Shuttle Camp. An outdoor display features launch vehicles and spacecraft. See p. 138.

Albuquerque (C-3)

NEW MEXICO MUSEUM OF NATURAL HISTORY & SCIENCE—Origins and geographical history of the Southwest are explored. A naturalist center and saltwater aquarium also are featured. See p. 142.

OLD TOWN—This site presents a visible record of Albuquerque's evolution from small town to big city. American Indians and artisans vend their handicrafts around the plaza. See p. 142.

RIO GRANDE ZOO—More than 1,000 animals representing some 250 species are housed here. See p. 142.

SANDIA PEAK AERIAL TRAMWAY—Visitors are transported above the deep canyons of the Sandia Mountains in the Cibola National Forest. See p. 143.

Angel Fire (B-4)

VIETNAM VETERANS NATIONAL MEMORIAL—A curvilinear structure is dedicated to Vietnam War casualties. The hilltop vantage affords views of the Sangre de Cristo Mountains and the Moreno Valley. See p. 144.

Aztec Ruins National Monument (A-2)

AZTEC RUINS NATIONAL MONUMENT—A monument marks one of the largest and best preserved Ancestral Puebloan ruins in the Southwest. See p. 144.

Bandelier National Monument (B-2)

BANDELIER NATIONAL MONUMENT—Remnants of an Ancestral Puebloan community established centuries ago include pueblo and cliff ruins as well as cave rooms hewn out of soft tuff rock. See p. 145.

Capulin Volcano National Monument (A-5)

CAPULIN VOLCANO NATIONAL MONUMENT—Created about 60,000 years ago when ash and cinders piled up around a volcano vent, this is one of the best examples of a volcanic cinder cone in the nation. See p. 146.

Carlsbad Caverns National Park (E-4)

CARLSBAD CAVERNS NATIONAL PARK—In the rugged foothills of the Guadalupe Mountains, the park's exhibits depict the geology, biology, history and archeology of the area. See p. 146.

Chaco Culture National Historical Park (B-2)

CHACO CULTURE NATIONAL HISTORICAL PARK—A thousand years ago the Chacoan people flourished in this high desert community. The well-preserved ruins of their ancient city remain. See p. 149.

Chama (A-3)

CUMBRES & TOLTEC SCENIC RAILROAD—Ride on the narrow-gauge railroad to explore the territory along the rugged San Juan and Sangre de Cristo mountain ranges. See p. 150.

Las Cruces (E-3)

NEW MEXICO FARM & RANCH HERITAGE MUSEUM—Visit a working cattle ranch and dairy farm to learn more about New Mexico's rural life and 3,000-year-old agricultural history. See p. 159.

Los Alamos (B-3)

BRADBURY SCIENCE MUSEUM—Exhibits interpret the depth of science and engineering capabilities, including that of the Manhattan Project. See p. 161.

Roswell (D-5)

ROSWELL MUSEUM AND ART CENTER—Historical art and artifacts of Southwestern culture are displayed. See p. 165.

Santa Fe (B-4)

MUSEUM OF INTERNATIONAL FOLK ART—Exhibits include miniature buildings, streets and marketplaces in village scenes from 100 countries. Also featured is Spanish colonial folk art. See p. 171.

PALACE OF THE GOVERNORS—Built in 1610, the adobe structure was the seat of government under Spanish, American Indian, Mexican and U.S. territorial rule until 1909, when it became the state history museum. See p. 171.

SAN MIGUEL MISSION CHURCH—One of the country's oldest churches, the mission is adorned with priceless ornaments and paintings. See p. 172.

Santa Teresa (F-3)

WAR EAGLES AIR MUSEUM—Featured are restored aircraft from World War II and jet fighters from the Korean War. See p. 175.

White Sands Missile Range (D-3)

WHITE SANDS MISSILE RANGE MUSEUM—With a flash of light and tremendous explosion, the Atomic Age was born here in 1945. Learn more about the top secret operations. See p. 181.

White Sands National Monument (E-3)

WHITE SANDS NATIONAL MONUMENT—White gypsum sands and dunes rise up to 60 feet above the Tularosa Valley. The site also features a visitor center and interpretive programs. See p. 181.

RECREATION AREAS

	MAP LOCATION	CAMPING	PICNICKING	HIKING TRAILS	BOATING	BOAT RAMP	BOAT RENTAL	FISHING	SWIMMING	PETS ON LEASH	BICYCLE TRAILS	WINTER SPORTS	VISITOR CENTER	LODGE/CABINS	FOOD SERVICE
NATIONAL PARKS (See place listings)															
Carlsbad Caverns (F-4) 46,776 acres. Southeast New Mexico.			●	●									●		●
Chaco Culture (B-2) 33,974 acres. Northwest New Mexico.		●	●	●						●	●		●		
NATIONAL FORESTS (See place listings)															
Carson 1,500,000 acres. North-central New Mexico.		●	●	●	●			●			●	●	●	●	
Cibola 1,630,221 acres. Central New Mexico.		●	●	●	●	●		●	●	●	●	●	●	●	●
Gila 3,321,000 acres. Southwestern New Mexico.		●	●	●	●	●	●	●	●	●			●		
Lincoln 1,103,466 acres. South-central New Mexico. Horse rental.		●	●	●				●		●	●	●		●	●
Santa Fe 1,568,820 acres. North-central New Mexico between the San Pedro Mountains and the Sangre de Cristo Mountains.		●	●	●				●		●	●	●	●		
NATIONAL CONSERVATION AREAS (See place listings)															
El Malpais (C-2) 376,000 acres. Central New Mexico.		●	●	●									●		
Valles Caldera (B-3) 89,000 acres 18 mi. w. of Los Alamos off SR 4. (See Los Alamos p. 161)			●	●				●				●			
ARMY CORPS OF ENGINEERS															
Abiquiu Lake (B-3) 4,015 acres 7 mi. n.w. of Abiquiu via US 84. Water skiing. (See Abiquiu p. 137)	❶	●	●			●	●	●	●	●			●		
Cochití Lake (B-3) 1,200 acres 5 mi. n. of Pea Blanca on SR 22. (See Cochití Pueblo p. 152)	❷	●	●	●	●	●		●	●	●			●		

RECREATION AREAS

	MAP LOCATION	CAMPING	PICNICKING	HIKING TRAILS	BOATING	BOAT RAMP	BOAT RENTAL	FISHING	SWIMMING	PETS ON LEASH	BICYCLE TRAILS	WINTER SPORTS	VISITOR CENTER	LODGE/CABINS	FOOD SERVICE
STATE															
Bluewater Lake (C-2) 2,105 acres 29 mi. n.w. of Grants off I-40.	3	•	•	•	•	•		•	•	•		•			•
Bottomless Lakes (D-5) 1,611 acres 16 mi. s.e. of Roswell via US 380, then 6 mi. s. on SR 409. *(See Roswell p. 165)*	4	•	•	•	•			•	•	•			•		
Brantley Lake (E-5) 3,000 acres 12 mi. n. of Carlsbad off US 285.	5	•	•		•	•		•		•			•		
Caballo Lake (E-3) 11,610 acres 14 mi. s. of Truth or Consequences off I-25. *(See Truth or Consequences p. 180)*	6	•	•		•	•		•	•	•					•
Cimarron Canyon (A-4) 33,000 acres 12 mi. e. of Eagle Nest via US 64. *(See Cimarron p. 151)*	7	•	•	•				•		•		•	•		
Clayton Lake (A-6) 417 acres 15 mi. n. of Clayton on SR 370. *(See Clayton p. 152)*	8	•	•		•	•		•		•			•		
Conchas Lake (B-5) 1,557 acres 31 mi. n.w. of Tucumcari via SR 104. *(See Tucumcari p. 180)*	9	•	•	•	•	•		•	•	•			•	•	•
Coyote Creek (B-4) 80 acres 14 mi. n.e. of Mora on SR 434.	10	•	•	•				•		•			•		
Elephant Butte Lake (D-3) 40,056 acres 5 mi. e. of Truth or Consequences off I-25. *(See Truth or Consequences p. 180)*	11	•	•		•	•	•	•	•	•				•	•
El Vado Lake (A-3) 113 acres 4 mi. n.e. of El Vado off SR 112.	12	•	•	•	•	•		•	•	•		•			
Fenton Lake (B-3) 700 acres 38 mi. w. of Los Alamos via SRs 4 and 126. Canoeing, cross-country skiing.	13	•	•	•				•		•		•			
Heron Lake (A-3) 4,107 acres 11 mi. w. of Tierra Amarilla via US 84 and SR 95.	14	•	•	•				•		•		•	•		
Hyde Memorial (B-4) 350 acres 8 mi. n.e. of Santa Fe on Hyde Park Rd. *(See Santa Fe p. 169)*	15	•	•	•						•		•			
Leasburg Dam (E-3) 140 acres 15 mi. n.w. of Las Cruces via I-25 and SR 185. Canoeing; playground.	16	•	•					•					•		
Manzano Mountains (C-3) 160 acres 13 mi. n.w. of Mountainair via SR 55.	17	•	•	•						•			•		
Morphy Lake (B-4) 65 acres 11 mi. n. of Las Vegas off SR 518. *(See Las Vegas p. 160)*	18	•	•	•	•			•		•		•			
Navajo Lake (A-2) 13,300 acres 23 mi. n.e. of Bloomfield on SR 511. *(See Bloomfield p. 145)*	19	•	•	•	•	•	•	•	•	•			•		
Oasis (C-6) 193 acres 5.7 mi. n. of Portales off SR 467. *(See Portales p. 163)*	20	•	•					•		•		•			
Oliver Lee Memorial (E-3) 180 acres 10 mi. s. on US 54, then 5 mi. e. on Dog Canyon Rd. *(See Alamogordo p. 138)*	21	•	•	•						•			•		
Percha Dam (E-2) 84 acres 21 mi. s. of Truth or Consequences via I-25. Playground.	22	•	•	•				•	•	•					
Red Rock (B-1) 640 acres on I-40 in Church Rock. Museum. *(See Church Rock p. 151)*	23	•	•							•			•	•	•
Santa Rosa Lake (C-5) 14,000 acres 7 mi. n. of Santa Rosa via access road. Water skiing; nature trail. *(See Santa Rosa p. 174)*	24	•	•	•	•	•		•	•	•			•		
Sen. Willie M. Chavez (C-3) 150 acres on the Rio Grande at Belen.	25	•	•					•		•	•		•		
Storrie Lake (B-4) 83 acres 5 mi. n. of Las Vegas off SR 518. Windsurfing. *(See Las Vegas p. 160)*	26	•	•	•	•	•		•	•	•		•			
Sugarite Canyon (A-5) 9,500 acres 10 mi. n.e. of Raton via SR 72. Historic. Canoeing, cross-country skiing, mountain climbing, snowmobiling. *(See Raton p. 164)*	27	•	•	•				•		•		•	•		
Sumner Lake (C-5) 5,425 acres 16 mi. n. of Fort Sumner on US 84.	28	•	•		•	•		•	•	•					•
Ute Lake (B-6) 633 acres 2 mi. s.w. of Logan on SR 540. *(See Tucumcari p. 180)*	29	•	•	•	•	•	•	•	•	•			•	•	
Villanueva (C-4) 1,679 acres 31 mi. s.w. of Las Vegas via I-25 and SR 3.	30	•	•	•				•	•	•			•		
OTHER															
Blue Hole (C-4) 50 acres .5 mi. e. of Park Lake on La Pradira Ln. in Santa Rosa. Scuba diving. *(See Santa Rosa p. 174)*	31		•	•				•	•				•		

RECREATION AREAS

	MAP LOCATION	CAMPING	PICNICKING	HIKING TRAILS	BOATING	BOAT RAMP	BOAT RENTAL	FISHING	SWIMMING	PETS ON LEASH	BICYCLE TRAILS	WINTER SPORTS	VISITOR CENTER	LODGE/CABINS	FOOD SERVICE
Chicosa Lake (B-5) 640 acres 9 mi. n.e. of Roy on SR 120.	32	•	•	•				•		•			•		
Fort Stanton (D-4) 23,000 acres 5 mi. w. of Lincoln on US 380. Caving; horse trails.	33	•	•	•				•							
Janes-Wallace Memorial (C-5) 1 mi. s. of Santa Rosa on SR 91. (See Santa Rosa p. 174)	34	•	•					•					•		
Lake Carlsbad (E-5) In Carlsbad on Park Dr. Water skiing. (See Carlsbad p. 146)	35	•	•		•	•		•	•		•				•
Orilla Verde (B-4) 2,840 acres 6 mi. n of Pilar on SR 570.	36	•	•	•	•	•		•					•		
Park Lake (C-4) In Santa Rosa. (See Santa Rosa p. 174)	37		•	•				•	•	•	•				
Perch Lake (C-5) 22 acres 2 mi. s. of Santa Rosa on SR 91. Scuba diving. (See Santa Rosa p. 174)	38		•	•				•	•						
Santa Cruz Lake (B-4) 2,543 acres 14 mi. e. of Española via SRs 76 and 4. Mountain biking.	39	•	•	•	•	•	•	•							
Valle Vidal (A-4) 100,000 acres 4 mi. n. on US 64, then 21 mi. n.w. on Valle Vidal Rd. following signs. (See Cimarron p. 151)	40	•	•	•				•		•					
Wild Rivers (A-4) 20,300 acres 5 mi. w. of Questa off SR 378.	41	•	•	•				•					•		

New Mexico Temperature Averages Maximum / Minimum
From the records of the National Weather Service

	JAN	FEB	MAR	APR	MAY	JUNE	JULY	AUG	SEPT	OCT	NOV	DEC
Albuquerque	47 / 23	53 / 27	59 / 32	70 / 41	80 / 51	89 / 60	92 / 65	90 / 63	83 / 58	72 / 45	57 / 32	47 / 25
Carlsbad	61 / 27	65 / 31	73 / 38	81 / 46	88 / 54	95 / 63	95 / 66	94 / 65	89 / 59	79 / 47	69 / 35	59 / 27
Clayton	47 / 19	50 / 22	55 / 25	66 / 36	74 / 46	83 / 55	87 / 60	86 / 60	80 / 51	69 / 40	60 / 28	49 / 21
Las Cruces	57 / 28	64 / 31	70 / 37	79 / 45	88 / 53	96 / 61	97 / 67	95 / 66	91 / 59	82 / 47	67 / 33	59 / 29
Raton	45 / 13	49 / 17	55 / 21	63 / 30	72 / 39	83 / 48	87 / 53	85 / 51	79 / 45	69 / 33	55 / 20	48 / 15
Roswell	55 / 21	61 / 25	68 / 31	78 / 42	86 / 50	94 / 60	95 / 64	93 / 62	86 / 54	77 / 42	69 / 29	57 / 22
Santa Fe	40 / 19	43 / 23	51 / 29	59 / 35	68 / 43	78 / 52	80 / 57	79 / 56	73 / 49	62 / 39	50 / 28	41 / 20

Points of Interest

ABIQUIU (B-3) elev. 6,063'

In the mid-18th century Abiquiu (AH-be-cue) was one of several settlements the Spanish government provided for *Genízaros,* people of mixed blood who were either the Spaniards' own prisoners or captives ransomed from the Comanches or Apaches and later released from slavery. By 1778 the community was a stop on the Old Spanish Trail, which led westward to an infant coastal hamlet called Los Angeles.

Abiquiu was the birthplace of Padre Antonio José Martínez, the priest credited with the establishment of the Southwest's first coeducational school. His lifelong crusade to educate his people took him to Taos in 1826, then into politics.

The area is known for its colorful, rugged rock formations and other scenic features. Abiquiu Lake *(see Recreation Chart),* 7 miles northwest via US 84, provides opportunities for water sports while controlling downstream flooding and sedimentation. The Carson and Santa Fe national forests *(see place listings p. 148 and 174)* surround the lake.

As anyone who has seen her landscapes would suspect, artist Georgia O'Keeffe spent winters and springs in Abiquiu and summers and autumns at nearby Ghost Ranch. Along US 84 are some of the views O'Keeffe captured in her work. Guided tours of the Georgia O'Keeffe Home and Studio are available by reservation 3 months in advance. Tours, which accommodate 12 people, require advanced payment and depart from the nearby Abiquiu Inn; phone (505) 685-4539. The artist's ashes were scattered at Pedernal, the flat-topped mountain to the south of Ghost Ranch.

GHOST RANCH is 12 mi. n.w. on US 84. Georgia O'Keeffe owned a summer house and painted familiar scenes at this 21,000-acre ranch, now a Presbyterian education center. The facility includes hiking trails, a meditation labyrinth and two museums. Horseback rides are offered June through August; phone for reservations. Guided tours of the landscapes that O'Keeffe explored and painted are given by appointment. Food is available, and picnicking is permitted. Daily 8-5. Grounds and hiking trails free. Tour $20. Phone (505) 685-4333 or (877) 804-4678.

Florence Hawley Ellis Museum of Anthropology is 12 mi. n.w. on US 84 at the Ghost Ranch Education and Retreat Center. Exhibits depict 12,000 years of civilization within the Chama-Rio Grande region. Contemporary Southwestern art also is displayed. Allow 30 minutes minimum. Tues.-Sat. 9-noon and 1-5 (also Sun.-Mon. 1-5, Memorial Day weekend-Labor Day). Admission $2; over 64 and under 14, $1. MC, VI. Phone (505) 685-4333 or (877) 804-4678.

Ruth Hall Museum of Paleontology is 12 mi. n.w. on US 84 at the Ghost Ranch Education and Retreat Center. The museum documents Ghost Ranch's rich fossil record, including the 1947 discovery of a small, predatory dinosaur named *Coelophysis.* Allow 30 minutes minimum. Tues.-Sat. 9-noon and 1-5 (also Sun.-Mon. 1-5, Memorial Day weekend-Labor Day). Admission $2; over 64 and under 14, $1. MC, VI. Phone (505) 685-4333 or (877) 804-4678.

ACOMA PUEBLO (C-2) elev. 6, 550'

One of the oldest continuously inhabited settlements in the country—evidence dates it from A.D. 1150—Acoma was well established when Francisco Vasquez de Coronado explored New Mexico in 1540. Inhabitants of Sky City, as the pueblo was known, worked fields on the plains 367 feet below their village and climbed back atop the mesa each night. Acoma afforded protection through decades of warfare, but the numerical superiority of the Spaniards proved too much. A final battle in 1599 vanquished the community.

Today only a few dozen Acomans live year-round on the mesa top; others live in nearby villages but return to Sky City for cultural observances. Visitors to the mesa must register at the Sky City Cultural Center and be accompanied by a guide.

About 3 miles northeast is Enchanted Mesa, which looms 430 feet above the surrounding plain. According to legend, this was an ancestral settlement, but access to it was wiped out by a violent storm, leaving several Acoma women and children to starve on the mesa top.

ACOMA PUEBLO (SKY CITY) is off I-40 exit 102, then 15 mi. s. on R.R. 30/32 to the Sky City Mesa. Occupied by the Acomans since the second century, this 367-foot-high mesa is topped by one of the largest adobe structures in North America, the 1629 Spanish mission San Esteban del Rey. Building materials, including great log beams hand cut on Mount Taylor some 30 miles north, were carried to the summit by Acoman laborers. Guided walking tours feature the pueblo, the plaza and the mission church with its ecclesiastic art, tapestries and hand-carved woodwork.

Visitors to the mesa must arrange for a guide at the [SAVE] Sky City Cultural Center, which features museum exhibits and displays of Acoma pottery. Videotaping is not allowed on the mesa; a permit for still photography may be acquired at the cultural center. Food is available. Allow 1 hour minimum. Daily 8-6, mid-May to mid-Oct.; 8-5, rest of year. Closed July 10-13, the first or second weekend in Oct. and other days without notice. Last tour departs 1 hour before closing. Guided tours $10; over 60, $9; ages 6-17, $7. Museum $4; over 60, $3; ages 6-17, $2. Still-camera photography fee $10. AX, DS, MC, VI. Phone (505) 469-1052 or (800) 747-0181.

ALAMOGORDO (E-4)
pop. 35,582, elev. 4,335'

A ready water supply from the looming Sacramento Mountains prompted the town's founding as a railroad division point in 1898. Alamogordo—Spanish for "fat cottonwood"—grew quickly as ranching, lumber production, farming and tourism were added to its assets. Nevertheless, modern development has been due primarily to the Holloman Air Force Base. Diversified industry, much of it related to space, also contributes to the economy.

The Air Force Missile Development Center conducts rocket and allied research at the base. The work done at the National Solar Observatory *(see attraction listing p. 177)* is an integral part of Holloman and the nearby White Sands Missile Range *(see place listing p. 180)*.

Tularosa Basin Historical Society Museum, 1301 N. White Sands Blvd., focuses on local history; phone (505) 434-4438. Leading eastward to Cloudcroft *(see place listing p. 152)*, US 82 passes through the state's only highway tunnel.

Alamogordo Chamber of Commerce and Aubrey Dunn Sr. Visitor Center: 1301 N. White Sands Blvd., Alamogordo, NM 88310; phone (505) 437-6120 or (800) 826-0294.

ALAMEDA PARK AND ZOO is at 1321 N. White Sands Blvd., jct. US 54 and 10th St. The 7-acre zoo is home to 90 species of American and exotic wildlife including herd animals, cougars, bears, wolves and birds. Shaded lawns, recreation facilities and a playground are offered. Picnicking is permitted. Daily 9-5; closed Jan. 1 and Dec. 25. Admission $2.20; over 60 and ages 3-11, $1.10. Phone (505) 439-4290.

NEW MEXICO MUSEUM OF SPACE HISTORY is 2 mi. e. of US 54/70. This large complex includes Stapp Air and Space Park, Astronaut Memorial Garden, International Space Hall of Fame and Shuttle Camp. Exhibits honor pioneers from many nations and include international space program items. A special display chronicles the X Prize competition that awarded $10 million for the first civilian spaceflight.

At the Clyde W. Tombaugh IMAX Dome Theater and Planetarium, films are projected on a 40-foot wraparound dome screen. An outdoor display features launch vehicles and spacecraft.

Allow 2 hours minimum. Daily 9-5; closed Dec. 25. IMAX films are shown daily on the hour 11-5 (also Fri.-Sat. at 6 p.m.), Memorial Day-Labor Day; schedule varies rest of year. Museum $2.50; over 59 and military with ID $2.25; ages 4-12, $2. IMAX Admission $6; over 59, military with ID and ages 13-17, $5.50; ages 4-12, $4.50. Phone (505) 437-2840 or (877) 333-6589.

OLIVER LEE MEMORIAL STATE PARK is 12 mi. s. on US 54. A green oasis flourishes here around the springs of Dog Canyon, a deep ravine on the west-facing flank of the Sacramento Mountains. The park features historical exhibits and the restored 19th-century house of rancher Oliver Milton Lee.

Park daily 24 hours. Visitor center daily 9-4. One-hour ranch house tours are given Sat.-Sun. at 3. Admission $5 per private vehicle. Phone (505) 437-8284. *See Recreation Chart and the AAA Southwestern CampBook.*

TOY TRAIN DEPOT is 1 mi. n. on US 70/54 to 1991 N. White Sands Blvd. Hundreds of models and toy train displays are housed in an old depot. Built in 1898, a narrow-gauge train ride runs outdoors through neighboring Alameda Park. Allow 30 minutes minimum. Wed.-Sun. noon-5. Last train departs 30 minutes before closing. Admission $3. Train $4; under 12, $3. AX, DS, MC, VI. Phone (505) 437-2855 or (888) 207-3564.

ALBUQUERQUE (C-3)
pop. 448,607, elev. 4,955'
See map page 140.

Commanding the wide valley between the Sandia Mountains and the sweeping plateau country paralleling the Rio Grande, metropolitan Albuquerque is New Mexico's big city. And at more than 5,000 feet, Albuquerque's elevation makes it one of the highest metropolitan areas in the United States.

The combination of elevation and low rainfall distinguishes Albuquerque's high desert climate, but

despite relatively little rainfall the area is hardly desolate. Wildlife abounds among the wetlands and cottonwoods along the Rio Grande, while in the nearby mountains increased levels of precipitation support forests of ponderosa pine, not to mention a winter ski area on Sandia Peak.

Albuquerque was founded in 1706 by 18 families from Bernalillo in search of greener pastures. Soon their flocks and crops were flourishing. The colonists laid out their town in traditional Spanish fashion, incorporating a central plaza bordered by a church, government buildings and homes. Due to the local climate and scarcity of wood, sun-baked adobe bricks made from mud and straw were the construction materials of choice.

In the mid-19th century the U.S. government established a series of forts to protect American settlers heading west, and Albuquerque became a major supply depot for these. The coming of the railroad in 1880 created a modern, more vigorous Albuquerque 2 miles east of the historic core. Although the old city languished, it did not lose its character, and the new city soon engulfed and later annexed Old Town *(see attraction listing p. 142)*.

Today Old Town is a quaint area of flat-roofed, adobe-style buildings with rounded edges and projected wooden roof beams called vigas. Brick paths and patios are tucked in among a variety of shops, galleries and restaurants. Visitors cannot help but notice the colorful clumps of dried chili peppers suspended in windows and beneath eaves. Called *ristras,* these hand-strung arrangements are hung for good luck and to welcome guests. Of course, chili peppers are not just for decoration. A favorite ingredient in many Southwestern dishes, chile, as the term appears on menus here, come in two colors—red and green—and are usually served as part of flavorful sauces for a range of dishes.

Within walking distance of Old Town are several museums, including the Albuquerque Museum of Art & History and the New Mexico Museum of Natural History & Science *(see attraction listings p. 141 and 142)*. An information center in Plaza Don Luis provides brochures and maps.

Albuquerque's Central Avenue runs through Old Town, but it is probably better known to out-of-towners as Historic Route 66. Called the "Mother Road" and the "Main Street of America," Route 66 once connected Chicago with Los Angeles and transported thousands of desperate people westward during the Great Depression.

Designated in 1926, this icon of American auto travel actually intersects itself in downtown Albuquerque thanks to a 1937 realignment that replaced a north-south segment through town with an east-west routing. During its golden era, a wave of whimsically designed motels, diners and service stations rose up along the road. Some still remain, such as a gas station on the pre-1937 segment at 2455 Isleta Blvd. sporting a mushroom-shaped canopy.

Another Route 66 landmark is the KiMo Theater at 423 Central Ave. N.W., an ornate 1927 building designed in the Pueblo Deco style as a venue for vaudeville acts. Wall sconces made to look like steer skulls along with Southwestern-themed murals and ornate plaster ceilings characterize its quirky interior.

Farther east on Route 66, just past the University of New Mexico campus *(see attraction listing p. 143)*, is Nob Hill, a commercial area noted for its eclectic cafés, diners and shops. Gateway arches outlined in neon lights span the roadway marking the eastern and western boundaries of the district, which boasts such architectural styles as Pueblo Revival, Streamline Moderne and Art Deco.

Making the leap from 20th-century pop culture to a culture hundreds of years older is no more difficult than a drive to one of New Mexico's 19 Indian pueblos, three of which are in the Albuquerque vicinity. The Sandia Pueblo is 15 miles north via I-25; its Bien Mur Indian Arts and Crafts Market, 1 mile east of I-25 exit 234, is one of the largest in the Southwest. Isleta Pueblo *(see place listing p. 158)* is 13 miles south and is widely known for its pottery and fresh bread. Santa Ana Pueblo, 16 miles north near Rio Rancho, dates to the 1500s. Be aware that some pueblos have strict rules regarding photography, sketching and videotaping. Contact the Indian Pueblo Cultural Center *(see attraction listing p. 141)* for further information about pueblo etiquette and for listings of events; phone (505) 843-7270.

Northwest of Albuquerque is Petroglyph National Monument, where more than 17,000 ancient Indian rock carvings—some as much as 3,000 years old—have been cut into the black volcanic rocks. The visitor center is west on I-40 to Unser Boulevard, then 3 miles north to Western Trail.

Frequently seen soaring above the monument's petroglyphs are the far more delicate shapes of hot-air balloons. Local wind and weather conditions create what is known as the "Albuquerque Box," an atmospheric effect enabling pilots to change direction by varying their altitude, making precision flying possible.

For this reason, hot-air balloonists come from all over the world to fly here, especially during the 9-day Albuquerque International Balloon Fiesta, held during the first week of October. Probably the most dramatic fiesta events are the mass ascensions during which some 700 colorful craft take to the sky all at once.

Another way to rise above Albuquerque and its environs is by way of a thrilling ride aboard the Sandia Peak Aerial Tramway *(see attraction listing p. 143)*. The 2.7-mile-long ride lifts passengers a total of 3,819 feet into the New Mexico sky, affording a panorama of more than 11,000 square miles of desert landscape.

A closer look at the spectacular high countryside is possible via a 62-mile scenic loop that follows I-40 east to Tijeras, SR 14 north to San Antonito, SR 536 west to Bernalillo and returns to Albuquerque via I-25. The section between San Antonito and Bernalillo crosses the crest of the Sandias, but because the most rugged 8 miles are unpaved, large trucks, trailers and RVs are prohibited. Drivers should heed posted signs.

The Turquoise Trail runs along the east side of the Sandias between Cedar Crest and La Cienega near Santa Fe on SRs 14 and 536; highlights include mountain scenery, a few ghost towns, thick pine and aspen forests and Sandia Crest (*see Cibola National Forest p. 151*). Madrid is one of several ghost towns that have been revitalized into quaint art communities with galleries and shops (*see place listing p. 161*).

Albuquerque Convention and Visitors Bureau: 20 First Plaza N.W., Suite 601, P.O. Box 26866, Albuquerque, NM 87125; phone (505) 842-9918 or (800) 733-9918.

Self-guiding tours: Brochures of driving tours through Albuquerque and nearby communities are available from the convention and visitors bureau.

Shopping areas: Winrock Shopping Center, 51 Winrock Center N.E., is home to Dillard's and other specialty merchants. Coronado Center, 6600 Menaul St. N.E., counts Foley's, JCPenney, Macy's, Mervyn's and Sears among its 160 stores. Cottonwood Mall, 10000 Coors Blvd. N.W., features Dillard's, Foley's, JCPenney and Mervyn's. The historic Nob Hill District, bounded by Washington Avenue and Girard Boulevard, offers some 130 shops, galleries and restaurants. Old Town Plaza,

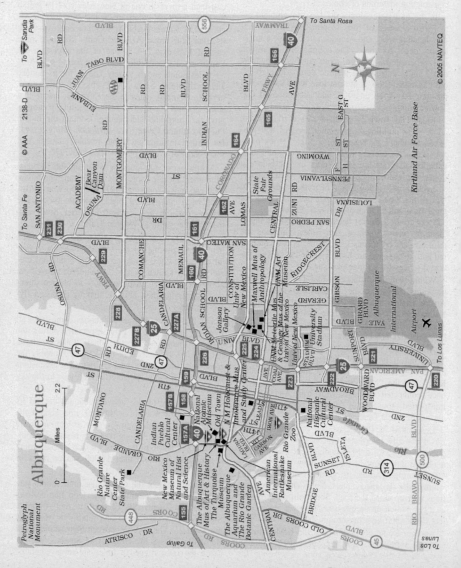

downtown off Central Avenue, offers a wide array of specialty stores and eateries.

THE ALBUQUERQUE AQUARIUM AND THE RIO GRANDE BOTANIC GARDEN are at 2601 N.W. Central Ave. Marine habitats of the Gulf of Mexico and other ecosystems are presented at the aquarium. Tanks contain stingrays, jellyfish, eels, sharks and other aquatic life. The botanic garden features Mediterranean and desert conservatories, a children's fantasy garden, water and plant exhibits, demonstration gardens, the PNM Butterfly Pavilion, a butterfly-hummingbird garden and the Rio Grande Heritage Farm.

Food is available. Allow 1 hour, 30 minutes minimum. Daily 9-5 (also Sat.-Sun. 5-6, June-Aug.); closed Jan. 1, Thanksgiving and Dec. 25. Last admission 30 minutes before closing. Admission $7; over 64 and ages 3-12, $3. Combination ticket with the Rio Grande Zoo $10; over 64 and ages 3-12, $5. MC, VI. Phone (505) 764-6200.

THE ALBUQUERQUE MUSEUM OF ART & HISTORY is at 2000 Mountain Rd. N.W. The museum features art of the Southwest and explores 400 years of Albuquerque history through permanent displays, exhibitions and guided walking tours of Old Town. The collection includes works from major New Mexican artists from the early 20th century to the present. Children's exhibits and a sculpture garden also are featured.

Guided tours are available. Allow 2 hours minimum. Tues.-Sun. 9-5. Thirty-minute gallery tours depart Tues.-Sun. at 2. Sculpture garden tours depart Tues.-Sat. at 10, Apr.-Oct. Old Town walking tours depart Tues.-Sun. at 11, mid-May to mid-Dec. Closed Jan. 1, Thanksgiving and Dec. 25. Admission $4; over 64, $2; ages 4-12, $1; free to all first Wed. of the month. MC, VI. Phone (505) 243-7255.

[SAVE] **AMERICAN INTERNATIONAL RATTLE-SNAKE MUSEUM** is at 202 San Felipe St. N.W. More than 30 species of rattlesnakes are displayed at the museum, which offers films and information about snakes and other reptiles. Artwork featuring snakes, herpetological fossils and skeletons, and other items also are featured. Allow 30 minutes minimum. Mon.-Sat. 10-6, Sun. 1-5. Admission $3.50; over 59, $3; ages 3-12, $2.50. AX, DS, MC, VI. Phone (505) 242-6569.

INDIAN PUEBLO CULTURAL CENTER is at 2401 12th St. N.W. The center depicts the history, art and culture of New Mexico's 19 American Indian pueblos. The 10,000-square-foot main museum features an extensive collection of artifacts and an in-depth film overview of the pueblos. A children's museum, open by appointment, offers hands-on learning about the Pueblo people. Ceremonial dances and craft demonstrations take place weekends. An exhibit gallery highlights the work of contemporary artists and craftsmen.

Food is available. Allow 30 minutes minimum. Museum open daily 9-5. Gallery daily 9-4:30. Closed Jan. 1, Memorial Day, July 4, Labor Day, Thanksgiving and Dec. 25. Museum $4; over 62 and students with ID, $3; ages 5-18, $1. Combination ticket for museum and gallery $6; over 62 and students with ID, $5; ages 5-18, $3. AX, DC, DS, MC, VI. Phone (505) 843-7270. *See color ad p. 141.*

NATIONAL ATOMIC MUSEUM is at 1905 Mountain Rd. N.W. The nation's official museum for the history and science of the Nuclear Age features replicas of the world's first two atomic weapons, Little Boy and Fat Man. Exhibits include The Manhattan Project; WW II and The Cold War; Secret No More—A Look Into Russia's Nuclear Weapon Museums; Waging Peace—The History of Arms Control; Seeing Is Healing—Nuclear Medicine; and Power Up—Nuclear Energy. History films are shown daily.

Allow 30 minutes minimum. Daily 9-5; closed Jan. 1, Easter, Thanksgiving and Dec. 25. Admission $5; over 60, military with ID and ages 7-18, $4. DS, MC, VI. Phone (505) 245-2137.

NATIONAL HISPANIC CULTURAL CENTER is at 1701 4th St. S.W. Mayan temples, Spanish haciendas and adobe pueblos influenced the architecture of this 51-acre site, which features an art museum, a theater complex, a library, a genealogy center and a Spanish language institute. The Roy E. Disney Center for Performing Arts offers a world-class stage for theatre, music, dance and media arts. Cultural programs and activities are offered throughout the year, many accompanied by children's events.

Food is available. Allow 30 minutes minimum. Museum open Tues.-Sun. 10-5. Library open Tues.-Sat. 10-5. Closed Jan. 1, Easter, Thanksgiving and Dec. 25. Museum admission $3; over 60, $2; under 16 free. MC, VI. Phone (505) 246-2261.

NEW MEXICO HOLOCAUST & INTOLERANCE MUSEUM AND STUDY CENTER is at 415 Central Ave. N.W., just w. of 4th St. Dedicated to combating hatred through education, the museum's documents, photographs and artifacts illustrate how ethnic intolerance engenders global conflict. Exhibits depict the Holocaust, Native American persecution, African-American Slavery, Armenian and Greek genocide, the Bataan Death March and the Nuremburg Trials. A library contains research materials. Guided tours are available. Allow 1 hour minimum. Tues.-Fri. 11-3, Sat. 11-4; closed national and Jewish holidays. Donations. Phone (505) 247-0606.

NEW MEXICO MUSEUM OF NATURAL HISTORY & SCIENCE is .5 mi. s. of I-40 on Rio Grande Blvd., then 2 blks. e. to 1801 Mountain Rd. N.W. The origins and geological history of the Southwest are explored through full-scale dinosaur models, a walk-through volcano, an ice age cave replica, a time machine and a fossil preparation area. A saltwater tide pool, a hands-on

naturalist center and botanical exhibits also are offered. The Lodestar Astronomy Center features planetarium shows and the Virtual Voyages simulation theater. The Lockheed Martin DynaTheater presents giant-screen film adventures to exotic locales.

Allow 1 hour minimum. Daily 9-5; closed Thanksgiving and Dec. 25. DynaTheater films are shown on the hour; other show times vary. Museum $6; over 59, $5; ages 3-12, $3. DynaTheater or planetarium shows $6; over 59, $5; ages 3-12, $3. Virtual Voyages $4; under 36 inches tall or under age 4 are not permitted. Combination tickets are available. DS, MC, VI. Phone (505) 841-2800 for the museum or (505) 841-5950 for the theaters.

OLD TOWN is 1 blk. n. of the 2000 blk. of Central Ave. N.W. (US 66) and .5 mi. s. of the I-40 Rio Grande Blvd. exit. The city's original settlement, founded in 1706, was named for the Duke of Albuquerque. Old Town is a visible record of the area's evolution from small village to big city. Shops and galleries in Old Town Plaza offer artwork, jewelry, food and specialty items. American Indians also sell their handicrafts around the plaza. The 1793 San Felipe de Neri Church, on the plaza's north side, represents an interesting mix of Victorian and basic adobe architecture.

An information booth in Plaza Don Luis provides free maps. Guided 1-hour walking tours of Old Town depart from the Albuquerque Museum of Art & History Tues.-Sun. at 11, mid-May to mid-Dec. Fee $4; over 54, $2; ages 4-12, $1. Phone (505) 243-7255.

RIO GRANDE NATURE CENTER STATE PARK is at 2901 Candelaria Rd. N.W. On the central Rio Grande flyway, the park provides a winter refuge for migrating Canada geese, sandhill cranes, ducks and other waterfowl. Trails along the Rio Grande River, classrooms, a library and visitor center exhibits are offered. Allow 30 minutes minimum. Park daily 8-5. Visitor center daily 10-5. Closed Jan. 1, Thanksgiving and Dec. 25. Admission $3 per private vehicle; exact change required. Phone (505) 344-7240.

RIO GRANDE ZOO is at 903 Tenth St. S.W. The zoo houses more than 1,000 animals representing some 250 species in a variety of naturalistic habitats. Popular residents include chimpanzees, gorillas, elephants, polar bears, giraffes, hippos, mountain lions, jaguars and zebras. Tropical America features toucans, spider monkeys, tamarins, tarantulas and colorful bromeliads. The 6-acre Africa Exhibit is home to warthogs, cheetahs, spotted hyenas and Marabou storks. Seal and sea lion feedings take place daily in a 350,000-gallon tank.

Food is available. Daily 9-5 (also Sat.-Sun. 5-6, June-Aug.); closed Jan. 1, Thanksgiving and Dec. 25. Last admission 30 minutes before closing. Admission $7; over 64 and ages 3-12, $3. Combination ticket with The Albuquerque Aquarium and The Rio Grande Botanic Garden $10; over 64 and ages 3-12,

$5. Under 13 must be with an adult. MC, VI. Phone (505) 764-6200.

SAN AGUSTÍN DE LA ISLETA MISSION—
see Isleta Pueblo p. 158

SANDIA CREST—
see Cibola National Forest p. 151.

SANDIA PEAK AERIAL TRAMWAY is off I-25 exit 234, then 6 mi. e. on Tramway Rd. The 2.7-mile tramway, one of the world's longest, transports visitors above the deep canyons and spectacular terrain of the western Sandia Mountains and the Cibola National Forest. A Forest Service visitor center is in the upper tram terminal. Restaurants operate at the base and summit.

Sandia Peak is a popular recreation spot. Skiers frequent the 10,378-foot peak from mid-December to mid-March. In summer 24 miles of trails are available for mountain biking. Bicycle rentals are available weekends and holidays, Memorial Day weekend through Labor Day, and in October during the Albuquerque International Balloon Fiesta.

Trams depart every 20-30 minutes daily 9-9, Memorial Day-Labor Day and during the balloon fiesta; Wed.-Mon. and holidays 9-8, Tues. 5-8, rest of year. The tram is closed for 10 days each April and October for maintenance.

Round-trip tram fare $15; over 61, $13; ages 5-12, $10. AX, DS, MC, VI. Phone (505) 856-7325 or (505) 856-6419.

SAVE **THE TURQUOISE MUSEUM** is at 2107 Central Ave. N.W. A mine tunnel provides entrance to this museum, which features rare turquoise specimens from around the world. Interactive silversmith and lapidary demonstrations are offered. Mon.-Sat. 10-5; closed Jan. 1, Thanksgiving and Dec. 25. Admission $4; over 59 and under 13, $3; family rate $10. AX, CB, DC, DS, MC, VI. Phone (505) 247-8650.

UNIVERSITY OF NEW MEXICO is 2 mi. e. on Central Ave. (US 66). The university occupies a 640-acre campus and enrolls approximately 27,000 students. College buildings feature Pueblo Revival architecture, and the grounds are designated as a National College Arboretum. Of particular interest are several museums and libraries as well as Popejoy Hall, home to ballet, musicals, lectures and the New Mexico Symphony Orchestra. Guided tours are available. Phone (505) 277-1989, or (505) 277-4569 for ticket information.

Geology Museum of the University of New Mexico is at 200 Yale Blvd. (Northrop Hall) in the Earth and Planetary Sciences Building. Various types of minerals, the geology of the earth and New Mexico fossils are depicted in more than 20 exhibits. Guided tours are offered by appointment. Allow 30 minutes minimum. Mon.-Fri. 8-noon and 1-4:30; closed holidays. Donations. Phone (505) 277-4204.

Jonson Gallery is at 1909 Las Lomas N.E. on the University of New Mexico campus. Modernist painter Raymond Jonson opened the gallery in 1950 for use as a residence, archive and repository for contemporary art. His work usually is displayed June through August; other artists are featured during the rest of the year. Allow 30 minutes minimum. Tues.-Fri. 9-4 (also Tues. 5-8 p.m.); closed holidays. Free. Phone (505) 277-4967.

Maxwell Museum of Anthropology is on Redondo Dr. just e. of University Blvd. on the University of New Mexico campus. The museum emphasizes native cultures of the American Southwest—including such groups as the Ancestral Puebloan—in its collections about early man. Changing exhibits also are presented. Tues.-Fri. 9-4, Sat. 10-4; closed holidays. Donations. Phone (505) 277-4405.

UNM Art Museum is at Cornell St. and Redondo Dr. N.E. on the University of New Mexico campus. Changing exhibits present paintings, prints and photography from the 19th century through contemporary periods as well as Southwestern artwork and artifacts. Tues.-Fri. 9-4, Sun. 1-4 (also Tues. 5-8 and during most events at Popejoy Hall); closed holidays. Free. Phone (505) 277-4001.

UNM Meteorite Museum is part of the Institute of Meteoritics on the first floor of the Earth and Planetary Sciences Building at 200 Yale Blvd. (Northrop Hall) on the University of New Mexico campus. Meteorites discovered throughout the world are displayed. The institute also is concerned with the teaching and research of space and planetary sciences. A brochure for self-guiding tours, available at the entrance, explains all specimens. Allow 30 minutes minimum. Mon.-Fri. 9-noon and 1-4; closed holidays. Donations. Phone (505) 277-1644.

RECREATIONAL ACTIVITIES

Hot Air Ballooning

- **Rainbow Ryders, Inc.** departs from various locations for flights over the Rio Grande Valley. Write to 11520 San Bernardino N.E., Albuquerque, NM 87106. Daily at dawn. Phone (505) 823-1111 or (800) 725-2477. *See color ad p. 138.*

White-water Rafting

- **Passageways** departs El Vado Ranch at the base of El Vado Dam and Lower Chama Canyon. Write to 916 Vassar N.E., Albuquerque, NM 87106. Daily May-Aug. Phone (505) 265-4542.

CASINOS

- **Isleta Casino and Resort** is at 11000 Broadway S.E. Mon.-Thurs. 8 a.m.-3 a.m., Fri.-Sun. 24 hours. Phone (505) 724-3800 or (800) 460-5686.
- **Sandia Casino** is at 30 Rainbow Rd. N.E. Mon.-Thurs. 8 a.m.-4 a.m., Fri.-Sun. 24 hours. Phone (505) 796-7500 or (800) 526-9366.

WINERIES

- **Anderson Valley Vineyards** is at 4920 Rio Grande Blvd. N.W. Tours are offered Wed.-Sun. noon-5; closed major holidays. Phone (505) 344-7266.

ANGEL FIRE (B-4) pop. 1,048, elev. 8,415'

In the Moreno Valley of the Sangre de Cristo Mountains, Angel Fire is a year-round resort area that offers boating, fishing, hunting, golfing, hiking, mountain bicycling and horseback riding in summer; and snowmobiling, snowboarding and skiing in winter.

Angel Fire Chamber of Commerce: 3407 SR 434, Centro Plaza, P.O. Box 547, Angel Fire, NM 87710; phone (505) 377-6661 or (800) 446-8117.

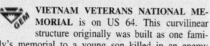 **VIETNAM VETERANS NATIONAL MEMORIAL** is on US 64. This curvilinear structure originally was built as one family's memorial to a young son killed in an enemy ambush in Vietnam. President Ronald Reagan proclaimed it a national memorial in November 1987. The chapel is dedicated to Vietnam War casualties. Its hilltop vantage affords views of the Sangre de Cristo Mountains and the broad Moreno Valley. Chapel daily 24 hours. Visitor center daily 9-5; closed Jan. 1, Thanksgiving and Dec. 25. Free. Phone (505) 377-6900.

APACHE-SITGREAVES NATIONAL FOREST— *see Arizona p. 40.*

ARTESIA (E-5) pop. 10,692, elev. 3,379'

Artesia was named for its huge underground water supply, which is pumped to the surface via numerous artesian wells. The water irrigates thousands of acres of area farmland.

Another underground resource—oil—was discovered in 1923. This, coupled with reserves of natural gas, has bolstered Artesia's economy and made it one of New Mexico's most productive oil centers. The city also claims what was once the first underground school in the country, built to shelter about 500 students and 2,000 other citizens in the event of a nuclear attack.

Greater Artesia Chamber of Commerce: 107 N. 1st St., P.O. Box 99, Artesia, NM 88211-0099; phone (505) 746-2744.

ARTESIA HISTORICAL MUSEUM AND ART CENTER is at 505 W. Richardson Ave. Two preserved houses built at the beginning of the 20th century contain historical and cultural displays. The museum, devoted to local heritage, displays equipment used in industrial development as well as such Western paraphernalia as saddles, barbed wire and clothing. The art center next to the museum offers traveling exhibits and work by area artists. Allow 30 minutes minimum. Tues.-Fri, 9-noon and 1-5, Sat. 1-5; closed holidays. Free. Phone (505) 748-2390.

AZTEC (A-2) pop. 6,378, elev. 5,623'

Pioneers founded the city in 1890 along the Animas River across from ancient Pueblo ruins.

Aztec Chamber of Commerce and Visitors Center: 110 N. Ash St., Aztec, NM 87410; phone (505) 334-9551 or (888) 838-9551. *See color ad.*

Self-guiding tours: Information on walking tours of the city's historic sites is available from the chamber of commerce.

AZTEC MUSEUM & PIONEER VILLAGE is at 125 N. Main St. The historical museum of northwest New Mexico consists of 14 original and replicated structures dating from the 1880s forward. The outdoor oil and gas exhibit depicts the history of the industry. Farm and ranch equipment used by early settlers also is displayed. Mon.-Sat. 9-5, day after Memorial Day-Labor Day; Mon.-Sat. 10-4, rest of year. Closed Jan. 1, Memorial Day, July 4, Labor Day, Veterans Day, Thanksgiving and Dec. 25. Admission $3; ages 11-17, $1. Phone (505) 334-9829.

AZTEC RUINS NATIONAL MONUMENT (A-2)

In the northwest corner of New Mexico, just north of Aztec on US 516 to Ruins Road, is one of the largest and best preserved Ancestral Pueblo ruins in the Southwest. The misnomer Aztec was applied by early settlers who incorrectly inferred the builders' identity. The largest of these sandstone pueblos, the West Ruin, was built about 1110; it contained nearly 450 rooms, some of which remain intact. Several smaller structures adjoin the main ruin.

A large ceremonial building, the Great Kiva, is the only reconstruction of its kind in North America. The visitor center features artifacts found during excavations. Daily 8-6, Memorial Day-Labor Day; 8-5, rest of year. Closed Jan. 1, Thanksgiving and Dec. 25. Admission (valid for 7 days) $4, under 17 free. AX, DS, MC, VI. Phone (505) 334-6174, ext. 30.

GEM BANDELIER NATIONAL MONUMENT (B-2)

Just 50 miles northwest of Santa Fe via US 285 to Pojoaque, then west on SR 502 and south on SR 4, this 50-square-mile monument is on the Pajarito Plateau in the rugged canyon and mesa country of northern New Mexico. Remnants of an Ancestral Puebloan community established 7 or 8 centuries ago include pueblo and cliff dwellings.

The most accessible sites consist of cave rooms hewn out of the soft tuff rock, houses built on the talus slopes and a circular community village. Bandelier also contains 23,267 acres of designated wilderness, including 70 miles of hiking trails. Free permits, required for overnight back-country travel, can be obtained at the visitor center. Pets or bicycles are not permitted on any trails in the monument.

In summer a variety of ranger-led activities are offered including guided walks, interpretive programs and craft demonstrations. The Nightwalk tour of archeological sites is conducted largely in silence so as to appreciate the nighttime solitude.

An introductory slide program and a small museum in the visitor center provide orientation to the area. A 1-hour self-guiding walking tour of the principal sites starts at the visitor center. Monument open daily dawn-dusk. Visitor center open daily 9-5:30, during DST (Memorial Day to Labor Day 8-6); 8-4:30, rest of year. Closed Jan. 1 and Dec. 25. Admission $10 per private vehicle, $5 per person arriving by other means. Visitor center free. Nightwalk tours $6. MC, VI. Phone (505) 672-3861, ext. 517 or (505) 672-0343. *See the AAA Southwestern CampBook.*

BELÉN (C-3) pop. 6,901, elev. 4,808′

Belén, which in Spanish means "Bethlehem," was founded by Capt. Don Diego Torres and Antonio Salazar in 1740. By the late 19th century, the farming community was a major hub on the Atchison, Topeka, and Santa Fe Railroad.

HARVEY HOUSE MUSEUM is at 104 N. First St. The building served as a restaurant for Santa Fe Railroad passengers 1910-39. Exhibits depict railroad and town history. A model train display and changing exhibits are offered. Allow 1 hour; 30 minutes minimum. Tues.-Sat. 12:30-3:30; closed holidays. Donations. Phone (505) 861-0581.

BERNALILLO (B-3) pop. 6,611, elev. 5,052′

Still essentially a Spanish and American Indian farming community and livestock shipping point, Bernalillo (bern-a-LEE-oh) nevertheless is growing as the Albuquerque metropolitan area expands northward along the Rio Grande. The first settlers—descendants of Bernal Díaz del Castillo, chronicler of Hernando Cortés' conquest of Mexico—arrived in 1698.

Remnants of times past remain. Northwest of Bernalillo is the pueblo of Santa Ana and the Spanish-American village of San Ysidro. At Santa Ana is one of the oldest missions in the United States. Open to visitors only a few days per year, it is believed to have been built by Spanish missionary Fray Juan de Rosas, who accompanied Juan de Oñate on his expedition to New Mexico in 1598.

Town of Bernalillo: 243 Camino del Pueblo, P.O. Box 1776, Bernalillo, NM 87004; phone (505) 867-1185 or (800) 252-0191.

CORONADO STATE MONUMENT is 2 mi. n.w. on SR 550 (old SR 44) to 485 Kuaua Rd. The 98-acre site includes ruins of the Tiwa pueblo of Kuaua. Lured by the Rio Grande River's fertile land, an ancient tribe first settled Kuaua around 1300. The area is named for Francisco Vasquez de Coronado, whose army camped here in 1540 while searching for the fabled Cities of Gold. A kiva excavated in the 1930s features many layers of pre-Columbian art, some of which is displayed in the visitor center.

Wed.-Mon. 8:30-5; closed major holidays. Admission $3, under 17 free. Combination ticket with Jémez State Monument *(see Jémez Springs p. 158)* $5. MC, VI. Phone (505) 867-5351.

BLOOMFIELD (A-2) pop. 6,417, elev. 5,453′

Bloomfield was settled about 1876 and quickly became a classic Wild West town, complete with a gang of rustlers headed by its own ex-sheriff. The gang operated openly, marketing stolen beef through its own butcher shop. After the gang's decline, outlawry found haven at Blancett's Saloon, which attracted gunmen from throughout the San Juan Basin.

That violent era passed unmourned. By the early 20th century residents were more interested in stimulating agriculture through irrigation, an endeavor that persists. Navajo Reservoir, 25 miles northeast via US 64 and SR 511, is the source of much of the area's irrigation water. Navajo Lake State Park, surrounding the reservoir in Navajo Dam, offers recreational opportunities *(see Recreation Chart and the AAA Southwestern CampBook).*

Bloomfield Chamber of Commerce: 224 W. Broadway Ave., Bloomfield, NM 87413; phone (505) 632-0880 or (800) 461-1245.

SALMON RUIN is 2 mi. w. on US 64. The 2-acre site was built in the late 11th century by people from the Chaco culture *(see Chaco Culture National Historical Park p. 149).* The C-shaped masonry complex measures 450 feet along the back wall and 150 feet along the arms. Some of the more than 1 million artifacts recovered are displayed in San Juan County Archaeological Research Center and Library, next to the ruin.

Picnicking is permitted. Mon.-Fri. 8-5, Sat.-Sun. 9-5, May-Oct.; Mon.-Fri. 8-5, Sat. 9-5, Sun. noon-5, rest of year. Closed Jan. 1, Easter, Thanksgiving and Dec. 25. Admission (includes Heritage Park) $3; over 64, $2; ages 6-16, $1. DS, MC, VI. Phone (505) 632-2013.

Heritage Park is 2 mi. w. on US 64 at 6131 US 64 at Salmon Ruin. Offering a glimpse into the lifestyles and cultures of the San Juan Valley, the park features Navajo log homes, Apache teepees and a Basketmaker pithouse—a semi-underground house that conserved heat in winter and remained cool in summer. Visitors can examine ancient figures etched into stone and view the unusual construction of the Salmon homestead, built about 1900. Phone (505) 632-2013.

CAPITAN (D-4) pop. 1,443, elev. 6,351'

Capitan began to flourish in 1897 when the El Paso and Northeastern Railway built a line to nearby coal reserves. After the mines were depleted and the railroad abandoned its branch, Capitan became a business center for farmers, ranchers and visitors to the recreation lands of Lincoln National Forest *(see place listing p. 160)*.

Capitan Chamber of Commerce: 433 Smokey Bear Blvd., P.O. Box 441, Capitan, NM 88316; phone (505) 354-2273.

SMOKEY BEAR HISTORICAL PARK is on US 380. Exhibits trace the history of Smokey Bear and the government's efforts to combat forest fires; a 10-minute film is shown several times per hour. Having survived a devastating fire in 1950, Smokey was found clinging to a burned tree in Lincoln National Forest and became the national symbol for wildfire prevention. He died in 1976 and is buried in the park. Picnicking is permitted. Daily 9-5; closed Jan. 1, Thanksgiving and Dec. 25. Admission $2; ages 7-12, $1. Phone (505) 354-2748.

CAPULIN VOLCANO NATIONAL MONUMENT (A-5)

Three miles north of US 64/87 and Capulin on SR 325, Capulin Volcano National Monument contains one of the best examples of a volcanic cinder cone in the nation. About 60,000 years ago ash, cinders and lava erupted and formed a classic cinder cone that stands more than 1,000 feet above the surrounding prairie. Today, a 2-mile road winds up the volcano, and trails lead into the crater and around the rim. The view from the summit includes the Rocky Mountains, volcanic features of the Raton-Clayton Volcanic Field, and the distant horizons of Colorado, Oklahoma and Texas.

The visitor center offers information and a 10-minute videotape program. Pets are not allowed on trails. Road to the crater rim, park and visitor center open daily 7:30-6:30, Memorial Day weekend-Labor Day; 8-4, rest of year. Closed Jan. 1, Thanksgiving and Dec. 25. Admission $5 per private vehicle, $3 per person arriving by other means. DS, MC, VI. Phone (505) 278-2201.

CARLSBAD (E-5) pop. 25,625, elev. 3,111'

The fields of cotton, alfalfa and vegetables that surround Carlsbad are made possible by the U.S. Bureau of Reclamation's system of dams and canals, which irrigates 25,000 acres. The city also benefits from the rich neighboring oil and gas fields and potash mines as well as its proximity to Carlsbad Caverns National Park *(see place listing p. 146)*. Lake Carlsbad *(see Recreation Chart)* offers fishing, boating and water sports.

Carlsbad Convention and Visitors Bureau: 302 S. Canal St., Carlsbad, NM 88220; phone (505) 887-6516 or (800) 221-1224.

CARLSBAD MUSEUM AND ART CENTER is 1 blk. w. of Canal St. (US 285) at 418 W. Fox St. in Halagueno Park. Established in 1931, this municipal museum houses local and regional history displays, archeological specimens, contemporary and Southwestern art, Peruvian and Pueblo pottery, and pioneer ranching artifacts. The McAdoo Room features paintings by the founders of the Taos Society of Artists. Changing exhibits spotlight local artists. Allow 1 hour minimum. Mon.-Sat. 10-5; closed holidays. Free. Phone (505) 887-0276.

LIVING DESERT ZOO AND GARDENS STATE PARK stands atop the Ocotillo Hills off US 285. Dedicated to the interpretation of the Chihuahuan Desert, this living museum displays some 40 native animal species and hundreds of succulents from around the world in indoor and outdoor settings. Endangered Mexican gray wolves are featured as part of a species conservation exhibit. Daily 8-8, Memorial Day weekend-Labor Day; 9-5, rest of year. Closed Dec. 25. Last admission 90 minutes before closing. Admission $5; ages 7-12, $3. MC, VI. Phone (505) 887-5516.

CARLSBAD CAVERNS NATIONAL PARK (E-4)

Elevations in the park range from 3,596 ft. in the southeastern corner to 6,368 ft. in the southwestern region. Refer to AAA maps for additional elevation information.

Carlsbad Caverns National Park is 20 miles southwest of Carlsbad off US 62/180. The park covers 46,776 acres in the rugged foothills of the Guadalupe Mountains, with miles of tunnels cutting through a Permian-age fossil reef. Among more than 100 known caves is Lechuguilla, thought to be the nation's deepest limestone cavern. The park's showpiece is Carlsbad Cavern, a series of enormous rooms that make up one of the world's largest caves.

Unlike most limestone caves that form when surface water flows through cracks in the rock, these passageways in the Guadalupe Mountains are the rare product of sulfuric acid. Oil deposits mixed with the water table to create an aggressive chemical that dissolved holes in the subterranean limestone. As the mountains rose over a period of 20 million years, the caves dried out, revealing the wonders of Carlsbad.

A steep, paved trail leads into the cavern's natural entrance, which measures 90 feet wide and 40 feet high. The cavern has more than 30 miles of surveyed subterranean corridors and great chambers. Formations range from small, delicate growths resembling plants to massive stalagmites, stalactites and columns. Many are tinted by iron and other minerals present in the limestone. Highlights include Bat Cave, Devil's Spring, Iceberg Rock, Green Lake Overlook and the Boneyard, a maze of limestone rock reminiscent of Swiss cheese.

The 8-acre Big Room, one of the most impressive chambers, has a 255-foot ceiling. Its clear pools contain limestone masses resembling lily pads. Other formations evoke an atmosphere of snow-banked forests, adding to the tranquil beauty of the cavern.

Every evening from mid-May to mid-October, hundreds of thousands of bats emerge from Carlsbad's uppermost chamber at dusk to feed on flying insects. Park rangers give a pre-flight talk in an amphitheater at the mouth of the cave. The flight outward lasts a half-hour to 2 hours; the bats return near dawn. During the day, bats hang head down from the walls and ceilings of a portion of the cavern not open to visitors.

General Information and Activities

The park is open all year, except Dec. 25. The visitor center is open daily 8-7 (cave tours are offered 8:30-5), Memorial Day weekend to mid-Aug.; 8-5, (cave tours are offered 8:30-3:30) rest of year. Visitors may explore Carlsbad Cavern on two self-guiding routes, the Natural Entrance and the Big Room, and return to the surface by elevator. The Big Room route is recommended for visitors who are short on time or who prefer a less strenuous walk.

A brief orientation is presented prior to touring. An audio guide provides descriptive commentary, and interpretive signs explain cavern features, history and geology. Alternative activities—including ranger talks, self-guiding nature trails and a desert automobile drive—are available for early arrivals.

Guided cave tours *(see below)* are led by park rangers and range from easy walks to difficult crawls and climbs. These tours fill quickly in the summer and are available by reservation only.

Exhibits at the visitor center depict the geology, biology, history and archeology of the cavern and surrounding area. Interpretive programs about bats are given at dusk at the cave entrance amphitheater from late May to late September. A half-mile, self-guiding desert nature trail begins near the cave entrance.

The 9.5-mile Walnut Canyon Desert Drive, a one-way loop drive over a graded gravel road, offers views of Rattlesnake Canyon and upper Walnut Canyon. A permit is required for overnight back-country trips; inquire at the visitor center for hiking information. *See Recreation Chart.*

The temperature underground is a constant 56 F. A sweater and flat-heeled shoes with rubber soles are recommended. Strollers are not permitted. Flash and time-exposure photography is allowed, but all photographs must be taken from paved trails. Food is available.

ADMISSION to the park area and the visitor center without entrance to the caves is free. Cave admission (valid for 3 days) including the Natural Entrance and Big Room self-guiding routes $6; ages 6-15, $3. Audio guide rental $3. DS, MC, VI.

PETS, except Seeing Eye dogs, are not permitted inside caves. The visitor center provides kennels for $4 per pet.

ADDRESS inquiries to the Superintendent, Carlsbad Caverns National Park, 3225 National Parks Hwy., Carlsbad, NM 88220; phone (505) 785-2232.

Points of Interest

CARLSBAD CAVERNS GUIDED TOURS depart from the visitor center. Offered in addition to two self-guiding tours of Carlsbad Cavern—the Natural Entrance and Big Room routes—these six guided tours are led by park rangers. Tours range from easy to difficult, and visitors must supply their own equipment for some routes. Sturdy hiking boots are required. **Note:** Guided cavern tours fill quickly in the summer and are available by reservation only. Departure times, tour length, fees, group size and age restrictions vary. Phone (800) 967-2283 for reservations.

Hall of the White Giant Tour departs from the Carlsbad Caverns Visitor Center. This strenuous 4-hour guided tour leads to a remote chamber. Participants must crawl long distances, squeeze through crevices such as the tight Matlock's Pinch and climb a slippery passage. Hiking boots or other sturdy shoes and four new AA batteries are required; gloves, long pants and knee pads are recommended. Headlamps are provided. The tour is limited to eight participants. Tours depart Sat. at 1. Fee (in addition to cavern admission) $20; ages 12-15, $10. Under 12 are not permitted. Reservations are required. DS, MC, VI. Phone (800) 967-2283.

King's Palace Tour departs from the underground rest area in Carlsbad Cavern. This 1.5-hour tour covers 1 mile and descends to the deepest part of the cave open to the public, 830 feet below the surface. Cave formations include helictites, draperies, columns and soda straws. The tour is limited to 75 participants. Tours are given daily at 10, 11, 2 and 3, Memorial Day weekend-Labor Day; at 10 and 2, rest of year. Fee (in addition to cavern admission) $8; ages 4-15, $4. Under 4 are not permitted. Reservations are required. DS, MC, VI. Phone (800) 967-2283.

Left Hand Tunnel Tour departs from the Carlsbad Caverns Visitor Center off US 62/180. This 2-hour lantern tour highlights cavern history and geology along a half-mile route. Sights along this easy tour include cave pools and fossils. Lanterns are provided; walking shoes are required. The tour is limited to 15 participants. Tours depart daily at 9. Fee (in addition to cavern admission) $7; ages 6-15, $3.50. Under 6 are not permitted. Reservations are required. DS, MC, VI. Phone (800) 967-2283.

Lower Cave Tour departs from the Carlsbad Caverns Visitor Center off US 62/180. Entered by ladder, this area of the cavern contains beautiful formations and evidence of early exploration. The Rookery is a showcase for cave pearls. The 3-hour tour involves climbing and heights and is moderately strenuous. Athletic shoes or hiking boots and four new AA batteries are required. The tour is limited to 12 participants. Tours depart Mon.-Fri. at 1. Fee (in addition to cavern admission) $20; ages 12-15, $10. Under 12 are not permitted. Reservations are required. DS, MC, VI. Phone (800) 967-2283.

Slaughter Canyon Cave Tour departs 23 mi. s.w. of the Carlsbad Caverns Visitor Center on US 62/180 to CR 418, following signs to the cave entrance. Dramatic formations in this undeveloped cave include the 89-foot-high Monarch, the sparkling Christmas Tree column and the delicate Chinese Wall.

An unpaved, 1-mile trail leads from the parking area to the cave, climbing 500 feet; allow 45 minutes to make this steep and strenuous climb. Hiking boots or other sturdy shoes, a two-D-cell battery flashlight and water are required. The 2-hour tour is limited to 25 participants. Tours are offered daily at 10 and 1, Memorial Day weekend-Labor Day; Sat.-Sun. at 10, rest of year. Hikers should arrive at the cave entrance 15 minute prior to departure time. Fee $15; ages 6-15, $7.50. Under 6 are not permitted. Reservations are required. DS, MC, VI. Phone (800) 967-2283.

Spider Cave Tour departs from the Carlsbad Caverns Visitor Center off US 62/180. This three-dimensional maze includes tight crawlways, canyonlike passages and bizarre formations. Highlights include the Mace and Medusa rooms and Cactus Spring. Hiking boots or other sturdy shoes and four AA batteries are required for this most strenuous tour; gloves, long pants, knee pads and water are recommended. Helmets and headlamps are provided. The 4-hour tour is limited to eight participants. Tours are given Sun. at 1. Fee $20; ages 12-15, $10. Under 12 are not permitted. Reservations are required. DS, MC, VI. Phone (800) 967-2283.

CARRIZOZO (D-4) pop. 1,036, elev. 5,426′

Once a shipping and commercial center for area ranches, Carrizozo is now a busy county seat and tourist center. In addition to its own parks and recreational facilities, it offers easy access to the northern portion of Lincoln National Forest (*see place listing p. 160*). Established in 1899 as a division point on the El Paso & Northeastern Railroad, the community takes its name from *carrizo*, a regional grass.

Nine miles northeast via US 54 and SR 349 is the ghost town of White Oaks. For 20 years after the original gold strike on nearby Baxter Mountain in 1880, White Oaks was a substantial community with stone buildings, two banks and two newspapers. Although White Oaks faded with the gold market in the 20th century, one of the first strikes—the Old Abe Mine—produced $3 million in gold until it closed around 1960.

Carrizozo Chamber of Commerce: P.O. Box 567, Carrizozo, NM 88301; phone (505) 648-2732.

VALLEY OF FIRES RECREATION AREA is 4 mi. w. on US 380. These 463 acres of *mal país*—badlands—were named for an American Indian account of ancient volcanic eruptions that created a valley of fires. The magma flowed from Little Black Peak 1,500 to 2,000 years ago, traveled some 44 miles and covered 127 square miles of the valley. A three-quarter-mile nature trail winds through the park; trail guides are available at the visitor center.

Tent and RV camping is permitted. Pets on leashes are permitted. Daily 24 hours. Visitor center daily 8-4. Admission $3 per person or $5 per private vehicle. Admission is half-price for Golden Age and Golden Access pass holders. Camping $7-$18. Further information is available from Carrizozo Travel Information Center; phone (505) 648-2241. *See the AAA Southwestern CampBook.*

CARSON NATIONAL FOREST

Elevations in the forest range from 6,000 ft. in the Pinon Juniper Tree region to 13,161 ft. at Wheeler Peak. Refer to AAA maps for additional elevation information.

In north central New Mexico, Carson National Forest encompasses 1,500,000 acres. Its scenic and recreational focus is in the districts that encompass the Sangre de Cristo and the San Juan mountains flanking the upper Rio Grande Valley.

Five wilderness areas—Wheeler Peak, Latir Peak, Cruces Basin, the northern portion of the Pecos and Chama wildernesses and an 8-mile-long section of the Rio Grande Wild River—preserve the region's pristine beauty. Wildlife abounds in the 100,000-acre Valle Vidal Unit.

Enchanted Circle Scenic Byway is an 84-mile drive offering panoramic views of the southern Rocky Mountains, including Wheeler Peak. It loops from Taos east to Eagle Nest, then north to Questa via SR 38, and south on SR 522 back to Taos.

The curved cliff side of Echo Amphitheater, 9 miles south of Canjilon on US 84, is a prime spot for photography. Summer and winter recreation is available. Trails for cycling, hiking, horseback riding, snowmobiling and cross-country skiing traverse the forest.

For further information contact Carson National Forest, 208 Cruz Alta Rd., Taos, NM 87571; phone (505) 758-6200. *See Recreation Chart.*

CASA BLANCA— *See Laguna Pueblo p. 158.*

CHACO CULTURE NATIONAL HISTORICAL PARK (B-2)

Located in northwestern New Mexico, the park can be reached via US 550/SR 44, exit at CR 7900—entry is about 3 miles southeast of Nageezi and approximately 50 miles west of Cuba. Follow signs to the park for 21 miles. (This route has 5 miles of paved road and 16 miles of dirt road.)

Chaco Culture National Historical Park preserves the remains of 13 major great houses, or monumental public buildings, and several thousand smaller sites that exemplify the culture of the Ancestral Puebloan people A.D. 850-1150.

By about A.D. 500 the Ancestral Puebloan people gradually exchanged their nomadic ways for agriculture and permanent settlements. They began to build Pueblo Bonito at the base of the northern canyon wall, 4 miles west of the headquarters area, during the mid-9th century. By the late 12th century Pueblo Bonito had attained a height of at least 4 stories and contained more than 600 rooms and kivas (ceremonial rooms).

In addition to the large public buildings, numerous smaller village sites in the canyon attest to the settlement's sizable and diverse populations, which were greater than those found in the area today. It is one of the most imposing cultural sites in the Southwest.

Not content with building great public buildings and an elaborate irrigation system of gates and canals that diverted runoff from summer storms into their cornfields, the Chacoans also constructed a vast road network. These straight, 30-foot-wide corridors linked the canyon settlements with more than 150 satellite communities, some as distant as Arizona, Colorado and Utah.

One route, the Great North Road, runs from Pueblo Alto near Pueblo Bonito to a point near Salmon Ruin *(see Bloomfield p. 145)* and may continue to Aztec Ruins National Monument *(see place listing p. 144).*

Another major achievement of the Chaco is a highly sophisticated solstice marker. High on the isolated Fajada Butte a sliver of noontime sunlight slashes between stone slabs onto two spiral petroglyphs, precisely timing the equinoxes and solstices by which the Chacoans planted their crops and scheduled their ceremonies. The butte is closed to the public due to its fragile condition.

Eventually Chaco's influence waned and new centers emerged at Aztec and Mesa Verde—by 1250 only the wind whispered among the colossal masonry walls of Pueblo Bonito and its sister cities. The people were assimilated into the existing populations in the Zuni, Hopi, Acoma, Rio Grande and Mesa Verde regions. Descendents continue to return to honor these sacred places.

Note: Due to the park's remote location and its extensive ruins and trails, it may be advisable to schedule 2 or 3 days for the visit. A full day is required for travel and to see a portion of the park. A second or third day is necessary to view the entire site.

Because Chaco is accessible only over dirt roads that are rough, towing trailers more than 30 feet long is not advised. Some sections of road may become impassable during inclement weather; phone ahead for current weather and road conditions. There are no services, food, gas or lodging available in the park. Campers must bring their own wood or charcoal. Drinking water and dump station facilities are available.

Self-guiding trails explore seven major sites, including Pueblo Bonito, Chetro Ketl, Pueblo del Arroyo, Casa Rinconada and three village sites. Allow 1 hour minimum per trail. Four other trails for day hiking lead into the back country; free permits, available at the visitor center and trailheads, are required.

Rangers conduct free 90-minute tours of the major Chacoan sites. An observatory provides a view of the evening sky. Picnicking and camping are permitted in designated areas.

CHACO CULTURE NATIONAL HISTORICAL PARK VISITOR CENTER is 1.5 mi. from the park entrance. A museum traces the history of the canyon and the cultures that developed it. Displays include artifacts of the Pueblo and Navajo peoples as well as various forms of pottery. Short films about the area are shown. Visitor center daily 8-5; closed Jan. 1, Thanksgiving and Dec. 25. Trails open daily dawn-dusk year-round. Admission (valid for 7 days) $8 per private vehicle, $4 per person arriving by other means. DS, MC, VI. Phone (505) 786-7014, ext. 240.

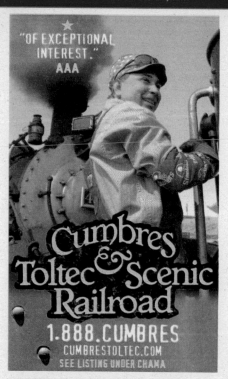

CHAMA (A-3) pop. 1,199, elev. 7,875'

Like the railroad that is its most popular attraction, Chama grew during the silver mining boom of the 1880s. The old railroad yards, shops, a roundhouse and one of the last coal tipples in the nation are relics of that era. In addition to tourism, lumber and outdoor recreation contribute to the town economy.

Chama Valley Chamber of Commerce: 2372 SR 17S, P.O. Box 306, Chama, NM 87520; phone (505) 756-2306 or (800) 477-0149.

CUMBRES & TOLTEC SCENIC RAILROAD is on SR 17. The railroad operates the New Mexico Express from Chama to Osier, Colo., where it connects with the Colorado Limited, which continues to Antonito, Colo. All-day trips on the vintage, narrow-gauge, coal-burning trains afford spectacular views of the rugged San Juan and Sangre de Cristo mountain ranges.

Osier, the old stagecoach stop, is the transfer and lunch point for those making the complete trip and returning by bus, as well as the turnaround point for passengers making the round trip to their point of origin.

AAA offices in New Mexico and Colorado can make reservations. Trains depart from Chama and Antonito Mon.-Thurs. and Sat.-Sun. at 10, Memorial Day weekend to mid-Oct. Excursions return to Chama about 4:30 and to Antonito about 5. Fare (includes lunch) $69.75; ages 2-11, $37. Reservations are suggested. AX, CB, DC, DS, MC, VI. Phone (505) 756-2151 in N.M., (719) 376-5483 in Colo., or (888) 286-2737. *See color ad.*

CHIMAYÓ (B-4) pop. 2,924, elev. 6,075'

The Spanish village of Chimayó is the home of the softly colored Chimayó blankets and rugs woven by Ortega family members. Throughout the village winding dirt roads lead past adobe houses. Vibrant colors decorate the village each autumn as the golden foliage of cottonwood trees provides a backdrop for garlands of red chili peppers drying in the sun.

Chimayó was settled in 1598 and for the next 100 years was the easternmost outpost of the Province of New Mexico, the frontier place of banishment. The reconquest of the rebellious Pueblo and Apache in 1692 initiated a new settlement in the western foothills of the Sangre de Cristo Mountains, and Spaniards were granted permission to settle along the Santa Cruz River.

In 1740 San Buenaventura de Chimayó—Chimayó of the Good Venture—was built. The plaza is one of the oldest of Spanish colonial origin surviving in the Southwest; many surrounding structures are homes of the settlers' descendants.

East of Chimayó on SR 76—a route known as the High Road to Taos—are two other well-known craft villages. Cordova maintains a tradition of excellence in woodcarving, in which the Lopez family is most prominent. Beyond Cordova, Truchas is the home of the Cordova family of master weavers. Visitors are welcome to browse during daylight hours in the workshops scattered throughout the villages.

Shopping areas: Galleria Plaza del Cerro, in the town center, offers crafts and other goods. Centinela Traditional Arts specializes in handwoven wool products.

EL SANTUARIO DE NUESTRO SEÑOR DE ESQUIPULAS is at the s.e. end of town via SR 76 and CR 98. In 1810 Bernardo Abeyta, a farmer, was praying and claimed to see a light emanating from the soil. Upon investigation he found a cross, which is now kept inside the chapel. Legend maintains that the earth surrounding this cross has healing power. Many pilgrims come to touch the dirt in a pit inside the chapel, where castoff crutches and braces line the walls. Daily 9-6, May-Sept.; 9-4, rest of year. Free. Phone (505) 351-4360.

CHURCH ROCK (B-1) pop. 1,077, elev. 6,765'

Church Rock, which received its name from a prominent sandstone formation, was called *Kinlitsoh sinili* by the Navajo, or "place of yellow houses." This small settlement was the unlikely site of a nuclear disaster in 1979, when a dam containing uranium waste collapsed, spilling millions of gallons of radioactive water into the Puerco River. New

Mexico banned uranium mining on Navajo land in 2005.

RED ROCK STATE PARK is off I-40 exit 26/33. Red sandstone cliffs provide a striking backdrop for this 640-acre park, which features hiking and nature trails, a rodeo arena, campgrounds and a museum. Archeological evidence of ancient Pueblo dwellings dates to the third century. Red Rock Museum traces prehistoric habitation and the modern-day culture of Zuni, Hopi and Navajo tribes through displays of artwork and crafts.

Picnicking is permitted. Daily 8-6, Memorial Day weekend-Labor Day; 8-4:30, rest of year. Park free. Museum by donation. Phone (505) 722-3829. *See Recreation Chart and the AAA Southwestern CampBook.*

CIBOLA NATIONAL FOREST

Elevations in the forest range from 6,500 ft. in the Magdalena district to 11,301 ft. at Mt. Taylor. Refer to AAA maps for additional elevation information.

The forest comprises scattered mountain ranges rising from the desert east and south of Albuquerque and stretching west to Arizona. Cibola National Forest's 1,630,221 acres encompass four wilderness areas: Sandia, Manzano, Apache Kid and The Withington. Recreational opportunities include camping, fishing and hiking. *See Recreation Chart.*

The rugged Canadian River Canyon west of Roy provides another type of beauty within Kiowa National Grassland. The forest also administers Black Kettle National Grassland, in neighboring western Oklahoma and the Texas panhandle. Camping and fishing center on the grassland's five lakes. Hunting is available in season, and there is skiing at Sandia Peak Ski Area.

A chairlift carries visitors to the northeastern face of Sandia Peak. The lift may be accessed via the Sandia Peak Aerial Tramway *(see attraction listing p. 143)* or by automobile, taking I-40 exit 175, north to SR 536. It operates weekends Memorial Day through mid-October and daily during the Albuquerque International Balloon Fiesta. It also transports mountain bikes for cyclists who wish to explore the peak's upper trails; phone (505) 242-9052.

SANDIA CREST is 16 mi. e. of Albuquerque on I-40, 6 mi. n. on SR 14, then 14 mi. n.w. on the Sandia Crest National Scenic Byway (SR 536). Paved and all-weather roads lead to an observation deck atop the 10,678-foot crest, where the panorama encompasses 15,000 square miles. A self-guiding nature trail begins here and loops for a half-mile. The byway is a 14-mile spur of the Turquoise Trail, the scenic stretch of SR 14 that links Albuquerque and Santa Fe. Volcanic rock formations, ghost towns and old mines are visible.

Snowboarding, downhill and cross-country skiing are available in winter; hiking and mountain biking are popular in summer. Equipment can be rented in both seasons. Food is available at the top of the crest. Parking $3. Phone (505) 281-3304 or (505) 242-0952.

 SANDIA PEAK AERIAL TRAMWAY— *see Albuquerque p. 143.*

CIMARRON (A-4) pop. 917, elev. 6,428'

Meaning "wild" or "untamed," Cimarron was fitting for both the brawling stream and the settlement that developed on its banks. Although Eagle Nest Lake ultimately tamed the river, nothing could contain the activities in town from the late 1860s to about 1880. The Las Vegas *Gazette* once reported, "Things are quiet in Cimarron; nobody has been killed in three days."

Clay Allison, Billy the Kid, Bob Ford and Black Jack Ketchum were among notorious part-time residents. Gunfights killed 26 men, and New Mexico's first printing press was dumped into the Cimarron River before the range wars ended and the town ceased to be a magnet for every outlaw in the Southwest.

Cimarron languished after losing the county seat to Springer in 1880 but revived in the early 1900s with the arrival of two railroads and the lumber industry. The modern-day city serves nearby ranches, some logging operations and a lively tourist trade. St. James Hotel, where Annie Oakley joined Buffalo Bill Cody's Wild West Show, and the old jail are among the buildings that stand as reminders of a boisterous past. Just 4 miles south on SR 21 is Philmont Scout Ranch *(see attraction listing)*, a high-adventure camp for more than 20,000 Boy Scouts each summer.

The 3,600-acre Maxwell National Wildlife Refuge, 30 miles east off I-25, supports sizable populations of eagles, hawks and falcons around its grasslands, lakes and farmland. As part of Carson National Forest, Valle Vidal *(see Recreation Chart)*, offers 100,000 acres of rugged back country for backpacking, hunting and fishing. It is 4 miles north on scenic US 64, then 21 miles northwest on Valle Vidal Road, following signs. Cimarron Canyon State Park, 12 miles west on US 64, features brown trout fishing, hiking and camping *(see Recreation Chart)*.

Cimarron Chamber of Commerce: 104 N. Lincoln Ave., P.O. Box 604, Cimarron, NM 87714; phone (505) 376-2417.

Self-guiding Tours: A walking tour map available from the chamber of commerce describes 14 historic buildings in the old town of Cimarron.

OLD AZTEC MILL MUSEUM is s. of US 64 in Old Town on SR 21. An 1864 building houses four floors of artifacts relating to county history. Included are American Indian arts and crafts, furnishings, historic items, vintage clothing and books. Placards explain the mill's original workings, which are partially intact. Allow 1 hour minimum. Mon.-Wed.

and Fri.-Sat. 9-5, Sun. 1-5, June-Aug.; Sat. 9-5, Sun. 1-5 in May and Sept. Admission $3; over 61 and under 12, $2. Phone (505) 376-2913.

PHILMONT SCOUT RANCH is 5 mi. s. off SR 21 at 17 Deer Run Rd. The 137,493-acre national camping center is operated by the National Council of the Boy Scouts of America. More than 20,000 Scouts from around the world visit each summer. Seton Memorial Library and Museum presents Southwestern art and history. Tours are available of Villa Philmonte, the summer home of Tulsa oilman Waite Philips, benefactor of Philmont Scout Ranch.

Library and museum daily 8-5, June-Aug.; Mon.-Fri. 8-5, rest of year. Villa tours depart every 30 minutes, 8-noon and 1-5, June-Aug.; by appointment rest of year. Last tour begins 30 minutes before closing. Donations. Phone (505) 376-2281.

CLAYTON (A-6) pop. 2,524, elev. 5,053′

So numerous were the herds of cattle driven through this small farming community in the mid-1880s that the Denver & Fort Worth Railroad established the settlement as a division point. As a railhead and trading center, Clayton underwent a Wild West phase. Celebrated train robber Black Jack Ketchum was hanged from a gallows enclosed in a stockade to foil yet another rescue by his gang.

Clayton, at the foot of the Rabbit Ear Mountains, is still a cattle town; some of the largest feedlots in the region are just to the north. It also is one of the world's largest producers of carbon dioxide, which is used for recovering oil in the Permian Basin in New Mexico and Texas.

Livestock studies are conducted at Clayton Livestock Research Center, 5 miles east in Kiowa Rita Blanca National Grasslands. The University of New Mexico and the U.S. Forest Service investigate problems related to the health, nutrition and management of cattle. Free 45- to 60-minute tours of the facility are available by appointment; phone (505) 374-2566.

Recreational opportunities abound at Clayton Lake State Park (see Recreation Chart and the AAA Southwestern CampBook), known for its excellent trout, walleye and bass fishing. Dinosaur tracks were discovered on the spillway of the dam in 1982; more than 500 such tracks have been plotted.

Clayton-Union County Chamber of Commerce: 1103 S. First St., P.O. Box 476, Clayton, NM 88415; phone (505) 374-9253 or (800) 390-7858.

THE HERZSTEIN MEMORIAL MUSEUM is at 23 S. 2nd St. Offering a glimpse into the local area's rich history, the collection is wide-ranging and includes pioneer artifacts, paintings and antique furniture. Allow 1 hour minimum. Tues.-Sun. 1-5; closed holidays. Donations. Phone (505) 374-2977.

CLOUDCROFT (E-4) pop. 749, elev. 8,663′

A flourishing resort and recreation center at the summit of the Sacramento Mountains, Cloudcroft offers skiing and snow play in winter and varied summer activities such as hiking and camping, especially in Lincoln National Forest (see place listing p. 160).

This high, wide country was settled when the Southern Pacific Railroad ran a spur from Alamogordo to tap the timber reserves in the Sacramento Mountains. To lure excursion passengers the railroad built an elaborate resort, The Lodge, in 1901. Though the last train arrived in 1947, the resort still operates. Today's visitors enjoy hiking, bicycling and skiing along trails where trains once traveled. Local artisans create a variety of crafts. In downtown, shopping, dining and entertainment are offered along historic Burro Avenue.

Sacramento Mountains Historical Museum on US 82 recalls the town's settlement days. Within the museum complex, the Cloudcroft Pioneer Village features historic buildings furnished in period, a granary, a barn and antique farm equipment.

Cloudcroft Chamber of Commerce: 1001 James Canyon Hwy., P.O. Box 1290, Cloudcroft, NM 88317; phone (505) 682-2733.

CLOVIS (C-6) pop. 32,667, elev. 4,266′

Clovis is located on the high plains of eastern New Mexico in the heart of cattle country, with ranching, farming, the dairy industry and the railroad comprising important components of the community's economic base. Eight miles to the west is Cannon Air Force Base, another important component of the local economy.

In rock 'n' roll circles, Clovis also is known for the Norman Petty Recording Studios where Buddy Holly recorded the 1957 hit, "Peggy Sue." The studios, still operating, are restored to their original 1950s appearance and feature music memorabilia and vintage recording equipment. Guided tours are available by appointment; phone (505) 763-3435.

Hillcrest Park, at 10th and Sycamore streets, encompasses a sunken garden, amusement rides for children, picnic areas and Hillcrest Zoo.

Clovis/Curry County Chamber of Commerce: 215 N. Main St., Clovis, NM 88101; phone (505) 763-3435 or (800) 261-7656.

COCHITÍ PUEBLO (B-3) elev. 5,258′

West of the Rio Grande River and a few miles southwest of Cochití Dam, this ancient Keresan pueblo retains few of its old landmarks. The mission church, San Buenaventura de Cochití, was built in 1628. The tribe leases land to the community of Cochití Lake, where a recreation area offers boating, camping, fishing and nature trails (see Recreation Chart). Visitors to the pueblo are welcome dawn to dusk. Drawing, painting, photography or tape recording are not permitted.

Kasha-Katuwe Tent Rocks National Monument, 5 miles west on Tribal Road 92, is named for the fanciful, teepeelike formations created by the effects of erosion on lava. A 2-mile hiking trail winds through the undeveloped site, which is reached via a dirt road.

COLUMBUS (F-2) pop. 1,765, elev. 4,064'

Just before dawn on March 9, 1916, the revolutionary activities of Pancho Villa and his 1,000 guerrillas spilled over the international border into drowsy Columbus and its military outpost—the first attack on U.S. soil since the War of 1812. The raiders seized livestock, burned the town and killed 18 Americans, eliciting immediate retaliation from President Woodrow Wilson.

Within a week Gen. John "Black Jack" Pershing marched his 6,000 troops, accompanied by motorized vehicles and airplanes, into Mexico to mark the first mechanized U.S. military action. Pershing's forces pursued the rebel leader for 11 months but never captured him; Villa was assassinated in 1923.

Columbus Chamber of Commerce: 214 W. Broadway Ave., P.O. Box 350, Columbus, NM 88029; phone (505) 531-2663, ask for the chamber.

COLUMBUS HISTORICAL SOCIETY MUSEUM is at jct. SRs 9 and 11 across from Pancho Villa State Park. Chronicling local history from the pioneer era to modern times, the museum is housed in a 1902 Southern Pacific Railroad depot that stood witness to Pancho Villa's raid on the city. This attack and the U.S. Army's subsequent retaliation is depicted with photographs, military artifacts and a 20-minute film. Displays include Mexican pottery and beads, pioneer implements and railroad memorabilia. Allow 30 minutes minimum. Daily 10-4, Sept.-May; 10-1, rest of year. Closed Dec. 25. Free. Phone (505) 531-2620.

PANCHO VILLA STATE PARK is 32 mi. s. at jct. SRs 9 and 11. The site of Pancho Villa's raid into American territory is preserved at the park, which commemorates the event with historical exhibits, including pre-WW I vehicles used by Gen. John Pershing's men in their pursuit of Villa. The 61-acre park includes a visitor center, buildings from Camp Furlong, nature trails, a playground and an exotic botanical garden with some 30 varieties of cacti. Daily 24 hours. Visitor center daily 8-5. Admission $5 per private vehicle. Camping $8-$14. Phone (505) 531-2711. *See the AAA Southwestern CampBook.*

CORONADO NATIONAL FOREST—

see Arizona p. 45.

DEMING (E-2) pop. 14,116, elev. 4,337'

Fields of cotton and chilies flourish in the seemingly riverless valley around Deming. The water that sustains them is the subsurface flow of the Mimbres River, which vanishes into the earth north of the city and reappears in a lake in the Mexican state of Chihuahua. Stock raising and some manufacturing augment the economy of this busy county seat, which also is a growing retirement center. Southeast the Little Florida (flo-REE-da) Mountains yield an abundance of agate, fire opal, jasper and semiprecious stones.

Deming-Luna County Chamber of Commerce and Visitors Center: 800 E. Pine St., P.O. Box 8, Deming, NM 88031; phone (505) 546-2674.

Self-guiding tours: A walking-tour brochure listing 16 historic buildings and sites is available from the chamber of commerce.

CITY OF ROCKS STATE PARK is 30 mi. n.w. via US 180, then 3 mi. n.e. on SR 61. Millions of years ago wind and water shaped volcanic rock into the curious monolithic formations that give this 680-acre park its name. The Mimbres Indians and Spanish conquistadors left evidence of their visits. A cactus garden, hiking trails, interpretive exhibits and visitor center also are featured. Picnicking and camping are permitted. Daily 7 a.m.-9 p.m. Visitor center daily 10-4. Admission $5 per private vehicle. Camping $10-$14. Phone (505) 536-2800. *See the AAA Southwestern CampBook.*

DEMING LUNA MIMBRES MUSEUM is at 301 S. Silver St. The museum depicts Southwest history with a 1853 customs house, pioneer artifacts, military items from early cavalry days through World War II, railroad and cowboy memorabilia, gems and minerals, and a Mimbres Indian pottery exhibit. The transportation annex features street scenes and antique automobiles representing Deming's past. A 53-foot mural illustrates county history. Mon.-Sat. 9-4, Sun. 1:30-4; closed Jan. 1, Easter, Thanksgiving and Dec. 25. Donations. Phone (505) 546-2382.

ROCKHOUND STATE PARK is 14 mi. s.e. off SR 11. Abundant agate and quartz crystals are found within this park on the western slope of the Florida Mountains. Up to 15 pounds of rock may be collected, making it a favorite spot for "rockhounds." Picnicking and camping are permitted. Daily 7-dusk. Admission $5 per private vehicle. Camping $10-$14. Phone (505) 546-6182. *See the AAA Southwestern CampBook.*

DULCE (A-3) pop. 2,623, elev. 6,769'

Dulce is the capital and principal town of Jicarilla Apache Indian Reservation. The Jicarillas (hek-a-REH-yas), whose name means "little baskets," are renowned for woven baskets and other ornate craftwork. Visitors may watch artisans at work at the Jicarilla Arts and Crafts Museum on the reservation.

The town, at the northeastern corner of the reservation, is a popular provision point with hunters and anglers. The 14,500-acre Horse Lake Mesa Game Park is one of the country's largest elk enclosures.

Jicarilla Apache Nation, Public Relations Department: P.O. Box 507, Dulce, NM 87528; phone (505) 759-3242.

EDGEWOOD (C-3) pop. 1,893, elev. 6,645'

A relative newcomer in state history, the farming community of Edgewood was settled in the 1930s.

[SAVE] **WILDLIFE WEST NATURE PARK** is off I-40 exit 187 to 87 W. Frontage Rd. The 122-acre habitat park contains animals and plants native to New Mexico. Trails allow visitors to see elk, Mexican wolves, whitetail deer, pronghorn antelope, foxes, raccoons, ducks, raptors and other birds. Hayrides are offered Saturday summer evenings prior to the Chuckwagon Dinner Show, which offers barbecue and Western musical entertainment.

Allow 1 hour, 30 minutes minimum. Park daily 10-6, Apr.-Oct.; noon-4, rest of year. Dinner show is offered Sat. at 7 p.m., mid-June through Labor Day. Closed Jan. 1 and Dec. 25. Admission $5; over 59 and ages 5-11, $4. Dinner show $16.50; over 59, $15.50; ages 5-11, $10. MC, VI. Phone (505) 281-7655.

EL MALPAIS NATIONAL MONUMENT—*see Grants p. 157.*

EL MORRO NATIONAL MONUMENT (C-1)

El Morro National Monument is 43 miles southwest of Grants via SR 53. The central features of the 1,278-acre monument are 200-foot-high Inscription Rock and the water hole fed by snowmelt and rainfall pouring off the rock. The Spanish called the sandstone mesa *El Morro*, meaning "the bluff" or "the headland."

Carved into the soft rock are centuries-old petroglyphs. The first known European inscription was left in 1605 by Juan de Oñate, governor and colonizer of New Mexico. Others include those of Gov. Manuel de Silva Nieto in 1629; a soldier in 1632; Don Diego de Vargas, leader of the 1692 reconquest; and Lt. Edward Beale, who passed by with a camel caravan in 1857. Other soldiers and settlers making their way west added their names and dates.

Two Ancestral Puebloan villages once thrived atop this mesa. Remains of an 800-room dwelling from about the 13th century have been partly excavated.

Self-guiding tours are available. A half-mile trail and a 2-mile trail take about 45 minutes and 1.5 hours, respectively. A small campground is available on a first-come, first-served basis. For further information contact the Superintendent, El Morro National Monument, HC61, P.O. Box 43, Ramah, NM 87321.

Visitor center daily 9-5; closed Jan. 1 and Dec. 25. Last admission for hiking trails 1 hour before closing. Schedule may be extended in summer; phone ahead. Admission $3; under 17 free. Phone (505) 783-4226.

ESPAÑOLA (B-3) pop. 9,688, elev. 5,589′

In the northern Rio Grande Valley between the Jémez Mountains and the Truchas Peaks, Española was founded in 1598 by the Spaniards as the first capital of New Mexico.

The town assumed its present role as a trading and distribution center when the Denver and Rio Grande Western Railroad built its Chili Line between Española and Antonito, Colo., in the late 1870s. In late summer garlands of *ristras*—strings of scarlet chilies drying in the sun—decorate houses and fences.

Española is the central point for visiting the eight northern pueblos and Hispanic villages selling arts and crafts, including Nambé, Picurís, Pojoaque, San Ildefonso, San Juan, Santa Clara, Taos and Tesuque (*see place listings*).

Española Valley Chamber of Commerce: 710 Paseo de Onate, P.O. Box 190, Española, NM 87532-0190; phone (505) 753-2831.

FARMINGTON (A-2) pop. 37,844, elev. 5,292′

Orchards replaced saloons and coal miners ousted card sharks as Farmington evolved into the major commerce and industrial center of the Four Corners region in northwestern New Mexico.

Navajo Mine, west of town, is one of the largest coal mining operations in the world. Its output fuels the adjacent Four Corners Power Plant, which in turn heats the waters used by windsurfers on nearby Morgan Lake. Anglers favor the San Juan River and Farmington and Jackson lakes.

West of town the vast Navajo Indian Reservation extends into Arizona. The convention and visitors bureau distributes a list of trading posts.

Forty miles south via SR 371 is the Bisti/De-Na-Zin Wilderness, an area of weirdly eroded hoodoos and slate-topped *mesitas*—geological formations made up of sandstone and shale that have become eroded by wind and rain. Angel Peak Recreation Area *(see Bloomfield in the AAA Southwestern CampBook)* lies 35 miles southeast via SR 550. Once considered by the Navajos as the dwelling place of sacred ones, the colorful sandstone formations crowning the peak were shaped over millions of years.

Changing exhibits by area artists are displayed at Farmington Civic Center and at San Juan College Fine Arts Center; the school has an enrollment of 6,200. The drama "Black River Traders" is performed mid-June to mid-August in the Lion's Wilderness Park, a natural sandstone amphitheater.

Farmington Convention and Visitors Bureau: 3041 E. Main St., Farmington, NM 87402; phone (505) 326-7602 or (800) 448-1240. *See color ad p. 154.*

FARMINGTON MUSEUM is at 3041 E. Main St. Permanent exhibits depict local history, including the region's oil and gas industry, through such items as clothing, photographs, tools and equipment. The facility hosts year-round lectures, educational programs and art shows highlighting regional heritage and culture. An atrium affords excellent views of the Animas River. Allow 30 minutes minimum. Mon.-Sat. 8-5; closed Jan. 1, Easter, Thanksgiving and Dec. 25. Admission $2, students with ID and under 7 free. DS, MC, VI. Phone (505) 599-1174.

E-3 Children's Museum is just n. of jct. Main and Orchard sts. Permanent and changing science exhibits encourage interactive learning for children. Allow 30 minutes minimum. Tues.-Sat. noon-5. Free. Phone (505) 599-1425 or (800) 448-1240.

FORT SUMNER (C-5) pop. 1,249, elev. 4,049′

The agricultural potential of the Pecos River bottomlands surrounding this quiet farming and ranching center so impressed Maj. James Carleton that in 1852 he recommended the site for an Army post. A decade later, as brigadier general, he realized his dream. He established Fort Sumner and made it the core of a permanent reservation for the Navajos and Apaches, whose resettlement was being supervised by Col. Kit Carson.

In 1864 Carson forced more than 8,600 Navajos to make the 400-mile Long Walk from Fort Defiance, Ariz., to the 1,024,000-acre reservation at Fort Sumner. The fort was abandoned in 1869, and the Navajos returned to their tribal lands.

Fort Sumner County Chamber of Commerce: 707 N. 4th St., P.O. Box 28, Fort Sumner, NM 88119; phone (505) 355-7705.

FORT SUMNER STATE MONUMENT is 3 mi. e. on US 60, then 3 mi. s. on Billy the Kid Rd. The site marks the former Bosque Redondo Indian Reservation where some 9,000 Navajo and Mescalero Apache Indians were interred in the 1860s after the U.S. government forced them from tribal lands. Troops led by Kit Carson marched the Navajo some 300 miles to the prison camp, a grueling ordeal that came to be known as "The Long Walk." Exhibits and artifacts at the Bosque Redondo Memorial recount 5 years of starvation, disease and forced labor before the Navajo were allowed to return to their homes.

Wed.-Mon. 8:30-5; closed major holidays. Admission $3, under 17 free. Phone (505) 355-2573, or (505) 355-2942 for museum.

FORT UNION NATIONAL MONUMENT (B-4)

Eight miles northwest of Watrous on SR 161 (off I-25 exit 366), ranks of chimneys are stark reminders of the days when Fort Union was one of the largest military posts on the Southwestern frontier. Fort Union was the chief quartermaster depot 1851-91 for all garrisons throughout the region as well as the primary station for troops assigned to protect settlers and Santa Fe Trail travelers.

The site was well chosen, for the two branches of the Santa Fe Trail—the Mountain Branch and the Cimarron—pass through the Fort Union Valley. In addition the remote location put the soldiers closer to the tribes and farther from towns which might distract them from their duties.

A group of log buildings west of Wolf Creek constituted the first Fort Union. For a decade it served as a way station on the Santa Fe Trail and as a headquarters for battling the Utes, Jicarilla Apaches, Comanches and Kiowas.

The outbreak of the Civil War abruptly turned the Army's attention away from these conflicts. The second Fort Union, an earthwork defense bastion, was built east of the creek in late 1861. It was constructed by local volunteers just before Confederate forces from Texas, eager to control Colorado's mineral resources and Fort Union's supplies, swept up the Rio Grande Valley. After their supply train was destroyed in the Battle of Glorieta, the Confederate troops retreated and headed for home.

The third fort, whose garrison, quartermaster depot and arsenal still stand today, dates from the mid-1860s. For the next 15 years the Indian wars occupied the military, while tons of goods flowed through the depot. Gradually local tribes were subdued. The Santa Fe Railway reached New Mexico in 1879, making travel safer. Fort Union was abandoned in 1891.

A self-guiding 1.2-mile trail explores 100 acres of adobe ruins. A visitor center with a museum relates fort history. Living-history demonstrations and other events are offered during summer. Daily 8-6, Memorial Day weekend-Labor Day; 8-4, rest of year. Closed Jan. 1, Thanksgiving and Dec. 25. Admission $3. Phone (505) 425-8025.

FOUR CORNERS MONUMENT—

see Window Rock, Ariz., p. 122.

GALLUP (B-1) pop. 20,209, elev. 6,508'

The Atchison, Topeka & Santa Fe Railway pushed into this red rock mesa region in 1881 to use area coal deposits for its engines. Until then mostly stockmen had lived in the area; Gallup was a stage stop consisting of a saloon/general store called the Blue Goose. Coal mining and the presence of the railroad attracted settlers from other nations, giving the city an especially cosmopolitan heritage.

The city is best known as the main trading center for most Navajos, whose vast reservation extends north and west into Arizona as well as for the residents of the nearby Zuni Pueblo *(see place listing p. 181)*. Gallup has more than 100 trading posts, shops and galleries. At many trading posts handmade articles ranging from rugs and baskets to turquoise jewelry are sold.

Gallup Development Commission: 230 S. Second St., P.O. Box 1270, Gallup, NM 87301; phone (505) 726-2045. *See color ad.*

GALLUP CULTURAL CENTER is at 201 E. Hwy. 66. Southwest American Indian history is presented within the setting of a restored Santa Fe Railroad depot. Audio-narrated exhibits include vintage photographs, sand paintings, ancient pottery and a 10-foot bronze statue honoring World War II Navajo code talkers. The Kiva Cinema presents films about American Indian culture. Guided tours are available. Picnicking is permitted. Food is available. Allow 30 minutes minimum. Mon.-Fri. 8-4. Free. Phone (505) 863-4131.

GILA CLIFF DWELLINGS NATIONAL MONUMENT (D-2)

Gila Cliff Dwellings National Monument is a 2-hour drive 44 miles north of Silver City via SR 15; vehicles pulling trailers 20 feet or longer should use SR 35 north from San Lorenzo. In this rough and desolate country near the west fork of the Gila (HEE-la) River, seven natural cavities indent the face of a cliff some 175 feet above the canyon floor. Five of these hollows contain rooms constructed during the late 13th century by people of the Mogollon culture—these remain the focus of the monument.

A 1-mile hiking trail loops from the contact station to the dwellings. Gila Visitor Center *(see Gila National Forest)* is 1.5 miles from the monument entrance. There are weekend activity programs in summer; a park ranger is on duty all year.

Guided 1-hour tours of the cliff dwellings are offered as part of admission. Pets are not permitted on the monument trail; free kennels are available. Park open daily 8-6, Memorial Day-Labor Day; 9-4, rest of year. Closed Dec. 25. Guided tours are given daily at 11 and 2; allow an extra 30 minutes to walk from the parking area to the departure point. Admission $3, family rate $10, under 16 free. Exact change is required and may be obtained at the visitor center. Trail guide brochures are available for 50c. Phone (505) 536-9461.

GILA NATIONAL FOREST

Elevations in the forest range from 4,000 ft. in the desert to 11,000 ft. at Whitewater Baldy. Refer to AAA maps for additional elevation information.

In southwestern New Mexico, Gila (HEE-la) National Forest occupies 3,321,000 acres of forest and rangeland. The smaller of its two units extends north from Lordsburg along the Big Burro Mountains. The main unit, north of Silver City *(see place listing p. 176)*, embraces the Black, Mogollon, Tularosa and Diablo mountains. These wild ranges and remote canyons were the stronghold of such Apache warriors as Geronimo and Mangas Coloradas.

Much of the Mogollon Mountains lies within the Gila Wilderness, the first area in the nation to be so designated. Instrumental in its 1924 establishment was Aldo Leopold, the forester and naturalist whose "Sand County Almanac" and other writings have become classics of environmental literature.

A plaque 8 miles south of Pleasanton on US 180 marks Leopold Vista Historical Monument. The Gila, Blue Range and Aldo Leopold wilderness areas as well as Gila Cliff Dwellings National Monument *(see place listing p. 156)*, lie north of Silver City.

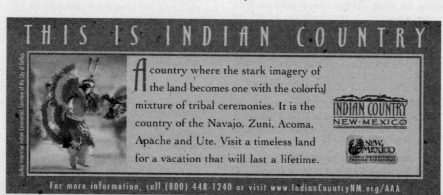

In the 1870s the region was the center of a mining boom, of which ghost towns and old mine structures are silent reminders. The 1-mile-long Catwalk National Recreation Trail passes through the steep walls of Whitewater Canyon. A metal suspension bridge carries hikers across a creek that once provided water to a nearby mill. Now a popular recreation area, it is reached via SR 174 from US 180.

The 110-mile Trail of the Mountain Spirits/Gila Cliff Dwellings Scenic Byway travels from Silver City east to San Lorenzo, through the Mimbres Valley, down Sapillo Creek, past Clinton P. Anderson Vista to Gila Cliff Dwellings National Monument, and returns to Silver City over the Pinos Altos Range. Overlooks along the byway provide perspective on the magnitude of the cliffs and the surrounding countryside.

There are numerous developed recreation areas in the forest. Stream and lake fishing and big game hunting are available in season. *See Recreation Chart.*

GILA VISITOR CENTER is 1 mi. s. of Gila Cliff Dwellings National Monument, 43 mi. n. of Silver City via SR 15; vehicles pulling trailers 20 feet or longer should use SR 35 north from San Lorenzo. Cultural artifacts and an exhibit about the Apache people and the Gila Wilderness are presented. A 15-minute videotape is shown. Visitor center daily 8-5, Memorial Day weekend-Labor Day; 8-4:30, rest of year. Closed Jan. 1 and Dec. 25. Free. Phone (505) 536-9461.

GRANTS (C-2) pop. 8,806, elev. 6,450′

Navajo rancher Paddy Martinez's curiosity about the odd yellow rock he found on Haystack Mountain about 10 miles west had far-reaching effects. The rock was uranium, and within months of the day he happened upon it in 1950, Grants was transformed from a farming community to a mining town.

With huge contracts from the Atomic Energy Commission for all the uranium they could produce, mining companies rushed to the area, which soon proved to contain one of the largest uranium reserves in the world. A 1982-83 recession forced the closure of mills and mines, bringing to an end a prosperous era.

Grants/Cibola County Chamber of Commerce: 100 N. Iron Ave., P.O. Box 297, Grants, NM 87020; phone (505) 287-4802 or (800) 748-2142.

EL MALPAIS NATIONAL MONUMENT AND NATIONAL CONSERVATION AREA is 25 mi. s. of I-40 via SRs 53 and 117. The monument preserves 114,000 acres of *mal país*, or badlands, a volcanic landscape of lava flows, cinder cones and lava tubes. Primitive camping, hiking, caving and mountain biking are permitted. Information is available at the National Park Information Center, 23 mi. south of Grants on SR 53; the Northwest New Mexico Visitor Center, off I-40 exit 85 in Grants; and the Bureau of Land Management Ranger Station, 9 mi. s. of I-40 on SR 117.

Note: Use heavy footgear and extreme care when walking on the sharp lava. Daily 24 hours; closed Jan. 1, Thanksgiving and Dec. 25. El Malpais Information Center daily 8:30-4:30. Northwest New Mexico Visitor Center daily 9-6, Apr.-Oct.; 8-5, rest of year. Free. Phone (505) 783-4774 or (505) 876-2783. *See Recreation Chart.*

Ice Cave and Bandera Volcano is 25 mi. s.w. of Grants on SR 53 at El Malpais National Monument. A partially collapsed lava tube formed the cave, which contains perpetual formations of ice. At an elevation of 8,000 feet, the temperature is a constant 31 F. The extinct Bandera Volcano, which erupted 10,000 years ago with massive lava flows, rises above the mountain valley. Self-guiding tours depart from the trading post south of SR 53.

Picnicking is permitted. Comfortable shoes are recommended. Allow 1 hour minimum. Daily 8-7, June-Sept.; 8-1 hour before dusk, rest of year. Admission $8.50; over 64, $7; ages 5-12, $4.25. AX, CB, DS, MC, VI. Phone (505) 783-4303 or (888) 423-2283.

NEW MEXICO MINING MUSEUM is 1 mi. w. off I-40 exit 85 at 100 N. Iron Ave. Exhibits chronicle the area's 1950 uranium discovery. Beneath the museum, reached by elevator, is a replica of a mine—complete with equipment. Allow 30 minutes minimum. Mon.-Sat. 9-4; closed Jan. 1, Thanksgiving and Dec. 25. Admission $3; over 59 and ages 7-18, $2. MC, VI. Phone (505) 287-4802 or (800) 748-2142.

HOBBS (E-6) pop. 28,657, elev. 3,621′

Oil and water mix in the economy of Hobbs, a modern city on the western edge of the flat Llano Estacado. Grasslands first attracted farmers and cattlemen to this streamless region in the early 20th century; one of them, James Hobbs, gave his name to the community. A vast underground reserve of water produced bountiful crops of cotton, alfalfa, vegetables and grain as well as a thriving cattle industry.

In 1928, however, the discovery of another kind of well changed pastoral Hobbs into a boomtown. Within a decade the city was the home of some 10,000 citizens, most associated with tapping the oil field that still produces 90 percent of the state's petroleum. Many oil companies operating in the area have headquarters in Hobbs.

World War II aircraft from the New Mexico Wing of the Confederate Air Force are displayed in the Flying Museum at Lea County Regional Airport. For history buffs, the Thelma Webber Southwest Heritage Room in Scarborough Memorial Library at the College of the Southwest, 6610 Lovington Highway, contains prehistoric American Indian artifacts, art pieces and pioneer collectibles.

Hobbs Chamber of Commerce: 400 N. Marland Blvd., Hobbs, NM 88240; phone (505) 397-3202 or (800) 658-6291.

LEA COUNTY COWBOY HALL OF FAME AND WESTERN HERITAGE CENTER is about 4 mi. n. to 5317 Lovington Hwy. (SR 18) on the New Mexico Junior College campus. Well-known ranchers and rodeo performers of Lea County are honored. Exhibits depict the cultures—American Indian to pioneer—that shaped the area for 150 years. Allow 30 minutes minimum. Mon.-Fri. 10-5, Sat. 1-5; closed holidays. Free. Phone (505) 392-5518.

ISLETA PUEBLO (C-3) elev. 4,887′

Thirteen miles south of Albuquerque in the Río Grande Valley, Isleta Pueblo was established in the 14th century. Its name in Spanish means "little island."

SAN AGUSTÍN DE LA ISLETA MISSION is s. of Isleta Blvd., following signs. The heavily buttressed structure was erected in 1613 by Spanish missionary Fray Juan de Salas. During the Pueblo Rebellion the mission was burned partially and then used as a corral. The church, restored after the 1692 reconquest, has been in constant use since. Tues.-Sat. 9-4. Donations. Phone (505) 869-3398.

JÉMEZ PUEBLO (B-3)
pop. 1,953, elev. 5,604′

When European explorers arrived in 1541, the Jémez nation was one of the most powerful pueblo cultures in the Southwest. With an estimated population of 30,000, the Towa-speaking people lived in numerous villages spread far across the high mountain mesas. Clashes between the two cultures eventually ensued and the Jémez defended their land for some 80 years. Eventually, their defenses—but not their traditions—were broken by gunfire.

Through perseverance Jémez traditions, religion and language remain alive. Today the tribe numbers about 3,400 members, many of whom live within the pueblo community of Walatowa.

DID YOU KNOW

Coyotes lived in New Mexico as long ago as 12,000 years.

Note: To preserve privacy and culture, the pueblo is closed to the public except for certain feast days throughout the year when colorful ceremonial dances are performed. Photography, tape recording, sketching or painting are prohibited.

The Walatowa Visitor Center at 7413 SR 4 presents cultural exhibits, photographs, pottery displays, a reconstructed field house and nature walks. On weekends Apr. 1-Oct. 15, the Jémez Red Rocks Open Air Market features traditional foods. For further information, including dates the pueblo is open to the public, phone the visitor center at (505) 834-7235.

The Jémez Mountain Trail (SR 44) is a scenic highway that runs through the Jémez and Zia serves between Cuba and San Ysidro.

JÉMEZ SPRINGS (B-3) pop. 375, elev. 6,200′

About 13 miles north of Jémez Pueblo, the hot mineral waters at Jémez Springs attracted Spanish explorers, Pueblo dwellers, cowboys, miners and pioneers. A bath house built here in the 1870s continues to serve weary travelers. Five miles north are the Soda Dam and Battleship Rock formations; there are picnic facilities at Battleship Rock, and trout fishing is available.

JÉMEZ STATE MONUMENT is 1 mi. n. on SR 4. The site preserves the 500-year-old stone ruins of Giusewa Pueblo, ancestral home of the present-day Jémez people. About 1621 the Spanish built the fortresslike San Jose de los Jémez Mission; its massive walls still stand. A visitor center offers a library, interpretive history exhibits and information about self-guiding tours. Special events are scheduled throughout the year. Wed.-Mon. 8:30-5; closed major holidays. Admission $3, under 17 free. Combination ticket with the Coronado State Monument $5 (see Bernalillo p. 145). MC, VI. Phone (505) 829-3530.

LAGUNA PUEBLO (C-2)
pop. 423, elev. 5,807′

Rich in American Indian history, Laguna Pueblo is divided into six villages, with Old Laguna Village having served as the capital since the early 1300s. Casa Blanca is a tourist and commercial center for the reservation, which is known for its traditional crafts, pottery and jewelry.

Spain's recognition of the pueblo in the late 1600s was followed, as was typical, by the construction of a mission. Completed in 1699, the Mission of the Pueblo of Laguna is a long, narrow stone structure notable for its bright and unusual interior design.

The pueblo can be visited dawn-dusk weekdays, although religious ceremonies are closed to the public during the summer. Photographing, sketching, painting or recording pueblo ceremonies are not permitted.

Governor of the Pueblo—Laguna: P.O. Box 194, Laguna, NM 87026; phone (505) 552-6654.

Shopping areas: Casa Blanca Commercial Center, off I-40, offers a number of stores featuring traditional American Indian crafts and wares.

CASINOS

- **Dancing Eagle Casino** is off I-40 exit 108. Fri.-Sun. 24 hours, Mon.-Thurs. 8 a.m.-4 a.m. Phone (505) 552-1111 or (877) 440-9969.

LAS CRUCES (E-3) pop. 74,267, elev. 3,908′

A little forest of crosses marking the graves of members of a caravan ambushed by Mescalero Apaches soon came to identify this spot on El Camino Real at the foot of the Organ Mountains. By the mid-19th century Las Cruces—the crosses—was a major supply point for mining operations and forts that protected the trade routes to Santa Fe and points west. The largest of these posts was Fort Selden in nearby Radium Springs (see place listing p. 163). In the Mesquite Street Historic District, parts of the original 1849 town still remain. Small adobes painted shades of pink, blue and green are found east of Main Street between Picacho and Lohman avenues.

The town's real foundation, however, is agriculture. Irrigated by the Rio Grande River, the surrounding Mesilla Valley is a leading producer of alfalfa, chilies, onions, corn, cotton and pecans. With a growing roster of manufacturers broadening the economic picture, the city is now the largest business center in southern New Mexico.

Las Cruces, home of New Mexico State University, balances agriculture and industry with education and the Space Age. About 19 miles northeast on US 70/82, then 4 miles south, is White Sands Missile Range where experimental rockets are tested (see place listing p. 180).

Las Cruces Convention and Visitors Bureau: 211 N. Water St., Las Cruces, NM 88001; phone (505) 541-2444 or (800) 343-7827.

BRANIGAN CULTURAL CENTER is on the north end of Downtown Mall at 500 N. Water St.

Traveling and permanent exhibits highlight regional history. Allow 30 minutes minimum. Mon.-Fri. 10-4:30, Sat. 9-1; closed holidays. Free. Phone (505) 541-2155.

Las Cruces Museum of Fine Art is at 490 N. Water St., next to the Branigan Cultural Center. The 5,000-square-foot gallery features changing exhibits of contemporary art, many featuring local artists. Allow 30 minutes minimum. Tues.-Fri. 10-4, Sat. 9-1. Free. Phone (505) 541-2137.

LAS CRUCES MUSEUM OF NATURAL HISTORY is in Mesilla Valley Mall at 700 S. Telshor Blvd. Permanent and temporary exhibits relate to the area's natural history, science and environment. More than 50 live animals and hands-on displays are included. Allow 30 minutes minimum. Mon.-Sat. 10-5 (also Fri. 5-8), Sun. 1-5; closed holidays. Donations. Phone (505) 522-3120.

NEW MEXICO FARM & RANCH HERITAGE MUSEUM is off I-25 exit 1, then 1.5 mi. e. to 4100 Dripping Springs Rd. New Mexico's rural life and 3,000-year-old farming history are presented with interactive displays and demonstrations. The 47-acre site includes a working cattle ranch as well as a dairy farm that offers feeding and milking demonstrations. Family life on a Southwest farm is depicted with museum exhibits, photographs, artifacts and audiovisual presentations. Picnicking is permitted. Food is available. Mon.-Sat. 9-5, Sun. noon-5. Admission $3; over 59, $2; ages 6-17, $1. Phone (505) 522-4100. See color ad.

UNIVERSITY MUSEUM is on the New Mexico State University campus in Kent Hall at Solano Dr. and University Ave. The museum on this 15,500-student campus presents changing exhibits about the archeology, history and culture of southern New Mexico and northern Mexico. Guided tours are available. Allow 30 minutes minimum. Tues.-Sat. noon-4; closed holidays. Donations. Phone (505) 646-3739.

LA UNION (F-3) elev. 3,795′

WINERIES

• **La Viña Winery** is off I-10 exit 2, 4 mi. w. to SR 28, then 1 mi. n. Tours and tastings are offered. Daily noon-5; closed major holidays. Tours are given at 11:30. Hours may vary; phone ahead. Phone (505) 882-7632.

LAS VEGAS (B-4) pop. 14,565, elev. 6,430′

The faint wagon wheel ruts still visible outside Las Vegas attest to the town's era as a mercantile center on the Santa Fe Trail. Las Vegas also was a military post until Fort Union *(see Fort Union National Monument p. 155)* was built. During the 1880s it was known as one of the roughest towns on the frontier, with such desperados as Billy the Kid and Doc Holliday frequenting the area.

The arrival of the Santa Fe Railroad in 1879 ushered in commercial activity and prosperity. Las Vegas soon became a major retail center. The townspeople embarked on a flurry of building and rebuilding, which utilized previously unavailable materials and established an array of architectural styles. The city boasts some 900 historic buildings, many of which are highlighted on walking and driving tours.

Outdoor recreation is available at Storrie Lake and Mora's Morphy Lake state parks *(see Recreation Chart and the AAA Southwestern CampBook)*, 5 and 25 miles north, respectively, off SR 518; and in the Sangre de Cristo Mountains, which rise to the west *(see Santa Fe National Forest p. 174)*.

Las Vegas-San Miguel Chamber of Commerce: 701 Grand Ave., P.O. Box 128, Las Vegas, NM 87701; phone (505) 425-8631 or (800) 832-5947.

Self-guiding tours: A brochure of walking and driving tours is available from the chamber of commerce.

CITY OF LAS VEGAS MUSEUM AND ROUGH RIDERS MEMORIAL COLLECTION is just n. of I-25 exit 345 at 727 N. Grand Ave. The museum commemorates the Rough Riders, the first U.S. volunteer cavalry division led by President Theodore Roosevelt in the Spanish-American War. Displayed are artifacts belonging to regiment members as well as exhibits depicting New Mexico territorial history. Allow 30 minutes minimum. Tues.-Sun. 10-4, May-Oct.; Tues.-Sat. 10-4, rest of year. Closed holidays. Donations. Phone (505) 454-1401, ext. 283.

LAS VEGAS NATIONAL WILDLIFE REFUGE is 6 mi. s.e. via SRs 104 and 281. Covering 8,672 acres of prairie bordered by the timbered canyons of the Gallinas River and Vegosa Creek, the refuge has more than 300 species of wildlife and is noted for its birds of prey. In season, bald eagles, hawks and kestrels are seen. Brochures, an auto loop map and nature-trail permits are available at the refuge office. Allow 1 hour minimum for the driving tour, 2 hours minimum for the nature trail. Auto loop drive open daily dawn-dusk (weather permitting). Office Mon.-Fri. 8-4:30; closed federal holidays. Free. Phone (505) 425-3581.

LINCOLN (D-4) elev. 5,715′

Lincoln's main street is lined with adobe houses and commercial structures dating from the late 19th century, when stock raising, farming, mining and the status of a frontier county seat sustained the village. But Lincoln's prominence in Billy the Kid lore is by far the town's most well-known aspect.

Billy was tried, convicted and sentenced to hang as retribution for a life of rustling and murder, but instead he killed his guards and escaped from Lincoln County Courthouse. Sheriff Pat Garrett tracked him to Fort Sumner, where two shots from his pistol ended the outlaw's story July 14, 1881.

LINCOLN STATE MONUMENT covers the half-mile stretch of town. Nearly a dozen 19th-century stone and adobe buildings are preserved as they appeared during the violent era of the Lincoln County War 1878-81. The Tunstall Store and the Lincoln County Courthouse Museum contain exhibits. Other buildings include the Montaño Store and the San Juan Mission Church.

Allow 1 hour minimum. Daily 8:30-4:30; closed major holidays. Admission $6, under 17 free with adult. Phone (505) 653-4372.

LINCOLN NATIONAL FOREST

Elevations in the forest range from 4,440 ft. at Grapevine Canyon to 11,580 ft. at Lookout Mountain. Refer to AAA maps for additional elevation information.

In south central New Mexico, most of the Sacramento, Jicarilla, Guadalupe and Capitan mountains lie within the three units of Lincoln National Forest. Covering 1,103,466 acres of pine, juniper and fir timber, the forest ranges from desert to subalpine terrain. The Smokey Bear Ranger District includes two wilderness areas offering pristine back country for horseback riding or hiking trips. The district office is located in the mountain community of Ruidoso *(see place listing p. 165)* which is a popular recreation and resort center.

The Smokey Bear Ranger District also was home to the original Smokey Bear, the living symbol of fire prevention. The Smokey Bear Historical Park in Capitan, north of Ruidoso, displays memorabilia about the tiny cub and information about wildfire prevention. In fire season from April through July, camping fires may be prohibited. Along the Billy the Kid Scenic Byway are a variety of communities, scenic vistas and attractions that make this an area well worth exploring.

The Sacramento Ranger District is located in and around the small village of Cloudcroft *(see place listing p. 152)*. Nestled high in the tall pines, Cloudcroft attracts many who want to escape the heat of the desert below and enjoy fresh, cool air. Recreation activities range from what is purported to be the highest 9-hole golf course in the country, to camping, hiking, mountain biking and some of the best hunting in the state—turkey, bear, elk and deer. The Sunspot Scenic Highway, SR 6563, offers spectacular views of the Tularosa Basin as well as of the dunes of White Sands National Monument *(see place listing p. 181)*.

The southern Guadalupe Ranger District embraces the relatively little-traveled, semiarid Guadalupe Mountains. A waterfall, uncommon to this region, is the focus of an oasis in the desert at Sitting Bull Falls Picnic Area, 49 miles northwest of Carlsbad via US 285, SR 137 and FR 276. Numerous caves can be explored; permits must be obtained at least 2 weeks in advance. Phone (505) 885-4181.

For further information contact the Lincoln Forest Supervisor's Office, 1101 New York Ave., Alamogordo, NM 88310; phone (505) 434-7200, or TTY (505) 434-7296. *See Recreation Chart.*

LOS ALAMOS (B-3) pop. 11,909, elev. 7,320′

In 1942 the federal government selected Los Alamos Ranch School as the top secret, maximum security site for the Manhattan Project, an atomic bomb research and testing program where Little Boy and Fat Man—the atomic bombs that ended World War II—were built. By 1945, when the first atomic device was detonated at Trinity Site *(see White Sands Missile Range p. 180)*, more than 3,000 civilian and military personnel were working at the laboratory.

Los Alamos National Laboratory continues to apply science to issues of national security, economic strength and energy security. Its staff of nearly 9,000 conducts extensive research about technology associated with nuclear weapons, deterrence and other defense applications, energy production, health, safety and environmental concerns, astrophysics and life sciences.

Explosions of another sort created the rugged setting that was so essential for maintaining the secrecy of the Manhattan Project. About a million years ago the volcanic vents that had built the Jémez Mountains issued 100 cubic miles of ash and pumice, then collapsed. The result is Valle Grande, one of the largest measured calderas on earth, covering 148 square miles, with a rim averaging 500 feet above its floor.

SR 4, about 15 miles west of Los Alamos, outlines the crater's southern curve and permits views into its vast, grassy bowl. The erupted ash hardened into a layer of tuff, the Pajarito Plateau, characterized by a remoteness that is protected by the finger canyons that serrate its edges. Within the plateau Bandelier National Monument *(see place listing p. 145)* contains extensive Ancestral Puebloan ruins. Guided hiking trips, wagon rides and van tours of Valles Caldera National Preserve *(see Recreation Chart)* offer a glimpse of the region's geology, archeology and wildlife; phone (505) 661-3333 for reservations.

Los Alamos County Chamber of Commerce and Visitor Center: 109 Central Park Sq., P.O. Box 460, Los Alamos, NM 87544; phone (505) 662-8105.

Self-guiding tours: A guidebook available at Los Alamos County Historical Museum *(see attraction listing)* outlines a walking tour of local history sites.

ART CENTER AT FULLER LODGE is at 2132 Central Ave. Changing exhibits showcase the work of northern New Mexico artists. The center occupies the south wing of Historic Fuller Lodge, which was home to the Los Alamos Ranch School prior to World War II. Allow 1 hour minimum. Mon.-Sat. 10-4; closed Jan. 1, July 4, Thanksgiving and Dec. 25. Free. Phone (505) 662-9331.

 BRADBURY SCIENCE MUSEUM is at 15th St. and Central Ave. More than 40 interactive exhibits interpret the history of Los Alamos National Laboratory and its contributions to modern science, research and technology. The museum focuses on the laboratory's role in the development of the Manhattan Project and its current mission of national security. Tues.-Sat. 10-5, Sun.-Mon. 1-5; closed Jan. 1, Thanksgiving and Dec. 25. Free. Phone (505) 667-4444.

LOS ALAMOS COUNTY HISTORICAL MUSEUM is next to Fuller Lodge on Central Ave. A restored log and stone cottage once served as the infirmary and guest house for the Los Alamos Ranch School. The museum details area history, including the Manhattan Project. Newspaper articles, military uniforms, photographs of bomb tests and changing exhibits are displayed. A Tewa ruin dating from the 14th century and a relocated homesteader's cabin are other highlights.

Mon.-Sat. 9:30-4:30, Sun. 11-5, Apr.-Oct.; Mon.-Sat. 10-4, Sun. 1-4, rest of year. Closed Jan. 1, Easter, Thanksgiving and Dec. 25. Donations. Phone (505) 662-6272 or (505) 662-4493.

MADRID (B-3) pop. 149, elev. 6,020′

Once a ghost town, Madrid (MAD-rid) is coming back to life as artists and merchants transform abandoned buildings into studios, galleries and shops. For nearly a century Madrid prospered as a coal mining town, supplying the military in Santa Fe and Las Vegas during the Civil War and producing commercially after the Santa Fe Railway reached neighboring Cerrillos in the 1880s. Madrid continued as a coal center until the 1950s, when the development of cheaper and cleaner fuels marked the beginning of its decline.

Coal was not the first prize for miners in the region. As early as 1,000 B.C., prehistoric people worked the Cerrillos turquoise mines with stone axes and antler picks. Perhaps the oldest mine in North America, Cerrillos provided a valuable trade commodity for the San Marcos and Santo Domingo pueblos. Cerrillos turquoise has been unearthed in Aztec jewelry. The Tiffany Company purchased mining rights in the late 1800s, extracting some $2 million worth of the stone.

SAVE **OLD COAL MINE MUSEUM** is at 2846 SR 14. This once bustling 1890s mining village became a ghost town when digging ceased in 1959. A restored railroad locomotive, mining equipment, vintage vehicles and various buildings, including the mine office and a machinist shop remain. Visitors may enter a portion of the mine shaft. The Engine House Theatre Melodrama presents classic melodramas in season.

Food is available. Allow 1 hour minimum. Daily 10-6; closed Dec. 25. Plays are offered Sat. at 3 and 7, Sun. and Mon. holidays at 3, Memorial Day to mid-Oct. Admission $4; over 60, $3; ages 6-11, $1. Melodrama $10; over 60, $8; under 12, $5. DS, MC, VI. Phone (505) 438-3780.

MESCALERO (E-4) pop. 1,233, elev. 6,600′

Mescalero is the largest town within the Mescalero Apache Reservation and serves as its headquarters. The 461,000-acre tract embraces the Sierra Blanca Mountains and their wealth of timber, grazing lands and scenic beauty. Among the last American Indians to lay down arms against the U.S. government, the tribe now operates as a federally chartered corporation.

Capitalizing on their land's recreational potential, the Mescaleros have developed a ski area and a major resort near Ruidoso *(see place listing p. 165)*. Information about ceremonials and recreational facilities is available from the community center; phone (505) 671-4494.

MESILLA (E-3) pop. 2,180, elev. 3,886′

Mesilla had its official beginning around 1848, when some residents of a nearby community that had become part of the United States by the Treaty of Guadalupe Hidalgo elected to move to the town in order to retain Mexican citizenship. They received a Mexican land grant in 1850, but in 1854 the Gadsden Purchase transferred nearly 30,000 square miles west of the Rio Grande River to the United States.

The combination of excellent farmland and strategic location spurred Mesilla's growth. By the time the Butterfield Trail Overland mail route established a major stage stop in 1858, Mesilla was the largest town in the southern part of New Mexico Territory, which then included present-day Arizona. By contrast, El Paso, Texas, and neighboring Las Cruces *(see place listing p. 159)* were mere hamlets. Billy the Kid was tried and sentenced in Mesilla, a former territorial capital.

The Mesilla Plaza, designated a state monument, hosts many local cultural events. Its surrounding buildings, which have been restored to their 19th-century appearance, now house shops and businesses.

Old Mesilla Visitors Center: 2231 Avenida de Masilla (SR 28), P.O. Box 116, Mesilla, NM 88046; phone (505) 647-9698.

NAMBÉ PUEBLO (B-3) elev. 6,058′

This settlement in the foothills of the Sangre de Cristo Mountains was established in the 1300s. Its name in the Tewa language means "people of the round earth."

NAMBÉ PUEBLO is 8 mi. s. of Española on US 84, then 2 mi. e. on SR 503. Fleeing drought, disease and Navajo invasions, the Pojoaque settled in the Rio Grande Valley and prospered until an 1890 smallpox epidemic decimated the population. A few survivors reclaimed the land in 1932, and today some 1,800 people live there. Above the pueblo, Nambé Falls Recreation Area is popular for camping, fishing, hiking, picnicking and boating. Pueblo Mon.-Fri. 8-5. Recreation area daily dawn-dusk. Pueblo free. Recreation area $5. Still-camera photography fee $10. Fishing fee $10. Phone (505) 455-2304 or (505) 455-2036.

OJO CALIENTE (B-3) elev. 6,257′

First enjoyed by American Indians, then by Spaniards, the Ojo Caliente Mineral Springs are still sought for their purported therapeutic properties. Fueled by a volcanic aquifer, five springs each supply a different mineral: iron, sodium sulphate, lithia, soda and arsenic.

Perhaps additional qualities are lent to the springs by virtue of their being sacred. According to Tewa tradition, the spiritual figure Poseyemo returns to the waters each year to visit her grandmother. The springs themselves were considered to be the windows between the outer world and the below world, where the people originated. The Spanish name, *Ojo Caliente*, means "hot eye." Numerous bath facilities and pools are open to the public; phone (505) 583-2233 or (800) 222-9162.

PECOS NATIONAL HISTORICAL PARK (B-4)

Two miles south of Pecos on SR 63, Pecos National Historical Park preserves the ruins of one of the largest ancient pueblos as well as two mission churches built by Franciscans in the 17th and 18th centuries. The American Indian population dwindled over the years because of famine, diseases, emigration and the changing needs of the mission. In 1838 the remaining Pecos people moved to Jémez Pueblo *(see place listing p. 158)*.

Visitors can walk through the ruins on a 1.2-mile self-guiding trail; guided 1- to 2-hour tours are available by reservation. A visitor center offers a film depicting Pecos' history and displays hand-carved furniture, artifacts from excavations, tin chandeliers and original artwork.

Picnicking is permitted. Allow 1 hour, 30 minutes minimum. Daily 8-6, Memorial Day weekend-Labor Day; 8-5, rest of year. Closed Jan. 1 and Dec. 25. Admission $3. Phone (505) 757-6414, ext. 1.

PICURÍS PUEBLO (B-4) elev. 7,320′

Once one of the largest Tewa pueblos, Picurís (or *We-Lai*) is now among the smallest. Tribal leaders estimate the number of "people of the hidden valley" at less than 300. Picurís pottery is known for its sparkling bronze finish, which comes from mica in the regional clay.

PICURÍS PUEBLO is about 7 mi. n.w. of Española off SR 75. Believed to have been established 1250-1300, the pueblo was a site of unrest during the revolts of the late 17th century. Mission of San Lorenzo, erected after the 1692 reconquest, has been in use for more than 2 centuries. The Picurís Pueblo Museum displays artifacts excavated from the pueblo. Food is available. Pueblo and museum daily 8-5. Fees apply for sketching, videotaping and still-camera photography. Phone (505) 587-2519.

PILAR (B-4) elev. 6,082'

The Rio Grande River flows through a deep gorge between Pilar and Taos, making this one of the state's prime white-water rafting areas. Hot springs along the river are testament to ongoing seismic activity on the Rio Grande Rift, which stretches from Colorado to Mexico.

RECREATIONAL ACTIVITIES
White-water Rafting

- **Big River Raft Trips** departs various locations. Write Box 16D, Pilar, NM 87531. Daily Apr.-Sept. Phone (505) 758-9711 or (800) 748-3760.
- [SAVE] **Far Flung Adventures** departs from Pilar Cafe. Write P.O. Box 707, El Prado, NM 87529. Daily late Apr.-Sept. 30. Phone (505) 758-2628 or (800) 359-2627.

PINOS ALTOS (E-2) elev. 6,997'

When John Birch bent to drink from Bear Creek in 1860, he found that the stream would satisfy more than just thirst—the gold glimmering in the water would assuage a hunger for wealth. News of riches spread quickly, and within 3 months Birchville, renamed Pinos Altos in 1866, emerged as a camp of 700 miners. In 1868 it was designated the seat of newly formed Grant County.

Pinos Altos, with a small population descended from its founders, retains the atmosphere of a 19th-century frontier town. The dirt streets, saloon, opera house and store have been restored or remain essentially as they existed in the 1860s. Pinos Altos Historical Museum, housed in an 1866 log cabin, preserves many items from the town's mining era.

Silver City/Grant County Chamber of Commerce—Pinos Altos: 201 N. Hudson St., Silver City, NM 88061; phone (505) 538-3785 or (800) 548-9378.

POJOAQUE PUEBLO (B-3) elev. 5,852'

At the joining of three rivers, Pojoaque (po-WALK-ee) was named "the water-drinking place" by Tewa travelers. Smallpox wiped out the settlement twice before it was abandoned in 1915. Tribal members returned in the 1930s, and casino gambling now fuels the local economy.

POJOAQUE PUEBLO is 8 mi. s. of Española on US 84 to SR 503 at 96 Cities of Gold Rd. The Pojoaque people's Tewa ancestors migrated to the Four Corners region in the first millennium. The Poeh Cultural Center, 78 Cities of Gold Rd., presents centuries of culture through art, archeological artifacts and history exhibits. Photography is not permitted. Daily 9-5. Cultural center Mon.-Fri. 8-5. Free. Phone (505) 455-1110.

PORTALES (D-6) pop. 11,131, elev. 4,009'

The discovery of shallow groundwater in 1890 ensured the prosperity of Portales. Wells irrigate thousands of acres of peanuts, sorghum, cotton and other crops that surround this commercial center. Dairy production and propagation of drought-resistant crops also are important.

Blackwater Draw Archaeological Site, 7 miles northeast via US 70 on SR 467, has yielded evidence of Paleo-Indian habitation stretching back more than 11,000 years. The 3,600-student Eastern New Mexico University, which occupies a 550-acre campus off US 70 at the south edge of town, maintains Blackwater Draw Museum on US 70. Roosevelt County Museum on campus traces more recent area history, focusing on the late 19th and early 20th centuries. If you are looking to generate some energy, drive past the Dalley Windmills, one of the largest such collections in the country; they are off SR 70 at 1506 S. Kilgore.

Various recreational pursuits are available at Oasis State Park *(see Recreation Chart and the AAA Southwestern CampBook)*, 5.7 miles north on SR 467, then 2 miles west.

Roosevelt County Chamber of Commerce: 100 S. Ave. A, Portales, NM 88130; phone (505) 356-8541 or (800) 635-8036.

RADIUM SPRINGS (E-3)
pop. 1,518, elev. 3,980'

As its name suggests, Radium Springs first became a travel destination for its hot mineral waters. The Apaches considered the springs sacred, and Chief Geronimo is said to have camped here. Soldiers from Fort Selden enjoyed a bathhouse near the springs' source, a rhyolite dome along the Rio Grande River. In the 1930s, the Santa Fe Railroad carried weekend travelers from El Paso to the Radium Hot Springs Resort. The temperature of the springs averaged 127 F.

FORT SELDEN STATE MONUMENT is at 1280 Ft. Selden Rd. The Mogollón farmed this site long before Civil War forces arrived. Crumbling adobe walls are all that remain of the 1865 fort, which protected travelers and settlers in the Mesilla Valley from desperados and Apache Indians. After the war, African-American "Buffalo Soldiers" occupied the fort. As a boy in the 1880s, Gen. Douglas MacArthur also lived here while his father served as post commander. A visitor center displays military artifacts.

Wed.-Mon. 8:30-5; closed major holidays. Living-history demonstrations are occasionally offered Sat.-Sun. 1-4, May 1-Sept. 15. Admission $3, under 17 free. Phone (505) 526-8911.

RATON (A-5) pop. 7,282, elev. 6,680'

In 1866 Uncle Dick Wootton, an enterprising man, completed 27 miles of road over Raton Pass, set up a tollgate at his ranch near the summit and charged $1.50 per wagon to use his improvement. As the Santa Fe Trail was the main route between the East and Southwest, he did well. It is said that his bank deposits consisted of whiskey kegs full of silver dollars.

By 1880 this pleasant watering hole 7 miles south of the summit of Raton Pass evolved into a thriving community. Raton based its economy on the railroad, commerce, cattle ranching and, later, the development of nearby coal reserves. These industries, along with outdoor recreation and the tourism generated by the ease of traveling I-25, continue to sustain Raton. The name, pronounced *ra-TONE*, means "rat" in Spanish.

The Victorian architecture along First Street preserves the atmosphere of Raton's 19th-century mining and railroad heyday. The 1890s Palace Hotel is at First and Cook streets.

Sugarite Canyon State Park *(see Recreation Chart and the AAA Southwestern CampBook)*, 10 miles northeast via SR 72, provides lakes and picnic sites.

Raton Chamber and Economic Development Council, Inc.: 100 Clayton Rd., P.O. Box 1211, Raton, NM 87740; phone (505) 445-3689 or (800) 638-6161.

Self-guiding tours: Brochures detailing tours of the city's historic district are available from the chamber and economic development council.

NRA WHITTINGTON CENTER is 4 mi. w. of I-25 exit 446 on US 64. A variety of gun ranges are available at the National Rifle Association's 33,300-acre shooting facility. An unaltered section of the Santa Fe Trail cuts through the complex. Allow 1 hour minimum. Daily 8-5; closed Dec. 25. Visitor center free. Gun ranges $15. Other fees may apply. AX, DS, MC, VI. Phone (505) 445-3615.

RATON MUSEUM is at 216 S. First St. Photographs, household articles, railroad and coal camp memorabilia and other items depict 19th-century life. Tues.-Sat. 9-5, Memorial Day-Labor Day; Wed.-Sat. 10-4, rest of year. Closed holidays. Free. Phone (505) 445-8979.

RED RIVER (A-4) pop. 484, elev. 8,650'

Gold drew early settlers to this former frontier town on the northeastern face of Wheeler Peak. Today's visitors are drawn by the prospect of fun. Skiing and snowmobiling are popular winter pursuits, while hiking, fishing and mountain biking lure summer guests.

Red River Chamber of Commerce: 100 E. Main St., P.O. Box 870, Red River, NM 87558; phone (505) 754-2366.

RECREATIONAL ACTIVITIES
Skiing

- **Enchanted Forest Cross Country Ski Area** is 3 mi. e. at 417 W. Main St. Daily mid-Nov. to late Mar. Phone (800) 966-9381.

- **Red River Ski & Snowboard Area** is at 400 Pioneer Rd. Write P.O. Box 900, Red River, NM 87558. Daily 9-4, late Nov.-late Mar. Phone (505) 754-2223.

RIO RANCHO (B-3) pop. 51,765, elev. 5,550'

The housing development of Rio Rancho Estates opened outside Albuquerque in the early 1960s. Lots were marketed to retirees from the midwest. By the time the community was incorporated in 1981, it numbered 10,000 residents and covered 72 square miles. Intel Corporation opened an office here in the 1980s, bringing younger home buyers. Now the largest private industrial employer in New Mexico, Intel employs more than 5,000 people in the manufacture of microchips and computer processors.

J&R VINTAGE AUTO MUSEUM is off I-25 exit 242, 2.4 mi. w. on US 550, then .5 mi. s. to 3650A SR 528. More than 60 restored vintage cars are displayed, including several that have competed in the Great American Race. Highlights include a 1902 Oldsmobile, a 1917 Marmon, a 1928 Model A Ford and a 1932 Packard. Allow 30 minutes minimum. Mon.-Sat. 10-6, Sun. 1-5, Memorial Day-Labor Day; Mon.-Sat. 10-5, rest of year. Closed Thanksgiving and Dec. 25. Admission $4; over 55, $3; ages 6-12, $1.50. DS, MC, VI. Phone (505) 867-1885.

RODEO (F-1) elev. 4,128'

In a line of ghost towns, Rodeo was one of the few survivors after the passing of the El Paso and Southwestern Railroad. The train line, built in 1952 to connect El Paso, Texas, with copper mines in Bisbee, Arizona, closed in 1952.

CHIRICAHUA GALLERY is on SR 80. Works by local artists and artisans include paintings, photographs, ceramics, basketry, woodwork, quilted items, leather work, silver jewelry and pottery. Allow 30 minutes minimum. Mon.-Sat. 10-4; closed Thanksgiving, Dec. 25 and Dec. 31. Free. Phone (505) 557-2225.

ROSWELL (D-5) pop. 45,293, elev. 3,573'

During the 16th century, Spanish explorers discovered the area's springs, an oasis in the scorching plains and desert. By the 1870s Roswell was an established crossroads and by 1891 residents realized that this abundance of water could sustain large herds of cattle and large fields of crops. By 1910 it was one of the most prosperous, fastest growing towns in New Mexico. Dr. Robert Goddard conducted rocketry experiments on the nearby prairie

1930-41; his work ultimately made possible man's venture into space. Outside New Mexico, Roswell is probably best noted for UFO sightings and an alleged spaceship crash in 1947.

Roswell's economy is based on agriculture, manufacturing and oil production. Some 6,000 students attend a branch of Eastern New Mexico University and the New Mexico Military Institute has an enrollment of 1,000. These schools as well as fine museums and a symphony add to the cultural life.

Ten miles east on US 380, Bottomless Lakes State Park *(see Recreation Chart and the AAA Southwestern CampBook)* offers water recreation.

Roswell Chamber of Commerce: 131 W. Second St., P.O. Drawer 70, Roswell, NM 88202; phone (505) 623-5695.

BITTER LAKE NATIONAL WILDLIFE REFUGE is 8 mi. e. via Pine Lodge Rd. The refuge occupies more than 24,000 acres of grassland, ponds and desert shrubs. A 7-mile drive tour offers glimpses of wintering waterfowl, sandhill cranes, roadrunners, quails, pheasants and 300 other species of birds. Salt Creek Wilderness can be entered only on foot or horseback; the access point is off US 70 near the Pecos River. The best time for wildlife viewing is October through February.

Daily 30 minutes before dawn to 30 minutes after dusk (weather permitting). Free. Phone (505) 622-6755.

INTERNATIONAL UFO MUSEUM & RESEARCH CENTER is at 114 N. Main St. The center is dedicated to the study of Unidentified Flying Objects (UFOs) thought to be from other planets. Exhibits include paintings, murals and dioramas depicting the purported 1947 crash of a UFO in Roswell along with other alleged sightings of alien beings and their spacecraft. On the premises is a research library with extensive works dealing with UFOs. Allow 1 hour, 30 minutes minimum. Daily 9-5. Admission $2; under 19, $1. Phone (505) 625-9495.

LT. GEN. DOUGLAS L. McBRIDE MUSEUM is at W. College Blvd. and N. Main St., on the campus of New Mexico Military Institute. Displays examine methods of waging war and preserving peace. Exhibits emphasize the service of New Mexicans and the institute's graduates throughout American history. Tues.-Fri. 8:30-11:30 and 1-3; closed holidays. Donations. Phone (505) 624-8220.

ROSWELL MUSEUM AND ART CENTER is in the Civic Center Plaza at 11th and Main sts. Known for its New Mexico modernism collection, the museum showcases Southwestern culture through historical artifacts and fine art. Highlights include works by Andrew Dasburg, Stuart Davis, Marsden Hartley, Victor Higgins and Georgia O'Keeffe. Roswell landscape artist Peter Hurd also is represented.

The Goddard wing has a re-creation of Dr. Robert Goddard's early laboratory with displays about rocketry and space. Traveling exhibits are shown regularly. The Robert H. Goddard Planetarium presents astronomy programs and multimedia presentations. Mon.-Sat. 9-5, Sun. and holidays 1-5; closed Jan. 1, Thanksgiving and Dec. 25. Free. Phone (505) 624-6744.

SPRING RIVER PARK AND ZOO is 1 mi. e. off US 285/Main St. on College Blvd., or 1 mi. n. of US 380/Second St. on Atkinson St. More than 140 animals and birds represent 50 species. Within the 36-acre zoo are a wooden-horse carousel, a miniature train ride and a children's fishing lake. Picnicking is permitted. Allow 1 hour minimum. Daily 10-dusk; closed Dec. 25. Free. Train rides 25c. Phone (505) 624-6760.

RUIDOSO (D-4) pop. 7,698, elev. 6,720′

With skiing in winter, golfing, riding, hiking and fishing in spring and summer, and the gilded beauty of the aspen highlighting autumn, Ruidoso is among the state's premier year-round mountain playgrounds. So popular is it during the summer that prospective visitors are advised to make reservations several months in advance for holiday weekends.

The town's setting is the timbered Sacramento Mountains within Lincoln National Forest *(see place listing p. 160)*. The community that now extends 10 miles along the Ruidoso River began in the 1890s as a tin-roofed trading post. The post's old waterwheel still stands on the main street.

The Billy the Kid Trail is an 84-mile National Scenic Byway offering sweeping mountain views and a glimpse into the desperado's past. Maps and information are available from the chamber of commerce.

Ruidoso Valley Chamber of Commerce and Visitors Center: 720 Sudderth Dr., Ruidoso, NM 88355; phone (505) 257-7395 or (800) 253-2255.

RECREATIONAL ACTIVITIES

Skiing

- **Ski Apache** is 16 mi. n.w. at the end of SR 532. Write P.O. Box 220, Ruidoso, NM 88355. Daily 8:45-4, Thanksgiving-early Apr. Phone (505) 336-4356 or (505) 257-9001 for ski conditions.

RUIDOSO DOWNS (D-4)
pop. 1,894, elev. 6,420′

From its humble origins in a mountain field in 1947, Ruidoso Downs Race Track has become a premier facility for Quarter Horse and Thoroughbred racing and one of the area's major attractions. The All-American Futurity is held Labor Day, the final day of the racing season. Tagged the world's richest Quarter Horse race—the purse exceeds $2 million—it is the final leg of Quarter Horse racing's Triple Crown. The first two, the Ruidoso Quarter Horse Futurity and the Rainbow Futurity, take place at Ruidoso Downs in June and July, respectively. Phone (505) 378-4431 or (505) 378-4140.

Note: Policies concerning admittance of children to pari-mutuel betting facilities vary. Phone for information.

THE HUBBARD MUSEUM OF THE AMERICAN WEST is 1 mi. e. of the racetrack off US 70. The museum displays horse-related items from the Anne C. Stradling Collection. Included are life-size models, saddles, wagons and carriages, harnesses and paintings. Kids Corner entices children with a mannequin horse. The Ruidoso Downs Hall of Fame displays photographs, videotapes, trophies and silks chronicling Quarter Horse racing. Outdoors is the monumental horse sculpture "Free Spirits at Noisy Water."

Allow 1 hour minimum. Daily 9-5; closed Thanksgiving and Dec. 25. Admission $6; over 59 and military with ID $5; ages 6-16, $2. AX, DS, MC, VI. Phone (505) 378-4142.

SALINAS PUEBLO MISSIONS NATIONAL MONUMENT (D-4)

Near Mountainair, Salinas Pueblo Missions National Monument contains three geographically and historically related pueblos and 17th-century Spanish Franciscan missions. The 1,071-acre park includes the former Gran Quivira National Monument and two former state monuments, Abó and Quarai.

Because there was no further resettlement after the Spaniards and the Tompiro and Tewa Indians abandoned the site in the late 17th century, the masonry ruins are remarkably intact. A visitor center on US 60 a block west of SR 55 offers a 15-minute orientation film and an exhibit depicting regional history. All three sites open daily 9-6, Memorial Day weekend-Labor Day; 9-5, rest of year. Visitor center daily 8-5. Closed Jan. 1, Thanksgiving and Dec. 25. Free. Phone (505) 847-2585.

ABÓ RUINS is 9 mi. w. of Mountainair on US 60, then .7 mi. n. on SR 513. Once a large pueblo, this Tompiro Indian village was abandoned in the 1670s. Ruins of the 1620 church San Gregorio de Abó, built in medieval style with a 40-foot-tall buttressed curtain wall, rise curiously out of the desert. Brochures, available at the visitor center, as well as interpretive trail markers offer information for self-guiding tours. Picnicking is permitted. Allow 1 hour minimum. Daily 9-6, Memorial Day weekend-Labor Day; 9-5, rest of year. Closed Jan. 1, Thanksgiving and Dec. 25. Phone (505) 847-2400.

GRAN QUIVIRA RUINS is 26 mi. s. of Mountainair on SR 55. Gran Quivira was one of the most populous pueblos of Salinas Province, with more than 2,000 inhabitants. The 20 limestone house mounds date 1300-1670; 300 rooms and six kivas can be viewed. Also preserved are 17th-century ruins from San Isidro and San Buenaventura. A visitor center displays artifacts and interpretive exhibits. Interpretive trail markers provide information for self-guiding tours. Picnicking is permitted. Allow 1 hour minimum. Daily 9-6, Memorial Day weekend-Labor

Day; 9-5, rest of year. Closed Jan. 1, Thanksgiving and Dec. 25. Phone (505) 847-2770.

QUARAI RUINS is 8 mi. n. of Mountainair on SR 55 and 1 mi. w. on a hard-surface road. The site preserves 10 large unexcavated pueblo house mounds and the remains of the 1630 church and convent of Nuestra Senora de La Purisma Concepción de Cuarac. The sandstone church has walls nearly 40 feet high. Another small church may date from 1820 or earlier. A museum displays a scale model of the older church and other exhibits. A brochure outlining self-guiding tours is available. Picnicking is permitted. Daily 9-6, Memorial Day weekend-Labor Day; 9-5, rest of year. Closed Jan. 1, Thanksgiving and Dec. 25. Phone (505) 847-2290.

SAN ANTONIO (D-3) elev. 4,568′

Founded in 1629 as a mission, San Antonio is a trading center for nearby farms and ranches. Corn and alfalfa thrive in the fields along the Rio Grande Valley. To the southeast, beyond the river valley, lies a 35-mile-wide, 90-mile-long stretch of merciless desert. In the days of El Camino Real the desert earned the name Jornada del Muerto—Journey of the Dead.

Some 21 miles south across the river from San Marcial is Valverde Battlefield, scene of the first Civil War engagement in New Mexico. Confederate forces led by Gen. H.H. Sibley beat back Union troops from nearby Fort Craig in a day-long battle in February 1862, and went on to occupy Albuquerque. Eroded remnants of the fort survive and are accessible by way of a 5-mile gravel road; however, the battlefield is not.

San Antonio is the birthplace of famed hotelier Conrad Hilton. The ruins of the Hilton family's mercantile boardinghouse and home are 1 mile south of US 380 west of SR 1.

BOSQUE DEL APACHE NATIONAL WILDLIFE REFUGE is 8 mi. s. of I-25 exit 139 at US 380 and SR 1. A 12-mile driving route and several interpretive trails thread through 57,000 acres of marsh, grasslands and desert uplands. A visitor center contains exhibits about the refuge's inhabitants, which include sandhill cranes, snow geese, ducks and more than 300 other bird species, as well as mammals, reptiles and amphibians. The Laura Jean Deal Desert Arboretum features one of the most complete collections of cacti, succulents and native trees and plants in the southwest.

Wildlife viewing is best late November through early February; plants are in bloom from April through August. Fishing and hunting are permitted in designated areas; restrictions apply. Allow 1 hour, 30 minutes minimum. Refuge daily 1 hour before dawn-1 hour after dusk. Visitor center Mon.-Fri. 7:30-4, Sat.-Sun. 8-4:30. Automobile route $3 per private vehicle. AX, DS, MC, VI. Phone (505) 835-1828.

SANDIA PARK (C-3) elev. 7,159′

Sandia Park is about 25 miles east of Albuquerque on the Turquoise Trail National Scenic Byway, a mountain route that passes through the Sandias and Cibola National Forest *(see place listing p. 151).*

TINKERTOWN MUSEUM is 1.5 mi. w. on SR 536 to 121 Sandia Crest Rd. The museum displays the life's work of New Mexican folk artist Ross Ward, whose carved and hand-painted miniatures include an animated Western town and a three-ring circus. A wall made of more than 50,000 glass bottles surrounds the museum. Daily 9-6, Apr.-Oct. Last admission 30 minutes before closing. Admission $3; over 62, $2.50; ages 4-16, $1. AX, DS, MC, VI. Phone (505) 281-5233.

SAN FELIPE PUEBLO (B-3)
pop. 2,080, elev. 5,130′

Founded in 1706, San Felipe Pueblo is the most culturally conservative of the Keresan-speaking communities. Villagers are protective of ancient traditions and invite visitors only during Green Corn Dances in May, when hundreds of men, women and children dance in traditional costumes. San Pedro's Day Festival in June also is a popular event.

CASINOS

- **San Felipe's Casino Hollywood** is at 25 Hagan Rd. Mon.-Thurs. 8 a.m.-4 a.m.; Fri.-Sun. 24 hours. Phone (505) 867-6700 or (877) 529-2946.

SAN ILDEFONSO PUEBLO (B-3)
pop. 458, elev. 5,550′

Twenty-three miles north of Santa Fe, this settlement sits in the shadow of Black Mesa. This natural mountain stronghold helped the Pueblo people withstand a Spanish attack in 1694.

SAN ILDEFONSO PUEBLO is 13 mi. s. of Española via SR 30/502. For nearly 100 years, this Tewa village has been at the center of a pueblo arts revival. It is best known as the home of Maria Martinez, celebrated potter and creator of the black-on-black pottery prized by collectors. Family members and other potters continue her tradition. A museum depicts pottery-making techniques. Shops on the main plaza display and sell artwork.

Daily 8-5; closed holidays. Hours may vary; phone ahead. Admission $5 per private vehicle. Fees for drawing $25, videotaping $20, still-camera photography $10. Phone (505) 455-3549.

SAN JUAN PUEBLO (B-3) elev. 5,660′

Juan de Oñate established the first Spanish capital of New Mexico here in 1598 at the Tewa settlement of *O'ke,* where villagers offered the explorer a hospitable welcome. Oñate named the pueblo San Juan de los Caballeros in honor of his horsemen. A traditional meeting ground, the pueblo became so powerful that only an *O'ke* native had the authority to declare war for the Pueblo Indians. Today, San Juan is one of the largest Tewa-speaking communities.

SAN JUAN PUEBLO is 4 mi. n.e. of Española off SR 68. Some 2,000 inhabitants of San Juan Pueblo—headquarters for the Eight Northern Indian Pueblos Council—maintain farms and produce red pottery, beadwork and embroidery. Ceremonial dances are held throughout the year and most are open to the public. Dance of the Matachines is performed Dec. 25. Inquire about photography restrictions. Daily dawn-dusk. Free. Photography fee $5. Phone (505) 852-4400.

SANTA CLARA PUEBLO (B-3) elev. 5,605′

In the 13th century, the Pajarito Plateau Indians carved their first dwellings into the cliffs above Santa Clara Canyon, where they hunted and farmed. Three hundred years later, drought forced the tribe to move east to the Río Grande Valley, site of Santa Clara Pueblo. The Puye Cliff Dwellings included some 740 rooms and ceremonial areas. The ruins were closed to the public after the 2000 Cerro Grande fire, which damaged 45,000 acres in northern New Mexico.

SANTA CLARA PUEBLO is 2 mi. s. of Española on SR 30. Established in 1550, this Tewa-speaking pueblo traces its ancestry to the Puye cliff dwellers. Santa Clara artists are noted for their glossy black and red pottery adorned with meticulously incised designs as well as for their paintings and sculpture. Daily 9-4. Free. Photography fee $5. Phone (505) 753-7326.

SANTA FE (B-4) pop. 62,203, elev. 6,989′
See map page 170.

Like the combination of green and red chile sauces on enchiladas served "Christmas style," Santa Fe represents a blend of cultures that have each added something to the distinctive flavor of this nearly 400-year-old city. Nowhere is that mixture more evident than in the Southwestern architectural style so closely associated with New Mexico's capital city.

Most experts agree that Santa Fe was once the site of Pueblo Indian villages that seem to have been abandoned centuries before the Spanish arrived in 1607. As they constructed churches, homes and government buildings, the Spanish colonists used the Indian method of adobe construction, which efficiently kept interiors cool in summer and warm in winter. They adapted the style by adding such innovations as mud-brick fireplaces and outdoor ovens. The "Oldest House" at 215 E. De Vargas St. is among the last surviving examples of a puddled adobe dwelling.

It is no accident that modern Santa Fe has retained its Spanish-Pueblo look. Strict ordinances enacted decades ago mandate the appearance of new buildings. In many parts of the city even fast food restaurants and convenience stores must be painted in officially sanctioned hues of brown and conform to the traditional adobe style.

One might expect the state capitol *(see attraction listing p. 172)* to deviate from the local architectural norm, but surprisingly it does not. Eschewing the columns and dome common to most state capitols, New Mexico's is a low, circular, three-story interpretation of the Indian adobe style. Completed in 1966 and affectionately called "the Roundhouse," the capitol's floor plan duplicates the shape of the Zia symbol from New Mexico's state flag.

Although the current capitol building is relatively new, Santa Fe is hardly a newcomer to the status of capital city. In fact, it is the oldest capital in North America and the second oldest city in the United States.

It was around 1609-10 that newly appointed governor Don Pedro de Peralta chose Santa Fe as the capital of the Spanish "Kingdom of New Mexico," thus making it the seat of power for all imperial holdings north of the Rio Grande. The Spanish penchant for long titles did not fail Peralta, who named his city La Villa Real de Santa Fé de San Francisco de Asis—the Royal City of the Holy Faith of St. Francis of Assisi.

In 1610 the San Miguel Mission Church *(see attraction listing p. 172)* was established to serve as headquarters for a second power in the region: the church. Franciscan fathers quickly fanned out to usher the local tribe members into the Christian fold; a 1617 report stated that 14,000 souls had been converted.

Time mercifully has shortened the city's name to Santa Fe, but the core of the original settlement—the Plaza—remains essentially intact. At its north edge Peralta's *palacio*—a monument to continuity of rule, if not of rulers—still stands. Four flags have flown over the building as a governmental center under Spain, Mexico, the Confederate States of America and the United States.

As it has been for nearly 4 centuries, the Plaza, the square block bounded by Lincoln Avenue, E. Palace Avenue, Santa Fe Trail and San Francisco Street, is a vital center of commerce, festivals and history. The Museum of New Mexico offers guided walking tours of the city, which depart from the blue gate of the Palace of the Governors *(see attraction listing p. 171)*; phone (505) 476-5109. Tours by Historic Walks of Santa Fe depart from La Fonda Hotel, 100 E. San Francisco St., or the Plaza Galeria, 72 E. San Francisco St.; phone (505) 986-8388.

Just north of the Plaza on East Palace Avenue is historic Sena Plaza, a secluded garden area surrounded by shops and restaurants. The plaza was once the courtyard of the prominent Sena family's large hacienda, which was temporarily used by the territorial legislature after the capitol burned in 1892.

Across East Palace Avenue from Sena Plaza is one of Santa Fe's most widely recognized landmarks—Cathedral of St. Francis of Assisi *(see attraction listing p. 170)*. Bordered by a tree-filled park, the cathedral is one of the few buildings downtown that was not designed in the adobe or territorial style. Its sharp, French Romanesque lines create a pleasing contrast to its rounded-edged neighbors, making it a picture postcard favorite.

By the time visitors have walked the short distance from the Plaza to Cathedral of St. Francis of Assisi, they will have undoubtedly seen an art gallery or two (or more). There are dozens scattered about Santa Fe's historic core and even more along Canyon Road, which runs southeast from downtown.

Painters and photographers have been drawn to Santa Fe because of its starkly beautiful scenery and undiffused Southwestern sunlight, but other kinds of artists have favored the area, too. In addition to painters Edward Hopper and Marsden Hartley, writers Willa Cather, Jack London, H.L. Mencken and Ezra Pound sought inspiration in Santa Fe, following in the footsteps of Gen. Lew Wallace, who published his novel "Ben-Hur" in 1880 while serving as territorial governor of New Mexico.

Composer Igor Stravinsky spent his summers in Santa Fe for more than a decade and often worked with the Santa Fe Opera *(see attraction listing p. 172).* Today the opera is one of the city's leading cultural offerings—thanks in part to its breathtaking modern theater, with its eye-catching, cable-suspended roofs that frame panoramas of the surrounding Jémez and Sangre de Cristo mountains.

Santa Fe's scenic location in a valley between these two mountain ranges, where nearby peaks rise up to 12,000 feet, can best be appreciated by automobile. The Santa Fe Scenic Byway follows SR 475 northeast through Little Tesuque Canyon to Hyde Memorial State Park *(see Recreation Chart and the AAA Southeastern CampBook)* and continues to the Santa Fe Ski Area. The loop is completed via FR 102 through Pacheco Canyon and SR 22, which

ends at Tesuque, about 6 miles north. Forest roads are not paved; check road conditions before starting.

Turquoise Trail (SRs 14 and 536) runs along the east side of the Sandias between Cedar Crest and La Cienega; highlights along this route include spectacular mountain scenery, a few ghost towns, thick pine and aspen forests and Sandia Crest *(see Cibola National Forest p. 151).*

Another interesting trip follows I-25 through Glorieta Pass to Pecos. There, SR 63 turns north to Cowles at the edge of Santa Fe National Forest's Pecos Wilderness, known for its trout fishing, big game hunting and large elk herds. Various area pueblos welcome visitors; check for hours and restrictions.

Santa Fe Convention and Visitors Bureau: 201 W. Marcy St., P.O. Box 909, Santa Fe, NM 87504-0909; phone (505) 955-6200 or (800) 777-2489.

Shopping areas: At 8380 Cerrillos Rd., Santa Fe Premium Outlets features more than 40 outlets, including Brooks Brothers, Jones New York and Nine West. Canyon Road is noted for its concentration of galleries, studios and shops.

ABOOT ABOUT/SANTA FE WALKS depart from the Hotel St. Francis at 210 Don Gaspar Ave. The 2-hour guided tours explore the history, culture and art of historic downtown as well as residential and art communities. Tours depart daily at 9:45 and 1:45. Phone for other tour times and departure points. Fee $10; over 64, $9; under 12 free. Phone (505) 988-2774.

ARCHDIOCESE OF SANTA FE MUSEUM is just s. of the Plaza at 223 Cathedral Pl. This museum depicts the Catholic church's history in Santa Fe and New Mexico. Exhibits include artifacts, furniture,

relics and other religious items. Allow 30 minutes minimum. Mon.-Fri. 9-4; closed holidays. Donations. Phone (505) 983-3811.

THE AWAKENING MUSEUM is just n.w. of the Plaza at 125 N. Guadalupe St. Four hundred wood panels, carved and painted by artist Jean-Claude Gaugy, cover the ceiling, walls and doors of the museum, which has been called "a Sistine Chapel in a contemporary idiom." Allow 30 minutes minimum. Daily 10-5; closed Thanksgiving and Dec. 25. Last admission 15 minutes before closing. Admission $3, under 12 free. AX, MC, VI. Phone (505) 989-7636.

CATHEDRAL OF ST. FRANCIS OF ASSISI is 1 blk. e. of the Plaza on Cathedral Pl. Built to serve Santa Fe's Catholic community, this was the first church in New Mexico to attain the status of cathedral basilica. The parish was founded in 1610; the present building dates to 1869. Archbishop J.B. Lamy, who inspired Willa Cather's novel "Death Comes for the Archbishop," is buried beneath the main altar beside missionary priests Fray Zarate and Fray Gerónimo

de la Lama. A collection of ecclesiastical art is displayed. Mon.-Sat. 6-6, Sun. 7-7. Services are held on Saturday night and throughout the day on Sunday. Free. Phone (505) 982-5619.

THE CENTER FOR CONTEMPORARY ARTS AND CCA CINEMATEQUE is at 1050 Old Pecos Tr. The center is a forum for contemporary art exhibits, independent and foreign films, theater, lectures and workshops. Allow 30 minutes minimum. Daily 10-6; closed holidays. Film times vary; phone ahead. Donations. Phone (505) 982-1338.

CRISTO REY CHURCH is at Canyon Rd. and Cristo Rey St. One of the largest adobe structures in the country, the church contains a hand-carved stone reredos dating from 1761. Daily 8-4. Free. Phone (505) 983-8528.

SAVE **EL RANCHO DE LAS GOLONDRINAS** is off I-25 exit 276, following signs to 334 Los Pinos Rd. The living-history museum's name means "The Ranch of the Swallows." It was once a stopping place on El Camino Real (The Royal Road)

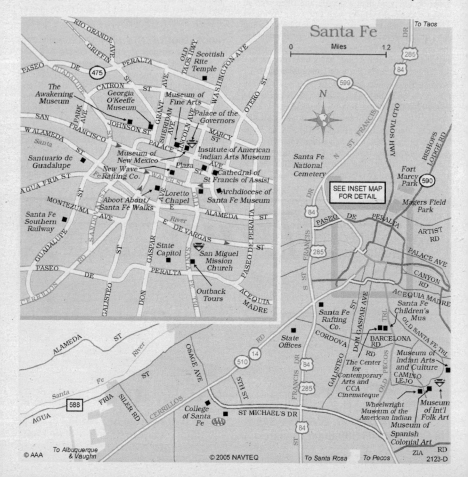

from Mexico City to Old Santa Fe. Exhibits depict Spanish colonial life in New Mexico. Restored buildings include an 18th-century *placita* house with a defensive tower as well as a mill, smithy, schoolhouse and church. A 1.5-mile path leads to the buildings.

Allow 1 hour, 30 minutes minimum. Wed.-Sun. 10-4, June-Sept. Guided tours are offered Wed.-Fri. at 10:30; reservations are required. Admission $5; over 62 and ages 13-18, $4; ages 5-12, $2. Admission for festivals and theme weekends $7; over 62 and ages 13-18, $5; ages 5-12, $3. Guided tours $10; ages 5-12, $7. AX, MC, VI. Phone (505) 471-2261.

GEORGIA O'KEEFFE MUSEUM is at 217 Johnson St. The artist's best-known works include many pieces inspired by New Mexico's stark beauty. Some 130 paintings, drawings and sculptures comprise the permanent collection, which spans 7 decades. A changing selection of at least 50 works is featured throughout the year. Special exhibits combine O'Keeffe's paintings with other works from the American Modernism Movement.

Allow 2 hours minimum. Daily 10-5 (also Fri. 5-8), mid-May through late Oct.; Thurs.-Tues. 10-5, rest of year. Closed Jan. 1, Easter, Thanksgiving and Dec. 25 and between some exhibits. Guided tours are offered at 10:30 and 2. Admission $8; over 60, $7; under 17 free; free to all Fri. 5-8. AX, MC, VI. Phone (505) 946-1000.

INSTITUTE OF AMERICAN INDIAN ARTS MUSEUM is at 108 Cathedral Pl. The museum displays paintings, sculpture, pottery, ceramics, beadwork and textiles of alumni, students and faculty of the Institute of American Indian Arts as well as new art forms created in the region. Allow 1 hour minimum. Mon.-Sat. 10-5, Sun. noon-5; closed Jan. 1, Easter, Thanksgiving and Dec. 25. Admission $4, over 62 and students with ID $2, under 16 free. AX, DS, MC, VI. Phone (505) 983-8900.

LORETTO CHAPEL is at 207 Old Santa Fe Tr. The "Miraculous Staircase" to the chapel's choir loft has two 360-degree turns and no visible means of support. An anonymous carpenter is said to have fashioned the spiral steps in 1878 using only wooden pegs. Legend suggests that St. Joseph, the patron saint of carpenters, inspired the work.

Allow 30 minutes minimum. Mon.-Sat. 9-6, Sun. 10:30-5, mid-May to mid-Oct.; Mon.-Sat. 9-5, Sun. 10:30-5, rest of year. Chapel may close for weddings. Admission $2.50; ages 7-12, $2. MC, VI. Phone (505) 982-0092.

LORETTO LINE TRAM TOURS departs near Loretto Chapel at 211 Old Santa Fe Tr. Passengers board an open-air tram for a guided 1.5-hour historical tour of Santa Fe. Tours depart daily on the hour 10-3, Apr.-Oct. Fare $14; under 12, $10. The parking lot a half-block east on Alameda charges a fee. Phone (505) 983-3701.

MUSEUM OF NEW MEXICO is comprised of four museums dealing with various phases and periods of Southwestern and international culture. Milner Plaza, which anchors the complex, features a paved labyrinth and performance circles. Food is available. Museums open Tues.-Sun. 10-5; closed Jan. 1, Easter, Thanksgiving and Dec. 25. Admission $7 per museum, under 17 free. Four-day pass for four museums (also includes the Museum of Spanish Colonial Art) $15. MC, VI. Phone (505) 476-1125 or (505) 827-6463 for recorded information.

Museum of Fine Arts is just off the Plaza at 107 W. Palace Ave. The museum, completed in 1917, houses contemporary and traditional American art. Changing exhibits focus on Southwestern artists from the 19th century to the present, including the Santa Fe and Taos masters. Allow 1 hour minimum. Tues.-Sun. 10-5; closed Jan. 1, Easter, Thanksgiving and Dec. 25. Admission $7, under 17 free. Four-day pass for the Museum of New Mexico's four facilities and the Museum of Spanish Colonial Art $15. Phone (505) 476-5072.

Museum of Indian Arts and Culture is on Museum Hill off Old Santa Fe Tr. The museum interprets Southwest American Indian culture. Objects from the Laboratory of Anthropology Collection include pottery, basketry, woven fabrics, jewelry and contemporary crafts. An exhibit details the comprehensive story of the Southwest's Navajo, Apache and Pueblo peoples in their own words and voices.

Allow 1 hour minimum. Tues.-Sun. 10-5; closed Jan. 1, Easter, Thanksgiving and Dec. 25. Admission $7, under 17 free. Four-day pass for the Museum of New Mexico's four facilities and the Museum of Spanish Colonial Art $15. Phone (505) 476-1269.

Museum of International Folk Art is on Museum Hill off Old Santa Fe Tr. Of the museum's 130,000 objects, the Girard Foundation Collection contains more than 106,000 items, including miniature buildings, streets and marketplaces in village scenes from 100 countries. The Hispanic Heritage Wing features Spanish colonial folk art; the Neutrogena Wing offers a behind-the-scenes look at museum storage; the Bartlett Wing presents changing exhibits.

Allow 1 hour minimum. Tues.-Sun. 10-5; closed Jan. 1, Easter, Thanksgiving and Dec. 25. Admission $7, under 17 free. Four-day pass for the Museum of New Mexico's four facilities and the Museum of Spanish Colonial Art $15. Phone (505) 476-1200.

Palace of the Governors is on the Plaza at 105 W. Palace Ave. Built in 1610, the Palace is considered one of the oldest public buildings in the United States. The long, low adobe structure with massive walls was the seat of government under Spanish, Pueblo Indian, Mexican and U.S. territorial rule until 1909, when it became the state history museum. Exhibits reflect the history of New Mexico and its varied cultures. The Palace Print Shop and Bindery features 19th-century printing presses and other equipment, all of which still operate.

The *portal*—porch—is a gathering place for local American Indian artisans. Guided 90-minute tours of the museum are available. Allow 2 hours minimum. Tues.-Sun. 10-5; closed Jan. 1, Easter, Thanksgiving and Dec. 25. Admission $7, under 17 free. Four-day pass for the Museum of New Mexico's four facilities and the Museum of Spanish Colonial Art $15. Phone (505) 476-5100.

MUSEUM OF SPANISH COLONIAL ART is 2 mi. s.e. of the Plaza at 750 Camino Lejo. Housed in a 1930 Pueblo Revival building designed by architect John Gaw Meem, the museum presents Hispanic-influenced art produced throughout the region since the start of Spanish colonization. The collection of some 3,000 objects includes painted images of saints, sculpture, textiles, metal work, ceramics, furniture and books. Allow 1 hour minimum. Tues.-Sun. 10-5; closed major holidays. Admission $6, under 16 free. Combination ticket with the Museum of New Mexico's four museums $15. AX, DS, MC, VI. Phone (505) 982-2226.

NEW MEXICO STATE CAPITOL is at Old Santa Fe Tr. and Paseo de Peralta, 4 blks. s. of the Plaza. The capitol building is designed in the shape of the state's official emblem, the Zia sun symbol, and features a collection of artwork and furnishings handcrafted by New Mexicans. Self-guiding tours are available Mon.-Fri. 7-7, Memorial Day-Labor Day; Mon.-Fri. 7-6, rest of year. Guided tours are offered Mon.-Sat. 10-2, June-July. Closed all holidays except Memorial Day and July 4. Free. Phone (505) 986-4589.

OUTBACK TOURS meets passengers at downtown hotels and the New Mexico and Santa Fe Visitors Information Center, 491 Old Santa Fe Tr. Destinations for guided safari tours of northern New Mexico sites include Taos, Bandelier National Monument, the Rocky Mountains, Georgia O'Keeffe country, the Turquoise Trail, the Jémez Mountains and Los Alamos. Off-road tours and tour-and-train outings also are offered. Tour lengths vary from 3 hours, 30 minutes to all-day trips. Departure times vary; closed Jan. 1 and Dec. 25. Fares $65-$96; under 11 and over 64, $60-$91. Reservations are recommended. AX, DS, MC, VI. Phone (888) 772-3274.

RANDALL DAVEY AUDUBON CENTER is 3 mi. e. of the Plaza at the end of Upper Canyon Rd. This 135-acre preserve in the Santa Fe Canyon hosts more 130 bird species as well as bears, bobcats, coyotes, deer and foxes. The site includes an education center and nature trails. The Historic Randall Davey House, originally an 1847 sawmill, was converted into a home by the noted painter. It contains his studio, antiques and art work. Allow 1 hour minimum. Daily 9-5; closed holidays. Guided house tours are offered Mon. at 2. Guided bird walks depart Sat. at 8:30. Audubon center $2; under 13, $1. House tours $5, under 13 free. MC, VI. Phone (505) 983-4609.

SAN MIGUEL MISSION CHURCH is 9 blks. s. of the Plaza at 401 Old Santa Fe Tr. at E. De Vargas St. The mission is one of the country's oldest churches in continual use. It was constructed in 1610, and although records of its early history were burned during the Pueblo Indian Rebellion of 1680, the thick, sturdy adobe walls remained unharmed. Stone buttresses later were added to strengthen the walls, tower and facade.

A bell cast in Spain in 1356 is displayed. It was used in churches in Spain and Mexico before being brought to Santa Fe by oxcart in the early 19th century. Priceless ornaments and paintings adorn the interior of the mission.

Mon.-Sat. 9-5, Sun. 10-4; closed Jan. 1, Good Friday, Easter, Thanksgiving and Dec. 25. Mass is given Sun. at 5. Admission $1, under 6 free. AX, MC, VI. Phone (505) 983-3974.

SANTA FE CHILDREN'S MUSEUM is 1 mi. s. of the Plaza at 1050 Old Pecos Tr. Geared to children ages 2-12, interactive exhibits focus on the arts, sciences and humanities. Among the highlights are an outdoor garden learning environment, bubble exhibits, a rock climbing wall and water works. Artists, scientists and environmental educators conduct hands-on activities; phone ahead for schedule. Wed.-Sat. 10-5, Sun. noon-5; closed holidays. Admission $4. AX, DS, MC, VI. Phone (505) 989-8359.

SANTA FE NATIONAL CEMETERY is 1.5 mi. n. of the Plaza on US 285 at 501 N. Guadalupe St. Originally the military post cemetery, the site contains the graves of soldiers from the Indian wars as well as those killed in the battles of Pigeon's Ranch and Valverde during the Civil War. It also is the final resting place for eight Congressional Medal of Honor recipients. Daily 6 a.m.-8 p.m. Free. Phone (505) 988-6400.

SANTA FE OPERA is 7 mi. n. on the w. side of US 84/285. Classical opera is presented in an open-air theater against the backdrop of the Sangre de Cristo mountains. Inquire about weather policies. Some 40 performances are offered in July and August. Box office open Mon.-Fri. 9-5. Tickets $24-$142. AX, DS, MC, VI. Phone (505) 986-5900 or (800) 280-4654.

SANTA FE SOUTHERN RAILWAY departs from Santa Fe Depot at 410 S. Guadalupe St. Sightseeing passengers travel the desert spur built by the Atchison, Topeka & Santa Fe Railway in 1880. Historic Lamy and the scenic Galisteo overlook are among the destinations for 2.5- to 4-hour excursions in vintage coaches or luxury cars. The Friday evening High Desert Highball and the Saturday night Campfire Barbecue trains are available April through October.

Food is usually available for purchase in Lamy, and picnicking is permitted. Scenic Day Trains depart daily, Apr.-Oct.; Tues., Thurs. and Sat.-Sun., rest of year. Departure times vary; phone for schedule. Day train $28-$55; over 59, $24-$50; ages 3-13,

$14-$42. Reservations are recommended. AX, DS, MC, VI. Phone (505) 989-8600 or (888) 989-8600. *See color ad p. 169.*

SANTUARIO DE GUADALUPE is 4 blks. w. of the Plaza at Agua Fria and Guadalupe sts. The 18th-century church is called the nation's oldest shrine dedicated to Our Lady of Guadalupe. A 1783 oil-on-canvas altar painting by Mexican baroque artist José Alzibar is considered among the finest oil paintings in the Spanish Southwest. Also included are the meditation chapel with religious woodcarvings, a pictorial history room and the Plants of the Holy Land botanical garden. An 18th-century mission is at the end of El Camino Real. Mon.-Fri. 9-4 (also Sat. 10-4, June-Aug.). Donations. Phone (505) 988-2027.

SCOTTISH RITE TEMPLE is on Washington Ave., 3 blks. n. of the Plaza. The Masonic building was inspired by the Court of the Lions at the Alhambra in Granada, Spain. Mon.-Fri. 9-noon and 2-4; closed holidays. Free. Phone (505) 982-4414.

SOUTHWEST SAFARIS departs from and returns to Santa Fe by airplane. Full-day air/land combination tours travel to the Grand Canyon, Monument Valley, Canyon de Chelly, Arches/Canyonlands and Mesa Verde. The expeditions include exploration of landmarks, pueblos, cliff dwellings and ruins. Regional geology, archeology and history are explained. Local scenic flights and half-day air/land adventures also are available. Tour lengths range from 1 to 8 hours; some include lunch. Fares $149-$599. Reservations are required. AX, DS, MC, VI. Phone (505) 988-4246 or (800) 842-4246. *See color ad p. 168.*

TESUQUE PUEBLO—*see place listing p. 179.*

WHEELWRIGHT MUSEUM OF THE AMERICAN INDIAN is 2 mi. s.e. of the plaza at 704 Camino Lejo. Reminiscent of an eight-sided Navajo hogan, the museum offers exhibits of historic and contemporary American Indian art with emphasis on the Southwest. Among the displays are pottery, jewelry, rugs and baskets. Mon.-Sat. 10-5, Sun. 1-5; closed Jan. 1, Thanksgiving and Dec. 25. Gallery tours are offered Mon.-Fri. at 2, Sat. at 1. Donations. Phone (505) 982-4636 or (800) 607-4636.

RECREATIONAL ACTIVITIES
White-water Rafting

- **Known World Guides** departs various locations. Write P.O. Box 428, Velarde, NM 87582. Daily Apr.-Sept. Other activities are available. Phone (505) 983-7756 or (800) 983-7756.

- **Kokopelli Rafting Adventures** departs from various locations. Write 551 W. Cordova Rd. #540, Santa Fe, NM 87505. Daily Apr.-Oct. Phone (505) 983-3734 or (800) 879-9035.

- **New Wave Rafting Co.** is at 1101 Cerrillos Rd. Write 70 CR 84B, Santa Fe, NM 87506. Daily Apr. 21-Labor Day. Phone (505) 984-1444 or (800) 984-1444.

- **Santa Fe Rafting Co.** is 1.5 mi. s.w. of the Plaza on Cerrillos Rd. Write P.O. Box 23525, Santa Fe, NM 87502-3525. Daily Apr.-Oct. Phone (505) 988-4914 or (888) 988-4914.

High-Altitude Health

Temples throbbing, gasping for breath and nauseated, you barely notice the scudding clouds or the spectacular view.

You might be suffering from Acute Mountain Sickness (AMS). Usually striking at around 8,000 feet (2,450 m) in altitude, AMS is your body's way of coping with the reduced oxygen and humidity of high altitudes. Among the symptoms are headaches, shortness of breath, loss of appetite, insomnia and lethargy. Some people complain of temporary weight gain or swelling in the face, hands and feet.

If your AMS is severe, you should stop ascending; you will recover in a few days. If the AMS is mild, a quick descent will end the suffering immediately.

Digital Archives

You can reduce the effect of high altitude by being in top condition. If you smoke or suffer from heart or lung ailments, consult your physician. Alcohol and certain drugs will intensify the symptoms.

A gradual ascent with a couple days of acclimatization is best if you have time. On the way up, eat light, nutritious meals and drink plenty of water. A spicy, high-carbohydrate diet may mitigate the effects of low oxygen and encourage you to drink more.

Other high-altitude health problems include sunburn and hypothermia. Dress in layers to protect yourself from the intense sun and wide fluctuations in temperature.

Finally, after you lounge in the sauna or whirlpool bath at your lodgings, remember to stand up carefully, for the heat has relaxed your blood vessels and lowered your blood pressure.

SANTA FE NATIONAL FOREST

Elevations in the forest range from 7,300 ft. to 13,101 ft. at Truchas Peak. Refer to AAA maps for additional elevation information.

In the north central part of the state, some 1,568,820 acres of forest and rangeland lie within Santa Fe National Forest. The southern Sangre de Cristo Range, with several 12,000- to 13,000-foot peaks, dominates the eastern half. Within the forest are Pecos Wilderness, the headwaters of the Pecos River and the Santa Fe River Basin winter sports area. The 18-mile trip along SR 63 between Cowles and Pecos provides outstanding views of the forest's eastern section.

In the portion west of the Rio Grande are the Jémez Mountains, San Pedro Parks Wilderness, Chama River Canyon Wilderness and Dome Wilderness. Developed recreation sites and day-use picnic areas are near streams, trailheads and other scenic highlights. Recreational opportunities include hiking, fishing, horseback riding and such winter sports as cross-country skiing and snowshoeing. Fees are required for some developed areas.

For information and maps contact the Supervisor, Santa Fe National Forest, P.O. Box 1689, Santa Fe, NM 87504; phone the Public Information Officer at (505) 438-7840. *See Recreation Chart.*

SANTA ROSA (C-5) pop. 2,744, elev. 4,599'

Santa Rosa is surrounded by parcels of land with property lines that were established by Spanish land grants. Many residents are descendents of the men who accompanied Francisco Vasquez de Coronado on his explorations of the area in 1540.

The town is in a semidesert area with artesian springs and lakes. Blue Hole, an artesian spring 87 feet deep and 60 feet in diameter, is a half-mile west of Park Lake. Stocked with goldfish, its 65-degree waters attract scuba divers; a diving permit is required. A city park at Perch Lake also offers scuba diving. *See Recreation Chart.*

Other nearby lakes, such as Park Lake and the lake in Janes-Wallace Memorial Park, yield large catches of trout, crappie and walleye *(see Recreation Chart)*. Channel cat are taken from the Pecos River. Rock Lake Trout Hatchery, 2 miles south of town on River Road, propagates rainbow trout and walleye.

Scenic SR 91 follows the Pecos River south for 10 miles to Puerto de Luna, one of several abandoned Spanish settlements in the area. A marker indicates where Coronado encamped to build a bridge across the river. Another pleasant drive leads to Santa Rosa Lake State Park *(see Recreation Chart)*, 7 miles north off SR 91. A .7-mile nature trail and other recreational facilities border the dam and reservoir.

Santa Rosa Visitors Information Center: 486 Historic Route 66, Santa Rosa, NM 88435; phone (505) 472-3763.

SANTA TERESA (F-3)
pop. 2,607, elev. 4,100′

Santa Teresa, on the southern border just west of El Paso, Texas, offers access to Mexico and the border town of Cuidad Juárez (HWAH-res). The border crossing station here is recommended only for travelers who plan to bypass Juárez and continue into Chihuahua; the crossing is in a rural area, off the beaten track for tourists. Banjercito offices here and at the 30-kilometer mark on the Juárez-Chihuahua Highway are the only local agencies that will process the paperwork necessary for vehicle travel into the interior.

Ciudad Juárez is accessed by several bridges. The Ysleta-Zaragoza Bridge (toll) on Zaragoza Avenue enters Mexico east of Ciudad Juárez. From US 54 south of I-10, the Cordova Bridge (Bridge of the Americas, or the "free bridge") enters Juárez via Avenida Lincoln.

The Santa Fe Street Bridge is the most convenient bridge to use if you are walking across the border for a day visit; there is plenty of parking on the U.S. side. Once across the border, Santa Fe Street becomes Avenida Juárez. The bridge is one way northbound for vehicles.

The Stanton Street Bridge (toll fee $2 per vehicle, 30 cents for pedestrians) is one way southbound, entering Juárez from Stanton Street in El Paso; once across the border the street becomes Avenida Lerdo.

Motorists returning to the United States from downtown Juárez must use the northbound-only Paseo del Norte Bridge (toll fee $2 per vehicle, 70 cents for pedestrians) via Avenida Juárez to Santa Fe Street, or the nontoll Bridge of the Americas via Avenida Lincoln. Lines are often long, especially at the free bridge. **Note:** Dollars or pesos are accepted when entering or departing Mexico or the United States. Baggage may be inspected at the customs offices.

Both Mexican and U.S. Border Protection offices are open 24 hours daily. AAA/CAA members can obtain Mexican auto insurance and make arrangements for bus tours of the city through the El Paso office of AAA Texas; phone (915) 778-9521.

U.S. and Canadian visitors must carry proof of citizenship. A valid U.S. or Canadian passport is the most convenient, since it serves as a photo ID and facilitates many transactions, such as cashing traveler's checks. The U.S., Canadian and Mexican governments also recognize a birth certificate, which must be a certified copy with a raised seal from the government agency that issued it. A driver's license, voter registration card or baptismal certificate is **not** proof of citizenship.

Note: Beginning Dec. 31, 2007, all American and Mexican citizens traveling to or from Mexico by air, land and sea will be required to show a passport or other accepted secure document in order to enter or re-enter the United States. This means that travelers who now use a certified birth certificate as proof of citizenship will need to obtain a passport. The new policy is designed to thwart terrorists from exploiting the relative ease of travel in North America.

All travelers who plan to visit the interior of Mexico or stay in the border area more than 72 hours also must obtain a Mexican-government tourist card. Tourist cards are available, with proof of citizenship, from Mexican government tourism offices, Mexican consulates in the U.S. and Canada or immigration offices at official points of entry.

For a more detailed explanation of border-crossing procedures and the requirements for temporary importation of vehicles, *see Border Information in the AAA Mexico TourBook.*

Mexico collects a tourist entry fee of 225 pesos (at press time, about $20 U.S.) from each person entering the country. The fee must be paid in order to have your tourist card validated if you plan to remain anywhere in Mexico for more than 72 hours, or stay less than 72 hours and travel beyond the 12-mile (20-kilometer) border zone. If arriving by land, the fee is paid at a branch of any bank operating in Mexico. Upon payment your tourist card is stamped with an official "Fee paid" designation. All visitors are required to produce verification of payment by showing the "Fee paid" stamp on their tourist card upon departing Mexico.

Visitors who limit their travel to destinations within the border zone, regardless of length of stay, are exempt. An exemption also applies to visitors staying more than 72 hours but limiting their visit to the destination/tourist route of Ciudad Juárez to Paquime, Chihuahua.

Note: The border region has experienced increased drug-related violence in the last year. Visitors should stick to established tourist areas during daylight hours. Avoid the area west of Avenida Juárez as it extends south toward Avenida 16 de Septiembre, especially after dark. If driving in the city, do not park in any area that appears to be restricted, as your license plates may be confiscated.

WAR EAGLES AIR MUSEUM is off I-10 exit 8, 7.5 mi. w. on Art Craft Rd. to Santa Teresa Airport. The 64,000-square-foot museum features restored aircraft from the World War II era and jet fighters used in the Korean Conflict. Fighters include the P-51 Mustang, the P-38 Lightning, the P-40 Warhawk, a twin-engine Invader bomber and a Fieseler Storch.

Among the 1950s jets are an F-86 Sabre, a T-33 Silver Star and MIG-15s. Additional displays feature a German observation plane, women aviators, flight equipment and vintage automobiles. Allow 1 hour minimum. Tues.-Sun. 10-4; closed holidays. Admission $5, over 64 and military with ID $4, under 12 free. MC, VI. Phone (505) 589-2000.

SANTO DOMINGO PUEBLO (B-3)
pop. 2,550, elev. 5,185′

Santo Domingo received its name in 1691 when missionaries began renaming New Mexican pueblos for Catholic saints. Keresan people had inhabited the site since the 1200s. The pueblo's actual location has changed over the years with flooding of the Río Grande. The town of Domingo became a stopover on the way to Pea Blanca during Spanish colonial times; it later served as a stage stop on the road between Albuquerque and Santa Fe. The 1883 Santo Domingo Trading Post is one of the largest in the area.

SANTO DOMINGO PUEBLO is off I-25 exit 259, then 2.5 mi. w. Because of their proximity to the ancient Cerrillos turquoise mines, the Keresan artisans of Santo Domingo earned a reputation for fine jewelry, beadwork and mosaics. Their *heishe* beads are prized today. A cultural center and small museum offer visitors a glimpse into tribal life and traditions. Some 350 artists gather for an arts and crafts festival on Labor Day weekend.

The Church of the Pueblo of Santo Domingo dates from 1886 and replaced a mission that was carried away by Rio Grande floodwaters. Records as well as paintings by American Indian artists can be seen. Photography, sketching and painting are not permitted. Daily 8-5; closed Jan. 1, Easter and Dec. 25. Donations. Phone (505) 465-2214.

SHIPROCK (A-1) pop. 8,150, elev. 4,900′

The geological formation Shiprock is within the Navajo Indian Reservation, 15 miles southwest via US 491 and Red Rock Road, from which it can be viewed. The basalt core of an old volcano, the rock rises more than 1,700 feet above the desert. At sunset it appears to shimmer and float.

Because the Navajo consider Shiprock to be a sacred place, the tribe does not permit climbers to scale it. Scenic Indian Route 33 runs between Shiprock and Red Rock on the Arizona border.

FOUR CORNERS MONUMENT—
see Window Rock, Ariz., p. 122.

SILVER CITY (E-1) pop. 10,545, elev. 5,938′

Silver City burgeoned with the discovery of silver in the late 1860s. Growth was reinforced by additional discoveries in the area, and the city became the county seat in late 1871. A lumber mill was set up to take advantage of nearby timberland; the mill and other businesses based on supplying the proliferating mines ensured that Silver City's existence would not be the brief, single-minded one of the typical mining town.

Permanence was declared with the establishment of Western New Mexico University in 1893—the same year the bottom dropped out of the silver market. As the mines closed and mining towns faded into history throughout the region, Silver City's economy regrouped around shipping and cattle ranching. The city is remembered as the boyhood home of William Bonney, who later gained notoriety as outlaw Billy the Kid.

Mining processes can be viewed from an open pit copper mine 15 miles east on SR 152. The huge pit, 1.7 miles across and 1,000 feet deep, has produced mountains of ore since the discovery of the deposits

in 1800. One of the largest operations of its type in the United States, Chino Mine shows evidence of Spanish and Mexican workings. Chino Mines Co. provides an observation point and a picnic area.

Twelve miles south on SR 90, another vast open-pit mine yields some 50,000 tons of copper ore a day from the original site of Tyrone. Built in 1915 by Phelps-Dodge Corp. to house miners and their families, it was a beautifully designed city until declining markets caused the closure of the mine in 1921. Reactivation in the mid-1960s resulted in a new Tyrone 4.5 miles south of Silver City.

Silver City provides access to the 110-mile Trail of the Mountain Spirits, which leads to Gila Cliff Dwellings National Monument *(see place listing p. 156)* via US 180 and SRs 152, 35 and 15, then crosses the Pinos Altos Range back to Silver City. Contact the visitor center at Gila National Forest *(see place listing p. 156)* at (505) 536-9344.

Silver City/Grant County Chamber of Commerce 201 N. Hudson St., Silver City, NM 88061; phone (505) 538-3785 or (800) 548-9378.

Self-guiding tours: Pocket guides for walking tours of the city's three historic neighborhoods, Capilla, Gospel Hill and the historic business district, may be purchased for 50c at the Silver City Museum.

SILVER CITY MUSEUM is at 312 W. Broadway St. Exhibits in this 1881 mansion explore the history of southwest New Mexico. Collections include 19th- and 20th-century regional history objects and photographs, Southwestern American Indian artifacts and items from an early 20th-century mining camp. Allow 1 hour minimum. Tues.-Fri. 9-4:30, Sat.-Sun. 10-4; closed Jan. 1, Easter, Thanksgiving and Dec. 24-25. Donations. Phone (505) 538-5921.

WESTERN NEW MEXICO UNIVERSITY MUSEUM is on campus .5 mi. s.w. of US 180 at 10th and West sts. in Fleming Hall. Extensive displays depict prehistoric Mimbres culture; artifacts include pottery, stone tools and jewelry. Also featured are Casas Grandes pottery, historical displays, mining items and traveling exhibits. Mon.-Fri. 9-4:30, Sat.-Sun. 10-4; closed university holidays. Donations. Phone (505) 538-6386.

SOCORRO (D-3) pop. 8,877, elev. 4,605′

Socorro was the biggest—and wildest—city in New Mexico during the 1880s. After the Panic of 1893 sent silver prices plunging, local mines produced zinc and other ores until these reserves became depleted. After most miners left, the remaining townspeople turned their energies to farming and stock raising.

A natural outgrowth of the mining era was the 1889 founding of the New Mexico School of Mines, later renamed New Mexico Institute of Mining and Technology.

Socorro County Chamber of Commerce: 101 Plaza, P.O. Box 743, Socorro, NM 87801; phone (505) 835-0424.

Self-guiding tours: A brochure outlining a walking tour of historic buildings and places, most within walking distance of the central plaza, is available from the chamber.

MINERAL MUSEUM is at Olive Ln. and Canyon Rd. at the New Mexico Institute of Mining and Technology. An extensive mineral collection includes more than 2,000 specimens indigenous to the region and from around the world as well as artifacts and memorabilia related to mining and minerals. Exhibits change periodically. Mon.-Fri. 8-noon and 1-5, Sat.-Sun. 10-3; closed holidays. Free. Phone (505) 835-5140.

SAN MIGUEL MISSION is n. of the plaza at 403 El Camino Real. The twin-steeple church, built 1819-21, is still in use. Its predecessor, constructed in the 1620s, was destroyed in the Pueblo Rebellion of 1680. A portion of one wall dates from 1598; hand-carved ceiling beams highlight the interior. Artifacts are displayed in the adjoining church office. Daily 8-6. Free. Phone (505) 835-1620.

VERY LARGE ARRAY (VLA) RADIO TELESCOPE is 52 mi. w. on US 60. One of the world's premier radio space observatories, the VLA telescope consists of 27 dish antennas, each weighing 230 tons and measuring 82 feet in diameter. For optimum tracking, they can be maneuvered along a Y-shaped grid of railroad tracks that stretch for miles across the desert floor. Self-guiding walking tours start at the visitor center, which provides an orientation film and educational exhibits. Allow 1 hour minimum. Daily 8:30-dusk. Free. Phone (505) 835-7000.

SPRINGER (B-5) pop. 1,285, elev. 5,832′

Springer was named for Frank Springer, who came to New Mexico from Iowa in 1873. Having settled in Cimarron, Springer was a prominent lawyer and paleontologist. His most lasting legacy is the Museum of New Mexico's Museum of Fine Arts *(see attraction listing p. 171)*, of which he was a founder.

The Santa Fe Trail Museum, housed in the old county courthouse at US 56 and US 85, displays household items, clothing, period furniture and the only electric chair used in New Mexico.

Springer Chamber of Commerce and Visitor Center: 516 Maxwell St., P.O. Box 323, Springer, NM 87747; phone (505) 483-2998.

STEINS (E-1) elev. 4,350′

STEINS RAILROAD GHOST TOWN is off I-10 exit 3. More than 15 pioneer buildings—including remnants of Hotel Steins, saloons, a bordello stand and several adobe and stone structures—have been restored to their original appearance. Many rooms, including the pioneer kitchen, are furnished in period.

A bottle collection and pioneer artifacts dating to the 1800s are among the historic displays. Antique corrals hold farm animals.

Guided tours are available. Picnicking is permitted. Allow 30 minutes minimum. Daily 9-7, late May-late Oct.; 9:30-5, rest of year. Closed Thanksgiving, the first 3 weeks in Dec. and Dec. 25. Admission $2.50, under 12 free. Phone (505) 542-9791.

SUNSPOT (E-4) elev. 9,200′

NATIONAL SOLAR OBSERVATORY is on Sacramento Peak. At an elevation of 9,200 feet, the research facility makes high-resolution observations of the sun. Exhibits and interactive displays are featured at the Sunspot Astronomy and Visitor Center. The observatory also offers views of the Tularosa Basin. A brochure and map are available for self-guiding tours that include the Grain Bin Dome and the Evans Solar Facility. Allow 1 hour minimum. Daily 10-6, May-Sept.; otherwise varies. Admission $3, over 54 and students with ID $1, under 10 free, family rate $5. Phone (505) 434-7000.

TAOS (A-4) pop. 4,700, elev. 6,952′

Spanish, American Indian and Anglo influences mingle yet remain distinct in Taos, which is actually three villages. Taos proper—legally Don Fernando de Taos—is the original Spanish town that is now a center of art and tourism. Pueblo de Taos, home of the conservative Taos Indians, remains much as it was before the Spanish conquest. Ranchos de Taos formerly was a farming community; its adobe mission church is one of the most frequently photographed structures in the state.

This cultural mix and a dramatic setting on a plateau between the Rio Grande and the western foot of the Sangre de Cristo Range have lured artists since the 19th century. The first to come were adventurous sketch and watercolor artists who arrived with railroad survey teams in search of inspiration. Many found their muses within the area's dramatic landscapes and indigenous communities.

It was painters Ernest Blumenschein and Bert Phillips who are credited with really getting the artistic ball rolling in Taos. Visiting the region in 1898, the two were forced to stop in Taos to repair a broken wagon wheel. They became enamored of the town and its surroundings during their brief stay, and eventually both settled here permanently. They spread the word about New Mexico's rugged beauty, and soon dozens of artists were heeding the city's siren song.

In 1915 Blumenschein, Phillips and others formed the Taos Society of Artists, which is noteworthy for the distinctive mark it has made on art in the United States. Although the city's fame as an artists' colony was established decades ago, artists and artisans, writers and musicians continue to uphold its reputation as a center of creativity, as can be seen by the number of art galleries, studios and shops that occupy the brown stucco buildings surrounding the town plaza.

Coincidentally, two of Taos's most influential promoters were transplanted New York socialites who fell in love with the area for similar reasons. Art connoisseur Mabel Dodge arrived here in 1918 and shortly after married Taos Indian Tony Luhan. It became her mission to share the local American Indian culture, which she had come to admire, with the luminaries of her day. Through persistent effort she was able to entice such notable figures as D.H. Lawrence, Georgia O'Keeffe and Ansel Adams to visit Taos. Both Lawrence and O'Keeffe eventually relocated to New Mexico.

The Mabel Dodge Luhan House is 2 blocks east of Taos Plaza. Guided walking tours of the city conducted by Taos Historic Walks begin at the Luhan House June through September. For reservations phone (505) 758-4020.

The second socialite to adopt Taos as her home was a glamorous Standard Oil heiress named Millicent Rogers. A fashion designer and collector of traditional Navajo and Pueblo Indian art, Rogers moved to Taos in 1947. Her work popularized American Indian fabrics and patterns along with the turquoise-and-silver jewelry so closely associated with "Santa Fe style." Samples of her extensive collection of Southwestern art can be seen at the Millicent Rogers Museum (see attraction listing p. 179).

An even more intimate encounter with Pueblo Indian culture is no farther away than Taos Pueblo (see attraction listing p. 179), less than 3 miles north of Taos Plaza. The often-photographed multi-storied adobe buildings have come to represent Southwest culture. The pueblo appears much as it did when Spanish explorers first reached the region more than 500 years ago, and sections of the structure may be up to a thousand years old.

Despite its age, the village is not a re-enactment but rather a living community of some 150 people dedicated to preserving ancient ways of life. Religious ceremonies are held throughout the year; many are open to visitors.

Relative newcomers to the Taos scene, young counterculture idealists arrived in the 1960s, establishing nearly 30 communes and earning Taos the reputation as a "hippie haven." This antiestablishment influx was portrayed in the 1969 independent movie, "Easy Rider," part of which was filmed in Taos. Many of the new arrivals stayed, enhancing the city's unconventional mystique.

Eight miles northwest on US 64 is one of the loftiest highway bridges in the nation. The three-span, continuous-truss bridge crosses Rio Grande Gorge some 650 feet above the river. Raised sidewalks and observation platforms permit views. Until its junction with I-25, US 64 also provides outstanding views of the region.

Farther north and east the mountainous skyline, extolled by author D.H. Lawrence as the most beautiful he had ever encountered, beckons outdoor enthusiasts to Carson National Forest (see place listing p. 148). Lawrence's ashes are enshrined on a knoll on his Kiowa Ranch, now a facility of the University of New Mexico, 15 miles north on scenic SR 522, then 5 miles east. The shrine can be visited only during daylight hours; check road conditions during or after inclement weather.

The proximity of the Rio Grande River makes Taos a popular starting point for river rafting. Outfitters are based in Taos and Santa Fe. Ski resorts are south and northeast of town. Wheeler Peak Wilderness Area is open in summer for camping, fishing and hiking. Phone (505) 776-2916 for snow conditions and year-round recreational activities.

Taos County Chamber of Commerce: 1139 Paseo del Pueblo Sur, P.O. Drawer I, Taos, NM 87571; phone (505) 758-3873 or (800) 732-8267.

ERNEST L. BLUMENSCHEIN HOME is 2 blks. w. of historic Taos Plaza on Ledoux St. The artist and co-founder of the original Taos Society of Artists made this his permanent home in 1919. Portions of the adobe house were built in 1797; other sections were added by Blumenschein. The restored 13-room house contains original furnishings and serves as a showcase for works by Ernest and Mary Blumenschein, their daughter, Helen, and other Taos painters. Daily 9-5, May-Oct.; otherwise varies. Admission $6; ages 6-16, $3; family rate $15. AX, DS, MC, VI. Phone (505) 758-0505.

SAVE **HARWOOD MUSEUM OF ART** is at 238 Ledoux St. Taos art from the 18th century to the present includes paintings, sculpture and Hispanic religious art. The Agnes Martin Gallery presents seven paintings by this foremost American abstract artist. Changing exhibits also are presented, with special attention given to Taos artists. The museum also houses the Southwest Research Center, which features an extensive collection of books written by authors who have ties to the region, particularly D.H. Lawrence. Tues.-Sat. 10-5, Sun. noon-5; closed holidays. Admission $7, senior citizens $6, under 12 free. MC, VI. Phone (505) 758-9826.

HISTORIC TAOS TROLLEY TOURS depart from the Taos Visitors Center at 1139 Paseo del Pueblo Sur. Visitors can choose between two narrated tours aboard a trolley-style bus. The Taos Pueblo Excursion makes a 1-hour visit to the centuries-old pueblo with stops at Historic Taos Plaza and San Francisco de Asis Church. The History and Culture Tour includes Taos Plaza, the Millicent Rogers Museum and the Martinez Hacienda.

Allow 3 hours minimum. Taos Pueblo Excursion departs Tues.-Sat. at 10:30 and 2, Sun.-Mon. at 10:30, May-Oct.; History and Culture Tour departs Sun.-Mon. at 2, May-Oct. Fare (includes admission to attractions) $33; ages 6-12, $10. Tickets may be purchased at Atira's Southwest in the old courthouse building on Taos Plaza. MC, VI. Phone (505) 751-0366.

KIT CARSON PARK is 2 blks. n. of Taos Plaza. The park contains the cemetery where Kit Carson, Padre Martinez and other historic figures are buried.

Picnicking is permitted. Daily 8-8, Apr.-Oct.; 8-5, rest of year. Free. Phone (505) 758-8234.

MARTINEZ HACIENDA is 2 mi. w. of Taos Plaza at 708 Ranchitos Rd. This restored *hacienda* was built in 1804 by Don Antonio Severino Martinez, a merchant and *alcalde*—mayor—of Taos. The fortresslike house has 21 rooms built around two large *placitas*, or patios. Furnished in period, it contains exhibits of Spanish colonial life and culture. Living-history demonstrations are presented periodically. Daily 9-5, Apr.-Oct.; otherwise varies. Admission $6; ages 6-16, $3; family rate $15. AX, DS, MC, VI. Phone (505) 758-1000.

SAVE **MILLICENT ROGERS MUSEUM** is 4 mi. n. of Taos Plaza near US 64. The adobe house displays the art, history and culture of the Southwest. It focuses on the American Indian, Hispanic and Anglo art of Taos and northern New Mexico. Also presented is one of the largest known pottery collections by Maria Martinez, an early 20th-century Pueblo artist whose career spanned some 85 years. Allow 1 hour minimum. Daily 10-5, Apr.-Oct.; Tues.-Sun. 10-5, rest of year. Closed Jan. 1, Easter, Sept. 30, Thanksgiving and Dec. 25. Admission $7; over 59 and students with ID $6; ages 6-16, $2; family rate $15. AX, DS, MC, VI. Phone (505) 758-2462.

PICURÍS PUEBLO—*see place listing p. 163.*

SAN FRANCISCO DE ASIS CHURCH is 4 mi. s. on SR 68. Completed in 1816, the heavily buttressed adobe structure exemplifies Franciscan Old World architecture and appears in works by photographer Ansel Adams and painter Georgia O'Keeffe. Its interior is adorned with art, images of saints and reredos. Henri Ault's mysterious, some say miraculous, luminescent painting, "The Shadow of the Cross," is displayed in the church hall.

Photography is not permitted inside the church. Allow 1 hour minimum. Mon.-Sat. 9-4, Sun. for services only. Church free. Admission for painting $3, under 10 free. MC, VI. Phone (505) 758-2754.

TAOS ART MUSEUM is at 227 Paseo del Pueblo Norte. Housed in the historic home of Russian-born artist Nicolai Fechin, the permanent collection includes paintings by the Taos Society of Artists and the Taos Moderns. The Fechin Home, designed and reconstructed in the 1930s, is considered an architectural masterpiece. It is filled with Fechin's hand-carved doors, windows, furniture and art. Allow 30 minutes minimum. Tues.-Sun. 10-5, June-Sept.; Wed.-Sun. 10-5, rest of year. Hours may vary; phone ahead. Admission $6; over 64 and students with ID $5; ages 6-16, $3. Phone (505) 758-2690.

TAOS PUEBLO is 2.6 mi. n. of Taos Plaza. Two multiple-storied adobe dwellings reflect a culture hundreds of years old. This picturesque pueblo at the base of the Sangre de Cristo Mountains is one of the oldest continuously inhabited communities in North America.

Ruins of the Mission San Gerónimo de Taos are near the entrance to the pueblo. Established about 1598, the mission was burned by the Pueblos in their 1680 rebellion, restored 25 years later and finally destroyed by U.S. troops during a revolt in 1847. A cemetery, sections of the massive walls and a portion of an original bell tower are all that remain; the cemetery is closed to the public. Guided tours of the pueblo are available. Allow 30 minutes minimum. Daily 8-4:30. Closed twice yearly for ceremonial activities. Admission $10, students with ID $5, under 12 free. Videotape and camera fee $5. Phone (505) 758-1028.

RECREATIONAL ACTIVITIES

Skiing

- **Taos Ski Valley** is in the Sangre de Cristo Mountains in Carson National Forest *(see place listing p. 148)*. Write Taos Ski Valley, P.O. Box 90, Taos Ski Valley, NM 87525. Other activities are offered. Daily Thanksgiving-early Apr. Phone (505) 776-2291 or (800) 992-7669.

White-water Rafting

- **Far Flung Adventures** departs from 15 SR 522N. Write P.O. Box 707, El Prado, NM 87529. Daily late Apr.-Sept. 30. Phone (505) 758-2628 or (800) 359-2627.

- **Los Rios River Runners** departs from various locations. Write P.O. Box 2734, Taos, NM 87571. Daily Mar.-Oct. Phone (505) 776-8854 or (800) 544-1181.

- **Native Sons Adventures** departs from 1033A Paseo de Pueblo Sur (US 68) or from Pilar, 14 mi. s. on US 68. Write 1033A Paseo de Pueblo Sur, Taos, NM 87571. Other activities are available. Daily May-Sept. and Dec.-Mar. Phone (800) 753-7559 to verify schedule.

TESUQUE PUEBLO (B-4) elev. 6,365′

Named by the Tewa-speaking people for the "village at the narrow place of the cottonwood trees," Tesuque (te-SOO-kay) rests in the foothills of the Sangre de Cristo Mountains. The pueblo is just south of Camel Rock, one of many unusual sandstone formations in the area.

TESUQUE PUEBLO is on US 84/285. Tewa-speaking people founded the present settlement in the late 17th century, although habitation dates to 1200 A.D. The 1915 San Diego Mission, designed in the shape of a crucifix, stands on the main plaza. The Pueblos, who have retained their traditional language and culture, hold a ceremonial Corn Dance the first Saturday in June and celebrate the Feast of San Diego on Nov. 12. The pueblo closes to the public on certain days; phone ahead. Free. Phone (505) 983-2667.

THREE RIVERS (D-3) elev. 4,568′

Watered by runoff from the surrounding mountains, the grazing lands of the upper Tularosa Valley attracted cattle barons in the 1870s. Three Rivers, once a railroad shipping point, maintains a ranching and farming economy.

THREE RIVERS PETROGLYPH SITE is 5 mi. e. on a paved road from US 54 following signs. A large group of prehistoric picture writings includes more than 21,000 individual petroglyphs. The Jornada branch of the Mogollon culture is thought to have inscribed them A.D. 900-1400. A trail links many petroglyph sites. Picnicking is permitted. Camping is available. Daily 24 hours. Admission $2 per private vehicle. Phone (505) 525-4300 or (505) 525-4400.

TRUTH OR CONSEQUENCES (E-2)
pop. 7,289, elev. 4,242′

Playing host to a live broadcast of the radio program "Truth or Consequences" changed not only Hot Springs' future but also its name. So pleased were residents with the publicity engendered by Ralph Edwards' popular show that they adopted the program's name in 1950.

The fire of the chilies—one of the Rio Grande Valley's major crops—is nearly matched by the 110 F of the thermal springs that bubble to the surface in Truth or Consequences. The mineral springs have been enjoyed for their legendary curative properties since the days when only the Apaches knew of them. Inevitably, popular bathhouses grew up around the springs in the early 20th century.

Elephant Butte Lake and Caballo Lake state parks offer water activities. *See Recreation Chart and the AAA Southwestern CampBook.*

Truth or Consequences Visitors Center: 211 Main St., Truth or Consequences, NM 87901; phone (505) 894-1968.

[SAVE] **GERONIMO SPRINGS MUSEUM** is 211 Main St. The museum houses American Indian artifacts, prehistoric Mimbres pottery, ranching, military and mining items, paleontological and geological finds, a reconstructed log cabin, Southwestern art and mementos of Ralph Edwards, originator of the "Truth or Consequences" radio show. Allow 1 hour, 30 minutes minimum. Mon.-Sat. 9-5; closed Jan. 1, July 4, Thanksgiving and Dec. 25. Admission $3, ages 6-18, $1.50. DS, MC, VI. Phone (505) 894-6600.

TUCUMCARI (C-5) pop. 5,989, elev. 4,086′

Established with the Rock Island Railroad in 1901, Tucumcari supposedly takes its name from the 4,999-foot Tucumcari Mountain once used by the Comanches as a lookout point, or *tucumcari.*

A more sentimental theory, however, traces the origin of the name to the legend of an ill-fated romance between the Apache warrior Tocom and Kari, the daughter of an Apache chief. When Tocom died in a fight for Kari's hand, Kari stabbed the victor, then herself. Witness to the tragic scene, her father also ended his life with a dagger, crying out "Tocom-Kari."

In the 1920s Tucumcari became the first stop in New Mexico for westbound travelers on the new federal highway, Route 66. The 2,448-mile road stretching between Chicago and Los Angeles was credited with connecting New Mexico to the rest of the nation. For some 40 years it was one of America's best known routes for commerce and leisure travel. The interstate highway system eventually supplanted Route 66, which was officially decertified in 1985. Landmarks from the heydays remain. In Tucumcari, neon-lit motor courts and a teepee shaped curios shop are among the more prominent sites.

The two Canadian River reservoirs that irrigate 45,000 acres around the city also provide water sports and other recreation. Conchas Lake is 31 miles northwest via SR 104; Ute Lake is 23 miles northeast via SR 54 at Logan. *See Recreation Chart and the AAA Southwestern CampBook.*

Tucumcari-Quay County Chamber of Commerce: 404 W. Route 66 Blvd., P.O. Drawer E, Tucumcari, NM 88401; phone (505) 461-1694 or (888) 664-7255.

TUCUMCARI HISTORICAL MUSEUM is at 416 S. Adams St. A 1903 schoolhouse contains three floors of regional artifacts and memorabilia. Thematic exhibits include a pioneer kitchen, general store, bunkhouse, courthouse room, barn, firehouse with a 1926 fire truck and a tribute to the Armed Forces. Native landscaping surrounds the museum and provides the setting for outdoor exhibits including a railroad caboose. Mon.-Sat. 8-5, Memorial Day to Labor Day; Mon.-Fri. 8-5, rest of year. Closed holidays. Admission $2; ages 6-15, 50c. Phone (505) 461-4201.

WHITE SANDS MISSILE RANGE (D-3)
pop. 2,616, elev. 4,295′

On July 16, 1945, in a remote section of White Sands Missile Range, the first man-made atomic explosion sent a huge multicolored cloud surging to an altitude of 40,000 feet. The resultant sloping crater at Trinity Site is mute evidence of man's transition to the Atomic Age.

With the advent of the Space Age, rocket testing took center stage. In the 1960s the desert proved ideal for testing the lunar module engines that propelled Apollo astronauts off the moon's surface. Today the missile range is known for its world-class test facilities. The U.S. Army as well as private industry and foreign nations conduct laser, radar and flight research here.

Vehicle passes are issued at the main gate; a valid driver's license, registration and proof of insurance are required. Photo ID is required for all car occupants. Trinity Site is open the first Saturdays in April and in October. Contact the Public Affairs Office, Bldg. 1782, White Sands Missile Range, NM 88002. Phone (505) 678-1134, or the Alamogordo Chamber of Commerce at (505) 437-6120 or (800) 826-0294.

WHITE SANDS MISSILE RANGE MUSEUM is 19 mi. n.e. of Las Cruces on US 70/80, then 4 mi. e. to just inside main gate. The history of the nation's missile program and the Atomic Age is presented with artifacts, displays and photographs depicting early rocket launches and the first atomic bomb test at Trinity Site. The accomplishments of noted scientists Dr. Wernher von Braun and Dr. Clyde Tombaugh also are highlighted. An outdoor park displays some 60 rockets and missiles.

Exhibits about Paleo-Indian culture as well as 19th-century mining and ranching also are offered. Picnicking is permitted. Allow 30 minutes minimum. Mon.-Fri. 8-4, Sat.-Sun. 10-3; closed major holidays. Missile park daily dawn-dusk. Free. Phone (505) 678-8824.

WHITE SANDS NATIONAL MONUMENT (E-3)

About 15 miles southwest of Alamogordo on US 70, White Sands National Monument is the source of rare gypsum sands that form snow-white dunes rising up to 60 feet above the Tularosa Basin floor.

Covering 275 square miles, the massive dunes are created when rain and melting snow dissolve gypsum from the surrounding mountains and carry it into the seasonal lake, or *playa*, of Lake Lucero. Desert heat evaporates the *playa*, causing gypsum crystals to form. Dry winds expose the crystals, eroding them into sand-sized particles that are blown into the dune field.

Much of the wide sea of dunes is bare of vegetation. However, a few species of plants exhibit remarkable adaptation to the shifting sands; the soaptree yucca can stretch its stem up to 30 feet to keep from being buried.

Drinking water is available only at the visitor center; covered picnic sites and restrooms are in the heart of the dunes area. Information about park facilities is broadcast continuously within 6 miles of the monument over AM 1610. A visitor center relates the origin and history of White Sands through exhibits and a video presentation that is shown every half hour.

On summer evenings guided walks are offered at 7 p.m.; narrated programs are presented at 8:30 p.m., earlier in August. Brochures describing four self-guiding walking tours also are available. On full-moon nights from June to August, the park remains open until 11 p.m. so visitors can witness the celestial light reflecting off the dunes.

The scenic 16-mile round-trip Dunes Drive can be entered daily 7 a.m.-9 p.m., Memorial Day weekend-Labor Day; 7 a.m.-dusk, rest of year. Visitor center is open daily 9-7, Memorial Day-Labor Day; 8-5, rest of year. Closed Dec. 25. Admission $3, under 17 free. Phone (505) 479-6124 or (505) 679-2599.

WHITES CITY (E-5) elev. 3,660'

James Larkin White first explored Carlsbad Caverns as a teenager, carving his name into the rock wall in 1898. He spent the rest of his life promoting the cave and succeeded in having it named a national park in 1930. Around that time, Charles White—no relation to James—bought a 120-acre homestead near the entrance to the caves, and Whites City became the base for a series of guano mining companies, all of which failed. The town today is a stopover for visitors to the national park.

MILLION DOLLAR MUSEUM is at entrance to Carlsbad Caverns National Park. The museum's 18 rooms contain exhibits about area history and include European doll houses, antique furniture, doll collections, a 1905 car, pioneer items, rifles, jukeboxes and American Indian artifacts. Daily 7 a.m.-9 p.m., May 15-Sept. 14; 7 a.m.-8 p.m., rest of year. Admission $3; over 61, $2.50; under 13, $2. AX, DS, MC, VI. Phone (505) 785-2291.

ZIA PUEBLO (B-3) pop. 646, elev. 5,470'

Once one of the largest of the Rio Grande pueblos with some 6,000 residents, Zia is now a community of less than 650 people. Zia potters are renowned for their geometric designs and plant and animal motifs on a white background; thin-walled pottery adorned with the Zia bird symbol is highly prized.

ZIA PUEBLO AND MISSION is off US 550 at 135 Capital Square Dr. Settled in the 13th century, the pueblo stands on a barren mesa where it blends almost invisibly with the natural terrain. New Mexico adopted the pueblo's ancient Zia sun symbol to adorn the state flag. The Zia Cultural Center sells and displays traditional crafts.

Photography is not allowed within some areas. A permit is required for fishing on Zia Lake. Daily dawn-dusk. Cultural center Mon.-Fri. 8-5. Closed during some ceremonial events. Free. Phone (505) 867-3304.

ZUNI PUEBLO (C-1) pop. 6,367, elev. 6,282'

About 30 miles south of Gallup *(see place listing p. 156)* via SRs 602 and 53, Zuni is the only surviving settlement of the Seven Cities of Cibola sought by Francisco Vasquez de Coronado in his quest for gold. It is among the largest of existing inhabited pueblos. Fray Marcos de Niza, bringing the first contact with Europeans in 1539, was followed by Coronado, Juan de Oñate and Franciscan padres, who found the people unresponsive to Christianity.

Long considered master carvers, the Zuni are renowned for their quality inlay jewelry of silver, jet, shell and turquoise, including needlepoint work of finely cut turquoise in silver, and for carved animal fetishes. Ancient rites and traditions are still preserved. Ceremonial dances are held throughout the year.

Photography, videotaping, sketching and hiking are allowed by permit only. Permission must be obtained from the Government of Zuni for hunting and fishing; phone (505) 782-7238. More information is available at the Zuni A:Shiwi A:wan Museum & Heritage Center; phone (505) 782-4403.

Share the

Happiest Celebration On Earth ...

and receive special benefits only when you book with AAA/CAA Travel!

The biggest Disney celebration ever brings you new attractions, shows and enchantment. And when you book a *AAA Vacations*® package to the *Walt Disney World*® Resort or *Disney Cruise Line*® vacation through your AAA/CAA Travel office, you'll enjoy special benefits and great values, too. Visit AAA/CAA Travel today and let the celebration begin!

aaa.com

Disneyland® Resort
Walt Disney World® Resort
Disney Cruise Line®

As to Disney properties/artwork:
©Disney 4058025CMC0103

Ships' Registry: The Bahamas
CST#1022229-50

START WITH AAA. FINISH FIRST.

Arizona

Organ Pipe Cactus
National Monument
©Ray Manley
SuperStock

AJO pop. 3,705

──────── WHERE TO STAY ────────

THE GUEST HOUSE INN

▼▼▼▼

Bed & Breakfast

All Year [BP]   1P: $79   2P: $89   XP: $15   Phone: 520/387-6133

Location: SR 85, 0.5 mi sw; from town plaza, take La Mina Ave and Hospital Dr. Located in a residential area. 700 Guest House Rd 85321. **Facility:** Built in 1925 as a house for the mine directors when they visited, the open rooms and two enclosed porches offer expansive rooms for today's guests. Designated smoking area. 4 one-bedroom standard units. 1 story, interior corridors. *Bath:* combo or shower only. **Parking:** on-site. **Terms:** office hours 9 am-8 pm, 3 day cancellation notice. **Amenities:** irons, hair dryers. **Guest Services:** TV in common area. **Cards:** DC, MC, VI.

LA SIESTA MOTEL

▼

Motel

All Year   1P: $53   2P: $53   Phone: 520/387-6569

Location: On SR 85, 1.8 mi n of town plaza. 2561 N Ajo-Gila Bend Hwy 85321. Fax: 520/387-3743. **Facility:** 12 one-bedroom standard units. 1 story, exterior corridors. *Bath:* combo or shower only. **Parking:** on-site. **Terms:** office hours 8 am-9 pm, cancellation fee imposed. **Amenities:** video library (fee). **Pool(s):** small heated outdoor. **Leisure Activities:** whirlpool, tennis court, horseshoes, shuffleboard. **Cards:** AX, CB, DC, DS, JC, MC, VI.

SOME UNITS

AMADO pop. 275

──────── WHERE TO STAY ────────

AMADO TERRITORY INN

AAA SAVE

▼▼▼▼

Bed & Breakfast

2/1-6/30 & 11/1-1/31	1P: $120-$135	2P: $120-$135
7/1-10/31	1P: $95-$105	2P: $95-$105

Phone: (520)398-8684

Location: I-19, exit 48, just e, then just s. Located on the grounds of the Territory Ranch. 3001 E Frontage Rd 85645 (PO Box 81). Fax: 520/398-8186. **Facility:** A two-story high stone fireplace, a sunny breakfast room looking across a dry wash and a roadrunner who comes to look at visitors may all charm you. Designated smoking area. 9 one-bedroom standard units. 2 stories (no elevator), interior corridors. *Bath:* shower only. **Parking:** on-site. **Terms:** office hours 7:30 am-9 pm, age restrictions may apply, 4 day cancellation notice, weekly rates available, package plans. **Amenities:** hair dryers. **Leisure Activities:** putting green, bicycles, horseshoes. *Fee:* massage. **Guest Services:** TV in common area, gift shop, complimentary evening beverages. **Cards:** AX, DS, MC, VI. **Special Amenities:** free full breakfast and free local telephone calls.

──────── WHERE TO DINE ────────

AMADO CAFE

▼▼▼

American

Lunch: $7-$11   **Dinner:** $12-$31   Phone: 520/398-9211

Location: I-19, exit 48, just e, then just s. 3001 E Frontage Rd 85645. **Hours:** 11:30 am-2 & 5-8 pm, Sun-2 pm. Closed: 1/1, 12/25; also Mon. **Reservations:** suggested. **Features:** The desert garden setting of this casual restaurant is just right for a lunch stop when traveling or for a more leisurely dinner. Casual dress; cocktails. **Parking:** on-site. **Cards:** AX, DS, MC, VI.

COW PALACE RESTAURANT
~~~ ~~~
Steak House
Cards: AX, DS, MC, VI.

Lunch: $6-$10   **Dinner:** $10-$20   **Phone:** 520/398-1999
Location: I-19, exit 48, just w, then just n. 28802 S Nogales Hwy 85645. **Hours:** 8 am-9 pm. Closed: 12/25.
Reservations: accepted. **Features:** Beyond grilled steaks, diners may order Mexican dishes, fresh crispy salads, baby back ribs and grilled or fried fish. Established more than 50 years ago, the restaurant has been a frequent stop for travelers heading south from Tucson. Casual dress; cocktails. **Parking:** on-site.

ANTHEM

──────── WHERE TO STAY ────────

HAMPTON INN AT ANTHEM   *Book at aaa.com*
(AAA) [SAVE]
~~~ ~~~ ~~~
Small-scale Hotel

	1P: $99-$129	2P: $99-$129
12/31-1/31	1P: $99-$129	2P: $99-$129
2/1-4/29 & 9/15-12/30	1P: $79-$129	2P: $79-$129
4/30-9/14	1P: $49-$79	2P: $49-$79

Phone: (623)465-7979

Location: I-17, exit 229 (Anthem Way), just w. 42415 N 41st Dr 85086. Fax: 623/465-9299. **Facility:** 76 one-bedroom standard units, some with whirlpools. 3 stories, interior corridors. *Bath:* combo or shower only. **Amenities:** video games (fee), high-speed Internet, voice mail, irons, hair dryers. **Pool(s):** heated outdoor. **Leisure Activities:** whirlpool, exercise room. **Guest Services:** sundries, coin laundry. **Business Services:** meeting rooms, business center. **Cards:** AX, CB, DC, DS, MC, VI.
Special Amenities: free expanded continental breakfast and free local telephone calls.

SOME UNITS

APACHE JUNCTION —*See Phoenix p. 311.*

BELLEMONT

──────── WHERE TO STAY ────────

BELLEMONT MICROTEL INN
~~~ ~~~
Small-scale Hotel

	1P: $54	2P: $54	XP: $10	F18
4/1-10/31	1P: $54	2P: $54	XP: $10	F18
2/1-3/31	1P: $33-$44	2P: $33-$44	XP: $10	F18
11/1-1/31	1P: $39	2P: $39	XP: $10	F18

Phone: (928)556-9599

Location: I-40, exit 185, just n. 12380 W Interstate Hwy 40 86015 (PO Box 16122). Fax: 928/556-8786. **Facility:** 60 one-bedroom standard units, some with efficiencies (no utensils). 2 stories (no elevator), interior corridors. *Bath:* combo or shower only. **Parking:** on-site. **Terms:** 1-3 night minimum stay, cancellation fee imposed, weekly rates available, package plans, $6 service charge, pets ($15 extra charge). **Amenities:** *Some:* irons, hair dryers. **Guest Services:** coin laundry. **Cards:** AX, DS, MC, VI.

SOME UNITS

BENSON pop. 4,711

──────── WHERE TO STAY ────────

BEST WESTERN QUAIL HOLLOW INN   *Book at aaa.com*
(AAA) [SAVE]
~~~ ~~~ ~~~
Motel

	1P: $80-$90	2P: $80-$90	XP: $5	F17
2/1-2/15 [ECP]	1P: $80-$90	2P: $80-$90	XP: $5	F17
2/16-1/31 [ECP]	1P: $65-$85	2P: $65-$85	XP: $5	F17

Phone: (520)586-3646

Location: I-10, exit 304, just s. 699 N Ocotillo Ave 85602. Fax: 520/586-7035. **Facility:** 89 one-bedroom standard units. 1-2 stories (no elevator), exterior corridors. *Bath:* combo or shower only. **Parking:** on-site. **Terms:** package plans, small pets only ($10 extra charge, in limited units). **Amenities:** video library (fee), high-speed Internet, irons, hair dryers. **Pool(s):** heated outdoor. **Leisure Activities:** whirlpool. **Guest Services:** coin laundry. **Business Services:** fax (fee). **Cards:** AX, CB, DC, DS, MC, VI. **Special Amenities:** free expanded continental breakfast and free local telephone calls.

SOME UNITS

DAYS INN   *Book at aaa.com*
(AAA) [SAVE]
~~~ ~~~ ~~~
Small-scale Hotel

	1P: $70-$80	2P: $80-$90	XP: $5	F5
2/1-2/20	1P: $70-$80	2P: $80-$90	XP: $5	F5
2/21-5/31 & 10/1-1/31	1P: $58-$65	2P: $63-$70	XP: $5	F5
6/1-9/30	1P: $50-$55	2P: $55-$60	XP: $5	F5

Phone: (520)586-3000

Location: I-10, exit 304, just n. 621 Commerce Dr 85602. Fax: 520/586-7000. **Facility:** 61 units. 60 one-bedroom standard units. 1 one-bedroom suite ($80-$100) with whirlpool. 2 stories (no elevator), interior corridors. *Bath:* combo or shower only. **Parking:** on-site. **Terms:** cancellation fee imposed. **Amenities:** hair dryers. *Some:* irons. **Pool(s):** heated outdoor. **Leisure Activities:** whirlpool. **Guest Services:** gift shop, coin laundry. **Cards:** AX, DC, DS, MC, VI. **Special Amenities:** free continental breakfast and free local telephone calls.

SOME UNITS

HOLIDAY INN EXPRESS   *Book at aaa.com*
(AAA) [SAVE]
~~~ ~~~ ~~~
Small-scale Hotel

	1P: $99-$139	2P: $99-$139	XP: $10	F18
2/1-4/1	1P: $99-$139	2P: $99-$139	XP: $10	F18
12/1-1/31	1P: $89-$129	2P: $89-$129	XP: $10	F18
4/2-8/31	1P: $72-$99	2P: $72-$99	XP: $10	F18
9/1-11/30	1P: $72-$89	2P: $72-$89	XP: $10	F18

Phone: 520/586-8800

Location: I-10, exit 302, just s. 630 S Village Loop 85602. Fax: 520/586-1370. **Facility:** 62 one-bedroom standard units, some with whirlpools. 2 stories, interior corridors. *Bath:* combo or shower only. **Parking:** on-site. **Terms:** 3 day cancellation notice-fee imposed, [ECP] meal plan available. **Amenities:** dual phone lines, voice mail, irons, hair dryers. *Some:* high-speed Internet. **Pool(s):** heated outdoor. **Leisure Activities:** exercise room. **Guest Services:** coin laundry. **Business Services:** meeting rooms, PC. **Cards:** AX, DC, DS, MC, VI. **Special Amenities:** free expanded continental breakfast and free local telephone calls.

SOME UNITS

SUPER 8 MOTEL *Book at aaa.com* **Phone: (520)586-1530**

2/1-2/17	1P: $69-$89	2P: $79-$109	XP: $12	F
10/1-1/31	1P: $50-$79	2P: $59-$89	XP: $8	F
2/18-5/31	1P: $49-$59	2P: $56-$79	XP: $8	F
6/1-9/30	1P: $45-$65	2P: $50-$70	XP: $6	F

Motel

Location: I-10, exit 304, just n. 855 N Ocotillo Ave 85602. Fax: 520/586-1534. **Facility:** 40 one-bedroom standard units. 2 stories (no elevator), exterior corridors. **Parking:** on-site. **Terms:** 3 day cancellation notice, [CP] meal plan available, pets ($10 deposit). **Pool(s):** outdoor. **Cards:** AX, DC, DS, MC, VI.

——— WHERE TO DINE ———

CHUTE-OUT STEAKHOUSE & SALOON Dinner: $8-$17 **Phone: 520/586-7297**

Steak House

Location: I-10, exit 304; center. 161 S Huachuca 85602. **Hours:** 4 pm-9 pm. Closed: 4/16, 11/23, 12/25. **Reservations:** accepted. **Features:** The casual, friendly atmosphere and Western motif set the stage for some down-home eating. Among appetizers is a plate of Texas toothpicks—fried strips of peppers and onions. Good entree choices include pasta preparations and mesquite-grilled meats and chicken. Casual dress; cocktails. **Parking:** on-site. **Cards:** AX, DS, MC, VI.

HORSE SHOE CAFE Lunch: $5-$9 Dinner: $5-$11 **Phone: 520/586-3303**

American

Location: Center. 154 E 4th St 85602. **Hours:** 6 am-9 pm. Closed: 11/23, 12/24, 12/25. **Reservations:** accepted. **Features:** Lending to the charm here are the old building as well as the Western murals by cowboy artist Vern Parker. The family-run eatery serves hearty portions of well-prepared entrees, sandwiches and soups. Breakfast sticky rolls are a local treat. Also worth trying are chili, the hearty turkey sandwich and the steak dinner. Casual dress; cocktails. **Parking:** on-site. **Cards:** AX, MC, VI.

MAGALY'S MEXICAN RESTAURANT Lunch: $5-$8 Dinner: $5-$8 **Phone: 520/586-2027**

Mexican

Location: I-10, exit 304, 0.5 mi s on Ocatilla Ave, then just w. 675 W 4th St 85602. **Hours:** 11 am-9 pm, Mon & Tues-8 pm. Closed major holidays; also Sun. **Features:** Friendly staff members serve economical and hearty Sonoran dishes prepared by the chef-owner. The neat and tidy room is decorated with Mexican handicrafts, which may be purchased. Casual dress; beer only. **Parking:** on-site. **Cards:** AX, MC, VI.

BISBEE pop. 6,090

——— WHERE TO STAY ———

AUDREY'S INN [AAA] [SAVE] **Phone: (520)227-6120**

All Year 1P: $95-$110 2P: $95-$110

Condominium

Location: Just ne of Main St; in historic district. 20 Brewery Ave 85603. Fax: 520/432-9022. **Facility:** In the early 1900s, a sporting gentlemen's club operated in the building that now houses modern suites and two-level units. Smoke free premises. 6 units. 3 one-bedroom standard units with kitchens. 3 one-bedroom suites with kitchens. 3 stories (no elevator), interior corridors. **Parking:** street. **Terms:** office hours 8 am-5 pm, off-site registration, check-in 4 pm, cancellation fee imposed. **Amenities:** voice mail, irons, hair dryers. **Guest Services:** coin laundry. **Cards:** MC, VI. **Special Amenities:** free local telephone calls.

CANYON ROSE SUITES [AAA] [SAVE] **Phone: (520)432-5098**

2/1-5/29 & 9/5-1/31	2P: $95-$200	XP: $10	F12
5/30-9/4	2P: $85-$180	XP: $10	F12

Classic Historic
Small-scale Hotel

Location: Corner of Shearer; in historic district. 27 Subway St 85603. Fax: 520/432-7670. **Facility:** Attractive rooms and modern conveniences are recent additions to this older building just off Main Street. Smoke free premises. 6 units. 5 one-bedroom standard units with kitchens. 1 one-bedroom suite with kitchen. 2 stories (no elevator), interior corridors. *Bath:* combo or shower only. **Parking:** street. **Terms:** office hours 8 am-8 pm, cancellation fee imposed, package plans. **Amenities:** video library, voice mail, irons, hair dryers. **Guest Services:** coin laundry. **Business Services:** meeting rooms. **Cards:** AX, DS, MC, VI. **Special Amenities:** free local telephone calls and early check-in/late check-out.

LA ESTANCIA BED & BREAKFAST **Phone: (520)432-5582**

All Year [BP] 1P: $75 2P: $85

Bed & Breakfast

Location: Corner of Brewery Ave; historic district; center. 7 Howell Ave 85603 (PO Box 908). **Facility:** Formerly a Western Union building, the large charming rooms are filled with antiques, have modern baths and open to a pleasant gallery courtyard. Designated smoking area. 4 one-bedroom standard units. 2 stories, interior/exterior corridors. *Bath:* combo or shower only. **Parking:** on-site. **Terms:** age restrictions may apply, 3 day cancellation notice-fee imposed, no pets allowed (owner's pet in premises). **Amenities:** high-speed Internet, hair dryers. **Cards:** MC, VI.

SAN JOSE LODGE [AAA] [SAVE] *Book at aaa.com* **Phone: (520)432-5761**

All Year 1P: $59-$95 2P: $75-$125 XP: $10 F10

Motel

Location: 1.5 mi s from jct SR 92. 1002 Naco Hwy 85603. Fax: 520/432-4302. **Facility:** 43 units. 39 one-bedroom standard units. 4 one-bedroom suites ($95-$150) with kitchens (no utensils). 1 story, exterior corridors. **Parking:** on-site. **Terms:** 3 day cancellation notice-fee imposed, pets ($10 extra charge). **Amenities:** voice mail. *Some:* irons, hair dryers. **Dining:** 7 am-9 pm, Sun-8 pm, cocktails. **Pool(s):** outdoor. **Business Services:** meeting rooms. **Cards:** AX, DC, DS, MC, VI. **Special Amenities:** free local telephone calls and early check-in/late check-out.

--------- The following lodging was either not evaluated or did not ---------
meet AAA rating requirements but is listed for your information only.

COPPER QUEEN HOTEL   Phone: 520/432-2216
[fyi]   Not evaluated. **Location:** Corner of Brewery Ave; in historic district. 11 Howell Ave 85603. Facilities, services, and decor characterize a mid-range property.

--------- **WHERE TO DINE** ---------

THE BREWERY STEAKHOUSE AND STOCK   **Dinner:** $8-$19   Phone: 520/432-3317
   EXCHANGE BAR   **Location:** Corner of Howell Ave; in historic district. 15 Brewery Gulch 85603. **Hours:** 5 pm-9 pm. Closed: 12/25;
▽▽ ▽▽   also Wed. **Reservations:** accepted. **Features:** The historic building sits just off Main Street, and guests
Steak House   enter the below-sidewalk-level restaurant by walking downstairs. The grill turns out prime rib, steaks, crispy
         salads and sandwiches. Casual dress; cocktails. **Parking:** street. **Cards:** MC, VI.   [Y] [K]

CAFE ROKA   **Dinner:** $14-$23   Phone: 520/432-5153
AAA   **Location:** SR 80, just n; in historic district; downtown. 35 Main St 85603. **Hours:** 5 pm-9 pm; seasonal hours may
         vary. Closed major holidays; also Mon & Tues. **Reservations:** suggested. **Features:** This popular eatery is
▽▽▽▽   located in a restored 1907 building with a central oval bar. The chef/owner serves up Italian and California
American cuisine excellently prepared using seasonal ingredients. Vegetarian entrees offered and meals include 4
         courses. Casual dress; cocktails. **Parking:** street. **Cards:** AX, MC, VI. **Historic**

WINCHESTER'S   **Lunch:** $7-$9   **Dinner:** $15-$21   Phone: 520/432-2216
▽▽ ▽▽   **Location:** Corner of Brewery Ave; in historic district; in Copper Queen Hotel. 11 Howell Ave 85603. **Hours:** 7-10:30
         am, 11-2:30 & 5:30-9 pm. **Reservations:** suggested. **Features:** Charming Victorian decor is one step into
American the past in the historic facility, but the dishes are strictly up-to-the-minute, prepared with the freshest
         ingredients. Seasonal patio seating is a fair-weather option. Casual dress; cocktails. **Parking:** street.
Cards: AX, DC, MC, VI. **Historic**   [Y]

--------- The following restaurants have not been evaluated by AAA ---------
but are listed for your information only.

CAFE CORNUCOPIA   Phone: 520/432-4820
[fyi]   Not evaluated. **Location:** In Historic District. 14 Main St 85603. **Features:** The small space of the sidewalk delicatessen does not limit the big taste from soups and sandwiches.

THE STRIPED STOCKING   Phone: 520/432-1832
[fyi]   Not evaluated. **Location:** Corner of Brewery and Howell aves; center. 1 Howell Ave 85603. **Features:** An intimate
         atmosphere, trained servers and such delectable dishes as pear and Gorgonzola salad, panko-encrusted
chicken breast with mustard-tarragon sauce and homemade chocolate ice cream make the restaurant an elegant option for
dinner.   [Y]

BLACK CANYON CITY pop. 2,697

--------- **WHERE TO DINE** ---------

KID CHILLEEN'S BAD ASS BBQ STEAKHOUSE   **Lunch:** $6-$11   **Dinner:** $10-$18   Phone: 623/374-5552
▽▽ ▽▽   **Location:** I-17, exit 244, just e. 33150 Coldwater Rd 85324. **Hours:** 11 am-10 pm, Fri-11 pm, Sat 7 am-11 pm,
         Sun 7 am-10 pm. Closed: 11/23, 12/25. **Reservations:** accepted. **Features:** Country barbecue, grilled
Steak House   steaks, roasted chicken and desserts are large enough to share. Live entertainment is featured on the
         weekends. Casual dress; cocktails. **Parking:** on-site. **Cards:** AX, DS, MC, VI.   [Y] [\]

BUCKEYE —See Phoenix p. 312.

BULLHEAD CITY pop. 33,769

--------- **WHERE TO STAY** ---------

BEST WESTERN BULLHEAD CITY INN   *Book at aaa.com*   Phone: (928)754-3000
AAA [SAVE]   All Year   1P: $69-$99   2P: $74-$99   XP: $5   F12
         Location: 1.8 mi s of Laughlin Bridge. 1126 Hwy 95 86429. Fax: 928/754-5234. **Facility:** 89 one-bedroom
▽▽▽▽   standard units. 2 stories (no elevator), exterior corridors. **Parking:** on-site. **Terms:** pets ($10 fee).
         Amenities: high-speed Internet, safes (fee), irons, hair dryers. **Pool(s):** small outdoor. **Leisure**
Small-scale Hotel   **Activities:** whirlpool. **Guest Services:** valet and coin laundry. **Business Services:** meeting rooms.
         Cards: AX, CB, DC, DS, JC, MC, VI. **Special Amenities:** free continental breakfast and free
newspaper.

SOME UNITS
[icons] [S₀] [🛏] [🍴] [🔊] [🏊] [🐾] [DATA PORT] [🔌] [💻] / [✗] [🖨] /
FEE

BUDGET HOST INN   Phone: 928/763-1002
AAA [SAVE]   All Year   1P: $60-$65   2P: $65-$75   XP: $5   F12
         Location: Jct SR 68, 3.2 mi s on SR 95. 1616 Hwy 95 86442. Fax: 928/763-2984. **Facility:** 118 one-bedroom
▽▽   standard units. 2 stories (no elevator), interior corridors. **Bath:** combo or shower only. **Parking:** on-site.
Motel   **Terms:** package plans, pets ($5 extra charge, in limited units). **Pool(s):** outdoor. **Cards:** AX, DC, DS,
         MC, VI. **Special Amenities:** free continental breakfast and free local telephone calls.

[icons] [S₀] [🛏] [🍴] [♿] [🏊] [🐾] [DATA PORT]
FEE

LAKE MOHAVE RESORT MOTEL

(AAA) (SAVE)
◇◇◇
Motel

All Year   1P: $85-$115   2P: $85-$115

Phone: (928)754-3245
XP: $10   F5

Location: Jct SR 95, 1.5 mi e on SR 68, 1 mi n, then 5.4 mi e; at Katherine Landing; in Lake Mead National Recreation area. At Katherine Landing; in Lake Mead National Recreation Area. 2690 E Katherine Spur Rd 86429. Fax: 928/754-1125. **Facility:** 49 one-bedroom standard units, some with efficiencies. 2 stories (no elevator), exterior corridors. **Bath:** combo or shower only. **Parking:** on-site. **Terms:** 3 day cancellation notice, pets ($10 extra charge). **Leisure Activities:** rental boats, marina, waterskiing, fishing, houseboats. **Business Services:** fax (fee). **Cards:** DS, MC, VI.

SOME UNITS
🐕 📶 ✕ 📷 / 🛗 🍳 ☕ /
FEE

——— WHERE TO DINE ———

BLACK BEAR DINER

◇◇ ◇◇
American

Lunch: $6-$9   **Dinner:** $8-$15   **Phone:** 928/763-2477

Location: 3.6 mi s of Laughlin Bridge. 1751 W Hwy 95, Suite 25 86442. **Hours:** 6 am-10 pm. **Features:** A homey decor and atmosphere characterizes the family-oriented restaurant. Familiar comfort foods, such as meatloaf with mashed potatoes and chicken-fried steak, are at the heart of the menu. The wait staff is chipper and pleasant. Casual dress; beer & wine only. **Parking:** on-site. **Cards:** AX, DC, DS, MC, VI.

COLIANNO'S ITALIAN RESTAURANT

◇◇ ◇◇
Italian

Lunch: $5-$18   **Dinner:** $9-$30   **Phone:** 928/758-7104

Location: 4.1 mi s of Laughlin Bridge. 1884 Hwy 95 86442. **Hours:** 11 am-10 pm. **Features:** The feeling here is decidedly Old World, complete with checkered tablecloths. The menu lists steak, seafood and pasta dishes, as well a specialty pizza. Carryout service is available from the on-premises delicatessen. Casual dress; cocktails. **Parking:** on-site. **Cards:** AX, DS, MC, VI.

🍸

EL PALACIO

◇◇ ◇◇
Mexican

Lunch: $4-$8   **Dinner:** $4-$13   **Phone:** 928/763-2494

Location: 4.1 mi s of Laughlin Bridge. 1885 Hwy 95 86442. **Hours:** 11 am-10 pm. Closed: 4/16, 9/4, 12/24, 12/25. **Reservations:** not accepted. **Features:** In addition to assorted Mexican steak and seafood dishes, the menu lists more familiar enchiladas, burritos and tamales. The atmosphere is festive, with bright and colorful appointments. Casual dress; cocktails. **Parking:** on-site. **Cards:** AX, DC, DS, MC, VI.

🍸

CAMERON pop. 978—See also GRAND CANYON NATIONAL PARK - SOUTH RIM.

——— WHERE TO STAY ———

CAMERON TRADING POST MOTEL, RESTAURANT & GIFT SHOP

Phone: 928/679-2231

(AAA) (SAVE)
◇◇ ◇◇
Small-scale Hotel

6/1-10/15	1P: $89-$119	2P: $89-$119
3/2-5/31	1P: $69-$99	2P: $69-$99
10/16-1/31	1P: $59-$79	2P: $59-$79
2/1-3/1	1P: $49-$69	2P: $49-$69

Location: 1 mi from the east gate turn off. US 89 86020 (PO Box 339). Fax: 928/679-2350. **Facility:** 66 units. 62 one-bedroom standard units. 4 one-bedroom suites ($99-$159). 2-3 stories (no elevator), exterior corridors. **Parking:** on-site. **Terms:** check-in 4 pm, [AP], [BP] & [MAP] meal plans available, small pets only (in smoking units). **Amenities:** voice mail. *Some:* irons, hair dryers. **Dining:** 6 am-10 pm. **Leisure Activities:** hiking trails. **Guest Services:** gift shop. **Cards:** AX, CB, DC, DS, JC, MC, VI. **Special Amenities:** free local telephone calls and preferred room (subject to availability with advance reservations). *(See color ad p 225)*

SOME UNITS
🅂🄳 🐕 📶 🐾 📠 ☕ / ✕ 🛗 /

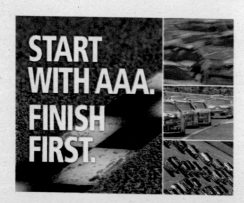

CAMP VERDE pop. 9,451

—— WHERE TO STAY ——

COMFORT INN-CAMP VERDE   *Book at aaa.com*   **Phone:** (928)567-9000

AAA SAVE   All Year   1P: $59-$139   2P: $59-$139   XP: $10   F18
Location: I-17, exit 287, just e, then just s. 340 N Goswick Way 86322 (PO Box 1325). **Fax:** 928/567-1828.
Facility: 85 one-bedroom standard units. 3 stories, interior corridors. *Bath:* combo or shower only. **Parking:**
on-site. **Terms:** [ECP] meal plan available, package plans, pets ($15 fee, in designated units).
Small-scale Hotel   **Amenities:** irons, hair dryers. **Pool(s):** heated outdoor. **Leisure Activities:** whirlpool. **Guest Services:**
sundries, coin laundry. **Business Services:** meeting rooms, fax (fee). **Cards:** AX, CB, DC, DS, JC, MC, VI.
Special Amenities: free continental breakfast and free local telephone calls.

DAYS INN & SUITES OF CAMP VERDE   *Book at aaa.com*   **Phone:** (928)567-3700

AAA SAVE   All Year   1P: $45-$85   2P: $45-$95   XP: $10   F17
Location: I-17, exit 287, just e, then just n. 1640 W Hwy 260 86322. **Fax:** 928/567-1822. **Facility:** 63 one-bedroom
standard units. 3 stories, interior corridors. *Bath:* combo or shower only. **Parking:** on-site. **Terms:** [ECP]
meal plan available, package plans, pets ($10 fee). **Amenities:** voice mail, hair dryers. *Some:* irons.
Small-scale Hotel   **Pool(s):** heated outdoor. **Leisure Activities:** whirlpool. **Guest Services:** complimentary laundry. **Business
Services:** meeting rooms, fax (fee). **Cards:** AX, CB, DC, DS, JC, MC, VI. **Special Amenities:** free
expanded continental breakfast and free local telephone calls.

SUPER 8 MOTEL-CAMP VERDE   *Book at aaa.com*   **Phone:** (928)567-2622

AAA SAVE   2/1-10/31   1P: $54-$129   2P: $59-$129   XP: $5   F14
            11/1-1/31   1P: $49-$129   2P: $54-$129   XP: $5   F14
Location: I-17, exit 287, just e. 1550 W Hwy 260 86322. **Fax:** 928/567-2622. **Facility:** 44 one-bedroom standard
units. 2 stories (no elevator), interior corridors. **Parking:** on-site. **Terms:** small pets only ($10 fee, with prior
Motel   approval). **Amenities:** video library. **Pool(s):** heated indoor. **Leisure Activities:** whirlpool. **Cards:** AX, CB,
DC, DS, JC, MC, VI. **Special Amenities:** free continental breakfast and free local telephone calls.

CAREFREE —*See Phoenix p. 312.*

CASA GRANDE pop. 25,224

—— WHERE TO STAY ——

BEST WESTERN CASA GRANDE   *Book at aaa.com*   **Phone:** (520)836-1600

AAA SAVE   2/1-4/30 & 9/1-1/31 [ECP]   1P: $90-$140   2P: $100-$150   XP: $5   F5
            5/1-8/31 [ECP]   1P: $70-$120   2P: $80-$130   XP: $5   F5
Location: I-10, exit 194 (SR 287), 1 mi w. Located across from Regional Medical Center. 665 Via Del Cielo 85222.
Fax: 520/836-7242. **Facility:** 81 one-bedroom standard units. 2 stories (no elevator), exterior corridors.
Small-scale Hotel   **Parking:** on-site. **Terms:** pets ($10 extra charge). **Amenities:** high-speed Internet, voice mail, irons, hair
dryers. **Pool(s):** heated outdoor. **Leisure Activities:** whirlpool, barbecue grill, exercise room. **Guest
Services:** coin laundry. **Cards:** AX, CB, DC, DS, JC, MC, VI. **Special Amenities:** free expanded continental breakfast and
free local telephone calls.

COMFORT INN

Book at aaa.com

AAA SAVE

3/16-4/30	1P: $75-$99	2P: $95-$99	XP: $5	F18
2/1-3/15	1P: $89-$99	2P: $99	XP: $5	F18
10/1-1/31	1P: $85-$89	2P: $90-$105	XP: $5	F18
5/1-9/30	1P: $75-$85	2P: $80-$85	XP: $5	F18

Phone: (520)421-9878

Small-scale Hotel **Location:** I-10, exit 194 (SR 287), 0.5 mi w. 2145 E Florence Blvd 85222. Fax: 520/421-2189. **Facility:** 65 one-bedroom standard units. 2 stories (no elevator), interior corridors. *Bath:* combo or shower only. **Parking:** on-site. **Terms:** 7 day cancellation notice. **Amenities:** irons, hair dryers. **Pool(s):** small heated outdoor. **Leisure Activities:** whirlpool, exercise room. **Guest Services:** coin laundry. **Business Services:** fax (fee). **Cards:** AX, CB, DC, DS, JC, MC, VI. **Special Amenities:** free expanded continental breakfast and free local telephone calls.

SOME UNITS

FRANCISCO GRANDE HOTEL & GOLF RESORT

Book at aaa.com

AAA SAVE

12/26-1/31	1P: $119-$169	2P: $119-$169	XP: $10	F
2/1-5/1	1P: $109-$169	2P: $109-$169	XP: $10	F
9/15-12/25	1P: $99-$129	2P: $99-$129	XP: $10	F
5/2-9/14	1P: $69-$109	2P: $69-$109	XP: $10	F

Phone: (520)836-6444

Large-scale Hotel **Location:** I-8, exit 172 (Thornton Rd), 3.5 mi n, then 4.2 mi w. 26000 W Gila Bend Hwy (SR 84) 85222. Fax: 520/381-8222. **Facility:** 84 units. 80 one-bedroom standard units. 4 one-bedroom suites ($159-$199) with kitchens. 2-8 stories, exterior corridors. *Bath:* combo or shower only. **Terms:** cancellation fee imposed, [BP] meal plan available, package plans. **Amenities:** DVD players, high-speed Internet (fee), voice mail, irons, hair dryers. **Dining:** 2 restaurants, 6 am-2 & 5-10 pm, cocktails. **Pool(s):** heated outdoor. **Leisure Activities:** whirlpool, driving range, exercise room, horseshoes, volleyball. *Fee:* golf-18 holes, massage. **Guest Services:** area transportation-within 5 mi. **Business Services:** conference facilities. *Fee:* administrative services, fax. **Cards:** AX, DS, MC, VI. *(See color ad p 191)*

SOME UNITS
FEE

HOLIDAY INN CASA GRANDE

Book at aaa.com

2/1-4/30	1P: $71-$99	2P: $71-$99	XP: $6	F18
5/1-1/31	1P: $69-$81	2P: $69-$81	XP: $6	F18

Phone: (520)426-3500

Small-scale Hotel **Location:** I-10, exit 194 (SR 287), 3.9 mi w. 777 N Pinal Ave 85222. Fax: 520/836-4728. **Facility:** 176 one-bedroom standard units, some with whirlpools. 4 stories, interior corridors. **Parking:** on-site. **Terms:** [BP] meal plan available, package plans. **Amenities:** voice mail, irons, hair dryers. **Pool(s):** heated outdoor. **Leisure Activities:** whirlpool, exercise room. **Guest Services:** coin laundry. **Business Services:** conference facilities. **Cards:** AX, CB, DC, DS, JC, MC, VI.

SOME UNITS
FEE

MOTEL 6 - 1263

Book at aaa.com

2/1-4/20	1P: $47-$57	2P: $53-$63	XP: $3	F17
12/16-1/31	1P: $39-$49	2P: $45-$55	XP: $3	F17
4/21-12/15	1P: $35-$45	2P: $41-$51	XP: $3	F17

Phone: 520/836-3323

Motel **Location:** I-10, exit 200. 4965 N Sunland Gin Rd 85222. Fax: 520/421-3094. **Facility:** 97 one-bedroom standard units. 2 stories (no elevator), exterior corridors. *Bath:* combo or shower only. **Parking:** on-site. **Terms:** small pets only. **Pool(s):** outdoor. **Guest Services:** coin laundry. **Cards:** AX, CB, DC, DS, MC, VI.

SOME UNITS
FEE FEE

SUPER 8 MOTEL

Book at aaa.com

AAA SAVE

2/1-2/15	1P: $99-$150	2P: $99-$150	XP: $5	F
1/1-1/31	1P: $59-$79	2P: $69-$89	XP: $5	F
2/16-5/31	1P: $59-$79	2P: $69-$79	XP: $5	F
6/1-12/31	1P: $49-$69	2P: $55-$79	XP: $5	F

Phone: 520/836-8800

Small-scale Hotel **Location:** I-10, exit 194 (SR 287), 0.6 mi w. 2066 E Florence Blvd 85222. Fax: 520/836-8800. **Facility:** 42 one-bedroom standard units. 2 stories (no elevator), interior corridors. *Bath:* combo or shower only. **Parking:** on-site. **Terms:** cancellation fee imposed, pets ($10 extra charge). **Amenities:** hair dryers. **Pool(s):** small outdoor. **Guest Services:** coin laundry. **Cards:** AX, CB, DC, DS, JC, MC, VI. **Special Amenities:** free continental breakfast and free local telephone calls.

SOME UNITS
FEE

——— **WHERE TO DINE** ———

BEDILLON'S CACTUS GARDEN RESTAURANT

Lunch: $6-$10   **Dinner:** $9-$19   **Phone: 520/836-2045**

American **Location:** I-10, exit 194 (SR 287), 3.8 mi w, then just n. 800 N Park Ave 85222. **Hours:** 11 am-2:30 & 5-9 pm, Fri & Sat-9:30 pm. Closed: 11/23, 12/25; also Sun. **Reservations:** accepted. **Features:** The 80-year-old restored home enables visitors to visit a Western museum, walk through a cactus garden and devour a fulfilling meal. Casual dress; cocktails. **Parking:** on-site. **Cards:** AX, DC, DS, MC, VI.

CAFE' DE MANUEL

Lunch: $6-$10   **Dinner:** $6-$13   **Phone: 520/421-3199**

Mexican **Location:** Jct SR 84 and 287, 0.4 mi n on SR 387 (Pinal Ave). 1300 N Pinal Ave 85222. **Hours:** 10:30 am-8 pm, Fri-9 pm, Sat 8 am-9 pm, Sun 8 am-8 pm. Closed: 4/16, 11/23, 12/25. **Reservations:** accepted. **Features:** The friendly, casual eatery serves fresh, traditional dishes. Made-to-order dishes, such as enchilada salad, creamed chimichanga and carne asada, are worth the wait. Weekend breakfasts include rellenos and eggs with machaca. Casual dress; cocktails. **Parking:** on-site. **Cards:** AX, DS, MC, VI.

CATALINA —*See Tucson p. 454.*

CAVE CREEK —*See Phoenix p. 313.*

CHAMBERS

——— WHERE TO STAY ———

CHIEFTAIN INN
Motel
(AAA) (SAVE)

			Phone: (928)688-2754	
7/1-9/30 [BP]	1P: $80-$125	2P: $90-$150	XP: $10	F16
4/1-6/30 [BP]	1P: $68-$110	2P: $77-$115	XP: $10	F16
2/1-3/31 & 10/1-1/31 [BP]	1P: $65-$105	2P: $75-$110	XP: $10	F16

Location: I-40, exit 333, just s at jct US 191 N. I-40 & 191 Interchange 86502 (PO Box 39). **Fax:** 928/688-2754. **Facility:** Smoke free premises. 52 one-bedroom standard units. 2 stories (no elevator), exterior corridors. **Parking:** on-site. **Terms:** small pets only ($10 extra charge). **Amenities:** voice mail, irons, hair dryers. **Dining:** Chieftain Restaurant, see separate listing. **Pool(s):** small heated outdoor. **Leisure Activities:** whirlpools. **Guest Services:** gift shop, coin laundry. **Business Services:** meeting rooms. **Cards:** AX, CB, DC, DS, JC, MC, VI. **Special Amenities:** free full breakfast and free local telephone calls.

——— WHERE TO DINE ———

CHIEFTAIN RESTAURANT
American
(AAA)

Lunch: $6-$10   **Dinner:** $8-$18   **Phone:** 928/688-2754
Location: I-40, exit 333, just s at jct US 191 N; in Chieftain Inn. I-40 & State 191 86502. **Hours:** 24 hours; 6 am-8 pm in winter. **Features:** Along a lonely stretch of highway, the breakfast, lunch and dinner restaurant serves hamburgers, hot open-faced sandwiches, soups and salads. The dinner menu also includes steaks. Casual dress. **Parking:** on-site. **Cards:** AX, CB, DC, DS, MC, VI.

CHANDLER —*See Phoenix p. 313.*

CHINLE pop. 5,366

——— WHERE TO STAY ———

BEST WESTERN CANYON DE CHELLY INN
Motel
(AAA) (SAVE)

		Phone: (928)674-5875	
5/1-10/31	2P: $99-$119	XP: $10	F12
2/1-4/30	2P: $89-$109	XP: $10	F12
11/1-1/31	2P: $79-$99	XP: $10	F12

Location: US 191, just e. 100 Main St, Rt 7 86503 (PO Box 295). **Fax:** 928/674-3715. **Facility:** 99 one-bedroom standard units. 2 stories (no elevator), exterior corridors. **Parking:** on-site. **Terms:** [AP] & [CP] meal plans available, pets ($40 deposit, $5 extra charge). **Amenities:** voice mail, irons, hair dryers. *Some:* high-speed Internet. **Dining:** Junction Restaurant, see separate listing. **Pool(s):** heated indoor. **Leisure Activities:** sauna, whirlpool. **Guest Services:** gift shop. **Business Services:** meeting rooms, PC. **Cards:** AX, CB, DC, DS, JC, MC, VI. **Special Amenities:** early check-in/late check-out. *(See color ad below)*

HOLIDAY INN CANYON DE CHELLY *Book at aaa.com*   **Phone:** (928)674-5000

| | 5/1-10/31 | 1P: $129 | 2P: $129 |
| | 2/1-4/30 & 11/1-1/31 | 1P: $89 | 2P: $89 |

Small-scale Hotel

Location: US 191, 2.5 mi e; at entrance to Canyon de Chelly National Monument. Indian Rt 7 86503 (PO Box 1889). Fax: 928/674-8264. **Facility:** 108 one-bedroom standard units. 2 stories (no elevator), interior corridors. *Bath:* combo or shower only. **Parking:** on-site. **Terms:** cancellation fee imposed, [BP] & [MAP] meal plans available. **Amenities:** voice mail, irons, hair dryers. **Dining:** Garcia's Restaurant, see separate listing. **Pool(s):** heated outdoor. **Leisure Activities:** exercise room. **Guest Services:** gift shop, complimentary laundry. **Business Services:** meeting rooms. **Cards:** AX, DC, DS, MC, VI. **Special Amenities:** free newspaper. *(See color ad below)*

SOME UNITS

THUNDERBIRD LODGE   **Phone:** (928)674-5841

| | 4/1-10/31 | 1P: $78-$110 | 2P: $82-$114 | XP: $4 | F |
| | 2/1-3/31 & 11/1-1/31 | 1P: $49-$65 | 2P: $53-$69 | XP: $4 | F |

Motel

Location: US 191, 3.5 mi e; just e of visitor center. Located in Canyon de Chelly National Monument. Indian Rt 7 86503-0548 (PO Box 548). Fax: 928/674-5844. **Facility:** Smoke free premises. 74 units. 73 one-bedroom standard units. 1 one-bedroom suite. 1 story, exterior corridors. **Parking:** on-site. **Terms:** package plans. **Amenities:** *Some:* irons, hair dryers. **Dining:** Thunder Bird Cafeteria, see separate listing. **Guest Services:** gift shop. **Business Services:** meeting rooms. **Cards:** AX, CB, DC, DS, MC, VI.

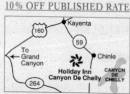

SOME UNITS

WHERE TO DINE

GARCIA'S RESTAURANT   **Lunch:** $5-$15   **Dinner:** $10-$24   **Phone:** 928/674-5000
Location: US 191, 2.5 mi e; at entrance to Canyon de Chelly National Monument; in Holiday Inn Canyon de Chelly. Indian Rt 7 86503. **Hours:** 6:30 am-10 pm, Sat & Sun from 5 pm; 7 am-1 & 5:30-9 pm in winter. Closed: 12/25. **Reservations:** not accepted. **Features:** The menu at this restaurant includes a variety of American and Mexican dishes. Casual dress. **Parking:** on-site. **Cards:** AX, CB, DC, DS, MC, VI.

American

(See color ad p 194)

JUNCTION RESTAURANT   **Lunch:** $5-$10   **Dinner:** $8-$18   **Phone:** 928/674-8443
Location: US 191, just e; in Best Western Canyon De Chelly Inn. 100 Main St, Rt #7 86503. **Hours:** 6:30 am-10 pm; to 9 pm off season. **Features:** Serving breakfast, lunch and dinner, the family restaurant lines up a good selection of beef, chicken and pork dishes, sandwiches and such Navajo favorites as mutton stew and fry

American

bread. Local Native American arts and crafts are displayed. The dining patio opens seasonally. Casual dress. **Parking:** on-site. **Cards:** AX, DS, MC, VI.

THUNDER BIRD CAFETERIA   **Lunch:** $6-$10   **Dinner:** $8-$20   **Phone:** 928/674-5841
Location: US 191, 3.5 mi e; just e of visitor center; in Thunderbird Lodge. Indian Rt 7 86503. **Hours:** 6:30 am-8:30 pm; to 8 pm in winter. **Features:** Among the cafeteria's comfort foods are some Mexican entrees and Navajo fry bread. Some steak and other dishes are prepared to order and delivered to the table. Casual

American

dress. **Parking:** on-site. **Cards:** AX, CB, DC, MC, VI.

CHLORIDE

WHERE TO STAY

SHEPS MINERS INN   **Phone:** (928)565-4251

All Year   1P: $35-$65   2P: $35-$65
Location: Jct 2nd St and Elkhart Ave. 9827 2nd St 86431 (PO Box 100). **Fax:** 928/565-3643. **Facility:** 11 one-bedroom standard units. 1 story, exterior corridors. *Bath:* shower only. **Parking:** on-site. **Terms:** 7 day cancellation notice, package plans. **Amenities:** video library. **Dining:** Yesterdays Restaurant, see separate

Motel

listing. **Guest Services:** TV in common area. **Cards:** AX, DS, MC, VI.

SOME UNITS

WHERE TO DINE

YESTERDAYS RESTAURANT   *Menu on aaa.com*   **Lunch:** $4-$7   **Dinner:** $8-$15   **Phone:** 928/565-4251
Location: Jct 2nd St and Elkhart Ave; in Sheps Miners Inn. 9827 2nd St 86431. **Hours:** 8 am-9 pm. **Features:** In a rustic setting off the beaten path, the three-meal restaurant presents a menu of varied sandwiches, soups and salads for lunch and several steak, seafood and pasta dishes for dinner. Casual dress; cocktails. **Parking:** on-site. **Cards:** AX, DS, MC, VI.

American

CLARKDALE pop. 3,422

WHERE TO DINE

SU CASA OF CLARKDALE   **Lunch:** $7-$12   **Dinner:** $7-$12   **Phone:** 928/634-2771
Location: Center. 1000 S Main St 86324. **Hours:** 11 am-9 pm. Closed: 4/16, 11/23, 12/25. **Reservations:** accepted. **Features:** Friendly service complements well-prepared dishes made to order from fresh ingredients. The comfortable eatery is welcoming to families. Casual dress; cocktails. **Parking:** on-site.

Mexican

Cards: MC, VI.

CORNVILLE pop. 3,335

WHERE TO DINE

THE KRAMERS AT THE MANZANITA RESTAURANT   **Dinner:** $14-$23   **Phone:** 928/634-8851
Location: 4.5 mi e of jct SR 89A. 11425 E Cornville Rd 86325. **Hours:** Open 2/1-7/1 & 8/1-1/31; 4 pm-8 pm. Closed: Mon & Tues. **Reservations:** suggested. **Features:** Kramers is a popular restaurant in a country setting. Casual dress; cocktails. **Parking:** on-site. **Cards:** MC, VI.

Continental

PAGE SPRINGS BAR & RESTAURANT   **Lunch:** $4-$9   **Dinner:** $12-$20   **Phone:** 928/634-9954
Location: From SR 179, 2.6 mi se. 1975 N Page Springs Rd 86325. **Hours:** 4 pm-9 pm, Fri-10 pm, Sat noon-10 pm, Sun noon-9 pm. Closed: 11/23, 12/25; also Mon & Tues. **Reservations:** suggested. **Features:** Make a reservation or wait in line for some of the best char-broiled steaks around. Overlooking the shaded Oak

Steak House

Creek, you can enjoy barbecue ribs, burgers or prime rib, and the homemade cobblers will top off a great meal. Casual dress; cocktails. **Parking:** on-site. **Cards:** MC, VI.

COTTONWOOD pop. 9,179

——— WHERE TO STAY ———

BEST WESTERN COTTONWOOD INN
AAA [SAVE]

Book at aaa.com

Motel

			Phone: (928)634-5575
3/1-5/31 & 9/1-1/31	1P: $79-$109	2P: $79-$109	XP: $10 F12
6/1-8/31	1P: $75-$109	2P: $75-$109	XP: $10 F12
2/1-2/28	1P: $69-$99	2P: $69-$99	XP: $10 F12

Location: On SR 89A, at SR 260. Located across from a shopping center. 993 S Main St 86326. Fax: 928/634-5576. **Facility:** 77 one-bedroom standard units. 1-2 stories (no elevator), exterior corridors. *Bath:* combo or shower only. **Parking:** on-site. **Terms:** [ECP] meal plan available, package plans, small pets only ($20 fee, in designated units). **Amenities:** voice mail, irons, hair dryers. *Some:* high-speed Internet. **Pool(s):** heated outdoor. **Leisure Activities:** whirlpool. **Guest Services:** coin laundry. **Business Services:** meeting rooms, PC. **Cards:** AX, CB, DC, DS, MC, VI. **Special Amenities:** free continental breakfast and free local telephone calls.

SOME UNITS

BUDGET INN & SUITES
AAA [SAVE]

Book at aaa.com

Motel

(See color ad below)

			Phone: (928)634-3678
2/1-5/31 & 9/1-12/31	1P: $59-$99	2P: $59-$99	XP: $6 F10
6/1-8/31 & 1/1-1/31	1P: $49-$89	2P: $54-$99	XP: $6 F10

Location: On SR 260, just e of jct SR 89A. 1089 Hwy 260 86326. Fax: 928/639-0407. **Facility:** 31 one-bedroom standard units. 2 stories (no elevator), exterior corridors. *Bath:* combo or shower only. **Parking:** on-site. **Terms:** cancellation fee imposed, [CP] meal plan available, small pets only ($10 extra charge). **Amenities:** high-speed Internet. *Some:* DVD players (fee). **Cards:** AX, DC, DS, MC, VI.

SOME UNITS

LITTLE DAISY MOTEL
AAA [SAVE]

Motel

			Phone: (928)634-7865
All Year	1P: $50-$55	2P: $50-$55	XP: $5

Location: On SR 89A, just n. 34 S Main St 86326. Fax: 928/639-3447. **Facility:** 20 units. 19 one- and 1 two-bedroom standard units, some with efficiencies or kitchens. 1 story, exterior corridors. *Bath:* combo or shower only. **Parking:** on-site. **Terms:** office hours 7 am-10 pm, weekly rates available, pets ($20 deposit, $5 extra charge). **Cards:** AX, DC, MC, VI. **Special Amenities:** free local telephone calls.

SOME UNITS

PINES MOTEL
AAA [SAVE]

Motel

			Phone: (928)634-9975
All Year	1P: $49-$59	2P: $54-$79	XP: $5 F12

Location: Jct SR 260, just nw on SR 89A, then just s. 920 S Camino Real 86326. Fax: 928/634-5557. **Facility:** 14 one-bedroom standard units. 2 stories (no elevator), exterior corridors. **Parking:** on-site. **Terms:** office hours 8 am-10 pm, weekly rates available, pets ($10 fee). **Amenities:** hair dryers. **Pool(s):** small heated outdoor. **Cards:** DS, MC, VI. **Special Amenities:** free local telephone calls.

SOME UNITS

QUALITY INN
AAA [SAVE]

Book at aaa.com

Motel

			Phone: (928)634-4207
2/1-10/31	1P: $69-$99	2P: $69-$99	XP: $10 D18
11/1-1/31	1P: $65-$79	2P: $65-$79	XP: $10 D18

Location: On SR 89A, 1.8 mi s of jct SR 260. Located across from the Verde Valley Medical Center. 301 W Hwy 89A 86326. Fax: 928/634-5764. **Facility:** 51 one-bedroom standard units. 2 stories (no elevator), exterior corridors. **Parking:** on-site. **Terms:** package plans, small pets only ($20 fee). **Amenities:** irons, hair dryers. **Dining:** 4 pm-9 pm, Fri & Sat-10 pm, cocktails. **Pool(s):** outdoor. **Leisure Activities:** whirlpool. **Business Services:** meeting rooms. **Cards:** AX, DC, DS, MC, VI. **Special Amenities:** free continental breakfast and free local telephone calls.

SOME UNITS

FEE FEE

SUPER 8 COTTONWOOD   *Book at aaa.com*   Phone: 928/639-1888

AAA SAVE
Motel

All Year   1P: $55-$67   2P: $60-$78
Location: On SR 89A, 0.4 mi nw of jct SR 260. 800 S Main St 86326. Fax: 928/639-2285. **Facility:** 52 one-bedroom standard units. 2 stories (no elevator), exterior corridors. *Bath:* combo or shower only. **Parking:** on-site. **Amenities:** hair dryers. **Pool(s):** small outdoor. **Leisure Activities:** whirlpool. **Cards:** AX, DC, DS, MC, VI. **Special Amenities:** free expanded continental breakfast and free local telephone calls.

SOME UNITS

THE VIEW MOTEL   Phone: 928/634-7581

AAA SAVE
Motel

All Year   1P: $48-$58   2P: $48-$58   XP: $5
Location: On SR 89A, 0.4 mi nw of jct SR 260. 818 S Main St 86326. Fax: 928/639-2101. **Facility:** 34 one-bedroom standard units. 1 story, exterior corridors. *Bath:* combo or shower only. **Parking:** on-site. **Terms:** weekly rates available, pets (dogs only, $3-$5 extra charge). **Pool(s):** heated outdoor. **Leisure Activities:** whirlpool, barbecues and deck areas. **Guest Services:** sundries. **Business Services:** fax (fee). **Cards:** AX, DS, MC, VI. **Special Amenities:** free local telephone calls and preferred room (subject to availability with advance reservations).

SOME UNITS
FEE

——— WHERE TO DINE ———

MAI THAI ON MAIN   Lunch: $7-$10   Dinner: $8-$13   Phone: 928/649-2999

AAA
Thai

Location: 0.5 mi n of E Cottonwood St on SR 89A; center. 157 S Main St 86326. **Hours:** 11:30 am-2:30 & 5-9 pm. Closed: 1/1, 11/23, 12/25; also Sun. **Reservations:** accepted. **Features:** Dishes ranging from classic pad thai to choices of curry, including panang, red, mussamon and green, are served by friendly and helpful staff members who guide guests through the heat levels. Many vegetarian dishes are on the menu. Casual dress; cocktails. **Parking:** on-site. **Cards:** AX, MC, VI.

NIC'S ITALIAN STEAK & CRAB HOUSE   Dinner: $8-$29   Phone: 928/634-9626

Steak House

Location: Center. 925 N Main St 86326. **Hours:** 5 pm-10 pm. Closed: 4/16, 11/23, 12/25. **Features:** Although the menu centers on steaks, guests also will find a nice selection of traditional pasta dishes and fresh seafood. Casual dress; cocktails. **Parking:** on-site. **Cards:** MC, VI.

SWEET JILL'S   Lunch: $6-$8   Dinner: $14-$22   Phone: 928/649-2779

American

Location: Jct SR 260, just nw on SR 89A, then just e. 1750 E Villa Dr 86326. **Hours:** 7 am-5 pm, Fri & Sat-9 pm. Closed major holidays; also Sun. **Reservations:** accepted. **Features:** Bright decor, including whimsical prints and murals, is done with flair. Creativity marks such dishes as fresh chicken curry salad. Hearty soups and breakfast options make this a great place to start the day. The staff is helpful. Casual dress; beer & wine only. **Parking:** on-site. **Cards:** AX, MC, VI.

DEWEY

——— WHERE TO DINE ———

YOUNG'S FARM RESTAURANT   Lunch: $5-$10   Dinner: $5-$10   Phone: 928/632-7272

Regional American

Location: On SR 169, just n of jct SR 69. Jct SR 69 & 169 86327. **Hours:** 7 am-3 pm, Fri & Sat-8 pm, Sun 7 am-6 pm; hours vary in summer. Closed: 1/1, 11/23, 12/25. **Features:** Great for groups or singles, you'll enjoy family dining with down-home-style food. Casual dress; wine only. **Parking:** on-site. **Cards:** AX, DS, MC, VI.

DOUGLAS pop. 14,312

——— WHERE TO STAY ———

MOTEL 6 #305   *Book at aaa.com*   Phone: 520/364-2457

Motel

All Year   1P: $34-$42   2P: $36-$46   XP: $6   F17
Location: 1.2 mi e of jct SR 191. 111 16th St (SR 80) 85607. Fax: 520/364-9332. **Facility:** 98 one-bedroom standard units. 2 stories (no elevator), exterior corridors. *Bath:* shower only. **Parking:** on-site. **Pool(s):** outdoor. **Guest Services:** coin laundry. **Business Services:** fax (fee). **Cards:** AX, DC, DS, MC, VI.

SOME UNITS
FEE   FEE

---

*——— The following lodging was either not evaluated or did not
meet AAA rating requirements but is listed for your information only. ———*

THE GADSDEN HOTEL   Phone: 520/364-4481

fyi
Historic
Small-scale Hotel

Did not meet all AAA rating requirements for locking devices in some guest rooms at time of last evaluation on 10/20/2004. **Location:** Center. 1046 G Ave 85607. Facilities, services, and decor characterize a basic property.

EAGAR pop. 4,033

——— WHERE TO STAY ———

BEST WESTERN SUNRISE INN *Book at aaa.com*
All Year   1P: $70   2P: $75   XP: $5   F12   **Phone:** (928)333-2540
Motel   **Location:** From jct SR 260, just n; from jct US 60, 1.5 mi s. 128 N Main St 85925. Fax: 928/333-4700. **Facility:** 41 one-bedroom standard units. 2 stories (no elevator), exterior corridors. **Parking:** on-site. **Terms:** 14 day cancellation notice, [CP], [ECP] & [MAP] meal plans available, pets ($10 fee). **Amenities:** voice mail, irons, hair dryers. **Leisure Activities:** sauna, exercise room. **Guest Services:** coin laundry. **Cards:** AX, DC, DS, MC, VI.

SOME UNITS

EHRENBERG pop. 1,357

——— WHERE TO STAY ———

BEST WESTERN FLYING J MOTEL *Book at aaa.com*
   Phone: (928)923-9711

1/6-1/31	1P: $189-$195	2P: $197-$199	XP: $10 F12
8/30-1/5	1P: $189-$195	2P: $195-$199	XP: $10 F12
4/16-8/29	1P: $159-$189	2P: $169-$190	XP: $10 F12
2/1-4/15	1P: $69-$119	2P: $79-$129	XP: $10 F12

Small-scale Hotel   **Location:** I-10, exit 1, just s; 0.5 mi e of the Colorado River. Located at Flying J Travel Plaza. S Frontage Rd 85334 (PO Box 260). Fax: 928/923-8335. **Facility:** 84 one-bedroom standard units. 2 stories (no elevator), interior corridors. **Parking:** on-site. **Terms:** [CP] meal plan available, pets ($10 fee, in limited units). **Amenities:** high-speed Internet, irons, hair dryers. **Pool(s):** outdoor. **Leisure Activities:** whirlpool, limited exercise equipment. **Guest Services:** coin laundry. **Business Services:** fax (fee). **Cards:** AX, CB, DC, DS, MC, VI. **Special Amenities:** free continental breakfast and free local telephone calls.

SOME UNITS

ELOY pop. 10,375

——— WHERE TO STAY ———

SUPER 8 MOTEL *Book at aaa.com*
Property failed to provide current rates   **Phone:** 520/466-7804
Motel   **Location:** I-10, exit 203 (Toltec Rd), just e, then just s. 3945 W Houser Rd 85231. Fax: 520/466-3431. **Facility:** 42 one-bedroom standard units. 2 stories (no elevator), exterior corridors. **Parking:** on-site. **Terms:** pets ($10 extra charge). **Pool(s):** heated outdoor. **Guest Services:** coin laundry.

SOME UNITS

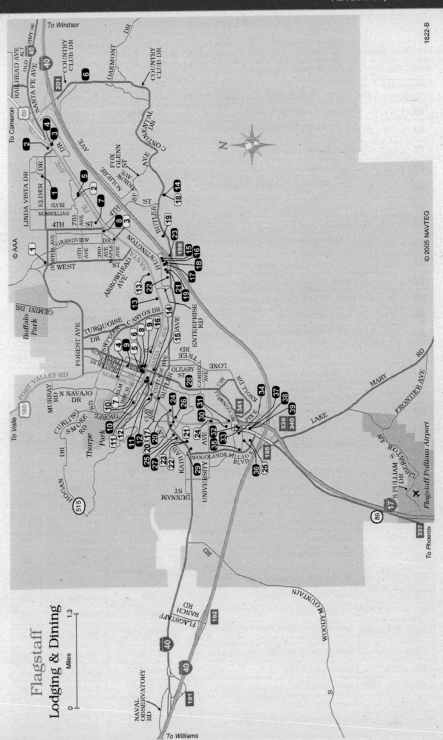

Flagstaff
Lodging & Dining

Miles

0   1.3

© 2005 NAVTEQ

1622-B

Flagstaff

This index helps you "spot" where approved accommodations and restaurants are located on the corresponding detailed maps. Lodging rate ranges are for comparison only and show the property's high season; rates are per night, unless only weekly (W) rates are available. Restaurant rate range is for dinner, unless only lunch (L) is served. Turn to the listing page for more detailed rate information and consult display ads for special promotions.

Spotter/Map Page Number	OA	FLAGSTAFF - Lodgings	Diamond Rating	Rate Range High Season	Listing Page
❶ / p. 199		Starlight Pines, A Bed & Breakfast	▽▽▽	$119-$149	214
❷ / p. 199	AAA	Super 8 Motel East Flagstaff - see color ad p 215, p 229	▽▽	$59-$149 SAVE	215
❸ / p. 199	AAA	Hampton Inn East - see color ad p 207	▽▽▽	$89-$189 SAVE	207
❹ / p. 199	AAA	Days Inn East - see color ad p 204	▽▽	$69-$169 SAVE	204
❺ / p. 199	AAA	Best Western Pony Soldier Inn and Suites - see color ad p 203	▽▽▽	$69-$119 SAVE	202
❻ / p. 199		Residence Inn by Marriott Flagstaff	▽▽▽	$99-$199	213
❼ / p. 199	AAA	Rodeway Inn East	▽▽	$55-$89 SAVE	213
❽ / p. 199	AAA	Travelodge-Grand Canyon/Flagstaff - see color ad p 201	▽▽	$40-$130 SAVE	216
❾ / p. 199		The Inn at 410 Bed & Breakfast	▽▽▽	$150-$210	209
❿ / p. 199	AAA	Super 8 Motel - see color ad p 214	▽▽	$49-$125 SAVE	215
⓫ / p. 199	AAA	Parkside Family Inn & Suites	▽	$29-$149 SAVE	211
⓬ / p. 199	AAA	Highland Country Inn	▽▽	$49-$109 SAVE	208
⓭ / p. 199	AAA	Best Western Kings House - see color ad p 202	▽▽	$65-$125 SAVE	202
⓮ / p. 199	AAA	Little America Hotel - see color ad p 210	▽▽▽	$129-$179 SAVE	210
⓯ / p. 199	AAA	Super 8-Lucky Lane	▽▽	$44-$109 SAVE	214
⓰ / p. 199	AAA	Howard Johnson Inn-Lucky Lane - see color ad p 209	▽▽	$44-$109 SAVE	209
⓱ / p. 199		Econo Lodge - see color ad p 206	▽▽	$89-$119	206
⓲ / p. 199	AAA	Quality Inn-Lucky Lane - see color ad p 211	▽▽	$44-$109 SAVE	212
⓳ / p. 199	AAA	Ramada Limited-Lucky Lane - see color ad p 213	▽▽	$44-$109 SAVE	212
⓴ / p. 199		Embassy Suites-Flagstaff/Grand Canyon	▽▽▽	$129-$179	206
㉑ / p. 199	AAA	Holiday Inn Express - see color ad p 208	▽▽▽	$79-$139 SAVE	209
㉒ / p. 199		Motel 6 Flagstaff-Butler Ave #301	▽	$39-$55	210
㉓ / p. 199	AAA	Travelodge Hotel	▽▽	$39-$179 SAVE	216
㉔ / p. 199	AAA	Budget Inn	▽▽	$49-$99 SAVE	203
㉕ / p. 199	AAA	Days Inn Route 66 - see color ad p 205, p 224	▽▽	$57-$129 SAVE	205
㉖ / p. 199	AAA	Econo Lodge-University	▽▽	$49-$109 SAVE	206
㉗ / p. 199	AAA	Travel Inn	▽	$33-$89 SAVE	215
㉘ / p. 199	AAA	The Inn at NAU	▽▽	$99-$109 SAVE	210
㉙ / p. 199	AAA	Radisson Woodlands Hotel Flagstaff - see color ad p 212	▽▽▽	$90-$150 SAVE	212
㉚ / p. 199	AAA	Fairfield Inn By Marriott - see color ad p 206	▽▽	$89-$129 SAVE	207
㉛ / p. 199	AAA	Quality Inn I-40/I-17	▽▽	$49-$99 SAVE	211
㉜ / p. 199	AAA	Hilton Garden Inn - see color ad p 208	▽▽▽	$119-$149 SAVE	208
㉝ / p. 199		Hampton Inn & Suites	▽▽▽	$99-$119	207
㉞ / p. 199	AAA	AmeriSuites (Flagstaff/Interstate Crossroads)	▽▽▽	$89-$129 SAVE	202

Spotter/Map Page Number	OA	**FLAGSTAFF - Lodgings (continued)**	Diamond Rating	Rate Range High Season	Listing Page
35 / p. 199		Motel 6-Flagstaff West #1000	◈	$39-$55	211
36 / p. 199	AAA	Sleep Inn	◈◈	$80-$130 SAVE	214
37 / p. 199	AAA	Days Inn I-40 - see color ad p 205	◈◈	$79-$129 SAVE	204
38 / p. 199	AAA	Ramada Limited West - see color ad p 212	◈◈	$59-$144 SAVE	213
39 / p. 199	AAA	Comfort Inn I-17/I-40 - see color ad p 203	◈◈◈	$79-$139 SAVE	204
		FLAGSTAFF - Restaurants			
1 / p. 199		Brandy's Restaurant & Bakery	◈◈	$8-$14	216
2 / p. 199		Mamma Luisa	◈◈	$8-$17	218
3 / p. 199		Salsa Brava East	◈◈	$8-$14	218
4 / p. 199	AAA	Josephine's	◈◈◈	$17-$25	217
5 / p. 199		Pesto Brothers Piazza	◈◈	$10-$20	218
6 / p. 199		Mountain Oasis International Restaurant	◈◈	$6-$18	218
7 / p. 199		Pasto	◈◈	$15-$25	218
8 / p. 199		Racha Thai	◈	$8-$14	218
9 / p. 199		Corea House	◈◈	$8-$17	217
10 / p. 199		Beaver Street Brewery & Whistle Stop Cafe	◈◈	$7-$18	216
11 / p. 199		La Bellavia	◈	$4-$8(L)	218
12 / p. 199		Macy's European Coffee House & Bakery	◈	$3-$8	218
13 / p. 199		China Star	◈	$5-$8	217
14 / p. 199		Dara Thai Restaurant	◈◈	$10-$13	217
15 / p. 199	AAA	Cottage Place Restaurant	◈◈◈	$17-$25	217
16 / p. 199		Kachina Restaurant	◈◈	$8-$18	218
17 / p. 199		Granny's Closet	◈◈	$7-$24	217
18 / p. 199	AAA	Western Gold Dining Room	◈◈◈	$22-$34	218
19 / p. 199	AAA	Black Bart's Steak House & Musical Revue	◈◈	$14-$30	216
20 / p. 199		Galaxy Diner	◈◈	$6-$14	217
21 / p. 199		Hiro's Sushi Bar & Japanese Restaurant	◈◈	$4-$20	217
22 / p. 199		Woodlands Cafe	◈◈	$10-$16	218
23 / p. 199		Sakura Restaurant - see color ad p 212	◈◈	$11-$17	218
24 / p. 199		Buster's	◈◈	$9-$18	217
25 / p. 199		Cilantro's Mexican Grill	◈◈	$6-$19	217

FLAGSTAFF pop. 52,894   (See map and index starting on p. 199)—*See also GRAND CANYON NATIONAL PARK - SOUTH RIM.*

——————— WHERE TO STAY ———————

AMERISUITES (FLAGSTAFF/INTERSTATE CROSSROADS)   *Book at aaa.com*

		Phone: (928)774-8042	**34**
5/26-9/5 [ECP]	1P: $89-$129	2P: $89-$129	XP: $10	F17
3/4-5/25 & 9/6-1/31 [ECP]	1P: $69-$109	2P: $69-$109	XP: $10	F17
2/1-3/3 [ECP]	1P: $59-$99	2P: $59-$99	XP: $10	F17

Location: I-40, exit 195, just n to Forest Meadows St, just w, then just s. 2455 S Beulah Blvd 86001. Small-scale Hotel **Fax:** 928/774-5524. **Facility:** 116 one-bedroom standard units. 5 stories, interior corridors. *Bath:* combo or shower only. **Parking:** on-site. **Amenities:** high-speed Internet, voice mail, irons, hair dryers. **Pool(s):** small heated indoor. **Leisure Activities:** whirlpool, exercise room. **Guest Services:** valet and coin laundry. **Business Services:** meeting rooms. **Cards:** AX, CB, DC, DS, MC, VI. **Special Amenities:** free full breakfast.

SOME UNITS
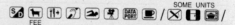

BEST WESTERN KINGS HOUSE   *Book at aaa.com*

		Phone: (928)774-7186	**13**
5/9-9/30	1P: $65-$119	2P: $69-$125	XP: $10	F16
3/1-4/30	1P: $49-$69	2P: $59-$79	XP: $10	F16
2/1-2/28 & 10/1-1/31	1P: $42-$69	2P: $45-$75	XP: $10	F16

Location: I-40, exit 198 (Butler Ave), just w, just n on Enterprise, then just w. 1560 E Route 66 86001. Motel **Fax:** 928/774-7188. **Facility:** 57 units. 56 one- and 1 two-bedroom standard units. 2 stories (no elevator), exterior corridors. **Parking:** on-site. **Terms:** cancellation fee imposed, [CP] meal plan available, small pets only ($10 extra charge). **Amenities:** voice mail, irons, hair dryers. *Some:* high-speed Internet. **Pool(s):** small heated outdoor. **Cards:** AX, DC, DS, MC, VI. **Special Amenities:** free continental breakfast and free local telephone calls. *(See color ad below)*

SOME UNITS

FEE

BEST WESTERN PONY SOLDIER INN AND SUITES   *Book at aaa.com*

		Phone: (928)526-2388	**5**
5/1-9/30 [ECP]	1P: $69-$119	2P: $79-$119	XP: $5	F18
2/1-4/30 & 10/1-1/31 [ECP]	1P: $49-$69	2P: $59-$79	XP: $5	F18

Location: I-40, exit 201, just n, then 1 mi w. 3030 E Route 66 86004. **Fax:** 928/527-8329. **Facility:** 75 units. 59 one-bedroom standard units. 15 one- and 1 two-bedroom suites ($79-$119). 2 stories (no elevator), interior Small-scale Hotel corridors. **Parking:** on-site. **Terms:** small pets only ($15 fee, in designated units). **Amenities:** voice mail, irons, hair dryers. *Some:* high-speed Internet. **Pool(s):** small heated indoor. **Leisure Activities:** whirlpool. **Business Services:** PC. **Cards:** AX, CB, DC, DS, JC, MC, VI. **Special Amenities:** free expanded continental breakfast and free newspaper. *(See color ad p 203)*

SOME UNITS
FEE

(See map and index starting on p. 199)

BUDGET INN

Motel

Phone: (928)774-5038 **24**

	5/1-8/31	1P: $49-$99	2P: $55-$99	XP: $5	F16
	9/1-10/31	1P: $39-$49	2P: $45-$59	XP: $5	F16
	2/1-4/30 & 11/1-1/31	1P: $29-$39	2P: $35-$45	XP: $5	F16

Location: I-40, exit 195, 1 mi n. 913 S Milton Rd 86001. Fax: 928/774-8232. **Facility:** 38 one-bedroom standard units. 2 stories (no elevator), exterior corridors. **Parking:** on-site. **Terms:** 3 day cancellation notice. **Amenities:** voice mail. *Some:* irons, hair dryers. **Pool(s):** small heated outdoor. **Leisure Activities:** whirlpool. **Cards:** AX, CB, DC, DS, MC, VI. **Special Amenities:** free local telephone calls.

SOME UNITS

(See map and index starting on p. 199)

COMFORT INN I-17/I-40 *Book at aaa.com* Phone: (928)774-2225 **39**
AAA SAVE 5/1-10/15 [ECP] 1P: $79-$139 2P: $79-$139 XP: $5 F18
◇◇◇◇ 2/1-4/30 & 10/16-1/31 [ECP] 1P: $59-$129 2P: $59-$129 XP: $5 F18
Location: I-40, exit 195, just n to Forest Meadows St, then 1 blk w. 2355 S Beulah Blvd 86001. **Fax:** 928/774-2225.
Facility: 85 one-bedroom standard units. 2 stories (no elevator), interior corridors. **Parking:** on-site.
Small-scale Hotel **Terms:** small pets only ($5 extra charge). **Amenities:** high-speed Internet, voice mail, irons, hair dryers.
Pool(s): small heated outdoor. **Leisure Activities:** whirlpools. **Guest Services:** coin laundry. **Business**
Services: PC. **Cards:** AX, CB, DC, DS, JC, MC, VI. **Special Amenities:** free expanded continental breakfast and free
newspaper. *(See color ad p 203)*

SOME UNITS
🅂🄳 🐾 🍴 🎥 🏊 🛐 📷 DATA PORT 💻 / ✕ 📶 🔲
FEE   FEE

DAYS INN EAST *Book at aaa.com* Phone: (928)527-1477 **4**
AAA SAVE 4/1-9/30 [CP] 1P: $69-$169 2P: $69-$169 XP: $10 F17
◇◇◇◇ 2/1-3/31 & 10/1-1/31 [CP] 1P: $39-$109 2P: $39-$109 XP: $10 F17
Location: I-40, exit 201, just n, 0.5 mi w on I-40 business loop, then just n. 3601 E Lockett Rd 86004.
Fax: 928/527-0228. **Facility:** 54 one-bedroom standard units. 3 stories, interior corridors. **Parking:** on-site.
Small-scale Hotel **Terms:** [CP] meal plan available, pets ($10 fee). **Amenities:** high-speed Internet, safes (fee), hair dryers.
Some: irons. **Pool(s):** small heated indoor. **Leisure Activities:** whirlpool. **Guest Services:** coin laundry.
Cards: AX, DC, DS, MC, VI. **Special Amenities:** free continental breakfast. *(See color ad below)*

SOME UNITS
🅂🄳 🐾 🍴 🏊 DATA PORT 💻 / ✕ 📶 /
FEE

DAYS INN I-40 *Book at aaa.com* Phone: (928)779-1575 **37**
AAA SAVE 7/1-10/31 1P: $79-$129 2P: $79-$129 XP: $5 F12
◇◇◇◇ 5/1-6/30 1P: $69-$129 2P: $69-$129 XP: $5 F12
2/1-4/30 & 11/1-1/31 1P: $39-$79 2P: $44-$79 XP: $5 F12
Location: I-40, exit 195, just n to Forest Meadows St, w to Beulah Blvd, just s, then w. 2735 S Woodlands Village Blvd
Small-scale Hotel 86001. **Fax:** 928/779-0044. **Facility:** 57 one-bedroom standard units. 2 stories (no elevator), interior
corridors. **Parking:** on-site. **Terms:** weekly rates available, [CP] meal plan available. **Amenities:** high-speed
Internet, voice mail, safes, hair dryers. *Some:* irons. **Leisure Activities:** whirlpool. **Guest Services:** coin laundry. **Cards:** AX,
DC, DS, MC, VI. **Special Amenities:** free continental breakfast and free local telephone calls. *(See color ad p 205)*

SOME UNITS
🅂🄳 🍴 🎥 DATA PORT 💻 / ✕ 📶 🔲

(See map and index starting on p. 199)

DAYS INN ROUTE 66   *Book at aaa.com*   Phone: (928)774-5221   **25**

AAA SAVE	5/1-9/3	1P: $57-$129	2P: $57-$129	XP: $10	F17
	9/4-10/31	1P: $45-$99	2P: $45-$99	XP: $10	F17
	2/1-4/30	1P: $42-$99	2P: $42-$99	XP: $10	F17
Motel	11/1-1/31	1P: $40-$99	2P: $40-$99	XP: $10	F17

Location: I-40, exit 195, 1.5 mi n on Milton Rd, then just w. 1000 W Route 66 86001. Fax: 928/774-4977. **Facility:** 157 one-bedroom standard units. 2 stories (no elevator), exterior corridors. **Parking:** on-site. **Terms:** [BP] meal plan available, small pets only ($10 extra charge, in limited units). **Amenities:** voice mail, hair dryers. *Some:* irons. **Pool(s):** heated outdoor. **Leisure Activities:** darts, pool table. *Fee:* game room. **Guest Services:** gift shop, coin laundry. **Business Services:** meeting rooms. **Cards:** AX, CB, DC, DS, JC, MC, VI. **Special Amenities:** free continental breakfast. *(See color ad below & p 224)*

(See map and index starting on p. 199)

ECONO LODGE — *Book at aaa.com*

▽▽▽ ▽▽▽

Small-scale Hotel

Phone: (928)774-7701 **17**

5/1-10/31	1P: $89-$98	2P: $95-$119	XP: $15	D14
3/1-4/30	1P: $68-$78	2P: $78-$88	XP: $10	D14
11/1-1/31	1P: $50-$70	2P: $60-$80	XP: $10	D14
2/1-2/28	1P: $50-$60	2P: $60-$70	XP: $10	D14

Location: I-40, exit 198 (Butler Ave), just n, then just e. 2480 E Lucky Ln 86004. Fax: 928/774-7855. **Facility:** 66 one-bedroom standard units. 3 stories, interior corridors. **Parking:** on-site. **Terms:** 7 day cancellation notice-fee imposed, [CP] meal plan available, small pets only ($10 extra charge). **Amenities:** voice mail. *Some:* irons, hair dryers. **Pool(s):** small heated indoor. **Leisure Activities:** whirlpool, limited exercise equipment. **Guest Services:** coin laundry. **Business Services:** PC. **Cards:** AX, CB, DC, DS, JC, MC, VI. *(See color ad below)*

[ASK] [SD] [🐕 FEE] [🛏] [🏊] [📷] [DATA PORT] / [✕] [📶] [📠] [📺] / SOME UNITS

ECONO LODGE-UNIVERSITY — *Book at aaa.com*

[AAA] [SAVE]

▽▽ ▽▽

Motel

Phone: (928)774-7326 **26**

5/2-8/31 [CP]	1P: $49-$109	2P: $49-$109	XP: $5	F18
9/1-11/1 [CP]	1P: $41-$79	2P: $45-$79	XP: $5	F18
2/1-5/1 & 11/2-1/31 [CP]	1P: $41-$59	2P: $45-$59	XP: $5	F18

Location: I-40, exit 195, 1.2 mi n. 914 S Milton Rd 86001. Fax: 928/774-7328. **Facility:** 67 one-bedroom standard units. 2 stories (no elevator), exterior corridors. **Parking:** on-site. **Terms:** pets (with prior approval). **Amenities:** *Some:* irons, hair dryers. **Pool(s):** small heated outdoor. **Cards:** AX, CB, DC, DS, MC, VI. **Special Amenities:** free continental breakfast and free local telephone calls.

[SD] [🐕] [🛏] [🏊] [📷] / [✕] [📠] [📺] / SOME UNITS

EMBASSY SUITES-FLAGSTAFF/GRAND CANYON — *Book at aaa.com*

▽▽▽

Small-scale Hotel

Phone: (928)774-4333 **20**

5/1-8/31 [BP]	1P: $129-$179	2P: $129-$179	XP: $10	F17
9/1-10/31 [BP]	1P: $119-$159	2P: $119-$159	XP: $10	F17
2/1-4/30 & 11/1-1/31 [BP]	1P: $99-$149	2P: $99-$149	XP: $10	F17

Location: I-40, exit 195, 1.5 mi n. Located adjacent to Northern Arizona University. 706 S Milton Rd 86001. Fax: 928/774-0216. **Facility:** 119 units. 117 one- and 2 two-bedroom suites. 3 stories, interior corridors. **Parking:** on-site. **Terms:** 2-3 night minimum stay - seasonal and/or weekends, cancellation fee imposed. **Amenities:** video games (fee), voice mail, irons, hair dryers. **Pool(s):** heated outdoor. **Leisure Activities:** whirlpool, exercise room. **Guest Services:** complimentary evening beverages, valet and coin laundry. **Business Services:** meeting rooms. **Cards:** AX, CB, DC, DS, JC, MC, VI.

[ASK] [SD] [🛏] [🍸] [📶] [🏊] [📷] [DATA PORT] [📠] [📺] / [✕] / SOME UNITS

(See map and index starting on p. 199)

FAIRFIELD INN BY MARRIOTT   *Book at aaa.com*   Phone: (928)773-1300   **30**

AAA SAVE

5/1-9/30	1P: $89-$129	2P: $89-$129
2/1-4/30 & 10/1-1/31	1P: $69-$89	2P: $69-$89

Small-scale Hotel

Location: I-40, exit 195, 0.5 mi n. 2005 S Milton Rd 86001. Fax: 928/773-1462. **Facility:** 131 one-bedroom standard units. 3 stories, interior/exterior corridors. **Parking:** on-site. **Terms:** 1-2 night minimum stay - weekends. **Amenities:** high-speed Internet, voice mail, irons, hair dryers. **Pool(s):** small heated outdoor. **Leisure Activities:** whirlpool, exercise room. **Guest Services:** valet laundry. **Business Services:** PC. **Cards:** AX, CB, DC, DS, JC, MC, VI. **Special Amenities:** free continental breakfast and free local telephone calls.
(See color ad p 206)

SOME UNITS

HAMPTON INN & SUITES   *Book at aaa.com*   Phone: (928)913-0900   **33**

Small-scale Hotel

5/26-10/31 [ECP]	1P: $99-$119	2P: $99-$119
3/17-5/25 [ECP]	1P: $79-$119	2P: $79-$119
2/1-3/16 & 11/1-1/31 [ECP]	1P: $75-$99	2P: $75-$99

Location: I-40, exit 195, just n to Forest Meadows St, just w, then just s. 2400 S Beulah Blvd 86001. Fax: 928/913-0800. **Facility:** 126 units. 87 one-bedroom standard units, some with whirlpools. 39 one-bedroom suites ($99-$159) with efficiencies. 5 stories, interior corridors. *Bath:* combo or shower only. **Parking:** on-site. **Terms:** 3 night minimum stay - seasonal and/or weekends. **Amenities:** high-speed Internet, dual phone lines, voice mail, irons, hair dryers. **Pool(s):** heated indoor. **Leisure Activities:** whirlpool, exercise room. **Guest Services:** valet and coin laundry. **Business Services:** meeting rooms, business center. **Cards:** AX, DC, DS, MC, VI.

SOME UNITS

HAMPTON INN EAST   *Book at aaa.com*   Phone: (928)526-1885   **3**

AAA SAVE

4/1-9/3 [ECP]	1P: $89-$189	2P: $89-$189	XP: $5 F17
9/4-10/31 [ECP]	1P: $79-$139	2P: $79-$139	XP: $5 F17
2/1-3/31 & 11/1-1/31 [ECP]	1P: $59-$109	2P: $59-$109	XP: $5 F17

Small-scale Hotel

Location: I-40, exit 201, 0.5 mi w on I-40 business loop, then just n. 3501 E Lockett Rd 86004. Fax: 928/526-9885. **Facility:** 50 units. 48 one-bedroom standard units. 2 one-bedroom suites. 3 stories, interior corridors. *Bath:* combo or shower only. **Parking:** on-site. **Terms:** 3 day cancellation notice-fee imposed. **Amenities:** high-speed Internet, voice mail, irons, hair dryers. **Pool(s):** small heated indoor. **Leisure Activities:** whirlpool, exercise room. **Guest Services:** valet laundry. **Cards:** AX, DS, MC, VI. **Special Amenities:** free expanded continental breakfast.
(See color ad below)

SOME UNITS

(See map and index starting on p. 199)

HIGHLAND COUNTRY INN

AAA SAVE

Motel

5/1-8/31	1P: $49-$109	2P: $49-$109	XP: $5	F16
9/1-10/31	1P: $39-$49	2P: $45-$55	XP: $5	F16
2/1-4/30 & 11/1-1/31	1P: $29-$39	2P: $35-$45	XP: $5	F16

Phone: (928)774-5041 **12**

Location: I-40, exit 195, 1.8 mi n on SR 89A (Milton Rd). 223 S Milton Rd 86001. Fax: 928/774-5651. **Facility:** 42 one-bedroom standard units. 2 stories (no elevator), exterior corridors. **Parking:** on-site. **Terms:** office hours 7:30 am-10:30 pm, 3 day cancellation notice. **Amenities:** voice mail. *Some:* irons, hair dryers. **Guest Services:** coin laundry. **Cards:** AX, DS, MC, VI. **Special Amenities:** free continental breakfast and free local telephone calls.

SOME UNITS

HILTON GARDEN INN   *Book at aaa.com*

AAA SAVE

Small-scale Hotel

All Year	1P: $119-$149	2P: $119-$149	

Phone: (928)226-8888 **32**

Location: I-40, exit 195, 0.5 mi n on Milton Rd, then just w. 350 W Forest Meadows St 86001. Fax: 928/556-9059. **Facility:** 90 one-bedroom standard units. 3 stories, interior corridors. *Bath:* combo or shower only. **Parking:** on-site. **Terms:** cancellation fee imposed, [BP] meal plan available, package plans. **Amenities:** video games (fee), high-speed Internet, dual phone lines, voice mail, irons, hair dryers. **Pool(s):** small heated indoor. **Leisure Activities:** sauna, whirlpool, exercise room. **Guest Services:** valet and coin laundry. **Business Services:** business center. **Cards:** AX, CB, DC, DS, JC, MC, VI. **Special Amenities:** free local telephone calls and free newspaper. *(See color ad below)*

SOME UNITS

(See map and index starting on p. 199)

HOLIDAY INN EXPRESS   *Book at aaa.com*   Phone: (928)714-1000   **21**

AAA SAVE

▽▽▽

Small-scale Hotel

5/1-9/7	1P: $79-$139	2P: $79-$139
9/8-1/31	1P: $69-$119	2P: $69-$119
2/1-4/30	1P: $59-$99	2P: $59-$99

Location: I-40, exit 198 (Butler Ave), just n, then just e. 2320 E Lucky Ln 86004. Fax: 928/779-2610. **Facility:** 156 units. 155 one-bedroom standard units. 1 one-bedroom suite. 5 stories, interior corridors. *Bath:* combo or shower only. **Parking:** on-site. **Terms:** [ECP] meal plan available, pets ($25 fee). **Amenities:** video games (fee), voice mail, irons, hair dryers. **Dining:** 6 am-10 & 5-10 pm, cocktails. **Pool(s):** heated indoor/outdoor. **Leisure Activities:** whirlpool, exercise room. *Fee:* game room. **Guest Services:** valet and coin laundry. **Business Services:** meeting rooms. **Cards:** AX, CB, DC, DS, MC, VI. **Special Amenities:** free expanded continental breakfast and free local telephone calls. *(See color ad p 208)*

SOME UNITS

[icons] S D 🐾 ⊤⊤⊤ ⛾ ⬚ ⬚ ≈ ✕ 📷 DATA PORT ⬚ / ✕ ⊟ ⬚ /
FEE

HOWARD JOHNSON INN-LUCKY LANE   Phone: (928)779-5121   **16**

AAA SAVE

▽▽▽

Motel

5/1-9/30	1P: $44-$99	2P: $54-$109	XP: $10 F17
2/1-4/30 & 10/1-1/31	1P: $39-$69	2P: $49-$79	XP: $10 F17

Location: I-40, exit 198 (Butler Ave), just n, then just e. Located in a commercial area. 2520 E Lucky Ln 86004 (PO Box 207, 86002). Fax: 928/774-3809. **Facility:** 70 one-bedroom standard units. 2 stories (no elevator), exterior corridors. **Parking:** on-site. **Terms:** $2 service charge, small pets only ($10 extra charge). **Amenities:** voice mail, irons, hair dryers. **Pool(s):** small heated outdoor. **Leisure Activities:** whirlpool. **Guest Services:** coin laundry. **Cards:** AX, CB, DC, DS, MC, VI. **Special Amenities:** free local telephone calls and free newspaper. *(See color ad below)*

SOME UNITS

[icons] S D 🐾 ⊤⊤⊤ ⬚ ≈ 📷 DATA PORT ⬚ / ✕ ⊟ ⬚ /
FEE

THE INN AT 410 BED & BREAKFAST   Phone: (928)774-0088   **9**

▽▽▽▽

Bed & Breakfast

All Year	1P: $150-$210	2P: $150-$210 XP: $25

Location: From historic town center, just n of Cherry. 410 N Leroux St 86001. Fax: 928/774-6354. **Facility:** A garden gazebo accents the grounds of this charming 1907 Craftsman home, which is comfortably furnished with antiques and touches of the Southwest. Smoke free premises. 9 units. 4 one-bedroom standard units. 5 one-bedroom suites, some with whirlpools. 2 stories (no elevator), interior/exterior corridors. *Bath:* combo or shower only. **Parking:** on-site. **Terms:** check-in 4 pm, 7 day cancellation notice-fee imposed, [BP] meal plan available. **Amenities:** video library, DVD players, CD players, high-speed Internet, hair dryers. *Some:* irons. **Guest Services:** complimentary evening beverages. **Business Services:** PC. **Cards:** MC, VI.

[icons] ASK ⚐⚐⚐ ✕ CTV VCR ⊘ ⊟ ⬚
FEE

(See map and index starting on p. 199)

THE INN AT NAU

Motel

Phone: 928/523-1616 **28**

5/26-9/4 [BP]	1P: $99-$109	2P: $99-$109	XP: $10	F12
2/1-3/17, 3/27-5/25 & 9/5-12/17 [BP]	1P: $79-$89	2P: $79-$89	XP: $10	F12

Location: I-40, exit 198 (Butler Ave), just n, 1 mi w on Butler Ave, then just s; in Northern Arizona University Campus. Bldg 33 @ San Francisco & McCreary 86011 (PO Box 5606). Fax: 928/523-1625. **Facility:** Smoke free premises. 19 units. 1 one- and 17 two-bedroom standard units. 1 one-bedroom suite. 1 story, interior corridors. *Bath:* combo or shower only. **Parking:** on-site. **Terms:** open 2/1-3/17 & 3/27-12/17, cancellation fee imposed. **Amenities:** high-speed Internet, safes, irons, hair dryers. **Dining:** 6:30 am-9 & 11:30-1:30 pm, Sat & Sun 7-11 am; dinner served only during spring & fall semester; 6 course meal on some Fri, seating at 6:30 pm. **Leisure Activities:** complimentary outdoor track (guest use only). *Fee:* olympic swimming & diving facilities. **Guest Services:** valet laundry. **Business Services:** meeting rooms, business center. **Cards:** AX, MC, VI. **Special Amenities:** free full breakfast and free local telephone calls.

LITTLE AMERICA HOTEL

Large-scale Hotel

Phone: (928)779-7900 **14**

4/28-10/28	1P: $129-$179	2P: $129-$179	XP: $10	F12
3/3-4/27 & 10/29-1/31	1P: $99-$149	2P: $99-$149	XP: $10	F12
2/1-3/2	1P: $89-$139	2P: $89-$139	XP: $10	F12

Facility: 247 units. 244 one-bedroom standard units. 1 one- and 2 two-bedroom suites with kitchens. 2 stories (no elevator), interior corridors. **Parking:** on-site. **Terms:** check-in 4 pm, [AP] meal plan available. **Location:** I-40, exit 198 (Butler Ave), just s. 2515 E Butler Ave 86004 (PO Box 3900, 86003). Fax: 928/779-7983. **Amenities:** video games (fee), high-speed Internet, voice mail, irons, hair dryers. **Dining:** 2 restaurants, 6 am-11 pm, cocktails, also, Western Gold Dining Room, see separate listing, entertainment. **Pool(s):** heated outdoor. **Leisure Activities:** whirlpool, hiking trails, playground, exercise room, horseshoes, volleyball. **Guest Services:** gift shop, valet and coin laundry, airport transportation-Flagstaff Airport, area transportation-train & bus station. **Business Services:** conference facilities. **Cards:** AX, CB, DC, DS, MC, VI. *(See color ad below)*

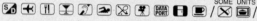

SOME UNITS

MOTEL 6 FLAGSTAFF-BUTLER AVE #301

Motel

Book at aaa.com

Phone: 928/774-1801 **22**

5/27-9/4	1P: $39-$49	2P: $45-$55	XP: $3	F17
2/1-5/26 & 9/5-1/31	1P: $36-$46	2P: $42-$52	XP: $3	F17

Location: I-40, exit 198 (Butler Ave), just n. 2010 E Butler Ave 86004. **Facility:** 149 one-bedroom standard units. 2 stories (no elevator), exterior corridors. *Bath:* combo or shower only. **Parking:** on-site. **Pool(s):** outdoor. **Guest Services:** coin laundry. **Cards:** AX, CB, DC, DS, MC, VI.

SOME UNITS

(See map and index starting on p. 199)

MOTEL 6-FLAGSTAFF WEST #1000   *Book at aaa.com*   Phone: 928/779-3757   **35**

	5/26-9/4	1P: $39-$49	2P: $45-$55	XP: $3	F17
	2/1-5/25 & 9/5-1/31	1P: $36-$46	2P: $42-$52	XP: $3	F17

Motel   **Location:** I-40, exit 195, just n to Forest Meadows St, w to Beulah Blvd, just s, then just w. 2745 S Woodlands Village 86001. Fax: 928/774-2137. **Facility:** 150 one-bedroom standard units. 3 stories, exterior corridors. *Bath:* combo or shower only. **Parking:** on-site, winter plug-ins. **Terms:** pets (in limited units, must be attended). **Amenities:** high-speed Internet. **Pool(s):** heated outdoor. **Guest Services:** coin laundry. **Business Services:** meeting rooms. **Cards:** AX, CB, DC, DS, MC, VI.

SOME UNITS
⬛⬛⬛⬛⬛⬛⬛⬛⬛ / ⬛ ⬛ ⬛ /

PARKSIDE FAMILY INN & SUITES   *Book at aaa.com*   Phone: (928)774-8820   **11**

	5/1-10/31 [BP]	1P: $29-$139	2P: $34-$149	XP: $5	F10
	2/1-4/30 [BP]	1P: $25-$49	2P: $29-$59	XP: $3	F10
	11/1-1/31 [BP]	1P: $20-$49	2P: $25-$59	XP: $3	F10

Motel   **Location:** I-40, exit 195, 2.5 mi n. 121 S Milton Rd 86001. Fax: 928/774-1004. **Facility:** 21 units. 19 one- and 2 two-bedroom standard units. 1 story, exterior corridors. *Bath:* combo or shower only. **Parking:** on-site. **Terms:** cancellation fee imposed, pets ($7 fee). **Amenities:** high-speed Internet. *Some:* DVD players. **Cards:** AX, DS, MC, VI. **Special Amenities:** free full breakfast and free local telephone calls.

SOME UNITS
⬛⬛⬛⬛⬛⬛ / ⬛ /
FEE

QUALITY INN I-40/I-17   *Book at aaa.com*   Phone: (928)774-8771   **31**

	6/1-10/31	1P: $49-$99	2P: $49-$99	
	2/1-5/31	1P: $39-$69	2P: $39-$69	
	11/1-1/31	1P: $39-$59	2P: $39-$59	

Small-scale Hotel   **Location:** I-40, exit 195, just n to Forest Meadows, then right. 2000 S Milton Rd 86001. Fax: 928/773-9382. **Facility:** 96 one-bedroom standard units. 2 stories (no elevator), interior corridors. *Bath:* combo or shower only. **Parking:** on-site. **Terms:** pets ($10 extra charge). **Amenities:** high-speed Internet, irons, hair dryers. **Pool(s):** heated outdoor. **Business Services:** PC. **Cards:** AX, CB, DC, DS, JC, MC, VI. **Special Amenities:** free expanded continental breakfast and free local telephone calls.

SOME UNITS
⬛⬛⬛⬛⬛⬛⬛⬛⬛ / ⬛ /
FEE

(See map and index starting on p. 199)

QUALITY INN-LUCKY LANE   *Book at aaa.com*   Phone: (928)226-7111   **18**
[AAA] [SAVE]   5/1-9/30   1P: $44-$99   2P: $54-$109   XP: $10   F17
2/1-4/30 & 10/1-1/31   1P: $39-$64   2P: $49-$79   XP: $10   F17
◆◆◆ ◆◆   **Location:** I-40, exit 198 (Butler Ave), just n. then just e. 2500 E Lucky Ln 86004 (PO Box 207, 86002).
Motel   Fax: 928/226-1660. **Facility:** 122 one-bedroom standard units. 2 stories (no elevator), exterior corridors.
Parking: on-site. **Terms:** $2 service charge, pets ($10 extra charge). **Amenities:** high-speed Internet, irons,
hair dryers. **Pool(s):** heated outdoor. **Guest Services:** coin laundry. **Cards:** AX, CB, DC, DS, MC, VI.
Special Amenities: free continental breakfast and free local telephone calls. *(See color ad p 211)*

SOME UNITS
[S▪D] [🛏] [▯◀] [🍴] [📶] [🐾] [🚐] [📺] [DATA PORT] [💻] / [✕] [🔒] [🖥] /
FEE

RADISSON WOODLANDS HOTEL FLAGSTAFF   *Book at aaa.com*   Phone: (928)773-8888   **29**
[AAA] [SAVE]   2/1-10/31   1P: $90-$150   2P: $90-$150   XP: $10   F17
11/1-1/31   1P: $80-$130   2P: $80-$130   XP: $10   F17
◆◆◆◆ ◆◆◆◆   **Location:** I-40, exit 195, 1.5 mi n on Milton Rd, then 0.5 mi w. 1175 W Route 66 86001. Fax: 928/773-1827.
Large-scale Hotel   **Facility:** 183 units. 168 one-bedroom standard units. 15 one-bedroom suites, some with whirlpools. 3-4
stories, interior corridors. *Bath:* combo or shower only. **Parking:** on-site. **Terms:** check-in 4 pm, package
plans, pets ($25 fee, in designated units). **Amenities:** video games (fee), voice mail, irons, hair dryers.
Dining: Sakura Restaurant, Woodlands Cafe, see separate listings. **Pool(s):** heated outdoor. **Leisure Activities:** sauna,
whirlpools, exercise room. **Guest Services:** valet and coin laundry. **Business Services:** conference facilities, business center.
Cards: AX, DC, DS, JC, MC, VI. *(See color ad below)*

SOME UNITS
[S▪D] [🐏] [▯◀] [🍴] [👶] [📶] [🐾] [✕📺] [🎥] [DATA PORT] [💻] / [✕] [VCR] [🔒] [🖥] /
FEE   FEE

RAMADA LIMITED-LUCKY LANE   *Book at aaa.com*   Phone: (928)779-3614   **19**
[AAA] [SAVE]   5/1-9/30   1P: $44-$99   2P: $54-$109   XP: $10   F17
2/1-4/30 & 10/1-1/31   1P: $39-$69   2P: $49-$79   XP: $10   F17
◆◆◆ ◆◆   **Location:** I-40, exit 198 (Butler Ave), just n. then just e. 2350 E Lucky Ln 86004 (PO Box 207, 86002).
Motel   Fax: 928/774-5834. **Facility:** 103 one-bedroom standard units. 2-3 stories (no elevator), exterior corridors.
Parking: on-site. **Terms:** $2 service charge, pets ($5 extra charge). **Amenities:** voice mail, irons, hair
dryers. **Pool(s):** small heated outdoor. **Guest Services:** coin laundry. **Cards:** AX, CB, DC, DS, MC, VI.
Special Amenities: free continental breakfast and free local telephone calls. *(See color ad p 213)*

SOME UNITS
[S▪D] [🛏] [▯◀] [🐾] [🚐] [📺] [🎥] [DATA PORT] [💻] / [✕] [🔒] [🖥] /
FEE

(See map and index starting on p. 199)

RAMADA LIMITED WEST   *Book at aaa.com*
AAA (SAVE)
| | 5/1-10/31 | 1P: $59-$139 | 2P: $64-$144 | XP: $5 | 38 F17 |
| | 2/1-4/30 & 11/1-1/31 | 1P: $44-$69 | 2P: $49-$79 | XP: $5 | F17 |

Phone: (928)773-1111

Location: I-40, exit 195, just n to Forest Meadows St, w to Beulah Blvd, just s, then w. 2755 S Woodlands Village Blvd 86001. Fax: 928/774-1449. **Facility:** 89 one-bedroom standard units. 2 stories (no elevator), exterior
Small-scale Hotel corridors. **Parking:** on-site. **Terms:** cancellation fee imposed, [CP] meal plan available, pets ($10 fee, in designated units). **Amenities:** high-speed Internet, voice mail, irons, hair dryers. **Pool(s):** heated outdoor. **Leisure Activities:** sauna, whirlpool, exercise room. **Guest Services:** coin laundry. **Business Services:** PC. **Cards:** AX, DC, DS, MC, VI. **Special Amenities:** free local telephone calls and free newspaper. *(See color ad p 212)*

SOME UNITS
🐾 🍴 ⊘ 🏊 ✕ 📷 DATA PORT ▯ 🖥 💻 / ✕ /
FEE

RESIDENCE INN BY MARRIOTT FLAGSTAFF   *Book at aaa.com*
| | 5/27-9/30 | 2P: $99-$199 | 6 |
| | 2/1-5/26 & 10/1-1/31 | 2P: $60-$179 | |

Phone: (928)526-5555

Motel   **Location:** I-40, exit 201, 0.5 mi s. 3440 N Country Club Dr 86004. Fax: 928/527-0328. **Facility:** 102 units. 78 one-bedroom standard units with kitchens. 24 two-bedroom suites ($89-$269) with kitchens. 2 stories (no elevator), interior/exterior corridors. *Bath:* combo or shower only. **Parking:** on-site. **Terms:** check-in 4 pm, cancellation fee imposed, [MAP] meal plan available, pets ($7.50 extra charge). **Amenities:** video games (fee), high-speed Internet, dual phone lines, voice mail, irons, hair dryers. **Pool(s):** heated outdoor. **Leisure Activities:** whirlpool, sports court. **Guest Services:** complimentary evening beverages: Mon-Thurs, valet and coin laundry. **Business Services:** meeting rooms. **Cards:** AX, CB, DC, DS, JC, MC, VI.

SOME UNITS
(ASK) 🐾 ♿ ⊘ 🏊 🛁 📷 DATA PORT ▯ 🖥 💻 / ✕ VCR /
FEE   FEE   FEE

RODEWAY INN EAST   *Book at aaa.com*
AAA (SAVE)
	6/1-1/31	1P: $55	2P: $89	XP: $10	7 F
	5/1-5/31	1P: $45	2P: $55	XP: $10	F
	4/1-4/30	1P: $35	2P: $45	XP: $10	F
	2/1-3/31	1P: $29	2P: $35	XP: $10	F

Phone: (928)526-2200

Small-scale Hotel **Location:** I-40, exit 201, 0.5 mi n; then 1.6 mi w. 2650 E Route 66 86004. Fax: 928/526-2200. **Facility:** 88 one-bedroom standard units. 2 stories (no elevator), exterior corridors. **Parking:** on-site. **Terms:** cancellation fee imposed, small pets only ($10 extra charge). **Amenities:** *Some:* irons, hair dryers. **Cards:** AX, CB, DC, DS, JC, MC, VI. **Special Amenities:** free continental breakfast and free local telephone calls.

SOME UNITS
S/D 🐾 DATA PORT / ✕ 💻 /
FEE

(See map and index starting on p. 199)

SLEEP INN   *Book at aaa.com*   Phone: 928/556-3000   **36**

(AAA) (SAVE)

[diamond diamond diamond diamond]

Motel

9/1-12/31	1P: $80-$125	2P: $85-$130
5/1-8/31	1P: $65-$115	2P: $70-$120
2/1-4/30 & 1/1-1/31	1P: $50-$75	2P: $55-$80

Location: I-40, exit 195, just n to Forest Meadows St, w to Beaulah Rd, just s, then just w. 2765 S Woodlands Village Blvd 86001. Fax: 928/774-1901. **Facility:** 58 one-bedroom standard units. 2 stories (no elevator), interior corridors. *Bath:* combo or shower only. **Parking:** on-site. **Terms:** cancellation fee imposed, weekly rates available, pets ($50 deposit). **Amenities:** hair dryers. *Some:* irons. **Pool(s):** small heated indoor. **Leisure Activities:** whirlpool. **Guest Services:** valet laundry. **Cards:** AX, DC, DS, MC, VI. **Special Amenities:** free continental breakfast and free local telephone calls.

SOME UNITS
[icon row] FEE / [icon row] /

STARLIGHT PINES, A BED & BREAKFAST   Phone: (928)527-1912   **1**

[diamond diamond diamond diamond]

Bed & Breakfast

All Year [BP]	1P: $119-$149	2P: $119-$149 XP: $30

Location: I-40, exit 201, 0.5 mi w on I-40 business loop, then just n. 3380 E Lockett Rd 86004. Fax: 928/527-4014. **Facility:** Bathrooms in this stately Victorian-style home feature vintage claw-foot tubs as well as showers with handmade soap; rooms have a fireplace or porch. Smoke free premises. 4 one-bedroom standard units. 2 stories (no elevator), interior corridors. **Parking:** on-site. **Terms:** check-in 4 pm, cancellation fee imposed. **Amenities:** high-speed Internet. *Some:* irons, hair dryers. **Cards:** AX, DS, MC, VI.

SOME UNITS
(ASK) [icon row] / [icon] /

SUPER 8-LUCKY LANE   Phone: (928)773-4888   **15**

(AAA) (SAVE)

[diamond diamond diamond]

Motel

5/1-9/30	1P: $44-$99	2P: $54-$109 XP: $10 F17
2/1-4/30 & 10/1-1/31	1P: $39-$69	2P: $49-$79 XP: $10 F17

Location: I-40, exit 198 (Butler Ave), just n, then just e. 2540 E Lucky Ln 86004. Fax: 928/774-0075. **Facility:** 70 one-bedroom standard units. 2 stories (no elevator), exterior corridors. **Parking:** on-site. **Terms:** $2 service charge, small pets only ($10 extra charge). **Amenities:** voice mail, irons, hair dryers. **Pool(s):** small heated indoor. **Leisure Activities:** whirlpool. **Guest Services:** coin laundry. **Special Amenities:** free local telephone calls and free newspaper.

SOME UNITS
[icon row] FEE / [icon row] /

(See map and index starting on p. 199)

SUPER 8 MOTEL   *Book at aaa.com*   Phone: (928)774-4581   **10**

AAA SAVE		1P: $49-$125	2P: $49-$125	XP: $10	F16
	5/1-8/31	1P: $49-$69	2P: $49-$79	XP: $10	F16
	9/1-10/31	1P: $39-$59	2P: $39-$69	XP: $10	F16
	2/1-4/30 & 11/1-1/31				

Motel   **Location:** I-40, exit 195, 1.5 mi n on SR 89A (Milton Rd), just w. 602 W Route 66 86001. Fax: 928/774-4581.
Facility: 66 one-bedroom standard units. 1-2 stories (no elevator), exterior corridors. **Parking:** on-site.
Terms: cancellation fee imposed, [ECP] meal plan available, package plans, ($10 extra charge).
Amenities: hair dryers. *Some:* irons. **Pool(s):** heated indoor. **Leisure Activities:** whirlpool. **Guest Services:** coin laundry.
Business Services: PC. **Cards:** AX, DC, DS, MC, VI. **Special Amenities:** free continental breakfast and free local
telephone calls. *(See color ad p 214)*

SOME UNITS

SUPER 8 MOTEL EAST FLAGSTAFF   *Book at aaa.com*   Phone: (928)526-0818   **2**

AAA SAVE	4/1-9/3 [CP]	1P: $59-$149	2P: $59-$149	XP: $10	F17
	9/4-10/31 [CP]	1P: $49-$99	2P: $49-$99	XP: $10	F17
	2/1-3/31 & 11/1-1/31 [CP]	1P: $39-$69	2P: $39-$69	XP: $10	F17

Motel   **Location:** I-40, exit 201, just n, 0.5 mi w on I-40 business loop, then just n. Located on a busy commercial street. 3725
Kasper Ave 86004. Fax: 928/526-8786. **Facility:** 89 one-bedroom standard units, some with whirlpools. 2
stories (no elevator), interior corridors. *Bath:* combo or shower only. **Parking:** on-site. **Terms:** pets ($20
extra charge, in limited units). **Amenities:** hair dryers. *Some:* irons. **Cards:** AX, DS, MC, VI. **Special Amenities:** free
continental breakfast and free newspaper. *(See color ad below & p 229)*

SOME UNITS

TRAVEL INN   Phone: 928/774-3381   **27**

AAA SAVE		1P: $33-$69	2P: $43-$89	XP: $10	F18
	5/1-10/31	1P: $30-$50	2P: $40-$60	XP: $10	F18
	2/1-4/30	1P: $26-$50	2P: $36-$60	XP: $10	F18
	11/1-1/31				

Motel   **Location:** I-40, exit 195, 1.2 mi n on Milton Rd, then just w. 801 W Route 66 86001. Fax: 928/774-1648. **Facility:** 48
units. 40 one- and 8 two-bedroom standard units. 2 stories (no elevator), exterior corridors. *Bath:* combo or
shower only. **Parking:** on-site. **Terms:** package plans, small pets only ($10 extra charge, in limited units).
Amenities: voice mail, hair dryers. *Some:* irons. **Leisure Activities:** sauna, whirlpool. **Business Services:** business center.
Cards: AX, DS, MC, VI. **Special Amenities:** free continental breakfast and free local telephone calls.

SOME UNITS

(See map and index starting on p. 199)

TRAVELODGE-GRAND CANYON/FLAGSTAFF   *Book at aaa.com*   Phone: 928/526-1399   **8**

AAA SAVE

5/1-10/31	1P: $40-$130	2P: $40-$130	XP: $10 F12
2/1-4/30	1P: $29-$79	2P: $29-$89	XP: $10 F12
11/1-1/31	1P: $29-$69	2P: $29-$79	XP: $10 F12

Motel   **Location:** I-40, exit 201, just n, then 1.7 mi w on I-40 business loop. 2610 E Route 66 86004. **Fax:** 928/527-8626. **Facility:** 85 one-bedroom standard units. 1-2 stories (no elevator); exterior corridors. **Parking:** on-site. **Terms:** small pets only ($10 extra charge). **Amenities:** hair dryers. *Some:* irons. **Dining:** 6 am-10 pm, cocktails. **Pool(s):** small heated outdoor. **Leisure Activities:** playground. **Guest Services:** coin laundry. **Cards:** AX, DC, DS, MC, VI. **Special Amenities:** free local telephone calls and early check-in/late check-out. *(See color ad p 201)*

SOME UNITS
SD [icons] FEE [icons] / [icons] VCR [icons] /

TRAVELODGE HOTEL   *Book at aaa.com*   Phone: 928/779-6944   **23**

AAA SAVE

5/1-11/4	1P: $39-$99	2P: $39-$179	XP: $10 F12
2/1-4/30 & 11/5-1/31	1P: $34-$79	2P: $34-$79	XP: $10 F12

Small-scale Hotel   **Location:** I-40, exit 198 (Butler Ave), just n. 2200 E Butler Ave 86004. **Fax:** 928/774-3990. **Facility:** 100 one-bedroom standard units. 3 stories, interior corridors. **Parking:** on-site. **Terms:** pets ($10 fee, in designated units). **Amenities:** voice mail, irons, hair dryers. **Dining:** 5:30 am-10 pm, cocktails. **Pool(s):** small heated indoor. **Leisure Activities:** saunas, whirlpool. **Guest Services:** coin laundry. **Cards:** AX, DC, DS, MC, VI. **Special Amenities:** free local telephone calls and preferred room (subject to availability with advance reservations).

SOME UNITS
SD [icons] FEE [icons] / [icons] /

The following lodging was either not evaluated or did not meet AAA rating requirements but is listed for your information only.

MOUNTAIN COUNTRY CONDOS   Phone: 928/214-0810

[fyi]   Not evaluated; management refused evaluation on 07/06/2005. **Location:** I-40, exit 201, 0.7 mi s on Country Club Dr, then just w. Located in a residential area. 2380 N Oakmont Dr 86004 (200 S Leroux, Suite 1, 86001). Facilities, services, and decor characterize a mid-range property.

--- WHERE TO DINE ---

BEAVER STREET BREWERY & WHISTLE STOP
CAFE   **Lunch:** $7-$10   **Dinner:** $7-$18   Phone: 928/779-0079   **10**

American   **Location:** I-40, exit 195, 2 mi n to Santa Fe Ave, just e, then just s. 11 S Beaver St #86001. **Hours:** 11:30 am-midnight. **Closed:** 1/1, 11/23, 12/25. **Reservations:** not accepted. **Features:** Among offerings at the casual restaurant are soups, fondues, salads, sandwiches and wood-fired pizzas, as well as a selection of entrees at dinner. Several ales and beers are brewed on the premises. Patio dining is a nice option in pleasant weather. Casual dress; cocktails. **Parking:** on-site. **Cards:** AX, DS, MC, VI.

BLACK BART'S STEAK HOUSE &
MUSICAL REVUE   **Dinner:** $14-$30   Phone: 928/779-3142   **19**

Steak House   **Location:** I-40, exit 198 (Butler Ave), just se. 2760 E Butler Ave 86004. **Hours:** 5 pm-9 pm; Fri & Sat-10 pm in summer. **Closed:** 1/1, 11/23, 12/24, 12/25; also Super Bowl Sun. **Reservations:** accepted. **Features:** A musical revue provides nightly entertainment in this rustic, casual restaurant. Oak-broiled steak, seafood, chicken and prime rib delight the palate. Casual dress; cocktails; entertainment. **Parking:** on-site. **Cards:** AX, DC, DS, MC, VI.

BRANDY'S RESTAURANT & BAKERY   **Lunch:** $5-$8   **Dinner:** $8-$14   Phone: 928/779-2187   **1**

American   **Location:** From Route 66, 0.8 mi n on 4th St, then just w; in strip mall. 1500 E Cedar Ave 86004. **Hours:** 6:30 am-9 pm, Sun & Mon-2:30 pm. **Reservations:** not accepted. **Features:** Famous for breakfast and baked goods, they also offer an extensive lunch menu and creative dinner options. Lunch sandwiches include tuna melts, Reubens, hamburgers, grilled salmon, grilled portabella and much more. Dinner dishes feature mahi mahi, Ahi tuna, steak, chicken and salmon as well as burgers and a limited sandwich list. Casual dress; wine only. **Parking:** on-site. **Cards:** MC, VI.

(See map and index starting on p. 199)

BUSTER'S
American
DC, DS, MC, VI.

Lunch: $5-$9   Dinner: $9-$18   Phone: 928/774-5155   24
Location: I-40, exit 195, 0.5 mi n; in Green Tree Village. 1800 S Milton Rd 86001. **Hours:** 11:30 am-10 pm. Closed: 11/23, 12/25. **Reservations:** accepted. **Features:** For casual dining in a lively atmosphere, the restaurant is a favorite. Salads and sandwiches are popular lunch offerings, while dinners typically revolve around steaks, chicken and a daily selection of fresh seafood. Casual dress; cocktails. **Parking:** on-site. **Cards:** AX, CB,

CHINA STAR
Chinese

Lunch: $6   Dinner: $5-$8   Phone: 928/774-8880   13
Location: 1.3 mi e. 1802 E Route 66 86004. **Hours:** 11 am-9 pm. Closed: 12/25. **Features:** Two large self-service tables display soups, salads, fruits and desserts, as well as a variety of chicken, beef and rice entrees, including moo goo gai pan. Parking is plentiful around the restaurant, which stands alone in front of a small shopping center. Casual dress. **Parking:** on-site. **Cards:** AX, DS, MC, VI.

CILANTRO'S MEXICAN GRILL
Mexican

Lunch: $7-$9   Dinner: $6-$19   Phone: 928/779-1271   25
Location: I-40, exit 195, just n to Forest Meadows St, w to Beaulah, just s to Woodlands Village Blvd, then just w. 2800 S Woodlands Blvd 86001. **Hours:** 7:30 am-9 pm. **Reservations:** accepted. **Features:** The restaurant prepares traditional Mexican dishes. Delicious desserts are large enough to share, so save room and order extra spoons. Casual dress. **Parking:** on-site. **Cards:** AX, DC, DS, MC, VI.

COREA HOUSE
Korean

Lunch: $7-$10   Dinner: $8-$17   Phone: 928/773-1122   9
Location: Historic town center. 115 E Aspen Ave 86001. **Hours:** 11 am-9 pm. **Reservations:** accepted. **Features:** A knowledgeable staff will help you choose from an extensive list of traditional Korean favorites. Casual dress; cocktails. **Parking:** street. **Cards:** MC, VI.

COTTAGE PLACE RESTAURANT
Continental

Dinner: $17-$25   Phone: 928/774-8431   15
Location: Just s of downtown; just w of Beaver St. 126 W Cottage Ave 86001. **Hours:** 5 pm-9:30 pm. Closed: Mon. **Reservations:** suggested. **Features:** Classical background music and a nice selection of international entrees enhance the fine dining in this resorted 1909 bungalow. Prix fixe dinner with wine paring is offered. Casual dress; beer & wine only. **Parking:** street. **Cards:** AX, MC, VI.

DARA THAI RESTAURANT
Thai

Lunch: $6-$8   Dinner: $10-$13   Phone: 928/774-8390   14
Location: Corner of W Phoenix Ave and S San Francisco St; downtown. 14 S San Francisco St 86001. **Hours:** 11 am-10 pm, Sat & Sun from noon. Closed: 11/23, 12/25. **Reservations:** accepted. **Features:** Friendly servers offer a nice selection of Thai dishes in a relaxed, unpretentious setting. Spice levels are adjusted to suit each diner's taste. Casual dress; cocktails. **Parking:** street. **Cards:** MC, VI.

GALAXY DINER
American

Lunch: $5-$8   Dinner: $6-$14   Phone: 928/774-2466   20
Location: I-40, exit 195, 1.5 mi n on Milton Rd, then just w. 931 W Hwy 66 86001. **Hours:** 6 am-9 pm, Fri & Sat-10 pm. Closed: 11/23, 12/25. **Reservations:** not accepted. **Features:** On the west side of town, the diner welcomes patrons with 1950s-era music and photographs of movie stars decorating the walls. On the menu are burgers, chicken-fried steak and roast beef. Shakes, malts and ice cream in a variety of flavors are among sweet choices. Casual dress; beer & wine only. **Parking:** on-site. **Cards:** AX, DS, MC, VI.

GRANNY'S CLOSET
American
Parking: on-site. **Cards:** AX, CB, DC, DS, MC, VI.

Lunch: $4-$8   Dinner: $7-$24   Phone: 928/774-8331   17
Location: I-40, exit 195, 1.9 mi n on SR 89A (Milton Rd). 218 W Route 66 86001. **Hours:** 11 am-midnight. **Reservations:** accepted. **Features:** Since 1974, the casual eatery has served traditional Italian entrees, such as lasagna and spaghetti, as well as steaks, seafood, sandwiches and burgers. Lighter munchies, including wings, nachos and a host of other favorites, are popular in the sports bar. Casual dress; cocktails.

HIRO'S SUSHI BAR & JAPANESE RESTAURANT
Japanese

Lunch: $4-$20   Dinner: $4-$20   Phone: 928/226-8030   21
Location: I-40, exit 195, 1 mi n on Milton Rd, just sw. 1312 S Plaza Way 86001. **Hours:** 11:30 am-2 & 5-9 pm, Fri & Sat-9:30 pm, Sun noon-9:30 pm. Closed major holidays. **Reservations:** not accepted. **Features:** Fresh sushi, tempura and other traditional dishes are served in a laid-back atmosphere. Casual dress; wine only. **Parking:** on-site. **Cards:** AX, DC, DS, MC, VI.

HORSEMEN LODGE
American

Dinner: $14-$30   Phone: 928/526-2655
Location: I-40, exit 201, 3.5 mi n. 8500 N Hwy 89 N 86002. **Hours:** 5 pm-close. Closed major holidays; also Sun. **Reservations:** not accepted. **Features:** Decorated with saddles, tack room items and mounted game trophies, the Old West-style steak house appeals to those seeking a glimpse and the taste of the Western past. Casual dress; cocktails. **Parking:** on-site. **Cards:** AX, MC, VI.

JOSEPHINE'S
American

Menu on aaa.com   Lunch: $7-$10   Dinner: $17-$25   Phone: 928/779-3400   4
Location: Just n of jct old Route 66. 503 N Humphrey's St 86001. **Hours:** 11 am-2:30 & 5:30-9 pm. Closed: for lunch Sat 11/1-5/31. **Reservations:** suggested. **Features:** The eclectic menu is a showcase for steak, seafood, chicken, lamb and pork dishes prepared with European, Asian, Pan American and Southwestern influences. The renovated historic home provides a casually comfortable setting. Casual dress; cocktails. **Parking:** on-site. **Cards:** AX, DS, MC, VI.

(See map and index starting on p. 199)

KACHINA RESTAURANT   Lunch: $6-$14   Dinner: $8-$18   Phone: 928/779-1944   16

Mexican

Location: Just e; downtown. 522 E Route 66 86001. **Hours:** 10 am-9 pm, Fri & Sat-9:30 pm, Sun 11 am-8 pm, Mon 10 am-8 pm. **Features:** The popular restaurant prepares varied enchiladas, burritos, tamales and other traditional Mexican dishes, as well as tempting daily specials. Casual dress; cocktails. **Parking:** on-site. **Cards:** AX, DS, MC, VI.

LA BELLAVIA   Lunch: $4-$8   Phone: 928/774-8301   11

American

Location: Just s of old Route 66; downtown. 18 Beaver St S 86001. **Hours:** 6:30 am-2 pm. Closed: 1/1, 11/23, 12/25. **Reservations:** accepted. **Features:** Cozy, comfortable family dining and daily specials are featured. Try the house specialty - Swedish oat pancake. Casual dress. **Parking:** street.

MACY'S EUROPEAN COFFEE HOUSE & BAKERY   Lunch: $3-$8   Dinner: $3-$8   Phone: 928/774-2243   12

Vegetarian

Location: Just s of Route 66; in historic town center. 14 S Beaver St 86001. **Hours:** 6 am-10 pm. Closed: 11/23, 12/25. **Features:** Patrons stop in for a quick bite or a specialty coffee. Fresh vegetarian offerings include sandwiches, soups and baked goods. Casual dress. **Parking:** street.

MAMMA LUISA   Dinner: $8-$17   Phone: 928/526-6809   2

Italian

Location: On US 180 and 89, just n of E Route 66; in Kachina Square Shopping Center. 2710 N Steves Blvd 86004. **Hours:** 4:30 pm-close. Closed: 11/23, 12/25. **Reservations:** suggested. **Features:** The small, cozy restaurant with red-checkered tablecloths appeals to those seeking a good Italian meal in an Old World atmosphere. Casual dress; cocktails. **Parking:** on-site. **Cards:** AX, DC, DS, MC, VI.

MOUNTAIN OASIS INTERNATIONAL RESTAURANT   Lunch: $6-$10   Dinner: $6-$18   Phone: 928/214-9270   6

International

Location: Route 66, just n on Beaver St, just e; downtown. 11 E Aspen Ave 86001. **Hours:** 11 am-9 pm, Fri & Sat-10 pm. Closed: 4/16, 11/23, 12/25. **Reservations:** accepted. **Features:** The "international" in the comfortable bistro's name describes the widely varied menu that covers Asian, Middle Eastern, Mediterranean and American fare. Vegetarian and vegan dishes share menu space with steak, fish, chicken and pasta preparations. Casual dress; cocktails. **Parking:** street. **Cards:** AX, DC, DS, MC, VI.

PASTO   Lunch: $7-$12   Dinner: $15-$25   Phone: 928/779-1937   7

Italian

Location: Route 66, just n on Leroux St; just e; downtown. 19 E Aspen St 86001. **Hours:** 11 am-2 & 5-9 pm, Fri-9:30 pm, Sat 5 pm-9:30 pm, Sun 5 pm-9 pm. Closed: 11/23, 12/24, 12/25; also Super Bowl Sun. **Reservations:** suggested. **Features:** In historic downtown, the casual yet elegant bistro features fine Italian food that has won much local praise. The menu lists beef, seafood, chicken and pasta choices. Rolled eggplant is the specialty of the house. Dressy casual; beer & wine only. **Parking:** street. **Cards:** AX, DS, MC, VI.

PESTO BROTHERS PIAZZA   Lunch: $4-$10   Dinner: $10-$20   Phone: 928/774-3020   5

Italian

Location: Corner of Birch and LeRoux sts; center. 120 N LeRoux St, Suite 104 86001. **Hours:** 11 am-2 & 5-9 pm, Fri & Sat-10 pm, Sun 5 pm-9 pm. Closed: 1/1, 11/23, 12/25. **Reservations:** suggested. **Features:** In a small indoor shopping center in the historic area downtown, the eatery focuses its menu on traditional dishes, including cannelloni, spaghetti and ravioli. Salads are large and delicious. Casual dress; cocktails. **Parking:** street. **Cards:** AX, MC, VI.

RACHA THAI   Lunch: $7-$8   Dinner: $8-$14   Phone: 928/774-0003   8

Thai

Location: Between Aspen and Birch; in historic downtown. 104 N San Francisco St 86001. **Hours:** 11 am-3:30 & 4:30-9 pm, Fri & Sat-10 pm, Sun 4:30 pm-9 pm. Closed: Mon. **Reservations:** accepted. **Features:** The cozy restaurant serves standard Thai cuisine. All dishes can be made vegetarian. Casual dress; cocktails. **Parking:** street. **Cards:** AX, MC, VI.

SAKURA RESTAURANT   Lunch: $5-$9   Dinner: $11-$17   Phone: 928/773-9118   23

Japanese

Location: I-40, exit 195, 1.5 mi on Milton Rd, then 0.5 mi w; in Radisson Woodlands Hotel Flagstaff. 1175 W Route 66 86001. **Hours:** 11:30 am-2 & 5-10 pm, Sun from 5 pm. Closed: 11/23, 12/25. **Reservations:** suggested. **Features:** Teppanyaki-style cooking is prepared in a traditional Japanese steak house atmosphere. Guests from several parties join together around the grill as the chef cooks individual meals. Casual dress; cocktails. **Parking:** on-site. **Cards:** AX, CB, DC, DS, JC, MC, VI. *(See color ad p 212)*

SALSA BRAVA EAST   Lunch: $6-$14   Dinner: $8-$14   Phone: 928/779-5293   3

Mexican

Location: I-40, exit 201, 0.5 mi n, then 2.7 mi w. 2220 E Route 66 86001. **Hours:** 11 am-9 pm, Fri-10 pm, Sat 8 am-10 pm, Sun 8 am-9 pm. Closed: 4/16, 11/23, 12/25. **Reservations:** not accepted. **Features:** On historic Route 66, the restaurant serves a variety of Mexican dishes. Be sure to try the Baja fish wraps for which this place is famous. Casual dress; cocktails. **Parking:** on-site. **Cards:** AX, DS, MC, VI.

WESTERN GOLD DINING ROOM   *Menu on aaa.com*   Lunch: $9   Dinner: $22-$34   Phone: 928/779-2741   18

American

Location: I-40, exit 198 (Butler Ave), just s; in Little America Hotel. 2515 E Butler Ave 86004. **Hours:** 11 am-2 & 5-10 pm, Sat from 5 pm, Sun 10 am-2 & 5-10 pm. **Reservations:** suggested. **Features:** Patrons who visit the attractive dining room are treated to a nice selection of American and Continental cuisine, including rack of lamb and chateaubriand. The restaurant appeals to travelers in search of an upscale dining experience. Casual dress; cocktails; entertainment. **Parking:** on-site. **Cards:** AX, CB, DC, DS, MC, VI.

WOODLANDS CAFE   Lunch: $5-$8   Dinner: $10-$16   Phone: 928/773-8888   22

American

Location: I-40, exit 195, 1.5 mi n on Milton Rd, then 0.5 mi w; in Radisson Woodlands Hotel Flagstaff. 1175 W Route 66 86001. **Hours:** 6 am-10 pm. **Reservations:** accepted. **Features:** A three meal menu is offered here with lunch dishes including salads, sandwiches and some pasta, seafood and Mexican dishes. Dinner has a larger selection including steak, seafood, pasta and Mexican entrees. Casual dress; cocktails. **Parking:** on-site. **Cards:** AX, CB, DC, DS, JC, MC, VI.

FLORENCE pop. 17,054

——— WHERE TO STAY ———

BLUE MIST MOTEL

Motel

Phone: 520/868-5875

| All Year | 1P: $45-$55 | 2P: $65-$75 | XP: $10 | D10 |

Location: On SR 79, at SR 287. 40 S Pinal Pkwy 85232. **Fax:** 520/868-0660. **Facility:** 22 one-bedroom standard units, some with efficiencies or kitchens. 1 story, exterior corridors. *Bath:* combo or shower only. **Parking:** on-site. **Terms:** cancellation fee imposed. **Amenities:** hair dryers. **Pool(s):** small outdoor. **Cards:** AX, DC, DS, MC, VI. **Special Amenities:** free local telephone calls and early check-in/late check-out.

SOME UNITS

RANCHO SONORA INN

Motel

Phone: (520)868-8000

| 10/1-1/31 [ECP] | 1P: $79 | 2P: $89 | XP: $10 | F10 |
| 2/1-9/30 [ECP] | 1P: $69 | 2P: $79 | XP: $10 | F10 |

Location: On SR 79, 5 mi s of SR 287. Located in a quiet desert area. 9198 N Hwy 79 85232. **Fax:** 520/868-8000. **Facility:** Designated smoking area. 11 units. 9 one-bedroom standard units. 2 one-bedroom suites ($95-$135) with kitchens. 1 story, exterior corridors. *Bath:* combo or shower only. **Parking:** on-site. **Terms:** 3 day cancellation notice, weekly rates available, pets ($10 fee). **Amenities:** irons, hair dryers. **Business Services:** fax (fee). **Cards:** AX, DS, MC, VI.

SOME UNITS

Drive
See
Stay
Play

DO IT ALL WITH AAA!

AAA is your complete travel resource. Access AAA's expert travel information services anywhere, anytime at aaa.com and get exclusive member benefits and savings, including the lowest online hotel rates! For personal, professional service, call or visit your local AAA office.

Do more with AAA.

aaa.com

*PRODUCTS AND SERVICES AVAILABLE THROUGH PARTICIPATING AAA AND CAA CLUBS.

FOREST LAKES

—— WHERE TO STAY ——

FOREST LAKES LODGE

AAA [SAVE]

Motel

	5/1-9/30 [CP]	1P: $45-$74	2P: $55-$74	Phone: (928)535-4727
	2/1-4/30 & 10/1-1/31 [CP]	1P: $45-$65	2P: $55-$65	XP: $10 F12
				XP: $10 F12

Location: On SR 260. Located in a quiet area. 876 AZ Hwy 260 85931. **Facility:** 20 one-bedroom standard units. 2 stories (no elevator), exterior corridors. **Parking:** on-site. **Terms:** weekly rates available, pets ($10 extra charge). **Leisure Activities:** playground. **Cards:** AX, MC, VI. **Special Amenities:** free continental breakfast and free local telephone calls.

SOME UNITS
[icons] FEE

FORT MOHAVE pop. 773

—— WHERE TO DINE ——

LOUIGI'S

[icons]

Italian

| **Lunch:** $6-$10 | **Dinner:** $10-$18 | **Phone:** 928/758-9432 |

Location: 7.2 mi s of Laughlin Bridge. 4360 Hwy 95 86426. **Hours:** 11:30 am-9 pm, Sat & Sun from 4 pm. **Features:** The menu at the small family restaurant centers on steak, seafood and pasta dishes. Service is friendly and prompt. Casual dress; cocktails. **Parking:** on-site. **Cards:** MC, VI.

[icons]

FOUNTAIN HILLS —See Phoenix p. 317.

GILA BEND pop. 1,980

—— WHERE TO STAY ——

AMERICA'S CHOICE INN & SUITES

[icons]

Motel

| | All Year | 1P: $59-$75 | 2P: $59-$75 | Phone: (928)683-6311 |

Location: I-8, exit 119, just nw. 2888 Butterfield Tr 85337 (PO Box 368). Fax: 928/683-2120. **Facility:** 62 one-bedroom standard units. 3 stories (no elevator), interior corridors. **Parking:** on-site. **Terms:** cancellation fee imposed, [CP] meal plan available, pets ($10 fee, $10 deposit). **Pool(s):** small heated outdoor. **Guest Services:** valet laundry. **Business Services:** fax (fee). **Cards:** AX, CB, DC, DS, MC, VI.

SOME UNITS
[ASK] [icons] FEE

BEST WESTERN SPACE AGE LODGE *Book at aaa.com*

AAA [SAVE]

[icons]

Motel

| | All Year | 1P: $65-$115 | 2P: $69-$119 | Phone: (928)683-2273 |
| | | | | XP: $5 F17 |

Location: Business Loop I-8; center. 401 E Pima St 85337 (PO Box C). Fax: 928/683-2273. **Facility:** 41 one-bedroom standard units. 1 story, exterior corridors. **Parking:** on-site. **Amenities:** irons, hair dryers. *Some:* high-speed Internet. **Dining:** 5 am-9 pm. **Pool(s):** outdoor. **Leisure Activities:** whirlpool. **Guest Services:** gift shop. **Business Services:** meeting rooms, PC, fax (fee). **Cards:** AX, CB, DC, DS, MC, VI. **Special Amenities:** free local telephone calls and early check-in/late check-out. *(See color ad below)*

SOME UNITS
[icons]

GILBERT —See Phoenix p. 318.

GLENDALE —See Phoenix p. 319.

GLOBE pop. 7,486

------ WHERE TO STAY ------

COMFORT INN AT ROUND MOUNTAIN PARK *Book at aaa.com* **Phone:** (928)425-7575

| | 2/1-6/30 | 1P: $79-$199 | 2P: $89-$209 | XP: $10 | F17 |
| | 7/1-1/31 | 1P: $59-$199 | 2P: $69-$209 | XP: $10 | F17 |

Small-scale Hotel **Location:** On US 60, 1 mi e of town. 1515 South St 85501. Fax: 928/425-4062. **Facility:** 52 one-bedroom standard units, some with whirlpools. 2 stories (no elevator), exterior corridors. **Parking:** on-site. **Terms:** cancellation fee imposed, [ECP] meal plan available, pets ($10 extra charge). **Amenities:** irons, hair dryers. **Pool(s):** outdoor. **Leisure Activities:** whirlpool. **Business Services:** PC. **Cards:** AX, CB, DC, DS, MC, VI.

SOME UNITS

ASK SD ▥ ▮|◆ ◢ ▧ DATA PORT ▯ ▭ ▱ / ⊠ /
FEE

DAYS INN *Book at aaa.com* **Phone:** (928)425-5500

All Year 1P: $59-$129 2P: $65-$129 XP: $7 F17

Small-scale Hotel **Location:** On US 60, 1.3 mi e of town. 1630 E Ash St 85501. Fax: 928/425-4146. **Facility:** 42 one-bedroom standard units. 2 stories (no elevator), exterior corridors. **Parking:** on-site. **Amenities:** irons, hair dryers. **Pool(s):** outdoor. **Leisure Activities:** whirlpool. **Business Services:** PC. **Cards:** AX, DC, DS, MC, VI. **Special Amenities:** free expanded continental breakfast and free local telephone calls.

SOME UNITS

SD ▮|◆ ◢ ▧ DATA PORT ▯ ▭ ▱ / ⊠ /

MOTEL 6 #4223 *Book at aaa.com* **Phone:** (928)425-5741

All Year 1P: $43-$50 2P: $43-$50 XP: $6 F17

Small-scale Hotel **Location:** On US 60, 1.3 mi e of town. 1699 E Ash St 85501. Fax: 928/402-8466. **Facility:** 78 units. 75 one-bedroom standard units, some with whirlpools. 3 one-bedroom suites. 2 stories (no elevator), interior/exterior corridors. *Bath:* combo or shower only. **Parking:** on-site. **Terms:** small pets only. **Pool(s):** outdoor. **Leisure Activities:** whirlpool. **Guest Services:** coin laundry. **Business Services:** meeting rooms. **Cards:** AX, DS, MC, VI.

SOME UNITS

ASK SD ▥ ▧ ◢ ▧ DATA PORT / ⊠ ▯ ▭ /

TRAVELODGE GLOBE **Phone:** (928)425-7008

All Year 1P: $65-$120 2P: $65-$120 XP: $10 D12

Small-scale Hotel **Location:** On US 60, 4 mi w of town. 2119 W Hwy 60 85501 (PO Box 1043, 85502). Fax: 928/425-6410. **Facility:** 45 one-bedroom standard units. 2 stories, interior corridors. *Bath:* combo or shower only. **Parking:** on-site. **Terms:** cancellation fee imposed, [ECP] meal plan available. **Amenities:** high-speed Internet, voice mail, irons, hair dryers. **Guest Services:** coin laundry. **Business Services:** meeting rooms. **Cards:** AX, DC, DS, MC, VI. **Special Amenities:** free expanded continental breakfast and free local telephone calls.

SOME UNITS

SD ▧ ◢ ▧ DATA PORT ▯ ▭ ▱ / ⊠ /

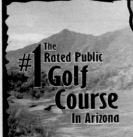

——— WHERE TO DINE ———

GUAYO'S ON THE TRAIL
Mexican

Lunch: $5-$10   **Dinner:** $6-$17   **Phone:** 928/425-9969
Location: Jct US 60, 1.3 mi n. 14239 S Hwy 188 85501. **Hours:** 10:30 am-9 pm. Closed: 11/23, 12/25; also Tues. **Features:** For an array of traditional favorites, including menudo and burritos, served in a friendly atmosphere, guests can visit the eatery, which has served locals for 38 years. Casual dress; cocktails. **Parking:** on-site. **Cards:** AX, DS, MC, VI.

GOLD CANYON

——— WHERE TO STAY ———

BEST WESTERN GOLD CANYON INN & SUITES   *Book at aaa.com*   **Phone:** (480)671-6000

2/1-4/27	1P: $116-$170	2P: $116-$170	XP: $10	F12
9/27-1/31	1P: $92-$146	2P: $92-$146	XP: $10	F12
4/28-5/14	1P: $76-$105	2P: $76-$105	XP: $10	F12
5/15-9/26	1P: $69-$105	2P: $69-$105	XP: $10	F12

Small-scale Hotel **Location:** US 60, exit Kings Ranch Rd, just n, then just e; 7 mi e of Apache Junction. 8333 E Sunrise Sky Dr 85218. **Fax:** 480/671-0013. **Facility:** 68 one-bedroom standard units, some with whirlpools. 2 stories, interior corridors. *Bath:* combo or shower only. **Parking:** on-site. **Terms:** cancellation fee imposed. **Amenities:** high-speed Internet, voice mail, irons, hair dryers. *Some:* dual phone lines. **Pool(s):** heated outdoor. **Leisure Activities:** whirlpool, billiards, exercise room. **Guest Services:** valet and coin laundry. **Business Services:** meeting rooms, PC. **Cards:** AX, DC, DS, MC, VI. **Special Amenities:** free expanded continental breakfast and free local telephone calls.

SOME UNITS

GOLD CANYON GOLF RESORT   **Phone:** (480)982-9090

2/1-5/18 & 1/1-1/31	1P: $235-$310	2P: $235-$310	XP: $10	F18
9/12-12/31	1P: $185-$260	2P: $185-$260	XP: $10	F18
5/19-9/11	1P: $135-$210	2P: $135-$210	XP: $10	F18

Resort
Large-scale Hotel **Location:** US 60, exit Kings Ranch Rd, 1 mi n. 6100 S Kings Ranch Rd 85219. **Fax:** 480/983-9554. **Facility:** Nestled against the Superstition Mountains, the resort offers spacious Mediterranean-style casitas overlooking the two golf courses. Designated smoking area. 99 units. 96 one-bedroom standard units, some with efficiencies and/or whirlpools. 3 one-bedroom suites ($300-$500). 1 story, exterior corridors. *Bath:* combo or shower only. **Parking:** valet and street. **Terms:** check-in 4 pm, 3 day cancellation notice-fee imposed, package plans, $7 service charge, small pets only ($75 extra charge). **Amenities:** voice mail, honor bars, irons, hair dryers. *Some:* DVD players. **Dining:** Kokopelli's, see separate listing. **Pool(s):** heated outdoor. **Leisure Activities:** whirlpool, hiking trails, exercise room, spa. *Fee:* golf-36 holes. **Guest Services:** valet laundry. **Business Services:** meeting rooms, PC. **Cards:** AX, DC, DS, MC, VI.

FEE

——— WHERE TO DINE ———

KOKOPELLI'S
American

Lunch: $10-$15   **Dinner:** $12-$29   **Phone:** 480/982-9090
Location: US 60, exit Kings Ranch Rd, 1 mi n; in Gold Canyon Golf Resort. 6100 S Kings Ranch Rd 85219. **Hours:** 6:30 am-9:30 pm. **Reservations:** accepted. **Features:** Views to the Superstition Mountains or over the adjacent golf course enhance the dining experience. The well-trained staff assists with choices of specialty steaks or preparations of seafood, chicken or veal. Gold Canyon mousse is a must for dessert. Dressy casual; cocktails. **Parking:** on-site and valet. **Cards:** AX, CB, DC, DS, MC, VI.

OPEN RANGE STEAKHOUSE
Steak House

Lunch: $5-$23   **Dinner:** $8-$24   **Phone:** 480/983-3020
Location: US 60, exit Kings Ranch Rd, 1.1 mi n. 6030 S King's Ranch Rd 85218. **Hours:** 11:30 am-9 pm. Closed: 7/4, 11/23, 12/25; also Mon. **Reservations:** accepted. **Features:** Cooked-to-order steaks, fresh seafood and a salad bar with fresh ingredients make the casual restaurant a good choice for dinner. Western decor characterizes the dining room. Casual dress; beer & wine only. **Parking:** on-site. **Cards:** MC, VI.

RED SAGE RESTAURANT
American

Lunch: $5-$10   **Dinner:** $7-$15   **Phone:** 480/671-0300
Location: US 60, exit Kings Ranch Rd, just n. 8330 E Sunrise Sky Dr 85219. **Hours:** 6 am-9 pm. Closed: 11/23, 12/25. **Features:** For ample portions of family-style food served in a friendly manner, it's hard to beat this eatery, a popular drop-in spot for locals. Casual dress; cocktails. **Parking:** on-site. **Cards:** AX, DS, MC, VI.

GOODYEAR —*See Phoenix p. 320.*

Grand Canyon National Park

GRAND CANYON NATIONAL PARK - SOUTH RIM —

See also CAMERON, FLAGSTAFF, WILLIAMS.—See also CAMERON, FLAGSTAFF, WILLIAMS.

——— WHERE TO STAY ———

BEST WESTERN GRAND CANYON SQUIRE INN   *Book at aaa.com*   **Phone:** (928)638-2681

(AAA) [SAVE]	3/16-10/15 & 12/16-1/31 [CP]	1P: $99-$190	2P: $99-$190	XP: $10	F12
	10/16-12/15 [CP]	1P: $75-$155	2P: $75-$155	XP: $10	F12
▽▽▽	2/1-3/15 [CP]	1P: $75-$145	2P: $75-$145	XP: $10	F12

Small-scale Hotel
Location: On SR 64, 2 mi s of South Rim entrance. 100 Hwy 64 86023 (PO Box 130, Hwy 64, GRAND CANYON NATIONAL PARK). Fax: 928/638-2782. **Facility:** 250 units. 248 one-bedroom standard units, some with whirlpools. 2 one-bedroom suites with whirlpools. 1-3 stories (no elevator), interior/exterior corridors. **Bath:** combo or shower only. **Parking:** on-site. **Terms:** check-in 4 pm, cancellation fee imposed. **Amenities:** voice mail, irons, hair dryers. *Some:* high-speed Internet. **Dining:** 2 restaurants, 6:30 am-10 pm; hours may vary off season, cocktails, also, Coronado Room, see separate listing. **Pool(s):** heated outdoor. **Leisure Activities:** sauna, whirlpool, 2 tennis courts, exercise room. *Fee:* bowling, massage, game room. **Guest Services:** gift shop, coin laundry. *Fee:* beauty salon. **Business Services:** conference facilities. **Cards:** AX, DC, DS, MC, VI. **Special Amenities:** free local telephone calls and preferred room (subject to availability with advance reservations). (*See color ad below*)

SOME UNITS

[icons] 🆔 ✈ 🍴 🍸 ⛱ 🏊 ⊠ 🏷 DATA PORT 🖥 / ⊠ 🚪 / FEE

CANYON PLAZA QUALITY INN & SUITES   *Book at aaa.com*   **Phone:** (928)638-2673

(AAA) [SAVE]	3/22-10/31 [CP]	1P: $119-$199	2P: $119-$199	XP: $10	F17
	11/1-1/31 [CP]	1P: $79-$199	2P: $79-$199	XP: $10	F17
▽▽▽	2/1-3/21 [CP]	1P: $79-$199	2P: $79-$199	XP: $10	F17

Small-scale Hotel
Location: On SR 64; 2 mi s of South Rim entrance. Located behind the Imax Theatre. Hwy 64 86023 (PO Box 520, GRAND CANYON). Fax: 928/638-9537. **Facility:** 232 units. 176 one-bedroom standard units. 56 one-bedroom suites ($119-$199). 3 stories, interior/exterior corridors. **Bath:** combo or shower only. **Parking:** on-site. **Terms:** cancellation fee imposed, [AP] & [BP] meal plans available. **Amenities:** video games (fee), high-speed Internet, irons, hair dryers. *Some:* honor bars. **Dining:** 6 am-10 pm; hours vary off season, cocktails. **Pool(s):** small heated outdoor. **Leisure Activities:** whirlpools. **Guest Services:** gift shop. **Business Services:** meeting rooms. **Cards:** AX, CB, DC, DS, JC, MC, VI. **Special Amenities:** free continental breakfast and free local telephone calls.

SOME UNITS

[icons] 🆔 🍴 🍸 ⛱ 🏊 ⊠ 🏷 DATA PORT 🖥 / ⊠ 🚪 🖥 /

EL TOVAR HOTEL

◆◆◆ Small-scale Hotel

All Year — 1P: $133-$310 — 2P: $133-$310 — XP: $11 — **Phone: 303/297-2757** — F16

Location: At Grand Canyon Village South Rim. (PO Box 699, GRAND CANYON NATIONAL PARK, 86023). Fax: 303/297-3175. **Facility:** Smoke free premises. 78 units. 66 one-bedroom standard units. 12 one-bedroom suites ($255-$310). 3 stories (no elevator), interior corridors. **Parking:** on-site. **Terms:** check-in 4 pm, no pets allowed ($8-$14 extra charge, kennels available). **Amenities:** CD players, voice mail, irons, hair dryers. **Dining:** El Tovar Hotel Dining Room, see separate listing. **Guest Services:** gift shop. **Cards:** AX, CB, DC, DS, JC, MC, VI.

SOME UNITS

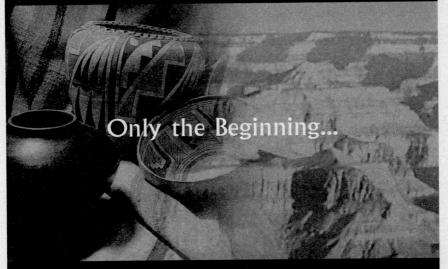

GRAND CANYON HOLIDAY INN EXPRESS & ARIZONA ROOMS   *Book at aaa.com*   Phone: 928/638-3000

Small-scale Hotel

Property failed to provide current rates

Location: On SR 64; 2 mi s of South Rim entrance. Hwy 64 86023 (PO Box 3245, GRAND CANYON). Fax: 928/638-0123. **Facility:** Smoke free premises. 194 units. 163 one-bedroom standard units. 24 one- and 7 two-bedroom suites, some with kitchens. 3 stories, interior corridors. *Bath:* combo or shower only. **Parking:** on-site. **Terms:** check-in 4 pm. **Amenities:** high-speed Internet, voice mail, irons, hair dryers. **Pool(s):** small heated indoor. **Leisure Activities:** whirlpools. *(See color ad below)*

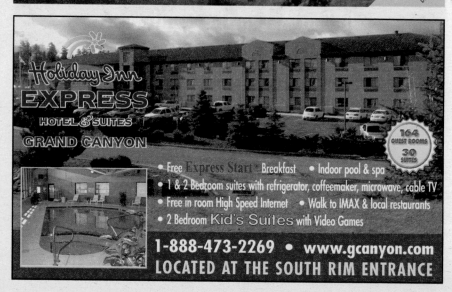

THE GRAND HOTEL *Book at aaa.com*

Phone: (928)638-3333

3/16-10/31 [BP]	1P: $139-$189	2P: $139-$189
2/1-3/15 & 11/1-1/31 [BP]	1P: $99-$149	2P: $99-$149

XP: $10   F17
XP: $10   F17

Small-scale Hotel **Location:** On SR 64; 2 mi s of South Rim entrance. Hwy 64 86023 (PO Box 3319, GRAND CANYON). **Fax:** 928/638-3131. **Facility:** 121 units. 120 one-bedroom standard units. 1 one-bedroom suite. 3 stories, interior corridors. *Bath:* combo or shower only. **Parking:** on-site. **Terms:** check-in 4 pm, 3 day cancellation notice-fee imposed, package plans, pets ($10 extra charge, in designated units). **Amenities:** voice mail, hair dryers. *Some:* irons. **Dining:** Canyon Star, see separate listing. **Pool(s):** small heated indoor. **Leisure Activities:** whirlpool, exercise room. **Guest Services:** gift shop, coin laundry. **Business Services:** meeting rooms. **Cards:** AX, CB, DC, DS, JC, MC, VI. *(See color ad p 228)*

SOME UNITS

(A$K) (S&) 🛏 📶 (Ⓣ) 📺 🍳 ➰ 🔌(DATA PORT) 🖥 / ⊠ 🛢 🖥 /
    FEE

KACHINA LODGE

Phone: 303/297-2757

All Year   1P: $130-$140   2P: $130-$140   XP: $9   F16

Small-scale Hotel **Location:** At Grand Canyon Village South Rim. (PO Box 699, GRAND CANYON NATIONAL PARK, 86023). **Fax:** 303/297-3175. **Facility:** Smoke free premises. 49 one-bedroom standard units. 2 stories, interior corridors. **Parking:** on-site. **Terms:** check-in 4 pm, no pets allowed ($8-$14 extra charge, kennels available). **Amenities:** CD players, safes, irons, hair dryers. **Business Services:** meeting rooms. **Cards:** AX, CB, DC, DS, JC, MC, VI.

🍽 ⊠ (DATA PORT) 🛢 🖥

MASWIK LODGE
Phone: 303/297-2757

3/17-11/27	1P: $83-$127	2P: $83-$127	XP: $9 F16
11/28-1/31	1P: $74-$127	2P: $74-$127	XP: $9 F16

Motel
Location: At Grand Canyon Village South Rim. (PO Box 699, GRAND CANYON NATIONAL PARK, 86023). **Fax:** 303/297-3175. **Facility:** Smoke free premises. 278 one-bedroom standard units. 2 stories (no elevator), exterior corridors. **Bath:** combo or shower only. **Parking:** on-site. **Terms:** open 3/17-1/31, check-in 4 pm, no pets allowed ($8-14 extra charge, kennels available). **Amenities:** *Some:* hair dryers. **Guest Services:** gift shop. **Cards:** AX, CB, DC, DS, JC, MC, VI.

RED FEATHER LODGE   *Book at aaa.com*
Phone: (928)638-2414

All Year	1P: $75-$145	2P: $75-$145 XP: $10 F17

Location: On SR 64; 2 mi s of South Rim entrance. Hwy 64 86023 (PO Box 1460, GRAND CANYON). **Fax:** 928/638-9216. **Facility:** 212 one-bedroom standard units. 2-3 stories, interior/exterior corridors. *Bath:* combo or shower only. **Parking:** on-site. **Terms:** check-in 4 pm, pets ($50 deposit, $10 extra charge, in Small-scale Hotel designated units). **Amenities:** video games (fee), voice mail. *Some:* hair dryers. **Dining:** 7 am-9 pm; hours may vary off season, wine/beer only. **Pool(s):** small heated outdoor. **Leisure Activities:** whirlpool, limited exercise equipment. **Cards:** AX, DC, DS, MC, VI. **Special Amenities:** free continental breakfast and free local telephone calls. *(See color ad p 228)*

SOME UNITS

THUNDERBIRD LODGE

Phone: 303/297-2757

All Year	1P: $130-$140	2P: $130-$140	XP: $9 F16

Location: At Grand Canyon Village South Rim. (PO Box 699, GRAND CANYON NATIONAL PARK, 86023). Fax: 303/297-3175. **Facility:** Smoke free premises. 55 one-bedroom standard units. 2 stories (no elevator), interior/exterior corridors. *Bath:* combo or shower only. **Parking:** on-site. **Terms:** check-in 4 pm, no pets allowed ($8-$14 extra charge, kennels available). **Amenities:** CD players, safes, irons, hair dryers. **Business Services:** meeting rooms. **Cards:** AX, CB, DC, DS, JC, MC, VI.

Small-scale Hotel

YAVAPAI LODGE

Phone: 303/297-2757

3/11-11/1	1P: $83-$127	2P: $83-$127	XP: $9 F16
11/22-1/2	1P: $72-$127	2P: $72-$127	XP: $9 F16
2/1-3/10	1P: $72-$83	2P: $72-$83	XP: $9 F16

Motel

Location: 1 mi e of Grand Canyon Village. Located in a quiet area. (PO Box 699, GRAND CANYON NATIONAL PARK, 86023). Fax: 303/297-3175. **Facility:** Smoke free premises. 358 one-bedroom standard units. 1-2 stories (no elevator), interior/exterior corridors. *Bath:* combo or shower only. **Parking:** on-site. **Terms:** open 2/1-11/1 & 11/22-1/2, check-in 4 pm, no pets allowed ($8-$14 extra charge, kennels available). **Amenities:** hair dryers. **Guest Services:** gift shop. **Cards:** AX, CB, DC, DS, JC, MC, VI.

SOME UNITS

──────── The following lodging was either not evaluated or did not ────────
meet AAA rating requirements but is listed for your information only.

BRIGHT ANGEL LODGE & CABINS

Phone: 303/297-2757

[fyi]   Not evaluated. **Location:** At Grand Canyon Village South Rim. (PO Box 699, GRAND CANYON NATIONAL PARK, 86023). Facilities, services, and decor characterize a basic property.

──────── **WHERE TO DINE** ────────

THE ARIZONA ROOM AT BRIGHT ANGEL LODGE   Lunch: $7-$12   Dinner: $12-$25   Phone: 928-638-2631

American

Location: At Grand Canyon Village South Rim; between Bright Angel Lodge & Cabins and Thunderbird Lodge. **Hours:** Open 2/15-12/31; 4:30 pm-10 pm; also 11:30 am-3 pm 3/1-4/30. **Features:** The menu of this popular restaurant with windows looking toward the canyon features a selection of steak, barbecue, chicken and seafood. Casual dress; cocktails. **Parking:** on-site. **Cards:** AX, DC, DS, JC, MC, VI.

CANYON STAR   Lunch: $5-$13   Dinner: $10-$25   Phone: 928/638-3333

Southwest American

Location: On SR 64; 2 mi s of South Rim entrance; in The Grand Hotel. Hwy 64 86023. **Hours:** 7 am-10 & 11:30-10 pm. **Reservations:** accepted. **Features:** Featuring a Southwestern menu with steaks and a seasonal buffet, this restaurant also entertains the guests with Native American dancers and singing cowboys. Casual dress; cocktails; entertainment. **Parking:** on-site. **Cards:** AX, DC, DS, MC, VI.

CORONADO ROOM   Dinner: $15-$28   Phone: 928/638-2681

American

Location: On SR 64, 2 mi s of South Rim entrance; in Best Western Grand Canyon Squire Inn. 100 Hwy 64 86023. **Hours:** 5 pm-10 pm; to 9 pm 11/1-2/28. **Reservations:** accepted. **Features:** Features a nice selection of steaks, seafood, pastas and Mexican dishes. Casual dress; cocktails. **Parking:** on-site. **Cards:** AX, DC, DS, MC, VI.

EL TOVAR HOTEL DINING ROOM   Lunch: $9-$16   Dinner: $17-$25   Phone: 928/638-2631

Continental

Location: At Grand Canyon Village South Rim; in El Tovar Hotel. **Hours:** 6:30-11 am, 11:30-2 & 5-10 pm. **Reservations:** suggested, for dinner. **Features:** A very attractive dining room is the setting for a nice selection of veal, beef, seafood, chicken and vegetarian entrees. Casual dress; cocktails. **Parking:** on-site. **Cards:** AX, DC, DS, JC, MC, VI. **Historic**

──────── The following restaurant has not been evaluated by AAA ────────
but is listed for your information only.

STEAK HOUSE AT THE GRAND CANYON

Phone: 928/638-2780

[fyi]   Not evaluated. **Location:** On SR 64. **Features:** Steaks, barbecue ribs and chicken prepared over an open juniper wood fire and served in a Western atmosphere.

GRAND CANYON NATIONAL PARK · NORTH RIM

──────── **WHERE TO STAY** ────────

──────── The following lodgings were either not evaluated or did not ────────
meet AAA rating requirements but are listed for your information only.

GRAND CANYON LODGE

Phone: 928/638-2611

[fyi]   Not evaluated. **Location:** In Grand Canyon National Park North Rim. (North Rim, GRAND CANYON NATIONAL PARK, 86052). Facilities, services, and decor characterize a mid-range property.

KAIBAB LODGE

Phone: 928/638-2389

[fyi]
Cottage
Did not meet all AAA rating requirements for some guest rooms at time of last evaluation on 06/08/2005. **Location:** 26 mi s of jct SR 67 and Alternate Rt US 89. SR 67 86003 (PO Box 2997, FLAGSTAFF). Facilities, services, and decor characterize a mid-range property.

The previous listings were for the Grand Canyon National Park.
This page resumes the alphabetical listings of cities in Arizona.

GREEN VALLEY —*See Tucson p. 454.*

GREER

———— **WHERE TO STAY** ————

———— *The following lodging was either not evaluated or did not* ————
meet AAA rating requirements but is listed for your information only.

RED SETTER INN & COTTAGES   **Phone: 928/735-7441**
[fyi]   Not evaluated. **Location:** Just sw. Located in the national forest. 8 Main St 85927 (PO Box 133). Facilities, services, and decor characterize an upscale property.

HEBER

———— **WHERE TO STAY** ————

BEST WESTERN SAWMILL INN   *Book at aaa.com*   **Phone: (928)535-5053**

AAA SAVE	5/1-10/31 [CP]	1P: $69-$99	2P: $69-$99	XP: $5	F17
▽▽▽▽	2/1-4/30 & 11/1-1/31 [CP]	1P: $59-$66	2P: $59-$66	XP: $5	F17

Location: 0.5 mi e of center. 1877 Hwy 260 85928 (PO Box 730). Fax: 928/535-4164. **Facility:** 43 one-bedroom standard units. 2 stories (no elevator), exterior corridors. *Bath:* combo or shower only. **Parking:** on-site. Small-scale Hotel   **Terms:** pets ($10 extra charge). **Amenities:** voice mail, irons, hair dryers. **Leisure Activities:** whirlpool. **Guest Services:** coin laundry. **Cards:** AX, CB, DC, DS, MC, VI.

SOME UNITS
[icons] FEE

HOLBROOK pop. 4,917

———— **WHERE TO STAY** ————

AMERICAN BEST INN   *Book at aaa.com*   **Phone: 928/524-2654**

AAA SAVE	6/1-9/30	1P: $32-$49	2P: $37-$57	XP: $5	F12
▽▽ ▽▽	5/1-5/31	1P: $32-$45	2P: $37-$53	XP: $5	F12
	2/1-4/30	1P: $32-$45	2P: $37-$49	XP: $5	F12
Motel	10/1-1/31	1P: $32-$41	2P: $37-$49	XP: $5	F12

Location: I-40, exit 289, 1 mi w. 2211 E Navajo Blvd 86025. Fax: 928/524-1496. **Facility:** 39 one-bedroom standard units. 2 stories (no elevator), exterior corridors. **Parking:** on-site. **Terms:** pets ($5 fee). **Amenities:** *Some:* irons, hair dryers. **Cards:** AX, DS, MC, VI. **Special Amenities:** free continental breakfast and free local telephone calls.

SOME UNITS
[icons] FEE

BEST WESTERN ADOBE INN   *Book at aaa.com*   **Phone: (928)524-3948**

AAA SAVE	3/1-10/31 [ECP]	1P: $54-$74	2P: $59-$79	XP: $5	F17
▽▽▽▽	2/1-2/28 & 11/1-1/31 [ECP]	1P: $44-$69	2P: $49-$74	XP: $5	F17

Location: I-40, exit 285, 1 mi w on US 180 (Hopi Dr). 615 W Hopi Dr 86025. Fax: 928/524-3612. **Facility:** 54 one-bedroom standard units. 2 stories (no elevator), exterior corridors. **Parking:** on-site. **Terms:** pets ($25 Motel   deposit). **Amenities:** high-speed Internet, irons, hair dryers. **Pool(s):** small heated outdoor. **Business Services:** PC. **Cards:** AX, CB, DC, DS, MC, VI. **Special Amenities:** free expanded continental breakfast and early check-in/late check-out. *(See color ad p 232)*

SOME UNITS
[icons] FEE

BEST WESTERN ARIZONIAN INN   *Book at aaa.com*   Phone: (928)524-2611

6/1-10/31	1P: $78-$90	2P: $85-$91	XP: $6 F18
11/1-1/31	1P: $73-$83	2P: $83-$90	XP: $6 F18
4/1-5/31	1P: $76-$88	2P: $83-$88	XP: $6 F18
2/1-3/31	1P: $71-$82	2P: $77-$82	XP: $6 F18

Small-scale Hotel **Location:** I-40, exit 289, 0.5 mi w. 2508 Navajo Blvd 86025. **Fax:** 928/524-2253. **Facility:** 70 one-bedroom standard units. 2 stories (no elevator), exterior corridors. **Parking:** on-site. **Terms:** cancellation fee imposed, weekly rates available, [CP] meal plan available, pets ($30 deposit). **Amenities:** high-speed Internet, voice mail, irons, hair dryers. **Pool(s):** small heated outdoor. **Business Services:** PC. **Cards:** AX, CB, DC, DS, MC, VI. **Special Amenities:** free local telephone calls and early check-in/late check-out. *(See color ad p 231)*

SOME UNITS

COMFORT INN   *Book at aaa.com*   Phone: (928)524-6131

5/1-10/31 [ECP]	1P: $55-$65	2P: $59-$75	XP: $5 F17
2/1-4/30 & 11/1-1/31 [ECP]	1P: $49-$59	2P: $59-$69	XP: $5 F17

Small-scale Hotel **Location:** I-40, exit 289, just w. 2602 E Navajo Blvd 86025. **Fax:** 928/524-2281. **Facility:** 61 one-bedroom standard units. 2 stories (no elevator), exterior corridors. **Parking:** on-site. **Terms:** [CP] meal plan available, pets ($10 fee). **Amenities:** high-speed Internet, irons, hair dryers. **Pool(s):** small heated outdoor. **Guest Services:** coin laundry. **Cards:** AX, DC, DS, MC, VI. **Special Amenities:** free continental breakfast and free local telephone calls.

SOME UNITS

DAYS INN   *Book at aaa.com*   Phone: 928/524-6949

6/1-10/31 [ECP]	1P: $55-$75	2P: $55-$75	XP: $6
2/1-5/31 [ECP]	1P: $45-$65	2P: $45-$65	XP: $6
11/1-1/31 [ECP]	1P: $40-$65	2P: $40-$65	XP: $6

Motel **Location:** I-40, exit 289, 0.3 mi w. 2601 Navajo Blvd 86025. **Fax:** 928/524-6665. **Facility:** 54 units. 53 one-bedroom standard units, some with whirlpools. 1 one-bedroom suite with whirlpool. 2 stories (no elevator), interior/exterior corridors. **Parking:** on-site. **Amenities:** video library (fee), hair dryers. *Some:* irons. **Pool(s):** small heated indoor. **Leisure Activities:** whirlpool. **Guest Services:** coin laundry. **Cards:** AX, CB, DC, DS, JC, MC, VI. **Special Amenities:** free expanded continental breakfast and free local telephone calls.

SOME UNITS

ECONO LODGE   *Book at aaa.com*

Small-scale Hotel

Phone: (928)524-1448

5/1-10/31 [ECP]	1P: $39-$45	2P: $45-$55	XP: $5 F17
2/1-4/30 & 11/1-1/31 [ECP]	1P: $35-$40	2P: $40-$45	XP: $5 F17

Location: I-40, exit 289, just w. 2596 E Navajo Blvd 86025. **Fax:** 928/524-1493. **Facility:** 63 one-bedroom standard units. 2 stories (no elevator), exterior corridors. **Parking:** on-site. **Terms:** pets ($10 fee). **Amenities:** *Some:* irons, hair dryers. **Pool(s):** small heated outdoor. **Guest Services:** coin laundry. **Cards:** AX, DC, DS, MC, VI. **Special Amenities:** free continental breakfast and free local telephone calls.

SOME UNITS

HOLBROOK HOLIDAY INN EXPRESS   *Book at aaa.com*

Motel

Phone: 928/524-1466

Property failed to provide current rates

Location: I-40, exit 286, just e. 1308 E Navajo Blvd 86025. **Fax:** 928/524-1788. **Facility:** 59 units. 57 one-bedroom standard units. 2 one-bedroom suites. 2 stories (no elevator), interior corridors. **Parking:** on-site. **Terms:** small pets only ($10 extra charge). **Amenities:** high-speed Internet, dual phone lines, voice mail, irons, hair dryers. **Pool(s):** small heated indoor. **Leisure Activities:** whirlpool. **Guest Services:** gift shop, coin laundry. **Business Services:** PC.

SOME UNITS

──── WHERE TO DINE ────

BUTTERFIELD STAGE CO. STEAK HOUSE   Dinner: $9-$26

Steak House

Phone: 928/524-3447

Location: I-40, exit 285, 1 mi e on US 180. 609 W Hopi Dr 86025. **Hours:** 4 pm-10 pm. **Reservations:** accepted. **Features:** Western decor and a nice selection of steaks are offered here. Soup and salad bar are also available. Casual dress; cocktails. **Parking:** on-site. **Cards:** DC, MC, VI.

MANDARIN BEAUTY RESTAURANT   Lunch: $4-$13   Dinner: $4-$13

Chinese

Phone: 928/524-3663

Location: I-40, exit 286, 1 mi e. 2218 E Navajo Blvd 86025. **Hours:** 11 am-9 pm. Closed major holidays. **Reservations:** not accepted. **Features:** The no-frills restaurant serves traditional Chinese dishes in a casual atmosphere. Casual dress; wine only. **Parking:** on-site. **Cards:** MC, VI.

MESA ITALIANA RESTAURANT   Lunch: $8   Dinner: $9-$17

Italian

Phone: 928/524-6696

Location: I-40, exit 286, 1.3 mi e. 2318 E Navajo Blvd 86025. **Hours:** 11 am-2 & 4-9 pm, Sat & Sun from 4 pm. **Closed:** 11/23, 12/25. **Reservations:** accepted. **Features:** Featuring a nice selection of traditional Italian dishes, the restaurant appeals to those looking for something different in a small Western town. A child's menu and carry-out service are available. Casual dress; cocktails. **Parking:** on-site. **Cards:** AX, DS, MC, VI.

JACOB LAKE

──── WHERE TO STAY ────

──── The following lodging was either not evaluated or did not meet AAA rating requirements but is listed for your information only.

JACOB LAKE INN

[fyi]

Phone: 928/643-7232

Not evaluated. **Location:** Jct SR 89A and 67 86002. Facilities, services, and decor characterize a basic property.

JEROME pop. 329

──── WHERE TO STAY ────

CONNOR HOTEL OF JEROME

Historic
Small-scale Hotel

Phone: (928)634-5006

All Year	1P: $85-$145	2P: $85-$145	XP: $10 F12

Location: Center. 164 Main St 86331. **Fax:** 928/649-0981. **Facility:** This historic hotel had full guestroom renovations and now offers charming rooms filled with period pieces and modern tiled baths. 10 one-bedroom standard units. 2 stories (no elevator), interior corridors. *Bath:* combo or shower only. **Parking:** street. **Terms:** office hours 8 am-9 pm, 3 day cancellation notice, package plans, pets (with prior approval). **Amenities:** CD players, voice mail, hair dryers. **Guest Services:** gift shop. **Cards:** AX, DS, MC, VI. **Special Amenities:** free local telephone calls.

SOME UNITS

JEROME GRAND HOTEL

Historic
Small-scale Hotel

Phone: 928/634-8200

All Year	1P: $100-$230	2P: $100-$230

Location: 0.3 mi s on SR 89A, just s on Cobblestone Rd; center. 200 Hill St 86331. **Fax:** 928/639-0299. **Facility:** This historic property, once a hospital, has been converted to a charming hotel with limited amenities but a fabulous view. 22 units. 21 one-bedroom standard units. 1 one-bedroom suite ($350-$450). 4 stories, interior corridors. *Bath:* combo, shower or tub only. **Parking:** on-site. **Terms:** 2 night minimum stay - weekends, package plans. **Amenities:** video library (fee), irons. **Dining:** The Asylum, see separate listing. **Guest Services:** gift shop. **Cards:** DS, MC, VI. **Special Amenities:** free continental breakfast.

SOME UNITS

────── WHERE TO DINE ──────

THE ASYLUM

American

Lunch: $8-$13   Dinner: $18-$26   Phone: 928/639-3197
Location: 0.3 mi s on SR 89A, just s on Cobblestone Rd; center; in Jerome Grand Hotel. 200 Hill St 86331. **Hours:** 11 am-3 & 5-9 pm. Closed: 10/1. **Reservations:** suggested. **Features:** Billed as "fun fine dining," the experience at the cozy restaurant includes relaxed service and spectacular views. The wide selection of wines, interesting sauces and creative combinations, such as roast maple leaf duck breast on green chili brown rice with plum serrano salsa, add up to "fine dining". Casual dress; cocktails. **Parking:** on-site. **Cards:** AX, DS, MC, VI.

JEROME BREWERY
Pizza

Lunch: $7-$10   Dinner: $7-$10   Phone: 928/639-8477
Location: Center. 111 Main St 86331. **Hours:** 11 am-9 pm. Closed: 4/16, 11/23, 12/25. **Features:** Although the pizza is famous locally, other menu items—including hearty sandwiches and tasty and filling soups and chili—also are worth trying. The upstairs loft area is a quieter seating option. This place no longer brews its own beers. Casual dress; cocktails. **Parking:** street. **Cards:** MC, VI.

─────── *The following restaurant has not been evaluated by AAA* ───────
but is listed for your information only.

JEROME PALACE/HAUNTED HAMBURGER   Phone: 928/634-0554
[fyi]   Not evaluated. **Location:** Center. 410 Clark St 86331. **Features:** Guests should arrive before they are hungry, as there is always a line waiting to wolf down the great burgers and comfort food. In a historic house overlooking the valley, the restaurant is a good spot to rest and recuperate after the steep street walking tour.

 Do you know the facts?

AAA publishes the Digest of Motor Laws to assist traveling motorists. Filled with facts and information, this one-of-a-kind compilation includes a comprehensive description of the laws that govern motor vehicle registration and operation in the United States and Canada. This guide has a new, easy-to-read format with graphics, state-by-state tax summary tables and detailed information on occupant protection laws, driver licensing laws, automated enforcement laws and motor vehicle fees and taxes.

You can easily locate various licensing and motor laws governing the states in which you are traveling. In addition to vehicle registration and operation laws, the Digest contains information and facts about alcohol laws, traffic safety laws and more.

Call your local club to obtain a copy of the Digest.

The book retails for $13.95.

KAYENTA pop. 4,922

─── WHERE TO STAY ───

BEST WESTERN WETHERILL INN *Book at aaa.com* Phone: (928)697-3231

5/1-10/15 [CP]	1P: $98-$113	2P: $98-$113	XP: $10	F12
2/1-4/30 & 10/16-1/31 [CP]	1P: $55-$75	2P: $55-$75	XP: $10	F12

AAA **SAVE**
◈◈◈◈
Small-scale Hotel

Location: US 163, 1 mi n of jct US 160. US 163 86033 (PO Box .175). Fax: 928/697-3233. **Facility:** 54 one-bedroom standard units. 2 stories (no elevator), exterior corridors. **Parking:** on-site. **Amenities:** voice mail, irons, hair dryers. *Some:* high-speed Internet. **Pool(s):** small heated indoor. **Guest Services:** gift shop. **Business Services:** PC. **Cards:** AX, CB, DC, DS, JC, MC, VI. **Special Amenities:** free continental breakfast and free local telephone calls. *(See color ad below)*

SOME UNITS

HAMPTON INN OF KAYENTA *Book at aaa.com* Phone: 928/697-3170

3/16-10/15 [BP]	1P: $79-$139	2P: $89-$139	XP: $10	F18
10/16-1/31 [BP]	1P: $59-$79	2P: $69-$79	XP: $10	F18
2/1-3/15 [BP]	1P: $59-$69	2P: $59-$69	XP: $10	F18

◈◈◈◈
Small-scale Hotel

Location: On US 160, just w. Hwy 160 86033 (PO Box 1219). Fax: 928/697-3189. **Facility:** 73 one-bedroom standard units. 3 stories, interior corridors. *Bath:* combo or shower only. **Parking:** on-site. **Terms:** 3 day cancellation notice-fee imposed, weekly rates available, package plans, pets ($20 fee). **Dining:** Reuben Heflin Restaurant, see separate listing. **Pool(s):** small heated outdoor. **Guest Services:** gift shop, coin laundry. **Business Services:** meeting rooms. **Cards:** AX, CB, DC, DS, MC, VI.

SOME UNITS

(ASK) [icons] FEE

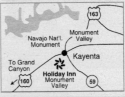

HOLIDAY INN-MONUMENT VALLEY *Book at aaa.com*   Phone: (928)697-3221

5/1-10/31	1P: $99-$159	2P: $99-$159	XP: $10	F19
2/1-4/30	1P: $79-$99	2P: $79-$99	XP: $10	F19
11/1-1/31	1P: $59-$89	2P: $59-$89	XP: $10	F19

Small-scale Hotel **Location:** Jct of US 160 and 163. (PO Box 307, 86033). Fax: 928/697-3349. **Facility:** 163 units. 155 one-bedroom standard units. 8 one-bedroom suites. 2 stories (no elevator), interior/exterior corridors. **Parking:** on-site. **Terms:** cancellation fee imposed. **Amenities:** voice mail, irons, hair dryers. **Pool(s):** heated outdoor, wading. **Leisure Activities:** exercise room. **Guest Services:** gift shop, coin laundry. **Cards:** AX, CB, DC, DS, JC, MC, VI.
(See color ad p 235)

SOME UNITS

(ASK) (SA) ▯ ⊘ ⇌ ⊗ (DATA PORT) ⊡ / ⊠ /

─────── **WHERE TO DINE** ───────

REUBEN HEFLIN RESTAURANT   Dinner: $7-$24   Phone: 928/697-3170

Location: On US 160, just w; in Hampton Inn of Kayenta. Hwy 160 86033. **Hours:** 5 pm-9 pm; to 10 pm 4/1-10/31.
Reservations: accepted. **Features:** The decor is decidedly Southwestern, with an exposed beam ceiling
Regional American and a warm fireplace. The menu centers on steak, seafood and Southwestern dishes. Casual dress.
Parking: on-site. **Cards:** AX, CB, DC, DS, MC, VI.

(&M)

KINGMAN pop. 20,069

─────── **WHERE TO STAY** ───────

1ST VALUE INN   Phone: 928/757-7122

AAA (SAVE)   All Year   1P: $35-$50   2P: $40-$70   XP: $6
Location: I-40, exit 53, just n. 3270 E Andy Devine Ave 86401. Fax: 928/757-8439. **Facility:** 70 one-bedroom
standard units. 2 stories (no elevator), exterior corridors. **Bath:** shower only. **Parking:** on-site. **Terms:** 7 day
Motel   cancellation notice. **Pool(s):** outdoor. **Cards:** AX, DS, MC, VI. **Special Amenities:** free local telephone
calls.

SOME UNITS

▯+ ⇌ ⊗ (DATA PORT) / ⊠ ▪ ⊡ /

BEST WESTERN A WAYFARER'S INN *Book at aaa.com*   Phone: (928)753-6271

AAA (SAVE)   4/1-10/31 [BP]   1P: $79-$94   2P: $85-$97   XP: $5 | F12
2/1-3/31 & 11/1-1/31 [BP]   1P: $75-$90   2P: $78-$94   XP: $5 | F12
Location: I-40, exit 53, 0.5 mi w on Route 66. 2815 E Andy Devine Ave 86401. Fax: 928/753-9608. **Facility:** 101
Small-scale Hotel units. 96 one-bedroom standard units. 5 one-bedroom suites ($160), some with efficiencies and/or
whirlpools. 2 stories (no elevator), exterior corridors. **Parking:** on-site. **Terms:** pets ($8 fee).
Amenities: high-speed Internet, voice mail, irons, hair dryers. **Pool(s):** heated outdoor. **Leisure
Activities:** whirlpool, exercise room. **Guest Services:** valet and coin laundry. **Business Services:** meeting rooms, PC, fax.
Cards: AX, CB, DC, DS, JC, MC, VI. **Special Amenities:** free full breakfast and free local telephone calls.
(See color ad below)

SOME UNITS

(SA) ⊗ ▯+ ⊘ ⇌ ⊗ (DATA PORT) ▪ ⊡ ⊡ / ⊠ /
FEE

BEST WESTERN KING'S INN & SUITES *Book at aaa.com*

AAA SAVE

WWWW

Small-scale Hotel

Phone: (928)753-6101

4/1-10/31 [ECP]	1P: $79-$94	2P: $85-$97	XP: $5 F17
2/1-3/31 & 11/1-1/31 [ECP]	1P: $75-$89	2P: $78-$94	XP: $5 F17

Location: I-40, exit 53, just w on Route 66. 2930 E Route 66 86401. Fax: 928/753-6192. **Facility:** 101 units. 95 one- and 3 two-bedroom standard units, some with whirlpools. 3 one-bedroom suites ($100-$125) with whirlpools, some with efficiencies. 2 stories (no elevator), interior corridors. *Bath:* combo or shower only. **Parking:** on-site. **Terms:** pets ($8 fee, in limited units). **Amenities:** high-speed Internet, voice mail, irons, hair dryers. **Pool(s):** heated outdoor. **Leisure Activities:** whirlpool, exercise room. **Guest Services:** valet and coin laundry. **Business Services:** meeting rooms. **Cards:** AX, CB, DC, DS, MC, VI. **Special Amenities:** free expanded continental breakfast and free local telephone calls.

SOME UNITS

[SD] [🛏] [⏱️+] [♿] [🌀] [🛶] [🎥] [DATA PORT] [🔌] [🍽] [💻] / [✕] /
FEE

BRUNSWICK HOTEL

AAA SAVE

WWWW

Historic
Small-scale Hotel

Phone: (928)718-1800

All Year	1P: $55-$66	2P: $55-$66	XP: $10 F7

Location: On Route 66; downtown. Located in the historic district. 315 E Andy Devine Ave 86401. Fax: 928/718-1801. **Facility:** Built in 1909, this hotel stirs up feelings of yesteryear. Each guest room decor is unique. Rooms vary from modest suites to compact "cowboy" units. Designated smoking area. 24 units. 15 one-bedroom standard units. 9 one-bedroom suites ($95). 3 stories, interior corridors. *Bath:* some shared or private, combo or shower only. **Parking:** street. **Terms:** cancellation fee imposed, small pets only ($10 extra charge, in limited units). **Dining:** Hubb's Bistro, see separate listing. **Guest Services:** valet and coin laundry. **Cards:** AX, CB, DC, DS, MC, VI. **Special Amenities:** free local telephone calls.

SOME UNITS

[SD] [🛏] [🍴] [♿] [✕] [DATA PORT] / [📺] [VCR] [🔌] [🍽] /
FEE

COMFORT INN *Book at aaa.com*

WW WW

Motel

Phone: (928)718-1717

5/16-9/15	1P: $60-$90	2P: $65-$95	XP: $5 F18
2/1-5/15 & 9/16-1/31	1P: $50-$75	2P: $55-$80	XP: $5 F18

Location: I-40, exit 53, just w on Route 66. 3129 E Andy Devine Ave 86401. Fax: 928/718-5668. **Facility:** 38 one-bedroom standard units. 3 stories, interior corridors. *Bath:* combo or shower only. **Parking:** on-site. **Terms:** [ECP] meal plan available. **Amenities:** high-speed Internet, irons, hair dryers. **Pool(s):** small heated indoor. **Leisure Activities:** whirlpool. **Guest Services:** valet and coin laundry. **Cards:** AX, CB, DC, DS, JC, MC, VI.

SOME UNITS

[ASK] [SD] [🍴] [♿] [🌀] [🛶] [🎥] [DATA PORT] [💻] / [✕] [🔌] [🍽] /

DAYS INN WEST *Book at aaa.com*

AAA SAVE

WW WW

Motel

Phone: (928)753-7500

All Year	1P: $39-$89	2P: $39-$89	XP: $5 F18

Location: I-40, exit 53, just w on Route 66. 3023 E Andy Devine Ave 86401. Fax: 928/753-1011. **Facility:** 60 one-bedroom standard units. 2 stories (no elevator), exterior corridors. **Parking:** on-site. **Terms:** small pets only ($10 extra charge). **Amenities:** high-speed Internet, hair dryers. **Pool(s):** small heated outdoor. **Leisure Activities:** whirlpool. **Guest Services:** coin laundry. **Cards:** AX, DC, DS, MC, VI. **Special Amenities:** free expanded continental breakfast and free local telephone calls.

SOME UNITS

[SD] [🛏] [⏱️+] [🛶] [🎥] [🔌] [🍽] / [✕] /
FEE

HILL TOP MOTEL

AAA SAVE

WW

Motel

Phone: (928)753-2198

4/14-9/3	1P: $42-$75	2P: $42-$75	XP: $6
2/1-4/13	1P: $38-$70	2P: $40-$70	XP: $6
9/4-1/31	1P: $34-$65	2P: $38-$65	XP: $6

Location: I-40, exit 53, 2 mi w on Route 66. 1901 E Andy Devine Ave 86401. Fax: 928/753-5985. **Facility:** 28 one-bedroom standard units. 1 story, exterior corridors. *Bath:* combo or shower only. **Parking:** on-site. **Terms:** 3 day cancellation notice-fee imposed, [AP] meal plan available, pets (dogs only, $5 extra charge). **Amenities:** high-speed Internet, hair dryers. **Pool(s):** small heated outdoor. **Guest Services:** coin laundry. **Business Services:** PC (fee). **Cards:** AX, DS, MC, VI. **Special Amenities:** free local telephone calls.

SOME UNITS

[SD] [🛏] [🍴+] [🛶] [🎥] [🔌] [🍽] / [✕] /
FEE

HOLIDAY INN EXPRESS HOTEL & SUITES

AAA SAVE

WWWW

Phone: (928)718-4343

4/1-10/31	1P: $81-$189	2P: $81-$189	XP: $10 F18
2/1-3/31 & 11/1-1/31	1P: $69-$76	2P: $76-$81	XP: $10 F18

Location: I-40, exit 53, just w on Route 66. 3031 E Andy Divine Ave 86401. Fax: 928/718-1422. **Facility:** 75 units. 73 one- and 2 two-bedroom standard units. 3 stories, interior corridors. *Bath:* combo or shower only. **Parking:** on-site. **Amenities:** high-speed Internet, voice mail, irons, hair dryers. **Pool(s):** heated indoor. **Leisure Activities:** whirlpool, exercise room. **Guest Services:** valet and coin laundry. **Business Services:** meeting rooms, business center. **Cards:** AX, DC, DS, MC, VI. **Special Amenities:** free expanded continental breakfast and free local telephone calls.

[SD] [🍴+] [♿] [🛶] [✕] [🎥] [DATA PORT] [🔌] [🍽] [💻]

KNIGHTS INN

AAA SAVE

WW WW

Motel

Phone: (928)753-3881

All Year	1P: $50-$120	2P: $80-$150	XP: $10 F8

Location: I-40, exit 48, just nw. 1225 W Beale St 86401. Fax: 928/753-2683. **Facility:** 35 one-bedroom standard units. 1 story, exterior corridors. **Parking:** on-site. **Terms:** 5 day cancellation notice-fee imposed. **Amenities:** hair dryers. **Cards:** AX, DS, MC, VI. **Special Amenities:** free local telephone calls and preferred room (subject to availability with advance reservations).

SOME UNITS

[🎥] [DATA PORT] / [✕] [🔌] [🍽] /

MOTEL 6 - 1114 *Book at aaa.com*

WW

Motel

Phone: 928/753-9222

5/26-9/4	1P: $45-$55	2P: $51-$61	XP: $3 F17
2/1-5/25 & 9/5-1/31	1P: $41-$51	2P: $47-$57	XP: $3 F17

Location: I-40, exit 48, just se on Business Loop I-40/US 93. 424 W Beale St 86401. Fax: 928/753-4791. **Facility:** 80 one-bedroom standard units. 2 stories (no elevator), exterior corridors. *Bath:* combo or shower only. **Parking:** on-site. **Terms:** small pets only. **Pool(s):** heated outdoor. **Guest Services:** coin laundry. **Cards:** AX, CB, DC, DS, MC, VI.

SOME UNITS

[SD] [🛏] [🍴+] [♿] [🌀] [🛶] [🎥] [DATA PORT] / [✕] /

MOTEL 6 - 1366
Motel
DC, DS, MC, VI.

Book at aaa.com
All Year — 1P: $37-$47 — 2P: $43-$53 — XP: $3 — F17
Location: I-40, exit 53, just e on Route 66. 3351 E Andy Devine Ave 86401. Fax: 928/757-2438. **Facility:** 118 one-bedroom standard units. 2 stories (no elevator), exterior corridors. *Bath:* combo or shower only. **Parking:** on-site. **Terms:** small pets only. **Pool(s):** heated outdoor. **Guest Services:** coin laundry. **Cards:** AX, CB,

SOME UNITS

QUALITY INN
Motel

Book at aaa.com

4/19-5/10 [BP]	1P: $90-$120	2P: $110-$150	XP: $10 — F16
2/1-4/18 [BP]	1P: $55-$70	2P: $64-$80	XP: $10 — F16
5/11-9/30 [BP]	1P: $54-$60	2P: $64-$80	XP: $10 — F16
10/1-1/31 [BP]	1P: $50-$60	2P: $56-$70	XP: $10 — F16

Phone: (928)753-4747

Location: I-40, exit 48, 2 mi e on Route 66. 1400 E Andy Devine Ave 86401. Fax: 928/753-5175. **Facility:** 98 one-bedroom standard units. 2 stories (no elevator), exterior corridors. **Parking:** on-site. **Terms:** small pets only ($10 fee, in limited units). **Amenities:** high-speed Internet, irons, hair dryers. **Pool(s):** heated outdoor. **Leisure Activities:** sauna, whirlpool, exercise room. **Guest Services:** coin laundry. **Business Services:** meeting rooms, PC, fax. **Cards:** AX, DC, DS, MC, VI.

SOME UNITS
FEE

RAMBLIN' ROSE MOTEL
Motel

All Year — 1P: $29-$75 — 2P: $29-$75 — XP: $5 — D15
Location: I-40, exit 48, 1.5 mi e on I-40 business loop (US 93 and Route 66). 1001 E Andy Devine Ave 86401. Fax: 928/753-4344. **Facility:** 35 one-bedroom standard units. 2 stories (no elevator), exterior corridors. *Bath:* combo or shower only. **Parking:** on-site. **Terms:** cancellation fee imposed, weekly rates available, package plans. **Pool(s):** outdoor. **Cards:** AX, DS, MC, VI. **Special Amenities:** free local telephone calls.

Phone: 928/753-5541

SOME UNITS

SUPER 8 MOTEL
Small-scale Hotel

Book at aaa.com

3/16-9/5	1P: $39-$159	2P: $49-$159	XP: $5 — F17
9/6-1/31	1P: $37-$68	2P: $44-$68	XP: $5 — F17
2/1-3/15	1P: $37-$49	2P: $44-$68	XP: $5 — F17

Phone: (928)757-4808

Location: I-40, exit 53, just e on Route 66. 3401 E Andy Devine Ave 86401. Fax: 928/681-3480. **Facility:** 60 one-bedroom standard units. 3 stories, interior corridors. **Parking:** on-site. **Terms:** cancellation fee imposed, small pets only ($10 extra charge, in limited units). **Leisure Activities:** pool privileges. **Guest Services:** coin laundry. **Cards:** AX, CB, DC, DS, MC, VI. **Special Amenities:** free continental breakfast and free local telephone calls.

SOME UNITS
FEE

TRAVELODGE
Motel

Book at aaa.com
All Year — 1P: $60-$90 — 2P: $60-$90 — XP: $5 — F17
Location: I-40, exit 53, just e on Route 66. 3275 E Andy Devine Ave 86401. Fax: 928/757-1010. **Facility:** 65 one-bedroom standard units. 2 stories (no elevator), exterior corridors. **Parking:** on-site. **Terms:** 3 day cancellation notice, [CP] meal plan available. **Amenities:** high-speed Internet, hair dryers. *Some:* irons. **Pool(s):** small heated outdoor. **Leisure Activities:** whirlpool. **Guest Services:** coin laundry. **Cards:** AX, CB, DC, DS, MC, VI. **Special Amenities:** free continental breakfast and free local telephone calls.

Phone: (928)757-1188

SOME UNITS

——— WHERE TO DINE ———

ABC RESTAURANT
Chinese

Lunch: $4-$10 — Dinner: $8-$14 — Phone: 928/753-6363
Location: I-40, exit 53, just sw. 2890 E Andy Devine Ave 86401. **Hours:** 9 am-10 pm. **Reservations:** accepted. **Features:** Chinese and American dishes can be ordered from the menu, and a Chinese buffet is available for both lunch and dinner. Casual dress; cocktails. **Parking:** on-site. **Cards:** AX, MC, VI.

DAMBAR STEAKHOUSE
Steak House

Lunch: $6-$10 — Dinner: $10-$20 — Phone: 928/753-3523
Location: I-40, exit 53, 1.2 mi e. 1960 E Andy Devine Ave 86401. **Hours:** 11 am-10 pm, Fri & Sat-11 pm. Closed: 9/4, 12/25. **Reservations:** suggested, weekends. **Features:** The menu incorporates a good selection of steak, ribs, sandwiches and salads. The atmosphere is friendly. Casual dress; cocktails. **Parking:** on-site. **Cards:** AX, DS, MC, VI.

HUBB'S BISTRO
American

Dinner: $16-$22 — Phone: 928/718-1800
Location: On Route 66; downtown; in Brunswick Hotel. 315 E Andy Devine Ave 86401. **Hours:** 5 pm-9 pm. Closed: 1/1, 12/25. **Reservations:** suggested. **Features:** This restaurant presents a menu of American beef, chicken, pork and seafood dishes. French and Asian influences are evident in the food. Casual dress; cocktails. **Parking:** street. **Cards:** AX, CB, DC, DS, MC, VI.

MATTINA'S RISTORANTE & STEAKHOUSE
Italian

Dinner: $12-$24 — Phone: 928/753-7504
Location: Between 3rd and 4th sts; downtown. 318 Oak St 86401. **Hours:** 5 pm-9 pm, Fri & Sat-10 pm. Closed major holidays; also Sun. **Reservations:** accepted. **Features:** Located in an intimate yet casual cottage in historic downtown, this family-owned and -operated bistro features aged premium steaks cut when ordered, as well as fresh seafood and Italian pasta dishes. The homemade tiramisu is a perennial favorite. Patio seating is also available. Casual dress; cocktails. **Parking:** street. **Cards:** AX, MC, VI.

KOHLS RANCH

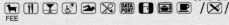

────── **WHERE TO STAY** ──────

KOHL'S RANCH LODGE

Phone: 928/478-4211

Property failed to provide current rates

Resort
Condominium

Location: Jct SR 87 and 260E, 16.6 mi e, just s. 202 S Kohl's Ranch Lodge Rd 85541 (HC 2 Box 96-K, PAYSON). Fax: 928/478-0353. **Facility:** Charming, attractively appointed lodge rooms and creekside cabins ranging from cozy to luxurious await guests at this high mountain resort. 67 units. 43 one-bedroom standard units, some with efficiencies. 24 cabins. 1 story, interior/exterior corridors. **Bath:** combo or shower only. **Parking:** on-site. **Terms:** check-in 4 pm, pets ($5 extra charge, in boarding kennel only). **Amenities:** video library (fee), DVD players, CD players, irons, hair dryers. **Pool(s):** heated outdoor. **Leisure Activities:** saunas, whirlpool, miniature golf, cross country skiing, recreation programs, hiking trails, playground, exercise room, basketball, horseshoes, shuffleboard, volleyball. **Fee:** horseback riding, game room. **Guest Services:** sundries, coin laundry. **Business Services:** meeting rooms, PC, fax (fee).

SOME UNITS

🐕 ⓘ ⓨ 🖐 🚗 ✕ DATA PORT 🛏 🖥 📺 / ✕ /
FEE

LAKE HAVASU CITY pop. 41,938

────── **WHERE TO STAY** ──────

BEST WESTERN LAKE PLACE INN   *Book at aaa.com*   **Phone: (928)855-2146**

AAA SAVE

Small-scale Hotel

5/1-10/31	1P: $69-$300	2P: $69-$300	XP: $10	F12
3/1-4/30	1P: $69-$250	2P: $69-$250	XP: $10	F12
2/1-2/28 & 11/1-1/31	1P: $69-$130	2P: $69-$130	XP: $10	F12

Location: 1 mi e of SR 95 via Swanson Ave; downtown. 31 Wing's Loop 86403. Fax: 928/855-3148. **Facility:** 40 one-bedroom standard units. 1-2 stories (no elevator), exterior corridors. **Parking:** on-site. **Terms:** 2 night minimum stay - weekends, package plans, pets ($5 extra charge). **Amenities:** high-speed Internet, voice mail, irons, hair dryers. **Pool(s):** heated outdoor. **Business Services:** fax (fee). **Cards:** AX, DC, DS, MC, VI. **Special Amenities:** free local telephone calls. *(See color ad p 240)*

SOME UNITS

🛏 ⓘ 🚗 CTV DATA PORT 📺 / ✕ 🛏 🖥 /
FEE

HAMPTON INN LAKE HAVASU   *Book at aaa.com*   **Phone: (928)855-4071**

All Year   1P: $79-$119   2P: $89-$129

Small-scale Hotel

Location: 0.5 mi n of London Bridge. 245 London Bridge Rd 86403. Fax: 928/855-2379. **Facility:** 162 one-bedroom standard units. 4 stories, interior corridors. **Bath:** combo or shower only. **Parking:** on-site. **Terms:** [ECP] meal plan available, package plans, small pets only ($10 extra charge). **Amenities:** high-speed Internet, voice mail, irons, hair dryers. **Pool(s):** heated outdoor. **Leisure Activities:** whirlpool, exercise room. **Fee:** bicycles. **Guest Services:** sundries, complimentary evening beverages: Mon-Thurs, coin laundry. **Business Services:** meeting rooms, business center. **Cards:** AX, CB, DC, DS, MC, VI.

SOME UNITS

ASK SD 🖐 🐕 🖐 ⊘ 🚗 ✕ ⓧ DATA PORT 🛏 🖥 📺 / ✕ /
FEE

THE HAVASU INN   **Phone: (928)855-7841**

All Year   1P: $59-$159   2P: $59-$159   XP: $10   F17

Motel

Location: At Riviera Blvd. 1700 N McCulloch 86403 (1700 N McCulloch Blvd). Fax: 928/855-9553. **Facility:** 90 one-bedroom standard units. 2 stories (no elevator), exterior corridors. **Parking:** on-site. **Terms:** package plans, small pets only ($100 deposit). **Amenities:** *Some:* high-speed Internet. **Pool(s):** heated outdoor. **Leisure Activities:** whirlpool. **Guest Services:** sundries. **Cards:** AX, CB, DC, DS, JC, MC, VI.

SOME UNITS

ASK SD 🐕 ⓘ 🚗 ⓧ DATA PORT / ✕ 🛏 🖥 /
FEE   FEE FEE

HOWARD JOHNSON EXPRESS INN & SUITES   *Book at aaa.com*   **Phone: (928)453-4656**

AAA SAVE

Small-scale Hotel

2/1-11/11 [CP]	1P: $89-$169	2P: $99-$179	XP: $10	D17
11/12-1/31 [CP]	1P: $89-$149	2P: $99-$159	XP: $10	D17

Location: 0.8 mi n of London Bridge. 335 London Bridge Rd 86403. Fax: 928/680-4561. **Facility:** 47 one-bedroom standard units, some with efficiencies. 2 stories (no elevator), interior corridors. **Bath:** combo or shower only. **Parking:** on-site, winter plug-ins. **Terms:** cancellation fee imposed, weekly rates available. **Amenities:** voice mail, irons, hair dryers. **Pool(s):** small heated indoor. **Leisure Activities:** whirlpool, boat and RV parking. **Guest Services:** coin laundry. **Business Services:** fax (fee). **Cards:** AX, CB, DC, DS, MC, VI. **Special Amenities:** free local telephone calls and free newspaper. *(See color ad below)*

SOME UNITS

SD ⓘ 🚗 ⓧ DATA PORT 🛏 🖥 📺 / ✕ /

ISLAND INN HOTEL *Book at aaa.com* Phone: (928)680-0606

5/1-10/31	1P: $75-$300	2P: $75-$300	XP: $10 F16
3/1-4/30	1P: $69-$250	2P: $69-$250	XP: $10 F16
2/1-2/28 & 11/1-1/31	1P: $69-$90	2P: $69-$90	XP: $10 F16

Small-scale Hotel **Location:** 0.7 mi w of London Bridge/SR 95. 1300 W McCulloch Blvd 86403. Fax: 928/680-4218. **Facility:** 117 units. 116 one-bedroom standard units. 1 one-bedroom suite. 4 stories, interior corridors. **Parking:** on-site. **Terms:** small pets only ($10 fee). **Amenities:** hair dryers. *Some:* irons. **Dining:** 7 am-10 pm, Fri & Sat-11 pm. **Pool(s):** heated outdoor. **Leisure Activities:** whirlpool. **Guest Services:** valet and coin laundry. **Business Services:** meeting rooms, fax (fee). **Cards:** AX, DC, DS, MC, VI.

SOME UNITS
ⓘ ⓘ ⓘ ⓘ / ⓘ ⓘ ⓘ ⓘ /
FEE

ISLAND SUITES *Book at aaa.com* Phone: (928)855-7333

2/1-5/31	1P: $99-$300	2P: $102-$300	XP: $10 F17
6/1-1/31	1P: $79-$300	2P: $82-$300	XP: $10 F17

Small-scale Hotel **Location:** Just s of jct McCulloch Blvd. 236 S Lake Havasu Ave 86403. Fax: 928/855-7676. **Facility:** 45 one-bedroom standard units with kitchens (utensil deposit required). 2 stories (no elevator), interior corridors. *Bath:* combo or shower only. **Parking:** on-site. **Terms:** cancellation fee imposed, pets ($10 fee). **Amenities:** voice mail, hair dryers. **Pool(s):** heated outdoor. **Leisure Activities:** whirlpool. **Business Services:** fax (fee). **Cards:** AX, DC, DS, MC, VI.

SOME UNITS
ⓢⓓ ⓘ ⓘ ⓘ ⓘ ⓘ ⓘ / ⓘ /
FEE

LAKE HAVASU CITY SUPER 8 Phone: 928/855-8844

All Year	1P: $45-$149	2P: $55-$169	XP: $5 F

Motel **Location:** Just w of SR 95, exit Palo Verde; 0.5 mi n of London Bridge. 305 London Bridge Rd 86403. Fax: 928/855-7132. **Facility:** 59 one-bedroom standard units. 3 stories (no elevator), interior corridors. **Parking:** on-site. **Terms:** 2-3 night minimum stay - seasonal, small pets only ($10 fee, in limited units). **Pool(s):** outdoor. **Leisure Activities:** whirlpool. **Business Services:** fax (fee). **Cards:** AX, DS, MC, VI.

SOME UNITS
ⒶⓈⓀ ⓢⓓ ⓘ ⓘ ⓘ ⓘ / ⓘ ⓘ /
FEE

LONDON BRIDGE RESORT   **Phone:** 928/855-0888

(AAA) (SAVE)   All Year   1P: $129-$359   XP: $10
◇◇◇◇◇   **Location:** SR 95, just sw, via Swanson Ave. Located at the London Bridge. 1477 Queens Bay 86403.
             Fax: 928/855-5404. **Facility:** 122 units. 4 one-bedroom standard units with efficiencies. 72 one- and 46 two-
             bedroom suites with efficiencies, some with whirlpools. 3 stories, interior corridors. *Bath:* combo or shower
Large-scale Hotel only. **Parking:** on-site. **Terms:** check-in 4 pm, [BP] meal plan available. **Amenities:** DVD players, video
             games (fee), CD players, voice mail, irons, hair dryers. **Dining:** 4 restaurants, 6 am-11 pm, cocktails,
nightclub. **Pool(s):** 3 heated outdoor. **Leisure Activities:** whirlpool, boat dock, fishing, lighted tennis court, playground, exercise
room. *Fee:* boats, canoes, paddleboats, waterskiing, scuba diving, snorkeling, charter fishing, golf-9 holes, massage. **Guest
Services:** gift shop, valet and coin laundry, area transportation-within 5 mi. **Business Services:** meeting rooms, business
center. **Cards:** AX, DC, DS, VI. **Special Amenities:** early check-in/late check-out and preferred room (subject to
availability with advance reservations).** *(See color ad below)*   SOME UNITS

[⑪] [☓] [🕭] [✍] [🏊] [☒] [VCR] [DATA PORT] [🔌] [🍴] [🛏] /[☒]/

MOTEL 6 LAKE HAVASU

Phone: 928/855-3200

AAA [SAVE] / Motel

5/1-10/31	1P: $55-$125	2P: $61-$131	XP: $6	F17
2/1-2/27	1P: $41-$96	2P: $47-$105	XP: $6	F17
2/28-4/30	1P: $83-$94	2P: $69-$99	XP: $6	F17
11/1-1/31	1P: $41-$47	2P: $47-$53	XP: $6	F17

Location: 0.3 mi n of London Bridge. 111 London Bridge Rd 86403. Fax: 928/855-3376. **Facility:** 30 one-bedroom standard units. 2 stories (no elevator), interior corridors. *Bath:* combo or shower only. **Parking:** on-site. **Business Services:** fax (fee). **Cards:** AX, DS, MC, VI.

SOME UNITS

NAUTICAL INN RESORT AND CONFERENCE
CENTER   *Book at aaa.com*

Phone: (928)855-2141

AAA [SAVE] / Motel

5/1-9/14	2P: $139-$499	XP: $20	F16
2/1-4/30 & 9/15-10/31	2P: $129-$379	XP: $20	F16
11/1-1/31	2P: $69-$189	XP: $20	F16

Location: 1.4 mi w of London Bridge/SR 95, follow signs. 1000 McCulloch Blvd 86403. Fax: 928/453-5808. **Facility:** 139 units. 134 one-bedroom standard units. 3 one- and 2 two-bedroom suites ($169-$499), some with efficiencies or kitchens. 2 stories (no elevator), exterior corridors. *Bath:* combo or shower only. **Parking:** on-site. **Terms:** check-in 4 pm, 2 night minimum stay - weekends, 3 day cancellation notice-fee imposed. **Amenities:** voice mail. *Some:* irons, hair dryers. **Dining:** 8 am-10 pm, cocktails. **Pool(s):** heated outdoor. **Leisure Activities:** whirlpool, boat dock, fishing, rental watercraft, playground. *Fee:* paddleboats, sailboats, golf-18 holes. **Guest Services:** gift shop. **Business Services:** conference facilities, fax (fee). **Cards:** AX, DC, DS, MC, VI.

SOME UNITS

RAMADA INN HAVASU   *Book at aaa.com*

Phone: (928)855-1111

AAA [SAVE] / Motel

3/1-5/31 [CP]	1P: $95-$299	2P: $95-$299	XP: $10	F17
6/1-8/31 [CP]	1P: $75-$199	2P: $75-$199	XP: $10	F17
2/1-2/28 & 9/1-1/31 [CP]	1P: $69-$199	2P: $69-$199	XP: $10	F17

Location: SR 95, just e on Swanson Ave, just s. 271 S Lake Havasu Ave 86403. Fax: 928/855-6228. **Facility:** 193 units. 190 one-bedroom standard units. 3 one-bedroom suites ($199-$299) with whirlpools. 3 stories (no elevator), exterior corridors. *Bath:* combo or shower only. **Parking:** on-site. **Terms:** cancellation fee imposed, $2 service charge, small pets only ($20 fee, $50 deposit). **Amenities:** voice mail, irons, hair dryers. **Dining:** 7 am-2 & 5-10 pm, cocktails, entertainment. **Pool(s):** heated outdoor. **Leisure Activities:** whirlpool. **Guest Services:** valet and coin laundry. **Business Services:** meeting rooms, fax (fee). **Cards:** AX, DC, DS, MC, VI. *(See color ad p 241)*.

SOME UNITS
FEE   FEE   FEE FEE

SANDS VACATION RESORT

Phone: 928/855-1388

Condominium

Property failed to provide current rates

Location: 1 mi e of SR 95, just n of McCulloch Blvd. 2040 Mesquite Ave 86403. Fax: 928/453-1802. **Facility:** Designated smoking area. 42 units. 36 one- and 6 two-bedroom suites with efficiencies. 2 stories (no elevator), exterior corridors. **Parking:** on-site. **Terms:** office hours 7 am-8 pm. **Amenities:** video library (fee), high-speed Internet, voice mail, hair dryers. **Pool(s):** small heated outdoor. **Leisure Activities:** whirlpool, exercise room. **Guest Services:** coin laundry. **Business Services:** fax (fee).

TRAVELODGE-LAKE HAVASU CITY   *Book at aaa.com*

Phone: (928)680-9202

AAA [SAVE] / Small-scale Hotel

3/1-4/30 [CP]	1P: $80-$160	2P: $80-$160	XP: $5	F17
5/1-10/31 [CP]	1P: $60-$160	2P: $60-$160	XP: $5	F17
2/1-2/28 [CP]	1P: $60-$125	2P: $60-$125	XP: $5	F17
11/1-1/31 [CP]	1P: $50-$90	2P: $50-$90	XP: $5	F17

Location: 1 mi n of London Bridge. 480 London Bridge Rd 86403. Fax: 928/680-1511. **Facility:** 41 units. 40 one-bedroom standard units. 1 one-bedroom suite with kitchen. 2 stories (no elevator), interior corridors. *Bath:* combo or shower only. **Parking:** on-site. **Terms:** 3 day cancellation notice-fee imposed, package plans, small pets only ($50 deposit, $5 extra charge). **Amenities:** voice mail, hair dryers. **Leisure Activities:** whirlpool. **Business Services:** fax. **Cards:** AX, DS, MC, VI. **Special Amenities:** free continental breakfast and free local telephone calls.
(See color ad below)

SOME UNITS
FEE   FEE

--------- **WHERE TO DINE** ---------

CASA SERRANO
Ⓐ
▽▽ ▽▽
Mexican

Lunch: $4-$8   **Dinner:** $5-$13   **Phone:** 928/854-5500
Location: Jct SR 95, just sw. 150 Swanson Ave 86403. **Hours:** 11 am-9 pm. Closed: 4/16, 9/4, 12/24, 12/25. **Features:** Friendly staffers welcome patrons into a brightly colored dining room. Fresh ingredients in the wide variety of dishes will satisfy the most discriminating diner. Casual dress; cocktails. **Parking:** on-site. **Cards:** AX, DC, DS, MC, VI.
🍸 ◣

FARRELL'S GOLDEN HORSESHOE STEAKHOUSE
▽▽▽ ▽▽▽
Steak House

Dinner: $10-$22   **Phone:** 928/764-3800
Location: SR 95, 6.1 mi n. 4501 N London Bridge Rd 86404. **Hours:** 4 pm-10 pm. Closed: 11/23, 12/25. **Features:** The Western theme is carried out in everything from buckets of peanuts on the table to such steak names as cowboy cut or cattle baron. Patrons can enjoy live entertainment while feasting on a choice of beef, seafood or pasta. Save room for the six-layer carrot cake. Casual dress; cocktails. **Parking:** on-site.
Cards: AX, DS, MC, VI.
🍸 ◣

JAVELINA CANTINA
▽▽▽ ▽▽▽
Mexican

Lunch: $5-$12   **Dinner:** $7-$15   **Phone:** 928/855-8226
Location: West side of London Bridge. 1420 McCulloch Blvd 86403. **Hours:** 11 am-10 pm, Fri & Sat-11 pm. Closed: 12/25. **Reservations:** accepted. **Features:** Adding to the trendy decor are curved metal dividers, brightly colored tile walls and plasma TVs mounted so diners can enjoy sports events. On the riverside patio, a misting system cools the summer heat so patrons can enjoy classic, freshly prepared south-of-the-border foods. Casual dress; cocktails. **Parking:** on-site. **Cards:** AX, DC, DS, MC, VI.
🍸

JUICY'S RIVER CAFE
▽▽ ▽▽
American

Lunch: $8-$10   **Dinner:** $9-$15   **Phone:** 928/855-8429
Location: Jct Lake Havasu Ave, 1.4 mi e, just n. 25 N Acoma 86403. **Hours:** 7 am-8 pm, Sun-2 pm. Closed: 11/23, 12/25. **Features:** Owner Mike Bradley stops by guests' tables to ensure they are satisfied with the hearty homemade food. For 23 years, diners have frequented the award-winning cafe for breakfast items, as well as a wide selection of sandwiches, salads and such specials as "Pop's favorite meatloaf.". Casual dress; beer & wine only. **Parking:** on-site. **Cards:** MC, VI.

KRYSTAL'S RESTAURANT
▽▽▽ ▽▽▽
Steak & Seafood

Dinner: $10-$40   **Phone:** 928/453-2999
Location: Just w of SR 95; 1.2 mi n of London Bridge. 460 El Camino Way 86403. **Hours:** 4 pm-10 pm. Closed: 12/25. **Reservations:** suggested. **Features:** Familiar selections of seafood, chicken and beef, including ribeye, filet mignon and prime rib cuts are simply prepared. Chicken comes barbecued or broiled, while dominant seafood choices range from shrimp scampi to mahi mahi to the fisherman's platter, a must for those with hearty appetites. There are hints of formalized service. Casual dress; cocktails. **Parking:** on-site. **Cards:** AX, MC, VI.
🍸 ◣

MONTANA STEAK HOUSE
▽▽▽ ▽▽▽
Steak House

Dinner: $11-$23   **Phone:** 928/855-3736
Location: 4.7 mi s of London Bridge; just off SR 95 on east side. 3301 Maricopa Ave 86406. **Hours:** 4 pm-9 pm, Fri & Sat-10 pm. Closed: 11/23, 12/25. **Reservations:** accepted. **Features:** Western decor sets the stage at the casual family restaurant. Steaks, including filet mignon, New York strip and rib-eye, are the house specialty. Meals come with the usual accompaniments of soup or salad and a starch. Casual dress; cocktails. **Parking:** on-site. **Cards:** AX, DC, DS, MC, VI.
🍸 ◣

THE POUR HOUSE
▽▽
American

Lunch: $4-$9   **Dinner:** $7-$20   **Phone:** 928/680-0063
Location: 1.3 mi e of London Bridge; center. 2093 McCulloch Blvd 86403. **Hours:** 6 am-9 pm; hours may vary in summer. Closed: 12/25. **Features:** One of the city's first eateries, this place is known for its breakfasts and ample portions of such lunch favorites as the half-pound burger, turkey avocado sandwich and sausage Parmesan sandwich. Pasta dishes and early-bird specials are among dinner offerings. Casual dress; cocktails. **Parking:** on-site. **Cards:** AX, DS, MC, VI.
🍸 ◣

SHUGRUE'S
▽▽ ▽▽
Steak & Seafood

Lunch: $7-$12   **Dinner:** $14-$29   **Phone:** 928/453-1400
Location: West side of London Bridge. 1425 McCulloch Blvd 86403. **Hours:** 11 am-9 pm, Fri & Sat-10 pm. Closed: 12/25. **Reservations:** suggested. **Features:** Overlooking the channel to Lake Havasu and London Bridge, the restaurant bakes pastries and bread on the premises. Fresh seafood is offered daily, and Pacific Rim dishes are available Thursday evenings. Casual dress; cocktails. **Parking:** on-site. **Cards:** AX, DS, MC, VI.
🍸

LITCHFIELD PARK —See Phoenix p. 322.

MARANA —See Tucson p. 456.

MARICOPA pop. 1,040

--------- **WHERE TO STAY** ---------

HARRAH'S AK-CHIN CASINO RESORT
▽▽▽▽
Large-scale Hotel

Book at aaa.com
All Year   1P: $55-$250   2P: $55-$250   XP: $10   **Phone:** (480)802-5000
Location: Jct SR 238, 4.5 mi s. 15406 Maricopa Rd 85239. Fax: 480/802-3009. **Facility:** Besides the casino, you may enjoy a palm tree-shaded courtyard and cool off in a pool with a swim-up cocktail bar. 146 units. 142 one-bedroom standard units. 4 one-bedroom suites with whirlpools. 2 stories, interior/exterior corridors. **Bath:** combo or shower only. **Parking:** on-site. **Terms:** check-in 4 pm, 3 day cancellation notice. **Amenities:** video games (fee), dual phone lines, voice mail, irons, hair dryers. **Pool(s):** heated outdoor. **Leisure Activities:** whirlpool, exercise room. **Guest Services:** gift shop. **Business Services:** conference facilities. **Cards:** AX, DC, DS, MC, VI.

SOME UNITS
🛰 🍴 24 ⏰ 🆓 ➿ 🏋 📠 💻 / ✕ 🛗 /

MESA —See Phoenix p. 323.

MONUMENT VALLEY, UTAH

-------- **WHERE TO STAY** --------

GOULDING'S TRADING POST & LODGE

Phone: (435)727-3231

AAA **SAVE**

	6/1-10/15	1P: $175	2P: $175	XP: $10	F8
	4/1-5/31	1P: $145	2P: $145	XP: $10	F8
	11/16-3/31	1P: $73-$118	2P: $73-$118	XP: $10	F8
	10/16-11/15	1P: $118	2P: $118	XP: $10	F8

Small-scale Hotel **Location:** Just n of Arizona border; 2 mi w of US 163. 1000 Main St 84536 (PO Box 360001, MONUMENT VALLEY, UT). Fax: 435/727-3344. **Facility:** Smoke free premises. 62 units. 60 one-bedroom standard units, some with efficiencies. 2 cabins. 2 stories (no elevator), exterior corridors. **Parking:** on-site. **Terms:** 3 day cancellation notice, [AP] meal plan available. **Amenities:** video library (fee), voice mail, irons, hair dryers. **Dining:** 7 am-9 pm; limited hours 11/15-3/15. **Pool(s):** heated indoor. **Leisure Activities:** museum, exercise room. **Guest Services:** gift shop, coin laundry. **Cards:** AX, DC, DS, JC, MC, VI.

SOME UNITS

⏹⏹⏹⏹⏹⏹⏹⏹⏹ / ⏹ /

MORMON LAKE

-------- **WHERE TO STAY** --------

-------- *The following lodging was either not evaluated or did not* --------
meet AAA rating requirements but is listed for your information only.

MORMON LAKE LODGE

Phone: 928/354-2227

fyi

Not evaluated. **Location:** I-17, exit 339, 30 mi s of Flagstaff via Lake Mary and Mormon Lake rds. Main St 86038 (PO Box 38012). Facilities, services, and decor characterize a basic property.

-------- **WHERE TO DINE** --------

MORMON LAKE LODGE STEAK HOUSE & SALOON

Lunch: $5-$8   **Dinner:** $9-$20   Phone: 928/354-2227

AAA
♦♦♦

Location: I-17, exit 339, 30 mi s of Flagstaff via Lake Mary and Mormon Lake rds; in Mormon Lake Lodge. **Hours:** 9 am-9 pm, Fri & Sat-10 pm. **Reservations:** suggested. **Features:** Among this steak house's menu items for the entire family are barbecue ribs, steak and chicken. The decor is rustic with a Western flair. Casual dress; cocktails. **Parking:** on-site and street. **Cards:** AX, DS, MC, VI.

Steak House

⏹ ⏹

NOGALES pop. 20,878

-------- **WHERE TO STAY** --------

BEST WESTERN SIESTA MOTEL

Book at aaa.com

Phone: (520)287-4671

AAA **SAVE**
♦♦♦

All Year   1P: $65-$70   2P: $70-$75   XP: $5   F16

Motel

Location: On Business Loop I-19, 1 mi n of International border. Located in a business area. 673 N Grand Ave 85621. Fax: 520/287-9616. **Facility:** 47 one-bedroom standard units. 2 stories (no elevator), exterior corridors. **Parking:** on-site. **Terms:** cancellation fee imposed, [CP] meal plan available, pets ($5 fee). **Amenities:** irons, hair dryers. *Some:* high-speed Internet. **Pool(s):** outdoor. **Leisure Activities:** whirlpool. **Cards:** AX, CB, DC, DS, MC, VI. **Special Amenities:** free continental breakfast and free local telephone calls. *(See color ad below)*

SOME UNITS

⏹⏹ ⏹⏹⏹⏹⏹⏹⏹⏹ / ⏹ /
FEE

HOLIDAY INN EXPRESS

Book at aaa.com

Phone: (520)281-0123

♦♦♦

All Year [ECP]   1P: $80-$123   2P: $80-$123

Small-scale Hotel

Location: I-19, exit 4, just w to Frank Reed, then just nw. 850 W Shell Rd 85621. Fax: 520/281-2005. **Facility:** 99 units. 96 one-bedroom standard units. 3 one-bedroom suites ($123-$225) with whirlpools. 3 stories, interior corridors. **Bath:** combo or shower only. **Parking:** on-site. **Terms:** cancellation fee imposed, package plans. **Amenities:** high-speed Internet, dual phone lines, voice mail, irons, hair dryers. **Pool(s):** outdoor. **Leisure Activities:** whirlpool, exercise room. **Guest Services:** gift shop, coin laundry. **Business Services:** meeting rooms. **Cards:** AX, DS, MC, VI.

SOME UNITS

ASK ⏹⏹⏹⏹⏹⏹⏹⏹⏹ / ⏹ /

MOTEL 6 NOGALES #71   *Book at aaa.com*   Phone: 520/281-2951

4/27-10/25	1P: $45-$55	2P: $51-$61	XP: $3	F17
2/1-4/26 & 10/26-1/31	1P: $41-$51	2P: $47-$57	XP: $3	F17

Motel

Location: I-19, exit 4, 0.9 mi e. 141 W Mariposa Rd 85621. **Fax:** 520/281-9592. **Facility:** 79 one-bedroom standard units. 2 stories (no elevator), exterior corridors. *Bath:* shower only. **Parking:** on-site. **Terms:** small pets only. **Pool(s):** outdoor. **Guest Services:** coin laundry. **Cards:** AX, CB, DC, DS, MC, VI.

SOME UNITS
FEE FEE

--------- WHERE TO DINE ---------

MR. C'S RESTAURANT AND SUPPER CLUB   **Lunch:** $7-$14   **Dinner:** $14-$32   Phone: 520/281-9000

Location: I-19, exit 4, 0.7 mi e to W Mastick Way, just s, then just w to top of hill. 282 W Viewpoint Dr 85621. **Hours:** 11:30 am-10:30 pm, Sat from 5 pm. Closed: 5/29, 11/23, 12/24, 12/25; also Sun.

Steak & Seafood   **Reservations:** accepted. **Features:** Views through tall windows in the hilltop eatery enhance meals that incorporate wonderfully tasty soups, hearty entrees and salads compiled from a bar filled with crispy ingredients. The staff is pleasant. Casual dress; cocktails. **Parking:** on-site. **Cards:** AX, DC, DS, MC, VI.

ORO VALLEY — *See Tucson p. 458.*

PAGE pop. 6,809

--------- WHERE TO STAY ---------

AMERICAS BEST VALUE INN   *Book at aaa.com*   Phone: (928)645-2858

5/1-8/20	1P: $49-$64	2P: $55-$69	XP: $5	F12
8/21-10/20	1P: $44-$59	2P: $44-$64	XP: $5	F12
10/21-1/31	1P: $39-$54	2P: $39-$59	XP: $5	F12
2/1-4/30	1P: $39-$49	2P: $39-$49	XP: $5	F12

Motel

Location: 1 mi e of US 89 via SR 89L, just n of Lake Powell Blvd. 75 S 7th Ave 86040 (PO Box 4450). **Fax:** 928/645-2890. **Facility:** 39 one-bedroom standard units. 2 stories (no elevator), exterior corridors. **Parking:** on-site. **Terms:** 3 day cancellation notice. **Amenities:** *Some:* irons, hair dryers. **Cards:** AX, CB, DC, DS, MC, VI. **Special Amenities:** free local telephone calls.

SOME UNITS

BEST WESTERN ARIZONA INN   *Book at aaa.com*   Phone: (928)645-2466

5/15-10/14 [CP]	1P: $79-$109	2P: $79-$109	XP: $5	F17
4/15-5/14 [CP]	1P: $74-$99	2P: $74-$99	XP: $5	F17
2/1-4/14 & 10/15-1/31 [CP]	1P: $44-$64	2P: $44-$64	XP: $5	F17

Small-scale Hotel

Location: 0.7 mi e of US 89 via SR 89L. 716 Rimview Dr 86040 (PO Box 250). **Fax:** 928/645-2053. **Facility:** 102 units. 100 one-bedroom standard units. 2 one-bedroom suites ($100-$175). 3 stories, interior corridors. **Parking:** on-site. **Terms:** pets ($10 extra charge). **Amenities:** irons, hair dryers. **Pool(s):** heated outdoor. **Leisure Activities:** whirlpool, exercise room. **Guest Services:** coin laundry. **Business Services:** meeting rooms. **Cards:** AX, DC, DS, MC, VI. *(See color ad below)*

FEE

SOME UNITS

BEST WESTERN AT LAKE POWELL   *Book at aaa.com*   Phone: 928/645-5988

4/1-10/31 [CP]	1P: $79-$129	2P: $79-$129	XP: $10	F12
2/1-3/31 & 11/1-1/31 [CP]	1P: $59-$99	2P: $59-$99	XP: $10	F12

Small-scale Hotel

Location: 0.8 mi e of US 89 via SR 89L. 208 N Lake Powell Blvd 86040 (PO Box 4899). **Fax:** 928/645-2578. **Facility:** 132 units. 129 one-bedroom standard units. 3 one-bedroom suites ($89-$179). 4 stories, interior corridors. **Parking:** on-site. **Terms:** check-in 3:30 pm, cancellation fee imposed. **Amenities:** irons, hair dryers. **Pool(s):** heated outdoor. **Leisure Activities:** whirlpool, exercise room. **Guest Services:** valet laundry. **Business Services:** meeting rooms. **Cards:** AX, CB, DC, DS, JC, MC, VI. **Special Amenities:** free local telephone calls. *(See color ad p 246)*

SOME UNITS

COURTYARD BY MARRIOTT   *Book at aaa.com*   **Phone: 928/645-5000**

7/1-9/30	1P: $99-$129	2P: $99-$129	XP: $10 F18
4/1-6/30	1P: $79-$109	2P: $79-$109	XP: $10 F18
10/1-1/31	1P: $69-$99	2P: $69-$99	XP: $10 F18
2/1-3/31	1P: $69-$89	2P: $69-$89	XP: $10 F18

Small-scale Hotel **Location:** On SR 89L, jct US 89. 600 Clubhouse Dr 86040 (PO Box 4150). Fax: 928/645-5004. **Facility:** 153 one-bedroom standard units. 2-4 stories, interior corridors. *Bath:* combo or shower only. **Parking:** on-site. **Amenities:** high-speed Internet, voice mail, irons, hair dryers. **Dining:** Pepper's, see separate listing. **Pool(s):** heated outdoor. **Leisure Activities:** whirlpool, exercise room. **Guest Services:** gift shop, valet and coin laundry. **Business Services:** meeting rooms. **Cards:** AX, DC, DS, JC, MC, VI. *(See color ad below)*

SOME UNITS

HOLIDAY INN EXPRESS   *Book at aaa.com*   **Phone: 928/645-9000**

5/1-8/20	1P: $59-$99	2P: $59-$99	XP: $10 F16
8/21-10/20	1P: $59-$79	2P: $59-$79	XP: $10 F16
2/1-4/30	1P: $49-$69	2P: $49-$69	XP: $10 F16
10/21-1/31	1P: $49-$59	2P: $49-$59	XP: $10 F16

Small-scale Hotel **Location:** On SR 89L, 1.5 mi e of US 89. 751 S Navajo Dr 86040 (PO Box 4450). Fax: 928/645-1605. **Facility:** 74 units. 71 one-bedroom standard units. 3 one-bedroom suites ($59-$119) with kitchens (no utensils). 3 stories, interior corridors. *Bath:* combo or shower only. **Parking:** on-site. **Terms:** 3 day cancellation notice. **Amenities:** voice mail, irons, hair dryers. **Pool(s):** small outdoor. **Guest Services:** coin laundry. **Cards:** AX, CB, DC, DS, JC, MC, VI. **Special Amenities:** free continental breakfast and free newspaper. *(See color ad p 247)*

SOME UNITS

LAKE POWELL DAYS INN & SUITES   *Book at aaa.com*   Phone: (928)645-2800

4/1-10/31 [CP]	1P: $69-$119	2P: $69-$119	XP: $7 F18
2/1-3/31 & 11/1-1/31 [CP]	1P: $49-$89	2P: $49-$89	XP: $7 F18

AAA **SAVE** ◇◇◇◇ Small-scale Hotel **Location:** On US 89, just s. 961 N Hwy 89 86040 (PO Box 3910). Fax: 928/645-2604. **Facility:** 82 units. 70 one-bedroom standard units, some with whirlpools. 12 one-bedroom suites. 3 stories, interior corridors. *Bath:* combo or shower only. **Parking:** on-site. **Terms:** small pets only ($10 extra charge). **Amenities:** safes (fee), hair dryers. **Pool(s):** heated outdoor. **Leisure Activities:** whirlpool. **Guest Services:** gift shop, coin laundry. **Business Services:** PC. **Cards:** AX, CB, DC, DS, JC, MC, VI. **Special Amenities:** free continental breakfast and free local telephone calls.

SOME UNITS

[icons: SD FEE, pets, ..., DATA PORT, ... / ✕ / ...]

Unforgettable Lake Powell Getaway.
Outstanding AAA Member Savings.

Visit beautiful Lake Powell for a vacation you'll never forget. Enjoy our lake-side resort lodging, fine dining with spectacular lake views, scenic tours and more, plus great new products and services. Call today – ask your AAA representative about our other great lodging and houseboat packages!

AAA Members get great rates at Lake Powell.

**Book our
AAA GETAWAY PACKAGE
for only:**

$108 per person per day

See our ad under Glen Canyon National Recreation Area, AZ in the "Points of Interest" section for great discounts on houseboat & powerboat rentals, and more!

Call: **1-888-272-3161**
and request **Code H30013**

• 3 nights at Lake Powell Resort
• Navajo Tapestry Scenic Cruise
• Colorado River Float Trip
• Dinner for 2 in the award winning Rainbow Room
• Retail voucher for $25
• Rate: $647 plus tax for 2; based on double occupancy

Lake Powell
RESORT
ARAMARK

www.lakepowell.com

Offer valid on arrivals January 1, 2006 through December 31, 2006. Total package price is $647. Extra person in the same room is an additional $149 (receives other package benefits). Offer is subject to availability. Advance reservations are required. Not valid with any other offer or discount. Valid on new reservations only. Cancel/change policy and schedule of fees are applicable. Energy surcharge, applicable taxes and other charges that may apply are not included. Offer is valid on standard rooms only. Can upgrade to Lakeview for a $20 upgrade fee per night, subject to availability. Lake Powell Resorts & Marinas, managed by ARAMARK, is an authorized concessioner of the National Park Service, Glen Canyon National Recreation Area. ARA703PgLdg

---

Stay Smart® In
Page-Lake Powell.

Free Breakfast Bar • Free Local Phone Calls
Priority Club® Rewards Program
Outdoor Pool • Jeep Tours/Scenic Flights-.5 mile
Lake Powell/Glen Canyon Dam/Boat Tours/Rafting-1 mile

I-40 to US-89 N to Page-1st Exit
I-40 to US-89 S to Page-2nd Exit
928 645-9000 or 1 800-Holiday

Holiday Inn
EXPRESS
Stay Smart®

751 S. Navajo Drive
Page, AZ 86040

www.hiexpress.com

LAKE POWELL RESORT AND MARINA

Phone: 928/645-2433

(AAA) (SAVE) All Year — 1P: $49-$139 — XP: $10 — F8

(fyi) Under major renovation, scheduled to be completed February 2006. **Last rated:** ▽▽▽ **Location:** 4 mi n of Glen Canyon Dam via US 89. 100 Lakeshore Dr 86040 (PO Box 1597). Fax: 928/645-1031. **Facility:** Located in the Glen Canyon National Recreation Area, this hotel provides direct access to all sorts of water sports on **Resort** Lake Powell. Smoke free premises. 348 units. 344 one-bedroom standard units. 4 one-bedroom suites. 2 **Large-scale Hotel** stories (no elevator), interior corridors. *Bath:* combo or shower only. **Parking:** on-site. **Terms:** cancellation fee imposed, package plans, small pets only ($75 deposit, $10 extra charge, with prior approval). **Amenities:** hair dryers. *Some:* irons. **Dining:** 11 am-10 pm, 5/1-10/31, also, Rainbow Room, see separate listing. **Pool(s):** 2 heated outdoor. **Leisure Activities:** sauna, whirlpool, rental boats, exercise room. *Fee:* marina, waterskiing, boat trips, river rafting, houseboats. **Guest Services:** gift shop, coin laundry, area transportation-Page. **Business Services:** meeting rooms, Cards: AX, DS, MC, VI. **Special Amenities: free local telephone calls and early check-in/late check-out.** *(See color ad p 52 & p 247)*

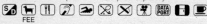
FEE

LINDA'S LAKE POWELL CONDOS

Phone: 928/353-4591

▽▽▽ Property failed to provide current rates
Location: 6 mi n on US 89. Located in Greenhaven. 1019 Tower Butte 86040 (PO Box 5292). Fax: 928/353-4200.
Condominium **Facility:** Smoke free premises. 40 one-bedroom standard units with kitchens. 2 stories (no elevator), exterior corridors. **Parking:** on-site. **Terms:** check-in 4 pm, small pets only ($100 deposit, in limited units). **Amenities:** *Some:* irons, hair dryers. **Leisure Activities:** whirlpool. **Guest Services:** complimentary laundry.

SOME UNITS

[icons] / VCR /
FEE

MOTEL 6-PAGE/LAKE POWELL #4013   *Book at aaa.com*

Phone: (928)645-5888

5/1-8/20	1P: $49-$59	2P: $54-$69	XP: $3	F12
8/21-10/20	1P: $43-$53	2P: $49-$59	XP: $3	F12
2/1-4/30 & 10/21-1/31	1P: $39-$49	2P: $39-$55	XP: $3	F12

Location: On Business Loop SR 89L, just e of US 89. 637 S Lake Powell Blvd 86040 (PO Box 4450). **Small-scale Hotel** Fax: 928/645-0009. **Facility:** 111 one-bedroom standard units. 3 stories, interior corridors. *Bath:* combo or shower only. **Parking:** on-site. **Terms:** 3 day cancellation notice, small pets only. **Amenities:** *Some:* irons, hair dryers. **Pool(s):** outdoor. **Guest Services:** coin laundry. **Cards:** AX, CB, DC, DS, MC, VI. **Special Amenities: free local telephone calls and preferred room (subject to availability with advance reservations).** *(See color ad below)*

SOME UNITS

[icons] / ⊠ /
FEE

QUALITY INN, AT LAKE POWELL   *Book at aaa.com*

Phone: (928)645-8851

4/15-10/15 [ECP]	1P: $89-$150	2P: $89-$150	XP: $10	D17
2/1-4/14 & 10/16-1/31 [ECP]	1P: $40-$90	2P: $40-$90	XP: $10	D17

Location: 0.8 mi e of US 89/SR 89L. 287 N Lake Powell Blvd 86040 (PO Box 1867). Fax: 928/645-2523. **Facility:** 129 one-bedroom standard units. 3 stories, interior corridors. **Parking:** on-site. **Terms:** small pets **Small-scale Hotel** only ($20 extra charge, in limited units). **Amenities:** irons, hair dryers. **Pool(s):** heated outdoor. **Guest Services:** valet and coin laundry. **Business Services:** meeting rooms, business center. **Cards:** AX, CB, DC, DS, MC, VI. *(See color ad p 249)*

SOME UNITS

[icons] / ⊠ [icons]
FEE — FEE FEE

SUPER 8 GATEWAY TO LAKE POWELL   *Book at aaa.com*

Phone: (928)645-5858

5/1-8/20	1P: $54-$84	2P: $54-$84	XP: $5	F12
8/21-10/20	1P: $49-$79	2P: $49-$79	XP: $5	F12
2/1-4/30 & 10/21-1/31	1P: $44-$54	2P: $44-$54	XP: $5	F12

Location: On SR 89L, just e of US 89. 649 S Lake Powell Blvd 86040 (PO Box 4450). Fax: 928/645-0335. **Small-scale Hotel** **Facility:** 101 one-bedroom standard units. 3 stories, interior corridors. *Bath:* combo or shower only. **Parking:** on-site. **Terms:** 3 day cancellation notice, small pets only ($10 fee). **Amenities:** irons, hair dryers. **Pool(s):** outdoor. **Leisure Activities:** exercise room. **Guest Services:** coin laundry. **Business Services:** PC. **Cards:** AX, CB, DC, DS, MC, VI. **Special Amenities: free continental breakfast and free local telephone calls.** *(See color ad p 249)*

SOME UNITS

[icons] / ⊠ [icons] /
FEE

——— WHERE TO DINE ———

THE DAM BAR & GRILLE

American

Lunch: $5-$11   **Dinner:** $8-$23   **Phone:** 928/645-2161

Location: 0.6 mi n of US 89 via SR 89L; in shopping center. 644 N Navajo Dr 86040. **Hours:** 3 pm-close; 11:30 am-10 pm 5/1-10/31. Closed: 12/25; also Sun off season. **Reservations:** accepted. **Features:** On the menu at the casual, sports-bar restaurant is a nice selection of steak, chicken, seafood and pasta dishes, as well as an assortment of sandwiches. Casual dress; cocktails. **Parking:** on-site. **Cards:** AX, MC, VI.

ITALIA'S FAMILY BUFFET

Italian

MC, VI.

Lunch: $7   **Dinner:** $11   **Phone:** 928/645-2706

Location: 1 mi s of US 89 via SR 89L, just ne of Lake Powell Blvd. 810 N Navajo Dr 86040. **Hours:** 11 am-close; call for winter hours. **Reservations:** not accepted. **Features:** The charming, family-oriented restaurant prepares traditional Italian dishes, including pasta and pizza. Fresh fish and seafood are featured on Fridays. Patio dining is a nice option in good weather. Casual dress; beer & wine only. **Parking:** on-site. **Cards:** DS,

KEN'S OLD WEST RESTAURANT & LOUNGE

Steak House

DS, MC, VI.

Dinner: $9-$20   **Phone:** 928/645-5160

Location: 0.8 mi e of US 89 via SR 89L, then just n. 718 Vista Ave 86040. **Hours:** 4 pm-close. Closed: 1/1, 11/23, 12/25; also Sun-Wed in winter. **Reservations:** accepted. **Features:** The restaurant features a selection of steak, seafood and prime rib entrees and a small salad bar. Live country and Western music each day lends to the upbeat atmosphere. Casual dress; cocktails; entertainment. **Parking:** on-site. **Cards:** AX, CB, DC,

MANDARIN GOURMET

Chinese

Lunch: $6-$16   **Dinner:** $6-$16   **Phone:** 928/645-5516

Location: Jct US 89. 683 Lake Powell Blvd 86040. **Hours:** 11 am-9:30 pm, Sat & Sun from 11:30 am. **Features:** Mandarin Gourmet offers a variety of traditional Chinese dishes in a casual atmosphere. Stop in for lunch and sample the extensive buffet. Casual dress. **Parking:** on-site. **Cards:** MC, VI.

PEPPER'S

Southwestern

(See color ad p 246)

Lunch: $7-$11   **Dinner:** $9-$23   **Phone:** 928/645-5000

Location: On SR 89L, jct US 89; in Courtyard by Marriott. 600 Clubhouse Dr 86040. **Hours:** 6 am-2 & 5-10 pm. **Reservations:** accepted. **Features:** Enlivened by Southwestern decor, the comfortable hotel restaurant prepares a nice variety of Southwestern and American entrees. The lunch buffet is good for diners in a bit of a hurry. Casual dress; cocktails. **Parking:** on-site. **Cards:** AX, CB, DC, DS, JC, MC, VI.

RAINBOW ROOM

American

Lunch: $7-$13   **Dinner:** $13-$24   **Phone:** 928/645-2433

Location: 4 mi n of Glen Canyon Dam via US 89; in Lake Powell Resort & Marina. 100 Lakeshore Dr 86040. **Hours:** 6 am-2 & 5-10 pm; 7 am-1:30 & 5-9 pm in winter. **Reservations:** not accepted. **Features:** The dining room affords beautiful views of Lake Powell from every table. The lunch buffet lines up cold cuts, Mexican dishes, fruits and salads, while the dinner menu centers on such choices as grilled pork loin chops, New York strip steak and farm-raised pine nut-crusted trout, as well as pasta. Casual dress; cocktails. **Parking:** on-site. **Cards:** AX, DC, DS, MC, VI. **(See color ad p 247)**

ZAPATA'S

Mexican

Lunch: $6-$12   **Dinner:** $6-$12   **Phone:** 928/645-9006

Location: 0.6 mi n of US 89 via SR 89L; in shopping center. 614 N Navajo Dr 86040. **Hours:** 11 am-10 pm. Closed: 1/1, 11/23, 12/25. **Reservations:** accepted. **Features:** The popular restaurant builds its menu on Sonoran favorites, such as chiles rellenos, enchiladas and fajitas. The patio opens seasonally. Casual dress; cocktails. **Parking:** on-site. **Cards:** MC, VI.

PARADISE VALLEY —See Phoenix p. 330.

PARKER pop. 3,140

——— WHERE TO STAY ———

BEST WESTERN PARKER INN   *Book at aaa.com*   Phone: 928/669-6060
AAA SAVE   All Year [CP]   1P: $64-$129   2P: $69-$129   XP: $5   F18
Location: SR 95, just e. 1012 Geronimo Ave 85344. **Fax:** 928/669-6204. **Facility:** 45 one-bedroom standard
Small-scale Hotel   units. 2 stories (no elevator), interior corridors. *Bath:* combo or shower only. **Parking:** on-site. **Terms:** small
pets only (in limited units). **Amenities:** high-speed Internet, voice mail, irons, hair dryers. **Pool(s):** outdoor.
Guest Services: coin laundry. **Business Services:** fax (fee). **Cards:** AX, DC, DS, MC, VI.
Special Amenities: free continental breakfast and free local telephone calls. *(See color ad below)*
SOME UNITS

KOFA INN   Phone: 928/669-2101
Property failed to provide current rates
Location: SR 95, just e. 1700 California Ave 85344. **Fax:** 928/669-6902. **Facility:** 41 one-bedroom standard
Motel   units. 1-2 stories (no elevator), exterior corridors. **Parking:** on-site. **Terms:** office hours 7 am-9 pm. **Pool(s):**
heated outdoor. **Business Services:** fax (fee).
SOME UNITS

——— WHERE TO DINE ———

PARKER STRIP GRILL   **Lunch:** $5-$16   **Dinner:** $5-$16   Phone: 928/667-4054
Location: Jct SR 95 and Riverside Dr. 10230 Harbor Dr 85344. **Hours:** 10 am-9 pm, Fri & Sat-10 pm. Closed:
American   12/25. **Features:** The restaurant resembles a '50s diner, but the well-prepared food is fresh in concept and
preparation. The fun decor takes many patrons back to their youth. Try one of the soda fountain delights,
including malts and banana splits. Casual dress; wine only. **Parking:** on-site. **Cards:** MC, VI.

PARKS pop. 1,137

——— WHERE TO DINE ———

RACK & BULL   **Lunch:** $7-$12   **Dinner:** $10-$25   Phone: 928/635-0200
Location: I-40, exit 178, just n. 2 N Park St 86018. **Hours:** 4 pm-9 pm, Fri & Sat-10 pm, Sun noon-8 pm. Closed:
American   1/1, 12/25; also Mon & Tues. **Features:** Tucked in a rural setting and surrounded by pine trees, the newly
constructed yet rustic-feeling restaurant is a delightful treat. Some pasta dishes complement a wide
memorabilia. Casual dress; cocktails. **Parking:** on-site. **Cards:** AX, MC, VI.

PAYSON pop. 13,620

-------- WHERE TO STAY --------

AMERICAS BEST VALUE INN
Book at aaa.com
Phone: (928)474-2283
(AAA) (SAVE)
All Year 1P: $45-$99 2P: $45-$99 XP: $5 D16
Location: On SR 87, 0.7 mi s of SR 260. 811 S Beeline Hwy 85541. Fax: 928/474-5448. **Facility:** 23 one-bedroom standard units. 2 stories (no elevator), interior/exterior corridors. Bath: combo or shower only. **Parking:** on-site. **Terms:** cancellation fee imposed, pets ($5 extra charge). **Amenities:** Some: hair dryers. **Cards:** AX, DS, MC, VI. **Special Amenities:** free local telephone calls.
Motel

SOME UNITS

FEE

BEST WESTERN PAYSON INN
Phone: (928)474-3241
(AAA) (SAVE)
5/1-10/31 [ECP] 1P: $89-$149 2P: $89-$149 XP: $10 F16
2/1-4/30 & 11/1-1/31 [ECP] 1P: $69-$149 2P: $69-$149 XP: $10 F16
Location: On SR 87, 0.6 mi n of SR 260. 801 N Beeline Hwy 85541. Fax: 928/472-6564. **Facility:** 99 units. 98 one-bedroom standard units. 1 two-bedroom suite. 2 stories (no elevator), exterior corridors. Bath: combo or shower only. **Parking:** on-site. **Terms:** package plans, small pets only ($10 extra charge). **Amenities:** high-speed Internet, irons, hair dryers. **Pool(s):** heated outdoor. **Leisure Activities:** whirlpool, exercise room.
Small-scale Hotel
Business Services: meeting rooms. Fee: PC, fax. **Cards:** AX, CB, DC, DS, MC, VI. **Special Amenities:** free continental breakfast and free local telephone calls. (See color ad below)

SOME UNITS

FEE

COMFORT INN
Book at aaa.com
Phone: (928)474-5241
(AAA) (SAVE)
All Year 1P: $52-$189 XP: $15 F15
Location: On SR 260, 0.8 mi e of SR 87. 809 E Hwy 260 85541. Fax: 928/472-6919. **Facility:** 39 one-bedroom standard units, some with whirlpools. 2 stories (no elevator), exterior corridors. **Parking:** on-site. **Terms:** [ECP] meal plan available, $2 service charge, pets ($10 extra charge, in limited units). **Amenities:** video library (fee), high-speed Internet, irons, hair dryers. **Pool(s):** heated outdoor. **Leisure Activities:** whirlpool. **Guest Services:** coin laundry. **Business Services:** fax (fee). **Cards:** AX, CB, DC, DS, MC, VI. **Special Amenities:** free continental breakfast and free local telephone calls. (See color ad p 253)
Motel

SOME UNITS

FEE

DAYS INN & SUITES   *Book at aaa.com*   Phone: (928)474-9800

All Year [ECP]   1P: $49-$129   2P: $59-$149   XP: $10   F12
Location: On SR 87, just s of SR 260. 301-A S Beeline Hwy 85541. Fax: 928/474-9700. Facility: 48 one-bedroom
standard units, some with whirlpools. 2 stories (no elevator), interior corridors. *Bath:* combo or shower only.
Parking: on-site. Terms: cancellation fee imposed, small pets only ($10 extra charge, in smoking units).
Small-scale Hotel Amenities: high-speed Internet, irons, hair dryers. *Some:* dual phone lines. Pool(s): heated indoor. Leisure
Activities: whirlpool. Guest Services: coin laundry. Business Services: fax (fee). Cards: AX, CB, DC, DS,
MC, VI. Special Amenities: free expanded continental breakfast and free newspaper.

SOME UNITS

HOLIDAY INN EXPRESS   *Book at aaa.com*   Phone: (928)472-7484

All Year [ECP]   1P: $69-$149   2P: $69-$149   XP: $10   F17
Location: On SR 87, just s of SR 260. 206 S Beeline Hwy 85541. Fax: 928/472-6283. Facility: 44 one-bedroom
standard units, some with whirlpools. 3 stories, interior corridors. Parking: on-site. Amenities: video library
(fee), high-speed Internet, voice mail, irons, hair dryers. Pool(s): heated indoor. Leisure
Small-scale Hotel Activities: whirlpool. Guest Services: coin laundry. Business Services: fax (fee). Cards: AX, CB, DC, DS,
MC, VI. Special Amenities: free expanded continental breakfast and free local telephone calls.

SOME UNITS

MAJESTIC MOUNTAIN INN   Phone: 928/474-0185

All Year   1P: $65-$150   2P: $65-$150
Location: On SR 260, 0.5 mi e of SR 87. 602 E Hwy 260 85541. Fax: 928/472-6097. Facility: 50 one-bedroom
standard units, some with whirlpools. 1-2 stories (no elevator), exterior corridors. Parking: on-site.
Small-scale Hotel Terms: office hours 7 am-10 pm, pets ($10 extra charge). Amenities: video library (fee), voice mail, irons,
hair dryers. *Some:* DVD players, CD players, high-speed Internet. Pool(s): heated outdoor. Business Services: meeting
rooms, PC. Cards: AX, CB, DC, DS, MC, VI. *(See color ad below)*

SOME UNITS

MOTEL 6 #4201   *Book at aaa.com*   Phone: 928/474-4526

All Year   1P: $35-$79   2P: $45-$85   XP: $6   F16
Location: On SR 87, 1.1 mi s of SR 260. 101 W Phoenix St 85541. Fax: 928/474-0263. Facility: 39 one-bedroom
Motel   standard units. 2 stories (no elevator), interior corridors. Parking: on-site. Terms: pets ($6 extra charge).
Cards: AX, CB, DC, DS, MC, VI.

SOME UNITS

PAYSONGLO LODGE
Phone: (928)474-2382

AAA [SAVE]

Small-scale Hotel

| 5/1-9/30 | 1P: $80-$92 | XP: $10 | F16 |
| 2/1-4/30 & 10/1-1/31 | 1P: $55-$81 | XP: $10 | F16 |

Location: On SR 87, 0.9 mi s of SR 260. 1005 S Beeline Hwy 85541. **Fax:** 928/474-1937. **Facility:** 46 one-bedroom standard units. 1-2 stories (no elevator), exterior corridors. **Parking:** on-site. **Terms:** [CP] meal plan available, small pets only (in smoking units). **Amenities:** voice mail, hair dryers. **Pool(s):** heated outdoor. **Leisure Activities:** whirlpool. **Cards:** AX, DS, MC, VI. **Special Amenities: free continental breakfast and free local telephone calls.**

SOME UNITS

WOODEN NICKEL CABINS
Phone: 928/478-4519

Cabin

| All Year | 1P: $110 | 2P: $110 | XP: $25 |

Location: 23 mi e on SR 260 from jct SR 87, then 0.7 mi n; just w of MM 275, follow signs. 165 Hunter Creek Dr 85541 (HC 2, Box 121C). **Fax:** 928/478-5015. **Facility:** 6 cabins. 2 stories (no elevator), exterior corridors. **Parking:** on-site. **Terms:** office hours 9 am-9 pm, 2 night minimum stay - weekends, 30 day cancellation notice-fee imposed. **Amenities:** video library. **Leisure Activities:** hiking trails, playground, horseshoes. **Cards:** AX, DS, MC, VI.

------- WHERE TO DINE -------

CUCINA PARADISO
Lunch: $7-$11   Dinner: $12-$19   Phone: 928/468-6500

Italian

Location: On SR 87, 0.5 mi n of SR 260. 512 N Beeline Hwy 85541. **Hours:** 11 am-2 & 4-8:30 pm. Closed: 1/1, 12/25; also Mon. **Reservations:** not accepted. **Features:** The pleasant trattoria-style restaurant serves rustic homemade Italian food. Included on the menu are hand-tossed pizzas cooked in wood-burning ovens, panini and traditional pasta preparations. Fish dishes are a favorite of the locals. A salad buffet is offered at lunch. Casual dress; cocktails. **Parking:** on-site. **Cards:** AX, DC, DS, MC, VI.

FARGO'S STEAKHOUSE
Lunch: $5-$9   Dinner: $10-$40   Phone: 928/474-7455

Steak House

Location: On SR 260, 0.5 mi e of SR 87. 620 E Hwy 260 85541. **Hours:** 11:30 am-9 pm, Fri & Sat 10 am-11:30 pm. Closed: 12/25. **Features:** The setting is much like a comfortable lakefront lodge, and the warm welcome from staff starts off a pleasant dining experience. Steaks and seafood may be combined in hearty meals. Casual dress; cocktails. **Parking:** on-site. **Cards:** AX, DS, MC, VI.

MAD DAWG'S & MEL'S BAR &
EATERY
Lunch: $6-$9   Dinner: $7-$22   Phone: 928/474-4391

AAA

American

Location: Jct SR 87, just w; center. 202 W Main St 85541. **Hours:** 7 am-9 pm, Fri & Sat-10 pm. Closed: 12/25. **Reservations:** accepted. **Features:** Fast becoming "the" place to gather, the charming old home is now lively with new owners who serve everything from hot breakfast to homemade soup to some of the best hot "dawgs" around. Ribs, chicken and steaks are not to be ignored. Casual dress; cocktails. **Parking:** on-site. **Cards:** AX, DS, MC, VI.

SESAME INN
Lunch: $6-$8   Dinner: $8-$14   Phone: 928/472-6888

Chinese

Location: On SR 260, just e of SR 87. 203 E Hwy 260 85541. **Hours:** 11 am-8:30 pm, Fri & Sat-9 pm, Sun-8 pm. Closed: 11/23, 12/25. **Reservations:** accepted. **Features:** Behind the simple storefront are the freshest ingredients, a most attractive decor and friendly servers. Mandarin, Hunan and Szechuan cuisine makes up the menu. Casual dress; cocktails. **Parking:** on-site. **Cards:** AX, CB, DC, MC, VI.

PEACH SPRINGS pop. 600

------- WHERE TO STAY -------

HUALAPAI LODGE   *Book at aaa.com*
Phone: (928)769-2230

AAA [SAVE]

Small-scale Hotel

| 4/1-10/31 | 1P: $85 | 2P: $95 | XP: $10 | F15 |
| 2/1-3/31 & 11/1-1/31 | 1P: $65 | 2P: $75 | XP: $10 | F15 |

Location: Center. 900 Route 66 86434 (PO Box 538). **Fax:** 928/769-2372. **Facility:** 57 one-bedroom standard units. 2 stories, interior corridors. *Bath:* combo or shower only. **Parking:** on-site. **Terms:** package plans. **Amenities:** voice mail, hair dryers. *Some:* irons. **Dining:** River Runner's, see separate listing. **Pool(s):** small heated outdoor. **Leisure Activities:** whirlpool, exercise room. **Guest Services:** gift shop, coin laundry. **Business Services:** meeting rooms. **Cards:** AX, CB, DC, DS, MC, VI. **Special Amenities: free local telephone calls.**
(See color ad p 227)

SOME UNITS

------- WHERE TO DINE -------

RIVER RUNNER'S
Lunch: $6-$12   Dinner: $6-$12   Phone: 928/769-2230

American

Location: Center; in Hualapai Lodge. 900 Route 66 86434. **Hours:** 7 am-9 pm; 7 am-2 & 5-7:30 pm in winter. **Features:** Traditional dishes are influenced by the local Native American population. For example, the Navajo taco has all the traditional taco fixings but is served on fry bread. Casual dress. **Parking:** on-site. **Cards:** AX, DS, MC, VI.

PEORIA —See Phoenix p. 330.

Destination Phoenix.

pop. 1,321,045

Rising from the centuries-old ashes of a once-thriving Hohokam Indian community, modern Phoenix is a city of diverse architectural styles.

From prehistoric ruins at the Pueblo Grande Museum, to Heritage Square's Victorian homes, to Frank Lloyd Wright's paragon of modernism Taliesin West, you can witness Phoenix's heritage manifested in timber, brick and stone.

Phoenix CVB

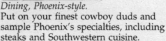
Dining, Phoenix-style.
Put on your finest cowboy duds and sample Phoenix's specialties, including steaks and Southwestern cuisine.

© Witold Skrypczak
SuperStock

Golfing in Phoenix.
Pack your clubs when you visit Phoenix; the city is home to some of the best golf courses in the nation.

Scottsdale CVB

Bank One Ballpark, Phoenix.
Phoenix's newest sports stadium sizzles with baseball fever when the championship Arizona Diamondbacks are in town. (See mention page 82)

See Vicinity map page 264

Phoenix

See Vicinity map pages 260 & 266

17

74

Cave Creek •

Carefree

60 *Surprise*

Youngtown •

Peoria •

Glendale •

Litchfield Park •

10

Goodyear

Buckeye

Tolleson

Tempe

60

Paradise Valley

Scottsdale

Mesa

Apache Junction

Gilbert

Fountain Hills

Native American arts and crafts, Phoenix. Purchase baskets, jewelry, Navajo rugs and other handicrafts at area shops.

See map pages 256 & 271

10 *Chandler*

Places included in this AAA Destination City:

David Moore
Scottsdale CVB

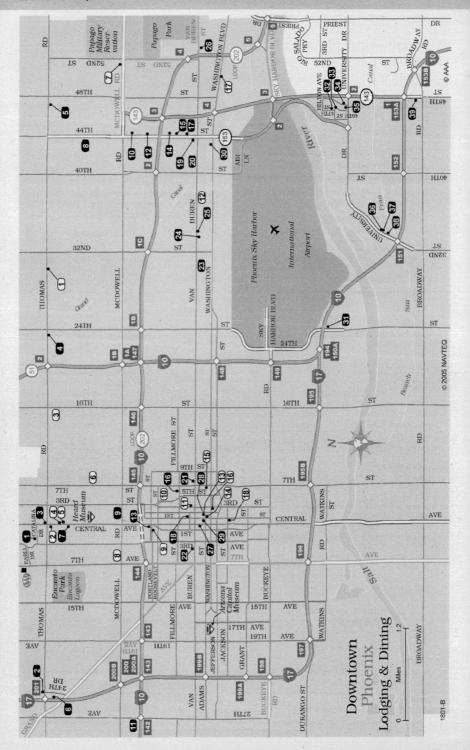

Downtown
Phoenix
Lodging & Dining

© 2005 NAVTEQ

1801-B

✈ Airport Accommodations

Spotter/Map Page Number	OA	PHOENIX SKY HARBOR INTERNATIONAL	Diamond Rating	Rate Range High Season	Listing Page
31 / p. 256	AAA	Best Western Airport Inn, 1 mi s of west entrance	◆◆	$99-$149 SAVE	276
33 / p. 256		Courtyard by Marriott Phoenix Airport, 0.5 mi s of east entrance	◆◆◆	$69-$239	276
30 / p. 256	AAA	Crowne Plaza Phoenix Airport, 0.7 mi n of east entrance	◆◆◆	$99-$159 SAVE	277
24 / p. 256	AAA	Days Inn-Airport, 1.5 mi n of east entrance	◆◆	$69-$99 SAVE	277
19 / p. 256	AAA	Doubletree Guest Suites-Phoenix, 1 mi n of east entrance	◆◆◆	$139-$249 SAVE	277
23 / p. 256	AAA	Econo Lodge Airport, exit east side to 153 N, 0.7 mi n, 1.7 mi w of airport	◆◆	$59-$89 SAVE	278
4 / p. 256	AAA	Embassy Suites Phoenix Airport at 24th St, 2.4 mi n of west entrance	◆◆◆	$129-$199 SAVE	278
10 / p. 256		Embassy Suites Phoenix Airport at 44th St, 1.5 mi n of east entrance	◆◆◆	$119-$229	278
8 / p. 256		Extended StayAmerica Phoenix/Airport/E Oak St,	◆◆	$90-$95	278
35 / p. 256	AAA	Fairfield Inn by Marriott Phoenix Airport, 0.5 mi s of east entrance	◆◆	$99-$139 SAVE	278
15 / p. 256		Hampton Inn Phoenix Airport North, 1.2 mi n of east airport entrance	◆◆◆	$139-$169	279
37 / p. 256		Hilton Garden Inn Phoenix Airport, 1.5 mi se of west entrance	◆◆◆	$209	279
32 / p. 256	AAA	Hilton Phoenix Airport, 0.5 mi s of east entrance	◆◆◆	$99-$249 SAVE	280
36 / p. 256		Holiday Inn Express Hotel & Suites, 1.5 mi se of west airport entrance	◆◆◆	Failed to provide	280
5 / p. 256	AAA	La Quinta Inn Phoenix Airport North, 2.3 mi n of east airport entrance	◆◆	$80-$120 SAVE	281
17 / p. 256		Radisson Hotel Phoenix Airport North, 1 mi n of east airport entrance	◆◆◆	$129-$239	281
38 / p. 256	AAA	Radisson Phoenix Airport Hotel, 3 mi se of west airport entrance; use I-10 E	◆◆◆	$179-$199 SAVE	281
20 / p. 256	AAA	Ramada Airport North, 1 mi n of east airport entrance	◆◆	$79-$100 SAVE	281
14 / p. 256		Residence Inn by Marriott Phoenix Airport,	◆◆◆	$109-$250	282
34 / p. 256	AAA	Sleep Inn Sky Harbor Airport, 0.5 mi s of east entrance	◆◆	$89-$169 SAVE	283
25 / p. 256	AAA	Super 8-Airport, 1.5 mi n of east airport entrance	◆◆	$59-$99 SAVE	283
14 / p. 271	AAA	AmeriSuites (Tempe/Phoenix Airport), 2.5 mi e of airport	◆◆	$109-$189 SAVE	357
39 / p. 256	AAA	Hampton Inn & Suites Phoenix Airport South/Tempe, 2.5 mi from east entrance	◆◆◆	$119-$179 SAVE	279
18 / p. 271		La Quinta Inn Phoenix (Sky Harbor South), 1 mi s of east airport entrance	◆◆◆	$125-$142	362
13 / p. 271	AAA	SpringHill Suites by Marriott Tempe Airport, 2.5 mi e of airport	◆◆◆	$80-$143 SAVE	364

Downtown Phoenix

This index helps you "spot" where approved accommodations and restaurants are located on the corresponding detailed maps. Lodging rate ranges are for comparison only and show the property's high season; rates are per night, unless only weekly (W) rates are available. Restaurant rate range is for dinner, unless only lunch (L) is served. Turn to the listing page for more detailed rate information and consult display ads for special promotions.

Spotter/Map Page Number	OA	DOWNTOWN PHOENIX - Lodgings	Diamond Rating	Rate Range High Season	Listing Page
1 / p. 256		Hampton Inn-Phoenix/Midtown - see color ad p 279	◆◆◆	$79-$159	279
2 / p. 256	AAA	Days Inn Phoenix I-17 & Thomas	◆◆	$69-$109 SAVE	277

Spotter/Map Page Number	OA	DOWNTOWN PHOENIX - Lodgings (continued)	Diamond Rating	Rate Range High Season	Listing Page
3 / p. 256	AAA	Hilton Suites-Phoenix	▽▽ ▽▽ ▽▽	$139-$249 SAVE	280
4 / p. 256	AAA	Embassy Suites Phoenix Airport at 24th St	▽▽ ▽▽ ▽▽	$129-$199 SAVE	278
5 / p. 256	AAA	La Quinta Inn Phoenix Airport North	▽▽ ▽▽	$80-$120 SAVE	281
6 / p. 256		La Quinta Inn Phoenix (Thomas Road) - see color ad p 295	▽▽ ▽▽ ▽▽	$91-$108	281
7 / p. 256	AAA	Wingate Inn Phoenix	▽▽ ▽▽ ▽▽	$99-$129 SAVE	283
8 / p. 256		Extended StayAmerica Phoenix/Airport/E Oak St	▽▽ ▽▽	$90-$95	278
9 / p. 256		Econo Lodge Inn & Suites-Downtown	▽▽ ▽▽	$69-$159	278
10 / p. 256		Embassy Suites Phoenix Airport at 44th St	▽▽ ▽▽ ▽▽	$119-$229	278
11 / p. 256	AAA	Comfort Inn I-10 West/Central	▽▽ ▽▽	$72 SAVE	276
12 / p. 256		Phoenix Airport Marriott	▽▽ ▽▽ ▽▽	$161-$246	281
13 / p. 256	AAA	Best Western Central Phoenix Inn	▽▽ ▽▽ ▽▽	$109-$229 SAVE	276
14 / p. 256		Residence Inn by Marriott Phoenix Airport	▽▽ ▽▽ ▽▽	$109-$250	282
15 / p. 256		Hampton Inn Phoenix Airport North	▽▽ ▽▽ ▽▽	$139-$169	279
16 / p. 256		Holiday Inn Express Hotel and Suites-Downtown/BankOne Ball Park	▽▽ ▽▽ ▽▽	$134-$149	280
17 / p. 256		Radisson Hotel Phoenix Airport North	▽▽ ▽▽ ▽▽	$129-$239	281
18 / p. 256	AAA	Ramada Inn Downtown Phoenix - see color ad p 282	▽▽ ▽▽ ▽▽	$89-$129 SAVE	282
19 / p. 256	AAA	Doubletree Guest Suites-Phoenix - see color ad p 277	▽▽ ▽▽ ▽▽	$139-$249 SAVE	277
20 / p. 256	AAA	Ramada Airport North	▽▽ ▽▽	$79-$100 SAVE	281
21 / p. 256	AAA	SpringHill Suites by Marriott	▽▽ ▽▽ ▽▽	$99-$169 SAVE	283
22 / p. 256	AAA	Budget Lodge Motel	▽▽ ▽▽	$45-$85 SAVE	276
23 / p. 256	AAA	Econo Lodge Airport	▽▽ ▽▽	$59-$89 SAVE	278
24 / p. 256	AAA	Days Inn-Airport	▽▽ ▽▽	$69-$99 SAVE	277
25 / p. 256	AAA	Super 8-Airport	▽▽ ▽▽	$59-$99 SAVE	283
26 / p. 256		Motel 6 Phoenix East #18	▽▽	$45-$61	281
27 / p. 256	AAA	Hotel San Carlos	▽▽ ▽▽ ▽▽	$119 SAVE	280
28 / p. 256	AAA	Hyatt Regency Phoenix	▽▽ ▽▽ ▽▽	$120-$245 SAVE	280
29 / p. 256	AAA	Wyndham Phoenix Hotel	▽▽ ▽▽ ▽▽	$169 SAVE	284
30 / p. 256	AAA	Crowne Plaza Phoenix Airport	▽▽ ▽▽ ▽▽	$99-$159 SAVE	277
31 / p. 256	AAA	Best Western Airport Inn - see color ad p 276	▽▽ ▽▽	$99-$149 SAVE	276
32 / p. 256	AAA	Hilton Phoenix Airport	▽▽ ▽▽ ▽▽	$99-$249 SAVE	280
33 / p. 256		Courtyard by Marriott Phoenix Airport	▽▽ ▽▽ ▽▽	$69-$239	276
34 / p. 256	AAA	Sleep Inn Sky Harbor Airport - see color ad p 283, p 302	▽▽ ▽▽	$89-$169 SAVE	283
35 / p. 256	AAA	Fairfield Inn by Marriott Phoenix Airport	▽▽ ▽▽	$99-$139 SAVE	278
36 / p. 256		Holiday Inn Express Hotel & Suites	▽▽ ▽▽ ▽▽	Failed to provide	280
37 / p. 256		Hilton Garden Inn Phoenix Airport	▽▽ ▽▽ ▽▽	$209	279
38 / p. 256	AAA	Radisson Phoenix Airport Hotel	▽▽ ▽▽ ▽▽	$179-$199 SAVE	281
39 / p. 256	AAA	Hampton Inn & Suites Phoenix Airport South/Tempe	▽▽ ▽▽ ▽▽	$119-$179 SAVE	279

Spotter/Map Page Number	OA	**DOWNTOWN PHOENIX** - Restaurants	Diamond Rating	Rate Range High Season	Listing Page
1 / p. 256		Bacchanal Restaurant	◆◆	$15-$22	284
2 / p. 256		Honey Bear's BBQ	◆	$4-$14	284
3 / p. 256	◆◆◆	**Barrio Cafe'**	◆◆	$12-$20	284
4 / p. 256		The Wild Thaiger	◆◆	$9-$14	285
5 / p. 256	◆◆◆	**Durant's**	◆◆◆	$21-$52	284
6 / p. 256		Coronado Cafe	◆◆	$9-$15	284
7 / p. 256		Indian Delhi Palace	◆◆	$7-$17	285
8 / p. 256		My Florist Cafe	◆◆◆	$6-$12	285
9 / p. 256		Portland's	◆◆◆	$9-$24	285
10 / p. 256		Fate	◆◆	$6-$13	284
11 / p. 256		Sam's Cafe at the Arizona Center	◆◆	$9-$16	285
12 / p. 256		Bill Johnson's Big Apple Restaurant	◆◆	$10-$16	284
13 / p. 256		Compass Restaurant	◆◆◆	$20-$30	284
14 / p. 256		Matador Restaurant	◆◆	$4-$25	285
15 / p. 256		Pizzeria Bianco	◆◆	$10-$20	285
16 / p. 256		Kincaid's Fish, Chop & Steakhouse	◆◆◆	$16-$26	285
17 / p. 256		Stockyards Restaurant & 1889 Saloon	◆◆	$16-$32	285
18 / p. 256		Alice Cooper'sTown	◆◆	$8-$15	284

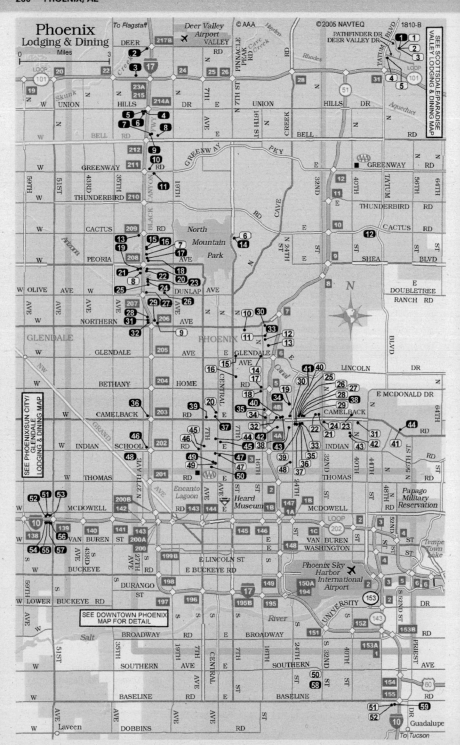

Phoenix
Lodging & Dining

© AAA

©2005 NAVTEQ

1810-B

Phoenix

This index helps you "spot" where approved accommodations and restaurants are located on the corresponding detailed maps. Lodging rate ranges are for comparison only and show the property's high season; rates are per night, unless only weekly (W) rates are available. Restaurant rate range is for dinner, unless only lunch (L) is served. Turn to the listing page for more detailed rate information and consult display ads for special promotions.

Spotter/Map Page Number	OA	PHOENIX - Lodgings	Diamond Rating	Rate Range High Season	Listing Page
1 / p. 260	AAA	JW Marriott Desert Ridge Resort & Spa	◇◇◇◇	$469-$599 SAVE	294
2 / p. 260		Days Inn-North Phoenix	◇◇	Failed to provide	290
3 / p. 260		Country Inn & Suites By Carlson	◇◇◇	$169-$219	290
4 / p. 260		Prime Hotel Phoenix North	◇◇	Failed to provide	298
5 / p. 260		Studio 6 Phoenix-Deer Valley #6030	◇◇	$63-$77	302
6 / p. 260	AAA	Sleep Inn Phoenix North - see color ad p 302	◇◇	$71-$143 SAVE	302
7 / p. 260	AAA	Best Western Bell Hotel - see color ad p 286	◇◇	$69-$139 SAVE	286
8 / p. 260		Motel 6 Phoenix-North #344	◇	$47-$63	296
9 / p. 260	AAA	Fairfield Inn by Marriott Phoenix North	◇◇	$109-$119 SAVE	292
10 / p. 260		La Quinta Inn Phoenix (North) - see color ad p 295	◇◇◇	$99-$116	294
11 / p. 260	AAA	Embassy Suites Phoenix North - see color ad p 291	◇◇◇	$159-$232 SAVE	291
12 / p. 260		Embassy Suites Phoenix-Scottsdale-A Golf Resort	◇◇◇	Failed to provide	291
13 / p. 260	AAA	Ramada Plaza Hotel and Suites - see color ad p 299	◇◇	$79-$130 SAVE	298
14 / p. 260	AAA	Pointe Hilton Tapatio Cliffs Resort	◇◇◇	$135-$299 SAVE	297
15 / p. 260		Candlewood Suites	◇◇	$66-$199	288
16 / p. 260		Extended Stay America Phoenix-Metro Center	◇◇	$75-$80	291
17 / p. 260	AAA	AmeriSuites (Phoenix/Metro Center)	◇◇◇	$79-$179 SAVE	286
18 / p. 260	AAA	Crowne Plaza Phoenix - see color ad p 290	◇◇◇	$99-$169 SAVE	290
19 / p. 260	AAA	Premier Inns	◇	$44-$109 SAVE	298
20 / p. 260	AAA	Homewood Suites Hotel - see color ad p 293	◇◇◇	$129-$159 SAVE	294
21 / p. 260		Four Points by Sheraton Phoenix Metrocenter	◇◇◇	Failed to provide	292
22 / p. 260		Comfort Suites by Choice Hotels	◇◇◇	$99-$149	289
23 / p. 260		MainStay Suites	◇◇◇	$89-$139	296
24 / p. 260		SpringHill Suites by Marriott-Metro Center	◇◇◇	$119-$140	302
25 / p. 260		TownePlace Suites by Marriott	◇◇	$140-$150	304
26 / p. 260		Homestead Studio Suites Hotel-Phoenix North/Metro Center	◇◇	$70-$75	294
27 / p. 260	AAA	Sheraton Crescent Hotel - see color ad p 301	◇◇◇	$119-$259 SAVE	301
28 / p. 260	AAA	Residence Inn by Marriott - see color ad p 300	◇◇◇	$122 SAVE	300
29 / p. 260	AAA	Best Western Phoenix I-17 MetroCenter Inn - see color ad p 288	◇◇	$79-$99 SAVE	288
30 / p. 260	AAA	Best Western InnSuites Hotel Phoenix Northern/Airport - see color ad p 287	◇◇◇	$89-$139 SAVE	287
31 / p. 260	AAA	Super 8 Motel-Phoenix Metro North	◇◇	$36-$85 SAVE	303
32 / p. 260		Motel 6 Phoenix-Northern Ave #1185	◇	$41-$57	296
33 / p. 260	AAA	Pointe Hilton Squaw Peak Resort	◇◇◇	$135-$299 SAVE	297
34 / p. 260	AAA	Arizona Biltmore Resort & Spa	◇◇◇	$445-$1845 SAVE	286

Spotter/Map Page Number	OA	PHOENIX - Lodgings (continued)	Diamond Rating	Rate Range High Season	Listing Page
35 / p. 260		Extended Stay Deluxe Phoenix-Biltmore	◆◆◆	$120-$125	292
36 / p. 260		Comfort Inn Black Canyon - see color ad p 289	◆◆	$79-$129	289
37 / p. 260		Maricopa Manor Bed & Breakfast Inn	◆◆◆	$159-$219	296
38 / p. 260		Embassy Suites Phoenix-Biltmore	◆◆◆	$199-$309	290
39 / p. 260		Red Roof Inn-Camelback	◆◆	$46-$51	300
40 / p. 260		Camelback Courtyard by Marriott	◆◆◆	$149-$219	288
41 / p. 260		The Ritz-Carlton, Phoenix	◆◆◆◆	$329-$519	300
42 / p. 260		Homewood Suites by Hilton	◆◆◆	$169-$219	294
43 / p. 260	AAA	**Phoenix Inn Suites** - see color ad p 297	◆◆◆	$109 [SAVE]	296
44 / p. 260	AAA	**Royal Palms Resort and Spa**	◆◆◆◆	$325 [SAVE]	301
45 / p. 260	AAA	**Holiday Inn Midtown Phoenix** - see color ad p 293	◆◆◆	$89-$139 [SAVE]	293
46 / p. 260		Motel 6 Phoenix-Black Canyon #1304	◆	$41-$57	296
47 / p. 260		Hilton Garden Inn	◆◆◆	$159	292
48 / p. 260		Comfort Suites Conference Center	◆◆	Failed to provide	290
49 / p. 260		Sunshine Hotel & Suites	◆◆	Failed to provide	303
50 / p. 260		Extended StayDeluxe (Phoenix/Midtown)	◆◆◆	$95-$100	292
51 / p. 260		Red Roof Inn	◆◆	$58-$75	298
52 / p. 260		Motel 6 Phoenix West #696	◆	$51-$67	296
53 / p. 260	AAA	**Holiday Inn West**	◆◆◆	$129 [SAVE]	293
54 / p. 260		Super 8 Motel-Phoenix	◆◆	$69-$199	303
55 / p. 260	AAA	**Phoenix West Inn**	◆◆	$69-$119 [SAVE]	297
56 / p. 260		Travelers Inn	◆◆	$49	304
57 / p. 260	AAA	**Hampton Inn Phoenix I-10 West** - see color ad p 279	◆◆◆	$69-$179 [SAVE]	292
58 / p. 260		The Legacy Golf Resort - see color ad p 295	◆◆◆	$139-$299	295
59 / p. 260	AAA	**Pointe South Mountain Resort**	◆◆◆◆	$399-$899 [SAVE]	297
		PHOENIX - Restaurants			
1 / p. 260		Ristorante Tuscany	◆◆◆◆	$16-$32	308
2 / p. 260		Meritage Steakhouse	◆◆◆	$16-$36	307
3 / p. 260	AAA	**Roy's Desert Ridge**	◆◆◆	$22-$28	308
4 / p. 260		Malee's Thai Bistro	◆◆	$10-$19	307
5 / p. 260		Salute Ristorante Italiano	◆◆◆	$14-$23	309
6 / p. 260		Different Pointe of View	◆◆◆◆	$28-$40	305
7 / p. 260		Pappadeaux Seafood Kitchen	◆◆◆	$13-$27	308
8 / p. 260		El Torito Grill	◆◆	$7-$15	305
9 / p. 260		Prickly Pear Deli & Winery	◆	$6-$7	308
10 / p. 260		Carlos O'Brien's Mexican Restaurant	◆	$8-$15	305
11 / p. 260		Lantana Grille	◆◆◆	$14-$26	306
12 / p. 260		Tutti Santi Ristorante	◆◆◆	$10-$18	309
13 / p. 260		Aunt Chilada's Hideaway	◆◆	$7-$16	304
14 / p. 260		Convivo Bistro	◆◆◆	$19-$25	305

Spotter/Map Page Number	OA	PHOENIX - Restaurants (continued)	Diamond Rating	Rate Range High Season	Listing Page
⑮ / p. 260		Sauce	◆◆	$5-$9	309
⑯ / p. 260		Christo's	◆◆	$11-$26	305
⑰ / p. 260		Richardson's	◆◆	$10-$26	308
⑱ / p. 260		Phoenix City Grille	◆◆	$12-$24	308
⑲ / p. 260		Wright's	◆◆◆◆	$21-$32	310
⑳ / p. 260		Panino on Central	◆◆◆	$13-$25	307
㉑ / p. 260		Zen 32	◆◆	$10-$20	310
㉒ / p. 260		Keegan's Grill	◆◆	$8-$15	306
㉓ / p. 260		Vincent on Camelback	◆◆◆	$29-$33	309
㉔ / p. 260		Tarbell's	◆◆◆	$14-$34	309
㉕ / p. 260		The Capital Grille	◆◆◆	$18-$33	305
㉖ / p. 260		The Bamboo Club	◆◆	$9-$22	304
㉗ / p. 260		Christopher's Fermier Brasserie	◆◆◆	$30-$50	305
㉘ / p. 260		Sam's Cafe	◆◆	$11-$20	309
㉙ / p. 260		Omaha Steakhouse	◆◆	$16-$32	307
㉚ / p. 260		Eddie Matney's	◆◆◆	$17-$29	305
㉛ / p. 260		Havana Cafe	◆◆	$10-$23	306
㉜ / p. 260		Greekfest	◆◆◆	$10-$30	306
㉝ / p. 260		Marco Polo Supper Club	◆◆◆	$15-$35	307
㉞ / p. 260		The Fish Market & Top of The Market	◆◆	$9-$34	305
㉟ / p. 260		Morton's of Chicago	◆◆◆	$20-$34	307
㊱ / p. 260		Nixon's	◆◆	$7-$12	307
㊲ / p. 260		Franco's Italian Caffe	◆◆◆	$11-$24	306
㊳ / p. 260		Tucchetti	◆◆	$10-$18	309
㊴ / p. 260		McCormick & Schmick's Seafood Restaurant	◆◆◆	$8-$27	307
㊵ / p. 260		Bistro 24	◆◆◆	$20-$35	304
㊶ / p. 260		T. Cook's	◆◆◆◆	$24-$32	309
㊷ / p. 260		Pronto Ristorante	◆◆	$9-$24	308
㊸ / p. 260		Postino Winecafe	◆◆	$8-$10	308
㊹ / p. 260		Pane Bianco	◆	$8-$10(L)	307
㊺ / p. 260	◬	**The Roman Table**	◆◆	$11-$27	308
㊻ / p. 260		The Fry Bread House	◆	$4-$7	306
㊼ / p. 260		Macayo's Mexican Kitchen Central	◆◆	$8-$14	306
㊽ / p. 260		Asi es La Vida - Such Is Life	◆◆	$7-$25	304
㊾ / p. 260		Alexis Grill	◆◆◆	$11-$25	304
㊿ / p. 260	◬	**Farm Kitchen at The Farm at South Mountain**	◆	$5-$9(L)	305
51 / p. 260		Rustler's Rooste	◆◆	$13-$31	309
52 / p. 260		Latitude 30	◆◆◆	$17-$29	306

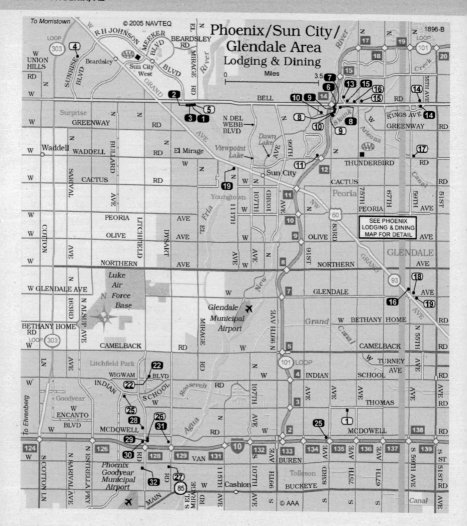

Phoenix Sun City/Glendale Area

This index helps you "spot" where approved accommodations and restaurants are located on the corresponding detailed maps. Lodging rate ranges are for comparison only and show the property's high season; rates are per night, unless only weekly (W) rates are available. Restaurant rate range is for dinner, unless only lunch (L) is served. Turn to the listing page for more detailed rate information and consult display ads for special promotions.

Spotter/Map Page Number	OA	SURPRISE - Lodgings	Diamond Rating	Rate Range High Season	Listing Page
1 / above		Days Inn & Suites	◆◆	$85-$175	355
2 / above	AAA	**Windmill Suites at Sun City West**	◆◆◆	$115-$157 SAVE	355
3 / above		Quality Inn & Suites	◆◆	$79-$129	355
		SURPRISE - Restaurants			
4 / above		Dillon's Grand	◆◆	$7-$18	355
5 / above		Desert Palms Restaurant	◆	$5-$14	355

Spotter/Map Page Number	OA	PEORIA - Lodgings	Diamond Rating	Rate Range High Season	Listing Page
6 / p. 264		Comfort Suites by Choice Hotels/Sports Complex	◈◈	$79-$169	330
7 / p. 264		Residence Inn by Marriott	◈◈◈	$90-$210	331
8 / p. 264		La Quinta Inn & Suites Phoenix (West/Peoria) - see color ad p 295	◈◈◈	$163-$180	331
9 / p. 264	⟨AAA⟩	**Hampton Inn**	◈◈◈	$69-$149 [SAVE]	331
10 / p. 264		Holiday Inn Express Hotel & Suites	◈◈◈	$129-$179	331
		PEORIA - Restaurants			
⑧ / p. 264		P.F. Chang's China Bistro	◈◈◈	$8-$18	331
⑨ / p. 264		Elephant Bar Restaurant	◈◈	$6-$15	331
⑩ / p. 264		Abuelo's Mexican Food Embassy	◈◈	$8-$16	331
⑪ / p. 264		Dillon's Restaurant	◈◈	$8-$17	331
		GLENDALE - Lodgings			
13 / p. 264	⟨AAA⟩	**Ramada Limited**	◈◈	$149 [SAVE]	320
14 / p. 264	⟨AAA⟩	**Quality Inn & Suites at Talavi - see color ad p 319**	◈◈◈	$79-$159 [SAVE]	319
15 / p. 264	⟨AAA⟩	**SpringHill Suites by Marriott**	◈◈◈	$159-$179 [SAVE]	320
16 / p. 264	⟨AAA⟩	**Best Western Phoenix-Glendale - see color ad p 319**	◈◈	$89-$119 [SAVE]	319
		GLENDALE - Restaurants			
⑭ / p. 264		Thee Pitt's "Again"	◈◈	$6-$20	320
⑮ / p. 264		Bill Johnson's Big Apple	◈◈	$10-$16	320
⑯ / p. 264		Rock Bottom Restaurant & Brewery	◈◈	$9-$20	320
⑰ / p. 264		Bistro di Napoli	◈◈	$9-$15	320
⑱ / p. 264		Aunt Pitty Pat's Kitchen	◈◈	$5-$8(L)	320
⑲ / p. 264		Haus Murphy's	◈◈	$9-$28	320
		YOUNGTOWN - Lodgings			
19 / p. 264	⟨AAA⟩	**Best Western Inn & Suites of Sun City - see color ad p 367**	◈◈	$99-$130 [SAVE]	367
		LITCHFIELD PARK - Lodgings			
22 / p. 264	⟨AAA⟩	**The Wigwam Resort - see color ad p 322**	◈◈◈◈	$549-$669 [SAVE]	322
		LITCHFIELD PARK - Restaurant			
㉒ / p. 264		Arizona Kitchen	◈◈◈◈	$20-$32	322
		TOLLESON - Lodgings			
25 / p. 264		Comfort Suites	◈◈	$99-$119	367
		GOODYEAR - Lodgings			
28 / p. 264		Hampton Inn & Suites	◈◈◈	$139-$179	321
29 / p. 264		Holiday Inn Express	◈◈◈	$139-$199	321
30 / p. 264		Residence Inn by Marriott	◈◈◈	$169-$299	321
31 / p. 264		Wingate Inn & Suites	◈◈◈	$139-$169	321
32 / p. 264		Best Western Phoenix Goodyear Inn	◈◈	$109-$149	320
		GOODYEAR - Restaurants			
㉕ / p. 264		Bella Luna Ristorante	◈◈	$7-$33	321
㉖ / p. 264		Macayo's Goodyear	◈◈	$8-$14	321
㉗ / p. 264		Bill Johnson's Big Apple Restaurant	◈◈	$10-$16	321
		PHOENIX - Restaurant			
① / p. 264		Macayo's Desert Sky	◈◈	$8-$14	306

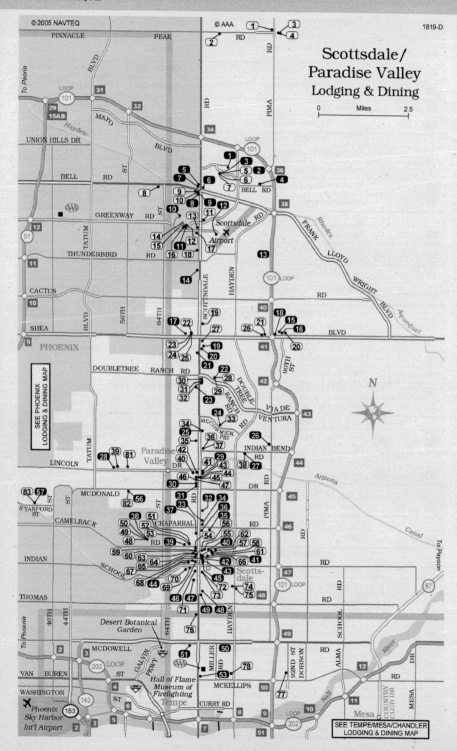

Scottsdale/
Paradise Valley
Lodging & Dining

✈ Airport Accommodations

Spotter/Map Page Number	OA	SCOTTSDALE	Diamond Rating	Rate Range High Season	Listing Page
12 / p. 266		Best Western Scottsdale Airpark Suites, at airport	◈◈◈	$99-$179	332
14 / p. 266		Fairfield Inn North Scottsdale, 1.5 mi sw of airport	◈◈	Failed to provide	336

Scottsdale/Paradise Valley and Vicinity

This index helps you "spot" where approved accommodations and restaurants are located on the corresponding detailed maps. Lodging rate ranges are for comparison only and show the property's high season; rates are per night, unless only weekly (W) rates are available. Restaurant rate range is for dinner, unless only lunch (L) is served. Turn to the listing page for more detailed rate information and consult display ads for special promotions.

Spotter/Map Page Number	OA	SCOTTSDALE - Lodgings	Diamond Rating	Rate Range High Season	Listing Page
1 / p. 266		Scottsdale Villa Mirage	◈◈◈	$158-$293	345
2 / p. 266		Hilton Garden Inn North	◈◈◈	$139-$219	338
3 / p. 266	AAA	**The Fairmont Scottsdale Princess**	◈◈◈◈◈	$369-$499 SAVE	337
4 / p. 266	AAA	**Scottsdale Marriott at McDowell Mountains**	◈◈◈◈	$249-$329 SAVE	344
5 / p. 266		SpringHill Suites by Marriott-Scottsdale North	◈◈◈	$199-$249	345
6 / p. 266		Residence Inn Scottsdale North	◈◈◈	$169-$239	343
7 / p. 266		Courtyard By Marriott/Scottsdale North	◈◈◈	Failed to provide	335
8 / p. 266	AAA	**Sleep Inn**	◈◈	$89-$139 SAVE	345
9 / p. 266	AAA	**Hampton Inn & Suites**	◈◈◈	$154-$204 SAVE	338
10 / p. 266		The Westin Kierland Villas	◈◈◈	$599	346
11 / p. 266	AAA	**The Westin Kierland Resort & Spa**	◈◈◈◈	$299-$569 SAVE	346
12 / p. 266		Best Western Scottsdale Airpark Suites - see color ad p 333	◈◈◈	$99-$179	332
13 / p. 266	AAA	**Wingate Inn & Suites** - see color ad p 346	◈◈◈	$150-$250 SAVE	346
14 / p. 266		Fairfield Inn North Scottsdale	◈◈	Failed to provide	336
15 / p. 266		Country Inn & Suites By Carlson	◈◈◈	$125-$155	335
16 / p. 266		TownePlace Suites by Marriott	◈◈	$99-$139	345
17 / p. 266		Extended Stay Deluxe Phoenix-Scottsdale	◈◈◈	$110-$115	336
18 / p. 266	AAA	**La Quinta Inn & Suites Phoenix (Scottsdale)** - see color ad p 295	◈◈◈	$141-$158 SAVE	340
19 / p. 266	AAA	**Comfort Inn of Scottsdale**	◈◈	$109-$129 SAVE	334
20 / p. 266	AAA	**Hampton Inn Scottsdale**	◈◈	$109-$119 SAVE	338
21 / p. 266		Homewood Suites by Hilton/Scottsdale	◈◈◈	Failed to provide	339
22 / p. 266	AAA	**Hyatt Regency Scottsdale Resort at Gainey Ranch**	◈◈◈◈	$330-$450 SAVE	340
23 / p. 266		Gainey Suites Hotel - see color ad p 337	◈◈◈	$219-$359 SAVE	337
24 / p. 266	AAA	**Scottsdale Resort & Conference Center -** see color ad p 344	◈◈◈◈	$199-$279 SAVE	345
25 / p. 266	AAA	**Millennium Resort Scottsdale, McCormick Ranch** - see color ad p 332	◈◈◈	$129-$279 SAVE	341
26 / p. 266	AAA	**The Inn at Pima, A Condominium Suite Hotel** - see color ad p 340	◈◈	$69-$189 SAVE	340
27 / p. 266		Scottsdale Resort & Athletic Club	◈◈◈	$249-$549	344
28 / p. 266	AAA	**Camelback Inn, A JW Marriott Resort & Spa**	◈◈◈◈◈	$299-$499 SAVE	334

Spotter/Map Page Number	OA	SCOTTSDALE - Lodgings (continued)	Diamond Rating	Rate Range High Season	Listing Page
29 / p. 266	AAA	Hilton Scottsdale Resort & Villas	◆◆◆◆	$139-$359 [SAVE]	339
30 / p. 266	AAA	Renaissance Scottsdale Resort - see color ad p 343	◆◆◆	$269-$369 [SAVE]	342
31 / p. 266	AAA	Residence Inn by Marriott, Scottsdale/Paradise Valley	◆◆◆	$139-$309 [SAVE]	343
32 / p. 266	AAA	DoubleTree Paradise Valley Resort-Scottsdale - see color ad p 336	◆◆◆	$169-$289 [SAVE]	336
33 / p. 266		Fairfield Inn-Downtown Scottsdale	◆◆	$119-$149	336
34 / p. 266	AAA	Chaparral Suites Resort - see color ad p 334	◆◆◆	$199-$219 [SAVE]	334
35 / p. 266		Hotel Waterfront Ivy	◆◆	$149-$209	339
36 / p. 266		Caleo Resort & Spa	◆◆◆	$309-$629	333
37 / p. 266	AAA	Days Inn Scottsdale Fashion Square - see color ad p 335	◆◆	$119-$189 [SAVE]	335
38 / p. 266	AAA	The Phoenician - see color ad p 341	◆◆◆◆◆	$675-$775 [SAVE]	341
39 / p. 266		Motel 6 Scottsdale #29	◆	$62-$78	341
40 / p. 266		Hampton Inn-Oldtown/Fashion Square Scottsdale - see color ad p 338	◆◆◆	$119-$179	338
41 / p. 266		Summerfield Suites by Wyndham-Scottsdale	◆◆◆	$179-$329	345
42 / p. 266	AAA	AmeriSuites (Scottsdale/Old Town)	◆◆◆	$129-$199 [SAVE]	332
43 / p. 266		Marriott Suites Scottsdale	◆◆◆	$209-$319	340
44 / p. 266		Ramada Limited Scottsdale	◆◆	Failed to provide	342
45 / p. 266		Hilton Garden Inn Scottsdale	◆◆◆	Failed to provide	338
46 / p. 266	AAA	Rodeway Inn of Scottsdale	◆◆	$69-$109 [SAVE]	343
47 / p. 266		Homestead Studio Suites Hotel-Phoenix-Scottsdale	◆◆	$90-$95	339
48 / p. 266		Comfort Suites by Choice Hotels-Old Town	◆◆	$130-$170	335
49 / p. 266	AAA	Holiday Inn Express Hotel & Suites-Scottsdale	◆◆◆	$109-$189 [SAVE]	339
50 / p. 266		3 Palms Resort Oasis	[fyi]	Failed to provide	332
51 / p. 266	AAA	Best Western Papago Inn & Resort - see color ad p 333	◆◆◆	$99-$159 [SAVE]	332
52 / p. 266	AAA	Hospitality Suite Resort	◆◆	$69-$129 [SAVE]	339
		SCOTTSDALE - Restaurants			
1 / p. 266		Michael's at the Citadel	◆◆◆◆	$19-$29	351
2 / p. 266		Thai Pan	◆◆	$8-$12	354
3 / p. 266		Mastro's Steakhouse	◆◆◆	$22-$40	351
4 / p. 266	AAA	Pane E Vino	◆◆◆	$18-$32	352
5 / p. 266		The Grill	◆◆	$24-$48	349
6 / p. 266		La Hacienda	◆◆◆◆	$22-$36	350
7 / p. 266	AAA	Marquesa	◆◆◆◆◆	$35-$46	351
8 / p. 266		Havana Patio Cafe	◆◆	$10-$18	350
9 / p. 266		The Coyote Grill	◆◆◆	$15-$25	349
10 / p. 266		Carlos O'Brien's Mexican Restaurant	◆◆	$8-$15	348
11 / p. 266		Barcelona	◆◆◆	$12-$30	347

Spotter/Map Page Number	OA	SCOTTSDALE - Restaurants (continued)	Diamond Rating	Rate Range High Season	Listing Page
12 / p. 266		NoRTH	◈◈◈	$11-$28	351
13 / p. 266		P.F. Chang's China Bistro at Kierland Commons	◈◈◈	$8-$18	352
14 / p. 266		Nellie Cashman's Monday Club Cafe'	◈◈◈	$17-$28	351
15 / p. 266		Deseo	◈◈◈◈	$27-$40	349
16 / p. 266		Brittlebush Bar & Grill	◈◈◈	$10-$12	348
17 / p. 266		Zinc Bistro	◈◈◈	$17-$29	355
18 / p. 266		Sapporo	◈◈◈	$15-$45	353
19 / p. 266		Macayo's Mexican Kitchen	◈◈	$8-$14	350
20 / p. 266		Jade Palace Chinese Restaurant	◈◈	$10-$22	350
21 / p. 266		Rock Bottom Brewery & Restaurant	◈◈	$9-$20	353
22 / p. 266		Claim Jumper	◈◈◈	$10-$21	348
23 / p. 266		Maria's When in Naples	◈◈◈	$14-$27	351
24 / p. 266		Eli's American Grille	◈◈	$7-$30	349
25 / p. 266		Sushi On Shea	◈◈	$9-$28	354
26 / p. 266		The Bamboo Club	◈◈	$9-$23	347
27 / p. 266		Oregano's Pizza Bistro	◈◈	$7-$22	352
28 / p. 266		Vu	◈◈◈◈	$27-$38	354
29 / p. 266		Sandolo Ristorante	◈◈	$12-$24	353
30 / p. 266		Bloom	◈◈◈	$15-$39	347
31 / p. 266		Garduno's Margarita Factory	◈◈	$10-$22	349
32 / p. 266		Thaifoon	◈◈◈	$8-$17	354
33 / p. 266		Palm Court	◈◈◈◈	$22-$34	352
34 / p. 266		Pinon Grill - see color ad p 332	◈◈◈	$18-$26	352
35 / p. 266		Remington's	◈◈◈	$19-$30	353
36 / p. 266		Roy's Scottsdale	◈◈◈	$17-$29	353
37 / p. 266		Ruth's Chris Steak House	◈◈◈	$21-$38	353
38 / p. 266		Eurasia Bistro & Bar	◈◈	$10-$24	349
39 / p. 266		The Chaparral	◈◈◈◈	$21-$35	348
40 / p. 266		The Other Place	◈◈	$15-$30	352
41 / p. 266		Fleming's Prime Steakhouse & Wine Bar	◈◈◈	$19-$34	349
42 / p. 266		The Quilted Bear	◈◈	$12-$25	352
43 / p. 266		Rancho Pinot	◈◈◈	$18-$29	352
44 / p. 266		Restaurant Hapa	◈◈◈	$18-$40	353
45 / p. 266		El Torito Grill	◈◈	$7-$15	349
46 / p. 266	◈◈◈	**Thai Thai Restaurant**	◈◈◈	$9-$15	354
47 / p. 266		Mancuso's Restaurant	◈◈◈	$20-$30	350
48 / p. 266	◈◈◈	**Mary Elaine's**	◈◈◈◈◈	$50-$60	351
49 / p. 266		Windows on the Green	◈◈◈	$20-$32	354
50 / p. 266	◈◈◈	**The Terrace Dining Room**	◈◈◈◈	$22-$40	354

Spotter/Map Page Number	OA	SCOTTSDALE - Restaurants (continued)	Diamond Rating	Rate Range High Season	Listing Page
51 / p. 266		La Madeleine French Bakery	◈	$7-$13	350
52 / p. 266		P.F. Chang's China Bistro	◈◈◈	$8-$18	352
53 / p. 266		Kona Grill	◈◈◈	$9-$24	350
54 / p. 266		Roaring Fork	◈◈◈	$16-$30	353
55 / p. 266		Suede	◈◈◈	$14-$24	354
56 / p. 266		Buckets	◈◈	$8-$19	348
57 / p. 266		Pasta Brioni	◈◈	$11-$65	352
58 / p. 266		Tequila Grill	◈◈	$12-$29	354
59 / p. 266		Ibiza Cafe & Wine Bar	◈◈	$8-$16	350
60 / p. 266		The Breakfast Club	◈◈	$6-$10(L)	348
61 / p. 266		Drift	◈◈	$7-$18	349
62 / p. 266		Bravo Bistro	◈◈	$15-$32	348
63 / p. 266		Cowboy Ciao Restaurant	◈◈◈	$14-$32	349
64 / p. 266		6th Avenue Bistrot	◈◈	$16-$25	347
65 / p. 266		Sea Saw	◈◈◈	$11-$22	354
66 / p. 266		Blue Agave Mexican Cantina	◈◈	$8-$13	348
67 / p. 266		Medizona	◈◈◈	$21-$29	351
68 / p. 266		Cafe' Blue	◈◈◈	$16-$32	348
69 / p. 266		Arcadia Farms	◈◈	$11-$14(L)	347
70 / p. 266		Old Town Tortilla Factory	◈◈	$12-$36	351
71 / p. 266		Malee's Thai On Main	◈◈	$11-$19	350
72 / p. 266		Pink Pony	◈◈	$10-$25	352
73 / p. 266		RA Sushi Bar Restaurant	◈◈	$11-$15	353
74 / p. 266		Twisted Vine	◈	$5-$8(L)	354
75 / p. 266		Carlsbad Tavern	◈◈	$10-$20	348
76 / p. 266		Los Sombreros	◈◈	$9-$14	350
77 / p. 266		Cholla	◈◈◈	$23-$30	348
78 / p. 266	ⒶⒶⒶ	**The Salt Cellar Restaurant**	◈◈	$24-$30	353
		PARADISE VALLEY - Lodgings			
56 / p. 266	ⒶⒶⒶ	**Sanctuary on Camelback Mountain**	◈◈◈◈	$165-$645 [SAVE]	330
57 / p. 266		Hermosa Inn	◈◈◈	Failed to provide	330
		PARADISE VALLEY - Restaurants			
81 / p. 266		El Chorro Lodge Restaurant	◈◈◈	$16-$62	330
82 / p. 266		Elements	◈◈◈◈	$18-$36	330
83 / p. 266		Lon's at the Hermosa	◈◈◈	$23-$35	330

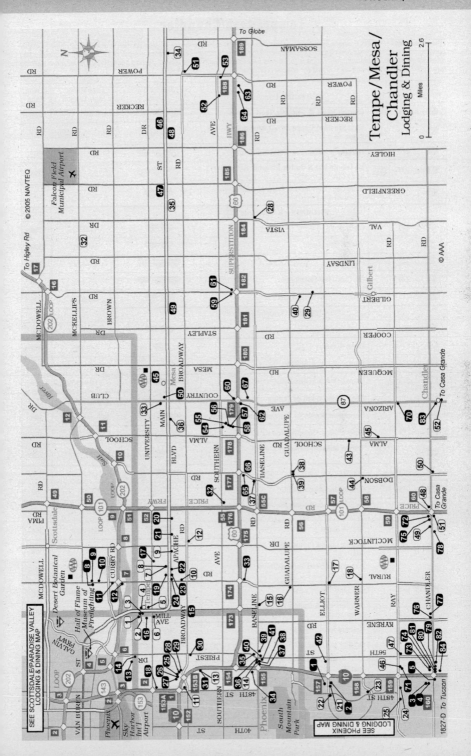

Tempe/Mesa/
Chandler
Lodging & Dining

© 2005 NAVTEQ

© AAA

1827-D

Tempe/Mesa/Chandler

This index helps you "spot" where approved accommodations and restaurants are located on the corresponding detailed maps. Lodging rate ranges are for comparison only and show the property's high season; rates are per night, unless only weekly (W) rates are available. Restaurant rate range is for dinner, unless only lunch (L) is served. Turn to the listing page for more detailed rate information and consult display ads for special promotions.

Spotter/Map Page Number	OA	PHOENIX - Lodgings	Diamond Rating	Rate Range High Season	Listing Page
1 / p. 271	AAA	Clarion Hotel @ Phoenix Tech Center	▽▽▽	$99-$159 SAVE	289
2 / p. 271	AAA	Best Western Grace Inn At Ahwatukee - see color ad p 287	▽▽	$109-$139	287
3 / p. 271	AAA	Holiday Inn Express Hotel & Suites	▽▽▽	$109-$119 SAVE	292
4 / p. 271	AAA	La Quinta Inn & Suites Phoenix (Chandler) - see color ad p 295	▽▽▽	$119-$136 SAVE	294
5 / p. 271		Extended StayAmerica Pheonix-Chandler-E Chandler Blvd	▽▽	$85-$90	291
		PHOENIX - Restaurants			
21 / p. 271		Caffe Boa	▽▽	$6-$23	304
22 / p. 271		Venice Restorante	▽▽	$10-$20	309
23 / p. 271		Ruffino	▽▽	$9-$21	308
24 / p. 271		RA Sushi-Bar-Restaurant	▽▽▽	$8-$18	308
25 / p. 271		Keegan's Grill & Taproom	▽▽	$8-$15	306
		TEMPE - Lodgings			
8 / p. 271		Executive Suites Extended Stay	▽▽	$89-$129	359
9 / p. 271		Motel 6 #1315	▽	$49-$65	362
10 / p. 271	AAA	Hampton Inn & Suites	▽▽▽	$139-$159 SAVE	359
11 / p. 271		Country Inn & Suites By Carlson	▽▽▽	$129-$159	357
12 / p. 271	AAA	Best Western Inn of Tempe	▽▽▽	$99-$129 SAVE	357
13 / p. 271	AAA	SpringHill Suites by Marriott Tempe Airport	▽▽▽	$80-$143 SAVE	364
14 / p. 271	AAA	AmeriSuites (Tempe/Phoenix Airport)	▽▽▽	$109-$189 SAVE	357
15 / p. 271	AAA	Tempe Mission Palms Hotel - see color ad p 303	▽▽▽	$219 SAVE	365
16 / p. 271		Courtyard by Marriott-Downtown Tempe	▽▽▽	$119-$208	358
17 / p. 271	AAA	Quality Inn Airport/ASU	▽▽	$94-$199 SAVE	362
18 / p. 271		La Quinta Inn Phoenix (Sky Harbor South) - see color ad p 295	▽▽▽	$125-$142	362
19 / p. 271		Tempe Super 8	▽▽	$59-$99	365
20 / p. 271	AAA	Econo Lodge/Tempe ASU - see color ad p 358	▽	$62-$72 SAVE	359
21 / p. 271	AAA	Ramada Limited Tempe-University - see color ad p 363	▽▽	$49-$99 SAVE	363
22 / p. 271		Days Inn Tempe/ASU	▽▽	Failed to provide	358
23 / p. 271	AAA	Comfort Inn & Suites Tempe/ASU - see color ad p 356	▽▽▽	$69-$129 SAVE	357
24 / p. 271	AAA	Holiday Inn - see color ad p 360	▽▽	$95-$116 SAVE	360
25 / p. 271	AAA	Quality Inn Tempe/Airport - see color ad p 362	▽▽	$99-$139 SAVE	363
26 / p. 271		Red Roof Inn Phoenix Airport	▽▽	$59-$75	364
27 / p. 271		Homestead Studio Suites Hotel-Phoenix/Airport/Tempe	▽▽▽	$90-$95	361
28 / p. 271	AAA	Sheraton Phoenix Airport Hotel	▽▽▽	$209-$239 SAVE	364
29 / p. 271		Comfort Suites Airport	▽▽	$99-$159	357

Spotter/Map Page Number	OA	TEMPE - Lodgings (continued)	Diamond Rating	Rate Range High Season	Listing Page
30 / p. 271	AAA	Fiesta Inn Resort - see color ad p 359	▽▽▽	$145-$165 SAVE	359
31 / p. 271	AAA	Wyndham Buttes Resort	▽▽▽	$239 SAVE	365
32 / p. 271		Hawthorn Suites - Tempe - see color ad p 360	▽▽▽	$89-$159	360
33 / p. 271		Embassy Suites Phoenix-Tempe	▽▽▽	$99-$259	359
34 / p. 271		Studio 6 Extended Stay #6031	▽▽	$63-$77	364
35 / p. 271		Residence Inn by Marriott	▽▽▽	$119-$229	364
36 / p. 271	AAA	AmeriSuites (Tempe/Arizona Mills)	▽▽▽	$79-$179 SAVE	356
37 / p. 271	AAA	Ramada Limited - see color ad p 363	▽▽	$64-$69 SAVE	363
38 / p. 271	AAA	InnSuites Hotels & Suites Tempe/Phoenix Airport - see color ad p 361	▽▽▽	$89-$119 SAVE	362
39 / p. 271		Candlewood Suites	▽▽▽	$86-$120	357
40 / p. 271		SpringHill Suites by Marriott	▽▽▽	Failed to provide	364
41 / p. 271		Holiday Inn Express/Tempe - see color ad p 361	▽▽	$99	361
42 / p. 271		Country Inn & Suites By Carlson	▽▽▽	$99-$110	358
		TEMPE - Restaurants			
1 / p. 271		Macayo Depot Cantina	▽▽	$8-$14	366
2 / p. 271		Gordon Biersch Brewery Restaurant	▽▽▽	$9-$23	366
3 / p. 271		Sammy's	▽▽	$8-$20	366
4 / p. 271		My Big Fat Greek Restaurant	▽▽	$5-$16	366
5 / p. 271		House of Tricks	▽▽	$16-$28	366
6 / p. 271		Casey Moore's Oyster House	▽▽	$9-$35	365
7 / p. 271		Tasty Kabob	▽▽	$10-$17	366
8 / p. 271		Pita Jungle	▽▽	$5-$12	366
9 / p. 271		The Firehouse Restaurant	▽▽	$10-$25	365
10 / p. 271		3 Margaritas	▽▽	$8-$12	365
11 / p. 271	AAA	George & Dragon II English Restaurant & Pub	▽▽	$10-$16	366
12 / p. 271		Royal Taj	▽▽	$7-$14	366
13 / p. 271		Top of the Rock Restaurant	▽▽▽	$26-$34	367
14 / p. 271		Claim Jumper	▽▽▽	$10-$20	365
15 / p. 271		Tom's BBQ Chicago Style	▽	$4-$13	367
16 / p. 271		Serrano's Mexican Restaurant	▽▽	$6-$10	366
17 / p. 271		John Henry's Continental Italian Cuisine	▽▽▽	$12-$25	366
18 / p. 271		Zipangu Sushi & Yakitori	▽▽	$9-$16	367
		MESA - Lodgings			
45 / p. 271		Phoenix Marriott Mesa	▽▽▽	$199	327
46 / p. 271	AAA	Windemere Hotel and Conference Center - see color ad p 328	▽▽	$109-$139 SAVE	328
47 / p. 271		Travelodge Suites Mesa	▽	$59-$109	328
48 / p. 271		Days Inn-East Mesa	▽	$69-$109	325
49 / p. 271	AAA	Best Western Mesa Inn	▽▽	$80-$100 SAVE	323
50 / p. 271	AAA	Best Western Mezona Inn - see color ad p 324	▽▽	$109-$149 SAVE	323

Spotter/Map Page Number	OA	MESA - Lodgings (continued)	Diamond Rating	Rate Range High Season	Listing Page
51 / p. 271	AAA	Arizona Golf Resort & Conference Center - see color ad p 323	◇◇◇	$169-$199 SAVE	323
52 / p. 271		Sleep Inn of Mesa	◇◇	Failed to provide	327
53 / p. 271	AAA	Best Western Superstition Springs Inn	◇◇	$119-$129 SAVE	324
54 / p. 271		Courtyard by Marriott	◇◇◇	$119-$199	324
55 / p. 271	AAA	La Quinta Inn & Suites Phoenix (Mesa West) - see color ad p 295	◇◇◇	$119-$136 SAVE	326
56 / p. 271		Residence Inn by Marriott Mesa	◇◇◇	$139-$214	327
57 / p. 271	AAA	Fairfield Inn by Marriott Phoenix Mesa	◇◇	$119 SAVE	325
58 / p. 271	AAA	Hilton Phoenix East/Mesa	◇◇◇	$159-$209 SAVE	325
59 / p. 271		Super 8 Motel-Mesa/Gilbert Rd - see color ad p 327	◇	$59-$81	327
60 / p. 271		Motel 6-Mesa South #1030	◇	$45-$61	327
61 / p. 271	AAA	Hampton Inn Phoenix/Mesa - see color ad p 325	◇◇◇	$129-$159 SAVE	325
62 / p. 271	AAA	Holiday Inn Hotel & Suites - see color ad p 326	◇◇◇	$119-$139 SAVE	326
63 / p. 271		Country Inn & Suites By Carlson	◇◇◇	$139-$159	324
64 / p. 271		La Quinta Inn & Suites Phoenix (Mesa East) - see color ad p 295	◇◇◇	$127-$144	326
65 / p. 271	AAA	Best Western Dobson Ranch Inn	◇◇	$125-$170 SAVE	323
66 / p. 271		Homestead Studio Suites Hotel Phoenix-Mesa	◇◇	$80-$85	326
67 / p. 271	AAA	Days Inn	◇◇	$79-$129 SAVE	324
		MESA - Restaurants			
32 / p. 271		Rancho de Tia Rosa	◇◇	$8-$15	329
33 / p. 271		Blue Adobe Grille	◇◇	$10-$20	329
34 / p. 271	AAA	The Weather Vane Restaurant	◇◇	$7-$14	329
35 / p. 271		Little Mesa Cafe	◇	$6-$12	329
36 / p. 271	AAA	The Landmark Restaurant	◇◇	$12-$25	329
37 / p. 271		Brunello Italian Restaurant	◇◇◇	$12-$25	329
38 / p. 271		Pink Pepper Thai Cuisine	◇◇	$8-$14	329
39 / p. 271		Serrano's Mexican Restaurant	◇◇	$6-$10	329
40 / p. 271	AAA	Flancer's Cafe	◇◇	$6-$21	329
		CHANDLER - Lodgings			
70 / p. 271	AAA	Best Western Inn of Chandler	◇◇	$79-$99 SAVE	313
71 / p. 271		Courtyard by Marriott	◇◇◇	Failed to provide	314
72 / p. 271		Residence Inn-Chandler Fashion Center	◇◇◇	$99-$199	315
73 / p. 271		Homewood Suites by Hilton	◇◇◇	$99-$239	314
74 / p. 271		Hampton Inn - see color ad p 279	◇◇◇	$119-$129	314
75 / p. 271		SpringHill Suites by Marriott-Fashion Center	◇◇◇	$140-$170	316
76 / p. 271	AAA	Comfort Inn	◇◇	$99-$119 SAVE	314
77 / p. 271		Hawthorn Suites Chandler	◇◇◇	$129-$169	314
78 / p. 271	AAA	Windmill Suites of Chandler	◇◇◇	$84-$149 SAVE	316
79 / p. 271	AAA	Fairfield Inn by Marriott Phoenix Chandler	◇◇	$107-$125 SAVE	314

Spotter/Map Page Number	OA	CHANDLER - Lodgings (continued)	Diamond Rating	Rate Range High Season	Listing Page
80 / p. 271		Southgate Motel	◆◆	Failed to provide	315
81 / p. 271		Park Plaza Phoenix/Chandler - see color ad p 315	◆◆◆	$109-$128	315
82 / p. 271		Chandler Super 8 - see color ad p 327	◆◆	$60-$75	313
83 / p. 271	AAA	San Marcos Resort and Conference Center	◆◆◆	$139-$219 SAVE	315
84 / p. 271		Red Roof Inn-Chandler	◆◆	$57-$74	315
		CHANDLER - Restaurants			
43 / p. 271		Citrus Cafe	◆◆◆	$16-$28	316
44 / p. 271		C-Fu Gourmet	◆	$8-$19	316
45 / p. 271		Saigon Pho & Seafood	◆	$5-$13	317
46 / p. 271		Z Tejas New American Cuisine	◆◆◆	$9-$19	317
47 / p. 271	AAA	56 East Bar & Kitchen	◆◆◆	$12-$26	316
48 / p. 271		P.F. Chang's China Bistro	◆◆◆	$7-$16	317
49 / p. 271		Abuelo's Mexican Food Embassy	◆◆	$7-$17	316
50 / p. 271		Cyclo Vietnamese Cuisine	◆◆	$5-$8	316
51 / p. 271		Kona Grill	◆◆◆	$9-$24	316
52 / p. 271		Serrano's Mexican Restaurant	◆◆	$6-$10	317
		GILBERT - Restaurants			
28 / p. 271		Cafe Sahara	◆◆	$8-$14	318
29 / p. 271	AAA	Joe's Real BBQ	◆	$6-$17	318

DOWNTOWN PHOENIX   (See map and index starting on p. 256)

──────── WHERE TO STAY ────────

BEST WESTERN AIRPORT INN   *Book at aaa.com*

(AAA) (SAVE)   Phone: (602)273-7251   **31**

	1/1-1/31	1P: $99-$149	2P: $99-$149	XP: $5	F17
	2/1-4/30 & 10/1-12/31	1P: $89-$139	2P: $89-$139	XP: $5	F17
	5/1-9/30	1P: $69-$99	2P: $69-$99	XP: $5	F17

Location: I-10, exit 150B westbound, just s; exit 151 (University Dr) eastbound, just n to I-10 westbound, 1 mi w to exit 150B (24th St), then just s. 2425 S 24th St 85034. Fax: 602/273-7180. **Facility:** 117 one-bedroom standard units, some with kitchens. 2 stories (no elevator); interior/exterior corridors. *Bath:* combo or shower only. **Parking:** on-site. **Terms:** check-in 4 pm, cancellation fee imposed, small pets only ($10 fee). **Amenities:** voice mail, irons, hair dryers. **Dining:** 6 am-10 pm, cocktails. **Pool(s):** heated outdoor. **Leisure Activities:** saunas, whirlpool. **Guest Services:** coin laundry, area transportation-bus depots. **Business Services:** meeting rooms, fax (fee). **Cards:** AX, CB, DC, DS, JC, MC, VI. **Special Amenities:** free local telephone calls and early check-in/late check-out. *(See color ad below)*

SOME UNITS

[SD FEE 🛬 🛏 ¶ ☂ ⊘ ⇌ 🎥 DATA-PORT 🖥 / ✕ 📱]

BEST WESTERN CENTRAL PHOENIX INN   *Book at aaa.com*

(AAA) (SAVE)   Phone: (602)252-2100   **13**

	1/1-1/31	1P: $109-$229	2P: $109-$229	XP: $10	F17
	2/1-5/31	1P: $99-$209	2P: $99-$209	XP: $10	F17
	10/1-12/31	1P: $89-$209	2P: $89-$209	XP: $10	F17
	6/1-9/30	1P: $74-$189	2P: $74-$189	XP: $10	F17

Small-scale Hotel **Location:** Just s of McDowell Rd. Located adjacent to the Margaret T. Hance Park. 1100 N Central Ave 85004. Fax: 602/340-1989. **Facility:** 107 units. 101 one-bedroom standard units. 6 one-bedroom suites ($149-$269) with whirlpools. 8 stories, interior corridors. *Bath:* combo or shower only. **Parking:** on-site. **Terms:** cancellation fee imposed, package plans. **Amenities:** high-speed Internet, voice mail, irons, hair dryers. **Dining:** 7 am-2 & 5-9 pm, Sun-11 am. **Pool(s):** heated outdoor. **Leisure Activities:** saunas, whirlpool, exercise room. **Guest Services:** coin laundry. **Business Services:** meeting rooms, PC, fax (fee). **Cards:** AX, DC, DS, MC, VI. **Special Amenities:** free expanded continental breakfast and free local telephone calls.

SOME UNITS

[SD ✈ ¶ ♿ ⊘ ⇌ ✕ DATA-PORT 🖥 / ✕ 📱]

BUDGET LODGE MOTEL

(AAA) (SAVE)   Phone: (602)254-7247   **22**

| | All Year | 1P: $45-$75 | 2P: $45-$85 | XP: $10 | D16 |

Motel   **Location:** Just w of Central Ave; center. 402 W Van Buren St 85003. Fax: 602/252-4730. **Facility:** 38 one-bedroom standard units. 2 stories (no elevator); interior/exterior corridors. *Bath:* combo or shower only. **Parking:** on-site. **Terms:** cancellation fee imposed. **Business Services:** fax. **Cards:** AX, DS, MC, VI. **Special Amenities:** free local telephone calls.

SOME UNITS

[🎥 / ✕ DATA-PORT 📱]

COMFORT INN I-10 WEST/CENTRAL   *Book at aaa.com*

(AAA) (SAVE)   Phone: (602)415-1623   **11**

| | 9/2-1/31 | 1P: $72 | 2P: $72 | XP: $10 | F12 |
| | 2/1-9/1 | 1P: $54 | 2P: $54 | XP: $10 | F12 |

Location: I-10, exit 27th Ave westbound, just n; exit 141 (35th Ave) eastbound, just n, 1 mi e on McDowell Rd, then s. 1344 N 27th Ave 85009. Fax: 602/415-1838. **Facility:** 65 units. 64 one-bedroom standard units. 1 one-bedroom suite. 3 stories, interior corridors. *Bath:* combo or shower only. **Parking:** on-site. **Terms:** cancellation fee imposed. **Amenities:** irons, hair dryers. **Pool(s):** heated outdoor. **Leisure Activities:** whirlpool. **Guest Services:** coin laundry. **Cards:** AX, CB, DC, DS, JC, MC, VI. **Special Amenities:** free continental breakfast and free local telephone calls.

SOME UNITS

[SD ♿ ⇌ 🎥 DATA-PORT 📱 🖥 / ✕]

COURTYARD BY MARRIOTT PHOENIX AIRPORT   *Book at aaa.com*

    Phone: (480)966-4300   **33**

| | All Year | 1P: $69-$239 | | | |

Small-scale Hotel **Location:** I-10, exit 151 (University Dr), 2 mi n, then just w. 2621 S 47th St 85034. Fax: 480/966-0198. **Facility:** 145 units. 133 one-bedroom standard units. 12 one-bedroom suites. 4 stories, interior corridors. *Bath:* combo or shower only. **Parking:** on-site. **Terms:** cancellation fee imposed, [BP] meal plan available, package plans. **Amenities:** high-speed Internet, dual phone lines, voice mail, irons, hair dryers. **Pool(s):** heated outdoor. **Leisure Activities:** whirlpool. **Guest Services:** valet and coin laundry. **Business Services:** meeting rooms, business center. **Cards:** AX, CB, DC, DS, JC, MC, VI.

SOME UNITS

[ASK SD ✈ ¶ ☂ 🔊M ♿ ⇌ 🔧 🎥 DATA-PORT 🖥 / ✕ 📱 FEE]

(See map and index starting on p. 256)

CROWNE PLAZA PHOENIX AIRPORT   *Book at aaa.com*   Phone: (602)273-7778   30

(AAA) (SAVE)

2/1-4/16	1P: $99-$159	2P: $99-$159	XP: $10 F12
4/17-5/28	1P: $89-$129	2P: $89-$129	XP: $10 F12
9/11-1/31	1P: $79-$129	2P: $79-$129	XP: $10 F12
5/29-9/10	1P: $69-$99	2P: $69-$99	XP: $10 F12

Small-scale Hotel **Location:** Loop 202, exit 2 (44th St), 0.7 mi s. 4300 E Washington St 85034. Fax: 602/275-5616. **Facility:** 299 one-bedroom standard units, some with whirlpools. 10 stories, interior corridors. *Bath:* combo or shower only. **Parking:** on-site. **Terms:** package plans, pets ($50 fee). **Amenities:** CD players, high-speed Internet, dual phone lines, voice mail, irons, hair dryers. *Some:* safes. **Dining:** 6 am-11 pm, cocktails. **Pool(s):** heated outdoor. **Leisure Activities:** whirlpool, exercise room. **Guest Services:** sundries, valet and coin laundry, area transportation-within 3 mi. **Business Services:** conference facilities, business center. **Cards:** AX, CB, DC, DS, JC, MC, VI.

SOME UNITS

[icons] FEE

DAYS INN-AIRPORT   *Book at aaa.com*   Phone: (602)244-8244   24

(AAA) (SAVE)

2/1-4/29 & 9/28-1/31	1P: $69-$89	2P: $79-$99	XP: $10 F18
4/30-6/3	1P: $59-$79	2P: $69-$89	XP: $10 F18
6/4-9/27	1P: $55-$69	2P: $65-$89	XP: $10 F18

Motel **Location:** Loop 202, exit 1C (32nd St), 0.6 mi s, then just e. 3333 E Van Buren St 85008. Fax: 602/244-8240. **Facility:** 219 units. 218 one-bedroom standard units. 1 one-bedroom suite ($139-$199) with efficiency (no utensils). 3 stories, interior/exterior corridors. **Parking:** on-site. **Terms:** check-in 4 pm, package plans, pets ($20 fee). **Amenities:** high-speed Internet, voice mail, safes (fee), hair dryers. *Some:* irons. **Dining:** 6 am-10 pm, cocktails. **Pool(s):** heated outdoor. **Leisure Activities:** whirlpool, exercise room. **Guest Services:** gift shop, valet and coin laundry, area transportation-hospital, bus station. **Business Services:** meeting rooms. *Fee:* PC, fax. **Cards:** AX, CB, DC, DS, MC, VI. **Special Amenities:** free local telephone calls and free newspaper.

SOME UNITS

[icons] FEE

DAYS INN PHOENIX I-17 & THOMAS   *Book at aaa.com*   Phone: (602)257-0801   2

(AAA) (SAVE)

2/1-4/30 [CP]	1P: $69-$109	2P: $69-$109	XP: $10 F17
12/26-1/31 [CP]	1P: $59-$99	2P: $69-$99	XP: $10 F17
10/1-12/25 [CP]	1P: $59-$99	2P: $59-$109	XP: $10 F17
5/1-9/30 [CP]	1P: $49-$89	2P: $49-$99	XP: $10 F17

Small-scale Hotel **Location:** I-17, exit 201 (Thomas Rd), just e. 2420 W Thomas Rd 85015. Fax: 602/258-5336. **Facility:** 146 one-bedroom standard units. 2 stories (no elevator), interior corridors. **Parking:** on-site. **Amenities:** voice mail, irons, hair dryers. **Pool(s):** heated outdoor. **Leisure Activities:** whirlpool. **Guest Services:** valet and coin laundry. **Business Services:** meeting rooms, fax (fee). **Cards:** AX, DC, DS, MC, VI. **Special Amenities:** free continental breakfast and free local telephone calls.

SOME UNITS

[icons]

DOUBLETREE GUEST SUITES-PHOENIX   *Book at aaa.com*   Phone: (602)225-0500   19

(AAA) (SAVE)

2/1-4/14 [BP]	1P: $139-$249	2P: $139-$249	XP: $10 F17
9/5-1/31 [BP]	1P: $119-$249	2P: $119-$249	XP: $10 F17
4/15-5/25 [BP]	1P: $119-$229	2P: $119-$229	XP: $10 F17
5/26-9/4 [BP]	1P: $79-$149	2P: $79-$149	XP: $10 F17

Small-scale Hotel **Location:** Loop 202, exit 2 (44th St), 0.5 mi s. 320 N 44th St Gateway Center 85008. Fax: 602/225-0957. **Facility:** 242 one-bedroom suites. 6 stories, exterior corridors. *Bath:* some combo or shower only. **Parking:** on-site. **Terms:** cancellation fee imposed, [AP] meal plan available, package plans. **Amenities:** dual phone lines, voice mail, safes, irons, hair dryers. *Fee:* video games, high-speed Internet. *Some:* CD players. **Dining:** 6 am-10 pm, Sat & Sun from 7 am, cocktails. **Pool(s):** heated outdoor. **Leisure Activities:** whirlpool, exercise room. **Guest Services:** gift shop, valet and coin laundry, area transportation-within 3 mi. **Business Services:** conference facilities, business center. **Cards:** AX, DC, DS, MC, VI. **Special Amenities:** free full breakfast and free newspaper. *(See color ad below)*

SOME UNITS

[icons] FEE

(See map and index starting on p. 256)

ECONO LODGE AIRPORT *Book at aaa.com* Phone: (602)273-1601 23

AAA SAVE

Motel

2/1-4/15 [CP]	1P: $59-$79	2P: $69-$89	XP: $10 F12
9/14-1/31 [CP]	1P: $49-$69	2P: $59-$79	XP: $10 F12
4/16-9/13 [CP]	1P: $39-$59	2P: $49-$69	XP: $10 F12

Location: Loop 202, exit 1C (32nd St), 0.6 mi s, then just w. 3037 E Van Buren 85008. Fax: 602/286-6358. **Facility:** 94 one-bedroom standard units, some with whirlpools. 2 stories (no elevator), exterior corridors. **Parking:** on-site. **Terms:** office hours 6 am-9 pm, cancellation fee imposed. **Amenities:** voice mail. **Pool(s):** heated outdoor. **Guest Services:** coin laundry. **Business Services:** meeting rooms, fax (fee). **Cards:** AX, DC, DS, MC, VI. **Special Amenities:** free continental breakfast and free local telephone calls.

SOME UNITS

⬛ ⬛ ⬛ ⬛ ⬛ / ⬛ /

ECONO LODGE INN & SUITES-DOWNTOWN *Book at aaa.com* Phone: (602)528-9100 9

Small-scale Hotel

9/1-1/31	1P: $69-$159	2P: $69-$159	XP: $10 F18
2/1-5/28	1P: $69-$139	2P: $69-$139	XP: $10 F18
5/29-8/31	1P: $59-$99	2P: $59-$99	XP: $10 F18

Location: Just e of Central Ave. 202 E McDowell Rd 85004. Fax: 602/258-7259. **Facility:** 48 units. 33 one-bedroom standard units. 15 one-bedroom suites. 3 stories, interior corridors. **Parking:** on-site. **Terms:** [CP] meal plan available, small pets only. **Amenities:** voice mail, hair dryers. **Pool(s):** heated outdoor. **Leisure Activities:** whirlpool. **Guest Services:** coin laundry, area transportation. **Business Services:** meeting rooms, fax (fee). **Cards:** AX, CB, DC, DS, JC, MC, VI.

SOME UNITS

ASK ⬛ ⬛ ⬛ ⬛ ⬛ ⬛ / ⬛ ⬛ ⬛ /

EMBASSY SUITES PHOENIX AIRPORT AT 24TH ST *Book at aaa.com* Phone: (602)957-1910 4

AAA SAVE

Small-scale Hotel

2/1-5/25	1P: $129-$199	2P: $129-$199	XP: $10 F18
9/7-1/31	1P: $119-$189	2P: $119-$189	XP: $10 F18
5/26-9/6	1P: $99-$109	2P: $99-$109	XP: $10 F18

Location: SR 51, exit 2, just e. 2333 E Thomas Rd 85016. Fax: 602/955-2861. **Facility:** 183 one-bedroom suites ($99-$199). 4 stories, exterior corridors. **Bath:** combo or shower only. **Parking:** on-site. **Terms:** cancellation fee imposed, [BP] meal plan available, pets ($15 extra charge). **Amenities:** voice mail, irons, hair dryers. **Fee:** video games, high-speed Internet. *Some:* dual phone lines. **Dining:** 11 am-11 pm, cocktails. **Pool(s):** heated outdoor. **Leisure Activities:** whirlpool, exercise room. **Guest Services:** gift shop, complimentary evening beverages, valet and coin laundry, area transportation-within 3 mi. **Business Services:** meeting rooms, PC (fee). **Cards:** AX, CB, DC, DS, JC, MC, VI. **Special Amenities:** free full breakfast and free newspaper.

SOME UNITS

⬛ ⬛ ⬛ ⬛ ⬛ ⬛ ⬛ ⬛ ⬛ ⬛ / ⬛ /
FEE

EMBASSY SUITES PHOENIX AIRPORT AT 44TH ST *Book at aaa.com* Phone: (602)244-8800 10

Small-scale Hotel

2/1-5/31 & 1/1-1/31 [BP]	1P: $119-$229	2P: $119-$229	XP: $10 F18
10/1-12/31 [BP]	1P: $109-$169	2P: $109-$169	XP: $10 F18
6/1-9/30 [BP]	1P: $79-$129	2P: $79-$129	XP: $10 F18

Location: Loop 202, exit 2 (44th St), 0.3 mi n. 1515 N 44th St 85008. Fax: 602/244-8114. **Facility:** 229 one-bedroom suites. 4 stories, exterior corridors. **Parking:** on-site. **Terms:** cancellation fee imposed, package plans. **Amenities:** voice mail, irons, hair dryers. **Fee:** video games, high-speed Internet. **Pool(s):** heated outdoor. **Leisure Activities:** whirlpool, exercise room. **Guest Services:** gift shop, valet and coin laundry, area transportation. **Business Services:** conference facilities, fax (fee). **Cards:** AX, DC, DS, MC, VI.

SOME UNITS

⬛ ⬛ ⬛ ⬛ ⬛ ⬛ ⬛ ⬛ ⬛ ⬛ / ⬛ VCR /
FEE

EXTENDED STAYAMERICA PHOENIX/AIRPORT/E OAK ST *Book at aaa.com* Phone: (602)225-2998 8

Small-scale Hotel

2/1-4/1 & 1/10-1/31	1P: $90	2P: $95	XP: $5 F17
10/1-1/9	1P: $60	2P: $65	XP: $5 F17
4/2-9/30	1P: $45	2P: $50	XP: $5 F17

Location: Loop 202, exit 2 (44th St), 1 mi n. 4357 E Oak St 85008. Fax: 602/275-7607. **Facility:** 134 one-bedroom standard units with efficiencies. 2 stories (no elevator), exterior corridors. **Bath:** combo or shower only. **Parking:** on-site. **Terms:** small pets only ($25 fee). **Amenities:** high-speed Internet (fee), dual phone lines, voice mail, irons, hair dryers. **Pool(s):** heated outdoor. **Leisure Activities:** exercise room. **Guest Services:** valet and coin laundry. **Business Services:** meeting rooms, fax. **Cards:** AX, DC, DS, MC, VI.

SOME UNITS

ASK ⬛ ⬛ ⬛ ⬛ ⬛ ⬛ ⬛ ⬛ ⬛ ⬛ / ⬛ /
FEE

FAIRFIELD INN BY MARRIOTT PHOENIX AIRPORT *Book at aaa.com* Phone: (480)829-0700 35

AAA SAVE

Small-scale Hotel

2/1-4/2 & 1/1-1/31	1P: $99-$139	2P: $99-$139	
4/3-5/28	1P: $99-$119	2P: $99-$119	
5/29-12/31	1P: $59-$109	2P: $59-$109	

Location: I-10, exit 151 (University Dr), 2 mi n, then e. 4702 E University Dr 85034. Fax: 480/829-8068. **Facility:** 90 one-bedroom standard units. 3 stories, interior corridors. **Parking:** on-site. **Terms:** cancellation fee imposed. **Amenities:** high-speed Internet, voice mail, irons, hair dryers. *Some:* dual phone lines. **Pool(s):** heated outdoor. **Leisure Activities:** whirlpool. **Guest Services:** valet and coin laundry. **Business Services:** fax. **Cards:** AX, CB, DC, DS, JC, MC, VI. **Special Amenities:** free continental breakfast and free local telephone calls.

SOME UNITS

⬛ ⬛ ⬛ ⬛ ⬛ ⬛ ⬛ ⬛ ⬛ / ⬛ ⬛ ⬛ /
FEE

(See map and index starting on p. 256)

HAMPTON INN & SUITES PHOENIX AIRPORT SOUTH/TEMPE   *Book at aaa.com*

Phone: (602)438-8688   **39**

	1P	2P	XP	
2/1-5/14 [ECP]	1P: $119-$169	2P: $129-$179	XP: $10	F17
9/15-1/31 [ECP]	1P: $109-$159	2P: $119-$169	XP: $10	F17
5/15-9/14 [ECP]	1P: $69-$109	2P: $79-$139	XP: $10	F17

Small-scale Hotel   **Location:** I-10, exit 153 (48th St/Broadway), just s; exit 153B (52nd St/Broadway) westbound, 0.4 mi w. 4234 S 48th St 85040. Fax: 602/431-8339. **Facility:** 107 one-bedroom standard units. 4 stories, interior corridors. *Bath:* combo or shower only. **Parking:** on-site. **Terms:** cancellation fee imposed, [MAP] meal plan available. **Amenities:** video games (fee), high-speed Internet, voice mail, irons, hair dryers. **Pool(s):** heated outdoor. **Leisure Activities:** whirlpool, limited exercise equipment. **Guest Services:** sundries, valet laundry, area transportation (fee)-within 5 mi. **Business Services:** meeting rooms, business center. **Cards:** AX, CB, DC, DS, MC, VI. **Special Amenities:** free expanded continental breakfast and free local telephone calls.

SOME UNITS

HAMPTON INN PHOENIX AIRPORT NORTH   *Book at aaa.com*

Phone: (602)267-0606   **15**

	1P	2P	XP	
1/1-1/31	1P: $139-$159	2P: $149-$169	XP: $10	F18
2/1-5/13	1P: $129-$149	2P: $139-$159	XP: $10	F18
9/10-12/31	1P: $99-$129	2P: $99-$129	XP: $10	F18
5/14-9/9	1P: $59-$89	2P: $59-$89	XP: $10	F18

Small-scale Hotel   **Location:** Loop 202, exit 2 (44th St), 0.3 mi s. Located across from the Chinese Cultural Center. 601 N 44th St 85008. Fax: 602/267-9767. **Facility:** 106 units. 96 one-bedroom standard units, some with whirlpools. 10 one-bedroom suites, some with whirlpools. 4 stories, interior corridors. *Bath:* combo or shower only. **Parking:** on-site. **Terms:** cancellation fee imposed, [ECP] meal plan available. **Amenities:** high-speed Internet, dual phone lines, voice mail, irons, hair dryers. **Pool(s):** heated outdoor. **Leisure Activities:** whirlpool, exercise room. **Guest Services:** sundries, valet and coin laundry, area transportation. **Business Services:** meeting rooms, business center. **Cards:** AX, CB, DC, DS, JC, MC, VI.

SOME UNITS

HAMPTON INN-PHOENIX/MIDTOWN   *Book at aaa.com*

Phone: (602)200-0990   **1**

	1P	2P	
2/1-4/15 & 9/16-1/31 [ECP]	1P: $79-$149	2P: $89-$159	
4/16-5/31 [ECP]	1P: $69-$109	2P: $79-$119	
6/1-9/15 [ECP]	1P: $59-$89	2P: $69-$99	

Small-scale Hotel   **Location:** Jct Thomas Rd, just n on Central Ave, then 0.3 mi w. Located opposite St. Joseph's Hospital/Barrow Institute. 160 W Catalina Dr 85013. Fax: 602/200-0999. **Facility:** 99 one-bedroom standard units. 4 stories, interior corridors. *Bath:* combo or shower only. **Parking:** on-site. **Terms:** 3 day cancellation notice. **Amenities:** video games (fee), high-speed Internet, dual phone lines, voice mail, irons, hair dryers. **Pool(s):** heated outdoor. **Leisure Activities:** whirlpool, exercise room. **Guest Services:** valet and coin laundry. **Business Services:** meeting rooms, PC, fax. **Cards:** AX, CB, DC, DS, MC, VI.
(See color ad below)

SOME UNITS

HILTON GARDEN INN PHOENIX AIRPORT   *Book at aaa.com*

Phone: (602)470-0500   **37**

	1P	2P	XP	
2/1-4/16	1P: $209	2P: $209	XP: $10	F18
4/17-5/29 & 9/5-1/31	1P: $159	2P: $159	XP: $10	F18
5/30-9/4	1P: $99-$109	2P: $99-$109	XP: $10	F18

Small-scale Hotel   **Location:** I-10, exit 151 (University Dr), just n. 3422 E Elwood St 85040. Fax: 602/470-0200. **Facility:** 93 units. 63 one-bedroom standard units, some with whirlpools. 30 one-bedroom suites ($120) with kitchens, some with whirlpools. 3 stories, interior corridors. *Bath:* combo or shower only. **Parking:** on-site. **Terms:** cancellation fee imposed, [AP], [BP] & [CP] meal plans available, package plans. **Amenities:** video games (fee), high-speed Internet, dual phone lines, voice mail, safes, irons, hair dryers. **Pool(s):** heated outdoor. **Leisure Activities:** whirlpool, exercise room. **Guest Services:** sundries, coin laundry, area transportation. **Business Services:** conference facilities, business center. **Cards:** AX, CB, DC, DS, JC, MC, VI.

SOME UNITS

(See map and index starting on p. 256)

HILTON PHOENIX AIRPORT Book at aaa.com Phone: (480)894-1600 32

AAA SAVE
▽▽▽▽

2/1-5/18	1P: $99-$249	2P: $99-$249	XP: $15	F18
9/10-1/31	1P: $89-$249	2P: $89-$249	XP: $15	F18
5/19-9/9	1P: $69-$159	2P: $69-$159	XP: $15	F18

Small-scale Hotel **Location:** I-10, exit 151 (University Dr), 2 mi n, then just w. 2435 S 47th St 85034. Fax: 480/921-7844. **Facility:** 261 units. 257 one-bedroom standard units. 4 one-bedroom suites with whirlpools. 4 stories, interior corridors. **Bath:** combo or shower only. **Parking:** on-site. **Terms:** cancellation fee imposed. **Amenities:** Some: high-speed Internet (fee), dual phone lines, voice mail, safes, honor bars, irons, hair dryers. **Dining:** 6 am-2 & 5-10 pm, Sun-9 pm, cocktails. **Pool(s):** heated outdoor. **Leisure Activities:** whirlpool, exercise room. Fee: massage. **Guest Services:** gift shop, valet laundry, area transportation-within 3 mi. **Business Services:** conference facilities, business center. **Cards:** AX, DC, DS, MC, VI.

HILTON SUITES-PHOENIX Book at aaa.com Phone: (602)222-1111 3

AAA SAVE
▽▽▽▽

2/1-5/4	1P: $139-$249	2P: $139-$249	XP: $10	D18
9/5-1/31	1P: $119-$209	2P: $119-$209	XP: $10	D18
5/5-5/25	1P: $99-$199	2P: $99-$199	XP: $10	D18
5/26-9/4	1P: $89-$169	2P: $89-$169	XP: $10	D18

Large-scale Hotel **Location:** Just e of Central Ave; in Phoenix Plaza. 10 E Thomas Rd 85012. Fax: 602/265-4841. **Facility:** 226 one-bedroom suites. 11 stories, interior corridors. **Bath:** combo or shower only. **Parking:** on-site (fee). **Terms:** cancellation fee imposed, package plans, pets ($100 deposit). **Amenities:** video games (fee), dual phone lines, voice mail, irons, hair dryers. Some: CD players, high-speed Internet (fee). **Dining:** 6 am-11 pm, Sat & Sun 7 am-11 & 5-11 pm, cocktails. **Pool(s):** heated indoor. **Leisure Activities:** sauna, whirlpool, exercise room. **Guest Services:** gift shop, valet and coin laundry, area transportation-within 2 mi. **Business Services:** meeting rooms, business center. **Cards:** AX, CB, DC, DS, JC, MC, VI. **Special Amenities:** free newspaper and early check-in/late check-out.

HOLIDAY INN EXPRESS HOTEL & SUITES Phone: 602/453-9900 36

▽▽▽▽

Property failed to provide current rates

Small-scale Hotel **Location:** I-10, exit 151 (University Dr), just n. 3401 E University Dr 85034. Fax: 602/453-0090. **Facility:** 114 one-bedroom standard units, some with whirlpools. 4 stories, interior corridors. **Bath:** combo or shower only. **Parking:** on-site. **Terms:** small pets only. **Amenities:** high-speed Internet, dual phone lines, voice mail, irons, hair dryers. **Pool(s):** heated outdoor. **Leisure Activities:** whirlpool, exercise room. **Guest Services:** sundries, complimentary evening beverages: Mon-Fri, valet and coin laundry, area transportation. **Business Services:** meeting rooms, business center.

HOLIDAY INN EXPRESS HOTEL AND SUITES-DOWNTOWN/BANKONE BALL PARK Book at aaa.com Phone: (602)452-2020 16

▽▽▽▽

2/1-4/2	1P: $134-$149	2P: $134-$149	XP: $10	F12
4/3-9/5	1P: $124-$134	2P: $124-$134	XP: $10	F12
9/6-1/31	1P: $119-$134	2P: $119-$134	XP: $10	F12

Small-scale Hotel **Location:** I-10, exit 145 (7th St), 0.5 mi s, then 1 blk w on Fillmore. 620 N 6th St 85004. Fax: 602/252-2909. **Facility:** 90 units. 88 one-bedroom standard units. 2 one-bedroom suites with whirlpools. 3 stories, interior corridors. **Bath:** combo or shower only. **Parking:** on-site. **Terms:** 10 day cancellation notice-fee imposed, [CP] meal plan available. **Amenities:** high-speed Internet, voice mail, irons, hair dryers. **Pool(s):** small heated outdoor. **Leisure Activities:** whirlpool, exercise room, sports court. **Guest Services:** valet and coin laundry. **Business Services:** meeting rooms, business center. **Cards:** AX, CB, DC, DS, JC, MC, VI.

HOTEL SAN CARLOS Book at aaa.com Phone: (602)253-4121 27

AAA SAVE
▽▽▽▽

1/1-1/31 [CP]	1P: $119	2P: $119
2/1-4/30 [CP]	1P: $109	2P: $109
9/1-12/31 [CP]	1P: $89	2P: $89
5/1-8/31 [CP]	1P: $69	2P: $69

Historic
Small-scale Hotel **Location:** Just n of Washington St; town center. 202 N Central Ave 85004. Fax: 602/253-6668. **Facility:** This historic hotel is charmingly appointed with themed suites, attractive guest rooms and updated baths. 121 units. 109 one-bedroom standard units. 12 one-bedroom suites ($169). 7 stories, interior corridors. **Bath:** combo or shower only. **Parking:** no self-parking. **Terms:** weekly rates available, package plans. **Amenities:** voice mail, irons. **Dining:** 11 am-9 pm. **Pool(s):** heated outdoor. **Guest Services:** gift shop, area transportation-Copper Square, barber shop, shoe repair. **Business Services:** meeting rooms. **Cards:** AX, CB, DC, DS, MC, VI. **Special Amenities:** free continental breakfast and free local telephone calls.

HYATT REGENCY PHOENIX Book at aaa.com Phone: (602)252-1234 28

AAA SAVE
▽▽▽▽

| 2/1-4/30 & 10/1-1/31 | 1P: $120-$245 | 2P: $120-$245 | XP: $25 | F18 |
| 5/1-9/30 | 1P: $90-$195 | 2P: $90-$195 | XP: $25 | F18 |

Large-scale Hotel **Location:** Just s of Monroe St; downtown; at Civic Plaza. 122 N 2nd St 85004. Fax: 602/254-9472. **Facility:** 712 units. 707 one-bedroom standard units. 1 one-, 3 two- and 1 three-bedroom suites, some with kitchens. 24 stories, interior corridors. **Bath:** combo or shower only. **Parking:** on-site (fee) and valet. **Terms:** cancellation fee imposed. **Amenities:** dual phone lines, voice mail, irons, hair dryers. Some: CD players, safes. Fee: DVD players. **Dining:** 3 restaurants, 6 am-2 am, cocktails, also, Compass Restaurant, see separate listing. **Pool(s):** small heated outdoor. **Leisure Activities:** whirlpool. **Guest Services:** gift shop, valet laundry, area transportation-Copper Square Dash. **Business Services:** conference facilities, business center. **Cards:** AX, CB, DC, DS, JC, MC, VI.

(See map and index starting on p. 256)

LA QUINTA INN PHOENIX AIRPORT NORTH · *Book at aaa.com* · Phone: (602)956-6500 · **5**

2/1-4/5	1P: $80-$120	2P: $80-$120	XP: $5	F17
1/1-1/31	1P: $70-$90	2P: $70-$90	XP: $5	F17
9/1-12/31	1P: $65-$85	2P: $65-$85	XP: $5	F17
4/6-8/31	1P: $60-$80	2P: $60-$80	XP: $5	F17

Small-scale Hotel **Location:** Just w of 48th St. 4727 E Thomas Rd 85018. Fax: 602/840-3317. **Facility:** 115 one-bedroom standard units. 2 stories, interior/exterior corridors. *Bath:* combo or shower only. **Parking:** on-site. **Terms:** cancellation fee imposed, small pets only. **Amenities:** voice mail, irons, hair dryers. **Pool(s):** heated outdoor. **Leisure Activities:** whirlpool, exercise room. **Guest Services:** coin laundry, area transportation-hospitals. **Business Services:** meeting rooms, fax (fee). **Cards:** AX, DC, DS, MC, VI. **Special Amenities:** free expanded continental breakfast and free local telephone calls.

SOME UNITS

LA QUINTA INN PHOENIX (THOMAS ROAD) · *Book at aaa.com* · Phone: (602)258-6271 · **6**

2/1-3/31 [CP]	1P: $91-$101	2P: $98-$108	XP: $7	F18
4/1-1/31 [CP]	1P: $62-$72	2P: $69-$79	XP: $7	F18

Motel **Location:** I-17, exit 201 (Thomas Rd), just e, then just s on east side of freeway. 2725 N Black Canyon Hwy 85009-1897. Fax: 602/340-9255. **Facility:** 139 units. 137 one-bedroom standard units. 2 one-bedroom suites. 2 stories (no elevator), exterior corridors. *Bath:* combo or shower only. **Parking:** on-site. **Terms:** small pets only. **Amenities:** video games (fee), voice mail, irons, hair dryers. **Pool(s):** heated outdoor. **Guest Services:** coin laundry, area transportation. **Business Services:** fax (fee). **Cards:** AX, CB, DC, DS, MC, VI. *(See color ad p 295)*

SOME UNITS

MOTEL 6 PHOENIX EAST #18 · *Book at aaa.com* · Phone: 602/267-8555 · **26**

3/3-4/15	1P: $45-$55	2P: $51-$61	XP: $3	F17
2/1-3/2	1P: $41-$51	2P: $47-$57	XP: $3	F17
4/16-1/31	1P: $39-$49	2P: $45-$55	XP: $3	F17

Motel **Location:** Loop 202 eastbound, exit 4 (52nd/Van Buren sts) just s, then just e. 5315 E Van Buren St 85008. Fax: 602/231-9115. **Facility:** 80 one-bedroom standard units. 2 stories (no elevator), exterior corridors. *Bath:* combo or shower only. **Parking:** on-site. **Terms:** small pets only. **Pool(s):** heated outdoor. **Business Services:** fax (fee). **Cards:** AX, CB, DC, DS, MC, VI.

SOME UNITS · FEE · FEE

PHOENIX AIRPORT MARRIOTT · *Book at aaa.com* · Phone: (602)273-7373 · **12**

2/1-5/13 & 1/1-1/31	1P: $161-$246	2P: $161-$246	XP: $10	F10
5/14-12/31	1P: $98-$170	2P: $98-$170	XP: $10	F10

Large-scale Hotel **Location:** Loop 202, exit 2 (44th St), just n. 1101 N 44th St 85008. Fax: 602/273-7333. **Facility:** 347 one-bedroom standard units. 12 stories, interior corridors. *Bath:* combo or shower only. **Parking:** on-site. **Terms:** check-in 4 pm. **Amenities:** high-speed Internet (fee), dual phone lines, voice mail, irons, hair dryers. **Pool(s):** heated outdoor. **Leisure Activities:** whirlpool, exercise room. **Guest Services:** gift shop, valet and coin laundry. **Business Services:** conference facilities, business center. **Cards:** AX, CB, DC, DS, JC, MC, VI.

SOME UNITS · FEE · FEE

RADISSON HOTEL PHOENIX AIRPORT NORTH · *Book at aaa.com* · Phone: (602)220-4400 · **17**

9/8-1/31	1P: $129-$229	2P: $139-$239	XP: $10	F18
2/1-4/13	1P: $149-$199	2P: $159-$209	XP: $10	F18
4/14-5/25	1P: $129-$179	2P: $139-$189	XP: $10	F18
5/26-9/7	1P: $99-$149	2P: $109-$159	XP: $10	F18

Location: Loop 202, exit 2 (44th St), 0.5 mi s. 427 N 44th St 85008. Fax: 602/231-8703. **Facility:** 210 units. 186 one-bedroom standard units. 24 one-bedroom suites. 7 stories, interior corridors. **Parking:** on-site. **Terms:** small pets only. **Amenities:** video games (fee), high-speed Internet, dual phone lines, voice mail, irons, hair dryers. *Some:* CD players. **Pool(s):** heated outdoor. **Leisure Activities:** whirlpool, exercise room. **Guest Services:** valet laundry, area transportation. **Business Services:** meeting rooms, administrative services (fee). **Cards:** AX, CB, DC, DS, JC, MC, VI.

SOME UNITS

RADISSON PHOENIX AIRPORT HOTEL · Phone: (602)437-8400 · **38**

2/1-4/16	1P: $179-$199	2P: $179-$199	XP: $10	D21
4/17-5/23 & 9/11-1/31	1P: $149-$169	2P: $149-$169	XP: $10	D21
5/24-9/10	1P: $129-$139	2P: $129-$139	XP: $10	D21

Small-scale Hotel **Location:** I-10, exit 151, just e on University Dr, then just s on Elmwood. 3333 E University Dr 85034. Fax: 602/470-0998. **Facility:** 159 units. 148 one-bedroom standard units. 11 one-bedroom suites ($179-$219), some with whirlpools. 6 stories, interior corridors. *Bath:* combo or shower only. **Parking:** on-site. **Terms:** cancellation fee imposed. **Amenities:** high-speed Internet, voice mail, irons, hair dryers. **Dining:** 6 am-10 pm, Sat & Sun from 7 am, cocktails. **Pool(s):** heated outdoor. **Leisure Activities:** whirlpool, exercise room. **Guest Services:** sundries, valet and coin laundry. **Business Services:** conference facilities, fax (fee). **Cards:** AX, CB, DC, DS, MC, VI.

SOME UNITS

RAMADA AIRPORT NORTH · *Book at aaa.com* · Phone: (602)275-5746 · **20**

2/1-4/30 & 1/1-1/31	1P: $79-$89	2P: $89-$100	XP: $10	F18
10/1-12/31	1P: $59-$69	2P: $69-$79	XP: $10	F18
5/1-9/30	1P: $49-$59	2P: $59-$69	XP: $10	F18

Small-scale Hotel **Location:** Loop 202, exit 2 to 44th St, 0.5 mi s, then just w. 4120 E Van Buren St 85008. Fax: 602/275-9488. **Facility:** 47 one-bedroom standard units. 2 stories (no elevator), exterior corridors. *Bath:* combo or shower only. **Parking:** on-site. **Terms:** cancellation fee imposed, [BP] meal plan available, package plans, $1 service charge. **Amenities:** safes (fee). *Some:* irons, hair dryers. **Pool(s):** outdoor. **Guest Services:** valet laundry. **Business Services:** meeting rooms. **Fee:** PC, fax. **Cards:** AX, CB, DC, DS, JC, MC, VI. **Special Amenities:** free expanded continental breakfast and free newspaper.

SOME UNITS

(See map and index starting on p. 256)

RAMADA INN DOWNTOWN PHOENIX   *Book at aaa.com*   Phone: (602)258-3411   **18**

	2/1-4/30	1P: $89-$129	2P: $89-$129	XP: $10	F18
	9/12-1/31	1P: $79-$119	2P: $79-$119	XP: $10	F18
	5/1-9/11	1P: $49-$99	2P: $49-$99	XP: $10	F18

Location: I-10, exit 145B (7th St), 0.7 mi s to Van Buren St, 0.4 mi w, then just n; downtown. 401 N 1st St 85004.
Small-scale Hotel Fax: 602/258-3171. **Facility:** 163 units. 161 one-bedroom standard units. 1 one- and 1 two-bedroom suites. 2-4 stories, interior/exterior corridors. *Bath:* combo or shower only. **Parking:** on-site. **Terms:** check-in 4 pm, package plans. **Amenities:** video games (fee), voice mail, irons, hair dryers. **Dining:** 6:30 am-2 & 5-10 pm, cocktails. **Pool(s):** heated outdoor. **Guest Services:** gift shop, coin laundry. **Business Services:** meeting rooms, fax (fee). **Cards:** AX, CB, DC, DS, MC, VI. *(See color ad below)*

RESIDENCE INN BY MARRIOTT PHOENIX AIRPORT   *Book at aaa.com*   Phone: (602)273-9220   **14**

	2/1-4/8	1P: $109-$250	2P: $109-$250
	4/9-5/20 & 9/10-1/31	1P: $99-$250	2P: $99-$250
	5/21-9/9	1P: $69-$150	2P: $69-$150

Small-scale Hotel **Location:** Loop 202, exit 152 (40th and 44th sts) eastbound; exit 152 (44th St) westbound, just s. 801 N 44th St 85008.
Fax: 602/273-7221. **Facility:** 200 units. 124 one-bedroom standard units with efficiencies. 56 one- and 20 two-bedroom suites with efficiencies. 4 stories, interior corridors. *Bath:* combo or shower only. **Parking:** on-site. **Terms:** [ECP] meal plan available, small pets only ($75 fee). **Amenities:** video games (fee), high-speed Internet, voice mail, irons, hair dryers. **Pool(s):** heated outdoor. **Leisure Activities:** whirlpool, exercise room, sports court. **Guest Services:** complimentary evening beverages: Mon-Thurs, valet and coin laundry. **Business Services:** meeting rooms, fax (fee). **Cards:** AX, CB, DC, DS, JC, MC, VI.

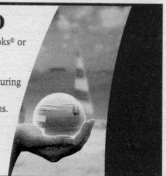

(See map and index starting on p. 256)

SLEEP INN SKY HARBOR AIRPORT   *Book at aaa.com*   Phone: (480)967-7100   **34**

(AAA) (SAVE)

	2/1-4/30	1P: $89-$169	2P: $99-$169	XP: $7	F17
	10/1-1/31	1P: $89-$129	2P: $99-$129	XP: $7	F17
	5/1-9/15	1P: $59-$89	2P: $65-$89	XP: $7	F17

Location: I-10, exit 151 (University Dr), 2 mi n, then just w. 2621 S 47th Pl 85034. Fax: 480/921-7400. **Facility:** 105

Small-scale Hotel   one-bedroom standard units. 3 stories, interior corridors. *Bath:* combo or shower only. **Parking:** on-site. **Terms:** small pets only ($25 fee). **Amenities:** high-speed Internet, voice mail, irons, hair dryers. **Pool(s):** heated outdoor. **Leisure Activities:** whirlpool. **Guest Services:** valet and coin laundry. **Business Services:** business center. **Cards:** AX, DC, DS, MC, VI. **Special Amenities:** free continental breakfast and free local telephone calls.
(See color ad below & p 302)

SOME UNITS

[icons]

SPRINGHILL SUITES BY MARRIOTT   *Book at aaa.com*   Phone: (602)307-9929   **21**

(AAA) (SAVE)

	2/1-3/31 [ECP]	1P: $99-$169	2P: $99-$169
	9/15-1/31 [ECP]	1P: $99-$149	2P: $99-$149
	4/1-6/1 [ECP]	1P: $79-$149	2P: $79-$149
	6/2-9/14 [ECP]	1P: $59-$89	2P: $59-$89

Small-scale Hotel   **Location:** I-10, exit 145 (7th St S), just s, then just e. 802 E Van Buren St 85006. Fax: 602/307-9964. **Facility:** 122 one-bedroom standard units. 6 stories, interior corridors. *Bath:* combo or shower only. **Parking:** on-site. **Amenities:** video games (fee), high-speed Internet, voice mail, irons, hair dryers. **Pool(s):** heated outdoor. **Leisure Activities:** whirlpool, exercise room. **Guest Services:** valet and coin laundry. **Business Services:** meeting rooms, business center. **Cards:** AX, CB, DC, DS, JC, MC, VI. **Special Amenities:** free continental breakfast and free local telephone calls.

SOME UNITS

[icons]

SUPER 8-AIRPORT   *Book at aaa.com*   Phone: (602)244-1627   **25**

(AAA) (SAVE)

	2/1-4/29	1P: $59-$79	2P: $69-$99	XP: $10	F18
	9/28-1/31	1P: $59-$69	2P: $69-$99	XP: $10	F18
	4/30-6/3	1P: $55-$69	2P: $59-$99	XP: $10	F18
	6/4-9/27	1P: $52-$65	2P: $59-$89	XP: $10	F18

Motel   **Location:** Loop 202, exit 1C (32nd St), 0.6 mi s, then just e. 3401 E Van Buren St 85008. Fax: 602/275-1126. **Facility:** 80 one-bedroom standard units. 2 stories (no elevator), interior/exterior corridors. *Bath:* combo or shower only. **Parking:** on-site. **Terms:** check-in 4 pm. **Leisure Activities:** pool and spa privileges. **Guest Services:** valet laundry, area transportation-hospital, bus terminal. **Business Services:** fax (fee). **Cards:** AX, CB, DC, DS, MC, VI. **Special Amenities:** free continental breakfast and free local telephone calls.

SOME UNITS

[icons]

WINGATE INN PHOENIX   *Book at aaa.com*   Phone: (602)716-9900   **7**

(AAA) (SAVE)

	2/1-4/15 [ECP]	1P: $99-$129	2P: $99-$129	XP: $10	F18
	9/17-1/31 [ECP]	1P: $79-$129	2P: $79-$129	XP: $10	F18
	4/16-5/19 [ECP]	1P: $79-$109	2P: $79-$109	XP: $10	F18
	5/20-9/16 [ECP]	1P: $69-$89	2P: $69-$89	XP: $10	F18

Small-scale Hotel   **Location:** I-10, exit 145 (7th St), just n to McDowell Rd, 0.4 mi w, then 0.7 mi n. Located in a commercial area. 2520 N Central Ave 85003. Fax: 602/716-9909. **Facility:** 107 units. 97 one-bedroom standard units. 10 one-bedroom suites. 4 stories, interior corridors. *Bath:* combo or shower only. **Parking:** on-site. **Amenities:** video games (fee), high-speed Internet, dual phone lines, voice mail, safes, irons, hair dryers. **Pool(s):** heated outdoor. **Leisure Activities:** whirlpool, exercise room. **Guest Services:** coin laundry, area transportation-within 5 mi. **Business Services:** meeting rooms, business center. **Cards:** AX, CB, DC, DS, JC, MC, VI. **Special Amenities:** free expanded continental breakfast and free newspaper.

SOME UNITS

[icons]

(See map and index starting on p. 256)

WYNDHAM PHOENIX HOTEL   *Book at aaa.com*   **Phone: (602)333-0000**   ㉙

⬥⬥⬥ SAVE	2/1-5/28 & 1/1-1/31	1P: $169	2P: $169	XP: $20	F
	9/11-12/31	1P: $149	2P: $149	XP: $20	F
〰〰〰	5/29-9/10	1P: $79	2P: $79	XP: $20	F

Location: Just w of 1st St; between 1st St and Central Ave; downtown. 50 E Adams St 85004. Fax: 602/333-5180.
Large-scale Hotel **Facility:** 530 units. 529 one-bedroom standard units. 1 two-bedroom suite ($109-$290) with kitchen. 19 stories, interior corridors. *Bath:* combo or shower only. **Parking:** on-site (fee) and valet. **Terms:** check-in 4 pm, 3 day cancellation notice. **Amenities:** high-speed Internet, dual phone lines, voice mail, irons, hair dryers. *Some:* CD players. *Fee:* DVD players. **Dining:** 2 restaurants, cocktails. **Pool(s):** heated outdoor. **Leisure Activities:** sauna. **Guest Services:** gift shop, valet laundry, area transportation-Copper Square Dash. **Business Services:** conference facilities, business center. **Cards:** AX, DC, DS, MC, VI. **Special Amenities:** free newspaper and preferred room (subject to availability with advance reservations).

SOME UNITS
🛫 🍽 ♿ 🚫 🏊 ✈ 📷 DATA PORT 💻 / ✖ VCR 🔲 🖵 /
FEE   FEE   FEE   FEE   FEE

───────── **WHERE TO DINE** ─────────

ALICE COOPER'STOWN   **Lunch:** $8-$15   **Dinner:** $8-$15   **Phone:** 602/253-7337   ⑱
〰〰 〰〰   **Location:** Just e of 2nd St; center. 101 E Jackson St 85004. **Hours:** 11 am-9 pm; closing hours vary on game days. Closed major holidays. **Features:** A short walk from the stadium, the barbecue eatery provides an
Regional American   unusual mix of hard rock and baseball camaraderie. Saucy sandwiches, Southwestern flavors and a wall-size TV make for an exciting meal. Casual dress; cocktails. **Parking:** street. **Cards:** AX, DC, MC, VI.

BACCHANAL RESTAURANT   **Dinner:** $15-$22   **Phone:** 602/224-9377   ①
〰〰 〰〰   **Location:** Jct 32nd St and E Thomas Rd, just w. 3015 E Thomas Rd 85016. **Hours:** 5 pm-9 pm, Fri & Sat-11 pm. Closed: 1/1, 11/23, 12/25; also 11/24, Sun & Mon. **Reservations:** accepted. **Features:** Named after the
Greek   ancient Greek god of wine and celebration, the restaurant offers plenty of each. Live music and a belly dancer are featured Tuesday through Saturday night, and a full bar is available. Well-prepared traditional Greek dishes, including soup and desserts, make up the menu. Guests should be prepared to join in the dancing at the lively night spot. Casual dress; cocktails. **Parking:** on-site. **Cards:** AX, MC, VI.   🍸 🚫

BARRIO CAFE'   **Lunch:** $7-$12   **Dinner:** $12-$20   **Phone:** 602/636-0240   ③
⬥⬥⬥   **Location:** Just s of Thomas Rd. 2814 N 16th St 85006. **Hours:** 11 am-2:30 & 5:30-10 pm, Sat 5:30 pm-10:30 pm, Sun 11 am-9 pm. Closed: 11/23, 12/25; also Mon. **Features:** The neat cafe in the heart of town serves what
〰〰 〰〰   the award-winning chef calls "Modern Mexican Cuisine." Using creative blends of traditional sauces, she enhances dishes such as enchiladas with chicken or fish grilled in banana leaf. Many vegetarian dishes are
Nouvelle Mexican   also offered. Casual dress; cocktails. **Parking:** on-site. **Cards:** AX, MC, VI.

BILL JOHNSON'S BIG APPLE RESTAURANT   **Lunch:** $6-$10 **Dinner:** $10-$16 **Phone:** 602/275-2107   ⑫
〰〰 〰〰   **Location:** Just e of 37th St. 3757 E Van Buren St 85008. **Hours:** 6 am-11 pm. Closed: 11/23, 12/25. **Features:** Casual Western decor, including wood shavings on the floor, does not detract from the hearty
Steak House   barbecue beef, pork and chicken that the popular local chain is known to serve. Casual dress; cocktails. **Parking:** on-site. **Cards:** AX, DS, MC, VI.   🚫

COMPASS RESTAURANT   **Lunch:** $10-$28   **Dinner:** $20-$30   **Phone:** 602/440-3166   ⑬
〰〰〰〰   **Location:** Just s of Monroe St; downtown; at Civic Plaza; in Hyatt Regency Phoenix. 122 N 2nd St 85004. **Hours:** 11:30 am-2 & 5:30-10 pm, Sun from 10 am. **Reservations:** suggested. **Features:** This revolving
American   restaurant on the 24th floor offers panoramic views of the city. Innovative presentations of seafood, beef, lamb and chicken combine artistic color with tempting accompaniments to make a delightful meal. Dressy casual; cocktails. **Parking:** on-site. **Cards:** AX, CB, DC, DS, JC, MC, VI.   ♿M 🍸

CORONADO CAFE   **Lunch:** $7-$11   **Dinner:** $9-$15   **Phone:** 602/258-5149   ⑥
〰〰 〰〰   **Location:** Between E Oak St and E Monte Vista Rd. 2201 N 7th St 85006. **Hours:** 11 am-3 pm, Fri & Sat-10 pm, Sun & Mon-3 pm. **Features:** In a small converted house, this local favorite serves Southwestern regional
Regional Mexican   Mexican and traditional favorites in a casual setting. Daily specials include meatloaf. Casual dress. **Parking:** on-site. **Cards:** AX, MC, VI.

DURANT'S   *Menu on aaa.com*   **Lunch:** $8-$19   **Dinner:** $21-$52   **Phone:** 602/264-5967   ⑤
⬥⬥⬥   **Location:** 0.8 mi n of McDowell Rd. 2611 N Central Ave 85004. **Hours:** 11 am-4 & 5-10 pm, Sat 5 pm-11 pm, Sun 4:30 pm-10 pm. Closed major holidays. **Reservations:** accepted. **Features:** For great steaks, a warm,
〰〰〰〰   friendly atmosphere and accomplished service, the restaurant fits the bill. The well-trained staff strives to provide guests a special dining experience. When entering from the parking area, diners may meet the grill
Steak House   chef as they walk through the kitchen itself. Casual dress; cocktails. **Parking:** valet. **Cards:** AX, CB, DC, DS, JC, MC, VI.   🍸 🚫

FATE   **Lunch:** $6-$13   **Dinner:** $6-$13   **Phone:** 602/254-6424   ⑩
〰〰 〰〰   **Location:** Just s of Roosevelt; downtown. 905 N 4th St 85004. **Hours:** 11 am-2 & 5-11 pm, Fri-3 am, Sat 5 pm-3 am. Closed major holidays; also Sun. **Reservations:** accepted. **Features:** The tiny house is home to fresh,
Asian   cooked-to-order vegetarian dishes, which may be coupled with a choice of shrimp, tofu or chicken. The curries are spicy and the salads crispy. Casual dress. **Parking:** on-site. **Cards:** AX, DS, MC, VI.

HONEY BEAR'S BBQ   **Lunch:** $4-$14   **Dinner:** $4-$14   **Phone:** 602/279-7911   ②
〰〰   **Location:** Jct Central Ave and Thomas Rd, just s. 2824 N Central Ave 85004. **Hours:** 10 am-9:30 pm, Sun-9 pm. Closed: 11/23, 12/25. **Features:** Barbecue sandwiches and popularly priced dinners are available at the
Barbecue   central Phoenix location. Casual dress; beer only. **Parking:** on-site. **Cards:** AX, DS, MC, VI.

(See map and index starting on p. 256)

INDIAN DELHI PALACE   Lunch: $7-$12   Dinner: $7-$17   Phone: 602/244-8181   ⑦
▼▼ ▼▼   **Location:** 0.5 mi e of SR 143. 5104 E McDowell Rd 85008. **Hours:** 11:30 am-10 pm. **Reservations:** accepted.
Features: The new building is inviting. Classic Indian cuisine includes freshly made sauces, hot breads and
Indian   spicy flavors. Local businesspeople favor the luncheon buffet. Casual dress; cocktails. **Parking:** on-site.
Cards: AX, DC, DS, MC, VI.

KINCAID'S FISH, CHOP & STEAKHOUSE   Lunch: $8-$16   Dinner: $16-$26   Phone: 602/340-0000   ⑯
▼▼▼▼   **Location:** Southwest corner of 3rd St and Washington; in Collier Center. Two S 3rd St 85004. **Hours:** 11:30 am-2:30
& 5-9 pm, Fri-9:30 pm, Sat 4 pm-9:30 pm, Sun 4 pm-9 pm. Closed major holidays. **Reservations:** accepted.
Steak & Seafood **Features:** Just steps away from art and sports venues, the restaurant prepares a good selection of
imported seafood, aged steaks and freshly prepared accompaniments. The eatery's warm atmosphere has
the feeling of a private club. Dressy casual; cocktails. **Parking:** on-site and street. **Cards:** AX, CB, DC, DS, JC, MC, VI.   ⛾

MATADOR RESTAURANT   Lunch: $4-$16   Dinner: $4-$25   Phone: 602-254-7563   ⑭
▼▼ ▼▼   **Location:** Jct E Adams and 1st sts. 125 E Adams St 85004. **Hours:** 7 am-11 pm. Closed: 4/16, 11/23, 12/25.
Reservations: accepted. **Features:** Offering fast service and Mexican, American and Greek selections, the
Mexican   downtown eatery is popular with the folks who work nearby. A full lounge is on site. The spacious dining
area displays Mexican appointments. Casual dress; cocktails. **Parking:** on-site (fee). **Cards:** AX, CB, DC,
DS, MC, VI.   ⛾ ⬎

MY FLORIST CAFE   Lunch: $6-$12   Dinner: $6-$12   Phone: 602/254-0333   ⑧
▼▼▼▼   **Location:** 0.4 mi w of Central Ave. 530 W McDowell Rd 85003. **Hours:** 7 am-midnight. **Reservations:** accepted.
Features: Sculptures add to the sleek, modern decor. Among choices are fresh salads, hearty sandwiches
American   and elegant desserts. Don't go home without checking out the baked goods at the Willo Bread bakery, just
off the entry. Casual dress; cocktails; entertainment. **Parking:** on-site. **Cards:** AX, MC, VI.

PIZZERIA BIANCO   Dinner: $10-$20   Phone: 602/258-8300   ⑮
▼▼ ▼▼   **Location:** I-10, exit 145 (7th St), 0.5 mi s, then just w. 623 E Adams St 85004. **Hours:** 5 pm-10 pm. Closed major
holidays; also Sun & Mon. **Features:** Freshly made, wood-fired pizza with a selection of custom-made
Pizza   toppings comes highly acclaimed at the casual restaurant. Casual dress; beer & wine only. **Parking:** on-site.
Cards: AX, MC, VI.   ⛾

PORTLAND'S   Lunch: $9-$14   Dinner: $9-$24   Phone: 602/795-7480   ⑨
▼▼▼▼   **Location:** Just w of Central Ave; downtown. 105 W Portland St 85003. **Hours:** 11 am-2 & 5-10 pm, Sat from 5 pm.
Closed major holidays; also Sun. **Reservations:** accepted. **Features:** Displaying upscale appointments, the
American   convenient downtown restaurant nurtures a relaxed atmosphere. The chef-owners prepare flavorful food
they dub "New American cuisine." Worth trying are ostrich tenderloin with sweet potato polenta or Australian
beef grilled to taste. Casual dress; cocktails. **Parking:** street. **Cards:** AX, DC, MC, VI.   ⛾

SAM'S CAFE AT THE ARIZONA CENTER   Lunch: $8-$13   Dinner: $9-$16   Phone: 602/252-3545   ⑪
▼▼ ▼▼   **Location:** Northwest corner of Van Buren and 3rd sts. 455 N 3rd St 85004. **Hours:** 11 am-10 pm, Sun-9 pm.
Closed: 7/4, 11/23, 12/25. **Reservations:** suggested. **Features:** Those who are hungry after shopping,
Southwestern   sports events or the theater will find that the restaurant's Southwestern delicacies fill a void. Applewood-
smoked pecan salmon, adovo chicken pasta and steaming fajitas are sure to satisfy the hungriest patrons.
Dressy casual; cocktails. **Parking:** street. **Cards:** AX, DS, MC, VI.   ⛾ ⬎

STOCKYARDS RESTAURANT & 1889 SALOON   Lunch: $8-$14   Dinner: $16-$32   Phone: 602/273-7378   ⑰
▼▼ ▼▼   **Location:** 0.5 mi e of 48th St. 5001 E Washington St 85034. **Hours:** 11 am-2 & 5-10 pm, Sat from 5 pm, Sun 4
pm-9 pm. Closed major holidays. **Reservations:** suggested. **Features:** Since 1947, this restaurant has
Steak House   been serving nice steaks, prime rib and other entrees. Completely renovated in 2004, the warm and inviting
dining room features an attractive stone dual-sided fireplace. Casual dress; cocktails. **Parking:** on-site.
Cards: AX, DC, DS, MC, VI.   ⛾

THE WILD THAIGER   Lunch: $7-$9   Dinner: $9-$14   Phone: 602/241-8995   ④
▼▼ ▼▼   **Location:** Just s of Thomas Rd. 2631 N Central Ave 85004. **Hours:** 11 am-3 & 5-9 pm, Fri & Sat-10 pm, Mon-3
pm, Sun 5 pm-9 pm. Closed major holidays. **Reservations:** accepted. **Features:** Patrons can satisfy their
Thai   inner "Thaiger." The friendly staff presents classic made-to-order dishes that are marked by attractive
presentation. Popular choices include hot pots that serve two, varied curries and such specialties as
tamarind shrimp. The casual setting is on a busy central avenue into the city. The small, nicely decorated spot has a large patio
on the street side for dining and smoking. Casual dress; cocktails. **Parking:** on-site. **Cards:** AX, CB, DC, DS, JC, MC, VI.

PHOENIX pop. 1,321,045 (See maps and indexes p. 260-263, 264-265, 271-272)

—————— WHERE TO STAY ——————

AMERISUITES (PHOENIX/METRO CENTER)   *Book at aaa.com*   Phone: (602)997-8800 **17**

(AAA) (SAVE)   All Year [ECP]   1P: $79-$169   2P: $89-$179   XP: $10   F18

▼▼▼▼   **Location:** I-17, exit 208 (Peoria Ave), just e, then 0.3 mi n. 10838 N 25th Ave 85029. Fax: 602/997-4218.

Small-scale Hotel **Facility:** 128 one-bedroom standard units. 4 stories, interior corridors. *Bath:* combo or shower only. **Parking:** on-site. **Terms:** cancellation fee imposed, small pets only ($10 extra charge). **Amenities:** voice mail, irons, hair dryers. **Fee:** video games, high-speed Internet. *Some:* dual phone lines. **Pool(s):** small heated outdoor. **Leisure Activities:** exercise room. **Guest Services:** valet and coin laundry, area transportation-within 5 mi. **Business Services:** meeting rooms, fax (fee). **Cards:** AX, CB, DC, DS, MC, VI. **Special Amenities:** free full breakfast.

SOME UNITS
🅂🄳 🛏 🛉 ♿ 🍽 📷 📠 🔌 ◻ 🖨 💻 / ✕ / 🆅🄲🅁 /
   FEE

ARIZONA BILTMORE RESORT & SPA   *Book at aaa.com*   Phone: (602)955-6600 **34**

(AAA) (SAVE)   2/1-5/24 & 1/1-1/31   1P: $445-$1845   2P: $445-$1845   XP: $20   F18

   9/12-12/31   1P: $375-$1295   2P: $375-$1295   XP: $20   F18

▼▼▼ ▼▼▼   5/25-9/11   1P: $195-$875   2P: $195-$875   XP: $20   F18

Resort   **Location:** Jct Camelback Rd, 0.5 mi n on 24th St, then 0.4 mi w. Located in a residential area. 2400 E Missouri 85016.

Large-scale Hotel   Fax: 602/381-7600. **Facility:** This venerable valley resort is noted for its attentive staff, buildings with Frank Lloyd Wright style, elegant guest rooms and over-size lawn chess. 739 units. 673 one-bedroom standard units. 66 one-bedroom suites ($295-$1845) with kitchens. 2-4 stories, interior/exterior corridors. *Bath:* combo or shower only. **Parking:** on-site and valet. **Terms:** check-in 4 pm, 7 day cancellation notice-fee imposed, package plans, small pets only ($50 fee, $100 deposit). **Amenities:** video games (fee), high-speed Internet, dual phone lines, voice mail, safes, honor bars, irons, hair dryers. **Dining:** 3 restaurants, 5:30 am-10 pm, cocktails, also, Wright's, see separate listing. **Pool(s):** 4 heated outdoor, 4 small heated outdoor. **Leisure Activities:** saunas, whirlpools, steamrooms, croquet, lawn chess, rental bicycles, hiking trails, jogging, exercise room, spa, sports court, volleyball. **Fee:** golf-36 holes, 7 lighted tennis courts. **Guest Services:** gift shop, area transportation (fee). **Business Services:** conference facilities, business center. **Cards:** AX, CB, DC, DS, MC, VI.

SOME UNITS
➕ 🛏 🍽 24🕐 📺 ♿ 🦺 ✕ 📷 📠 / ✕ / 🆅🄲🅁 💻 /
FEE FEE   FEE

BEST WESTERN BELL HOTEL   *Book at aaa.com*   Phone: (602)993-8300 **7**

(AAA) (SAVE)   2/1-4/15 [ECP]   1P: $69-$139   2P: $69-$139   XP: $5   F12

   10/1-1/31 [ECP]   1P: $59-$109   2P: $59-$109   XP: $5   F12

▼▼▼ ▼▼▼   4/16-9/30 [ECP]   1P: $54-$84   2P: $54-$84   XP: $5   F12

   Location: I-17, exit 212, just e, then just n. 17211 N Black Canyon Hwy 85023. Fax: 602/863-2163. **Facility:** 100

Small-scale Hotel one-bedroom standard units. 2 stories (no elevator), exterior corridors. **Parking:** on-site. **Terms:** 1-4 night minimum stay - seasonal, pets (small dogs only, $10 extra charge). **Amenities:** high-speed Internet, voice mail, irons, hair dryers. **Pool(s):** heated outdoor. **Leisure Activities:** whirlpool. **Guest Services:** valet and coin laundry. **Business Services:** PC. **Cards:** AX, CB, DC, DS, JC, MC, VI. **Special Amenities:** free expanded continental breakfast and early check-in/late check-out. *(See color ad below)*

SOME UNITS
🅂🄳 🛏 🛉 📶 🍽 📷 🔌 ◻ 🖨 💻 / ✕ /
   FEE

(See maps and indexes p. 260-263, 264-265, 271-272)

BEST WESTERN GRACE INN AT AHWATUKEE

Book at aaa.com

Phone: (480)893-3000 **2**

2/1-4/20	1P: $109-$129	2P: $119-$139	XP: $10	F18
4/21-5/28 & 9/16-1/31	1P: $89-$119	2P: $99-$129	XP: $10	F18
5/29-9/15	1P: $79-$109	2P: $89-$119	XP: $10	F18

Location: I-10, exit 157, just w on Elliot Rd, then just s. 10831 S 51st St 85044. Fax: 480/496-8303. **Facility:** 160 units. 152 one-bedroom standard units. 8 one-bedroom suites with efficiencies. 6 stories, interior corridors. **Parking:** on-site. **Terms:** 2-3 night minimum stay - seasonal, cancellation fee imposed, package plans. **Amenities:** voice mail, irons, hair dryers. *Some:* high-speed Internet. **Dining:** 6 am-2 & 5-10 pm; to 9 pm in summer, cocktails. **Pool(s):** heated outdoor. **Leisure Activities:** whirlpool, lighted tennis court. **Guest Services:** gift shop, valet and coin laundry, area transportation-within 5 mi. **Business Services:** conference facilities, fax (fee). **Cards:** AX, DC, DS, MC, VI. **Special Amenities:** free local telephone calls and preferred room (subject to availability with advance reservations).
(See color ad below)

Small-scale Hotel

SOME UNITS

BEST WESTERN INNSUITES HOTEL PHOENIX NORTHERN/AIRPORT

Book at aaa.com

Phone: (602)997-6285 **30**

2/1-4/2 [BP]	1P: $89-$139	2P: $89-$139	XP: $10	F18
9/17-1/31 [BP]	1P: $79-$129	2P: $79-$129	XP: $10	F18
4/3-5/27	1P: $79-$129	2P: $79-$129	XP: $10	F18
5/28-9/16 [BP]	1P: $69-$99	2P: $69-$99	XP: $10	F18

Location: Loop 51, 0.3 mi w. 1615 E Northern Ave 85020. Fax: 602/943-1407. **Facility:** 104 units. 73 one-bedroom standard units. 31 one-bedroom suites ($89-$169), some with efficiencies and/or whirlpools. 2 stories (no elevator), exterior corridors. *Bath:* combo or shower only. **Parking:** on-site. **Terms:** weekly rates available, pets ($25 fee). **Amenities:** video games (fee), high-speed Internet, dual phone lines, voice mail, irons, hair dryers. **Pool(s):** heated outdoor. **Leisure Activities:** whirlpool, limited exercise equipment. **Guest Services:** sundries, complimentary evening beverages, valet and coin laundry. **Business Services:** meeting rooms, PC. **Cards:** AX, CB, DC, DS, JC, MC, VI. **Special Amenities:** free full breakfast and free room upgrade (subject to availability with advance reservations).
(See color ad below)

Small-scale Hotel

FEE

SOME UNITS

(See maps and indexes p. 260-263, 264-265, 271-272)

BEST WESTERN PHOENIX I-17 METROCENTER INN

Phone: (602)864-6233 **29**

2/1-4/30 & 11/1-1/31 [BP]   1P: $79-$89   2P: $89-$99   XP: $5   F17
5/1-10/31 [BP]   1P: $64-$69   2P: $69-$74   XP: $5   F17

Location: I-17, exit 206 (Northern Ave), just e, then just n; on east side of freeway. 8101 N Black Canyon Hwy 85021. Fax: 602/995-7503. **Facility:** 147 one-bedroom standard units. 3 stories, exterior corridors. **Parking:** on-

Small-scale Hotel   site. **Terms:** pets ($25 fee). **Amenities:** high-speed Internet, voice mail, irons, hair dryers. **Pool(s):** small heated outdoor. **Leisure Activities:** whirlpool. **Guest Services:** valet laundry. **Business Services:** meeting rooms, fax (fee). **Cards:** AX, CB, DC, DS, MC, VI. **Special Amenities: free expanded continental breakfast and free newspaper.** *(See color ad below)*

CAMELBACK COURTYARD BY MARRIOTT   *Book at aaa.com*

Phone: (602)955-5200   **40**

2/1-4/29   1P: $149-$219
9/10-1/31   1P: $129-$189
Small-scale Hotel   4/30-5/27   1P: $119-$179
5/28-9/9   1P: $79-$119

Location: Jct 20th St and Camelback Rd. Located in Town and Country Shopping Center. 2101 E Camelback Rd 85016. Fax: 602/955-1101. **Facility:** 155 units. 144 one-bedroom standard units. 11 one-bedroom suites ($89-$239). 4 stories, interior corridors. *Bath:* combo or shower only. **Parking:** on-site. **Amenities:** high-speed Internet, dual phone lines, voice mail, irons, hair dryers. **Pool(s):** heated outdoor. **Leisure Activities:** whirlpool, exercise room. **Guest Services:** valet and coin laundry. **Business Services:** meeting rooms, fax. **Cards:** AX, DC, DS, JC, MC, VI.

CANDLEWOOD SUITES   *Book at aaa.com*

Phone: (602)861-4900   **15**

2/1-4/30   1P: $66-$199
9/20-1/31   1P: $50-$90
Small-scale Hotel   5/1-9/19   1P: $40-$80

Location: I-17, exit 208 (Peoria Ave), just e, then 0.4 mi n. 11411 N Black Canyon Hwy 85029. Fax: 602/861-4940. **Facility:** 98 units. 74 one-bedroom standard units with efficiencies. 24 one-bedroom suites with efficiencies. 3 stories, interior corridors. *Bath:* combo or shower only. **Parking:** on-site. **Terms:** office hours 7 am-11 pm, cancellation fee imposed, small pets only ($75 fee). **Amenities:** video library, CD players, high-speed Internet, dual phone lines, voice mail, irons, hair dryers. **Pool(s):** heated outdoor. **Leisure Activities:** whirlpool, exercise room. **Guest Services:** sundries, valet and coin laundry. **Business Services:** fax. **Cards:** AX, CB, DC, DS, JC, MC, VI.

(See maps and indexes p. 260-261, 264-265, 271-272)

CLARION HOTEL @ PHOENIX TECH CENTER   *Book at aaa.com*   Phone: (480)893-3900

2/1-4/15	1P: $99-$149	2P: $109-$159	XP: $10 F18
4/16-6/3 & 9/29-1/31	1P: $79-$99	2P: $89-$109	XP: $10 F18
6/4-9/28	1P: $59-$79	2P: $69-$89	XP: $10 F18

Small-scale Hotel   **Location:** I-10, exit 157 (Elliot Rd), just w, just n on 51st St, then just e. Located in a residential area. 5121 E La Puenta Ave 85044. Fax: 480/496-0815. **Facility:** 188 units. 186 one-bedroom standard units. 2 one-bedroom suites ($119-$189). 4 stories, exterior corridors. **Parking:** on-site. **Terms:** cancellation fee imposed, [BP] meal plan available, package plans, pets ($25 fee, must be attended). **Amenities:** voice mail, irons, hair dryers. **Pool(s):** heated outdoor. **Leisure Activities:** whirlpool, exercise room. **Guest Services:** valet and coin laundry, area transportation-within 5 mi. **Business Services:** meeting rooms, business center. **Cards:** AX, DC, DS, MC, VI. **Special Amenities:** free expanded continental breakfast and early check-in/late check-out.

SOME UNITS

COMFORT INN BLACK CANYON   *Book at aaa.com*   Phone: (602)242-8011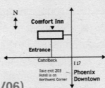

2/1-4/18	1P: $79-$129	2P: $79-$129	XP: $10 F12
10/1-1/31	1P: $69-$109	2P: $69-$109	XP: $10 F12
4/19-9/30	1P: $59-$99	2P: $59-$99	XP: $10 F12

Small-scale Hotel   **Location:** I-17, exit 203 (Camelback Rd), just n on west side of freeway. 5050 N Black Canyon Hwy 85017. Fax: 602/249-1988. **Facility:** 153 units. 143 one-bedroom standard units, some with whirlpools. 10 one-bedroom suites. 3 stories, exterior corridors. *Bath:* combo or shower only. **Parking:** on-site. **Terms:** weekly rates available, pets ($25 fee, in limited units). **Amenities:** voice mail, irons, hair dryers. **Pool(s):** heated outdoor. **Leisure Activities:** whirlpool. *Fee:* game room. **Guest Services:** valet and coin laundry. **Business Services:** meeting rooms. **Cards:** AX, DC, DS, MC, VI. *(See color ad below)*

SOME UNITS

COMFORT SUITES BY CHOICE HOTELS   *Book at aaa.com*   Phone: (602)861-3900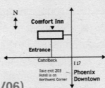

2/1-3/31 [ECP]	1P: $99-$149	2P: $99-$149	XP: $10 F17
10/1-1/31 [ECP]	1P: $69-$99	2P: $69-$99	XP: $10 F17
4/1-9/30 [ECP]	1P: $49-$89	2P: $49-$89	XP: $10 F17

Small-scale Hotel   **Location:** I-17, exit 208 (Peoria Ave), just e, just s on 25th Ave, then 0.3 mi w on W Beryl Ave. 10210 N 26th Dr 85021. Fax: 602/861-9300. **Facility:** 60 one-bedroom standard units. 3 stories, interior corridors. *Bath:* combo or shower only. **Parking:** on-site. **Terms:** cancellation fee imposed, pets ($25-$50 fee). **Amenities:** video library, voice mail, irons, hair dryers. **Pool(s):** small heated indoor. **Leisure Activities:** whirlpool, limited exercise equipment. **Guest Services:** valet and coin laundry. **Business Services:** meeting rooms, fax (fee). **Cards:** AX, DC, DS, MC, VI.

SOME UNITS

(See maps and indexes p. 260-263, 264-265, 271-272)

COMFORT SUITES CONFERENCE CENTER *Book at aaa.com* Phone: 602/279-3211 48
Property failed to provide current rates
Location: I-17, exit 201 (Thomas Rd), just w to 27th Ave, just n, then 0.7 mi nw. 3210 NW Grand Ave 85017.
Small-scale Hotel **Fax:** 602/230-2145. **Facility:** 167 one-bedroom suites. 4 stories, exterior corridors. *Bath:* combo or shower
only. **Parking:** on-site. **Terms:** pets ($25 fee). **Amenities:** voice mail, irons, hair dryers. **Pool(s):** heated
outdoor. **Leisure Activities:** whirlpool, limited exercise equipment. **Guest Services:** complimentary evening beverages, coin
laundry. **Business Services:** meeting rooms.

SOME UNITS

COUNTRY INN & SUITES BY CARLSON *Book at aaa.com* Phone: (623)879-9000 3

3/1-3/31	1P: $169-$219	2P: $169-$219	XP: $10	F18
2/1-2/28	1P: $149-$199	2P: $149-$199	XP: $10	F18
9/1-1/31	1P: $119-$169	2P: $119-$169	XP: $10	F18
4/1-8/31	1P: $109-$159	2P: $109-$159	XP: $10	F18

Small-scale Hotel
Location: I-17, exit 215A (Rose Garden Ln), just w to 27th Ave, 0.4 mi s, then just w on Frontage Rd. 20221 N 29th Ave 85027.
Fax: 623/476-1000. **Facility:** 126 units. 63 one-bedroom standard units. 63 one-bedroom suites ($119-$219), some with
whirlpools. 4 stories, interior corridors. *Bath:* combo or shower only. **Terms:** check-in 4 pm, [ECP] meal plan
available. **Amenities:** video games (fee), high-speed Internet, voice mail, irons, hair dryers. *Some:* dual phone lines. **Pool(s):**
heated outdoor. **Leisure Activities:** whirlpool, exercise room. **Guest Services:** valet and coin laundry, area transportation.
Business Services: meeting rooms, PC. **Cards:** AX, DC, DS, MC, VI.

SOME UNITS

CROWNE PLAZA PHOENIX *Book at aaa.com* Phone: (602)943-2341 18

1/2-1/31	1P: $99-$169	2P: $99-$169	XP: $10	F17
2/1-4/2	1P: $99-$164	2P: $99-$164	XP: $10	F17
10/2-1/1	1P: $79-$139	2P: $79-$139	XP: $10	F17
4/3-10/1	1P: $59-$139	2P: $59-$139	XP: $10	F17

Small-scale Hotel **Location:** I-17, exit 208 (Peoria Ave), just e, then just n on 25th Ave. 2532 W Peoria Ave 85029. **Fax:** 602/371-8470.
Facility: 249 one-bedroom standard units. 4 stories, interior corridors. *Bath:* combo or shower only. **Parking:** on-site. **Terms:** cancellation fee imposed, [AP], [BP] & [CP] meal plans available, pets ($25 fee). **Amenities:** CD
players, voice mail, irons, hair dryers. *Fee:* video games, high-speed Internet. **Dining:** 6 am-10 pm, cocktails. **Pool(s):** heated
outdoor, small heated indoor. **Leisure Activities:** whirlpools, exercise room. **Guest Services:** gift shop, valet and coin laundry,
area transportation-within 5 mi. **Business Services:** conference facilities, business center. **Cards:** AX, DC, DS, MC, VI.
Special Amenities: free local telephone calls and free newspaper. *(See color ad below)*

SOME UNITS

FEE   FEE

DAYS INN-NORTH PHOENIX *Book at aaa.com* Phone: 623/434-5500 2
Property failed to provide current rates
Location: I-17, exit 215B (Deer Valley Rd), just w. 21636 N 26th Ave 85027. **Fax:** 623/869-9726. **Facility:** 70 one-
bedroom standard units, some with whirlpools. 2 stories (no elevator), interior corridors. *Bath:* combo or
Small-scale Hotel shower only. **Parking:** on-site. **Amenities:** voice mail, hair dryers. **Pool(s):** small outdoor. **Leisure
Activities:** whirlpool. **Guest Services:** coin laundry. **Business Services:** fax (fee).

SOME UNITS

EMBASSY SUITES PHOENIX-BILTMORE *Book at aaa.com* Phone: (602)955-3992 38

2/1-3/30 & 9/10-1/31 [BP]	1P: $199-$309	2P: $199-$309	XP: $20	F18
3/31-5/25 [BP]	1P: $219-$259	2P: $219-$259	XP: $20	F18
5/26-9/9 [BP]	1P: $129-$169	2P: $129-$169	XP: $20	F18

Small-scale Hotel **Location:** Just n of Camelback Rd, on 26th St. Located adjacent to Biltmore Fashion Park. 2630 E Camelback Rd
85016. **Fax:** 602/955-6479. **Facility:** 232 one-bedroom suites. 5 stories, interior corridors. **Parking:** on-site and valet.
Terms: cancellation fee imposed, small pets only ($25 fee). **Amenities:** video games (fee), dual phone lines, voice mail, irons,
hair dryers. **Dining:** Omaha Steakhouse, see separate listing. **Pool(s):** heated outdoor. **Leisure Activities:** whirlpool, exercise
room. **Guest Services:** complimentary evening beverages, valet and coin laundry, area transportation. **Business Services:**
meeting rooms, fax (fee). **Cards:** AX, CB, DC, DS, JC, MC, VI.

SOME UNITS

FEE   FEE

(See maps and indexes p. 260-263, 264-265, 271-272)

EMBASSY SUITES PHOENIX NORTH *Book at aaa.com*   **Phone:** 602/375-1777   **11**

	2/1-4/30 [BP]	1P: $159-$222	2P: $169-$232	XP: $10 F18
	10/1-11/13 [BP]	1P: $139-$189	2P: $149-$199	XP: $10 F18
	11/14-2/28 [BP]	1P: $119-$166	2P: $129-$176	XP: $10 F18
	5/1-9/30 [BP]	1P: $129-$155	2P: $139-$165	XP: $10 F18

Large-scale Hotel **Location:** I-17, exit 211, just e. 2577 W Greenway Rd 85023. Fax: 602/993-5963. **Facility:** 314 units. 311 one- and 3 two-bedroom standard units, some with whirlpools. 3 stories, exterior corridors. *Bath:* combo or shower only. **Parking:** on-site. **Terms:** pets ($50 deposit). **Amenities:** dual phone lines, voice mail, irons, hair dryers. *Fee:* video games, high-speed Internet. **Dining:** 6:30 am-2 & 5-10 pm, Sat & Sun from 7 am, cocktails. **Pool(s):** heated outdoor, wading. **Leisure Activities:** whirlpool, lighted tennis court, exercise room. **Guest Services:** gift shop, complimentary evening beverages, valet and coin laundry. **Business Services:** conference facilities. **Cards:** AX, CB, DC, DS, MC, VI. **Special Amenities:** free full breakfast and free newspaper. *(See color ad below)*

SOME UNITS

🅂🄳 🐾 🍴 🍸 ♿ 📷 ⊠ 🎥 📠 🛏 🖥 💻 /⊠/
FEE

EMBASSY SUITES PHOENIX-SCOTTSDALE-A GOLF   **Phone:** 602/765-5800   **12**
RESORT   *Book at aaa.com*

Property failed to provide current rates

Location: Just s of Cactus; just w of Tatum. 4415 E Paradise Village Pkwy S 85032. Fax: 602/765-5890. Large-scale Hotel **Facility:** 270 one-bedroom suites. 6 stories, interior corridors. *Bath:* combo or shower only. **Parking:** on-site. **Amenities:** dual phone lines, voice mail, safes, irons, hair dryers. *Fee:* video games, high-speed Internet. **Pool(s):** heated outdoor. **Leisure Activities:** whirlpool, exercise room. *Fee:* golf-18 holes. **Guest Services:** gift shop, complimentary evening beverages, valet and coin laundry, area transportation. **Business Services:** meeting rooms, PC.

SOME UNITS

🍴 🍸 ♿M ♿ 📷 ⊠ 🎥 📠 🛏 🖥 💻 /⊠/

EXTENDED STAYAMERICA PHEONIX-CHANDLER-E   **Phone:** (480)753-6700   **5**
CHANDLER BLVD   *Book at aaa.com*

2/1-4/16 & 1/19-1/31	1P: $85	2P: $90	XP: $5 F17
10/1-1/18	1P: $70	2P: $75	XP: $5 F17
4/17-9/30	1P: $55	2P: $60	XP: $5 F17

Small-scale Hotel **Location:** I-10, exit 160 (Chandler Blvd), just w. 5035 E Chandler Blvd 85048. Fax: 480/753-6800. **Facility:** 129 one-bedroom standard units with efficiencies. 2 stories (no elevator), exterior corridors. *Bath:* combo or shower only. **Parking:** on-site. **Terms:** cancellation fee imposed, small pets only ($25 extra charge). **Amenities:** high-speed Internet (fee), voice mail, irons, hair dryers. **Pool(s):** heated outdoor. **Leisure Activities:** exercise room. **Guest Services:** valet and coin laundry. **Business Services:** fax (fee). **Cards:** AX, DC, DS, MC, VI.

SOME UNITS

Ⓐ🅂🄳 🐾 🍴 ♿ ⊠ 🎥 📠 🛏 🖥 💻 /⊠/
FEE

EXTENDED STAY AMERICA PHOENIX-METRO   **Phone:** (602)870-2999   **16**
CENTER   *Book at aaa.com*

2/1-4/3 & 1/18-1/31	1P: $75	2P: $80	XP: $5 F17
10/1-1/17	1P: $60	2P: $65	XP: $5 F17
4/4-9/30	1P: $45	2P: $50	XP: $5 F17

Small-scale Hotel **Location:** I-17, exit 208 (Peoria Ave), just e, then 0.3 mi n; on east side of freeway. 11211 N Black Canyon Hwy 85029. Fax: 602/870-2992. **Facility:** 133 one-bedroom standard units. 2 stories (no elevator), exterior corridors. *Bath:* combo or shower only. **Parking:** on-site. **Terms:** office hours 7 am-11 pm, cancellation fee imposed, small pets only ($25-$75 deposit). **Amenities:** high-speed Internet (fee), dual phone lines, voice mail, irons, hair dryers. **Pool(s):** small heated outdoor. **Leisure Activities:** exercise room. **Guest Services:** valet and coin laundry. **Cards:** AX, DC, DS, JC, MC, VI.

SOME UNITS

Ⓐ🅂🄳 🐾 🍴 ♿ ⊠ 🎥 📠 🛏 🖥 💻 /⊠/
FEE

(See maps and indexes p. 260-263, 264-265, 271-272)

EXTENDED STAY DELUXE PHOENIX-BILTMORE *Book at aaa.com*   **Phone: (602)265-6800** **35**

	2/1-4/2 & 1/16-1/31	1P: $120	2P: $125	XP: $5	F17
	10/1-1/15	1P: $80	2P: $85	XP: $5	F17
Small-scale Hotel	4/3-9/30	1P: $70	2P: $75	XP: $5	F17

Location: Jct SR 51, just w on Camelback Rd, then just n. 5235 N 16th St 85016. Fax: 602/265-1114. **Facility:** 111 one-bedroom standard units with efficiencies. 3 stories, interior corridors. *Bath:* combo or shower only. **Parking:** on-site. **Terms:** cancellation fee imposed, pets ($25 extra charge). **Amenities:** high-speed Internet (fee), voice mail, irons, hair dryers. *Some:* DVD players (fee). **Pool(s):** heated outdoor. **Leisure Activities:** whirlpool, exercise room. **Guest Services:** valet and coin laundry. **Cards:** AX, DC, DS, MC, VI.

EXTENDED STAYDELUXE (PHOENIX/MIDTOWN) *Book at aaa.com*   **Phone: (602)279-9000** **50**

	2/1-3/31 & 1/17-1/31	1P: $95	2P: $100	XP: $5	F17
	10/1-1/16	1P: $70	2P: $75	XP: $5	F17
Small-scale Hotel	4/1-9/30	1P: $60	2P: $65	XP: $5	F17

Location: Just w of Central Ave; between Indian School and Thomas rds. 217 W Osborn Rd 85013. Fax: 602/277-0900. **Facility:** 129 units. 100 one-bedroom standard units with efficiencies. 29 one-bedroom suites with efficiencies. 3 stories, interior corridors. *Bath:* combo or shower only. **Terms:** cancellation fee imposed, small pets only. **Amenities:** dual phone lines, voice mail, irons, hair dryers. *Fee:* video games, high-speed Internet, safes. **Pool(s):** heated outdoor. **Leisure Activities:** exercise room. **Guest Services:** valet and coin laundry. **Business Services:** meeting rooms, fax. **Cards:** AX, DC, DS, MC, VI.

FAIRFIELD INN BY MARRIOTT PHOENIX NORTH *Book at aaa.com*   **Phone: (602)548-8888** **9**

	2/1-4/29 & 1/1-1/31	1P: $109-$119	2P: $109-$119	
	4/30-5/27	1P: $99-$109	2P: $99-$109	
	5/28-12/31	1P: $69-$79	2P: $69-$79	

Location: I-17, exit 212, just e, then just n; on east side of freeway. 17017 N Black Canyon Hwy 85023. Small-scale Hotel Fax: 602/548-9553. **Facility:** 66 one-bedroom standard units. 3 stories, interior corridors. **Parking:** on-site. **Amenities:** high-speed Internet, irons, hair dryers. **Pool(s):** small heated outdoor. **Leisure Activities:** whirlpool. **Guest Services:** valet and coin laundry. **Business Services:** PC. **Cards:** AX, CB, DC, DS, JC, MC, VI. **Special Amenities:** free continental breakfast and free local telephone calls.

FOUR POINTS BY SHERATON PHOENIX
METROCENTER *Book at aaa.com*   **Phone: 602/997-5900** **21**

Property failed to provide current rates

Location: I-17, exit 208 (Peoria Ave), 0.3 mi w to 28th Dr, just s, then just e. Located at Metrocenter. 10220 N Metro Small-scale Hotel Pkwy E 85051. Fax: 602/943-6156. **Facility:** 284 units. 276 one-bedroom standard units. 8 one-bedroom suites. 5 stories, interior corridors. *Bath:* shower only. **Parking:** on-site. **Amenities:** dual phone lines, voice mail, irons, hair dryers. *Some: Fee:* high-speed Internet. **Pool(s):** heated outdoor. **Leisure Activities:** sauna, whirlpool, lighted tennis court, exercise room. **Guest Services:** gift shop, valet laundry, area transportation. **Business Services:** conference facilities, business center.

HAMPTON INN PHOENIX I-10 WEST *Book at aaa.com*   **Phone: (602)484-7000** **57**

| | 2/1-5/31 [ECP] | 1P: $69-$169 | 2P: $79-$179 | |
| | 6/1-1/31 [ECP] | 1P: $59-$169 | 2P: $69-$169 | |

Location: I-10, exit 139 (51st Ave), just sw. 5152 W Latham St 85043. Fax: 602/484-4377. **Facility:** 123 one-bedroom standard units. 3 stories, interior corridors. *Bath:* combo or shower only. **Parking:** on-site. Small-scale Hotel **Amenities:** high-speed Internet, voice mail, irons, hair dryers. **Pool(s):** heated outdoor. **Leisure Activities:** whirlpool. **Guest Services:** valet and coin laundry. **Business Services:** meeting rooms, fax (fee). **Cards:** AX, DC, DS, MC, VI. **Special Amenities:** free expanded continental breakfast and free local telephone calls. *(See color ad p 279)*

HILTON GARDEN INN *Book at aaa.com*   **Phone: (602)279-9811** **47**

	2/1-5/31 & 1/1-1/31	1P: $159	2P: $159	XP: $10	F18
	9/16-12/31	1P: $119	2P: $119	XP: $10	F18
Small-scale Hotel	6/1-9/15	1P: $89	2P: $89	XP: $10	F18

Location: 0.3 mi s of Indian School Rd, just w on Clarendon Ave. Located in a commercial area. 4000 N Central 85012. Fax: 602/285-2932. **Facility:** 156 one-bedroom standard units. 3-7 stories, interior corridors. *Bath:* combo or shower only. **Parking:** on-site. **Terms:** cancellation fee imposed. **Amenities:** video games (fee), high-speed Internet, dual phone lines, voice mail, irons, hair dryers. **Pool(s):** heated outdoor. **Leisure Activities:** whirlpool. **Guest Services:** gift shop, valet and coin laundry. **Business Services:** conference facilities, business center. **Cards:** AX, CB, DC, DS, JC, MC, VI.

HOLIDAY INN EXPRESS HOTEL & SUITES *Book at aaa.com*   **Phone: (480)785-8500** **3**

	2/1-4/30	1P: $109-$119	2P: $109-$119	XP: $10	F18
	9/1-1/31	1P: $99-$109	2P: $99-$109	XP: $10	F18
	5/1-8/31	1P: $79-$89	2P: $79-$89	XP: $10	F18

Location: I-10, exit 160 (Chandler Blvd), just w. 15221 S 50th St 85044. Fax: 480/785-7377. **Facility:** 125 units. Small-scale Hotel 123 one-bedroom standard units. 2 one-bedroom suites. 4 stories, interior corridors. *Bath:* combo or shower only. **Parking:** on-site. **Terms:** small pets only. **Amenities:** high-speed Internet, voice mail, irons, hair dryers. *Some:* dual phone lines. **Pool(s):** heated outdoor. **Leisure Activities:** whirlpool, exercise room. **Business Services:** meeting rooms, fax. **Cards:** AX, CB, DC, DS, JC, MC, VI. **Special Amenities:** free continental breakfast and free local telephone calls.

(See maps and indexes p. 260-263, 264-265, 271-272)

HOLIDAY INN MIDTOWN PHOENIX   *Book at aaa.com*   Phone: (602)200-8888   **45**

(AAA) (SAVE)	2/1-4/16	1P: $89-$139	2P: $89-$139	XP: $10 F18
	4/17-5/25 & 9/18-1/31	1P: $79-$129	2P: $79-$129	XP: $10 F18
	5/26-9/17	1P: $59-$99	2P: $59-$99	XP: $10 F18

Location: 0.3 mi n of Indian School Rd. 4321 N Central Ave 85012. Fax: 602/200-8800. **Facility:** 183 one-
Small-scale Hotel   bedroom standard units. 3-4 stories, exterior corridors. **Parking:** on-site. **Amenities:** high-speed Internet,
voice mail, irons, hair dryers. **Dining:** 6 am-10 pm, cocktails. **Pool(s):** heated outdoor. **Leisure
Activities:** whirlpool, exercise room. **Guest Services:** valet and coin laundry, area transportation-within 5 mi. **Business
Services:** meeting rooms, fax (fee). **Cards:** AX, DC, DS, MC, VI. **Special Amenities:** free newspaper and early check-in/late
check-out. *(See color ad below)*

SOME UNITS

[amenity icons]

HOLIDAY INN WEST   *Book at aaa.com*   Phone: (602)484-9009   **53**

(AAA) (SAVE)	2/1-4/16	1P: $129	2P: $129
	4/17-5/28 & 9/7-1/31	1P: $119	2P: $119
	5/29-9/6	1P: $99	2P: $99

Location: I-10, exit 139 (51st Ave), just n. 1500 N 51st Ave 85043. Fax: 602/484-0108. **Facility:** 144 units. 141
Small-scale Hotel   one-bedroom standard units. 3 one-bedroom suites with whirlpools. 4 stories, interior corridors. *Bath:* combo
or shower only. **Parking:** on-site. **Terms:** cancellation fee imposed, [BP] & [CP] meal plans available,
package plans, 19% service charge, pets ($25 fee). **Amenities:** video games (fee), high-speed Internet, voice mail, irons, hair
dryers. **Dining:** 6 am-9 pm, cocktails. **Pool(s):** small heated outdoor. **Leisure Activities:** whirlpool, exercise room. **Guest
Services:** valet laundry. **Business Services:** conference facilities, fax (fee). **Cards:** AX, CB, DC, DS, JC, MC, VI.

SOME UNITS

[amenity icons]

(See maps and indexes p. 260-263, 264-265, 271-272)

HOMESTEAD STUDIO SUITES HOTEL-PHOENIX NORTH/METRO CENTER   *Book at aaa.com*   **Phone:** (602)944-7828   **26**

Motel

	1P: $70	2P: $75	XP: $5	F17
2/1-4/2 & 1/9-1/31				
10/2-1/8	1P: $55	2P: $60	XP: $5	F17
4/3-10/1	1P: $40	2P: $45	XP: $5	F17

Location: I-17, exit 207, 0.7 mi e. 2102 W Dunlap Ave 85021. Fax: 602/944-7831. **Facility:** 141 one-bedroom standard units with efficiencies. 2 stories (no elevator), exterior corridors. **Bath:** combo or shower only. **Parking:** on-site. **Terms:** cancellation fee imposed, pets ($75 fee). **Amenities:** video games (fee), voice mail, irons. **Guest Services:** coin laundry. **Cards:** AX, DC, DS, MC, VI.

SOME UNITS

HOMEWOOD SUITES BY HILTON   *Book at aaa.com*   **Phone:** (602)508-0937   **42**

Small-scale Hotel

2/1-4/30 [BP]	1P: $169-$209	2P: $179-$219	XP: $10	F18
5/1-5/31 & 9/5-1/31 [BP]	1P: $129-$169	2P: $139-$179	XP: $10	F18
6/1-9/4 [BP]	1P: $79-$119	2P: $89-$129	XP: $10	F18

Location: Just e of 20th St. 2001 E Highland Ave 85016. Fax: 602/508-0854. **Facility:** 124 units. 116 one- and 8 two-bedroom suites ($79-$209) with kitchens. 4 stories, interior corridors. **Bath:** combo or shower only. **Parking:** on-site. **Terms:** cancellation fee imposed, pets. **Amenities:** video games (fee), high-speed Internet, voice mail, irons, hair dryers. **Pool(s):** small heated outdoor. **Leisure Activities:** exercise room, basketball. **Guest Services:** sundries, complimentary evening beverages: Mon-Thurs, coin laundry, area transportation. **Business Services:** meeting rooms, business center. **Cards:** AX, MC, VI.

SOME UNITS

HOMEWOOD SUITES HOTEL   *Book at aaa.com*   **Phone:** (602)674-8900   **20**

Small-scale Hotel

2/1-3/26	1P: $129-$159	2P: $139-$159	XP: $10	F16
3/27-5/21 & 9/11-1/31	1P: $99-$129	2P: $109-$129	XP: $10	F16
5/22-9/10	1P: $79-$99	2P: $79-$99	XP: $10	F16

Location: I-17, exit 208 (Peoria Ave), just e, just s on 25th Ave, then just w. 2536 W Beryl Ave 85015. Fax: 602/674-8901. **Facility:** 126 units. 117 one- and 9 two-bedroom suites with efficiencies. 5 stories, interior corridors. **Bath:** combo or shower only. **Parking:** on-site. **Terms:** cancellation fee imposed, pets ($50 fee, $200 deposit). **Amenities:** high-speed Internet, dual phone lines, voice mail, irons, hair dryers. **Pool(s):** heated outdoor. **Leisure Activities:** exercise room, sports court. **Guest Services:** sundries, complimentary evening beverages: Mon-Thurs, valet and coin laundry. **Business Services:** meeting rooms, business center. **Cards:** AX, DC, DS, MC, VI. **Special Amenities:** free full breakfast and free newspaper. *(See color ad p 293)*

SOME UNITS

JW MARRIOTT DESERT RIDGE RESORT & SPA   *Book at aaa.com*   **Phone:** (480)293-5000   **1**

Resort
Large-scale Hotel

2/1-5/7	1P: $469-$599	2P: $469-$599
9/6-1/31	1P: $419-$529	2P: $419-$529
5/8-6/14	1P: $419-$499	2P: $419-$499
6/15-9/5	1P: $169-$259	2P: $169-$259

Location: SR 101, exit 31 (Tatum Blvd), 0.4 mi n to Deer Valley, then 0.5 mi e. 5350 E Marriott Dr 85054. Fax: 480/293-3600. **Facility:** The destination resort has activities for families or groups, a tri-level lobby open to a courtyard with pools, water play areas and a flowing "river". 950 units. 869 one-bedroom standard units. 81 one-bedroom suites ($319-$3500), some with whirlpools. 6 stories, interior corridors. **Bath:** combo or shower only. **Parking:** on-site (fee) and valet. **Terms:** check-in 4 pm, 7 day cancellation notice-fee imposed, package plans. **Amenities:** CD players, dual phone lines, voice mail, safes, honor bars, irons, hair dryers. **Fee:** video games, high-speed Internet. **Some:** DVD players, fax. **Dining:** 4 restaurants, 7 am-1 am, cocktails, also, Meritage Steakhouse, Ristorante Tuscany, Roy's Desert Ridge, see separate listings. **Pool(s):** 5 heated outdoor. **Leisure Activities:** saunas, whirlpools, steamrooms, waterslide, lazy river water ride, recreation programs, hiking trails, jogging, spa. **Fee:** golf-36 holes, 8 lighted tennis courts, bicycles. **Guest Services:** gift shop, complimentary laundry, area transportation-Desert Ridge Mall. **Business Services:** conference facilities, business center. **Cards:** AX, CB, DC, DS, JC, MC, VI. **Special Amenities:** free newspaper.

SOME UNITS

LA QUINTA INN & SUITES PHOENIX (CHANDLER)   *Book at aaa.com*   **Phone:** (480)961-7700   **4**

Small-scale Hotel

| 2/1-4/30 & 1/13-1/31 [CP] | 1P: $119-$129 | 2P: $126-$136 | XP: $7 | F18 |
| 5/1-1/12 [CP] | 1P: $89-$99 | 2P: $96-$106 | XP: $7 | F18 |

Location: I-10, exit 160 (Chandler Blvd), just w, then just n. Located in a light-commercial area. 15241 S 50th St 85044. Fax: 480/961-7705. **Facility:** 117 units. 113 one-bedroom standard units. 4 one-bedroom suites ($119-$179). 4 stories, interior corridors. **Bath:** combo or shower only. **Parking:** on-site. **Terms:** small pets only. **Amenities:** video games (fee), high-speed Internet, voice mail, irons, hair dryers. **Pool(s):** heated outdoor. **Leisure Activities:** whirlpool, exercise room. **Guest Services:** valet and coin laundry. **Business Services:** meeting rooms, fax. **Cards:** AX, CB, DC, DS, MC, VI. **Special Amenities:** free expanded continental breakfast and free local telephone calls. *(See color ad p 295)*

SOME UNITS

LA QUINTA INN PHOENIX (NORTH)   *Book at aaa.com*   **Phone:** (602)993-0800   **10**

Small-scale Hotel

| 2/1-3/31 [CP] | 1P: $99-$109 | 2P: $106-$116 | XP: $7 | F18 |
| 4/1-1/31 [CP] | 1P: $79-$89 | 2P: $86-$96 | XP: $7 | F18 |

Location: I-17, exit 211, just e. 2510 W Greenway Rd 85023. Fax: 602/789-9172. **Facility:** 145 units. 144 one-bedroom standard units. 1 one-bedroom suite with whirlpool. 2 stories (no elevator), exterior corridors. **Bath:** combo or shower only. **Parking:** on-site. **Terms:** small pets only. **Amenities:** video games (fee), voice mail, irons, hair dryers. **Some:** high-speed Internet. **Pool(s):** heated outdoor, wading. **Leisure Activities:** whirlpool, 2 lighted tennis courts, exercise room. **Guest Services:** valet and coin laundry. **Business Services:** meeting rooms. **Cards:** AX, CB, DC, DS, MC, VI. *(See color ad p 295)*

SOME UNITS

(See maps and indexes p. 260-263, 264-265, 271-272)

THE LEGACY GOLF RESORT   *Book at aaa.com*   **Phone:** (602)305-5500 [58]

▼▼▼▼ All Year   1P: $139-$299

Resort Condominium

Location: I-10, exit 155 (Baseline Rd), 2.4 mi w, then 0.4 mi n. 6808 S 32nd St 85042. Fax: 602/305-5501. **Facility:** Elegant rooms and baths await you in the contemporary desert setting along with a golf course designed by Gary Panks. 328 units. 164 one-bedroom standard units with efficiencies. 164 one-bedroom suites with kitchens and whirlpools. 2 stories (no elevator), exterior corridors. **Parking:** on-site. **Terms:** check-in 4 pm, cancellation fee imposed, package plans. **Amenities:** DVD players, dual phone lines, voice mail, safes, irons, hair dryers. *Fee:* video library, high-speed Internet. *Some:* CD players. **Pool(s):** heated outdoor, wading. **Leisure Activities:** whirlpools, 2 lighted tennis courts, hiking trails, jogging, playground, exercise room, shuffleboard, volleyball. *Fee:* golf-18 holes, bicycles, massage. **Guest Services:** complimentary laundry, **Business Services:** meeting rooms, fax (fee). **Cards:** AX, DC, DS, MC, VI. *(See color ad below)*

SOME UNITS

(ASK) (S🐕🏠) (🍴) (🛋️) (🏊) (✕) (VCR) (🐾) (DATA PORT) (📦) (🍳) (☕) /✕/

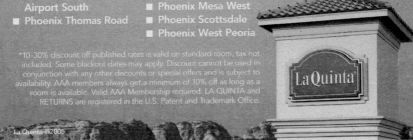

(See maps and indexes p. 260-263, 264-265, 271-272)

MAINSTAY SUITES · *Book at aaa.com* · Phone: (602)395-0900 · 23

2/1-3/31 [ECP]	1P: $89-$139	2P: $89-$139	XP: $10 F18
10/1-1/31 [ECP]	1P: $79-$119	2P: $79-$119	XP: $10 F18
4/1-4/30 [ECP]	1P: $69-$99	2P: $69-$99	XP: $10 F18
5/1-9/30 [ECP]	1P: $59-$89	2P: $59-$89	XP: $10 F18

Small-scale Hotel

Location: I-17, exit 207, just e, then 0.4 mi n. 9455 N Black Canyon Hwy 85021. Fax: 602/395-1900. **Facility:** 87 one-bedroom standard units with efficiencies. 3 stories, interior corridors. *Bath:* combo or shower only. **Parking:** on-site. **Terms:** small pets only ($150 fee). **Amenities:** high-speed Internet, voice mail, irons, hair dryers. **Pool(s):** heated outdoor. **Leisure Activities:** whirlpool, exercise room. **Guest Services:** valet and coin laundry. **Business Services:** PC, fax (fee). **Cards:** AX, CB, DC, DS, JC, MC, VI.

MARICOPA MANOR BED & BREAKFAST INN · *Book at aaa.com* · Phone: (602)274-6302 · 37

2/1-4/30 & 12/21-1/31 [ECP]	1P: $159-$209	2P: $159-$219	XP: $25 F12
9/16-12/20 [ECP]	1P: $109-$169	2P: $109-$179	XP: $25 F12
5/1-9/15 [ECP]	1P: $89-$169	2P: $89-$179	XP: $25 F12

Bed & Breakfast

Location: Just n of Camelback Rd, w of Central Ave. Located in a residential area. 15 W Pasadena Ave 85013. Fax: 602/266-3904. **Facility:** This Spanish mission home built in 1928 has elegantly decorated one or two-bedroom suites with patios and some with a gas or wood-burning fireplace. Designated smoking area. 7 units. 3 one-bedroom suites, some with whirlpools. 4 one-bedroom suites, some with whirlpools. 1 story, interior/exterior corridors. *Bath:* combo or shower only. **Parking:** on-site. **Terms:** office hours 8 am-10 pm, check-in 4 pm, age restrictions may apply, 14 day cancellation notice-fee imposed, no pets allowed (owner's pet on premises). **Amenities:** video library, CD players, high-speed Internet, irons, hair dryers. *Some:* DVD players. **Pool(s):** outdoor. **Leisure Activities:** whirlpool. **Business Services:** fax. **Cards:** AX, CB, DC, DS, MC, VI.

MOTEL 6 PHOENIX-BLACK CANYON #1304 · *Book at aaa.com* · Phone: 602/277-5501 · 46

2/1-4/24	1P: $41-$51	2P: $47-$57	XP: $3 F17
4/25-1/31	1P: $35-$45	2P: $41-$51	XP: $3 F17

Motel

Location: I-17, exit 202 (Indian School Rd), just w. 4130 N Black Canyon Hwy 85017. Fax: 602/274-9724. **Facility:** 351 one-bedroom standard units. 2-4 stories, exterior corridors. *Bath:* combo or shower only. **Parking:** on-site. **Pool(s):** 3 heated outdoor. **Leisure Activities:** whirlpool. **Guest Services:** coin laundry. **Business Services:** fax (fee). **Cards:** AX, CB, DC, DS, MC, VI.

MOTEL 6 PHOENIX-NORTH #344 · *Book at aaa.com* · Phone: 602/993-2353 · 8

2/1-4/30	1P: $47-$57	2P: $53-$63	XP: $3 F17
9/5-1/31	1P: $39-$49	2P: $45-$55	XP: $3 F17
5/1-5/25	1P: $37-$47	2P: $43-$53	XP: $3 F17
5/26-9/4	1P: $36-$46	2P: $42-$52	XP: $3 F17

Motel

Location: I-17, exit 212A, just e. 2330 W Bell Rd 85023. Fax: 602/548-3461. **Facility:** 139 one-bedroom standard units. 2 stories (no elevator), exterior corridors. *Bath:* combo or shower only. **Parking:** on-site. **Terms:** small pets only. **Pool(s):** small heated outdoor. **Guest Services:** coin laundry. **Cards:** AX, CB, DC, DS, MC, VI.

MOTEL 6 PHOENIX-NORTHERN AVE #1185 · *Book at aaa.com* · Phone: 602/995-7592 · 32

2/1-4/24	1P: $41-$51	2P: $47-$57	XP: $3 F17
4/25-1/31	1P: $35-$45	2P: $41-$51	XP: $3 F17

Motel

Location: I-17, exit 206, just w, then just s. Located in a commercial area. 8152 N Black Canyon Hwy 85051. Fax: 602/995-9592. **Facility:** 142 one-bedroom standard units. 4 stories, exterior corridors. *Bath:* combo or shower only. **Parking:** on-site. **Pool(s):** heated outdoor. **Guest Services:** coin laundry. **Cards:** AX, CB, DC, DS, MC, VI.

MOTEL 6 PHOENIX WEST #696 · *Book at aaa.com* · Phone: 602/272-0220 · 52

2/1-4/24	1P: $51-$61	2P: $57-$67	XP: $3 F17
11/9-1/31	1P: $41-$51	2P: $47-$57	XP: $3 F17
4/25-11/8	1P: $39-$49	2P: $45-$55	XP: $3 F17

Motel

Location: I-10, exit 139, just n to McDowell, just w, then just s. 1530 N 52nd Dr 85043. Fax: 602/278-4210. **Facility:** 147 one-bedroom standard units. 3 stories, exterior corridors. *Bath:* combo or shower only. **Parking:** on-site. **Terms:** pets (with prior approval). **Pool(s):** heated outdoor. **Business Services:** fax (fee). **Cards:** AX, CB, DC, DS, MC, VI.

PHOENIX INN SUITES · *Book at aaa.com* · Phone: (602)956-5221 · 43

2/1-4/30 & 1/1-1/31 [ECP]	1P: $109	2P: $109	XP: $10 F17
9/16-12/31 [ECP]	1P: $89	2P: $89	XP: $10 F17
5/1-9/15 [ECP]	1P: $69	2P: $69	XP: $10 F17

Small-scale Hotel

Location: Just sw of Camelback Rd and 24th St. 2310 E Highland Ave 85016. Fax: 602/468-7220. **Facility:** 120 units. 117 one-bedroom standard units, some with whirlpools. 3 one-bedroom suites. 4 stories, interior corridors. *Bath:* combo or shower only. **Parking:** on-site. **Terms:** check-in 4 pm, package plans. **Amenities:** high-speed Internet, voice mail, irons, hair dryers. **Pool(s):** heated outdoor. **Leisure Activities:** whirlpool, exercise room. **Guest Services:** sundries, coin laundry, area transportation-within 3 mi. **Business Services:** meeting rooms, PC, fax (fee). **Cards:** AX, CB, DC, DS, MC, VI. **Special Amenities:** free expanded continental breakfast and free local telephone calls. (See color ad p 297)

(See maps and indexes p. 260-263, 264-265, 271-272)

PHOENIX WEST INN

AAA SAVE · ▼▼

Small-scale Hotel

Phone: (602)269-1919 🔢 55

F

All Year 1P: $69-$89 2P: $79-$119 XP: $10

Location: I-10, exit 139 (51st Ave), just s, just w on Latham St, then just n. 1241 N 53rd Ave 85043. Fax: 602/269-7409. **Facility:** 126 one-bedroom standard units. 3 stories, exterior corridors. **Parking:** on-site. **Terms:** cancellation fee imposed, [CP] meal plan available. **Amenities:** irons, hair dryers. **Pool(s):** outdoor. **Guest Services:** coin laundry. **Business Services:** meeting rooms, fax (fee). **Cards:** AX, CB, DC, DS, JC, MC, VI. **Special Amenities:** free continental breakfast and early check-in/late check-out.

SOME UNITS

POINTE HILTON SQUAW PEAK RESORT

AAA SAVE · ▼▼▼

Resort
Large-scale Hotel

Book at aaa.com   **Phone: (602)997-2626** 🔢 33

2/1-5/21	1P: $135-$299	2P: $135-$299	XP: $25	F17
1/8-1/31	1P: $149-$269	2P: $149-$269	XP: $25	F17
9/11-1/7	1P: $89-$229	2P: $89-$229	XP: $15	F17
5/22-9/10	1P: $79-$149	2P: $79-$149	XP: $15	F17

Location: Loop 51, exit Glendale Ave, 0.4 mi w, then 0.6 mi n. 7677 N 16th St 85020 (7600 N 16th St, Suite 130). Fax: 602/997-2391. **Facility:** This resort's one-bedroom suites and one- and two-bedroom casitas are on extensive grounds featuring shaded, landscaped pool areas and courtyards. 563 units. 508 one- and 55 two-bedroom suites. 3-4 stories, exterior corridors. **Bath:** combo or shower only. **Parking:** on-site. **Terms:** check-in 4 pm, 3 day cancellation notice-fee imposed, package plans, pets ($150 deposit). **Amenities:** dual phone lines, voice mail, honor bars, irons, hair dryers. *Fee:* video games, high-speed Internet. **Dining:** 6 am-10 pm, cocktails, also, Lantana Grille, see separate listing. **Pool(s):** 8 heated outdoor, wading. **Leisure Activities:** saunas, whirlpools, steamrooms, waterslide, lazy river rafting, recreation programs, spa. *Fee:* 18-hole putting course, 4 lighted tennis courts. **Guest Services:** gift shop, valet and coin laundry, area transportation (fee)-Biltmore Shopping Center. **Business Services:** conference facilities, business center. **Cards:** AX, CB, DC, DS, JC, MC, VI.

SOME UNITS

POINTE HILTON TAPATIO CLIFFS RESORT

AAA SAVE · ▼▼▼

Resort
Large-scale Hotel

Book at aaa.com   **Phone: (602)866-7500** 🔢 14

2/1-5/21	1P: $135-$299	2P: $135-$299	XP: $25	F17
1/8-1/31	1P: $149-$269	2P: $149-$269	XP: $25	F17
9/11-1/7	1P: $89-$229	2P: $89-$229	XP: $15	F17
5/22-9/10	1P: $79-$149	2P: $79-$149	XP: $15	F17

Location: I-17, exit 207 (Dunlap Ave), 3 mi e, then 2 mi n. 11111 N 7th St 85020. Fax: 602/993-0276. **Facility:** On extensive, nicely landscaped, hillside grounds, these one-bedroom suites are in several buildings; many have views across the valley. 585 one-bedroom suites. 2-5 stories, exterior corridors. **Bath:** combo or shower only. **Parking:** on-site. **Terms:** check-in 4 pm, 3 day cancellation notice-fee imposed, package plans, pets ($75 deposit). **Amenities:** high-speed Internet (fee), dual phone lines, voice mail, honor bars, irons, hair dryers. *Some: Fee:* DVD players. **Dining:** 4 restaurants, 6:30 am-11 pm, cocktails, also, Different Pointe of View, see separate listing, entertainment. **Pool(s):** 8 heated outdoor. **Leisure Activities:** sauna, whirlpools, steamroom, waterslide, recreation programs, rental bicycles, hiking trails, jogging, spa. *Fee:* golf-18 holes, 2 lighted tennis courts, exercise room. **Guest Services:** gift shop, valet and coin laundry. **Business Services:** conference facilities, business center. **Cards:** AX, CB, DC, DS, JC, MC, VI.

SOME UNITS

POINTE SOUTH MOUNTAIN RESORT

AAA SAVE · ▼▼ ▼▼

Resort
Large-scale Hotel

Book at aaa.com   **Phone: (602)438-9000** 🔢 59

2/1-4/30	1P: $399-$899	2P: $399-$899	XP: $25	F18
9/6-1/31	1P: $319-$619	2P: $319-$619	XP: $25	F18
5/1-5/31	1P: $279-$579	2P: $279-$579	XP: $25	F18
6/1-9/5	1P: $179-$429	2P: $179-$429	XP: $25	F18

Location: I-10, exit 155 (Baseline Rd), just w, then just s. 7777 S Pointe Pkwy 85044. Fax: 602/659-6535. **Facility:** Water plays a key role at this six-acre property, which features fountains, adult and children's pools, a waterslide and a simulated lazy river. 640 one-bedroom suites, some with whirlpools. 2-5 stories (no elevator), exterior corridors. **Bath:** combo or shower only. **Parking:** on-site. **Terms:** check-in 4 pm, cancellation fee imposed, [AP] meal plan available, package plans, $16 service charge. **Amenities:** video games (fee), CD players, high-speed Internet, dual phone lines, voice mail, honor bars, irons, hair dryers. **Dining:** 4 restaurants, 6 am-1 am, cocktails, also, Latitude 30, Rustler's Rooste, see separate listings, entertainment. **Pool(s):** 6 heated outdoor. **Leisure Activities:** whirlpools, steamrooms, oasis water park, 6 lighted tennis courts, racquetball court, recreation programs, croquet, rental bicycles, hiking trails, jogging, spa, basketball, volleyball. *Fee:* golf-18 holes, horseback riding, game room. **Guest Services:** gift shop, valet and coin laundry, area transportation-Arizona Mills. **Business Services:** conference facilities, business center. **Cards:** AX, DC, DS, MC, VI.

SOME UNITS

(See maps and indexes p. 260-261, 264-265, 271-272)

PREMIER INNS

Phone: (602)943-2371 **19**

Motel

2/1-4/1 & 1/1-1/31	1P: $44-$94	2P: $50-$109
4/2-12/31	1P: $35-$65	2P: $39-$79

Location: I-17, exit 208 (Peoria Ave), 0.3 mi w to 28th Dr, just s, just e on Metro Pkwy E, then just n on 27th Ave. 10402 Black Canyon Fwy 85051. Fax: 602/943-5847. **Facility:** 253 one-bedroom standard units. 2 stories (no elevator), exterior corridors. **Parking:** on-site. **Terms:** cancellation fee imposed, [CP] meal plan available, pets (with prior approval). **Amenities:** voice mail. **Pool(s):** outdoor, heated outdoor, wading. **Leisure Activities:** whirlpool. **Fee:** game room. **Guest Services:** coin laundry. **Business Services:** meeting rooms, fax. **Cards:** AX, MC, VI. **Special Amenities:** free room upgrade and preferred room (each subject to availability with advance reservations).

SOME UNITS
FEE FEE

PRIME HOTEL PHOENIX NORTH   *Book at aaa.com*

Phone: 602/978-2222 **4**

Small-scale Hotel

Property failed to provide current rates

Location: I-17, exit 214A (Union Hills Dr), just w. 2641 W Union Hills Dr 85027. Fax: 602/978-9139. **Facility:** 166 units. 150 one-bedroom standard units. 16 one-bedroom suites. 2 stories, interior corridors. **Parking:** on-site. **Terms:** small pets only. **Amenities:** video games (fee), high-speed Internet, voice mail, irons, hair dryers. **Pool(s):** heated outdoor. **Leisure Activities:** whirlpool. **Guest Services:** valet laundry. **Business Services:** meeting rooms, fax (fee).

SOME UNITS
FEE

RAMADA PLAZA HOTEL AND SUITES   *Book at aaa.com*

Phone: (602)866-7000 **13**

Small-scale Hotel

2/1-4/16 [BP]	1P: $79-$130	2P: $79-$130	XP: $20	F17
10/13-1/31 [BP]	1P: $79-$119	2P: $79-$119	XP: $20	F17
9/8-10/12 [BP]	1P: $79-$109	2P: $79-$109	XP: $20	F17
4/17-9/7 [BP]	1P: $69-$99	2P: $69-$99	XP: $10	F17

Location: I-17, exit 209 (Cactus Rd), just w, then just s. 12027 N 28th Dr 85029. Fax: 602/504-9832. **Facility:** Designated smoking area. 171 units. 163 one-bedroom standard units. 8 one-bedroom suites ($85-$199). 4 stories, interior corridors. **Bath:** combo or shower only. **Parking:** on-site. **Terms:** package plans, pets ($25 fee). **Amenities:** voice mail, irons, hair dryers. **Dining:** 6:30 am-10 & 5-10 pm, Fri & Sat-midnight, cocktails. **Pool(s):** outdoor. **Leisure Activities:** whirlpool, exercise room. **Guest Services:** valet laundry. **Business Services:** meeting rooms. **Cards:** AX, CB, DC, DS, JC, MC, VI. **Special Amenities:** free full breakfast and free local telephone calls. *(See color ad p 299)*

FEE

RED ROOF INN   *Book at aaa.com*

Phone: (602)233-8004 **51**

Small-scale Hotel

2/1-3/25	1P: $58-$69	2P: $65-$75	XP: $6	F18
3/26-10/21	1P: $55-$61	2P: $61-$68	XP: $6	F18
1/1-1/31	1P: $51-$60	2P: $57-$67	XP: $6	F18
10/22-12/31	1P: $51-$58	2P: $57-$65	XP: $6	F18

Location: I-10, exit 139 (51st Ave), just n, just e on McDowell Rd, then just s. 5215 W Willetta 85043. Fax: 602/233-2360. **Facility:** 133 units. 129 one-bedroom standard units. 4 one-bedroom suites. 4 stories, interior corridors. **Bath:** combo or shower only. **Parking:** on-site. **Terms:** small pets only (limit 1). **Amenities:** video games (fee), voice mail. **Pool(s):** heated outdoor. **Business Services:** fax (fee). **Cards:** AX, CB, DC, DS, MC, VI.

SOME UNITS

(See maps and indexes p. 260-263, 264-265, 271-272)

RED ROOF INN-CAMELBACK — *Book at aaa.com* — Phone: (602)264-9290 — **39**

	2/1-4/14	1P: $46	2P: $51	XP: $5	F18
	9/30-1/31	1P: $44	2P: $48	XP: $5	F18
Small-scale Hotel	4/15-6/29	1P: $42	2P: $46	XP: $5	F18
	6/30-9/29	1P: $40	2P: $45	XP: $5	F18

Location: I-17, exit 203 (Camelback Rd), 1.8 mi e. 502 W Camelback Rd 85013. Fax: 602/264-3068. **Facility:** 107 one-bedroom standard units. 4 stories, interior corridors. **Parking:** on-site. **Terms:** cancellation fee imposed, small pets only. **Pool(s):** heated outdoor. **Leisure Activities:** whirlpool. **Guest Services:** coin laundry. **Business Services:** meeting rooms. **Cards:** AX, DC, DS, MC, VI.

SOME UNITS
(ASK) (S★) (🐄) (🛋) (📷) (DATA PORT) / (⊠) (📶) (📷) /

RESIDENCE INN BY MARRIOTT — *Book at aaa.com* — Phone: (602)864-1900 — **28**

(AAA) (SAVE)

	2/1-4/16 [BP]	1P: $122	2P: $122	XP: $10	F17
	9/10-1/31 [BP]	1P: $109	2P: $109	XP: $10	F17
	4/17-5/27 [BP]	1P: $99	2P: $99	XP: $10	F17
Small-scale Hotel	5/28-9/9 [BP]	1P: $79	2P: $79	XP: $10	F17

Location: I-17, exit 207 (Dunlap Ave), just w, then 0.8 mi s. 8242 N Black Canyon Hwy 85051. Fax: 602/995-8251. **Facility:** 168 units. 140 one-bedroom standard units with efficiencies. 20 one- and 8 two-bedroom suites with efficiencies. 2 stories (no elevator), interior/exterior corridors. *Bath:* combo or shower only. **Parking:** on-site. **Terms:** weekly rates available, pets ($75 fee). **Amenities:** voice mail, irons, hair dryers. *Some:* dual phone lines. **Pool(s):** heated outdoor. **Leisure Activities:** whirlpool, playground, sports court. **Guest Services:** complimentary evening beverages: Mon-Thurs, valet and coin laundry. **Business Services:** meeting rooms, fax (fee). **Cards:** AX, DS, MC, VI. **Special Amenities:** free full breakfast and free newspaper. *(See color ad below)*

SOME UNITS
(S★) (🛋 FEE) (🛢M) (🔲) (📷) (🏊) (♿) (⊠) (📷) (DATA PORT) (📶) (📷) (📺) /(⊠) /

THE RITZ-CARLTON, PHOENIX — *Book at aaa.com* — Phone: (602)468-0700 — **41**

	2/1-4/30	1P: $329-$519	
	5/1-5/25 & 9/5-1/31	1P: $259-$429	
Large-scale Hotel	5/26-9/4	1P: $159-$299	

Location: Southeast corner of Camelback Rd and 24th St. Located across from Biltmore Fashion Park. 2401 E Camelback Rd 85016. Fax: 602/468-0793. **Facility:** This elegant, service-oriented hotel across from the Biltmore Fashion Square has well-appointed guest rooms and large meeting spaces. 281 units. 279 one-bedroom standard units. 2 one-bedroom suites ($449-$3000), some with efficiencies and/or whirlpools. 11 stories, interior corridors. *Bath:* combo or shower only. **Parking:** on-site (fee) and valet. **Terms:** cancellation fee imposed, package plans, pets ($150 deposit). **Amenities:** CD players, dual phone lines, voice mail, safes, honor bars, irons, hair dryers. *Fee:* video games, high-speed Internet. *Some:* DVD players (fee). **Dining:** Bistro 24, see separate listing. **Pool(s):** heated outdoor. **Leisure Activities:** saunas, jogging, exercise room. *Fee:* massage. **Guest Services:** gift shop, valet laundry. **Business Services:** conference facilities, business center. **Cards:** AX, CB, DC, DS, JC, MC, VI.

SOME UNITS
(🆓 FEE) (🐄 FEE) (🍴) (24T) (Y) (🛢M) (🔲) (🛋) (⊠) (📷) (DATA PORT) /(⊠) (VCR FEE) (📶) (📷) /

(See maps and indexes p. 260-263, 264-265, 271-272)

ROYAL PALMS RESORT AND SPA   *Book at aaa.com*   Phone: 602/840-3610   **44**

◆◆◆ SAVE   2/1-5/31 & 9/12-1/31   1P: $325   2P: $325   XP: $25   F16
6/1-9/11   1P: $135   2P: $135   XP: $25   F16
▽▽▽▽ ▽▽▽▽   **Location:** Just e of 52nd St. Located in a quiet residential area. 5200 E Camelback Rd 85018. Fax: 602/840-6927.
Large-scale Hotel **Facility:** A hideaway by Camelback Mountain, the property has extensive grounds, varied meeting spaces and Mediterranean-style rooms, many with private patios. Designated smoking area. 117 units. 78 one-bedroom standard units. 39 one-bedroom suites. 2 stories, interior/exterior corridors. *Bath:* combo or shower only. **Parking:** valet and street. **Terms:** 7 day cancellation notice-fee imposed, package plans, $22 service charge, small pets only ($100 fee). **Amenities:** video games (fee), CD players, dual phone lines, voice mail, safes, honor bars, irons, hair dryers. *Some:* DVD players (fee), fax. **Dining:** 10 am-6 pm, also, T. Cook's, see separate listing. **Pool(s):** heated outdoor. **Leisure Activities:** whirlpools, steamrooms, croquet, exercise room, spa. **Guest Services:** valet laundry. **Business Services:** meeting rooms, business center. **Cards:** AX, CB, DC, DS, JC, MC, VI.

SOME UNITS

🛏️ 🍴 24↑ 🍸 🚹 🏊 ⊗ ⊠ DATA PORT 💻 / VCR 📠 🖨️ /
FEE   FEE

SHERATON CRESCENT HOTEL   *Book at aaa.com*   Phone: (602)943-8200   **27**

◆◆◆ SAVE   2/1-5/13   1P: $119-$259   2P: $119-$259   XP: $10   F18
9/5-1/31   1P: $105-$229   2P: $105-$229   XP: $10   F18
▽▽▽▽   5/14-9/4   1P: $75-$199   2P: $75-$199   XP: $10   F18
Large-scale Hotel **Location:** I-17, exit 207 (Dunlap Ave), just e. 2620 W Dunlap Ave 85021. Fax: 602/371-2857. **Facility:** 342 units. 340 one-bedroom standard units. 2 one-bedroom suites with whirlpools. 8 stories, interior corridors. *Bath:* combo or shower only. **Parking:** on-site. **Terms:** cancellation fee imposed, [AP] meal plan available, small pets only. **Amenities:** dual phone lines, voice mail, safes, irons, hair dryers. *Fee:* video games, high-speed Internet. **Dining:** 6:30 am-10 pm, cocktails. **Pool(s):** heated outdoor. **Leisure Activities:** saunas, whirlpool, waterslide, 2 lighted tennis courts, racquetball courts, playground, basketball, horseshoes, volleyball. *Fee:* golf. **Guest Services:** gift shop, valet laundry, area transportation-within 5 mi & local businesses. **Business Services:** conference facilities, PC. **Cards:** AX, CB, DC, DS, JC, MC, VI. **Special Amenities:** free newspaper and early check-in/late check-out. *(See color ad below)*

SOME UNITS

🅂🄳 ✈️ 🛏️ 🍴 🍸 ♿M 🚹 🎣 🏊 📶 ⊗ 🎥 DATA PORT 💻 / ⊠ VCR 📠 🖨️ /
FEE   FEE

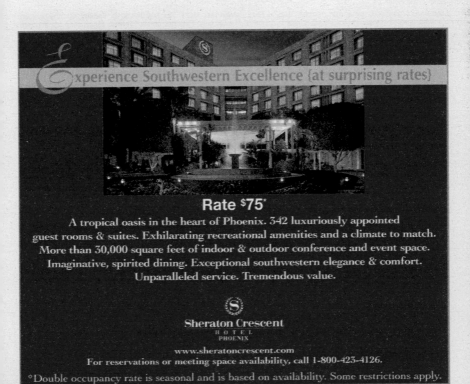

(See maps and indexes p. 260-263, 264-265, 271-272)

SHERATON WILD HORSE PASS RESORT & SPA — Book at aaa.com

(AAA) [SAVE]

Resort
Large-scale Hotel

Phone: (602)225-0100

	1P:	2P:	XP:	
2/1-5/24	$275-$300	$275-$300	$30	F16
9/7-1/31	$250-$300	$250-$300	$30	F16
5/25-9/6	$125-$140	$125-$140	$30	F16

Location: I-10, exit 162, 2.4 mi w. 5594 W Wild Horse Pass Blvd 85020-4000 (PO Box 94000, 85070-4000). Fax: 602/225-0300. Facility: Wild horses roam the desert areas nearby, while the property's extensive grounds offer views of the mountains and golf course. Designated smoking area. 500 units. 474 one-bedroom standard units. 26 one-bedroom suites ($380-$1050), some with whirlpools. 4 stories, interior corridors. Bath: combo or shower only. Parking: on-site and valet. Terms: 7 day cancellation notice-fee imposed, package plans, pets (small dogs only). Amenities: dual phone lines, voice mail, safes, honor bars, irons, hair dryers. Fee: video games, high-speed Internet. Some: CD players. Dining: 3 restaurants, 6:30 am-11 pm, also, Kai, see separate listing. Pool(s): 5 heated outdoor, wading. Leisure Activities: saunas, whirlpools, steamrooms, waterslide, recreation programs, hiking trails, jogging, spa. Fee: golf-36 holes, 2 lighted tennis courts, balloon rides, horseback riding. Guest Services: gift shop, valet laundry, area transportation-casino. Business Services: conference facilities, business center. Cards: AX, CB, DC, DS, JC, MC, VI. Special Amenities: free newspaper and free room upgrade (subject to availability with advance reservations).

SLEEP INN PHOENIX NORTH — Book at aaa.com

(AAA) [SAVE]

Small-scale Hotel

Phone: (602)504-1200 [6]

	1P:	2P:	XP:	
2/1-5/21	$71-$143	$71-$143	$10	F18
9/10-1/31	$71-$125	$71-$125	$10	F18
5/22-9/9	$49-$125	$49-$125	$10	F18

Location: I-17, exit 214A, just w, then just s. 18235 N 27th Ave 85053. Fax: 602/504-6100. Facility: 61 one-bedroom standard units. 2 stories, interior corridors. Bath: combo or shower only. Parking: on-site. Terms: cancellation fee imposed, [ECP] meal plan available, small pets only ($15 extra charge). Amenities: high-speed Internet, voice mail, irons, hair dryers. Pool(s): small heated outdoor. Leisure Activities: whirlpool, exercise room. Guest Services: coin laundry. Business Services: meeting rooms, fax (fee). Cards: AX, CB, DC, DS, MC, VI. Special Amenities: free expanded continental breakfast and free local telephone calls. (See color ad below)

SPRINGHILL SUITES BY MARRIOTT-METRO CENTER — Book at aaa.com

Small-scale Hotel

Phone: (602)943-0010 [24]

	1P:	2P:	
10/1-1/31 [ECP]	$119-$140	$119-$140	
2/1-4/29 [ECP]	$140	$140	
4/30-7/1 [ECP]	$119	$119	
7/2-9/30 [ECP]	$79	$79	

Location: I-17, exit 207, just e, then 0.3 mi n. 9425 N Black Canyon Hwy 85021. Fax: 602/943-0010. Facility: 81 one-bedroom standard units. 3 stories, interior corridors. Bath: combo or shower only. Parking: on-site. Terms: cancellation fee imposed. Amenities: high-speed Internet, voice mail, irons, hair dryers. Pool(s): heated outdoor. Leisure Activities: whirlpool, exercise room. Guest Services: valet laundry. Business Services: PC, fax (fee). Cards: AX, DC, DS, MC, VI.

STUDIO 6 PHOENIX-DEER VALLEY #6030 — Book at aaa.com

Small-scale Hotel

Phone: 602/843-1151 [5]

	1P:	2P:	XP:	
2/1-3/25	$63-$73	$67-$77	$4	F17
3/26-1/31	$45-$55	$49-$59	$4	F17

Location: I-17, exit 214A (Union Hills Dr), just w, then just s. 18405 N 27th Ave 85053. Fax: 602/843-6302. Facility: 141 one-bedroom standard units with efficiencies. 2 stories (no elevator), exterior corridors. Bath: combo or shower only. Parking: on-site. Terms: office hours 7 am-8 pm, small pets only ($10 extra charge). Amenities: voice mail, irons. Guest Services: coin laundry. Business Services: fax (fee). Cards: AX, CB, DC, DS, MC, VI.

(See maps and indexes p. 260-263, 264-265, 271-272)

SUNSHINE HOTEL & SUITES **Book at aaa.com** Phone: 602/604-4900 **49**

Property failed to provide current rates

Small-scale Hotel

Location: Just n of Osborn Rd, 0.5 mi s of Indian School; downtown. 3600 N 2nd Ave 85013. Fax: 602/265-6331. **Facility:** 276 one-bedroom standard units, some with whirlpools. 6-10 stories, interior/exterior corridors. *Bath:* combo or shower only. **Parking:** on-site. **Terms:** small pets only ($25 fee). **Amenities:** video games (fee), high-speed Internet, voice mail, irons, hair dryers. **Pool(s):** 2 heated outdoor, 2 small heated outdoor. **Leisure Activities:** whirlpool, putting green, lighted tennis court, playground, basketball, shuffleboard, volleyball. **Guest Services:** coin laundry. **Business Services:** conference facilities, business center.

SOME UNITS

SUPER 8 MOTEL-PHOENIX **Book at aaa.com** Phone: (602)415-0888 **54**

	1P	2P	XP	
2/1-5/1	1P: $69-$199	2P: $79-$199	XP: $5	F14
10/1-1/31	1P: $69-$199	2P: $69-$199	XP: $5	F14
5/2-9/30	1P: $69-$99	2P: $69-$99	XP: $5	F14

Small-scale Hotel

Location: I-10, exit 139 (51st Ave), just s to Latham Rd, then just w. 1242 N 53rd Ave 85043. Fax: 602/455-4888. **Facility:** 67 one-bedroom standard units. 2 stories (no elevator), interior corridors. *Bath:* combo or shower only. **Parking:** on-site. **Terms:** [CP] meal plan available, pets ($10 extra charge, in limited units). **Pool(s):** small heated outdoor. **Guest Services:** coin laundry. **Business Services:** fax (fee). **Cards:** AX, DC, DS, MC, VI.

SOME UNITS

SUPER 8 MOTEL-PHOENIX METRO NORTH **Book at aaa.com** Phone: (602)995-8451 **31**

Motel

All Year [CP] 1P: $36-$79 2P: $42-$85 D18

Location: I-17, exit 206 (Northern Ave), just w, then just n on west side of freeway. 8130 N Black Canyon Hwy 85051. Fax: 602/995-8496. **Facility:** 121 units. 119 one-bedroom standard units. 2 one-bedroom suites. 2 stories (no elevator), exterior corridors. **Parking:** on-site. **Terms:** 7 day cancellation notice. **Pool(s):** heated outdoor. **Leisure Activities:** whirlpool. **Guest Services:** coin laundry. **Cards:** AX, CB, DC, DS, MC, VI. **Special Amenities:** free continental breakfast and free local telephone calls.

SOME UNITS

(See maps and indexes p. 260-263, 264-265, 271-272)

TOWNEPLACE SUITES BY MARRIOTT   *Book at aaa.com*   **Phone:** (602)943-9510   ㉕

	2/1-4/30 [ECP]	1P: $140-$150	2P: $140-$150
	10/1-1/31 [ECP]	1P: $100-$150	2P: $100-$150
Small-scale Hotel	5/1-7/1 [ECP]	1P: $100-$120	2P: $100-$120
	7/2-9/30 [ECP]	1P: $80-$90	2P: $80-$90

Location: I-17, exit 207, just e, then 0.3 mi n. 9425 N Black Canyon Hwy 85021. Fax: 602/943-7654. **Facility:** 94 units. 68 one-bedroom standard units with efficiencies. 4 one- and 22 two-bedroom suites with kitchens. 3 stories, interior corridors. *Bath:* combo or shower only. **Parking:** on-site. **Terms:** cancellation fee imposed, pets ($75 fee). **Pool(s):** heated outdoor. **Leisure Activities:** exercise room. **Guest Services:** valet and coin laundry. **Business Services:** fax. **Cards:** AX, DC, DS, MC, VI.

SOME UNITS

(ASK) (SD) ▦ ⊞ ⬢ ⬤ ▦ 🛢 ▦ ▭ / ⊠ /
FEE

TRAVELERS INN   **Phone:** (602)233-1988   ㊇
	All Year	1P: $49	2P: $49	XP: $10
				F12

Small-scale Hotel   **Location:** I-10, exit 139 (51st Ave), just sw. Located in a commercial area. 5102 W Latham St 85043. Fax: 602/278-4598. **Facility:** 128 units. 125 one-bedroom standard units. 3 one-bedroom suites ($79). 3 stories, exterior corridors. **Parking:** on-site. **Terms:** package plans, pets ($10 extra charge). **Amenities:** voice mail. **Pool(s):** heated outdoor. **Leisure Activities:** whirlpool. **Guest Services:** coin laundry. **Cards:** AX, CB, DC, DS, JC, MC, VI.

SOME UNITS

(ASK) (SD) ⊞ ⊞ ⬤ ▦ ▦ / ⊠ /
FEE

───── *The following lodgings were either not evaluated or did not* ─────
meet AAA rating requirements but are listed for your information only.

COURTYARD BY MARRIOTT PHOENIX NORTH   **Phone:** 602/944-7373
   [fyi]   Did not meet all AAA rating requirements for some property operations at time of last evaluation on
            05/24/2005. **Location:** I-17, exit 207, just e, then 0.4 mi n. 9631 N Black Canyon Hwy 85021. Facilities, services, and
Small-scale Hotel   decor characterize a mid-range property.

POINTE AT TAPATIO CLIFFS   **Phone:** 480/515-2300
   [fyi]   Did not meet all AAA rating requirements for locking devices in some guest rooms at time of last evaluation
            on 05/11/2004. **Location:** Jct 7th St and Dunlap Ave, 1.1 mi ne. 10410 N Cave Creek Rd 85020. Facilities, services,
Condominium   and decor characterize a mid-range property.

─────── **WHERE TO DINE** ───────

ALEXIS GRILL   **Lunch:** $6-$13   **Dinner:** $11-$25   **Phone:** 602/279-0982   ㊾
                     Location: Just n of Osborne Rd. 3550 N Central Ave 85012. **Hours:** 11 am-9 pm, Fri-10 pm, Sat 4 pm-10 pm.
   Northern   Closed major holidays; also Sun. **Reservations:** suggested. **Features:** Whether for a business lunch,
   Italian   intimate dinner or celebration, the friendly staff and eclectic foods prepared with Mediterranean flair are
                     certain to delight. The signature rack of lamb is highly recommended. Dressy casual; cocktails. **Parking:** on-
                     site. **Cards:** AX, DC, DS, MC, VI.
                                                                                         ⛉ ⬤

ASI ES LA VIDA - SUCH IS LIFE   **Lunch:** $7-$10   **Dinner:** $7-$25   **Phone:** 602/952-1255   ㊽
                     Location: 0.5 mi n of Thomas. 3602 N 24th St 85016. **Hours:** 11 am-10 pm. Closed: 1/1, 11/23, 12/24, 12/25.
   South Mexican   **Reservations:** suggested. **Features:** Flavors from southern Mexico delight palates in the intimate mid-town
                     eatery. Although the names of dishes may be unfamiliar, the friendly staff will assist with good descriptions.
                     Casual dress; cocktails. **Parking:** on-site. **Cards:** AX, MC, VI.
                                                                                         ⬤

AUNT CHILADA'S HIDEAWAY   **Lunch:** $5-$9   **Dinner:** $7-$16   **Phone:** 602/944-1286   ⑬
                     Location: Loop 51, exit Glendale Ave, 0.4 mi w to 16th St, 0.6 mi to Morten, then just e. 7330 N Dreamy Draw Dr
                     85020. **Hours:** 11 am-10 pm, Fri & Sat-11 pm, Sun 9 am-11 pm. Closed: 11/23, 12/25.
   Mexican   **Reservations:** accepted. **Features:** Colorful decor, Mexican memorabilia and several patios enhance the
                     rooms of the historic, hacienda-style building. Guests can select from traditional favorites, such as
                     chimichangas, enchiladas and the house specialty fajitas. Live entertainment is on hand Wednesdays and Fridays. Catering
                     service is available. Casual dress; cocktails. **Parking:** on-site and street. **Cards:** AX, MC, VI.
                                                                                         ⛉ ⬤

THE BAMBOO CLUB   **Lunch:** $7-$22   **Dinner:** $9-$22   **Phone:** 602/955-1288   ㉖
                     Location: Just e of 24th St; in Biltmore Fashion Park, 2nd level, east end. 2596 E Camelback Rd 85016. **Hours:** 11
                     am-10 pm, Fri & Sat-11 pm. Closed: 11/23, 12/25. **Reservations:** suggested. **Features:** Pacific Rim and
   Pacific Rim   Asian specialties are at the heart of the menu at this high-energy restaurant on the upper level of Biltmore
                     Fashion Square Mall. Casual dress; cocktails. **Parking:** on-site. **Cards:** AX, CB, DC, DS, MC, VI.

BISTRO 24   **Lunch:** $8-$20   **Dinner:** $20-$35   **Phone:** 602/952-2424   ㊵
                     Location: Southeast corner of Camelback Rd and 24th St; in The Ritz-Carlton, Phoenix. 2401 E Camelback Rd 85016.
                     Hours: 6:30 am-9 pm, Fri & Sat-10 pm, Sun & Mon-3 pm. **Reservations:** suggested. **Features:** A
   French   seasonally changing menu in this upscale bistro features the freshest of ingredients served by friendly and
                     attentive wait staff. Patio dining is available seasonally. Casual dress; cocktails. **Parking:** valet. **Cards:** AX,
   CB, DC, DS, JC, MC, VI.
                                                                                         ⛉

CAFFE BOA   **Lunch:** $6-$23   **Dinner:** $6-$23   **Phone:** 480/893-3331   ㉑
                     Location: I-10, exit 157, 1 blk w; in Ahwatukee Shopping Center. 5063 E Elliott Rd 85044. **Hours:** 11 am-10 pm, Fri-
                     11 pm, Sat 5 pm-11 pm, Sun 5 pm-10 pm. Closed: 11/23, 12/25. **Reservations:** accepted.
   Italian   **Features:** Upscale presentations are a highlight. The menu lists pasta dishes, as well as preparations of
                     beef, chicken and seafood. Indoor and outdoor seating is offered. Dressy casual; cocktails. **Parking:** on-
   site. **Cards:** AX, MC, VI.
                                                                                         ⛉

(See maps and indexes p. 260-263, 264-265, 271-272)

THE CAPITAL GRILLE
Lunch: $8-$15   Dinner: $18-$33   Phone: 602/952-8900   ⑤

▼▼▼▼
Steak House

Location: Jct Camelback Rd and 26th St, just e; in Biltmore Fashion Park. 2502 E Camelback Rd, Suite 199 85016. **Hours:** 11 am-3 & 5-10 pm, Fri & Sat from 5 pm, Sun 4 pm-9 pm. Closed: 11/23, 12/25. **Reservations:** accepted. **Features:** One of the new breed of trendy steakhouses, the well-appointed restaurant serves excellent prime beef. It also is home to a lively lounge scene. Lending to the decor are original-looking artwork, rich mahogany paneling and matching chairs, crisp white linens and silenced tables. Dressy casual; cocktails. **Parking:** on-site. **Cards:** AX, CB, DC, DS, MC, VI.

CARLOS O'BRIEN'S MEXICAN RESTAURANT
Lunch: $6-$10   Dinner: $8-$15   Phone: 602/274-5881   ⑩

▼▼
Mexican

Location: SR 51, exit Northern Ave, 1.4 mi w. 1133 E Northern Ave 85020. **Hours:** 11 am-11 pm, Fri & Sat-midnight. Closed: 4/16, 11/23, 12/25. **Reservations:** accepted. **Features:** The cavernous restaurant serves predictable Tex-Mex fare. Both the food and the margaritas make this spot popular with the locals. Casual dress; cocktails. **Parking:** on-site. **Cards:** AX, DS, MC, VI.

CHRISTOPHER'S FERMIER BRASSERIE
Lunch: $30-$50   Dinner: $30-$50   Phone: 602/522-2344   ㉗

▼▼▼
French

Location: Just e of 24th St; in Biltmore Fashion Park. 2584 E Camelback Rd 85016. **Hours:** 11 am-3 & 5-10 pm. Closed major holidays; also Super Bowl Sun. **Reservations:** suggested. **Features:** The upstairs location is convenient, and pleasant staff welcome patrons to a special dining experience. Regional American influences combine with classic French preparations. Indulge in the hot and cold chocolate dessert. Dressy casual. **Parking:** on-site. **Cards:** AX, CB, DC, DS, JC, MC, VI.

CHRISTO'S
Lunch: $9-$15   Dinner: $11-$26   Phone: 602/264-1784   ⑯

▼▼
Italian

Location: Just s of Maryland Ave. 6327 N 7th St 85014. **Hours:** 11 am-2:30 & 5:30-10 pm, Sat 5:30 pm-10:30 pm. Closed: 1/1, 11/23, 12/25; also Sun. **Reservations:** suggested. **Features:** The popular restaurant serves an excellent variety of traditional Italian dishes, including fettuccine monte casino, chicken Florentine and shrimp diavolo. Casual dress; cocktails. **Parking:** on-site. **Cards:** AX, DC, DS, MC, VI.

CONVIVO BISTRO
Lunch: $7-$11   Dinner: $19-$25   Phone: 602/997-7676   ⑭

▼▼
International

Location: Northwest corner of 16th St and Glendale Ave. 7000 N 16th St #140 85020. **Hours:** 11:30 am-2 & 5-9 pm, Fri & Sat-10 pm. Closed: 11/23, 12/25; also Sun & Mon. **Reservations:** suggested. **Features:** The restaurant's name and menu have changed, but the basic concept remains the same. Chef Beeson uses Continental methods and regional ingredients to produce flavorful dishes, such as the must-try roasted corn and lobster tamale starter. Varied meat, seafood and vegetarian specialties employ local and organically grown ingredients. The atmosphere is casual. Casual dress; cocktails. **Parking:** on-site. **Cards:** AX, MC, VI.

DIFFERENT POINTE OF VIEW
Dinner: $28-$40   Phone: 602/866-6350   ⑥

▼▼▼ ▼▼▼
French

Location: I-17, exit 207 (Dunlap Ave), 3 mi e, then 2 mi n; in Pointe Hilton Tapatio Cliffs Resort. 11111 N 7th St 85020. **Hours:** 6 pm-10 pm. Closed: Sun & Mon 6/1-10/1. **Reservations:** suggested. **Features:** While dining on the French-influenced Mediterranean cuisine served in a grand manner, guests can take in panoramic views of the city. The restaurant boasts an award-winning, international wine list. Casual dress; cocktails; entertainment. **Parking:** valet. **Cards:** AX, CB, DC, DS, JC, MC, VI.

EDDIE MATNEY'S
Lunch: $10-$15   Dinner: $17-$29   Phone: 602/957-3214   ㉚

▼▼▼
Mediterranean

Location: Northwest corner of Camelback Rd and 24th St; 1st floor of Northern Trust Bank Tower. 2398 E Camelback Rd 85016. **Hours:** 11:30 am-2:30 & 5-10 pm, Fri-11 pm, Sat 5 pm-11 pm. Closed major holidays; also Sun. **Reservations:** suggested. **Features:** Contemporary French Mediterranean cuisine, including salads and preparations of chicken, seafood, steak and veal, is the highlight of the meal. The wine list is extensive. Smoking is permitted on the patio. Dressy casual; cocktails; entertainment. **Parking:** valet. **Cards:** AX, DC, DS, MC, VI.

EL TORITO GRILL
Lunch: $4-$12   Dinner: $7-$15   Phone: 602/997-9511   ⑧

▼▼
Regional Mexican

Location: I-10, exit 208 (Peoria Ave), 0.3 mi w to 28th Dr, just s, then 0.3 mi e. 10047 N Metro Pkwy E 85051. **Hours:** 11 am-10 pm, Fri & Sat-11 pm. Closed: 11/23, 12/25. **Reservations:** accepted. **Features:** Beyond the classic Mexican dishes, guests can look for innovative dishes created with Afro-Cuban and Spanish elements reminiscent of Veracruz. Casual dress; cocktails. **Parking:** on-site. **Cards:** AX, MC, VI.

FARM KITCHEN AT THE FARM AT
SOUTH MOUNTAIN   *Menu on aaa.com*   Lunch: $5-$9   Phone: 602/276-6360   ㊿

AAA
▼
American

Location: I-10, exit 151 (University Dr), 1.4 mi s, then just s of Southern Ave. 6106 S 32nd St 85042. **Hours:** Open 2/1-5/30 & 9/15-1/31; 8 am-3 pm. Closed: 11/23, 12/25; also Mon. **Reservations:** accepted. **Features:** Dining outdoors is a picnic, with meals in a basket given to patrons who can seek refuge under canvas awnings or shady trees. Picnic tables with checked cloths are on brick patios. Cool salads and warming soups share menu space with scrumptious pies, cookies and cakes. Casual dress. **Parking:** on-site. **Cards:** AX, MC, VI.

THE FISH MARKET & TOP OF THE MARKET
Lunch: $7-$18   Dinner: $9-$34   Phone: 602/277-3474   ㉞

▼▼
Seafood

Location: Just e of 16th St. 1720 E Camelback Rd 85016. **Hours:** 11 am-9:30 pm, Fri & Sat-10 pm, Sun noon-9:30 pm. Closed: 11/23, 12/25. **Reservations:** suggested. **Features:** Seafood from around the world—from shellfish to fish to sushi—is used to make the restaurant's tasty dishes. Preparation styles include several grilling, steaming and smoking options. The lively atmosphere appeals to young and old. Casual dress; cocktails. **Parking:** on-site. **Cards:** AX, DC, DS, MC, VI.

(See maps and indexes p. 260-263, 264-265, 271-272)

FRANCO'S ITALIAN CAFFE
Italian

Lunch: $8-$14   **Dinner:** $11-$24   **Phone:** 602/381-1155   (37)
Location: Jct E Camelback Rd and 25th St; in Camelback Esplanade. 2501 E Camelback Rd 85016. **Hours:** 11:30 am-2:30 & 5:30-10 pm, Sat from 5 pm. Closed: 12/25; also Sun. **Features:** On the upscale restaurant's menu are wood-fired pizza and pasta dishes, as well as land and sea specialties. Casual dress; cocktails. **Parking:** on-site (fee) and street. **Cards:** AX, MC, VI.

THE FRY BREAD HOUSE
Regional Specialty

Lunch: $4-$7   **Dinner:** $4-$7   **Phone:** 602/351-2345   (46)
Location: Just n of Indian School Rd. 4140 N 7th Ave 85013. **Hours:** 10 am-7 pm, Fri & Sat-8 pm. Closed major holidays; also Sun. **Features:** For something unusual, try fry-bread tacos with any of varied fillings. A true Native American food, they are tasty and satisfying. The honey-covered dessert fry bread is decadent. Casual dress. **Parking:** on-site. **Cards:** DS, MC, VI.

GREEKFEST
Greek

Lunch: $7-$14   **Dinner:** $10-$30   **Phone:** 602/265-2990   (32)
Location: Jct Camelback Rd and 19th St, just e. 1940 E Camelback Rd 85016. **Hours:** 8 am-2:30 & 5-10 pm. Closed: 1/1, 11/23, 12/25; also Sun. **Reservations:** suggested. **Features:** Traditional Greek favorites, starting with flaming saganaki made from tasty kasseri cheese, are served in a taverna setting. Scrumptious salads, souvlaki and moussaka can be followed by baklava and strong Greek coffee. A good selection of wines is offered. Dressy casual; cocktails. **Parking:** on-site. **Cards:** AX, CB, DC, DS, MC, VI.

HAVANA CAFE
Cuban

Lunch: $6-$12   **Dinner:** $10-$23   **Phone:** 602/952-1991   (31)
Location: 0.5 mi w of 42nd St. 4225 E Camelback Rd 85018. **Hours:** 11 am-9:30 pm, Fri & Sat-10 pm, Sun 4 pm-9:30 pm. Closed major holidays. **Features:** The small eatery presents a varied menu of Cuban, Spanish and South American dishes. The efficient wait staff will gladly describe any and all foods. Casual dress; cocktails. **Parking:** on-site. **Cards:** AX, DC, DS, MC, VI.

KAI
Regional Southwestern

Dinner: $23-$35   **Phone:** 602/225-0100
Location: I-10, exit 162, 2.4 mi w; in Sheraton Wild Horse Pass Resort & Spa. 5594 W Wild Horse Pass Blvd 85020. **Hours:** 5:30 pm-9:30 pm, Fri & Sat-10 pm. Closed: Sun, Mon & last 3 weeks of August. **Reservations:** suggested. **Features:** Using Native American indigenous foods, chefs Sandy Garcia and Janos Wilder have created a seasonally changing menu. Meats, game and seafood are enhanced by vegetable and herb sauces, some of which were developed from native seeds. Dressy casual; cocktails. **Parking:** on-site and valet. **Cards:** AX, CB, DC, DS, JC, MC, VI.

KEEGAN'S GRILL
American

Lunch: $7-$10   **Dinner:** $8-$15   **Phone:** 602/955-6616   (22)
Location: Just w of 32nd St. 3114 E Camelback Rd 85016. **Hours:** 11 am-midnight, Thurs-Sat to 1 am, Sun 8 am-10 pm. Closed major holidays. **Reservations:** accepted. **Features:** Patrons are treated like family in the neighborhood pub, which serves great sandwiches, freshly made soups and the house specialty: tender baby back ribs. Casual dress; cocktails. **Parking:** on-site. **Cards:** AX, MC, VI.

KEEGAN'S GRILL & TAPROOM
American

Lunch: $7-$10   **Dinner:** $8-$15   **Phone:** 480/705-0505   (25)
Location: I-10, exit 159 (Ray Rd), 0.5 mi w. 4723 E Ray Rd 85044. **Hours:** 11 am-10 pm, Fri & Sat-11 pm, Sun 8 am-10 pm. Closed major holidays. **Reservations:** accepted. **Features:** The sports bar prepares great food, from soups and hearty sandwiches to barbecue ribs, seafood and steaks. Friendly staff members welcome patrons as neighbors. Save room for one of the lush desserts. Casual dress; cocktails. **Parking:** on-site. **Cards:** AX, MC, VI.

LANTANA GRILLE
American

Lunch: $9-$15   **Dinner:** $14-$26   **Phone:** 602/997-5850   (11)
Location: Loop 51, exit Glendale Ave, 0.4 mi w, then 0.6 mi n; in Pointe Hilton Squaw Peak Resort. 7677 N 16th St 85020. **Hours:** 6 am-10 pm, Fri & Sat-11 pm. **Reservations:** accepted. **Features:** The popular and attractive restaurant has patio dining in seasonal weather, a friendly staff and food cooked with a Southwestern touch. Casual dress; cocktails. **Parking:** on-site. **Cards:** AX, CB, DC, DS, JC, MC, VI.

LATITUDE 30
California

Dinner: $17-$29   **Phone:** 602/431-6472   (52)
Location: I-10, exit 155 (Baseline Rd), just w, then just s; in Pointe South Mountain Resort. 7777 S Pointe Pkwy 85044. **Hours:** 5 pm-10 pm. Closed: Sun & Mon. **Reservations:** suggested. **Features:** Elegant surroundings, friendly staff and innovative dishes designed by chef Stephen Stromberg make this a "trip for a meal out of this world." Asian influences are noted in such dishes as citrus-crusted halibut with Himalayan red rice and swirled green tea cheesecake. Dressy casual; cocktails. **Parking:** on-site. **Cards:** AX, CB, DC, DS, MC, VI.

MACAYO'S DESERT SKY
Mexican

Lunch: $7-$9   **Dinner:** $8-$14   **Phone:** 623/873-0313   (1)
Location: 0.5 mi w of 75th Ave; adjacent to Desert Sky Mall. 7829 W Thomas Rd 85033. **Hours:** 11 am-11 pm. Closed: 11/23, 12/25. **Reservations:** accepted. **Features:** Families enjoy the colorful, casual atmosphere while enjoying a nice selection of Mexican entrees, many made with chiles from the owner's farm near Tucson. Casual dress; cocktails. **Parking:** on-site. **Cards:** AX, DC, DS, MC, VI.

MACAYO'S MEXICAN KITCHEN CENTRAL
Mexican

Lunch: $6-$9   **Dinner:** $8-$14   **Phone:** 602/264-6141   (47)
Location: Just n of Indian School Rd. 4001 N Central Ave 85012. **Hours:** 11 am-11 pm, Fri & Sat-midnight. Closed: 11/23, 12/25. **Features:** In one of the original restaurants opened by the Johnson family and inside the colorful Aztec-style exterior, you will still find the house specialty chimichangas and other Mexican classics. Casual dress; cocktails. **Parking:** on-site. **Cards:** AX, CB, DC, DS, JC, MC, VI.

(See maps and indexes p. 260-263, 264-265, 271-272)

MALEE'S THAI BISTRO   **Lunch:** $8-$14   **Dinner:** $10-$19   **Phone:** 480/342-9220 ④

Thai

Location: Loop 101, exit 31 (Tatum Blvd), just n; in The District at Desert Ridge Marketplace. 21001 N Tatum Blvd 85050. **Hours:** 11:30 am-2:30 & 4:30-9 pm, Sat & Sun noon-10 pm. Closed: 11/23, 12/25. **Reservations:** suggested. **Features:** The decor with decorative glass fixtures emulating jellyfish brings a whimsical touch to the new eatery's sushi bar. Widely varied dishes appeal both to the eye and palate. Friendly staff help guests select from among stir-fries, curries, soups and house features. Casual dress; cocktails. **Parking:** on-site. **Cards:** AX, DC, MC, VI.

MARCO POLO SUPPER CLUB   **Dinner:** $15-$35   **Phone:** 602/468-0100 �33

Northern
Italian

Location: Just e of 24th St. 2621 E Camelback Rd 85016. **Hours:** 5 pm-10 pm, Fri & Sat-11 pm. Closed: 7/4, 11/23, 12/25; also Sun. **Reservations:** suggested. **Features:** It all happens upstairs in the upscale dining room. Guests are entertained as they ponder a wide wine selection and a choice of elegant Asia-influenced dishes or hearty Italian fare, none of which disappoints the discriminating palate. Dressy casual; cocktails; entertainment. **Parking:** valet. **Cards:** AX, DC, DS, MC, VI.

MCCORMICK & SCHMICK'S SEAFOOD RESTAURANT   **Lunch:** $7-$13   **Dinner:** $8-$27   **Phone:** 602/468-1200 ㊴

Seafood

Location: Southeast corner of 24th St and Camelback Rd; in Camelback Esplanade. 2575 E Camelback Rd 85016. **Hours:** 11 am-11 pm, Sat from 5 pm, Sun 5 pm-10 pm. Closed: 12/25. **Reservations:** accepted. **Features:** This place is all about seafood, which is imported from all over the world. Among good choices are Washington state oysters, Maine clams, delicate Hawaiian escolar and tuna from Ecuador. The clublike decor is cozy, and expert staff provide able assistance. Casual dress; cocktails. **Parking:** on-site (fee) and valet. **Cards:** AX, DC, DS, MC, VI.

THE MELTING POT   **Dinner:** $35-$49   **Phone:** 480/704-9206

Fondue

Location: I-10, exit 159, 2 mi w; in Mountain Park Pavilion. 3626 E Ray Rd 85044. **Hours:** 5 pm-10 pm, Fri-11 pm, Sat 4 pm-11 pm, Sun 4 pm-10 pm. Closed: 11/23, 12/25. **Reservations:** suggested. **Features:** In addition to several types of cheese fondue, the restaurant offers three types of broths in which to simmer beef, chicken, seafood and garden-fresh vegetables. Not to be forgotten are the sumptuous chocolate dips. Casual dress; cocktails. **Parking:** on-site. **Cards:** AX, DC, DS, MC, VI.

MERITAGE STEAKHOUSE   **Dinner:** $16-$36   **Phone:** 480/293-5000 ②

Steak House

Location: SR 101, exit 31 (Tatum Blvd), 0.4 mi n to Deer Valley, then 0.5 mi e; JW Marriott Desert Ridge Resort & Spa. 5350 E Marriott Dr 85004. **Hours:** 11 am-2 & 5:30-10 pm. **Reservations:** suggested. **Features:** With classic style, the steaks and chops are grilled to perfection and the seafood is delicately sauced. Crisp salads and sides including sauteed asparagus or mushrooms round out your meal served by attentive and courteous staff. Casual dress; cocktails. **Parking:** on-site and valet. **Cards:** AX, CB, DC, DS, JC, MC, VI.

MORTON'S OF CHICAGO   **Dinner:** $20-$34   **Phone:** 602/955-9577 �35

Steak House

Location: Southeast corner of Camelback Rd and 24th St. 2501 E Camelback Rd 85016. **Hours:** 5:30 pm-11 pm, Sun 5 pm-10 pm. Closed major holidays. **Reservations:** suggested. **Features:** The popular steak house chain is known for "big food and big prices." The dining room has an open kitchen and a wall of celebrity photographs. In addition to USDA prime aged beef, the menu includes some seafood, including lobster. Dressy casual; cocktails. **Parking:** on-site. **Cards:** AX, DC, DS, MC, VI.

NIXON'S   **Lunch:** $7-$12   **Dinner:** $7-$12   **Phone:** 602/852-0900 ㊱

American

Location: Just e of jct Camelback Rd and 24th St; in Camelback Esplanade. 2501 E Camelback Rd, Suite 40 85016. **Hours:** 11 am-10 pm, Sat 4 pm-11 pm. Closed: 1/1, 11/23, 12/25; also Sun. **Features:** The popular after-work eatery displays a wide range of political memorabilia, including protest posters and a scrolling tickertape. Offerings include burgers, sandwiches, pizza and chicken. Casual dress; cocktails. **Parking:** on-site and valet. **Cards:** AX, MC, VI.

OMAHA STEAKHOUSE   **Lunch:** $9-$23   **Dinner:** $16-$32   **Phone:** 602/553-8970 ㉙

American

Location: Just n of Camelback Rd, on 26th St; in Embassy Suites Phoenix-Biltmore. 2630 E Camelback Rd 85020. **Hours:** 11 am-10 pm, Fri & Sat-11 pm. **Reservations:** accepted. **Features:** This traditional steak house with a semi-casual atmosphere features certified Mid-Western corn-fed beef. Pasta, seafood, lamb and pork are also on the varied menu. Casual dress; cocktails. **Parking:** on-site. **Cards:** AX, CB, DC, DS, MC, VI.

PANE BIANCO   **Lunch:** $8-$10   **Phone:** 602/234-2100 ㊹

Specialty

Location: 0.4 mi n of Indian School Rd. 4404 N Central Ave 85012. **Hours:** 11 am-3 pm. Closed major holidays; also Sun & Mon. **Features:** The take-out spot offers just four sandwich and two salad choices—such as tuna with red onion, gaeta olives and arugula on focaccia—but the quality is excellent. Why not have an upscale lunch in a brown bag (albeit a fun and classy one with handles)? A complimentary mini-dessert is a custom caramel. Imported bottled beverages are available. Casual dress. **Parking:** on-site. **Cards:** MC, VI.

PANINO ON CENTRAL   **Lunch:** $7-$10   **Dinner:** $13-$25   **Phone:** 602/336-1198 ⑳

International

Location: Just n of Camelback Rd. 5202 N Central Ave 85012. **Hours:** 11 am-3 & 5:30-10 pm, Sat from 5:30 pm, Sun 11 am-2:30 pm; Sunday brunch. Closed major holidays. **Reservations:** accepted. **Features:** Chef Alonzo presents attractive dishes with creative flavor blends, such as Caribbean grilled chicken and the lemon basil mousse dessert. Dressy casual; cocktails. **Parking:** on-site. **Cards:** AX, DC, MC, VI.

(See maps and indexes p. 260-263, 264-265, 271-272)

PAPPADEAUX SEAFOOD KITCHEN   **Lunch:** $7-$15   **Dinner:** $13-$27   **Phone:** 602/331-3434   (7)
▼▼▼▼   **Location:** I-17, exit 208 (Peoria Ave), just e, then 0.6 mi n on Frontage Rd. 11051 N Black Canyon Hwy 85029.
Cajun   **Hours:** 11 am-10 pm, Fri-11 pm, Sat noon-11 pm, Sun noon-10 pm. Closed: 11/23, 12/25. **Features:** Just a touch above the usual is found at the eatery, where friendly, smiling staffers assist guests through a meal of hearty Cajun dishes, such as Louisiana seafood gumbo, fried shrimp and pasta Mardi Gras. Sweet potato pecan pie is sumptuous. Casual dress; cocktails. **Parking:** on-site. **Cards:** AX, MC, VI.

PHOENIX CITY GRILLE   **Lunch:** $8-$12   **Dinner:** $12-$24   **Phone:** 602/266-3001   (18)
▼▼ ▼▼ ◆◆   **Location:** 0.8 mi n of Camelback Rd. 5816 N 16th St 85016. **Hours:** 11 am-10 pm, Fri & Sat-11 pm, Sun 10 am-9 pm. Closed: 11/23, 12/25. **Reservations:** accepted. **Features:** The friendly neighborhood place is comfortable. Capable servers offer traditional salads, sandwiches, pasta and chicken. Cedar-plank salmon
American   is a favorite, and mesquite-smoked barbecue back pork ribs are lean and tasty. Casual dress; **Parking:** on-site. **Cards:** AX, DC, MC, VI.

POSTINO WINECAFE   **Lunch:** $8-$10   **Dinner:** $8-$10   **Phone:** 602/852-3939   (43)
▼▼ ▼▼   **Location:** 0.5 mi n of Indian School on 40th St, just w. 3939 E Campbell Ave 85018. **Hours:** 11 am-11 pm. Closed: 1/1, 11/23, 12/25; also Sun. **Features:** The light fare served in the recycled post office building incorporates Mediterranean blends and flavors, such as bruschetta toppings of roasted artichoke or ricotta with
American   pistachios. The varied sandwich and salad menu continues through the evening. Casual dress; beer & wine only. **Parking:** on-site. **Cards:** AX, DC, MC, VI.

PRICKLY PEAR DELI & WINERY   **Lunch:** $4-$7   **Dinner:** $6-$7   **Phone:** 602/995-2241   (9)
▼▼   **Location:** I-17, exit 206, just e to 23rd Ave, then just n. 2308 W Northern Ave 85021. **Hours:** 7 am-4 pm, Wed-8 pm, Sat 8 am-2 pm. Closed major holidays; also Sun. **Features:** The mid-town breakfast and lunch stop employs a friendly staff and prepares hearty sandwiches, homemade soups and an interesting selection of
American   egg dishes, breads and cereals. The location is bright and sunny. On Wednesday nights, guests can sample from an Italian buffet. Casual dress; wine only. **Parking:** on-site. **Cards:** AX, DS, MC, VI.

PRONTO RISTORANTE   **Lunch:** $5-$15   **Dinner:** $9-$24   **Phone:** 602/956-4049   (42)
▼▼ ▼▼   **Location:** Jct Camelback Rd, 0.5 mi s on 40th St, then just w. 3950 E Campbell Ave 85018. **Hours:** 11:30 am-2:30 & 5-10 pm, Sat & Sun from 5 pm. **Reservations:** suggested. **Features:** Small, charming and intimate, the
Italian   neighborhood eatery is a local favorite. Antipasto is a must. Valet parking is available on Friday and Saturday nights. Dressy casual; cocktails. **Parking:** on-site. **Cards:** AX, DC, DS, MC, VI.

RA SUSHI-BAR-RESTAURANT   **Lunch:** $7-$9   **Dinner:** $8-$18   **Phone:** 480/940-1111   (24)
▼▼ ▼▼   **Location:** I-10, exit 159, just w. 4921 E Ray Rd 85044. **Hours:** 11 am-11 pm. Closed: 11/23, 12/25.
Sushi   **Features:** Tucked into a busy shopping center, the upscale sushi bar offers a selection of innovatively designed seafood dishes served by a casual, efficient staff. Try spinach gyoza to start. To end, the signature tempura cinnamon ice cream will serve three or four folks. Casual dress; cocktails. **Parking:** on-site. **Cards:** AX, DC, DS, MC, VI.

RICHARDSON'S   **Lunch:** $8-$14   **Dinner:** $10-$26   **Phone:** 602/265-5886   (17)
▼▼ ▼▼   **Location:** Jct 16th St. 1582 E Bethany Home Rd 85016. **Hours:** 11 am-midnight, Sat & Sun from 10 am. Closed: 11/23, 12/25. **Reservations:** accepted. **Features:** High-energy crowds, friendly service and great Southwestern and New Mexican food are hallmarks of the laid-back but lively restaurant. Chilies ranging
Southwestern   from mild to hot are used in the varied dishes. Also on the menu are such specialties as chorizo-stuffed pork chop and Sandia chicken, as well as pizza made in a wood-fired oven. A copper bar and Pueblo-style booths distinguish the dining space. Casual dress; cocktails. **Parking:** on-site. **Cards:** AX, CB, DC, DS, MC, VI.

RISTORANTE TUSCANY   **Dinner:** $16-$32   **Phone:** 480/293-3737   (1)
▼▼◆ ▼▼◆   **Location:** SR 101, exit 31 (Tatum Blvd), 0.4 mi n to Deer Valley, then 0.5 mi e; in JW Marriott Desert Ridge Resort & Spa. 5350 E Marriott Dr 85044. **Hours:** 6 pm-10 pm. **Reservations:** suggested. **Features:** Chef Davies brings
Regional   a wonderful delicacy to hearty, country-style Tuscan dishes. The staff is well-trained and attentive. Guests
Italian   may enjoy the display kitchen during the meal or opt for a table overlooking a lake and distant mountains. Dressy casual; cocktails. **Parking:** on-site and valet. **Cards:** AX, CB, DC, DS, JC, MC, VI.

THE ROMAN TABLE   *Menu on aaa.com*   **Lunch:** $6-$12   **Dinner:** $11-$27   **Phone:** 602/234-0333   (45)
(AAA)   **Location:** I-10, exit 144, 2.2 mi n. 4221 N 7th Ave 85013. **Hours:** 11 am-2 & 5-10 pm, Sat from 5 pm, Sun 5 pm-9 pm. Closed: 4/16, 12/25. **Reservations:** suggested. **Features:** Diners can choose from more than 10
▼▼ ▼▼   varieties of fresh, hand-tossed pizza baked in a brick oven. Other menu favorites include ravioli, gnocchi
Italian   and sauteed salmon over penne in a light tomato sauce. Dressy casual; cocktails. **Parking:** on-site. **Cards:** AX, DC, DS, MC, VI.

ROY'S DESERT RIDGE   **Dinner:** $22-$28   **Phone:** 480/419-7697   (3)
(AAA)   **Location:** SR 101, exit 31 (Tatum Blvd), 0.4 mi n to Deer Valley, then 0.5 mi e; in JW Marriott Desert Ridge Resort & Spa. 5350 E Marriott Dr 85004. **Hours:** 5 pm-10 pm, Fri & Sat-11 pm. Closed: 11/23, 12/25.
▼▼◆▼▼   **Reservations:** suggested. **Features:** An attractive setting and tropical motif blend well with friendly and
Hawaiian   attentive service. Widely varied seafood dishes, which change based on availability, are expertly prepared. Examples might include basil-seared ono, herb-crusted yellowtail and butterfish. Chocolate souffle is a house specialty. Dressy casual; cocktails. **Parking:** on-site and valet. **Cards:** AX, CB, DC, DS, JC, MC, VI.

RUFFINO   **Lunch:** $5-$11   **Dinner:** $9-$21   **Phone:** 480/893-8544   (23)
▼▼ ▼▼   **Location:** I-10, exit 158, 0.5 mi w. 4902 E Warner Rd 85044. **Hours:** 11:30 am-3 & 5-10 pm, Fri-11 pm, Sat 5 pm-11 pm, Sun 4 pm-10 pm. Closed: 12/25; also Super Bowl Sun. **Reservations:** suggested. **Features:** A quiet and relaxing space in a busy city awaits you at Ruffino. They are known for the seafood specialties as well
Italian   as more traditional dishes such as rigatoni bolognese or veal saltimbocca. Casual dress; cocktails. **Parking:** on-site. **Cards:** AX, DC, DS, MC, VI.

(See maps and indexes p. 260-263, 264-265, 271-272)

RUSTLER'S ROOSTE
Steak House
▼▼ ▼▼

Dinner: $13-$31   **Phone:** 602/438-9000   [51]
Location: I-10, exit 155 (Baseline Rd), just w, then just s; in Pointe South Mountain Resort. 7777 S Pointe Pkwy 85044. **Hours:** 5 pm-10 pm, Sun 10 am-2 pm. **Reservations:** suggested. **Features:** Overlooking the city, the popular Western-style restaurant prepares a nice selection of steak, seafood and barbecue specialties. A band performs nightly. Casual dress; cocktails; entertainment. **Parking:** on-site. **Cards:** AX, CB, DC, DS, JC, MC, VI.

SALUTE RISTORANTE ITALIANO
Italian
▼▼▼ ▼▼▼

Lunch: $14-$23   **Dinner:** $14-$23   **Phone:** 480/502-5575   [5]
Location: Loop 101, exit 31 (Tatum Blvd); in Desert Ridge Mall. 21001 N Tatum Blvd, Suite 38-1320 85050. **Hours:** 11:30 am-2:30 & 5-9 pm, Fri & Sat-9 pm. **Closed:** 1/1, 11/23, 12/25. **Reservations:** suggested, weekends. **Features:** Part of a small Phoenix-area chain that specializes in Italian cuisine, the restaurant is in Desert Ridge Mall on the north side of the city. Excellent entrees center on veal, chicken, beef, seafood, vegetarian ingredients and pasta. Patio seating is an option for those who want to enjoy the out-of-doors in the cool of the evening. Casual dress; cocktails. **Parking:** on-site. **Cards:** AX, CB, DC, DS, MC, VI.

SAM'S CAFE
Regional American
▼▼▼ ▼▼▼

Lunch: $10-$13   **Dinner:** $11-$20   **Phone:** 602/954-7100   [28]
Location: Just e of 24th St; in Biltmore Fashion Park, 2nd level east end. 2566 E Camelback Rd 85016. **Hours:** 11 am-10 pm, Sun-9 pm. **Closed:** 11/23, 12/25. **Reservations:** suggested. **Features:** The bustling eatery lays out a tempting selection of Southwestern-style entrees. Casual dress; cocktails. **Parking:** on-site. **Cards:** AX, DC, DS, MC, VI.

SAUCE
Italian
▼▼ ▼▼

Lunch: $5-$9   **Dinner:** $5-$9   **Phone:** 602/216-2400   [15]
Location: Jct 7th St; northeast corner. 742 E Glendale Ave 85020. **Hours:** 11 am-9 pm, Fri & Sat-10 pm. Closed major holidays. **Features:** The restaurant's selections could be characterized as "gourmet fast food." Among choices are sausage and caramelized onion or chicken and broccoli rabe pizzas. Lasagna and fresh salads also are on the menu. A clean modern decor with indoor seating makes a fun dining experience. Casual dress; wine only. **Parking:** on-site. **Cards:** AX, DS, MC, VI.

TARBELL'S
American
▼▼▼ ▼▼▼

Dinner: $14-$34   **Phone:** 602/955-8100   [24]
Location: Just e of 32nd Ave. 3213 E Camelback Rd 85018. **Hours:** 5 pm-10 pm, Sun-9 pm. Closed major holidays. **Reservations:** suggested. **Features:** The lively restaurant's monthly changing selection of creative dishes are complemented with 100 percent organic local produce and a variety of poultry, fish and beef. An open kitchen allows glimpses of the preparation process. Children are accommodated. Dressy casual; cocktails. **Parking:** on-site and valet. **Cards:** AX, CB, DC, DS, JC, MC, VI.

T-BONE STEAKHOUSE
Steak House
▼▼

Dinner: $11-$25   **Phone:** 602/276-0945
Location: 1.5 mi s of Baseline Rd. 10037 S 19th Ave 85041. **Hours:** 5 pm-10 pm, Fri & Sat-11 pm. Closed: 11/23, 12/24, 12/25. **Features:** The friendly staff serves mesquite-broiled steaks and chicken. The dining room and outdoor patio afford panoramic views of the city skyline, city lights and Camelback mountain range. Casual dress; cocktails. **Parking:** on-site. **Cards:** AX, CB, DC, DS, MC, VI.

T. COOK'S
American
▼▼▼ ▼▼▼

Lunch: $10-$16   **Dinner:** $24-$32   **Phone:** 602/808-0766   [41]
Location: Just e of 52nd St; in Royal Palms Resort and Spa. 5200 E Camelback Rd 85018. **Hours:** 6-10 am, 11-2 & 5:30-10 pm; Sunday brunch from 10 am. **Reservations:** suggested. **Features:** Accomplished staffers serve a nice selection of Mediterranean entrees, including wood-burning rotisserie items, in elegant surroundings. Patio seating is an option. Dressy casual; cocktails. **Parking:** valet. **Cards:** AX, CB, DC, DS, MC, VI.

TUCCHETTI
Italian
▼▼ ▼▼

Lunch: $7-$10   **Dinner:** $10-$18   **Phone:** 602/957-0222   [38]
Location: Just e of 20th St; in Town & Country Mall. 2135 E Camelback Rd 85016. **Hours:** 11:30 am-9 pm, Fri-10 pm, Sat 4 pm-10 pm, Sun 4 pm-9 pm. **Closed:** 11/23, 12/25. **Reservations:** accepted. **Features:** Bright decor, a friendly staff and an attractive, help-yourself salad bar are just the beginning of the dining experience. Traditional entrees and pizzas baked on stone are top choices in the busy eatery. Casual dress; cocktails. **Parking:** on-site. **Cards:** AX, DC, DS, MC, VI.

TUTTI SANTI RISTORANTE
Italian
▼▼▼ ▼▼▼

Lunch: $8-$12   **Dinner:** $10-$18   **Phone:** 602/216-0336   [12]
Location: Between E Washington and E Jefferson sts. 7575 N 16th St 85254. **Hours:** 11:30 am-2 & 5-10 pm, Fri & Sat-11 pm, Sun 5 pm-10 pm. **Reservations:** accepted. **Features:** Vaulted ceilings, large framed artwork, fresh pasta and an outdoor terrace distinguish the family-operated local favorite. Dressy casual; cocktails. **Parking:** on-site. **Cards:** AX, DS, MC, VI.

VENICE RESTORANTE
Italian
▼▼ ▼▼

Lunch: $7-$12   **Dinner:** $10-$20   **Phone:** 480/961-9350   [22]
Location: I-10, exit 157 (Elliot Rd), 0.5 mi w; in Ahwatukee Mercado Plaza. 4240 E Ahwatukee Dr 85044. **Hours:** 11:30 am-11 pm, Sat from 5 pm, Sun 5 pm-9 pm. Closed major holidays. **Reservations:** accepted. **Features:** The homemade pasta, specialties of duck ravioli and rich tiramisu are all reasons to visit this friendly, neighborhood bistro. Easy parking is offered at the shopping plaza location. Casual dress; cocktails. **Parking:** on-site. **Cards:** AX, MC, VI.

VINCENT ON CAMELBACK
Southwest French
▼▼▼ ▼▼▼

Lunch: $13-$16   **Dinner:** $29-$33   **Phone:** 602/224-0225   [23]
Location: Just w of 40th St, on the north side of Camelback Rd. 3930 E Camelback Rd 85018. **Hours:** 11 am-2 & 5-10 pm, Fri-10:30 pm, Sat 5 pm-10:30 pm. Closed major holidays; also Sun & Mon 5/1-9/30. **Reservations:** suggested. **Features:** Prepared with a French flair, the fresh seafood, lobster, veal, duck confit, rack of lamb, beef and cornish hen all are attractively presented. Attentive, accomplished service is achieved in each of several intimate dining rooms, which are surrounded by fresh orchids. Dressy casual; cocktails. **Parking:** valet. **Cards:** AX, CB, DC, DS, MC, VI.

(See maps and indexes p. 260-263, 264-265, 271-272)

WRIGHT'S   **Dinner:** $21-$32   **Phone:** 602/381-7668   ⑲
▼▼▼▼ ▼▼▼▼ **Location:** Jct Camelback Rd, 0.5 mi n on 24th St, then 0.4 mi w; in Arizona Biltmore Resort & Spa. 2400 E Missouri
American   85016. **Hours:** 6 pm-10 pm. **Reservations:** suggested. **Features:** Elegant, attentive servers bring eye-pleasing and palate-satisfying dishes that take advantage of seasonally fresh ingredients. Menu selections range from the freshest seafood to aged steaks. The signature chocolate souffle is worth the wait. Dressy casual; cocktails. **Parking:** valet. **Cards:** AX, CB, DC, DS, JC, MC, VI.

ZEN 32   **Lunch:** $7-$15   **Dinner:** $10-$20   **Phone:** 602/954-8700   ㉑
▼▼ ▼▼   **Location:** Northwest corner of E Camelback Rd and 32nd St; in The Biltmore Plaza. 3160 E Camelback Rd 85016.
Japanese   **Hours:** 11 am-midnight, Sat & Sun from 4:30 pm. Closed major holidays. **Reservations:** accepted. **Features:** In addition to items from the sushi bar, the restaurant presents a grilled fusion menu. Dishes range from teriyaki chicken and yaki soba noodles to grilled salmon and New York steak. Casual dress; cocktails. **Parking:** on-site. **Cards:** AX, DC, MC, VI.

─────── *The following restaurant has not been evaluated by AAA* ───────
but is listed for your information only.

MIRACLE MILE DELICATESSEN   **Phone:** 602/776-0992
[fyi]   Not evaluated. **Location:** Just w of N 20th St; in Camelback Colonade Shopping Center. 1949 E Camelback, Suite 160 85016. **Features:** Since 1949 this establishment has been serving up delicious hot pastrami and corned beef sandwiches along with other deli favorites and daily entree specials.

Do you know the facts?

AAA publishes the Digest of Motor Laws to assist traveling motorists. Filled with facts and information, this one-of-a-kind compilation includes a comprehensive description of the laws that govern motor vehicle registration and operation in the United States and Canada. This guide has a new, easy-to-read format with graphics, state-by-state tax summary tables and detailed information on occupant protection laws, driver licensing laws, automated enforcement laws and motor vehicle fees and taxes.

You can easily locate various licensing and motor laws governing the states in which you are traveling. In addition to vehicle registration and operation laws, the Digest contains information and facts about alcohol laws, traffic safety laws and more.

Call your local club to obtain a copy of the Digest.

The book retails for $13.95.

The Phoenix Vicinity

APACHE JUNCTION pop. 31,814

—— WHERE TO STAY ——

APACHE JUNCTION MOTEL

AAA SAVE

Motel

			Phone: 480/982-7702	
2/1-3/31 [CP]	1P: $58-$64	2P: $64-$69	XP: $6	D10
12/22-1/31 [CP]	1P: $48-$58	2P: $58-$64	XP: $6	D10
10/1-12/21	1P: $40-$45	2P: $45-$50	XP: $5	D10
4/1-9/30	1P: $38-$43	2P: $43-$48	XP: $5	D10

Location: US 60, exit 195, 2 mi n, then just w. 1680 W Apache Tr 85220. Fax: 480/671-5287. **Facility:** 15 one-bedroom standard units. 1 story, exterior corridors. *Bath:* shower only. **Parking:** on-site. **Terms:** 3 day cancellation notice-fee imposed, weekly rates available, small pets only ($5-$20 fee, no cats). **Guest Services:** airport transportation (fee)-Phoenix Sky Harbor & Goldwater International airports. **Cards:** AX, DS, MC, VI. **Special Amenities:** free continental breakfast and free local telephone calls.

SOME UNITS

APACHE JUNCTION SUPER 8   *Book at aaa.com*

AAA SAVE

Small-scale Hotel

			Phone: (480)288-8888	
2/1-3/31 [ECP]	1P: $94-$109	2P: $99-$114	XP: $5	F12
10/31-1/31 [ECP]	1P: $74-$84	2P: $79-$84	XP: $5	F12
4/1-4/30 [ECP]	1P: $64-$79	2P: $69-$84	XP: $5	F12
5/1-10/30 [ECP]	1P: $54-$69	2P: $59-$74	XP: $5	F12

Location: US 60, exit 196 (Idaho Rd/SR 88 E), just n. 251 E 29th Ave 85219. Fax: 480/288-0648. **Facility:** 60 one-bedroom standard units, some with whirlpools. 2 stories (no elevator), interior/exterior corridors. *Bath:* combo or shower only. **Parking:** on-site. **Terms:** cancellation fee imposed, weekly rates available, small pets only ($50 deposit, in designated units, no cats). **Amenities:** hair dryers. **Pool(s):** heated outdoor. **Leisure Activities:** whirlpool. **Guest Services:** coin laundry. **Cards:** AX, CB, DC, DS, JC, MC, VI. **Special Amenities:** free expanded continental breakfast and free local telephone calls.

SOME UNITS

EXPRESS INN   *Book at aaa.com*

AAA SAVE

Small-scale Hotel

			Phone: 480/982-9200	
2/1-4/27	1P: $116-$132	2P: $116-$132	XP: $10	F12
9/27-1/31	1P: $88-$110	2P: $88-$110	XP: $10	F12
4/28-9/26	1P: $69-$85	2P: $69-$85	XP: $10	F12

Location: US 60, exit 195, 2 mi n to W Apache Tr, then 0.4 mi e. 1101 W Apache Tr 85220. Fax: 480/671-6183. **Facility:** 40 one-bedroom standard units, some with whirlpools. 2 stories (no elevator), interior/exterior corridors. *Bath:* combo or shower only. **Parking:** on-site. **Terms:** office hours 6:30 am-10 pm. **Amenities:** high-speed Internet, dual phone lines, irons, hair dryers. **Pool(s):** heated outdoor. **Leisure Activities:** whirlpool. **Guest Services:** coin laundry. **Business Services:** meeting rooms. **Cards:** AX, DC, DS, MC, VI.

SOME UNITS

—— WHERE TO DINE ——

BARLEEN ARIZONA OPRY DINNER SHOW

American

Dinner: $23   **Phone:** 480/982-7991

Location: US 60, exit Tomahawk Rd, 1 mi n, then 0.5 mi e. 2275 Old West Hwy 85219. **Hours:** Open 11/12-1/31; 6:30 pm seating. **Closed:** 12/24, 12/25; also Sun. **Reservations:** suggested. **Features:** Three generations perform country-style entertainment and serve roast beef dinners. Casual dress. **Parking:** on-site. **Cards:** DS, MC, VI.

DIRTWATER SPRINGS

Steak House

Lunch: $4-$11   **Dinner:** $8-$18   **Phone:** 480/983-3478

Location: Center. 586 W Apache Tr 85220. **Hours:** 11 am-10 pm. **Closed:** 12/25. **Features:** Steaks and ribs are favorites, but diners shouldn't miss the classic Mexican-style dishes. The casual decor incorporates Western and hunting elements, including mounted animal heads. Casual dress; cocktails. **Parking:** on-site. **Cards:** DS, MC, VI.

FEED BAG RESTAURANT

American

Lunch: $5-$13   **Dinner:** $6-$13   **Phone:** 480/983-3521

Location: US 60, exit 196 (Idaho Rd/SR 88 E), 1.7 mi n to Old W Highway, just w, then just s. 300 S Phelps Dr 85220. **Hours:** 6 am-9 pm. **Closed:** 11/23, 12/25. **Features:** Fresh decor, ample portions of home-style food and smiling servers make the restaurant a popular place with the locals. Casual dress. **Parking:** on-site. **Cards:** AX, DS, MC, VI.

MINING CAMP RESTUARANT & TRADING POST

American

Dinner: $18   **Phone:** 480/982-3181

Location: US 60, exit 196 (Idaho Rd/SR 88), 2.2 mi n to Apache Tr, 2.9 mi ne, then 1 mi e and n; via Nodak Rd and Mining Camp St, follow signs. 6100 E Mining Camp St 85219. **Hours:** 4 pm-9 pm, Sun from noon. **Closed:** Mon-Thurs 6/6-9/30. **Features:** Established in 1961, the restaurant sits at the base of the Superstition Mountains and serves all-you-can-eat meals family style. Dinner includes roast chicken and dressing, baked ham and barbecue ribs, along with side dishes. Constructed of rough-hewn Ponderosa pine, the setting resembles an early mining camp cook shanty. Casual dress; beer & wine only. **Parking:** on-site. **Cards:** AX, DS, MC, VI.

BUCKEYE pop. 6,537

——— WHERE TO STAY ———

DAYS INN-BUCKEYE   *Book at aaa.com*   **Phone:** 623/386-5400

▼▼ ▼▼   Property failed to provide current rates
Small-scale Hotel   **Location:** I-10, exit 114 (Miller Rd), just sw. 25205 W Yuma Rd 85326. **Fax:** 623/386-4988. **Facility:** 60 one-bedroom standard units. 2 stories (no elevator), exterior corridors. **Bath:** combo or shower only. **Parking:** on-site. **Terms:** pets ($10 extra charge). **Amenities:** hair dryers. **Pool(s):** outdoor. **Leisure Activities:** whirlpool. **Guest Services:** coin laundry. **Business Services:** fax (fee).

SOME UNITS
🚐 ⌨ 🐾 🎥 DATA PORT 🛢 🖥 /✕ 📺 /
FEE

CAREFREE pop. 2,927

——— WHERE TO STAY ———

THE BOULDERS RESORT & GOLDEN DOOR SPA   *Book at aaa.com*   **Phone:** (480)488-9009

AAA SAVE	12/15-1/31	1P: $575	2P: $575	XP: $25	F16
▼▼▼ ▼▼▼	2/1-5/20	1P: $549	2P: $549	XP: $25	F16
	9/8-12/14	1P: $499	2P: $499	XP: $25	F16
	5/21-9/7	1P: $199	2P: $199	XP: $25	F16

Resort
Large-scale Hotel   **Location:** Scottsdale Rd, 11 mi n of Bell Rd. 34631 N Tom Darlington Dr 85377. **Fax:** 480/488-6799. **Facility:** Nestled in the Sonoran desert, the distinctive resort uses the natural topography of dramatic boulders in its design along with oversized casita rooms. Smoke free premises. 160 units. 157 one-bedroom standard units. 3 one-bedroom suites. 1-2 stories, exterior corridors. **Parking:** on-site and valet. **Terms:** check-in 4 pm, 21 day cancellation notice, [BP] & [MAP] meal plans available, $30 service charge, pets ($100 fee). **Amenities:** CD players, dual phone lines, voice mail, safes, honor bars, irons, hair dryers. *Fee:* video games, high-speed Internet. *Some:* DVD players. **Dining:** 6 restaurants, 6 am-10 pm, cocktails, also, Latilla Dining Room, see separate listing, entertainment. **Pool(s):** 3 heated outdoor. **Leisure Activities:** saunas, whirlpools, steamrooms, recreation programs in summer, rental bicycles, hiking trails, jogging, exercise room, spa. *Fee:* golf-36 holes, 8 tennis courts, balloon rides, bi-plane rides, aerobic instruction, guided hiking, rock climbing, jeep and hummer tours, flat water river floats, night vision stargazing, geology tour, horseback riding. **Guest Services:** gift shop, valet laundry, area transportation-within 5 mi. **Business Services:** conference facilities, business center. **Cards:** AX, DC, DS, JC, MC, VI.

SOME UNITS
✈ 🐑 🍽 24 Y 🏊 🐾 ✂ ✕ VCR 🎥 DATA PORT 🖥 / 🛢 🖥 /
FEE FEE

CAREFREE RESORT & VILLAS   *Book at aaa.com*   **Phone:** (480)488-5300

AAA SAVE	2/1-4/23	1P: $199-$239	2P: $199-$239	XP: $10	F
▼▼ ▼▼	9/11-1/31	1P: $129-$199	2P: $129-$199	XP: $10	F
	4/24-5/29	1P: $129-$179	2P: $129-$179	XP: $10	F
	5/30-9/10	1P: $79-$109	2P: $79-$109	XP: $10	F

Resort
Large-scale Hotel   **Location:** SR 101, exit 36 (Pima Rd), 12.2 mi n to Cave Creek Rd, 1 mi w, then 0.4 mi n. 37220 Mule Train Rd 85377. **Fax:** 480/488-5779. **Facility:** Spacious rooms in the main building or expansive condominium units that are very well appointed give this property appeal. 410 units. 238 one-bedroom standard units. 172 one-bedroom suites, some with efficiencies, kitchens and/or whirlpools. 1-3 stories, interior/exterior corridors. **Bath:** combo or shower only. **Parking:** on-site and valet. **Terms:** check-in 4 pm, cancellation fee imposed, package plans, $12 service charge, pets ($50 fee). **Amenities:** voice mail, irons, hair dryers. *Some:* DVD players, CD players, honor bars. *Fee:* video games, high-speed Internet. **Dining:** 2 restaurants, 7 am-10 pm, cocktails. **Pool(s):** 3 heated outdoor. **Leisure Activities:** whirlpools, steamroom, putting green, recreation programs in summer, rental bicycles, hiking trails, jogging, exercise room, spa, horseshoes. *Fee:* 6 lighted tennis courts, jeep tours, hot air balloon, horseback riding. **Guest Services:** gift shop, valet laundry, area transportation-within 3 mi. **Business Services:** conference facilities, business center. **Cards:** AX, CB, DC, DS, JC, MC, VI. *(See color ad below)*

SOME UNITS
S D ✈ 🐑 🍽 Y 🏊 🐾 ✕ DATA PORT 🖥 /✕ 🛢 🖥 /
FEE FEE

WHERE TO DINE

ENGLISH ROSE TEA ROOM   **Lunch: $6-$10**   **Phone: 480/488-4812**

▼▼▼▼   **Location:** From Tom Darlington Blvd, just e on Wampum, then just n; center. 201 Easy St, #103 85377. **Hours:** Open 2/1-6/29 & 10/2-1/31; 10 am-5 pm. Closed: 1/1, 11/23, 12/24, 12/25; also Sun. **Reservations:** required.
Specialty   **Features:** The setting is tiny in space, but the charming decor is classic tea room. The friendly staff even have a selection of hats guests may wear to make their luncheon or high tea a special dining experience.
Casual dress. **Parking:** street. **Cards:** AX, DC, DS, MC, VI.

LATILLA DINING ROOM   **Dinner: $29-$36**   **Phone: 480/488-9009**

▼▼▼▼▼   **Location:** Scottsdale Rd, 11 mi n of Bell Rd; in The Boulders Resort & Golden Door Spa-A Wyndham Luxury Resort. 34631 N Tom Darlington Dr 85377. **Hours:** 6 pm-10 pm. **Reservations:** suggested. **Features:** Highly
Regional American   imaginative and innovative preparations of regional favorites make up the menu. The sophisticated dining room is the renowned resort's premier place for enjoying upscale cuisine. Dressy casual; cocktails;
entertainment. **Parking:** on-site and valet. **Cards:** AX, CB, DC, DS, JC, MC, VI.   Ⓨ

CAVE CREEK pop. 3,728

WHERE TO STAY

CAVE CREEK TUMBLEWEED HOTEL   **Phone: 480/488-3668**

AAA SAVE	2/1-4/30 & 1/1-1/31	1P: $109-$199	2P: $109-$199	XP: $10	F18
▼▼ ▼▼	5/1-7/5 & 9/1-12/31	1P: $89-$179	2P: $89-$179	XP: $10	F18

Motel   **Location:** Jct Scottsdale Rd/Tom Darlington Rd, 1.3 mi w. 6333 E Cave Creek Rd 85327 (PO Box 312). Fax: 480/595-1719. **Facility:** 24 one-bedroom standard units, some with efficiencies. 2 stories (no elevator), exterior corridors. **Parking:** on-site. **Terms:** open 9/1-1/31 & 2/1-7/5, office hours 7 am-10 pm, 14 day cancellation notice, pets ($75 deposit). **Amenities:** voice mail, hair dryers. **Pool(s):** outdoor. **Business Services:** meeting rooms. **Cards:** AX, DS, MC, VI.

SOME UNITS
🛏️ 🍽️ 🏊 📽️ / ✕ 🗄️ 🖼️ 🖵 /
FEE

WHERE TO DINE

EL ENCANTO MEXICAN RESTAURANT   **Lunch: $6-$9**   **Dinner: $10-$15**   **Phone: 480/488-1752**

▼▼▼▼   **Location:** Center. 6248 E Cave Creek Rd 85331. **Hours:** 8 am-10 pm. Closed: 11/23, 12/25.
Mexican   **Reservations:** accepted. **Features:** An outdoor dining area features a mission-style garden setting with pond and lots of shade trees. Southwestern, Mexican and Sonoran Mexican cuisine is featured in this relaxing oasis in this scenic Western town. Casual dress; cocktails. **Parking:** on-site. **Cards:** AX, DC, DS,
MC, VI.   Ⓨ

THE HORNY TOAD   **Lunch: $6-$12**   **Dinner: $9-$21**   **Phone: 480/488-9542**

▼▼▼ ▼▼   **Location:** Jct Scottsdale Rd/Tom Darlington Rd, 0.8 mi w. 6738 E Cave Creek Rd 85331. **Hours:** 11 am-10 pm, Fri & Sat-11 pm. Closed: 11/23, 12/25. **Features:** Built like a Western barn, the restaurant has fun decor that fits
American   the casual, friendly service. Guests can savor freshly prepared dishes and generously sized desserts. The patio is open when the weather permits. Casual dress; cocktails. **Parking:** on-site. **Cards:** AX, DC, DS,
MC, VI.   Ⓨ

TONTO BAR & GRILL   **Lunch: $10-$26**   **Dinner: $10-$26**   **Phone: 480/488-0698**

▼▼▼   **Location:** Jct Carefree Hwy, 2.4 mi n on Cave Creek Rd, just w; at Rancho Manana Golf Resort. 5736 E Rancho Manana Blvd 85331. **Hours:** 11 am-9 pm. Closed: 11/23, 12/25. **Reservations:** suggested. **Features:** The
American   casual setting, in an old dude ranch, and views of a golf course do not detract from the upscale, eclectic cuisine that award-winning chef Flatt prepares. The seasonally changing menu takes advantage of the best
regional foods available. Dressy casual; cocktails. **Parking:** on-site. **Cards:** AX, DC, DS, MC, VI.   Ⓨ

CHANDLER pop. 176,581   (See map and index starting on p. 271)

WHERE TO STAY

BEST WESTERN INN OF CHANDLER   *Book at aaa.com*   **Phone: 480/814-8600**   🆖

AAA SAVE	2/1-3/31 & 1/1-1/31	1P: $79	2P: $99	XP: $10
▼▼ ▼▼	4/1-4/30	1P: $69	2P: $89	XP: $10
	5/1-12/31	1P: $59	2P: $89	XP: $10

Small-scale Hotel   **Location:** Just s of Ray Rd. 950 N Arizona Ave 85225. Fax: 480/814-1198. **Facility:** 48 one-bedroom standard units, some with whirlpools. 2 stories (no elevator), exterior corridors. *Bath:* combo or shower only. **Parking:** on-site. **Amenities:** high-speed Internet, voice mail, irons, hair dryers. **Pool(s):** small outdoor. **Leisure Activities:** whirlpool. **Cards:** AX, DC, DS, MC, VI. **Special Amenities:** free continental breakfast and free newspaper.

SOME UNITS
♿ 🅿️ 🏊 📽️ DATA PORT 🖵 / ✕ 🗄️ 🖼️ /

CHANDLER SUPER 8   *Book at aaa.com*   **Phone: (480)961-3888**   🆖

▼▼ ▼▼	1/12-1/31 [ECP]	1P: $60-$69	2P: $66-$75	XP: $6	F17
	2/1-4/1 [ECP]	1P: $60-$66	2P: $66-$72	XP: $6	F17
Small-scale Hotel	4/2-1/11 [ECP]	1P: $53-$60	2P: $59-$66	XP: $6	F17

Location: I-10, exit 160 (Chandler Blvd). 7171 W Chandler Blvd 85226. Fax: 480/961-3888. **Facility:** 73 one-bedroom standard units. 2 stories (no elevator), interior corridors. **Parking:** on-site. **Terms:** pets ($5 extra charge). **Amenities:** safes (fee). **Pool(s):** heated outdoor. **Guest Services:** valet and coin laundry. **Business Services:** fax (fee). **Cards:** AX, CB, DC, DS, JC, MC, VI. *(See color ad p 327)*

SOME UNITS
ASK 🆂🅳 🛏️ 🍽️ 🏊 🐾 📽️ DATA PORT / ✕ 🗄️ 🖼️ /
FEE   FEE   FEE FEE

(See map and index starting on p. 271)

COMFORT INN — *Book at aaa.com*

Phone: (480)705-8882 — **76**

2/1-4/16 [BP]	1P: $99-$119	2P: $99-$119	XP: $10 — F18
9/1-1/31 [BP]	1P: $79-$109	2P: $79-$109	XP: $10 — F18
4/17-8/31 [BP]	1P: $69-$89	2P: $69-$89	XP: $10 — F18

Location: I-10, exit 160 (Chandler Blvd), 1.5 mi e, then just n. 255 N Kyrene Rd 85226. Fax: 480/705-6697. **Small-scale Hotel** Facility: 70 one-bedroom standard units. 3 stories, interior corridors. Bath: combo or shower only. Parking: on-site. Terms: package plans, small pets only. Amenities: high-speed Internet, voice mail, irons, hair dryers. Pool(s): small heated outdoor. Guest Services: coin laundry. Business Services: fax. Cards: AX, CB, DC, DS, JC, MC, VI. Special Amenities: free full breakfast and free local telephone calls.

SOME UNITS

COURTYARD BY MARRIOTT — *Book at aaa.com*

Phone: 480/763-9500 — **71**

Property failed to provide current rates

Location: I-10, exit 159, just e on Ray Rd, then just s. 920 N 54th St 85226. Fax: 480/763-9600. **Small-scale Hotel** Facility: 156 units. 152 one-bedroom standard units, some with whirlpools. 4 one-bedroom suites. 3 stories, interior corridors. Bath: combo or shower only. Parking: on-site. Amenities: high-speed Internet, dual phone lines, voice mail, irons, hair dryers. Pool(s): heated outdoor. Leisure Activities: whirlpool, exercise room. Guest Services: valet and coin laundry. Business Services: meeting rooms. Fee: PC, fax.

SOME UNITS

FAIRFIELD INN BY MARRIOTT PHOENIX CHANDLER — *Book at aaa.com*

Phone: (480)940-0099 — **79**

2/1-4/30	1P: $107-$125	2P: $107-$125
9/12-1/31	1P: $80-$107	2P: $80-$107
5/1-5/27	1P: $71-$107	2P: $71-$107
5/28-9/11	1P: $53-$71	2P: $53-$71

Small-scale Hotel Location: I-10, exit 160 (Chandler Blvd), just e, then s on Southgate Dr. 7425 W Chandler Blvd 85226. Fax: 480/940-7336. Facility: 66 one-bedroom standard units. 3 stories, interior corridors. Parking: on-site. Amenities: high-speed Internet, irons, hair dryers. Pool(s): heated outdoor. Leisure Activities: whirlpool. Guest Services: valet and coin laundry. Business Services: PC, fax (fee). Cards: AX, CB, DC, DS, MC, VI. Special Amenities: free continental breakfast and free local telephone calls.

SOME UNITS

HAMPTON INN — *Book at aaa.com*

Phone: (480)753-5200 — **74**

2/1-4/30 & 1/1-1/31 [BP]	1P: $119-$129	2P: $119-$129
10/1-12/31 [BP]	1P: $79-$99	2P: $79-$99
5/1-9/30 [BP]	1P: $69-$89	2P: $69-$89

Small-scale Hotel Location: I-10, exit 160 (Chandler Blvd), just e. 7333 W Detroit St 85226. Fax: 480/753-5100. Facility: 101 one-bedroom standard units, some with whirlpools. 6 stories, interior corridors. Bath: combo or shower only. Parking: on-site. Terms: cancellation fee imposed. Amenities: video games (fee), high-speed Internet, voice mail, irons, hair dryers. Some: dual phone lines. Pool(s): small heated outdoor. Leisure Activities: whirlpool. Guest Services: valet laundry. Business Services: meeting rooms. Cards: AX, CB, DC, DS, JC, MC, VI. *(See color ad p 279)*

SOME UNITS — FEE   FEE

HAWTHORN SUITES CHANDLER — *Book at aaa.com*

Phone: (480)705-8881 — **77**

2/1-4/14 [BP]	1P: $129-$169	2P: $129-$169
4/15-6/9 & 9/11-1/31 [BP]	1P: $99-$139	2P: $99-$139
6/10-9/10 [BP]	1P: $89-$119	2P: $89-$119

Small-scale Hotel Location: I-10, exit 160 (Chandler Blvd), 1.5 mi e. 5858 W Chandler Blvd 85226. Fax: 480/785-1451. Facility: 100 units. 90 one- and 10 two-bedroom suites with efficiencies. 2 stories (no elevator), interior corridors. Bath: combo or shower only. Parking: on-site. Terms: cancellation fee imposed, small pets only ($25 fee). Amenities: high-speed Internet, dual phone lines, voice mail, irons, hair dryers. Some: DVD players (fee). Pool(s): heated outdoor. Leisure Activities: whirlpool. Guest Services: sundries, valet and coin laundry. Business Services: meeting rooms, PC. Cards: AX, CB, DC, DS, JC, MC, VI.

SOME UNITS — FEE   FEE   FEE

HOLIDAY INN AT OCOTILLO — *Book at aaa.com*

Phone: 480/203-2121

2/1-5/31	1P: $149-$249	2P: $149-$249
9/1-1/31	1P: $132-$232	2P: $132-$232
6/1-8/31	1P: $102-$202	2P: $102-$202

Location: I-10, exit 164 (Queen Creek Rd), 5.5 mi e, 1.1 mi s on Alma School Rd, then just w. 1200 W Ocotillo Rd **Small-scale Hotel** 85248. Fax: 480/203-2122. Facility: Designated smoking area. 106 units. 97 one-bedroom standard units. 9 one-bedroom suites ($202-$249) with whirlpools. 4 stories, interior corridors. Bath: combo or shower only. Parking: on-site. Amenities: high-speed Internet, dual phone lines, voice mail, irons, hair dryers. Dining: 6 am-10 pm, cocktails. Pool(s): heated outdoor. Leisure Activities: whirlpool, exercise room. Guest Services: sundries, valet and coin laundry, area transportation-within 5 mi. Business Services: meeting rooms, business center. Cards: AX, DS, MC, VI. Special Amenities: free newspaper and early check-in/late check-out.

HOMEWOOD SUITES BY HILTON — *Book at aaa.com*

Phone: (480)753-6200 — **73**

1/1-1/31	1P: $99-$239	2P: $99-$239	XP: $10 — F18
2/1-12/31	1P: $79-$219	2P: $79-$219	XP: $10 — F18

Small-scale Hotel Location: I-10, exit 160 (Chandler Blvd), 0.4 mi e, n on 54th St, then just w. 7373 W Detroit St 85226. Fax: 480/753-6222. Facility: 83 units. 78 one- and 5 two-bedroom suites ($79-$219) with efficiencies. 3 stories, interior corridors. Bath: combo or shower only. Parking: on-site. Terms: cancellation fee imposed, pets (small dogs only, with prior approval). Amenities: video games (fee), high-speed Internet, dual phone lines, voice mail, irons, hair dryers. Pool(s): heated outdoor. Leisure Activities: whirlpool, exercise room. Guest Services: sundries, complimentary evening beverages: Mon-Thurs, valet and coin laundry, area transportation. Business Services: meeting rooms, business center. Cards: AX, CB, DC, DS, JC, MC, VI.

SOME UNITS

(See map and index starting on p. 271)

PARK PLAZA PHOENIX/CHANDLER   *Book at aaa.com*   Phone: (480)961-4444   81

▼▼▼
2/1-4/28 & 1/1-1/31	1P: $109-$118	2P: $119-$128	XP: $10
9/9-12/31	1P: $95-$118	2P: $105-$128	XP: $10
4/29-9/8	1P: $62-$80	2P: $72-$90	XP: $10

Small-scale Hotel   **Location:** I-10, exit 160 (Chandler Blvd), just e, then just s on Southgate Dr. Located in a commercial area. 7475 W Chandler Blvd 85226. Fax: 480/940-0269. **Facility:** 159 units. 140 one-bedroom standard units. 19 one-bedroom suites. 4 stories, interior corridors. **Parking:** on-site. **Terms:** cancellation fee imposed. **Amenities:** video games (fee), voice mail, irons, hair dryers. *Some:* high-speed Internet. **Pool(s):** heated outdoor. **Leisure Activities:** whirlpool, exercise room. **Guest Services:** valet and coin laundry. **Business Services:** meeting rooms. **Cards:** AX, CB, DC, DS, MC, VI. *(See color ad below)*

SOME UNITS
(ASK) (SD) (dog) (fork) (swim) (film) (DATA PORT) (TV) / (X) /

RED ROOF INN-CHANDLER   *Book at aaa.com*   Phone: (480)857-4969   84

▼▼▼ ▼▼▼
2/1-3/30 & 1/1-1/31	1P: $57-$69	2P: $61-$74	XP: $7 F18
3/31-10/30	1P: $48-$62	2P: $53-$69	XP: $5 F18
10/31-12/31	1P: $40-$59	2P: $46-$65	XP: $6 F18

Small-scale Hotel   **Location:** I-10, exit 160 (Chandler Blvd), just e, then s on Southgate Dr. 7400 W Boston St 85226. Fax: 480/857-4979. **Facility:** 131 units. 127 one-bedroom standard units. 4 one-bedroom suites. 4 stories, interior corridors. *Bath:* combo or shower only. **Parking:** on-site. **Terms:** small pets only. **Amenities:** video games (fee), voice mail. **Pool(s):** heated outdoor. **Business Services:** meeting rooms, fax (fee). **Cards:** AX, CB, DC, DS, MC, VI.

SOME UNITS
(dog) (fork) (&M) (film) (DATA PORT) / (X) (phone) (TV) /

RESIDENCE INN-CHANDLER FASHION CENTER   *Book at aaa.com*   Phone: (480)782-1551   72

▼▼▼
All Year	1P: $99-$199	2P: $99-$199	

Small-scale Hotel   **Location:** I-10, exit 160 (Chandler Blvd), 4.2 mi e, just n on N Metro Blvd, then just e. Located across from the Chandler Fashion Center Mall. 200 N Federal St 85226. Fax: 480/726-6785. **Facility:** 102 units. 30 one-bedroom standard units with kitchens. 51 one- and 21 two-bedroom suites with kitchens. 3 stories, interior corridors. *Bath:* combo or shower only. **Parking:** on-site. **Terms:** 14 day cancellation notice, [BP] meal plan available, small pets only ($75 fee). **Amenities:** high-speed Internet, dual phone lines, voice mail, irons, hair dryers. **Pool(s):** small heated outdoor. **Leisure Activities:** whirlpool, exercise room, sports court. **Guest Services:** valet and coin laundry. **Business Services:** meeting rooms. **Cards:** AX, CB, DC, DS, JC, MC, VI.

SOME UNITS
(ASK) (SD) (dog) (fork/FEE) (&M) (film) (swim) (X) (film) (DATA PORT) (phone) (cup) (TV) / (X) (phone) (VCR) /

SAN MARCOS RESORT AND CONFERENCE CENTER   *Book at aaa.com*   Phone: (480)812-0900   83

(AAA) (SAVE)
▼▼▼
1/1-1/31	1P: $139-$219	2P: $139-$219	XP: $10 F17
2/1-5/31 & 10/1-12/31	1P: $129-$209	2P: $129-$209	XP: $10 F17
6/1-9/30	1P: $79-$129	2P: $79-$129	XP: $10 F17

Large-scale Hotel   **Location:** Just s on Arizona Ave from jct Chandler Blvd, just w on Buffalo St; in historic downtown. 1 San Marcos Pl 85225. Fax: 480/963-6777. **Facility:** 295 units. 293 one-bedroom standard units. 2 one-bedroom suites ($159-$439) with whirlpools. 4 stories, exterior corridors. **Parking:** on-site. **Terms:** 3 day cancellation notice-fee imposed, package plans, $7 service charge, pets ($100 deposit). **Amenities:** high-speed Internet, dual phone lines, voice mail, irons, hair dryers. **Dining:** 2 restaurants, 6:30 am-10 pm, cocktails. **Pool(s):** 2 heated outdoor. **Leisure Activities:** whirlpool, spa. *Fee:* golf-18 holes, 2 lighted tennis courts. **Guest Services:** gift shop, valet laundry, area transportation-within 5 mi. **Business Services:** conference facilities, business center. **Cards:** AX, CB, DC, DS, MC, VI. **Special Amenities:** free newspaper.

SOME UNITS
(SD) (dog) (fork/FEE) (Y) (swim) (tennis/FEE) (X) (film) (DATA PORT) (TV) / (X) (phone) (cup) /

SOUTHGATE MOTEL   *Book at aaa.com*   Phone: 480/940-0308   80

▼▼▼
Property failed to provide current rates

Motel   **Location:** I-10, exit 160 (Chandler Blvd), just e, then just s on Southgate Dr. 7445 W Chandler Blvd 85226. Fax: 480/705-9019. **Facility:** 49 one-bedroom standard units. 2 stories (no elevator), exterior corridors. *Bath:* combo or shower only. **Parking:** on-site. **Terms:** pets ($10 fee). **Amenities:** *Some:* hair dryers. **Pool(s):** heated outdoor. **Guest Services:** coin laundry.

SOME UNITS
(dog) (fork/FEE) (film) (swim) (film) (phone) (cup) / (X) (DATA PORT) (TV) /

(See map and index starting on p. 271)

SPRINGHILL SUITES BY MARRIOTT-FASHION
CENTER   *Book at aaa.com*   Phone: (480)726-7666   **75**

	2/1-5/21 [BP]	1P: $140-$170	2P: $140-$170
	7/1-1/31 [BP]	1P: $120-$140	2P: $120-$140
Small-scale Hotel	5/22-6/30 [BP]	1P: $110-$130	2P: $110-$130

Location: I-10, exit 160 (Chandler Blvd), 4.2 mi e, then just n. Located across from the Chandler Fashion Center Mall. 225 N Metro Blvd 85226. Fax: 480/726-7666. **Facility:** 101 one-bedroom standard units. 3 stories, interior corridors. *Bath:* combo or shower only. **Parking:** on-site. **Terms:** cancellation fee imposed. **Amenities:** high-speed Internet, dual phone lines, voice mail, irons, hair dryers. *Some:* DVD players. **Pool(s):** heated outdoor. **Leisure Activities:** whirlpool, exercise room. **Guest Services:** valet and coin laundry. **Business Services:** meeting rooms. **Cards:** AX, DC, DS, MC, VI.

SOME UNITS

(ASK) (Sᴅ) (GM) (⊡) (⬚) (🚲) (✕⃘) (DATA PORT) (🛏) (🖨) (💻) / (✕) (VCR) /

WINDMILL SUITES OF CHANDLER   *Book at aaa.com*   Phone: (480)812-9600   **78**

AAA (SAVE)   All Year [ECP]   1P: $84-$149   2P: $84-$149   XP: $10   F18

Location: I-10, exit 160 (Chandler Blvd), 4 mi e. Located at the Chandler Fashion Center Mall. 3535 W Chandler Blvd 85226. Fax: 480/812-8911. **Facility:** Smoke free premises. 127 one-bedroom suites, some with whirlpools. 3 stories, interior corridors. *Bath:* combo or shower only. **Parking:** on-site. **Terms:** check-in 4 pm, cancellation
Small-scale Hotel fee imposed. **Amenities:** voice mail, irons, hair dryers. *Some:* dual phone lines. **Pool(s):** heated outdoor. **Leisure Activities:** whirlpool, barbecue grill, bicycles, limited exercise equipment. **Guest Services:** valet and coin laundry, area transportation-within 5 mi. **Business Services:** meeting rooms, PC. **Cards:** AX, DC, DS, MC, VI. **Special Amenities:** free expanded continental breakfast and free local telephone calls.

(Sᴅ) (🐄) (🍴) (👨‍🦽) (🚲) (✕⃘) (✕) (✕⃘) (DATA PORT) (🛏) (🖨)

———— WHERE TO DINE ————

56 EAST BAR & KITCHEN   **Lunch:** $9-$15   **Dinner:** $12-$26   **Phone:** 480/705-5602   **47**

AAA   **Location:** I-10, exit 159 (Ray Rd), 0.5 mi e to 75th St, just s to Dublin, then just w. 7131 W Ray Rd, Suite 45 85226. **Hours:** 11 am-2 & 5-10 pm. Closed: 11/23, 12/25; also Sun. **Features:** In a shopping plaza, the martini bar and restaurant serves flavorful drinks along with dishes on its tasty menu. Among favorites is the apple pork chop with sweetened onions atop garlic mashed potatoes. Save room for chocolate banana fritters with
American   vanilla bean gelato for dessert and an after-dinner drink. The friendly staff offers suggestions regarding martinis and dinner entrees. Casual dress; cocktails. **Parking:** on-site. **Cards:** MC, VI.

(GM) (◥)

ABUELO'S MEXICAN FOOD EMBASSY   **Lunch:** $7-$17   **Dinner:** $7-$17   **Phone:** 480/855-0960   **49**

Location: SR 101 Expwy Loop, exit 160 (Chandler Blvd), 0.4 mi w. 3440 W Chandler Blvd 85226. **Hours:** 11 am-10 pm, Fri & Sat-11 pm. Closed: 11/23, 12/24, 12/25. **Features:** The charming decor is reminiscent of a Mexican hacienda, with plants, statues and folk art. Representative of the upscale menu's distinctive
Regional Mexican   combinations are mesquite-grilled, bacon-wrapped shrimp. Fresh herb flavors and ingredients enhance each menu item. Casual dress; cocktails. **Parking:** on-site. **Cards:** AX, DC, DS, MC, VI.

(◥)

C-FU GOURMET   **Lunch:** $5-$7   **Dinner:** $8-$19   **Phone:** 480/899-3888   **44**

Location: Southwest corner of Warner and Dobson rds. 2051 W Warner Rd 85224. **Hours:** 10:30 am-2:30 & 4:30-9 pm, Fri & Sat-9:30 pm. **Reservations:** accepted. **Features:** Among favorites are moo goo gai pan and
Chinese   chicken lo mein, as well as a few American dishes. All are reasonably priced. Casual dress; cocktails. **Parking:** on-site. **Cards:** AX, MC, VI.

(◥)

CITRUS CAFE   **Dinner:** $16-$28   **Phone:** 480/899-0502   **43**

Location: 0.6 mi s of Elliot Rd; in Alma School Shops Plaza. 2330 N Alma School Rd 85224. **Hours:** 5 pm-close, Sun 4 pm-8 pm. Closed major holidays; also Mon. **Reservations:** suggested. **Features:** Tucked into a simple shopping plaza, the cozy, intimate bistro presents French fare with polish and elan. Traditional onion
French   soup, escargots, layered cheesecake and creme brulee are among Gallic favorites prepared from the freshest ingredients. Dressy casual; cocktails. **Parking:** on-site. **Cards:** AX, DS, MC, VI.

CYCLO VIETNAMESE CUISINE   **Lunch:** $5-$8   **Dinner:** $5-$8   **Phone:** 480/963-4490   **50**

Location: Just e of Dobson Rd. 1919 W Chandler Blvd, Suite 2 85224. **Hours:** 11 am-3 & 5-9 pm, Fri & Sat-10 pm. Closed: 1/1, 11/23, 12/25; also Sun & 7/1-7/15. **Features:** In a small shopping plaza, the eatery has
Vietnamese   food bursting with flavor and freshness. Dishes such as chicken pineapple curry and jasmine tea-scented creme brulee made without eggs are sure to please. Local chefs often visit on Monday evenings to relax and enjoy the savory foods. Casual dress; beer & wine only. **Parking:** on-site. **Cards:** MC, VI.

KEEGAN'S GRILL   **Lunch:** $7-$11   **Dinner:** $8-$20   **Phone:** 480/814-0003

Location: I-10, exit 164 (Queen Creek Rd), 5.2 mi e. 1095 W Queen Creek Rd 85248. **Hours:** 11 am-10 pm, Fri & Sat-11 pm. Closed major holidays. **Reservations:** accepted. **Features:** A decor featuring witty quotes painted on the walls and huge wooden columns welcomes diners to the bistro. Friendly staff members serve
American   dishes ranging from such comfort foods as meatloaf and barbecue ribs to more eclectic creations, including prosciutto-wrapped shrimp and Pacific Rim grilled chicken salad. Casual dress; cocktails. **Parking:** on-site. **Cards:** AX, MC, VI.

(◥)

KONA GRILL   **Lunch:** $6-$12   **Dinner:** $9-$24   **Phone:** 480/792-1711   **51**

Location: Just w of Loop 101; in Chandler Fashion Square Mall. 3111 W Chandler Blvd 85226. **Hours:** 11 am-11 pm, Fri & Sat-midnight, Sun-9 pm. Closed: 11/23, 12/25. **Features:** In the busy Chandler Fashion Square Mall,
Pacific Rim   the restaurant prepares Pacific Rim cuisine, including fresh salads, poultry and seafood. A large sushi bar entices devotees of raw creations. Outdoor seating is an option. Casual dress; cocktails. **Parking:** on-site. **Cards:** AX, DC, DS, MC, VI.

(GM) (◥) (◥)

(See map and index starting on p. 271)

P.F. CHANG'S CHINA BISTRO   **Lunch:** $7-$16   **Dinner:** $7-$16   **Phone:** 480/899-0472   48
Location: Loop 101 (Price Rd), exit Chandler Blvd, just e; across from Chandler Fashion Center. 3255 W Chandler Blvd 85226. **Hours:** 11 am-11 pm, Fri & Sat-midnight. Closed: 11/23, 12/25. **Reservations:** accepted.
Regional Chinese   **Features:** Asian fusion cuisine from major regions harmoniously and artfully blends fresh ingredients based on Chinese fan and t'sai principles. The intimate but casual dining room provides a culturally stimulating environment of sculptures and murals. Casual dress; cocktails. **Parking:** on-site. **Cards:** AX, DC, DS, MC, VI.

SAIGON PHO & SEAFOOD   **Lunch:** $5-$8   **Dinner:** $5-$13   **Phone:** 480/786-8828   45
Location: Jct Warner Rd, 0.5 mi s. 1381 N Alma School Rd 85224. **Hours:** 11 am-9 pm. Closed major holidays.
Vietnamese   **Features:** Dishes are prepared with fresh vegetables, herbs, beef, seafood, chicken and pork. From hot pot soups to fresh fish pulled from an on-site tank, the casual storefront eatery's offerings are infused with Eastern flavors. Casual dress. **Parking:** on-site. **Cards:** MC, VI.

SERRANO'S MEXICAN RESTAURANT   **Lunch:** $6-$10   **Dinner:** $6-$10   **Phone:** 480/899-3318   52
Location: 3 mi e on Chandler Blvd from jct SR 101, 0.3 mi s. 141 S Arizona Ave 85224. **Hours:** 11 am-10 pm, Sun-9 pm. Closed major holidays. **Reservations:** accepted. **Features:** Bring family and friends to enjoy the
Regional Mexican   complimentary warm bean dip, salsa and chips that are just the beginning of an exciting taste adventure in Sonoran style Mexican food. Several large dining rooms and a private function space are available. Casual dress; cocktails. **Parking:** on-site. **Cards:** AX, DC, DS, MC, VI.

Z TEJAS NEW AMERICAN CUISINE   **Lunch:** $7-$10   **Dinner:** $9-$19   **Phone:** 480/893-7550   46
Location: I-10, exit 158, just e. 7221 W Ray Rd 85226. **Hours:** 11 am-10 pm, Fri & Sat-11 pm. Closed: 11/23, 12/25. **Reservations:** accepted. **Features:** The young, friendly staff welcomes diners with smiles.
Southwestern   Attractively presented entrees are prepared in a Southwestern style with influences from Texas, Louisiana and Arizona. Banana cream pie is among the show-stopping desserts. Casual dress; cocktails. **Parking:** on-site. **Cards:** AX, CB, DC, DS, JC, MC, VI.

FOUNTAIN HILLS pop. 20,235

———— **WHERE TO STAY** ————

COMFORT INN   *Book at aaa.com*   **Phone:** (480)837-5343

2/1-4/30 [ECP]	1P: $99-$139	2P: $109-$139	XP: $10	F18
10/1-1/31 [ECP]	1P: $79-$109	2P: $89-$119	XP: $10	F18
5/1-9/30 [ECP]	1P: $49-$79	2P: $59-$79	XP: $10	F18

Small-scale Hotel   **Location:** 0.5 mi w of SR 87 (Beeline Hwy). 17105 E Shea Blvd 85268. Fax: 480/837-9146. **Facility:** 48 one-bedroom standard units, some with whirlpools. 2 stories, interior corridors. *Bath:* combo or shower only. **Parking:** on-site. **Amenities:** irons, hair dryers. **Pool(s):** heated outdoor. **Leisure Activities:** whirlpool. **Guest Services:** coin laundry, area transportation-Mayo Clinic. **Business Services:** PC. **Cards:** AX, CB, DC, DS, JC, MC, VI. **Special Amenities:** free expanded continental breakfast and free local telephone calls.   SOME UNITS

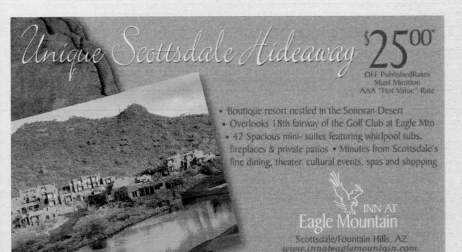

COPPERWYND RESORT AND CLUB   *Book at aaa.com*   Phone: (480)333-1900

(AAA) [SAVE]   2/1-5/15 & 1/1-1/31   1P: $299-$439
                9/16-12/31   1P: $259-$439
▼▼▼▼ ▼▼▼▼   5/16-9/15   1P: $149-$239

Resort   **Location:** Loop 101, exit 41, 7.6 mi e on Shea Blvd, 1.1 mi n on Palisades Blvd, then 0.8 mi w. Located in a secluded
Large-scale Hotel   area. 13225 N Eagle Ridge Dr 85268. Fax: 480/333-1901. **Facility:** An intimate hideaway with elegantly
                furnished rooms, surrounded by the desert with mountain views, golf club and city lights below. Designated
smoking area. 42 units. 32 one-bedroom standard units. 5 two- and 5 three-bedroom suites with kitchens. 2
stories (no elevator), exterior corridors. **Bath:** combo or shower only. **Parking:** on-site. **Terms:** check-in 4 pm, 3 day cancellation
notice-fee imposed, package plans, $18 service charge. **Amenities:** dual phone lines, voice mail, irons, hair dryers. *Some:* CD
players, fax, safes. **Dining:** Alchemy at CopperWynd, see separate listing. **Pool(s):** 2 heated outdoor. **Leisure
Activities:** whirlpools, steamrooms, hiking trails, jogging, spa. *Fee:* golf-18 holes, 9 lighted tennis courts. **Guest Services:** gift
shop, valet laundry, area transportation-within 5 mi. **Business Services:** meeting rooms. **Cards:** AX, DC, DS, MC, VI.
Special Amenities: free local telephone calls and free newspaper.

SOME UNITS

[S🅳] [📶] [⛏] [🅰] [➳] [🚲] [⊠] [⊗] [🎦] [DATA PORT] [🛏] [🖥] / [VCR] [🖨] /
                            FEE

INN AT EAGLE MOUNTAIN   *Book at aaa.com*   Phone: (480)816-3000

(AAA) [SAVE]   2/1-4/10   1P: $199-$259   2P: $199-$259   XP: $10   F12
                4/11-5/29 & 10/1-1/31   1P: $149-$199   2P: $149-$199   XP: $10   F12
▼▼▼ ▼▼   5/30-9/30 [CP]   1P: $99-$149   2P: $99-$149   XP: $10   F12

Small-scale Hotel   **Location:** Loop 101, exit 41, 7.3 mi e on Shea Blvd, 0.3 mi e on Eagle Mountain Pkwy, then just w. 9800 N Summer Hill
                Blvd 85268. Fax: 480/816-3090. **Facility:** Designated smoking area. 42 units. 31 one-bedroom standard units
with whirlpools. 11 one-bedroom suites with whirlpools. 2 stories (no elevator), exterior corridors. **Parking:**
on-site. **Terms:** 3 day cancellation notice, package plans. **Amenities:** video library (fee), voice mail, irons, hair dryers. *Some:*
DVD players. **Dining:** 6:30-10:30 am & 5-9 pm; closed 6/1-10/1. **Pool(s):** heated outdoor. **Leisure Activities:** whirlpool. **Guest
Services:** gift shop, valet laundry. **Business Services:** meeting rooms. **Cards:** AX, DC, DS, MC, VI. **Special Amenities:** free
expanded continental breakfast and free local telephone calls. *(See color ad p 317)*

SOME UNITS

[S🅳] [📶] [⛏] [➳] [🚲] [VCR] [🎦] [DATA PORT] [🛏] [🖥] / [🖨] /
                        FEE

--------- **WHERE TO DINE** ---------

ALCHEMY AT COPPERWYND   Lunch: $10-$15   Dinner: $20-$34   Phone: 480/333-1880
(AAA)   **Location:** Loop 101, exit 41, 7.6 mi e on Shea Blvd, 1.1 mi n on Palisades Blvd, then 0.8 mi e; in CopperWynd Resort
▼▼▼ ▼▼   and Club. 13225 N Eagle Ridge Dr 85268. **Hours:** 6:30 am-2 & 5-9 pm. **Reservations:** suggested.
Nouvelle   **Features:** This upscale eatery has accomplished staff, fabulous views over the east valley and some of the
American   most attractive and delicious contemporary American cuisine in the area. Dressy casual; cocktails. **Parking:**
                on-site. **Cards:** AX, CB, DC, DS, JC, MC, VI.   [Y]

LA PIAZZA   Dinner: $9-$18   Phone: 480/837-1878
▼▼ ▼▼   **Location:** Scottsdale Rd, 13 mi e on Shea Blvd, then 1.3 mi n. 11865 N Saguaro Blvd 85268. **Hours:** 5 pm-9 pm.
Italian   Closed: 1/1, 11/23, 12/25; also Mon & Sun 6/1-8/31. **Reservations:** suggested. **Features:** Selections of
MC, VI.   chicken, seafood, steak, veal, pork, pasta and salad are available. Enjoy patio dining as you indulge in
                Tuscan peasant bread and homemade desserts. Casual dress; cocktails. **Parking:** on-site. **Cards:** AX, DS,

GILBERT pop. 109,697   (See map and index starting on p. 271)

--------- **WHERE TO DINE** ---------

CAFE SAHARA   Lunch: $4-$6   Dinner: $8-$14   Phone: 480/633-1217 (28)
▼▼ ▼▼   **Location:** US 60, exit 184, 0.3 mi s; southeast corner of Val Vista Ave and E Baseline Rd; in Lake View Village
Middle Eastern Shopping Center. 3641 E Baseline Rd, Suite Q100 85234. **Hours:** 11 am-3 & 5-9 pm, Sat from noon. Closed:
                5/29, 9/4; also Sun. **Reservations:** accepted. **Features:** The small restaurant offers a taste of the Middle
to be a main course. Casual dress. **Parking:** on-site. **Cards:** DC, MC, VI.
                East. On the menu are chicken, beef, lamb and vegetarian dishes. The delicious gyro salad is large enough

JOE'S REAL BBQ   *Menu on aaa.com*   Lunch: $6-$17   Dinner: $6-$17   Phone: 480/503-3805 (29)
(AAA)   **Location:** US 60, exit 189 (Gilbert Rd), 2.1 mi s. 301 N Gilbert Rd 85234. **Hours:** 11 am-9 pm. Closed: 4/16, 11/23,
▼▼   12/25. **Features:** Pecan-grilled meats, barbecue beans, root beer made on site and fresh desserts are
Barbecue   favorites. The serve-yourself setting and optional patio seating lend to a fun atmosphere. Casual dress.
                Parking: street. **Cards:** AX, DS, MC, VI.

Pick a destination. Any destination.

Wherever you're headed, there's always a Choice hotel that fits your travel plans and budget. Book in advance and as a AAA/CAA member, you'll save at any of our over 3,500 Choice hotels across the U.S.* Plus, it's easy to earn nights or flights with our reward programs. Just contact your local AAA/CAA office, call 800.228.1AAA or visit choicehotels.com to book.

CHOICE HOTELS
INTERNATIONAL®

choicehotels.com
800.228.1AAA

We'll see you there.

CHOICE HOTELS INTERNATIONAL®

We'll see you there.

CHOICE HOTELS INTERNATIONAL®

Visit your local AAA/CAA office or call **800.228.1AAA** to book your next stay.

🛰️ 🅐🅐 TourBookMark

Lodging Listing Symbols

Member Values (see pgs. 12-13)

- 🅐🅐🅐 Official Appointment
- SAVE Offers lowest public rate or minimum 10% discount
- ASK May offer discount
- S🔟 Offers senior discount
- fyi Informational listing only

Member Services

- ✈ Airport transportation
- 🐾 Pets allowed
- 🍴 Restaurant on premises
- 🍴+ Restaurant off premises (walking distance)
- 24🍴 24-hour room service
- 🍸 Cocktail lounge
- 🧒 Child care

Accessibility Features

- &M Accessibility features
- 🚿 Roll-in showers
- 🎧 Hearing impaired equipment

Leisure Activities

- 🎰 Full service casino
- 🏊 Pool
- 💪 Health club on premises
- 💪+ Health club off premises
- 🎯 Recreational activities

In-Room Amenities

- ⊠ Non-smoking rooms
- VCR VCR
- 📺 Movies
- DATA PORT Data port/modem line
- 🧊 Refrigerator
- 🍽 Microwave
- ☕ Coffee maker
- AC No air conditioning
- TV No TV
- CTV No cable TV
- ☎ No telephones

Safety Features (see page 24)
(Mexico and Caribbean only)

- S Sprinklers
- D Smoke detectors

Call property for detailed information about fees & restrictions relating to the lodging listing symbols.

CHOICE HOTELS
INTERNATIONAL ®

Your trip across America starts here.

CHOICE HOTELS
INTERNATIONAL ®

choicehotels.com
800.228.1AAA

We'll see you there.

CHOICE HOTELS INTERNATIONAL®

GLENDALE pop. 218,812 (See map and index starting on p. 264)

──── WHERE TO STAY ────

BEST WESTERN PHOENIX-GLENDALE   *Book at aaa.com*   Phone: (623)939-9431   **16**

AAA SAVE	3/5-4/5 [ECP]	1P: $89-$119	2P: $89-$119	XP: $10	F17
▼▼ ▼▼	2/1-3/4 [ECP]	1P: $64-$99	2P: $64-$99	XP: $7	F17
	4/6-1/31 [ECP]	1P: $59-$79	2P: $59-$79	XP: $7	F17

Small-scale Hotel   **Location:** I-17, exit 205 (Glendale Ave), 4.3 mi w, then just n. Located adjacent to the historic downtown. 7116 N 59th Ave 85301. Fax: 623/937-3137. **Facility:** 78 units. 76 one-bedroom standard units. 2 one-bedroom suites ($79-$139). 2 stories (no elevator), exterior corridors. **Parking:** on-site. **Terms:** pets ($10 deposit). **Pool(s):** heated outdoor. **Guest Services:** coin laundry. **Business Services:** meeting rooms, fax. **Cards:** AX, CB, DC, DS, JC, MC, VI. **Special Amenities:** free expanded continental breakfast and free newspaper. *(See color ad below)*

SOME UNITS

[icons] FEE

QUALITY INN & SUITES AT TALAVI   *Book at aaa.com*   Phone: (602)896-8900   **14**

AAA SAVE	2/1-4/2	1P: $79-$159	2P: $79-$159	XP: $12	F18
▼▼ ▼▼	11/5-1/31	1P: $79-$109	2P: $79-$109	XP: $12	F18
	4/3-11/4	1P: $69-$99	2P: $69-$99	XP: $12	F18

Small-scale Hotel   **Location:** Loop 101, exit 14 (Bell Rd), 3.4 mi e. 5511 W Bell Rd 85308. Fax: 602/896-8991. **Facility:** 74 units. 71 one-bedroom standard units. 3 one-bedroom suites. 3 stories, interior corridors. **Bath:** combo or shower only. **Parking:** on-site. **Terms:** [CP] meal plan available. **Amenities:** dual phone lines, voice mail, irons, hair dryers. **Pool(s):** small heated outdoor. **Leisure Activities:** whirlpool. **Guest Services:** gift shop, valet laundry. **Business Services:** meeting rooms, fax (fee). **Cards:** AX, CB, DC, DS, JC, MC, VI. **Special Amenities:** free continental breakfast and free local telephone calls. *(See color ad below)*

SOME UNITS

[icons]

(See map and index starting on p. 264)

RAMADA LIMITED   *Book at aaa.com*   **Phone:** (623)412-2000 🔢 **13**

AAA SAVE

3/1-3/31	1P: $149	2P: $149	XP: $5	F17
2/1-2/28 & 4/1-5/31	1P: $71	2P: $71	XP: $5	F17
6/1-1/31	1P: $53	2P: $53	XP: $5	F17

Location: Loop 101, exit 14 (Bell Rd), 0.3 mi e, then just n on 79th Ave. Located at Arrowhead Towne Center. 7885 W
Small-scale Hotel Arrowhead Towne Ctr Dr 85308. Fax: 623/412-5522. **Facility:** 60 one-bedroom standard units. 2 stories (no
elevator), exterior corridors. *Bath:* combo or shower only. **Parking:** on-site. **Terms:** cancellation fee
imposed, [ECP] meal plan available, small pets only ($10 extra charge). **Amenities:** high-speed Internet, voice mail, irons, hair
dryers. **Pool(s):** heated outdoor. **Leisure Activities:** whirlpool, exercise room. **Guest Services:** valet and coin laundry.
Business Services: fax. **Cards:** AX, CB, DC, DS, JC, MC, VI. **Special Amenities:** free expanded continental breakfast and
free local telephone calls.

SOME UNITS

(icons) 🅂🄳 🛏 🍽️ 🛋️ ⊘ 🏊 📷 DATA PORT 🖥 🖨 ☕ / ✕ / FEE

SPRINGHILL SUITES BY MARRIOTT   *Book at aaa.com*   **Phone:** (623)878-6666 🔢 **15**

AAA SAVE

2/1-4/10	1P: $159-$169	2P: $169-$179
10/2-1/31	1P: $149-$159	2P: $169-$179
5/11-10/1	1P: $119-$129	2P: $129-$139
4/11-5/10	1P: $119	2P: $119-$129

Small-scale Hotel **Location:** Loop 101, exit 14 (Bell Rd), 0.3 mi e. Located adjacent to Arrowhead Towne Center. 7810 W Bell Rd 85308.
Fax: 623/878-6611. **Facility:** 89 one-bedroom standard units. 4 stories, interior corridors. *Bath:* combo or
shower only. **Parking:** on-site. **Terms:** cancellation fee imposed. **Amenities:** high-speed Internet, voice mail, irons, hair dryers.
Pool(s): small heated outdoor. **Leisure Activities:** whirlpool. **Guest Services:** valet and coin laundry. **Business Services:** fax.
Cards: AX, DC, DS, MC, VI. **Special Amenities:** free continental breakfast and free local telephone calls.

SOME UNITS

(icons) 🍽️ 🛋️ ⊘ 🏊 ✖️ 📷 DATA PORT 🖥 🖨 ☕ / ✕ /

─────── **WHERE TO DINE** ───────

AUNT PITTY PAT'S KITCHEN   **Lunch:** $5-$8   **Phone:** 623/931-0838 🔢 **18**

American

Cards: MC, VI.

Location: Just n of jct Glendale Rd. 7123 N 58th Ave 85301. **Hours:** 7 am-2 pm, Sat-3 pm. Closed: 1/1, 11/23,
12/25; also Sun. **Reservations:** accepted. **Features:** In the Catlin Court Historic District, the tea room
prepares breakfasts that may entice folks to get up early for omelets or pancakes. Fresh soups are hearty
and filling when paired with one of the many luncheon sandwich choices. Casual dress. **Parking:** on-site.

BILL JOHNSON'S BIG APPLE   **Lunch:** $6-$10   **Dinner:** $10-$16   **Phone:** 623/776-1900 🔢 **15**

Steak House

Location: Loop 101, exit 14 (Bell Rd), 1.1 mi e. 7322 W Bell Rd 85308. **Hours:** 6 am-11 pm. Closed: 12/25.
Features: The locally popular barbecue and steak house offers a casual atmosphere, friendly service and
hearty portions of the signature barbecue beef, chicken and pork. Save room for fresh fruit pie, which is
large enough to share. Casual dress; cocktails. **Parking:** on-site. **Cards:** AX, DS, MC, VI.

BISTRO DI NAPOLI   **Lunch:** $7-$15   **Dinner:** $9-$15   **Phone:** 602/298-6767 🔢 **17**

Italian

Location: I-17, exit 210B (Thunderbird Rd), 3.8 mi w. 5830 W Thunderbird Rd 85306. **Hours:** 11 am-9 pm, Fri-9:30
pm, Sat 4:30 pm-9:30 pm. Closed major holidays; also Sun. **Features:** The trained chef cooks classic Italian
comfort foods using fresh ingredients. The easy style of service fits the casual atmosphere, in which families
are welcomed. Casual dress; cocktails. **Parking:** on-site. **Cards:** AX, DS, MC, VI.

HAUS MURPHY'S   **Lunch:** $6-$15   **Dinner:** $9-$28   **Phone:** 623/939-2480 🔢 **19**

German

Location: Just e of Grand Ave (US 60); center. 5739 W Glendale Ave 85301. **Hours:** 11:30 am-9 pm, Sun 1 pm-8
pm. Closed: 1/1, 12/25. **Reservations:** suggested. **Features:** As is the case in many favorite neighborhood
pubs, the walls are covered in photographs and memorabilia, the hearty food is freshly prepared and a
selection of German beers is available to wash down the crispy schnitzels and plump sausages. Casual
dress; cocktails. **Parking:** street. **Cards:** AX, DS, MC, VI.

🍸

ROCK BOTTOM RESTAURANT & BREWERY   **Lunch:** $6-$12   **Dinner:** $9-$20   **Phone:** 623/878-8822 🔢 **16**

American

Location: Loop 101, exit 14 (Bell Rd), 0.5 mi e. 7640 W Bell Rd 85308. **Hours:** 11 am-10 pm, Fri & Sat-11 pm.
Closed: 12/25. **Reservations:** accepted. **Features:** Besides the house-brewed beers, guests find innovative
foods such as alder-smoked salmon, jambalaya and barbeque ribs. Energy infuses the atmosphere and the
staff is friendly. Casual dress; cocktails. **Parking:** on-site. **Cards:** AX, DC, DS, MC, VI.

🍸 ⑤

THEE PITT'S "AGAIN"   **Lunch:** $6-$20   **Dinner:** $6-$20   **Phone:** 602/996-7488 🔢 **14**

Barbecue

Location: From Bell Rd, take 55th Ave n, then e; opposite Honeywell. 5558 W Bell Rd 85308. **Hours:** 11 am-9 pm.
Closed: 11/23, 12/25; also Mon. **Features:** Patrons can sample award-winning barbecue that has a distinct
flavor. In addition to the standard Memphis-style pork, chicken, brisket and sausage pit-cooked over
mesquite, the menu lists burgers, salads and sides, including coleslaw, potato salad, beans and corn on the
cob. The diner displays colorful pig artwork. Casual dress; beer & wine only. **Parking:** on-site. **Cards:** AX, DS, MC, VI.

♿ M

GOODYEAR pop. 18,911   (See map and index starting on p. 264)

─────── **WHERE TO STAY** ───────

BEST WESTERN PHOENIX GOODYEAR INN   *Book at aaa.com*   **Phone:** (623)932-3210 🔢 **32**

1/1-1/31	1P: $109-$149	2P: $109-$149	XP: $10	F12
2/1-5/2	1P: $99-$139	2P: $99-$139	XP: $10	F12
9/18-12/31	1P: $79-$109	2P: $79-$109	XP: $10	F12
5/3-9/17	1P: $69-$99	2P: $69-$99	XP: $10	F12

Motel

Location: I-10, exit 128, 0.8 mi s. 55 N Litchfield Rd 85338. Fax: 623/932-1530. **Facility:** 85 units. 78 one-bedroom standard units. 7
one-bedroom suites with whirlpools. 2 stories (no elevator), interior/exterior corridors. **Parking:** on-site. **Terms:** check-in 4 pm,
[BP] meal plan available, small pets only ($10 extra charge). **Amenities:** voice mail, irons, hair dryers. *Some:* high-speed
Internet. **Pool(s):** heated outdoor. **Guest Services:** coin laundry. **Business Services:** meeting rooms, PC, fax (fee).
Cards: AX, CB, DC, DS, JC, MC, VI.

SOME UNITS

(icons) ASK 🅂🄳 🛏 🍽️ 🍸 🏊 📷 DATA PORT 🖥 🖨 ☕ / ✕ / FEE

(See map and index starting on p. 264)

HAMPTON INN & SUITES   *Book at aaa.com*   Phone: (623)536-1313   28
▼▼▲▼▼   2/1-4/22   1P: $139-$179
          9/11-1/31   1P: $119-$159
Small-scale Hotel   4/23-6/8   1P: $109-$149
          6/9-9/10   1P: $99-$129
Location: I-10, exit 128, 0.5 mi n. 2000 N Litchfield Rd 85338. Fax: 623/536-1414. **Facility:** 110 units. 80 one-bedroom standard units, some with whirlpools. 30 one-bedroom suites with efficiencies and whirlpools. 3 stories, interior corridors. *Bath:* combo or shower only. **Parking:** on-site. **Terms:** check-in 4 pm, pets ($25 deposit). **Amenities:** high-speed Internet, dual phone lines, voice mail, irons, hair dryers. **Pool(s):** small heated outdoor. **Leisure Activities:** whirlpool, exercise room, sports court. **Guest Services:** sundries, coin laundry. **Business Services:** meeting rooms, business center. **Cards:** AX, CB, DC, DS, JC, MC, VI.

SOME UNITS

(ASK) 🛏️ 🍽️ 🖧M 🛏️ 🏊 ⊠ 📷 [DATA PORT] 🖥️ / ⊠ [VCR] 🔌 🖨️ /
          FEE

HOLIDAY INN EXPRESS   *Book at aaa.com*   Phone: (623)535-1313   29
▼▼▲▼▼   2/1-4/22 [ECP]   1P: $139-$199   2P: $139-$199
          9/11-1/31 [ECP]   1P: $119-$159   2P: $119-$159
Small-scale Hotel   4/23-6/8 [ECP]   1P: $109-$149   2P: $109-$149
          6/9-9/10 [ECP]   1P: $99-$129   2P: $99-$129
Location: I-10, exit 128, just n. 1313 N Litchfield Rd 85338. Fax: 623/535-0950. **Facility:** 90 units. 85 one-bedroom standard units, some with whirlpools. 5 one-bedroom suites with whirlpools. 3 stories, interior corridors. *Bath:* combo or shower only. **Parking:** on-site. **Terms:** check-in 4 pm, cancellation fee imposed, small pets only ($25 deposit). **Amenities:** high-speed Internet, dual phone lines, voice mail, irons, hair dryers. **Pool(s):** heated outdoor. **Leisure Activities:** whirlpool, exercise room. **Guest Services:** coin laundry. **Business Services:** meeting rooms, fax. **Cards:** AX, CB, DC, DS, JC, MC, VI.

SOME UNITS

(ASK) [S/D] 🛏️ 🍽️ 🛏️ 🏊 📷 [DATA PORT] 🖥️ / ⊠ 🔌 🖨️ /
          FEE   FEE FEE

RESIDENCE INN BY MARRIOTT   *Book at aaa.com*   Phone: (623)866-1313   30
▼▼▲▼▼   2/1-4/22 [BP]   1P: $169-$299   2P: $169-$299
          4/23-6/8 & 9/11-1/31 [BP]   1P: $149-$229   2P: $149-$229
Small-scale Hotel   6/9-9/10 [BP]   1P: $139-$219   2P: $139-$219
Location: I-10, exit 128, 0.6 mi n. 2020 N Litchfield Rd 85338. Fax: 623/245-1414. **Facility:** 78 units. 30 one-bedroom standard units with efficiencies, some with whirlpools. 39 one- & 9 two-bedroom suites with efficiencies, some with whirlpools. 3 stories, interior corridors. *Bath:* some combo or shower only. **Parking:** on-site. **Terms:** pets ($75 fee). **Amenities:** high-speed Internet, dual phone lines, voice mail, irons, hair dryers. **Pool(s):** small heated outdoor. **Leisure Activities:** whirlpool, exercise room, sports court. **Guest Services:** sundries, complimentary evening beverages: Mon-Thurs, coin laundry. **Business Services:** meeting rooms, fax. **Cards:** AX, CB, DC, DS, JC, MC, VI.

SOME UNITS

(ASK) [S/D] 🛏️ 🍽️ 🛏️ 🏊 ⊠ 📷 [DATA PORT] 🔌 🖨️ 🖥️ / ⊠ /
          FEE

WINGATE INN & SUITES   *Book at aaa.com*   Phone: 623/547-1313   31
▼▼▲▼▼   2/1-4/22 [ECP]   1P: $139-$169   2P: $139-$169
          9/11-1/31 [ECP]   1P: $119-$149   2P: $119-$149
Small-scale Hotel   4/23-9/10 [ECP] 1P: $109-$139   2P: $109-$139
          6/9-9/10 [ECP]   1P: $99-$129   2P: $99-$129
Location: I-10, exit 129 (Dysart Rd), just n. 1188 N Dysart Rd 85338. Fax: 623/547-9933. **Facility:** 100 units. 64 one-bedroom standard units, some with whirlpools. 36 one-bedroom suites ($129-$169) with whirlpools. 4 stories, interior corridors. *Bath:* combo or shower only. **Parking:** on-site. **Terms:** pets ($25 deposit). **Amenities:** video games (fee), high-speed Internet, dual phone lines, voice mail, safes, irons, hair dryers. *Some:* DVD players, CD players. **Pool(s):** small heated outdoor. **Leisure Activities:** whirlpool, exercise room. **Guest Services:** sundries, coin laundry. **Business Services:** meeting rooms, business center. **Cards:** AX, DC, DS, MC, VI.

SOME UNITS

(ASK) [S/D] 🛏️ 🍽️ 🛏️ 🏊 📷 [DATA PORT] 🔌 🖨️ 🖥️ / ⊠ /
          FEE

——————— **WHERE TO DINE** ———————

BELLA LUNA RISTORANTE   **Lunch:** $7-$10   **Dinner:** $7-$33   Phone: 623/535-4642   25
▼▼ ▼▼   **Location:** I-10, exit 128, 1.9 mi n. 14175 Indian School Rd 85338. **Hours:** 11 am-10 pm, Sat from 3 pm. Closed:
Italian   11/23, 12/25. **Features:** Italian dishes freshly made to entice you include shrimp and crab in a fra diavolo sauce over linguine or veal cutlet in a special white wine sauce with onions and peas. The light and delicate preparations are served by friendly staff in a modern setting. Dressy casual; cocktails. **Parking:** on-site.
Cards: AX, CB, DC, DS, JC, MC, VI.
                                                                                                              🍸

BILL JOHNSON'S BIG APPLE RESTAURANT   **Lunch:** $6-$10   **Dinner:** $10-$16   Phone: 623/882-8288   27
▼▼ ▼▼   **Location:** I-10, exit 129 (Dysart Rd), just n. 1330 N Dysart Rd 85338. **Hours:** 6 am-11 pm, Fri & Sat-midnight.
Steak House   Closed: 11/23, 12/25. **Features:** The popular, casual barbecue and steak house has several locations in the valley. Signature barbecue beef, chicken and pork favorites are dished in hearty portions. Desserts and fresh fruit pies are large enough to share. Service is friendly. Casual dress; cocktails. **Parking:** on-site.
Cards: AX, DS, MC, VI.
                                                                                                              🖊️

MACAYO'S GOODYEAR   **Lunch:** $8-$14   **Dinner:** $8-$14   Phone: 623/209-7000   26
▼▼ ▼▼   **Location:** I-10, exit 128, just n. 1417 N Litchfield Rd 85338. **Hours:** 11 am-11 pm, Fri & Sat-midnight. Closed:
Mexican   11/23, 12/25. **Features:** These popular local eateries employ friendly and efficient staffers who serve traditional and "light" dishes flavored with their own chili peppers, which are grown near Tucson. Casual dress; cocktails. **Parking:** on-site. **Cards:** AX, DS, MC, VI.
                                                                                                              🍸

LITCHFIELD PARK pop. 3,810 (See map and index starting on p. 264)

──────── WHERE TO STAY ────────

THE WIGWAM RESORT *Book at aaa.com* Phone: (623)935-3811 **22**

(AAA) (SAVE)	1/4-1/31	1P: $549-$669	2P: $549-$669	XP: $25	F17
	2/1-5/24	1P: $499-$619	2P: $499-$619	XP: $25	F17
◊◊◊ ◊◊◊	9/7-1/3	1P: $399-$499	2P: $399-$499	XP: $25	F17
	5/25-9/6	1P: $229-$309	2P: $229-$309	XP: $25	F17

Resort
Large-scale Hotel
Location: I-10, exit 128 (Litchfield Rd), 2.4 mi n, then 0.4 mi e. 300 Wigwam Blvd 85340. Fax: 623/935-3737. **Facility:** Celebrating 75 years, this resort offers enticements ranging from a golf course by Trent Jones Sr. to spacious grounds and updated rooms. Designated smoking area. 331 units. 321 one-bedroom standard units, some with whirlpools. 8 one- and 2 two-bedroom suites. 2 stories (no elevator), exterior corridors. *Bath:* combo or shower only. **Parking:** on-site and valet. **Terms:** check-in 4 pm, 7 day cancellation notice-fee imposed, $15 service charge, small pets only ($25 deposit). **Amenities:** video games (fee), high-speed Internet, dual phone lines, voice mail, safes, honor bars, irons, hair dryers. *Some: Fee:* DVD players. **Dining:** 4 restaurants, 6:30 am-10 pm, cocktails, also, Arizona Kitchen, see separate listing, entertainment. **Pool(s):** 2 heated outdoor, wading. **Leisure Activities:** saunas, whirlpools, steamrooms, waterslide, recreation programs, croquet, bicycles, jogging, playground, exercise room, spa, shuffleboard, volleyball. *Fee:* golf-54 holes, 9 lighted tennis courts, horseback riding. **Guest Services:** gift shop, valet laundry. **Business Services:** conference facilities, business center. **Cards:** AX, DC, DS, JC, MC, VI. Affiliated with A Preferred Hotel. *(See color ad below)*

SOME UNITS

(S/D) (⊀) (🐕) (¶) (24) (▽) (fi) (⚷) (⌇) (☒) (🎥) (DATA PORT) (▭) / (🔊) /
FEE FEE FEE

──────── WHERE TO DINE ────────

ARIZONA KITCHEN **Lunch:** $7-$15 **Dinner:** $20-$32 Phone: 623/935-3811 **22**

◊◊◊ ◊◊◊
Southwest American
Location: I-10, exit 128 (Litchfield Rd), 2.4 mi n, then 0.4 mi e; in The Wigwam Resort. 300 Wigwam Blvd 85340. **Hours:** 6:30 am-2 & 5:30-9:30 pm, Fri & Sat-10 pm. Closed: Sun & Mon 6/1-9/30. **Reservations:** suggested. **Features:** Arizona territorial decor punctuates the attractive, upscale dining room, which serves as a theater setting for the display kitchen. Imaginative cooking techniques go into the preparation of memorable Southwestern cuisine, such as guajillo-chile-rubbed veal chop and pepita-crusted ahi tuna. Dressy casual; cocktails. **Parking:** valet. **Cards:** AX, CB, DC, DS, MC, VI.

(▽)

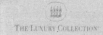

MESA pop. 396,375 (See map and index starting on p. 271)

―――― WHERE TO STAY ――――

ARIZONA GOLF RESORT & CONFERENCE CENTER *Book at aaa.com* Phone: (480)832-3202 **51**

2/1-4/14 [BP]	1P: $169-$189	2P: $179-$199	XP: $25	F16
10/1-1/31 [BP]	1P: $139-$179	2P: $149-$199	XP: $25	F16
4/15-5/31 [BP]	1P: $149-$159	2P: $159-$169	XP: $25	F16
6/1-9/30 [BP]	1P: $119-$139	2P: $129-$149	XP: $25	F16

Resort
Large-scale Hotel
Location: 1.3 mi n of US 60 (Superstition Frwy), exit 188 (Power Rd); southeast corner of Broadway and Power rds; entrance on Broadway Rd. 425 S Power Rd 85206. Fax: 480/981-0151. **Facility:** This golf resort is a complex of well-landscaped grounds with multiple buildings containing a variety of rooms and suites. 186 units. 88 one-bedroom standard units. 98 one-bedroom suites ($169-$359), some with efficiencies or kitchens. 2 stories (no elevator), exterior corridors. **Bath:** combo or shower only. **Parking:** on-site. **Terms:** package plans. **Amenities:** voice mail, safes, irons, hair dryers. **Fee:** video games, high-speed Internet. **Dining:** 6 am-10 pm, cocktails. **Pool(s):** heated outdoor. **Leisure Activities:** whirlpools, bicycles, exercise room, basketball, volleyball. **Fee:** golf-18 holes, driving range. **Guest Services:** gift shop, valet and coin laundry. **Business Services:** conference facilities, business center. **Cards:** AX, CB, DC, DS, JC, MC, VI. **Special Amenities:** free full breakfast and free newspaper. *(See color ad below)* SOME UNITS

BEST WESTERN DOBSON RANCH INN *Book at aaa.com* Phone: (480)831-7000 **65**

2/1-3/31 [BP]	1P: $125-$170	2P: $125-$170	XP: $5	F12
10/1-1/31 [BP]	1P: $100-$130	2P: $100-$130	XP: $5	F12
4/1-4/30 [BP]	1P: $86-$100	2P: $86-$100	XP: $5	F12
5/1-9/30 [BP]	1P: $62-$75	2P: $62-$75	XP: $5	F12

Small-scale Hotel
Location: Just s of US 60 (Superstition Frwy), exit 177 (Dobson Rd). 1666 S Dobson Rd 85202. Fax: 480/831-7000. **Facility:** 213 units. 200 one-bedroom standard units. 13 one-bedroom suites, some with whirlpools. 2 stories, interior/exterior corridors. **Parking:** on-site. **Terms:** check-in 4 pm, package plans. **Amenities:** video games (fee), voice mail, irons, hair dryers. **Some:** high-speed Internet, dual phone lines. **Pool(s):** heated outdoor. **Leisure Activities:** whirlpools, exercise room. **Guest Services:** gift shop, valet and coin laundry. **Business Services:** conference facilities, PC. **Cards:** AX, CB, DC, DS, JC, MC, VI. **Special Amenities:** free full breakfast and free local telephone calls. SOME UNITS

BEST WESTERN MESA INN *Book at aaa.com* Phone: (480)964-8000 **49**

3/1-4/15	1P: $80-$90	2P: $90-$100	XP: $5	F15
2/1-2/28 & 1/1-1/31	1P: $70-$80	2P: $80-$90	XP: $5	F15
4/16-12/31	1P: $50-$60	2P: $60-$70	XP: $5	F15

Location: 2 mi n of US 60 (Superstition Frwy), exit Stapley Dr, 0.5 mi e. 1625 E Main St 85203. Fax: 480/835-1272. Small-scale Hotel **Facility:** 100 one-bedroom standard units. 2 stories (no elevator), exterior corridors. **Bath:** combo or shower only. **Parking:** on-site. **Terms:** [CP] meal plan available, small pets only ($10 fee). **Amenities:** voice mail, irons, hair dryers. **Some:** high-speed Internet. **Pool(s):** heated outdoor. **Leisure Activities:** whirlpool. **Guest Services:** complimentary evening beverages: Mon-Fri, coin laundry. **Business Services:** fax. **Cards:** AX, CB, DC, DS, JC, MC, VI. **Special Amenities:** free continental breakfast and early check-in/late check-out. SOME UNITS

FEE

BEST WESTERN MEZONA INN *Book at aaa.com* Phone: (480)834-9233 **50**

2/17-4/1 [ECP]	1P: $109-$149	2P: $109-$149	XP: $5	F18
1/1-1/31 [ECP]	1P: $89-$119	2P: $89-$119	XP: $5	F18
2/1-2/16 [ECP]	1P: $79-$109	2P: $79-$109	XP: $5	F18
4/2-12/31 [ECP]	1P: $59-$89	2P: $59-$89	XP: $5	F18

Small-scale Hotel
Location: Just e of Country Club Dr; downtown. 250 W Main St 85201. Fax: 480/844-7920. **Facility:** 128 one-bedroom standard units. 2 stories (no elevator), exterior corridors. **Parking:** on-site. **Terms:** package plans, small pets only (in designated units). **Amenities:** voice mail, irons, hair dryers. **Pool(s):** heated outdoor. **Leisure Activities:** whirlpool. **Guest Services:** coin laundry. **Business Services:** meeting rooms, PC. **Cards:** AX, CB, DC, DS, JC, MC, VI. **Special Amenities:** free expanded continental breakfast and free room upgrade (subject to availability with advance reservations). *(See color ad p 324)* SOME UNITS

(See map and index starting on p. 271)

BEST WESTERN SUPERSTITION SPRINGS INN
AAA SAVE VVVV — *Book at aaa.com* — Phone: (480)641-1164 **53**

2/1-4/14 [ECP]	1P: $119	2P: $129	XP: $10 F17
10/1-1/31 [ECP]	1P: $89-$109	2P: $89-$109	XP: $10 F17
4/15-5/31 [ECP]	1P: $79-$89	2P: $79-$89	XP: $10 F17
6/1-9/30 [ECP]	1P: $59-$69	2P: $59-$69	XP: $10 F17

Small-scale Hotel **Location:** Just n of US 60 (Superstition Frwy), exit 188 (Power Rd); northwest corner of Power Rd and Hampton Ave. Located next to Superstition Springs Mall and Leisure World. 1342 S Power Rd 85206. Fax: 480/641-7253. **Facility:** 58 one-bedroom units. 2 stories (no elevator); exterior corridors. *Bath:* combo or shower only. **Parking:** on-site. **Terms:** package plans, small pets only ($10 extra charge, in designated units). **Amenities:** irons, hair dryers. **Leisure Activities:** whirlpool, exercise room. **Guest Services:** valet and coin laundry. **Business Services:** PC. **Cards:** AX, CB, DC, DS, MC, VI. **Special Amenities:** free expanded continental breakfast and free local telephone calls.

SOME UNITS
(icons) FEE

COUNTRY INN & SUITES BY CARLSON
VVVV — *Book at aaa.com* — Phone: (480)641-8000 **63**

2/1-5/31 & 1/1-1/31 [ECP]	1P: $139-$159	2P: $139-$159	XP: $10 F18
9/1-12/31 [ECP]	1P: $99-$119	2P: $99-$119	XP: $10 F18
6/1-8/31 [ECP]	1P: $89-$109	2P: $89-$109	XP: $10 F18

Small-scale Hotel **Location:** Just s of US 60 (Superstition Frwy), exit 188 (Power Rd), just sw. 6650 E Superstition Springs Blvd 85206. Fax: 480/641-9600. **Facility:** 126 units. 73 one-bedroom standard units. 53 one-bedroom suites ($109-$159), some with whirlpools. 4 stories, interior corridors. *Bath:* combo or shower only. **Parking:** on-site. **Terms:** check-in 4 pm. **Amenities:** high-speed Internet, dual phone lines, voice mail, irons, hair dryers. *Some:* heated outdoor. **Leisure Activities:** whirlpool, exercise room. **Guest Services:** sundries, valet and coin laundry, area transportation. **Business Services:** meeting rooms, business center. **Cards:** AX, DC, DS, MC, VI.

SOME UNITS
(icons)

COURTYARD BY MARRIOTT
VVVV — Phone: (480)461-3000 **54**

2/1-4/29	1P: $119-$199	2P: $119-$199
4/30-5/27 & 9/10-1/31	1P: $79-$149	2P: $79-$149
5/28-9/9	1P: $59-$109	2P: $59-$109

Small-scale Hotel **Location:** US 60 (Superstition Frwy), exit 178 (Alma School Rd), 0.4 mi n, just e on Southern Ave, then just s. 1221 S Westwood Ave 85210. Fax: 480/461-0179. **Facility:** 149 units. 138 one-bedroom standard units. 11 one-bedroom suites ($119-$199). 3 stories, interior corridors. *Bath:* combo or shower only. **Parking:** on-site. **Terms:** [BP] meal plan available, package plans. **Amenities:** high-speed Internet, voice mail, irons, hair dryers. *Some:* DVD players (fee). **Pool(s):** heated outdoor. **Leisure Activities:** whirlpool, exercise room. **Guest Services:** valet and coin laundry, area transportation. **Business Services:** meeting rooms, PC (fee). **Cards:** AX, CB, DC, DS, JC, MC, VI.

SOME UNITS
(icons) VCR FEE

DAYS INN
AAA SAVE VVVV — *Book at aaa.com* — Phone: (480)844-8900 **67**

2/1-4/15	1P: $79-$129	2P: $79-$129
4/16-1/31	1P: $49-$89	2P: $49-$89

Small-scale Hotel **Location:** US 60 (Superstition Frwy), exit 179 (Country Club Dr), just s, then just e. 333 W Juanita 85210. Fax: 480/844-0973. **Facility:** 123 units. 122 one-bedroom standard units. 1 two-bedroom suite with kitchen. 3 stories, interior corridors. *Bath:* combo or shower only. **Parking:** on-site. **Terms:** pets ($10 fee). **Amenities:** safes (fee), hair dryers. **Pool(s):** heated outdoor. **Leisure Activities:** sauna, whirlpool, exercise room. **Guest Services:** coin laundry. **Business Services:** meeting rooms. **Cards:** AX, CB, DC, DS, MC, VI. **Special Amenities:** free expanded continental breakfast and free room upgrade (subject to availability with advance reservations).

SOME UNITS
(icons) FEE

(See map and index starting on p. 271)

DAYS INN-EAST MESA   *Book at aaa.com*   **Phone:** (480)981-8111    **48**

	2/1-4/10	1P: $69-$99	2P: $69-$109	XP: $6	F12
	10/1-1/31	1P: $59-$89	2P: $59-$89	XP: $6	F12
Motel	4/11-9/30	1P: $59-$79	2P: $59-$79	XP: $6	F12

Location: 0.5 mi e of Higley Rd. 5531 E Main St 85205. **Fax:** 480/396-8027. **Facility:** 61 units. 60 one-bedroom standard units. 1 one-bedroom suite ($89-$129). 2 stories (no elevator), exterior corridors. **Parking:** on-site. **Terms:** cancellation fee imposed, package plans, small pets only ($5 extra charge). **Amenities:** hair dryers. *Some:* irons. **Pool(s):** small heated outdoor. **Leisure Activities:** whirlpool. **Business Services:** fax (fee). **Cards:** AX, DC, DS, MC, VI.

SOME UNITS

(ASK) (SD) 🐾 🚷 ⊟ / ⊠ (DATA PORT) 🖥 🖵 /
FEE

FAIRFIELD INN BY MARRIOTT PHOENIX MESA   *Book at aaa.com*   **Phone:** 480/668-8000   **57**

	2/1-4/11	1P: $119	2P: $119
	4/12-5/28 & 9/11-1/31	1P: $89	2P: $89
	5/29-9/10	1P: $69	2P: $69

Small-scale Hotel **Location:** Just n of US 60 (Superstition Frwy), exit 178 (Alma School Rd), just e on Grove St, then just s. 1405 S Westwood Ave 85210. **Fax:** 480/668-7313. **Facility:** 64 one-bedroom standard units. 3 stories, interior corridors. *Bath:* combo or shower only. **Terms:** [ECP] meal plan available. **Amenities:** high-speed Internet, irons, hair dryers. **Pool(s):** small heated outdoor. **Leisure Activities:** whirlpool. **Guest Services:** valet laundry. **Business Services:** PC. **Cards:** AX, DS, MC, VI. **Special Amenities:** free expanded continental breakfast and free local telephone calls.

SOME UNITS

(SD) (♿) 🚷 ➡ 🛠 📷 (DATA PORT) 🖵 / ⊠ ⊟ 🖥 /

HAMPTON INN PHOENIX/MESA   *Book at aaa.com*   **Phone:** (480)926-3600   **61**

	1/1-1/31 [BP]	1P: $129-$139	2P: $139-$159	XP: $10	F18
	2/1-4/30 [BP]	1P: $119-$129	2P: $129-$139	XP: $10	F18
	5/1-5/31 [BP]	1P: $109-$119	2P: $119-$129	XP: $10	F18
	6/1-12/31 [BP]	1P: $89-$99	2P: $99-$109	XP: $10	F18

Small-scale Hotel **Location:** US 60 (Superstition Frwy), exit 182 (Gilbert Rd), just ne. 1563 S Gilbert Rd 85204. **Fax:** 480/926-4892. **Facility:** 116 one-bedroom standard units. 4 stories, interior corridors. *Bath:* combo or shower only. **Parking:** on-site. **Terms:** cancellation fee imposed. **Amenities:** video games (fee), high-speed Internet, dual phone lines, voice mail, irons, hair dryers. **Pool(s):** heated outdoor. **Leisure Activities:** whirlpool. **Guest Services:** valet and coin laundry. **Business Services:** meeting rooms, fax (fee). **Cards:** AX, CB, DC, DS, JC, MC, VI. **Special Amenities:** free expanded continental breakfast and free local telephone calls. *(See color ad below)*

SOME UNITS

(SD) 🍴 (♿) ➡ 🛠 📷 (DATA PORT) ⊟ 🖵 / ⊠ 🖥 /

HILTON PHOENIX EAST/MESA   *Book at aaa.com*   **Phone:** (480)833-5555   **58**

	2/1-4/14	1P: $159-$209
	4/15-5/26 & 9/5-1/31	1P: $119-$169
	5/27-9/4	1P: $89-$129

Large-scale Hotel **Location:** US 60 (Superstition Frwy), exit 178 (Alma School Rd), just n, then just e. Located across from the Fiesta Mall. 1011 W Holmes Ave 85210. **Fax:** 480/649-1886. **Facility:** 260 units. 219 one-bedroom standard units. 41 one-bedroom suites ($119-$239), some with whirlpools. 8 stories, interior corridors. *Bath:* combo or shower only. **Parking:** on-site. **Terms:** package plans. **Amenities:** video games (fee), high-speed Internet, dual phone lines, voice mail, irons, hair dryers. **Dining:** 6:30 am-10 pm, cocktails. **Pool(s):** heated outdoor. **Leisure Activities:** whirlpools, exercise room. **Guest Services:** gift shop, valet laundry, area transportation-within 3 mi. **Business Services:** conference facilities, business center. **Cards:** AX, CB, DC, DS, JC, MC, VI. **Special Amenities:** free newspaper and early check-in/late check-out.

SOME UNITS

(SD) 🍴 (♿) ➡ 📷 (DATA PORT) ⊟ 🖵 / ⊠ (VCR) /
FEE

(See map and index starting on p. 271)

HOLIDAY INN HOTEL & SUITES *Book at aaa.com* Phone: (480)964-7000 **62**

AAA SAVE
▽▼▽▼

	2/1-4/15	1P: $119-$139
	1/9-1/31	1P: $99-$109
	9/11-1/8	1P: $79-$89
	4/16-9/10	1P: $65-$75

Large-scale Hotel **Location:** US 60 (Superstition Frwy), exit 179, just s. 1600 S Country Club Dr 85210. Fax: 480/833-6419. **Facility:** 246 units. 163 one-bedroom standard units. 83 one-bedroom suites. 6 stories, interior/exterior corridors. *Bath:* combo or shower only. **Parking:** on-site. **Terms:** cancellation fee imposed, [BP] meal plan available, small pets only ($25 fee). **Amenities:** video games (fee), high-speed Internet, dual phone lines, voice mail, irons, hair dryers. **Dining:** 6 am-2 & 5-10 pm, cocktails. **Pool(s):** heated outdoor. **Leisure Activities:** whirlpool, exercise room. **Guest Services:** gift shop, valet and coin laundry, area transportation-within 5 mi. **Business Services:** conference facilities, PC. **Cards:** AX, DC, DS, MC, VI. **Special Amenities:** free newspaper and early check-in/late check-out. *(See color ad below)*

SOME UNITS

HOMESTEAD STUDIO SUITES HOTEL PHOENIX-MESA *Book at aaa.com* Phone: (480)752-2266 **66**

▽▼▽▼

	2/1-4/16 & 1/10-1/31	1P: $80	2P: $85	XP: $5	F17
	9/24-1/9	1P: $60	2P: $65	XP: $5	F17
	4/17-9/23	1P: $50	2P: $55	XP: $5	F17

Small-scale Hotel **Location:** Just s of US 60 (Superstition Frwy), exit 177 (Dobson Rd). 1920 W Isabella 85202. Fax: 480/752-7865. **Facility:** 124 one-bedroom standard units with efficiencies. 2 stories (no elevator), exterior corridors. *Bath:* combo or shower only. **Parking:** on-site. **Terms:** office hours 6 am-8 pm, cancellation fee imposed, weekly rates available, pets ($75 fee). **Amenities:** voice mail, irons. **Guest Services:** coin laundry. **Cards:** AX, DC, DS, MC, VI.

SOME UNITS

LA QUINTA INN & SUITES PHOENIX (MESA EAST) *Book at aaa.com* Phone: (480)654-1970 **64**

▽▼▽▼

| | 2/1-4/30 & 1/15-1/31 [CP] | 1P: $127-$137 | 2P: $134-$144 | XP: $7 | F18 |
| | 5/1-1/14 [CP] | 1P: $92-$102 | 2P: $99-$109 | XP: $7 | F18 |

Small-scale Hotel **Location:** US 60 (Superstition Frwy), exit 187 (Superstition Springs Blvd) eastbound, just se; exit 188 (Power Rd) westbound, just sw. 6530 E Superstition Springs Blvd 85206. Fax: 480/654-1973. **Facility:** 107 units. 101 one-bedroom standard units. 6 one-bedroom suites ($119-$179). 6 stories, interior corridors. *Bath:* combo or shower only. **Parking:** on-site. **Terms:** small pets only. **Amenities:** video games (fee), high-speed Internet, voice mail, irons, hair dryers. *Some:* dual phone lines. **Pool(s):** heated outdoor. **Leisure Activities:** whirlpool, exercise room. **Guest Services:** valet and coin laundry, area transportation. **Business Services:** meeting rooms. **Cards:** AX, CB, DC, DS, MC, VI. *(See color ad p 295)*

SOME UNITS

LA QUINTA INN & SUITES PHOENIX (MESA WEST) *Book at aaa.com* Phone: (480)844-8747 **55**

AAA SAVE
▽▼▽▼

	2/1-4/30 [CP]	1P: $119-$129	2P: $126-$136	XP: $7	F18
	1/1-1/31 [CP]	1P: $104-$114	2P: $111-$121	XP: $7	F18
	10/1-12/31 [CP]	1P: $93-$103	2P: $100-$110	XP: $7	F18
	5/1-9/30 [CP]	1P: $69-$79	2P: $76-$86	XP: $7	F18

Small-scale Hotel **Location:** US 60 (Superstition Frwy), exit 178 (Alma School Rd), just n, then just e. 902 W Grove Ave 85210. Fax: 480/844-8850. **Facility:** 125 units. 118 one-bedroom standard units. 7 one-bedroom suites ($99-$149). 7 stories, interior corridors. *Bath:* combo or shower only. **Parking:** on-site. **Terms:** small pets only. **Amenities:** video games (fee), high-speed Internet, voice mail, irons, hair dryers. *Some:* dual phone lines. **Pool(s):** heated outdoor. **Leisure Activities:** whirlpool, exercise room. **Guest Services:** valet and coin laundry. **Business Services:** meeting rooms, fax (fee). **Cards:** AX, CB, DC, DS, MC, VI. **Special Amenities:** free expanded continental breakfast and free local telephone calls. *(See color ad p 295)*

SOME UNITS

(See map and index starting on p. 271)

MOTEL 6-MESA SOUTH #1030   *Book at aaa.com*   Phone: 480/834-0066   **60**

2/1-4/15	1P: $45-$55	2P: $51-$61	XP: $3 F17
4/16-5/25 & 10/6-1/31	1P: $39-$49	2P: $45-$55	XP: $3 F17
5/26-10/5	1P: $33-$43	2P: $39-$49	XP: $3 F17

Motel   **Location:** US 60 (Superstition Frwy), exit 179 (Country Club Dr), northeast corner. Located adjacent to Golf Land Amusement Park. 1511 S Country Club Dr 85210. Fax: 480/969-6313. **Facility:** 91 one-bedroom standard units. 2 stories (no elevator), exterior corridors. **Bath:** combo or shower only. **Parking:** on-site. **Terms:** pets (must be attended). **Pool(s):** heated outdoor. **Cards:** AX, CB, DC, DS, MC, VI.

SOME UNITS
FEE FEE

PHOENIX MARRIOTT MESA   *Book at aaa.com*   Phone: (480)898-8300   **45**

2/1-4/29	1P: $199	2P: $199
4/30-5/27 & 9/10-1/31	1P: $151	2P: $151
5/28-9/9	1P: $104	2P: $104

Large-scale Hotel   **Location:** US 60 (Superstition Frwy), exit 180 (Mesa Dr), 2 mi n, just w on Main St, then just n. 200 N Centennial Way 85201. Fax: 480/964-9279. **Facility:** 275 units. 265 one-bedroom standard units. 10 one-bedroom suites ($174-$259). 12 stories, interior corridors. **Bath:** combo or shower only. **Parking:** on-site. **Terms:** cancellation fee imposed, [AP] meal plan available, package plans. **Amenities:** dual phone lines, voice mail, irons, hair dryers. **Fee:** video games, high-speed Internet. **Some:** CD players. **Pool(s):** heated outdoor. **Leisure Activities:** whirlpool, exercise room. **Guest Services:** gift shop, valet and coin laundry. **Business Services:** conference facilities, business center. **Cards:** AX, DC, DS, MC, VI.

SOME UNITS

RESIDENCE INN BY MARRIOTT MESA   *Book at aaa.com*   Phone: (480)610-0100   **56**

2/1-4/30	1P: $139-$214
9/3-1/31	1P: $109-$149
5/1-9/2	1P: $89-$109

Small-scale Hotel   **Location:** US 60 (Superstition Frwy), exit 178 (Alma School Rd), just n, then just e. 941 W Grove Ave 85210. Fax: 480/610-6490. **Facility:** 117 units. 48 one-bedroom standard units with efficiencies. 48 one- and 21 two-bedroom suites with efficiencies. 3 stories, interior corridors. **Bath:** combo or shower only. **Parking:** on-site. **Terms:** cancellation fee imposed, pets ($75 fee). **Amenities:** video library, high-speed Internet, dual phone lines, voice mail, irons, hair dryers. **Some:** DVD players (fee). **Pool(s):** heated outdoor. **Leisure Activities:** whirlpool, exercise room, sports court. **Guest Services:** sundries, complimentary evening beverages: Mon-Thurs, valet and coin laundry. **Business Services:** meeting rooms, business center. **Cards:** AX, DC, DS, JC, MC, VI.

SOME UNITS
FEE   FEE

SLEEP INN OF MESA   *Book at aaa.com*   Phone: 480/807-7760   **52**

Property failed to provide current rates

Small-scale Hotel   **Location:** US 60 (Superstition Frwy), exit 188 (Power Rd), 0.8 mi n, then 0.4 mi w to mall entrance. Located at the west end of Superstition Springs Mall. 6347 E Southern Ave 85206. Fax: 480/807-2646. **Facility:** 84 units. 83 one-bedroom standard units. 1 one-bedroom suite. 3 stories, interior corridors. **Bath:** combo or shower only. **Parking:** on-site. **Terms:** small pets only ($25 fee, in designated units). **Amenities:** irons, hair dryers. **Pool(s):** small heated outdoor. **Leisure Activities:** whirlpool, limited exercise equipment. **Guest Services:** valet and coin laundry. **Business Services:** PC.

SOME UNITS
FEE

SUPER 8 MOTEL-MESA/GILBERT RD   *Book at aaa.com*   Phone: (480)545-0888   **59**

2/1-4/1 & 1/12-1/31 [ECP]	1P: $59-$75	2P: $65-$81	XP: $6 F17
4/2-1/11 [ECP]	1P: $50-$56	2P: $56-$62	XP: $6 F17

Small-scale Hotel   **Location:** US 60 (Superstition Frwy), exit 182 (Gilbert Rd), 1 blk n. 1550 S Gilbert Rd 85204. Fax: 480/545-0888. **Facility:** 72 units. 69 one-bedroom standard units. 3 one-bedroom suites. 3 stories, interior corridors. **Bath:** combo or shower only. **Parking:** on-site. **Terms:** pets ($5 extra charge). **Amenities:** high-speed Internet, safes (fee). **Pool(s):** heated outdoor. **Leisure Activities:** whirlpool. **Guest Services:** coin laundry. **Business Services:** fax (fee). **Cards:** AX, CB, DC, DS, JC, MC, VI. *(See color ad below)*

SOME UNITS
FEE   FEE FEE

(See map and index starting on p. 271)

TRAVELODGE SUITES MESA   *Book at aaa.com*   Phone: (480)832-5961 **47**

	2/1-4/15	1P: $59-$79	2P: $89-$109	XP: $10	F12
	9/16-1/31	1P: $49-$69	2P: $59-$79	XP: $10	F12
Small-scale Hotel	4/16-9/15	1P: $29-$49	2P: $39-$59	XP: $5	F12

Location: US 60 (Superstition Frwy), exit 185 (Greenfield Rd), 2 mi n, then just w. 4244 E Main St 85205. Fax: 480/830-9274. **Facility:** 74 one-bedroom standard units, some with efficiencies (no utensils) and/or whirlpools. 2 stories (no elevator), exterior corridors. *Bath:* combo or shower only. **Parking:** on-site. **Terms:** weekly rates available, package plans, pets ($10 extra charge, in designated units). **Amenities:** safes (fee), irons, hair dryers. **Pool(s):** heated outdoor. **Leisure Activities:** whirlpool. **Guest Services:** valet and coin laundry. **Business Services:** fax (fee). **Cards:** AX, CB, DC, DS, JC, MC, VI.

SOME UNITS

(ASK) (S◊) 🐾 🛏✈ (&) 🏊 (🎥) (DATA PORT) 🖥 🖨 🖵 / ✕ /
FEE

WINDEMERE HOTEL AND CONFERENCE CENTER   *Book at aaa.com*   Phone: (480)985-3600 **46**

	2/1-3/31	1P: $109-$129	2P: $119-$139	XP: $10	F12
	4/1-5/31	1P: $89-$109	2P: $99-$119	XP: $10	F12
	10/1-1/31	1P: $69-$99	2P: $79-$109	XP: $10	F12
Small-scale Hotel	6/1-9/30	1P: $59-$79	2P: $69-$89	XP: $10	F12

Location: 0.7 mi e of Higley Rd. 5750 E Main St 85205. Fax: 480/832-1230. **Facility:** 114 one-bedroom standard units, some with efficiencies (no utensils) and/or whirlpools. 2 stories (no elevator), exterior corridors. **Parking:** on-site. **Terms:** package plans, small pets only. **Amenities:** voice mail, irons, hair dryers. **Dining:** 10 am-10 pm. **Pool(s):** heated outdoor. **Leisure Activities:** whirlpool. **Guest Services:** valet and coin laundry. **Business Services:** conference facilities, fax. **Cards:** AX, CB, DC, DS, JC, MC, VI. **Special Amenities:** free expanded continental breakfast and free room upgrade (subject to availability with advance reservations). *(See color ad below)*

SOME UNITS

(S◊) 🐾 🍴 🛏 🏊 ♿ (🎥) (DATA PORT) 🖥 🖨 🖵 / ✕ /

(See map and index starting on p. 271)

───── *The following lodging was either not evaluated or did not* ─────
meet AAA rating requirements but is listed for your information only.

WESTGATE @ PAINTED MOUNTAIN   **Phone:** 480/654-3611
[fyi]   Not evaluated. **Location:** Loop 202 E, exit 12 (McKellips Rd), 9.1 mi e. Adjacent to golf course. 6302 E McKellips Rd 85215. Facilities, services, and decor characterize a mid-range property.

───── **WHERE TO DINE** ─────

BLUE ADOBE GRILLE   **Lunch:** $5-$10   **Dinner:** $10-$20   **Phone:** 480/962-1000   33
          Location: US 60 (Superstition Frwy), exit 179 (Country Club Dr), 2.1 mi n. 144 N Country Club Dr 85201. **Hours:** 11
Mexican   am-9 pm, Fri & Sat-10 pm. Closed major holidays. **Reservations:** suggested, Fri & Sat. **Features:** A new addition to the Southwestern dining scene, the restaurant prepares regional cuisine using red and green chilies from New Mexico. Bold flavors infuse the interesting and diverse menu, which lists such tempting dishes as the honey pork tamale, pecan-roasted chicken quesadilla and tenderloin chiles rellenos. Casual dress; cocktails.
Parking: on-site. **Cards:** AX, CB, DC, DS, MC, VI.

BRUNELLO ITALIAN RESTAURANT   **Lunch:** $7-$15   **Dinner:** $12-$25   **Phone:** 480/897-0140   37
          Location: Loop 100, exit Dobson Rd, 0.8 mi e. 1954 S Dobson Rd 85202. **Hours:** 11:30 am-2:30 & 5-10 pm, Fri-11
Italian   pm, Sat 5 pm-11 pm, Sun 4 pm-9:30 pm. Closed: 11/23, 12/25. **Reservations:** suggested. **Features:** Serving classic fare such as cannelloni Florentine and osso buco, the intimate eatery's polished staff brings guests a fine-dining experience. Patio seats overlook a small lake. Casual dress; cocktails.
Parking: on-site. **Cards:** AX, DC, DS, MC, VI.

FLANCER'S CAFE   **Lunch:** $6-$21   **Dinner:** $6-$21   **Phone:** 480/926-9077   40
          Location: US 60, (Superstition Frwy), exit 182, 1.6 mi s. 610 N Gilbert Rd, Suite 300 85234. **Hours:** 10:30 am-9 pm.
Deli/Subs   Closed: 11/23, 12/25. **Features:** The cafe's sandwiches are not made; they're created. And incredible
Sandwiches   sandwiches they are, too. Try the award-winning green chile turkey prepared with avocado slices, sizzling bacon and zippy green chile mayonnaise or the perfect prickly pear with a chicken breast baked in prickly pear glaze. Everything from the breads to the desserts is homemade and delicious. Pizza, pasta and salads also figure on the menu. Casual dress; beer & wine only. **Parking:** on-site. **Cards:** AX, DC, DS, MC, VI.

THE LANDMARK RESTAURANT   **Lunch:** $7-$11   **Dinner:** $12-$25   **Phone:** 480/962-4652   36
          Location: US 60 (Superstition Frwy), exit 179 (Country Club Dr), 2 mi n, then 0.5 mi w. 809 W Main St 85201.
          Hours: 11 am-9 pm, Sun-7 pm. Closed: 7/4, 11/23, 12/25. **Features:** Dine in a restored church building
American   amid Victorian decor. A varied menu and a large soup and salad bar are featured as well as an extensive display of Mesa historical photographs. Casual dress; cocktails. **Parking:** on-site. **Cards:** AX, DS, MC, VI.

LITTLE MESA CAFE   **Lunch:** $4-$12   **Dinner:** $6-$12   **Phone:** 480/830-6201   35
          Location: US 60 (Superstition Frwy), exit 184 (Val Vista Rd), then just e. 3929 E Main St 85206. **Hours:** 6 am-
American   8 pm, Sun from 7 am; hours vary in summer. Closed: 12/25. **Features:** Some patrons might just start with the home-baked pies, which are as good as Grandma's, before digging into fresh salad and such dishes as chicken-fried steak and center-cut pork chops. The casual decor and smiling servers put guests at ease.
Casual dress. **Parking:** on-site. **Cards:** AX, DC, DS, MC, VI.

PINK PEPPER THAI CUISINE   **Lunch:** $7-$12   **Dinner:** $8-$14   **Phone:** 480/839-9009   38
          Location: US 60 (Superstition Frwy), exit 177 (Dobson Rd) 1.6 mi s. 1941 W Guadalupe Rd 85202. **Hours:** 11 am-
          2:30 & 4:30-10 pm, Sun from 4:30 pm. Closed: 11/23, 12/25. **Reservations:** accepted. **Features:** A wide
Thai   selection of dishes—including the nicely spiced jumping shrimp with vegetables—demonstrates the chef's expertise. Soft decor colors are a pleasant backdrop for the vivid flavors of the food. Casual dress; cocktails.
Parking: on-site. **Cards:** AX, CB, DS, JC, MC, VI.

RANCHO DE TIA ROSA   **Lunch:** $5-$12   **Dinner:** $8-$15   **Phone:** 480/659-8787   32
          Location: Just e of Val Vista Dr. 3129 E McKellips Rd 85213. **Hours:** 11 am-9 pm, Sat from 11:30 am. Closed
Mexican   major holidays; also Sun & Mon. **Features:** Four acres of grounds encompass the restaurant and greenhouses where organic produce is grown for the kitchen. A taqueria for take-out service is at the entrance, while the main building includes a front courtyard with seating, an indoor dining room and patio seating. Casual dress; cocktails. **Parking:** on-site. **Cards:** AX, MC, VI.
                                                      ⛫Ⓜ Ⓨ

SERRANO'S MEXICAN RESTAURANT   **Lunch:** $6-$10   **Dinner:** $6-$10   **Phone:** 480/756-2992   39
          Location: US 60 (Superstition Frwy), exit 177 (Dobson Rd), 1.6 mi s. 1955 W Guadalupe Rd 85202. **Hours:** 11 am-10
          pm, Sun-9 pm. Closed major holidays. **Features:** For 25 years, the Serrano family has served freshly
Regional Mexican   prepared and tasty food. The charming decor incorporates bird cages and murals of exotic birds. Classic selections include chiles rellenos and seafood enchiladas. Casual dress; cocktails. **Parking:** on-site.
Cards: AX, DC, DS, MC, VI.
                                                            Ⓨ

THE WEATHER VANE RESTAURANT   **Lunch:** $6-$10   **Dinner:** $7-$14   **Phone:** 480/830-2721   34
          Location: 0.7 mi e of Power Rd, on south side of Main St; in Weather Vane Plaza. 7303 E Main St, Suite 115 85207.
          Hours: 11 am-9 pm. Closed: 11/23, 12/25. **Features:** Families that patronize the informal restaurant can
American   choose from chicken, pork, seafood and prime rib dishes, as well as numerous sandwiches and the specialty meatloaf. Casual dress; cocktails. **Parking:** on-site. **Cards:** DS, MC, VI.

PARADISE VALLEY pop. 13,664   (See map and index starting on p. 266)

─────── WHERE TO STAY ───────

HERMOSA INN   *Book at aaa.com*   Phone: 602/955-8614   **57**
▼▼▼▼   Property failed to provide current rates
Small-scale Hotel   **Location:** 1 mi s of Lincoln Dr; corner of Stanford Dr. Located in a residential area. 5532 N Palo Cristi Rd 85253. Fax: 602/955-8299. **Facility:** Designated smoking area. 35 units. 31 one-bedroom standard units, some with whirlpools. 4 two-bedroom suites with kitchens. 1 story, exterior corridors. *Bath:* combo or shower only. **Parking:** on-site. **Terms:** small pets only ($50 fee). **Amenities:** DVD players, CD players, high-speed Internet, voice mail, safes, honor bars, irons, hair dryers. *Some:* dual phone lines. **Dining:** Lon's at the Hermosa, see separate listing. **Pool(s):** heated outdoor. **Leisure Activities:** whirlpools, tennis court. *Fee:* massage. **Guest Services:** valet laundry. **Business Services:** meeting rooms.

SOME UNITS

🛏️ 🍽️ 📺 🐕 📶 ✖️ ✖️ VCR 📹 DATA PORT 💻 / 🖨️ /
FEE

SANCTUARY ON CAMELBACK MOUNTAIN   *Book at aaa.com*   Phone: (480)948-2100   **56**
AAA SAVE   All Year   1P: $165-$645   2P: $165-$645   XP: $30   F
▼▼▼▼ ▼▼▼▼   **Location:** US 101, exit McDonald Dr, 3.9 mi w. 5700 E McDonald Dr 85253. Fax: 480/483-7314. **Facility:** This quiet retreat offers luxurious rooms and amenities, some with fireplaces and panoramic views; a first-class spa is featured. Designated smoking area. 98 units. 45 one-bedroom standard units. 53 one-bedroom
Resort   suites, some with kitchens. 1 story, exterior corridors. *Bath:* combo or shower only. **Parking:** on-site and
Large-scale Hotel   valet. **Terms:** check-in 4 pm, 7 day cancellation notice, package plans. **Amenities:** DVD players, CD players, high-speed Internet, dual phone lines, voice mail, safes, honor bars, irons, hair dryers. **Dining:** Elements, see separate listing. **Pool(s):** heated outdoor, 2 small heated outdoor, lap. **Leisure Activities:** whirlpools, steamrooms, 5 tennis courts, recreation programs, rental bicycles, hiking trails, spa. **Guest Services:** gift shop, valet laundry. **Business Services:** conference facilities, business center. **Cards:** AX, CB, DC, DS, MC, VI.

SOME UNITS

🛏️ 🍽️ ♿ 🐕 📶 ✖️ ✖️ 📹 DATA PORT 💻 / VCR 🖨️ /
FEE

─────── *The following lodging was either not evaluated or did not* ───────
meet AAA rating requirements but is listed for your information only.

MARBEYA CONDOMINIUMS   Phone: 480/515-2300
(fyi)   Not evaluated. **Location:** 1.7 mi w of Scottsdale Rd on Shea Blvd, just s. Located in a residential area. 10401 N 52nd St 85253. Facilities, services, and decor characterize a mid-range property.

─────── WHERE TO DINE ───────

EL CHORRO LODGE RESTAURANT   Dinner: $16-$62   Phone: 480/948-5170   **81**
▼▼▼▼   **Location:** 2 mi w of Scottsdale Rd; on north side of Lincoln Dr. 5550 E Lincoln Dr 85253. **Hours:** 11 am-2 & 5:30-10
Steak & Seafood   pm, Sat from 5:30 pm, Sun 9 am-2 & 5-10 pm; seasonal hours vary. **Reservations:** suggested. **Features:** The small, charming restaurant has a nice selection of prime rib, lamb and fresh seafood preparations. Sticky buns are a specialty. Outdoor seating is a pleasant option with a warming fireplace on chilly nights. Casual dress; cocktails. **Parking:** on-site and valet. **Cards:** AX, CB, DC, DS, JC, MC, VI.   📺

ELEMENTS   Lunch: $11-$24   Dinner: $18-$36   Phone: 480/607-2300   **82**
▼▼▼ ▼▼▼   **Location:** US 101, exit McDonald Dr, 3.9 mi w; in Sanctuary on Camelback Mountain. 5700 E McDonald Dr 85253.
American   **Hours:** 7-10:30 am, 11:30-2 & 6-9:45 pm; Sunday brunch. **Reservations:** suggested. **Features:** Using local farm-fresh organic vegetables and a wide selection of meats and seafood, Chef McMillon creates monthly menus that satisfy the gourmet in all of us. Stunning views of the valley and sunsets enhance the experience. Dressy casual; cocktails. **Parking:** valet. **Cards:** AX, DC, DS, MC, VI.   📺

LON'S AT THE HERMOSA   Lunch: $10-$15   Dinner: $23-$35   Phone: 602/955-7878   **83**
▼▼▼   **Location:** 1 mi s of Lincoln Dr; corner of Stanford Dr; in Hermosa Inn. 5532 N Palo Cristi Rd 85253. **Hours:** 11:30
American   am-2 & 6-10 pm, Sat from 6 pm, Sun from 10 am. Closed: 1/1, 7/4. **Reservations:** suggested. **Features:** Coming here for dinner is like returning to the "home ranch" in Arizona territorial days. The excellent menu selection centers on natural and organic foods, some grown on the premises. Choices include seafood, steak and fowl preparations, delivered with casual, yet attentive, service. Casual dress; cocktails. **Parking:** on-site and valet. **Cards:** AX, CB, DC, DS, MC, VI.   📺

PEORIA pop. 108,364   (See map and index starting on p. 264)

─────── WHERE TO STAY ───────

COMFORT SUITES BY CHOICE HOTELS/SPORTS
COMPLEX   *Book at aaa.com*   Phone: (623)334-3993   **6**
▼▼▼ ▼▼   2/1-4/30 [ECP]   1P: $79-$169   2P: $79-$169   XP: $5   F18
    10/1-1/31 [ECP]   1P: $79-$129   2P: $79-$129   XP: $5   F18
Small-scale Hotel   5/1-9/30 [ECP]   1P: $55-$89   2P: $55-$89   XP: $5   F18
Location: Loop 101, exit 14 (Bell Rd), just e to 83rd Ave, just s, then just w. 8473 W Paradise Ln 85382. Fax: 623/334-3993. **Facility:** 79 one-bedroom standard units. 3 stories, interior corridors. *Bath:* combo or shower only. **Parking:** on-site. **Terms:** pets ($50 fee). **Amenities:** high-speed Internet, voice mail, irons, hair dryers. **Pool(s):** heated outdoor. **Leisure Activities:** whirlpool. **Guest Services:** coin laundry. **Business Services:** meeting rooms, fax (fee). **Cards:** AX, DC, DS, MC, VI.

SOME UNITS

ASK SD 🛏️ 🍽️ ♿ 📋 🐕 📶 📹 DATA PORT 📶 💻 / ✖️ /
FEE   FEE

(See map and index starting on p. 264)

HAMPTON INN *Book at aaa.com* Phone: (623)486-9918 **9**

(AAA) (SAVE)

2/1-3/30	1P: $69-$149	2P: $69-$149
3/31-5/30 & 9/21-1/31	1P: $69-$89	2P: $69-$89
5/31-9/20	1P: $49-$79	2P: $49-$79

Small-scale Hotel **Location:** Loop 101, exit 14 (Bell Rd), just s to 83rd Ave, just s, then just w. Located across from Peoria Sports Complex. 8408 W Paradise Ln 85382. Fax: 623/486-4842. **Facility:** 112 one-bedroom standard units, some with whirlpools. 5 stories, interior corridors. *Bath:* combo or shower only. **Parking:** on-site. **Terms:** [ECP] meal plan available, package plans. **Amenities:** video games (fee), high-speed Internet, dual phone lines, voice mail, irons, hair dryers. **Pool(s):** heated outdoor. **Leisure Activities:** whirlpool, exercise room. **Guest Services:** sundries, coin laundry. **Business Services:** meeting rooms, PC, fax (fee). **Cards:** AX, CB, DC, DS, MC, VI. **Special Amenities:** free expanded continental breakfast and free local telephone calls.

SOME UNITS

HOLIDAY INN EXPRESS HOTEL & SUITES *Book at aaa.com* Phone: (623)853-1313 **10**

2/1-3/31 [ECP]	1P: $129-$179	2P: $129-$179
9/1-1/31 [ECP]	1P: $99-$159	2P: $99-$159
4/1-6/30 [ECP]	1P: $99-$149	2P: $99-$149
7/1-8/31 [ECP]	1P: $89-$129	2P: $89-$129

Small-scale Hotel **Location:** Loop 101, exit 14 (Bell Rd), just w, then just s. Located in a busy commercial area. 16771 N 84th Ave 85382. Fax: 623/853-8888. **Facility:** 98 units. 90 one-bedroom standard units. 8 one-bedroom suites, some with whirlpools. 4 stories, interior corridors. *Bath:* combo or shower only. **Parking:** on-site. **Terms:** check-in 4 pm, small pets only ($50 deposit). **Amenities:** video games (fee), high-speed Internet, dual phone lines, voice mail, irons, hair dryers. *Some:* DVD players (fee). **Pool(s):** small heated outdoor. **Leisure Activities:** exercise room. **Guest Services:** valet and coin laundry. **Business Services:** meeting rooms, fax (fee). **Cards:** AX, CB, DC, DS, JC, MC, VI.

SOME UNITS

FEE

LA QUINTA INN & SUITES PHOENIX (WEST/PEORIA) *Book at aaa.com* Phone: (623)487-1900 **8**

3/1-3/31 [CP]	1P: $163-$173	2P: $170-$180	XP: $7	F18
2/1-2/28 & 1/1-1/31 [CP]	1P: $114-$124	2P: $123-$133	XP: $7	F18
4/1-12/31 [CP]	1P: $89-$99	2P: $96-$106	XP: $7	F18

Small-scale Hotel **Location:** Loop 101, exit 14 (Bell Rd), just e, then just s. Located adjacent to Peoria Sports Complex. 16321 N 83 Ave 85382. Fax: 623/487-1919. **Facility:** 108 units. 103 one-bedroom standard units. 5 one-bedroom suites ($119-$179). 5 stories, interior corridors. *Bath:* combo or shower only. **Parking:** on-site. **Terms:** small pets only. **Amenities:** video games (fee), high-speed Internet, voice mail, irons, hair dryers. **Pool(s):** heated outdoor. **Leisure Activities:** whirlpool, exercise room. **Guest Services:** coin laundry. **Business Services:** meeting rooms, fax. **Cards:** AX, CB, DC, DS, MC, VI. *(See color ad p 295)*

SOME UNITS

RESIDENCE INN BY MARRIOTT *Book at aaa.com* Phone: (623)979-2074 **7**

All Year 1P: $90-$210 2P: $90-$210

Small-scale Hotel **Location:** Loop 101, exit 14 (Bell Rd), just e, just s on 83rd Ave, then just w. Located across from Peoria Sports Complex. 8435 W Paradise Ln 85382. Fax: 623/979-2074. **Facility:** 90 units. 45 one-bedroom standard units with efficiencies. 45 two-bedroom suites with efficiencies. 3 stories, interior corridors. *Bath:* combo or shower only. **Parking:** on-site. **Terms:** 14 day cancellation notice, [BP] meal plan available, pets ($75 fee). **Amenities:** high-speed Internet, voice mail, irons, hair dryers. **Pool(s):** heated outdoor. **Leisure Activities:** whirlpool, exercise room, sports court. **Guest Services:** complimentary evening beverages: Mon-Thurs, coin laundry. **Business Services:** meeting rooms, fax. **Cards:** AX, CB, DC, DS, JC, MC, VI.

SOME UNITS

FEE

———— WHERE TO DINE ————

ABUELO'S MEXICAN FOOD EMBASSY **Lunch:** $7-$9 **Dinner:** $8-$16 Phone: 623/878-8282 **10**

Mexican **Location:** Loop 101, exit 14 (Bell Rd), just e to 83rd Ave, 0.4 mi s to Stadium Way, just w, then just s. 16092 N Arrowhead Fountains Ctr Dr 85382. **Hours:** 11 am-10 pm, Fri & Sat-11 pm. Closed: 11/23, 12/24, 12/25. **Features:** The charming setting is reminiscent of a Mexican hacienda, with plants, statues, folk art and full-size wall murals, as done by Diego Rivera. Representative of the upscale menu's distinctive choices is mesquite-grilled, bacon-wrapped shrimp. Fresh herb flavors and ingredients enhance each menu item. Casual dress; cocktails. **Parking:** on-site. **Cards:** AX, DS, MC, VI.

DILLON'S RESTAURANT **Lunch:** $6-$12 **Dinner:** $8-$17 Phone: 623/979-5353 **11**

American **Location:** Loop 101, exit 12, just w. 8706 W Thunderbird Rd 85381. **Hours:** 11 am-9 pm, Fri & Sat-10 pm. Closed: 12/25. **Features:** The barbecue on the restaurant's menu is popular with local folks. Friendly, young servers bring out a selection of grilled meat, poultry and fish dishes. The attractive surroundings have a "country cottage" feel. Casual dress; cocktails. **Parking:** on-site. **Cards:** AX, DS, MC, VI.

ELEPHANT BAR RESTAURANT **Lunch:** $6-$15 **Dinner:** $6-$15 Phone: 623/776-0100 **9**

American **Location:** Loop 101, exit 14 (Bell Rd), just e, then just s. 16160 N 83rd Ave 85382. **Hours:** 11 am-10 pm, Fri & Sat-11 pm. Closed: 11/23, 12/25. **Features:** Going on safari was never this much fun. Guests who unwind amid the bright jungle decor can sample fresh California cuisine prepared with Pacific Rim influences. Casual dress; cocktails. **Parking:** on-site. **Cards:** AX, DC, DS, MC, VI.

P.F. CHANG'S CHINA BISTRO **Lunch:** $8-$18 **Dinner:** $8-$18 Phone: 623/412-3335 **8**

Chinese **Location:** Just s of Bell Rd. 16170 N 83rd Ave 85382. **Hours:** 11 am-11 pm, Fri & Sat-midnight. Closed: 11/23, 12/25. **Reservations:** accepted. **Features:** Upscale decor enhances a relaxed atmosphere in the trendy and busy eatery. The attentive staff serves varied Chinese dishes. Casual dress; cocktails. **Parking:** on-site. **Cards:** AX, DS, MC, VI.

SCOTTSDALE pop. 202,705   (See map and index starting on p. 266)

——— WHERE TO STAY ———

3 PALMS RESORT OASIS   **Phone:** 480/941-1202   **50**

(fyi)   Property failed to provide current rates
                          Under major renovation, scheduled to be completed December 2005. **Last rated:** ♥♥ **Location:** Just w of
Small-scale Hotel   Hayden Rd, on south side of McDowell Rd. Located across from El Dorado Parkway. 7707 E McDowell Rd 85257.
Fax: 480/990-7873. **Facility:** 116 units. 96 one-bedroom standard units. 20 one-bedroom suites, some with
efficiencies and/or whirlpools. 2 stories (no elevator), exterior corridors. *Bath:* combo or shower only. **Parking:** on-site.
Amenities: video games (fee), high-speed Internet, dual phone lines, voice mail, hair dryers. *Some:* irons. **Pool(s):** heated
outdoor. **Leisure Activities:** whirlpool, playground, exercise room. **Guest Services:** complimentary evening beverages, valet
and coin laundry. **Business Services:** meeting rooms, business center.

SOME UNITS
🍴 🍸 📶 ♿ 🏊 ✕ 📹 [DATA PORT] 🛏 📠 ☕ / ✕ /

AMERISUITES (SCOTTSDALE/OLD TOWN)   *Book at aaa.com*   **Phone:** (480)423-9944   **42**

AAA (SAVE)	2/1-4/15	1P: $129-$199	2P: $129-$199	XP: $10	F18
♦♦♦	4/16-5/28	1P: $99-$139	2P: $99-$139	XP: $10	F18
	9/9-1/31	1P: $79-$109	2P: $79-$109	XP: $10	F18
	5/29-9/8	1P: $59-$89	2P: $59-$89	XP: $10	F18

Small-scale Hotel   **Location:** Just e of Scottsdale Rd. 7300 E 3rd Ave 85251. Fax: 480/423-2991. **Facility:** 128 one-bedroom
standard units. 6 stories, interior corridors. *Bath:* combo or shower only. **Parking:** on-site. **Terms:** weekly
rates available, package plans, small pets only. **Amenities:** high-speed Internet, voice mail, irons, hair dryers. *Fee:* video
games, safes. *Some:* dual phone lines. **Pool(s):** heated outdoor. **Leisure Activities:** exercise room. **Guest Services:** coin
laundry, area transportation-within 5 mi. **Business Services:** meeting rooms, fax (fee). **Cards:** AX, CB, DC, DS, JC, MC, VI.
Special Amenities: free full breakfast.

SOME UNITS
(S🐕) 🐾 🍴 ⚖M ♿ 🏊 VCR 📹 [DATA PORT] 🛏 📠 ☕ / ✕ /

BEST WESTERN PAPAGO INN & RESORT   *Book at aaa.com*   **Phone:** (480)947-7335   **51**

AAA (SAVE)	2/1-3/31	1P: $99-$159	2P: $99-$159	XP: $10	F14
♦♦♦	12/31-1/31	1P: $89-$139	2P: $89-$139	XP: $10	F14
	10/1-12/30	1P: $59-$99	2P: $59-$99	XP: $10	F14
	4/1-9/30	1P: $59-$89	2P: $59-$89	XP: $10	F14

Small-scale Hotel   **Location:** From Scottsdale Rd, just w. Located in a busy commercial area. 7017 E McDowell Rd 85257.
Fax: 480/994-0692. **Facility:** 56 units. 54 one-bedroom standard units. 2 one-bedroom suites with
efficiencies. 2 stories (no elevator), exterior corridors. **Parking:** on-site. **Terms:** 3 day cancellation notice, small pets only.
Amenities: voice mail, irons, hair dryers. *Some:* high-speed Internet. **Pool(s):** heated outdoor. **Leisure Activities:** sauna,
exercise room. **Guest Services:** gift shop, valet and coin laundry. **Business Services:** meeting rooms, fax (fee). **Cards:** AX,
CB, DC, DS, JC, MC, VI. **Special Amenities:** free local telephone calls and free newspaper. *(See color ad p 333)*

SOME UNITS
(S🐕) 🐾 🍸 🏊 📹 [DATA PORT] 🛏 ☕ / ✕ 🖨 /

BEST WESTERN SCOTTSDALE AIRPARK SUITES   *Book at aaa.com*   **Phone:** (480)951-4000   **12**

	2/1-4/14	1P: $99-$179	2P: $99-$179	XP: $10	F18
♦♦♦	9/15-1/31	1P: $79-$179	2P: $79-$179	XP: $10	F18
	4/15-5/18	1P: $89-$149	2P: $89-$149	XP: $10	F18
Small-scale Hotel	5/19-9/14	1P: $79-$109	2P: $79-$109	XP: $10	F18

Location: 0.8 mi n of Thunderbird Rd; 0.5 mi e of Scottsdale Rd. Located at Scottsdale Municipal Airport. 7515 E Butherus Dr 85260.
Fax: 480/483-9046. **Facility:** 120 units. 4 one-bedroom standard units. 116 one-bedroom suites. 4 stories, exterior corridors.
Parking: on-site. **Terms:** cancellation fee imposed, [BP] meal plan available, pets ($10 extra charge). **Amenities:** dual phone
lines, voice mail, irons, hair dryers. **Pool(s):** heated outdoor. **Leisure Activities:** whirlpool, exercise room. **Guest Services:**
sundries, valet and coin laundry, area transportation. **Business Services:** meeting rooms, PC, fax (fee). **Cards:** AX, CB, DC,
DS, JC, MC, VI. *(See color ad p 333)*

SOME UNITS
(ASK) (S🐕) 🐾 🍴 📺 🚭 🏊 📹 [DATA PORT] 🛏 📠 ☕ / ✕ /
FEE

(See map and index starting on p. 266)

CALEO RESORT & SPA   *Book at aaa.com*   Phone: (480)945-7666   36

	2/1-4/30	1P: $309-$629	2P: $309-$629	XP: $15	F17
	5/1-5/28 & 9/5-1/31	1P: $209-$479	2P: $209-$479	XP: $15	F17
Small-scale Hotel	5/29-9/4	1P: $109-$319	2P: $109-$319	XP: $15	F17

Location: Southeast corner of Scottsdale and Chaparral rds. 4925 N Scottsdale Rd 85251. Fax: 480/946-4056. **Facility:** Designated smoking area. 204 units. 197 one-bedroom standard units. 7 one-bedroom suites, some with whirlpools. 2 stories (no elevator), interior corridors. *Bath:* combo or shower only. **Parking:** on-site. **Terms:** 2-3 night minimum stay - seasonal and/or weekends, 3 day cancellation notice-fee imposed. **Amenities:** high-speed Internet, dual phone lines, voice mail, honor bars, irons, hair dryers. **Pool(s):** heated outdoor. **Leisure Activities:** whirlpool, waterslide, exercise room, spa. **Guest Services:** gift shop, valet laundry, area transportation. **Business Services:** conference facilities, business center. **Cards:** AX, DC, DS, MC, VI.

SOME UNITS

(ASK) ⊞ ⍟ ♈ 🐕 🗑 🚀 🖾 ☒ 🎥 [DATA PORT] 💻 / 📺 /
FEE

(See map and index starting on p. 266)

CAMELBACK INN, A JW MARRIOTT RESORT & SPA   *Book at aaa.com*

Phone: (480)948-1700   **28**

(AAA) (SAVE)

9/5-1/31	1P: $299-$499	2P: $299-$499
2/1-4/29	1P: $419-$489	2P: $419-$489
4/30-6/11	1P: $299-$399	2P: $299-$399
6/12-9/4	1P: $149-$219	2P: $149-$219

Classic Resort Large-scale Hotel **Location:** 0.5 mi e of Tatum Blvd; north side of Lincoln Dr. 5402 E Lincoln Dr 85253. Fax: 480/951-8469. **Facility:** A classic resort on 120 scenic acres, the hotel boasts elegant Southwestern decor with mountain views; a recent renovation resulted in posh upgrades. 453 units. 422 one-bedroom standard units. 31 one-bedroom suites ($750-$2500), some with efficiencies. 1-2 stories, exterior corridors. **Parking:** on-site and valet. **Terms:** check-in 4 pm, 7 day cancellation notice-fee imposed, [BP] meal plan available. **Amenities:** CD players, dual phone lines, voice mail, safes, honor bars, irons, hair dryers. *Fee:* video games, high-speed Internet. *Some:* DVD players (fee). **Dining:** 6 restaurants, 6:30 am-10 pm, cocktails, also, The Chaparral, see separate listing, entertainment. **Pool(s):** 2 heated outdoor, lap. **Leisure Activities:** saunas, whirlpools, steamrooms, pitch and putt, rental bicycles, hiking trails, playground, spa, basketball, shuffleboard. *Fee:* golf-36 holes, 6 tennis courts (5 lighted), horseback riding. **Guest Services:** gift shop, complimentary and valet laundry, area transportation (fee). **Business Services:** conference facilities, business center. **Cards:** AX, CB, DC, DS, JC, MC, VI. **Special Amenities: free newspaper and preferred room (subject to availability with advance reservations).**

SOME UNITS

(icons) FEE · FEE · FEE

CHAPARRAL SUITES RESORT   *Book at aaa.com*

Phone: (480)949-1414   **34**

(AAA) (SAVE)

2/1-3/31 [BP]	1P: $199-$209	2P: $209-$219	XP: $10	F17
9/12-1/31 [BP]	1P: $159-$199	2P: $169-$209	XP: $10	F17
4/1-5/31 [BP]	1P: $149-$159	2P: $159-$169	XP: $10	F17
6/1-9/11 [BP]	1P: $99	2P: $109	XP: $10	F17

Small-scale Hotel **Location:** At Chaparral Rd. 5001 N Scottsdale Rd 85250. Fax: 480/947-2675. **Facility:** 311 units. 308 one- and 3 two-bedroom suites, some with whirlpools. 4 stories, exterior corridors. **Parking:** on-site. **Terms:** cancellation fee imposed, package plans, pets (small dogs only, $25 fee). **Amenities:** video games (fee), high-speed Internet, voice mail, safes, irons, hair dryers. **Dining:** 11 am-11 pm, cocktails. **Pool(s):** 2 heated outdoor. **Leisure Activities:** whirlpools, exercise room. **Guest Services:** gift shop, complimentary evening beverages, valet and coin laundry. **Business Services:** conference facilities, business center. **Cards:** AX, DC, DS, MC, VI. **Special Amenities: free full breakfast and free newspaper.** *(See color ad below)*

SOME UNITS

(icons) FEE · FEE

COMFORT INN OF SCOTTSDALE   *Book at aaa.com*

Phone: (480)596-6559   **19**

(AAA) (SAVE)

2/1-4/1	1P: $109-$129	2P: $109-$129
4/2-5/13 & 9/9-1/31	1P: $69-$89	2P: $69-$99
5/14-9/8	1P: $49-$69	2P: $49-$69

Small-scale Hotel **Location:** Just e of Scottsdale Rd; just s of Shea Blvd; on north side of Gold Dust Ave. Located in a light-commercial area. 7350 E Gold Dust Ave 85258. Fax: 480/596-0554. **Facility:** 123 one-bedroom standard units, some with whirlpools. 3 stories, interior corridors. **Bath:** combo or shower only. **Parking:** on-site. **Terms:** [ECP] meal plan available, package plans. **Amenities:** video games (fee), high-speed Internet, voice mail, irons, hair dryers. **Pool(s):** heated outdoor. **Leisure Activities:** whirlpool, exercise room. **Guest Services:** valet and coin laundry. **Business Services:** meeting rooms, business center. **Cards:** AX, CB, DC, DS, MC, VI. **Special Amenities: free expanded continental breakfast and free local telephone calls.**

SOME UNITS

(icons)

(See map and index starting on p. 266)

COMFORT SUITES BY CHOICE HOTELS-OLD TOWN *Book at aaa.com* Phone: (480)946-1111 48

▼▼ ▼▼▼▼

Small-scale Hotel

3/1-3/31 [ECP]	1P: $130-$170	2P: $130-$170	XP: $10	F18
2/1-2/28 [ECP]	1P: $90-$120	2P: $90-$120	XP: $10	F18
10/1-1/31 [ECP]	1P: $70-$110	2P: $70-$110	XP: $10	F18
4/1-9/30 [ECP]	1P: $50-$90	2P: $50-$90	XP: $10	F18

Location: N of Thomas Rd; just e of Scottsdale Rd. 3275 N Drinkwater Blvd 85251. Fax: 480/874-1641. **Facility:** 60 one-bedroom standard units. 3 stories, interior corridors. *Bath:* combo or shower only. **Parking:** on-site. **Terms:** cancellation fee imposed. **Amenities:** irons, hair dryers. **Pool(s):** heated indoor. **Leisure Activities:** whirlpools, limited exercise equipment. **Guest Services:** coin laundry. **Business Services:** PC, fax. **Cards:** AX, DC, DS, MC, VI.

SOME UNITS

(ASK) (S/D) 🐾 (L/M) 🐕 ➤ 🎦 (DATA PORT) 🔲 📠 💻 / 🗙 (VCR) /

COUNTRY INN & SUITES BY CARLSON *Book at aaa.com* Phone: (480)314-1200 15

▼▼ ▼▼▼▼

Small-scale Hotel

2/1-3/31	1P: $125-$155		XP: $10	F18
4/1-5/31	1P: $85-$115		XP: $10	F18
9/15-1/31	1P: $90-$110		XP: $10	F18
6/1-9/14	1P: $65-$85		XP: $10	F18

Location: Loop 101, exit 41, just e on Shea Blvd, then just n. 10801 N 89th Pl 85260. Fax: 480/314-7367. **Facility:** 163 units. 72 one-bedroom standard units. 91 one-bedroom suites, some with whirlpools. 3 stories, interior corridors. *Bath:* combo or shower only. **Parking:** on-site. **Terms:** check-in 4 pm, [ECP] meal plan available, package plans, small pets only ($50 fee, with prior approval). **Amenities:** video games (fee), high-speed Internet, voice mail, irons, hair dryers. **Pool(s):** heated outdoor, wading. **Leisure Activities:** whirlpool, exercise room. **Guest Services:** valet and coin laundry, area transportation. **Business Services:** meeting rooms, fax (fee). **Cards:** AX, DS, MC, VI.

SOME UNITS

(ASK) (S/D) 🐾 (¶+) 🐕 🕮 ➤ 🎦 (DATA PORT) 🔲 📠 💻 / 🗙 /
FEE

COURTYARD BY MARRIOTT SCOTTSDALE/MAYO CLINIC *Book at aaa.com* Phone: 480/860-4000

▼▼ ▼▼▼▼

Small-scale Hotel

2/1-4/15	1P: $189
4/16-5/27 & 9/10-1/31	1P: $169
5/28-9/9	1P: $119

Location: Loop 101, exit 41, 5.8 mi e; at Mayo Clinic entrance. 13444 E Shea Blvd 85259. Fax: 480/860-4308. **Facility:** 124 units. 112 one-bedroom standard units. 12 one-bedroom suites ($149-$219). 2 stories, interior corridors. *Bath:* combo or shower only. **Parking:** on-site. **Amenities:** high-speed Internet, voice mail, irons, hair dryers. **Pool(s):** heated outdoor. **Leisure Activities:** whirlpool, exercise room. **Guest Services:** sundries, valet and coin laundry, area transportation, beauty salon. **Business Services:** meeting rooms. **Cards:** AX, DC, DS, MC, VI.

SOME UNITS

(¶+) 🍴 🕮 🕮 🖪 ➤ 🎦 (DATA PORT) 💻 / 🗙 🔲 📠 /

COURTYARD BY MARRIOTT/SCOTTSDALE NORTH *Book at aaa.com* Phone: 480/922-8400 7

▼▼ ▼▼▼▼

Small-scale Hotel

Property failed to provide current rates

Location: Just n of Frank Lloyd Wright Blvd. 17010 N Scottsdale Rd 85255. Fax: 480/948-3481. **Facility:** 153 units. 147 one-bedroom standard units, some with whirlpools. 6 one-bedroom suites. 3 stories, interior corridors. *Bath:* combo or shower only. **Parking:** on-site. **Amenities:** video games (fee), high-speed Internet, voice mail, irons, hair dryers. **Pool(s):** small heated outdoor. **Leisure Activities:** whirlpool, exercise room. **Guest Services:** sundries, valet and coin laundry, area transportation. **Business Services:** meeting rooms, PC.

SOME UNITS

(¶+) 🍴 🕮 🖪 ➤ 🎦 (DATA PORT) 💻 / 🗙 🔲 📠 /

DAYS INN SCOTTSDALE FASHION SQUARE *Book at aaa.com* Phone: (480)947-5411 37

(AAA) (SAVE)
▼▼ ▼▼
Motel

2/1-4/15 & 1/1-1/31 [CP]	1P: $119-$189	2P: $119-$189	XP: $10	F17
4/16-12/31 [CP]	1P: $104-$165	2P: $104-$165	XP: $10	F17

Location: Just n of Camelback Rd. Located at north side of Scottsdale Fashion Square Shopping Ctr. 4710 N Scottsdale Rd 85251. Fax: 480/946-1324. **Facility:** 167 one-bedroom standard units. 2 stories (no elevator), exterior corridors. *Bath:* combo or shower only. **Parking:** on-site. **Terms:** package plans. **Amenities:** voice mail, safes (fee), irons, hair dryers. **Pool(s):** heated outdoor. **Leisure Activities:** whirlpool, lighted tennis court, volleyball. **Guest Services:** valet and coin laundry, area transportation-within 4 mi. **Business Services:** meeting rooms, fax (fee). **Cards:** AX, CB, DC, DS, JC, MC, VI. **Special Amenities:** free continental breakfast and early check-in/late check-out.** *(See color ad below)*

SOME UNITS

(S/D) (¶+) 🕮 ➤ ✚ 🗙 🎦 (DATA PORT) 🔲 💻 / 🗙 📠 /

(See map and index starting on p. 266)

DOUBLETREE PARADISE VALLEY RESORT-SCOTTSDALE
Book at aaa.com

Phone: (480)947-5400   **32**

2/1-4/30	1P: $169-$289	2P: $169-$289	XP: $15 F18
5/1-6/17	1P: $119-$219	2P: $119-$219	XP: $15 F18
9/10-1/31	1P: $99-$189	2P: $99-$189	XP: $15 F18
6/18-9/9	1P: $75-$129	2P: $75-$129	XP: $15 F18

Resort
Large-scale Hotel

Location: Just n of Chaparral Rd; on east side of Scottsdale Rd. 5401 N Scottsdale Rd 85250. Fax: 480/946-1524. **Facility:** Near restaurants and shops, the resort offers Southwestern-style rooms with Sweet Dreams beds and custom pillows, a pool area and children's programs. 378 one-bedroom standard units, some with whirlpools. 2 stories, exterior corridors. *Bath:* combo or shower only. **Parking:** on-site. **Terms:** check-in 4 pm, 3 day cancellation notice-fee imposed, package plans, small pets only ($75 fee). **Amenities:** dual phone lines, voice mail, honor bars, irons, hair dryers. *Fee:* video games, high-speed Internet. **Dining:** 6 am-11 pm, cocktails, entertainment. **Pool(s):** 2 heated outdoor. **Leisure Activities:** saunas, whirlpools, steamrooms, putting green, playground, volleyball. *Fee:* 2 lighted tennis courts, racquetball court, massage. **Guest Services:** gift shop, valet laundry, area transportation-within 2 mi. **Business Services:** conference facilities, business center. **Cards:** AX, DC, DS, MC, VI. **Special Amenities:** free newspaper.
(See color ad below)

SOME UNITS

EXTENDED STAY DELUXE PHOENIX-SCOTTSDALE
Book at aaa.com

Phone: (480)483-1333   **17**

2/1-4/2 & 1/16-1/31	1P: $110	2P: $115	XP: $5 F17
10/1-1/15	1P: $75	2P: $80	XP: $5 F17
4/3-9/30	1P: $70	2P: $75	XP: $5 F17

Small-scale Hotel

Location: From jct Scottsdale Rd, just w on Shea Blvd, then just n. Located in the Agua Caliente Center. 10660 N 69th St 85254. Fax: 480/483-8811. **Facility:** 105 one-bedroom standard units with efficiencies. 3 stories, interior corridors. *Bath:* combo or shower only. **Parking:** on-site. **Terms:** cancellation fee imposed, small pets only ($100 fee). **Amenities:** high-speed Internet (fee), voice mail, irons, hair dryers. **Pool(s):** heated outdoor. **Leisure Activities:** whirlpool, exercise room. **Guest Services:** valet and coin laundry. **Business Services:** fax. **Cards:** AX, DC, DS, MC, VI.

SOME UNITS

FAIRFIELD INN-DOWNTOWN SCOTTSDALE
Book at aaa.com

Phone: (480)945-4392   **33**

2/1-4/1	1P: $119-$139	2P: $119-$149	
10/1-1/31	1P: $79-$129	2P: $79-$129	
4/2-5/31	1P: $79-$89	2P: $79-$89	
6/1-9/30	1P: $59-$69	2P: $59-$69	

Small-scale Hotel

Location: Just n of Chaparral Rd. 5101 N Scottsdale Rd 85250. Fax: 480/947-3044. **Facility:** 218 one-bedroom standard units. 2 stories (no elevator), exterior corridors. *Bath:* combo or shower only. **Parking:** on-site. **Terms:** package plans. **Amenities:** video games (fee), voice mail, irons, hair dryers. **Pool(s):** heated outdoor. **Leisure Activities:** whirlpool, exercise room. **Guest Services:** coin laundry. **Business Services:** meeting rooms, PC, fax. **Cards:** AX, CB, DC, DS, JC, MC, VI.

SOME UNITS

FAIRFIELD INN NORTH SCOTTSDALE
Book at aaa.com

Phone: 480/483-0042   **14**

Property failed to provide current rates

Small-scale Hotel

Location: Just s of Thunderbird Rd; on west side of Scottsdale Rd. 13440 N Scottsdale Rd 85254. Fax: 480/483-3715. **Facility:** 132 one-bedroom standard units. 3 stories, interior/exterior corridors. **Parking:** on-site. **Amenities:** high-speed Internet, voice mail, irons, hair dryers. **Pool(s):** heated outdoor. **Leisure Activities:** whirlpool. **Guest Services:** valet and coin laundry. **Business Services:** PC, fax.

SOME UNITS

(See map and index starting on p. 266)

THE FAIRMONT SCOTTSDALE PRINCESS
Book at aaa.com Phone: (480)585-4848 **3**

(AAA) [SAVE]

▽▽◇▽◇ ▽▽◇▽

2/1-4/2	1P: $369-$499	2P: $369-$499	XP: $30 F18
4/3-5/24	1P: $239-$399	2P: $239-$399	XP: $30 F18
9/22-1/31	1P: $239-$359	2P: $239-$359	XP: $30 F18
5/25-9/21	1P: $139-$229	2P: $139-$229	XP: $30 F18

Resort
Large-scale Hotel

Location: 0.6 mi n of Bell Rd, 0.5 mi e of Scottsdale Rd; on south side of Princess Dr. 7575 E Princess Dr 85255. Fax: 480/585-0086. **Facility:** A 450-acre luxury resort which offers balcony or terraces from each unit. It is the site of the PGA's Phoenix Open and the ATP tennis tournament. 651 units. 576 one-bedroom standard units. 75 one-bedroom suites. 1-4 stories, interior/exterior corridors. *Bath:* combo or shower only. **Parking:** on-site and valet. **Terms:** check-in 4 pm, 14 day cancellation notice-fee imposed, small pets only ($30 extra charge). **Amenities:** CD players, dual phone lines, voice mail, safes, honor bars, irons, hair dryers. *Fee:* video games, high-speed Internet. *Some:* fax. **Dining:** 6 am-9 pm, cocktails, also, The Grill, La Hacienda, Marquesa, see separate listings, entertainment. **Pool(s):** 4 heated outdoor. **Leisure Activities:** saunas, whirlpools, steamrooms, waterslide, fishing; recreation programs, squash-1 court, rental bicycles, hiking trails, jogging, spa, basketball, horseshoes, shuffleboard, volleyball. *Fee:* golf-36 holes, 7 tennis courts (6 lighted), racquetball court. **Guest Services:** gift shop, valet laundry, beauty salon. **Business Services:** conference facilities, business center. **Cards:** AX, CB, DC, DS, JC, MC, VI.

SOME UNITS

[icons: S/D FEE FEE ⊞ 24 Y π &M ⓕ 🖊 🕯 🛏 📠 DATA PORT 💻 / ✕ VCR FEE 🖥 📷 /]

FOUR SEASONS RESORT SCOTTSDALE AT
TROON NORTH   *Book at aaa.com*
Phone: (480)515-5700

(AAA) [SAVE]

▽▽◇▽◇ ▽▽◇▽

2/1-5/31	1P: $495-$4500	2P: $495-$4500	XP: $30 F17
9/1-1/31	1P: $445-$4500	2P: $445-$4500	XP: $30 F17
6/1-8/31	1P: $185-$2500	2P: $185-$2500	XP: $30 F17

Resort
Large-scale Hotel

Location: SR 101, exit 36 (Pima Rd), 4.7 mi n, 2 mi e on Happy Valley, then 1.5 mi n on Alma School Rd. 10600 E Crescent Moon Dr 85262. Fax: 480/515-5599. **Facility:** Well-designed landscaping seamlessly blends the resort with its desert surroundings, allowing for striking views from the Territorial-style casitas. Smoke free premises. 210 units. 188 one-bedroom standard units. 22 one-bedroom suites. 1-3 stories, exterior corridors. **Parking:** on-site (fee) and valet. **Terms:** check-in 4 pm, 7 day cancellation notice-fee imposed, small pets only. **Amenities:** video library, DVD players, CD players, dual phone lines, voice mail, safes, honor bars, irons, hair dryers. *Fee:* video games, high-speed Internet. *Some:* fax. **Dining:** 3 restaurants, 7 am-10 pm, also, Acacia, see separate listing, entertainment. **Pool(s):** 2 heated outdoor, wading. **Leisure Activities:** whirlpool, steamrooms, recreation programs, rental bicycles, hiking trails, spa, horseshoes. *Fee:* golf-36 holes, 2 lighted tennis courts, jeep tours, hot air ballooning, kids club, horseback riding. **Guest Services:** gift shop, complimentary and valet laundry, area transportation (fee), beauty salon. **Business Services:** conference facilities, business center. **Cards:** AX, CB, DC, DS, JC, MC, VI.

SOME UNITS

[icons: 🔗 FEE 🐾 ⊞ 24 Y &M ⓕ 🖊 🛏 📠 ✕ VCR 📷 DATA PORT 💻 / 🖥 📠 /]

GAINEY SUITES HOTEL   *Book at aaa.com*
Phone: (480)922-6969 **23**

(AAA) [SAVE]

▽▽◇▽◇ ▽▽◇▽

1/1-1/31 [ECP]	1P: $219-$359
2/1-5/26 [ECP]	1P: $209-$359
9/11-12/31 [ECP]	1P: $179-$315
5/27-9/10 [ECP]	1P: $95-$185

Small-scale Hotel

Location: Just e of Scottsdale Rd. 7300 E Gainey Suites Dr 85258. Fax: 480/922-1689. **Facility:** 162 units. 48 one-bedroom standard units with efficiencies. 83 one- and 31 two-bedroom suites with efficiencies. 2-3 stories, interior corridors. *Bath:* combo or shower only. **Parking:** on-site. **Terms:** cancellation fee imposed. **Amenities:** video games (fee), CD players, high-speed Internet, dual phone lines, voice mail, safes, irons, hair dryers. **Pool(s):** heated outdoor. **Leisure Activities:** whirlpool, jogging. **Guest Services:** sundries, complimentary evening beverages, valet and coin laundry, area transportation-within 5 mi. **Business Services:** conference facilities, PC. **Cards:** AX, CB, DC, DS, JC, MC, VI. **Special Amenities:** free expanded continental breakfast and free newspaper. *(See color ad below)*

SOME UNITS

[icons: S/D 🍴 & 🛏 📠 FEE DATA PORT 🖥 📠 💻 / ✕ /]

(See map and index starting on p. 266)

HAMPTON INN & SUITES *Book at aaa.com*
Phone: (480)348-9280 **9**

2/1-4/9	1P: $154-$194	2P: $164-$204
4/10-5/14 & 9/1-1/31	1P: $114-$154	2P: $124-$164
5/15-8/31	1P: $84-$124	2P: $94-$124

Small-scale Hotel **Location:** Just s of Bell Rd, just w. 16620 N Scottsdale Rd 85254. Fax: 480/348-9281. **Facility:** 123 units. 83 one-bedroom standard units. 40 one-bedroom suites with efficiencies, some with whirlpools. 3 stories, interior/exterior corridors. *Bath:* combo or shower only. **Parking:** on-site. **Terms:** [ECP] meal plan available, package plans. **Amenities:** video games (fee), high-speed Internet, dual phone lines, voice mail, irons, hair dryers. **Pool(s):** heated outdoor, wading. **Leisure Activities:** whirlpool, exercise room. **Guest Services:** sundries, valet and coin laundry, area transportation-within 5 mi. **Business Services:** meeting rooms, business center. **Cards:** AX, CB, DC, DS, MC, VI. **Special Amenities: free expanded continental breakfast and free local telephone calls.**

SOME UNITS

HAMPTON INN-OLDTOWN/FASHION SQUARE SCOTTSDALE *Book at aaa.com*
Phone: (480)941-9400 **40**

2/1-3/31 [ECP]	1P: $119-$169	2P: $129-$179
4/1-5/27 [ECP]	1P: $89-$129	2P: $99-$139
9/10-1/31 [ECP]	1P: $89-$119	2P: $99-$129
5/28-9/9 [ECP]	1P: $59-$89	2P: $69-$99

Small-scale Hotel **Location:** Scottsdale Rd, just e on Camelback Rd, just s on 75th St. 4415 N Civic Center Plaza 85251. Fax: 480/675-5240. **Facility:** 126 one-bedroom standard units. 5 stories, interior/exterior corridors. *Bath:* combo or shower only. **Parking:** on-site. **Terms:** package plans, pets ($50 fee). **Amenities:** voice mail, irons, hair dryers. **Pool(s):** small heated outdoor. **Guest Services:** valet and coin laundry. **Business Services:** meeting rooms, fax (fee). **Cards:** AX, CB, DC, DS, JC, MC, VI. *(See color ad below)*

SOME UNITS

HAMPTON INN SCOTTSDALE *Book at aaa.com*
Phone: (480)443-3233 **20**

2/1-4/2	1P: $109-$119	2P: $109-$119
9/11-1/31	1P: $79-$119	2P: $79-$119
4/3-5/14	1P: $79-$89	2P: $79-$89
5/15-9/10	1P: $49-$59	2P: $49-$59

Small-scale Hotel **Location:** Just s of Shea Blvd. 10101 N Scottsdale Rd 85253. Fax: 480/443-9149. **Facility:** 130 one-bedroom standard units, some with whirlpools. 2 stories, interior corridors. *Bath:* combo or shower only. **Parking:** on-site. **Terms:** [ECP] meal plan available, package plans. **Amenities:** video games (fee), high-speed Internet, voice mail, irons, hair dryers. **Pool(s):** heated outdoor. **Leisure Activities:** whirlpool, exercise room. **Guest Services:** valet and coin laundry, area transportation-within 5 mi. **Business Services:** meeting rooms, business center. **Cards:** AX, CB, DC, DS, MC, VI. **Special Amenities: free expanded continental breakfast and free local telephone calls.**

SOME UNITS

HILTON GARDEN INN NORTH *Book at aaa.com*
Phone: (480)515-4944 **2**

2/1-3/31	1P: $139-$219	2P: $139-$219	XP: $10 F18
4/1-5/22 & 9/16-1/31	1P: $99-$149	2P: $99-$149	XP: $10 F18
5/23-9/15	1P: $59-$99	2P: $59-$99	XP: $10 F18

Small-scale Hotel **Location:** Loop 101, exit 36 (Pima Rd/Princess Dr), just w. 8550 E Princess Dr 85255. Fax: 480/515-4954. **Facility:** 122 units. 117 one-bedroom standard units, some with whirlpools. 5 one-bedroom suites ($99-$259) with whirlpools. 3 stories, interior corridors. *Bath:* combo or shower only. **Parking:** on-site. **Terms:** [BP] & [ECP] meal plans available, package plans. **Amenities:** video games (fee), voice mail, irons, hair dryers. **Pool(s):** heated outdoor, wading. **Leisure Activities:** whirlpool, putting green, exercise room. **Guest Services:** coin laundry, area transportation. **Business Services:** meeting rooms, business center. **Cards:** AX, CB, DC, DS, JC, MC, VI.

SOME UNITS

HILTON GARDEN INN SCOTTSDALE *Book at aaa.com*
Phone: 480/481-0400 **45**

Property failed to provide current rates

Small-scale Hotel **Location:** Just e of Scottsdale Rd. 7324 E Indian School Rd 85251. Fax: 480/481-0800. **Facility:** 200 units. 186 one-bedroom standard units, some with whirlpools. 14 one-bedroom suites with whirlpools. 7 stories, interior corridors. *Bath:* combo or shower only. **Parking:** on-site. **Amenities:** video games (fee), high-speed Internet, dual phone lines, voice mail, irons, hair dryers. **Pool(s):** heated outdoor. **Leisure Activities:** whirlpool, exercise room. **Guest Services:** sundries, valet and coin laundry. **Business Services:** meeting rooms, business center.

SOME UNITS

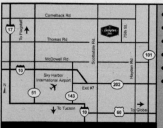

(See map and index starting on p. 266)

HILTON SCOTTSDALE RESORT & VILLAS   *Book at aaa.com*   Phone: (480)948-7750   29

(AAA) (SAVE)

2/1-5/14 & 9/12-1/31	1P: $139-$359	2P: $139-$359	XP: $10	F18
5/15-9/11	1P: $89-$199	2P: $89-$199	XP: $10	F18

Location: Loop 101, exit 45, 2.1 mi w on McDonald Dr, then 0.3 mi n. 6333 N Scottsdale Rd 85250. Fax: 480/948-2232. **Facility:** Modern and sophisticated decor is highlighted in the lobby and framed by high
Large-scale Hotel ceilings and picture windows. Rooms overlook a beautiful pool area. 185 units. 184 one-bedroom standard units. 1 one-bedroom suite ($169-$359) with whirlpool. 2-3 stories, interior corridors. *Bath:* combo or shower only. **Parking:** on-site and valet. **Terms:** check-in 4 pm, 3 day cancellation notice-fee imposed. [AP] meal plan available, package plans, pets ($25 fee, $75 deposit). **Amenities:** dual phone lines, voice mail, safes, honor bars, irons, hair dryers. *Fee:* video games, high-speed Internet. **Dining:** 3 restaurants, 6 am-midnight, cocktails. **Pool(s):** heated outdoor, wading. **Leisure Activities:** saunas, whirlpool, steamrooms, rental bicycles. *Fee:* massage. **Guest Services:** gift shop, valet laundry, beauty salon. **Business Services:** conference facilities, business center. **Cards:** AX, CB, DC, DS, JC, MC, VI. **Special Amenities:** free newspaper.

SOME UNITS

HOLIDAY INN EXPRESS HOTEL & SUITES-SCOTTSDALE   *Book at aaa.com*   Phone: (480)675-7665   49

(AAA) (SAVE)

2/1-4/17 [ECP]	1P: $109-$189	2P: $109-$189	XP: $10	F18
9/12-1/31 [ECP]	1P: $79-$129	2P: $79-$129	XP: $10	F18
4/18-9/11 [ECP]	1P: $69-$109	2P: $69-$109	XP: $10	F18

Location: Northeast corner of Scottsdale Rd and Earll Dr. 3131 N Scottsdale Rd 85251. Fax: 480/675-8666.
Small-scale Hotel **Facility:** 170 units. 170 one-bedroom, some with kitchens (no utensils) and/or whirlpools. 3 stories, interior corridors. *Bath:* combo or shower only. **Parking:** on-site. **Terms:** check-in 4 pm, small pets only ($50 deposit, in smoking units). **Amenities:** video games (fee), voice mail, irons, hair dryers. **Pool(s):** heated outdoor. **Leisure Activities:** whirlpool, exercise room. **Guest Services:** sundries, complimentary evening beverages, valet and coin laundry, area transportation-within 3 mi. **Business Services:** meeting rooms, business center. **Cards:** AX, CB, DC, DS, JC, MC, VI. **Special Amenities:** free expanded continental breakfast and free newspaper.

SOME UNITS

HOMESTEAD STUDIO SUITES HOTEL-PHOENIX-SCOTTSDALE   *Book at aaa.com*   Phone: (480)994-0297   47

3/1-4/2	1P: $90	2P: $95	XP: $5	F17
2/1-2/28	1P: $85	2P: $90	XP: $5	F17
9/24-1/31	1P: $70	2P: $75	XP: $5	F17
Small-scale Hotel 4/3-9/23	1P: $50	2P: $55	XP: $5	F17

Location: Just w of Scottsdale Rd on Goldwater, just s. 3560 N Marshall Way 85251. Fax: 480/994-9036. **Facility:** 120 one-bedroom standard units with efficiencies. 2 stories (no elevator), exterior corridors. *Bath:* combo or shower only. **Parking:** on-site. **Terms:** office hours 6 am-10 pm, cancellation fee imposed, small pets only ($25 extra charge). **Amenities:** voice mail, irons, hair dryers. **Pool(s):** small heated outdoor. **Guest Services:** coin laundry. **Business Services:** fax. **Cards:** AX, DC, DS, MC, VI.

SOME UNITS

HOMEWOOD SUITES BY HILTON/SCOTTSDALE   *Book at aaa.com*   Phone: 480/368-8705   21

Property failed to provide current rates

Location: 0.5 mi s of Shea Blvd. 9880 N Scottsdale Rd 85253. Fax: 480/368-8725. **Facility:** 114 units. 111 one-
Small-scale Hotel and 3 two-bedroom suites with efficiencies. 3 stories, interior corridors. *Bath:* combo or shower only. **Parking:** on-site. **Amenities:** video games (fee), high-speed Internet, dual phone lines, voice mail, irons, hair dryers. **Pool(s):** small heated outdoor. **Leisure Activities:** exercise room, basketball. **Guest Services:** sundries, complimentary evening beverages: Mon-Thurs, coin laundry, area transportation. **Business Services:** meeting rooms, business center.

SOME UNITS

HOSPITALITY SUITE RESORT   *Book at aaa.com*   Phone: (480)949-5115   53

(AAA) (SAVE)

2/1-3/31	1P: $69-$89	2P: $89-$129	XP: $10	F16
4/1-5/15 & 10/1-1/31	1P: $59-$79	2P: $79-$99	XP: $10	F16
5/16-9/30	1P: $49-$69	2P: $59-$79	XP: $10	F16

Location: Just n of McKellips Rd; on east side of Scottsdale Rd. Located in a busy commercial area. 409 N Scottsdale
Small-scale Hotel Rd 85257. Fax: 480/941-8014. **Facility:** 210 units. 86 one-bedroom standard units with efficiencies. 123 one-and 1 two-bedroom suites with kitchens. 2-3 stories, exterior corridors. *Bath:* combo or shower only. **Parking:** on-site. **Terms:** package plans, pets (small dogs only, $200 deposit). **Amenities:** video games (fee), voice mail, irons, hair dryers. **Dining:** 6 am-10 pm, cocktails. **Pool(s):** heated outdoor, 2 small heated outdoor. **Leisure Activities:** whirlpool, 2 lighted tennis courts, barbecues, table tennis, pool table, basketball, horseshoes, shuffleboard. **Guest Services:** complimentary evening beverages, valet and coin laundry, area transportation-within 5 mi. **Business Services:** PC, fax (fee). **Cards:** AX, CB, DC, DS, MC, VI. **Special Amenities:** free full breakfast and free local telephone calls.

SOME UNITS

HOTEL WATERFRONT IVY   Phone: (480)994-5282   35

2/1-4/15 [BP]	1P: $149-$209	2P: $149-$209	XP: $10	F18
4/16-5/20 [BP]	1P: $109-$159	2P: $109-$159	XP: $10	F18
Motel 9/17-1/31 [BP]	1P: $99-$149	2P: $99-$149	XP: $10	F18
5/21-9/16 [BP]	1P: $69-$109	2P: $69-$109	XP: $10	F18

Location: 0.3 mi e of Scottsdale Rd. Located in a quiet residential area. 7445 E Chaparral Rd 85250. Fax: 480/994-5625. **Facility:** 105 units. 38 one- and 20 two-bedroom standard units, some with kitchens. 37 one-bedroom suites with kitchens. 2 stories (no elevator), exterior corridors. *Bath:* combo or shower only. **Parking:** on-site. **Terms:** check-in 4 pm. **Amenities:** voice mail, irons, hair dryers. *Fee:* video games, safes. *Some:* CD players. **Pool(s):** 4 small outdoor, small heated outdoor. **Leisure Activities:** whirlpool, 2 tennis courts, playground, exercise room. *Fee:* bicycles. **Guest Services:** complimentary evening beverages, valet and coin laundry. **Business Services:** meeting rooms, fax (fee). **Cards:** AX, DC, DS, MC, VI.

SOME UNITS

(See map and index starting on p. 266)

HYATT REGENCY SCOTTSDALE RESORT AT GAINEY RANCH *Book at aaa.com*

Phone: (480)991-3388 **22**

2/1-5/29 & 12/22-1/31	1P: $330-$450	2P: $330-$450	XP: $10	F18
9/15-12/21	1P: $265-$385	2P: $265-$385	XP: $10	F18
5/30-9/14	1P: $139-$199	2P: $139-$199	XP: $10	F18

Resort
Large-scale Hotel

Location: Loop 101, exit 43, 2.6 mi w on Via de Ventura. 7500 E Doubletree Ranch Rd 85258. Fax: 480/483-5550. **Facility:** The resort has a man-made beach, waterslide, spa, tennis courts, golf course and family-friendly activities; a Learning Center has cultural programs. Designated smoking area. 490 units. 454 one-bedroom standard units. 1 one- and 35 two-bedroom suites, some with whirlpools. 4 stories, interior/exterior corridors. **Bath:** combo or shower only. **Parking:** on-site and valet. **Terms:** check-in 4 pm, 3 day cancellation notice-fee imposed, $12 service charge. **Amenities:** video library, high-speed Internet (fee), dual phone lines, voice mail, safes, honor bars, irons, hair dryers. **Some:** DVD players, CD players. **Dining:** 4 restaurants, 6 am-10:30 pm, cocktails, also, Sandolo Ristorante, Vu, see separate listings, entertainment. **Pool(s):** 2 heated outdoor, 8 small heated outdoor. **Leisure Activities:** saunas, whirlpools, steamrooms, waterslide, man-made sandy beach at 1 pool, recreation programs, Lost Dutchman's Mine, bicycles, playground, spa. **Fee:** golf-27 holes, 4 lighted tennis courts. **Guest Services:** gift shop, valet laundry, area transportation-within 3 mi. **Business Services:** conference facilities, business center. **Cards:** AX, CB, DC, DS, JC, MC, VI.

SOME UNITS

(icons) FEE / VCR FEE

THE INN AT PIMA, A CONDOMINIUM SUITE HOTEL *Book at aaa.com*

Phone: (480)948-3800 **26**

8/29-1/31	1P: $69-$189	2P: $69-$189
2/1-4/27	1P: $99-$179	2P: $99-$179
4/28-8/28	1P: $59-$99	2P: $59-$99

Condominium

Location: 0.4 mi n of Indian Bend Rd; on west side of Pima Rd. 7330 N Pima Rd 85258. Fax: 480/443-3374. **Facility:** 121 units. 70 one-bedroom standard units. 51 one-bedroom suites with kitchens. 2 stories, interior/exterior corridors. **Bath:** combo or shower only. **Parking:** on-site. **Terms:** [ECP] meal plan available, package plans, pets ($10 extra charge, in designated units). **Amenities:** video games (fee), high-speed Internet, voice mail, irons, hair dryers. **Some:** CD players. **Pool(s):** heated outdoor, wading. **Leisure Activities:** sauna, whirlpool, card room, library, picnic and grill areas, bicycles, exercise room. **Guest Services:** sundries, complimentary evening beverages, coin laundry, area transportation-within 5 mi. **Business Services:** conference facilities, business center. **Cards:** AX, CB, DC, DS, MC, VI. **Special Amenities:** free expanded continental breakfast and free newspaper. *(See color ad below)*

SOME UNITS

(icons) FEE / (icons)

LA QUINTA INN & SUITES PHOENIX (SCOTTSDALE) *Book at aaa.com*

Phone: (480)614-5300 **18**

2/1-4/30 & 1/2-1/31 [CP]	1P: $141-$151	2P: $148-$158	XP: $7	F18
5/1-1/1 [CP]	1P: $89-$99	2P: $96-$106	XP: $7	F18

Small-scale Hotel

Location: Loop 101, exit Shea Blvd, northeast corner. 8888 E Shea Blvd 85260. Fax: 480/614-5333. **Facility:** 140 units. 135 one-bedroom standard units. 5 one-bedroom suites. 3 stories, interior corridors. **Bath:** combo or shower only. **Parking:** on-site. **Terms:** [ECP] meal plan available. **Amenities:** video games (fee), high-speed Internet, voice mail, irons, hair dryers. **Some:** dual phone lines. **Pool(s):** heated outdoor. **Leisure Activities:** whirlpool, exercise room. **Guest Services:** valet and coin laundry, area transportation-within 5 mi. **Business Services:** meeting rooms, fax (fee). **Cards:** AX, CB, DC, DS, MC, VI. **Special Amenities:** free expanded continental breakfast and free local telephone calls. *(See color ad p 295)*

SOME UNITS

(icons) / (icons)

MARRIOTT SUITES SCOTTSDALE *Book at aaa.com*

Phone: (480)945-1550 **43**

2/1-4/29	1P: $209-$319	2P: $209-$319
4/30-5/28	1P: $169-$279	2P: $169-$279
9/10-1/31	1P: $169-$239	2P: $169-$239
5/29-9/9	1P: $89-$159	2P: $89-$159

Small-scale Hotel

Location: Just e of Scottsdale Rd. 7325 E 3rd Ave 85251. Fax: 480/945-2005. **Facility:** 251 one-bedroom suites. 8 stories, interior corridors. **Parking:** on-site (fee) and valet. **Terms:** check-in 4 pm, cancellation fee imposed, [AP], [BP], [CP], [ECP] & [MAP] meal plans available. **Amenities:** high-speed Internet (fee), dual phone lines, voice mail, irons, hair dryers. **Pool(s):** heated outdoor. **Leisure Activities:** saunas, whirlpool, exercise room. **Guest Services:** sundries, valet and coin laundry. **Business Services:** meeting rooms, business center. **Cards:** AX, CB, DC, DS, JC, MC, VI.

SOME UNITS

(icons) / (icons) VCR FEE

(See map and index starting on p. 266)

MILLENNIUM RESORT SCOTTSDALE, MCCORMICK
RANCH   *Book at aaa.com*   **Phone:** (480)948-5050   25

AAA [SAVE]

2/1-4/30	1P: $129-$279	2P: $129-$279	XP: $20	F17
1/1-1/31	1P: $99-$279	2P: $99-$279	XP: $20	F17
10/1-12/31	1P: $89-$169	2P: $89-$169	XP: $20	F17
5/1-9/30	1P: $69-$149	2P: $69-$149	XP: $20	F17

Large-scale Hotel **Location:** 0.8 mi n of Indian Bend Rd. 7401 N Scottsdale Rd 85253. Fax: 480/991-5572. **Facility:** 176 units. 122 one-bedroom standard units. 3 one-, 14 two- and 37 three-bedroom suites ($159-$569), some with kitchens. 3 stories, interior corridors. **Parking:** on-site. **Terms:** check-in 4 pm, package plans, $9 service charge, small pets only ($50 deposit). **Amenities:** dual phone lines, voice mail, irons, hair dryers. *Some:* video games (fee), high-speed Internet. **Dining:** 6 am-midnight, cocktails, also, Pinon Grill, see separate listing. **Pool(s):** heated outdoor. **Leisure Activities:** whirlpool, canoeing, paddleboats, boat dock, fishing, kayak, lighted tennis court, bicycles, exercise room, volleyball. *Fee:* golf-36 holes, massage. **Guest Services:** gift shop, valet laundry, area transportation-golf & spa. **Business Services:** conference facilities, PC. **Cards:** AX, CB, DC, DS, JC, MC, VI. **Special Amenities:** free newspaper. *(See color ad p 332)*

SOME UNITS

MOTEL 6 SCOTTSDALE #29   *Book at aaa.com*   **Phone:** 480/946-2280   39

2/1-4/16	1P: $62-$72	2P: $68-$78	XP: $3	F17
4/17-5/3	1P: $55-$65	2P: $61-$71	XP: $3	F17
5/4-1/31	1P: $49-$59	2P: $55-$65	XP: $3	F17

Motel **Location:** Just w of Scottsdale Rd. 6848 E Camelback Rd 85251. Fax: 480/949-7583. **Facility:** 122 one-bedroom standard units. 2 stories (no elevator), exterior corridors. *Bath:* combo or shower only. **Parking:** on-site. **Pool(s):** heated outdoor. **Guest Services:** coin laundry. **Business Services:** fax (fee). **Cards:** AX, CB, DC, DS, MC, VI.

SOME UNITS

THE PHOENICIAN   *Book at aaa.com*   **Phone:** (480)941-8200   38

AAA [SAVE]

2/1-6/15	1P: $675-$775	2P: $675-$775	XP: $50	F18
9/18-1/31	1P: $585-$685	2P: $585-$685	XP: $50	F18
6/16-9/17	1P: $375-$425	2P: $375-$425	XP: $25	F18

Resort
Large-scale Hotel **Location:** 0.5 mi w of 64th St. 6000 E Camelback Rd 85251. Fax: 480/947-4311. **Facility:** Tucked at the base of Camelback Mountain, this resort with its tropical lagoon, pools reflecting the tiered building and elegant rooms awaits you. 654 units. 581 one-bedroom standard units, some with whirlpools. 64 one-, 6 two- and 3 three-bedroom suites ($950-$1950), some with kitchens and/or whirlpools. 3-4 stories, interior/exterior corridors. **Parking:** valet and street. **Terms:** check-in 4 pm, 7 day cancellation notice-fee imposed, package plans, small pets only (in casitas). **Amenities:** CD players, high-speed Internet (fee), dual phone lines, voice mail, safes, honor bars, irons, hair dryers. *Some:* DVD players (fee), fax. **Dining:** 4 restaurants, 6:30 am-10:30 pm, cocktails, also, Mary Elaine's, The Terrace Dining Room, Windows on the Green, see separate listings, entertainment. **Pool(s):** 7 heated outdoor, 2 small heated outdoor, 2 wading. **Leisure Activities:** saunas, whirlpools, steamrooms, waterslide, grass tennis court, recreation programs, lawn bowling, croquet, rental bicycles, hiking trails, jogging, playground, spa, basketball, volleyball. *Fee:* golf-27 holes, 12 tennis courts (11 lighted). **Guest Services:** gift shop, valet laundry, area transportation (fee). **Business Services:** conference facilities, business center. **Cards:** AX, CB, DC, DS, JC, MC, VI. **Special Amenities:** free newspaper and free room upgrade (subject to availability with advance reservations). *(See color ad below)*

SOME UNITS

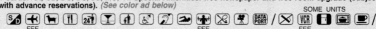

(See map and index starting on p. 266)

RADISSON FORT MCDOWELL RESORT & CASINO   Phone: 480/836-5300

[fyi]

	2/1-4/20	1P: $189-$249	2P: $199-$249
	9/8-1/31	1P: $149-$199	2P: $149-$199
Small-scale Hotel	4/21-5/29	1P: $139-$189	2P: $139-$189
	5/30-9/7	1P: $99-$139	2P: $99-$139

Too new to rate. **Location:** SR 87 to Fort McDowell Rd, then left. 10438 N Fort McDowell Rd 85264. Fax: 480/836-8545. **Amenities:** 250 units. **Terms:** $10 service charge. **Cards:** AX, MC, VI. *(See color ad below)*

RAMADA LIMITED SCOTTSDALE   *Book at aaa.com*   Phone: 480/994-9461   [44]

▽▽ ▽▽   Property failed to provide current rates

Motel   **Location:** Just w of Scottsdale Rd; just n of Indian School Rd; on south side of 5th Ave. 6935 5th Ave 85251.
Fax: 480/947-1695. **Facility:** 92 one-bedroom standard units. 3 stories, exterior corridors. **Parking:** on-site.
Terms: small pets only ($15 extra charge). **Amenities:** voice mail, irons, hair dryers. **Pool(s):** heated
outdoor. **Leisure Activities:** exercise room. **Guest Services:** coin laundry. **Business Services:** *Fee:* PC, fax.

SOME UNITS

🛏 [📶+] 🍽 [📺] [DATA PORT] 🔌 🖥 / ⊠ 🖨 /
FEE

RENAISSANCE SCOTTSDALE RESORT   *Book at aaa.com*   Phone: (480)991-1414   [30]

[AAA] [SAVE]

	2/1-4/29	1P: $269-$369	2P: $269-$369	XP: $10
	4/30-6/11 & 9/5-1/31	1P: $219-$319	2P: $219-$319	XP: $10
	6/12-9/4	1P: $129-$189	2P: $129-$189	XP: $10

▽▽▽ ▽▽▽

Resort
Large-scale Hotel

Location: Just n of McDonald Dr; on west side of Scottsdale Rd. Located adjacent to the Borgata Shopping Village. 6160 N Scottsdale Rd 85253. Fax: 480/951-3350. **Facility:** The spacious grounds, spread over 25 acres, are a combination of desert landscaping and wide, tree-shaded lawns. 171 units. 64 one-bedroom standard units. 106 one-bedroom suites with whirlpools, some with kitchens. 1 vacation home. 1 story, exterior corridors. *Bath:* combo or shower only. **Parking:** on-site. **Terms:** check-in 4 pm, cancellation fee imposed, package plans, small pets only ($75 deposit). **Amenities:** voice mail, safes, honor bars, irons, hair dryers. *Fee:* video games, high-speed Internet. **Dining:** 3 restaurants, 7 am-10 pm, cocktails. **Pool(s):** 2 heated outdoor. **Leisure Activities:** whirlpools, water aerobics, putting green, croquet, table tennis, soft tip darts, jogging, shuffleboard. *Fee:* 4 tennis courts (2 lighted), massage. **Guest Services:** gift shop, valet laundry, area transportation-within 5 mi. **Business Services:** conference facilities, business center. **Cards:** AX, DC, DS, MC, VI. *(See color ad p 343)*

SOME UNITS

🛏 🍽 [24] [Y] [GM] [🐕] 🌀 ➤ ⊠ [DATA PORT] 🖥 / ⊠ [VCR] 🔌 🖨 /
FEE   FEE

(See map and index starting on p. 266)

RESIDENCE INN BY MARRIOTT, SCOTTSDALE/PARADISE VALLEY   *Book at aaa.com*   Phone: (480)948-8666   **31**

(AAA) (SAVE)
◇◇◇
2/1-4/2   1P: $139-$309
4/3-5/28 & 9/11-1/31   1P: $129-$239
5/29-9/10   1P: $79-$149

Small-scale Hotel **Location:** Just n of McDonald Dr. 6040 N Scottsdale Rd 85253. Fax: 480/443-4869. **Facility:** 122 units. 94 one-bedroom standard units with efficiencies. 28 two-bedroom suites with efficiencies. 2 stories (no elevator), interior/exterior corridors. *Bath:* combo or shower only. **Parking:** on-site. **Terms:** pets ($75 fee). **Amenities:** video games (fee), high-speed Internet, voice mail, irons, hair dryers. **Pool(s):** heated outdoor. **Leisure Activities:** whirlpool, barbecue grills, exercise room, sports court. **Guest Services:** complimentary evening beverages: Mon-Thurs, valet and coin laundry. **Business Services:** meeting rooms, fax (fee). **Cards:** AX, CB, DC, DS, MC, VI.

SOME UNITS

[S🅳] [📞] [🕩+] [24🅝] [🅕M] [♿] [🖉] [🏊] [✕] [🎥] [DATA PORT] [🅱] [🍴] [💻] /✕/
FEE

RESIDENCE INN SCOTTSDALE NORTH   *Book at aaa.com*   Phone: (480)563-4120   **6**

◇◇◇
2/1-4/29 & 1/1-1/31 [ECP]   1P: $169-$239   2P: $169-$239
9/11-12/31 [ECP]   1P: $129-$199   2P: $129-$199
4/30-9/10 [ECP]   1P: $89-$199   2P: $89-$199

Small-scale Hotel **Location:** SR 101, exit 34 (Scottsdale Rd), 1.1 mi s, then just e on 17050 N. 17011 N Scottsdale Rd 85255. Fax: 480/563-9470. **Facility:** 120 units. 51 one-bedroom standard units with efficiencies. 56 one- and 13 two-bedroom suites, some with efficiencies or kitchens. 3 stories, interior corridors. *Bath:* combo or shower only. **Parking:** on-site. **Terms:** small pets only ($75 fee). **Amenities:** video games (fee), high-speed Internet, dual phone lines, voice mail, irons, hair dryers. *Some:* DVD players. **Pool(s):** heated outdoor. **Leisure Activities:** whirlpool, exercise room, sports court. **Guest Services:** complimentary evening beverages: Mon-Thurs, valet and coin laundry, area transportation. **Business Services:** meeting rooms, PC, fax (fee). **Cards:** AX, CB, DC, DS, JC, MC, VI.

SOME UNITS

[A$K] [S🅳] [📞] [🕩+] [♿] [🏊] [✕] [🎥] [DATA PORT] [🅱] [🍴] [💻] /✕/ [VCR]
FEE

RODEWAY INN OF SCOTTSDALE   *Book at aaa.com*   Phone: (480)946-3456   **46**

(AAA) (SAVE)
▽▽
2/1-4/27   1P: $69-$89   2P: $79-$109
4/28-8/28   1P: $49-$79   2P: $59-$89
8/29-1/31   1P: $49-$69   2P: $54-$74

Motel **Location:** Just w of Scottsdale Rd, on north side of Indian School Rd. 7110 E Indian School Rd 85251. Fax: 480/874-0492. **Facility:** 65 units. 61 one-bedroom standard units. 4 one-bedroom suites. 2 stories (no elevator), exterior corridors. *Bath:* combo or shower only. **Parking:** on-site. **Terms:** [ECP] meal plan available, small pets only ($10 extra charge, in designated units). **Amenities:** hair dryers. *Some:* irons. **Pool(s):** heated outdoor. **Leisure Activities:** whirlpool. **Guest Services:** coin laundry. **Business Services:** PC, fax (fee). **Cards:** AX, CB, DC, DS, MC, VI. **Special Amenities: free continental breakfast and free local telephone calls.**

SOME UNITS

[S🅳] [📞] [🕩+] [♿] [🖉] [🏊] [✕] [🎥] [DATA PORT] [🅱] [🍴] [💻] /✕/
FEE

(See map and index starting on p. 266)

SCOTTSDALE MARRIOTT AT MCDOWELL MOUNTAINS   Book at aaa.com   Phone: (480)502-3836

2/1-4/29	1P: $249-$329	
4/30-6/11 & 9/5-1/31	1P: $189-$279	
6/12-9/4	1P: $119-$139	

Small-scale Hotel   **Location:** Loop 101, exit 36 (Princess Dr), just w to N Perimeter Dr, then 0.6 mi s. 16770 N Perimeter Dr 85260. Fax: 480/502-0653. **Facility:** All rooms have a balcony or patio and many overlook the courtyard at this property adjacent to the TPC Scottsdale Desert Golf Course. 270 one-bedroom suites. 4 stories, interior corridors. *Bath:* combo or shower only. **Parking:** on-site and valet. **Terms:** cancellation fee imposed, [BP] meal plan available, small pets only ($50 fee). **Amenities:** dual phone lines, voice mail, irons, hair dryers. *Fee:* video games, high-speed Internet. **Dining:** 6:30 am-2 & 5:30-10 pm, cocktails. **Pool(s):** heated outdoor. **Leisure Activities:** saunas, whirlpool, billiards, exercise room. **Guest Services:** gift shop, valet and coin laundry, area transportation-within 5 mi. **Business Services:** meeting rooms, business center. **Cards:** AX, CB, DC, DS, JC, MC, VI.

SOME UNITS

SCOTTSDALE RESORT & ATHLETIC CLUB   Book at aaa.com   Phone: (480)344-0600   27

2/1-4/30	1P: $249-$549	XP: $20	F12
10/1-1/31	1P: $149-$359	XP: $20	F12
5/1-9/30	1P: $119-$279	XP: $20	F12

Small-scale Hotel   **Location:** 1.5 mi e of Scottsdale Rd. 8235 E Indian Bend Rd 85250. Fax: 480/344-0650. **Facility:** Designated smoking area. 56 units. 28 one-bedroom standard units. 28 one-bedroom suites ($359-$1100) with kitchens and whirlpools. 2 stories (no elevator), exterior corridors. *Bath:* combo or shower only. **Parking:** on-site. **Terms:** cancellation fee imposed, package plans. **Amenities:** DVD players, CD players, high-speed Internet, voice mail, irons, hair dryers. **Dining:** Eurasia Bistro & Bar, see separate listing. **Pool(s):** heated outdoor. **Leisure Activities:** whirlpool, 11 lighted tennis courts. **Guest Services:** valet and coin laundry. **Business Services:** meeting rooms, business center. **Cards:** AX, DS, MC, VI.

(See map and index starting on p. 266)

SCOTTSDALE RESORT & CONFERENCE CENTER *Book at aaa.com* — Phone: (480)991-9000 [24]

AAA SAVE

	2/1-4/30	1P: $199-$279	2P: $199-$279	XP: $10	F12
	9/7-12/20	1P: $169-$219	2P: $169-$219	XP: $10	F12
	12/21-1/31	1P: $99-$129	2P: $99-$129	XP: $10	F12
	5/1-9/6	1P: $99-$119	2P: $99-$119	XP: $10	F12

Resort
Large-scale Hotel

Location: Just w of Hayden; just e of Scottsdale Rd. 7700 E McCormack Pkwy 85258. Fax: 480/596-7422. **Facility:** A recent, extensive renovation enhanced the hacienda-style rooms, shaded courtyards and spacious public areas with gracious appointments. 326 units. 311 one-bedroom standard units. 15 one-bedroom suites, some with kitchens (no utensils) and/or whirlpools. 2-3 stories, interior/exterior corridors. *Bath:* combo or shower only. **Parking:** on-site and valet. **Terms:** cancellation fee imposed, $12 service charge. **Amenities:** dual phone lines, voice mail, honor bars, irons, hair dryers. *Fee:* video games, high-speed Internet. **Dining:** Palm Court, see separate listing. **Pool(s):** 2 heated outdoor. **Leisure Activities:** saunas, whirlpools, steamroom, pool tables, rental bicycles, jogging, exercise room, spa, sports court, basketball, horseshoes, volleyball. *Fee:* 4 lighted tennis courts. **Guest Services:** sundries, valet laundry. **Business Services:** conference facilities, business center. **Cards:** AX, DC, DS, MC, VI. **Special Amenities:** free local telephone calls and free newspaper. *(See color ad p 344)*

SOME UNITS

SCOTTSDALE VILLA MIRAGE *Book at aaa.com* — Phone: 480/473-4000 [1]

	2/1-4/15	1P: $158-$293	2P: $158-$293
	4/16-5/31 & 10/1-1/31	1P: $113-$225	2P: $113-$225
	6/1-9/30	1P: $90-$149	2P: $90-$149

Condominium

Location: Loop 101, exit 34 eastbound, 0.7 mi s on Scottsdale Rd, then 0.8 mi e; exit 38 westbound, 2 mi w on Frank Lloyd Wright Blvd, 0.5 mi n on Scottsdale Rd, then 0.8 mi e. 7887 E Princess Blvd 85255. Fax: 480/473-4010. **Facility:** These garden-style condominiums are pleasantly appointed and convenient to shopping, local attractions and sports centers. 224 units. 96 one-bedroom standard units. 96 one- and 32 two-bedroom suites with kitchens and whirlpools. 3 stories (no elevator), exterior corridors. *Bath:* combo or shower only. **Parking:** on-site. **Terms:** check-in 4 pm. **Amenities:** video library (fee), DVD players, voice mail, irons, hair dryers. *Some:* CD players. **Pool(s):** heated outdoor, wading. **Leisure Activities:** saunas, whirlpools, steamrooms, 2 lighted tennis courts, recreation programs, playground, exercise room, basketball. *Fee:* massage, game room. **Guest Services:** gift shop, valet and coin laundry. **Business Services:** meeting rooms. **Cards:** AX, DC, DS, MC, VI.

SOME UNITS

SLEEP INN *Book at aaa.com* — Phone: (480)998-9211 [8]

AAA SAVE

	2/1-4/15	1P: $89-$129	2P: $99-$139
	4/16-5/30 & 10/20-1/31	1P: $54-$89	2P: $59-$99
	5/31-10/19	1P: $49-$69	2P: $54-$79

Small-scale Hotel

Location: Just s of Bell Rd. 16630 N Scottsdale Rd 85254. Fax: 480/607-2893. **Facility:** 107 one-bedroom standard units. 3 stories, interior corridors. *Bath:* combo or shower only. **Parking:** on-site. **Terms:** [ECP] meal plan available, package plans, small pets only ($10 extra charge). **Amenities:** video games (fee), high-speed Internet, voice mail, irons, hair dryers. **Pool(s):** small heated outdoor. **Leisure Activities:** whirlpool, exercise room. **Guest Services:** valet and coin laundry, area transportation-within 5 mi. **Business Services:** meeting rooms, PC. **Cards:** AX, CB, DC, DS, MC, VI. **Special Amenities:** free expanded continental breakfast and free local telephone calls.

SOME UNITS

SPRINGHILL SUITES BY MARRIOTT-SCOTTSDALE NORTH *Book at aaa.com* — Phone: (480)922-8700 [5]

	2/1-4/29	1P: $199-$249	2P: $199-$249
	4/30-5/27 & 9/10-1/31	1P: $159-$199	2P: $159-$199
	5/28-9/9	1P: $99-$109	2P: $99-$109

Small-scale Hotel

Location: Just n of Frank Lloyd Wright Blvd. Located in a commercial area. 17020 N Scottsdale Rd 85255. Fax: 480/948-2276. **Facility:** 123 one-bedroom standard units. 4 stories, interior corridors. *Bath:* combo or shower only. **Parking:** on-site. **Amenities:** video games (fee), high-speed Internet, voice mail, irons, hair dryers. **Pool(s):** heated outdoor. **Leisure Activities:** whirlpool. **Guest Services:** sundries, valet and coin laundry, area transportation. **Business Services:** meeting rooms, PC, fax (fee). **Cards:** AX, CB, DC, DS, JC, MC, VI.

SOME UNITS

SUMMERFIELD SUITES BY WYNDHAM-SCOTTSDALE *Book at aaa.com* — Phone: (480)946-7700 [41]

	2/1-4/2 [BP]	1P: $179-$329	2P: $179-$329
	9/18-1/31 [BP]	1P: $129-$329	2P: $129-$329
	4/3-5/31 [BP]	1P: $129-$279	2P: $129-$279
	6/1-9/17 [BP]	1P: $89-$219	2P: $89-$219

Small-scale Hotel

Location: 0.3 mi e of Scottsdale Rd. 4245 N Drinkwater Blvd 85251. Fax: 480/946-7711. **Facility:** 164 units. 96 one- and 68 two-bedroom suites ($89-$329) with kitchens. 3 stories (no elevator), exterior corridors. *Bath:* combo or shower only. **Parking:** on-site. **Terms:** check-in 4 pm, small pets only ($150-$200 fee). **Amenities:** DVD players, dual phone lines, voice mail, irons, hair dryers. *Fee:* video library, high-speed Internet. **Pool(s):** heated outdoor. **Leisure Activities:** whirlpool, exercise room. **Guest Services:** sundries, complimentary evening beverages: Mon-Thurs, valet and coin laundry, area transportation. **Business Services:** meeting rooms. **Cards:** AX, CB, DC, DS, JC, MC, VI.

SOME UNITS

TOWNEPLACE SUITES BY MARRIOTT *Book at aaa.com* — Phone: 480/551-1100 [16]

Small-scale Hotel

Location: Loop 101, exit Shea Blvd, just e to 90th St, then just n. 10740 N 90th St 85260. Fax: 480/551-1300. **Facility:** 131 units. 91 one-bedroom standard units with efficiencies. 6 one- and 34 two-bedroom suites with efficiencies. 3 stories, interior corridors. *Bath:* combo or shower only. **Parking:** on-site. **Terms:** pets ($75 fee). **Amenities:** high-speed Internet, voice mail, irons, hair dryers. **Pool(s):** small heated outdoor. **Leisure Activities:** exercise room. **Guest Services:** valet and coin laundry. **Business Services:** business center.

SOME UNITS

(See map and index starting on p. 266)

THE WESTIN KIERLAND RESORT & SPA *Book at aaa.com* Phone: (480)624-1000 11

AAA SAVE	2/1-5/25	1P: $299-$569	2P: $299-$569	XP: $50	F17
◇◇◇◇	9/11-12/31	1P: $269-$549	2P: $269-$549	XP: $50	F17
	1/1-1/31	1P: $309-$609	2P: $309-$508	XP: $50	F17
	5/26-9/10	1P: $169-$309	2P: $169-$309	XP: $50	F17

Resort
Large-scale Hotel
Location: 0.5 mi w of Scottsdale Rd. 6902 E Greenway Pkwy 85254. Fax: 480/624-1001. **Facility:** The views across the lagoon to the golf course are amazing and add a special ambiance to this new resort in North Scottsdale. 735 units. 714 one-bedroom standard units. 21 one-bedroom suites ($499-$2500), some with whirlpools. 11 stories, interior corridors. **Parking:** on-site and valet. **Terms:** check-in 4 pm, 7 day cancellation notice-fee imposed, package plans. **Amenities:** dual phone lines, voice mail, safes, honor bars, irons, hair dryers. *Fee:* video games, high-speed Internet. *Some:* DVD players, CD players. **Dining:** 5 restaurants, 6 am-11 pm, cocktails, also, Deseo, Nellie Cashman's Monday Club Cafe', see separate listings. **Pool(s):** 2 heated outdoor. **Leisure Activities:** saunas, whirlpools, steamrooms, waterslide, lazy river, La Bauve Golf School, playground, exercise room, spa. *Fee:* golf-27 holes, 2 lighted tennis courts, game room. **Guest Services:** gift shop. **Business Services:** conference facilities, business center. **Cards:** AX, CB, DC, DS, JC, MC, VI.

SOME UNITS

[icons] FEE / ⊠ /

THE WESTIN KIERLAND VILLAS *Book at aaa.com* Phone: (480)624-1700 10

◇◇◇	2/1-5/26	2P: $599
	9/17-1/31	2P: $537
Condominium	5/27-9/16	2P: $327

Location: Jct Scottsdale Rd, 0.8 mi w on Greenway Pkwy, just n. 15620 N Clubgate Dr 85254. Fax: 480/624-1701. **Facility:** Spacious, elegant rooms have upscale baths, full kitchens and balconies or patios; a family pool and an adult pool are among the amenities. Designated smoking area. 186 one-bedroom suites with whirlpools, some with efficiencies or kitchens. 3-4 stories, exterior corridors. **Parking:** on-site. **Terms:** check-in 4 pm, 3 day cancellation notice-fee imposed. **Amenities:** video library (fee), DVD players, CD players, dual phone lines, voice mail, safes, irons, hair dryers. **Pool(s):** 2 heated outdoor, wading. **Leisure Activities:** sauna, whirlpools, steamroom, waterslide, exercise room. *Fee:* golf-27 holes, 2 lighted tennis courts. **Guest Services:** sundries, complimentary laundry, area transportation. **Business Services:** business center. **Cards:** AX, DC, DS, MC, VI.

[icons] ASK [icons]

WINGATE INN & SUITES *Book at aaa.com* Phone: 480/922-6500 13

AAA SAVE	2/1-4/9 & 9/10-1/31 [ECP]	1P: $150-$250	2P: $150-$250	XP: $10	F17
◇◇◇◇	4/10-5/22 [ECP]	1P: $130-$230	2P: $130-$230	XP: $10	F17
	5/23-9/9 [ECP]	1P: $110-$190	2P: $110-$190	XP: $10	F17

Location: Loop 101, exit 39 (Raintree Dr), just w, then 0.3 mi s. 14255 N 87th St 85260. Fax: 480/922-6502.
Small-scale Hotel
Facility: Designated smoking area. 117 units. 88 one-bedroom standard units, some with efficiencies and/or whirlpools. 28 one- and 1 two-bedroom suites with efficiencies, some with whirlpools. 4 stories, interior corridors. *Bath:* combo or shower only. **Parking:** on-site. **Amenities:** video games (fee), high-speed Internet, dual phone lines, voice mail, safes, irons, hair dryers. *Some:* DVD players. **Pool(s):** heated outdoor. **Leisure Activities:** whirlpool, putting green, exercise room. **Guest Services:** sundries, coin laundry, area transportation-within 3 mi. **Business Services:** meeting rooms, business center. **Cards:** AX, CB, DC, DS, MC, VI. **Special Amenities:** free expanded continental breakfast and free local telephone calls. *(See color ad below)*

[icons]

(See map and index starting on p. 266)

——— *The following lodgings were either not evaluated or did not* ———
meet AAA rating requirements but are listed for your information only.

KIERLAND VILLAS CONDOMINIUMS   Phone: 480/515-2300
[fyi]   Not evaluated. **Location:** Jct Scottsdale Rd and Greenway Pkwy, 0.5 mi w, then just n. 15221 N Clubgate 85254.
          Facilities, services, and decor characterize an upscale property.

MONTANA DEL SOL   Phone: 480/515-2300
[fyi]   Did not meet all AAA rating requirements for locking devices in some guest rooms at time of last evaluation
              on 10/31/2001. **Location:** Loop 101, exit 38 (Bell Rd), 0.7 mi w. 8245 E Bell Rd 85260. Facilities, services, and decor
Condominium   characterize a mid-range property.

RAINTREE RESORT CASITAS   Phone: 480/515-2300
[fyi]   Did not meet all AAA rating requirements for locking devices in some guest rooms at time of last evaluation
              on 10/31/2001. **Location:** Loop 101, exit 39 (Raintree Dr), 0.4 mi e. 9100 E Raintree Dr 85260. Facilities, services,
Condominium   and decor characterize a mid-range property.

THE SCOTTSDALE PLAZA RESORT   Phone: 480/948-5000
[fyi]   Not evaluated. **Location:** Just n of Indian Bend Rd. 7200 N Scottsdale Rd 85253. Facilities, services, and decor
          characterize an upscale property.

THE VILLAGE AT STONECREEK   Phone: 480/515-2300
[fyi]   Did not meet all AAA rating requirements for locking devices in some guest rooms at time of last evaluation
              on 10/24/2002. **Location:** Just n, on Tatum Blvd at Shea Blvd, just e. 4850 E Desert Cove Ave 85254. Facilities,
Condominium   services, and decor characterize a mid-range property.

——— **WHERE TO DINE** ———

6TH AVENUE BISTROT   **Dinner:** $16-$25   Phone: 480/947-6022   (64)
▼▼▼▼   **Location:** Just w of Scottsdale Rd. 7150 E 6th Ave 85251. **Hours:** Open 2/1-6/30 & 9/1-1/31; 5 pm-9 pm, Fri &
          Sat-10 pm. Closed: 11/23, 12/25; also Sun 4/1-10/31. **Reservations:** accepted. **Features:** The intimate
French   bistro serves beautifully presented dishes with rich flavors and yet a light touch with sauces. On the menu
          are traditional foods, such as lamb shank, as well as delicate fish, including escolar. Casual dress; cocktails.
Parking: street. **Cards:** AX, MC, VI.

ACACIA   **Dinner:** $29-$40   Phone: 480/515-5700
▼▼▼ ▼▼▼   **Location:** SR 101, exit 36 (Pima Rd), 4.7 mi n, 2 mi e on Happy Valley, then 1.5 mi n on Alma School Rd; in Four
          Seasons Resort Scottsdale at Troon North. 10600 E Crescent Moon Dr 85255. **Hours:** 6 pm-10 pm.
Steak & Seafood **Reservations:** suggested. **Features:** The sophisticated, contemporary decor employs aspects of Arizona
          ranch living. An expert in layering flavors, the chef prepares innovative regional American cuisine from
specialty meats and seafood. Dressy casual; cocktails; entertainment. **Parking:** valet. **Cards:** AX, CB, DC, DS, JC, MC, VI.

                                                                                      [Y]

ARCADIA FARMS   **Lunch:** $11-$14   Phone: 480/941-5665   (69)
▼▼ ▼▼   **Location:** Just w of Scottsdale Rd. 7014 E First Ave 85251. **Hours:** 11 am-3 pm. Closed: 1/1, 11/23, 12/25.
          Reservations: suggested. **Features:** The cheery garden decor delights guests' eyes in this popular eatery
American in mid-Scottsdale. Lush salads, thick sandwiches and desserts tempt any appetite. Patio seating is an
          option. Dressy casual; wine only. **Parking:** valet and street. **Cards:** MC, VI.

THE BAMBOO CLUB   **Lunch:** $7-$22   **Dinner:** $9-$23   Phone: 480/998-1287   (26)
▼▼ ▼▼   **Location:** Loop 101, exit 41, just w. 8624 E Shea Blvd 85260. **Hours:** 11 am-10 pm, Fri & Sat-11 pm. Closed:
          11/23, 12/25. **Reservations:** suggested. **Features:** Varied dishes of the popular bistro's dynamic cuisine
Pacific Rim delight the palate with flavors and textures blended in recipes from such places as Korea, Thailand, Japan
          and China. Service is gracious. Casual dress; cocktails. **Parking:** on-site. **Cards:** AX, CB, DC, DS, MC, VI.

                                                                                  [Y] [⬒]

BARCELONA   **Lunch:** $6-$12   **Dinner:** $12-$30   Phone: 480/603-0370   (11)
▼▼▼▼   **Location:** Just e of Scottsdale Rd. 15440 E Greenway-Hayden Loop 85260. **Hours:** 11 am-11 pm, Sat 4 pm-
          midnight. Closed: 11/23, 12/25; also Sun. **Reservations:** suggested. **Features:** Diners enter the modern
Regional Spanish dining room through the massive wood doors of a former hacienda. An immense hand-decorated, domed
          ceiling dominates this area. Favorites include paella and smoked salmon. Dressy casual; cocktails;
entertainment. **Parking:** on-site and valet. **Cards:** AX, CB, DC, DS, JC, MC.

                                                                                  [Y] [⬒]

BLOOM   **Lunch:** $9-$15   **Dinner:** $15-$39   Phone: 480/922-5666   (30)
▼▼▼▼   **Location:** Just s of Doubletree Ranch Rd; in New Shops at Gainey Village. 8877 N Scottsdale Rd, Suite 402 85253.
          Hours: 11 am-2:30 & 5-9:30 pm, Fri & Sat-10:30 pm. Closed major holidays. **Reservations:** suggested.
American **Features:** Beautifully presented and cooked to delight the palate are dishes such as marinated Chinese
          chicken salad and wood-grilled center cut pork chop with caramelized apples. Sophisticated decor and
attentive service add finishing touches to the dining experience. Casual dress; cocktails. **Parking:** on-site. **Cards:** AX, CB, DC,
DS, JC, MC, VI.

(See map and index starting on p. 266)

BLUE AGAVE MEXICAN CANTINA
Mexican

Lunch: $8-$13   Dinner: $8-$13   Phone: 480/429-1123   66

Location: Just n of Indian School Rd, just w on 3rd Ave. 4280 Drinkwater Blvd 85251. **Hours:** 11 am-midnight, Fri & Sat-1 am, Sun-11 pm. Closed major holidays. **Reservations:** accepted. **Features:** The cantina is not the usual Mexican eatery, and its owners define the experience as "Mexican without borders." Dishes such as red chili ahi tuna and filet mignon enchiladas blend creative ingredients and savory flavors. The fried, tortilla-wrapped banana dessert is luscious. Casual dress; cocktails. **Parking:** on-site. **Cards:** AX, CB, DC, DS, MC, VI.

BRAVO BISTRO
Italian

Lunch: $9-$14   Dinner: $15-$32   Phone: 480/481-7614   62

Location: Loop 101, exit 46 (Chaparral Rd), 2.1 mi w to Scottsdale Rd, then 0.8 mi s. 4327 N Scottsdale Rd 85251. **Hours:** 5 pm-11 pm, Wed-Fri also 11:30 am-2 pm. **Reservations:** suggested. **Features:** Close to excellent shopping and scenic historic Scottsdale, the intimate eatery serves both Italian- and Mediterranean-inspired cuisine. Examples include lobster ravioli, penne with wild mushrooms, paella and Israeli couscous. Dressy casual; cocktails. **Parking:** valet. **Cards:** AX, DC, DS, MC, VI.

THE BREAKFAST CLUB
Specialty

Lunch: $6-$10   Phone: 480/222-2582   60

Location: Northwest corner of Stetson and Scottsdale Rd. 4400 N Scottsdale Rd 85251. **Hours:** 6 am-3 pm, Sat & Sun from 8 am. Closed: 11/23, 12/25. **Features:** Breakfast choices will satisfy any sleepy person wanting to jump-start the day. Friendly, wide-awake staffers quickly serve fresh coffee, eggs of any style, juices and homemade baked goods. Lunch salads and sandwiches are hearty. Casual dress. **Parking:** on-site. **Cards:** AX, DS, MC, VI.

BRITTLEBUSH BAR & GRILL
American

Lunch: $10-$12   Dinner: $10-$12   Phone: 480/624-1000   16

Location: 0.5 mi w of Scottsdale Rd; in Westin Kierland Resort & Spa. 6902 E Greenway Pkwy 85254. **Hours:** 11 am-7 pm. Closed: 1/1. **Reservations:** suggested. **Features:** Dine while overlooking the golf greens at this relaxed eatery located at the golf shop at the Westin Kierland Resort. Friendly service, hearty salads and sandwiches with luscious soups entice everyone. Casual dress; cocktails. **Parking:** on-site. **Cards:** AX, CB, DC, DS, JC, MC, VI.

BUCKETS
American

Lunch: $8-$19   Dinner: $8-$19   Phone: 480/994-8484   56

Location: Loop 101, exit 46 (Chaparral Rd), 2.1 mi w to Scottsdale Rd, 0.6 mi s to Shoeman Ln, then just e. 7216 E Shoeman Ln 85251. **Hours:** 11 am-10 pm. Closed major holidays. **Features:** On the surface, the eatery may look like another neighborhood bar. It is. However, the delightful surprise is that the food is taken as seriously as the drinks. While diners can get the standard sandwiches and chicken wings, fish tacos are done perfectly and buckets of shrimp, fish or chicken provide this place the reason for the name. Plasma TVs and outdoor seating are elements of the experience. Casual dress; cocktails. **Parking:** on-site. **Cards:** AX, MC, VI.

CAFE' BLUE
Continental

Dinner: $16-$32   Phone: 480/946-6555   68

Location: Just s of Camelback Rd. 4175 N Goldwater Blvd 85251. **Hours:** 5:30 pm-10 pm. Closed major holidays. **Reservations:** suggested. **Features:** The Old Town area eatery's soft blue lighting and upscale decor enhance dishes designed by chef/owner Jim Valli. Widely varied sauces enliven preparations of beef, seafood, lamb and poultry. Casual dress; cocktails. **Parking:** on-site. **Cards:** AX, DC, DS, MC, VI.

CARLOS O'BRIEN'S MEXICAN RESTAURANT
Mexican

Lunch: $6-$10   Dinner: $8-$15   Phone: 480/367-0469   10

Location: Just w of Scottsdale Rd. 7111 E Bell Rd 85254. **Hours:** 11 am-11 pm, Fri & Sat-midnight. Closed: 4/16, 11/23, 12/25. **Reservations:** accepted. **Features:** The family restaurant serves the classic favorites that most enjoy: fajitas, enchiladas and Spanish chicken. Attentive servers take guests through the meal, from chips and salsa to the sweet desserts, which are served in ample portions. Casual dress; cocktails. **Parking:** on-site. **Cards:** AX, DC, DS, MC, VI.

CARLSBAD TAVERN
Southwestern

Lunch: $8-$11   Dinner: $10-$20   Phone: 480/970-8164   75

Location: Just s of Osborn. 3313 N Hayden Rd 85251. **Hours:** 11 am-2 am, Sun from 1 pm. Closed: 4/16, 11/23, 12/24, 12/25. **Features:** There are no bats here, just great regional dishes served by helpful staff. A newspaper menu offers horoscopes and fun reading along with such choices as tequila shrimp and flan with prickly pear sauce. Casual dress; cocktails. **Parking:** on-site. **Cards:** AX, DS, MC, VI.

THE CHAPARRAL
American

Dinner: $21-$35   Phone: 480/948-1700   39

Location: 0.5 mi e of Tatum Blvd; north side of Lincoln Dr; in Camelback Inn, A JW Marriott Resort & Spa. 5402 E Lincoln Dr 85253. **Hours:** 6 pm-10 pm, Fri & Sat-11 pm. Closed: Mon & Tues. **Reservations:** suggested. **Features:** Dining in a relaxed but elegant setting. Enjoy innovative preparations of lobster as well as signature dishes of beef Wellington. Upscale coffee service is provided with whipped cream and chocolate. Dressy casual; cocktails; entertainment. **Parking:** on-site and valet. **Cards:** AX, CB, DC, DS, JC, MC, VI.

CHOLLA
Regional Steak & Seafood

Dinner: $23-$30   Phone: 480/850-7736   77

Location: SR 101, exit 50 (McKellips Rd), just ne; in Casino Arizona. 524 N 92nd St 85256. **Hours:** 5 pm-11 pm, Fri & Sat-midnight. Closed: 11/23, 12/25. **Reservations:** suggested. **Features:** This fine-dining establishment features well-prepared steak, seafood and specialty items. Worth mentioning are the fresh greens salad and knowledgeable service staff. Dressy casual; cocktails. **Parking:** on-site and valet. **Cards:** AX, DC, DS, MC, VI.

CLAIM JUMPER
International

Lunch: $10-$21   Dinner: $10-$21   Phone: 480/951-6111   22

Location: Just w of jct N Scottsdale Rd and E Shea Blvd; in Scottsdale Promenade. 7000 E Shea Blvd 85254. **Hours:** 11 am-10 pm, Fri & Sat-11 pm. Closed: 7/4, 11/23, 12/25. **Features:** The distinctive restaurant chain offers something for everyone. Entrees span the spectrum from Oriental to Italian to American cuisine. Sandwiches and salads are among lighter-fare choices. Come hungry because the portions are huge. To top off the meal, try a piece of home-baked pie or cake. The six-layer chocolate mother-lode cake is a meal in itself. Casual dress; cocktails. **Parking:** on-site. **Cards:** AX, DC, DS, MC, VI.

(See map and index starting on p. 266)

COWBOY CIAO RESTAURANT
Lunch: $7-$14   Dinner: $14-$32   Phone: 480/946-3111   (63)
American
Location: Just e of Scottsdale Rd; downtown. 7133 E Stetson Dr 85251. **Hours:** 11:30 am-2:30 & 5-10 pm, Fri & Sat-11 pm, Sun & Mon 5 pm-10 pm. **Closed:** 11/23, 12/25. **Reservations:** suggested. **Features:** Eclectic, artsy decor sets the stage for fun dining. Among "wine-friendly" dishes are peppercorn-seared sea bass with pan-fried penne and pig and pudding, a preparation of pulled pork in chipotle and balsamic barbecue sauce over chili grits. Try warm bread pudding or Mexican chocolate pot de creme for a satisfying meal-ender. Casual dress; cocktails. **Parking:** street. **Cards:** AX, CB, DC, DS, MC, VI.

THE COYOTE GRILL
Lunch: $5-$9   Dinner: $15-$25   Phone: 480/922-8424   (9)
Southwestern
Location: Just w of Scottsdale Rd. 7077 E Bell Rd 85254. **Hours:** 11 am-3 & 4-9 pm, Fri & Sat-10 pm. **Closed:** 11/23, 12/25. **Reservations:** suggested. **Features:** The contemporary eatery sports a copper and stone decor. Guests who unwind in the dining room or on the covered patio can sample innovative Southwestern-style dishes with a selection from an extensive inventory of tequilas. The friendly, well-trained staff is knowledgeable about such dishes as crispy crab cakes, the 20-ounce garlic porterhouse and chicken and asparagus fettuccine. Casual dress; cocktails; entertainment. **Parking:** on-site. **Cards:** AX, CB, DC, DS, JC, MC, VI.

DESEO
Dinner: $27-$40   Phone: 480/624-1000   (15)
Nouvelle Latino
Location: 0.5 mi w of Scottsdale Rd; in The Westin Kierland Resort & Spa. 6902 E Greenway Pkwy 85254. **Hours:** 6 pm-10 pm. **Closed:** 11/23; also Sun-Tues 6/1-9/15. **Reservations:** suggested. **Features:** With influences spanning the Caribbean and South America, Chef Rodriguez prepares a savory selection of ceviches, creative seafood entrees and Kobe beef. The open kitchen allows for interaction among diners and chefs. Dressy casual; cocktails. **Parking:** on-site and valet. **Cards:** AX, CB, DC, DS, JC, MC, VI.

DRIFT
Dinner: $7-$18   Phone: 480/949-8454   (61)
Polynesian
Location: Jct Scottsdale Rd, just e on Camelback Rd, then just s. 4341 N 75th St 85251. **Hours:** 5 pm-10 pm, Thurs-Sat to 11 pm. **Closed:** 11/23, 12/25, 12/26. **Features:** South Sea Islands decor is a draw for the young crowd. The trendy lounge serves an interesting fusion of foods, such as roasted pork loin with mango-chutney rice and noodle bowls savory with cilantro and Thai chili garlic shrimp. Casual dress; cocktails. **Parking:** street. **Cards:** AX, DS, MC, VI.

ELI'S AMERICAN GRILLE
Lunch: $7-$10   Dinner: $7-$30   Phone: 480/948-9800   (24)
American
Location: Jct Scottsdale Rd and E Shea Blvd, 2 blks w. 7000 E Shea Blvd 85254. **Hours:** 11 am-midnight, Fri & Sat-1 am. **Closed:** 11/23, 12/25. **Reservations:** not accepted. **Features:** Large portions of sandwiches, steaks, chicken and some seafood dishes are served in the restaurant, where viewing sports is a main attraction. Dressy casual; cocktails; entertainment. **Parking:** on-site and valet. **Cards:** AX, MC, VI.

EL TORITO GRILL
Lunch: $5-$12   Dinner: $7-$15   Phone: 480/948-8376   (45)
Regional Mexican
Location: Just s of Lincoln Ave. 6200 N Scottsdale Rd 85253. **Hours:** 11 am-10 pm, Fri & Sat-11 pm. **Closed:** 11/23, 12/25. **Reservations:** accepted. **Features:** Homemade Mexican favorites span from classic preparations to specialties from the country's central regions. Spicy taqueria-style tacos and carnitas michoacan (marinated pork) are tasty choices. Service is friendly and casual. Casual dress; cocktails. **Parking:** on-site. **Cards:** AX, MC, VI.

EURASIA BISTRO & BAR
Lunch: $7-$10   Dinner: $10-$24   Phone: 480/991-1571   (38)
Pacific Rim
Location: 1.5 mi e of Scottsdale Rd; in Scottsdale Resort & Athletic Club. 8225 E Indian Bend Rd 85250. **Hours:** 11 am-9 pm, Sat from 10:30 am, Sun 9:30 am-2 pm, Mon 5 pm-9 pm. **Closed:** 1/1, 11/23, 12/25. **Reservations:** accepted. **Features:** For a casual meal between tennis matches or an intimate dinner, the bistro offers upscale dishes with regional and Pacific Rim touches. Hearty soups, wrap sandwiches and grilled steaks are among choices. Casual dress; cocktails. **Parking:** on-site. **Cards:** AX, MC, VI.

FLEMING'S PRIME STEAKHOUSE & WINE BAR
Dinner: $19-$34   Phone: 480/596-8265   (41)
Steak House
Location: Just s of Lincoln Dr. 6333 N Scottsdale Rd 85250. **Hours:** 5 pm-10 pm, Fri & Sat 5:30 pm-10:30 pm. **Closed:** 11/23, 12/25. **Reservations:** suggested. **Features:** The warm, clubby atmosphere is the ideal setting for perfectly grilled steaks and seafood. Side dishes come in hearty portions, and salads are fresh and crisp. More than 100 wine selections are available. Casual dress; cocktails. **Parking:** on-site and valet. **Cards:** AX, DC, DS, MC, VI.

GARDUNO'S MARGARITA FACTORY
Lunch: $6-$10   Dinner: $10-$22   Phone: 480/607-9222   (31)
Mexican
Location: Just s of Doubletree Ranch Rd; n of McCormick Ranch Rd; in Shops of Gainey Village. 8787 N Scottsdale Rd 85251. **Hours:** 11 am-10 pm, Fri & Sat-11 pm, Sun 10:30 am-10 pm. **Closed:** 11/23, 12/25. **Reservations:** accepted. **Features:** A real tequila distillery is on display in the "new age" New Mexican restaurant. More than 350 varieties of margaritas are made from 160 tequilas. Fashioned after a 200-year-old hacienda, the festive, spaciously open dining room is a lively setting for a special occasion. Casual dress; cocktails; entertainment. **Parking:** on-site. **Cards:** AX, DC, DS, MC, VI.

THE GRILL
Lunch: $9-$12   Dinner: $24-$48   Phone: 480/585-4848   (5)
Steak & Seafood
Location: 0.6 mi n of Bell Rd, 0.5 mi e of Scottsdale Rd; on south side of Princess Dr; in The Fairmont Scottsdale Princess. 7575 E Princess Dr 85253. **Hours:** 6 am-9 pm, Fri & Sat-10 pm. **Closed:** for dinner Sun & Mon 7/5-9/4. **Reservations:** suggested. **Features:** Overlooking the TPC golf course at the Fairmont Princess, the upscale casual restaurant presents a menu of prime, dry-aged steaks and fresh seafood. The well-trained staff delivers attentive, expert service. Dressy casual; cocktails. **Parking:** on-site. **Cards:** AX, CB, DC, DS, JC, MC, VI.

(See map and index starting on p. 266)

HAVANA PATIO CAFE **Lunch:** $5-$8 **Dinner:** $10-$18 **Phone:** 480/991-1496 ⑧

Cuban

Location: 1 mi w of Scottsdale Rd. 6245 E Bell Rd 85254. **Hours:** 11 am-9:30 pm, Fri & Sat-10 pm, Sun 4 pm-9:30 pm. Closed major holidays. **Reservations:** accepted. **Features:** Fresh Latin flavors and elements from Cuba and Spain infuse palate-pleasing dishes. The garden atmosphere is delightfully casual. A gluten-free menu is available upon request. Casual dress; cocktails. **Parking:** on-site. **Cards:** AX, CB, DC, DS, JC, MC, VI.

IBIZA CAFE & WINE BAR **Lunch:** $8-$11 **Dinner:** $8-$16 **Phone:** 480/421-2492 (59)

American

Location: Just s of Camelback Rd. 4400 N Scottsdale Rd 85251. **Hours:** 11 am-2 & 4:30-11 pm. Closed: 1/1, 11/23, 12/25; also Sun. **Reservations:** accepted. **Features:** Casual decor, smiling service and delectable food in smaller tapas servings make the cafe an attractive option. Wine selections are extensive, and some nights bottles are half-price. Casual dress; cocktails. **Parking:** on-site. **Cards:** AX, DC, DS, MC, VI.

JADE PALACE CHINESE RESTAURANT **Lunch:** $5-$9 **Dinner:** $10-$22 **Phone:** 480/391-0607 ⑳

Chinese

Location: Shea Blvd, exit off SR 101, 0.4 mi e. 9160 E Shea Blvd 85260. **Hours:** 11 am-9:30 pm, Fri & Sat-10:30 pm. Closed: 7/4, 11/23. **Reservations:** accepted. **Features:** In a strip mall across from the hospital, the restaurant is a friendly place to dine. On the menu are traditional favorites, as well as specialty dinners and healthy choices. Reasonably priced lunches include soup, crab puff, spring roll and fried rice. Casual dress; cocktails. **Parking:** on-site. **Cards:** AX, CB, DC, DS, MC, VI.

KONA GRILL **Lunch:** $6-$12 **Dinner:** $9-$24 **Phone:** 480/429-1100 (53)

Pacific Rim

Location: Just w of Scottsdale Rd; in Scottsdale Fashion Square, ground level. 7014 E Camelback Rd 85251. **Hours:** 11 am-11 pm, Fri & Sat-midnight, Sun-9 pm. Closed: 11/23, 12/25. **Features:** The lively restaurant sits amid the shops of Scottsdale Fashion Square. The menu centers on Pacific Rim cuisine, and a sushi bar gazes right into a colorful built-in-the-wall fish tank. Some specialty items are Oriental salad, macadamia nut chicken and pan-seared ahi. Happy hour takes place in the second-floor lounge. Casual dress; cocktails. **Parking:** on-site. **Cards:** AX, DC, DS, MC, VI.

LA HACIENDA **Dinner:** $22-$36 **Phone:** 480/585-4848 ⑥

Traditional Mexican

Location: 0.6 mi n of Bell Rd, 0.5 mi e of Scottsdale Rd; on south side of Princess Dr; in The Fairmont Scottsdale Princess. 7575 E Princess Dr 85255. **Hours:** 6 pm-10 pm. Closed: Wed. **Reservations:** suggested. **Features:** In a 19th-century Mexican ranch house, the restaurant is on the grounds of the luxurious Fairmont Princess Resort. Sophisticated specialties include spit-roasted suckling pig, grilled seafood and seasonal preparations of beef and chicken. Strolling mariachis enhance the dining experience. Dressy casual; cocktails; entertainment. **Parking:** valet. **Cards:** AX, CB, DC, DS, JC, MC, VI.

LA MADELEINE FRENCH BAKERY **Lunch:** $4-$10 **Dinner:** $7-$13 **Phone:** 480/945-1663 (51)

French

Location: Loop 101, exit 46 (Chaparral Rd), 2.1 mi w to Scottsdale Rd, 0.5 mi s, then just w; in Scottsdale Fashion Square Mall. 7014 E Camelback Rd, Suite 562 85251. **Hours:** 8 am-9 pm, Fri & Sat-10 pm, Sun-7 pm. Closed: 1/1, 11/23, 12/25. **Features:** After a long day of shopping, the French bakery provides a perfect respite. Guests can peruse the pastry case at the entry to make a mental note for dessert then go through the line to choose from an array of soups, salads and quiches or have something created from the menu. Breakfast is served all day. Casual dress; beer & wine only. **Parking:** on-site. **Cards:** AX, DS, MC, VI.

LOS SOMBREROS **Dinner:** $9-$14 **Phone:** 480/994-1799 (76)

Mexican

Location: Just s of Thomas St. 2534 N Scottsdale Rd 85257. **Hours:** 5 pm-9 pm, Fri & Sat-10 pm. Closed major holidays; also Mon. **Reservations:** accepted. **Features:** This small, colorful Mexican restaurant specializes in authentic Mexican marketplace cuisine. Casual dress; cocktails. **Parking:** on-site. **Cards:** AX, DC, DS, MC, VI.

MACAYO'S MEXICAN KITCHEN **Lunch:** $6-$9 **Dinner:** $8-$14 **Phone:** 480/596-1181 ⑲

Mexican

Location: Just n of Shea Blvd. 11107 N Scottsdale Rd 85254. **Hours:** 11 am-11 pm, Fri & Sat-midnight. Closed: 11/23, 12/25. **Features:** The cheerful and bright Mexican decor welcomes you to try great chimichangas said to be invented by the owners. Other classic dishes are flavored with chilis grown on their own farm in southern Arizona. Casual dress; cocktails. **Parking:** on-site. **Cards:** AX, CB, DC, DS, JC, MC, VI.

MALEE'S THAI ON MAIN **Lunch:** $8-$12 **Dinner:** $11-$19 **Phone:** 480/947-6042 (71)

Regional Thai

Location: Just s of Indian School Rd, just w of Scottsdale Rd; on south side of Main St. 7131 E Main St 85251. **Hours:** 11:30 am-2:30 & 5-9:30 pm, Fri & Sat 5 pm-10 pm, Sun 5 pm-9 pm. Closed major holidays. **Reservations:** suggested. **Features:** The food at this casual, popular restaurant is a showcase for interesting combinations of flavors and sauces. Yum woon sen blends chicken, shrimp, cilantro and lime. In the heart of the Old Scottsdale art district, this place also offers patio seating, weather permitting. Casual dress; cocktails. **Parking:** street. **Cards:** AX, DC, MC, VI.

MANCUSO'S RESTAURANT **Dinner:** $20-$30 **Phone:** 480/948-9988 ㊼

Continental

Location: Just n of McDonald Dr; in Borgata Shopping Plaza. 6166 N Scottsdale Rd 85253. **Hours:** 5 pm-10 pm. Closed major holidays. **Reservations:** suggested. **Features:** Reminiscent of a medieval castle, the restaurant offers a romantic setting. The impeccable wait staff presents innovative Continental cuisine that reflects Italian and French influences. Dressy casual; cocktails. **Parking:** on-site. **Cards:** AX, DC, DS, MC, VI.

(See map and index starting on p. 266)

MARIA'S WHEN IN NAPLES

Italian

Dinner: $14-$27   **Phone:** 480/991-6887   (23)

Location: Just w of jct N Scottsdale Rd and E Shea Blvd; in Scottsdale Promenade. 7000 E Shea Blvd, Suite 1010 85254. **Hours:** 5 pm-close. Closed: 9/4, 11/23, 12/25; also Mon. **Reservations:** suggested. **Features:** An area fixture for 13 years, the restaurant specializes in Italian food, including such favorites as the bruschetta di salmone appetizer, several choices of pasta and a complete selection of dishes utilizing beef, chicken, seafood, veal and vegetables. This place is praised for its tiramisu, a great way to complete the meal. Casual dress; cocktails. **Parking:** on-site and valet. **Cards:** AX, DC, DS, MC, VI.

MARQUESA

Mediterranean

Dinner: $35-$46   **Phone:** 480/585-4848   (7)

Location: 0.6 mi n of Bell Rd, 0.5 mi e of Scottsdale Rd; on south side of Princess Dr; in The Fairmont Scottsdale Princess. 7575 E Princess Dr 85255. **Hours:** Open 2/1-6/25 & 9/22-1/31; 6 pm-10 pm; Sunday brunch 10:30 am-2:30 pm. Closed: Mon & Tues. **Reservations:** required. **Features:** Enjoy contemporary Mediterranean cuisine with a Catalan influence amid surrounding of casual elegance. Fine dining is offered both indoors and outdoors, weather permitting. Semi-formal attire; cocktails; entertainment. **Parking:** on-site and valet. **Cards:** AX, CB, DC, DS, JC, MC, VI.

MARY ELAINE'S

French

Dinner: $50-$60   **Phone:** 480/423-2444   (48)

Location: 0.5 mi w of 64th St; in The Phoenician. 6000 E Camelback Rd 85251. **Hours:** 6 pm-10 pm, Fri & Sat-11 pm. Closed: Sun & Mon. **Reservations:** suggested. **Features:** The professionally trained staff attends effortlessly to diners' every need. The focus is on first-class dining in classical elegance. Artistic presentations of creative and innovative courses use the freshest and finest of ingredients. Prix fixe and wine-pairing menus now are offered. Semi-formal attire; cocktails; entertainment. **Parking:** on-site and valet. **Cards:** AX, CB, DC, DS, JC, MC, VI.

MASTRO'S STEAKHOUSE

Steak House

Dinner: $22-$40   **Phone:** 480/585-9500   (3)

Location: Loop 101, exit 36 (Pima Rd), 3.7 mi n; in La Mirada Shopping Center. 8852 E Pinnacle Peak Rd 85260. **Hours:** 5 pm-10:30 pm, Fri & Sat-11 pm. Closed: 11/23, 12/25. **Reservations:** suggested. **Features:** For a purely sophisticated dining experience, it doesn't get much better than Mastro's. Perfect for special occasions, this is where the well-heeled go to see and be seen. Hand-cut USDA prime steaks are served by an attentive staff that anticipates every need. Live entertainment provides the willing an opportunity to dance. Dressy casual; cocktails; entertainment. **Parking:** on-site and valet. **Cards:** AX, DC, DS, MC, VI.

MEDIZONA

Southwestern

Dinner: $21-$29   **Phone:** 480/947-9500   (67)

Location: 2 blks n of Indian School Rd on Scottsdale Rd, just e; center. 7217 E 4th Ave 85251. **Hours:** 6 pm-10 pm. Closed major holidays; also Sun 6/1-9/1. **Reservations:** suggested. **Features:** A bistro setting with bright colors and eclectic details greet you as you enter an intimate room to indulge in a unique dining experience in which you may savor Mediterranean-influenced Southwestern dishes. Casual dress; cocktails. **Parking:** on-site. **Cards:** AX, DC, MC, VI.

MICHAEL'S AT THE CITADEL

American

Lunch: $8-$15   **Dinner:** $19-$29   **Phone:** 480/515-2575   (1)

Location: Loop 101, exit 36 (Pima Rd), 5 mi n to Pinnacle Peak Rd; northwest corner. 8700 E Pinnacle Peak Rd 85255. **Hours:** 11 am-2 & 6-10 pm, Sat from 6 pm, Sun from 10 am. Closed: 5/29, 9/4. **Reservations:** suggested. **Features:** The award-winning restaurant has a popular brunch and eclectic dinner menu with silver spoon appetizers and desserts. The atmosphere is comfortable and classy, with a fireplace inside and excellent sunset views outside. Service is professional and personalized. Dressy casual; cocktails. **Parking:** on-site. **Cards:** AX, CB, DC, DS, MC, VI.

MOSAIC

Continental

Dinner: $26-$38   **Phone:** 480/563-9600

Location: Loop 101, exit 36 (Pima Rd), 4.7 mi n, 2 mi e on Happy Valley Rd, then 1.3 mi n on Alma School Rd. 10600 E Jomax Rd 85255. **Hours:** 5:30 pm-9 pm, Fri & Sat-9:30 pm. Closed major holidays; also Sun & Mon. **Reservations:** suggested. **Features:** The chef-owner presents creative blends of fresh organic foods paired with imported seafood, specialty meats and vegetarian ingredients. Examples include seared California sculpin and mesquite-smoked tenderloin of beef. Dressy casual; cocktails. **Parking:** on-site. **Cards:** AX, CB, DC, DS, JC, MC, VI.

NELLIE CASHMAN'S MONDAY CLUB CAFE'

Nouvelle American

Lunch: $9-$14   **Dinner:** $17-$28   **Phone:** 480/624-1000   (14)

Location: 0.5 mi w of Scottsdale Rd; in The Westin Kierland Resort & Spa. 6902 E Greenway Pkwy 85254. **Hours:** 6 am-3 & 5-9 pm, Fri & Sat-10 pm. **Reservations:** accepted. **Features:** The namesake's history is worth reading at the comfortable cafe. Casually modern surroundings afford views to the courtyard, and artful dish presentations contribute to an enjoyable dining experience. Casual dress; cocktails. **Parking:** valet. **Cards:** AX, CB, DC, DS, JC, MC, VI.

NORTH

Nouvelle Italian

Lunch: $8-$13   **Dinner:** $11-$28   **Phone:** 480/948-2055   (12)

Location: Just w on Greenway Pkwy; in Kierland Commons Shopping Mall. 15024 N Scottsdale Rd #160 85254. **Hours:** 11 am-10 pm, Sun noon-9 pm. Closed: 1/1, 11/23, 12/25. **Reservations:** accepted. **Features:** In the trendy Kierland shopping district, the upscale, modern eatery delights palates with fresh, innovative, Italian-based creations. Wood-fired pizza is a nice beginning. Casual dress; cocktails. **Parking:** street. **Cards:** AX, CB, DC, DS, JC, MC, VI.

OLD TOWN TORTILLA FACTORY

Mexican

Dinner: $12-$36   **Phone:** 480/945-4567   (70)

Location: Just w of Goldwater Blvd. 6910 E Main St 85251. **Hours:** 5 pm-9 pm, Fri & Sat-10 pm. **Features:** Menu items range from traditional enchiladas and tamales to more refined steak and seafood dishes. This place prides itself on its varied margaritas and homemade tortillas. Casual dress; cocktails. **Parking:** on-site. **Cards:** AX, DS, MC, VI.

(See map and index starting on p. 266)

OREGANO'S PIZZA BISTRO
Pizza

Lunch: $6-$14   **Dinner:** $7-$22   **Phone:** 480/348-0500   27
Location: Just e of Scottsdale Rd. 7215 E Shea Blvd 85260. **Hours:** 11 am-9 pm, Fri & Sat-10 pm. Closed: 11/23, 12/25. **Features:** The high-energy eatery, with its young and attentive wait staff, serves hearty, oversized portions of delicious pizza, salads, pasta and "baked" sandwiches. The patio is the happening spot. Casual dress; wine only. **Parking:** on-site. **Cards:** AX, DC, DS, MC, VI.

THE OTHER PLACE
American

Dinner: $15-$30   **Phone:** 480/948-7910   40
Location: Just w of Scottsdale Rd. 7101 E Lincoln Dr 85253. **Hours:** 5 pm-9 pm, Fri & Sat-10 pm. **Reservations:** suggested. **Features:** Decorated in a Southwestern motif, the converted ranch house has offered guests a graceful dining experience for 35 years. The menu lists a nice selection of steak, prime rib cuts, chicken and some seafood. Casual dress; cocktails. **Parking:** on-site and valet. **Cards:** AX, DC, DS, MC, VI.

PALM COURT
American

Lunch: $8-$25   **Dinner:** $22-$34   **Phone:** 480/596-7700   33
Location: Just w of Hayden; just e of Scottsdale Rd; in Scottsdale Resort & Conference Center. 7700 E McCormick Pkwy 85258. **Hours:** 7 am-2 & 5-10 pm. **Reservations:** suggested. **Features:** The fine dining restaurant features a practiced staff that provides attentive, formal service. You'll find an eclectic selection of menu choices ranging from tableside-prepared salads to deftly prepared steaks. A perfect setting for a special occasion treat. Dressy casual; cocktails. **Parking:** on-site and valet. **Cards:** AX, CB, DC, DS, JC, MC, VI.

PANE E VINO
AAA
Italian

Dinner: $18-$32   **Phone:** 480/473-7900   4
Location: Loop 101, exit 36 (Pima Rd), 3.7 mi n; in La Mirada Shopping Center. 8900 E Pinnacle Peak Rd 85255. **Hours:** 5 pm-11 pm, Fri & Sat-midnight. Closed major holidays. **Reservations:** suggested. **Features:** Tucked in the interior of an upscale strip mall, the restaurant prepares classic Italian cuisine. Lending to the ambience are dim lighting, mirrors and art deco stylings. Entertainment in the adjoining lounge provides the opportunity for further nighttime enjoyment. Semi-formal attire; cocktails; entertainment. **Parking:** on-site. **Cards:** AX, DC, MC, VI.

PASTA BRIONI
Italian

Lunch: $9-$17   **Dinner:** $11-$65   **Phone:** 480/994-0028   57
Location: Just s of Indian School Rd. 4416 N Miller Rd 85251. **Hours:** 11 am-2 & 4-midnight, Sat & Sun from 4 pm. **Reservations:** suggested. **Features:** This small family restaurant features freshly made sandwiches, pizza and salads in a casual setting. Dressy casual; cocktails. **Parking:** on-site. **Cards:** AX, DC, DS, MC, VI.

P.F. CHANG'S CHINA BISTRO
Regional Chinese

Lunch: $6-$10   **Dinner:** $8-$18   **Phone:** 480/949-2610   52
Location: At Scottsdale Rd; in Scottsdale Fashion Square; ground level exterior entrance; south side of mall. 7014 E Camelback Rd 85251. **Hours:** 11 am-11 pm, Fri & Sat-midnight. Closed: 11/23, 12/25. **Reservations:** accepted. **Features:** A young, friendly staff serves an excellent variety of regional Chinese dishes in this busy, popular restaurant. Casual dress; cocktails. **Parking:** on-site. **Cards:** AX, DC, DS, MC, VI.

P.F. CHANG'S CHINA BISTRO AT KIERLAND COMMONS
Regional Chinese

Lunch: $6-$13   **Dinner:** $8-$18   **Phone:** 480/367-2999   13
Location: 1 mi s of Bell Rd at Scottsdale Rd. 7132 E Greenway Pkwy 85254. **Hours:** 11 am-11 pm, Fri & Sat-midnight. Closed: 11/23, 12/25. **Reservations:** accepted. **Features:** Upscale decor enhances the appeal of the relaxed dining room. Varied Chinese dishes are prepared and served by friendly, helpful staff members. Casual dress; cocktails. **Parking:** on-site. **Cards:** AX, DC, DS, MC, VI.

PINK PONY
Steak House

Lunch: $6-$10   **Dinner:** $10-$25   **Phone:** 480/945-6697   72
Location: Just s of Indian School Rd; center of Old Town. 3831 N Scottsdale Rd 85251. **Hours:** 11 am-3 & 5-10:30 pm, Sat & Sun from 5 pm. Closed: 7/4, 11/23, 12/25. **Reservations:** accepted. **Features:** The local institution has served its clientele for more than 50 years. The menu centers on grilled steaks and family-style dishes. Casual dress; cocktails. **Parking:** valet and street. **Cards:** AX, CB, DC, DS, JC, MC, VI.

PINON GRILL
Southwestern

Lunch: $9-$13   **Dinner:** $18-$26   **Phone:** 480/948-5050   34
Location: 0.8 mi n of Indian Bend Rd; in Millennium Resort Scottsdale, McCormick Ranch. 7401 N Scottsdale Rd 85253. **Hours:** 6 am-10 pm, Fri & Sat-11 pm. **Reservations:** suggested. **Features:** Two seating options are offered: the intimate dining room or the patio, which affords a view over the lake to the golf course. Distinctive Southwestern Rim preparations of chicken, seafood, veal, steak and wild game are accompanied by succulent vegetables and sauces. Dressy casual; cocktails. **Parking:** valet. **Cards:** AX, CB, DC, DS, JC, MC, VI.
(See color ad p 332)

THE QUILTED BEAR
American

Lunch: $5-$12   **Dinner:** $12-$25   **Phone:** 480/948-7760   42
Location: Southwest corner of Scottsdale Rd and Lincoln Dr; in Lincoln Plaza Shopping Center. 6316 N Scottsdale Rd 85253. **Hours:** 7 am-10 pm, Sun 8 am-9 pm. **Reservations:** accepted. **Features:** The familiar family restaurant serves a nice selection of salads, sandwiches and entrees. The garden atmosphere is cheerful and inviting. Casual dress; cocktails. **Parking:** on-site. **Cards:** AX, DC, DS, MC, VI.

RANCHO PINOT
American

Dinner: $18-$29   **Phone:** 480/367-8030   43
Location: Just s of Lincoln Dr; in Lincoln Plaza Shopping Center. 6208 N Scottsdale Rd 85253. **Hours:** 5:30 pm-10 pm; hours vary in summer. **Reservations:** suggested. **Features:** Taking advantage of seasonally fresh items, the menu changes frequently to bring diners an excellent variety of fresh meat, poultry and seafood. The high-energy dining room looks into the open kitchen, where chefs use mesquite-grill cooking for many dishes. Casual dress; cocktails. **Parking:** on-site. **Cards:** AX, DC, DS, MC, VI.

(See map and index starting on p. 266)

RA SUSHI BAR RESTAURANT   **Lunch:** $6-$10   **Dinner:** $11-$15   **Phone:** 480/990-9256   73
Location: Corner of 1st St; in historic downtown. 3815 N Scottsdale Rd 85251. **Hours:** 11 am-11 pm. Closed: 11/23, 12/25. **Reservations:** not accepted. **Features:** Fresh sushi creations are the specialty at the busy, bistro-style restaurant. Crunchy tempura is available for the less daring. Artful, tasty creations can be accented with seaweed, squid salad or rice. Casual dress; cocktails. **Parking:** on-site and valet. **Cards:** AX, DC, DS, MC, VI.

Sushi

REMINGTON'S   **Lunch:** $12-$18   **Dinner:** $19-$30   **Phone:** 480/951-5101   35
Location: Just n of Indian Bend Rd; in The Scottsdale Plaza Resort. 7200 N Scottsdale Rd 85253. **Hours:** 11 am-2 & 5-10 pm, Sat & Sun from 5 pm. **Reservations:** accepted. **Features:** New American cuisine—including mesquite-grilled chicken and braised veal osso buco—pairs with hearty classic vegetable accompaniments. The well-trained staff assists patrons through any celebration or casual dinner. The patio opens when the weather permits. Dressy casual; cocktails. **Parking:** on-site. **Cards:** AX, CB, DC, DS, JC, MC, VI.

American

RESTAURANT HAPA   **Dinner:** $18-$40   **Phone:** 480/998-8220   44
Location: Just n of McDonald Dr; in Lincoln Village Plaza. 6204 N Scottsdale Rd 85253. **Hours:** 5:30 pm-10 pm. Closed major holidays; also Sun. **Reservations:** suggested. **Features:** Creative dishes prepared by chef-owner James McDevitt tantalize guests of the intimate eatery, which is tucked in the back of a shopping plaza. Fresh ingredients, sauces with an Asian influence and fabulous desserts add up to a great dining experience. Casual dress; cocktails. **Parking:** on-site. **Cards:** AX, MC, VI.

American

ROARING FORK   **Dinner:** $16-$30   **Phone:** 480/947-0795   54
Location: Southwest corner of Chaparral and Scottsdale rds. 4800 N Scottsdale Rd 85251. **Hours:** 5 pm-9 pm, Fri & Sat-10 pm. Closed: 7/4, 11/23, 12/25. **Reservations:** suggested. **Features:** Known for the excellent quality of award-winning chef McGrath's food, the larger, upscale restaurant is ideal for any special occasion. Service is consistently friendly and accomplished, and such signature dishes as salmon cooked "campfire style" are good choices. Dressy casual; cocktails. **Parking:** on-site. **Cards:** AX, DC, DS, MC, VI.

West American

ROCK BOTTOM BREWERY & RESTAURANT   **Lunch:** $6-$10   **Dinner:** $9-$20   **Phone:** 480/998-7777   21
Location: Loop 101, exit Shea Blvd, just w. 8668 E Shea Blvd 85260. **Hours:** 11 am-1 am. Closed: 12/25. **Reservations:** accepted. **Features:** Guests can check out the "birthdays" of the microbrews and then enjoy any of a number of snacks and other heartier offerings. Chili is "awesome," and mile-high carrot cake is scrumptious. Casual dress; cocktails. **Parking:** on-site. **Cards:** AX, DC, DS, MC, VI.

American

ROY'S SCOTTSDALE   **Dinner:** $17-$29   **Phone:** 480/905-1155   36
Location: At Indian Bend Rd; in Scottsdale Shopping Center. 7001 N Scottsdale Rd 85253. **Hours:** 5 pm-10 pm, Sun-9 pm. Closed: 7/4, 11/23, 12/25. **Reservations:** suggested. **Features:** Enjoy fusion of fresh Pacific seafood, French sauces and Asian seasonings. The ever-changing menu has many entrees, grilled salmon, barbecue lamb rack and signature dessert, chocolate souffle. Casual dress; cocktails. **Parking:** on-site. **Cards:** AX, DC, DS, MC, VI.

Pacific Rim

RUTH'S CHRIS STEAK HOUSE   **Dinner:** $21-$38   **Phone:** 480/991-5988   37
Location: Northeast corner of jct Scottsdale and Indian Bend rds; in Seville Strip Center. 7001 N Scottsdale Rd 85253. **Hours:** 5 pm-10 pm, Fri & Sat-10:30 pm, Sun 4 pm-9:30 pm. Closed: 11/23, 12/25. **Reservations:** suggested. **Features:** The main fare is steak, which is prepared from several cuts of prime beef and cooked to perfection, but the menu also lists lamb, chicken and seafood dishes. Guests should come hungry because the side dishes, which are among the a la carte offerings, could be a meal by themselves. Upscale atmosphere and subdued lighting enhance special occasions or romantic evenings on the town. Dressy casual; cocktails. **Parking:** on-site. **Cards:** AX, DC, DS, MC, VI.

Steak House

THE SALT CELLAR RESTAURANT   *Menu on aaa.com*   **Dinner:** $24-$30   **Phone:** 480/947-1963   78
Location: McDowell Rd, just s. 550 N Hayden Rd 85257. **Hours:** 5 pm-11 pm, Fri & Sat-midnight. Closed: 12/25. **Reservations:** suggested. **Features:** The popular, underground cellar restaurant carries a large selection of fish and shellfish, as well as the "turf" to accompany it. Casual dress; cocktails. **Parking:** on-site. **Cards:** AX, MC, VI.

Seafood

SANDOLO RISTORANTE   **Dinner:** $12-$24   **Phone:** 480/991-3388   29
Location: Loop 101, exit 43, 2.6 mi w on Via de Ventura; in Hyatt Regency Scottsdale Resort at Gainey Ranch. 7500 E Doubletree Ranch Rd 85258. **Hours:** 5:30 pm-10:30 pm. Closed: 11/23, 12/25. **Reservations:** suggested. **Features:** The Italian restaurant adds special features, such as singing servers and a complimentary gondola ride after dinner. Among well-prepared entrees are osso buco, veal scaloppine, mushroom-stuffed ravioli and sauteed shrimp in pasta. Dressy casual; cocktails; entertainment. **Parking:** on-site and valet. **Cards:** AX, CB, DC, DS, MC, VI.

Italian

SAPPORO   **Dinner:** $15-$45   **Phone:** 480/607-1114   18
Location: Just n of Thunderbird Rd. 14344 N Scottsdale Rd 85254. **Hours:** 4 pm-10 pm, Fri & Sat-11 pm. Closed: 11/23, 12/25. **Reservations:** suggested. **Features:** Seated amid a trendy decor with waterfalls and jellyfish tanks, patrons can indulge their whims for sushi and Pacific Rim foods. The knowledgeable wait staff provides guidance through a large selection of fish and Kobe beef. Casual dress; cocktails. **Parking:** on-site. **Cards:** AX, DC, DS, MC, VI.

Japanese

(See map and index starting on p. 266)

SEA SAW   **Dinner:** $11-$22   **Phone:** 480/481-9463   65
▼▼▼▼
Nouvelle
Japanese
Location: Just w of Scottsdale Rd; center. 7133 E Stetson Dr 85251. **Hours:** 5:30 pm-10 pm, Fri & Sat-11 pm. Closed: 11/23, 12/25. **Reservations:** suggested. **Features:** Chef Fukuda introduces something new with "izakaya," wine-friendly, Japanese-style tapas. Called "tapanese," the flavorful dishes include such choices as seared tuna with roasted beet puree. To enjoy the separate tasting menu, reservations are required. This unusual, high-energy place is not the normal idea of a restaurant. Casual dress; cocktails. **Parking:** street.
Cards: AX, DC, DS, MC, VI.

SUEDE   **Dinner:** $14-$24   **Phone:** 480/970-6969   55
▼▼▼▼
American
Location: From Scottsdale Rd, just e on Camelback Rd to Buckboard, just s, then just e. 7333 E Indian Plaza 85251. **Hours:** 5 pm-midnight, Sat 7 pm-1 am, Sun 9 pm-1 am. Closed: 11/23, 12/25, 12/26; also Mon. **Reservations:** accepted. **Features:** The trendy lounge and restaurant has a distinctive high-tech decor and serves great food with a fusion flair. Often a starting point for crowds headed to surrounding nightclubs, the eatery employs friendly servers and offers live entertainment. Casual dress; cocktails; entertainment. **Parking:** street.
Cards: AX, MC, VI.

SUSHI ON SHEA   **Lunch:** $9-$14   **Dinner:** $9-$28   **Phone:** 480/483-7799   25
▼▼▼ ▼▼▼
Japanese
Location: Just w of Scottsdale Rd. 7000 E Shea Blvd, #1510 85254. **Hours:** 11 am-2 & 5-10 pm, Fri & Sat-11 pm, Sun & Mon 5 pm-10 pm. Closed: 11/23, 12/24, 12/25. **Reservations:** accepted. **Features:** The casually elegant decor includes two saltwater aquariums and an expansive sushi bar. Patrons can enjoy fresh sushi, tempura, noodles and specialty dishes, such as chicken katsu or sesame-crusted salmon. Casual dress; cocktails. **Parking:** on-site. **Cards:** AX, DC, DS, JC, MC, VI.

TEQUILA GRILL   **Lunch:** $12-$29   **Dinner:** $12-$29   **Phone:** 480/941-1800   58
▼▼▼ ▼▼▼
Southwestern
Location: Just e of Camelback and N Scottsdale rds to 75th St, then just s. 4363 N 75th St 85251. **Hours:** 11 am-10 pm, Fri-11 pm, Sat 5 pm-11 pm, Mon 4 pm-10 pm. Closed major holidays; also Sun. **Reservations:** accepted. **Features:** The grill offers an "eclectic tour" with its distinctive architecture and Southwestern fusion menu. Entrees range from quesadillas to pizza and pasta, with an array of chef's specialties also available. A torch-lit patio welcomes those who wish to dine outdoors. Casual dress; cocktails. **Parking:** on-site.
Cards: AX, DC, DS, MC, VI.

⟁ ⟍

THE TERRACE DINING ROOM   **Lunch:** $12-$20   **Dinner:** $22-$40   **Phone:** 480/423-2530   50
ⒶⒶⒶ
▼▼▼ ▼▼▼
Steak & Seafood
Location: 0.5 mi w of 64th St; in The Phoenician. 6000 E Camelback Rd 85251. **Hours:** 6 am-10 pm. **Reservations:** suggested. **Features:** Specialty foods prepared with an Italian flair include seafood choices from around the world, as well as pasta, lamb, steak, rich soups and salads, such as one with wild greens. Live entertainment enhances the Sunday brunch. The elegant dining area incorporates indoor and covered patio seating. Dressy casual; cocktails; entertainment. **Parking:** on-site and valet. **Cards:** AX, CB, DC, DS, JC, MC, VI.

⟁M ⟁

THAIFOON   **Lunch:** $8-$14   **Dinner:** $8-$17   **Phone:** 480/998-0011   32
▼▼▼
Asian
Location: Just s of Doubletree Ranch Rd; in Shops at Gainey Village. 8777 N Scottsdale Rd 85253. **Hours:** 11 am-10 pm. Closed: 11/23, 12/25. **Reservations:** accepted. **Features:** Thai/Asian cuisine with fresh, exotic ingredients is a healthy dining alternative. Among favorites are lemon grass chicken satay and sizzling beef. Creative salad choices and wok items can be shared, so bring a friend. Dressy casual; cocktails. **Parking:** on-site. **Cards:** AX, DS, MC, VI.

⟁

THAI PAN   **Lunch:** $6-$9   **Dinner:** $8-$12   **Phone:** 480/513-7471   2
▼▼▼ ▼▼
Regional Thai
Location: Just e of Scottsdale Rd. 7605 Pinnacle Peak Rd, Suite 2 85255. **Hours:** 11 am-8 pm, Fri & Sat-10 pm. Closed: Sun. **Features:** Orders are taken at the counter of the modern and trendy restaurant and prepared fresh to diners' specifications. Hot sauces in three degrees of spiciness are at each table. Casual dress; beer & wine only. **Parking:** on-site. **Cards:** AX, DS, MC, VI.

THAI THAI RESTAURANT   **Lunch:** $8-$14   **Dinner:** $9-$15   **Phone:** 480/778-9901   46
ⒶⒶⒶ
▼▼▼
Thai
Location: Just n of McDonald Dr; in the Borgata Shopping Plaza. 6166 N Scottsdale Rd 85253. **Hours:** 11 am-3 & 5-9:30 pm, Fri & Sat 11:30 am-10 pm, Sun noon-9 pm; hours may vary in summer. Closed: 11/23, 12/25. **Reservations:** accepted. **Features:** Chef Chai uses only fresh herbs and choice vegetables to complement such dishes as Thai beef salad, coconut shrimp and lemon grass with eggplant. He and his wife Phen treat patrons to a relaxed and delectable dining experience. Casual dress; cocktails. **Parking:** on-site. **Cards:** MC, VI.

TWISTED VINE   **Lunch:** $5-$8   **Phone:** 480/663-7873   74
▼▼▼
American
Location: Just s of Osborn Rd. 3360 N Hayden Rd #116 85251. **Hours:** 10 am-2:30 pm; hours may vary. Closed major holidays; also Sat & Sun. **Reservations:** accepted. **Features:** The delicatessen is good for take-out, but dining in with the friendly staff makes for a pleasant stop. Salads and made-to-order sandwiches taste fresh, and homemade desserts are not to be missed. Patio tables are available. Casual dress. **Parking:** on-site. **Cards:** AX, DS, MC, VI.

VU   **Dinner:** $27-$38   **Phone:** 480/991-3388   28
▼▼▼ ▼▼▼
American
Location: Loop 101, exit 43, 2.6 mi w on Via de Ventura; in Hyatt Regency Scottsdale Resort at Gainey Ranch. 7500 E Doubletree Ranch Rd 85258. **Hours:** 5:30 pm-10:30 pm, Fri & Sat-11 pm. **Reservations:** accepted. **Features:** The room is warm and elegant and the service is smooth and polished, but it is Chef Bradley's food that deserves the attention. Contemporary steaks and seafood are his mild way to speak of explosive flavors and combinations that delight the palate. Kobe short ribs with cornichons, horseradish and sea salt melt in your mouth. Salmon, John Dory and black bass may be on a given menu, all with sauces to tempt you. Dressy casual; cocktails. **Parking:** on-site and valet. **Cards:** AX, CB, DC, DS, JC, MC, VI.

⟁

WINDOWS ON THE GREEN   **Dinner:** $20-$32   **Phone:** 480/423-2530   49
▼▼▼
Southwestern
Location: 0.5 mi w of 64th St; in The Phoenician. 6000 E Camelback Rd 85251. **Hours:** 5 pm-10 pm. Closed: Tues & Wed. **Reservations:** suggested. **Features:** In addition to the sweeping view of the golf course, patrons should be prepared to savor innovative food preparations that employ many Southwestern-inspired accompaniments. The menu changes seasonally, and patio seating is an option. Casual dress; cocktails. **Parking:** on-site. **Cards:** AX, CB, DC, DS, JC, MC, VI.

⟁

(See map and index starting on p. 266)

ZINC BISTRO
▼▼▼
French

Lunch: $17-$29   **Dinner:** $17-$29   **Phone:** 480/603-0922   (17)
Location: Just w of jct N Scottsdale Rd and Greenway-Hayden Loop; in Kierland Mall. 15034 N Scottsdale Rd, Suite 140 85254. **Hours:** 11 am-10 pm, Fri & Sat-midnight. Closed: 11/23, 12/25. **Features:** In Kierland Commons Shopping Mall on the north side, the French bistro prepares steak, roasted pork, lamb, chicken, seafood and some pasta dishes. A nice selection of salads and sandwiches appeals to those who want a lighter meal. Casual dress; cocktails. **Parking:** street. **Cards:** AX, DC, MC, VI.   ⓨ

The following restaurants have not been evaluated by AAA but are listed for your information only.

DU JOUR RESTAURANT   **Phone:** 480/603-1066
[fyi]   Not evaluated. **Location:** Jct Shea Blvd, just s on 116th St. 10585 N 114th St 85251. **Features:** The on-campus training facility for students of the Arizona Culinary Institute, the dining room overlooks the bakery kitchen where mouthwatering goodies are prepared.

L'ACADEMIE CAFE   **Phone:** 480/425-3111
[fyi]   Not evaluated. **Location:** On the east side of Scottsdale Rd, at 5th Ave; in the Galleria. 4301 N Scottsdale Rd 85250. **Features:** Prior to graduation, Scottsdale Culinary Institute's students put their talents to the test here. The friendly and accomplished staff offers guests a selection of sophisticated sandwiches and entrees, as well as pastry delights.

L'ECOLE RESTAURANT   **Phone:** 480/425-3111
[fyi]   Not evaluated. **Location:** Just e of Hayden Rd. 8100 E Camelback Rd 85251. **Features:** Diners can sample prix fixe lunches and sophisticated entrees at the original Scottsdale Culinary Institute student kitchen. The student staff is trained and affable.

SURPRISE pop. 30,848   (See map and index starting on p. 264)

—— WHERE TO STAY ——

DAYS INN & SUITES   *Book at aaa.com*   **Phone:** (623)933-4000   ❶
▼▼▼▼
Small-scale Hotel

	1P: $85-$175	2P: $85-$175	XP: $10	F17
2/1-4/30 [CP]				
9/16-1/31 [CP]	1P: $70-$165	2P: $70-$165	XP: $10	F17
5/1-9/15 [CP]	1P: $60-$155	2P: $60-$155	XP: $10	F17

Location: US 60 (Grand Ave), 1.1 mi e, then just s on Greasewood St. 12477 W Bell Rd 85374. Fax: 623/933-4003. **Facility:** 60 units. 43 one-bedroom standard units, some with whirlpools. 17 one-bedroom suites. 3 stories, interior corridors. *Bath:* combo or shower only. **Parking:** on-site. **Terms:** small pets only ($10 fee). **Amenities:** video library (fee), irons, hair dryers. **Pool(s):** heated outdoor. **Leisure Activities:** whirlpool. **Guest Services:** coin laundry. **Business Services:** fax (fee). **Cards:** AX, DS, MC, VI.

SOME UNITS
(ASK) (SD) 🛏 🍴 (⛬) 🏊 📷 (DATA PORT) 🔒 🖥 / ✕ (VCR) 🖨 /
        FEE   FEE

QUALITY INN & SUITES   *Book at aaa.com*   **Phone:** (623)583-3500   ❸
▼▼
Small-scale Hotel

	1P: $79-$129	2P: $79-$129	XP: $10	F
2/1-4/15 & 10/1-1/31				
4/16-5/31	1P: $55-$99	2P: $55-$99	XP: $10	F
6/1-9/30	1P: $50-$95	2P: $50-$95	XP: $10	F

Location: US 60 (Grand Ave), 1.1 mi e on Bell Rd, then just s. 16741 N Greasewood St 85374. Fax: 623/583-4356. **Facility:** Designated smoking area. 69 units. 67 one-bedroom standard units. 2 one-bedroom suites ($99-$159). 3 stories, interior corridors. *Bath:* combo or shower only. **Parking:** on-site. **Terms:** [BP] meal plan available, package plans. **Amenities:** voice mail, irons, hair dryers. *Fee:* high-speed Internet, safes. **Pool(s):** heated indoor. **Leisure Activities:** whirlpool, limited exercise equipment. **Guest Services:** coin laundry. **Business Services:** meeting rooms, fax (fee). **Cards:** AX, DC, DS, MC, VI.

SOME UNITS
(ASK) (SD) 🍴 (⛬) 🏊 ✕ 🎣 (DATA PORT) 🖥 / 🔒 🖨 /

WINDMILL SUITES AT SUN CITY WEST   *Book at aaa.com*   **Phone:** 623/583-0133   ❷
(AAA) (SAVE)
▼▼▼▼
Small-scale Hotel

	1P: $115-$157		XP: $10	F18
2/1-3/31 [CP]				
10/1-1/31 [CP]	1P: $85-$149		XP: $10	F18
4/1-4/30 [CP]	1P: $95-$110		XP: $10	F18
5/1-9/30 [CP]	1P: $76-$89		XP: $10	F18

Location: US 60 (Grand Ave), 1 mi e. 12545 W Bell Rd 85374. Fax: 623/583-8366. **Facility:** Smoke free premises. 127 one-bedroom suites. 3 stories, interior corridors. *Bath:* combo or shower only. **Parking:** on-site. **Terms:** check-in 4 pm, cancellation fee imposed, package plans, small pets only. **Amenities:** high-speed Internet, voice mail, irons, hair dryers. **Pool(s):** heated outdoor. **Leisure Activities:** whirlpool, lending library, bicycles, limited exercise equipment. **Guest Services:** valet and coin laundry. **Business Services:** meeting rooms, PC, fax (fee). **Cards:** AX, DC, DS, MC, VI. **Special Amenities:** free expanded continental breakfast and free local telephone calls.

SOME UNITS
(SD) 🛏 🍴 (⛬) 🍽 🏊 ✕ ✕ 🎣 (DATA PORT) 🔒 🖨 / (VCR) /

—— WHERE TO DINE ——

DESERT PALMS RESTAURANT
▼▼▼
American

Lunch: $4-$8   **Dinner:** $5-$14   **Phone:** 623/583-8740   (5)
Location: Jct US 60 (Grand Ave), 1.2 mi e. 12425 W Bell Rd 85374. **Hours:** 6 am-9 pm. Closed major holidays. **Features:** From breakfast to dinner, the friendly staff offer smiles and pleasant service in the casual and popular eatery. Angus beef and broasted chicken are featured items. Casual dress; wine only. **Parking:** on-site. **Cards:** DS, MC, VI.

DILLON'S GRAND
▼▼ ▼▼
American

Lunch: $7-$11   **Dinner:** $7-$18   **Phone:** 623/584-8494   (4)
Location: Jct Bell Rd, 3 mi nw on Grande Ave, 1 mi sw on Sunrise, then 0.4 mi nw. 19900 N Remington Dr 85374. **Hours:** 11 am-9 pm, Sat & Sun from 7 am. Closed: 12/25. **Features:** The barbecue is popular with local folks. Friendly, young servers bring out a selection of grilled meat, poultry and fish dishes, along with hearty desserts of a size to share. The attractive dining room overlooks a golf course and pools with waterfalls. Casual dress; cocktails. **Parking:** on-site. **Cards:** AX, DS, MC, VI.   ⓨ

TEMPE pop. 158,625   (See map and index starting on p. 271)

—————— **WHERE TO STAY** ——————

AMERISUITES (TEMPE/ARIZONA MILLS)   *Book at aaa.com*   **Phone:** (480)831-9800   **36**

AAA SAVE	9/16-1/31	1P: $79-$179	2P: $79-$179	XP: $10	F18
	2/1-4/15	1P: $129-$169	2P: $129-$169	XP: $10	F18
	4/16-5/31	1P: $109-$129	2P: $109-$129	XP: $10	F18
	6/1-9/15	1P: $69-$99	2P: $69-$99	XP: $10	F18

Small-scale Hotel **Location:** I-10, exit 155 (Baseline Rd), 0.4 mi e. Located adjacent to Arizona Mills Mall Outlet Center. 1520 W Baseline Rd 85283. Fax: 480/831-9292. **Facility:** 128 one-bedroom standard units. 6 stories, interior corridors. *Bath:* combo or shower only. **Parking:** on-site. **Terms:** cancellation fee imposed, pets ($10 extra charge). **Amenities:** video games (fee), high-speed Internet, voice mail, irons, hair dryers. *Some:* dual phone lines. **Pool(s):** small heated outdoor. **Leisure Activities:** exercise room. **Guest Services:** coin laundry, area transportation-within 5 mi. **Business Services:** meeting rooms, business center. **Cards:** AX, CB, DC, DS, MC, VI. **Special Amenities:** free full breakfast.

SOME UNITS

(See map and index starting on p. 271)

AMERISUITES (TEMPE/PHOENIX AIRPORT)

AAA (SAVE)
▼▼▼▼▼▼

Book at aaa.com

Phone: (480)804-9544   **14**

9/11-1/31 [ECP]	1P: $109-$189	2P: $109-$189	XP: $10	F18
2/1-4/13 [ECP]	1P: $139-$169	2P: $139-$169	XP: $10	F18
4/14-5/18 [ECP]	1P: $109-$139	2P: $109-$139	XP: $10	F18
5/19-9/10 [ECP]	1P: $79-$109	2P: $79-$109	XP: $10	F18

Small-scale Hotel Location: Just w of Priest Dr. 1413 W Rio Salado Pkwy 85281. Fax: 480/804-9548. **Facility:** 125 one-bedroom standard units. 6 stories, interior corridors. *Bath:* combo or shower only. **Parking:** on-site. **Terms:** pets ($10 extra charge). **Amenities:** high-speed Internet, dual phone lines, voice mail, irons, hair dryers. *Fee:* video games, safes. **Pool(s):** heated outdoor. **Leisure Activities:** exercise room. **Guest Services:** valet and coin laundry, area transportation-within 5 mi. **Business Services:** meeting rooms, fax (fee). **Cards:** AX, DC, DS, MC, VI. **Special Amenities:** free full breakfast.

SOME UNITS
[icons] FEE

BEST WESTERN INN OF TEMPE

AAA (SAVE)
▼▼▼▼▼▼

Book at aaa.com

Phone: (480)784-2233   **12**

2/1-4/15 [CP]	1P: $99-$129	2P: $99-$129	XP: $5	F17
1/1-1/31 [CP]	1P: $99-$119	2P: $99-$119	XP: $5	F17
9/1-12/31 [CP]	1P: $89-$99	2P: $89-$99	XP: $5	F17
4/16-8/31 [CP]	1P: $69-$79	2P: $69-$79	XP: $5	F17

Small-scale Hotel Location: SR 202 Loop (Red Mountain Frwy), exit 7, just s. 670 N Scottsdale Rd 85281. Fax: 480/784-2299. **Facility:** 103 one-bedroom standard units, some with whirlpools. 4 stories, interior corridors. *Bath:* combo or shower only. **Parking:** on-site. **Terms:** 15 day cancellation notice, small pets only ($20 deposit, in smoking units). **Amenities:** voice mail, irons, hair dryers. *Some:* high-speed Internet. **Pool(s):** lap. **Leisure Activities:** whirlpools, exercise room. **Guest Services:** valet laundry, area transportation (fee)-within 5 mi. **Business Services:** meeting rooms, fax (fee). **Cards:** AX, CB, DC, DS, JC, MC, VI. **Special Amenities:** free continental breakfast and free local telephone calls.

SOME UNITS
[icons] FEE   FEE FEE

CANDLEWOOD SUITES

▼▼▼▼▼

Book at aaa.com

Phone: (480)777-0440   **39**

2/1-4/30	1P: $86-$120	2P: $86-$120
5/1-5/31 & 9/11-1/31	1P: $66-$100	2P: $66-$100
6/1-9/10	1P: $46-$70	2P: $46-$70

Small-scale Hotel Location: I-10, exit 155 (Baseline Rd), 0.5 mi e; just e of Priest Dr. 1335 W Baseline Rd 85283. Fax: 480/777-5858. **Facility:** 122 units. 98 one-bedroom standard units with efficiencies. 24 one-bedroom suites with efficiencies. 3 stories, interior corridors. *Bath:* combo or shower only. **Parking:** on-site. **Terms:** office hours 7 am-11 pm, weekly rates available, small pets only ($75-$150 fee). **Amenities:** video library, CD players, dual phone lines, voice mail, irons, hair dryers. **Pool(s):** heated outdoor. **Leisure Activities:** whirlpool, exercise room. **Guest Services:** sundries, complimentary and valet laundry. **Business Services:** fax. **Cards:** AX, CB, DC, DS, JC, MC, VI.

SOME UNITS
[icons] FEE

COMFORT INN & SUITES TEMPE/ASU

AAA (SAVE)
▼▼▼▼▼▼

Book at aaa.com

Phone: (480)966-7202   **23**

2/1-4/15 & 9/1-1/31	1P: $69-$129	2P: $69-$129	XP: $5	F18
4/16-5/31	1P: $69-$109	2P: $69-$109	XP: $5	F18
6/1-8/31	1P: $49-$69	2P: $49-$69	XP: $5	F18

Location: SR 202 Loop (Red Mountain Frwy), exit 7 (Rural Rd S), 1.5 mi s, then just e. 1031 E Apache Blvd 85281. **Small-scale Hotel** Fax: 480/829-9340. **Facility:** 72 units. 71 one-bedroom standard units, some with whirlpools. 1 one-bedroom suite. 3 stories, interior corridors. *Bath:* combo or shower only. **Parking:** on-site. **Terms:** cancellation fee imposed, small pets only ($50 deposit). **Amenities:** voice mail, irons, hair dryers. *Some:* high-speed Internet. **Pool(s):** small heated outdoor. **Leisure Activities:** sauna, whirlpool, exercise room. **Guest Services:** valet and coin laundry. **Business Services:** meeting rooms, business center. **Cards:** AX, CB, DC, DS, JC, MC, VI. **Special Amenities: free continental breakfast and free local telephone calls.** *(See color ad p 356)*

SOME UNITS
[icons] FEE

COMFORT SUITES AIRPORT

▼▼▼ ▼▼▼

Book at aaa.com

Phone: (480)446-9500   **29**

2/1-4/30 & 12/31-1/31 [ECP]	1P: $99-$149	2P: $109-$159	XP: $10	F17
10/1-12/30 [ECP]	1P: $89-$119	2P: $99-$129	XP: $10	F17
5/1-9/30 [ECP]	1P: $69-$109	2P: $79-$119	XP: $10	F17

Small-scale Hotel Location: I-10, exit 153B (Broadway Rd). 1625 S 52nd St 85281. Fax: 480/446-8080. **Facility:** 92 one-bedroom standard units, some with whirlpools. 3 stories, interior corridors. *Bath:* combo or shower only. **Parking:** on-site. **Amenities:** high-speed Internet, voice mail, irons, hair dryers. *Some:* safes. **Pool(s):** heated outdoor. **Leisure Activities:** whirlpool, exercise room. **Guest Services:** valet and coin laundry. **Business Services:** fax (fee). **Cards:** AX, CB, DC, DS, JC, MC, VI.

SOME UNITS
[icons]

COUNTRY INN & SUITES BY CARLSON

▼▼▼▼▼

Book at aaa.com

Phone: (480)858-9898   **11**

2/1-4/15 [CP]	1P: $129-$159	2P: $129-$159	XP: $10	F18
4/16-5/31 [CP]	1P: $109-$139	2P: $109-$139	XP: $10	F18
9/1-1/31 [CP]	1P: $99-$119	2P: $99-$119	XP: $10	F18
6/1-8/31 [CP]	1P: $89-$109	2P: $89-$109	XP: $10	F18

Small-scale Hotel Location: SR 202 Loop (Red Mountain Frwy), exit 7, just n. 808 N Scottsdale Rd 85281. Fax: 480/784-2246. **Facility:** 83 units. 68 one-bedroom standard units, some with whirlpools. 15 one-bedroom suites ($89-$139). 4 stories, interior corridors. *Bath:* combo or shower only. **Parking:** on-site. **Terms:** cancellation fee imposed. **Amenities:** dual phone lines, voice mail, irons, hair dryers. *Fee:* video games, high-speed Internet. **Pool(s):** heated outdoor. **Leisure Activities:** whirlpool, exercise room. **Guest Services:** valet and coin laundry, area transportation. **Business Services:** meeting rooms, fax (fee). **Cards:** AX, DC, DS, MC, VI.

SOME UNITS
[icons] FEE FEE

(See map and index starting on p. 271)

COUNTRY INN & SUITES BY CARLSON   *Book at aaa.com*   Phone: (480)345-8585   **42**

2/1-3/31 [ECP]	1P: $99-$110	2P: $99-$110	XP: $10 F18
4/1-5/31 & 9/16-1/31 [ECP]	1P: $90-$100	2P: $90-$100	XP: $10 F18
6/1-9/15 [ECP]	1P: $72-$90	2P: $72-$90	XP: $10 F18

Small-scale Hotel   **Location:** I-10, exit 157, just e. 1660 W Elliot Rd 85283. Fax: 480/345-7461. **Facility:** 139 units. 71 one-bedroom standard units. 68 one-bedroom suites ($81-$117), some with efficiencies. 3 stories, exterior corridors. **Parking:** on-site. **Terms:** pets ($50 deposit). **Amenities:** video games (fee), voice mail, irons, hair dryers. *Some:* dual phone lines. **Pool(s):** heated outdoor, wading. **Leisure Activities:** whirlpool. **Guest Services:** complimentary evening beverages: Mon-Thurs, valet and coin laundry, area transportation. **Business Services:** meeting rooms, fax (fee). **Cards:** AX, DC, DS, MC, VI.

SOME UNITS
(ASK) 🛡 ➡️ 🛏 🍴 📷 🏊 💪 🎦 DATA PORT 🔲 🖥 🔲 /✕/
FEE

COURTYARD BY MARRIOTT-DOWNTOWN TEMPE   *Book at aaa.com*   Phone: (480)966-2800   **16**

2/1-4/30	1P: $119-$208	2P: $119-$208
5/1-5/28	1P: $109-$180	2P: $109-$180
9/10-1/31	1P: $109-$161	2P: $109-$161
5/29-9/9	1P: $79-$113	2P: $79-$113

Small-scale Hotel

Location: SR 143 (Hohokam Expwy), exit University Dr, 2.2 mi e, then 0.3 mi n. 601 S Ash Ave 85281. Fax: 480/829-8446. **Facility:** 160 units. 155 one-bedroom standard units, some with whirlpools. 5 one-bedroom suites. 3 stories, interior corridors. *Bath:* combo or shower only. **Parking:** on-site. **Terms:** cancellation fee imposed, package plans. **Amenities:** high-speed Internet, dual phone lines, voice mail, irons, hair dryers. **Pool(s):** heated outdoor. **Leisure Activities:** whirlpool. **Guest Services:** valet and coin laundry. **Business Services:** meeting rooms, business center. **Cards:** AX, DC, DS, MC, VI.

SOME UNITS
(ASK) 🛡 ➡️ 🍴 🏊 📷 🏊 💪 🎦 DATA PORT 🔲 /✕ 🔲 🖥 /
FEE

DAYS INN TEMPE/ASU   *Book at aaa.com*   Phone: 480/968-7793   **22**

Property failed to provide current rates

Small-scale Hotel   **Location:** 0.4 mi e of Rural Rd. Located in a commercial area. 1221 E Apache Blvd 85281. Fax: 480/966-4450. **Facility:** 102 one-bedroom standard units, some with whirlpools. 2 stories (no elevator), exterior corridors. **Parking:** on-site. **Amenities:** voice mail, hair dryers. *Some:* high-speed Internet, irons. **Pool(s):** heated outdoor. **Guest Services:** coin laundry. **Business Services:** PC, fax (fee).

SOME UNITS
➡️ 🍴 🏊 💪 🎦 DATA PORT 🔲 /✕ 🔲 🖥 /

(See map and index starting on p. 271)

ECONO LODGE/TEMPE ASU   *Book at aaa.com*   Phone: (480)966-5832   **20**

AAA [SAVE]

2/1-4/15	1P: $62	2P: $72	XP: $5	F7
10/1-1/31	1P: $42	2P: $52	XP: $5	F7
4/16-9/30	1P: $32	2P: $42	XP: $5	F7

Motel   **Location:** Loop 101, exit Broadway southbound, just e to Price Rd, then just s; exit Rio Salado Pkwy northbound, just s. 2101 E Apache Blvd 85281. Fax: 480/966-5832. **Facility:** 40 one-bedroom standard units. 2 stories (no elevator), exterior corridors. **Parking:** on-site. **Terms:** small pets only ($10 extra charge). **Amenities:** hair dryers. **Pool(s):** small outdoor. **Guest Services:** coin laundry. **Business Services:** fax (fee). **Cards:** AX, DC, DS, MC, VI. **Special Amenities:** free local telephone calls. *(See color ad p 358)*

SOME UNITS
FEE

EMBASSY SUITES PHOENIX-TEMPE   *Book at aaa.com*   Phone: (480)897-7444   **33**

9/5-1/31 [BP]	1P: $99-$249	2P: $99-$259	XP: $10	F18
2/1-4/13 [BP]	1P: $139-$219	2P: $139-$229	XP: $10	F18
4/14-5/25 [BP]	1P: $119-$189	2P: $119-$199	XP: $10	F18
5/26-9/4 [BP]	1P: $89-$119	2P: $89-$129	XP: $10	F18

Small-scale Hotel   **Location:** US 60 (Superstition Frwy), exit 174 (Rural Rd), just s. 4400 S Rural Rd 85282. Fax: 480/897-6112. **Facility:** 224 one-bedroom suites ($89-$259). 2-3 stories, exterior corridors. **Bath:** combo or shower only. **Parking:** on-site. **Terms:** cancellation fee imposed. **Amenities:** voice mail, irons, hair dryers. **Fee:** video games, high-speed Internet. **Pool(s):** heated indoor. **Leisure Activities:** sauna, whirlpool, exercise room. **Fee:** game room. **Guest Services:** gift shop, complimentary evening beverages, valet and coin laundry. **Business Services:** meeting rooms, business center. **Cards:** AX, CB, DC, DS, JC, MC, VI.

SOME UNITS

EXECUTIVE SUITES EXTENDED STAY   *Book at aaa.com*   Phone: (480)947-3711   **8**

2/1-3/31 [BP]	1P: $89-$129	2P: $89-$129	XP: $10	F12
4/1-5/15 & 10/1-1/31 [BP]	1P: $69-$99	2P: $69-$99	XP: $10	F12
5/16-9/30 [BP]	1P: $49-$79	2P: $49-$79	XP: $10	F12

Small-scale Hotel   **Location:** SR 202 Loop (Red Mountain Frwy), exit 7, 0.6 mi n. 1635 N Scottsdale Rd 85281. Fax: 480/949-7902. **Facility:** 140 units. 3 one-bedroom standard units, some with efficiencies. 137 one-bedroom suites ($59-$129), some with efficiencies. 3 stories (no elevator), exterior corridors. **Bath:** combo or shower only. **Parking:** on-site. **Terms:** weekly rates available, package plans. **Amenities:** voice mail, safes, irons, hair dryers. **Pool(s):** heated outdoor. **Leisure Activities:** whirlpool, putting green, exercise room. **Guest Services:** complimentary laundry. **Business Services:** meeting rooms, fax (fee). **Cards:** AX, DC, DS, MC, VI.

SOME UNITS

[ASK] [S/D]

FIESTA INN RESORT   *Book at aaa.com*   Phone: (480)967-1441   **30**

AAA [SAVE]

2/1-4/15	1P: $145-$165	2P: $145-$165	XP: $10	F12
4/16-5/31	1P: $129-$149	2P: $129-$149	XP: $10	F12
10/1-1/31	1P: $139	2P: $139	XP: $10	F12
6/1-9/30	1P: $85-$105	2P: $85-$105	XP: $10	F12

Large-scale Hotel   **Location:** I-10, exit 153 (Broadway Rd), 0.5 mi e. 2100 S Priest Dr 85282. Fax: 480/967-0224. **Facility:** 270 units. 269 one-bedroom standard units. 1 one-bedroom suite. 3 stories, exterior corridors. **Bath:** combo or shower only. **Parking:** on-site. **Terms:** cancellation fee imposed, [AP], [BP] & [CP] meal plans available, package plans. **Amenities:** video games (fee), voice mail, irons, hair dryers. *Some:* dual phone lines. **Dining:** 6:30 am-10 pm, cocktails. **Pool(s):** heated outdoor. **Leisure Activities:** whirlpool, 3 lighted tennis courts, bicycles, exercise room. **Guest Services:** gift shop, valet laundry, area transportation-within 5 mi. **Business Services:** conference facilities, business center. **Cards:** AX, CB, DC, DS, MC, VI. **Special Amenities:** free local telephone calls and free newspaper. *(See color ad below)*

SOME UNITS

[S/D]

HAMPTON INN & SUITES   *Book at aaa.com*   Phone: (480)675-9799   **10**

AAA [SAVE]

2/1-4/15 [BP]	1P: $139-$159	2P: $139-$159
4/16-5/31 & 9/13-1/31 [BP]	1P: $109-$129	2P: $109-$129
6/1-9/12 [BP]	1P: $89-$109	2P: $89-$109

Small-scale Hotel   **Location:** SR 202 Loop (Red Mountain Frwy), exit 7, 0.5 mi n. 1429 N Scottsdale Rd 85281. Fax: 480/675-9879. **Facility:** 160 units. 80 one-bedroom standard units. 80 one-bedroom suites, some with efficiencies. 1-3 stories, exterior corridors. **Bath:** combo or shower only. **Parking:** on-site. **Terms:** cancellation fee imposed, small pets only ($50 fee). **Amenities:** high-speed Internet, voice mail, irons, hair dryers. **Pool(s):** 2 heated outdoor. **Leisure Activities:** 3 lighted tennis courts, exercise room, sports court. **Guest Services:** sundries, valet and coin laundry, area transportation-within 5 mi. **Business Services:** meeting rooms, business center. **Cards:** AX, CB, DC, DS, JC, MC, VI. **Special Amenities:** free full breakfast and free local telephone calls.

SOME UNITS

[S/D]   [VCR]
FEE

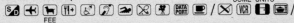

(See map and index starting on p. 271)

HAWTHORN SUITES - TEMPE   *Book at aaa.com*   Phone: (480)633-2744   **32**
▼▼▼▼	2/1-4/30 [ECP]	1P: $89-$149	2P: $99-$159	XP: $10	F13
	1/1-1/31 [ECP]	1P: $85-$105	2P: $95-$115	XP: $10	F13
Small-scale Hotel	10/1-12/31 [ECP]	1P: $79-$99	2P: $89-$109	XP: $10	F13
	5/1-9/30 [ECP]	1P: $59-$79	2P: $69-$89	XP: $10	F13

Location: Loop 101, exit Southern Ave/Baseline Rd; at southeast corner. 2301 E Southern Ave 85282. Fax: 480/633-2743. **Facility:** 68 one-bedroom standard units with efficiencies. 3 stories, interior corridors. *Bath:* combo or shower only. **Parking:** on-site. **Terms:** cancellation fee imposed, pets ($25-$100 extra charge). **Amenities:** video library, high-speed Internet, voice mail, safes (fee), irons, hair dryers. **Pool(s):** small heated outdoor. **Leisure Activities:** whirlpool, exercise room. **Guest Services:** valet and coin laundry. **Business Services:** business center. **Cards:** AX, CB, DC, DS, MC, VI. *(See color ad below)*

SOME UNITS

(A$K) (S⬤) 🛏 (⏸↕) (⬛M) (⬛) (⊘) (⇌) (VCR) (⛽) (DATA PORT) 🖥 📠 💻 / (✕) /
FEE

HOLIDAY INN   *Book at aaa.com*   Phone: (480)968-3451   **24**
AAA SAVE	2/1-4/2	1P: $95-$116	2P: $95-$116	XP: $10	F19
▼▼▼▼	10/1-1/31	1P: $69-$116	2P: $69-$116	XP: $10	F19
	4/3-5/14	1P: $69-$89	2P: $69-$89	XP: $10	F19
Small-scale Hotel	5/15-9/30	1P: $59-$69	2P: $59-$69	XP: $10	F19

Location: US 60 (Superstition Frwy), exit 174 (Rural Rd), 2 mi n. Located at southeast area of Arizona State University Campus. 915 E Apache Blvd 85281. Fax: 480/968-6262. **Facility:** 190 units. 189 one-bedroom standard units. 1 one-bedroom suite. 4 stories, interior corridors. *Bath:* combo or shower only. **Parking:** on-site. **Terms:** package plans. **Amenities:** high-speed Internet, voice mail, irons, hair dryers. **Dining:** 6 am-2 & 5-10 pm, cocktails. **Pool(s):** heated outdoor. **Leisure Activities:** whirlpool, exercise room. **Guest Services:** gift shop, valet and coin laundry, area transportation-within 5 mi. **Business Services:** meeting rooms, business center. **Cards:** AX, CB, DC, DS, JC, MC, VI. *(See color ad below)*

SOME UNITS

(S⬤) (⤚) 🐾 🛏 (🍴) (Y) (⬛) (⊘) (⇌) (⛽) (DATA PORT) 🖥 💻 / (✕) 📠 /

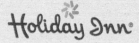
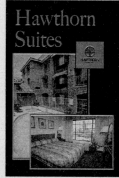

(See map and index starting on p. 271)

HOLIDAY INN EXPRESS/TEMPE   *Book at aaa.com*   Phone: (480)820-7500   **41**
Small-scale Hotel
1/1-1/31 [CP]	1P: $99	2P: $99	XP: $10	F18
2/1-4/30 [CP]	1P: $89	2P: $89	XP: $10	F18
10/1-12/31 [CP]	1P: $69	2P: $69	XP: $10	F18
5/1-9/30 [CP]	1P: $59	2P: $59	XP: $10	F18

Location: I-10, exit 155 (Baseline Rd), 0.4 mi e, then just s. 5300 S Priest Dr 85283. Fax: 480/730-6626. **Facility:** 159 one-bedroom standard units. 4 stories, interior corridors. **Parking:** on-site. **Terms:** cancellation fee imposed, small pets only ($5 extra charge). **Amenities:** high-speed Internet, voice mail, irons, hair dryers. *Some:* dual phone lines. **Pool(s):** heated outdoor. **Leisure Activities:** whirlpool, exercise room. **Guest Services:** valet laundry. **Business Services:** meeting rooms, fax. **Cards:** AX, DC, DS, MC, VI. *(See color ad below)*

HOMESTEAD STUDIO SUITES
HOTEL-PHOENIX/AIRPORT/TEMPE   *Book at aaa.com*   Phone: (480)557-8880   **27**
Small-scale Hotel
2/1-4/23 & 1/9-1/31	1P: $90	2P: $95	XP: $5	F17
9/24-1/8	1P: $70	2P: $75	XP: $5	F17
4/24-9/23	1P: $60	2P: $65	XP: $5	F17

Location: I-10, exit 153 (Broadway Rd), 0.3 mi ne, just nw on S 52nd St, then just w. 2165 W 15th St 85281. Fax: 480/921-7900. **Facility:** 95 units. 71 one-bedroom standard units with efficiencies. 24 one-bedroom suites with efficiencies. 3 stories, interior corridors. *Bath:* combo or shower only. **Parking:** on-site. **Terms:** office hours 6:30 am-10:30 pm, cancellation fee imposed, small pets only ($25 extra charge). **Amenities:** video games (fee), high-speed Internet, dual phone lines, voice mail, irons, hair dryers. **Pool(s):** small heated outdoor. **Leisure Activities:** exercise room. **Guest Services:** sundries, valet and coin laundry. **Business Services:** fax (fee). **Cards:** AX, DC, DS, MC, VI.

Stay Smart® In Tempe-Phoenix.

Complimentary deluxe breakfast bar
Complimentary local phone calls
Free High Speed Internet
Complimentary "USA Today"
Heated pool & jacuzzi • Centrally located
Within 5 mi. of Phoenix Sky Harbor Airport
Walking distance to Arizona Mills Mall

1-4 Guests
$89.00 1-1-06 - 4-30-06
$59.00 5-1-06 - 9-30-06
$69.00 10-1-06 - 12-31-06 Per Night

For Reservations Call
800-822-4334
1-480-820-7500 or 1-800-HOLIDAY
E-mail:holidayinntempe@aol.com
Website: www.hiexpress.com/tempeaz

Holiday Inn EXPRESS Stay Smart®
Tempe-Phoenix
5300 S. Priest
Tempe, AZ 85283

www.innsuites.com

InnSuites HOTELS & SUITES

$59.99 Studio 1-4 People April - Sept.

TEMPE/PHOENIX
1651 W. Baseline Rd., at I-10
Tempe, AZ 85283
(480) 897-7900
(800) 841-4242

FREE Healthy Hot Breakfast Buffet
Afternoon Social Hour
• High Speed Internet in Suite
• Free Monthly First Wednesday BBQ
• Free Newspaper
• Free HBO/ESPN and More
• Free Airport Transportation
• AZ Mills Shopping

ASK FOR AAA DISCOUNT & FAMILY SUITE
VISIT ALL INNSUITES® LOCATIONS: Tempe/Phoenix Airport • Phoenix/Scottsdale • Tucson City Center
Tucson Catalina Foothills • Yuma Castle Dome • Ontario Airport/Los Angeles • Albuquerque

Family/Executive Suite

1-888-INNSUITES   1-800-842-4242

(See map and index starting on p. 271)

INNSUITES HOTELS & SUITES TEMPE/PHOENIX
AIRPORT   *Book at aaa.com*

	2/1-4/1 [BP]	1P: $89-$119	2P: $89-$119	Phone: (480)897-7900 **38**
	4/2-5/27 & 9/15-1/31 [BP]	1P: $79-$109	2P: $79-$109	XP: $10 F18
	5/28-9/14 [BP]	1P: $69-$89	2P: $69-$89	XP: $10 F18
				XP: $10 F18

Location: I-10, exit 155 (Baseline Rd), just e. 1651 W Baseline Rd 85283. Fax: 480/491-1008. **Facility:** 160 units.
Small-scale Hotel 90 one-bedroom standard units, some with efficiencies and/or whirlpools. 70 one-bedroom suites ($79-$149), some with efficiencies and/or whirlpools. 2 stories (no elevator), exterior corridors. *Bath:* combo or shower only. **Parking:** on-site. **Terms:** weekly rates available, pets ($25 fee). **Amenities:** video games (fee), high-speed Internet, dual phone lines, voice mail, irons, hair dryers. **Dining:** 6 am-10 & 5-10 pm; hours extended in winter. **Pool(s):** heated outdoor. **Leisure Activities:** whirlpool, putting green, 2 lighted tennis courts, playground, exercise room, basketball, volleyball. **Guest Services:** complimentary evening beverages, coin laundry, area transportation-Arizona Mills Mall. **Business Services:** meeting rooms, business center. **Cards:** AX, CB, DC, DS, JC, MC, VI. **Special Amenities:** free full breakfast.
(See color ad p 361)

SOME UNITS

LA QUINTA INN PHOENIX (SKY HARBOR SOUTH)   *Book at aaa.com*

2/1-3/31 [CP]	1P: $125-$135	2P: $132-$142	Phone: (480)967-4465 **18**
4/1-5/31 [CP]	1P: $99-$109	2P: $106-$116	XP: $7 F18
1/1-1/31 [CP]	1P: $95-$105	2P: $102-$112	XP: $7 F18
6/1-12/31 [CP]	1P: $63-$73	2P: $70-$80	XP: $7 F18

Small-scale Hotel
Location: I-10, exit 153 (Broadway Rd) eastbound; exit 153A (University Dr) westbound, 0.8 mi n; on south side of University Dr; east side of SR 143 (Hohokam Expwy). 911 S 48th St 85281. Fax: 480/921-9172. **Facility:** 128 units. 125 one-bedroom standard units. 3 one-bedroom suites. 3 stories, exterior corridors. *Bath:* combo or shower only. **Parking:** on-site. **Terms:** small pets only. **Amenities:** video games (fee), voice mail, irons, hair dryers. **Pool(s):** heated outdoor. **Leisure Activities:** putting green, exercise room. **Guest Services:** coin laundry. **Business Services:** fax (fee). **Cards:** AX, CB, DC, DS, MC, VI.
(See color ad p 295)

SOME UNITS

MOTEL 6 #1315   *Book at aaa.com*

2/1-4/15	1P: $49-$59	2P: $55-$65	Phone: 480/945-9506 **9**
1/1-1/31	1P: $45-$55	2P: $51-$61	XP: $3 F17
4/16-12/31	1P: $39-$49	2P: $45-$55	XP: $3 F17

Motel
Location: Loop 202(Red Mountain Frwy), exit 7, 0.6 mi n. 1612 N Scottsdale Rd 85281. Fax: 480/970-4763.
Facility: 100 one-bedroom standard units. 2 stories (no elevator), exterior corridors. *Bath:* combo or shower only. **Parking:** on-site. **Terms:** small pets only. **Pool(s):** small heated outdoor. **Guest Services:** coin laundry. **Business Services:** fax (fee). **Cards:** AX, CB, DC, DS, MC, VI.

SOME UNITS

QUALITY INN AIRPORT/ASU   *Book at aaa.com*

12/30-1/31 [BP]	1P: $94-$199	2P: $94-$199	Phone: (480)774-2500 **17**
2/1-5/15 [BP]	1P: $89-$149	2P: $89-$149	XP: $10 F18
10/1-12/29 [BP]	1P: $79-$109	2P: $79-$109	XP: $10 F18
5/16-9/30 [BP]	1P: $69-$99	2P: $69-$99	XP: $10 F18

Small-scale Hotel **Location:** 0.5 mi e of Rural Rd. 1375 E University Dr 85281. Fax: 480/929-0524. **Facility:** Smoke free premises. 52 one-bedroom standard units. 3 stories, interior corridors. *Bath:* combo or shower only. **Parking:** on-site. **Amenities:** high-speed Internet, voice mail, irons, hair dryers. **Pool(s):** small heated outdoor. **Guest Services:** coin laundry. **Business Services:** fax. **Cards:** AX, CB, DC, DS, MC, VI. **Special Amenities:** free full breakfast and free local telephone calls.

SOME UNITS

(See map and index starting on p. 271)

QUALITY INN TEMPE/AIRPORT

 Motel

Phone: (480)967-3000   25

2/1-3/31	1P: $99-$139	2P: $109-$139	XP: $10 F17
10/1-1/31	1P: $89-$99	2P: $89-$99	XP: $10 F17
4/1-5/31	1P: $79-$89	2P: $79-$89	XP: $10 F17
6/1-9/30	1P: $59-$69	2P: $59-$69	XP: $10 F17

Location: I-10, exit 153 (Broadway Rd), 0.3 mi ne. Located in a business and industrial park area. 1550 S 52nd St 85281. Fax: 480/966-9568. **Facility:** 100 one-bedroom standard units, some with whirlpools. 2 stories (no elevator), exterior corridors. **Parking:** on-site. **Terms:** [CP] meal plan available, package plans, pets ($10 fee). **Amenities:** irons. **Pool(s):** heated outdoor. **Leisure Activities:** whirlpool. **Guest Services:** coin laundry. **Business Services:** fax (fee). **Cards:** AX, CB, DC, DS, JC, MC, VI. **Special Amenities: free expanded continental breakfast and free room upgrade (subject to availability with advance reservations).** *(See color ad p 362)*

SOME UNITS

RAMADA LIMITED   *Book at aaa.com*

Phone: (480)413-1188   37

11/1-1/31	1P: $64	2P: $69	XP: $10 F17
2/1-4/30	1P: $59	2P: $64	XP: $10 F17
5/1-10/31	1P: $54	2P: $59	XP: $10 F17

Small-scale Hotel

Location: I-10, exit 155 (Baseline Rd), just e. 1701 W Baseline Rd 85283. Fax: 480/413-1266. **Facility:** 119 units. 116 one-bedroom standard units. 3 one-bedroom suites. 3 stories, exterior corridors. *Bath:* combo or shower only. **Parking:** on-site. **Terms:** weekly rates available, small pets only ($15 fee). **Amenities:** high-speed Internet, voice mail, irons, hair dryers. **Pool(s):** small heated outdoor. **Leisure Activities:** whirlpool. **Guest Services:** coin laundry. **Business Services:** fax (fee). **Cards:** AX, DC, DS, MC, VI. **Special Amenities: free expanded continental breakfast and free newspaper.** *(See color ad below)*

SOME UNITS

RAMADA LIMITED TEMPE-UNIVERSITY   *Book at aaa.com*

Phone: (480)736-1700   21

2/1-3/31	1P: $49-$99	2P: $49-$99	XP: $10 F18
4/1-1/31	1P: $49-$59	2P: $49-$59	XP: $10 F18

Motel

Location: US 60 (Superstition Frwy), exit 175, 1.9 mi n on McClintock Dr, then 0.3 mi e. 1915 E Apache Blvd 85281. Fax: 480/736-9030. **Facility:** 56 units. 54 one-bedroom standard units. 2 one-bedroom suites ($69-$139) with whirlpools. 2 stories (no elevator), exterior corridors. **Parking:** on-site. **Terms:** weekly rates available, [ECP] meal plan available, pets ($25 deposit). **Amenities:** voice mail, irons, hair dryers. **Pool(s):** outdoor. **Leisure Activities:** whirlpool. **Business Services:** meeting rooms. **Cards:** AX, CB, DC, DS, JC, MC, VI. **Special Amenities: free expanded continental breakfast and free local telephone calls.** *(See color ad below)*

SOME UNITS

(See map and index starting on p. 271)

RED ROOF INN PHOENIX AIRPORT *Book at aaa.com* Phone: (480)449-3205 26

2/1-3/25	1P: $59-$70	2P: $64-$75	XP: $5	F18
1/1-1/31	1P: $51-$61	2P: $56-$67	XP: $5	F18
3/26-12/31	1P: $49-$59	2P: $54-$64	XP: $5	F18

Small-scale Hotel **Location:** I-10, exit 153 (Broadway Rd), just nw on S 52nd St, then just w. 2135 W 15th St 85281. Fax: 480/449-3235. **Facility:** 125 units. 123 one-bedroom standard units. 2 one-bedroom suites. 3 stories, interior corridors. *Bath:* combo or shower only. **Parking:** on-site. **Terms:** small pets only. **Amenities:** video games (fee), voice mail. **Pool(s):** heated outdoor. **Leisure Activities:** whirlpool. **Guest Services:** coin laundry. **Business Services:** fax (fee). **Cards:** AX, CB, DC, DS, MC, VI.

SOME UNITS
FEE FEE

RESIDENCE INN BY MARRIOTT *Book at aaa.com* Phone: 480/756-2122 35

2/1-4/29 [BP]	1P: $119-$229	2P: $119-$229	
4/30-5/27 & 9/10-1/31 [BP]	1P: $99-$199	2P: $99-$199	
5/28-9/9 [BP]	1P: $79-$139	2P: $79-$139	

Small-scale Hotel **Location:** I-10, exit 155 (Baseline Rd), 0.4 mi e, then just n. 5075 S Priest Dr 85282. Fax: 480/345-2802. **Facility:** 126 units. 94 one-bedroom standard units with efficiencies. 32 two-bedroom suites with kitchens. 2 stories (no elevator), interior/exterior corridors. *Bath:* combo or shower only. **Parking:** on-site. **Terms:** pets ($75 fee). **Amenities:** high-speed Internet, voice mail, irons, hair dryers. *Some:* DVD players (fee). **Pool(s):** heated outdoor. **Leisure Activities:** whirlpool, exercise room, sports court. **Guest Services:** complimentary evening beverages: Mon-Thurs, valet and coin laundry. **Business Services:** meeting rooms, fax (fee). **Cards:** AX, CB, DC, DS, JC, MC, VI.

SOME UNITS
FEE FEE

SHERATON PHOENIX AIRPORT HOTEL *Book at aaa.com* Phone: 480/967-6600 28

2/1-4/15	1P: $209-$239	2P: $209-$239	XP: $10	F16
4/16-5/27 & 9/10-1/31	1P: $169-$199	2P: $169-$199	XP: $10	F16
5/28-9/9	1P: $119-$149	2P: $119-$149	XP: $10	F16

Large-scale Hotel **Location:** I-10, exit 153B Broadway Rd westbound; exit 153A 48th St eastbound, 0.3 mi ne. Located in a business and industrial park area. 1600 S 52nd St 85281. Fax: 480/829-9427. **Facility:** Smoke free premises. 210 one-bedroom standard units. 4 stories, interior corridors. *Bath:* combo or shower only. **Parking:** on-site. **Terms:** cancellation fee imposed, small pets only (in limited units). **Amenities:** dual phone lines, voice mail, irons, hair dryers. *Fee:* video games, high-speed Internet. *Some:* fax. **Dining:** 6 am-10:30 pm, cocktails. **Pool(s):** heated outdoor. **Leisure Activities:** whirlpool, exercise room. *Fee:* massage. **Guest Services:** gift shop, valet laundry, area transportation-within 3 mi. **Business Services:** meeting rooms, business center. **Cards:** AX, CB, DC, DS, JC, MC, VI. **Special Amenities:** free newspaper.

SOME UNITS
FEE

SPRINGHILL SUITES BY MARRIOTT *Book at aaa.com* Phone: 480/752-7979 40

Property failed to provide current rates

Location: I-10, exit 155 (Baseline Rd), southeast corner of Baseline Rd and Priest Dr. Located across from Arizona Mills Mall Outlet Center. 5211 S Priest Dr 85283. Fax: 480/752-2288. **Facility:** 121 one-bedroom standard units. 3 stories, interior corridors. *Bath:* combo or shower only. **Parking:** on-site. **Amenities:** high-speed Internet, voice mail, irons, hair dryers. **Pool(s):** small heated outdoor. **Leisure Activities:** whirlpool, exercise room. **Guest Services:** valet and coin laundry, area transportation. **Business Services:** meeting rooms, fax (fee).

SOME UNITS

SPRINGHILL SUITES BY MARRIOTT TEMPE AIRPORT *Book at aaa.com* Phone: (480)968-8222 13

All Year 1P: $80-$143 2P: $80-$143

Location: Just w of Priest Dr. 1601 W Rio Salado Pkwy 85281. Fax: 480/968-4114. **Facility:** 99 one-bedroom standard units. 6 stories, interior corridors. *Bath:* combo or shower only. **Parking:** on-site. **Amenities:** high-speed Internet, dual phone lines, voice mail, irons, hair dryers. **Pool(s):** heated outdoor. **Leisure Activities:** whirlpool, exercise room. **Guest Services:** valet and coin laundry, airport transportation-Sky Harbor International Airport, area transportation-within 3 mi. **Business Services:** meeting rooms, fax (fee). **Cards:** AX, CB, DC, DS, JC, MC, VI. **Special Amenities:** free expanded continental breakfast and free local telephone calls.

SOME UNITS

STUDIO 6 EXTENDED STAY #6031 *Book at aaa.com* Phone: 602/414-4470 34

2/1-3/25	1P: $63-$73	2P: $67-$77	XP: $4	F17
3/26-12/31	1P: $45-$55	2P: $49-$59	XP: $4	F17

Small-scale Hotel **Location:** I-10, exit 155 (Baseline Rd), just w, then 0.4 mi n. 4909 S Wendler Dr 85282. Fax: 602/414-4466. **Facility:** 149 one-bedroom standard units with efficiencies. 2 stories (no elevator), exterior corridors. *Bath:* combo or shower only. **Parking:** on-site. **Terms:** check-in 4 pm, pets ($10 extra charge). **Amenities:** voice mail, irons. **Pool(s):** outdoor. **Guest Services:** coin laundry. **Cards:** AX, CB, DC, DS, MC, VI.

SOME UNITS
FEE

(See map and index starting on p. 271)

TEMPE MISSION PALMS HOTEL *Book at aaa.com* Phone: (480)894-1400 🔟5️⃣

1/1-1/31	1P: $219	2P: $219	XP: $10 F18
2/1-5/25	1P: $209	2P: $209	XP: $10 F18
9/10-12/31	1P: $179	2P: $179	XP: $10 F18
5/26-9/9	1P: $109	2P: $109	XP: $10 F18

Small-scale Hotel **Location:** Just e of Mill Ave, 0.3 mi n of University Dr; downtown. 60 E 5th St 85281. Fax: 480/968-7677. **Facility:** 303 units. 297 one-bedroom standard units. 6 one-bedroom suites ($279-$419), some with whirlpools. 4 stories, interior corridors. *Bath:* combo or shower only. **Parking:** on-site and valet. **Terms:** 3 day cancellation notice-fee imposed, $10 service charge, small pets only ($125 fee). **Amenities:** video games (fee), CD players, dual phone lines, voice mail, irons, hair dryers. **Dining:** 6:30 am-2 & 6-10 pm, cocktails. **Pool(s):** heated outdoor. **Leisure Activities:** whirlpools, lighted tennis court, exercise room. **Guest Services:** gift shop, valet laundry, area transportation (fee)-within 5 mi. **Business Services:** conference facilities, business center. **Cards:** AX, CB, DC, DS, JC, MC, VI. **Special Amenities:** free local telephone calls and free newspaper. *(See color ad p 303)*

SOME UNITS

TEMPE SUPER 8 *Book at aaa.com* Phone: (480)967-8891 1️⃣9️⃣

2/1-4/2 & 10/2-1/31	1P: $59-$99	2P: $59-$99	XP: $5 F18
4/3-10/1	1P: $39-$69	2P: $39-$69	XP: $5 F18

Motel **Location:** Just e of Rural Rd. Located on a busy commercial area. 1020 E Apache Blvd 85281. Fax: 480/968-7868. **Facility:** 55 one-bedroom standard units. 2 stories (no elevator), exterior corridors. **Parking:** on-site. **Terms:** weekly rates available, pets ($15 fee, in designated units). **Pool(s):** heated outdoor. **Leisure Activities:** whirlpool. **Business Services:** fax (fee). **Cards:** AX, DS, MC, VI.

SOME UNITS

WYNDHAM BUTTES RESORT *Book at aaa.com* Phone: (602)225-9000 3️⃣1️⃣

2/1-4/15	1P: $239	2P: $239	XP: $10 F16
9/10-1/31	1P: $219	2P: $219	XP: $10 F16
4/16-5/20	1P: $189	2P: $189	XP: $10 F16
5/21-9/9	1P: $119	2P: $119	XP: $10 F16

Resort Small-scale Hotel **Location:** I-10, exit 153 (Broadway Rd) westbound, 0.8 mi w to 48th St, then 0.3 mi s; exit 48th St eastbound, 0.5 mi s. 2000 Westcourt Way 85282. Fax: 602/438-8622. **Facility:** Hillside location overlooking the valley. Extensive and beautiful desert landscaping. Stream/waterfall fed interconnecting pools. 353 units. 344 one-bedroom standard units. 9 one-bedroom suites, some with whirlpools. 4 stories, interior corridors. **Parking:** valet and street. **Terms:** [BP] meal plan available, $5 service charge, pets ($25 fee). **Amenities:** video games (fee), dual phone lines, voice mail, honor bars, irons, hair dryers. *Some:* CD players. *Fee:* DVD players, high-speed Internet. **Dining:** 2 restaurants, 6 am-midnight, cocktails, also, Top of the Rock Restaurant, see separate listing, entertainment. **Pool(s):** 2 heated outdoor, small heated outdoor. **Leisure Activities:** sauna, whirlpools, steamrooms, waterslide, 4 lighted tennis courts, exercise room, spa, basketball, horseshoes, volleyball. **Guest Services:** gift shop, valet laundry. **Business Services:** conference facilities, business center. **Cards:** AX, DC, DS, JC, MC, VI.

SOME UNITS

——— WHERE TO DINE ———

3 MARGARITAS Lunch: $7-$11 Dinner: $8-$12 Phone: 480/829-5737 🔟

Location: US 60 (Superstition Frwy), exit 174 (Rural Rd), 1.6 mi n. 1717 S Rural Rd 85281. **Hours:** 11 am-11 pm. Closed major holidays. **Reservations:** accepted. **Features:** The bright decor, with lots of color and south-of-the-border flavor, is welcoming to the whole family. Well-prepared traditional dishes and low-fat options make for hearty and healthy dining. Casual dress; cocktails. **Parking:** on-site. **Cards:** AX, DC, DS, MC, VI.

Mexican

CASEY MOORE'S OYSTER HOUSE Lunch: $5-$9 Dinner: $9-$35 Phone: 480/968-9935 6️⃣

Location: Jct Mill Ave, just w on University, then just s. 850 S Ash Ave 85281. **Hours:** 11 am-2 am. **Reservations:** suggested. **Features:** Built in 1910, the historic house now is a showcase for a casual eatery that serves more than seafood. On the menu are such salads as spinach berry, a selection of classic sandwiches and Creole- and Southwestern-influenced dishes, including chipotle chicken and Cajun-style shrimp. Dressy casual; cocktails. **Parking:** on-site. **Cards:** AX, CB, DC, DS, JC, MC, VI. **Historic**

American

CLAIM JUMPER Lunch: $8-$13 Dinner: $10-$20 Phone: 480/831-8200 1️⃣4️⃣

Location: I-10, exit 160 (Baseline Rd), just e. 1530 W Baseline Rd 85283. **Hours:** 11 am-10 pm, Fri & Sat-11 pm. Closed: 7/4, 11/23, 12/25. **Features:** A Western mining theme and family-style portions attract diners to the busy eatery. Choices range from California rolls and crunchy spinach salad to steaks and rotisserie chicken. Save room for the six-layer chocolate mother lode cake. Casual dress; cocktails. **Parking:** on-site. **Cards:** AX, CB, DS, MC, VI.

American

THE FIREHOUSE RESTAURANT Lunch: $6-$11 Dinner: $10-$25 Phone: 480/966-4531 9️⃣

Location: Just w of McClintock. 1639 E Apache Blvd 85281. **Hours:** 11 am-10 pm, Fri & Sat-11 pm, Sun 4:30 pm-9:30 pm. Closed major holidays; also 7/3, 11/23. **Reservations:** accepted. **Features:** Patrons are surrounded by 35 years of firehouse memorabilia in the converted fire station. Steaks are cooked to perfection, and pleasant staffers are helpful. Casual dress; cocktails. **Parking:** on-site. **Cards:** DC, DS, MC, VI.

Steak House

(See map and index starting on p. 271)

GEORGE & DRAGON II ENGLISH RESTAURANT & PUB

Traditional English

Lunch: $6-$10   **Dinner:** $10-$16   **Phone:** 602/470-0018   ⑪
Location: I-10, exit 153 (48th St/Broadway Rd) eastbound, just s; exit 153B (52nd St/Broadway Rd) westbound, 0.4 mi w. 4230 S 48th St 85040. **Hours:** 7 am-1 am. Closed: 12/25. **Features:** The English-owned and operated establishment prepares traditional dishes, including Cornish pasties, shepherd's pie and blackberry and apple crumble with Bird's custard. Lending to the classic pub feel are two dozen draft and 50 bottled beers. Casual dress; cocktails. **Parking:** on-site. **Cards:** AX, DS, MC, VI.

GORDON BIERSCH BREWERY RESTAURANT

American

MC, VI.

Lunch: $8-$14   **Dinner:** $9-$23   **Phone:** 480/736-0033   ②
Location: Northwest corner of 5th St and S Mill Ave. 420 S Mill Ave 85281. **Hours:** 11 am-11 pm, Thurs-midnight, Fri & Sat-1 am. Closed: 11/23, 12/25. **Reservations:** accepted. **Features:** From the upstairs location in the heart of downtown, guests can watch passersby enjoy meals prepared from the freshest ingredients. Custom microbrews are worth sampling. Casual dress; cocktails. **Parking:** street. **Cards:** AX, DC, DS,

HOUSE OF TRICKS

American

Lunch: $7-$12   **Dinner:** $16-$28   **Phone:** 480/968-1114   ⑤
Location: Just e of Mill Ave. 114 E 7th St 85281. **Hours:** 11 am-10 pm. Closed major holidays; also Sun & 7/17-7/31. **Reservations:** suggested. **Features:** Visitors to the "house" can dine on a pleasant shaded patio or inside the quaint bungalow. Offerings include freshly prepared salads, hearty sandwiches and grilled rib-eye or seafood. Casual dress; cocktails. **Parking:** on-site and street. **Cards:** AX, CB, DC, DS, MC, VI.

JOHN HENRY'S CONTINENTAL ITALIAN CUISINE

Italian

Lunch: $7-$13   **Dinner:** $12-$25   **Phone:** 480/730-9009   ⑰
Location: I-10, exit Elliot Rd, 2.5 mi e; corner of Elliot and Rural rds. 909 E Elliot Rd 85284. **Hours:** 11:30 am-2:30 & 5-10 pm, Fri 11 am-11 pm, Sat 5 pm-11 pm, Sun 5 pm-10 pm. Closed: 7/4, 11/23, 12/25. **Reservations:** suggested. **Features:** Although the restaurant is not at the racetrack, horse racing sets the theme. Formally clad servers help diners smooth their way through dinner selections. The lounge is a popular stopping-off place for locals. Casual dress; cocktails; entertainment. **Parking:** on-site. **Cards:** AX, DC, DS, MC, VI.

MACAYO DEPOT CANTINA

Mexican

Lunch: $6-$9   **Dinner:** $8-$14   **Phone:** 480/966-6677   ①
Location: I-10, exit 153 (Broadway Rd), 2 mi e to Mill Ave, 1.5 mi n to 3rd St, then 0.3 mi w. 300 S Ash 85281. **Hours:** 11 am-11 pm, Fri & Sat-midnight. Closed: 11/23, 12/25. **Reservations:** accepted. **Features:** The colorfully furnished Mexican-style eatery occupies an old railroad depot station. The high-volume, energetic atmosphere suits the college crowd that frequents this popular place. Casual dress; cocktails; entertainment. **Parking:** on-site. **Cards:** AX, DC, DS, MC, VI.

MY BIG FAT GREEK RESTAURANT

Greek

Lunch: $5-$16   **Dinner:** $5-$16   **Phone:** 480/966-5883   ④
Location: Downtown. 525 S Mill Ave 85281. **Hours:** 11 am-11 pm, Fri & Sat-midnight. Closed: 1/1, 11/23, 12/25. **Features:** Named after a hit film, the restaurant prepares fun and creative Greek dishes that are sure to entice. Casual dress. **Parking:** on-site and street. **Cards:** AX, DS, MC, VI.

PITA JUNGLE

Mediterranean

DC, DS, MC, VI.

Lunch: $5-$12   **Dinner:** $5-$12   **Phone:** 480/804-0234   ⑧
Location: Just e of jct Rural Rd and Apache Blvd. 1250 E Apache Blvd, Suite 110 85282. **Hours:** 9 am-10 pm. Closed major holidays. **Features:** The atmosphere is super-casual in the dining area and on the patio. On the menu is a wide variety of hot and cold pita wraps, pizza, falafel, spanakopita, salads and burgers, as well as natural, healthful vegetarian offerings. Casual dress; beer & wine only. **Parking:** on-site. **Cards:** AX,

ROYAL TAJ

Indian

Lunch: $7-$14   **Dinner:** $7-$14   **Phone:** 480/967-5234   ⑫
Location: Just e of McClintock Dr. 1845 E Broadway Rd 85282. **Hours:** 11 am-2:30 & 5-10 pm, Sat & Sun 11 am-3 & 5-10 pm. **Reservations:** accepted. **Features:** Traditional specialties include a variety of curry dishes. The casual eatery's friendly servers offer clear explanations of the many foods offered. Casual dress; cocktails. **Parking:** on-site. **Cards:** AX, DC, DS, MC, VI.

SAMMY'S

American

Lunch: $5-$9   **Dinner:** $8-$20   **Phone:** 480/967-6444   ③
Location: Just w of Mill Ave; 0.3 mi n of University Dr. 414 S Mill 85281. **Hours:** 11 am-10 pm, Fri & Sat-midnight, Sun noon-10 pm. **Features:** Conveniently located close to Arizona State University, this casual eatery provides soups, pastas, sandwiches and wraps. Local favorites include their wood-fired pizzas and the large variety of salads. Casual dress; cocktails. **Parking:** street. **Cards:** AX, DS, MC, VI.

SERRANO'S MEXICAN RESTAURANT

Regional Mexican

Lunch: $6-$10   **Dinner:** $6-$10   **Phone:** 480/345-0044   ⑯
Location: Just s of Guadalupe Rd. 6440 S Rural Rd 85283. **Hours:** 11 am-10 pm, Sun-9 pm. Closed major holidays. **Reservations:** accepted. **Features:** This spot is a pleasant stop for lunch or dinner. The restaurant's bean dip starter warms up diners. Traditional dishes are prepared with fresh ingredients, and service is friendly. Casual dress; cocktails. **Parking:** on-site. **Cards:** AX, DC, DS, MC, VI.

TASTY KABOB

Persian

Cards: AX, DS, MC, VI.

Lunch: $7-$9   **Dinner:** $10-$17   **Phone:** 480/966-0260   ⑦
Location: 0.4 mi e of Rural Rd. 1250 E Apache Blvd 85281. **Hours:** Closed: Mon. **Reservations:** accepted, weekends. **Features:** The small eatery is an excellent choice for Persian foods. The owner not only works as the friendly hostess but also prepares the delectable desserts. Diners can choose from varied kebabs or try walnuts in pomegranate sauce with chicken or beef. Casual dress; cocktails. **Parking:** on-site.

(See map and index starting on p. 271)

TOM'S BBQ CHICAGO STYLE
▼

Barbecue

Lunch: $4-$13   **Dinner:** $4-$13   **Phone:** 480/820-0728   ⑮

Location: I-10, exit 155, just e of Mill Ave. 115 E Baseline Rd 85283-1288. **Hours:** 10:30 am-9 pm, Sun 11 am-8 pm. Closed major holidays. **Features:** The unpretentious strip-mall eatery displays Chicago memorabilia and serves barbecue beef brisket, pulled pork, smoked chicken, rib tips, sides and more. Sunday is all-you-can-eat day. Casual dress; beer only. **Parking:** on-site. **Cards:** AX, CB, DC, DS, MC, VI.

TOP OF THE ROCK RESTAURANT
▼▼▼▼

American

Dinner: $26-$34   **Phone:** 602/431-2370   ⑬

Location: I-10, exit 153 (Broadway Rd) westbound, 0.8 mi w to 48th St, then 0.3 mi s; exit 48th St eastbound, 0.5 mi s; in Wyndham Buttes Resort. 2000 Westcourt Way 85282. **Hours:** 5:30 pm-10 pm, Sun 10 am-2 pm. **Reservations:** suggested. **Features:** The fine-dining establishment treats guests to mountaintop panoramic views. Solid rock juts up and around the casually elegant dining room. An open kitchen affords a hint of what lies in store. Dressy casual; cocktails. **Parking:** on-site and valet. **Cards:** AX, CB, DC, DS, JC, MC, VI.   ☒

ZIPANGU SUSHI & YAKITORI
▼▼◆ ▼◆

Japanese

Lunch: $6-$9   **Dinner:** $9-$16   **Phone:** 480/839-3924   ⑱

Location: I-10, exit 158 (Warner Rd), 2.5 mi e; in Landis Cyclery Plaza. 1006 Warner Rd, #113 85284. **Hours:** 11 am-2 & 5-9:30 pm, Fri-10 pm, Sat noon-3 & 5-10 pm. Closed major holidays; also Sun. **Reservations:** accepted. **Features:** The clean, modern look of fresh wood and the cool blues of fish tanks contribute to a calming decor. Among offerings are freshly prepared tempura, yakitori and tasty grilled chicken and seafood dishes. Casual dress; wine only. **Parking:** on-site. **Cards:** AX, DS, MC, VI.

TOLLESON pop. 4,974   (See map and index starting on p. 264)

─── **WHERE TO STAY** ───

COMFORT SUITES   *Book at aaa.com*
▼▼◆ ▼◆

Small-scale Hotel

Phone: (623)936-6000   ㉕

	1P: $99-$109	2P: $109-$119	XP: $10	F18
2/1-4/30 & 11/1-1/31				
9/1-10/31	1P: $89-$99	2P: $99-$109	XP: $10	F18
5/1-8/31	1P: $79-$89	2P: $89-$99	XP: $10	F18

Location: I-10, exit 135 (83rd Ave), just n, then just w. 8421 W McDowell Rd 85353. **Fax:** 623/936-2631. **Facility:** 60 units. 59 one-bedroom standard units, some with whirlpools. 1 two-bedroom suite. 2 stories (no elevator), interior corridors. **Bath:** combo or shower only. **Parking:** on-site. **Terms:** cancellation fee imposed, [ECP] meal plan available. **Amenities:** high-speed Internet, voice mail, irons, hair dryers. **Pool(s):** small heated outdoor. **Leisure Activities:** whirlpool, exercise room. **Guest Services:** coin laundry. **Business Services:** meeting rooms, fax (fee). **Cards:** AX, CB, DC, DS, JC, MC, VI.

SOME UNITS

ⓐⓢⓚ Ⓢⓓ 🛡️ 🍴 ⅃Ⓜ ♿ 🏊 🎥 📶 🛡️ 🍽️ 💻 / ☒ ⓋⒸⓇ /

YOUNGTOWN pop. 3,010   (See map and index starting on p. 264)

─── **WHERE TO STAY** ───

BEST WESTERN INN & SUITES OF SUN CITY   *Book at aaa.com*
Ⓐ Ⓐ Ⓐ ⓢⓐⓥⓔ
▼▼◆ ▼◆

Small-scale Hotel

Phone: (623)933-8211   ⑲

	1P: $99-$125	2P: $105-$130	XP: $5	F17
2/1-4/30 [ECP]				
12/21-1/31 [ECP]	1P: $85-$115	2P: $90-$120	XP: $5	F17
10/1-12/20 [ECP]	1P: $70-$100	2P: $75-$105	XP: $5	F17
5/1-9/30 [ECP]	1P: $59-$95	2P: $65-$105	XP: $5	F17

Location: On US 60, just se of 113th Ave. 11201 Grand Ave 85363. **Fax:** 623/933-5062. **Facility:** 96 one-bedroom standard units, some with efficiencies and/or whirlpools. 2 stories (no elevator), interior/exterior corridors. **Bath:** combo or shower only. **Parking:** on-site. **Terms:** weekly rates available, small pets only (in limited units). **Amenities:** voice mail, irons, hair dryers. *Some:* high-speed Internet, dual phone lines. **Pool(s):** heated outdoor. **Guest Services:** coin laundry. **Business Services:** PC, fax (fee). **Cards:** AX, CB, DC, DS, MC, VI. **Special Amenities:** free expanded continental breakfast and free local telephone calls. *(See color ad below)*

SOME UNITS

Ⓢⓓ 🐾 🍴 📷 🚭 🏊 🎥 📶 🛡️ 🍽️ 💻 / ☒ /

PINETOP-LAKESIDE pop. 3,582

──────── WHERE TO STAY ────────

BEAR MOUNTAIN INN & SUITES
Book at aaa.com

AAA [SAVE]
◆◆◆ ◆◆
Small-scale Hotel

5/26-9/30	1P: $59-$109	2P: $59-$109	XP: $5
2/1-5/25 & 10/1-1/31	1P: $49-$99	2P: $49-$99	XP: $5

Phone: (928)368-6600
F14
F14

Location: On SR 260. Located in Lakeside. 1637 White Mountain Blvd 85929. **Fax:** 928/368-6600. **Facility:** 52 one-bedroom standard units. 2 stories (no elevator), interior corridors. **Parking:** on-site. **Terms:** package plans, small pets only (in designated units). **Amenities:** hair dryers. **Leisure Activities:** whirlpool. **Business Services:** meeting rooms. **Cards:** AX, DS, MC, VI. **Special Amenities:** free expanded continental breakfast and free local telephone calls.

SOME UNITS
[icons]

BEST WESTERN INN OF PINETOP
Book at aaa.com

AAA [SAVE]
◆◆◆ ◆◆
Motel

All Year [BP]	1P: $90	2P: $95	XP: $10

Phone: (928)367-6667
F17

Location: On SR 260. Located in Pinetop. 404 E White Mountain Blvd 85935 (PO Box 1528, PINETOP). **Fax:** 928/367-6672. **Facility:** 42 units. 41 one-bedroom standard units. 1 two-bedroom suite with kitchen. 2 stories (no elevator), exterior corridors. **Parking:** on-site. **Terms:** pets ($10 fee). **Amenities:** high-speed Internet, voice mail, irons, hair dryers. **Leisure Activities:** whirlpool. **Cards:** AX, DC, DS, MC, VI. **Special Amenities:** free continental breakfast and free newspaper.

SOME UNITS
[icons] FEE

HOLIDAY INN EXPRESS
Book at aaa.com

AAA [SAVE]
◆◆◆ ◆◆
Small-scale Hotel

6/1-9/30	1P: $89-$169	2P: $89-$169	
4/1-5/31	1P: $79-$169	2P: $79-$169	
2/1-3/31	1P: $99-$149	2P: $99-$149	
10/1-1/31	1P: $79-$149	2P: $79-$149	

Phone: (928)367-6077

Location: On SR 260. Located in Pinetop. 431 E White Mountain Blvd 85935. **Fax:** 928/367-3220. **Facility:** 40 one-bedroom standard units. 2 stories, interior corridors. **Parking:** on-site. **Terms:** [BP] meal plan available, pets ($20 fee). **Amenities:** high-speed Internet, voice mail, irons, hair dryers. **Leisure Activities:** sauna, whirlpool, exercise room. **Guest Services:** coin laundry. **Business Services:** meeting rooms, PC. **Cards:** AX, CB, DC, DS, JC, MC, VI. **Special Amenities:** free full breakfast. *(See color ad below)*

SOME UNITS
[icons] FEE

HON-DAH RESORT CASINO & CONFERENCE CENTER

AAA [SAVE]
◆◆◆ ◆◆
Large-scale Hotel

All Year	1P: $79-$109	2P: $79-$109	XP: $10

Phone: 928/369-0299
F

Location: Jct SR 260 and 73. Located in the White Mountain Apache Reservation. 777 Hwy 260 85935. **Fax:** 928/369-7504. **Facility:** The surrounding acres of wooded reservation, cool weather and outdoor sports are as enticing as the casino and large rooms at this mountain lodge. 128 one-bedroom standard units, some with whirlpools. 2 stories, interior corridors. **Bath:** combo or shower only. **Parking:** on-site. **Terms:** check-in 4 pm, package plans. **Amenities:** voice mail, irons, hair dryers. **Dining:** 2 restaurants, 6 am-10:30 pm, cocktails, nightclub, entertainment. **Pool(s):** heated outdoor. **Leisure Activities:** sauna, whirlpool, hiking trails. **Fee:** game room. **Guest Services:** gift shop, coin laundry. **Business Services:** conference facilities, PC. **Cards:** AX, DC, DS, MC, VI.

SOME UNITS
[icons]

LAZY OAKS RESORT

◆◆ ◆◆
Cottage

All Year	2P: $69-$126	XP: $9

Phone: 928/368-6203

Location: Jct SR 260, 0.8 mi s on Rainbow Lake Dr, then 0.6 mi w. Located in Lakeside. 1075 Larson Rd 85929. **Facility:** 15 cottages. 1 story, exterior corridors. **Bath:** combo or shower only. **Parking:** on-site. **Terms:** office hours 8:30 am-9 pm, 21 day cancellation notice-fee imposed, weekly rates available, small pets only (with prior approval). **Leisure Activities:** rental boats, fishing, bicycles, horseshoes. **Guest Services:** coin laundry.

[icons]

MOUNTAIN HACIENDA LODGE

◆◆ ◆◆
Motel

2/1-2/28	1P: $52-$59	2P: $59-$62	XP: $5
3/1-1/31	1P: $49	2P: $52	XP: $5

Phone: 928/367-4146
F17
F17

Location: On SR 260. Located in Pinetop. 1023 E White Mountain Blvd 85935. **Fax:** 928/367-0291. **Facility:** 24 one-bedroom standard units. 2 stories (no elevator), exterior corridors. **Parking:** on-site. **Amenities:** *Some:* hair dryers. **Leisure Activities:** playground. **Fee:** miniature golf. **Business Services:** fax (fee). **Cards:** AX, DS, MC, VI.

SOME UNITS
[icons]

MOUNTAIN HAVEN INN

Phone: (928)367-2101

▼▼ ▼▼
Motel

All Year | 1P: $54-$119 | 2P: $54-$119

Location: On SR 260. Located in Pinetop. 1120 E White Moutain Blvd 85935. **Facility:** Smoke free premises. 10 units. 6 one-bedroom standard units. 2 one- and 2 two-bedroom suites ($79-$119) with kitchens. 1-2 stories (no elevator), exterior corridors. **Parking:** on-site. **Terms:** office hours 10 am-5 pm, 2-3 night minimum stay - seasonal and/or weekends, 7 day cancellation notice-fee imposed, package plans, no pets allowed (owner's pets on premises). **Amenities:** irons, hair dryers. **Leisure Activities:** horseshoes. **Guest Services:** gift shop. **Cards:** MC, VI.

SOME UNITS
(ASK) (S/D) (✕) (X) (▦) / (VCR) (🖥) (📶) /

NORTHWOODS RESORT

Phone: 928/367-2966

▼▼▼ ▼▼▼
Cottage

Property failed to provide current rates

Location: On SR 260. Located in Pinetop; in a quiet area. 165 E White Mountain Blvd 85935 (PO Box 397-R, PINETOP). Fax: 928/367-2969. **Facility:** Several wooded acres, complete with a fire pit, surround these studios and one- to four-bedroom housekeeping cottages with wood or gas fireplaces. 14 units. 4 vacation homes and 10 cottages, some with whirlpools. 1-2 stories, exterior corridors. **Parking:** on-site. **Terms:** office hours 9 am-9 pm, pets ($12 extra charge, with prior approval). **Leisure Activities:** whirlpool, hiking trails, playground, basketball, horseshoes, volleyball. **Guest Services:** coin laundry. **Business Services:** fax.

SOME UNITS
(🐾) (✕) (X) (📷) (🖥) (📶) (▦) / (✕) /
FEE

ROUNDHOUSE RESORT

Phone: 928/369-4848

▼▼ ▼▼
Condominium

Property failed to provide current rates

Location: 2.4 mi w on SR 260 from jct SR 73, 1.6 mi n. 5829 Buck Springs Rd 85935 (PO Box 1468, PINETOP). Fax: 928/369-4500. **Facility:** 59 units. 5 one-bedroom standard units with kitchens. 43 one- and 11 two-bedroom suites with kitchens. 1-2 stories (no elevator), interior/exterior corridors. **Terms:** check-in 4 pm. **Amenities:** video library (fee), voice mail, irons, hair dryers. **Pool(s):** heated indoor. **Leisure Activities:** whirlpool, playground, exercise room, horseshoes, volleyball. **Guest Services:** coin laundry. **Business Services:** meeting rooms, PC.

SOME UNITS
(🏊) (✕) (VCR) (🖥) (📶) (▦) / (✕) /

SUPER 8 MOTEL   *Book at aaa.com*

Phone: 928/367-3161

(AAA) (SAVE)
▼▼▼ ▼▼▼
Small-scale Hotel

All Year | 1P: $125-$150 | 2P: $125-$150 | XP: $5 | F12

Location: On SR 260, east end of town. Located in Pinetop. 1202 E White Mountain Blvd 85935 (PO Box 1819, PINETOP). Fax: 928/367-2445. **Facility:** 41 one-bedroom standard units, some with whirlpools. 2 stories (no elevator), interior corridors. **Terms:** cancellation fee imposed, weekly rates available, [ECP] meal plan available, pets ($25 extra charge). **Amenities:** hair dryers. **Pool(s):** small heated indoor. **Leisure Activities:** whirlpool, exercise room. **Guest Services:** coin laundry. **Cards:** AX, CB, DC, DS, MC, VI.

SOME UNITS
(S/D) (🐾) (🏊) (📷) (DATA PORT) (🖥) / (✕) (📶) /
FEE

TIMBER LODGE

Phone: (928)367-4463

▼▼
Motel

2/1-9/30 | 1P: $59 | 2P: $69
10/1-1/31 | 1P: $54 | 2P: $59

Location: On SR 260. Located in Pinetop. 1078 E White Mountain Blvd 85935. Fax: 928/367-4462. **Facility:** 29 one-bedroom standard units. 1-2 stories (no elevator), exterior corridors. *Bath:* combo or shower only. **Parking:** on-site. **Terms:** weekly rates available, package plans, pets ($5-$10 extra charge). **Cards:** AX, DS, JC, MC, VI.

SOME UNITS
(ASK) (S/D) (🐾) (✕) (X) (DATA PORT) (🖥) (📶) / (▦) /
FEE

WOODLAND INN & SUITES

Phone: (928)367-3636

(AAA) (SAVE)
▼▼▼ ▼▼▼
Motel

12/16-1/31 [ECP] | 1P: $99-$149 | 2P: $99-$149 | XP: $5 | F18
5/21-9/30 [ECP] | 1P: $79-$139 | 2P: $79-$139 | XP: $5 | F18
2/1-5/20 & 10/1-12/15 [ECP] | 1P: $69-$99 | 2P: $69-$99 | XP: $5 | F18

Location: On SR 260. Located in Pinetop. 458 E White Mountain Blvd 85935. Fax: 928/367-1543. **Facility:** 42 one-bedroom standard units. 2 stories (no elevator), interior corridors. **Parking:** on-site. **Terms:** 3 day cancellation notice-fee imposed, small pets only ($10 extra charge). **Amenities:** voice mail, irons, hair dryers. *Some:* DVD players (fee). **Leisure Activities:** whirlpool. **Business Services:** PC, fax. **Cards:** AX, CB, DC, DS, JC, MC, VI. **Special Amenities:** free expanded continental breakfast and free local telephone calls.

SOME UNITS
(S/D) (🐾) (DATA PORT) (🖥) (📶) (▦) / (✕) (VCR) /
FEE   FEE

─────── **WHERE TO DINE** ───────

THE CHALET RESTAURANT

Dinner: $8-$25   **Phone:** 928/367-1514

▼▼▼ ▼▼▼
American

Location: On SR 260; in Lakeside. 348 W White Mountain Blvd 85929. **Hours:** 5 pm-9 pm. Closed: 11/23, 12/25; also Sun & Mon. **Features:** An attractive country decor greets guests at the casual restaurant, which appeals to both locals and travelers. The menu has a variety of steak, seafood and chicken selections. Sushi bar is available on Tuesday and Friday nights. Casual dress; cocktails. **Parking:** on-site. **Cards:** AX, MC, VI.

(🍽) (📶)

CHARLIE CLARK'S

Dinner: $11-$28   **Phone:** 928/367-4900

▼▼ ▼▼
Steak House

Location: On SR 260; in Pinetop. 1701 E White Mountain Blvd 85935. **Hours:** 4:45 pm-10 pm; hours vary in winter. Closed: 4/16. **Reservations:** suggested. **Features:** An informal, Western atmosphere characterizes the popular, long-established restaurant. Prime rib, seafood and mesquite-broiled steak are included among entree selections. Lunch is served in the bar and on the patios. Casual dress; cocktails. **Parking:** on-site. **Cards:** AX, DC, DS, MC, VI.

(🍽)

THE CHRISTMAS TREE RESTAURANT

Dinner: $12-$50   **Phone:** 928/367-3107

▼▼ ▼▼
American

Location: Just s of jct SR 260; in Lakeside. 455 N Woodland Rd 85929. **Hours:** Open 2/1-10/20 & 11/26-1/31; 5 pm-9 pm. Closed: Mon & Tues. **Reservations:** suggested. **Features:** The holiday decor is fittingly festive at the restaurant, a favorite with locals and families. On the menu is a nice variety of beef, chicken and seafood entrees, all served with homemade cinnamon rolls. The house specialty is chicken and dumplings. Casual dress; cocktails. **Parking:** on-site. **Cards:** DS, MC, VI.

(🍽) (X) (📶)

EL RANCHO RESTAURANT   Lunch: $5-$8   Dinner: $8-$16   Phone: 928/367-4557

Mexican

Location: On SR 260; in Pinetop. 1523 E White Mountain Blvd 85935. **Hours:** 11 am-9 pm; seasonal hours may vary. Closed: 4/16, 11/23, 12/25. **Reservations:** accepted. **Features:** Chavez family recipes go back 60 years, but the friendly staff and owners of today contribute to a pleasant family dining experience. After noshing on traditional dishes, guests can savor flan or churros for dessert. Casual dress; cocktails. **Parking:** on-site. **Cards:** AX, DS, MC, VI.

MOUNTAIN THAI RESTAURANT   Lunch: $7-$10   Dinner: $7-$10   Phone: 928/368-4166

Thai

Location: W on SR 260; in Lakeside. 2741 Hwy 260 85929. **Hours:** Open 12/1-1/31; 11 am-8:30 pm, Sun 11:30 am-7:30 pm. Closed: 4/16; also Mon. **Features:** In a ramshackle little building not without its charms is this spot for true Thai cuisine. Noi has brought back authentic recipes from her native Thailand, including delicious yom wun sen, a spicy dish of clear bean thread noodles with cucumbers and cabbage. It tastes better than it sounds! Delicious soups are made with lemon grass and coconut milk. Everything is homemade, right down to the coconut ice cream. Casual dress; beer & wine only. **Parking:** on-site. **Cards:** AX, DS, MC, VI.

PHINEAS T'S   Lunch: $5-$11   Dinner: $10-$30   Phone: 928/367-7400

American

Location: On SR 260; in Pinetop. 1450 E White Mountain Blvd 85935. **Hours:** 11 am-10 pm. **Reservations:** accepted. **Features:** Haute cuisine offered in an upscale setting with casual, friendly service is not typical of the dining in this getaway town. However, Phineas T's offers just that if you're craving refinement and creativity and a carefully prepared selection of beef, game and seafood. Dressy casual; cocktails. **Parking:** on-site. **Cards:** AX, DC, DS, MC, VI.

THE VILLAGE DELI   Lunch: $3-$6   Dinner: $3-$6   Phone: 928/367-3354

Deli/Subs
Sandwiches

Location: On SR 260; in Ponderosa Village; in Pinetop. 476 White Mountain Blvd, Suites 1 & 2 85935. **Hours:** to 8 pm 6/1-9/30. Closed: 11/23, 12/25; also Sun. **Features:** Looking for a quick bite and a little bit of '60s memorabilia? The delicatessen—its walls brimming with pictures of Marilyn Monroe, Elvis Presley and vintage Coca-Cola signs—fills the bill. It serves a nice array of standard sandwiches and hot dogs. Casual dress. **Parking:** on-site. **Cards:** MC, VI.

PRESCOTT pop. 33,938

——— **WHERE TO STAY** ———

BEST WESTERN PRESCOTTONIAN MOTEL   ***Book at aaa.com***   Phone: (928)445-3096

Motel

| | 4/1-10/31 [BP] | 1P: $79-$129 | 2P: $89-$139 | XP: $10 | F12 |
| | 2/1-3/31 & 11/1-1/31 [BP] | 1P: $69-$99 | 2P: $79-$109 | XP: $10 | F12 |

Location: On SR 89, just s of jct SR 69. 1317 E Gurley St 86301. Fax: 928/778-2976. **Facility:** 121 units. 118 one-bedroom standard units. 1 one- and 2 two-bedroom suites ($139-$279). 2-3 stories (no elevator), exterior corridors. **Parking:** on-site. **Terms:** package plans. **Amenities:** voice mail, irons, hair dryers. **Pool(s):** small heated outdoor. **Leisure Activities:** whirlpool. **Guest Services:** valet and coin laundry. **Business Services:** meeting rooms. **Cards:** AX, CB, DC, DS, JC, MC, VI.

COMFORT INN OF PRESCOTT

Book at aaa.com

Phone: (928)778-5770

4/1-10/14	1P: $79-$139	2P: $79-$139	XP: $10	D18
2/1-3/31	1P: $59-$79	2P: $59-$79	XP: $10	D18
10/15-1/31	1P: $59	2P: $79	XP: $10	D18

Motel

Location: On SR 89, 1.5 mi s of town center. 1290 White Spar Rd 86303. Fax: 928/771-9373. **Facility:** 61 one-bedroom standard units, some with efficiencies. 2 stories (no elevator), exterior corridors. *Bath:* combo or shower only. **Parking:** on-site. **Terms:** cancellation fee imposed, [ECP] meal plan available, pets ($10 extra charge). **Amenities:** high-speed Internet, irons, hair dryers. **Leisure Activities:** hot tub. **Cards:** AX, CB, DC, DS, MC, VI. **Special Amenities:** free continental breakfast and free local telephone calls. *(See color ad p 370)*

SOME UNITS

- Suites with fireplaces & whirlpool spa available.
- Fitness center, pool & spa
- Deluxe continental breakfast
- All amenities in rooms
- 2 blocks from the new Gateway Mall
- Anniversary packages
- Special golf packages
- Close to recreation activities

1·800·223·3449 • 928·717·1200

3645 Lee Circle Prescott, Arizona 86301

www.forestvillas.com

Published rates all year for AAA members
Single/Double Occupancy

FOREST VILLAS HOTEL

Nov. 1-April 14= **$70**   April 15-Oct. 31= **$87** Sun-Thurs

Holiday and special events rates may be higher

FOREST VILLAS HOTEL *Book at aaa.com*

AAA **(SAVE)**
◆◆◆◆◆

Small-scale Hotel

Phone: (928)717-1200

4/15-10/31 [ECP]	1P: $95-$208	2P: $95-$208	XP: $10	F12
2/1-4/14 & 11/1-1/31 [ECP]	1P: $87-$208	2P: $87-$208	XP: $10	F12

Location: Jct SR 69, just n on Lee Blvd, then just e. 3645 Lee Cir 86301. **Fax:** 928/717-1400. **Facility:** 62 units. 61 one-bedroom standard units, some with whirlpools. 1 one-bedroom suite ($135-$208) with whirlpool. 2 stories, interior corridors. *Bath:* combo or shower only. **Parking:** on-site. **Terms:** cancellation fee imposed. **Amenities:** voice mail, irons, hair dryers. **Pool(s):** heated outdoor. **Leisure Activities:** whirlpool, exercise room. **Guest Services:** valet and coin laundry. **Business Services:** meeting rooms. **Cards:** AX, DC, DS, MC, VI. **Special Amenities:** free expanded continental breakfast and free local telephone calls. *(See color ad p 371)*

SOME UNITS
FEE

HAMPTON INN *Book at aaa.com*

AAA **(SAVE)**
◆◆◆◆◆

Small-scale Hotel

Phone: (928)443-5500

4/1-10/27 [ECP]	1P: $95-$159	2P: $95-$159	
10/28-1/31 [ECP]	1P: $89-$139	2P: $89-$139	
2/1-3/31 [ECP]	1P: $85-$139	2P: $85-$138	

Location: Jct SR 69 and Lee Blvd. 3453 Ranch Dr 86303. **Fax:** 928/443-5505. **Facility:** 76 units. 73 one-bedroom standard units, some with whirlpools. 3 one-bedroom suites. 3 stories, interior corridors. *Bath:* combo or shower only. **Parking:** on-site. **Amenities:** voice mail, irons, hair dryers. *Some:* dual phone lines. **Pool(s):** heated indoor, wading. **Leisure Activities:** whirlpool, hiking trails, exercise room. **Guest Services:** valet and coin laundry. **Business Services:** meeting rooms, PC. **Cards:** AX, DC, DS, JC, MC, VI. **Special Amenities:** free expanded continental breakfast and free local telephone calls. *(See color ad p 371)*

SOME UNITS
FEE FEE

HASSAYAMPA INN *Book at aaa.com*

◆◆◆

Historic
Small-scale Hotel

Phone: (928)778-9434

All Year	1P: $99-$229	2P: $109-$229	XP: $15	F13

Location: Corner of Marina; downtown. 122 E Gurley St 86301. **Fax:** 928/445-8590. **Facility:** This historic inn dates from 1927 with cozy rooms, stenciled, beamed lobby ceiling and original manual elevator, giving you the charm of yesteryear. 67 units. 54 one-bedroom standard units. 13 one-bedroom suites ($129-$229), some with whirlpools. 3 stories, interior corridors. *Bath:* combo or shower only. **Parking:** on-site. **Terms:** 3 day cancellation notice. **Amenities:** voice mail, irons, hair dryers. **Dining:** Peacock Room, see separate listing. **Leisure Activities:** exercise room. **Guest Services:** valet laundry. **Business Services:** meeting rooms, fax (fee). **Cards:** AX, CB, DC, DS, MC, VI. *(See color ad below)*

SOME UNITS

HOLIDAY INN EXPRESS PRESCOTT *Book at aaa.com*

AAA **(SAVE)**
◆◆◆

Small-scale Hotel

Phone: (928)445-8900

4/1-10/31 [ECP]	1P: $79-$129	2P: $79-$129	XP: $10	F13
2/1-3/31 & 11/1-1/31 [ECP]	1P: $78-$95	2P: $78-$95	XP: $10	F13

Location: Jct SR 69 and Lee Blvd. 3454 Ranch Dr 86303. **Fax:** 928/778-2629. **Facility:** 76 units. 73 one-bedroom standard units. 3 one-bedroom suites. 3 stories, interior corridors. *Bath:* combo or shower only. **Parking:** on-site. **Terms:** cancellation fee imposed. **Amenities:** dual phone lines, voice mail, irons, hair dryers. *Some:* high-speed Internet. **Pool(s):** heated indoor. **Leisure Activities:** sauna, whirlpool, exercise room. **Guest Services:** valet and coin laundry. **Business Services:** meeting rooms, PC, fax (fee). **Cards:** AX, DC, DS, MC, VI. **Special Amenities:** free expanded continental breakfast and free local telephone calls.

HOTEL ST. MICHAEL

◆◆

Historic
Small-scale Hotel

Phone: (928)776-1999

All Year [BP]	1P: $59-$99	2P: $59-$99	XP: $15	F12

Location: Center; across from Courthouse Square. 205 W Gurley St 86303. **Fax:** 928/776-7318. **Facility:** Across from the courthouse square, the 103-year-old building is filled with charm and offers pleasant guest rooms and modern baths. 72 units. 71 one-bedroom standard units. 1 one-bedroom suite ($99-$119). 3 stories, interior corridors. *Bath:* combo or shower only. **Parking:** on-site. **Terms:** 2 night minimum stay - seasonal and/or weekends, weekly rates available, package plans. **Amenities:** *Some:* high-speed Internet. **Guest Services:** gift shop. **Business Services:** meeting rooms. **Cards:** AX, DS, MC, VI.

SOME UNITS

HOTEL VENDOME *Book at aaa.com*   **Phone:** 928/776-0900

Property failed to provide current rates

♦♦♦
Historic
Small-scale Hotel

Location: S of Gurley St; downtown. 230 S Cortez St 86303. Fax: 928/771-0395. **Facility:** This small, historic hotel is a short distance from the old courthouse square and has two porches where you may rock as you watch passersby. Designated smoking area. 21 one-bedroom standard units. 2 stories (no elevator), interior corridors. *Bath:* combo or shower only. **Parking:** on-site. **Terms:** office hours 7 am-10 pm. **Business Services:** fax (fee).

MOTEL 6 #0166 *Book at aaa.com*   **Phone:** 928/776-0160

5/26-9/4	1P: $45-$55	2P: $51-$61	XP: $3 F17
9/5-10/30	1P: $41-$51	2P: $47-$57	XP: $3 F17
2/1-5/25 & 10/31-1/31	1P: $39-$49	2P: $45-$55	XP: $3 F17

♦
Motel

Location: 0.4 mi e of jct SR 89; center. 1111 E Sheldon St 86301. Fax: 928/445-4188. **Facility:** 79 one-bedroom standard units. 2 stories (no elevator), exterior corridors. *Bath:* shower only. **Parking:** on-site. **Terms:** pets (with prior approval). **Pool(s):** heated outdoor. **Guest Services:** coin laundry. **Cards:** AX, CB, DC, DS, MC, VI.

SOME UNITS

PLEASANT STREET INN BED & BREAKFAST   **Phone:** (928)445-4774

All Year [BP]   1P: $110-$150   2P: $110-$150

♦♦♦
Bed & Breakfast

Location: Just s of Gurley St; downtown. 142 S Pleasant St 86303. Fax: 928/445-4774. **Facility:** Built in 1906 and renovated in 1991, this two-story Victorian house offers a "pleasant" stay just three blocks from Courthouse Plaza. Designated smoking area. 4 units. 2 one-bedroom standard units. 2 one-bedroom suites. 2 stories (no elevator), interior corridors. *Bath:* combo or shower only. **Parking:** on-site. **Terms:** age restrictions may apply, 7 day cancellation notice-fee imposed. **Amenities:** hair dryers. **Guest Services:** complimentary evening beverages. **Cards:** AX, DS, MC, VI.

PRESCOTT CABIN RENTALS   **Phone:** (928)778-9573

3/1-12/31	1P: $116-$249	2P: $116-$249	XP: $20
2/1-2/28 & 1/1-1/31	1P: $106-$239	2P: $106-$239	XP: $20

♦♦
Motel

Location: Jct SR 89, 5 mi e on SR 69, 0.4 mi s on dirt/gravel road. Located in a quiet rural area. 5555 Onyx Dr 86303 (PO Box 4301, 86302). Fax: 928/443-0873. **Facility:** Designated smoking area. 9 units. 4 one-bedroom standard units, some with whirlpools. 4 one- and 1 three-bedroom suites with kitchens and whirlpools. 1 story, exterior corridors. **Parking:** on-site. **Terms:** office hours 7 am-8 pm, 2 night minimum stay, cancellation fee imposed, package plans, pets ($10 extra charge). **Amenities:** video library, irons, hair dryers. *Some:* DVD players, CD players. **Leisure Activities:** hiking trails, playground. **Fee:** massage. **Cards:** AX, DS, MC, VI. *(See color ad below)*

SOME UNITS

PRESCOTT PINES INN BED & BREAKFAST   **Phone:** (928)445-7270

AAA [SAVE]

All Year   1P: $79-$119   2P: $79-$119

♦♦
Motel

Location: On SR 89, 1.3 mi s of center. 901 White Spar Rd 86303. Fax: 928/778-3665. **Facility:** Designated smoking area. 12 units. 9 one- and 2 two-bedroom standard units, some with kitchens. 1 cottage ($279). 1 story, exterior corridors. *Bath:* combo or shower only. **Parking:** on-site. **Terms:** office hours 7:30 am-9 pm, 7 day cancellation notice, [BP] meal plan available. **Amenities:** voice mail. **Guest Services:** gift shop. **Business Services:** fax (fee). **Cards:** AX, DS, MC, VI. **Special Amenities:** free local telephone calls and early check-in/late check-out.

SOME UNITS

PRESCOTT RESORT & CONFERENCE CENTER

Phone: (928)776-1666

4/1-10/31	1P: $99-$119	2P: $109-$129	XP: $10	F18
2/1-3/31 & 11/1-1/31	1P: $79-$99	2P: $89-$109	XP: $10	F18

Small-scale Hotel **Location:** On SR 69, just e of SR 89. 1500 Hwy 69 86301. Fax: 928/776-8544. **Facility:** With a scenic view of Prescott valley, the elegantly decorated public areas also house many gallery paintings and sculptures. 160 units. 79 one-bedroom standard units. 81 one-bedroom suites. 5 stories, interior corridors. **Parking:** on-site. **Terms:** 2-3 night minimum stay - seasonal, cancellation fee imposed, package plans. **Amenities:** irons, hair dryers. **Dining:** Thumb Butte Dining Room, see separate listing. **Pool(s):** heated indoor. **Leisure Activities:** sauna, whirlpool, exercise room. *Fee:* massage, game room. **Guest Services:** gift shop, valet laundry, beauty salon. **Business Services:** conference facilities, business center. **Cards:** AX, DC, DS, JC, MC, VI. *(See color ad p 373)*

SOME UNITS

PRESCOTT SUPER 8 MOTEL   *Book at aaa.com*

Phone: (928)776-1282

5/1-10/31	1P: $52-$62	2P: $56-$66	XP: $5	F12
2/1-4/30 & 11/1-1/31	1P: $46-$56	2P: $51-$61	XP: $5	F12

Motel **Location:** 0.4 mi e of jct SR 89. 1105 Sheldon St 86301. Fax: 928/778-6736. **Facility:** 70 one-bedroom standard units. 2 stories (no elevator), interior corridors. **Parking:** on-site. **Terms:** [CP] meal plan available, pets ($10 fee). **Amenities:** safes (fee). **Pool(s):** heated outdoor. **Guest Services:** coin laundry. **Cards:** AX, CB, DC, DS, MC, VI. **Special Amenities:** free continental breakfast and free local telephone calls.

SOME UNITS

FEE   FEE

QUALITY INN & SUITES AND CONFERENCE CENTER   *Book at aaa.com*

Phone: (928)777-0770

5/16-10/15	1P: $89-$199	2P: $99-$209	XP: $10	F
2/1-5/15 & 10/16-1/31	1P: $79-$129	2P: $89-$179	XP: $10	F

Small-scale Hotel **Location:** On SR 69, 3.6 mi e of jct SR 89. 4499 Hwy 69 86301. Fax: 928/777-0064. **Facility:** 82 units. 54 one-bedroom standard units, some with whirlpools. 28 one-bedroom suites with whirlpools. 2 stories, interior corridors. *Bath:* combo or shower only. **Parking:** on-site. **Terms:** package plans, small pets only ($25 fee). **Amenities:** high-speed Internet, voice mail, irons, hair dryers. **Dining:** 11 am-9 pm, cocktails. **Pool(s):** heated indoor. **Leisure Activities:** whirlpool, hiking trails, exercise room. **Guest Services:** gift shop, valet and coin laundry, beauty salon. **Business Services:** meeting rooms. **Cards:** AX, CB, DC, DS, MC, VI.

SOME UNITS

FEE

SPRINGHILL SUITES BY MARRIOTT   *Book at aaa.com*

Phone: (928)776-0998

5/26-10/8	1P: $109-$145	2P: $109-$145	
4/1-5/25 & 10/9-1/31	1P: $89-$129	2P: $89-$129	
2/1-3/31	1P: $79-$119	2P: $79-$119	

Small-scale Hotel **Location:** On SR 89, at Marina St. 200 E Sheldon St 86301. Fax: 928/776-0998. **Facility:** 105 units. 102 one-bedroom standard units. 3 one-bedroom suites with whirlpools. 3 stories, interior corridors. *Bath:* combo or shower only. **Parking:** on-site. **Terms:** [BP] meal plan available. **Amenities:** high-speed Internet, dual phone lines, voice mail, irons, hair dryers. **Pool(s):** small heated indoor. **Leisure Activities:** whirlpool, exercise room. **Guest Services:** valet and coin laundry. **Business Services:** meeting rooms, business center. **Cards:** AX, CB, DC, DS, JC, MC, VI. *(See color ad below)*

SOME UNITS

——— WHERE TO DINE ———

ACME FISH COMPANY — Lunch: $9-$14 — Dinner: $10-$20 — Phone: 928/541-0221
Location: Just w of Montezuma. 220 W Gurley St 86303. **Hours:** 11 am-10 pm. Closed: 11/23, 12/25.
Features: This is a fun, relaxing type of restaurant with a raw bar and five fresh daily catches. Prices are reasonable and service is friendly. Casual dress; cocktails. **Parking:** street. **Cards:** AX, MC, VI.

Seafood

AMERICAN JAZZ GRILLE — Dinner: $15-$25 — Phone: 928/443-9292
Location: Just n of Gurley St. 129 1/2 N Cortez 86303. **Hours:** 5 pm-11 pm. Closed: 12/25; also Sun & Mon.
Features: The place for live jazz, this restaurant has some enticing specials such as chili shrimp and barbecue red snapper. Four sauce choices provide diners with creative options. Casual dress; cocktails; entertainment. **Parking:** street. **Cards:** AX, MC, VI.

American

EL GATO AZUL — Lunch: $9-$15 — Dinner: $10-$20 — Phone: 928/445-1070
Location: Just e of Granite. 316 W Goodwin 86303. **Hours:** 11 am-10 pm, Fri & Sat from 8 am, Sun 8 am-3 pm.
Closed: 12/25. **Features:** Enjoy leisurely lunches by the creek or cozy patio or terrace dining. Rotating tapas and wine selections in late afternoon and nightly features are available. Casual dress; cocktails.
Parking: street. **Cards:** AX, MC, VI.

Argentine

GURLEY ST GRILL — Lunch: $7-$10 — Dinner: $10-$22 — Phone: 928/445-3388
Location: Just w of SR 89. 230 W Gurley St 86301. **Hours:** 11 am-10 pm. Closed: 11/23, 12/25; also day after Labor Day. **Features:** Dine in the lively atmosphere of a resorted 1901 red brick building on pizza, burgers, steak, pasta, seafood and spit-roasted chicken. Casual dress; cocktails. **Parking:** street. **Cards:** AX, DS, MC, VI. **Historic**

American

MURPHY'S RESTAURANT — Lunch: $8-$15 — Dinner: $17-$46 — Phone: 928/445-4044
Location: Downtown. 201 N Cortez 86301. **Hours:** 11 am-3 & 4-10 pm, Fri & Sat-11 pm; Sunday brunch.
Closed: 12/25; also day after Labor Day. **Reservations:** suggested. **Features:** Restored to depict the era in which it was built, the historic 1890 mercantile now accommodates this restaurant, which serves mesquite-broiled seafood, steak and prime rib. Breads are baked daily on the premises. Diners who join a "professional" beer drinkers club can try the more than 60 domestic and imported varieties this spot offers. Dressy casual; cocktails. **Parking:** street. **Cards:** AX, DS, MC, VI. **Historic**

American

N'AWLINS — Lunch: $7-$12 — Dinner: $10-$20 — Phone: 928/541-1400
Location: Just n of Gurley St. **Hours:** 11 am-10 pm. Closed: 11/23, 12/25. **Features:** The eatery offers live Blues music on Tuesday, Friday and Saturday and other groups throughout the summer. There's a good variety of menu items and daily specials are always available. Casual dress; cocktails; entertainment.
Parking: street. **Cards:** AX, MC, VI.

Creole

THE OFFICE RESTAURANT & BAR — Lunch: $7-$14 — Dinner: $7-$14 — Phone: 928/445-1211
Location: Just n of Gurley St; center. 128 N Cortez 86301. **Hours:** 10:45 am-10 pm. Closed: 12/25.
Features: Patrons won't fool anyone by saying, "I'm going to the office," but they will find a nice selection of Southwestern dishes, including tortilla soup thick with chicken and burgers with toppings from caramelized onions to green chile. The warm "cookie" dessert is to tempting to share. Casual dress; cocktails. **Parking:**
Southwestern
street. **Cards:** AX, DS, MC, VI.

THE PALACE RESTAURANT AND SALOON — Lunch: $6-$11 — Dinner: $13-$37 — Phone: 928/541-1996
Location: Just s of Gurley St; downtown. 120 S Montezuma St 86301. **Hours:** 11 am-9:30 pm, Fri & Sat-10:30 pm.
Closed: 12/25. **Reservations:** accepted. **Features:** You will enjoy casual, relaxed dining in Arizona's oldest bar and amid a resorted 1880s decor. Casual dress; cocktails. **Parking:** street. **Cards:** AX, DS, MC, VI.

American

PEACOCK ROOM

▽▽▽▽
American

Lunch: $5-$10   **Dinner:** $14-$28   **Phone:** 928/778-9434
Location: Corner of Marina; downtown; in Hassayampa Inn. 122 E Gurley St 86301. **Hours:** 7 am-2 & 5-9 pm, Sun 7 am-1 & 5-9 pm. **Reservations:** suggested. **Features:** In a historic 1927 hotel, the elegant dining room is named for what was once a brightly colored tile wall entry called Peacock Alley. The sophisticated menu lists pasta, steak, seafood and veal dishes, in addition to other specialties. Casual dress; cocktails. **Parking:** on-site. **Cards:** AX, CB, DC, DS, MC, VI. **Historic (See color ad p 372)**

PRESCOTT BREWING COMPANY

ⒶⒶⒶ
▽▽ ▽▽
▽▽
American

Lunch: $6-$15   **Dinner:** $6-$15   **Phone:** 928/771-2795
Location: Between Cortez and Montezuma sts; downtown. 130 W Gurley St, Suite A 86301. **Hours:** 11 am-10 pm, Fri & Sat-11 pm. Closed: 5/29, 11/23, 12/25. **Reservations:** accepted, Sun-Thurs. **Features:** An on-site brewery and in-house bakery are among offerings at the casual restaurant. The brew pub includes a smoking section. Casual dress; cocktails. **Parking:** street. **Cards:** AX, DS, MC, VI.

THE ROSE RESTAURANT   *Menu on aaa.com*

ⒶⒶⒶ
▽▽▽ ▽▽
Continental

Dinner: $15-$32   **Phone:** 928/777-8308
Location: Just s of Gurley St. 234 S Cortez St 86303. **Hours:** 5 pm-9 pm. Closed: Mon & Tues. **Reservations:** suggested. **Features:** A restored Victorian house from the late 1890s is the setting for intimate dining. The menu blends an excellent selection of beef, pasta, veal, chicken and vegetarian entrees with distinctive sauces and seasonings. Patio dining is available in season. Casual dress; cocktails. **Parking:** on-site. **Cards:** AX, CB, DC, DS, MC, VI.

TAJ MAHAL

▽▽ ▽▽
Northern Indian

Lunch: $8-$15   **Dinner:** $8-$15   **Phone:** 928/445-5752
Location: On SR 69, 1.2 mi e; in Frontier Village Center. 1781 E Hwy 69 86301. **Hours:** 11 am-2:30 & 5-9 pm, Sat & Sun 11:30 am-3 & 5-9 pm. **Reservations:** accepted. **Features:** The new owner has refurbished the dining room and enhanced the menu with North Indian traditional dishes, such as chicken tikka and lamb madras. Casual dress; cocktails. **Parking:** on-site. **Cards:** AX, DS, MC, VI.

THUMB BUTTE DINING ROOM

▽▽▽▽
American

Lunch: $7-$12   **Dinner:** $16-$32   **Phone:** 928/776-1666
Location: On SR 69, just e of SR 89; in Prescott Resort, Conference Center & Casino. 1500 Hwy 69 86301. **Hours:** 6:30 am-3:30 & 4-9 pm, Fri & Sat-9:30 pm. **Reservations:** accepted. **Features:** A nice selection of chicken, steak and pasta is served with a hilltop view of Prescott or the valley. Casual dress; cocktails. **Parking:** on-site. **Cards:** AX, CB, DC, DS, MC, VI.

PRESCOTT VALLEY pop. 23,535

——— WHERE TO STAY ———

DAYS INN/PRESCOTT VALLEY   *Book at aaa.com*

ⒶⒶⒶ [SAVE]
▽▽▽ ▽▽
Motel

All Year	1P: $69-$120	2P: $79-$120	XP: $10 F18

Phone: (928)772-8600

Location: On SR 69; corner of Windsong Rd. 7875 E Hwy 69 86314. **Fax:** 928/772-0942. **Facility:** 78 units. 75 one-bedroom standard units. 3 one-bedroom suites. 2 stories (no elevator), exterior corridors. *Bath:* combo or shower only. **Parking:** on-site. **Terms:** [CP] meal plan available, pets ($50 deposit). **Amenities:** voice mail, hair dryers. **Pool(s):** heated outdoor. **Leisure Activities:** whirlpool. **Guest Services:** coin laundry. **Cards:** AX, CB, DC, DS, JC, MC, VI. **Special Amenities:** free expanded continental breakfast and free local telephone calls.

SOME UNITS

SUPER 8 MOTEL   *Book at aaa.com*

ⒶⒶⒶ [SAVE]
▽▽▽
Small-scale Hotel

3/16-10/1	1P: $55	2P: $75	XP: $10 F12
2/1-3/15 & 10/2-1/31	1P: $45	2P: $55	XP: $10 F12

Phone: (928)775-5888

Location: 0.4 mi w of Robert Rd. 7801 E Hwy 69 86314. **Fax:** 928/775-8740. **Facility:** 57 one-bedroom standard units, some with whirlpools. 2 stories (no elevator), interior corridors. **Parking:** on-site. **Pool(s):** small heated outdoor. **Guest Services:** coin laundry. **Cards:** AX, DS, MC, VI. **Special Amenities:** free continental breakfast and free local telephone calls.

SOME UNITS

——— WHERE TO DINE ———

GARCIA'S MEXICAN RESTAURANT

▽▽ ▽▽
Mexican

Lunch: $5-$10   **Dinner:** $6-$14   **Phone:** 928/759-9499
Location: Jct SR 69, just n on Centre Ct, then just e; behind theatre. 2992 Park Ave, Suite B 86314. **Hours:** 11 am-10 pm, Fri & Sat-11 pm. Closed: 11/23, 12/25. **Reservations:** not accepted. **Features:** The eatery, which has a fresh new look, serves classic preparations of all the favorites, including fajitas, burritos and tacos. The chicken enchilada with sour cream is excellent. Also on the menu are some lighter options. Casual dress; cocktails. **Parking:** on-site. **Cards:** AX, MC, VI.

TARA THAI II

▽▽
Thai

Lunch: $8-$16   **Dinner:** $9-$17   **Phone:** 928/772-3249
Location: Just w of Prescott Hwy; west side of town. 6170 E Hwy 69 86314. **Hours:** 11 am-3 & 5-9 pm, Sat & Sun from noon. Closed: 11/23, 12/25. **Reservations:** suggested. **Features:** Fresh, cooked-to-order food makes up the menu at the modest eatery. Widely varied curries and specialties come with fragrantly scented rice and crispy vegetables. Homemade ice cream is a perfect end to the meal. Dressy casual. **Parking:** on-site. **Cards:** DS, MC, VI.

ZEKE'S EATIN' PLACE

▽▽ ▽▽
American

Lunch: $6-$12   **Dinner:** $8-$22   **Phone:** 928/775-9832
Location: SR 69, just n. 2960 N Centre Ct 86314. **Hours:** 6:30 am-9 pm, Fri-10 pm, Sat 7 am-10 pm, Sun 7 am-9 pm. Closed: 11/23, 12/24, 12/25. **Features:** Given the ample portion sizes, guests must be mindful of how much entree they eat if they want to try the six-layer carrot or chocolate cakes. Such dishes as country-fried steak with mashed potatoes are sure to fill. Casual dress; cocktails. **Parking:** on-site. **Cards:** AX, DS, MC, VI.

QUARTZSITE pop. 3,354

———— WHERE TO STAY ————

SUPER 8 MOTEL-QUARTZSITE *Book at aaa.com* **Phone:** 928/927-8080

▼▼
Motel

1/1-1/31	1P: $125-$135	2P: $125-$135	
2/1-12/31	1P: $65-$90	2P: $75-$100	XP: $5 F12

Location: I-10, exit 17, just s to Frontage Rd, then 0.6 mi w. 2050 W Dome Rock Rd 85359 (PO Box 4444). Fax: 928/927-9233. **Facility:** 52 one-bedroom standard units. 2 stories (no elevator), interior corridors. *Bath:* combo or shower only. **Parking:** on-site. **Terms:** pets ($5 extra charge). **Amenities:** voice mail. **Guest Services:** coin laundry. **Business Services:** fax (fee). **Cards:** AX, DS, MC, VI.

SOME UNITS
(ASK) 🐾 📶 💲 (DATA PORT) / ✖ 🛢 📠 /
FEE

RIO RICO

———— WHERE TO STAY ————

ESPLENDOR RESORT AT RIO RICO *Book at aaa.com* **Phone:** (520)281-1901

▼▼▼▼
Resort
Large-scale Hotel

2/1-5/31 & 9/16-1/31	1P: $139-$250	XP: $25 F12	
6/1-9/15	1P: $99-$149	XP: $25 F12	

Location: I-19, exit 17 (Rio Rico Dr), 0.5 mi w. Located in a quiet area. 1069 Camino Caralampi 85648. Fax: 520/281-7132. **Facility:** High over the Santa Cruz River Valley, this resort blends old Southwest style and modern conveniences. 180 units. 179 one-bedroom standard units. 1 one-bedroom suite ($250-$550). 2-3 stories (no elevator), exterior corridors. *Bath:* combo or shower only. **Parking:** on-site. **Terms:** check-in 4 pm, cancellation fee imposed, [MAP] meal plan available, package plans, small pets only ($25 fee). **Amenities:** voice mail, irons, hair dryers. *Fee:* video games, high-speed Internet. **Dining:** San Cayetano, see separate listing. **Pool(s):** heated outdoor. **Leisure Activities:** sauna, whirlpool, hiking trails. *Fee:* golf-18 holes, 4 lighted tennis courts, horseback riding, massage. **Guest Services:** gift shop, valet laundry, area transportation (fee). **Business Services:** conference facilities. **Cards:** AX, DC, DS, MC, VI.

SOME UNITS
(ASK) (SD) ➕ 🐾 🍴 🍷 (&M) (&) 🛥 👨‍👧 ✖ 💲 (DATA PORT) 🛢 📠 / ✖ /
FEE FEE   FEE

———— WHERE TO DINE ————

SAN CAYETANO **Lunch:** $9-$15 **Dinner:** $21-$38 **Phone:** 520/377-7311

▼▼▼
Regional American

Location: I-19, exit 17 (Rio Rico Dr), 0.5 mi w; in Esplendor Resort at Rio Rico. 1069 Camino Caralampi 85648. **Hours:** 6 am-9:30 pm. **Reservations:** suggested. **Features:** Diners appreciate the casual atmosphere and stunning views across the valley to the mountains beyond. Specialties include steaks, seafood, sandwiches and soups. Casual dress; cocktails. **Parking:** on-site. **Cards:** AX, DC, DS, MC, VI.

SAFFORD pop. 9,232

———— WHERE TO STAY ————

BEST WESTERN DESERT INN *Book at aaa.com* **Phone:** (928)428-0521

(AAA) (SAVE)
▼▼▼ ▼▼
Motel

All Year [ECP]	1P: $60-$70	2P: $65-$75	XP: $5 F14

Location: US 191, 1 mi w on US 70. 1391 W Thatcher Blvd 85546. Fax: 928/428-7653. **Facility:** 70 units. 65 one-bedroom standard units. 5 one-bedroom suites, some with efficiencies. 2 stories (no elevator), exterior corridors. **Parking:** on-site. **Terms:** small pets only ($6 extra charge). **Amenities:** voice mail, irons, hair dryers. *Some:* high-speed Internet. **Pool(s):** small heated outdoor. **Guest Services:** coin laundry. **Business Services:** fax (fee). **Cards:** AX, CB, DC, DS, JC, MC, VI. **Special Amenities:** early check-in/late check-out and preferred room (subject to availability with advance reservations).

SOME UNITS
(SD) 🐾 🍴 🛥 💲 (DATA PORT) 🛢 📠 / ✖ 📠 /
FEE

COMFORT INN *Book at aaa.com* **Phone:** 928/428-5851

▼▼▼
Motel

Property failed to provide current rates

Location: US 191, 1.3 mi w on US 70. 1578 W Thatcher Blvd 85546. Fax: 928/428-4968. **Facility:** 44 one-bedroom standard units. 2 stories (no elevator), exterior corridors. **Parking:** on-site. **Terms:** small pets only ($10 extra charge). **Amenities:** high-speed Internet, voice mail, irons, hair dryers. **Pool(s):** heated outdoor. **Guest Services:** valet laundry. **Business Services:** fax (fee).

SOME UNITS
🐾 🍴 🛥 💲 (DATA PORT) 🛢 📠 / ✖ /
FEE

DAYS INN **Phone:** (928)428-5000

(AAA) (SAVE)
▼▼▼ ▼▼
Motel

All Year [CP]	1P: $70-$135	2P: $80-$150	XP: $10 F17

Location: US 191, 0.5 mi e. 520 E Hwy 70 85546. Fax: 928/428-7510. **Facility:** 43 units. 41 one-bedroom standard units. 2 one-bedroom suites ($135-$165). 2 stories (no elevator), exterior corridors. *Bath:* combo or shower only. **Parking:** on-site. **Terms:** 30 day cancellation notice-fee imposed, package plans, pets ($10 extra charge). **Amenities:** voice mail, hair dryers. **Pool(s):** small outdoor. **Leisure Activities:** whirlpool, adjacent recreation complex, batting cages & miniature golf, limited exercise equipment. **Guest Services:** valet and coin laundry. **Business Services:** PC, fax (fee). **Cards:** AX, CB, DC, DS, MC, VI. **Special Amenities:** free continental breakfast and free local telephone calls.

SOME UNITS
(SD) 🐾 🍴 (&M) (&) 🔔 🛥 ✖ (DATA PORT) 🛢 📠 💲 / ✖ /
FEE

ECONO LODGE *Book at aaa.com* **Phone:** (928)348-0011

▼▼
Motel

All Year	1P: $46	2P: $51	XP: $5 F18

Location: Just e of jct US 191 and 70. 225 E Hwy 70 85546. Fax: 928/348-7764. **Facility:** 40 one-bedroom standard units. 2 stories (no elevator), exterior corridors. **Parking:** on-site. **Terms:** office hours 6 am-11 pm. **Pool(s):** outdoor. **Leisure Activities:** whirlpool. **Guest Services:** complimentary laundry. **Business Services:** fax. **Cards:** AX, DS, MC, VI.

SOME UNITS
(ASK) (SD) 🐾 🛥 💲 (DATA PORT) 🛢 📠 / ✖ /

QUALITY INN & SUITES   *Book at aaa.com*   Phone: (928)428-3200

All Year   1P: $60-$195   2P: $85-$215   XP: $25   F17
Small-scale Hotel   **Location:** US 191, 0.5 mi e. 420 E Hwy 70 85546. Fax: 928/428-3288. **Facility:** 102 units. 98 one-bedroom standard units, some with whirlpools. 4 one-bedroom suites, some with whirlpools. 1-3 stories, interior/exterior corridors. **Bath:** combo or shower only. **Parking:** on-site. **Terms:** pets ($10 extra charge). **Amenities:** video library (fee), voice mail, irons, hair dryers. **Pool(s):** heated indoor. **Leisure Activities:** saunas, whirlpools, exercise room, horseshoes, shuffleboard. **Guest Services:** sundries, valet and coin laundry. **Business Services:** conference facilities, PC, fax (fee). **Cards:** AX, CB, DC, DS, JC, MC, VI.

SOME UNITS

--------- *The following lodging was either not evaluated or did not* ---------
meet AAA rating requirements but is listed for your information only.

THE OLNEY HOUSE   Phone: 928/428-5118

[fyi]   **Not evaluated. Location:** 0.4 mi s of US 70. 1104 Central Ave 85546. Facilities, services, and decor characterize a basic property.

--------- WHERE TO DINE ---------

BRICK'S STEAKS & MORE   **Lunch:** $5-$8   **Dinner:** $9-$17   Phone: 928/348-8111
Steak House   **Location:** 3.6 mi s of jct US 70 and 191. 4367 S Hwy 191 85546. **Hours:** 11 am-9 pm. Closed major holidays; also Sun. **Reservations:** accepted. **Features:** Hearty portions, grilled steaks and fruit cobblers are popular with locals who often drop in to celebrate a birthday. Casual dress; cocktails. **Parking:** on-site. **Cards:** AX, DS, MC, VI.

CHALO'S LA CASA REYNOSO   **Lunch:** $5-$7   **Dinner:** $5-$13   Phone: 928/348-9889
Mexican   **Location:** US 70, just s. 611 S 6th Ave 85546. **Hours:** 11 am-10 pm. Closed major holidays; also Tues. **Reservations:** accepted. **Features:** Everyone greets everyone in the family eatery, which employs a friendly staff. Such familiar favorites as burritos and fajitas are served in hearty portions. Chicken rellenos and the homemade green chili are noteworthy. Casual dress; cocktails. **Parking:** street. **Cards:** AX, DC, DS, MC, VI.

MANOR HOUSE   **Lunch:** $6-$10   **Dinner:** $6-$13   Phone: 928/428-7148
American   **Location:** US 191, 0.5 mi e. 415 E Hwy 70 85546. **Hours:** 5:30 am-9 pm, Fri & Sat-10 pm, Sun-7 pm. Closed: 12/25. **Reservations:** accepted. **Features:** The family-style warmth offered by the staff reflects the owner's friendly manner. Hearty dinners include Mexican, pasta and seafood dishes. The regulars often opt for Grandma's meatloaf or chicken Kiev. Casual dress; cocktails. **Parking:** on-site. **Cards:** AX, DC, MC, VI.

ST. JOHNS pop. 3,269

--------- WHERE TO STAY ---------

DAYS INN   Phone: (928)337-4422
Motel   All Year   1P: $60-$75   2P: $75-$85   XP: $5   F12
Location: Center. 125 E Commercial St 85936 (PO Box 2370). Fax: 928/337-4126. **Facility:** 39 one-bedroom standard units. 1-2 stories (no elevator), exterior corridors. **Bath:** combo or shower only. **Parking:** on-site. **Terms:** [CP] meal plan available, package plans, small pets only ($5 fee). **Amenities:** voice mail, hair dryers. **Guest Services:** coin laundry. **Business Services:** meeting rooms, PC. **Cards:** AX, DC, DS, MC, VI.

SOME UNITS

ST. MICHAELS pop. 1,295

--------- WHERE TO STAY ---------

NAVAJOLAND DAYS INN   *Book at aaa.com*   Phone: 928/871-5690
Small-scale Hotel   All Year   1P: $70-$95   2P: $70-$95   F17
Location: From jct SR 12, 1.5 mi w. 392 W Hwy 264 86511 (PO Box 905). Fax: 928/871-5699. **Facility:** 73 units. 65 one-bedroom standard units. 8 one-bedroom suites ($90). 2 stories (no elevator), exterior corridors. **Bath:** combo or shower only. **Parking:** on-site. **Terms:** pets ($15 extra charge). **Amenities:** irons, hair dryers. **Dining:** 24 hours. **Pool(s):** heated indoor. **Leisure Activities:** sauna, whirlpool, exercise room. **Guest Services:** gift shop, coin laundry. **Business Services:** meeting rooms. **Cards:** AX, CB, DC, DS, MC, VI. **Special Amenities:** free local telephone calls.

SOME UNITS

SAN CARLOS pop. 3,716

--------- WHERE TO STAY ---------

BEST WESTERN APACHE GOLD HOTEL   *Book at aaa.com*   Phone: 928/475-7600
Large-scale Hotel   Property failed to provide current rates
Location: From jct SR 77 S, 4.2 mi e. US Hwy 70 85550 (PO Box 1200). Fax: 928/475-7601. **Facility:** The many activities available, pleasant rooms and higher elevation make this a great place to visit for families or groups. 146 units. 144 one- and 2 two-bedroom standard units, some with whirlpools. 2 stories, interior corridors. **Bath:** combo or shower only. **Parking:** on-site. **Amenities:** video games (fee), irons, hair dryers. **Pool(s):** heated outdoor. **Leisure Activities:** sauna, whirlpool, playground, exercise room, basketball, volleyball. **Fee:** golf-18 holes. **Guest Services:** gift shop, coin laundry. **Business Services:** conference facilities. *(See color ad p 221)*

SOME UNITS

SCOTTSDALE —See Phoenix p. 332.

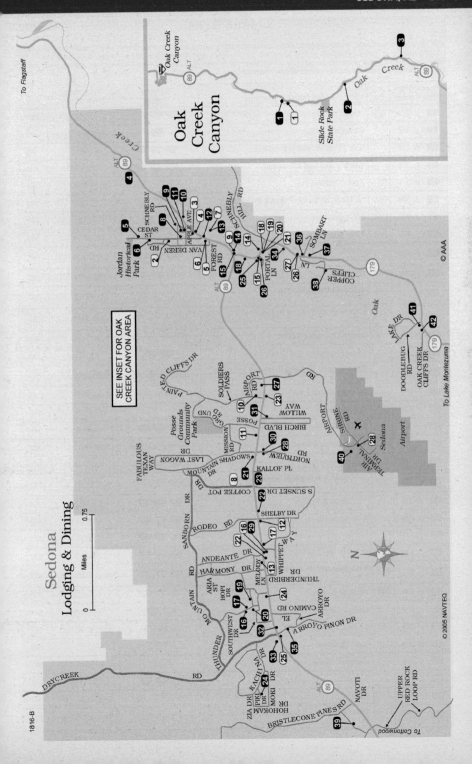

Sedona
Lodging & Dining

Sedona Area

This index helps you "spot" where approved accommodations and restaurants are located on the corresponding detailed maps. Lodging rate ranges are for comparison only and show the property's high season; rates are per night, unless only weekly (W) rates are available. Restaurant rate range is for dinner, unless only lunch (L) is served. Turn to the listing page for more detailed rate information and consult display ads for special promotions.

Spotter/Map Page Number	OA	SEDONA - Lodgings	Diamond Rating	Rate Range High Season	Listing Page
1 / p. 379	AAA	**Junipine Resort** - see color ad p 392	◆◆◆	$170-$360 SAVE	392
2 / p. 379		Slide Rock Lodge	◆	$79-$125	399
3 / p. 379		Briar Patch Inn Bed & Breakfast	◆◆◆	$189-$379	388
4 / p. 379		Wishing Well Bed & Breakfast	◆◆◆	$225-$235	400
5 / p. 379	AAA	**Apple Orchard Inn**	◆◆◆	$139-$205 SAVE	385
6 / p. 379	AAA	**"A Touch of Sedona"-Bed & Breakfast**	◆◆◆	$155-$205 SAVE	385
8 / p. 379	AAA	**Iris Garden Inn**	◆◆	$74-$125 SAVE	392
9 / p. 379	AAA	**Rose Tree Inn**	◆◆	$95-$135 SAVE	396
10 / p. 379	AAA	**Best Western Arroyo Roble Hotel & Creekside Villas** - see color ad p 386	◆◆◆	$129-$339 SAVE	385
11 / p. 379	AAA	**Matterhorn Inn** - see color ad p 395	◆◆◆	$89-$159 SAVE	395
12 / p. 379	AAA	**Orchards Inn of Sedona** - see color ad p 398	◆◆◆	$119-$199 SAVE	395
13 / p. 379	AAA	**L'Auberge de Sedona Resort** - see color ad p 398	◆◆◆	$189-$319 SAVE	394
14 / p. 379	AAA	**Amara Creekside Resort**	◆◆◆◆	$179-$459 SAVE	384
15 / p. 379		Cedars Resort on Oak Creek	◆◆	$99-$149	389
16 / p. 379	AAA	**Casa Sedona Bed and Breakfast Inn** - see color ad p 389	◆◆◆	$195-$300 SAVE	389
17 / p. 379	AAA	**Alma de Sedona Inn** - see color ad p 384	◆◆◆◆	$189-$305 SAVE	384
18 / p. 379	AAA	**Sedona Motel**	◆◆	$89-$109 SAVE	397
19 / p. 379		Boots & Saddles Romantic Bed & Breakfast	◆◆◆	$150-$245	388
20 / p. 379	AAA	**Adobe Grand Villas** - see color ad p 383	◆◆◆◆	$399-$900 SAVE	382
21 / p. 379		Hampton Inn	◆◆◆	$109-$179	391
22 / p. 379	AAA	**Sedona Rouge Hotel & Spa** - see color ad p 397	◆◆◆	$279-$309 SAVE	397
23 / p. 379		The Lodge at Sedona	◆◆◆	$155-$325	394
24 / p. 379		A Territorial House Traditional Old West B&B	◆◆◆	$125-$215	385
25 / p. 379		Los Abrigados Resort & Spa	◆◆◆	$225	395
26 / p. 379	AAA	**El Portal Sedona** - see color ad p 390	◆◆◆	$225-$495 SAVE	390
27 / p. 379	AAA	**Best Western Inn of Sedona** - see color ad p 387	◆◆◆	$164-$209 SAVE	387
28 / p. 379	AAA	**Villas of Sedona**	◆◆◆	$175-$225 SAVE	400
29 / p. 379		Sedona Super 8	◆◆	$85-$109	398
30 / p. 379	AAA	**Sedona Springs Resort**	◆◆◆	$115-$250 SAVE	397
31 / p. 379	AAA	**Baby Quail Inn**	◆◆	$79-$110 SAVE	385
32 / p. 379	AAA	**Kokopelli Suites** - see color ad p 393	◆◆◆	$109-$239 SAVE	393
33 / p. 379		Southwest Inn at Sedona	◆◆◆	$110-$310	399
34 / p. 379	AAA	**The Inn on Oak Creek** - see color ad p 391	◆◆◆	$200-$295 SAVE	392
35 / p. 379	AAA	**Sedona Real Inn & Suites** - see color ad p 382	◆◆◆	$135-$319 SAVE	397

Spotter/Map Page Number	OA	SEDONA - Lodgings (continued)	Diamond Rating	Rate Range High Season	Listing Page
36 / p. 379	AAA	Comfort Inn	◆◆	$89-$169 SAVE	389
37 / p. 379	AAA	Quality Inn-King's Ransom	◆◆	$79-$189 SAVE	396
38 / p. 379		Creekside Inn at Sedona	◆◆◆	$175-$285	390
39 / p. 379		Sedona Summit Resort	◆◆◆	$140-$300	397
40 / p. 379	AAA	Sky Ranch Lodge - see color ad p 398	◆◆	$75-$250 SAVE	398
41 / p. 379		Radisson Poco Diablo Resort - see color ad p 396	◆◆◆	Failed to provide	396
42 / p. 379	AAA	Villas at Poco Diablo	◆◆◆	$135-$155 SAVE	399
		SEDONA - Restaurants			
1 / p. 379		Junipine Cafe	◆◆	$10-$24	401
2 / p. 379		Takashi Japanese Restaurant	◆◆	$15-$22	403
3 / p. 379		Oaxaca Restaurant	◆◆	$10-$16	402
4 / p. 379		The Orchards Bar & Grill	◆◆	$8-$20	402
5 / p. 379	AAA	Cowboy Club	◆◆	$10-$40	401
6 / p. 379	AAA	The Silver Saddle Room	◆◆◆	$15-$39	403
7 / p. 379	AAA	L'Auberge de Sedona Restaurant	◆◆◆◆	$25-$40	402
8 / p. 379		Peking Inn	◆◆	$8-$13	402
9 / p. 379		Gallery on Oak Creek	◆◆◆	$12-$40	401
10 / p. 379		Judi's Restaurant	◆◆	$12-$25	401
11 / p. 379		The Heartline Cafe	◆◆◆	$15-$26	401
12 / p. 379		Dahl & DiLuca Ristorante Italiano	◆◆◆	$11-$28	401
13 / p. 379		Casa Rincon & Tapas Cantina	◆◆	$5-$22	401
14 / p. 379		Robert's Creekside Cafe & Grill	◆◆◆	$16-$22	403
15 / p. 379		Steaks & Sticks	◆◆◆	$16-$30	403
16 / p. 379		Spices	◆◆	$15-$22	403
17 / p. 379	AAA	Pietros	◆◆◆	$15-$26	402
18 / p. 379		The Secret Garden Cafe	◆◆	$8-$16(L)	403
19 / p. 379		El Rincon Restaurante Mexicano	◆◆	$8-$15	401
20 / p. 379		Oak Creek Brewery & Grill	◆◆◆	$11-$26	402
21 / p. 379	AAA	Rene At Tlaquepaque	◆◆◆	$17-$35	402
22 / p. 379		Savannah's	◆◆◆	$14-$34	403
23 / p. 379		Monsoon in the Red Rocks	◆◆	$7-$10	402
24 / p. 379		Keiser's West	◆◆	$10-$20	401
25 / p. 379		Rainbow's End Relics	◆◆	$14-$28	402
26 / p. 379		Shugrue's Hillside Grill	◆◆	$15-$35	403
27 / p. 379		Javelina Cantina	◆◆	$10-$16	401
28 / p. 379		Sedona Airport Restaurant	◆◆	$11-$22	403

SEDONA pop. 10,192 (See map and index starting on p. 379)

—— **WHERE TO STAY** ——

ADOBE GRAND VILLAS

All Year [BP]   1P: $399-$900

Bed & Breakfast

Phone: (928)203-7616 [20]
XP: $35

Location: Jct SR 179, 2 mi w on SR 89A, just nw on Tortilla and Southwest drs, then just nw. Located in a West Sedona residential area. 35 Hozoni Dr 86336. Fax: 928/284-0767. **Facility:** A boutique-style B&B with spacious, uniquely furnished villas offering appointments befitting the highest standards of luxury. Designated smoking area. 15 one-bedroom standard units with whirlpools. 2 stories (no elevator), exterior corridors. **Parking:** onsite. **Terms:** office hours 7 am-7 pm, 2 night minimum stay - weekends, 15 day cancellation notice-fee imposed, package plans. **Amenities:** video library, DVD players, CD players, high-speed Internet, voice mail, safes, irons, hair dryers. **Pool(s):** small heated outdoor. **Leisure Activities:** whirlpool, steamroom, hiking trails. *Fee:* massage. **Guest Services:** gift shop. **Business Services:** meeting rooms, PC. **Cards:** AX, DS, MC, VI. *(See color ad p 383)*

(See map and index starting on p. 379)

ADOBE HACIENDA BED & BREAKFAST *Book at aaa.com* **Phone:** (928)284-2020
All Year [BP] 1P: $179-$239 2P: $189-$249 XP: $10
Location: Jct SR 89A, 7.5 mi s on SR 179. Located in the Village of Oak Creek. 10 Rojo Dr 86351.
Bed & Breakfast Fax: 928/284-0247. **Facility:** Guest rooms reflect varied Southwest themes and some have golf-course views; the flagstone patio is a nice place to relax. Smoke free premises. 5 units. 4 one-bedroom standard units, some with whirlpools. 1 one-bedroom suite. 1 story, exterior corridors. **Parking:** on-site. **Terms:** check-in 4 pm, 10 day cancellation notice-fee imposed, package plans. **Amenities:** video library, CD players, irons, hair dryers. **Leisure Activities:** *Fee:* massage. **Guest Services:** complimentary laundry. **Business Services:** fax. **Cards:** AX, DS, MC, VI. [X] [VCR] [▢]

ADOBE VILLAGE GRAHAM INN *Book at aaa.com* **Phone:** (928)284-1425
(AAA) [SAVE] All Year [BP] 1P: $189-$499 2P: $189-$499 XP: $20
Location: Jct SR 179, just w on Bell Rock Rd. Located in Village of Oak Creek. 150 Canyon Circle Dr 86351.
Fax: 928/284-0767. **Facility:** A contemporary inn with views of Red Rocks, a sculpture garden, rooms beautifully and individually decorated, and some with balconies. Designated smoking area. 11 units. 10 one-
Bed & Breakfast bedroom standard units, some with whirlpools. 1 one-bedroom suite ($369-$499) with whirlpool. 2 stories (no elevator), interior/exterior corridors. *Bath:* combo or shower only. **Parking:** on-site. **Terms:** office hours 7 am-7 pm, 2 night minimum stay - weekends, 15 day cancellation notice-fee imposed, package plans. **Amenities:** video library, CD players, irons, hair dryers. *Some:* voice mail, safes. **Pool(s):** small outdoor. **Leisure Activities:** whirlpool, bicycles. **Guest Services:** gift shop, complimentary evening beverages. **Cards:** AX, DS, MC, VI. *(See color ad p 383)*
SOME UNITS
[≈] [X] [VCR] [DATA PORT] / [▢] [▢] [▢] [▢] /

ALMA DE SEDONA INN **Phone:** 928/282-2737 [17]
(AAA) [SAVE] All Year 2P: $189-$305 XP: $25
Location: Jct SR 179, 3 mi w on SR 89A, then 3 blks nw via Tortilla and Southwest drs. Located in a quiet residential area. 50 Hozoni Dr 86336. Fax: 928/203-4141. **Facility:** Guest rooms at this pueblo-style inn are elegantly appointed and have balconies or patios, some with views of the area's scenic red rocks. Smoke free
Bed & Breakfast premises. 12 one-bedroom standard units, some with whirlpools. 2 stories (no elevator), exterior corridors. *Bath:* combo or shower only. **Parking:** on-site. **Terms:** office hours 8 am-7 pm, age restrictions may apply, 15 day cancellation notice-fee imposed, package plans. **Amenities:** CD players, voice mail, hair dryers. **Pool(s):** heated outdoor. **Guest Services:** gift shop, complimentary evening beverages. **Business Services:** fax (fee). **Cards:** MC, VI. **Special Amenities:** free full breakfast and free local telephone calls. *(See color ad below)*
[SD] [♿] [≈] [X] [▢] [▢]

AMARA CREEKSIDE RESORT *Book at aaa.com* **Phone:** (928)282-4828 [14]
(AAA) [SAVE] 3/2-6/30 1P: $179-$459 2P: $179-$459 XP: $20 F18
9/1-1/31 1P: $179-$409 2P: $179-$409 XP: $20 F18
2/1-3/1 & 7/1-8/31 1P: $159-$409 2P: $159-$409 XP: $20 F18
Location: Jct SR 179, 0.4 mi ne; center. 310 N Hwy 89A 86336. Fax: 928/282-4825. **Facility:** Upscale, modern
Small-scale Hotel lodgings on Oak Creek offer elegant, Zen-inspired appointments; a central garden courtyard is adorned with sculptures and flowers. 100 units. 96 one-bedroom standard units, some with whirlpools. 4 one-bedroom suites ($299-$459) with whirlpools. 2 stories, interior corridors. *Bath:* combo or shower only. **Parking:** on-site and valet. **Terms:** check-in 4 pm, 3 day cancellation notice-fee imposed. **Amenities:** video library, DVD players, CD players, high-speed Internet, voice mail, irons, hair dryers. **Dining:** Gallery on Oak Creek, see separate listing. **Pool(s):** heated outdoor. **Leisure Activities:** whirlpool, exercise room. *Fee:* massage. **Guest Services:** valet laundry, airport transportation-Sedona Airport, area transportation-within 3 mi. **Business Services:** conference facilities, business center. **Cards:** AX, CB, DC, DS, JC, MC, VI. **Special Amenities:** free local telephone calls and free newspaper.
SOME UNITS
[✈] [¶] [24] [♿] [≈] [X] [DATA PORT] [▢] [▢] / [X] /

(See map and index starting on p. 379)

APPLE ORCHARD INN
AAA SAVE
▽▽▽▽
Bed & Breakfast

Phone: (928)282-5328   **5**

All Year [BP]   2P: $139-$205
Location: Jct SR 179, 0.3 mi ne on SR 89A, then 0.5 mi n. Located in Uptown Sedona. 656 Jordan Rd 86336. Fax: 928/204-0044. **Facility:** Idyllic setting against a backdrop of Wilson and Steamboat rock formations. Beautifully decorated - two units with gas fireplaces. Smoke free premises. 7 one-bedroom standard units, some with whirlpools. 2 stories (no elevator), interior corridors. **Parking:** on-site. **Terms:** office hours 8 am-6 pm, age restrictions may apply, 30 day cancellation notice-fee imposed. **Amenities:** video library, hair dryers. **Leisure Activities:** whirlpool, cooling pool with waterfall. *Fee:* massage. **Business Services:** fax. **Cards:** AX, DS, MC, VI. **Special Amenities:** free full breakfast and preferred room (subject to availability with advance reservations).

A TERRITORIAL HOUSE TRADITIONAL OLD WEST
B&B   *Book at aaa.com*
▽▽▽▽
Bed & Breakfast

Phone: (928)204-2737   **24**
F

All Year   2P: $125-$215   XP: $25
Location: Jct SR 179, 3.2 mi w on SR 89A, just n on Dry Creek Rd, then 0.4 mi w on Kachina Dr. 65 Piki Dr 86336. Fax: 928/204-2230. **Facility:** On shaded grounds in a quiet, secluded setting, this B&B offers guest rooms which are individually decorated in a territorial theme. Designated smoking area. 4 units. 3 one- and 1 two-bedroom standard units, some with whirlpools. 2 stories (no elevator), interior corridors. *Bath:* combo or shower only. **Parking:** on-site. **Terms:** office hours 7:30 am-9 pm, check-in 4 pm, 7 day cancellation notice-fee imposed, [BP] meal plan available, package plans. **Amenities:** video library, CD players, hair dryers. *Some:* irons. **Leisure Activities:** whirlpool. *Fee:* massage. **Guest Services:** complimentary evening beverages. **Business Services:** PC, fax. **Cards:** DS, MC, VI.

SOME UNITS

"A TOUCH OF SEDONA"-BED & BREAKFAST
AAA SAVE
▽▽▽▽
Bed & Breakfast

Phone: (928)282-6462   **6**
F11

All Year   2P: $155-$205   XP: $15
Location: Jct SR 179, 0.4 mi ne on SR 89A, then just w. Located in Uptown Sedona in a residential area. 595 Jordan Rd 86336. Fax: 928/282-1534. **Facility:** Beverages and snacks are available around-the-clock at this modern home offering nicely decorated rooms and one suite with a private hot tub. Designated smoking area. 5 one-bedroom standard units, some with efficiencies (no utensils). 1 story, interior/exterior corridors. *Bath:* combo or shower only. **Parking:** on-site. **Terms:** office hours 10 am-9 am, check-in 4 pm, 10 day cancellation notice-fee imposed, [BP] meal plan available, package plans. **Amenities:** irons, hair dryers. **Leisure Activities:** whirlpool. *Fee:* massage. **Guest Services:** gift shop, complimentary evening beverages, valet laundry. **Business Services:** fax. **Cards:** AX, DS, MC, VI.

SOME UNITS

BABY QUAIL INN
AAA SAVE
▽▽▽▽
Motel

Phone: 928/282-2835   **31**

All Year   1P: $79-$110   2P: $79-$110
Location: Jct SR 179, 1.3 mi w on SR 89A, just s. Located in a residential area. 50 Willow Way 86336. Fax: 928/282-0535. **Facility:** Smoke free premises. 12 one-bedroom standard units. 2 stories (no elevator), exterior corridors. *Bath:* combo or shower only. **Parking:** on-site. **Terms:** office hours 8 am-10 pm, 3 day cancellation notice-fee imposed, package plans. **Amenities:** video library. **Leisure Activities:** whirlpool. **Business Services:** fax (fee). **Cards:** DS, MC, VI. **Special Amenities:** free continental breakfast and free local telephone calls.

BEST WESTERN ARROYO ROBLE HOTEL &
CREEKSIDE VILLAS   *Book at aaa.com*
AAA SAVE
▽▽▽▽
Small-scale Hotel

Phone: (928)282-4001   **10**

2/1-11/30   1P: $129-$339   2P: $129-$339   XP: $10   F12
12/1-1/31   1P: $89-$339   2P: $89-$339   XP: $10   F12
Location: Jct SR 179, 0.5 mi nw. 400 N Hwy 89A 86336. Fax: 928/282-4001. **Facility:** 65 units. 57 one-bedroom standard units, some with whirlpools. 7 two-bedroom suites with kitchens and whirlpools. 1 vacation home. 5 stories, exterior corridors. *Bath:* combo or shower only. **Parking:** on-site. **Terms:** [ECP] meal plan available, package plans. **Amenities:** high-speed Internet, irons, hair dryers. **Pool(s):** 2 heated outdoor, heated indoor. **Leisure Activities:** sauna, whirlpools, steamroom, exercise room. *Fee:* 2 lighted tennis courts, racquetball courts. **Guest Services:** coin laundry. **Business Services:** meeting rooms, fax (fee). **Cards:** AX, DC, DS, MC, VI. **Special Amenities:** free expanded continental breakfast and free newspaper. *(See color ad p 386)*

SOME UNITS

(See map and index starting on p. 379)

BEST WESTERN INN OF SEDONA

Book at aaa.com

Phone: (928)282-3072 **27**

9/1-10/31 [ECP]	1P: $164-$209	2P: $164-$209	XP: $10	F12
7/1-8/31 [ECP]	1P: $144-$199	2P: $144-$199	XP: $10	F12
2/1-6/30 [ECP]	1P: $139-$199	2P: $139-$199	XP: $10	F12
11/1-1/31 [ECP]	1P: $134-$169	2P: $134-$169	XP: $10	F12

Small-scale Hotel Location: Jct SR 179, 1.2 mi w. 1200 W Hwy 89A 86336. Fax: 928/282-7218. **Facility:** 110 one-bedroom standard units. 1-3 stories (no elevator), exterior corridors. *Bath:* combo or shower only. **Parking:** on-site. **Terms:** cancellation fee imposed, package plans, pets ($10 extra charge, in limited units). **Amenities:** video games (fee), voice mail, irons, hair dryers. **Pool(s):** heated outdoor. **Leisure Activities:** whirlpool, exercise room. **Guest Services:** valet laundry, area transportation-within 3 mi. **Business Services:** meeting rooms, PC, fax (fee). **Cards:** AX, CB, DC, DS, JC, MC, VI. **Special Amenities:** free expanded continental breakfast and free local telephone calls. *(See color ad below)*

SOME UNITS

(See map and index starting on p. 379)

BOOTS & SADDLES ROMANTIC BED & BREAKFAST

Phat Phone: (928)282-1944 **19**

Bed & Breakfast

All Year [BP]   1P: $150-$230   2P: $165-$245   XP: $25
Location: Jct SR 179, 2.7 mi w on SR 89A, n on Tortilla Dr, 1 blk w on Southwest Dr, 1 blk n on Hozoni Dr, then just e. 2900 Hopi Dr 86336. **Facility:** The casual Western decor of this property lends a fun ambience to its guest rooms, all of which have gas fireplaces and either a patio or balcony. Designated smoking area. 4 one-bedroom standard units with whirlpools. 2 stories (no elevator), interior/exterior corridors. **Parking:** on-site. **Terms:** office hours 7 am-10 pm, check-in 4 pm, age restrictions may apply, 15 day cancellation notice-fee imposed, package plans. **Amenities:** video library, CD players, irons, hair dryers. **Leisure Activities:** whirlpool, bicycles. **Guest Services:** gift shop, complimentary evening beverages. **Business Services:** fax. **Cards:** AX, DS, MC, VI.

(ASK) ⊠ VCR DATA PORT 📶

BRIAR PATCH INN BED & BREAKFAST

Phone: (928)282-2342 **3**
F5

Cottage

All Year [BP]   1P: $189-$379   2P: $189-$379   XP: $25
Location: Jct SR 179, 3.5 mi ne. Located in Oak Creek Canyon. 3190 N Hwy 89A 86336. Fax: 928/282-2399. **Facility:** Classical music is performed six mornings a week at this B&B on nine tree-shaded acres bordering Oak Creek; a massage gazebo is on the grounds. Smoke free premises. 18 units. 1 vacation home and 17 cottages, some with whirlpools. 1 story, exterior corridors. *Bath:* combo or shower only. **Parking:** on-site. **Terms:** office hours 7:30 am-8 pm, 2 night minimum stay - weekends, 14 day cancellation notice-fee imposed. **Amenities:** CD players. **Leisure Activities:** fishing. *Fee:* massage. **Guest Services:** gift shop. **Business Services:** meeting rooms. **Cards:** AX, MC, VI.

SOME UNITS
⊠ ☎ 📶 💻 / W /

CANYON VILLA BED & BREAKFAST INN OF SEDONA

Phone: (928)284-1226

Bed & Breakfast

All Year [BP]   1P: $189-$324   2P: $198-$334   XP: $25
Location: Jct SR 179, just w on Bell Rock Blvd, then just n. Located in Village of Oak Creek. 40 Canyon Circle Dr 86351. Fax: 928/284-2114. **Facility:** A nearby desert provides outdoor interest at this upscale Spanish-Mission compound overlooking the Red Rocks. Smoke free premises. 11 one-bedroom standard units, some with whirlpools. 2 stories (no elevator), interior/exterior corridors. **Parking:** on-site. **Terms:** office hours 7:30 am-7 pm, 2-3 night minimum stay - seasonal and/or weekends, age restrictions may apply, 14 day cancellation notice-fee imposed. **Amenities:** CD players, irons, hair dryers. **Pool(s):** heated outdoor. **Leisure Activities:** library. **Guest Services:** gift shop, complimentary evening beverages, concierge service. **Business Services:** PC. **Cards:** AX, DC, DS, MC, VI. **Special Amenities:** free full breakfast and free local telephone calls. *(See color ad below)*

SOME UNITS
🍴 🏊 ⊠ 📷 DATA PORT / 📶 💻 /

(See map and index starting on p. 379)

CASA SEDONA BED AND BREAKFAST INN

AAA (SAVE)

▼▼▼ ▼▼▼

Bed & Breakfast

Phone: (928)282-2938   **16**

All Year   1P: $195-$300   2P: $195-$300   XP: $30
Location: Jct SR 179, 3 mi w on SR 89A, then 3 blks nw via Tortilla Dr, Southwest Dr to Hozoni Dr. Located in a quiet residential area. 55 Hozoni Dr 86336. Fax: 928/282-2259. **Facility:** Decor at this Southwest-style inn ranges from cowboy gear to lace; all rooms feature a balcony, patio or terrace. Smoke free premises. 16 one-bedroom standard units, some with whirlpools. 1-2 stories (no elevator), interior/exterior corridors. **Parking:** on-site. **Terms:** office hours 7:30 am-7:30 pm, age restrictions may apply, 14 day cancellation notice-fee imposed, package plans. **Amenities:** video library, CD players, high-speed Internet, irons, hair dryers. **Leisure Activities:** whirlpool, hiking trails. *Fee:* massage. **Guest Services:** gift shop, complimentary evening beverages. **Business Services:** fax (fee). **Cards:** MC, VI. **Special Amenities:** free full breakfast and preferred room (subject to availability with advance reservations).** *(See color ad below)*

🛁 ✕ ✕ VCR DATA/PORT 🔌

CEDARS RESORT ON OAK CREEK

▼▼▼ ▼▼

Motel

Phone: 928/282-7010   **15**
F12

All Year   1P: $99   2P: $149   XP: $10
Location: Jct SR 179, southeast corner. 20 W Hwy 89A 86339 (P O Box 292). Fax: 928/282-5372. **Facility:** Smoke free premises. 38 one-bedroom standard units. 1-2 stories (no elevator), exterior corridors. *Bath:* combo or shower only. **Parking:** on-site. **Terms:** [CP] meal plan available. **Amenities:** voice mail, irons, hair dryers. **Pool(s):** heated outdoor. **Leisure Activities:** whirlpool, fishing. **Business Services:** PC, fax (fee). **Cards:** AX, DC, DS, MC, VI.

A$K S/D 🏊 ✕ DATA/PORT 🔌 📺

COMFORT INN

AAA (SAVE)

▼▼▼ ▼▼

Small-scale Hotel

Book at aaa.com   Phone: (928)282-3132   **36**
2/13-5/31   1P: $89-$159   2P: $99-$169   XP: $10   F
6/1-10/31   1P: $79-$129   2P: $89-$139   XP: $10   F
2/1-2/12 & 11/1-1/31   1P: $69-$110   2P: $79-$120   XP: $10   F
Location: 0.7 mi s of jct SR 89A. 725 Hwy 179 86336. Fax: 928/203-9432. **Facility:** Designated smoking area. 53 units. 52 one-bedroom standard units. 1 one-bedroom suite. 2 stories (no elevator), interior corridors. *Bath:* combo or shower only. **Parking:** on-site. **Terms:** [CP] meal plan available, package plans. **Amenities:** irons, hair dryers. **Pool(s):** heated outdoor. **Leisure Activities:** whirlpool. **Business Services:** meeting rooms, fax (fee). **Cards:** AX, CB, DC, DS, JC, MC, VI. **Special Amenities:** free expanded continental breakfast and free local telephone calls.

SOME UNITS

S/D 🛁 ♿ 🏊 ✕ 📺 / 🔌 /

(See map and index starting on p. 379)

CREEKSIDE INN AT SEDONA

All Year [BP] ▼▼▼▼
Phone: (928)282-4992 [38]

Bed & Breakfast

2P: $175-$285   XP: $25

Location: Jct SR 89A, 0.7 mi s on SR 179, then just w. 99 Copper Cliffs Dr 86336. Fax: 928/282-0091. **Facility:** The sights and sounds of Oak Creek, which runs along its grounds, give this inn a soothing ambience. 6 one-bedroom standard units with whirlpools. 1 story, interior/exterior corridors. **Parking:** on-site. **Terms:** office hours 7 am-6 pm, 2 night minimum stay - weekends, age restrictions may apply, 10 day cancellation notice-fee imposed. **Amenities:** CD players, voice mail, hair dryers. *Some:* DVD players. **Leisure Activities:** fishing, hiking trails. **Business Services:** fax. **Cards:** AX, DS, MC, VI.

SOME UNITS
[ASK] [✕] [DATA PORT] [▣] / [🅟] [▯] [▭] /

DESERT QUAIL INN   *Book at aaa.com*

[AAA] [SAVE] ▼▼▼
Phone: (928)284-1433

Motel

2/1-5/31 & 9/1-11/15	1P: $84-$134	2P: $89-$139	XP: $10	F13
6/1-8/31 & 11/16-1/31	1P: $64-$124	2P: $69-$129	XP: $10	F13

Location: Jct Bell Rock Blvd, 0.9 mi s. Located across from factory outlet center. 6626 Hwy 179 86351. Fax: 928/284-0487. **Facility:** 41 units. 40 one-bedroom standard units, some with whirlpools. 1 one-bedroom suite ($134-$169) with kitchen and whirlpool. 2 stories (no elevator), exterior corridors. *Bath:* combo or shower only. **Parking:** on-site. **Terms:** office hours 7 am-10 pm, 2 night minimum stay, small pets only ($10 extra charge, with prior approval, in designated units). **Amenities:** irons, hair dryers. **Pool(s):** small heated outdoor. **Guest Services:** complimentary laundry. **Business Services:** fax (fee). **Cards:** AX, DC, DS, MC, VI.

SOME UNITS
[S/D] [🛏] [↑↓] [🛁] [🐾] [🏊] [DATA PORT] [▯] [▣] / [✕] [▭] /
FEE

EL PORTAL SEDONA   *Book at aaa.com*

[AAA] [SAVE] ▼▼▼▼
All Year
Phone: (928)203-9405 [26]

Bed & Breakfast

2P: $225-$495   XP: $25   D16

Location: Jct SR 89A, just s on SR 179, then just w. 95 Portal Ln 86336. Fax: 928/203-9401. **Facility:** Built to replicate southwest buildings of the early 1900s, guestrooms graciously surround a courtyard, each with elegant appointments and spacious baths. Designated smoking area. 12 units. 11 one-bedroom standard units, some with whirlpools. 1 one-bedroom suite with whirlpool. 2 stories (no elevator), interior/exterior corridors. *Bath:* combo or shower only. **Parking:** on-site. **Terms:** 15 day cancellation notice-fee imposed, package plans, pets (in designated units). **Amenities:** video library, DVD players, CD players, high-speed Internet, voice mail, irons, hair dryers. **Leisure Activities:** *Fee:* massage. **Guest Services:** complimentary evening beverages, valet laundry, airport transportation-Sedona Airport, area transportation-within 5 mi. **Business Services:** PC, fax. **Cards:** AX, DS, MC, VI. **Special Amenities:** free local telephone calls and free newspaper. *(See color ad below)*

[✈] [🛏] [↑↓] [🛁] [♿] [✕] [VCR] [DATA PORT] [▯]

ENCHANTMENT RESORT   *Book at aaa.com*

[AAA] [SAVE] ▼▼▼ ▼▼
Phone: (928)282-2900

Resort
Large-scale Hotel

2/1-6/17 & 9/1-1/6	1P: $425	2P: $425	XP: $50	F12
6/18-8/31 & 1/7-1/31	1P: $325	2P: $325	XP: $50	F12

Location: Jct SR 179, 3.5 mi w on SR 89A, 5 mi n on Dry Creek Rd and FR 152C. Located in a quiet rural area. 525 Boynton Canyon Rd 86336. Fax: 928/282-9249. **Facility:** Tucked into spectacular Boynton canyon with overhanging red rock cliffs, you find rooms and one- to two-bedroom suites in adobe style casitas. 236 units. 168 one-bedroom standard units. 62 one-bedroom suites ($425-$1250) with efficiencies. 6 vacation homes. 1 story, exterior corridors. *Bath:* combo or shower only. **Parking:** on-site. **Terms:** check-in 4 pm, 2-3 night minimum stay - seasonal and/or weekends, 7 day cancellation notice, package plans, $18 service charge. **Amenities:** video games (fee), CD players, high-speed Internet, dual phone lines, voice mail, safes, honor bars, irons, hair dryers. **Dining:** 2 restaurants, 6 am-9 pm, cocktails, also, The Yavapai Restaurant, see separate listing. **Pool(s):** 5 heated outdoor, heated indoor. **Leisure Activities:** saunas, whirlpools, putting green, tennis instruction, recreation programs, croquet, bocci, rental bicycles, hiking trails, spa, sports court, basketball, volleyball. *Fee:* 7 tennis courts. **Guest Services:** gift shop, complimentary and valet laundry, airport transportation-Sedona Airport. **Business Services:** conference facilities, business center. **Cards:** AX, DC, DS, MC, VI.

SOME UNITS
[✈] [🍴] [24] [Y] [🛁] [🏊] [♿] [✕] [🎦] [DATA PORT] [▯] / [✕] [▯] [▭] /
FEE

(See map and index starting on p. 379)

HAMPTON INN *Book at aaa.com* Phone: (928)282-4700 **21**

Small-scale Hotel
| 2/1-11/30 | 1P: $109-$179 | 2P: $109-$179 |
| 12/1-1/31 | 1P: $89-$159 | 2P: $89-$159 |

Location: Jct SR 179, 2 mi w. 1800 W Hwy 89A 86336. Fax: 928/282-0004. **Facility:** 56 one-bedroom standard units, some with whirlpools. 2 stories, interior corridors. *Bath:* combo or shower only. **Parking:** on-site. **Terms:** cancellation fee imposed. **Amenities:** video games (fee), high-speed Internet, dual phone lines, voice mail, irons, hair dryers. **Pool(s):** heated outdoor. **Leisure Activities:** whirlpool. **Guest Services:** valet laundry. **Business Services:** meeting rooms, PC, fax (fee). **Cards:** AX, CB.

SOME UNITS

HILTON SEDONA RESORT & SPA *Book at aaa.com* Phone: (928)284-4040

Resort
Large-scale Hotel
| All Year | 1P: $139-$299 | 2P: $139-$299 | XP: $20 | F18 |

Location: Jct SR 89A, 7.3 mi s on SR 179. Located in Village of Oak Creek. 90 Ridge Trail Dr 86351. Fax: 928/284-6940. **Facility:** Beautiful Red Rock views. All rooms with patio and fireplace. Two large pool areas, one with two levels- "mushroom fountain" and cascading waterfall. Designated smoking area. 219 units. 48 one-bedroom standard units. 171 one-bedroom suites ($159-$319), some with efficiencies and/or whirlpools. 3 stories, interior corridors. *Bath:* combo or shower only. **Parking:** on-site. **Terms:** check-in 4 pm, 2 night minimum stay - weekends, 3 day cancellation notice-fee imposed, package plans, small pets only ($50 fee). **Amenities:** dual phone lines, voice mail, safes, honor bars, irons, hair dryers. *Fee:* video games, high-speed Internet. **Dining:** 2 restaurants, 6:30 am-10 pm. **Pool(s):** 3 heated outdoor. **Leisure Activities:** whirlpools, kids camp in summer, hiking trails, spa, volleyball. *Fee:* golf-18 holes, 3 lighted tennis courts. **Guest Services:** gift shop, valet and coin laundry. **Business Services:** conference facilities, business center. **Cards:** AX, CB, DC, DS, JC, MC, VI. **Special Amenities:** free newspaper. *(See color ad below)*

SOME UNITS

FEE   FEE

You'll find all kinds of ways to relax at Sedona's only full-service spa & golf resort. Against a skyline of towering red cliffs, the Hilton Sedona Resort & Spa holds something for everyone. Tee off in the fresh air with on-site championship golf. Renew yourself at The Hilton Spa, our full-service spa, salon and fitness center. Drive into one of three refreshing pools and spas. Just make advance reservations with a call to Hilton's dedicated AAA number, **1-800-916-2221**, or your local AAA travel office, and request "Plan Code AA." Or visit us online at **hilton.com**.

$139-$279*
per room per night

Hilton HHonors

90 Ridge Trail Drive
Sedona, AZ 86351
928-284-4040

Hilton
Sedona Resort & Spa

Rates subject to availability, single/double occupancy for standard room. Valid AAA membership card required for reservation and check-in. *Offer valid from 2/1/06-1/31/07. ©2006 Hilton Hospitality, Inc.

Romantic Rooms with Running Water

THE INN ON OAK CREEK

Four Diamond Award

· Privacy · Comfort ·
· Location · Culinary Delights ·
(928) 282-7896 • (800) 499-7896
www.innonoakcreek.com

■ Sedona, Arizona ■

(See map and index starting on p. 379)

THE INN ON OAK CREEK

(AAA) (SAVE) ▼▼▼▼
Bed & Breakfast

All Year **Location:** Jct SR 89A, 0.5 mi s. 556 Hwy 179 86336. Fax: 928/282-0696. **Facility:** Located on Oak Creek with creekside park. All rooms with fireplaces and whirlpools. Walking distance to shops and galleries. Check-in 3-6 pm. Smoke free premises. 11 units. 9 one-bedroom standard units with whirlpools. 2 one-bedroom suites with whirlpools. 2 stories (no elevator), interior corridors. **Parking:** on-site. **Terms:** office hours 8 am-8 pm, age restrictions may apply, 7 day cancellation notice-fee imposed. **Amenities:** video library, hair dryers. *Some:* CD players. **Guest Services:** gift shop, complimentary laundry, airport transportation-Sedona Airport. **Business Services:** PC, fax. **Cards:** AX, DS, MC, VI. **Special Amenities: free local telephone calls and early check-in/late check-out.** *(See color ad p 391)*

Phone: (928)282-7896 34
2P: $200-$295 XP: $20

✈ ⓘ ✕ VCR 📷 DATA/PORT

IRIS GARDEN INN

(AAA) (SAVE) ▼▼▼▼
Motel

All Year **Location:** Jct SR 179, 0.3 mi ne on SR 89A, just n. Located in Uptown Sedona. 390 Jordan Rd 86336. Fax: 928/282-7054. **Facility:** Smoke free premises. 8 one-bedroom standard units, some with kitchens. 1 story, exterior corridors. *Bath:* combo or shower only. **Parking:** on-site. **Terms:** office hours 8 am-7:30 pm, 3 day cancellation notice-fee imposed. **Amenities:** voice mail, hair dryers. **Guest Services:** complimentary laundry. **Cards:** DS, MC, VI. **Special Amenities: free local telephone calls and early check-in/late check-out.**

Phone: (928)282-2552 8
1P: $74-$125 2P: $74-$125

S/D ⓘ &M 📷 ✕ 📶 🖥 📟

JUNIPINE RESORT

(AAA) (SAVE) ▼▼▼▼
Condominium

Book at aaa.com

3/4-11/12 1P: $170-$360 2P: $170-$360 XP: $25 F12
2/1-3/3 & 11/13-1/31 1P: $125-$310 2P: $125-$310 XP: $25 F12
Location: Jct SR 179, 9 mi ne. Located in a quiet area. 8351 N Hwy 89A 86336. Fax: 928/282-7402. **Facility:** In a wooded area along Oak Creek Canyon, the property has large, two-bedroom condominiums with fireplaces and outdoor decks (some have hot tubs). 40 two-bedroom standard units with kitchens. 1-2 stories (no elevator), exterior corridors. **Parking:** on-site. **Terms:** 7 day cancellation notice, package plans. **Amenities:** video library (fee), DVD players, CD players, high-speed Internet, voice mail, irons, hair dryers. **Dining:** Junipine Cafe, see separate listing. **Leisure Activities:** hiking trails, basketball, horseshoes. *Fee:* fishing. **Guest Services:** gift shop, coin laundry. **Cards:** AX, DS, MC, VI. **Special Amenities: free newspaper.** *(See color ad below)*

Phone: (928)282-3375 1
SOME UNITS

ⓘ &M 📷 ✕ AC VCR 🖥 📶 📟 /✕

KOKOPELLI INN

(AAA) (SAVE) ▼▼▼
Motel

Book at aaa.com

All Year **Location:** Jct Bell Rock Blvd, just s. Located in Village of Oak Creek. 6465 Hwy 179 86351. Fax: 928/284-9460. **Facility:** 42 one-bedroom standard units, some with whirlpools. 2 stories (no elevator), exterior corridors. **Parking:** on-site. **Terms:** office hours 7 am-10 pm, cancellation fee imposed, [CP] meal plan available. **Amenities:** safes, hair dryers. **Pool(s):** heated outdoor. **Guest Services:** gift shop. **Cards:** AX, CB, DC, DS, JC, MC, VI. *(See color ad p 394)*

Phone: (928)284-1100
1P: $89-$165 2P: $89-$165 XP: $10 F12

SOME UNITS
ⓘ 🏊 VCR 📷 DATA/PORT 📶 📟 /✕

(See map and index starting on p. 379)

KOKOPELLI SUITES   *Book at aaa.com*

AAA SAVE · ◇◇◇ Motel

Phone: (928)204-1146   **32**

| 2/1-5/31 & 9/1-11/10 [ECP] | 1P: $109-$239 | 2P: $119-$239 | XP: $10 | F12 |
| 6/1-8/31 & 11/11-1/31 [ECP] | 1P: $99-$239 | 2P: $109-$239 | XP: $10 | F12 |

Location: Jct SR 179, 3 mi w. Located in the business section of West Sedona. 3119 W Hwy 89A 86336. **Fax:** 928/204-5851. **Facility:** 46 units. 45 one-bedroom standard units, some with whirlpools. 1 one-bedroom suite with kitchen. 2 stories (no elevator), exterior corridors. *Bath:* combo or shower only. **Parking:** on-site. **Terms:** office hours 7 am-10 pm, 2 night minimum stay - seasonal, 3 day cancellation notice, package plans. **Amenities:** voice mail, safes, hair dryers. **Pool(s):** heated outdoor. **Leisure Activities:** whirlpool. **Guest Services:** coin laundry. **Business Services:** fax (fee). **Cards:** AX, CB, DC, DS, MC, VI. **Special Amenities:** free expanded continental breakfast and free newspaper. *(See color ad below)*

SOME UNITS

(See map and index starting on p. 379)

LA QUINTA INN SEDONA *Book at aaa.com*

AAA SAVE ▽▽▽▽ 💎

3/1-5/31 & 9/1-1/31 [CP]	1P: $109-$125	2P: $109-$125	XP: $20	F18
6/1-8/31 [CP]	1P: $105-$125	2P: $105-$125	XP: $20	F18
2/1-2/28 [CP]	1P: $105-$120	2P: $105-$120	XP: $20	F18

Phone: (928)284-0711

Small-scale Hotel

Location: Jct Bell Rock Blvd, just s. Located in Village of Oak Creek. 6176 Hwy 179 86351. Fax: 928/284-3760. **Facility:** 103 one-bedroom standard units. 2 stories, interior corridors. *Bath:* combo or shower only. **Parking:** on-site. **Terms:** cancellation fee imposed, small pets only. **Amenities:** voice mail, irons, hair dryers. **Pool(s):** heated outdoor. **Leisure Activities:** whirlpool. **Guest Services:** coin laundry. **Cards:** AX, DC, DS, MC, VI. **Special Amenities:** free continental breakfast.

SOME UNITS

L'AUBERGE DE SEDONA RESORT *Book at aaa.com*

AAA SAVE ▽▽▽▽ 💎💎

	All Year	1P: $189-$319	2P: $189-$319	XP: $20	F12

Phone: (928)282-1661 🔟🄔

Small-scale Hotel

Location: Jct SR 179, just ne on SR 89A to L'Auberge Ln; east side of SR 89A, just n down the hill. Located in a secluded area. 301 L Ln 86336 (PO Box B, 86339). Fax: 928/282-2885. **Facility:** Along Oak Creek. Lodge and individual cottages on several acres of landscaped and tree-shaded grounds. King canopy beds in most rooms, fireplace in cottages. Country French decor. 58 units. 25 one-bedroom standard units. 33 cottages ($269-$619), some with whirlpools. 1-2 stories (no elevator), interior/exterior corridors. *Bath:* combo or shower only. **Parking:** on-site and valet. **Terms:** 1-3 night minimum stay - weekends, 14 day cancellation notice, package plans, pets ($75 fee, in designated units). **Amenities:** video library, CD players, voice mail, safes, honor bars, irons, hair dryers. **Pool(s):** heated outdoor. **Leisure Activities:** whirlpool, fishing, recreation programs, hiking trails. *Fee:* yoga & Pilates on the lawn, stargazing with an astronomer, massage. **Guest Services:** gift shop, complimentary evening beverages: Fri, valet laundry. **Business Services:** meeting rooms, PC, fax (fee). **Cards:** AX, DC, DS, MC, VI. **Special Amenities:** free newspaper and preferred room (subject to availability with advance reservations). *(See color ad p 398)*

SOME UNITS

THE LODGE AT SEDONA

▽▽▽ 💎

	All Year	1P: $155-$315	2P: $165-$325	XP: $35

Phone: (928)204-1942 🔢🄛

Bed & Breakfast

Location: Jct SR 179, 1.8 mi w on SR 89A, then just s. Located in a secluded area. 125 Kallof Pl 86336. Fax: 928/204-2128. **Facility:** An elegant Mission-style inn sits on three acres with warmly decorated public areas, many units with gas fireplaces and most with private decks. Designated smoking area. 14 one-bedroom standard units, some with whirlpools. 1-2 stories (no elevator), interior/exterior corridors. *Bath:* combo or shower only. **Parking:** on-site. **Terms:** office hours 7 am-9 pm, check-in 4 pm, 2 night minimum stay - weekends, age restrictions may apply, 14 day cancellation notice-fee imposed, [BP] meal plan available, pets (dogs only, $200 deposit, $35 extra charge). **Amenities:** video library, CD players, irons, hair dryers. *Some:* DVD players. **Leisure Activities:** sports court, horseshoes. *Fee:* massage. **Guest Services:** gift shop, complimentary evening beverages. **Business Services:** PC, fax. **Cards:** DS, MC, VI.

SOME UNITS

(See map and index starting on p. 379)

LOS ABRIGADOS RESORT & SPA *Book at aaa.com*   Phone: (928)282-1777 25

Resort
Condominium

All Year   1P: $225   2P: $225
Location: Jct SR 89A, just s on SR 179, just w. Adjacent to Tlaquepaque. 160 Portal Ln 86336. Fax: 928/282-2614.
Facility: Surrounded by 22 acres along Oak Creek and with many recreation options, the attractive suites, some with fireplaces and outdoor spas, await you. 40 units. 38 one- and 2 two-bedroom suites with efficiencies, some with whirlpools. 2 stories (no elevator), exterior corridors. *Bath:* combo or shower only.
Parking: on-site. **Terms:** check-in 4 pm, 3 day cancellation notice-fee imposed. **Amenities:** DVD players, video games (fee), CD players, voice mail, irons, hair dryers. **Pool(s):** 2 heated outdoor. **Leisure Activities:** saunas, whirlpools, steamrooms, fishing, 2 lighted tennis courts, recreation programs in summer, playground, exercise room, spa, sports court, basketball, horseshoes, volleyball. *Fee:* miniature golf. **Guest Services:** gift shop, coin laundry, area transportation (fee). **Business Services:** meeting rooms, PC, fax (fee). **Cards:** AX, DC, DS, MC, VI.

SOME UNITS

MATTERHORN INN   Phone: (928)282-7176 11

Motel

2/1-5/31 & 9/1-11/12   1P: $89-$159   2P: $89-$159   XP: $10   F5
6/1-8/31   1P: $79-$139   2P: $79-$139   XP: $10   F5
11/13-1/31   1P: $69-$139   2P: $69-$139   XP: $10   F5
Location: Jct SR 179, just ne on SR 89A; uptown. Located in a central shopping district. 230 Apple Ave 86336. Fax: 928/282-0727. **Facility:** 23 one-bedroom standard units. 2 stories (no elevator), exterior corridors.
Parking: on-site. **Terms:** office hours 8 am-10 pm, package plans, small pets only ($10, in designated units). **Amenities:** CD players, voice mail, irons, hair dryers. **Pool(s):** small heated outdoor. **Leisure Activities:** whirlpool. **Business Services:** PC, fax (fee). **Cards:** AX, MC, VI. **Special Amenities:** free local telephone calls and preferred room (subject to availability with advance reservations).** *(See color ad below)*

FEE

ORCHARDS INN OF SEDONA *Book at aaa.com*   Phone: (928)282-1661 12

Small-scale Hotel

All Year [CP]   1P: $119-$199   2P: $119-$199   XP: $20   F12
Location: Jct SR 179, just ne of SR 179, off SR 89A. Located in Uptown Sedona shopping area. 254 Hwy 89A 86336 (PO Box B, 86339). Fax: 928/282-1064. **Facility:** Designated smoking area. 41 units. 40 one-bedroom standard units. 1 one-bedroom suite. 3 stories (no elevator), exterior corridors. **Parking:** on-site.
Terms: office hours 9 am-5 pm, 1-3 night minimum stay - seasonal and/or weekends, 14 day cancellation notice, package plans. **Amenities:** voice mail, safes, irons, hair dryers. *Some:* DVD players. **Pool(s):** heated outdoor. **Leisure Activities:** whirlpool. **Guest Services:** valet laundry. **Business Services:** fax (fee). **Cards:** AX, DC, DS, MC, VI. **Special Amenities:** free continental breakfast and free newspaper. *(See color ad p 398)*

SOME UNITS

 / /

(See map and index starting on p. 379)

THE PENROSE BED & BREAKFAST

AAA [SAVE]
▼▼▼▼

Bed & Breakfast

Phone: (928)284-3030

All Year [BP]   1P: $155-$225   2P: $180-$250   XP: $25   F12
Location: Jct SR 179, just w on Bell Rock Blvd, then 0.3 mi n. 250 Red Butte Dr 86351. Fax: 928/284-9611. **Facility:** Located near Bell Rock, this quiet B&B is an ideal stop for those seeking red rock views and friendly hosts. Smoke free premises. 5 one-bedroom standard units, some with whirlpools. 2 stories (no elevator), interior corridors. **Bath:** combo or shower only. **Parking:** on-site. **Terms:** 2 night minimum stay - weekends, 10 day cancellation notice-fee imposed, package plans. **Amenities:** video library, DVD players, CD players, high-speed Internet, voice mail, hair dryers. **Business Services:** fax. **Cards:** MC, VI. **Special Amenities:** free full breakfast and free local telephone calls.

QUALITY INN-KING'S RANSOM   *Book at aaa.com*

AAA [SAVE]
▼▼ ◆◆

Small-scale Hotel

Phone: (928)282-7151   37

2/13-5/31 & 9/1-1/31   1P: $79-$189   2P: $79-$189   XP: $10   F17
2/1-2/12 & 6/1-8/31   1P: $69-$149   2P: $69-$149   XP: $10   F17
Location: 0.7 mi s of jct SR 89A. 771 Hwy 179 86336 (PO Box 180, 86339). Fax: 928/282-5208. **Facility:** 101 units. 100 one-bedroom standard units, some with whirlpools. 1 one-bedroom suite with whirlpool. 2 stories (no elevator), interior/exterior corridors. **Bath:** combo or shower only. **Parking:** on-site. **Terms:** package plans, pets ($15 fee). **Amenities:** irons, hair dryers. **Dining:** 7 am-10 pm, cocktails. **Pool(s):** heated outdoor. **Leisure Activities:** whirlpool, hiking trails, shuffleboard. **Business Services:** meeting rooms. **Cards:** AX, CB, DC, DS, MC, VI. **Special Amenities:** free local telephone calls and free newspaper.

SOME UNITS
[S🅳] [🛏] [🍽] [🏊] [🖾] [DATA PORT] [▣] / [✕] [🛏] /
FEE

RADISSON POCO DIABLO RESORT

▼▼▼

Resort
Large-scale Hotel

Phone: 928/282-7333   41

Property failed to provide current rates

Location: Jct SR 179, 2 mi s of SR 89A. 1752 S Hwy 179 86336. Fax: 928/282-9712. **Facility:** The resort's multiple buildings are spread across several acres of grounds featuring gardens and a courtyard pool; 41 units have a fireplace. Smoke free premises. 137 one-bedroom standard units, some with whirlpools. 1-2 stories (no elevator), exterior corridors. **Bath:** combo or shower only. **Parking:** on-site. **Terms:** check-in 4 pm, pets ($50 fee). **Amenities:** video games (fee), high-speed Internet, voice mail, irons, hair dryers. **Pool(s):** heated outdoor. **Leisure Activities:** whirlpools, 4 tennis courts (2 lighted), racquetball court, hiking trails, playground, exercise room, basketball. *Fee:* massage. **Guest Services:** valet and coin laundry. **Business Services:** conference facilities, PC (fee). *(See color ad below)*

[🛏] [🍽] [🍸] [🖾] [🚭] [🏊] [✕] [✕] [🐾] [DATA PORT] [🛏] [▣]
FEE

THE RIDGE ON SEDONA GOLF RESORT-CLUB
SUNTERRA   *Book at aaa.com*

▼◆◆▼

Condominium

Phone: (928)284-1200

All Year   1P: $140-$300   2P: $140-$300
Location: Jct SR 89A, 7.4 mi s on SR 179, just w on Ridge Trail Dr, then just s. 55 Sunridge Cir 86351. Fax: 928/284-1777. **Facility:** The resort's pueblo-style buildings offer attractively furnished suites or standard rooms; some overlook the golf course and some have red-rock views. 236 units. 102 one-bedroom standard units. 134 one-bedroom suites with kitchens and whirlpools. 2 stories (no elevator), exterior corridors. **Bath:** combo or shower only. **Parking:** on-site. **Terms:** check-in 4 pm, 2 night minimum stay - seasonal, cancellation fee imposed. **Amenities:** CD players, voice mail, irons, hair dryers. *Fee:* video library, safes. *Some:* DVD players. **Pool(s):** 2 heated outdoor. **Leisure Activities:** whirlpools, horseshoes. **Guest Services:** gift shop, coin laundry. **Business Services:** fax (fee). **Cards:** AX, DS, MC, VI.

SOME UNITS
[ASK] [🍽] [🖾] [🏊] [🛏] [🛏] [🖥] [▣] / [✕] [VCR]

ROSE TREE INN

AAA [SAVE]
▼▼ ◆◆

Motel

Phone: 928/282-2065   9

All Year   1P: $95-$135   2P: $95-$135   XP: $10   F16
Location: Jct SR 179, 0.4 mi ne on SR 89A, just nw on Apple, then just ne. Located in a quiet area. 376 Cedar St 86336. **Facility:** Smoke free premises. 5 one-bedroom standard units, some with kitchens. 1 story, exterior corridors. **Bath:** combo or shower only. **Parking:** on-site. **Terms:** office hours 8 am-10 pm, no pets allowed (owner's pet on premises). **Amenities:** video library, CD players, hair dryers. *Some:* irons. **Guest Services:** complimentary laundry. **Business Services:** PC, fax (fee). **Cards:** AX, MC, VI. **Special Amenities:** free local telephone calls.

[✕] [VCR] [🔒] [🛏] [🖥] [▣]

(See map and index starting on p. 379)

SEDONA MOTEL
Phone: (928)282-7187 **18**

AAA (SAVE)
▼▼▼

Motel

2/1-5/31 & 9/1-10/31	1P: $89-$99	2P: $89-$109	XP: $10 F12
6/1-8/31 & 11/1-1/31	1P: $79-$89	2P: $79-$99	XP: $10 F12

Location: Jct SR 89A, just s. Located in a busy area. 218 Hwy 179 86336. Fax: 928/282-6757. **Facility:** Designated smoking area. 16 units. 14 one-bedroom standard units. 2 one-bedroom suites. 1 story, exterior corridors. **Parking:** on-site. **Terms:** office hours 8:30 am-9 pm. **Amenities:** safes, irons, hair dryers. **Cards:** DS, MC, VI. **Special Amenities:** free full breakfast and free local telephone calls.

(SD) (ii+) (X) (◉) (▤) (▣) (▢)

SEDONA REAL INN & SUITES   *Book at aaa.com*
Phone: (928)282-1414 **35**

AAA (SAVE)
▼▼▼▼

Small-scale Hotel

3/5-11/26 & 12/24-1/31 [ECP]	2P: $135-$319	XP: $10 F12
2/1-3/4 & 11/27-12/23 [ECP]	2P: $99-$259	XP: $10 F12

Location: Jct SR 179, 3.4 mi w on SR 89A, just sw. Located in West Sedona. 95 Arroyo Pinon 86340 (PO Box 4161). Fax: 928/282-0900. **Facility:** 47 units. 45 one-bedroom standard units, some with whirlpools. 2 one- and 1 two-bedroom suites, some with kitchens and/or whirlpools. 2 stories (no elevator), exterior corridors. **Parking:** on-site. **Terms:** office hours 6 am-midnight, 2-3 night minimum stay - seasonal and/or weekends, package plans, small pets only ($20 fee). **Amenities:** high-speed Internet, voice mail, safes, irons, hair dryers. **Pool(s):** heated outdoor. **Leisure Activities:** whirlpool, exercise room. **Guest Services:** valet and coin laundry. **Business Services:** meeting rooms. **Cards:** AX, DS, MC, VI. **Special Amenities:** free expanded continental breakfast and free local telephone calls. *(See color ad p 382)*

SOME UNITS

(SD) (🐾) (ii+) (🏊) (VCR) (◉) (DATA PORT) (▤) (▣) (▢) / (X) /
FEE

SEDONA ROUGE HOTEL & SPA   *Book at aaa.com*
Phone: (928)203-4111 **22**

AAA (SAVE)
▼▼▼▼

Small-scale Hotel

3/1-10/31	1P: $279	2P: $309	XP: $25 F
2/1-2/28 & 11/1-12/31	1P: $249	2P: $279	XP: $25 F

Location: Jct SR 179, 2 mi w. 2250 W Hwy 89A 86336. Fax: 928/203-9094. **Facility:** 77 one-bedroom standard units, some with whirlpools. 2-3 stories, interior/exterior corridors. *Bath:* combo or shower only. **Parking:** on-site. **Terms:** 3 day cancellation notice-fee imposed, pets ($25 fee, $100 deposit). **Amenities:** high-speed Internet, voice mail, irons, hair dryers. *Some:* DVD players. **Dining:** 7 am-10 pm, cocktails. **Pool(s):** small heated outdoor. **Leisure Activities:** whirlpools, steamroom, exercise room, spa. **Guest Services:** gift shop, valet laundry, airport transportation-Sedona Airport, area transportation-within 5 mi. **Business Services:** meeting rooms, PC, fax (fee). **Cards:** AX, DS, MC, VI. **Special Amenities:** free newspaper and free room upgrade (subject to availability with advance reservations). *(See color ad below)*

(SD) (✈) (🐾) (ii) (🏊) (X) (X) (DATA PORT) (▤) (▣) (▢)
FEE

SEDONA SPRINGS RESORT   *Book at aaa.com*
Phone: (928)204-3400 **30**

AAA (SAVE)
▼▼▼▼

Condominium

All Year	1P: $115-$250

Location: Jct SR 179, 1.6 mi s on SR 89A, then just e. Located in West Sedona. 55 Northview Rd 86336 (PO Box 2252, 86339). Fax: 928/204-3250. **Facility:** An apartment-style complex surrounding a central courtyard with pools, many of these spacious units have garden-style whirlpool baths and showers. Smoke free premises. 75 units. 35 one-bedroom standard units. 35 one- and 5 two-bedroom suites with kitchens and whirlpools. 2 stories (no elevator), exterior corridors. **Parking:** on-site. **Terms:** office hours 7 am-10 pm, check-in 4 pm, 14 day cancellation notice-fee imposed. **Amenities:** CD players, voice mail, irons, hair dryers. *Fee:* video library, safes. **Pool(s):** heated outdoor, heated indoor. **Leisure Activities:** whirlpools, miniature golf, gas grills, playground, exercise room. *Fee:* game room. **Guest Services:** coin laundry. **Cards:** AX, DC, DS, MC, VI.

(SD) (🐾) (X) (X) (VCR) (◉) (DATA PORT) (▤) (▣) (▢)

SEDONA SUMMIT RESORT   *Book at aaa.com*
Phone: (928)204-3100 **39**

▼▼▼▼

Condominium

All Year	1P: $140-$300 2P: $140-$300

Location: Jct SR 179, 3.8 mi w on SR 89A, then just s on Bristlecone Pine Dr. 4055 Navoti Dr 86336. Fax: 928/204-3937. **Facility:** The Sante Fe-style buildings offer some red rock views; lodgings include spacious suites or standard rooms in a garden setting with a lush courtyard. 230 units. 115 one-bedroom standard units. 115 one-bedroom suites with kitchens and whirlpools. 1-2 stories (no elevator), exterior corridors. *Bath:* combo or shower only. **Parking:** on-site. **Terms:** check-in 4 pm, cancellation fee imposed, 12% service charge. **Amenities:** video library (fee), DVD players, voice mail, safes, irons, hair dryers. *Some:* CD players. **Pool(s):** 3 heated outdoor, wading. **Leisure Activities:** whirlpools, exercise room. **Guest Services:** gift shop, coin laundry. **Business Services:** PC. **Cards:** AX, DS, MC, VI.

SOME UNITS

(ASK) (SD) (👶) (🐾) (VCR) (◉) (DATA PORT) (▤) (▣) (▢) / (X) /

(See map and index starting on p. 379)

SEDONA SUPER 8 *Book at aaa.com*

			Phone: (928)282-1533	**29**
2/14-11/30	1P: $85-$109	2P: $85-$109	XP: $10	F12
2/1-2/13 & 12/1-1/31	1P: $69-$85	2P: $69-$85	XP: $10	F12

Small-scale Hotel **Location:** Jct SR 179, 2.4 mi w. 2545 W Hwy 89A 86336. Fax: 928/282-2033. **Facility:** 66 one-bedroom standard units, some with whirlpools. 3 stories, interior corridors. **Parking:** on-site. **Terms:** cancellation fee imposed, package plans, small pets only ($10-$25 extra charge, in designated units). **Amenities:** *Some:* irons, hair dryers. **Pool(s):** heated outdoor. **Guest Services:** coin laundry. **Business Services:** meeting rooms. **Cards:** AX, DC, DS, MC, VI.

SOME UNITS

SKY RANCH LODGE

			Phone: 928/282-6400	**40**
All Year	1P: $75-$250	2P: $75-$250	XP: $10	F11

Motel **Location:** Jct SR 179, 1 mi w on SR 89A, then 1 mi s on west side. Airport Rd 86339 (PO Box 2579). Fax: 928/282-7682. **Facility:** 94 units. 92 one-bedroom standard units. 2 cottages ($189-$250). 1-2 stories (no elevator), exterior corridors. **Parking:** on-site. **Terms:** office hours 7 am-10 pm, check-in 4 pm, package plans, pets ($10 fee). **Amenities:** voice mail, hair dryers. *Some:* irons. **Pool(s):** heated outdoor. **Leisure Activities:** whirlpool. **Guest Services:** gift shop, coin laundry. **Cards:** AX, MC, VI. *(See color ad below)*

SOME UNITS

(See map and index starting on p. 379)

SLIDE ROCK LODGE
Phone: (928)282-3531 **2**

Motel

All Year 1P: $79-$125 2P: $79-$125
Location: Jct SR 179, 6.6 mi n. 6401 N Hwy 89A 86336. Fax: 928/282-2850. **Facility:** 20 one-bedroom standard units. 1 story, exterior corridors. *Bath:* shower only. **Parking:** on-site. **Terms:** office hours 8 am-8 pm, 2 night minimum stay - weekends, 3 day cancellation notice-fee imposed, weekly rates available. **Leisure Activities:** hiking trails. *Fee:* fishing. **Guest Services:** sundries. **Cards:** AX, DS, MC, VI.

SOME UNITS
(ASK) (SD) (☎) / (✕) /

SOUTHWEST INN AT SEDONA *Book at aaa.com*
Phone: (928)282-3344 **33**

Small-scale Hotel

All Year [ECP] 1P: $110-$310 2P: $110-$310 XP: $10 F12
Location: Jct SR 179, 3.5 mi w. Located in West Sedona. 3250 W Hwy 89A 86336. Fax: 928/282-0267. **Facility:** Smoke free premises. 28 units. 24 one-bedroom standard units, some with whirlpools. 4 one-bedroom suites ($190-$350). 2 stories (no elevator), exterior corridors. **Parking:** on-site. **Terms:** office hours 7 am-10 pm, 2 night minimum stay - seasonal and/or weekends, package plans. **Amenities:** voice mail, irons, hair dryers. *Some:* CD players. **Pool(s):** small heated outdoor. **Leisure Activities:** whirlpool, exercise room. **Guest Services:** gift shop. **Business Services:** meeting rooms, PC (fee). **Cards:** AX, DC, DS, MC, VI.

(ASK) (SD) (┼┤) (🏊) (✕) (VCR) (📷) (DATA PORT) (📶) (▭)

THE VIEWS INN SEDONA *Book at aaa.com*
Phone: (928)284-2487

Motel

9/1-1/31	2P: $80-$150	XP: $5 F13
3/2-5/31	2P: $75-$140	XP: $5 F13
2/1-3/1 & 6/1-8/31	2P: $65-$125	XP: $5 F13

Location: Jct Bell Rock Blvd, 0.9 mi s on SR 179, just e. 65 E Cortez Dr 86351. Fax: 928/284-2495. **Facility:** 39 one-bedroom standard units, some with whirlpools. 2 stories (no elevator), exterior corridors. **Parking:** on-site. **Terms:** office hours 7 am-11 pm, cancellation fee imposed, package plans, pets ($5 extra charge, in designated units). **Amenities:** safes, irons, hair dryers. **Pool(s):** outdoor. **Business Services:** fax (fee). **Cards:** AX, DS, MC, VI. **Special Amenities: free continental breakfast and free local telephone calls.** *(See color ad below)*

SOME UNITS
(SD) (🐾) (┼┤) (🏊) (✕) (▭) / (📶) (📠)
FEE FEE FEE

VILLAGE LODGE
Phone: (928)284-3626

Motel

All Year 1P: $49-$59 2P: $49-$59
Location: Jct SR 179, just w. Located in Village of Oak Creek. 78 Bell Rock Blvd 86351 (105 Bell Rock Plaza). Fax: 928/284-3629. **Facility:** Designated smoking area. 17 units. 12 one-bedroom standard units, some with whirlpools. 5 one-bedroom suites ($79-$89). 2 stories (no elevator), interior/exterior corridors. **Parking:** on-site. **Terms:** office hours 8 am-8 pm, cancellation fee imposed, weekly rates available, small pets only (in designated units). **Amenities:** hair dryers. **Cards:** AX, CB, DC, DS, JC, MC, VI. **Special Amenities: free local telephone calls and early check-in/late check-out.**

SOME UNITS
(SD) (🐾) (┼┤) (✕) (📶) / (📠) (▭) /

VILLAS AT POCO DIABLO
Phone: (928)204-3300 **42**

Condominium

All Year 1P: $135-$155
Location: On SR 179, 2 mi s of jct SR 89A. Located in a quiet area. 1752 S Hwy 179 86336 (PO Box 2252, 86339). Fax: 928/204-3250. **Facility:** Nestled between a rocky creek and a resort golf course, these spacious villas offer shady retreats from desert heat and welcome views. Smoke free premises. 33 units. 16 one-bedroom standard units with efficiencies and whirlpools. 17 one-bedroom suites with efficiencies and whirlpools. 1 story, exterior corridors. **Parking:** on-site. **Terms:** office hours 8 am-5 pm, off-site registration, check-in 4 pm, 14 day cancellation notice-fee imposed. **Amenities:** video library (fee), voice mail, irons, hair dryers. **Pool(s):** heated outdoor. **Leisure Activities:** whirlpool, basketball. *Fee:* 4 tennis courts (2 lighted). **Guest Services:** coin laundry. **Business Services:** fax (fee). **Cards:** AX, DC, DS, MC, VI.

(SD) (🏊) (🎿) (✕) (✕) (VCR) (📷) (📶) (📠) (▭)

(See map and index starting on p. 379)

VILLAS OF SEDONA   *Book at aaa.com*   Phone: (928)204-3400   **28**

AAA (SAVE)   All Year   2P: $175-$225
◇◇◇◇   **Location:** Jct SR 179, 1.6 mi w on SR 89A, then just s. Located in West Sedona. 55 Northview Rd 86336 (PO Box
Condominium   2252, 86339). Fax: 928/204-3250. **Facility:** An apartment-style complex surrounding a central courtyard and
pool and spacious townhome units, most having private, outdoor whirlpools. 40 units. 17 one- and 23 two-
bedroom suites with kitchens. 2 stories (no elevator), exterior corridors. **Parking:** on-site. **Terms:** office
hours 7 am-10 pm, check-in 4 pm, 14 day cancellation notice-fee imposed. **Amenities:** DVD players, CD
players, voice mail, irons, hair dryers. *Fee:* video library, safes. **Pool(s):** heated outdoor, heated indoor. **Leisure
Activities:** sauna, whirlpool, putting green, gas grills, playground, exercise room. *Fee:* game room. **Guest Services:** gift shop,
coin laundry. **Business Services:** meeting rooms. **Cards:** AX, DC, DS, MC, VI.

WILDFLOWER INN   *Book at aaa.com*   Phone: (928)284-3937

AAA (SAVE)   2/1-5/31 & 9/1-11/10 [ECP]   1P: $89-$159   2P: $99-$159   XP: $10   F12
◇◇◇◇   6/1-8/31 [ECP]   1P: $79-$139   2P: $89-$139   XP: $10   F12
Motel   11/11-1/31 [ECP]   1P: $69-$129   2P: $79-$129   XP: $10   F12
Location: Jct SR 179 and Bell Rock Blvd. Located in Village of Oak Creek. 6086 Hwy 179 86351. Fax: 928/284-3314.
Facility: Designated smoking area. 29 one-bedroom standard units, some with whirlpools. 2 stories (no
elevator), exterior corridors. **Parking:** on-site. **Terms:** office hours 7 am-10 pm, 2 night minimum stay -
seasonal, package plans. **Guest Services:** coin laundry. **Business Services:** fax. **Cards:** AX, CB, DC, DS, MC, VI.
Special Amenities: free expanded continental breakfast and early check-in/late check-out. *(See color ad below)*

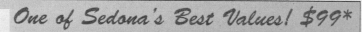

WISHING WELL BED & BREAKFAST   Phone: (928)282-4914   **4**

◇◇◇◇   All Year [BP]   1P: $225   2P: $235
Bed & Breakfast   **Location:** Jct SR 179, 1 mi ne; on top of hill at end of driveway. 995 N Hwy 89A 86336. Fax: 928/204-9766.
Facility: All rooms at this intimate B&B have a fireplace; four rooms also feature private hot tubs on
individual patios. Smoke free premises. 5 one-bedroom standard units, some with whirlpools. 2 stories,
interior/exterior corridors. **Bath:** combo or shower only. **Parking:** on-site. **Terms:** 2 night minimum stay, age restrictions may
apply, 14 day cancellation notice-fee imposed. **Amenities:** irons, hair dryers. **Guest Services:** TV in common area. **Business
Services:** fax. **Cards:** AX, DS, MC, VI.

SOME UNITS

(See map and index starting on p. 379)

—— WHERE TO DINE ——

CASA RINCON & TAPAS CANTINA   Lunch: $5-$22   Dinner: $5-$22   Phone: 928/282-4849   [13]
▼▼ ▼▼   Location: Jct SR 179, 2.5 mi n. 2620 W Hwy 89A 86339. Hours: 11:30 am-9 pm. Reservations: accepted.
Mexican   Features: The classic dishes are well-prepared, staff is friendly and the stage in the lounge is often used for evening entertainment. Casual dress; cocktails. Parking: on-site. Cards: MC, VI.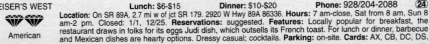

COWBOY CLUB   Lunch: $7-$18   Dinner: $10-$40   Phone: 928/282-4200   [5]
◍◍◍   Location: SR 179, 0.5 mi n. 241 N Hwy 89A 86336. Hours: 11 am-4 & 5-10 pm. Closed: 11/23, 12/25.
▼▼ ▼▼   Reservations: accepted. Features: This popular, bustling place exudes an informal Western atmosphere.
American   Many of the varied Southwestern dishes are based on buffalo meat. Casual dress; cocktails. Parking: on-site. Cards: AX, DS, MC, VI.

CUCINA RUSTICA   Dinner: $12-$26   Phone: 928/284-3010
◍◍◍   Location: Just s of Bell Rock Rd. 7000 Hwy 179, Suite 126A 86351. Hours: 5 pm-close.
▼▼▼ ▼▼▼   Reservations: suggested. Features: Boasting a decor akin to that of an elegant seaside villa, the new
Mediterranean   eatery prepares such hearty dishes as marinated and grilled pork loin and roast chicken in lemon-garlic sauce. Casual dress; cocktails. Parking: on-site. Cards: AX, CB, MC, VI.

DAHL & DILUCA RISTORANTE ITALIANO   Dinner: $11-$28   Phone: 928/282-5219   [12]
▼▼▼ ▼▼▼   Location: Jct SR 179, 3 mi w; in West Sedona. 2321 W Hwy 89A 86336. Hours: 5 pm-10 pm. Closed: 12/25; also
Italian   Super Bowl Sun. Reservations: suggested. Features: Examples of the refined, yet casual, restaurant's traditional entrees include piatto Milanese and linguine carbonara. Entertainment is offered nightly. Casual dress; cocktails. Parking: on-site. Cards: AX, DC, DS, MC, VI.

EL RINCON RESTAURANTE MEXICANO   Lunch: $4-$15   Dinner: $8-$15   Phone: 928/282-4648   [19]
▼▼ ▼▼   Location: Just s of jct SR 179 and 89A; in Tlaquepaque Plaza. Hwy 179 at the Bridge 86339. Hours: 11 am-9 pm.
Mexican   Closed: 1/1, 12/25. Reservations: suggested. Features: The casual eatery serves freshly prepared classics and specialty chimichangas that are robust meals for hungry art shoppers. Casual dress; cocktails. Parking: on-site. Cards: AX, DS, MC, VI.

GALLERY ON OAK CREEK   Lunch: $9-$15   Dinner: $12-$40   Phone: 928/282-4828   [9]
▼▼▼ ▼▼▼   Location: Jct SR 179, 0.4 mi ne; in Amara Creekside Resort. 310 N Hwy 89 A 86336. Hours: 7 am-10 pm.
Regional American   Reservations: accepted. Features: Wide windows overlooking the garden and Oak Creek make for an attractive setting. The attentive staff assists patrons as they consider dishes chef Alan McClean has designed, such as Thai salmon with forbidden rice and tandoori chicken brochette. Made from the freshest of ingredients, his dishes range from comfort food to exotic. Casual dress; cocktails. Parking: on-site. Cards: AX, CB, DC, DS, JC, MC, VI.

THE HEARTLINE CAFE   Lunch: $7-$13   Dinner: $15-$26   Phone: 928/282-0785   [11]
▼▼▼▼   Location: On SR 89A, 1.5 mi s of jct SR 179. 1610 W Hwy 89A 86336. Hours: 11 am-3 & 5-close.
American   Reservations: suggested. Features: The warm, intimate interior and pleasant wait staff complement the imaginative selection of Southwestern cuisine. The wine list is extensive. Dressy casual; cocktails. Parking: on-site. Cards: AX, DC, DS, MC, VI.

JAVELINA CANTINA   Lunch: $10-$16   Dinner: $10-$16   Phone: 928/282-1313   [27]
▼▼▼ ▼▼▼   Location: SR 89A, 0.8 mi s; in Hillside Courtyard and Marketplace, Bldg F ground level. 671 Hwy 179 86336.
Southwestern   Hours: 11:30 am-9:30 pm; hours may vary in winter. Closed: 11/23, 12/25. Reservations: accepted.
Features: Enjoy relaxed dining with views of the Red Rock from inside or the coverd patio. Large portions with fresh ingredients are served in a festive atmosphere. Casual dress; cocktails. Parking: on-site. Cards: AX, DC, MC, VI.

JUDI'S RESTAURANT   Lunch: $7-$12   Dinner: $12-$25   Phone: 928/282-4449   [10]
▼▼ ▼▼   Location: Jct SR 179, 1 mi w on SR 89A; northeast corner. 40 Soldier Rd 86336. Hours: 11:30 am-9 pm, Sun from
American   4:30 pm. Closed: 1/1, 12/25. Reservations: suggested. Features: Antiques and beamed ceilings contribute to the comfortable, cozy atmosphere. The menu centers on chicken, pasta, seafood and steak dishes. A favorite choice is barbecue baby back ribs. Casual dress; cocktails. Parking: on-site. Cards: AX, DC, DS, MC, VI.

JUNIPINE CAFE   Lunch: $6-$11   Dinner: $10-$24   Phone: 928/282-7406   [1]
▼▼ ▼▼   Location: Jct SR 179, 9 mi n; in Junipine Resort. 8351 N Hwy 89A 86336. Hours: 7:30 am-8 pm, Fri & Sat-9 pm;
American   seasonal hours may vary. Closed: 12/25. Reservations: suggested. Features: This cozy eatery serves a nice variety of beef, chicken and pasta. Outdoor dining is available weather permitting. Casual dress; cocktails. Parking: on-site. Cards: AX, MC, VI.

KEISER'S WEST   Lunch: $6-$15   Dinner: $10-$20   Phone: 928/204-2088   [24]
▼▼▼▼   Location: On SR 89A, 2.7 mi w of jct SR 179. 2920 W Hwy 89A 86336. Hours: 7 am-close, Sat from 8 am, Sun 8
American   am-2 pm. Closed: 1/1, 12/25. Reservations: suggested. Features: Locally popular for breakfast, the restaurant draws in folks for its eggs Judi dish, which outsells its French toast. For lunch or dinner, barbecue and Mexican dishes are hearty options. Dressy casual; cocktails. Parking: on-site. Cards: AX, CB, DC, DS, MC, VI.

(See map and index starting on p. 379)

L'AUBERGE DE SEDONA RESTAURANT

Lunch: $9-$27   Dinner: $25-$40   Phone: 928/282-1661   [7]

Location: Just n on SR 89A from jct SR 179, then e. 301 L'Auberge Ln 86336. **Hours:** 7:30 am-9 pm; seasonal hours may vary. **Reservations:** suggested. **Features:** The newly renovated restaurant offers elegant surroundings and formal service. Chef Brunacci offers a la carte and five-course prix fixe meals for dinner with modern international elements. The Terrace allows for seasonal creekside dining. Dressy casual; cocktails. **Parking:** on-site. **Cards:** AX, CB, DC, DS, MC, VI.

Continental

MANDARIN HOUSE

Lunch: $6-$8   Dinner: $8-$22   Phone: 928/284-9088

Location: Just s of Bell Rock Blvd; in Village of Oak Creek. 6486 Hwy 179 #114 86351. **Hours:** 11 am-9 pm, Fri & Sat-10 pm. **Closed:** 11/23, 12/25. **Reservations:** accepted. **Features:** The family-oriented restaurant employs a friendly staff. The menu centers on traditional Mandarin and Szechwan dishes prepared from the freshest ingredients. Glazed fruit desserts are wonderful with ice cream on the side. Casual dress; cocktails. **Parking:** on-site. **Cards:** AX, DS, MC, VI.

Regional Chinese

MARIA'S RESTAURANT & CANTINA

Lunch: $8-$15   Dinner: $10-$22   Phone: 928/284-3739

Location: 0.5 mi s of Bell Rock Blvd; in Village of Oak Creek. 6446 Hwy 179 86351. **Hours:** 11 am-9 pm. **Closed:** 4/16, 12/25. **Reservations:** accepted. **Features:** Located in the village of Oak Creek, this eatery offers classic Mexican dishes along with specialty appetizers such as "rattlesnake eggs," which are cheese-stuffed jalapenos that test your tongue for pepper-hot heat. Casual dress; cocktails. **Parking:** on-site. **Cards:** AX, DS, MC, VI.

Mexican

MONSOON IN THE RED ROCKS

Lunch: $7-$10   Dinner: $7-$10   Phone: 928/203-0012   [23]

Location: Jct SR 179, 1.3 mi w. 1350 W Hwy 89A 86336. **Hours:** 11:30 am-9 pm, Fri & Sat-10 pm. **Closed:** 11/23, 12/24, 12/25. **Reservations:** accepted. **Features:** The Asian cafe, with its sushi and martini bars, brings an eclectic dining experience to Sedona. Classic sushi, specialty rolls and such dishes as Thai spicy shrimp satisfy guests' yearnings for this food style. Casual dress; cocktails. **Parking:** on-site. **Cards:** AX, MC, VI.

Asian

OAK CREEK BREWERY & GRILL

Lunch: $9-$17   Dinner: $11-$26   Phone: 928/282-3300   [20]

Location: Jct SR 89A, 0.3 mi s on SR 179; in Tlaquepaque Village. 333 Hwy 179 86336. **Hours:** 11 am-9 pm. **Closed:** 11/23, 12/25. **Reservations:** accepted. **Features:** The microbrewery's owner, who trained in Germany, designs the prize-winning, freshly brewed beers. Accompaniments include hearty sandwiches, crisp salads, pizza, steaks and ribs. Desserts are awesome. Casual dress; cocktails. **Parking:** on-site. **Cards:** AX, DS, MC, VI.

American

OAXACA RESTAURANT

Lunch: $6-$12   Dinner: $10-$16   Phone: 928/282-4179   [3]

Location: Jct Apple Rd and SR 89A. 321 N Hwy 89A 86336. **Hours:** 8 am-9 pm. **Closed:** 12/25. **Features:** The family-friendly place serves dishes from the Mexican region of the same name. For more than 20 years, the family has prepared foods, being conscious of dietary concerns, using vegetable oils and no additives. Casual dress; cocktails. **Parking:** on-site. **Cards:** AX, DS, MC, VI.

Mexican

THE ORCHARDS BAR & GRILL

Lunch: $8-$12   Dinner: $8-$20   Phone: 928/282-7200   [4]

Location: Center. 254 N Hwy 89A 86339. **Hours:** 7 am-9 pm. **Reservations:** accepted. **Features:** From the start to the finish of the day, the popular eatery serves such well-cooked dishes as eggs Benedict, hearty burgers, sandwiches and regional Mexican fare. The staff is friendly. Casual dress; cocktails. **Parking:** street. **Cards:** AX, DS, MC, VI.

Regional American

PEKING INN

Lunch: $7-$10   Dinner: $8-$13   Phone: 928/282-3118   [8]

Location: Jct SR 179, 2 mi w on SR 89A; in West Sedona at Bashas' Shopping Center. 164-H Coffee Pot Dr 86336. **Hours:** 11 am-9:30 pm. **Closed:** 11/23. **Reservations:** accepted. **Features:** Served in the attractive restaurant is a large selection of a la carte dishes, as well as complete luncheons and dinners. Lunch and dinner buffets are locally popular. Casual dress; cocktails. **Parking:** on-site. **Cards:** MC, VI.

Chinese

PIETROS

Dinner: $15-$26   Phone: 928/282-2525   [17]

Location: SR 179, 2.8 mi w. 2445 W Hwy 89A 86336. **Hours:** 5 pm-9 pm, Fri & Sat-10 pm. **Reservations:** required. **Features:** Diners who unwind in the casual bistro atmosphere can savor classic Italian cuisine, vegetarian dishes or the specialty rack of lamb. The seasonally changing menu incorporates distinctive fusion elements. Casual dress; cocktails. **Parking:** on-site. **Cards:** AX, CB, DC, DS, MC, VI.

International

RAINBOW'S END RELICS

Lunch: $6-$19   Dinner: $14-$28   Phone: 928/282-1593   [25]

Location: Jct SR 179, 3.1 mi w. 3235 W Hwy 89A 86340. **Hours:** 11 am-2 & 5-9 pm, Fri-10 pm, Sat 5 pm-10 pm, Sun 5 pm-9 pm. **Closed:** 1/1, 11/23, 12/25. **Reservations:** accepted. **Features:** Antiques and memorabilia surround the dining room, where the pleasant staff serves guests. The eatery is known for prime steaks, barbecue and seafood. Casual dress; cocktails. **Parking:** on-site. **Cards:** AX, DC, DS, MC, VI.

Steak House

RENE AT TLAQUEPAQUE

Lunch: $8-$14   Dinner: $17-$35   Phone: 928/282-9225   [21]

Location: SR 89A, 0.3 mi s on SR 179; in Tlaquepaque Village, Bldg B-118. 336 Hwy 179 B-118 86336. **Hours:** 11:30 am-2:30 & 5:30-8:30 pm, Fri & Sat-9 pm; seasonal hours vary. **Closed:** 12/25. **Reservations:** suggested. **Features:** Tucked into the upscale, art-filled shopping plaza, the quietly elegant dining room is where diners are treated to attentive service and Continental and American favorites. Entertainers perform on weekends. Casual dress; cocktails. **Parking:** on-site. **Cards:** AX, MC, VI.

Continental

(See map and index starting on p. 379)

ROBERT'S CREEKSIDE CAFE & GRILL **Lunch:** $8-$11 **Dinner:** $16-$22 **Phone:** 928/282-3671 14
Southwest Continental
Location: Just s of jct SR 89A. 251 Hwy 179 86336. **Hours:** 11 am-4 & 5-9 pm. **Reservations:** suggested. **Features:** Overlooking Oak Creek, the cafe prepares such dishes as mahi mahi with guajillo chile sauce. The staff is attentive and friendly. The recipe for the popular peach cobbler is freely shared. Beef, pork and chicken are infused with lively Southwestern flavors. Casual dress; cocktails. **Parking:** on-site. **Cards:** AX, DS, MC, VI.

SASAKI JAPANESE CUISINE & SUSHI BAR **Dinner:** $14-$47 **Phone:** 928/284-1757
Specialty
Location: Jct SR 179, just w. 65 Bell Rock Blvd 86351. **Hours:** 5 pm-close. **Reservations:** suggested. **Features:** The contemporary eatery reflects tasteful Oriental decor. Listed on the menu are a wide variety of sushi offerings, as well as a large selection of Japanese dishes. Dressy casual; cocktails. **Parking:** on-site. **Cards:** AX, DS, MC, VI.

SAVANNAH'S **Dinner:** $14-$34 **Phone:** 928/282-7959 22
American
Location: Jct SR 179, 2.5 mi w. 2611 W Hwy 89A 86336. **Hours:** 5 pm-10 pm. **Reservations:** suggested. **Features:** Although prime steaks are the specialty, the chef-owner also infuses regional flavors into such dishes as roasted red pepper fettuccine and crispy spinach with calamari. The warm, intimate atmosphere is perfect for special occasions. Dressy casual; cocktails. **Parking:** on-site. **Cards:** AX, DS, MC, VI.

THE SECRET GARDEN CAFE **Lunch:** $8-$16 **Phone:** 928/203-9564 18
American
Location: Jct SR 89A, 0.3 mi s; on north end of Tlaquepaque. 336 Hwy 179 86336. **Hours:** 9 am-5 pm, Sun from 11 am. Closed: 1/1, 11/23, 12/25. **Features:** Just off the Tlaquepaque courtyard, the casual eatery serves fresh salads, homemade soups and such innovative sandwiches as the ahi tuna wrap. The dessert showcase holds mile-high carrot or chocolate cake, pies and other delicacies that will tempt even a staunch dieter. Casual dress; cocktails. **Parking:** on-site. **Cards:** AX, DS, MC, VI.

SEDONA AIRPORT RESTAURANT **Lunch:** $6-$10 **Dinner:** $11-$22 **Phone:** 928/282-3576 28
Regional American
Location: SR 179, 1 mi w on SR 89A, 1.3 mi s. 1185 Airport Rd 86336. **Hours:** 7 am-9 pm. Closed: 11/23, 12/25. **Reservations:** accepted. **Features:** Traditional foods with Southwestern flavors and pleasant garnishes are enjoyed while you watch planes take off and land at the local airport with red rock cliffs in the background. Casual dress; cocktails. **Parking:** on-site. **Cards:** MC, VI.

SHUGRUE'S HILLSIDE GRILL **Lunch:** $7-$16 **Dinner:** $15-$35 **Phone:** 928/282-5300 26
American
Location: Jct SR 89A, 0.8 mi s; in Hillside Courtyard and Marketplace, Bldg D upper level. 671 Hwy 179 86336. **Hours:** 11:30 am-3 & 5-9:30 pm. Closed: 12/25. **Reservations:** suggested. **Features:** The hillside location features large picture windows looking toward the mountains and an inviting seasonal deck. The specialty is seafood although the menu also includes selections of beef, lamb and chicken. Casual dress; cocktails; entertainment. **Parking:** on-site. **Cards:** AX, DC, MC, VI.

THE SILVER SADDLE ROOM **Dinner:** $15-$39 6
AAA
Steak House
Location: SR 179, 0.5 mi n. 241 N Hwy 89A 86336. **Hours:** 5 pm-10 pm. Closed: 11/23, 12/25. **Reservations:** suggested. **Features:** The comfortably elegant room invites diners to slow down, relax and enjoy wonderfully prepared grilled steaks and game. The smiling staff provides accomplished service. Dressy casual; cocktails. **Parking:** on-site. **Cards:** AX, DS, MC, VI.

SPICES **Lunch:** $8-$10 **Dinner:** $15-$22 **Phone:** 928/204-9117 16
Continental
Location: Jct SR 179, 2.4 mi w. 2545 W Hwy 89A 86340. **Hours:** 7 am-9 pm. Closed: 11/23, 12/25. **Reservations:** accepted. **Features:** Charming country-casual decor contributes to an interesting setting in which to enjoy Continental cuisine classics, including steak, pasta and seafood specialties. Casual dress; cocktails. **Parking:** on-site. **Cards:** AX, DS, MC, VI.

STEAKS & STICKS **Dinner:** $16-$30 **Phone:** 928/204-7849 15
Steak House
Location: Jct SR 89A, just s on SR 179, just w. 160 Portal Ln 86336. **Hours:** 5 pm-10 pm. **Reservations:** suggested. **Features:** Upscale decor characterizes the warm interior, where tender Angus steaks, savory seafood and delectable desserts await. Attentive staff members serve meals with smiles and ease. Dressy casual; cocktails. **Parking:** on-site. **Cards:** AX, DS, MC, VI.

TAKASHI JAPANESE RESTAURANT **Lunch:** $9-$15 **Dinner:** $15-$22 **Phone:** 928/282-2334 2
Japanese
Location: Jct SR 89A, 0.4 mi n; in north Uptown Sedona area. 465 Jordan Rd 86336. **Hours:** 11:30 am-1:30 & 5-9 pm, Sat & Sun from 5 pm. Closed: 11/23, 12/25; also Mon. **Reservations:** suggested. **Features:** Enjoy an excellent selection of Japanese appetizers, entrees and sushi surrounded by an attractive decor. Sake and Japanese beer are available. Outdoor dining is offered weather permitting. Casual dress; cocktails. **Parking:** on-site. **Cards:** AX, CB, DC, MC, VI.

THE YAVAPAI RESTAURANT **Lunch:** $12-$18 **Dinner:** $23-$38 **Phone:** 928/204-6000
American
Location: Jct SR 179, 3.5 mi w on SR 89A, 5 mi n on Dry Creek Rd and FR 152C; in Enchantment Resort. 525 Boynton Canyon Rd 86336. **Hours:** 6:30 am-9 pm. **Reservations:** required. **Features:** While taking in stunning views of Boynton Canyon, patrons can savor such dishes as sesame-crusted and grilled ahi tuna and cold-smoked buffalo tenderloin. The elegant service and decor complete a truly distinguished dining experience. Dressy casual; cocktails. **Parking:** on-site. **Cards:** AX, CB, DC, DS, MC, VI.

SELIGMAN pop. 456

———— WHERE TO STAY ————

CANYON LODGE

(AAA) [SAVE]
◊◊◊◊
Motel

Phone: (928)422-3255

All Year   1P: $42-$47   2P: $47-$50   XP: $7   D11
Location: I-40, exit 121, 1 mi n, then 0.7 mi e on Route 66. 114 E Chino Ave 86337 (PO Box 766). Fax: 928/422-3600. **Facility:** 16 one-bedroom standard units. 2 stories (no elevator), exterior corridors. *Bath:* combo or shower only. **Parking:** on-site. **Terms:** cancellation fee imposed, [CP] meal plan available, pets ($10 extra charge, in limited units). **Amenities:** hair dryers. *Some:* irons. **Leisure Activities:** recreation room, limited exercise equipment. **Cards:** AX, DC, DS, MC, VI.

SOME UNITS

HISTORIC ROUTE 66 MOTEL

(AAA) [SAVE]
◊◊◊◊
Motel

Phone: 928/422-3204

All Year   1P: $47-$57   2P: $52-$67   XP: $5   F
Location: I-40, exit 121, 1 mi n, then just e. 500 W Route 66 86337 (PO Box 5). Fax: 928/422-3581. **Facility:** 16 one-bedroom standard units. 1 story, exterior corridors. *Bath:* combo or shower only. **Parking:** on-site. **Terms:** cancellation fee imposed. **Cards:** AX, CB, DC, DS, MC, VI.

SOME UNITS

SHOW LOW pop. 7,695

———— WHERE TO STAY ————

BEST WESTERN PAINT PONY LODGE   *Book at aaa.com*

(AAA) [SAVE]
◊◊◊◊
Motel

Phone: (928)537-5773

5/1-10/2 [ECP]   1P: $89-$199   2P: $94-$204   XP: $5   F17
2/1-4/30 & 10/3-1/31 [ECP]   1P: $79-$139   2P: $84-$144   XP: $5   F17
Location: On US 60 and SR 260. 581 W Deuce of Clubs Ave 85901. Fax: 928/537-5766. **Facility:** 50 units. 49 one-bedroom standard units, some with whirlpools. 1 one-bedroom suite ($139-$204). 2 stories (no elevator), exterior corridors. **Parking:** on-site. **Terms:** cancellation fee imposed, $1 service charge, pets ($10 fee). **Amenities:** video library (fee), irons, hair dryers. *Some:* high-speed Internet. **Business Services:** fax (fee). **Cards:** AX, CB, DC, DS, JC, MC, VI. **Special Amenities:** free expanded continental breakfast and free newspaper.

SOME UNITS

DAYS INN   *Book at aaa.com*

(AAA) [SAVE]
◊◊◊◊
Motel

Phone: (928)537-4356

All Year   1P: $62-$85   2P: $65-$85   XP: $10   F13
Location: On US 60 and SR 260. 480 W Deuce of Clubs Ave 85901. Fax: 928/537-8692. **Facility:** 122 one-bedroom standard units, some with whirlpools. 2 stories (no elevator), interior/exterior corridors. *Bath:* combo or shower only. **Parking:** on-site. **Terms:** pets ($10 fee). **Amenities:** hair dryers. **Dining:** 6 am-9 pm, Fri & Sat-11 pm; seasonal hours may vary. **Pool(s):** small heated outdoor. **Guest Services:** coin laundry. **Business Services:** fax (fee). **Cards:** AX, DC, DS, MC, VI. **Special Amenities:** free local telephone calls and free newspaper.

SOME UNITS

HOLIDAY INN EXPRESS   *Book at aaa.com*

◊◊◊◊
Small-scale Hotel

Phone: 928/537-5115

Property failed to provide current rates
Location: On US 60 and SR 260. 151 W Deuce of Clubs Ave 85901. Fax: 928/537-2929. **Facility:** 71 units. 68 one-bedroom standard units, some with whirlpools. 3 one-bedroom suites with whirlpools. 2-3 stories, interior corridors. *Bath:* combo or shower only. **Parking:** on-site. **Amenities:** voice mail, irons, hair dryers. **Pool(s):** small heated indoor. **Leisure Activities:** whirlpool, exercise room. **Guest Services:** coin laundry. **Business Services:** meeting rooms.

SOME UNITS

K C MOTEL   *Book at aaa.com*

(AAA) [SAVE]
◊◊◊◊
Motel

Phone: (928)537-4433

5/30-9/30 [CP]   1P: $52-$69   2P: $56-$74   XP: $5   D18
2/1-5/29 & 10/1-1/31 [CP]   1P: $49-$56   2P: $52-$58   XP: $5   D18
Location: On US 60 and SR 260. 60 W Deuce of Clubs 85901. Fax: 928/537-0106. **Facility:** 35 one-bedroom standard units, some with whirlpools. 1-2 stories (no elevator), exterior corridors. **Parking:** on-site. **Leisure Activities:** whirlpool. **Business Services:** fax. **Cards:** AX, DS, MC, VI. **Special Amenities:** free continental breakfast and free local telephone calls.

SOME UNITS

KIVA MOTEL

(AAA) [SAVE]
◊◊◊
Motel

Phone: (928)537-4542

All Year   1P: $42-$45   2P: $48-$58   XP: $10   D20
Location: On US 60 and SR 260. 261 E Deuce of Clubs Ave 85901. Fax: 928/537-1024. **Facility:** 20 one-bedroom standard units. 1 story, exterior corridors. *Bath:* combo or shower only. **Parking:** on-site. **Terms:** 3 day cancellation notice, pets (small dogs only, $5 extra charge). **Amenities:** hair dryers. **Leisure Activities:** sauna, whirlpool. **Business Services:** fax. **Cards:** AX, DS, MC, VI. **Special Amenities:** free local telephone calls.

SOME UNITS

MOTEL 6 #4102   *Book at aaa.com*   Phone: 928/537-7694
Motel
| | 5/1-10/31 | 1P: $50 | 2P: $60-$74 | XP: $5 | F12 |
| | 2/1-4/30 & 11/1-1/31 | 1P: $45-$50 | 2P: $50-$65 | XP: $5 | F12 |

Location: Just e of jct SR 260. Located in a commercial area. 1941 E Deuce of Clubs Ave 85901. Fax: 928/537-1373. **Facility:** 42 one-bedroom standard units, some with whirlpools. 2 stories (no elevator), exterior corridors. **Parking:** on-site. **Terms:** small pets only. **Guest Services:** coin laundry. **Business Services:** fax (fee). **Cards:** AX, DC, DS, MC, VI.

SOME UNITS
(ASK) (S🌀) 🐾 📺 (DATA PORT) / ✕ 🍴 🖥 /

SLEEP INN   *Book at aaa.com*   Phone: (928)532-7323
(AAA) (SAVE)
Small-scale Hotel
| | 5/16-10/1 | 1P: $79-$99 | 2P: $89-$115 | XP: $10 | F18 |
| | 2/1-5/15 & 10/2-1/31 | 1P: $69-$89 | 2P: $74-$99 | XP: $10 | F18 |

Location: On SR 260, 0.5 mi w of US 60. 1751 W Deuce of Clubs Ave 85901. Fax: 928/537-3304. **Facility:** 70 one-bedroom standard units. 3 stories, interior corridors. *Bath:* combo or shower only. **Terms:** [ECP] meal plan available, pets ($10 extra charge). **Amenities:** video library (fee). *Some:* high-speed Internet, irons, hair dryers. **Pool(s):** heated indoor. **Leisure Activities:** whirlpool. **Guest Services:** coin laundry, airport transportation-Show Low Airport. **Business Services:** meeting rooms, fax (fee). **Cards:** AX, CB, DC, DS, JC, MC, VI.

SOME UNITS
(S🌀) ✈ 🛏 (GM) 🦽 🚭 🐎 🛅 📺 (DATA PORT) / ✕ (VCR) 🍴 🖥 📺 /
       FEE   FEE

——— WHERE TO DINE ———

BRANDING IRON STEAKHOUSE   Lunch: $7-$15   Dinner: $7-$30   Phone: 928/537-5151
Steak House

Location: Jct US 60 and SR 260. 1261 E Deuce of Clubs 85901. **Hours:** 11 am-9 pm, Fri-10 pm, Sat 4 pm-10 pm, Sun 4 pm-9 pm. **Closed:** 12/25. **Reservations:** suggested. **Features:** A wide selection of broiled beef cuts, along with fish and lobster dishes, gives everyone a favorite choice. Freshly baked bread is served warm, and fixings from the fresh salad bar complete the meal. Casual dress; cocktails. **Parking:** on-site.
Cards: AX, DC, DS, MC, VI.   🍸 ✕

LICANO'S MEXICAN STEAKHOUSE   Lunch: $4-$9   Dinner: $7-$15   Phone: 928/537-8220
Mexican

Location: On US 60 and SR 260; center. 573 W Deuce of Clubs 85902. **Hours:** 11 am-9:30 pm. **Closed:** 4/16, 12/25. **Reservations:** accepted. **Features:** The attractive dining room resembles that of a steakhouse, but the classic dishes of Mexico are what are warm and filling here. Guests can count on pleasant service with a friendly smile. Cocktails. **Parking:** on-site. **Cards:** MC, VI.   🍸

PAT'S PLACE   Lunch: $4-$8   Dinner: $6-$16   Phone: 928/537-2337
(AAA)
American

Location: 0.4 mi w of jct SR 260. 981 E Deuce of Clubs Ave 85901. **Hours:** 6 am-8:30 pm, Fri & Sat-9 pm. **Closed:** 11/23, 12/24, 12/25; also Mothers' Day. **Reservations:** accepted. **Features:** Guests are greeted as neighbors at the friendly eatery. Dishes ranging from hot and cold sandwiches to baked chicken and pizza are prepared to order. From breakfast to dinner, this is a comfortable stop. Casual dress; wine only. **Parking:** street. **Cards:** AX, DS, MC, VI.

SIERRA VISTA pop. 37,775

——— WHERE TO STAY ———

BEST WESTERN MISSION INN   *Book at aaa.com*   Phone: (520)458-8500
(AAA) (SAVE)
Motel
| | All Year | 1P: $65-$75 | 2P: $69-$80 | XP: $5 | F17 |

Location: Just w of jct SR 90 and 92. 3460 E Fry Blvd 85635. Fax: 520/459-3070. **Facility:** 40 one-bedroom standard units. 2 stories (no elevator), exterior corridors. **Parking:** on-site. **Terms:** [ECP] meal plan available, small pets only ($5 extra charge). **Amenities:** high-speed Internet, irons, hair dryers. **Pool(s):** heated outdoor. **Guest Services:** coin laundry. **Cards:** AX, CB, DC, DS, JC, MC, VI. **Special Amenities:** free expanded continental breakfast and free local telephone calls. *(See color ad below)*

SOME UNITS
(S🌀) 🛏 🍴 (GM) 🚭 📺 (DATA PORT) 🍴 🖥 📺 / ✕
       FEE

COMFORT INN & SUITES
Book at aaa.com

WWWW

Small-scale Hotel

| 1/1-1/31 | 1P: $109-$149 | 2P: $129-$169 | XP: $10 | F16 |
| 2/1-12/31 | 1P: $99-$109 | 2P: $129 | XP: $10 | F16 |

Phone: (520)459-0515

Location: Just w of jct SR 90 and 92. 3500 E Fry Blvd 85635. Fax: 520/459-3312. **Facility:** 65 one-bedroom standard units. 3 stories, interior corridors. *Bath:* combo or shower only. **Parking:** on-site. **Terms:** cancellation fee imposed. **Amenities:** voice mail, irons, hair dryers. **Pool(s):** small heated outdoor. **Leisure Activities:** whirlpool, exercise room. **Guest Services:** coin laundry. **Business Services:** PC. **Cards:** AX, DC, DS, MC, VI.

SOME UNITS

(ASK) (S) (D) (YI+) (&M) (☐) (🏊) (🎥) (DATA PORT) (☐) (☐) (☐) / (✕) /

FAIRFIELD INN & SUITES

WWWW

Small-scale Hotel

All Year | 1P: $84-$104 | 2P: $84-$104

Phone: (520)439-5900

Location: Jct SR 90, 1.5 mi s on SR 92. Located at the Sierra Vista Mall. 3855 El Mercado Loop 85635. Fax: 520/439-5905. **Facility:** 67 one-bedroom standard units. 3 stories, interior corridors. *Bath:* combo or shower only. **Parking:** on-site. **Terms:** [ECP] meal plan available. **Amenities:** high-speed Internet, voice mail, irons, hair dryers. *Some:* CD players. **Pool(s):** heated outdoor. **Leisure Activities:** whirlpool, exercise room. **Guest Services:** valet and coin laundry. **Business Services:** meeting rooms, PC. **Cards:** AX, DC, DS, MC, VI.

SOME UNITS

(ASK) (S) (D) (YI+) (🏊) (🎥) (DATA PORT) (☐) / (✕) (☐) (☐) /

GATEWAY STUDIO SUITES

WWWW

Small-scale Hotel

Property failed to provide current rates

Phone: 520/458-5555

Location: Just s of Fry Ave and se of Main. 203 S Garden Ave 85635. Fax: 520/458-2129. **Facility:** 83 one-bedroom standard units with efficiencies. 3 stories, interior corridors. *Bath:* combo or shower only. **Parking:** on-site. **Amenities:** high-speed Internet, voice mail, irons, hair dryers. **Pool(s):** small heated outdoor. **Leisure Activities:** whirlpool, exercise room. **Guest Services:** coin laundry. **Business Services:** meeting rooms, PC.

SOME UNITS

(✈) (YI+) (&) (☐) (🏊) (🎥) (DATA PORT) (☐) (☐) (☐) / (✕) /

QUALITY INN
Book at aaa.com

(AAA) (SAVE)
WWWW

Small-scale Hotel

All Year | 1P: $69-$89 | 2P: $79-$99 | XP: $5 | F17

Phone: (520)458-7900

Location: On SR 92, 1 mi s of jct SR 90. 1631 S Hwy 92 85635. Fax: 520/459-2603. **Facility:** 103 one-bedroom standard units. 2 stories (no elevator), interior corridors. **Parking:** on-site. **Terms:** 14 day cancellation notice-fee imposed, [ECP] meal plan available, pets ($10 extra charge). **Amenities:** high-speed Internet, voice mail, irons, hair dryers. **Pool(s):** outdoor. **Leisure Activities:** whirlpool. **Guest Services:** valet and coin laundry. **Cards:** AX, CB, DC, DS, JC, MC, VI. **Special Amenities:** free expanded continental breakfast and free local telephone calls. *(See color ad below)*

SOME UNITS

(S) (D) (🛏) (🏊) (📶) (🎥) (DATA PORT) (☐) (☐) (☐) / (✕) /
FEE

RAMSEY CANYON.COM BED & BREAKFAST

WWW

Bed & Breakfast

Property failed to provide current rates

Phone: 520/366-0500

Location: Jct SR 90, 6 mi s on SR 92, then 3.1 mi w. 76 Ramsey Canyon Rd 85615. Fax: 520/366-0600. **Facility:** Smoke free premises. 4 units. 3 one-bedroom standard units. 1 cottage. 2 stories (no elevator), interior/exterior corridors. *Bath:* some shared or private, shower only. **Parking:** on-site. **Terms:** check-in 4 pm, age restrictions may apply. **Leisure Activities:** hiking trails. **Guest Services:** TV in common area, complimentary laundry.

SOME UNITS

(✕) (W) (Z) / (☐) (☐) (☐) /

RAMSEY CANYON INN BED & BREAKFAST

WWW

Bed & Breakfast

All Year | 1P: $130-$200 | 2P: $130-$200

Phone: 520/378-3010

Location: Jct SR 90, 5.9 mi s on SR 92, then 3.5 mi w. 29 E Ramsey Canyon Rd 85615. Fax: 520/803-0819. **Facility:** At the entrance to the Nature Conservancy Park, this charming inn has attractive rooms and well-stocked baths. Designated smoking area. 9 units. 6 one-bedroom standard units. 3 one-bedroom suites ($150-$225) with kitchens. 2 stories (no elevator), interior/exterior corridors. *Bath:* combo or shower only. **Parking:** on-site. **Terms:** office hours 8 am-5 pm, 2 night minimum stay, 14 day cancellation notice-fee imposed, weekly rates available, [BP] meal plan available, package plans. **Leisure Activities:** hiking trails. **Cards:** MC, VI.

SOME UNITS

(ASK) (✕) (W) / (K) (Z) (☐) (☐) (☐) /

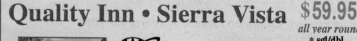

SIERRA SUITES *Book at aaa.com*   Phone: (520)459-4221
(AAA) (SAVE)   All Year [ECP]   1P: $83-$95   2P: $83-$95   XP: $5   F12
▼▼▼▼   **Location:** Jct SR 90 and 92, 2.2 mi w. 391 E Fry Blvd 85635. Fax: 520/459-8449. **Facility:** 100 units. 96 one-
Small-scale Hotel bedroom standard units. 4 one-bedroom suites. 2 stories (no elevator), exterior corridors. **Parking:** on-site.
Terms: package plans, small pets only ($30 fee, in designated units). **Amenities:** video games (fee), voice
mail, irons, hair dryers. **Pool(s):** heated outdoor. **Leisure Activities:** whirlpool, exercise room. **Guest
Services:** valet and coin laundry. **Business Services:** meeting rooms, PC. **Cards:** AX, DS, MC, VI.
Special Amenities: free expanded continental breakfast and free local telephone calls. *(See color ad below)*

SOME UNITS
[S𝐃] [🛏] [📶+] [🏊] [📷] [DATA PORT] [🔒] [🍽] [🖥] /[✕]/
FEE

SUN CANYON INN   Phone: (520)459-0610
▼▼ ▼▼   All Year   1P: $71   2P: $81   XP: $10   F14
Small-scale Hotel **Location:** Just n of Fry Blvd; just e of Main Main Gate to Fort Huachuca. 260 N Garden Ave 85635.
Fax: 520/459-5178. **Facility:** 80 one-bedroom standard units, some with whirlpools. 4 stories, interior
corridors. *Bath:* combo or shower only. **Parking:** on-site. **Terms:** cancellation fee imposed, [BP] meal plan
available. **Amenities:** video library (fee), high-speed Internet, voice mail, irons, hair dryers. **Pool(s):** heated outdoor. **Leisure
Activities:** whirlpool, exercise room. **Guest Services:** complimentary evening beverages: Mon-Fri, coin laundry. **Business
Services:** meeting rooms, PC. **Cards:** AX, DC, DS, MC, VI.

SOME UNITS
(ASK) [S𝐃] [🍴] [🍷] [🎣] [🏊] [📷] [DATA PORT] [🔒] [🖥] /[✕]/ [VCR]
FEE

SUPER 8 MOTEL *Book at aaa.com*   Phone: (520)459-5380
(AAA) (SAVE)   All Year   1P: $44-$54   2P: $49-$59   XP: $5   F12
▼▼▼   **Location:** Jct Business SR 90 and Fry Blvd, then just e of main gate to Fort Huachuca. 100 Fab Ave 85635.
Motel   Fax: 520/459-6052. **Facility:** 52 one-bedroom standard units. 2 stories (no elevator), exterior corridors.
Parking: on-site. **Terms:** [CP] meal plan available, pets (small dogs only, $10 fee). **Amenities:** safes (fee).
Pool(s): heated outdoor. **Guest Services:** coin laundry. **Cards:** AX, CB, DC, DS, MC, VI.
Special Amenities: free continental breakfast and free local telephone calls.

SOME UNITS
[S𝐃] [🛏] [📶+] [🛁] [🏊] [📷] [🔒] [🖥] /[✕] [DATA PORT] [🖥] /
FEE

THE WESTERN MOTEL   Phone: 520-458-4303
(AAA) (SAVE)   All Year   1P: $38-$42   2P: $45-$50   XP: $7   F8
▼▼▼   **Location:** 0.4 mi e of main entrance to Fort Huachuca. 43 W Fry Blvd 85635. Fax: 520/459-4197. **Facility:** 25 one-
Motel   bedroom standard units, some with efficiencies. 1 story, exterior corridors. **Parking:** on-site.
Amenities: *Some:* hair dryers. **Cards:** AX, CB, DC, DS, JC, MC, VI. **Special Amenities: free local
telephone calls and free room upgrade (subject to availability with advance reservations).**

SOME UNITS
[S𝐃] [📷] [DATA PORT] [🔒] [🖥] /[✕]/

WINDEMERE HOTEL & CONFERENCE CENTER *Book at aaa.com*   Phone: (520)459-5900
▼▼▼   All Year   1P: $139   2P: $139   XP: $10   F18
Location: 1.5 mi s of jct SR 90. 2047 S Hwy 92 85635. Fax: 520/458-1347. **Facility:** 149 units. 146 one-bedroom
Small-scale Hotel standard units. 3 one-bedroom suites ($175-$195), some with whirlpools. 3 stories, interior corridors.
Parking: on-site. **Terms:** check-in 4 pm, pets ($50 deposit). **Amenities:** video games (fee), voice mail,
irons, hair dryers. **Pool(s):** heated outdoor. **Leisure Activities:** whirlpool. **Guest Services:** complimentary evening beverages,
valet and coin laundry. **Business Services:** conference facilities. **Cards:** AX, CB, DC, DS, MC, VI.

SOME UNITS
(ASK) [S𝐃] [🛏] [🍴] [🍷] [🏊] [📶+] [📷] [DATA PORT] [🔒] [🍽] [🖥] /[✕]/
FEE

WHERE TO DINE

THE BREAD BASKET

Bakery/Desserts

Lunch: $4-$7 Phone: 520/458-8580

Location: Jct Fry Blvd, just s on Business SR 90 (Buffalo Soldier Tr), just e. 355 W Wilcox Dr 85635. **Hours:** 6 am-5 pm, Sat-noon. Closed major holidays; also Sun. **Features:** The small bakery serves a Continental breakfast, in addition to warm, hearty lunches from 11 am to 2 pm. Casual dress. **Parking:** on-site.

COUNTRY HOUSE FAMILY RESTAURANT

American

Lunch: $5-$8 **Dinner: $7-$13** Phone: 520/378-4400

Location: Jct SR 90 (Fry Blvd), 4.5 mi s. 4373 S Hwy 92 85635. **Hours:** 7 am-9 pm, Fri & Sat-10 pm. Closed: 12/25. **Features:** The warm "cottage" atmosphere is charming, and the friendly staff welcomes diners as family. Classic foods such as hearty burgers, grilled pork chops and country-fried steak can be enjoyed. The owners have been here since 1996. Casual dress; cocktails. **Parking:** on-site. **Cards:** AX, DS, MC, VI.

LA CASITA MEXICAN RESTAURANT & CANTINA

Mexican

Lunch: $6-$8 **Dinner: $6-$19** Phone: 520/458-2376

Location: 2.1 mi w of jct SR 90/92. 465 E Fry Blvd 85635. **Hours:** 11 am-9 pm, Fri & Sat-10 pm, Sun-8 pm. Closed major holidays. **Reservations:** suggested. **Features:** Cheerful Mexican decor pleases the eye, and traditional dishes satisfy the hunger at this popular spot. Casual dress; cocktails. **Parking:** on-site. **Cards:** AX, DS, MC, VI.

THE MESQUITE TREE RESTAURANT

American
MC, VI.

Dinner: $10-$19 Phone: 520/378-2758

Location: SR 92, 7 mi s of jct SR 90. 6398 S Hwy 92 85635. **Hours:** 5 pm-9 pm, Sun-8 pm. Closed major holidays; also 12/24 & Mon. **Reservations:** suggested. **Features:** The casual restaurant presents a diverse menu of steaks, prime rib, barbecue foods and seafood, chicken and pasta dishes. When the weather is nice, guests can request a seat on the patio. Casual dress; cocktails. **Parking:** on-site. **Cards:** AX, DC, DS,

SNOWFLAKE pop. 4,460

WHERE TO STAY

COMFORT INN

Small-scale Hotel

Book at aaa.com

All Year 1P: $59-$119 2P: $59-$119 XP: $5 F18
Phone: (928)536-3888

Location: SR 77, just s of town. 2055 S Main 85937. Fax: 928/536-3888. **Facility:** 64 one-bedroom standard units, some with whirlpools. 2 stories (no elevator), interior corridors. *Bath:* combo or shower only. **Parking:** on-site. **Terms:** check-in 4 pm, cancellation fee imposed, [CP] meal plan available. **Amenities:** irons, hair dryers. **Pool(s):** small heated indoor. **Leisure Activities:** whirlpool, exercise room. **Guest Services:** coin laundry. **Business Services:** meeting rooms. **Cards:** AX, CB, DC, DS, JC, MC, VI.

SOME UNITS

SONOITA pop. 826

WHERE TO STAY

The following lodging was either not evaluated or did not meet AAA rating requirements but is listed for your information only.

SONOITA INN

[fyi]

Phone: 520/455-5935

Not evaluated. **Location:** Center. 3243 Hwy 82 85637 (PO Box 99). Facilities, services, and decor characterize a mid-range property.

WHERE TO DINE

SONOITA WINE COUNTRY CAFE

American
MC, VI.

Lunch: $8-$10 **Dinner: $8-$17** Phone: 520/455-5282

Location: SR 82, just e of jct SR 83. 3266 Hwy 82 85637. **Hours:** 11 am-3 pm, Thurs-Sat also 5 pm-9 pm, Sun 11 am-4 pm. Closed: 1/1, 11/23, 12/25; also Mon. **Reservations:** suggested. **Features:** Dining is delightful in the colorful country atmosphere, which incorporates bright tablecloths and floor-to-ceiling wine racks. Guests are treated to views across the desert. Casual dress; cocktails. **Parking:** on-site. **Cards:** AX, DS,

SPRINGERVILLE pop. 1,972

WHERE TO STAY

The following lodging was either not evaluated or did not meet AAA rating requirements but is listed for your information only.

SUPER 8 MOTEL

[fyi]

Phone: 928/333-2655

Not evaluated. **Location:** On US 60/180. 138 W Main St 85938 (PO Box 1568). Facilities, services, and decor characterize a basic property.

SUMMERHAVEN

——— WHERE TO DINE ———

MOUNT LEMMON CAFE
AAA **▽▽▽**
Regional American

Lunch: $6-$20
Phone: 520/576-1234

Location: Village center; adjacent to post office. 12976 N Sabino Pkwy 85619. **Hours:** 10 am-4 pm, Sat & Sun 9 am-5 pm. **Features:** Just beyond the ski area, the eatery prepares Pennsylvania Dutch cooking at its hearty best. Among offerings are freshly made soups and house-smoked meats and poultry. The pies will make "shoo fly" a part of the guest's dining vocabulary. Casual dress. **Parking:** street. **Cards:** AX, DC, DS, MC, VI.   [AC]

SURPRISE — See Phoenix p. 355.

TAYLOR pop. 3,176

——— WHERE TO STAY ———

SILVER CREEK INN
AAA **SAVE**
▽▽▽ ◆◆
Motel

All Year   1P: $50-$59   2P: $53-$69   XP: $5   F18
Phone: 928/536-2600
Location: On SR 77. 825 N Main St 85939 (PO Box 980). Fax: 928/536-3250. **Facility:** 42 one-bedroom standard units. 2 stories (no elevator), exterior corridors. **Parking:** on-site. **Terms:** small pets only ($10 extra charge). **Amenities:** hair dryers. **Leisure Activities:** sauna, whirlpool. **Cards:** AX, DC, DS, MC, VI.

SOME UNITS
[S🛏/D] [🐾] [🍽] [DATA PORT] [⬛] [🖥] [💻] / [✕] [VCR] /
FEE   FEE

TEMPE — See Phoenix p. 356.

TOLLESON — See Phoenix p. 367.

TOMBSTONE pop. 1,504

——— WHERE TO STAY ———

BEST WESTERN LOOKOUT LODGE   *Book at aaa.com*
AAA **SAVE**
▽▽▽ ▽▽▽
Small-scale Hotel

2/1-5/31 & 9/1-10/31   1P: $86-$95   2P: $86-$95   XP: $10   F12
6/1-8/31 & 11/1-1/31   1P: $75-$82   2P: $75-$82   XP: $10   F12
Phone: (520)457-2223
Location: On SR 80, 1 mi n. Located in a quiet area. 801 US Hwy 80 W 85638 (PO Box 787). Fax: 520/457-3870. **Facility:** 40 one-bedroom standard units. 2 stories (no elevator), exterior corridors. **Parking:** on-site. **Terms:** 2 night minimum stay - seasonal, [AP] & [BP] meal plans available, pets ($20 extra charge). **Amenities:** irons, hair dryers. **Pool(s):** heated outdoor. **Business Services:** Fee: PC, fax. **Cards:** AX, CB, DC, DS, JC, MC, VI. **Special Amenities:** free local telephone calls. *(See color ad below)*

SOME UNITS
[S🛏/D] [🛏] [🏊] [DATA PORT] [💻] / [✕] [📶] /
FEE   FEE FEE

CURLY BILL'S BED & BREAKFAST
AAA **SAVE**
▽▽▽ ▽▽▽
Bed & Breakfast

2/1-5/31 & 9/1-1/1 [BP]   1P: $78-$150   2P: $78-$150   XP: $15   F12
6/1-8/31 & 1/2-1/31 [BP]   1P: $52-$150   2P: $52-$150   XP: $15   F12
Phone: (520)457-3858
Location: Just e; town center. Located in a quiet residential area. 210 N Ninth St 85638 (PO Box 746). Fax: 520/457-9419. **Facility:** Designated smoking area. 4 one-bedroom standard units. 1 story, interior corridors. **Bath:** some shared or private, combo or shower only. **Parking:** street. **Terms:** check-in 4 pm, 7 day cancellation notice-fee imposed, [CP] meal plan available, no pets allowed (owner's pets on premises). **Amenities:** video library. *Some:* CD players, hair dryers. **Leisure Activities:** whirlpool, barbecue and picnic area, jeep tours, hiking trails. **Guest Services:** complimentary evening beverages. **Cards:** MC, VI. **Special Amenities:** free local telephone calls and preferred room (subject to availability with advance reservations).

SOME UNITS
[S🛏/D] [✕] [✕] [☎] / [📶] [VCR]

TOMBSTONE MOTEL *Book at aaa.com* Phone: (520)457-3478
AAA SAVE All Year [ECP] 1P: $49-$69 2P: $59-$79 XP: $10 F12
◆◆◆ **Location:** On SR 80; between 5th and 6th sts. 502 E Fremont St 85638 (PO Box 0837). Fax: 520/457-9017.
◆ **Facility:** 37 units. 36 one-bedroom standard units. 1 two-bedroom suite ($109-$140). 2 stories (no elevator),
Motel exterior corridors. *Bath:* combo or shower only. **Parking:** on-site. **Terms:** office hours 7:30 am-10 pm, pets
($25 deposit, in designated units). **Amenities:** *Some:* irons, hair dryers. **Leisure Activities:** barbecue grill.
Guest Services: coin laundry. **Business Services:** meeting rooms, fax. **Cards:** AX, DS, MC, VI.
Special Amenities: free expanded continental breakfast and free local telephone calls.

SOME UNITS
🛏 🍴 📺 DATA PORT / ✕ 🛁 🖥 📶 /
FEE

TRAIL RIDERS INN Phone: 520/457-3573
AAA SAVE All Year 1P: $45 2P: $55 XP: $5 F
◆ **Location:** Just e; center. 13 N 7th St 85638. Fax: 520/457-3049. **Facility:** 15 one-bedroom standard units. 1
Motel story, exterior corridors. *Bath:* combo or shower only. **Parking:** on-site. **Terms:** office hours 5:30 am-8 pm,
small pets only ($5 extra charge). **Amenities:** *Some:* hair dryers. **Pool(s):** small heated outdoor. **Leisure
Activities:** hot tub, gas barbecue grill. **Cards:** MC, VI. **Special Amenities:** free local telephone calls and
preferred room (subject to availability with advance reservations).

SOME UNITS
🛏 🛏 🏊 / ✕ DATA PORT 🖥 /
FEE

————— WHERE TO DINE —————

THE LAMPLIGHT ROOM Lunch: $6-$9 Dinner: $7-$17 Phone: 520/457-3716
◆◆◆ **Location:** Just e of SR 80; center. 108 N Fourth St 85638. **Hours:** 11:30 am-8 pm, Fri & Sat-9 pm, Sun-7 pm.
American **Closed:** 12/25. **Reservations:** accepted. **Features:** The charming territorial-style home has been converted
to a friendly place for dining. A split menu lists classic Mexican dishes and such upscale options as roasted
pork loin and chicken cordon bleu. The three dining rooms are furnished differently, with cloth table covers in
one room and simple wooden tables with brightly colored Mexican details in the other two. Guests may order foods from either
menu in any of the rooms. Casual dress; cocktails. **Parking:** on-site. **Cards:** AX, DS, MC, VI.

🍸

THE LONGHORN RESTAURANT Lunch: $6-$10 Dinner: $10-$25 Phone: 520/457-3405
AAA **Location:** Corner of 5th St; in historic district. 501 E Allen 85638. **Hours:** 8 am-8 pm. **Closed:** 11/23, 12/25.
◆◆ **Features:** This corner eatery is popular with locals and tourists, serving a good selection of steak,
American sandwiches and Mexican entrees in an Old West decor. Casual dress; beer & wine only. **Parking:** street.
Cards: MC, VI.

O.K. CAFE Lunch: $6-$9 Phone: 520/457-3980
◆◆ **Location:** Northeast corner of Third and Allen St; center. 220 E Allen St 85638. **Hours:** 7 am-2 pm. **Closed:** 1/1,
American 11/23, 12/24, 12/25. **Features:** The popular eatery can be crowded during breakfast and lunch. Foods are
prepared from scratch, and the coffee is said to be the best in town. Hefty buffalo burgers are a specialty.
Casual dress. **Parking:** street. **Cards:** DS, MC, VI.

TORTILLA FLAT

──────── **WHERE TO DINE** ────────

TORTILLA FLAT SALOON
◆
American
MC, VI.

Lunch: $4-$10   **Dinner:** $4-$10   **Phone:** 520/457-3980
Location: Center. 1 Main St (SR 88) 85290. **Hours:** 9 am-6 pm, Sat & Sun 8 am-7 pm. Closed: 11/23, 12/25.
Features: Representative of robust fare are half-pound "burgers" and varied Mexican dishes, such as enchiladas and "killer chili" served in a sourdough bowl. The saloon awaits drivers who make the picturesque trip up SR 88 from Apache Junction. Casual dress; cocktails. **Parking:** street. **Cards:** DS,

TUBAC pop. 949

──────── **WHERE TO STAY** ────────

TUBAC GOLF RESORT
◆◆◆◆
Resort
Small-scale Hotel

		1P: $155-$345	2P: $155-$345	XP: $15	F18
9/28-1/31		1P: $155-$335	2P: $155-$335	XP: $15	F18
2/1-4/16		1P: $120-$225	2P: $120-$225	XP: $15	F18
4/17-6/4		1P: $99-$200	2P: $99-$200	XP: $15	F18
6/5-9/27					

Phone: (520)398-2211
Location: I-19, exit 40, on east side, then 2 mi s. Located in a quiet area. 1 Otero Rd 85646 (PO Box 1297).
Fax: 520/398-9261. **Facility:** Set on several acres of well-landscaped grounds, the nicely furnished rooms and suites have some fireplaces. Designated smoking area. 62 units. 43 one-bedroom standard units, some with whirlpools. 19 one-bedroom suites, some with efficiencies and/or whirlpools. 1 story, exterior corridors. *Bath:* combo or shower only. **Parking:** on-site. **Terms:** office hours 6 am-midnight, 2-3 night minimum stay - seasonal and/or weekends, 7 day cancellation notice-fee imposed, package plans, pets ($25 fee). **Amenities:** CD players, voice mail, irons, hair dryers. *Some:* DVD players (fee), high-speed Internet. **Dining:** Stables Dining Room, see separate listing. **Pool(s):** heated outdoor. **Leisure Activities:** whirlpool, 4 tennis courts, hiking trails, exercise room, horseshoes, volleyball. *Fee:* golf-18 holes, bicycles. **Guest Services:** coin laundry. **Business Services:** meeting rooms, business center. **Cards:** AX, DC, DS, MC, VI.

──────── **WHERE TO DINE** ────────

SHELBY'S BISTRO
◆◆
Regional American

Lunch: $8-$13   **Dinner:** $11-$22   **Phone:** 520/398-8075
Location: I-19, exit 34, just e to Frontage Rd, just n to Plaza Rd, then just e. 19 Tubac Rd-Mercado de Baca 85646. **Hours:** 11 am-4 & 5-9 pm, Sun-Tues to 4 pm. Closed: 11/23, 12/25. **Reservations:** accepted.
Features: Tucked into a courtyard, the brightly decorated bistro serves fresh salads, hearty sandwiches, a selection of steaks and pastas as well as yummy desserts. Patio seating overlooks a fountain. Casual dress; cocktails. **Parking:** on-site. **Cards:** AX, MC, VI.

STABLES DINING ROOM
◆◆◆
American
MC, VI. **Historic**

Lunch: $9-$12   **Dinner:** $18-$29   **Phone:** 520/398-2678
Location: I-19, exit 40, on east side, 2 mi s; in Tubac Golf Resort. 1 Otero Rd 85646. **Hours:** 6 am-10 pm.
Reservations: suggested. **Features:** Built in the original Otero ranch stables, the attractive dining is bedecked in ranch decor. Varied Southwestern and traditional American dishes are served in a dining room that offers a view over the 18-hole golf course. Casual dress; cocktails. **Parking:** on-site. **Cards:** AX, DS,

TUBA CITY pop. 8,225

──────── **WHERE TO STAY** ────────

QUALITY INN
AAA SAVE
◆◆◆
Small-scale Hotel

Book at aaa.com

4/1-10/31		1P: $95-$100	2P: $105-$110	XP: $10	F18
2/1-3/31 & 11/1-1/31		1P: $75-$80	2P: $85-$90	XP: $10	F18

Phone: (928)283-4545
Location: 1 mi n of US 160. Located adjacent to historic Tuba Trading Post. Main St & Moenave Rd 86045 (PO Box 247). Fax: 928/283-4144. **Facility:** 80 units. 78 one-bedroom standard units. 2 one-bedroom suites ($110-$170). 2 stories (no elevator), interior corridors. **Parking:** on-site. **Terms:** cancellation fee imposed, small pets only ($20 deposit, in limited units). **Amenities:** irons, hair dryers. **Dining:** 6 am-9 pm, Sat & Sun from 7 am. **Guest Services:** gift shop, coin laundry. **Business Services:** PC. **Cards:** AX, DC, DS, MC, VI. *(See color ad p 228)*

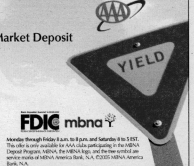

Destination Tucson
pop. 486,699

Visitors searching for variety will find it in Tucson.

Nestled in a dry valley surrounded by four mountain ranges, Tucson is a magnet for lovers of the outdoors thanks to its various recreation options. What's more, preservation of the local environment is taken seriously here. Tohono Chul Park and Tucson Mountain Park are just two of the protected sites that show off the area's distinctive desert setting.

© Gibson Stock Photography

Tucson skyline. Looking at its modern skyline, Tucson's nickname "the Old Pueblo" hardly seems appropriate.

Gill Kenny / Metropolitan Tucson CVB

Horseback riding in Tucson. Take in Tucson's breathtaking scenery on horseback, just as the early settlers did.

Fred Hood / Metropolitan Tucson CVB

Old Town Artisans, Tucson. If hiking and horseback riding aren't your speed, hunt for arts and crafts made by Native Americans and Arizonans at this collection of emporiums. (See mention page 116)

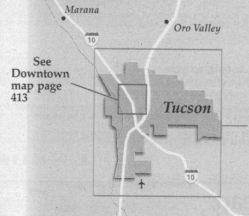

Catalina

Marana

Oro Valley

See Downtown map page 413

Tucson

See Vicinity map page 417

Green Valley

Fred Hood / Metropolitan Tucson CVB

Hiking in Sabino Canyon, Tucson. Hikers can make a day of picnicking, swimming and exploring in this beautiful section of Coronado National Forest. (See mention page 113)

Places included in this AAA Destination City:

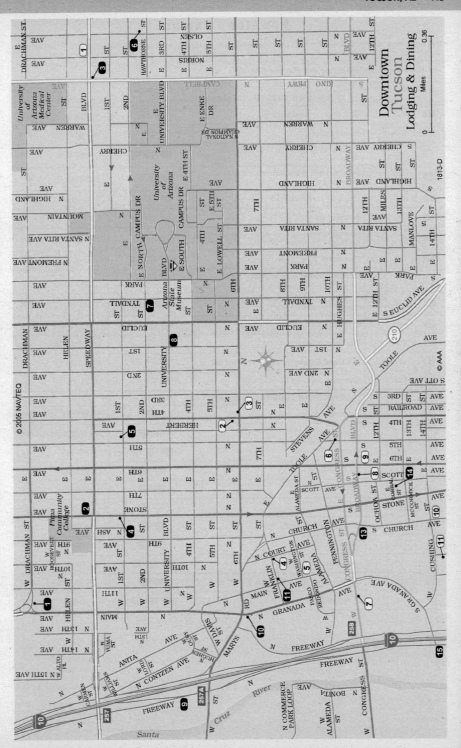

Downtown
Tucson
Lodging & Dining

Downtown Tucson

This index helps you "spot" where approved accommodations and restaurants are located on the corresponding detailed maps. Lodging rate ranges are for comparison only and show the property's high season; rates are per night, unless only weekly (W) rates are available. Restaurant rate range is for dinner, unless only lunch (L) is served. Turn to the listing page for more detailed rate information and consult display ads for special promotions.

Spotter/Map Page Number	OA	DOWNTOWN TUCSON - Lodgings	Diamond Rating	Rate Range High Season	Listing Page
❶ / p. 413	AAA	Best Western Executive Inn	◈◈	$69-$89 SAVE	423
❷ / p. 413	AAA	Econo Lodge	◈	$34-$199 SAVE	424
❸ / p. 413		Four Points by Sheraton Tucson University Plaza	◈◈◈	$259-$269	424
❹ / p. 413	AAA	Best Western Royal Sun Inn & Suites - see color ad p 423	◈◈◈	$89-$159 SAVE	423
❺ / p. 413		Catalina Park Inn Bed and Breakfast	◈◈◈	$86-$166	424
❻ / p. 413	AAA	Adobe Rose Inn	◈◈◈	$100-$185 SAVE	423
❼ / p. 413	AAA	Marriott University Park Hotel - see color ad p 425	◈◈◈	$194-$259 SAVE	425
❽ / p. 413		Peppertrees Inn	◈◈◈	Failed to provide	425
❾ / p. 413	AAA	Ramada Limited Tucson West - see color ad p 440	◈◈	$94 SAVE	426
❿ / p. 413	AAA	InnSuites Hotels & Suites Tucson City Center - see color ad p 424	◈◈	$99-$155 SAVE	425
⓫ / p. 413		El Presidio Bed & Breakfast Inn	◈◈◈	$110-$140	424
⓭ / p. 413	AAA	The Hotel Arizona	◈◈◈	$152-$189 SAVE	425
⓮ / p. 413	AAA	The Royal Elizabeth Bed & Breakfast Inn	◈◈◈	$145-$215 SAVE	426
⓯ / p. 413	AAA	Riverpark Inn - see color ad p 426	◈◈◈	$99-$169 SAVE	426
		DOWNTOWN TUCSON - Restaurants			
① / p. 413		Trident Grill & Bar	◈	$13-$18	428
② / p. 413		Delectables	◈◈	$6-$14	427
③ / p. 413		Athens' on 4th Ave	◈◈◈	$11-$20	427
④ / p. 413		El Charro Cafe	◈◈	$12-$22	427
⑤ / p. 413		Cafe a'la C'art	◈◈	$7-$9(L)	427
⑥ / p. 413		Cup Cafe'	◈◈	$10-$20	427
⑦ / p. 413		Garcia's Mexican Restaurant	◈◈	$7-$15	428
⑧ / p. 413		Cafe Poca Cosa	◈◈	$15-$19	427
⑨ / p. 413		Barrio Food & Drink	◈◈◈	$14-$32	427
⑩ / p. 413		Cushing Street Bar & Restaurant	◈◈	$10-$21	427
⑪ / p. 413		El Minuto Cafe	◈◈◈	$6-$12	427

The Interstate is 50!

Celebrate the Interstate

... Forever Changing America's Freedom to Travel, From Sea to Shining Sea

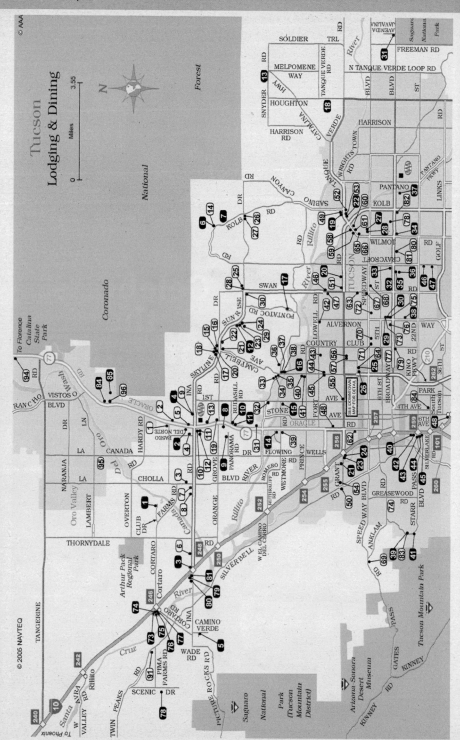

Tucson
Lodging & Dining

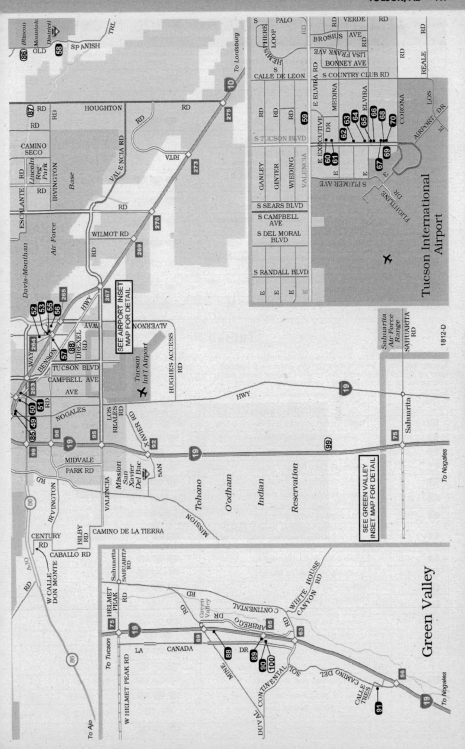

✈ Airport Accommodations

Spotter/Map Page Number	OA	TUCSON INTERNATIONAL	Diamond Rating	Rate Range High Season	Listing Page
64 / p. 416	AAA	**AmeriSuites (Tucson/Airport), just n of entrance**	▽▽▽	$79-$189 SAVE	428
69 / p. 416		Best Western Inn at the Airport, at entrance of terminal	fyi	$129-$189	428
63 / p. 416		Clarion Hotel Tucson Airport, just n of airport	▽▽▽	$99-$129	430
65 / p. 416	AAA	**Comfort Suites, just n of entrance**	▽▽	$59-$159 SAVE	430
61 / p. 416	AAA	**Country Inn & Suites By Carlson Tucson-Airport, 0.4 mi n of entrance**	▽▽▽	$119-$129 SAVE	431
60 / p. 416		Courtyard by Marriott-Tucson Airport, 0.6 mi n of entrance	▽▽▽	$209	431
70 / p. 416	AAA	**Embassy Suites Hotel @ Tucson International Airport, at entrance**	▽▽▽	$179-$279 SAVE	433
67 / p. 416	AAA	**Fairfield Inn by Marriott at Tucson Airport, just n of airport**	▽▽▽	$139 SAVE	433
66 / p. 416		Hampton Inn Tucson Airport, just n of airport	▽▽▽	$119-$159	435
62 / p. 416	AAA	**Holiday Inn Express Hotel & Suites Tucson Airport, just n of entrance**	▽▽▽	$129-$159 SAVE	435
68 / p. 416	AAA	**La Quinta Inn & Suites Tucson Airport, just n of airport**	▽▽▽	$106-$123 SAVE	437
59 / p. 416	AAA	**Quality Inn at Tucson Airport, 1 mi ne of airport**	▽▽	$99-$180 SAVE	440

Tucson

This index helps you "spot" where approved accommodations and restaurants are located on the corresponding detailed maps. Lodging rate ranges are for comparison only and show the property's high season; rates are per night, unless only weekly (W) rates are available. Restaurant rate range is for dinner, unless only lunch (L) is served. Turn to the listing page for more detailed rate information and consult display ads for special promotions.

Spotter/Map Page Number	OA	TUCSON - Lodgings	Diamond Rating	Rate Range High Season	Listing Page
1 / p. 416	AAA	**Omni Tucson National Golf Resort & Spa**	▽▽▽▽	$169-$439 SAVE	440
2 / p. 416		Country Inn & Suites By Carlson	▽▽▽	$109-$139	431
3 / p. 416		Motel 6 Tucson North #1127	▽	$69-$85	440
4 / p. 416	AAA	**Westward Look Resort -** see color ad p 445	▽▽▽	$149-$319 SAVE	445
5 / p. 416		Coyote Crossing Bed & Breakfast	▽▽▽	$110-$135	432
6 / p. 416	AAA	**Loews Ventana Canyon Resort -** see color ad p 439	▽▽▽▽	$179-$379 SAVE	439
7 / p. 416	AAA	**The Lodge At Ventana Canyon**	▽▽▽▽	$199-$549 SAVE	438
8 / p. 416	AAA	**Best Western InnSuites Hotel & Suites Tucson-Catalina Foothills -** see color ad p 429	▽▽▽	$99-$149 SAVE	429
9 / p. 416		Agave Grove Bed & Breakfast Inn	▽▽▽	$95-$175	428
10 / p. 416	AAA	**TownePlace Suites by Marriott**	▽▽▽	$129-$179 SAVE	443
11 / p. 416		Hampton Inn & Suites	▽▽▽	$159-$229	434
12 / p. 416	AAA	**The Westin La Paloma Resort & Spa -** see color ad p 444	▽▽▽▽	$299-$489 SAVE	444
13 / p. 416		Jeremiah Inn Bed & Breakfast	▽▽▽	$90-$130	436
14 / p. 416		Comfort Suites at Tucson Mall	▽▽	$150	431
15 / p. 416		Holiday Inn Express Suites-Tucson Mall	▽▽▽	$199-$229	435
16 / p. 416	AAA	**Windmill Suites at St. Philip's Plaza**	▽▽▽	$105-$165 SAVE	445
17 / p. 416	AAA	**Casa Luna Bed and Breakfast**	▽▽▽	$160-$300 SAVE	429
18 / p. 416		Indian Hill Bed & Breakfast	▽▽▽	$110-$150	436
19 / p. 416	AAA	**Comfort Suites Tanque Verde/Sabino Canyon**	▽▽	$149-$179 SAVE	431
20 / p. 416		Sheraton Tucson Hotel & Suites	▽▽▽	$269-$289	442

Spotter/Map Page Number	OA	TUCSON - Lodgings (continued)	Diamond Rating	Rate Range High Season	Listing Page
21 / p. 416		Super 8 Motel-Tucson	◆◆	$125-$145	443
22 / p. 416	AAA	Ramada Inn & Suites Foothills Resort - see color ad p 441	◆◆	$99-$199 SAVE	441
23 / p. 416	AAA	Hampton Inn North - see color ad p 434	◆◆◆	$89-$149 SAVE	434
24 / p. 416	AAA	Rodeway Inn I-10 & Grant Rd	◆◆	$129-$139 SAVE	442
25 / p. 416	AAA	Arizona Inn	◆◆◆◆	$169-$3200 SAVE	428
26 / p. 416	AAA	La Posada Del Valle Bed & Breakfast	◆◆◆	$129-$169 SAVE	437
27 / p. 416	AAA	Radisson Suites Tucson	◆◆◆	$139-$199 SAVE	441
28 / p. 416		Residence Inn by Marriott - see color ad p 442	◆◆	$139-$189	442
29 / p. 416	AAA	Lodge on the Desert	◆◆◆	$189-$289 SAVE	438
30 / p. 416		Clarion Hotel-Randolph Park	◆◆	$89-$164	430
31 / p. 416		The SunCatcher	◆◆◆	$135-$185	443
32 / p. 416	AAA	Viscount Suite Hotel	◆◆◆	$125-$135 SAVE	444
33 / p. 416	AAA	Embassy Suites Tucson-Williams Center	◆◆◆	$129-$249 SAVE	433
34 / p. 416	AAA	La Quinta Inn Tucson (East) - see color ad p 437	◆◆◆	$99-$116 SAVE	437
35 / p. 416		Residence Inn by Marriott Williams Centre	◆◆◆	$169-$249	442
36 / p. 416		Courtyard By Marriott-Tucson Williams Centre	◆◆◆	$180-$189	431
37 / p. 416	AAA	Hilton-Tucson East - see color ad p 435	◆◆◆	$59-$259 SAVE	435
38 / p. 416	AAA	DoubleTree Hotel at Reid Park	◆◆◆	$129-$289 SAVE	432
39 / p. 416		JW Marriott Starr Pass Resort & Spa	◆◆◆◆	$299-$499	436
40 / p. 416		Motel 6 Tucson-Congress Street #50	◆	$69-$85	440
41 / p. 416		Starr Pass Golf Suites	◆◆◆	$179-$309	442
42 / p. 416	AAA	Travelodge	◆	$89-$110 SAVE	443
43 / p. 416		La Quinta Inn Downtown - see color ad p 437	◆◆◆	$99-$119	437
44 / p. 416	AAA	Super 8	◆◆	$100-$160 SAVE	443
45 / p. 416		Motel 6 Tucson-22nd Street #1196	◆	$69-$85	439
46 / p. 416	AAA	Econo Lodge Inn & Suites	◆	$80-$105 SAVE	433
47 / p. 416	AAA	Super 8 Central East	◆	$89-$99 SAVE	443
48 / p. 416		Econo Lodge	◆	$69-$99	432
49 / p. 416	AAA	Lazy 8 Motel - see color ad p 438	◆	$39-$52 SAVE	438
50 / p. 416	AAA	Americas Best Value Inn-Tucson	◆	$139 SAVE	428
51 / p. 416		Motel 6 Tucson-Benson Hwy South #271	◆	$69-$85	439
52 / p. 416	AAA	Holiday Inn-Palo Verde - see color ad p 436	◆◆◆	$99-$114 SAVE	436
53 / p. 416	AAA	Days Inn	◆◆	$95-$115 SAVE	432
55 / p. 416		Fairfield Inn by Marriott	◆◆	$59-$124	433
56 / p. 416		Red Roof Inn-Tucson South	◆	$58-$74	441
57 / p. 416		Studio 6 Extended Stay #6002	◆◆	$63-$77	443
58 / p. 416		Hacienda del Desierto	◆◆◆	$145-$250	434
59 / p. 416	AAA	Quality Inn at Tucson Airport	◆◆	$99-$180 SAVE	440
60 / p. 416		Courtyard by Marriott-Tucson Airport	◆◆◆	$209	431
61 / p. 416	AAA	Country Inn & Suites By Carlson Tucson-Airport	◆◆◆	$119-$129 SAVE	431
62 / p. 416	AAA	Holiday Inn Express Hotel & Suites Tucson Airport	◆◆◆	$129-$159 SAVE	435
63 / p. 416		Clarion Hotel Tucson Airport - see color ad p 430	◆◆◆	$99-$129	430
64 / p. 416	AAA	AmeriSuites (Tucson/Airport)	◆◆◆	$79-$189 SAVE	428
65 / p. 416	AAA	Comfort Suites	◆◆	$59-$159 SAVE	430

Spotter/Map Page Number	OA	**TUCSON** - Lodgings (continued)	Diamond Rating	Rate Range High Season	Listing Page
66 / p. 416		Hampton Inn Tucson Airport - see color ad p 434	▽▽▽	$119-$159	435
67 / p. 416	ⒶⒶⒶ	**Fairfield Inn by Marriott at Tucson Airport**	▽▽▽	$139 ⓈⒶⓋⒺ	433
68 / p. 416	ⒶⒶⒶ	**La Quinta Inn & Suites Tucson Airport** - see color ad p 437	▽▽▽	$106-$123 ⓈⒶⓋⒺ	437
69 / p. 416		Best Western Inn at the Airport	[fyi]	$129-$189	428
70 / p. 416	ⒶⒶⒶ	**Embassy Suites Hotel @ Tucson International Airport** - see color ad p 433	▽▽▽	$179-$279 ⓈⒶⓋⒺ	433
		TUCSON - Restaurants			
1 / p. 416		Michelangelo Ristorante Italiano	▽▽▽	$8-$23	451
2 / p. 416		Metropolitan Grill	▽▽▽	$12-$21	451
3 / p. 416		Mosaic Cafe Dos	▽▽	$8-$13	451
4 / p. 416		Tohono Chul Park Tea Room	▽▽	$7-$11(L)	453
5 / p. 416		Macayo Mexican Kitchen del Norte	▽▽	$9-$14	450
6 / p. 416		La Parrilla Suiza	▽▽	$7-$15	450
7 / p. 416		Gavi Italian Restaurant	▽▽	$10-$25	449
8 / p. 416		Old Pueblo Grille Foothills Mall	▽▽▽	$14-$20	451
9 / p. 416	ⒶⒶⒶ	**The Gold Room** - see color ad p 445	▽▽▽▽	$19-$35	449
10 / p. 416		Sauce	▽▽	$7-$9	452
11 / p. 416		Bluefin Seafood Bistro	▽▽▽	$16-$28	447
12 / p. 416		Wildflower	▽▽▽	$14-$27	454
13 / p. 416		Hi Falutin Western Grill	▽▽	$8-$18	449
14 / p. 416	ⒶⒶⒶ	**The Ventana Room**	▽▽▽▽▽	$75-$105	454
15 / p. 416		Anthony's In The Catalinas	▽▽▽	$24-$40	446
16 / p. 416		Soleil	▽▽	$16-$25	453
17 / p. 416		RA Sushi-Bar-Restaurant	▽	$8-$18	452
18 / p. 416		NoRTH	▽▽	$11-$28	451
19 / p. 416		El Charro Cafe North	▽	$12-$22	448
20 / p. 416		Firebirds Rocky Mountain Grill	▽▽	$9-$23	448
21 / p. 416		Fleming's Prime Steakhouse & Wine Bar	▽▽▽	$20-$34	449
22 / p. 416		Terra Cotta	▽▽	$11-$23	453
23 / p. 416		Janos - see color ad p 444	▽▽▽▽	$22-$110	449
24 / p. 416		J Bar-A Latin Grill	▽▽	$13-$18	449
25 / p. 416		Bazil's	▽▽	$12-$20	446
26 / p. 416		Sonora Bay Restaurant & Cantina	▽▽	$7-$14	453
27 / p. 416		Risky Business	▽▽	$7-$21	452
28 / p. 416		Papagayo Mexican Restaurant & Catina	▽▽	$8-$20	452
29 / p. 416		The Grill at Hacienda del Sol	▽▽▽	$24-$42	449
30 / p. 416		Trattoria Pina	▽▽	$8-$25	453
31 / p. 416		Chantilly Tea Room	▽▽	$14-$17	447
32 / p. 416		Capriccio Bistro & Bar	▽▽	$10-$16	447
33 / p. 416		Sullivan's Steakhouse	▽▽▽	$18-$28	453
34 / p. 416		P. F. Chang's China Bistro	▽▽▽	$9-$13	452
35 / p. 416		Bistro Zin	▽▽▽	$14-$38	446
36 / p. 416		El Corral	▽	$9-$17	448
37 / p. 416		Acacia at St. Philips	▽▽▽	$16-$32	446
38 / p. 416		Vivace Restaurant	▽▽	$12-$26	454
39 / p. 416		The Keys	▽▽	$7-$14	449
40 / p. 416		Aladdin Middle Eastern Restuarant	▽▽	$10-$14	446

Spotter/Map Page Number	OA	**TUCSON** - Restaurants (continued)	Diamond Rating	Rate Range High Season	Listing Page
41 / p. 416		Ghini's French Caffe	◈◈	$6-$9(L)	449
42 / p. 416		Le Rendez-vous	◈◈	$19-$33	450
43 / p. 416		Cody's Beef 'n Beans	◈◈	$11-$18	447
44 / p. 416		Beyond Bread	◈◈	$5-$8	446
45 / p. 416	◈◈◈	**Pastiche Modern Eatery**	◈◈◈	$11-$22	452
46 / p. 416		Firecracker!	◈◈	$15-$21	448
47 / p. 416		McMahon's Steakhouse	◈◈	$18-$36	450
48 / p. 416		La Parrilla Suiza	◈◈	$6-$10	450
49 / p. 416		The Eclectic Cafe	◈◈	$7-$12	448
50 / p. 416		Teresa's Mosaic Cafe	◈◈	$8-$13	453
51 / p. 416		Buddy's Grill	◈◈	$10-$19	447
52 / p. 416		Olive Tree Restaurant	◈◈◈	$14-$27	451
53 / p. 416		Fuego	◈◈◈	$9-$22	449
54 / p. 416		Rusty's Family Restaurant & Sports Grill	◈◈	$9-$18	452
55 / p. 416		Sher-E-Punjab	◈◈	$7-$12	453
56 / p. 416		Kingfisher	◈◈◈	$15-$22	450
57 / p. 416		Nonie	◈◈	$7-$17	451
58 / p. 416		Dakota Cafe & Catering Company	◈◈◈	$9-$25	448
59 / p. 416		Pinnacle Peak Restaurant	◈	$10-$17	452
60 / p. 416		China Thai	◈◈	$5-$14	447
61 / p. 416		City Grill	◈◈◈	$15-$21	447
62 / p. 416		La Fuente Restaurant	◈◈	$10-$18	450
63 / p. 416		Red Sky Cafe	◈◈	$15-$23	452
64 / p. 416		Main Dining Room at the Arizona Inn	◈◈	$20-$30	450
65 / p. 416	◈◈◈	**Jonathan's Cork**	◈◈◈	$12-$24	449
66 / p. 416		Lotus Garden	◈◈	$9-$20	450
67 / p. 416		Smokin' "A Bar-B-Q Place"	◈	$5-$14	453
68 / p. 416		Oregano's Pizza Bistro	◈◈	$6-$20	451
69 / p. 416		Evangelo's	◈◈◈	$25-$30	448
70 / p. 416		Cuvee World Bistro	◈◈◈	$10-$19	447
71 / p. 416		The Dish	◈◈◈	$17-$35	448
72 / p. 416		Feast	◈◈	$8-$18	448
73 / p. 416		Lodge on the Desert	◈◈◈	$14-$28	450
74 / p. 416		Daisy Mae's Steakhouse	◈◈	$14-$22	447
75 / p. 416		Old Pueblo Grill	◈◈◈	$14-$20	451
76 / p. 416		Claim Jumper Restaurants	◈◈	$10-$25	447
77 / p. 416		Zemam's	◈	$8-$10	454
78 / p. 416		Delhi Palace	◈◈	$7-$12	448
79 / p. 416		Elle, A Wine Country Restaurant	◈◈◈	$12-$22	448
80 / p. 416		The Bamboo Club Asian Bistro	◈◈	$9-$23	446
81 / p. 416		Metro Grill Park Place	◈◈◈	$12-$18	450
82 / p. 416		Mona Lisa Italian Restaurant	◈◈	$12-$18	451
83 / p. 416		Primo	◈◈◈◈	$23-$27	452
84 / p. 416		Mi Nidito Family Restaurant	◈◈	$5-$11	451
85 / p. 416		Silver Saddle Steakhouse	◈◈	$15-$25	453
86 / p. 416		Saguaro Corners Restaurant	◈◈	$12-$26	452
87 / p. 416		Tucson McGraw's Original Cantina	◈◈	$8-$21	453

Spotter/Map Page Number	OA	TUCSON - Restaurants (continued)	Diamond Rating	Rate Range High Season	Listing Page
(88) / p. 416	(AAA)	CattleTown Steakhouse & Saloon	◇	$12-$30	447
		MARANA - Lodgings			
(73) / p. 416		Best Western Continental Inn	◇◇	$149-$199	456
(74) / p. 416	(AAA)	Days Inn & Suites-Tucson/Marana	◇◇	$49-$169 [SAVE]	456
(75) / p. 416	(AAA)	Ramada Limited & Suites	◇◇	$149-$199 [SAVE]	457
(76) / p. 416		Holiday Inn Express	◇◇◇	$159-$199	457
(77) / p. 416		Super 8 Motel	◇◇	$69-$109	458
(78) / p. 416		Lazy K Bar Guest Ranch	◇◇◇	$225-$385	457
(79) / p. 416		Comfort Inn I-10 & Ina	◇◇	$70-$150	456
(80) / p. 416		Red Roof Inn Tucson North	◇◇	$54-$73	458
(81) / p. 416		Travelodge	◇◇	$90-$150	458
		MARANA - Restaurant			
(91) / p. 416		Li'l Abner's Steakhouse	◇◇	$12-$29	458
		ORO VALLEY - Lodgings			
(84) / p. 416		Holiday Inn Express Suites	◇◇◇	Failed to provide	458
(85) / p. 416	(AAA)	Hilton Tucson El Conquistador Golf & Tennis Resort	◇◇◇◇	$179-$299 [SAVE]	458
		ORO VALLEY - Restaurants			
(94) / p. 416		Cibaria Cucina Italiana	◇◇	$11-$20	459
(95) / p. 416		Cien Anos-Mexican Grill	◇◇◇	$11-$25	459
(96) / p. 416		The Last Territory	◇◇	$13-$21	459
		GREEN VALLEY - Lodgings			
(88) / p. 416		Holiday Inn Express	◇◇	Failed to provide	455
(89) / p. 416	(AAA)	Baymont Inn & Suites	◇◇◇	$94-$144 [SAVE]	454
(90) / p. 416	(AAA)	Best Western Green Valley - see color ad p 455	◇◇◇	$89-$124 [SAVE]	455
(91) / p. 416	(AAA)	Inn at San Ignacio - see color ad p 455	◇◇◇	$129-$149 [SAVE]	456
		GREEN VALLEY - Restaurants			
(99) / p. 416		Agave at Desert Diamond Casino	◇◇	$11-$22	456
(100) / p. 416		Lavender	◇◇◇	$11-$22	456

DOWNTOWN TUCSON   (See map and index starting on p. 413)

------- WHERE TO STAY -------

ADOBE ROSE INN
(AAA) (SAVE)

Phone: (520)318-4644   **6**

	1P: $100-$185	2P: $100-$185	XP: $20
2/1-5/31 & 9/1-1/31 [BP]			
6/1-8/31 [BP]	1P: $75-$125	2P: $75-$125	XP: $20

Bed & Breakfast

Location: I-10, exit 257 (Speedway Blvd), 2.5 mi e, then just s. Located in a quiet residential area. 940 N Olsen Ave 85719. Fax: 520/318-4644. **Facility:** This adobe home built in 1933 has a charming, brick-faced courtyard shaded with tall trees; some rooms have fireplaces. Smoke free premises. 6 units. 5 one-bedroom standard units. 1 one-bedroom suite with kitchen. 1-2 stories (no elevator), interior/exterior corridors. *Bath:* combo or shower only. **Parking:** on-site. **Terms:** check-in 4 pm, age restrictions may apply, 14 day cancellation notice. **Amenities:** high-speed Internet, hair dryers. *Some:* irons. **Pool(s):** small outdoor. **Leisure Activities:** whirlpool. **Business Services:** fax. **Cards:** AX, MC, VI. **Special Amenities:** free full breakfast and free local telephone calls.

SOME UNITS

BEST WESTERN EXECUTIVE INN   *Book at aaa.com*
(AAA) (SAVE)

Phone: (520)791-7551   **1**

	1P: $69-$79	2P: $79-$89	XP: $10	F12
2/1-5/31				
6/1-9/30 & 10/1-1/31	1P: $55-$79	2P: $65-$89	XP: $10	F12

Small-scale Hotel

Location: I-10, exit 257 (Speedway Blvd), 0.4 mi e to Main St, then 0.3 mi n. 333 W Drachman St 85705. Fax: 520/623-7803. **Facility:** 129 units. 124 one-bedroom standard units. 5 one-bedroom suites ($99-$169) with efficiencies. 2 stories (no elevator), interior corridors. **Parking:** on-site. **Terms:** [ECP] meal plan available, pets ($25-$35 fee). **Amenities:** voice mail, irons, hair dryers. *Some:* high-speed Internet. **Pool(s):** heated outdoor. **Leisure Activities:** whirlpool. **Guest Services:** coin laundry. **Business Services:** meeting rooms, fax (fee). **Cards:** AX, CB, DC, DS, MC, VI. **Special Amenities:** free expanded continental breakfast and free local telephone calls.

SOME UNITS

BEST WESTERN ROYAL SUN INN & SUITES   *Book at aaa.com*
(AAA) (SAVE)

Phone: (520)622-8871   **4**

2/1-3/31	1P: $89-$159	2P: $89-$159	XP: $10	F14
8/1-1/31	1P: $79-$139	2P: $79-$139	XP: $10	F14
4/1-5/31	1P: $79-$119	2P: $79-$119	XP: $10	F14
6/1-7/31	1P: $69-$109	2P: $69-$109	XP: $10	F14

Motel

Location: I-10, exit 257 (Speedway Blvd), 0.8 mi e, then just s. 1015 N Stone Ave 85705. Fax: 520/623-2267. **Facility:** Designated smoking area. 79 units. 59 one-bedroom standard units. 20 one-bedroom suites with whirlpools. 2 stories (no elevator), exterior corridors. **Parking:** on-site. **Terms:** cancellation fee imposed. **Amenities:** video library (fee), DVD players, high-speed Internet, voice mail, irons, hair dryers. **Dining:** 6 am-10 pm. **Pool(s):** heated outdoor. **Leisure Activities:** whirlpool, exercise room. **Business Services:** meeting rooms, fax. **Cards:** AX, CB, DC, DS, JC, MC, VI. **Special Amenities:** free continental breakfast and free newspaper. *(See color ad below)*

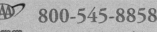

(See map and index starting on p. 413)

CATALINA PARK INN BED AND BREAKFAST   **Phone:** 520/792-4541   **5**
▼▼▼▼   2/1-7/10 & 8/15-1/31 [BP]   1P: $86-$166   2P: $86-$166   XP: $25
Bed & Breakfast   **Location:** I-10, exit 257 (Speedway Blvd), 1 mi e to 5th Ave, just s, then just e. Located in the West University Historic District. 309 E 1st St 85705. **Fax:** 520/792-4541. **Facility:** The house, dating from 1927, is near the historic district, surrounded by shady gardens with arbors and patios, and has attractively appointed rooms. Designated smoking area. 6 one-bedroom standard units, some with whirlpools. 1-2 stories (no elevator), interior/exterior corridors. *Bath:* combo, shower or tub only. **Parking:** street. **Terms:** open 2/1-7/10 & 8/15-1/31, office hours 8 am-9 pm, check-in 4 pm, age restrictions may apply, 14 day cancellation notice-fee imposed. **Amenities:** voice mail, irons, hair dryers. **Guest Services:** complimentary evening beverages. **Business Services:** PC, fax (fee). **Cards:** AX, DS, MC, VI.

SOME UNITS
[✕] / [VCR] [DATA PORT]

ECONO LODGE   *Book at aaa.com* ●   **Phone:** 520/622-6714   **2**
Ⓐ Ⓐ Ⓐ [SAVE]   All Year   1P: $34-$169   2P: $38-$199   XP: $4   F17
▼▼▼   **Location:** I-10, exit 257 (St Mary Blvd) eastbound, just e, then just n. 1136 N Stone Ave 85705. **Fax:** 520/617-0505.
Motel   **Facility:** 48 one-bedroom standard units. 3 stories (no elevator), exterior corridors. *Bath:* combo or shower only. **Parking:** on-site. **Terms:** [CP] meal plan available, small pets only ($10 fee, $20 deposit). **Pool(s):** small outdoor. **Business Services:** fax (fee). **Cards:** AX, CB, DC, DS, JC, MC, VI. **Special Amenities:** free continental breakfast and free local telephone calls.

SOME UNITS
[S][D] [🐾] [🛏] [🎥] [DATA PORT] / [✕] [📶]
FEE

EL PRESIDIO BED & BREAKFAST INN   **Phone:** (520)623-6151   **11**
▼▼▼▼   2/1-5/31 & 10/2-1/31 [BP]   1P: $110-$140   2P: $110-$140   XP: $25   D10
          6/1-10/1 [BP]   1P: $85-$100   2P: $85-$100   XP: $25   D10
Classic Historic Bed & Breakfast   **Location:** I-10, exit 258 (Congress St), 0.3 mi e, 0.3 mi n on Granada Ave, then just e on Franklin. Located in El Presidio Historic District. 297 N Main Ave 85701. **Fax:** 520/623-3860. **Facility:** An 1886 Victorian adobe with a quiet courtyard garden, nicely decorated rooms and suites, and within walking distance of museums and art district. Smoke free premises. 4 one-bedroom standard units, some with efficiencies. 1 story, interior/exterior corridors. *Bath:* combo or shower only. **Parking:** street. **Terms:** check-in 4 pm, 2 night minimum stay - seasonal, 14 day cancellation notice, weekly rates available, package plans. **Amenities:** video library, hair dryers. **Business Services:** fax.

SOME UNITS
[🛏][✕][📺] / [VCR] [📶] [🖥] [🖨] /
FEE

FOUR POINTS BY SHERATON TUCSON
    UNIVERSITY PLAZA   *Book at aaa.com*   **Phone:** (520)327-7341   **3**
▼▼▼▼   12/31-1/31   1P: $259-$269   2P: $259-$269   XP: $15   F17
          2/1-4/29   1P: $249-$269   2P: $249-$269   XP: $15   F17
Small-scale Hotel   9/3-12/30   1P: $229-$249   2P: $229-$249   XP: $15   F17
          4/30-9/2   1P: $154-$164   2P: $154-$164   XP: $15   F17
Location: Southeast corner of Speedway Blvd and Campbell Ave. 1900 E Speedway Blvd 85719. **Fax:** 520/327-0276. **Facility:** 150 units. 149 one-bedroom standard units. 1 one-bedroom suite. 7 stories, interior corridors. *Bath:* combo or shower only. **Parking:** on-site. **Amenities:** video games (fee), high-speed Internet, dual phone lines, voice mail, irons, hair dryers. **Pool(s):** heated outdoor. **Leisure Activities:** whirlpool, exercise room. **Guest Services:** coin laundry. **Business Services:** meeting rooms, fax. **Cards:** AX, DS, MC, VI.

SOME UNITS
[ASK] [S][D] [🍴] [🍷] [ⓂM] [🛜] [🏊] [🎥] [DATA PORT] [🖥] / [✕] [📶] /
FEE

(See map and index starting on p. 413)

THE HOTEL ARIZONA   *Book at aaa.com*    Phone: (520)624-8711   **13**

2/1-3/26	1P: $152-$189	2P: $152-$189	XP: $10 F18
3/27-5/14	1P: $134-$169	2P: $134-$169	XP: $10 F18
5/15-1/31	1P: $98-$169	2P: $98-$169	XP: $10 F18

Location: I-10, exit 258 (Broadway Blvd/Congress St), just e. Located adjacent to Tucson Convention Center. 181 W Broadway 85701. Fax: 520/624-9963. **Facility:** 307 units. 304 one-bedroom standard units. 3 one-bedroom
Large-scale Hotel suites. 12 stories, interior corridors. *Bath:* combo or shower only. **Parking:** on-site (fee). **Terms:** cancellation fee imposed, package plans, pets ($50 fee). **Amenities:** video games (fee), dual phone lines, voice mail, irons, hair dryers. **Dining:** 6 am-2 & 5-10 pm, cocktails. **Pool(s):** heated outdoor. **Guest Services:** gift shop, valet and coin laundry, area transportation-within 5 mi. **Business Services:** conference facilities, business center. **Cards:** AX, CB, DC, DS, JC, MC, VI.

SOME UNITS

INNSUITES HOTELS & SUITES TUCSON CITY
CENTER   *Book at aaa.com*   Phone: (520)622-3000   **10**

2/1-3/31 [BP]	1P: $99-$155	2P: $119-$155	XP: $10 F18
9/16-1/31 [BP]	1P: $79-$139	2P: $79-$139	XP: $10 F18
4/1-5/31 [BP]	1P: $89-$119	2P: $89-$119	XP: $10 F18
6/1-9/15 [BP]	1P: $79-$99	2P: $79-$99	XP: $10 F18

Small-scale Hotel **Location:** I-10, exit 258 (Broadway Blvd/Congress St), just e, then 0.4 mi n. 475 N Granada Ave 85701. Fax: 520/882-4100. **Facility:** 267 units. 221 one-bedroom standard units, some with kitchens. 46 one-bedroom suites ($99-$199), some with kitchens and/or whirlpools. 2-4 stories, interior/exterior corridors. **Parking:** on-site. **Terms:** weekly rates available, pets ($50 fee, in smoking units). **Amenities:** video games (fee), high-speed Internet, voice mail, irons, hair dryers. **Dining:** 6:30-10 am, 11-2 & 5-9 pm; seasonal hours vary, cocktails. **Pool(s):** heated outdoor. **Leisure Activities:** whirlpool, exercise room, volleyball. **Guest Services:** complimentary evening beverages, valet and coin laundry. **Business Services:** meeting rooms, business center. **Cards:** AX, CB, DC, DS, JC, MC, VI. **Special Amenities:** free full breakfast. *(See color ad p 424)*

SOME UNITS

MARRIOTT UNIVERSITY PARK HOTEL   *Book at aaa.com*   Phone: 520/792-4100   **7**

2/1-4/3	1P: $194-$259	2P: $194-$259
4/4-5/12 & 9/8-1/31	1P: $159-$209	2P: $159-$209
5/13-9/7	1P: $94-$124	2P: $94-$124

Location: I-10, exit 257 (Speedway Blvd), 1.2 mi e to Euclid Ave, then just s. 880 E 2nd St 85719.
Large-scale Hotel Fax: 520/882-4100. **Facility:** 250 units. 233 one-bedroom standard units. 17 one-bedroom suites, some with whirlpools. 9 stories, interior corridors. *Bath:* combo or shower only. **Parking:** on-site. **Terms:** cancellation fee imposed, package plans. **Amenities:** high-speed Internet (fee), dual phone lines, voice mail, irons, hair dryers. **Dining:** 6:30 am-10 pm, cocktails. **Pool(s):** small heated outdoor. **Leisure Activities:** sauna, whirlpool, exercise room. *Fee:* massage. **Guest Services:** gift shop, valet laundry. **Business Services:** conference facilities, business center. **Cards:** AX, DC, DS, MC. **Special Amenities:** free newspaper. *(See color ad below)*

SOME UNITS

PEPPERTREES INN   Phone: 520/622-7167   **8**

Property failed to provide current rates

Location: I-10, exit 257 (Speedway Blvd), 1.5 mi e, 0.3 mi s on Euclid Ave, then just w. 724 E University Blvd 85719-
Bed & Breakfast 5045. Fax: 520/622-7167. **Facility:** Southwestern guest houses and two territorial homes dating from 1905 surround a flagstone patio and blue-tiled fountain; special diet meals available. Designated smoking area. 6 units. 3 one-bedroom standard units. 1 one- and 2 two-bedroom suites with kitchens. 1-2 stories (no elevator), interior/exterior corridors. *Bath:* combo or shower only. **Parking:** on-site. **Terms:** office hours 8 am-8 pm. **Amenities:** video library, CD players, high-speed Internet, voice mail, irons, hair dryers. *Some:* DVD players. **Leisure Activities:** *Fee:* massage. **Business Services:** fax.

SOME UNITS

(See map and index starting on p. 413)

RAMADA LIMITED TUCSON WEST   *Book at aaa.com*   Phone: (520)622-6491   **9**

(AAA) [SAVE]   2/1-3/31 [ECP]   1P: $94   2P: $94

▽▽ ▽▽   4/1-4/30 [ECP]   1P: $84   2P: $84

            10/1-1/31 [ECP]   1P: $74   2P: $74

Motel   5/1-9/30 [ECP]   1P: $59   2P: $59

Location: I-10, exit 257 (St. Mary's Rd/Speedway Blvd), just s. 665 N Freeway 85745. Fax: 520/798-3669. **Facility:** 132 units. 130 one-bedroom standard units. 2 one-bedroom suites. 2 stories (no elevator), exterior corridors. **Parking:** on-site. **Amenities:** video games (fee), voice mail, irons, hair dryers. *Some:* high-speed Internet. **Pool(s):** heated outdoor. **Leisure Activities:** bicycles. **Guest Services:** coin laundry. **Business Services:** PC, fax (fee). **Cards:** AX, CB, DC, DS, JC, MC, VI. *(See color ad p 440)*

SOME UNITS

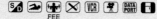

RIVERPARK INN   *Book at aaa.com*   Phone: (520)622-6611   **15**

(AAA) [SAVE]   2/13-3/26 [BP]   1P: $99-$169   2P: $99-$169   XP: $10   F17

▽▽ ▽▽   3/27-5/14 [BP]   1P: $89-$159   2P: $89-$159   XP: $10   F17

            9/5-1/31 [BP]   1P: $79-$149   2P: $79-$149   XP: $10   F17

Small-scale Hotel 5/15-9/4 [BP]   1P: $69-$139   2P: $69-$139   XP: $10   F17

Location: I-10, exit 158 (Broadway Blvd/Congress St), just w, then 0.4 mi s. 350 S Freeway 85745. Fax: 520/622-8143. **Facility:** 174 units. 168 one-bedroom standard units. 6 one-bedroom suites ($129-$199). 2 stories (no elevator), interior/exterior corridors. *Bath:* combo or shower only. **Parking:** on-site. **Terms:** open 2/13-1/31, pets ($35 fee). **Amenities:** video games (fee), high-speed Internet, dual phone lines, voice mail, safes, irons, hair dryers. **Dining:** 11 am-10 pm. **Pool(s):** heated outdoor. **Leisure Activities:** whirlpool, table tennis, croquet, bicycles, exercise room. **Guest Services:** valet and coin laundry. **Business Services:** meeting rooms, fax (fee). **Cards:** AX, CB, DC, DS, MC, VI. **Special Amenities:** free full breakfast and free local telephone calls. *(See color ad below)*

SOME UNITS

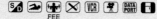

FEE

THE ROYAL ELIZABETH BED & BREAKFAST INN   Phone: 520/670-9022   **14**

(AAA) [SAVE]   2/1-5/31 & 9/1-1/31 [BP]   1P: $145-$215   2P: $145-$215   XP: $25   F8

▽▽ ▽▽   6/1-8/31 [BP]   1P: $105-$155   2P: $105-$155   XP: $25   F8

Historic Bed **Location:** I-10, exit 258 (Broadway Blvd/Congress St), 1.1 mi e, then just s. 204 S Scott Ave 85701.
& Breakfast Fax: 928/833-9974. **Facility:** Built in 1878, this Victorian adobe home with its large rooms, has been beautifully restored and is decorated with period pieces and antiques. Designated smoking area. 6 units. 5 one-bedroom standard units, some with whirlpools. 1 one-bedroom suite. 1 story, interior corridors. *Bath:* combo or shower only. **Parking:** on-site. **Terms:** 7 day cancellation notice-fee imposed, weekly rates available. **Amenities:** video library, high-speed Internet, safes, hair dryers. *Some:* DVD players. **Pool(s):** small heated outdoor. **Leisure Activities:** whirlpool. *Fee:* massage. **Guest Services:** complimentary evening beverages, valet laundry. **Business Services:** fax. **Cards:** AX, DS, MC, VI. **Special Amenities:** free full breakfast and free local telephone calls.

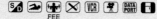

FEE

(See map and index starting on p. 413)

──────── **WHERE TO DINE** ────────

ATHENS' ON 4TH AVE   **Dinner:** $11-$20   **Phone:** 520/624-6886   ③
WWWW
Greek
Location: Northeast corner of 6th St and 4th Ave; center. 500 N 4th Ave #6 85705. **Hours:** 5 pm-10 pm. Closed: 1/1, 12/24, 12/25; also Sun. **Reservations:** accepted. **Features:** Chef-owner Andreas Delfakis thoughtfully prepares traditional Greek dishes, including moussaka, dolmades and chicken souvlaki. Casual dress; cocktails. **Parking:** on-site. **Cards:** AX, DC, DS, MC, VI.

BARRIO FOOD & DRINK   **Lunch:** $7-$13   **Dinner:** $14-$32   **Phone:** 520/629-0191   ⑨
WWWW
Southwest
American
Location: I-10, exit 258 (Broadway Blvd/Congress St), 0.8 mi e, then just s. 135 S 6th Ave 85701. **Hours:** 11 am-10 pm, Fri & Sat-midnight, Sun 5 pm-9 pm. Closed: Sun 5 pm-9 pm. **Reservations:** suggested. **Features:** At the hip downtown eatery, patrons can savor Southwestern sauces, the freshest ingredients and flavorful accompaniments. Choices range from small to large plates, depending on appetite and occasion. Plan to have dessert, such as chocolate caramel custard. It's worth it. Casual dress; cocktails. **Parking:** on-site and street. **Cards:** AX, DC, MC, VI.

CAFE A'LA C'ART   **Lunch:** $7-$9   **Phone:** 520/628-8533   ⑤
WW
American
Location: Broadway Blvd/Congress St, just n on Granada, just e on Paseo Redondo, just n on Main Ave to Washington, then just e; on grounds of Tucson Art Museum. 150 N Main Ave 85701. **Hours:** 11 am-3 pm. Closed major holidays; also Sat, Sun & 12/24-1/1. **Features:** Tucked into the side garden of the museum is this delightful luncheon cafe, which is open only for lunch on weekdays. The chef-owner prepares creative salads and sandwiches, such as grilled salmon on focaccia with chipotle sauce. Desserts are not to be missed. Casual dress. **Parking:** on-site. **Cards:** MC, VI.

CAFE POCA COSA   **Lunch:** $10-$11   **Dinner:** $15-$19   **Phone:** 520/622-6400   ⑧
WW
Mexican
Location: I-10, exit 258 (Broadway Blvd/Congress St), 0.6 mi e; in The Santa Rita Hotel & Suites. 88 E Broadway Blvd 85701. **Hours:** Open 2/1-7/14 & 8/6-1/31; 11 am-9 pm, Fri & Sat-10 pm. Closed major holidays; also Sun. **Reservations:** suggested. **Features:** The brightly colored surroundings and an open patio are settings for the young and pleasant staff to serve you from an interesting variety of regional Mexican cuisine. The blackboard menu changes twice daily. Casual dress; cocktails. **Parking:** on-site. **Cards:** MC, VI.

CUP CAFE'   **Lunch:** $5-$8   **Dinner:** $10-$20   **Phone:** 520/798-1618   ⑥
WW
American
Location: I-10, exit 258 (Broadway Blvd/Congress St), 0.7 mi e to 5th Ave, then just n; in Hotel Congress. 311 E Congress 85701. **Hours:** 7 am-10 pm, Fri & Sat-10 pm. **Reservations:** accepted. **Features:** This a popular place for breakfast, but the crispy salads, hearty sandwiches and steak dinners have their own following in the lunch and dinner crowds. Homemade desserts spinning in a display case tantalize taste buds. Casual dress; cocktails. **Parking:** on-site. **Cards:** AX, DS, MC, VI. **Classic**   Ⓜ

CUSHING STREET BAR & RESTAURANT   **Lunch:** $7-$12   **Dinner:** $10-$21   **Phone:** 520/622-7984   ⑩
WW
American
Location: I-10, exit 258 (Broadway Blvd/Congress St), 0.5 mi e to Church Ave, just s, then just w. 198 W Cushing St 85701. **Hours:** 11 am-9 pm, Fri & Sat-10 pm. Closed: Sun & Mon. **Reservations:** accepted. **Features:** The historic house is now an upscale eatery with an eclectic and casual decor featuring items from a French mansion in Mexico City. Southwestern flavors enhance such traditional offerings as roasted pork loin and shrimp quesadillas. Patio seating is available. Dressy casual; cocktails. **Parking:** on-site. **Cards:** AX, MC, VI.   ◥

DELECTABLES   **Lunch:** $6-$14   **Dinner:** $6-$14   **Phone:** 520/884-9289   ②
WW
International
Location: Just n of 6th St. 533 N Fourth Ave 85705. **Hours:** 11 am-9 pm, Fri & Sat-11 pm. Closed major holidays. **Reservations:** accepted. **Features:** Lively at lunch, the eatery presents a menu of casual, European, gourmet-style dishes. In addition to salads and sandwiches, choices include many vegetarian creations. Casual dress; cocktails. **Parking:** on-site. **Cards:** AX, DC, DS, MC, VI.

EL CHARRO CAFE   **Lunch:** $6-$10   **Dinner:** $12-$22   **Phone:** 520/622-1922   ④
WW
Mexican
Location: I-10, exit 257A (St. Mary's Rd), 0.7 mi e, then just s; in El Presidio Historic District. 311 N Court Ave 85701. **Hours:** 11 am-9 pm, Fri & Sat-10 pm. Closed major holidays. **Reservations:** accepted. **Features:** El Charro's is a busy, popular restaurant operated by the same family since 1922. Several small dining areas and an outdoor cantina add to the charm. Casual dress; cocktails. **Parking:** street. **Cards:** AX, DC, DS, MC, VI.   ▼

EL MINUTO CAFE   **Lunch:** $5-$12   **Dinner:** $6-$12   **Phone:** 520/882-4145   ⑪
WWWW
Mexican
Location: I-10, exit 258 (Broadway Blvd/Congress St), 0.4 mi e on Broadway Blvd, just s on Church Ave, then just w on Cushing. 354 S Main Ave 85701. **Hours:** 11 am-10 pm, Fri & Sat-11 pm. Closed: 4/16, 11/23, 12/25. **Reservations:** accepted. **Features:** A short distance from the convention center, this family-owned eatery serves traditional dishes such as chicken or beef enchiladas. The cheese crisps with toppings such as carne seca or green chiles are popular. Casual dress; cocktails. **Parking:** on-site. **Cards:** AX, DC, DS, MC, VI.

(See map and index starting on p. 413)

GARCIA'S MEXICAN RESTAURANT   **Lunch:** $6-$12   **Dinner:** $7-$15   **Phone:** 520/628-1956   (7)

Mexican

MC, VI.

Location: I-10, exit 258 (Broadway Blvd/Congress St), just e. 419 W Congress 85701. **Hours:** 11 am-9 pm, Fri & Sat-10 pm. Closed: 11/23, 12/25. **Reservations:** accepted. **Features:** In a historic train station dating from 1912, the eatery offers traditional dishes with friendly service. Such dishes as chicken and spinach quesadillas satisfy those looking for a lighter meal. Casual dress; cocktails. **Parking:** on-site. **Cards:** AX, MC, VI.

TRIDENT GRILL & BAR   **Lunch:** $6-$8   **Dinner:** $13-$18   **Phone:** 520/795-5755   (1)

American

Location: Just e of Campbell Ave. 2033 E Speedway 85719. **Hours:** 11 am-1 am. Closed: 4/16, 11/23; also 12/24-1/1. **Features:** A nautical theme, a pool table and warm, friendly servers lend to the atmosphere. These aspects combine with good sandwiches and salads, such as the applewood BLT and Brown Derby cobb, and grilled steaks to make the eatery popular with area college students. Casual dress; cocktails. **Parking:** on-site. **Cards:** AX, DS, MC, VI.

TUCSON pop. 486,699   (See map and index starting on p. 416)

——— WHERE TO STAY ———

AGAVE GROVE BED & BREAKFAST INN   **Phone:** (520)797-3400   (9)

2/1-4/30 & 10/1-1/31 [BP]	1P: $95-$175	2P: $95-$175	XP: $20	D18
5/1-9/30 [BP]	1P: $70-$130	2P: $70-$130	XP: $20	D18

Bed & Breakfast

Location: I-10, exit 250 (Orange Grove Rd), 3 mi e to La Canada, 0.4 mi s, then 0.6 mi e. Located in a quiet residential area. 800 W Panorama Rd 85704. Fax: 520/797-0980. **Facility:** A wide patio enhances the charming ambience of this inn, which is convenient to shopping, attractions and many restaurants. Designated smoking area. 4 one-bedroom standard units, some with whirlpools. 1 story, exterior corridors. **Bath:** combo or shower only. **Parking:** on-site. **Terms:** 14 day cancellation notice-fee imposed, package plans. **Amenities:** video library, hair dryers. **Pool(s):** outdoor. **Leisure Activities:** whirlpool. **Guest Services:** complimentary evening beverages. **Business Services:** fax. **Cards:** AX, DS, MC, VI.

SOME UNITS

AMERICAS BEST VALUE INN-TUCSON   *Book at aaa.com*   **Phone:** (520)884-5800   (50)

2/1-2/14	1P: $139	2P: $139	XP: $5	F18
2/15-3/31 & 1/21-1/31	1P: $59	2P: $69	XP: $5	F18
4/1-1/20	1P: $43	2P: $50	XP: $5	F18

Motel

Location: I-10, exit 262, just s. 810 E Benson Hwy 85713. Fax: 520/624-2681. **Facility:** 99 one-bedroom standard units. 2 stories (no elevator), exterior corridors. **Parking:** on-site. **Terms:** small pets only ($25 deposit). **Pool(s):** heated outdoor. **Guest Services:** coin laundry. **Business Services:** fax (fee). **Cards:** AX, CB, DC, DS, MC, VI. **Special Amenities:** free continental breakfast and early check-in/late check-out.

SOME UNITS

AMERISUITES (TUCSON/AIRPORT)   *Book at aaa.com*   **Phone:** (520)295-0405   (64)

2/1-4/30	1P: $79-$179	2P: $89-$189	XP: $10	F16
10/1-1/31	1P: $79-$129	2P: $89-$139	XP: $10	F16
5/1-9/30	1P: $69-$89	2P: $79-$99	XP: $10	F16

Small-scale Hotel

Location: Just n of Tucson International Airport. 6885 S Tucson Blvd 85706. Fax: 520/295-9140. **Facility:** 122 one-bedroom standard units. 5 stories, interior corridors. **Bath:** combo or shower only. **Parking:** on-site. **Terms:** cancellation fee imposed, [BP] meal plan available. **Amenities:** voice mail, irons, hair dryers. *Fee:* video games, high-speed Internet, safes. **Pool(s):** heated outdoor. **Leisure Activities:** exercise room. **Guest Services:** coin laundry, area transportation-within 5 mi. **Business Services:** meeting rooms, fax (fee). **Cards:** AX, CB, DC, DS, JC, MC, VI. **Special Amenities:** free full breakfast.

SOME UNITS

ARIZONA INN   *Book at aaa.com*   **Phone:** (520)325-1541   (25)

All Year	1P: $169-$3200	2P: $169-$3200	XP: $15	F10

Historic Large-scale Hotel

Location: I-10, exit 257 (Speedway Blvd), 2.5 mi e, 0.5 mi n on Campbell Ave, then just e. Located in a quiet residential area. 2200 E Elm St 85719. Fax: 520/881-5830. **Facility:** This historic property has kept the integrity of the early 1900s-style rooms, but with elegant appointments and lush, expansive gardens. 88 units. 86 one-bedroom standard units. 16 one- and 1 two-bedroom suites. 3 vacation homes, some with whirlpools. 2 stories, exterior corridors. **Bath:** combo or shower only. **Parking:** on-site and valet. **Terms:** 3 day cancellation notice-fee imposed, package plans. **Amenities:** video library, DVD players, high-speed Internet, voice mail, irons, hair dryers. **Dining:** 2 restaurants, 6 am-midnight, cocktails, also, Main Dining Room at the Arizona Inn, see separate listing, entertainment. **Pool(s):** heated outdoor. **Leisure Activities:** saunas, 2 lighted tennis courts, badminton, table tennis, croquet; tennis instruction, bicycles, exercise room. *Fee:* massage. **Guest Services:** gift shop, valet laundry. **Business Services:** meeting rooms, business center. **Cards:** AX, DC, MC, VI. **Special Amenities:** free newspaper.

SOME UNITS

BEST WESTERN INN AT THE AIRPORT   **Phone:** (520)746-0271   (69)

2/1-3/31	1P: $129-$189	2P: $129-$189
9/1-1/31	1P: $89-$129	2P: $89-$129
4/1-5/31	1P: $89-$109	2P: $89-$109
6/1-8/31	1P: $69-$99	2P: $69-$99

(fyi)

Small-scale Hotel

Under major renovation, scheduled to be completed September 2005. Last rated: ♦♦ **Location:** At entrance to Tucson International Airport. 7060 S Tucson Blvd 85706. Fax: 520/889-7391. **Facility:** 149 one-bedroom standard units. 2-3 stories, interior corridors. **Parking:** on-site. **Terms:** small pets only ($25 fee). **Amenities:** voice mail, irons, hair dryers. **Pool(s):** heated outdoor. **Leisure Activities:** whirlpool, putting green, lighted tennis court, exercise room, horseshoes, volleyball. **Guest Services:** coin laundry. **Business Services:** meeting rooms, fax (fee). **Cards:** AX, DC, DS, MC, VI.

SOME UNITS

(See map and index starting on p. 416)

BEST WESTERN INNSUITES HOTEL & SUITES
TUCSON-CATALINA FOOTHILLS   Book at aaa.com

			Phone: (520)297-8111			**8**
(AAA) (SAVE)	2/1-4/15 [BP]	1P: $99-$149	2P: $99-$149	XP: $10		F18
▽▽▽▽	4/16-5/31 & 9/1-1/31 [BP]	1P: $89-$109	2P: $89-$109	XP: $10		F18
	6/1-8/31 [BP]	1P: $69-$89	2P: $69-$89	XP: $10		F18

Location: I-10, exit 250 (Orange Grove Rd), 4 mi e, then just s. 6201 N Oracle Rd 85704. Fax: 520/297-2935.
Small-scale Hotel **Facility:** 159 units. 114 one-bedroom standard units, some with whirlpools. 45 one-bedroom suites ($99-
$149) with efficiencies, some with whirlpools. 2 stories (no elevator), exterior corridors. **Parking:** on-site.
Terms: weekly rates available, small pets only ($25 fee). **Amenities:** video games (fee), high-speed Internet, dual phone lines,
voice mail, irons, hair dryers. **Pool(s):** heated outdoor. **Leisure Activities:** whirlpool, 2 lighted tennis courts, exercise room.
Guest Services: complimentary evening beverages, coin laundry, airport transportation-Tucson International Airport, area
transportation-within 5 mi. **Business Services:** meeting rooms, PC. **Cards:** AX, CB, DC, DS, JC, MC, VI. **Special Amenities:**
free expanded continental breakfast and free room upgrade (subject to availability with advance reservations).
(See color ad below)

SOME UNITS

FEE

CASA LUNA BED AND BREAKFAST

			Phone: (520)577-4943		**17**
(AAA) (SAVE)	2/1-5/31 & 1/1-1/31 [BP]	1P: $160-$300	2P: $160-$300	XP: $30	D18
▽▽▽▽	9/1-12/31 [BP]	1P: $140-$280	2P: $140-$280	XP: $30	D18
	6/1-8/31 [BP]	1P: $100-$240	2P: $100-$240	XP: $30	D18

Location: Jct Campbell Ave, 2.7 mi e on River Rd, 0.5 mi n on Pontatoc, then just w. 4210 N Saranac Dr 85718.
Bed & Breakfast Fax: 520/615-5097. **Facility:** This desert-view facility has a separate guest house, modern baths and a
charming courtyard with shady terraces, a pool and a fountain. Designated smoking area. 5 one-bedroom
standard units, some with whirlpools. 1-2 stories, interior/exterior corridors. *Bath:* combo or shower only. **Parking:** on-site. **Terms:** 2
night minimum stay, age restrictions may apply, 14 day cancellation notice-fee imposed, package plans. **Amenities:** video
library, CD players, hair dryers. *Some:* DVD players. **Pool(s):** outdoor. **Leisure Activities:** whirlpool. **Business Services:**
meeting rooms, fax. **Cards:** MC, VI. **Special Amenities: free full breakfast and free local telephone calls.**

CASA TIERRA ADOBE B&B INN

			Phone: (520)578-3058	
(AAA) (SAVE)	2/1-4/30 & 12/1-1/31 [BP]	1P: $165-$325	2P: $165-$325	
▽▽▽▽	5/1-11/30 [BP]	1P: $150-$275	2P: $150-$275	

Location: I-10, exit 257 (Speedway Blvd and Gates Pass), 9.5 mi w, 3.8 mi nw on Kinney, 1.4 mi w on Milewide, then
0.7 mi s on unpaved road. Located in a quiet secluded area. 11155 W Calle Pima 85743. Fax: 520/578-8445.
Bed & Breakfast **Facility:** This charming adobe home with a central interior courtyard is in a desert setting 3.5 miles west of
the Arizona-Sonora Desert Museum. 4 units. 3 one-bedroom standard units. 1 two-bedroom suite. 1 story,
exterior corridors. *Bath:* combo or shower only. **Parking:** on-site. **Terms:** office hours 9 am-7 pm, check-in 4 pm, 2 night
minimum stay, age restrictions may apply, 14 day cancellation notice-fee imposed, weekly rates available. **Amenities:** CD
players, irons, hair dryers. **Leisure Activities:** whirlpools, exercise room. **Guest Services:** TV in common area. **Business
Services:** PC, fax. **Cards:** AX, DS, MC, VI. **Special Amenities: free full breakfast and free local telephone calls.**

(See map and index starting on p. 416)

CLARION HOTEL-RANDOLPH PARK   *Book at aaa.com*

Small-scale Hotel

10/1-1/31 [BP]	1P: $89-$159	2P: $94-$164	XP: $5
2/1-3/31 [BP]	1P: $99-$149	2P: $109-$154	XP: $5
4/1-5/14 [BP]	1P: $89-$129	2P: $94-$134	XP: $5
5/15-9/30 [BP]	1P: $69-$105	2P: $74-$109	XP: $5

Phone: (520)795-0330   **30**   F18 / F18 / F18 / F18

Location: Jct Campbell Ave, 2.2 mi e on Broadway, then just n. 102 N Alvernon 85711. Fax: 520/326-2111. **Facility:** 157 units. 149 one-bedroom standard units, some with efficiencies (no utensils). 7 one- and 1 two-bedroom suites ($89-$159) with kitchens (no utensils). 3 stories, interior/exterior corridors. **Parking:** on-site. **Terms:** 3 day cancellation notice, pets ($25 fee). **Amenities:** voice mail, irons, hair dryers. **Pool(s):** heated outdoor. **Leisure Activities:** whirlpool, exercise room, shuffleboard. **Guest Services:** complimentary evening beverages, coin laundry. **Business Services:** meeting rooms, business center. **Cards:** AX, CB, DC, DS, MC, VI.

SOME UNITS

CLARION HOTEL TUCSON AIRPORT   *Book at aaa.com*

Small-scale Hotel

2/1-3/31	1P: $99-$129	2P: $99-$129	
4/1-5/31 & 9/1-1/31	1P: $79-$89	2P: $79-$89	XP: $5
6/1-8/31	1P: $55-$79	2P: $55-$79	

Phone: (520)746-3932   **63**   F

Location: Just n of Tucson International Airport. 6801 S Tucson Blvd 85706. Fax: 520/889-9934. **Facility:** 189 units. 188 one-bedroom standard units. 1 one-bedroom suite. 2 stories (no elevator), interior corridors. *Bath:* combo or shower only. **Parking:** on-site. **Amenities:** voice mail, safes (fee), irons, hair dryers. *Some:* high-speed Internet. **Pool(s):** heated outdoor. **Leisure Activities:** whirlpool, exercise room. **Guest Services:** complimentary evening beverages, coin laundry, area transportation. **Business Services:** meeting rooms, business center. **Cards:** AX, DC, DS, MC, VI. *(See color ad below)*

SOME UNITS

COMFORT SUITES   *Book at aaa.com*

Small-scale Hotel

All Year [ECP]	1P: $59-$159

Phone: (520)295-4400   **65**   XP: $10   F18

Location: Just n of Tucson International Airport. 6935 S Tucson Blvd 85706. Fax: 520/295-4497. **Facility:** 82 one-bedroom standard units. 3 stories, interior corridors. **Terms:** small pets only ($25 fee). **Amenities:** voice mail, irons, hair dryers. **Pool(s):** outdoor. **Leisure Activities:** whirlpool, limited exercise equipment. **Guest Services:** coin laundry, area transportation-within 5 mi. **Business Services:** PC, fax (fee). **Cards:** AX, DC, DS, MC, VI.

SOME UNITS

(See map and index starting on p. 416)

COMFORT SUITES AT TUCSON MALL
Book at aaa.com Phone: (520)888-6676 **14**

▼▼▼

2/1-3/1	1P: $150	2P: $150	XP: $10	F17
3/2-4/15	1P: $109	2P: $109	XP: $10	F17
4/16-5/31	1P: $99	2P: $99	XP: $10	F17
6/1-1/31	1P: $69-$89	2P: $69-$89	XP: $10	F17

Small-scale Hotel

Location: I-10, exit 254 (Prince Rd), 1.9 mi e, then 1.2 mi ne. 515 W Auto Mall Dr 85705. Fax: 520/888-6617. **Facility:** 87 units. 86 one-bedroom standard units, some with whirlpools. 1 one-bedroom suite with whirlpool. 3 stories, interior corridors. *Bath:* combo or shower only. **Parking:** on-site. **Terms:** [ECP] meal plan available, pets ($10 fee). **Amenities:** high-speed Internet, voice mail, irons, hair dryers. *Fee:* video games, safes. **Pool(s):** heated outdoor. **Leisure Activities:** whirlpool, exercise room. **Guest Services:** complimentary evening beverages: Tues-Thurs, coin laundry. **Business Services:** meeting rooms, fax (fee). **Cards:** AX, DC, DS, MC, VI.

SOME UNITS
(ASK) (SD) 🐾 (&) 🏊 📷 (DATA PORT) 🛗 📺 📶 / (✕) /
FEE

COMFORT SUITES TANQUE VERDE/SABINO CANYON
Book at aaa.com Phone: (520)298-2300 **19**

AAA (SAVE)
▼▼▼ ▼▼▼

2/1-2/28	1P: $149-$169	2P: $159-$179
1/1-1/31	1P: $109-$169	2P: $119-$179
3/1-4/15	1P: $79-$109	2P: $89-$119
4/16-12/31	1P: $69-$99	2P: $79-$109

Small-scale Hotel **Location:** Jct Grand Rd, 0.4 mi ne. 7007 E Tanque Verde Rd 85715. Fax: 520/298-6756. **Facility:** 90 one-bedroom standard units. 2 stories, exterior corridors. **Parking:** on-site. **Terms:** pets ($25 fee). **Amenities:** video games (fee), voice mail, irons, hair dryers. **Pool(s):** heated outdoor. **Leisure Activities:** whirlpool. **Guest Services:** complimentary evening beverages: Mon-Thurs, coin laundry. **Business Services:** meeting rooms, fax (fee). **Cards:** AX, CB, DC, DS, JC, MC, VI. **Special Amenities:** free continental breakfast and free local telephone calls.

SOME UNITS
(SD) 🐾 🏊 📶 📷 (DATA PORT) 🛗 📺 📶 / (✕) /
FEE

COUNTRY INN & SUITES BY CARLSON
Book at aaa.com Phone: (520)575-9255 **2**

▼▼▼

2/1-4/30 & 1/1-1/31 [ECP]	1P: $109-$139	2P: $109-$139	XP: $10	F18
10/1-12/31 [ECP]	1P: $89-$109	2P: $89-$109	XP: $10	F18
5/1-9/30 [ECP]	1P: $79-$99	2P: $79-$99	XP: $10	F18

Small-scale Hotel **Location:** SR 77 (Oracle Rd), just n of Ina Rd. 7411 N Oracle Rd 85704. Fax: 520/575-8671. **Facility:** 156 units. 65 one-bedroom standard units. 91 one-bedroom suites, some with kitchens. 2-3 stories, exterior corridors. *Bath:* combo or shower only. **Parking:** on-site. **Terms:** small pets only ($25 fee). **Amenities:** video games (fee), high-speed Internet, voice mail, irons, hair dryers. **Pool(s):** heated outdoor. **Leisure Activities:** whirlpool, putting green. **Guest Services:** coin laundry, area transportation. **Business Services:** meeting rooms, fax (fee). **Cards:** AX, DC, DS, MC, VI.

SOME UNITS
(ASK) (SD) ✈ 🐾 (&M) (&) 📷 🏊 📶 📷 (DATA PORT) 🛗 📺 📶 / (✕) /
FEE

COUNTRY INN & SUITES BY CARLSON TUCSON-AIRPORT
Book at aaa.com Phone: (520)741-9000 **61**

AAA (SAVE)
▼▼▼ ▼▼▼

2/1-3/31	1P: $119-$129	2P: $119-$129
4/1-4/30	1P: $99-$119	2P: $99-$119
5/1-8/31	1P: $69-$89	2P: $99-$119
9/1-1/31	1P: $89-$99	2P: $89-$99

Small-scale Hotel **Location:** 0.4 mi n of Tucson International Airport entrance. 6681 S Tucson Blvd 85706. Fax: 520/741-9100. **Facility:** 83 units. 62 one-bedroom standard units. 21 one-bedroom suites ($70-$169). 3 stories, interior corridors. *Bath:* combo or shower only. **Parking:** on-site. **Terms:** 3 day cancellation notice-fee imposed, package plans. **Amenities:** voice mail, irons, hair dryers. **Pool(s):** heated outdoor. **Leisure Activities:** whirlpool, exercise room. **Guest Services:** complimentary evening beverages: Mon-Thurs, coin laundry, area transportation-within 5 mi. **Business Services:** meeting rooms, business center. **Cards:** AX, DC, DS, MC, VI. **Special Amenities:** free expanded continental breakfast and free local telephone calls.

SOME UNITS
(SD) ✈ (&M) (&) 🏊 📷 (DATA PORT) 📺 / (✕) (VCR) 🛗 📶 /
FEE

COURTYARD BY MARRIOTT-TUCSON AIRPORT
Book at aaa.com Phone: (520)573-0000 **60**

▼▼▼ ▼▼

9/10-1/31	1P: $209	2P: $209	XP: $10	F
2/1-4/29	1P: $199	2P: $199	XP: $10	F
4/30-5/27	1P: $159	2P: $159	XP: $10	F
5/28-9/9	1P: $119	2P: $119	XP: $10	F

Small-scale Hotel **Location:** On Tucson Blvd, 0.6 mi n of Tucson International Airport entrance. 2505 E Executive Dr 85706. Fax: 520/573-0470. **Facility:** 149 units. 137 one-bedroom standard units. 12 one-bedroom suites. 3 stories, interior corridors. *Bath:* combo or shower only. **Parking:** on-site. **Terms:** cancellation fee imposed, package plans. **Amenities:** high-speed Internet, dual phone lines, voice mail, irons, hair dryers. **Pool(s):** heated outdoor. **Leisure Activities:** whirlpool, exercise room. **Guest Services:** valet and coin laundry, area transportation. **Business Services:** meeting rooms. *Fee:* PC, fax. **Cards:** AX, CB, DC, DS, MC, VI.

SOME UNITS
(ASK) (SD) ✈ 🍴 (&M) (&) 📷 🏊 📷 (DATA PORT) 📺 / (✕) (VCR) 🛗 📶 /
FEE

COURTYARD BY MARRIOTT-TUCSON WILLIAMS CENTRE
Book at aaa.com Phone: (520)745-6000 **36**

▼▼▼ ▼▼

2/1-5/20	1P: $180-$189
9/10-1/31	1P: $152-$159
5/21-9/9	1P: $104-$109

Small-scale Hotel **Location:** Jct Campbell Ave, 3.8 mi e on Broadway, then just s. 201 S Williams Blvd 85711. Fax: 520/745-2393. **Facility:** 153 units. 147 one-bedroom standard units. 6 one-bedroom suites. 3 stories, interior corridors. *Bath:* combo or shower only. **Parking:** on-site. **Terms:** cancellation fee imposed, [BP] meal plan available. **Amenities:** high-speed Internet, voice mail, irons, hair dryers. **Pool(s):** small heated outdoor. **Leisure Activities:** whirlpool, exercise room. **Guest Services:** coin laundry, area transportation. **Business Services:** meeting rooms, fax (fee). **Cards:** AX, DC, DS, MC, VI.

SOME UNITS
(ASK) (SD) 🍴 (&M) (&) 🏊 📷 (DATA PORT) 📺 / (✕) 🛗 📶 /

(See map and index starting on p. 416)

COYOTE CROSSING BED & BREAKFAST
Phone: (520)744-3285 **5**

2/1-5/31 & 10/1-1/31 [ECP] 1P: $110-$130 2P: $115-$135 XP: $25 D12
6/1-6/30 & 8/1-9/30 [ECP] 1P: $75-$95 2P: $80-$100 XP: $25 D12

Bed & Breakfast **Location:** I-10, exit 248 (Ina Rd), 2.3 mi w, just s to Tres Casas, then just w. Located in a quiet residential area. 6985 N Camino Verde 85743. Fax: 520/744-5161. **Facility:** Surrounded by cactus gardens, this comfortable, modern Arizona ranch home overlooks the city of Tucson and backs up to the Saguaro National Forest. Designated smoking area. 4 one-bedroom standard units, some with whirlpools. 1 story, interior/exterior corridors. *Bath:* combo or shower only. **Parking:** on-site. **Terms:** open 2/1-6/30 & 8/1-1/31, office hours 6 am-9 pm, check-in 4 pm, 2 night minimum stay - seasonal and/or weekends, 7 day cancellation notice-fee imposed. **Amenities:** video library, hair dryers. **Pool(s):** heated outdoor. **Leisure Activities:** whirlpool. **Guest Services:** gift shop, complimentary evening beverages. **Cards:** AX, DS, MC, VI.

SOME UNITS
[S/D] [⊷] [✕] [☎] [🛏] [💻] / [VCR] [📷] /

DAYS INN *Book at aaa.com*
Phone: (520)747-8988 **53**

[AAA] [SAVE] 2/1-2/15 1P: $95-$105 2P: $105-$115 XP: $6 F
2/16-4/1 1P: $65-$75 2P: $75-$85 XP: $6 F
6/2-1/31 1P: $49-$59 2P: $59-$69 XP: $6 F
4/2-6/1 1P: $55-$60 2P: $60-$65 XP: $6 F

Small-scale Hotel **Location:** I-10, exit 264 westbound; exit 264B eastbound, just n. 4855 S Palo Verde 85714. Fax: 520/747-8428. **Facility:** 65 one-bedroom standard units. 2 stories (no elevator), exterior corridors. *Bath:* combo or shower only. **Parking:** on-site. **Terms:** package plans. **Amenities:** high-speed Internet, hair dryers. **Pool(s):** small outdoor. **Leisure Activities:** whirlpool. **Guest Services:** coin laundry. **Business Services:** fax (fee). **Cards:** AX, CB, DC, DS, JC, MC, VI. **Special Amenities:** free continental breakfast and free local telephone calls.

SOME UNITS
[S/D] [♿] [⊷] [✱] [DATA PORT] / [✕] [🛏] [📷] /

DOUBLETREE HOTEL AT REID PARK *Book at aaa.com*
Phone: (520)881-4200 **38**

[AAA] [SAVE] 2/1-4/22 & 1/1-1/31 1P: $129-$289 XP: $10 F18
9/11-12/31 1P: $84-$179 XP: $10 F18
4/23-9/10 1P: $74-$139 XP: $10 F18

Large-scale Hotel **Location:** I-10, exit 259 (22nd St), 4 mi e, then just n. 445 S Alvernon Way 85711. Fax: 520/323-5225. **Facility:** 295 units. 292 one-bedroom standard units. 3 one-bedroom suites. 2-9 stories, interior/exterior corridors. *Bath:* combo or shower only. **Parking:** on-site. **Terms:** cancellation fee imposed, package plans, small pets only ($50 fee). **Amenities:** high-speed Internet, voice mail, irons, hair dryers. *Some: Fee:* DVD players. *Dining:* 2 restaurants, 6:30 am-11 pm, cocktails. **Pool(s):** heated outdoor. **Leisure Activities:** whirlpool, 3 lighted tennis courts, exercise room. *Fee:* massage. **Guest Services:** gift shop, valet laundry. **Business Services:** conference facilities, business center. **Cards:** AX, MC, VI. **Special Amenities:** free newspaper and preferred room (subject to availability with advance reservations).

SOME UNITS
[S/D] [⊷] [🐾] [🍽] [♿] [🌐] [⊷] [✕] [✱] [DATA PORT] [💻] / [✕] [VCR] [🛏] /
FEE   FEE FEE

ECONO LODGE *Book at aaa.com*
Phone: (520)623-5881 **48**

2/1-2/20 1P: $69-$89 2P: $79-$99 XP: $10 F16
1/1-1/31 1P: $39-$89 2P: $39-$89 XP: $5 F16
2/21-12/31 1P: $39-$49 2P: $49-$69 XP: $5 F16

Motel **Location:** I-10, exit 261 (4th-6th Ave), just n. 3020 S 6th Ave 85713. Fax: 520/623-5881. **Facility:** 88 one-bedroom standard units. 2 stories (no elevator), exterior corridors. **Parking:** on-site. **Terms:** [CP] meal plan available. **Amenities:** voice mail. **Pool(s):** outdoor. **Leisure Activities:** whirlpool. **Guest Services:** coin laundry. **Business Services:** fax (fee). **Cards:** AX, DS, MC, VI.

SOME UNITS
[A$K] [S/D] [⊷] [✱] [DATA PORT] / [✕] [🛏] [💻] /
FEE FEE

(See map and index starting on p. 416)

ECONO LODGE INN & SUITES *Book at aaa.com*   **Phone:** (520)747-1440   **46**

△△△ SAVE   2/1-2/18   1P: $80-$100   2P: $85-$105   XP: $5   F17
          2/19-3/31   1P: $55-$85   2P: $60-$90   XP: $5   F17
◇◇◇   4/1-1/31   1P: $40-$60   2P: $50-$65   XP: $5   F17
          Location: I-10, exit 265 (Alvernon Way), 4.4 mi n and e, follow Golf Links Rd at jct, then 0.7 mi n. 1440 S Craycroft Rd
Small-scale Hotel   85711. Fax: 520/750-0144. **Facility:** 67 one-bedroom standard units, some with efficiencies (no utensils). 2 stories (no elevator), exterior corridors. *Bath:* combo or shower only. **Parking:** on-site. **Terms:** cancellation fee imposed. **Amenities:** high-speed Internet, voice mail. *Some:* hair dryers. **Pool(s):** outdoor. **Guest Services:** coin laundry. **Business Services:** PC, fax. **Cards:** AX, CB, DC, DS, JC, MC, VI. **Special Amenities:** free continental breakfast and free local telephone calls.

SOME UNITS

⬛ 🛗 🍴 ♿ 🚐 ⚡ 📠 🖥 / ✕ 🖨 💻 /

EMBASSY SUITES HOTEL @ TUCSON
INTERNATIONAL AIRPORT *Book at aaa.com*   **Phone:** (520)573-0700   **70**

△△△ SAVE   1/1-1/31   1P: $179-$279   2P: $179-$279   XP: $10   F18
          2/1-12/31   1P: $110-$189   2P: $110-$189   XP: $10   F18
◇◇◇◇   **Location:** At entrance to Tucson International Airport. 7051 S Tucson Blvd 85706. Fax: 520/741-9645. **Facility:** 204 one-bedroom suites. 3 stories, exterior corridors. *Bath:* combo or shower only. **Parking:** on-site.
Small-scale Hotel   **Terms:** cancellation fee imposed, package plans, small pets only ($25 deposit). **Amenities:** voice mail, irons, hair dryers. *Fee:* video games, high-speed Internet. **Dining:** 6 am-10 pm, Fri & Sat 7 am-11 pm, cocktails. **Pool(s):** heated outdoor. **Leisure Activities:** sauna, whirlpool, exercise room. **Guest Services:** gift shop, complimentary evening beverages, coin laundry, area transportation-within 5 mi. **Business Services:** meeting rooms, fax (fee). **Cards:** AX, CB, DC, DS, JC, MC, VI. **Special Amenities:** free full breakfast. *(See color ad below)*

SOME UNITS

⬛ ✈ 🐾 🍴 ♿ 🚐 ✕ 📠 🖥 🖨 💻 / ✕ /
FEE

EMBASSY SUITES TUCSON-WILLIAMS CENTER *Book at aaa.com*   **Phone:** (520)745-2700   **33**

△△△ SAVE   2/1-3/31 [BP]   1P: $129-$249   2P: $129-$249   XP: $10   F18
          9/16-1/31 [BP]   1P: $89-$199   2P: $89-$199   XP: $10   F18
◇◇◇◇   4/1-5/31 [BP]   1P: $89-$189   2P: $89-$189   XP: $10   F18
          6/1-9/15 [BP]   1P: $69-$129   2P: $69-$129   XP: $10   F18
Small-scale Hotel   **Location:** Jct Campbell Ave, 3.9 mi e. 5335 E Broadway 85711. Fax: 520/790-9232. **Facility:** 142 one-bedroom suites. 3 stories (no elevator), exterior corridors. *Bath:* combo or shower only. **Parking:** on-site. **Amenities:** voice mail, irons, hair dryers. *Fee:* video games, high-speed Internet. **Pool(s):** heated outdoor. **Leisure Activities:** whirlpool, exercise room. **Guest Services:** sundries, complimentary evening beverages, coin laundry, area transportation-within 5 mi. **Business Services:** meeting rooms, fax (fee). **Cards:** AX, CB, DC, DS, JC, MC, VI. **Special Amenities:** free full breakfast and free newspaper.

SOME UNITS

♿ 🚐 ✕ 📠 🖥 🖨 💻 / ✕ /

FAIRFIELD INN BY MARRIOTT *Book at aaa.com*   **Phone:** 520/747-7474   **55**

◇◇◇   All Year [ECP]   1P: $59-$119   2P: $69-$124   XP: $5   F
          Location: I-10, exit 264 westbound; exit 264B eastbound, just n. 4850 S Hotel Dr 85714. Fax: 520/747-5468.
Small-scale Hotel   **Facility:** 66 one-bedroom standard units. 3 stories, interior corridors. **Parking:** on-site. **Terms:** 3 day cancellation notice. **Amenities:** high-speed Internet, irons, hair dryers. **Pool(s):** heated outdoor. **Leisure Activities:** whirlpool. **Business Services:** fax. **Cards:** AX, CB, DC, DS, MC, VI.

SOME UNITS

ASK ⬛ 🚐 ✕ 📠 💻 / ✕ 🖨 🖨 /

FAIRFIELD INN BY MARRIOTT AT TUCSON
AIRPORT *Book at aaa.com*   **Phone:** (520)295-8800   **67**

△△△ SAVE   2/1-4/2   1P: $139   2P: $139
          4/3-4/30   1P: $109   2P: $109
◇◇◇   5/1-8/31   1P: $79-$89   2P: $79-$89
          9/1-1/31   1P: $69-$89   2P: $69-$89
Small-scale Hotel   **Location:** Just n of Tucson International Airport. 6955 S Tucson Blvd 85706. Fax: 520/295-8898. **Facility:** 86 one-bedroom standard units. 3 stories, interior corridors. *Bath:* combo or shower only. **Parking:** on-site. **Terms:** 3 day cancellation notice-fee imposed. **Amenities:** high-speed Internet, dual phone lines, voice mail, irons, hair dryers. **Pool(s):** small heated outdoor. **Leisure Activities:** whirlpool, exercise room. **Guest Services:** coin laundry, airport transportation-Tucson International Airport. **Business Services:** meeting rooms, business center. **Cards:** AX, CB, DC, DS, JC, MC, VI. **Special Amenities:** free expanded continental breakfast and free local telephone calls.

SOME UNITS

⬛ ✈ 🍴 ♿ 🚐 ✕ 📠 💻 / ✕ 🖨 🖨 /

(See map and index starting on p. 416)

HACIDENDA DEL DESIERTO

Phone: (520)298-1764 [58]

10/1-1/31	1P: $145-$245	2P: $150-$250	XP: $20
2/1-5/31	1P: $140-$230	2P: $145-$235	XP: $20
6/1-9/30	1P: $115-$175	2P: $120-$180	XP: $20

Bed & Breakfast **Location:** Jct Houghton Rd, 2 mi e on Escalante Rd, 1.3 mi s on Old Spanish Tr, then just w on Camino del Desierto Rd, through security gates. 11770 E Rambling Tr 85747. Fax: 520/722-4558. **Facility:** The quiet location near the eastern Saguaro National Park allows you to catch sight of small desert creatures as you lounge on the porch or patio. 4 units. 2 one-bedroom standard units, some with kitchens. 1 one- and 1 two-bedroom suites, some with efficiencies or kitchens. 1 story, exterior corridors. *Bath:* combo or shower only. **Parking:** on-site. **Terms:** check-in 4 pm, 2 night minimum stay - seasonal, 14 day cancellation notice-fee imposed. [ECP] meal plan available. **Amenities:** video library, DVD players, hair dryers. *Some:* irons. **Leisure Activities:** whirlpool, hiking trails. **Guest Services:** gift shop. **Business Services:** fax (fee). **Cards:** AX, DS, MC, VI.

(ASK) [X] (VCR) [symbols]

HAMPTON INN & SUITES *Book at aaa.com*

Phone: 520/618-8000 [11]

2/1-4/30 [BP]	1P: $159-$199	2P: $169-$229	XP: $10	F18
10/1-1/31 [BP]	1P: $119-$169	2P: $129-$179	XP: $10	F18
5/1-9/30 [BP]	1P: $99-$119	2P: $109-$129	XP: $10	F18

Small-scale Hotel **Location:** I-10, exit 250 (Orange Grove Rd), 4 mi e, then 0.5 mi s. 5950 N Oracle Rd 85704. Fax: 520/618-8055. **Facility:** 109 units. 70 one-bedroom standard units. 39 one-bedroom suites with kitchens, some with whirlpools. 3 stories, interior corridors. *Bath:* combo or shower only. **Parking:** on-site. **Amenities:** video games (fee), high-speed Internet, dual phone lines, voice mail, irons, hair dryers. **Pool(s):** heated outdoor. **Leisure Activities:** whirlpool, exercise room. **Guest Services:** sundries, complimentary evening beverages: Mon-Thurs, coin laundry. **Business Services:** meeting rooms, fax. **Cards:** AX, CB, DC, DS, JC, MC, VI.

SOME UNITS

HAMPTON INN NORTH *Book at aaa.com*

Phone: (520)206-0602 [23]

(AAA) (SAVE)

2/1-4/29	1P: $89-$149	2P: $89-$149
9/28-1/31	1P: $89-$119	2P: $89-$119
4/30-9/27	1P: $79-$109	2P: $79-$109

Small-scale Hotel **Location:** I-10, exit 256 (Grant Rd), just w. 1375 W Grant Rd 85745. Fax: 520/206-0610. **Facility:** 91 one-bedroom standard units, some with whirlpools. 5 stories, interior corridors. *Bath:* combo or shower only. **Parking:** on-site. **Terms:** [ECP] meal plan available, package plans, small pets only (in designated units). **Amenities:** video games (fee), high-speed Internet, voice mail, irons, hair dryers. **Pool(s):** heated outdoor. **Leisure Activities:** whirlpool. **Guest Services:** coin laundry. **Business Services:** meeting rooms, PC, fax. **Cards:** AX, CB, DC, DS, MC, VI. **Special Amenities:** free expanded continental breakfast and free local telephone calls. *(See color ad below)*

SOME UNITS

(See map and index starting on p. 416)

HAMPTON INN TUCSON AIRPORT   *Book at aaa.com*   Phone: (520)918-9000 66

Small-scale Hotel

2/1-3/31	1P: $119-$149	2P: $129-$159
9/6-1/31	1P: $89-$129	2P: $99-$139
4/1-4/29	1P: $89-$119	2P: $99-$129
4/30-9/5	1P: $69-$99	2P: $79-$109

Location: Just n of Tucson International Airport. 6971 S Tucson Blvd 85706. Fax: 520/889-4002. **Facility:** 126 one-bedroom standard units. 4 stories, interior corridors. *Bath:* combo or shower only. **Parking:** on-site. **Amenities:** video games (fee), high-speed Internet, voice mail, irons, hair dryers. **Pool(s):** small heated outdoor. **Leisure Activities:** whirlpool, exercise room. **Guest Services:** coin laundry, area transportation. **Business Services:** fax. **Cards:** AX, CB, DC, DS, MC, VI. *(See color ad p 434)*

SOME UNITS

(ASK) (S/D) 🛫 (🍴) 🏊 📷 (DATA PORT) 🔌 📷 📺 / ⊠ /

HILTON-TUCSON EAST   *Book at aaa.com*   Phone: (520)721-5600 37

AAA SAVE

Large-scale Hotel

All Year	1P: $59-$239	2P: $79-$259

Location: 0.5 mi e of Kolb Rd. 7600 E Broadway 85710. Fax: 520/721-5696. **Facility:** 233 units. 224 one-bedroom standard units. 9 one-bedroom suites. 7 stories, interior corridors. *Bath:* combo or shower only. **Parking:** on-site. **Terms:** cancellation fee imposed, [BP] & [CP] meal plans available, package plans. **Amenities:** video games (fee), dual phone lines, voice mail, irons, hair dryers. *Some:* CD players. **Dining:** 6 am-2 & 5-10 pm, Sat & Sun from 6:30 am, cocktails. **Pool(s):** heated outdoor. **Leisure Activities:** whirlpool, exercise room. **Guest Services:** gift shop, valet laundry, area transportation-within 3 mi. **Business Services:** conference facilities, business center. **Cards:** AX, CB, DC, DS, JC, MC, VI. **Special Amenities:** early check-in/late check-out and free room upgrade (subject to availability with advance reservations).** *(See color ad below)*

SOME UNITS

(S/D) (🍴) ⓜ (♿) 📷 🏊 📷 (DATA PORT) 📺 / ⊠ 🔌 📷 /
FEE FEE

HOLIDAY INN EXPRESS HOTEL & SUITES TUCSON
AIRPORT   *Book at aaa.com*   Phone: 520/889-6600 62

AAA SAVE

Small-scale Hotel

2/1-4/30	1P: $129-$159	2P: $129-$159	XP: $10	F18
1/1-1/31	1P: $119-$149	2P: $119-$149	XP: $10	F18
10/1-12/31	1P: $89-$119	2P: $89-$119	XP: $10	F18
5/1-9/30	1P: $79-$109	2P: $79-$109	XP: $10	F18

Location: 0.5 mi n of entrance to Tucson International Airport. 2548 E Medina Rd 85706. Fax: 520/889-6168. **Facility:** 97 units. 91 one-bedroom standard units. 6 one-bedroom suites. 3 stories, interior corridors. *Bath:* combo or shower only. **Parking:** on-site. **Terms:** [ECP] meal plan available, small pets only ($50 deposit). **Amenities:** video games (fee), high-speed Internet, voice mail, irons, hair dryers. **Pool(s):** heated outdoor. **Leisure Activities:** whirlpool, exercise room. **Guest Services:** coin laundry, area transportation-within 5 mi. **Business Services:** business center. **Cards:** AX, CB, DC, DS, JC, MC, VI. **Special Amenities:** free expanded continental breakfast and free local telephone calls.

SOME UNITS

(S/D) 🛫 🛏 (🍴) ⓜ (♿) 🏊 📷 (DATA PORT) 📺 / ⊠ 🔌 📷 /
FEE

HOLIDAY INN EXPRESS SUITES-TUCSON MALL   *Book at aaa.com*   Phone: (520)202-5000 15

Small-scale Hotel

2/1-2/11	1P: $199	2P: $209-$229	XP: $10	F18
2/12-3/31	1P: $139-$149	2P: $149-$169	XP: $10	F18
4/1-5/31	1P: $119-$149	2P: $129-$159	XP: $10	F18
6/1-1/31	1P: $89-$129	2P: $99-$139	XP: $10	F18

Location: Just w of N 1st Ave. 620 E Wetmore Rd 85705. Fax: 520/202-5050. **Facility:** Designated smoking area. 105 units. 103 one-bedroom standard units, some with whirlpools. 2 one-bedroom suites ($179-$299) with efficiencies. 3 stories, interior corridors. *Bath:* combo or shower only. **Parking:** on-site. **Amenities:** video games (fee), high-speed Internet, dual phone lines, voice mail, safes, irons, hair dryers. **Pool(s):** heated outdoor. **Leisure Activities:** whirlpool, exercise room. **Guest Services:** coin laundry. **Business Services:** meeting rooms, business center. **Cards:** AX, DC, DS, MC, VI.

(ASK) (S/D) (🍴) (♿) 🏊 ⊠ 📷 (DATA PORT) 🔌 📷 📺

(See map and index starting on p. 416)

HOLIDAY INN-PALO VERDE *Book at aaa.com*

Phone: (520)746-1161   52

AAA [SAVE]
▽▽◆◇▽▽

2/1-4/2	1P: $99-$114	2P: $99-$114
9/12-1/31	1P: $76-$114	2P: $76-$114
4/3-5/14	1P: $76-$109	2P: $76-$109
5/15-9/11	1P: $69-$89	2P: $69-$89

Small-scale Hotel **Location:** I-10, exit 264 westbound; exit 264B eastbound, 0.5 mi n. 4550 S Palo Verde Blvd 85714. Fax: 520/741-1170. **Facility:** 301 units. 250 one-bedroom standard units. 51 one-bedroom suites ($79-$209). 3-6 stories, interior/exterior corridors. *Bath:* combo or shower only. **Parking:** on-site. **Terms:** cancellation fee imposed, [AP], [BP], [CP] & [ECP] meal plans available, package plans. **Amenities:** video games (fee), high-speed Internet, voice mail, irons, hair dryers. **Dining:** 6 am-2 & 5-10 pm, Sat & Sun 7 am-1 & 5-10 pm, cocktails. **Pool(s):** heated outdoor. **Leisure Activities:** whirlpool, lighted tennis court, exercise room. *Fee:* massage. **Guest Services:** gift shop, coin laundry. **Business Services:** conference facilities, PC, fax (fee). **Cards:** AX, CB, DC, DS, JC, MC, VI. **Special Amenities:** free newspaper. *(See color ad below)*

SOME UNITS
[icons] / FEE

INDIAN HILL BED & BREAKFAST

Phone: 520/760-4200   18

▽▽◆◇▽▽

2/1-5/31 & 10/1-1/31	1P: $110-$140	2P: $120-$150	XP: $15 F12
6/1-9/30	1P: $90-$120	2P: $100-$130	XP: $15 F12

Bed & Breakfast **Location:** Jct of Speedway, 1.2 mi n on Houghton, just w on Tanque Verde, then 0.7 mi n. 2955 N Tomahawk Tr 85749. Fax: 520/760-5042. **Facility:** Oversized rooms filled with custom designed furnishings offer you a comfortable stay. Some rooms have private gardens with lounging swing sets. Designated smoking area. 4 units. 3 one-bedroom standard units. 1 one-bedroom suite. 1 story, interior/exterior corridors. *Bath:* shower only. **Parking:** on-site. **Terms:** 3 day cancellation notice-fee imposed. **Amenities:** video library, DVD players, CD players, hair dryers. **Business Services:** fax. **Cards:** DS, MC, VI.

SOME UNITS
[icons] / FEE

JEREMIAH INN BED & BREAKFAST

Phone: (520)749-3072   13

▽▽◆◇▽▽

All Year [BP]   1P: $90-$120   2P: $100-$130   F6

Bed & Breakfast **Location:** Jct Grant Rd, 3.6 mi ne on Tanque Verde Rd, 3.7 mi ne on Catalina Hwy, then just w. Located in a quiet residential area. 10921 E Snyder Rd 85749. **Facility:** A contemporary home with Southwestern architecture located in a peaceful desert setting right at the foothills of the Catalina Mountains. Smoke free premises. 4 units. 3 one- and 1 two-bedroom standard units. 1 story, interior corridors. **Parking:** on-site. **Amenities:** video library, hair dryers. *Some:* DVD players. **Pool(s):** small outdoor. **Leisure Activities:** whirlpool. **Guest Services:** complimentary laundry. **Cards:** AX, DS, MC, VI.

SOME UNITS
[icons] / VCR /

JW MARRIOTT STARR PASS RESORT & SPA *Book at aaa.com*

Phone: (520)792-3500   39

▽▽◆◇▽▽ ▽▽◆◇▽▽

2/1-4/16	1P: $299-$499	2P: $299-$499
4/17-5/28 & 9/11-1/31	1P: $229-$399	2P: $229-$399
5/29-9/10	1P: $129-$249	2P: $129-$249

Large-scale Hotel **Location:** I-10, exit 259 (Star Pass Blvd), 4.8 mi w. 3800 W Starr Pass Blvd 85745. Fax: 520/792-3351. **Facility:** Carved out of the hillside looking south across the valley toward Mexico, this elegant setting highlights the comfortable upscale rooms and spacious baths. 575 units. 560 one-bedroom standard units. 15 one-bedroom suites. 6 stories, interior corridors. **Parking:** valet. **Terms:** check-in 4 pm, 7 day cancellation notice, package plans. **Amenities:** CD players, dual phone lines, voice mail, safes, honor bars, irons, hair dryers. *Fee:* video games, high-speed Internet. **Dining:** Primo, see separate listing. **Pool(s):** heated outdoor. **Leisure Activities:** sauna, whirlpools, steamroom, 2 tennis courts, exercise room, spa. *Fee:* golf-27 holes. **Guest Services:** gift shop, complimentary laundry, area transportation. **Business Services:** conference facilities, business center. **Cards:** AX, CB, DC, DS, JC, MC, VI.

SOME UNITS
[icons] / [icon] /

(See map and index starting on p. 416)

LA POSADA DEL VALLE BED & BREAKFAST   Phone: (520)795-3840   **26**

AAA [SAVE]   2/1-6/23 & 9/1-1/31   2P: $129-$169
▽▽▽▽   6/24-8/31   2P: $89-$119
Location: I-10, exit 257 (Speedway Blvd), 2.4 mi e, then 0.5 mi n. Located in a residential area along a busy
Bed & Breakfast   thoroughfare. 1640 N Campbell Ave 85719. Fax: 520/795-0876. **Facility:** This Joessler-designed adobe home
dating from 1929 has guest quarters decorated with period furniture and surrounds attractive gardens.
Smoke free premises. 6 units. 5 one-bedroom standard units. 1 cottage. 1 story, exterior corridors. **Parking:**
on-site. **Terms:** office hours 8 am-9 pm, check-in 3:30 pm, age restrictions may apply, 14 day cancellation notice-fee imposed,
package plans. **Amenities:** video library, hair dryers. **Guest Services:** complimentary evening beverages. **Business Services:**
fax (fee). **Cards:** AX, MC, VI. **Special Amenities:** free full breakfast and free local telephone calls.

SOME UNITS
[⊹] [✕] [▦] / [VCR] [✆] [🛏] [🖳] [🖵] /
FEE

LA QUINTA INN & SUITES TUCSON AIRPORT   *Book at aaa.com*   Phone: (520)573-3333   **68**

AAA [SAVE]   4/1-4/30 [CP]   1P: $106-$116   2P: $113-$123   XP: $7   F18
▽▽▽▽   2/1-3/31 [CP]   1P: $105-$115   2P: $112-$122   XP: $7   F18
5/1-1/31 [CP]   1P: $89-$99   2P: $96-$106   XP: $7   F18
Location: Just n of Tucson International Airport. 7001 S Tucson Blvd 85706. Fax: 520/573-7710. **Facility:** 143
Small-scale Hotel   units. 135 one-bedroom standard units. 8 one-bedroom suites ($109-$156). 4 stories, interior corridors.
Bath: combo or shower only. **Parking:** on-site. **Terms:** small pets only. **Amenities:** video games (fee), high-
speed Internet, voice mail, irons, hair dryers. **Pool(s):** heated outdoor. **Leisure Activities:** whirlpool, exercise room. **Guest
Services:** coin laundry. **Business Services:** meeting rooms, fax (fee). **Cards:** AX, CB, DC, DS, MC, VI. **Special Amenities:**
free expanded continental breakfast and free local telephone calls. *(See color ad below)*

SOME UNITS
[✦] [🛏] [¶†] [&M] [♿] [⊘] [➘] [▦] [DATA PORT] [🖳] / [✕] [🛏] [🖳] /

LA QUINTA INN DOWNTOWN   *Book at aaa.com*   Phone: (520)624-4455   **43**

▽▽▽▽   2/1-3/31   1P: $99-$119   2P: $99-$119
10/1-1/31   1P: $79-$99   2P: $79-$99
Small-scale Hotel   4/1-9/30   1P: $59-$89   2P: $59-$89
Location: I-10, exit 259 (Starr Pass Blvd), just w. 750 Starr Pass Blvd 85713. Fax: 520/624-3172. **Facility:** 98 units.
97 one-bedroom standard units. 1 one-bedroom suite ($79-$129). 2 stories, interior corridors. *Bath:* combo or shower only.
Parking: on-site. **Amenities:** voice mail, safes, irons, hair dryers. **Pool(s):** heated outdoor. **Leisure Activities:** whirlpool. **Guest
Services:** coin laundry. **Business Services:** fax (fee). **Cards:** AX, CB, DC, DS, MC, VI. *(See color ad below)*

SOME UNITS
[A$K] [S⊘D] [🛏] [¶†] [♿] [⊘] [➘] [▦] [DATA PORT] [🖳] / [✕] [🛏] [🖳] /
FEE   FEE

LA QUINTA INN TUCSON (EAST)   *Book at aaa.com*   Phone: (520)747-1414   **34**

AAA [SAVE]   2/1-3/31 [CP]   1P: $99-$109   2P: $106-$116   XP: $7   F18
▽▽▽▽   4/1-1/31 [CP]   1P: $67-$77   2P: $74-$84   XP: $7   F18
Location: Just e of Wilmot Rd. 6404 E Broadway 85710. Fax: 520/745-6903. **Facility:** 140 one-bedroom
Small-scale Hotel   standard units. 2 stories (no elevator), exterior corridors. *Bath:* combo or shower only. **Parking:** on-site.
Terms: small pets only. **Amenities:** video games (fee), voice mail, irons, hair dryers. *Some:* high-speed
Internet. **Pool(s):** heated outdoor. **Leisure Activities:** whirlpool. **Guest Services:** coin laundry. **Business
Services:** meeting rooms, fax (fee). **Cards:** AX, CB, DC, DS, MC, VI. **Special Amenities:** free expanded continental
breakfast and free local telephone calls. *(See color ad below)*

SOME UNITS
[🛏] [¶†] [➘] [⊹] [▦] [DATA PORT] [🖳] / [✕] [🛏] [🖳] /
FEE   FEE

(See map and index starting on p. 416)

LAZY 8 MOTEL
AAA SAVE

2/1-4/18	1P: $39-$46	2P: $45-$52	XP: $5 F12
4/19-6/1	1P: $35-$45	2P: $40-$50	XP: $5 F12
12/2-1/31	1P: $37-$47	2P: $39-$49	XP: $5 F12
6/2-12/1	1P: $35-$45	2P: $37-$42	XP: $5 F12

Phone: (520)622-3336 [49]

Motel **Location:** I-10, exit 261, south side on frontage road; just e of 6th Ave. 314 E Benson Hwy 85713. Fax: 520/882-5496. **Facility:** 48 one-bedroom standard units, some with efficiencies or kitchens. 1-2 stories (no elevator), exterior corridors. *Bath:* combo or shower only. **Parking:** on-site. **Terms:** [ECP] meal plan available. **Amenities:** voice mail. *Some:* hair dryers. **Pool(s):** heated outdoor. **Guest Services:** coin laundry. **Cards:** AX, DS, MC, VI. **Special Amenities:** free expanded continental breakfast and free local telephone calls. *(See color ad below)*

SOME UNITS
(icons)

THE LODGE AT VENTANA CANYON
AAA SAVE

2/1-4/18	1P: $199-$549	2P: $199-$549	XP: $25 F17
5/1-5/21 & 9/8-1/31	1P: $149-$449	2P: $149-$449	XP: $25 F17
5/22-9/7	1P: $79-$185	2P: $79-$185	XP: $25 F17

Phone: (520)577-4000 [7]

Resort
Large-scale Hotel **Location:** I-10, exit 256 (Grant Rd), 8.6 mi e to Tanque Verde Rd, 0.6 mi e to Sabino Canyon Rd, 2 mi n, then 3.2 mi on Kolb Rd. Located in a residential resort area. 6200 N Clubhouse Ln 85750. Fax: 520/577-4063. **Facility:** This resort at the foot of the Catalina Mountains has spacious rooms, luxurious baths, and all are provided in an intimate setting. 50 units. 32 one-bedroom standard units with efficiencies. 15 one- and 3 two-bedroom suites with efficiencies. 2 stories, interior/exterior corridors. *Bath:* combo or shower only. **Parking:** on-site and valet. **Terms:** check-in 4 pm, 1-3 night minimum stay - seasonal, 21 day cancellation notice-fee imposed, package plans, $20 service charge, small pets only ($50 fee). **Amenities:** CD players, high-speed Internet (fee), voice mail, safes, honor bars, irons, hair dryers. **Dining:** 6 am-10 pm, cocktails. **Pool(s):** heated outdoor. **Leisure Activities:** whirlpool, 12 lighted tennis courts, croquet, jogging, exercise room. *Fee:* golf-36 holes, bicycles, massage. **Guest Services:** gift shop, valet laundry, area transportation-within 3 mi. **Business Services:** meeting rooms, PC. **Cards:** AX, DC, DS, MC, VI.

SOME UNITS
(icons)
FEE FEE

LODGE ON THE DESERT   *Book at aaa.com*
AAA SAVE

2/1-4/15 [ECP]	1P: $189-$289	2P: $189-$289	XP: $15 F18
4/16-5/14 & 9/18-1/31 [ECP]	1P: $129-$202	2P: $129-$202	XP: $15 F18
5/15-9/17 [ECP]	1P: $89-$134	2P: $89-$134	XP: $15 F18

Phone: (520)325-3366 [29]

Small-scale Hotel **Location:** I-10, exit 258 (Broadway Blvd/Congress St), 4 mi e, then just n. 306 N Alvernon Way 85711. Fax: 520/327-5834. **Facility:** Designated smoking area. 35 units. 31 one-bedroom standard units. 4 one-bedroom suites, some with kitchens (no utensils). 1-2 stories (no elevator), exterior corridors. **Parking:** on-site. **Terms:** cancellation fee imposed, pets ($50 deposit, $15 extra charge). **Amenities:** irons, hair dryers. **Dining:** Lodge on the Desert, see separate listing. **Pool(s):** heated outdoor. **Guest Services:** valet laundry. **Business Services:** meeting rooms. **Cards:** AX, DC, DS, MC, VI. **Special Amenities:** free expanded continental breakfast.

SOME UNITS
(icons)
FEE

(See map and index starting on p. 416)

LOEWS VENTANA CANYON RESORT · *Book at aaa.com* · Phone: (520)299-2020 · **6**

AAA SAVE

2/1-5/13	1P: $179-$379	2P: $179-$379	XP: $25 F17
9/13-1/31	1P: $169-$359	2P: $169-$359	XP: $25 F17
5/14-9/12	1P: $99-$249	2P: $99-$249	XP: $25 F17

Resort
Large-scale Hotel

Location: I-10, exit 256 (Grant Rd), 8.6 mi e, 0.6 mi ne on Tanque Verde Rd, 2 mi n on Sabino Canyon Rd, then 3.5 mi n on Kolb Rd. Located in a quiet area. 7000 N Resort Dr 85750. Fax: 520/299-6832. **Facility:** The elegant building, reminiscent of Frank L. Wright, sits at the base of the Catalina Mountains and is surrounded by full resort facilities. 398 units. 379 one-bedroom standard units. 19 one-bedroom suites ($249-$3500), some with whirlpools. 3-4 stories, interior/exterior corridors. *Bath:* combo or shower only. **Parking:** valet and street. **Terms:** 1-4 night minimum stay - seasonal and/or weekends, 7 day cancellation notice-fee imposed. **Amenities:** CD players, high-speed Internet (fee), dual phone lines, voice mail, safes, honor bars, irons, hair dryers. *Some:* DVD players. **Dining:** 4 restaurants, 6 am-10 pm, cocktails, also, The Ventana Room, see separate listing, entertainment. **Pool(s):** 2 heated outdoor. **Leisure Activities:** saunas, whirlpools, steamrooms, PAR course, recreation programs, rental bicycles, hiking trails, playground, spa, basketball. *Fee:* golf-36 holes, 8 lighted tennis courts. **Guest Services:** gift shop, valet laundry, area transportation-within 2 mi. **Business Services:** conference facilities, business center. **Cards:** AX, DC, DS, JC, MC, VI. *(See color ad below)*

SOME UNITS

MOTEL 6 TUCSON-22ND STREET #1196 · *Book at aaa.com* · Phone: 520/624-2516 · **45**

2/1-2/16	1P: $69-$79	2P: $75-$85	XP: $3 F17
2/17-4/2	1P: $39-$49	2P: $45-$55	XP: $3 F17
12/2-1/31	1P: $38-$48	2P: $44-$54	XP: $3 F17
4/3-12/1	1P: $35-$45	2P: $41-$51	XP: $3 F17

Motel

Location: I-10, exit 259 (Starr Pass Blvd), just w, then just s on frontage road. 1222 S Freeway Rd 85713. Fax: 520/624-1697. **Facility:** 98 one-bedroom standard units. 3 stories, exterior corridors. *Bath:* combo or shower only. **Parking:** on-site. **Terms:** small pets only. **Pool(s):** small outdoor. **Guest Services:** coin laundry. **Business Services:** fax (fee). **Cards:** AX, CB, DC, DS, MC, VI.

SOME UNITS

MOTEL 6 TUCSON-BENSON HWY SOUTH #271 · *Book at aaa.com* · Phone: 520/628-1264 · **51**

2/1-2/16	1P: $69-$79	2P: $75-$85	XP: $3 F17
2/17-4/2	1P: $44-$54	2P: $50-$60	XP: $3 F17
4/3-1/31	1P: $35-$45	2P: $41-$51	XP: $3 F17

Motel

Location: I-10, exit 262, 0.3 mi se. 1031 E Benson Hwy 85713. Fax: 520/624-1731. **Facility:** 145 one-bedroom standard units. 2 stories (no elevator), exterior corridors. *Bath:* shower only. **Parking:** on-site. **Pool(s):** heated outdoor. **Guest Services:** coin laundry. **Business Services:** fax (fee). **Cards:** AX, CB, DC, DS, MC, VI.

SOME UNITS

(See map and index starting on p. 416)

MOTEL 6 TUCSON-CONGRESS STREET #50   *Book at aaa.com*   Phone: 520/628-1339   **40**

	2/1-2/16	1P: $69-$79	2P: $75-$85	XP: $3	F17
	2/17-4/2	1P: $41-$51	2P: $47-$57	XP: $3	F17
Motel	4/3-1/31	1P: $38-$48	2P: $44-$54	XP: $3	F17

Location: I-10, exit 258 (Broadway Blvd/Congress St), 0.7 mi s on west side of interstate. 960 S Freeway 85745. Fax: 520/624-1848. **Facility:** 111 one-bedroom standard units. 2 stories (no elevator), exterior corridors. *Bath:* shower only. **Parking:** on-site. **Terms:** small pets only. **Pool(s):** heated outdoor. **Guest Services:** coin laundry. **Business Services:** fax (fee). **Cards:** AX, CB, DC, DS, MC, VI.

SOME UNITS

MOTEL 6 TUCSON NORTH #1127   *Book at aaa.com*   Phone: 520/744-9300   **3**

	2/1-2/16	1P: $69-$79	2P: $75-$85	XP: $3	F17
	2/17-4/2	1P: $49-$59	2P: $55-$65	XP: $3	F17
Motel	4/3-12/15	1P: $36-$46	2P: $42-$52	XP: $3	F17
	12/16-1/31	1P: $34-$44	2P: $40-$50	XP: $3	F17

Location: I-10, exit 248 (Ina Rd), just e to Camino de Oeste. 4630 W Ina Rd 85741. Fax: 520/744-2439. **Facility:** 118 one-bedroom standard units. 2 stories, interior corridors. *Bath:* combo or shower only. **Parking:** on-site. **Pool(s):** heated outdoor. **Guest Services:** coin laundry. **Business Services:** fax (fee). **Cards:** AX, CB, DC, DS, MC, VI.

SOME UNITS
FEE   FEE

OMNI TUCSON NATIONAL GOLF RESORT & SPA   *Book at aaa.com*   Phone: (520)297-2271   **1**

	9/1-1/31	1P: $169-$439	2P: $169-$439	XP: $25	F18
	2/1-4/30	1P: $259-$399	2P: $259-$399	XP: $25	F18
	5/1-5/31	1P: $169-$289	2P: $169-$289	XP: $25	F18
	6/1-8/31	1P: $109-$219	2P: $109-$219	XP: $25	F18

Resort   **Location:** I-10, exit 246 (Cortaro Rd), 3.5 mi e, then n on Shannon Rd. 2727 W Club Dr 85742. Fax: 520/297-7544.
Large-scale Hotel   **Facility:** Set on several manicured acres, the resort's guest rooms, suites and haciendas overlook a golf course; an extensive health spa is on site. 167 units. 143 one-bedroom standard units. 24 one-bedroom suites ($139-$399) with kitchens. 1-2 stories (no elevator), exterior corridors. **Parking:** on-site and valet. **Terms:** check-in 4 pm, 7 day cancellation notice-fee imposed, package plans, $12 service charge, small pets only ($75 fee). **Amenities:** video games (fee), CD players, dual phone lines, voice mail, honor bars, irons, hair dryers. *Some:* high-speed Internet. **Dining:** 3 restaurants, 6:30 am-11 pm, cocktails. **Pool(s):** 2 heated outdoor. **Leisure Activities:** saunas, whirlpools, steamrooms, golf-36 holes, croquet, pool tables, spa, sports court, basketball, horseshoes, volleyball. *Fee:* 4 lighted tennis courts. **Guest Services:** gift shop, valet laundry. **Business Services:** conference facilities, business center. **Cards:** AX, CB, DC, DS, JC, MC, VI.

SOME UNITS
FEE   FEE   FEE

QUALITY INN AT TUCSON AIRPORT   *Book at aaa.com*   Phone: (520)294-2500   **59**

	2/1-2/15	1P: $99-$150	2P: $110-$180
	2/16-3/31	1P: $89-$140	2P: $99-$150
	1/11-1/31	1P: $69-$99	2P: $79-$110
	4/1-1/10	1P: $49-$69	2P: $59-$79

Small-scale Hotel   **Location:** 1 mi ne of Tucson International Airport; just e of Tucson Blvd. 2803 E Valencia Rd 85706. Fax: 520/741-0851. **Facility:** 97 units. 92 one-bedroom standard units. 5 one-bedroom suites ($79-$150). 3 stories, interior/exterior corridors. **Parking:** on-site. **Terms:** small pets only. **Amenities:** high-speed Internet, irons, hair dryers. **Pool(s):** heated outdoor. **Leisure Activities:** whirlpool. **Guest Services:** coin laundry, area transportation-within 5 mi. **Business Services:** meeting rooms, fax (fee). **Cards:** AX, CB, DC, DS, MC, VI. **Special Amenities:** free expanded continental breakfast and free local telephone calls.

SOME UNITS
FEE

(See map and index starting on p. 416)

RADISSON SUITES TUCSON

Phone: (520)721-7100   **27**

2/1-4/30	1P: $139-$199	2P: $139-$199	XP: $10 F17
5/1-5/25 & 9/4-1/31	1P: $89-$149	2P: $89-$149	XP: $10 F17
5/26-9/3	1P: $69-$109	2P: $69-$109	XP: $10 F17

Location: Just e of Wilmot Rd. 6555 E Speedway Blvd 85710. Fax: 520/721-1991. **Facility:** 299 one-bedroom suites, some with whirlpools. 5 stories, exterior corridors. **Parking:** on-site. **Terms:** cancellation fee imposed, [BP] meal plan available, package plans, small pets only ($50 fee). **Amenities:** voice mail, irons, hair dryers. **Dining:** 6 am-11 pm, Sat & Sun from 7 am, cocktails. **Pool(s):** heated outdoor. **Leisure Activities:** whirlpool, exercise room. *Fee:* game room. **Guest Services:** gift shop, valet and coin laundry, area transportation-within 5 mi. **Business Services:** conference facilities, PC, fax (fee). **Cards:** AX, CB, DC, DS, MC, VI. **Special Amenities:** free newspaper and preferred room (subject to availability with advance reservations).

Large-scale Hotel

SOME UNITS

RAMADA INN & SUITES FOOTHILLS RESORT   *Book at aaa.com*

Phone: (520)886-9595   **22**

2/1-3/31 [ECP]	1P: $99-$199	2P: $99-$199	XP: $12 F16
4/1-5/31 & 10/1-1/31 [ECP]	1P: $79-$129	2P: $79-$129	XP: $12 F16
6/1-9/30 [ECP]	1P: $49-$89	2P: $49-$89	XP: $12 F16

Location: Jct Campbell Ave, 5.5 mi e on Grant Rd, then just ne. 6944 E Tanque Verde Rd 85715. Fax: 520/721-8466. **Facility:** 113 units. 52 one-bedroom standard units. 61 one-bedroom suites. 2 stories, exterior corridors. **Parking:** on-site. **Terms:** cancellation fee imposed, small pets only ($25 fee). **Amenities:** high-speed Internet, voice mail, safes (fee), irons, hair dryers. **Pool(s):** heated outdoor. **Leisure Activities:** saunas, whirlpool. **Guest Services:** complimentary evening beverages, coin laundry. **Business Services:** meeting rooms. *Fee:* PC, fax. **Cards:** AX, CB, DC, DS, JC, MC, VI. **Special Amenities:** free expanded continental breakfast and free local telephone calls.

Small-scale Hotel

(See color ad below)

SOME UNITS

RED ROOF INN-TUCSON SOUTH   *Book at aaa.com*

Phone: (520)571-1400   **56**

2/1-3/14	1P: $58-$69	2P: $63-$74	XP: $5 F18
3/15-12/31	1P: $45-$58	2P: $50-$63	XP: $5 F18
1/1-1/31	1P: $46-$53	2P: $51-$58	XP: $5 F18

Motel

Location: I-10, exit 264 westbound; exit 264B eastbound. 3704 E Irvington Rd 85714. Fax: 520/519-0051. **Facility:** 118 one-bedroom standard units. 2 stories, exterior corridors. *Bath:* combo or shower only. **Parking:** on-site. **Terms:** small pets only. **Amenities:** video games (fee), voice mail. **Pool(s):** heated outdoor. **Leisure Activities:** whirlpool. **Business Services:** fax (fee). **Cards:** AX, CB, DC, DS, MC, VI.

SOME UNITS

(See map and index starting on p. 416)

RESIDENCE INN BY MARRIOTT   *Book at aaa.com*
Phone: (520)721-0991   **28**

2/1-4/30 [BP]	1P: $139-$189	2P: $139-$189
5/1-1/31 [BP]	1P: $99-$139	2P: $99-$139

Small-scale Hotel **Location:** Just e of Wilmot Rd. 6477 E Speedway Blvd 85710. Fax: 520/290-8323. **Facility:** 128 one-bedroom standard units with efficiencies. 2 stories, exterior corridors. *Bath:* combo or shower only. **Parking:** on-site. **Terms:** check-in 4 pm, 10 day cancellation notice, pets ($75 fee). **Amenities:** video library, high-speed Internet, voice mail, irons, hair dryers. **Pool(s):** heated outdoor. **Leisure Activities:** whirlpool, exercise room, sports court. **Guest Services:** sundries, complimentary evening beverages: Mon-Thurs, coin laundry. **Business Services:** meeting rooms, business center. **Cards:** AX, CB, DC, DS, JC, MC, VI. *(See color ad below)*

SOME UNITS
(ASK) [🛏] [⛉] [📶] [🏊] [✕] [🎥] [DATA PORT] [🔌] [📺] [▤] [✕] (VCR) / FEE

RESIDENCE INN BY MARRIOTT WILLIAMS CENTRE   *Book at aaa.com*
Phone: (520)790-6100   **35**

2/1-4/15	1P: $169-$249	2P: $169-$249
4/16-5/13 & 9/10-1/31	1P: $99-$189	2P: $99-$189
5/14-9/9	1P: $69-$129	2P: $69-$129

Small-scale Hotel **Location:** Jct Campbell Ave, 3.8 mi e on Broadway Blvd, then just s and just e on Williams Centre. 5400 E Williams Cir 85711. Fax: 520/790-6107. **Facility:** 120 units. 53 one-bedroom standard units with efficiencies. 54 one- and 13 two-bedroom suites with efficiencies. 4 stories, interior corridors. *Bath:* combo or shower only. **Parking:** on-site. **Terms:** check-in 4 pm, weekly rates available, pets ($75 fee). **Amenities:** high-speed Internet, voice mail, irons, hair dryers. **Pool(s):** heated outdoor. **Leisure Activities:** whirlpool, exercise room, sports court. **Guest Services:** sundries, coin laundry, area transportation. **Business Services:** meeting rooms, fax (fee). **Cards:** AX, CB, DC, DS, JC, MC, VI.

SOME UNITS
(ASK) (S/D) [🛏] [🍴] [⛥M] [⛉] [📶] [🏊] [✕] [🎥] [DATA PORT] [🔌] [📺] [▤] /[✕] FEE

RODEWAY INN I-10 & GRANT RD   *Book at aaa.com*
Phone: (520)622-7791   **24**

2/1-2/11 [CP]	1P: $129	2P: $139	XP: $10	F18
2/12-4/1 [CP]	1P: $79	2P: $89	XP: $10	F18
7/30-1/31 [CP]	1P: $69	2P: $79	XP: $10	F18
4/2-7/29 [CP]	1P: $59	2P: $69	XP: $10	F18

Motel **Location:** I-10, exit 256 (Grant Rd), just w. 1365 W Grant Rd 85745. Fax: 520/629-0201. **Facility:** 147 one-bedroom standard units. 2 stories (no elevator), exterior corridors. **Parking:** on-site. **Terms:** 15 day cancellation notice, pets ($10 fee, in smoking units). **Dining:** 6 am-10 & 5-9 pm, Sun 7 am-9 pm. **Pool(s):** heated outdoor. **Leisure Activities:** whirlpool, exercise room. **Guest Services:** coin laundry. **Business Services:** meeting rooms, PC, fax (fee). **Cards:** AX, DC, DS, MC, VI. **Special Amenities:** free continental breakfast and free local telephone calls.

SOME UNITS
(S/D) [⊷] [🛏] [🍴] [📺] [📶] [🏊] [DATA PORT] [🔌] [📺] /[✕] FEE

SHERATON TUCSON HOTEL & SUITES   *Book at aaa.com*
Phone: (520)323-6262   **20**

12/31-1/31	1P: $269-$289	2P: $269-$289	XP: $15	F17
2/1-4/29	1P: $259-$279	2P: $259-$279	XP: $15	F17
9/3-12/30	1P: $229-$249	2P: $229-$249	XP: $15	F17
4/30-9/2	1P: $164-$184	2P: $164-$184	XP: $15	F17

Location: Jct Campbell Ave, 3.6 mi e. 5151 E Grant Rd 85712. Fax: 520/325-2989. **Facility:** 216 units. 81 one-bedroom standard units. 135 one-bedroom suites. 4 stories, interior/exterior corridors. *Bath:* combo or shower only. **Parking:** on-site. **Terms:** small pets only. **Amenities:** dual phone lines, voice mail, irons, hair dryers. *Fee:* video games, high-speed Internet. **Pool(s):** heated outdoor. **Leisure Activities:** sauna, whirlpool, steamroom, sports court. **Guest Services:** gift shop, valet and coin laundry. **Business Services:** conference facilities, business center. **Cards:** AX, DS, MC, VI.

SOME UNITS
(ASK) (S/D) [🛏] [🍴] [⛥M] [⛉] [📶] [🏊] [✕] [🎥] [DATA PORT] [🔌] [📺] [▤] /[✕] [🔌] / FEE

STARR PASS GOLF SUITES   *Book at aaa.com*
Phone: (520)670-0500   **41**

2/1-5/16	1P: $179-$309	2P: $179-$309
10/1-1/31	1P: $119-$179	2P: $119-$179
5/17-9/30	1P: $89-$139	2P: $89-$139

Small-scale Hotel **Location:** I-10, exit 259 (Starr Pass Blvd), 3.8 mi w. 3645 W Starr Pass Blvd 85745. Fax: 520/670-0427. **Facility:** Designated smoking area. 80 units. 40 one-bedroom standard units. 40 two-bedroom suites with efficiencies. 1 story, exterior corridors. **Parking:** on-site. **Terms:** office hours 6 am-midnight, check-in 4 pm, 7 day cancellation notice-fee imposed. **Amenities:** voice mail, irons, hair dryers. *Fee:* video library, high-speed Internet. **Pool(s):** heated outdoor. **Leisure Activities:** whirlpool, 2 tennis courts, hiking trails, exercise room. *Fee:* golf-27 holes. **Business Services:** meeting rooms, PC. **Cards:** AX, DC, DS, MC, VI.

[🍴] [📺] [🏊] [✕] [✕] (VCR) [🎥] [🔌] [📺] [▤]

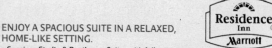

(See map and index starting on p. 416)

STUDIO 6 EXTENDED STAY #6002 — *Book at aaa.com* — Phone: 520/746-0030 — 57
▼▼▼ ◆
Motel

	1P: $63-$73	2P: $67-$77	XP: $4	F17
2/1-3/25				
3/26-1/31	1P: $44-$54	2P: $48-$58	XP: $4	F17

Location: I-10, exit 264A eastbound; exit 264B westbound, just s, then just nw on Julian Dr. 4950 S Outlet Center Dr 85706. Fax: 520/741-7403. **Facility:** 120 one-bedroom standard units with efficiencies. 2 stories (no elevator), exterior corridors. *Bath:* combo or shower only. **Parking:** on-site. **Terms:** office hours 7 am-8 pm, pets ($10 extra charge). **Amenities:** voice mail. **Pool(s):** small heated outdoor. **Guest Services:** coin laundry. **Cards:** AX, CB, DC, DS, MC, VI.

SOME UNITS

THE SUNCATCHER — Phone: (520)885-0200 — 31
▼▼▼
Bed & Breakfast

| 2/1-6/23 & 9/1-1/31 | 2P: $135-$185 |
| 6/24-8/31 | 2P: $95-$125 |

Location: Jct of Kolb Rd, 6.4 mi e on Broadway, just n on gravel road. Located in a quiet residential area. 105 N Avenida Javalina 85748. **Facility:** This contemporary home sits in a desert setting, has mountain views from the poolside and guest rooms are furnished in style of famous hotels. Designated smoking area. 4 one-bedroom standard units, some with whirlpools. 1 story, interior/exterior corridors. *Bath:* combo or shower only. **Parking:** on-site. **Terms:** office hours 10 am-6 pm. **Amenities:** video library, DVD players, hair dryers. **Pool(s):** heated outdoor. **Leisure Activities:** whirlpool, hiking trails, jogging. **Guest Services:** complimentary evening beverages. **Business Services:** PC, fax. **Cards:** AX, MC, VI.

SUPER 8 — *Book at aaa.com* — Phone: (520)791-9282 — 44
◆◆◆ SAVE
▼▼▼ ◆
Motel

2/1-2/16 [ECP]	1P: $100-$160	2P: $110-$160	XP: $5	F17
1/1-1/31 [ECP]	1P: $49-$120	2P: $55-$140	XP: $5	F17
6/1-12/31 [ECP]	1P: $39-$79	2P: $45-$85	XP: $5	F17
2/17-5/31 [ECP]	1P: $55-$75	2P: $64-$80	XP: $5	F17

Location: I-10, exit 259 (Starr Pass Blvd), just w. 715 W Starr Pass Blvd 85713. Fax: 520/798-1458. **Facility:** 68 one-bedroom standard units, some with whirlpools. 2 stories (no elevator), exterior corridors. **Parking:** on-site. **Amenities:** irons, hair dryers. **Pool(s):** outdoor. **Leisure Activities:** whirlpool. **Guest Services:** coin laundry. **Business Services:** fax (fee). **Cards:** AX, CB, DC, DS, MC, VI. **Special Amenities:** free continental breakfast and free local telephone calls.

SOME UNITS

SUPER 8 CENTRAL EAST — Phone: 520/790-6021 — 47
◆◆◆ SAVE
▼▼
Motel

2/1-2/15	1P: $89-$99	2P: $89-$99	XP: $10
2/16-3/31	1P: $59-$69	2P: $69	XP: $10
4/1-1/31	1P: $45-$49	2P: $49-$59	XP: $5

Location: I-10, exit 265 (Alvernon Way), 4.4 mi n and e on Alvernon Golflinks Rd, then 0.4 mi n. 1990 S Craycroft Rd 85711. Fax: 520/790-6074. **Facility:** 41 one-bedroom standard units. 2 stories (no elevator), exterior corridors. **Parking:** on-site. **Terms:** pets ($25 fee, $5 extra charge). **Pool(s):** small outdoor. **Guest Services:** coin laundry. **Business Services:** fax (fee). **Cards:** AX, CB, DC, DS, JC, MC, VI. **Special Amenities:** free continental breakfast and free local telephone calls.

SOME UNITS

SUPER 8 MOTEL-TUCSON — *Book at aaa.com* — Phone: (520)620-6500 — 21
▼▼ ▼▼
Motel

2/1-2/15	1P: $125-$145	2P: $125-$145	XP: $10	F11
2/16-3/31	1P: $75-$95	2P: $75-$95	XP: $5	F11
9/16-1/31	1P: $65-$75	2P: $65-$75	XP: $5	F11
4/1-9/15	1P: $60-$70	2P: $60-$70	XP: $5	F11

Location: I-10, exit 256 (Grant Rd), 0.3 mi w. 1550 W Grant Rd 85745. Fax: 520/903-0225. **Facility:** 65 one-bedroom standard units. 2 stories (no elevator), exterior corridors. *Bath:* combo or shower only. **Parking:** on-site. **Pool(s):** small outdoor. **Leisure Activities:** whirlpool. **Guest Services:** coin laundry. **Business Services:** fax (fee). **Cards:** AX, DC, DS, MC, VI.

SOME UNITS

TOWNEPLACE SUITES BY MARRIOTT — *Book at aaa.com* — Phone: (520)292-9697 — 10
◆◆◆ SAVE
▼▼▼ ◆
Small-scale Hotel

2/1-4/30 & 1/1-1/31	1P: $129-$179
9/1-12/31	1P: $99-$129
5/1-8/31	1P: $89-$119

Location: Jct Orange Grove Rd, 0.5 mi s on Oracle Rd, then just e. 405 W Rudasill Rd 85704. Fax: 520/292-9884. **Facility:** 77 units. 57 one-bedroom standard units with efficiencies. 4 one- and 16 two-bedroom suites with efficiencies. 3 stories, interior corridors. *Bath:* combo or shower only. **Parking:** on-site. **Terms:** cancellation fee imposed, pets ($75 fee). **Amenities:** video library (fee), high-speed Internet, dual phone lines, voice mail, irons, hair dryers. **Pool(s):** small heated outdoor. **Leisure Activities:** exercise room. **Guest Services:** coin laundry. **Business Services:** fax. **Cards:** AX, DC, DS, MC, VI. **Special Amenities:** free continental breakfast and free local telephone calls.

SOME UNITS

TRAVELODGE — *Book at aaa.com* — Phone: (520)622-8089 — 42
◆◆◆ SAVE
▼▼
Motel

2/1-2/15	1P: $89-$99	2P: $99-$110	XP: $6	F12
2/16-3/31	1P: $59-$64	2P: $64-$69	XP: $6	F12
1/1-1/31	1P: $49-$54	2P: $54-$59	XP: $6	F12
4/1-12/31	1P: $44-$49	2P: $49-$54	XP: $6	F12

Location: I-10, exit 259 (22nd St), just w, then just n. 1000 S Freeway 85745. Fax: 520/798-3940. **Facility:** 42 one-bedroom standard units. 2 stories (no elevator), interior corridors. **Parking:** on-site. **Terms:** [CP] meal plan available, package plans, pets ($10 extra charge). **Amenities:** hair dryers. **Guest Services:** coin laundry. **Business Services:** fax (fee). **Cards:** AX, CB, DC, DS, JC, MC, VI. **Special Amenities:** free continental breakfast and free local telephone calls.

SOME UNITS

(See map and index starting on p. 416)

VISCOUNT SUITE HOTEL *Book at aaa.com* Phone: 520/745-6500  32

AAA SAVE	2/1-4/30 [BP]	1P: $125-$135	2P: $125-$135	XP: $10	F12
	1/1-1/31 [BP]	1P: $105-$115	2P: $105-$115	XP: $10	F12
▽▽▽	10/1-12/31 [BP]	1P: $95-$105	2P: $95-$105	XP: $10	F12
	5/1-9/30 [BP]	1P: $79-$89	2P: $79-$89	XP: $10	F12

Small-scale Hotel **Location:** Just e of Swan Rd. 4855 E Broadway 85711. Fax: 520/790-5114. **Facility:** 216 units. 215 one- and 1 two-bedroom suites. 4 stories, interior corridors. **Parking:** on-site. **Amenities:** video games (fee), high-speed Internet, dual phone lines, voice mail, irons, hair dryers. **Dining:** 6 am-11 pm, Sat & Sun from 7 am, cocktails. **Pool(s):** heated outdoor. **Leisure Activities:** whirlpool, exercise room. **Guest Services:** gift shop, valet and coin laundry. **Business Services:** meeting rooms, fax (fee). **Cards:** AX, CB, DC, DS, MC, VI. **Special Amenities:** free full breakfast.

SOME UNITS

(icons)

THE WESTIN LA PALOMA RESORT & SPA *Book at aaa.com* Phone: (520)742-6000 12

AAA SAVE	1/1-1/31	1P: $299-$489	2P: $299-$489	XP: $30	F18
	2/1-5/24	1P: $279-$469	2P: $279-$469	XP: $30	F18
▽▽▽▽	9/10-12/31	1P: $229-$389	2P: $229-$389	XP: $30	F18
	5/25-9/9	1P: $109-$269	2P: $109-$269	XP: $30	F18

Resort
Large-scale Hotel **Location:** From SR 77 (Oracle Rd), 4.6 mi e on Ina Rd via Skyline and Sunrise drs, just s on Via Palomita. 3800 E Sunrise Dr 85718. Fax: 520/577-5878. **Facility:** Several acres of grounds in an attractive desert setting. Balconies and patios. Beautiful pool area with waterfall, pond, swim up bar and waterslide. Designated smoking area. 487 units. 471 one-bedroom standard units. 16 one-bedroom suites ($229-$1399), some with whirlpools. 3 stories, exterior corridors. **Bath:** combo or shower only. **Parking:** on-site (fee) and valet. **Terms:** check-in 4 pm, 7 day cancellation notice-fee imposed, [AP], [BP], [CP], [ECP] & [MAP] meal plans available, package plans, $11 service charge, pets (small dogs only). **Amenities:** dual phone lines, voice mail, safes, honor bars, irons, hair dryers. *Fee:* video games, high-speed Internet. *Some:* DVD players. **Dining:** 6 restaurants, 6:30 am-10 pm, cocktails, also, Janos, see separate listing. **Pool(s):** 2 heated outdoor, wading. **Leisure Activities:** saunas, whirlpools, steamrooms, waterslide, table tennis, playground, spa, volleyball. *Fee:* golf-27 holes, 10 lighted tennis courts, racquetball court. **Guest Services:** gift shop, valet laundry. **Business Services:** conference facilities, business center. **Cards:** AX, CB, DC, DS, JC, MC, VI. **Special Amenities:** free local telephone calls and free newspaper. *(See color ad below)*

SOME UNITS

(icons) FEE FEE FEE

(See map and index starting on p. 416)

WESTWARD LOOK RESORT

Book at aaa.com   Phone: (520)297-1151   **4**

2/1-5/20	1P: $149-$319	2P: $149-$319	XP: $25 F17
9/18-1/31	1P: $139-$269	2P: $139-$269	XP: $25 F17
5/21-9/17	1P: $79-$199	2P: $79-$199	XP: $25 F17

Location: I-10, exit 248 (Ina Rd), 6 mi e, then just n on Westward Look Dr. Located in a quiet area. 245 E Ina Rd 85704. Fax: 520/297-9023. **Facility:** This full service resort on 80 acres has fabulous views of the Catalina Mountains, pools are surrounded by trees and flowers, in a relaxed ambiance. 244 one-bedroom standard units. 1-2 stories (no elevator), exterior corridors. *Bath:* combo or shower only. **Parking:** on-site and valet. **Terms:** check-in 4 pm, 7 day cancellation notice-fee imposed, $12 service charge, small pets only ($75 fee). **Amenities:** video games (fee), high-speed Internet, voice mail, honor bars, irons, hair dryers. **Dining:** 2 restaurants, 6 am-11 pm, cocktails, also, The Gold Room, see separate listing. **Pool(s):** 3 heated outdoor. **Leisure Activities:** whirlpools, nature programs, hiking trails, jogging, exercise room, spa, sports court, basketball, horseshoes, shuffleboard, volleyball. *Fee:* 8 lighted tennis courts, horseback riding. **Guest Services:** gift shop, valet laundry. **Business Services:** conference facilities, business center. **Cards:** AX, CB, DC, DS, JC, MC, VI. **Special Amenities:** free newspaper and preferred room (subject to availability with advance reservations). *(See color ad below)*

Resort
Large-scale Hotel

SOME UNITS

WINDMILL SUITES AT ST. PHILIP'S PLAZA

Book at aaa.com   Phone: (520)577-0007   **16**

2/1-3/31	1P: $105-$165	2P: $105-$165	XP: $10 F18
4/1-5/31	1P: $89-$135	2P: $89-$135	XP: $10 F18
10/1-1/31	1P: $105-$115	2P: $105-$115	XP: $10 F18
6/1-9/30	1P: $69-$89	2P: $69-$89	XP: $10 F18

Small-scale Hotel **Location:** I-10, exit 254 (Prince Rd), 4 mi e, then 1 mi n. 4250 N Campbell Ave 85718. Fax: 520/577-0045. **Facility:** 122 one-bedroom suites, some with whirlpools. 3 stories, interior corridors. *Bath:* combo or shower only. **Parking:** on-site. **Terms:** check-in 4 pm, cancellation fee imposed. **Amenities:** voice mail, irons, hair dryers. **Pool(s):** heated outdoor. **Leisure Activities:** whirlpool, lending library, bicycles, limited exercise equipment. **Guest Services:** coin laundry. **Business Services:** meeting rooms, business center. **Cards:** AX, DC, DS, MC, VI. **Special Amenities:** free expanded continental breakfast and free local telephone calls.

SOME UNITS

(See map and index starting on p. 416)

──────── *The following lodgings were either not evaluated or did not* ────────
meet AAA rating requirements but are listed for your information only.

CANYON RANCH   **Phone: 520/749-9000**
[fyi]　　　Not evaluated. **Location:** 8600 E Rockcliff Rd 85749. Facilities, services, and decor characterize an upscale property.

HOLIDAY INN EXPRESS-GRANT RD   **Phone: 520/624-3200**
[fyi]　　　Did not meet all AAA rating requirements for some property operations at time of last evaluation on
12/09/2004. **Location:** I-10, exit 256 (Grant Rd), just w. 1560 W Grant Rd 85745. Facilities, services, and decor
Small-scale Hotel　characterize a mid-range property.

HOTEL CONGRESS   **Phone: 520/622-8848**
[fyi]　　　Did not meet all AAA rating requirements for some guest rooms at time of last evaluation on 01/18/2005.
Location: I-10, exit 258, 0.7 mi e to 5th Ave, then just n. 311 E Congress 85701. Facilities, services, and decor
Classic　characterize a basic property.
Small-scale Hotel

QUALITY INN TUCSON AIRPORT   **Phone: 520/623-7792**
[fyi]　　　Not evaluated. **Location:** I-10, exit 262, just s. 1025 E Benson Hwy 85713. Facilities, services, and decor characterize
a mid-range property. *(See color ad p 441)*

TANQUE VERDE RANCH   **Phone: 520/296-6275**
[fyi]　　　Not evaluated. **Location:** 14301 E Speedway 85748. Facilities, services, and decor characterize an upscale property.

──────── **WHERE TO DINE** ────────

ACACIA AT ST. PHILIPS　　　　**Lunch:** $7-$12　　　**Dinner:** $16-$32　　　**Phone:** 520/232-0101　　(37)
▼▼▼▼ ▼▼▼▼　**Location:** Jct River Rd; in St. Philips Plaza. 4340 N Campbell Ave 85718. **Hours:** 11 am-2 & 5-10 pm. Closed: 7/4,
11/23, 12/25. **Reservations:** suggested. **Features:** Chef Albert Hall has opened a charming facility with
American　creative dishes such as wok-charred salmon with ginger-plum and sambal sauce. The attentive staff will
make sure you are carefully served and on pleasant evenings, an open air patio overlooks a shady
courtyard. Dressy casual; cocktails. **Parking:** on-site. **Cards:** AX, DS, MC, VI.

ALADDIN MIDDLE EASTERN RESTUARANT　　　**Lunch:** $10-$14　　　**Dinner:** $10-$14　　**Phone:** 520/320-0468　　(40)
▼▼ ▼▼　**Location:** Just n of Prince Rd. 3699 N Campbell Ave 85719. **Hours:** 11 am-10 pm, Sun-9 pm. Closed major
holidays; also 12/24 & Mon. **Reservations:** accepted. **Features:** Among freshly prepared Middle East
Middle Eastern　dishes are hummus, tabbouleh, chicken or beef kebabs and other regional specialties. Wednesday night
centers on Persian foods. Casual dress; cocktails. **Parking:** on-site. **Cards:** AX, DS, MC, VI.

ANTHONY'S IN THE CATALINAS　　　　　**Dinner:** $24-$40　　　　　**Phone:** 520/299-1771　　(15)
▼▼▼▼ ▼▼▼▼　**Location:** I-10, exit 250 (Orange Grove Rd), 7 mi e to Skyline Dr, 0.5 mi e, then just n. 6440 N Campbell Ave 85718.
Hours: 5:30 pm-10 pm. Closed major holidays. **Reservations:** suggested. **Features:** In a desert setting
Continental　with city and mountain views, the pleasant dining room becomes a window to the world. A comprehensive
selection of wines complements well-presented dishes offered with accomplished service. Dressy casual;
cocktails. **Parking:** on-site and valet. **Cards:** AX, CB, DC, DS, MC, VI.

THE BAMBOO CLUB ASIAN BISTRO　　　**Lunch:** $7-$22　　　**Dinner:** $9-$23　　　**Phone:** 520/514-9665　　(80)
▼▼ ▼▼　**Location:** Just w of Wilmot; in Park Place Mall. 5870 E Broadway #524 85711. **Hours:** 11 am-10 pm, Fri & Sat-11
pm. Closed: 11/23, 12/25. **Reservations:** suggested. **Features:** Dynamic cuisine incorporating recipes from
Pacific Rim　such places as Korea, Japan, China and Thailand is found at the popular bistro. Pleasant service and
exciting decor supply the finishing touches. Casual dress; cocktails. **Parking:** on-site and valet. **Cards:** AX,
CB, DC, DS, MC, VI.

BAZIL'S　　　　　　　　　**Dinner:** $12-$20　　　　　　　**Phone:** 520/577-3322　　(25)
▼▼▼▼　**Location:** Northeast corner of Sunrise Dr and Swan. 4777 E Sunrise Dr, Suite 119 85718. **Hours:** 5 pm-10 pm.
Closed major holidays. **Reservations:** suggested. **Features:** Family members pride themselves on their
Regional　years of friendly service, and the warm ambience of the dining room is a perfect setting. Wonderful
Italian　traditional dishes, such as chicken rollatine or veal piccatti, are popular choices. Casual dress; cocktails.
Parking: on-site. **Cards:** AX, DS, MC, VI.

BEYOND BREAD　　　　　　**Lunch:** $5-$8　　　**Dinner:** $5-$8　　　**Phone:** 520/322-9965　　(44)
▼▼▼ ▼▼▼　**Location:** Just s of Ft Lowell. 3026 N Campbell 85719. **Hours:** 6:30 am-8 pm, Sat from 7 am, Sun 7 am-6 pm.
Closed major holidays. **Reservations:** not accepted. **Features:** The popular place prepares hearty
American　breakfasts, homemade soups and luncheon sandwiches to please any taste. Recently moved into a larger
location, the eatery features upscale decor that allows for a friendly display of breads and pastries. Casual
dress. **Parking:** on-site. **Cards:** AX, DS, MC, VI.

BISTRO ZIN　　　　　　　**Lunch:** $9-$13　　　**Dinner:** $14-$38　　　**Phone:** 520/299-7799　　(35)
▼▼▼▼　**Location:** 2.2 mi e of jct Oracle Rd. 1865 E River Rd 85718. **Hours:** 11:30 am-2:30 & 5-11:30 pm, Sat & Sun from
5 pm. Closed major holidays. **Reservations:** suggested. **Features:** The high energy of this popular eatery is
American　apparent from the moment you enter. The burgundy and black background provides an intimate setting for
the smooth service and beautifully presented dishes. Dressy casual; cocktails. **Parking:** on-site. **Cards:** AX,
DC, DS, MC, VI.

(See map and index starting on p. 416)

BLUEFIN SEAFOOD BISTRO
Seafood

Lunch: $8-$13   Dinner: $16-$28   Phone: 520/531-8500   11
Location: Just s of Ina Rd; in Casas Adobes. 7053 N Oracle Rd 85718. **Hours:** 11 am-midnight, Sun 10 am-9 pm. Closed major holidays. **Reservations:** accepted. **Features:** Diners may sit upstairs to overlook the courtyard or downstairs near the bar. Delightful selections of fresh fish range from wild salmon to ahi tuna to a variety of shellfish, prepared with various toppings and cooking styles. Dressy casual; cocktails. **Parking:** on-site. **Cards:** AX, CB, DC, DS, JC, MC, VI.

BUDDY'S GRILL
American

Lunch: $7-$12   Dinner: $10-$19   Phone: 520/795-2226   51
Location: Just e of Swan Rd. 4821 E Grant Rd 85712. **Hours:** 9 am-10 pm. Closed: 7/4, 11/23, 12/25. **Reservations:** accepted. **Features:** A casual eatery where everyone is "family". From breakfast omelets to over-sized burgers with red potato salad to roast prime rib, the classic comfort foods are freshly prepared and tasty. Casual dress; cocktails. **Parking:** on-site. **Cards:** MC, VI.

CAPRICCIO BISTRO & BAR
Italian

Dinner: $10-$16   Phone: 520/887-2333   32
Location: Just s of River Rd. 4825 N First Ave 85718. **Hours:** 5:30 pm-9 pm. Closed major holidays; also Sun. **Reservations:** accepted. **Features:** Italian food that incorporates regional American flavors and all with flair. The bistro's smoking bar is popular for meeting and greeting. Build-your-own pasta allows for any number of combinations. Casual dress; cocktails. **Parking:** on-site. **Cards:** AX, DC, DS, MC, VI.

CATTLETOWN STEAKHOUSE & SALOON
Steak House

Lunch: $5-$14   Dinner: $12-$30   Phone: 520/295-1141   88
Location: I-10, exit 264B (Irvington), just w to Country Club Rd, then 1 mi s. 3141 E Drexel Rd 85706. **Hours:** 11 am-10 pm, Fri & Sat-11 pm. Closed: 11/23, 12/25. **Reservations:** not accepted. **Features:** The Western theme is obvious to guests as they drive up and file inside. Mesquite-grilled steaks, seafood choices and friendly service contribute to a hearty family dinner or "howdy pardner" business lunch. Casual dress; cocktails. **Parking:** on-site. **Cards:** AX, DC, DS, MC, VI.

CHANTILLY TEA ROOM
Specialty

Lunch: $8-$10   Dinner: $14-$17   Phone: 520/622-3303   31
Location: Jct River Rd, just n on Oracle Rd, then just e. 5185 N Genematas Dr 85704. **Hours:** 11 am-4 pm. Closed: Sun & Mon. **Reservations:** required. **Features:** Elegant duchess tea service, with tiered trays of delectable morsels, is one option at the popular luncheon spot; a reservation is required. Salads, quiche, soup and sandwiches round out the menu. Dressy casual. **Parking:** on-site. **Cards:** MC, VI.

CHINA THAI
Chinese

Lunch: $5-$7   Dinner: $5-$14   Phone: 520/885-6860   60
Location: Just sw of Grant Rd. 6502 E Tanque Verde 85715. **Hours:** 11 am-9:30 pm, Fri & Sat-10 pm. **Reservations:** accepted. **Features:** The eastside restaurant's name gives some insight into its menu, which blends Thai and Chinese cuisine. Dishes made from fresh ingredients can be adapted to vegetarian and the spice level of curries and other dishes adjusted to the diner's taste. Casual dress; cocktails. **Parking:** on-site. **Cards:** AX, DS, MC, VI.

CITY GRILL
American

Lunch: $10-$15   Dinner: $15-$21   Phone: 520/733-1111   61
Location: Between Pima and Grant rds. 6464 E Tanque Verde Rd 85715. **Hours:** 11 am-10 pm, Fri & Sat-10:30 pm. Closed: 12/25. **Reservations:** suggested. **Features:** The casual atmosphere, welcoming attitude toward children and wide selection of foods make this a popular dining destination for city residents. Casual dress; cocktails. **Parking:** on-site. **Cards:** AX, CB, DC, DS, MC, VI.

CLAIM JUMPER RESTAURANTS
American

Lunch: $8-$13   Dinner: $10-$25   Phone: 520/795-2900   76
Location: 0.7 mi e of Country Club Rd. 3761 E Broadway Blvd 85716. **Hours:** 11 am-10 pm, Fri & Sat-11 pm. Closed: 11/23, 12/25. **Features:** A Western mining theme and family-style portions attract diners to this busy eatery. A wide range of foods are available from California rolls and crunchy spinach salad to steaks and rotisserie chicken. Save room for the six-layer chocolate motherlode cake. Casual dress; cocktails. **Parking:** on-site. **Cards:** AX, DS, MC, VI.

CODY'S BEEF 'N BEANS
Steak House

Lunch: $6-$11   Dinner: $11-$18   Phone: 520/322-9475   43
Location: Just w of Country Club Rd. 2708 E Ft Lowell 85716. **Hours:** 11 am-9 pm. Closed major holidays; also Sun, 12/24. **Features:** The Cody burger gets raves from the locals but the tender grilled steaks are mouthwatering and flavorful. All the sides you might want, from onion rings to cole slaw, make for a satisfying meal in this small eatery with its Western bunkhouse decor. Casual dress; beer & wine only. **Parking:** on-site. **Cards:** AX, DS, MC, VI.

CUVEE WORLD BISTRO
International

Lunch: $7-$13   Dinner: $10-$19   Phone: 520/881-7577   70
Location: I-10, exit 257 (Speedway Blvd), 3.6 mi e. 3352 E Speedway Blvd 85716. **Hours:** 11 am-10 pm, Fri-midnight, Sat 4:30 pm-midnight. Closed: 7/4, 11/23, 12/25; also Sun. **Reservations:** suggested. **Features:** Polished service, an upscale dining room and innovative blending of world elements and cuisine styles set the bistro apart. Seasonal menus take advantage of fresh foods, as exemplified in such dishes as wasabi ahi with ginger risotto nuggets. Casual dress; cocktails. **Parking:** on-site. **Cards:** AX, DC, DS, MC, VI.

DAISY MAE'S STEAKHOUSE
Steak House

Dinner: $14-$22   Phone: 520/792-8888   74
Location: I-10, exit 257 (Speedway Blvd/St. Mary's Rd), 2 mi w on St. Mary's Rd. 2735 W Anklam Rd 85745. **Hours:** 4 pm-10 pm, Sun-9 pm. Closed: 11/23, 12/25. **Reservations:** accepted. **Features:** Steaks are cooked just as patrons prefer in the casual eatery. Many folks lend to the decor by signing $1 bills and having them hung on the wall. Casual dress; cocktails. **Parking:** on-site. **Cards:** AX, DS, MC, VI.

(See map and index starting on p. 416)

DAKOTA CAFE & CATERING COMPANY
Lunch: $8-$11 **Dinner:** $9-$25 **Phone:** 520/298-7188 **58**

American

Location: Jct Campbell Ave, 5.6 mi e on Grant Rd, then just s. 6541 E Tanque Verde Rd 85715. **Hours:** 11 am-9 pm, Fri & Sat-10 pm. Closed major holidays; also Sun. **Reservations:** suggested. **Features:** In Trail Dust Town, the casually decorated dining room and patio seating are pleasant backdrops for exciting meals. Chef Carl Hendrick takes seriously his heart-healthy dishes, vegetarian choices and daily fresh fish items. Using cooking styles and food elements from around the world, he blends interesting ingredients in such dishes as tempura-coconut shrimp with mango chutney and pork tenderloin filled with poblano chiles, spinach and white cheddar cheese. Casual dress; cocktails. **Parking:** on-site. **Cards:** AX, CB, DC, MC, VI.

DELHI PALACE
Lunch: $6-$9 **Dinner:** $7-$12 **Phone:** 520/296-8585 **78**

Indian

Location: Jct Wilmot, 0.5 mi e. 6751 E Broadway Blvd 85710. **Hours:** 11:30 am-2:30 & 5-10 pm. Closed: 1/1, 11/23, 12/25; also 12/31. **Reservations:** accepted. **Features:** Local businesspeople come in for the popular lunch buffet; the well-presented evening dinners are every bit as good. Food choices center on traditional preparations of tandoori, curry, seafood and vegetarian ingredients. Desserts are made on the premises, and kulfi is excellent. Casual dress; cocktails. **Parking:** on-site. **Cards:** AX, MC, VI.

THE DISH
Dinner: $17-$35 **Phone:** 520/326-1714 **71**

American

Location: I-10, exit 257 (Speedway Blvd/St. Mary's Rd), 3.2 mi e; at RumRunner. 3200 E Speedway Blvd 85716. **Hours:** 5 pm-9 pm, Fri & Sat-10 pm. Closed major holidays; also Sun & Mon. **Reservations:** suggested. **Features:** The intimate dining space does not intimidate the chef, who serves big-time flavors. The attentive staff assists with meal choices and may offer tastes of wines. Casual dress; wine only. **Parking:** on-site. **Cards:** AX, DC, MC, VI.

THE ECLECTIC CAFE
Lunch: $7-$12 **Dinner:** $7-$12 **Phone:** 520/885-2842 **49**

American

Location: Jct Grant Rd, 0.5 mi ne. 7053 E Tanque Verde Rd 85715. **Hours:** 11 am-9 pm, Sat from 8 am, Sun 8 am-8 pm. Closed: 11/23, 12/25. **Features:** The storefront eatery has pizzazz. On the menu are innovative foods ranging from "warm" salads made with spicy or cooked meats and cool veggies to hearty sandwiches and a good selection of Mexican classics. Casual dress; wine only. **Parking:** on-site. **Cards:** AX, DC, MC, VI.

EL CHARRO CAFE NORTH
Lunch: $6-$10 **Dinner:** $12-$22 **Phone:** 520/615-1922 **19**

Mexican

Location: Jct N Oracle Rd. 100 W Orange Grove Rd 85704. **Hours:** 11 am-9 pm, Fri & Sat-10 pm. Closed major holidays. **Features:** From the family serving Tucson for over 80 years, you can expect the best in classic Mexican food preparations. The carne seca is a house specialty though the temptingly spiced tamales and enchiladas are popular. Casual dress; cocktails. **Parking:** on-site. **Cards:** AX, DS, MC, VI.

EL CORRAL
Dinner: $9-$17 **Phone:** 520/299-6092 **36**

Steak House

Location: I-10, exit 254 (Prince Rd), 0.4 mi e, 1 mi n on Campbell Ave, then just e. 2201 E River Rd 85718. **Hours:** 5 pm-10 pm, Fri-Sun from 4:30 pm. Closed: 11/23, 12/25. **Features:** Built in the late 1800s, the historic adobe ranch house is a nice spot for casual dining. Reservations are not accepted. Casual dress; cocktails. **Parking:** on-site. **Cards:** AX, DC, DS, MC, VI. **Historic**

ELLE, A WINE COUNTRY RESTAURANT
Lunch: $7-$15 **Dinner:** $12-$22 **Phone:** 520/327-0500 **79**

Regional American

Location: I-10, exit 258 (Broadway Blvd/Congress St), 3.1 mi e to Country Club Rd, then just s. 3048 E Broadway Blvd 85716. **Hours:** 11 am-10 pm, Sat from 4:30 pm, Sun 10 am-9 pm. Closed: 7/4, 11/23, 12/25. **Reservations:** suggested. **Features:** Food and wine pairings from a recently expanded list give diners the feel they are in northern California. Attentive service accompanies a variety of dishes, including a selection of pastas, seafood such as grilled salmon with fennel and carrots, and New York steak with roasted potatoes and blue cheese butter. Two patios provide ample outdoor seating in pleasant weather. Casual dress; cocktails. **Parking:** on-site. **Cards:** AX, DS, MC, VI.

EVANGELO'S
Dinner: $25-$30 **Phone:** 520/792-3055 **69**

Continental
DS, MC, VI.

Location: I-10, exit 157 (Speedway Blvd), 4.6 mi w. 4405 W Speedway Blvd 85745. **Hours:** 5 pm-10 pm. Closed: 1/1. **Reservations:** suggested. **Features:** High in the foothills west of the city, the restaurant presents an eclectic menu that features European and Mediterranean cuisine. Service is friendly and attentive. The tapas and cigar bar allows for intimate dining. Semi-formal attire; cocktails. **Parking:** on-site. **Cards:** AX,

FEAST
Lunch: $6-$14 **Dinner:** $8-$18 **Phone:** 520/326-9363 **72**

American

Location: Just e of Alvernon. 4122 E Speedway 85712. **Hours:** 11 am-9 pm. Closed: 7/4, 11/23, 12/25; also Mon. **Reservations:** not accepted. **Features:** Although take-out is a segment of the business, the dine-in option offers friendly staff who see to patrons' every need. The menu centers on upscale dishes, such as cream of asparagus soup, a salad that includes curried chicken, and vegetarian offerings. Casual dress; beer & wine only. **Parking:** on-site. **Cards:** AX, DC, DS, MC, VI.

FIREBIRDS ROCKY MOUNTAIN GRILL
Lunch: $7-$13 **Dinner:** $9-$23 **Phone:** 520/577-0747 **20**

American

Location: Jct Campbell Ave; northwest corner; in La Encantada Plaza. 2985 E Skyline Dr 85718. **Hours:** 11 am-10 pm, Fri & Sat-11 pm. Closed: 11/23, 12/25. **Features:** Lending to the busy meet-and-greet eatery's cozy charm are upscale mountain-lodge appointments, huge fireplaces and comfortable sofas and chairs for pre-dinner drinks. On the menu is a wide selection of hickory-grilled steaks and seafood. Casual dress; cocktails. **Parking:** on-site. **Cards:** AX, DC, DS, MC, VI.

FIRECRACKER!
Lunch: $7-$15 **Dinner:** $15-$21 **Phone:** 520/318-1118 **46**

Pacific Rim

Location: Southeast corner of Swan and Ft Lowell rds. 2990 N Swan Rd 85712. **Hours:** 11 am-10 pm, Fri & Sat-10:30 pm. Closed: 11/23, 12/25. **Reservations:** accepted. **Features:** The exciting flavors of Asia and the Pacific combine with Southwestern elements to bring patrons a distinctive dining experience. An open display kitchen is one design highlight of the popular eatery. Casual dress; cocktails. **Parking:** on-site. **Cards:** AX, DC, DS, MC, VI.

(See map and index starting on p. 416)

FLEMING'S PRIME STEAKHOUSE & WINE BAR   Dinner: $20-$34   Phone: 520/529-5017   21
Steak House
Location: Southwest corner of Skyline and Campbell Ave. 6360 N Campbell Ave 85718. **Hours:** 5 pm-10 pm, Fri & Sat-10:30 pm. **Closed:** 11/23, 12/25. **Reservations:** accepted. **Features:** The upscale, energetic restaurant is new to the city. Although steaks are featured, side dishes are ample and meant to be shared. More than 100 by-the-glass wines allow for sampling, and an attentive staff helps make it all memorable. Casual dress; cocktails. **Parking:** on-site and valet. **Cards:** AX, CB, DC, DS, JC, MC, VI.

FUEGO   Dinner: $9-$22   Phone: 520/886-1745   53
Southwest American
Location: I-10, exit 256 (Grant Rd), 8.8 mi e, then 0.7 mi e. 6958 E Tanque Verde Rd 85715. **Hours:** 5 pm-9 pm, Fri-Sun to 10 pm. **Closed:** 5/29, 7/4, 12/25. **Reservations:** suggested. **Features:** Fuego means "fire," a theme that recurs in the kitchen and when dishes are flambeed tableside. Chef Alan Zeman's thoughtful preparations of seafood, game and beef reflect a Southwestern influence. Casual dress; cocktails. **Parking:** on-site. **Cards:** AX, DC, MC, VI.

GAVI ITALIAN RESTAURANT   Lunch: $9-$20   Dinner: $10-$25   Phone: 520/219-9200   7
Italian
Location: Northwest corner of Ina Rd and La Cholla; in Foothills Mall. 7401 N La Cholla 85741. **Hours:** 11:30 am-10 pm, Fri & Sat-11 pm. **Closed:** 7/4, 11/23, 12/25. **Reservations:** accepted. **Features:** The upbeat decor incorporates European bicycle and soccer team jerseys, and the fresh taste of the amply plated food will delight any sports enthusiast. Casual dress; cocktails. **Parking:** on-site. **Cards:** AX, DC, MC, VI.

GHINIS FRENCH CAFFE   Lunch: $6-$9   Phone: 520/326-9095   41
French
Location: Just w of Campbell Ave. 1803 E Prince Rd 85719. **Hours:** 6:30 am-3 pm, Sun 8 am-2 pm. **Closed:** 7/4, 11/23, 12/25; also Mon. **Features:** The busy bistro's breakfast omelets and luncheon salads are prepared in the French country style. Menu offerings are treats either for a celebration or a relaxed meal with friends. Casual dress; beer & wine only. **Parking:** on-site. **Cards:** AX, DC, DS, MC, VI.

THE GOLD ROOM   Lunch: $8-$16   Dinner: $19-$35   Phone: 520/297-1151   9
American
Location: I-10, exit 248 (Ina Rd), 6 mi e, then just n on Westward Look Dr; in Westward Look Resort. 245 E Ina Rd 85704. **Hours:** 6 am-2 & 5:30-10 pm; Sunday brunch 9/16-6/16. **Reservations:** suggested. **Features:** The view over the valley below, which is particularly breathtaking at night, complements the fine-dining experience at the sophisticated restaurant. Sonoran Desert spices and flavors infuse classic and contemporary cuisine. Friday and Saturday theme-night dinners, such as a selection of lobster dishes or mariachi music with inspired dishes, are popular and may change in concept seasonally. Dressy casual; cocktails. **Parking:** valet. **Cards:** AX, CB, DC, DS, MC, VI. *(See color ad p 445)*

THE GRILL AT HACIENDA DEL SOL   Dinner: $24-$42   Phone: 520/529-3500   29
Continental
Location: Jct SR 77 (Oracle Rd), 5.4 mi e on Ina Rd/Skyline/Sunrise drs, 0.5 mi s to Via Alcade, then just nw; in Hacienda Del Sol Guest Ranch Resort. 5601 N Hacienda del Sol Rd 85718. **Hours:** 5:30 pm-10 pm; Sunday brunch 10 am-2 pm. **Reservations:** suggested. **Features:** Both in the main dining room and on the patio, the charming ambience of old Tucson is apparent in the decor. Seasonal menu offerings are prepared with the freshest ingredients and show innovative flavor combinations. Servers are accomplished. Dressy casual; cocktails. **Parking:** on-site and valet. **Cards:** AX, CB, DC, DS, JC, MC, VI.

HI FALUTIN WESTERN GRILL   Lunch: $7-$18   Dinner: $8-$18   Phone: 520/297-0518   13
American
Location: From jct Ina Rd, 0.5 mi s. 6780 N Oracle Rd 85704. **Hours:** 11 am-9 pm, Fri & Sat-10 pm. **Closed:** 1/1, 11/23, 12/25. **Features:** The charming Western decor is bright and fun; don't hesitate to wear your cowboy hat. Hearty and pleasing "eats" range from cattle boss pot roast to flat-iron rib-eye. Stetson-clad servers are friendly and helpful. Casual dress; cocktails. **Parking:** on-site. **Cards:** AX, DC, DS, MC, VI.

JANOS   Dinner: $22-$110   Phone: 520/615-6100   23
Southwest French
Location: From SR 77 (Oracle Rd), 4.6 mi e on Ina Rd via Skyline and Sunrise drs, just s on Via Palomita; in The Westin La Paloma Resort & Spa. 3770 E Sunrise Dr 85718. **Hours:** 5:30 pm-9 pm, Fri & Sat-9:30 pm. Closed major holidays; also Sun. **Reservations:** suggested. **Features:** Although Janos is noted for its innovative French-inspired Southwestern cuisine, the accomplished service adds a special element to the dining experience. The chef-owner often chats with guests. Dressy casual; cocktails. **Parking:** valet. **Cards:** AX, CB, DC, MC, VI. *(See color ad p 444)*

J BAR-A LATIN GRILL   Dinner: $13-$18   Phone: 520/615-6100   24
Caribbean
Location: 1.3 mi e of Campbell Ave via Skyline Dr; adjacent to the Westin La Paloma. 3770 E Sunrise Dr 85718. **Hours:** 5 pm-9:30 pm. Closed major holidays; also Sun. **Reservations:** accepted. **Features:** This is the place to "meet and greet" in town. The chef's high-energy, delectable food makes this spot popular with the young set. Casual dress; cocktails. **Parking:** on-site and valet. **Cards:** AX, CB, DC, MC, VI.

JONATHAN'S CORK   Dinner: $12-$24   Phone: 520/296-1631   65
Steak & Seafood
Location: Jct Speedway Blvd, 0.5 mi ne. 6320 E Tanque Verde Rd 85715. **Hours:** 5 pm-9:30 pm, Fri & Sat-10 pm. Closed major holidays; also 12/24. **Reservations:** accepted. **Features:** Chef Landeen flavors his dishes with a Southwestern flair and then may stop by tables with a greeting and to ask about the meal. The dining room is appointed in a casual ranch style. Casual dress; cocktails. **Parking:** on-site. **Cards:** AX, DC, MC, VI.

THE KEYS   Lunch: $7-$12   Dinner: $7-$14   Phone: 520/888-8084   39
American
Location: Just w of Oracle Rd; across from the Tucson Mall. 445 W Wetmore Rd 85705. **Hours:** 11 am-10 pm. **Closed:** 12/25. **Reservations:** accepted. **Features:** The lively atmosphere complements the young and friendly staff. Dishes reflect Florida flavors and Southwestern elements. Live weekend entertainment and a dance floor beckon to the city's younger crowd. Casual dress; cocktails. **Parking:** on-site. **Cards:** AX, DC, DS, MC, VI.

(See map and index starting on p. 416)

KINGFISHER
▼▼▼
Regional American

Lunch: $7-$12   Dinner: $15-$22   Phone: 520/323-7739   56

Location: I-10, exit 256 (Grant Rd), 3.5 mi e. 2564 E Grant Rd 85716. **Hours:** 11 am-midnight, Sat & Sun from 5 pm. Closed major holidays. **Reservations:** suggested. **Features:** Diners can expect a large selection of fresh fish, as well as pasta, beef and chicken selections. A summer menu centers on regional cuisine. Casual dress; cocktails. **Parking:** on-site. **Cards:** AX, CB, DC, DS, JC, MC, VI.

LA FUENTE RESTAURANT
▼▼▼▼
Mexican

Lunch: $6-$8   Dinner: $10-$18   Phone: 520/623-8659   62

Location: I-10, exit 256 (Grant Rd), 0.9 mi e, then 0.5 mi s. 1749 N Oracle Rd 85705. **Hours:** 11 am-9 pm, Fri-10 pm, Sat noon-10 pm. Closed: 11/23, 12/25. **Reservations:** accepted. **Features:** Hanging plants and weekend jazz or mariachi music lend to the colorful atmosphere at the laid-back restaurant, which has served the area for more than 40 years. The Mexican fare is tasty, and the Sunday champagne brunch from 11 am to 2 pm is a treat. Casual dress; cocktails; entertainment. **Parking:** on-site. **Cards:** AX, DC, DS, MC, VI.

LA PARRILLA SUIZA
▼▼▼ ▼▼▼
Mexican

Lunch: $7-$15   Dinner: $7-$15   Phone: 520/572-7200   6

Location: I-10, exit 248 (Ina Rd), 0.5 mi e. 4250 W Ina Rd 85741. **Hours:** 11 am-10 pm, Fri & Sat-11 pm. Closed: 11/23, 12/25. **Reservations:** accepted. **Features:** Bright decor—with a high-peaked ceiling and open bar—lends to a fresh setting in which to savor central Mexican cuisine. Pleasant servers assist patrons through the meal. During the winter season, mariachi music enlivens the place on weekends. Casual dress; cocktails. **Parking:** on-site. **Cards:** AX, DC, DS, MC, VI.

LA PARRILLA SUIZA
▼▼▼ ▼▼▼
Mexican

Lunch: $6-$10   Dinner: $6-$10   Phone: 520/624-4300   48

Location: 0.5 mi s of Fort Lowell Rd. 2720 N Oracle Rd 85705. **Hours:** 11 am-10 pm, Fri & Sat-11 pm. Closed: 11/23, 12/25. **Reservations:** accepted. **Features:** The casual atmosphere and friendly, efficient wait staff contribute to a pleasant outing at the locally popular eatery. Styled as Mexico City cuisine, traditional dishes are prepared with a continental flair. Casual dress; cocktails. **Parking:** on-site. **Cards:** AX, DS, MC, VI.

LE RENDEZ-VOUS
▼▼▼
French

Lunch: $8-$14   Dinner: $19-$33   Phone: 520/323-7373   42

Location: Jct Oracle Rd, 4 mi e. 3844 E Fort Lowell Rd 85716. **Hours:** 11:30 am-2 & 6-10 pm, Sat & Sun from 5:30 pm. Closed: 1/1, 11/23, 12/25; also Mon. **Reservations:** required. **Features:** Patrons of the small, charming restaurant are served elegantly prepared French dishes by the attentive and well-trained wait staff. Casual dress; cocktails. **Parking:** on-site. **Cards:** AX, CB, DC, DS, MC, VI.

LODGE ON THE DESERT
▼▼▼
American

Lunch: $8-$14   Dinner: $14-$28   Phone: 520/325-3366   73

Location: I-10, exit 258 (Broadway Blvd/Congress St), 4 mi e, then just n; in Lodge on the Desert. 306 N Alvernon Way 85711. **Hours:** 11 am-2 & 5-9 pm, Sat & Sun from 5 pm. **Reservations:** suggested. **Features:** The brightly appointed Southwestern dining room and covered patio are highlights at the modest yet sophisticated restaurant. The seasonal menu prepared by Chef Jeff Taffer includes some outstanding homemade desserts. Casual dress; cocktails. **Parking:** on-site. **Cards:** AX, CB, DC, DS, MC, VI.

LOTUS GARDEN
◆◆ ◆◆
Chinese

Lunch: $7-$8   Dinner: $9-$20   Phone: 520/298-3351   66

Location: I-10, exit 257 (Speedway Blvd), 7 mi e. 5975 E Speedway Blvd 85712. **Hours:** 11:30 am-10 pm, Fri & Sat-11 pm. Closed: 7/4, 11/23, 12/25. **Reservations:** suggested. **Features:** Although the restaurant's focus is on preparing Cantonese and Szechuan cuisine, the owners now also offer monthly wine tastings with special foods. The contemporary decor is refreshing, and a patio is available for al fresco dining. Casual dress; cocktails. **Parking:** on-site. **Cards:** AX, CB, DC, DS, JC, MC, VI.

MACAYO MEXICAN KITCHEN DEL NORTE
◆◆◆ ◆◆◆
Mexican

Lunch: $6-$8   Dinner: $9-$14   Phone: 520/742-2141   5

Location: Jct Ina Rd, just n. 7360 N Oracle Rd 85704. **Hours:** 11 am-10 pm, Fri & Sat-11 pm. Closed: 11/23, 12/25. **Reservations:** suggested. **Features:** With the third generation preparing meals, the long-established, family-run restaurant offers Sonoran Mexican dishes made with flair and chiles from the owner's farm near Tucson. Casual dress; cocktails. **Parking:** on-site. **Cards:** AX, DC, DS, MC, VI.

MAIN DINING ROOM AT THE ARIZONA INN
▼▼▼
Continental

Lunch: $7-$20   Dinner: $20-$30   Phone: 520/325-1541   64

Location: I-10, exit 257 (Speedway Blvd), 2.5 mi e, 0.5 mi n on Campbell Ave, then just e; in Arizona Inn. 2200 E Elm St 85719. **Hours:** 6:30-10 am, 11:30-2 & 6-10 pm. **Reservations:** suggested. **Features:** The historic inn is a nice spot for refined dining. Diners can savor preparations of seafood, beef and lamb in the formal dining room or on the outside patio, when weather permits. Dressy casual; cocktails; entertainment. **Parking:** on-site. **Cards:** AX, DC, MC, VI.

MCMAHON'S STEAKHOUSE
▼▼▼
Steak House

Lunch: $9-$16   Dinner: $18-$36   Phone: 520/327-7463   47

Location: I-10, exit 256 (Grant Rd), 5.6 mi e, then 0.7 mi n. 2959 N Swan Rd 85712. **Hours:** 11:30 am-10 pm, Sat & Sun 5 pm-11 pm. Closed: 5/29, 7/4, 9/4. **Reservations:** suggested. **Features:** An elegant curving wine cellar and extensive art collection greet diners in the upscale dining room. The accomplished, friendly wait staff serves excellent choice steaks, chops and appetizers. Dressy casual; cocktails; entertainment. **Parking:** valet. **Cards:** AX, CB, DC, DS, MC, VI.

METRO GRILL PARK PLACE
▼▼▼
American

Lunch: $7-$15   Dinner: $12-$18   Phone: 520/571-7111   81

Location: Just w of Wilmot; southside of Park Place Mall. 5870 E Broadway Blvd #520 85711. **Hours:** 11 am-10 pm, Fri & Sat-10:30 pm. Closed: 12/25. **Reservations:** accepted. **Features:** Stop in here to have a great meal before or after shopping. The freshly prepared dishes include pastas, beef, roasted chicken and seafood. Save room for the white chocolate creme brulee. Casual dress; cocktails. **Parking:** on-site and valet. **Cards:** AX, DC, DS, MC, VI.

(See map and index starting on p. 416)

METROPOLITAN GRILL   **Lunch:** $7-$10   **Dinner:** $12-$21   **Phone:** 520/531-1212   (2)
American
Location: I-10, exit 248 (Ina Rd), 5 mi e, then 1 mi n; in Plaza Escondida Shopping Center. 7892 N Oracle Rd 85704. **Hours:** 11 am-10 pm, Fri & Sat-10:30 pm. Closed: 12/25. **Reservations:** suggested. **Features:** Popular with locals and families, the high-energy, upscale eatery presents a wide selection of pizzas and entrees cooked over a wood fire. Casual dress; cocktails. **Parking:** on-site. **Cards:** AX, DC, DS, MC, VI.

MICHELANGELO RISTORANTE ITALIANO   **Lunch:** $7-$13   **Dinner:** $8-$23   **Phone:** 520/297-5775   (1)
Italian
Location: I-10, exit 248 (Ina Rd), then 1 mi n on SR 77 (Oracle Rd). 420 W Magee Rd 85704. **Hours:** 11 am-10 pm. Closed: 1/1, 11/23, 12/25; also Sun & 2 weeks in summer. **Reservations:** not accepted. **Features:** The family-owned-and-operated restaurant serves a large selection of classic dishes from veal Marsala to chicken Toscanini served with artichokes and mushrooms over cheese tortellini. Homemade desserts are too tempting to miss. Patio seating is available. Casual dress; cocktails. **Parking:** on-site. **Cards:** AX, MC, VI.

MI NIDITO FAMILY RESTAURANT   **Lunch:** $5-$11   **Dinner:** $5-$11   **Phone:** 520/622-5081   (84)
Mexican
Location: I-10, exit 259 (Starr Pass Blvd), 0.8 mi e on 22nd St, then 1.2 mi s; northeast corner of 29th St and 4th Ave. 1813 S 4th Ave 85713. **Hours:** 11 am-10:30 pm, Fri & Sat-2 am. Closed major holidays; also Mon & Tues. **Features:** Mi Nidito means "little nest," and guests will be cozy in this one. Hearty portions are served in the bright, welcoming dining room in south Tucson. In the Clinton booth, patrons can taste a dish named after the former president during his visit in 1999. Casual dress; wine only. **Parking:** on-site. **Cards:** AX, DS, MC, VI.

MONA LISA ITALIAN RESTAURANT   **Lunch:** $4-$9   **Dinner:** $12-$18   **Phone:** 520/751-7447   (82)
Italian
Location: Just w of Kolb. 7026 E Broadway Blvd 85710. **Hours:** 11 am-9 pm, Fri & Sat-10 pm, Sun 8 am-9 pm. Closed major holidays; also Mon. **Features:** The Puccia family has operated this small, casual eatery for five years. Everything is made fresh — from the portabella stuffed ravioli to the fettucine Mona Lisa with shrimp, scallops and sun-dried tomatoes. From classics like veal saltimbocca to the wide array of pastries and baked goods in the bakery case, you can be sure to find just what soothes your appetite. Casual dress; beer & wine only. **Parking:** on-site. **Cards:** AX, MC, VI.

MOSAIC CAFE DOS   **Lunch:** $6-$10   **Dinner:** $8-$13   **Phone:** 520/297-8470   (3)
Mexican
Location: Just n of Ina Rd. 7350 N La Cholla Blvd 85741. **Hours:** 7:30 am-9 pm, Sun-2 pm. Closed major holidays. **Features:** Diners come for delicious, freshly cooked foods; friendly and helpful staff; and the fun of watching tortillas patted out and cooked right in front of their eyes. Casual dress; cocktails. **Parking:** on-site. **Cards:** MC, VI.

NONIE   **Dinner:** $7-$17   **Phone:** 520/319-1965   (57)
Creole
Location: I-10, exit 256 (Grant Rd), 3.4 mi e. 2526 E Grant Rd 85716. **Hours:** 5 pm-9 pm, Fri & Sat-10 pm. Closed: 4/16, 11/23, 12/25; also Mon. **Reservations:** suggested, weekends. **Features:** The spicy fragrances of gumbo and jambalaya greet diners as they enter the New Orleans-style bistro. The casual atmosphere, friendly service and made-from-scratch Cajun food are hallmarks of the chef-owners, Chris and Suzy Leonard. Casual dress; cocktails. **Parking:** on-site. **Cards:** AX, CB, DC, DS, JC, MC, VI.

NORTH   **Lunch:** $7-$13   **Dinner:** $11-$28   **Phone:** 520/299-1600   (18)
Nouvelle Italian
Location: Jct Campbell Ave; northwest corner; in La Encantada Plaza. 2995 E Skyline Dr 85718. **Hours:** 11 am-3 & 5-10 pm, Fri & Sat-11 pm, Sun noon-9 pm. Closed: 1/1, 11/23, 12/25. **Reservations:** accepted. **Features:** Robust Northern Italian foods and attentive servers are hallmarks. Huge windows afford views across the valley. Diners can choose from a wide selection of wines and martinis. Casual dress; cocktails. **Parking:** on-site. **Cards:** AX, DS, MC, VI.

OLD PUEBLO GRILL   **Lunch:** $10-$14   **Dinner:** $14-$20   **Phone:** 520/326-6000   (75)
Regional American
Location: Just n of Broadway Blvd. 60 N Alvernon Way 85711. **Hours:** 11 am-10 pm, Fri & Sat-10:30 pm. Closed: 12/25. **Reservations:** accepted. **Features:** Whether on the outside walled patio or inside among large cactus plants, you'll enjoy innovative foods with Southwestern flair served by bright young staff. Casual dress; cocktails; entertainment. **Parking:** on-site. **Cards:** AX, CB, DC, DS, JC, MC, VI.

OLD PUEBLO GRILLE FOOTHILLS MALL   **Lunch:** $7-$14   **Dinner:** $14-$20   **Phone:** 520/297-1999   (8)
Regional American
Location: I-10, exit 248 (Ina Rd), 3.5 mi e; west side of Foothills Mall. 7401 N La Cholla Blvd 85741. **Hours:** 11 am-10 pm, Fri & Sat-10:30 pm. Closed: 12/25. **Reservations:** suggested. **Features:** A pleasant post-shopping stop, the restaurant employs friendly, attentive servers. The atmosphere is casually upscale, and dishes are attractively presented. Casual dress; cocktails. **Parking:** on-site. **Cards:** AX, CB, DC, DS, MC, VI.

OLIVE TREE RESTAURANT   **Lunch:** $7-$15   **Dinner:** $14-$27   **Phone:** 520/298-1845   (52)
Greek
Location: I-10, exit 256 (Grant Rd), 9 mi e, then just ne; in Santa Fe Square. 7000 E Tanque Verde Rd 85715. **Hours:** 11:30 am-2 & 5-9 pm, Fri & Sat-10 pm, Sun 5 pm-9 pm. Closed major holidays. **Reservations:** suggested. **Features:** Traditional Greek dishes, along the lines of shish kebab and moussaka, as well as dishes such as cinnamon chicken and fresh, grilled salmon are served in the intimate dining room, which looks out over the courtyard. Dressy casual; cocktails. **Parking:** on-site. **Cards:** AX, CB, DC, DS, MC, VI.

OREGANO'S PIZZA BISTRO   **Lunch:** $6-$20   **Dinner:** $6-$20   **Phone:** 520/327-8955   (68)
Italian
Location: 0.6 mi w of Craycroft. 4900 E Speedway 85712. **Hours:** 11 am-9 pm, Fri & Sat-10 pm. Closed: 11/23, 12/25. **Features:** The high-energy bistro employs a young and attentive wait staff that serves hearty, oversized portions of delicious food. Offerings range from pizza and salads to pasta and "baked" sandwiches. The patio can be the happening place. Casual dress; cocktails. **Parking:** on-site. **Cards:** AX, DS, MC, VI.

(See map and index starting on p. 416)

PAPAGAYO MEXICAN RESTAURANT & CATINA   Lunch: $5-$8   Dinner: $8-$20   Phone: 520/577-6055   [28]
Mexican
Location: Northeast corner of Sunrise Dr and Swan. 4717 E Sunrise Dr 85718. **Hours:** 11:30 am-9 pm, Sun from noon. Closed: 4/16, 12/25. **Reservations:** suggested. **Features:** Three generations have placed their mark on the popular eatery, which serves traditional dishes made with a Southwestern flair. Enhancing the bright decor is a large entry mural, an unsigned De Grazia original. Casual dress; cocktails. **Parking:** on-site.
Cards: AX, CB, DC, DS, JC, MC, VI.

PASTICHE MODERN EATERY   *Menu on aaa.com*   Lunch: $9-$16   Dinner: $11-$22   Phone: 520/325-3333   [45]
American
Location: Just s of Fort Lowell Rd. 3025 N Campbell Ave 85719. **Hours:** 11:30 am-midnight, Sat & Sun from 4:30 pm. Closed: 1/1, 12/24, 12/25. **Reservations:** suggested. **Features:** The decor, featuring interesting modern art, sets a backdrop for quiet dining. Local products factor significantly in classic yet creative dishes. Barbecue pork with tamarind sauce, thyme-covered sea bass and fried jalapeno ravioli entice guests to try new flavors. Casual dress; cocktails. **Parking:** on-site. **Cards:** AX, DC, DS, MC, VI.

P. F. CHANG'S CHINA BISTRO   Lunch: $7-$13   Dinner: $9-$13   Phone: 520/615-8788   [34]
Regional Chinese
Location: Just w of jct Campbell Ave. 1805 E River Rd 85718. **Hours:** 11 am-11 pm, Fri & Sat-midnight. Closed: 11/23, 12/25. **Reservations:** accepted. **Features:** Regional Chinese and Pacific Rim cuisine is served in a sophisticated setting. Casual dress; cocktails. **Parking:** on-site. **Cards:** AX, CB, DC, DS, JC, MC, VI.

PINNACLE PEAK RESTAURANT   Dinner: $10-$17   Phone: 520/296-0911   [59]
Steak House
Location: Jct Campbell Ave, 5.6 mi e on Grant Rd, then just s. 6541 E Tanque Verde Rd 85715. **Hours:** 5 pm-10 pm, Sat & Sun from 4:30 pm. Closed: 11/23, 12/25. **Reservations:** not accepted. **Features:** In a Western town with a small town square, shops and an opera house, the popular restaurant continues the Western theme in its decor and menu. Diners can count on reliable, down-home fare. Reservations are not accepted. Casual dress; cocktails; entertainment. **Parking:** on-site. **Cards:** AX, DC, DS, MC, VI.

PRIMO   Dinner: $23-$27   Phone: 520/791-6071   [83]
Regional Italian
Location: I-10, exit 259 (Star Pass Blvd), 4.8 mi w; in JW Marriott Starr Pass Resort & Spa. 3800 W Starr Pass Blvd 85745. **Hours:** 6 pm-10 pm. **Reservations:** suggested. **Features:** Chef Melissa Kelly brings a fresh approach to Italian cuisine from delicate side dishes like sauteed baby spinach to the whole roast Mediterranean sea bass with steamed cockles. Luscious desserts vie to bring your attention back to the table from the southern views over the distant valley. Dressy casual; cocktails. **Parking:** valet. **Cards:** AX, CB, DC, DS, JC, MC, VI.

RA SUSHI-BAR-RESTAURANT   Lunch: $6-$13   Dinner: $8-$18   Phone: 520/615-3970   [17]
Sushi
Location: Jct Campbell Ave, northwest corner; in La Encatada Plaza. 2905 E Skyline Dr, Suite 289 85718. **Hours:** 11 am-11 pm. Closed: 12/25. **Features:** The "hip meet-and-greet" place prepares fresh and innovative sushi and a selection of bento box meals that make lunch a treat. The gyoza are spicy and delicious, and any of the tempura selections will be sure to please. Casual dress; cocktails. **Parking:** on-site. **Cards:** AX, DC, DS, MC, VI.

RED SKY CAFE   Lunch: $9-$16   Dinner: $15-$23   Phone: 520/326-5454   [63]
American
Location: Just s of Ft. Lowell. 2900 N Swan Rd 85712. **Hours:** 11 am-10 pm, Sun from 10:30 am. Closed: 7/4, 12/25. **Reservations:** accepted. **Features:** Friendly and accomplished service in the intimate dining room rounds out an upscale meal experience. Salads like the Jamaican jerk chicken come with edible orchids. Entrees include grilled Boston cod in parchment with roasted garlic potatoes. Delectable vegetarian options include pastas and risottos. Casual dress; cocktails. **Parking:** on-site. **Cards:** AX, DS, MC, VI.

RISKY BUSINESS   Lunch: $4-$10   Dinner: $7-$21   Phone: 520/577-0021   [27]
American
Location: Southwest corner of Kolb and E Sunrise. 6866 E Sunrise Dr 85750. **Hours:** 11 am-midnight. Closed: 11/23, 12/25. **Reservations:** not accepted. **Features:** The northeast location is full of brightly colored walls, mountain views and such tasty dishes as peppered roast beef sandwich, down-home meatloaf, Greek pasta salad and build-your-own pizza. Casual dress; cocktails. **Parking:** on-site. **Cards:** AX, DC, DS, MC, VI.

RUSTY'S FAMILY RESTAURANT & SPORTS GRILL   Lunch: $6-$9   Dinner: $9-$18   Phone: 520/623-3363   [54]
American
Location: I-10, exit 256, 1.1 mi w. 2075 W Grant Rd 85745. **Hours:** 10 am-midnight. Closed: 12/25. **Reservations:** accepted. **Features:** Depending on the patron's mood, the front sports bar with banners and TVs is a good place for sandwiches or burgers and the larger dining room is welcoming to families or groups. Both offer friendly service. Casual dress; cocktails. **Parking:** on-site. **Cards:** AX, MC, VI.

SAGUARO CORNERS RESTAURANT   Lunch: $6-$13   Dinner: $12-$26   Phone: 520/886-5424   [86]
Steak House
Location: Jct Hougnton Rd, 3 mi s. 3750 S Old Spanish Tr 85730. **Hours:** noon-2:30 & 5-9:30 pm, Sun noon-9:30 pm. Closed: 12/25; also Mon & 8/1-8/15. **Reservations:** accepted. **Features:** Serving Tucson for more than 40 years, the family feeds the wildlife as well as the public. Patrons can savor steak while watching quail and rabbits in the outdoor garden. Casual dress; cocktails. **Parking:** on-site. **Cards:** AX, DC, DS, MC, VI.

SAUCE   Lunch: $5-$9   Dinner: $7-$9   Phone: 520/297-8575   [10]
Italian
Location: Just s of Ina Rd. 7117 N Oracle Rd 85718. **Hours:** 11 am-9 pm, Fri & Sat-10 pm. Closed major holidays. **Features:** The restaurant's selections could be characterized as "gourmet fast food." Among choices are sausage and caramelized onion or chicken and broccoli rabe pizzas. Lasagna and fresh salads also are on the menu. A clean modern decor with patio or indoor seating adds to a fun dining experience. Casual dress; wine only. **Parking:** on-site. **Cards:** AX, DS, MC, VI.

(See map and index starting on p. 416)

SHER-E-PUNJAB Lunch: $7-$12   Dinner: $7-$12   Phone: 520/624-9393 ⑤⑤
♦♦ ♦♦ **Location:** Just e of 1st Ave. 853 E Grant Rd 85719. **Hours:** 11 am-2:30 & 5-10 pm. Closed: 11/23, 12/25.
Features: The storefront is simple, but the neat, tidy decor welcomes guests to experience the "home-style
Indian cuisine of India." Try crisp samosa appetizers full of meat or vegetables. Fragrant curries include chicken,
lamb, seafood and beef. Casual dress; wine only. **Parking:** on-site. **Cards:** AX, DS, MC, VI.

SILVER SADDLE STEAKHOUSE Lunch: $6-$10   Dinner: $15-$25   Phone: 520/622-6253 ⑧⑤
♦♦ ♦♦ **Location:** I-10, exit 261, southside on Frontage Rd, then just e of 6th Ave. 310 E Benson Hwy 85713. **Hours:** 11 am-
9:30 pm, Fri-10 pm, Sat 2 pm-10 pm, Sun 1 pm-10 pm. Closed: 4/16, 11/23, 12/25.
Steak House **Reservations:** suggested. **Features:** Mesquite wood not only imparts a delicate flavor to meats but also
plays a key role in the decor. The popular grill's bar top is the huge trunk of a mesquite tree that came from
Trincheros, Mexico. The friendly staff keeps beverages filled and lets patrons in on all the extras, from sandwiches to vaquero
grande, a 1.5-pound T-bone. Casual dress; cocktails. **Parking:** on-site. **Cards:** AX, DS, MC, VI. 🍸 ◫

SMOKIN' "A BAR-B-Q PLACE" Lunch: $5-$14   Dinner: $5-$14   Phone: 520/327-7888 ⑥⑦
♦♦ **Location:** Northwest corner of Speedway Blvd and Swan. 4699 E Speedway Blvd 85712. **Hours:** 11 am-10 pm.
Closed: 11/23, 12/25. **Features:** Hearty beef, pork and poultry sandwiches vie with fresh salads and pies,
Barbecue resulting in quick and tasty meals. Casual dress; wine only. **Parking:** on-site. **Cards:** AX, DS, MC, VI.

SOLEIL Lunch: $7-$12   Dinner: $16-$25   Phone: 520/299-3345 ⑯
♦♦♦♦♦♦ **Location:** Jct Campbell Ave, northeast corner. 3001 E Skyline Dr 85718. **Hours:** 11 am-2 & 5-9:30 pm, Fri & Sat-
10 pm, Sun 10:30 am-3 & 5-9:30 pm; Sunday brunch. Closed: 1/1, 11/23, 12/25. **Reservations:** suggested.
International **Features:** High in the foothills and surrounded by art galleries, the restaurant affords breathtaking views
across the valley. Inspired contemporary cuisine with innovative flavors blends well with the wide selection
of wines, as well as samplings from the champagne bar. Dressy casual; cocktails. **Parking:** on-site. **Cards:** AX, CB, DC, DS,
MC, VI.

SONORA BAY RESTAURANT & CANTINA Lunch: $5-$9   Dinner: $7-$14   Phone: 520/615-1818 ㉖
♦♦♦♦♦♦ **Location:** Jct Kolb Rd; southwest corner. 6910 E Sunrise Dr 85750. **Hours:** 11 am-9 pm, Fri-10 pm, Sat 4 pm-10
pm, Sun 4 pm-9 pm. Closed major holidays; also 7/22-7/30. **Reservations:** accepted. **Features:** The patios
Mexican are meeting places where good food and cool beverages can be enjoyed. Try the Mexican barbecue beef or
broiled shrimp for a new taste. Classic dishes like enchiladas, ceviche and burritos are available. Casual
dress; cocktails. **Parking:** on-site. **Cards:** AX, DS, MC, VI. 🍸

SULLIVAN'S STEAKHOUSE Lunch: $10-$20   Dinner: $18-$28   Phone: 520/299-4275 ㉝
♦♦♦♦♦♦ **Location:** Just e of Campbell Ave. 1785 E River Rd 85718. **Hours:** 11 am-2 & 5:30-11 pm, Sat & Sun from 5 pm.
Closed: 11/23, 12/25. **Reservations:** suggested. **Features:** Sophisticated service enhances everything from
Steak House the shellfish and seafood starters to the tender steaks, veal and lamb chops. Delicate souffles are among
lush, freshly prepared desserts. A cigar-friendly bar is separate from the dining room. Casual dress;
cocktails. **Parking:** on-site and valet. **Cards:** AX, DC, DS, MC, VI. 🍸

TERESA'S MOSAIC CAFE Lunch: $6-$10   Dinner: $8-$13   Phone: 520/624-4512 ㊿
♦♦♦♦ **Location:** I-10, exit 256 (Grant Rd), 1 mi w; northwest corner of Silver Mosaic and Grand rds. 2455 N Silver Mosaic Rd
85745. **Hours:** 7:30 am-9 pm, Sun-2 pm. Closed major holidays. **Reservations:** accepted. **Features:** Atop a
Mexican hill, the friendly spot serves freshly made tortillas, which diners may watch being made as they enjoy one of
the many classic Mexican dishes. Casual dress; cocktails. **Parking:** on-site. **Cards:** MC, VI.

TERRA COTTA Lunch: $10-$23   Dinner: $11-$23   Phone: 520/577-8100 ㉒
♦♦♦♦♦♦ **Location:** Jct SR 77 (Oracle Rd), 3.9 mi w on Ina Rd, merging to Skyline Dr, then to Sunrise Dr. 3500 E Sunrise Dr
85718. **Hours:** 11:30 am-10 pm. Closed: 5/29, 11/23, 12/25. **Reservations:** suggested. **Features:** Soft,
Southwest desert colors mix with natural textures of brick, copper and stone to create a quietly warm interior, while the
Southwestern courtyard affords clear views to the Catalina foothills. Diners can request casual indoor or outdoor patio
seating before selecting dishes from a menu of contemporary Southwestern cuisine and gourmet wood-fired
pizzas. Ingredients are fresh and plate presentations attractive. Tapas can be enjoyed in the bar. Attentiveness marks the well-
trained service teams. Casual dress; cocktails. **Parking:** on-site. **Cards:** AX, CB, DC, DS, MC, VI.

TOHONO CHUL PARK TEA ROOM Lunch: $7-$11   Phone: 520/797-1222 ④
♦♦♦♦ **Location:** Jct Oracle Rd, just w on Ina Rd, then just n. 7366 N Paseo Del Norte 85704. **Hours:** 8 am-5 pm. Closed
major holidays. **Features:** Surrounded by Tohono Chul Park, the refreshing stopping place affords desert
American garden views. Breakfasts and luncheons are locally popular, and afternoon tea, complete with scones, is
served daily. Casual dress; wine only. **Parking:** on-site. **Cards:** AX, MC, VI.

TRATTORIA PINA Lunch: $6-$11   Dinner: $8-$25   Phone: 520/577-6992 ㉚
♦♦♦♦ **Location:** Just s of Sunrise. 5541 N Swan Rd 85718. **Hours:** 11:30 am-2:30 & 5-10 pm, Sat from 4:30 pm.
Closed: 1/1, 7/4, 12/25; also Sun. **Reservations:** accepted. **Features:** Near the base of the Catalina
Italian Mountains, the intimate eatery has a charming patio and display kitchen. On the menu are hearty pasta
dishes, wood-fired oven pizzas and a wide variety of veal, lamb, beef and seafood preparations. Dressy
casual; cocktails. **Parking:** on-site. **Cards:** AX, MC, VI. ◫

TUCSON MCGRAW'S ORIGINAL CANTINA Lunch: $7-$11   Dinner: $8-$21   Phone: 520/885-3088 ⑧⑦
♦♦ ♦♦ **Location:** 0.6 mi n of jct Irvington Rd. 4110 S Houghton Rd 85730. **Hours:** 11 am-10 pm. Closed: 4/16, 11/23,
12/25. **Reservations:** not accepted. **Features:** Perched on a hill overlooking the valley south of the city is a
American casual eatery with "see forever" views. Representative of good home-style cooking are mesquite-barbecue
dishes, which locals have enjoyed for 20 years. Servers are friendly. Casual dress; cocktails. **Parking:**
site. **Cards:** AX, DC, MC, VI. ◫

(See map and index starting on p. 416)

THE VENTANA ROOM   *Menu on aaa.com*   **Dinner: $75-$105**   **Phone: 520/615-5494**   14

AAA

▽AAA▽ ▽AAA▽ ▽AAA▽ ▽AAA▽

Continental

Location: I-10, exit 256 (Grant Rd), 8.6 mi e, 0.6 mi ne on Tanque Verde Rd, 2 mi n on Sabino Canyon Rd, then 3.5 mi n on Kolb Rd; in Loews Ventana Canyon Resort. 7000 N Resort Dr 85715. **Hours:** Open 3/1-7/31 & 9/1-1/31; 6 pm-9 pm, Fri & Sat-10 pm. Closed: Sun & Mon. **Reservations:** suggested. **Features:** The elegant setting is a favorite choice for sophisticated dining and spectacular city views. Chef Trosch's intriguing degustation menu ($75-$105) lines up seasonal specialties and signature desserts in beautiful presentations. Complex in flavor in texture, examples might include braided salmon with Yukon gold potatoes and loup de mer with fennel and gnocchi. The competent staff works together to provide seamless service, and the head waiter can describe any dish and recommend wine pairings. Semi-formal attire; cocktails. **Parking:** valet. **Cards:** AX, CB, DC, DS, JC, MC, VI.

VIVACE RESTAURANT   **Lunch: $7-$12**   **Dinner: $12-$26**   **Phone: 520/795-7221**   38

▽AAA▽ ▽AAA▽ ▽AAA▽

Italian

Location: I-10, exit 254 (Prince Rd), 4.2 mi e, then 1.2 mi n. 4310 N Campbell 85718. **Hours:** 11:30 am-9 pm, Fri & Sat-10 pm. Closed: Sun. **Reservations:** suggested. **Features:** The restaurant's location in popular St. Philip's Plaza incorporates patio seating. Contemporary Italian dishes are made with the freshest mix of ingredients. Casual dress; cocktails. **Parking:** on-site. **Cards:** AX, DC, DS, MC, VI.

WILDFLOWER   **Lunch: $6-$15**   **Dinner: $14-$27**   **Phone: 520/219-4230**   12

▽AAA▽ ▽AAA▽ ▽AAA▽

American

synthesis of Asian, MC, VI.

Location: Just s of Ina Rd. 7037 N Oracle Rd 85718. **Hours:** 11 am-3 & 5-9 pm, Fri & Sat-10 pm, Sun 5 pm-9 pm. Closed major holidays. **Reservations:** suggested. **Features:** In keeping with the restaurant's name, the modern, trendy decor includes oversize photographs of brightly colored flowers, as well as flowers incorporated into some plate presentations. Delectable meat and seafood dishes are prepared in a French and New American cooking styles. Casual dress; cocktails. **Parking:** on-site. **Cards:** AX, DC, DS,

⊻

ZEMAM'S   **Lunch: $8-$10**   **Dinner: $8-$10**   **Phone: 520/323-9928**   77

▽AAA▽

Ethiopian

Location: Just e of Tucson Blvd. 2731 E Broadway Blvd 85716. **Hours:** 11 am-2:30 & 4-9:30 pm. Closed: 1/1, 11/23, 12/25; also Mon. **Features:** Spicy Ethiopian dishes are served in a casual atmosphere with leisurely service. Forks are offered, but the traditional style of eating with fingers is always acceptable. Casual dress. **Parking:** on-site. **Cards:** MC, VI.

The Tucson Vicinity

CATALINA pop. 7,025

——— **WHERE TO STAY** ———

SUPER 8 MOTEL-TUCSON/CATALINA   *Book at aaa.com*   **Phone: 520/818-9500**

▽AAA▽ ▽AAA▽

Motel

Property failed to provide current rates

Location: 4.6 mi n of Tangerine Rd. 15691 N Oracle Rd 85739. Fax: 520/818-9600. **Facility:** 50 one-bedroom standard units. 2 stories (no elevator), interior/exterior corridors. *Bath:* combo or shower only. **Parking:** on-site. **Terms:** pets ($10 fee). **Amenities:** voice mail, irons, hair dryers. **Pool(s):** small outdoor. **Guest Services:** coin laundry. **Business Services:** meeting rooms.

SOME UNITS

🛏 FEE ♿ 🏊 📷 [DATA PORT] 🛢 🖨 💻 / ⊠ /

——— *The following lodging was either not evaluated or did not meet AAA rating requirements but is listed for your information only.* ———

MIRAVAL LIFE IN BALANCE RESORT   **Phone: 520/825-4000**

[fyi]

Not evaluated. **Location:** 5000 E Via Estancia Miraval 85739. Facilities, services, and decor characterize an upscale property.

——— **WHERE TO DINE** ———

MI TIERRA RESTAURANTE   **Lunch: $6-$10**   **Dinner: $10-$17**   **Phone: 520/825-3040**

▽AAA▽ ▽AAA▽

Mexican

Location: 5.3 mi n of Tangerine Rd. 16238 N Oracle Rd 85739. **Hours:** 11 am-9 pm, Sun from noon, Mon from 4 pm. Closed: 11/23, 12/25. **Features:** The friendly staff, bright Mexican decor and traditional Sonoran dishes warm diners' heart and satisfy their craving for a "comfort" meal. Casual dress; cocktails. **Parking:** on-site. **Cards:** AX, DC, DS, MC, VI.

◣

GREEN VALLEY pop. 17,283   (See map and index starting on p. 416)

——— **WHERE TO STAY** ———

BAYMONT INN & SUITES   *Book at aaa.com*   **Phone: (520)399-3736**   89

AAA [SAVE]

▽AAA▽ ▽AAA▽ ▽AAA▽

Small-scale Hotel

11/1-1/31	1P: $94-$134	2P: $104-$144	XP: $10	F17
2/1-3/31	1P: $89-$129	2P: $99-$139	XP: $10	F17
4/1-5/31	1P: $64-$89	2P: $74-$99	XP: $10	F17
6/1-10/31	1P: $64-$84	2P: $74-$94	XP: $10	F17

Location: I-19, exit 65, just w. 90 W Esperanza Blvd 85614. Fax: 520/399-3744. **Facility:** 58 one-bedroom standard units. 2 stories, interior corridors. *Bath:* combo or shower only. **Parking:** on-site. **Terms:** package plans, small pets only ($50 deposit). **Amenities:** voice mail, irons, hair dryers. **Pool(s):** heated outdoor. **Leisure Activities:** whirlpool, exercise room. **Guest Services:** coin laundry. **Business Services:** meeting rooms. **Cards:** AX, CB, DC, DS, MC, VI. **Special Amenities:** free expanded continental breakfast and free local telephone calls.

SOME UNITS

[S⬦] 🛏 🍴 FEE 📷 🍸 🏊 📷 [DATA PORT] 💻 / ⊠ 🛢 🖨 /

(See map and index starting on p. 416)

BEST WESTERN GREEN VALLEY   *Book at aaa.com*   Phone: (520)625-2250   **90**

AAA SAVE	2/1-4/15	1P: $89-$119	2P: $94-$124	XP: $5	F16
	4/16-5/31	1P: $79-$99	2P: $84-$104	XP: $5	F16
	10/1-1/31	1P: $69-$89	2P: $74-$84	XP: $5	F16
	6/1-9/30	1P: $54-$79	2P: $59-$84	XP: $5	F16

Small-scale Hotel **Location:** I-19, exit 65, just w, then just s. 111 S La Canada Dr 85614. Fax: 520/625-0215. **Facility:** 107 one-bedroom standard units. 2 stories (no elevator), interior corridors. **Parking:** on-site. **Terms:** weekly rates available, package plans, small pets only ($10 extra charge). **Amenities:** voice mail, irons, hair dryers. *Some:* high-speed Internet. **Dining:** Lavender, see separate listing. **Pool(s):** heated outdoor. **Leisure Activities:** whirlpool, exercise room. **Guest Services:** coin laundry. **Business Services:** meeting rooms, PC. **Cards:** AX, CB, DC, DS, JC, MC, VI. **Special Amenities:** free local telephone calls and early check-in/late check-out. *(See color ad below)* SOME UNITS

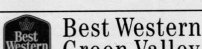

HOLIDAY INN EXPRESS   *Book at aaa.com*   Phone: 520/625-0900   **88**

Property failed to provide current rates

Small-scale Hotel **Location:** I-19, exit 69 (Duval Mine Rd), west side of interstate, then just s. 19200 S I-19 Frontage Rd 85614. Fax: 520/393-0522. **Facility:** 60 one-bedroom standard units, some with whirlpools. 3 stories, interior corridors. *Bath:* combo or shower only. **Parking:** on-site. **Terms:** pets ($80-$100 extra charge, in limited units). **Amenities:** high-speed Internet (fee), voice mail, irons, hair dryers. **Pool(s):** small heated indoor. **Leisure Activities:** whirlpool. **Guest Services:** coin laundry. SOME UNITS

(See map and index starting on p. 416)

INN AT SAN IGNACIO   *Book at aaa.com*   Phone: (520)393-5700   **91**

AAA [SAVE]   2/1-4/30 & 12/1-1/31   1P: $129-$149   2P: $129-$149   XP: $20   F17
             9/1-11/30   1P: $119-$139   2P: $119-$139   XP: $20   F17
             5/1-8/31   1P: $89-$109   2P: $89-$109   XP: $20   F17

Condominium   **Location:** I-19, exit 56, 0.5 mi n on Frontage Rd, 0.3 mi w on Calle Tres, then just n on Camino Del Sol, follow signs. 1861 W Demetrie Loop 85614. Fax: 520/393-1915. **Facility:** In a residential area, duplexes have large, well-appointed rooms, some with washers and dryers; a heated pool and golf course are among the amenities. Designated smoking area. 85 units. 43 one-bedroom standard units. 42 one-bedroom suites ($119-$199) with kitchens. 1 story, exterior corridors. *Bath:* combo or shower only. **Parking:** on-site. **Terms:** office hours 7 am-8 pm, weekly rates available, package plans. **Amenities:** video library, voice mail, irons, hair dryers. **Pool(s):** heated outdoor. **Leisure Activities:** whirlpool, gas barbecue grills. **Fee:** golf-72 holes. **Guest Services:** area transportation-within 5 mi. **Business Services:** meeting rooms. **Cards:** AX, DS, MC, VI. **Special Amenities:** free local telephone calls. *(See color ad p 455)*

──────── **WHERE TO DINE** ────────

AGAVE AT DESERT DIAMOND CASINO   **Lunch:** $10-$15   **Dinner:** $11-$22   Phone: 520/393-2720   **99**

Regional American   **Location:** I-19, exit 80, just e; in Desert Diamond Casino. 1100 W Pima Mine Rd 85629. **Hours:** 11 am-10 pm; to 9 pm 5/1-10/31. **Reservations:** suggested. **Features:** After a show or an evening in the casino, patrons can relax and enjoy friendly service and such dishes as Sea of Cortez cabrilla with cremini and green chiles. Chargrilled steaks are a specialty. Dressy casual; cocktails. **Parking:** on-site and valet. **Cards:** AX, DS, MC, VI.

GRILL AT QUAIL CREEK   **Lunch:** $6-$12   **Dinner:** $10-$18   Phone: 520/393-5806

American   **Location:** I-19, exit 63, 3.9 mi n on Continental Rd/Old Nogales Hwy, then 1.5 mi s. 1490 N Quail Range Loop #3 85614. **Hours:** 11 am-3 & 4-8 pm, Sun-3 pm. Closed: Mon 6/1-9/1. **Reservations:** accepted. **Features:** Attractive prairie decor surrounds the dining room, where guests eat overlooking the golf course. Friendly servers bring out freshly made and attractively presented beef, pork and seafood dishes. Casual dress; cocktails. **Parking:** on-site. **Cards:** AX, DS, MC, VI.

LAVENDER   **Lunch:** $8-$15   **Dinner:** $11-$22   Phone: 520/648-0205   **100**

French   **Location:** I-19, exit 65, just w, then just s; in Best Western Green Valley. 111 S La Canada Dr 85614. **Hours:** 7-10 am, 11-3 & 5-8 pm, Sun 8 am-2 pm. **Reservations:** suggested. **Features:** A surprise is in store at this modest bistro. The classically trained chef has adapted recipes using regional ingredients to create dishes that blend flavors and textures. Enjoyable dishes include Australian lamb with Moroccan couscous and sun-dried tomatoes or grilled ahi tuna with white corn relish. Casual dress; cocktails. **Parking:** on-site. **Cards:** AX, MC, VI.

MARANA pop. 13,556   (See map and index starting on p. 416)

──────── **WHERE TO STAY** ────────

BEST WESTERN CONTINENTAL INN   *Book at aaa.com*   Phone: (520)579-1099   **73**

             2/1-2/18   1P: $149-$179   2P: $159-$199   XP: $10   F16
             2/19-4/30 & 10/1-1/31   1P: $89-$99   2P: $99-$139   XP: $10   F16
Small-scale Hotel   5/1-9/30   1P: $69-$79   2P: $79-$89   XP: $10   F16

Location: I-10, exit 246 (Cortaro Rd), just w. 8425 N Cracker Barrel Rd 85743. Fax: 520/579-6938. **Facility:** 65 one-bedroom standard units. 3 stories, interior corridors. *Bath:* combo or shower only. **Parking:** on-site. **Terms:** cancellation fee imposed, [CP] meal plan available. **Amenities:** high-speed Internet, voice mail, irons, hair dryers. **Pool(s):** small outdoor. **Leisure Activities:** whirlpool, exercise room. **Guest Services:** coin laundry. **Business Services:** PC. **Cards:** AX, DC, DS, MC, VI.

SOME UNITS

COMFORT INN I-10 & INA   *Book at aaa.com*   Phone: (520)579-7202   **79**

             2/1-2/28   1P: $70-$150   2P: $75-$150
             1/1-1/31   1P: $65-$95   2P: $65-$95
Small-scale Hotel   3/1-4/30   1P: $65-$85   2P: $65-$85
             5/1-12/31   1P: $39-$60   2P: $40-$60

Location: I-10, exit 248 (Ina Rd), just w. 4930 W Ina Rd 85743. Fax: 520/579-3894. **Facility:** 60 units. 55 one-bedroom standard units. 5 one-bedroom suites with whirlpools. 3 stories, interior corridors. *Bath:* combo or shower only. **Parking:** on-site. **Terms:** 7 day cancellation notice. **Amenities:** irons, hair dryers. *Some:* high-speed Internet. **Pool(s):** small outdoor. **Leisure Activities:** whirlpool, exercise room. **Guest Services:** coin laundry. **Business Services:** meeting rooms, fax (fee). **Cards:** AX, DC, DS, MC, VI.

SOME UNITS

DAYS INN & SUITES-TUCSON/MARANA   *Book at aaa.com*   Phone: (520)744-6677   **74**

AAA [SAVE]   . All Year [ECP]   1P: $49-$169   2P: $49-$169

Small-scale Hotel   **Location:** I-10, exit 246 (Cortaro Rd), just w. 8370 N Cracker Barrel Rd 85743. Fax: 520/744-8779. **Facility:** 62 units. 59 one-bedroom standard units, some with whirlpools. 3 one-bedroom suites ($79-$189). 3 stories, interior corridors. *Bath:* combo or shower only. **Parking:** on-site. **Terms:** cancellation fee imposed. **Amenities:** high-speed Internet, irons, hair dryers. **Pool(s):** heated outdoor. **Leisure Activities:** whirlpool. **Guest Services:** coin laundry. **Business Services:** meeting rooms. **Cards:** AX, CB, DC, DS, JC, MC, VI. **Special Amenities:** free expanded continental breakfast and free local telephone calls.

SOME UNITS

(See map and index starting on p. 416)

HOLIDAY INN EXPRESS
Phone: 520/572-4777   **76**

2/1-2/28 & 1/1-1/31	1P: $159-$189	2P: $169-$199	XP: $10 F18
9/1-12/31	1P: $99-$129	2P: $109-$149	XP: $10 F18
3/1-8/31	1P: $89-$119	2P: $99-$129	XP: $10 F18

Small-scale Hotel   **Location:** I-10, exit 246 (Cortaro Rd), just w, then just n. 8373 N Cracker Barrel Rd 85743. Fax: 520/572-4666. **Facility:** 83 one-bedroom standard units, some with whirlpools. 3 stories, interior corridors. *Bath:* combo or shower only. **Parking:** on-site. **Amenities:** high-speed Internet, dual phone lines, voice mail, irons, hair dryers. **Pool(s):** small heated outdoor. **Leisure Activities:** whirlpool, exercise room. **Guest Services:** coin laundry. **Business Services:** meeting rooms, PC, fax (fee). **Cards:** AX, CB, DC, DS, MC, VI.

SOME UNITS

LAZY K BAR GUEST RANCH
Phone: (520)744-3050   **78**

2/1-4/30 [AP]	1P: $225-$250	2P: $340-$385	XP: $95 F3
10/1-1/31 [AP]	1P: $200-$250	2P: $320-$340	XP: $95 F3
5/1-5/31 & 9/1-9/30 [AP]	1P: $160-$185	2P: $230-$265	XP: $70 F3

Ranch   **Location:** I-10, exit 246 (Cortaro Rd), 1 mi w, 1.8 mi nw on Silverbell Rd, 0.5 mi sw on Continental Reserve Loop Rd/Coachline Blvd, then 0.7 mi nw on Pima Farms Rd. Located in the foothills of Sombrero Peak. 8401 N Scenic Dr 85743. Fax: 520/744-7628. **Facility:** Visit the typical Western horse corral, this ranch offers many other recreational facilities and outdoor activities. Designated smoking area. 24 units. 18 one-bedroom standard units. 6 one-bedroom suites ($305-$485), some with efficiencies and/or whirlpools. 1 story, exterior corridors. **Parking:** on-site. **Terms:** open 2/1-5/31 & 9/1-1/31, office hours 8 am-9 pm, age restrictions may apply, 30 day cancellation notice, package plans. **Amenities:** video library. **Pool(s):** heated outdoor. **Leisure Activities:** whirlpool, recreation programs, hiking trails, horseback riding, playground, horseshoes, shuffleboard. *Fee:* massage. **Guest Services:** TV in common area, gift shop, coin laundry. **Business Services:** conference facilities. **Cards:** DS, MC, VI.

SOME UNITS

RAMADA LIMITED & SUITES   *Book at aaa.com*
Phone: (520)572-4235   **75**

2/1-2/28	1P: $149-$189	2P: $159-$199	XP: $10 F12
3/1-5/31 & 12/23-1/31	1P: $79-$99	2P: $79-$99	XP: $10 F12
6/1-12/22	1P: $59-$79	2P: $59-$79	XP: $10 F12

Small-scale Hotel   **Location:** I-10, exit 246 (Cortaro Rd), just w, then just n. 6020 W Hospitality Rd 85743. Fax: 520/572-2175. **Facility:** 65 units. 63 one-bedroom standard units. 2 one-bedroom suites ($89-$209) with kitchens. 3 stories, interior corridors. *Bath:* combo or shower only. **Parking:** on-site. **Terms:** [CP] meal plan available, small pets only ($10 extra charge, with prior approval). **Amenities:** high-speed Internet, voice mail, irons, hair dryers. **Pool(s):** small heated indoor. **Leisure Activities:** whirlpool, exercise room. **Guest Services:** coin laundry. **Business Services:** meeting rooms, fax (fee). **Cards:** AX, CB, DC, DS, JC, MC, VI. **Special Amenities:** free expanded continental breakfast and free local telephone calls.

SOME UNITS

FEE

(See map and index starting on p. 416)

RED ROOF INN TUCSON NORTH *Book at aaa.com* Phone: (520)744-8199 **80**

	2/1-4/1	1P: $54-$68	2P: $59-$73	XP: $5	F18
	11/26-1/31	1P: $45-$60	2P: $50-$65	XP: $5	F18
Small-scale Hotel	4/2-11/25	1P: $42-$57	2P: $47-$62	XP: $5	F18

Location: I-10, exit 248 (Ina Rd), just w. 4940 W Ina Rd 85743. Fax: 520/744-7782. **Facility:** 133 one-bedroom standard units. 4 stories, interior corridors. *Bath:* combo or shower only. **Parking:** on-site. **Terms:** small pets only. **Amenities:** video games (fee), voice mail. **Pool(s):** heated outdoor. **Guest Services:** coin laundry. **Business Services:** fax (fee). **Cards:** AX, CB, DC, DS, MC, VI.

SOME UNITS

SUPER 8 MOTEL *Book at aaa.com* Phone: 520/572-0300 **77**

| | 2/1-3/31 & 1/1-1/31 | 1P: $69-$89 | 2P: $89-$109 | XP: $10 | F |
| Small-scale Hotel | 4/1-12/31 | 1P: $59-$69 | 2P: $79-$89 | XP: $10 | F |

Location: I-10, exit 246 (Cortaro Rd), just w. 8351 N Cracker Barrel Rd 85743. Fax: 520/572-9071. **Facility:** 67 one-bedroom standard units, some with whirlpools. 2 stories (no elevator), interior corridors. *Bath:* combo or shower only. **Parking:** on-site. **Terms:** pets ($20 deposit, must remain caged). **Amenities:** voice mail, hair dryers. *Some:* irons. **Pool(s):** small outdoor. **Leisure Activities:** whirlpool. **Guest Services:** coin laundry. **Business Services:** fax (fee). **Cards:** AX, DC, DS, MC, VI.

SOME UNITS

TRAVELODGE *Book at aaa.com* Phone: (520)744-3382 **81**

	2/1-2/28	1P: $90-$150	2P: $90-$150	
	1/1-1/31	1P: $65-$95	2P: $65-$95	
	3/1-4/30	1P: $75-$90	2P: $75-$90	
Small-scale Hotel	5/1-12/31	1P: $49-$65	2P: $50-$70	

Location: I-10, exit 248 (Ina Rd), just w. 4910 W Ina Rd 85743. Fax: 520/744-4116. **Facility:** 69 units. 68 one-bedroom standard units, some with whirlpools. 1 one-bedroom suite. 2 stories (no elevator), exterior corridors. *Bath:* combo or shower only. **Parking:** on-site. **Terms:** small pets only ($10 extra charge). **Amenities:** voice mail, irons, hair dryers. *Some:* high-speed Internet. **Pool(s):** small outdoor. **Leisure Activities:** whirlpool. **Guest Services:** coin laundry. **Business Services:** fax (fee). **Cards:** AX, DC, DS, MC, VI.

SOME UNITS

——— WHERE TO DINE ———

LI'L ABNER'S STEAKHOUSE **Dinner:** $12-$29 Phone: 520/744-2800 **91**

Steak House

Location: I-10, exit 246 (Cortaro Rd), 0.9 mi w, then 1.3 mi n. 8500 N Silverbell Rd 85743. **Hours:** 5 pm-10 pm, Fri & Sat-11 pm. Closed: 11/23, 12/24, 12/25. **Reservations:** accepted. **Features:** An area institution, the restaurant grills steaks, ribs and chicken on an outdoor pit. Young servers are energetic. The wooden building sports years of guest graffiti on the walls. Casual dress; cocktails; entertainment. **Parking:** on-site. **Cards:** AX, MC, VI.

ORO VALLEY pop. 29,700 (See map and index starting on p. 416)

——— WHERE TO STAY ———

HILTON TUCSON EL CONQUISTADOR GOLF & TENNIS RESORT *Book at aaa.com* Phone: (520)544-5000 **85**

	1/7-1/31	1P: $179-$299	2P: $179-$299	XP: $20	F18
	2/1-5/21	1P: $179-$279	2P: $179-$279	XP: $20	F18
	9/10-1/6	1P: $109-$199	2P: $109-$199	XP: $20	F18
Resort	5/22-9/9	1P: $79-$169	2P: $79-$169	XP: $20	F18

Large-scale Hotel

Location: I-10, exit 248 (Ina Rd), 5.4 mi e, then 4.4 mi n. Located in a quiet area. 10000 N Oracle Rd 85737. Fax: 520/544-1228. **Facility:** This large resort at the base of the Catalina Mountains has spacious rooms around a landscaped pool area brightened by vibrant yellow umbrellas. 428 units. 328 one-bedroom standard units. 100 one-bedroom suites, some with whirlpools. 1-3 stories, interior/exterior corridors. *Bath:* combo or shower only. **Parking:** on-site and valet. **Terms:** check-in 4 pm, cancellation fee imposed, package plans, small pets only ($50 deposit, in designated units). **Amenities:** video games (fee), dual phone lines, voice mail, safes, honor bars, irons, hair dryers. *Some:* fax. *Fee:* DVD players. **Dining:** 3 restaurants, 7 am-11 pm, cocktails, also, The Last Territory, see separate listing, entertainment. **Pool(s):** 3 heated outdoor, wading. **Leisure Activities:** whirlpools, waterslide, plunge pool with waterfall, rental bicycles, horseshoes, volleyball. *Fee:* golf-45 holes, 31 lighted tennis courts, racquetball courts, horseback riding, massage. **Guest Services:** gift shop, valet laundry, area transportation-golf club. **Business Services:** conference facilities, business center. **Cards:** AX, CB, DC, DS, JC, MC, VI. **Special Amenities:** free newspaper.

SOME UNITS

HOLIDAY INN EXPRESS SUITES *Book at aaa.com* Phone: 520/202-4000 **84**

Property failed to provide current rates

Small-scale Hotel

Location: 3.9 mi n from jct Ina Rd. 10150 N Oracle Rd 85737. Fax: 520/202-4040. **Facility:** Smoke free premises. 89 units. 88 one-bedroom standard units, some with whirlpools. 1 one-bedroom suite with kitchen and whirlpool. 2 stories, interior corridors. *Bath:* combo or shower only. **Parking:** on-site. **Amenities:** video games (fee), dual phone lines, voice mail, safes, irons, hair dryers. **Pool(s):** small heated outdoor. **Leisure Activities:** whirlpool, exercise room. **Guest Services:** coin laundry. **Business Services:** meeting rooms, business center.

SOME UNITS

(See map and index starting on p. 416)

—————— The following lodging was either not evaluated or did not ——————
meet AAA rating requirements but is listed for your information only.

VISTOSO RESORT CASITAS
Phone: 520/797-4496

fyi

Not evaluated. **Location:** Jct Tangerine Rd, 2.2 mi n on Rancho Vistoso Blvd, then just w. 655 W Vistoso Highlands Dr 85737. Facilities, services, and decor characterize a mid-range property.

—————— WHERE TO DINE ——————

CIBARIA CUCINA ITALIANA   **Lunch:** $7-$9   **Dinner:** $11-$20   Phone: 520/825-2900   **94**

♦♦ ♦♦

Italian

Location: 1 mi n of Tangerine Rd; in Rancho Vistoso Plaza. 12985 N Oracle Rd, Suite 165 85737. **Hours:** 11 am-2:30 & 4:30-9 pm, Sun 10 am-2 & 4:30-9 pm. Closed: 12/25; also Mon. **Features:** Friendly owners welcome diners, assist in dinner choices and carefully prepare a large variety of pasta entrees, as well as a selection of veal, seafood and chicken dishes. Casual dress; cocktails. **Parking:** on-site. **Cards:** AX, DS, MC, VI.

CIEN ANOS-MEXICAN GRILL   **Lunch:** $5-$9   **Dinner:** $11-$25   Phone: 520/877-8153   **95**

♦♦♦

Continental

Location: Jct Lambert Ln. 10325 N La Canada Dr 85739. **Hours:** 11:30 am-2:30 & 5-10 pm, Wed from 5 pm. Closed major holidays; also Sun. **Reservations:** accepted. **Features:** An upscale bistro atmosphere sets the stage for some delicious dining. Dishes such as grilled shrimp with Chihuahua cheese and pork tenderloin with mango, tamarind and jalapeno chutney are prepared in the sophisticated style of Mexico City's Continental cuisine. Casual dress; cocktails. **Parking:** on-site. **Cards:** AX, MC, VI.

THE LAST TERRITORY   **Dinner:** $13-$21   Phone: 520/544-5000   **96**

♦♦ ♦♦

Steak House

Location: I-10, exit 248 (Ina Rd), 5.4 mi e, then 4.4 mi n; in Hilton Tucson El Conquistador Golf & Tennis Resort. 10000 N Oracle Rd 85737. **Hours:** 5 pm-10 pm. Closed: Mon. **Reservations:** accepted. **Features:** Casual Western decor and saloon-style entertainment provide a lively atmosphere at this informal restaurant. The menu lists selections of steak and chicken, as well as Southwestern dishes. Casual dress; cocktails; entertainment.
Parking: on-site. **Cards:** AX, CB, DC, DS, JC, MC, VI.

Arizona-Sonora Desert Museum / Gill Kenny / Metropolitan Tucson Convention and Visitors Bureau

This ends listings for the Tucson Vicinity.
The following page resumes the alphabetical listings of cities in Arizona.

WICKENBURG pop. 5,082

———— WHERE TO STAY ————

AMERICINN   *Book at aaa.com*
◊◊◊ ◊◊◊

11/2-1/31	1P: $73-$79	2P: $81-$86	XP: $10 F12
2/1-5/31	1P: $69-$73	2P: $71-$86	XP: $10 F12
6/1-11/1	1P: $59-$68	2P: $65-$74	XP: $10 F12

Small-scale Hotel   **Location:** 1.3 mi se on US 60. 850 E Wickenburg Way 85390. Fax: 928/684-1118. **Facility:** 29 one-bedroom standard units. 2 stories (no elevator), interior corridors. *Bath:* combo or shower only. **Parking:** on-site. **Terms:** 5 day cancellation notice, pets ($6 extra charge). **Amenities:** hair dryers. **Pool(s):** heated outdoor. **Leisure Activities:** whirlpool. **Business Services:** fax. **Cards:** AX, CB, DC, DS, JC, MC, VI.

Phone: (928)684-5461

SOME UNITS
(ASK) (S/D) 🐕 🍴 📶 🐾 🎬 📠 💻 🖨 / ✕ / DATA PORT /
FEE

BEST WESTERN RANCHO GRANDE   *Book at aaa.com*
◊◊◊ ◊◊◊

2/1-5/31 & 1/1-1/31	1P: $73-$105	2P: $78-$111	XP: $5 F16
10/1-12/31	1P: $65-$96	2P: $70-$102	XP: $5 F16
6/1-9/30	1P: $59-$91	2P: $64-$97	XP: $5 F16

Small-scale Hotel   **Location:** On US 60; center. 293 E Wickenburg Way 85390. Fax: 928/684-7380. **Facility:** 78 units. 68 one-bedroom standard units, some with efficiencies. 10 one-bedroom suites ($109-$119) with kitchens. 1-2 stories (no elevator), exterior corridors. *Bath:* combo or shower only. **Parking:** on-site. **Terms:** [CP] meal plan available, pets ($8 extra charge). **Amenities:** irons, hair dryers. *Some:* high-speed Internet. **Pool(s):** heated outdoor. **Leisure Activities:** whirlpool, playground, horseshoes, volleyball. **Guest Services:** valet laundry. **Business Services:** fax (fee). **Cards:** AX, CB, DC, DS, MC, VI. *(See color ad below)*

Phone: (928)684-5445

SOME UNITS
(ASK) (S/D) ➤ 🐕 🍴 📶 🐾 ✕ 🎬 DATA PORT 💻 / ✕ 🖨 /
FEE

LOS VIAJEROS INN
◊◊◊ ◊◊◊

2/1-5/15	1P: $75	2P: $95-$110	XP: $10 F3
5/16-5/31	1P: $75	2P: $85-$100	XP: $10 F3
9/1-1/31	1P: $70-$85	2P: $72-$90	XP: $10 F3
6/1-8/31	1P: $68-$75	2P: $68-$75	XP: $10 F3

Small-scale Hotel   **Location:** 1 mi n of jct US 60 and 93. 1000 N Tegner Rd 85390. Fax: 928/684-7112. **Facility:** 57 one-bedroom standard units. 2 stories (no elevator), exterior corridors. *Bath:* combo or shower only. **Parking:** on-site. **Terms:** [CP] meal plan available. **Pool(s):** heated outdoor. **Leisure Activities:** whirlpool. **Guest Services:** valet laundry. **Business Services:** meeting rooms, fax (fee). **Cards:** AX, DC, DS, MC, VI.

Phone: 928/684-7099

SOME UNITS
(ASK) (S/D) 🍴 📶 🐾 🎬 DATA PORT 💻 🖨 / ✕ VCR 🖨 /

SUPER 8 MOTEL
◊◊◊ ◊◊◊

All Year	1P: $65-$75	2P: $70-$80	XP: $5 F12

Motel   **Location:** 1 mi n of US 60 and 93. 975 N Tegner St 85390. Fax: 928/684-0878. **Facility:** 40 one-bedroom standard units. 2 stories (no elevator), interior/exterior corridors. *Bath:* combo or shower only. **Parking:** on-site. **Terms:** [CP] meal plan available, pets ($10 extra charge). **Amenities:** hair dryers. **Guest Services:** coin laundry. **Business Services:** meeting rooms, fax (fee). **Cards:** AX, CB, DC, DS, JC, MC, VI.

Phone: 928/684-0808

SOME UNITS
(ASK) (S/D) 🐕 📶 DATA PORT / ✕ 📠 🖨 💻 /
FEE

—————— **WHERE TO DINE** ——————

ANITA'S COCINA

Mexican

Lunch: $5-$10   **Dinner:** $5-$10   Phone: 928/684-5777

Location: Just n of US 60; center. 57 N Valentine 85358. **Hours:** 11 am-9 pm. Closed major holidays.
Features: Popular with the locals, the casual eatery serves hearty portions of such classic dishes as cheese enchiladas with rice and beans and chiles rellenos. Casual dress; cocktails. **Parking:** street.
Cards: MC, VI.

GOLD NUGGET RESTAURANT

American

Lunch: $5-$14   **Dinner:** $7-$30   Phone: 928/684-0648

Location: On US 60, just se of jct US 60 and 93; center. 222 E Wickenburg Way 85390. **Hours:** 7 am-9 pm.
Features: Beef, chicken and fish entrees are served in the coffee shop and in the historical landmark dining rooms, which are appointed with turn-of-the-20th-century furnishings. Casual dress; cocktails. **Parking:** on-site. **Cards:** AX, MC, VI.

THE MARCH HARE RESTAURANT

American

Lunch: $5-$7   **Dinner:** $13-$20   Phone: 928/684-0223

Location: Just w of jct US 60 and 93. 170 Wickenburg Way 85390. **Hours:** Open 2/1-6/30 & 9/1-1/31; 11 am-2 pm; Fri also 5:30 pm-8 pm 11/1-4/30. Closed major holidays; also Sun & Mon. **Reservations:** accepted.
Features: Sprightly names on the menu come from Alice in Wonderland, but the hearty homemade soups and rolls are completely down to earth and go well with luncheon sandwiches and salads. When the restaurant is open seasonally for dinner, guests might find poached or baked salmon, herb pork roast or a luscious turkey dinner on the menu. Casual dress. **Parking:** street.

WILLCOX pop. 3,733

—————— **WHERE TO STAY** ——————

BEST WESTERN PLAZA INN   *Book at aaa.com*

Small-scale Hotel

Phone: (520)384-3556

| All Year | 1P: $63-$89 | 2P: $63-$89 | XP: $10 | F12 |

Location: I-10, exit 340, just s. 1100 W Rex Allen Dr 85643. **Fax:** 520/384-2679. **Facility:** 91 one-bedroom standard units, some with whirlpools. 2 stories (no elevator), exterior corridors. *Bath:* combo or shower only.
Parking: on-site. **Terms:** [AP] meal plan available, package plans, pets ($15 extra charge). **Amenities:** irons, hair dryers. **Dining:** 6 am-10 & 5-9 pm, cocktails. **Pool(s):** heated outdoor. **Guest Services:** coin laundry. **Business Services:** meeting rooms, PC, fax (fee). **Cards:** AX, CB, DC, DS, MC, VI. **Special Amenities:** free continental breakfast and free local telephone calls. *(See color ad below)*

SOME UNITS

DAYS INN   *Book at aaa.com*

Motel

Phone: (520)384-4222

| All Year | 1P: $45-$50 | 2P: $52-$65 | | F12 |

Location: I-10, exit 340, just s. Located adjacent to a shopping center. 724 N Bisbee Ave 85643. **Fax:** 520/384-3785.
Facility: 73 one-bedroom standard units. 2 stories (no elevator), exterior corridors. **Parking:** on-site.
Terms: [ECP] meal plan available, pets ($5 extra charge). **Amenities:** hair dryers. **Pool(s):** outdoor. **Guest Services:** coin laundry. **Business Services:** fax (fee). **Cards:** AX, DC, MC, VI. **Special Amenities:** free continental breakfast and free local telephone calls.

SOME UNITS

MOTEL 6 WILLCOX #410   *Book at aaa.com*

Motel

Phone: 520/384-2201

| 5/27-1/31 | 1P: $35-$45 | 2P: $41-$51 | XP: $3 | F17 |
| 2/1-5/26 | 1P: $33-$43 | 2P: $39-$43 | XP: $3 | F17 |

Location: I-10, exit 340, just s. 921 N Bisbee Ave 85643. **Fax:** 520/384-0192. **Facility:** 96 one-bedroom standard units. Exterior corridors. *Bath:* shower only. **Parking:** on-site. **Terms:** small pets only. **Pool(s):** heated outdoor. **Guest Services:** coin laundry. **Business Services:** fax (fee). **Cards:** AX, CB, DC, DS, MC, VI.

SOME UNITS

SUPER 8 MOTEL   *Book at aaa.com*   Phone: 520/384-0888
All Year [CP]   1P: $50-$55   2P: $55-$60   XP: $5   F12
Small-scale Hotel   Location: I-10, exit 340, just n. 1500 W Ft. Grant Rd 85643. Fax: 520/384-4485. **Facility:** 50 one-bedroom standard units. 2 stories (no elevator), interior corridors. *Bath:* combo or shower only. **Parking:** on-site. **Pool(s):** heated indoor. **Leisure Activities:** whirlpool. **Guest Services:** coin laundry. **Business Services:** fax (fee). **Cards:** AX, DC, DS, MC, VI.

SOME UNITS

(ASK) (S/D) (T+) (&M) (◎) (➰) (◼) (DATA PORT) (◻) / (✕) (◫) (▭) /

─────── **WHERE TO DINE** ───────

DESERT ROSE CAFE   *Menu on aaa.com*   Lunch: $5-$8   Dinner: $10-$24   Phone: 520/384-0514
Location: I-10, exit 336, 3 mi se. 706 S Haskell Ave 85643. **Hours:** 7 am-9 pm, Sun-3 pm. Closed: 1/1, 12/24, 12/25. **Reservations:** accepted. **Features:** Friendly staff and bright decor welcome patrons to the locally popular cafe. Freshly prepared dishes incorporate creative elements, such as roasted peppers and guacamole on grilled burgers. Casual dress; cocktails. **Parking:** on-site. **Cards:** AX, DS, MC, VI.

Regional American

(◣)

SALSA FIESTA   Lunch: $7-$13   Dinner: $7-$13   Phone: 520/384-4233
Location: I-10, exit 340, just s. 1201 W Rex Allen Dr 85643. **Hours:** 11 am-8:30 pm. **Reservations:** accepted.
Mexican   **Features:** Bright, cheerful decor matches the friendly service at the small eatery, which serves "big" taste in the traditional dishes of Northern Mexico. Fun Mexican artifacts are displayed. Casual dress; cocktails. **Parking:** on-site. **Cards:** AX, DS, MC, VI.

WILLIAMS pop. 2,842—See also *GRAND CANYON NATIONAL PARK - SOUTH RIM.*

─────── **WHERE TO STAY** ───────

AMERICAS BEST VALUE INN OF WILLIAMS   *Book at aaa.com*   Phone: (928)635-2202
5/1-8/31	1P: $49-$65	2P: $55-$69	XP: $5	F
2/1-4/30	1P: $45-$50	2P: $50-$65	XP: $5	F
9/1-10/31	1P: $35-$47	2P: $39-$53	XP: $5	F
11/1-1/31	1P: $31-$44	2P: $35-$48	XP: $5	F

Motel
Location: I-40, exit 161, 0.9 mi e. 1001 W Route 66 86046. Fax: 928/635-9202. **Facility:** 34 units. 33 one-bedroom standard units. 1 two-bedroom suite ($90-$130). 1 story, interior/exterior corridors. *Bath:* combo or shower only. **Parking:** on-site. **Terms:** [CP] meal plan available, package plans. **Amenities:** *Some:* irons, hair dryers. **Pool(s):** small heated outdoor. **Leisure Activities:** whirlpool. **Business Services:** PC. **Cards:** AX, DS, MC, VI.

SOME UNITS

(ASK) (S/D) (➰) (◼) (◻) / (✕) (▭) /

A TERRY RANCH HOUSE BED & BREAKFAST   Phone: (928)635-4171
All Year   2P: $125-$210
Bed & Breakfast   **Location:** I-40, exit 165 (Grand Canyon), 1 mi s on Business Loop 40, then just w on Rodeo Rd. Located in a residential area. 701 Quarterhorse Rd 86046. Fax: 928/635-2488. **Facility:** This beautifully decorated log cabin-style residence provides comfortable rooms and public areas and features three rooms with a fireplace. Smoke free premises. 4 one-bedroom standard units, some with whirlpools. 1 story, interior/exterior corridors. **Parking:** on-site. **Terms:** check-in 4 pm, age restrictions may apply, 7 day cancellation notice-fee imposed. **Amenities:** video library, CD players, hair dryers. *Some:* irons. **Cards:** AX, DS, MC, VI.

(✈) (T+) (✕) (VCR) (◼) (☎)

BEST WESTERN INN OF WILLIAMS   *Book at aaa.com*   Phone: (928)635-4400
6/1-9/15 [CP]	1P: $109-$149	2P: $109-$149	XP: $10	F15
9/16-1/31 [CP]	1P: $99-$149	2P: $99-$149	XP: $10	F15
3/16-5/31 [CP]	1P: $99-$129	2P: $99-$129	XP: $10	F15
2/1-3/15 [CP]	1P: $79-$109	2P: $79-$109	XP: $10	F15

Small-scale Hotel   **Location:** I-40, exit 161, just e. 2600 W Route 66 86046 (PO Box 275). Fax: 928/635-4488. **Facility:** Smoke free premises. 79 one-bedroom standard units. 2 stories (no elevator), interior corridors. *Bath:* combo or shower only. **Parking:** on-site. **Amenities:** video library, voice mail, irons, hair dryers. *Some:* high-speed Internet. **Pool(s):** heated outdoor. **Leisure Activities:** whirlpool. **Guest Services:** gift shop, coin laundry. **Business Services:** meeting rooms. **Cards:** AX, DC, DS, MC, VI. **Special Amenities:** free continental breakfast and free newspaper. *(See color ad p 224)*

(&) (◎) (➰) (✕) (VCR) (◼) (DATA PORT) (◻)

CANYON COUNTRY INN

Phone: (928)635-2349

(AAA) [SAVE]

Motel

3/16-10/15	1P: $39-$80	2P: $45-$80
2/1-3/15 & 10/16-12/31	1P: $35-$69	2P: $39-$69

Location: I-40, exit 163, 0.5 mi s, then just w on Railroad Ave (I-40 business loop). 442 W Route 66 86046. **Fax:** 928/635-9898. **Facility:** Smoke free premises. 13 one-bedroom standard units. 2 stories (no elevator), interior/exterior corridors. **Parking:** on-site. **Terms:** open 2/1-12/31, [ECP] meal plan available, package plans. **Amenities:** *Some:* irons, hair dryers. **Cards:** AX, DS, MC, VI. **Special Amenities: free expanded continental breakfast and free local telephone calls.**

SOME UNITS

THE CANYON MOTEL

Phone: (928)635-9371

(AAA) [SAVE]

Motel

All Year [CP]	1P: $39-$74	2P: $39-$74

Location: I-40, exit 165 (Grand Canyon), 1 mi s on Business Loop 40, then just w. 1900 E Rodeo Rd/Route 66 86046. **Fax:** 928/635-4138. **Facility:** 23 units. 21 one- and 2 two-bedroom standard units. 1 story, exterior corridors. *Bath:* combo or shower only. **Parking:** on-site. **Terms:** cancellation fee imposed, weekly rates available, package plans, $1 service charge, small pets only ($7 extra charge, must be attended). **Amenities:** video library. *Some:* irons, hair dryers. **Pool(s):** small heated indoor. **Leisure Activities:** board games, playing cards, swing set, gas grills, hiking trails, horseshoes. **Guest Services:** area transportation-within 3 mi. **Business Services:** PC (fee). **Cards:** DS, MC, VI. **Special Amenities: free continental breakfast and free local telephone calls.**

SOME UNITS

FEE

DAYS INN

Book at aaa.com

Phone: (928)635-4051

(AAA) [SAVE]

Motel

5/16-9/15 [ECP]	1P: $68-$128	2P: $68-$128	XP: $10	F17
9/16-10/15 [ECP]	1P: $52-$99	2P: $52-$99	XP: $5	F17
2/1-5/15 & 10/16-1/31 [ECP]	1P: $52-$68	2P: $52-$68	XP: $5	F17

Location: I-40, exit 161, just e. 2488 W Route 66 86046. **Fax:** 928/635-4411. **Facility:** 73 one-bedroom standard units, some with whirlpools. 2 stories (no elevator), interior corridors. **Parking:** on-site. **Terms:** cancellation fee imposed, pets ($20 deposit). **Amenities:** voice mail, safes, hair dryers. *Some:* irons. **Pool(s):** small heated indoor. **Leisure Activities:** whirlpool. **Guest Services:** coin laundry. **Cards:** AX, CB, DC, DS, MC, VI. **Special Amenities: free continental breakfast and free local telephone calls.**

SOME UNITS

FEE

ECONO LODGE

Book at aaa.com

Phone: (928)635-4085

(AAA) [SAVE]

Motel

10/1-10/31	1P: $45-$90	2P: $45-$90	XP: $5	F18
4/1-9/30	1P: $45-$80	2P: $45-$80	XP: $5	F18
2/1-3/31	1P: $35-$60	2P: $35-$60	XP: $5	F18
11/1-1/31	1P: $35-$55	2P: $35-$55	XP: $5	F18

Location: I-40, exit 163, 0.5 mi s, then just e. 302 E Route 66 86046. **Fax:** 928/635-1326. **Facility:** 38 units. 37 one-bedroom standard units. 1 one-bedroom suite ($120-$180). 2 stories (no elevator), exterior corridors. *Bath:* combo or shower only. **Parking:** on-site. **Terms:** cancellation fee imposed, [CP] meal plan available. **Amenities:** high-speed Internet, voice mail. **Cards:** AX, CB, DC, DS, JC, MC, VI. **Special Amenities: free continental breakfast and free local telephone calls.**

SOME UNITS

EL RANCHO MOTEL

Phone: (928)635-2552

(AAA) [SAVE]

Motel

5/20-10/15	1P: $52-$63	2P: $57-$73	XP: $5	F13
10/16-1/31	1P: $30-$45	2P: $35-$58	XP: $5	F13
4/1-5/19	1P: $40-$48	2P: $45-$49	XP: $5	F13
2/1-3/31	1P: $30-$38	2P: $33-$39	XP: $5	F13

Location: I-40, exit 163, 0.6 mi s, then just e. 617 E Route 66 86046. **Fax:** 928/635-4173. **Facility:** 25 units. 23 one-bedroom standard units. 2 one-bedroom suites ($75-$115). 2 stories (no elevator), exterior corridors. **Parking:** on-site. **Terms:** office hours 8 am-10:30 pm, cancellation fee imposed, small pets only ($5 extra charge, in limited units). **Amenities:** video library (fee). *Some:* irons, hair dryers. **Pool(s):** heated outdoor. **Cards:** AX, DS, MC, VI. **Special Amenities: free local telephone calls and early check-in/late check-out.** *(See color ad p 462)*

SOME UNITS

FEE

FAIRFIELD INN BY MARRIOTT

Book at aaa.com

Phone: (928)635-9888

Small-scale Hotel

5/1-9/30	1P: $69-$99	2P: $69-$99	XP: $5	F17
2/1-4/30 & 10/1-1/31	1P: $49-$79	2P: $49-$79	XP: $5	F17

Location: I-40, exit 161, just n. 1029 N Grand Canyon Blvd 86046. **Fax:** 928/635-2235. **Facility:** 80 one-bedroom standard units. 2 stories (no elevator), interior corridors. *Bath:* combo or shower only. **Parking:** on-site. **Amenities:** high-speed Internet, irons, hair dryers. **Pool(s):** small heated outdoor. **Leisure Activities:** whirlpool. **Business Services:** meeting rooms. **Cards:** AX, DC, DS, JC, MC, VI.

SOME UNITS

GRAND CANYON COUNTRY INN

Book at aaa.com

Phone: (928)635-4045

(AAA) [SAVE]

Small-scale Hotel

All Year	1P: $49-$99	2P: $49-$99	XP: $5

Location: I-40, exit 161, 1 mi e. 911 Route 66 86046. **Fax:** 928/635-9060. **Facility:** Smoke free premises. 77 units. 76 one- and 1 two-bedroom standard units. 2 stories, interior corridors. *Bath:* combo or shower only. **Parking:** on-site. **Terms:** [CP] meal plan available. **Amenities:** *Some:* irons, hair dryers. **Pool(s):** heated indoor. **Leisure Activities:** whirlpool. **Guest Services:** coin laundry. **Business Services:** PC. **Cards:** AX, CB, DC, DS, MC, VI. **Special Amenities: free local telephone calls.** *(See color ad p 464)*

SOME UNITS

GRAND CANYON RAILWAY HOTEL

Phone: (928)635-4010

(AAA) (SAVE)

Small-scale Hotel

| | 4/1-10/14 | 1P: $139 | 2P: $139 | XP: $10 | F16 |
| | 2/1-3/31 & 10/15-1/31 | 1P: $89 | 2P: $89 | XP: $10 | F16 |

Location: I-40, exit 163, 0.5 mi s. Located at historic Williams Depot. 235 N Grand Canyon Blvd 86046. **Fax:** 928/635-2180. **Facility:** 297 units. 287 one-bedroom standard units. 10 one-bedroom suites ($119-$199). 2 stories, interior corridors. *Bath:* combo or shower only. **Parking:** on-site. **Terms:** cancellation fee imposed, [AP] & [BP] meal plans available, package plans, pets (in kennels only). **Amenities:** irons, hair dryers. **Dining:** 2 restaurants, 6:30 am-9 pm, cocktails. **Pool(s):** heated indoor. **Leisure Activities:** whirlpool, exercise room. *Fee:* game room. **Guest Services:** gift shop. **Business Services:** meeting rooms. **Cards:** AX, DS, MC, VI. (See color ad p 227)

SOME UNITS

🐾 🍴 🍸 📶 ⬇ 🏊 ✕ 🎥 [DATA PORT] 🖥 / ✕ 📶 🖥 /

HIGHLANDER MOTEL

Phone: (928)635-2541

AAA [SAVE]

Motel

	1P: $65-$70	2P: $75-$85	XP: $5	F12
5/1-10/31	1P: $45-$50	2P: $50-$55	XP: $5	F12
3/1-4/30	1P: $35-$40	2P: $45-$50	XP: $5	F12
11/1-1/31	1P: $30-$35	2P: $40-$45	XP: $5	F12
2/1-2/28				

Location: I-40, exit 161, 1.3 mi e. 533 W Route 66 86046. Fax: 928/635-0609. **Facility:** 12 one-bedroom standard units. 1 story, exterior corridors. **Parking:** on-site. **Terms:** package plans, small pets only ($5 fee).
Cards: AX, DS, MC, VI. **Special Amenities:** free local telephone calls and early check-in/late check-out.

SOME UNITS

[S/D] [🛏] [▥▸] [▥] / [✕] /
FEE

HOLIDAY INN WILLIAMS   *Book at aaa.com*

Phone: (928)635-4114

AAA [SAVE]

Small-scale Hotel

All Year   1P: $69-$159   2P: $69-$159

Location: I-40, exit 163, just s. 950 N Grand Canyon Blvd 86046. Fax: 928/635-2700. **Facility:** 120 units. 113 one-bedroom standard units. 7 one-bedroom suites. 2 stories (no elevator), interior corridors. *Bath:* combo or shower only. **Parking:** on-site. **Terms:** $3 service charge. **Amenities:** high-speed Internet, voice mail, irons, hair dryers. **Dining:** Doc Holiday Steak House, see separate listing. **Pool(s):** heated indoor. **Leisure Activities:** whirlpool. **Guest Services:** gift shop, coin laundry. **Business Services:** meeting rooms.
Cards: AX, DC, DS, MC, VI. **Special Amenities:** free newspaper and early check-in/late check-out. *(See color ad p 229)*

SOME UNITS

[🐾] [🍽] [&M] [🖐] [📷] [🏊] [🎥] [DATA PORT] [▥] / [✕] [🔒] [▥] /

HOWARD JOHNSON EXPRESS INN   *Book at aaa.com*

Phone: (928)635-9561

AAA [SAVE]

Small-scale Hotel

5/1-8/31 [CP]	1P: $49-$69	2P: $59-$99	XP: $6	F12
9/1-10/31 [CP]	1P: $49-$59	2P: $59-$79	XP: $6	F12
2/1-4/30 & 11/1-1/31 [CP]	1P: $29-$59	2P: $39-$69	XP: $6	F12

Location: I-40, exit 163, just s. 511 N Grand Canyon Blvd 86046. Fax: 928/635-9565. **Facility:** 56 one-bedroom standard units. 2 stories (no elevator), interior corridors. **Parking:** on-site. **Terms:** cancellation fee imposed. **Amenities:** voice mail, irons, hair dryers. **Pool(s):** small heated indoor. **Leisure Activities:** whirlpool.
Cards: AX, DC, DS, MC, VI. **Special Amenities:** free continental breakfast and free local telephone calls.
(See color ad p 464)

SOME UNITS

[S/D] [▥▸] [📷] [🏊] [🎥] [DATA PORT] [▥] / [✕] [🔒] /

MOTEL 6 - 4010   *Book at aaa.com*

Phone: (928)635-9000

AAA [SAVE]

Motel

6/1-7/31	1P: $64-$84	2P: $70-$99	XP: $6	F17
3/1-5/31 & 8/1-1/31	1P: $39-$69	2P: $45-$75	XP: $6	F17
2/1-2/28	1P: $31-$41	2P: $35-$45	XP: $4	F17

Location: I-40, exit 161, 1 mi e. 831 W Route 66 86046. Fax: 928/635-2300. **Facility:** 52 units. 51 one-bedroom standard units. 1 one-bedroom suite with kitchen (no utensils). 2 stories (no elevator), interior corridors. **Parking:** on-site. **Terms:** small pets only. **Amenities:** *Some:* irons, hair dryers. **Pool(s):** small heated indoor. **Leisure Activities:** whirlpool. **Guest Services:** coin laundry. **Cards:** AX, DC, DS, MC, VI.

SOME UNITS

[S/D] [🛏] [▥▸] [🏊] [🎥] [DATA PORT] [▥] / [✕] [🔒] [▥] /

MOUNTAIN COUNTRY LODGE BED & BREAKFAST

Phone: 928/635-4341

Bed & Breakfast

Property failed to provide current rates

Location: I-40, exit 161, 1.4 mi s; jct S 5th St. 437 W Route 66 86046. Fax: 928/635-4341. **Facility:** Smoke free premises. 8 units. 7 one- and 1 two-bedroom standard units. 1-2 stories (no elevator), interior/exterior corridors. *Bath:* combo or shower only. **Parking:** on-site.

SOME UNITS

[✕] [☎] / [🔒] /

MOUNTAINSIDE INN

AAA SAVE

Small-scale Hotel

Phone: 928/635-4431

2/1-9/30	1P: $59-$99	2P: $69-$109	XP: $10	F18
10/1-1/31	1P: $49-$89	2P: $59-$99	XP: $10	F18

Location: I-40, exit 163, 0.6 mi s. 642 E Route 66 86046. Fax: 928/635-2292. **Facility:** 96 units. 95 one-bedroom standard units. 1 one-bedroom suite. 2 stories (no elevator), exterior corridors. **Parking:** on-site. **Terms:** weekly rates available, [AP] & [MAP] meal plans available, package plans, pets ($50 deposit, dogs only, in designated units). **Amenities:** voice mail, irons, hair dryers. **Dining:** 7 am-9:30 & 5-9 pm, cocktails. **Pool(s):** small heated outdoor. **Leisure Activities:** whirlpool. **Business Services:** PC. **Cards:** AX, DS, MC, VI.

SOME UNITS

QUALITY INN MOUNTAIN RANCH RESORT   *Book at aaa.com*

AAA SAVE

Small-scale Hotel

Phone: (928)635-2693

5/16-9/30	1P: $79-$109	2P: $79-$109	XP: $10	F17
3/15-5/15	1P: $59-$99	2P: $59-$99	XP: $10	F17
10/1-10/31	1P: $59-$89	2P: $45-$110	XP: $10	F17

Location: I-40, exit 171 (Deer Farm Rd), just s. Located in a scenic country area. 6701 E Mountain Ranch Rd 86046. Fax: 928/635-4188. **Facility:** 73 one-bedroom standard units. 2 stories (no elevator), exterior corridors. **Bath:** combo or shower only. **Parking:** on-site. **Terms:** open 3/15-10/31, small pets only ($25 fee). **Amenities:** video library (fee), irons, hair dryers. **Dining:** The Ranch Bar & Grill, see separate listing. **Pool(s):** small heated outdoor. **Leisure Activities:** whirlpool, putting green, 2 tennis courts, sports court, horseshoes. *Fee:* horseback riding, exercise room. **Guest Services:** gift shop. **Business Services:** meeting rooms. **Cards:** AX, CB, DC, DS, JC, MC, VI. **Special Amenities:** free local telephone calls and free newspaper.

SOME UNITS

RODEWAY INN   *Book at aaa.com*

AAA SAVE

Motel

Phone: (928)635-1412

3/1-8/31	1P: $49-$150	2P: $60-$150	XP: $10	F18
2/1-2/28 & 9/1-1/31	1P: $35-$99	2P: $45-$110	XP: $10	F18

Location: I-40, exit 163, just s. 750 N Grand Canyon Blvd 86046. Fax: 928/635-1507. **Facility:** 19 units. 17 one-bedroom standard units. 2 one-bedroom suites ($100-$150). 2 stories (no elevator), interior corridors. **Parking:** on-site. **Terms:** cancellation fee imposed, [CP] meal plan available. **Amenities:** high-speed Internet, voice mail, irons, hair dryers. **Cards:** DS, MC, VI. **Special Amenities:** free continental breakfast and free local telephone calls.

SOME UNITS

RODEWAY INN   *Book at aaa.com*

AAA SAVE

Motel

Phone: (928)635-2619

3/15-9/14 [CP]	1P: $45-$65	2P: $45-$75	XP: $8	D16
9/15-1/31 [CP]	1P: $29-$49	2P: $29-$59	XP: $8	D16
2/1-3/14 [CP]	1P: $35-$45	2P: $35-$55	XP: $8	D16

Location: I-40, exit 163, 0.5 mi s, then just e. 334 E Route 66 86046. Fax: 928/635-2610. **Facility:** 24 one-bedroom standard units. 1-2 stories (no elevator), exterior corridors. **Parking:** on-site. **Terms:** 7 day cancellation notice, small pets only ($8 fee, in designated units). **Amenities:** high-speed Internet, irons, hair dryers. **Cards:** AX, CB, DC, DS, MC, VI. **Special Amenities:** free continental breakfast and free local telephone calls.

SOME UNITS

SUPER 8 MOTEL WILLIAMS EAST   *Book at aaa.com*

Small-scale Hotel

Phone: (928)635-4700

3/31-1/31	1P: $55-$105	2P: $58-$145
2/1-3/30	1P: $51-$90	2P: $54-$105

Location: I-40, exit 165 (Grand Canyon), 1 mi s. 2001 E Route 66 86046. Fax: 928/635-4700. **Facility:** 40 one-bedroom standard units. 2 stories (no elevator), interior corridors. **Parking:** on-site. **Terms:** cancellation fee imposed, package plans. **Amenities:** *Some:* irons, hair dryers. **Pool(s):** small heated outdoor. **Cards:** AX, DC, DS, MC, VI.

SOME UNITS

TRAVELODGE WILLIAMS   *Book at aaa.com*

AAA SAVE

Motel

Phone: (928)635-2651

5/1-1/31	1P: $49-$99	2P: $49-$99	XP: $5	F
3/1-4/30	1P: $49-$89	2P: $49-$89	XP: $5	F
2/1-2/28	1P: $39-$69	2P: $39-$69	XP: $5	F

Location: I-40, exit 163, 0.5 mi s, then just e. 430 E Route 66 86046. Fax: 928/635-4296. **Facility:** 41 units. 37 one-bedroom standard units. 4 one-bedroom suites ($59-$169). 2 stories (no elevator), exterior corridors. **Bath:** combo or shower only. **Parking:** on-site. **Terms:** package plans, pets (dogs only, $7.50 extra charge). **Amenities:** hair dryers. *Some:* irons. **Pool(s):** small heated outdoor. **Leisure Activities:** whirlpool. **Cards:** AX, DC, DS, MC, VI. **Special Amenities:** free continental breakfast and free local telephone calls.

SOME UNITS

------- WHERE TO DINE -------

CRUISERS CAFE 66

American

Lunch: $6-$13   Dinner: $7-$13   Phone: 928/635-2445

Location: At Route 66 and 3rd; in historic downtown. 233 W Route 66 86046. **Hours:** 11 am-10 pm; from 3 pm in winter. **Closed:** 11/23, 12/25. **Reservations:** accepted. **Features:** The pleasant family restaurant prepares a variety of Mexican, steak and chicken dishes in a setting reminiscent of the 1950s. Casual dress; cocktails. **Parking:** street. **Cards:** AX, DS, MC, VI.

DOC HOLIDAY STEAK HOUSE

American

Dinner: $7-$20   Phone: 928/635-4114

Location: I-40, exit 163, just s; in Holiday Inn Williams. 950 N Grand Canyon Blvd 86046. **Hours:** 6 am-10 & 4-10 pm. **Closed:** 12/25. **Reservations:** accepted. **Features:** The restaurant presents a complete three-meal menu, with dinner items ranging from steaks to sandwiches. A salad bar also is available. Casual dress; cocktails. **Parking:** on-site. **Cards:** AX, CB, DC, DS, MC, VI.

MISS KITTY'S STEAK HOUSE
Dinner: $10-$22   **Phone:** 928/635-4431
Steak House
Location: I-40, exit 163, 0.6 mi s, then just e; in Ramada Inn. 642 E Route 66 86046. **Hours:** 5 pm-10 pm. **Features:** Great steaks, some seafood selections and a salad bar are among food offerings. Live entertainment is provided on some nights. Casual dress; cocktails. **Parking:** on-site. **Cards:** AX, DC, DS, MC, VI.

OLD SMOKEY'S RESTAURANT & PANCAKE HOUSE
Lunch: $3-$7   **Phone:** 928/635-1915
American
Location: I-40, exit 163, 0.5 mi s. 624 W Route 66 86046. **Hours:** 6 am-1:30 pm. Closed: 12/25. **Features:** Breakfast is served anytime during business hours, and lunch offerings include a variety of sandwiches. The decor has a decidedly 1950s style. Casual dress. **Parking:** street. **Cards:** AX, MC, VI.

PANCHO MCGILLICUDDY'S
Lunch: $6-$13   **Dinner:** $6-$13   **Phone:** 928/635-4150
Mexican
Location: I-40, exit 163, 0.5 mi s. 141 Railroad Ave 86046. **Hours:** 11 am-10 pm; to 9 pm in winter. Closed: 11/23, 12/25. **Reservations:** accepted. **Features:** The historic property is decorated in an attractive Western decor. The casual family restaurant's menu of authentic Mexican dishes includes fajitas, enchiladas and chiles rellenos. Casual dress; cocktails. **Parking:** on-site. **Cards:** AX, DS, MC, VI.

PINE COUNTRY RESTAURANT
Lunch: $4-$7   **Dinner:** $7-$12   **Phone:** 928/635-9718
American
Location: Cross street Route 66; downtown. 107 N Grand Canyon Blvd 86046. **Hours:** 5:30 am-9 pm. Closed: 11/23, 12/25. **Reservations:** accepted. **Features:** Home-style cooking is at the heart of the relaxed restaurant's menu. No meal is complete without a piece of one of the delicious, homemade pies. Casual dress. **Parking:** on-site and street. **Cards:** AX, DS, MC, VI.

THE RANCH BAR & GRILL
Dinner: $9-$24   **Phone:** 928/635-2693
American
Location: I-40, exit 171 (Deer Farm Rd), just s; in Quality Inn Mountain Ranch Resort. 6701 E Mountain Ranch Rd 86046. **Hours:** Open 3/15-10/31; 5 pm-9 pm. **Features:** Cordial and knowledgable servers contribute to the casual style here with menu offerings of steak, seafood and pasta dishes. Casual dress; cocktails. **Parking:** on-site. **Cards:** AX, DC, DS, MC, VI.

ROD'S STEAK HOUSE   *Menu on aaa.com*
Lunch: $6-$10   **Dinner:** $10-$22   **Phone:** 928/635-2671
Steak & Seafood
Location: Center. 301 E Rt 66 86046. **Hours:** 11 am-9:30 pm. Closed: 11/23, 12/24, 12/25; also Sun. **Reservations:** accepted. **Features:** Since 1946, the restaurant has served its specialty steaks, as well as seafood and chicken dishes, to travelers along historic Route 66. A must-try is the sugar-dipped charred steak, a surprising delight. Casual dress; cocktails. **Parking:** on-site. **Cards:** AX, DC, MC, VI.

ROSA'S CANTINA
Lunch: $6-$14   **Dinner:** $8-$18   **Phone:** 928/635-0708
Mexican
Location: I-40, exit 163, 0.5 mi s. 411 N Grand Canyon Blvd 86046. **Hours:** 11 am-9 pm, Sun-3 pm. Closed: Mon. **Features:** Friendly service and good Mexican food—including enchiladas, tamales and rellenos—are the fare here. Portions are large so no one goes away hungry. Casual dress; cocktails. **Parking:** on-site. **Cards:** AX, DS, MC, VI.

WINDOW ROCK pop. 3,059

——— WHERE TO STAY ———

QUALITY INN NAVAJO NATION CAPITAL   *Book at aaa.com*   **Phone:** (928)871-4108

4/1-10/31	1P: $70	2P: $80	XP: $10	F18
2/1-3/31 & 11/1-1/31	1P: $65	2P: $75	XP: $10	F18

Small-scale Hotel
Location: Center. 48 W Hwy 264 86515 (PO Box 2340). Fax: 928/871-5466. **Facility:** 56 one-bedroom standard units. 2 stories (no elevator), exterior corridors. **Parking:** on-site. **Terms:** small pets only ($50 deposit). **Amenities:** high-speed Internet, voice mail, irons, hair dryers. **Dining:** Dine' Restaurant, see separate listing. **Business Services:** meeting rooms, PC. **Cards:** AX, CB, DC, DS, MC, VI. *(See color ad p 66)*
SOME UNITS

——— WHERE TO DINE ———

DINE' RESTAURANT
Lunch: $6-$8   **Dinner:** $10-$14   **Phone:** 928/871-4108
Regional American
Location: Center; in Quality Inn Navajo Nation Capital. 48 W Hwy 264 86515. **Hours:** 6 am-9 pm, Sat & Sun 7 am-6 pm. **Features:** Near the center of town and a museum, the family-centered hotel restaurant offers three meals daily. On the dinner menu is a variety of selections, including steak and seafood, Mexican entrees, Navajo mutton stew and fry bread. Casual dress. **Parking:** on-site. **Cards:** AX, DC, DS, MC, VI.

WINSLOW pop. 9,520

——— WHERE TO STAY ———

BEST WESTERN ADOBE INN   *Book at aaa.com*   **Phone:** (928)289-4638

5/1-10/16 [BP]	1P: $85-$125	2P: $90-$130	XP: $5	F12
2/1-4/30 & 10/17-1/31 [BP]	1P: $75-$100	2P: $85-$105	XP: $5	F12

Small-scale Hotel
Location: I-40, exit 253. 1701 N Park Dr 86047. Fax: 928/289-5514. **Facility:** 72 one-bedroom standard units. 2 stories (no elevator), interior corridors. **Bath:** combo or shower only. **Parking:** on-site. **Terms:** 30 day cancellation notice, pets ($10 extra charge). **Amenities:** irons, hair dryers. **Dining:** Adobe Inn Restaurant, see separate listing. **Pool(s):** heated indoor. **Leisure Activities:** whirlpool. **Business Services:** meeting rooms, PC. **Cards:** AX, CB, DC, DS, MC, VI. **Special Amenities:** free full breakfast and free local telephone calls.
SOME UNITS

DAYS INN   *Book at aaa.com*

(AAA) (SAVE)

▼▼ ▼▼

Small-scale Hotel

Phone: (928)289-1010

	1P: $56	2P: $60	XP: $5	D18
2/1-9/9				
9/10-1/31	1P: $50	2P: $55	XP: $5	D18

Location: I-40, exit 252, just s. 2035 W Hwy 66 86047. Fax: 928/289-5778. **Facility:** 64 one-bedroom standard units, some with whirlpools. 2 stories (no elevator), interior corridors. *Bath:* combo or shower only. **Parking:** on-site. **Terms:** [MAP] meal plan available, small pets only ($10 fee). **Amenities:** *Some:* irons, hair dryers. **Pool(s):** small heated indoor. **Leisure Activities:** whirlpool. **Guest Services:** coin laundry. **Cards:** AX, CB, DC, DS, JC, MC, VI. **Special Amenities:** free continental breakfast and free local telephone calls.

SOME UNITS

[S🄳] [🐾] [♿] [🏊] [📹] [DATA PORT] / [✕] /
FEE

ECONO LODGE   *Book at aaa.com*

(AAA) (SAVE)

▼▼ ▼▼

Small-scale Hotel

Phone: (928)289-4687

| All Year [CP] | 1P: $49-$89 | 2P: $59-$119 | XP: $5 | F18 |

Location: I-40, exit 253. 1706 N Park Dr 86047. Fax: 928/289-9377. **Facility:** 72 one-bedroom standard units. 2 stories (no elevator), exterior corridors. **Parking:** on-site. **Terms:** weekly rates available, small pets only ($5 fee). **Amenities:** *Some:* irons, hair dryers. **Pool(s):** small outdoor. **Guest Services:** coin laundry. **Cards:** AX, CB, DC, DS, JC, MC, VI. **Special Amenities:** free continental breakfast and free local telephone calls.

SOME UNITS

[S🄳] [🐾] [⊞] [🏊] [📹] [DATA PORT] [▦] / [✕] [🛢] [▣] /
FEE

HOLIDAY INN EXPRESS-WINSLOW   *Book at aaa.com*

▼▼▼▼

Small-scale Hotel

Phone: 928/289-2960

| All Year | 1P: $89-$99 | 2P: $99-$109 | XP: $10 | F16 |

Location: I-40, exit 255, just n. 816 Transcon Ln 86047. Fax: 928/289-2947. **Facility:** 52 units. 50 one-bedroom standard units. 2 one-bedroom suites. 2 stories (no elevator), interior corridors. *Bath:* combo or shower only. **Parking:** on-site. **Terms:** [ECP] meal plan available, small pets only ($10 extra charge). **Amenities:** high-speed Internet, dual phone lines, voice mail, irons, hair dryers. **Pool(s):** small heated indoor. **Leisure Activities:** whirlpool. **Guest Services:** coin laundry. **Cards:** AX, CB, DC, DS, JC, MC, VI.

SOME UNITS

[ASK] [S🄳] [🐾] [⊞] [♿] [🏊] [📹] [DATA PORT] [🛢] [▦] [▣] / [✕] /
FEE

LA POSADA HOTEL

▼▼▼▼

Historic
Small-scale Hotel

Phone: (928)289-4366

| All Year | 1P: $89-$129 | 2P: $89-$129 | |

Location: I-40, exit 253, 1 mi s to Route 66 (2nd St), then just e; in historic downtown. 303 E 2nd St 86047. Fax: 928/289-3873. **Facility:** This restored historic hotel, built to resemble a fabulous Spanish hacienda, is tastefully decorated and has well-tended grounds. Smoke free premises. 37 units. 33 one-bedroom standard units, some with whirlpools. 4 one-bedroom suites ($149-$175), some with whirlpools. 2 stories (no elevator), interior corridors. *Bath:* combo or shower only. **Parking:** on-site. **Terms:** 3 day cancellation notice-fee imposed, pets ($10 extra charge). **Amenities:** irons, hair dryers. *Some:* DVD players. **Dining:** The Turquoise Room, see separate listing. **Leisure Activities:** game room. **Guest Services:** gift shop. **Business Services:** meeting rooms. **Cards:** AX, CB, DC, DS, JC, MC, VI.

SOME UNITS

[🐾] [🍴] [🍽] [&M] [♿] [✕] [🅩] / [VCR] [🛢] /
FEE

MOTEL 6 WINSLOW #4012   *Book at aaa.com*

(AAA) (SAVE)

▼▼ ▼▼

Motel

Phone: (928)289-9581

| All Year | 1P: $35-$51 | 2P: $39-$57 | XP: $6 | F17 |

Location: I-40, exit 253, just s on N Park Dr, then just w. Located across from shopping center. 520 W Desmond St 86047. Fax: 928/289-5642. **Facility:** 55 one-bedroom standard units. 2 stories (no elevator), interior corridors. *Bath:* combo or shower only. **Parking:** on-site. **Terms:** small pets only (limit 1). **Pool(s):** small heated indoor. **Leisure Activities:** whirlpool. **Cards:** AX, DC, DS, MC, VI.

SOME UNITS

[S🄳] [🐾] [⊞] [♿] [🏊] [📹] [DATA PORT] / [✕] /
FEE

SUPER 8 MOTEL

(AAA) (SAVE)

▼▼ ▼▼

Motel

Phone: (928)289-4606

| 6/1-9/30 | 1P: $51-$69 | 2P: $59-$79 | XP: $6 | F12 |
| 2/1-5/31 & 10/1-1/31 | 1P: $45-$55 | 2P: $51-$61 | XP: $6 | F12 |

Location: I-40, exit 252, just e on Route 66. 1916 W Third St 86047. Fax: 928/289-4606. **Facility:** 46 one-bedroom standard units. 2 stories (no elevator), interior corridors. *Bath:* combo or shower only. **Parking:** on-site. **Terms:** [CP] meal plan available, package plans, pets ($10 fee, with prior approval). **Amenities:** *Some:* irons, hair dryers. **Cards:** AX, CB, DC, DS, JC, MC, VI. **Special Amenities:** free continental breakfast and free local telephone calls.

SOME UNITS

[S🄳] [🐾] [⊞] [📹] [DATA PORT] / [✕] [🛢] /
FEE

—————— WHERE TO DINE ——————

ADOBE INN RESTAURANT

▼

American

Dinner: $8-$19   **Phone:** 928/289-4638

Location: I-40, exit 253; in Best Western Adobe Inn. 1701 N Park Dr 86047. **Hours:** 4 pm-9 pm; Fri-10 pm in winter; Fri-10 pm in summer. **Reservations:** accepted. **Features:** In the Best Western, the family-oriented restaurant presents a menu of steak, seafood, such comfort foods as chicken fried steak, some Mexican dishes and sandwiches. Casual dress; cocktails. **Parking:** on-site. **Cards:** AX, CB, DC, DS, JC, MC, VI.

[🍽]

CASA BLANCA CAFE'

▼▼ ▼▼

Mexican

Lunch: $4-$10   **Dinner:** $4-$10   **Phone:** 928/289-4191

Location: On Historic Route 66 (2nd St) and North Leonard. 1201 E 2nd St 86047. **Hours:** 11 am-9 pm, Sun 11:30 am-8 pm. Closed: 11/23, 12/25. **Reservations:** accepted. **Features:** A local favorite, the restaurant serves tasty Mexican food in a casual atmosphere. Casual dress; wine only. **Parking:** on-site. **Cards:** AX, DS, MC, VI.

THE TURQUOISE ROOM

▼▼ ▼▼

American

Lunch: $6-$12   **Dinner:** $9-$17   **Phone:** 928/289-2888

Location: I-40, exit 253, 1 mi s to Route 66 (2nd St), then just e; in historic downtown; in La Posada Hotel. 303 E 2nd St 86047. **Hours:** 7 am-2 & 5-9 pm. **Reservations:** accepted. **Features:** Eight hand-painted glass and tin chandeliers grace the restaurant's high beamed ceilings. Elk, quail, salmon, beef, lamb and pork, flavored with home-grown herbs, are always on the menu. Southwestern cuisine is another option, as are boxed lunches, which include fresh grilled and chilled salmon, herb-roasted chicken breast and fresh breads. Casual dress; cocktails. **Parking:** on-site. **Cards:** AX, CB, DC, DS, JC, MC, VI.

[🍽]

YOUNGTOWN —*See Phoenix p. 367.*

YUMA pop. 77,515

---------- WHERE TO STAY ----------

BEST WESTERN CORONADO MOTOR HOTEL   Book at aaa.com   Phone: (928)783-4453

AAA SAVE	8/31-9/3 [BP]	1P: $99-$119	2P: $115-$150	XP: $10	F12
	9/4-1/31 [BP]	1P: $82-$92	2P: $89-$129	XP: $10	F12
	2/1-4/1 [BP]	1P: $72-$92	2P: $79-$129	XP: $10	F12
Motel	4/2-8/30 [BP]	1P: $62-$82	2P: $69-$129	XP: $10	F12

Location: I-8, exit 4th Ave eastbound, 0.5 mi s; exit 1 (Giss Pkwy) westbound, 1 mi w. 233 4th Ave 85364. Fax: 928/782-7487. **Facility:** 86 units. 65 one-bedroom standard units, some with kitchens and/or whirlpools. 21 one-bedroom suites ($89-$175), some with kitchens and/or whirlpools. 1-2 stories (no elevator), exterior corridors. **Bath:** combo or shower only. **Parking:** on-site. **Terms:** cancellation fee imposed, package plans. **Amenities:** video library, high-speed Internet, dual phone lines, voice mail, safes, irons, hair dryers. **Dining:** Yuma Landing Restaurant, see separate listing. **Pool(s):** outdoor, small heated outdoor. **Leisure Activities:** whirlpool. **Guest Services:** coin laundry. **Business Services:** fax. **Cards:** AX, CB, DC, DS, JC, MC, VI. **Special Amenities:** free full breakfast and free room upgrade (subject to availability with advance reservations). *(See color ad below)*

SOME UNITS

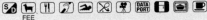

BEST WESTERN INNSUITES HOTEL & SUITES
YUMA   Book at aaa.com   Phone: (928)783-8341

AAA SAVE	2/1-4/30 [BP]	1P: $99-$169	2P: $99-$169	XP: $10	F18
	10/1-1/31 [BP]	1P: $89-$159	2P: $89-$159	XP: $10	F18
	7/1-9/30 [BP]	1P: $79-$149	2P: $79-$149	XP: $10	F18
Small-scale Hotel	5/1-6/30 [BP]	1P: $69-$139	2P: $69-$139	XP: $10	F18

Location: I-8, exit 2 (16th St/US 95), just ne. 1450 Castle Dome Ave 85365. Fax: 928/783-1349. **Facility:** 166 units. 119 one-bedroom standard units, some with whirlpools. 47 one-bedroom suites ($99-$179) with efficiencies, some with whirlpools. 2-3 stories (no elevator), exterior corridors. **Parking:** on-site. **Terms:** weekly rates available, pets ($25 fee). **Amenities:** high-speed Internet, dual phone lines, voice mail, irons, hair dryers. **Dining:** 6:30 am-10 & 5-10 pm; hours vary off season, cocktails. **Pool(s):** heated outdoor. **Leisure Activities:** whirlpool, 2 lighted tennis courts, guest library, exercise room, basketball. **Guest Services:** sundries, complimentary evening beverages, coin laundry. **Business Services:** meeting rooms, PC, fax. **Cards:** AX, CB, DC, DS, JC, MC, VI. **Special Amenities:** free full breakfast. *(See color ad below)*

SOME UNITS

FEE

CLARION SUITES   *Book at aaa.com*

▽▽▽▽ ▽▽▽▽

Small-scale Hotel

All Year [ECP]   1P: $117-$212   2P: $137-$284   XP: $20

Location: I-8, exit 2 (16 St/US 95) eastbound, 1 mi w, then 1.3 mi s; exit 3 (SR 280) westbound, 0.5 mi s, then 2 mi w. 2600 S 4th Ave 85364. Fax: 928/341-1152. **Facility:** 163 one-bedroom suites ($117-$400), some with whirlpools. 3 stories, exterior corridors. *Bath:* combo or shower only. **Parking:** on-site. **Terms:** pets (small dogs only, $25 extra charge). **Amenities:** video games (fee), voice mail, irons, hair dryers. *Some:* high-speed Internet. **Pool(s):** heated outdoor. **Leisure Activities:** whirlpool. **Guest Services:** complimentary evening beverages, coin laundry. **Business Services:** meeting rooms, PC, fax (fee). **Cards:** AX, CB, DC, DS, JC, MC, VI.

Phone: (928)726-4830
XP: $20   F17

SOME UNITS

[ASK] [SD] [🐾] [🍴] [⬅M] [&] [🏊] [🏄] [🎥] [DATA PORT] [🔌] [📷] [💻] / [✕] /
FEE

COMFORT INN   *Book at aaa.com*

▽▽▽▽ ▽▽▽▽

Small-scale Hotel

2/1-4/30 & 1/1-1/31 [ECP]   1P: $109-$159   2P: $129-$179   XP: $10   F18
9/1-12/31 [ECP]   1P: $99-$149   2P: $109-$159   XP: $10   F18
5/1-8/31 [ECP]   1P: $79-$99   2P: $99-$109   XP: $10   F18

Location: I-8, exit 2 (16th St/US 95), just w. 1691 S Riley Ave 85365. Fax: 928/782-0744. **Facility:** 81 one-bedroom standard units, some with whirlpools. 3 stories, interior corridors. *Bath:* combo or shower only. **Terms:** 7 day cancellation notice, pets ($10 extra charge). **Amenities:** dual phone lines, voice mail, irons, hair dryers. **Pool(s):** heated outdoor. **Leisure Activities:** whirlpool. **Guest Services:** valet and coin laundry. **Business Services:** meeting rooms, fax (fee). **Cards:** AX, DC, DS, MC, VI.

Phone: (928)782-1200

SOME UNITS

[ASK] [SD] [🐾] [🍴] [⬅M] [&] [🏊] [🏄] [🎥] [DATA PORT] [🔌] [💻] / [✕] [📷]
FEE

DAYS INN   *Book at aaa.com*

(AAA) [SAVE]
▽▽▽▽ ▽▽

Motel

2/1-3/31   1P: $80-$100   2P: $80-$100   XP: $5   F12
9/1-1/31   1P: $60-$100   2P: $60-$100   XP: $5   F12
4/1-8/31   1P: $60-$70   2P: $60-$70   XP: $5   F12

Location: I-8, exit 2 (16th St/US 95), just e. 1671 E 16th St 85365. Fax: 928/782-7609. **Facility:** 64 one-bedroom standard units, some with whirlpools. 2 stories (no elevator), exterior corridors. **Parking:** on-site. **Amenities:** hair dryers. *Some:* irons. **Pool(s):** small outdoor. **Leisure Activities:** whirlpool. **Guest Services:** coin laundry. **Business Services:** fax (fee). **Cards:** AX, CB, DC, DS, JC, MC, VI. **Special Amenities:** free continental breakfast and free local telephone calls.

Phone: (928)329-7790

SOME UNITS

[SD] [🍴] [⬅M] [&] [🏊] [🎥] [🔌] / [✕]

FAIRFIELD INN BY MARRIOTT   *Book at aaa.com*

▽▽▽ ▽▽

Small-scale Hotel

2/1-6/3 & 1/1-1/31   1P: $104-$114
10/1-12/31   1P: $89-$99
6/4-9/30   1P: $84-$94

Location: I-8, exit 2 (16th St/US 95), e to Sunridge Dr, then just s. 1801 S Sunridge Dr 85365. Fax: 928/345-1818. **Facility:** 64 one-bedroom standard units. 3 stories, interior corridors. *Bath:* combo or shower only. **Parking:** on-site. **Amenities:** high-speed Internet, voice mail, irons, hair dryers. **Pool(s):** heated outdoor. **Leisure Activities:** whirlpool, exercise room. **Guest Services:** valet and coin laundry. **Business Services:** fax (fee). **Cards:** AX, DC, DS, JC, MC, VI.

Phone: 928/345-1800

SOME UNITS

[ASK] [SD] [✈] [🍴] [⬅M] [&] [🏊] [🎥] [DATA PORT] [💻] / [✕] [🔌] [📷]
FEE FEE

HAMPTON INN

[fyi]

Property failed to provide current rates
Too new to rate, opening scheduled for November 2005. **Location:** I-8, exit 2 (16th St), just ne. 1600 E 16th St 85365. **Amenities:** 64 units.

Phone: 928/329-5600

HOLIDAY INN

▽▽▽▽ ▽▽▽▽

Small-scale Hotel

Property failed to provide current rates
Location: I-8, exit 2, 0.4 mi e on 16th St, just s on Pacific Ave, then just w. 1901 E 18th St 85364. Fax: 928/782-9301. **Facility:** 121 one-bedroom standard units, some with whirlpools. 4 stories, interior corridors. *Bath:* combo or shower only. **Parking:** on-site. **Terms:** small pets only ($10 extra charge). **Amenities:** high-speed Internet, voice mail, irons, hair dryers. **Pool(s):** heated outdoor. **Leisure Activities:** whirlpool, exercise room. **Guest Services:** sundries, coin laundry, area transportation. **Business Services:** meeting rooms, business center.

Phone: 928/782-9300

[✈] [🐾] [🍴] [⬅M] [🏊] [✕] [🎥] [DATA PORT] [🔌] [💻] [📷]
FEE

HOWARD JOHNSON INN   *Book at aaa.com*   Phone: (928)344-1420

(AAA) [SAVE]
2/1-4/30	1P: $91-$120	XP: $10	F
9/1-1/31	1P: $80-$99	XP: $10	F
5/1-8/31	1P: $70-$89	XP: $10	F

Small-scale Hotel   **Location:** I-8, exit 3E (SR 280 S), 1 mi s to 32nd St, then 2 mi w. Located across from shopping centers. 3181 S 4th Ave 85364. **Fax:** 928/341-0158. **Facility:** 120 one-bedroom standard units. 2 stories (no elevator), exterior corridors. *Bath:* combo or shower only. **Parking:** on-site. **Terms:** pets ($10 extra charge). **Amenities:** voice mail, irons, hair dryers. **Pool(s):** heated outdoor. **Leisure Activities:** whirlpool. **Guest Services:** complimentary evening beverages: Mon-Sat, except holidays, valet and coin laundry. **Business Services:** fax (fee). **Cards:** AX, CB, DC, DS, JC, MC, VI. **Special Amenities:** free local telephone calls and free newspaper. *(See color ad p 470)*

SOME UNITS

🐕 🍴 ♿ 🏊 📶 📷 [DATA PORT] 📠 📺 💻 / ⊠ /
FEE   FEE

LA FUENTE INN & SUITES   *Book at aaa.com*   Phone: (928)329-1814

(AAA) [SAVE]
| 6/1-12/31 [BP] | 1P: $83-$193 | 2P: $93-$225 | XP: $10 | F12 |
| 2/1-5/31 & 1/1-1/31 [BP] | 1P: $110-$130 | 2P: $120-$150 | XP: $10 | F12 |

Small-scale Hotel   **Location:** I-8, exit 2 (16th St/US 95), just e. 1513 E 16th St 85365. **Fax:** 928/343-2671. **Facility:** 97 units. 50 one-bedroom standard units. 47 one-bedroom suites, some with efficiencies and/or whirlpools. 2 stories (no elevator), exterior corridors. **Parking:** on-site. **Amenities:** video library (fee), high-speed Internet, dual phone lines, voice mail, irons, hair dryers. **Pool(s):** heated outdoor. **Leisure Activities:** whirlpool, exercise room. **Guest Services:** complimentary evening beverages, coin laundry. **Business Services:** meeting rooms, PC, fax (fee). **Cards:** AX, DC, DS, MC, VI. **Special Amenities:** free full breakfast and free local telephone calls. *(See color ad below)*

SOME UNITS

[S/D] ✈ 🍴 🏊 [VCR] 📷 [DATA PORT] 📠 📺 💻 / ⊠ /

MICROTEL INN & SUITES   *Book at aaa.com*   Phone: (928)345-1777

♦♦♦
11/1-1/31 [CP]	1P: $76-$140	2P: $76-$140
2/1-4/30 [CP]	1P: $74-$140	2P: $74-$140
5/1-10/31 [CP]	1P: $54-$130	2P: $54-$130

Small-scale Hotel   **Location:** I-8, exit 12 (Fortuna Rd), just s, then w on Frontage Rd. 11274 S Fortuna Rd, Suite H 85367. **Fax:** 928/305-9341. **Facility:** Smoke free premises. 110 units. 109 one-bedroom standard units, some with whirlpools. 1 one-bedroom suite with efficiency. 3 stories, interior corridors. *Bath:* combo or shower only. **Parking:** on-site. **Terms:** small pets only. **Amenities:** high-speed Internet, irons, hair dryers. **Pool(s):** heated outdoor. **Leisure Activities:** whirlpool. **Guest Services:** coin laundry. **Business Services:** meeting rooms, fax (fee). **Cards:** AX, DC, DS, MC, VI.

SOME UNITS

[ASK] 🐕 🍴 ♿ 🏊 📶 ⊠ 📷 [DATA PORT] / 📠 📺 💻 /
FEE

MOTEL 6 YUMA EAST #1031 *Book at aaa.com* Phone: 928/782-9521

Motel

2/1-4/15	1P: $47-$57	2P: $53-$63	XP: $3 F17
11/24-1/31	1P: $39-$49	2P: $45-$55	XP: $3 F17
4/16-11/23	1P: $37-$47	2P: $43-$53	XP: $3 F17

Location: I-8, exit 2 (16th St/US 95), just e. 1445 E 16th St 85365. Fax: 928/343-4941. **Facility:** 122 one-bedroom standard units. 2 stories, exterior corridors. *Bath:* combo or shower only. **Parking:** on-site. **Terms:** small pets only. **Pool(s):** small heated outdoor. **Guest Services:** coin laundry. **Business Services:** fax (fee). **Cards:** AX, CB, DC, DS, MC, VI.

SOME UNITS

OAK TREE INN Phone: (928)539-9000

Small-scale Hotel

1/1-1/31 [BP]	1P: $99-$109	2P: $99-$109	XP: $10 F18
9/1-12/31 [BP]	1P: $89-$99	2P: $99-$109	XP: $10 F18
2/1-4/30 [BP]	1P: $99	2P: $109	XP: $10 F18
5/1-8/31 [BP]	1P: $79-$89	2P: $85-$95	XP: $10 F18

Location: I-8, exit 2 (16th St/US 95), just e, then just s. Located in a commercial area. 1730 Sunridge Dr 85364. Fax: 928/539-0693. **Facility:** Smoke free premises. 119 one-bedroom standard units. 2 stories (no elevator), interior corridors. *Bath:* combo or shower only. **Parking:** on-site. **Terms:** 7 day cancellation notice, small pets only ($10 extra charge). **Amenities:** high-speed Internet, irons, hair dryers. **Pool(s):** heated outdoor. **Leisure Activities:** whirlpool, exercise room. **Guest Services:** coin laundry. **Business Services:** meeting rooms, fax (fee). **Cards:** AX, DC, DS, MC, VI.

SOME UNITS
FEE

QUALITY INN AIRPORT *Book at aaa.com* Phone: (928)726-4721

Small-scale Hotel

2/1-5/31	1P: $99-$149	XP: $10 F18
6/1-1/31	1P: $79-$149	XP: $10 F18

Location: I-8, exit 3E (SR 280), 1.2 mi s, then 1.9 mi w. 711 E 32nd St 85365. Fax: 928/344-0452. **Facility:** 80 one-bedroom standard units, some with efficiencies. 2 stories (no elevator), exterior corridors. *Bath:* combo or shower only. **Parking:** on-site. **Terms:** age restrictions may apply, weekly rates available, pets ($25 fee, with prior approval). **Amenities:** high-speed Internet, irons, hair dryers. **Dining:** 6 am-10 pm, cocktails. **Pool(s):** heated outdoor. **Guest Services:** complimentary evening beverages, valet and coin laundry. **Business Services:** meeting rooms, fax (fee). **Cards:** AX, DC, DS, MC, VI. **Special Amenities:** free expanded continental breakfast and free local telephone calls. *(See color ad below)*

SOME UNITS
FEE

RAMADA INN CHILTON CONFERENCE CENTER *Book at aaa.com* Phone: (928)344-1050

Small-scale Hotel

All Year [BP]	1P: $84-$109	2P: $94-$119	XP: $10 F17

Location: I-8 business loop, 2.3 mi s of jct US 95. 300 E 32nd St 85364. Fax: 928/344-4877. **Facility:** 121 one-bedroom standard units. 2 stories (no elevator), exterior corridors. **Parking:** on-site. **Terms:** check-in 3:30 pm, package plans, $5 service charge, pets ($10 fee). **Amenities:** voice mail, irons, hair dryers. *Some Fee:* DVD players. **Dining:** 6-9 am, 11:30-1:30 & 5-9 pm, cocktails. **Pool(s):** heated outdoor. **Leisure Activities:** whirlpool. **Guest Services:** valet and coin laundry, area transportation-bus & train terminal. **Business Services:** meeting rooms, fax (fee). **Cards:** AX, CB, DC, DS, JC, MC, VI. **Special Amenities:** free expanded continental breakfast and free local telephone calls.

SOME UNITS
FEE FEE FEE

SHILO INN HOTEL-YUMA *Book at aaa.com* Phone: (928)782-9511

Small-scale Hotel

All Year [BP]	1P: $113-$190	2P: $113-$190	XP: $12 F12

Location: I-8, exit 2 (16th St/US 95), just ne. 1550 S Castle Dome Rd 85365. Fax: 928/783-1538. **Facility:** 134 units. 133 one-bedroom standard units, some with kitchens. 1 one-bedroom suite with kitchen. 4 stories, interior corridors. *Bath:* combo or shower only. **Parking:** on-site. **Terms:** package plans, pets ($10 extra charge). **Amenities:** video games (fee), voice mail, irons, hair dryers. **Dining:** 6 am-10 pm, cocktails. **Pool(s):** heated outdoor. **Leisure Activities:** sauna, whirlpool, steamroom, exercise room. **Guest Services:** valet and coin laundry. **Business Services:** conference facilities, fax. **Cards:** AX, CB, DC, DS, JC, MC, VI.

SOME UNITS
FEE

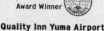

SPRINGHILL SUITES BY MARRIOTT

Book at aaa.com

Phone: (928)783-7853

Small-scale Hotel

2/1-6/4	1P: $139	2P: $139
10/1-1/31	1P: $129	2P: $129
6/5-9/30	1P: $109	2P: $109

Location: I-8, exit 2 (16th St/US 95), 0.5 mi e to Sunridge Dr, 0.3 mi s, then just e. 1825 E 18th St 85365. Fax: 928/783-7854. **Facility:** 80 one-bedroom standard units. 3 stories, interior corridors. *Bath:* combo or shower only. **Parking:** on-site. **Amenities:** high-speed Internet, voice mail, irons, hair dryers. **Pool(s):** heated outdoor. **Leisure Activities:** whirlpool, exercise room. **Guest Services:** sundries, coin laundry. **Business Services:** meeting rooms, PC, fax. **Cards:** AX, CB, DC, DS, JC, MC, VI.

SOME UNITS

YUMA CABANA MOTEL

Phone: (928)783-8311

Motel

2/1-3/31 [CP]	1P: $56-$72	2P: $64-$80	XP: $5 F19
1/1-1/31 [CP]	1P: $51-$64	2P: $57-$72	XP: $5 F19
4/1-4/30 [CP]	1P: $49-$58	2P: $55-$69	XP: $5 F19
5/1-12/31 [CP]	1P: $42-$48	2P: $47-$58	XP: $5 F19

Location: I-8, exit 2 (16th St/US 95), 1 mi w, then 0.5 mi s. 2151 S 4th Ave 85364. Fax: 928/783-1126. **Facility:** 63 units. 59 one-bedroom standard units. 4 one-bedroom suites ($80-$89) with efficiencies. 2 stories (no elevator), interior corridors. *Bath:* shower only. **Parking:** on-site. **Terms:** pets ($6 extra charge). **Amenities:** high-speed Internet, hair dryers. **Pool(s):** heated outdoor. **Leisure Activities:** shuffleboard. **Guest Services:** coin laundry. **Business Services:** fax (fee). **Cards:** AX, CB, DC, DS, JC, MC, VI. **Special Amenities:** free continental breakfast and free local telephone calls. *(See color ad below)*

SOME UNITS

YUMA SUPER 8 MOTEL

Book at aaa.com

Phone: (928)782-2000

Small-scale Hotel

1/1-1/31 [ECP]	1P: $109-$159	2P: $119-$169	XP: $10 F18
2/1-4/30 [ECP]	1P: $99-$149	2P: $119-$169	XP: $10 F18
9/1-12/31 [ECP]	1P: $89-$139	2P: $99-$149	XP: $10 F18
5/1-8/31 [ECP]	1P: $69-$89	2P: $89-$99	XP: $10 F18

Location: I-8, exit 2 (16th St/US 95), just w. 1688 S Riley Ave 85365. Fax: 928/782-6657. **Facility:** 82 one-bedroom standard units. 3 stories, interior corridors. *Bath:* combo or shower only. **Parking:** on-site. **Terms:** 7 day cancellation notice, pets ($10 extra charge). **Amenities:** voice mail. **Pool(s):** heated outdoor. **Leisure Activities:** whirlpool. **Guest Services:** valet and coin laundry. **Business Services:** fax (fee). **Cards:** AX, DC, DS, MC, VI.

SOME UNITS

——— WHERE TO DINE ———

BRITAIN'S FARM CHUCKWAGON & STEAK HOUSE **Lunch:** $6-$8 **Dinner:** $8-$16 **Phone:** 928/782-4699
◈◈ ◈◈ **Location:** Jct 4th Ave, 2.6 mi s on 8th St, 0.6 mi w on Ave C, then 0.4 mi s. 4330 W Riverside Dr 85364. **Hours:** 11
Steak House am-9 pm. Closed major holidays; also Sun-Tues. **Reservations:** accepted. **Features:** A whole family
experience, a meal at the eatery might incorporate a visit to an antique car museum and a petting zoo.
Grilled steak and homemade pies are served in hearty portions. Casual dress; cocktails. **Parking:** on-site.
Cards: MC, VI.

THE CROSSING RESTAURANT **Lunch:** $7-$12 **Dinner:** $7-$15 **Phone:** 928/726-5551
◈◈◈ **Location:** I-8, exit 2 (16th St), 1 mi w, then 1.5 mi s. 2690 S 4th Ave 85364. **Hours:** 11 am-9:30 pm, Sun-8:30 pm.
American Closed: 7/4, 12/25. **Reservations:** accepted. **Features:** The owners of this local institution use the freshest
ingredients for their hearty, family-style meals. Flame-broiled chicken and the open-faced hot prime
sandwich are popular choices. Casual dress; wine only. **Parking:** on-site. **Cards:** AX, DS, MC, VI.

DON QUIJOTE-MEXICAN & AMERICAN FOOD **Lunch:** $5-$9 **Dinner:** $5-$20 **Phone:** 928/342-3313
◈◈ **Location:** I-8, exit 12 (Fortuna Rd), 0.4 mi s. 11411 S Fortuna Rd #214 85367. **Hours:** 11 am-8 pm. Closed: 11/23,
Mexican 12/25; also Mon. **Features:** The casual, family-focused restaurant's menu includes a wide selection of
Mexican and American dishes. Casual dress; cocktails. **Parking:** on-site. **Cards:** MC, VI.

EL PAPPAGALLO MEXICAN RESTAURANT **Lunch:** $6-$10 **Dinner:** $10-$15 **Phone:** 928/343-9451
◈◈ ◈◈ **Location:** I-8, exit 2 (16th St/US 95), 2.5 mi w, then just n. 1401 S Ave B 85364. **Hours:** 11 am-9 pm, Fri & Sat-9:30
Mexican pm. Closed: 11/23, 12/25. **Features:** In this small, casual restaurant, family recipes are used in the food
preparation, and the smiling wait staff can help with suggestions. Casual dress; cocktails. **Parking:** on-site.
Cards: AX, CB, DC, DS, MC, VI.

HUNTER STEAKHOUSE **Lunch:** $7-$20 **Dinner:** $17-$29 **Phone:** 928/782-3637
◈◈ ◈◈ **Location:** Jct n of 24th St. 2355 S 4th Ave 85364. **Hours:** 11:30 am-2 & 4:30-9 pm, Fri-10 pm, Sat 4:30 pm-10
Steak House pm, Sun 4:30 pm-9 pm; hours may vary in summer. Closed: 12/25. **Reservations:** accepted.
Features: Tender steaks, succulent prime rib and some seafood dishes are among choices sure to satisfy
everyone. Warm interior colors and the smiling, attentive staff round out the dining experience. Casual
dress; cocktails. **Parking:** on-site. **Cards:** AX, DC, DS, MC, VI.

JULIEANNA'S PATIO CAFE **Lunch:** $6-$10 **Dinner:** $15-$25 **Phone:** 928/317-1961
◈◈◈ **Location:** I-8, exit 3 (SR 280), 0.5 mi s, 3.7 mi w on 24th St, then just s on 19th Ave; at Pichacho Mountain Medical
American Center. 1951 W 25th St 85364. **Hours:** 11 am-2 & 5-9 pm, Sat from 5 pm; seasonal hours vary. Closed major
holidays; also Mon & Sun except Mother's Day, Father's Day & Easter. **Reservations:** accepted.
Features: The cafe has a colorfully decorated dining room and a large, outdoor patio with brightly painted,
wrought-iron furnishings and metal sculptures. Casual dress; cocktails. **Parking:** on-site. **Cards:** AX, DC, DS, MC, VI.

MANDARIN GARDEN **Lunch:** $7-$12 **Dinner:** $9-$18 **Phone:** 928/342-6336
◈◈ ◈◈ **Location:** I-8, exit 14 (Foothills), just s, then 0.6 mi w. 12415 S Frontage Rd 85367. **Hours:** 11 am-9 pm.
Chinese **Reservations:** accepted. **Features:** The buffet here is popular with locals but a wide selection of foods such
as kung pao shrimp, Hunan pork ribs or chicken with black bean sauce is offered. Casual dress; cocktails.
Parking: on-site. **Cards:** AX, DS, MC, VI.

MANDARIN PALACE **Lunch:** $6-$8 **Dinner:** $8-$14 **Phone:** 928/344-2805
◈◈ **Location:** I-8, exit 2 (16th St/US 95) southbound, 0.5 mi w, then 2 mi s on Arizona Ave; exit 3 northbound, 1 mi s, then 2
Chinese mi w on I-8 business loop. 350 E 32nd St 85364. **Hours:** 11 am-9 pm, Fri & Sat-10 pm. **Reservations:** accepted.
Features: Mandarin and Szechuan cuisine dominates the offerings; a limited selection of American entrees
are also available. A lunch buffet is offered weekdays 11 am-2 pm. Casual dress; cocktails. **Parking:** on-
site. **Cards:** AX, DC, DS, MC, VI.

MOSTLY MUFFINS BAKERY & CAFE **Lunch:** $4-$8 **Phone:** 928/783-7484
◈◈ **Location:** I-8, exit 2 (16th St/US 95), 2.4 mi w. 2451 W 16th St 85364. **Hours:** 5:30 am-5 pm, Sat-2:30 pm.
Specialty Closed: 12/25; also Sun. **Features:** In the wee hours of the morning, muffin makers are busy making treats
for breakfast and hearty sandwiches and soups for lunch. A casual atmosphere, good coffee and muffins
from low-fat to decadent help diners start their day. Casual dress. **Parking:** on-site. **Cards:** AX, MC, VI.

RIVER CITY GRILL **Lunch:** $8-$12 **Dinner:** $10-$24 **Phone:** 928/782-7988
◈◈ ◈◈ **Location:** I-8, exit 1 (Giss Pkwy), 1 mi w. 600 W Third St 85364. **Hours:** 11:30 am-2 & 5-9 pm, Fri-10 pm, Sat 5
Seafood pm-10 pm, Sun 5 pm-9 pm. Closed: 7/4, 11/23, 12/25. **Reservations:** accepted. **Features:** Bright, eclectic
decor sets a tone for excitement. Fresh fish are sent from the Northwest. Try wild salmon with polenta
blueberry jus or mustard-crusted halibut, but don't get so full that you don't leave room for dessert, such as
chocolate bread pudding. Fresh sushi is another option. Casual dress; cocktails. **Parking:** on-site. **Cards:** AX, CB, DC, DS, JC,
MC, VI.

YUMA LANDING RESTAURANT **Lunch:** $5-$9 **Dinner:** $7-$15 **Phone:** 928/782-7427
ⒶⒶⒶ **Location:** I-8, exit 4th Ave eastbound, 0.5 mi s; exit 1 (Giss Pkwy) westbound, 1 mi w; in Best Western Coronado Motor
◈◈ ◈◈ Hotel. 195 4th Ave 85364. **Hours:** 6 am-9 pm, Fri & Sat-midnight. **Reservations:** accepted. **Features:** On the
American historic site of the first plane landing in Arizona in 1911, the restaurant displays early city memorabilia
throughout its dining rooms. Representative of the diverse selection of American, Mexican and Italian
entrees are barbecue ribs, beef fritter and liver and onions. Casual dress; cocktails. **Parking:** on-site.
Cards: AX, CB, DC, DS, JC, MC, VI. **Historic** *(See color ad p 469)*

ABIQUIU

———— WHERE TO STAY ————

CASA DEL RIO
▽▼▽▼▽
Bed & Breakfast

Phone: (505)753-2035
All Year   1P: $99-$119   2P: $109-$129   XP: $25   F
Location: 2.3 mi n from jct US 285, then just e on gated drive. Hwy 84, MM 199.46 87510 (PO Box 702). Fax: 505/753-2035. **Facility:** Nestled at the base of cliffs showing Georgia O'Keeffe's pink hues, the modern residence has quiet patios, a trickling fountain and a meditation room. 4 one-bedroom standard units. 1 story, interior/exterior corridors. *Bath:* shower only. **Parking:** on-site. **Terms:** check-in 4 pm, age restrictions may apply, 21 day cancellation notice, pets (horses only). **Amenities:** hair dryers. *Some:* irons. **Leisure Activities:** hiking trails. **Guest Services:** gift shop. **Business Services:** PC, fax. **Cards:** MC, VI.

SOME UNITS
(ASK) [🐴] [♿] [✕] [🔥] [📶] [🔒] / [💻] /

———— *The following lodging was either not evaluated or did not meet AAA rating requirements but is listed for your information only.* ————

GHOST RANCH B&B
[fyi]

Phone: 505/685-4333
Not evaluated. **Location:** HC 77, Box 11 87510. Facilities, services, and decor characterize a basic property.

ACOMITA

———— WHERE TO STAY ————

SKY CITY HOTEL AND CONFERENCE CENTER
(AAA) [SAVE]
▽▼▽▼▽
Small-scale Hotel

Phone: 505/552-6123
All Year   1P: $67-$92   2P: $72-$97   XP: $5
Location: I-40, exit 102, just n. (PO Box 310, ACOMA PUEBLO, 87034). Fax: 505/552-6431. **Facility:** 134 one-bedroom standard units. 3 stories, interior corridors. *Bath:* combo or shower only. **Parking:** on-site. **Terms:** cancellation fee imposed. **Amenities:** video games (fee), irons, hair dryers. **Dining:** 6 am-midnight, Thurs-Sat to 2 am, cocktails. **Pool(s):** heated outdoor. **Leisure Activities:** whirlpool, putting green, exercise room. **Guest Services:** gift shop. **Business Services:** conference facilities. **Cards:** AX, CB, DC, DS, MC, VI. *(See color ad p 543)*

SOME UNITS
[S♦] [🍴] [🍸] [♿M] [♿] [📷] [🏊] [✕] [🎥] [📶] [💻] / [✕] /

ALAMOGORDO pop. 35,582

———— WHERE TO STAY ————

BEST WESTERN DESERT AIRE INN   *Book at aaa.com*
(AAA) [SAVE]
▽▼▽▼▽
Small-scale Hotel

Phone: (505)437-2110
4/1-9/30 [CP]   1P: $60-$110   2P: $70-$110   XP: $5   F12
2/1-3/31 & 10/1-1/31 [CP]   1P: $50-$100   2P: $60-$100   XP: $5   F12
Location: 1.5 mi s of jct US 54/70 and 82. Located in a commercial area. 1021 S White Sands Blvd 88310. Fax: 505/437-1898. **Facility:** 99 one-bedroom standard units, some with kitchens and/or whirlpools. 2 stories (no elevator), exterior corridors. **Parking:** on-site. **Terms:** pets ($10 fee, $50 deposit). **Amenities:** voice mail, irons, hair dryers. **Pool(s):** heated outdoor. **Leisure Activities:** sauna, whirlpool. *Fee:* game room. **Guest Services:** valet and coin laundry. **Business Services:** meeting rooms, fax. **Cards:** AX, DC, DS, JC, MC, VI. **Special Amenities:** free continental breakfast and early check-in/late check-out.

SOME UNITS
[S♦] [🐴] [🍴] [📷] [🏊] [✕] [🎥] [📶] [🔒] [🛗] [💻] / [✕] /
FEE

COMFORT INN & SUITES   *Book at aaa.com*
(AAA) [SAVE]
▽▼▽▼▽
Small-scale Hotel

Phone: (505)434-4200
All Year [BP]   1P: $73-$120   2P: $81-$128   XP: $8   F18
Location: 1.5 mi s of jct US 54/70 and 82. 1020 S White Sands Blvd 88310. Fax: 505/437-8872. **Facility:** 91 one-bedroom standard units. 2 stories (no elevator), exterior corridors. **Parking:** on-site. **Amenities:** high-speed Internet, voice mail, irons, hair dryers. **Pool(s):** heated outdoor. **Leisure Activities:** whirlpool, exercise room. **Guest Services:** valet and coin laundry. **Business Services:** meeting rooms, fax. **Cards:** AX, DC, DS, MC, VI. **Special Amenities:** free full breakfast and free local telephone calls.

SOME UNITS
[S♦] [🍴] [🏊] [🎥] [📶] [🔒] [🛗] [💻] / [✕] /

HAMPTON INN   *Book at aaa.com*
▽▼▽
Small-scale Hotel

Phone: 505/439-1782
Property failed to provide current rates
Location: 1.6 mi s of jct US 54/70 and 82. 1295 Hamilton Rd 88310. Fax: 505/439-5680. **Facility:** 70 one-bedroom standard units. 3 stories, interior corridors. *Bath:* combo or shower only. **Parking:** on-site. **Amenities:** video games (fee), high-speed Internet, voice mail, irons, hair dryers. **Pool(s):** heated indoor. **Leisure Activities:** whirlpool, exercise room. **Guest Services:** valet and coin laundry. **Business Services:** meeting rooms, fax.

SOME UNITS
[🍴] [♿] [🏊] [🎥] [📶] [💻] / [✕] /

HOLIDAY INN EXPRESS-ALAMOGORDO   *Book at aaa.com*
▽▼▽▼▽
Small-scale Hotel

Phone: (505)437-7100
All Year [CP]   1P: $63-$85   2P: $63-$85
Location: 1.6 mi s of jct US 54/70 and 82. 1401 S White Sands Blvd 88310 (1000 Markey St, Bldg 1, Suite 100, PORTSMOUTH, NH, 03801). Fax: 505/443-0251. **Facility:** 106 one-bedroom standard units. 2 stories (no elevator), interior corridors. **Parking:** on-site. **Terms:** pets ($50 deposit, $10 extra charge). **Amenities:** high-speed Internet, irons, hair dryers. **Pool(s):** heated outdoor. **Guest Services:** valet and coin laundry. **Business Services:** meeting rooms, fax. **Cards:** AX, CB, DC, DS, JC, MC, VI.

SOME UNITS
(ASK) [S♦] [🐴] [🍴] [♿M] [📷] [🏊] [🎥] [📶] [💻] / [✕] /
FEE

SUPER 8 MOTEL-ALAMOGORDO
Phone: (505)439-2741

◊◊◊ ◊◊◊   All Year   1P: $49-$71   2P: $55-$79   XP: $6   F12
Location: Just s of jct US 54/70 and 82. Located across from the mall and adjacent to the fairgrounds. 3204 N White
Small-scale Hotel   Sands Blvd 88310. Fax: 505/439-2741. **Facility:** 57 one-bedroom standard units. 2 stories (no elevator),
interior corridors. **Parking:** on-site. **Terms:** small pets only (in smoking units, with prior approval).
Amenities: high-speed Internet, voice mail, hair dryers. **Guest Services:** coin laundry. **Business Services:** PC, fax (fee).
Cards: AX, CB, DC, DS, JC, MC, VI.

SOME UNITS
(A$K) (S⌀) (🐾) (📶) (🎥) / (✕) (🖥)/
FEE

WHITE SANDS MOTEL
Phone: 505/437-2922

◊◊◊ (SAVE)   All Year   1P: $35-$40   2P: $45-$50   XP: $5   D12
Location: 1.6 mi s of jct US 54/70 and 82. 1101 S White Sands Blvd 88310. Fax: 505/443-8365. **Facility:** 25 one-
◊◊◊   bedroom standard units. 1 story, exterior corridors. *Bath:* combo or shower only. **Parking:** on-site. **Business
◊   Services:** fax. **Cards:** AX, CB, DC, DS, JC, MC, VI. **Special Amenities:** free continental breakfast and
Motel   free local telephone calls.

SOME UNITS
(S⌀) (📶) (🎥) (🖥) / (✕) (🖥)/

———— **WHERE TO DINE** ————

PEPPER'S GRILL
Lunch: $6-$10   Dinner: $11-$25   Phone: 505/437-9717
◊◊◊   **Location:** On US 70 and 54; north end of town. 3200 N White Sands Blvd 88310. **Hours:** 11 am-2 & 5-9 pm.
Steak House   Closed major holidays; also Sun. **Reservations:** accepted. **Features:** One of the city's finer restaurants, the
grill prepares great steaks. here. Try the white cap: filet mignon topped with a portobello mushroom and
spectacular sauce. The setting is almost one of fine dining, and service, provided by staff members attired in
black and white, is cheerful. While it is still mainly a steakhouse, this place has the feel of a special-occasion spot at night.
Casual dress; beer & wine only. **Parking:** on-site. **Cards:** AX, DS, MC, VI.

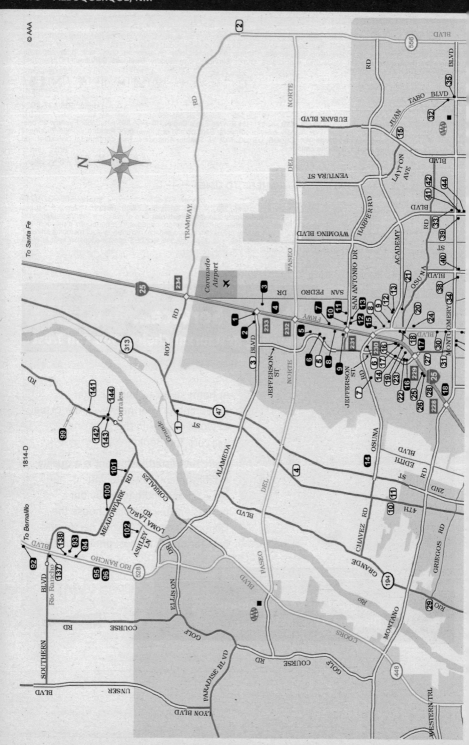

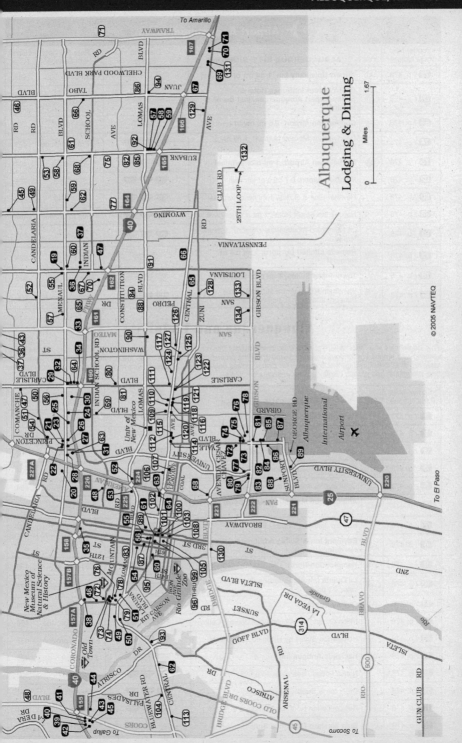

Albuquerque
Lodging & Dining

✈ Airport Accommodations

Spotter/Map Page Number	OA	ALBUQUERQUE INT'L SUNPORT	Diamond Rating	Rate Range High Season	Listing Page
77 / p. 478	AAA	Airport University Inn, 1 mi nw of terminal	◆◆◆	$59-$105 SAVE	487
85 / p. 478	AAA	Best Western InnSuites Hotel & Suites-Airport Albuquerque, just nw of terminal	◆◆	$119-$159 SAVE	490
84 / p. 478	AAA	Comfort Inn-Airport, 0.5 mi nw of terminal	◆◆	$59-$109 SAVE	492
74 / p. 478		Courtyard by Marriott (Airport), 1 mi nw of terminal	◆◆◆	Failed to provide	493
75 / p. 478	AAA	Fairfield Inn Airport, 1 mi n of terminal	◆◆◆	$59-$98 SAVE	495
82 / p. 478		Hampton-Airport, 0.7 mi s of terminal	◆◆◆	$79-$109	495
80 / p. 478		Hawthorn Inn & Suites, 1 mi nw of terminal	◆◆◆	$69-$149	496
88 / p. 478		Holiday Inn Select Hotel, 1 mi w of terminal	◆◆◆	Failed to provide	497
81 / p. 478		La Quinta Inn Albuquerque (Airport), 1 mi nw of terminal	◆◆◆	$82-$112	499
72 / p. 478	AAA	Ramada Limited (Airport), 1 mi nw of terminal	◆◆	$45-$70 SAVE	504
78 / p. 478	AAA	TownePlace Suites, 1 mi n of terminal	◆◆◆	$59-$109 SAVE	505
87 / p. 478		Wyndham Albuquerque at International Sunport, at airport, 0.3 mi w of terminal	◆◆◆	Failed to provide	506

Albuquerque and Vicinity

This index helps you "spot" where approved accommodations and restaurants are located on the corresponding detailed maps. Lodging rate ranges are for comparison only and show the property's high season; rates are per night, unless only weekly (W) rates are available. Restaurant rate range is for dinner, unless only lunch (L) is served. Turn to the listing page for more detailed rate information and consult display ads for special promotions.

Spotter/Map Page Number	OA	ALBUQUERQUE - Lodgings	Diamond Rating	Rate Range High Season	Listing Page
1 / p. 478		Ramada Limited	◆◆◆	$69-$79	503
2 / p. 478		Holiday Inn Express Hotel & Suites	◆◆◆	$86	497
3 / p. 478		Comfort Inn & Suites by Choice Hotels	◆◆◆	$65-$90	492
4 / p. 478		Motel 6 Albuquerque North #1290	◆	$39-$55	501
5 / p. 478		Courtyard by Marriott Journal Center	◆◆◆	Failed to provide	494
6 / p. 478	AAA	Albuquerque Marriott Pyramid North - see color ad p 488	◆◆◆	$99-$189 SAVE	488
7 / p. 478		Howard Johnson Express Inn	◆◆	$60-$75	497
8 / p. 478	AAA	Baymont Inn & Suites Albuquerque North - see color ad p 489	◆◆◆	$63-$80 SAVE	489
9 / p. 478	AAA	Hampton Inn-North	◆◆◆	$84-$94 SAVE	496
10 / p. 478	AAA	La Quinta Inn Albuquerque (North) - see color ad p 499	◆◆◆	$79-$109 SAVE	499
11 / p. 478	AAA	Quality Suites	◆◆◆	$79-$99 SAVE	503
12 / p. 478		Hilton Garden Inn Albuquerque Journal Center	◆◆◆	Failed to provide	496
13 / p. 478		Homewood Suites by Hilton-Journal Center	◆◆◆	Failed to provide	497
14 / p. 478	AAA	Hacienda Antigua Inn	◆◆◆	$149-$189 SAVE	495
15 / p. 478		Nativo Lodge - see color ad p 502	◆◆◆	$169-$179	502
16 / p. 478		Drury Inn & Suites-Albuquerque	◆◆◆	$86-$148	494
17 / p. 478		Residence Inn North by Marriott	◆◆◆	Failed to provide	504
18 / p. 478	AAA	Best Western Executive Suites	◆◆◆	$74-$154 SAVE	490

Spotter/Map Page Number	OA	ALBUQUERQUE - Lodgings (continued)	Diamond Rating	Rate Range High Season	Listing Page
19 / p. 478	AAA	Sheraton Albuquerque Uptown - see color ad p 504	◈◈◈	$89-$199 SAVE	504
20 / p. 478	AAA	ClubHouse Inn & Suites - see color ad p 492	◈◈◈	$74-$109 SAVE	492
21 / p. 478		La Quinta Suites Midtown/University - see color ad p 499	◈◈◈	$79-$129	500
22 / p. 478		Super 8 Motel of Albuquerque	◈◈	$45-$125	505
23 / p. 478		Comfort Inn-Midtown	◈◈	$49-$110	492
24 / p. 478		Candlewood Suites	◈◈◈	$59-$109	492
25 / p. 478	AAA	AmeriSuites (Albuquerque/Midtown)	◈◈◈	$109-$139 SAVE	488
26 / p. 478		Days Inn Midtown	◈◈	$39-$109	494
27 / p. 478		MCM Elegante Hotel	◈◈◈	$109-$139	500
28 / p. 478		Fairfield Inn by Marriott - see color ad p 495	◈◈◈	Failed to provide	495
29 / p. 478	AAA	Radisson Hotel & Conference Center - see color ad p 503	◈◈◈	$129-$179 SAVE	503
30 / p. 478	AAA	Albuquerque Inn & Suites (Now known as Equus Hotel Suites)	◈◈	$69-$109 SAVE	487
31 / p. 478		Hilton Albuquerque	◈◈◈	$69-$175	496
32 / p. 478	AAA	Econo Lodge Midtown	◈◈	$50-$60 SAVE	494
33 / p. 478	AAA	La Quinta Inn Albuquerque (I-40 East) - see color ad p 499	◈◈	$65-$100 SAVE	499
34 / p. 478		Hampton Inn University-Midtown	◈◈◈	$63-$109	496
35 / p. 478	AAA	Quality Inn & Suites Albuquerque Downtown	◈◈	$48-$95 SAVE	503
36 / p. 478	AAA	AmeriSuites (Albuquerque/Uptown)	◈◈◈	$79-$119 SAVE	489
37 / p. 478		Homewood Suites by Hilton-Uptown	◈◈◈	$79-$159	497
38 / p. 478	AAA	Best Western Rio Grande Inn - see color ad p 491	◈◈◈	$93-$123 SAVE	491
39 / p. 478		La Quinta Inn & Suites Albuquerque (West) - see color ad p 499	◈◈◈	$99-$129	500
40 / p. 478		Days Inn West	◈◈	$46-$85	494
41 / p. 478		Red Roof Inn	◈◈	$42-$59	504
42 / p. 478		Holiday Inn Express-West	◈◈◈	$59-$129	497
43 / p. 478		Super 8 Motel West (Albuquerque)	◈◈	$45-$125	505
44 / p. 478	AAA	Comfort Inn West	◈◈	$59-$79 SAVE	493
45 / p. 478	AAA	Motel 76	◈◈	$31-$52 SAVE	501
46 / p. 478		Hotel Albuquerque at Old Town	◈◈◈	$89-$254	497
47 / p. 478		The Albuquerque Marriott Hotel	◈◈◈	$94-$175	487
48 / p. 478		Sun Village Corporate Suites	◈◈◈	Failed to provide	505
49 / p. 478	AAA	Econo Lodge Old Town	◈◈	$45-$130 SAVE	494
50 / p. 478	AAA	Monterey Non-Smokers Motel-Old Town - see color ad p 501	◈◈	$42-$65 SAVE	501
51 / p. 478	AAA	Bottger Mansion of Old Town	◈◈◈	$115-$174 SAVE	491
52 / p. 478	AAA	Plaza Inn Albuquerque - see color ad p 502	◈◈	$109-$129 SAVE	502
53 / p. 478	AAA	Albuquerque Embassy Suites Hotel & Conference Center - see color ad p 488	◈◈◈	$99-$750 SAVE	487
54 / p. 478	AAA	Brittania & W E Mauger Estate Bed & Breakfast	◈◈◈	$89-$229 SAVE	491
55 / p. 478		Albuquerque Doubletree Hotel	◈◈◈	Failed to provide	487

Spotter/Map Page Number	OA	ALBUQUERQUE - Lodgings (continued)	Diamond Rating	Rate Range High Season	Listing Page
56 / p. 478	AAA	Hyatt Regency Albuquerque - see color ad p 498	◆◆◆◆	$99-$185 SAVE	498
57 / p. 478	AAA	Days Inn-Hotel Circle	◆◆	$65 SAVE	494
58 / p. 478		GuestHouse Inn & Suites	◆◆	$45-$95	495
59 / p. 478	AAA	Holiday Inn Express	◆◆◆	$69 SAVE	496
60 / p. 478		The Hotel Blue	◆◆◆	Failed to provide	497
61 / p. 478	AAA	La Posada de Albuquerque - see color ad p 498	fyi	$99-$153 SAVE	499
62 / p. 478	AAA	Sandia Peak Inn	◆◆	$40-$99 SAVE	504
63 / p. 478	AAA	Econo Lodge Downtown/University	◆◆	$39-$69 SAVE	494
64 / p. 478	AAA	Stardust Inn	◆	$49-$79 SAVE	505
65 / p. 478	AAA	Luxury Inn - see color ad p 500	◆◆	$40-$70 SAVE	500
66 / p. 478		Ambassador Inn	◆◆	Failed to provide	488
67 / p. 478		Super 8 Motel East	◆◆	$45-$125	505
68 / p. 478		Motel 6 #1349	◆	$41-$57	501
69 / p. 478	AAA	Best Western American Motor Inn	◆◆	$99-$169 SAVE	489
70 / p. 478	AAA	Comfort Inn East - see color ad p 493	◆◆	$44-$99 SAVE	492
71 / p. 478		Motel 6 Albuquerque East #49	◆	$35-$51	501
72 / p. 478	AAA	Ramada Limited (Airport)	◆◆	$45-$70 SAVE	504
73 / p. 478	AAA	Sleep Inn Airport	◆◆	$70 SAVE	505
74 / p. 478		Courtyard by Marriott (Airport)	◆◆◆	Failed to provide	493
75 / p. 478	AAA	Fairfield Inn Airport	◆◆	$59-$98 SAVE	495
76 / p. 478		Holiday Inn Express	◆◆◆	$77-$102	496
77 / p. 478	AAA	Airport University Inn	◆◆	$59-$105 SAVE	487
78 / p. 478	AAA	TownePlace Suites	◆◆	$59-$109 SAVE	505
79 / p. 478	AAA	Quality Suites-Airport/University	◆◆	$65-$99 SAVE	503
80 / p. 478		Hawthorn Inn & Suites	◆◆◆	$69-$149	496
81 / p. 478		La Quinta Inn Albuquerque (Airport) - see color ad p 499	◆◆◆	$82-$112	499
82 / p. 478		Hampton-Airport	◆◆◆	$79-$109	495
83 / p. 478		Country Inn & Suites - see color ad p 493	◆◆	$49-$89	493
84 / p. 478	AAA	Comfort Inn-Airport - see color ad p 487	◆◆	$59-$109 SAVE	492
85 / p. 478	AAA	Best Western InnSuites Hotel & Suites-Airport Albuquerque - see color ad p 490	◆◆	$119-$159 SAVE	490
86 / p. 478		Hilton Garden Inn Albuquerque Airport	◆◆◆	Failed to provide	496
87 / p. 478		Wyndham Albuquerque at International Sunport	◆◆◆	$79-$119	506
88 / p. 478		Holiday Inn Select Hotel	◆◆◆	Failed to provide	497
89 / p. 478	AAA	AmeriSuites (Albuquerque/Airport)	◆◆◆	$72-$125 SAVE	488
		ALBUQUERQUE - Restaurants			
1 / p. 478		El Pinto	◆◆	$7-$20	510
2 / p. 478		The County Line of Albuquerque	◆◆	$8-$20	509
3 / p. 478		Designer's Cafe	◆◆	$8-$15	509

Spotter/Map Page Number	OA	ALBUQUERQUE - Restaurants (continued)	Diamond Rating	Rate Range High Season	Listing Page
④ / p. 478		Casa de Benavidez New Mexican Restaurant	▽▽	$7-$14	508
⑤ / p. 478		Cafe' Voila	▽▽	$15-$22	508
⑥ / p. 478		Cajun Kitchen	▽▽	$8-$15	508
⑦ / p. 478		Vic's Daily Cafe	▽▽	$6-$8(L)	518
⑧ / p. 478		Gin Mill Restaurant & Tavern	▽▽	$6-$16	511
⑨ / p. 478		Garduno's of Mexico Restaurant & Cantina	▽▽	$9-$17	510
⑩ / p. 478		Luigi's Italian Restaurant & Pizzeria	▽▽	$7-$13	513
⑪ / p. 478		Sadie's Dining Room	▽▽	$8-$15	516
⑫ / p. 478	◈	**Trombino's Bistro Italiano**	▽▽▽	$8-$22	518
⑬ / p. 478		Scarpa's	▽▽	$6-$9	517
⑭ / p. 478		Fox and Hound Smokehouse & Tavern	▽▽	$7-$15	510
⑮ / p. 478		Mykonos Cafe & Taverna	▽▽▽	$7-$15	514
⑯ / p. 478		P.F. Chang's China Bistro	▽▽▽	$9-$18	515
⑰ / p. 478		Rockfish Seafood Grill	▽▽	$7-$16	516
⑱ / p. 478		Perennials Restaurant	▽▽	$6-$15	515
⑲ / p. 478		Mimi's Cafe	▽▽	$10-$15	513
⑳ / p. 478		Saigon Restaurant	▽▽	$5-$9	516
㉑ / p. 478		Monroe's Restaurant	▽▽	$8-$13	514
㉒ / p. 478		Jersey Jack's	▽	$6-$8	512
㉓ / p. 478		Santa Fe Peppers	▽	$5-$7	517
㉔ / p. 478		Siam Cafe	▽▽	$6-$9	517
㉕ / p. 478		Texas Land & Cattle Steak House	▽▽	$11-$25	517
㉖ / p. 478		Champ River Brewing Company	▽▽	$8-$17	508
㉗ / p. 478		Landry's Seafood House	▽▽	$14-$19	512
㉘ / p. 478		Dickey's Barbecue Pit	▽▽	$8-$19	509
㉙ / p. 478		Geezamboni's Restaurant	▽▽	$10-$20	510
㉚ / p. 478		Azuma	▽▽	$7-$19	507
㉛ / p. 478		Taste of China	▽▽	$7-$8	517
㉜ / p. 478		Flying Star Cafe	▽▽	$7-$10	510
㉝ / p. 478		Quarters Bar-B-Que	▽▽	$10-$24	515
㉞ / p. 478		Chez Axel	▽▽	$11-$21	508
㉟ / p. 478		Il Vicino	▽▽	$7-$9	512
㊱ / p. 478		Zea Rotisserie Restaurant	▽▽	$8-$19	518
㊲ / p. 478		China Star Super Buffet	▽▽	$8	508
㊳ / p. 478		Assets Grille & Brewery Co.	▽▽	$6-$20	507
㊴ / p. 478		Cafe' O	▽	$6-$9	507
㊵ / p. 478		Weck's	▽▽	$5-$8(L)	518
㊶ / p. 478		Yen Ching	▽▽	$7-$16	518
㊷ / p. 478		India Palace	▽▽	$8-$20	512
㊸ / p. 478		Pancho's Mexican Buffet	▽	$5-$7	515

Spotter/Map Page Number	OA	ALBUQUERQUE - Restaurants (continued)	Diamond Rating	Rate Range High Season	Listing Page
44 / p. 478		The Range Cafe	◆◆	$5-$16	516
45 / p. 478		Ortega's Mexican Restaurant & Grill	◆◆	$6-$9	514
46 / p. 478		Garcia's Kitchen	◆◆	$4-$9	510
47 / p. 478		East Ocean Chinese Seafood Restaurant	◆◆	$6-$12	509
48 / p. 478		Mimmo's Ristorante & Pizzeria	◆	$6-$15	514
49 / p. 478		Bread and Wine	◆◆	$16-$25	507
50 / p. 478		Hello Deli	◆◆	$5-$7(L)	511
51 / p. 478		Panza Llena Cafe	◆◆	$4-$6(L)	515
52 / p. 478		Robb's Ribbs	◆◆	$7-$15	516
53 / p. 478		Hurricane's Cafe'	◆◆	$4-$8	511
54 / p. 478		Milly's Restaurant	◆	$5-$7(L)	513
55 / p. 478		Cheese & Coffee Gourmet Deli	◆	$6-$8(L)	508
56 / p. 478		Richard's Mexican Restaurant	◆◆	$5-$8(L)	516
57 / p. 478		Louie's Pub & Grill	◆◆	$5-$8	513
58 / p. 478		Taco Sal	◆◆	$5-$7	517
59 / p. 478		Ho-Lo-Ma Chinese Restaurant	◆◆	$5-$11	511
60 / p. 478		Classic Grill	◆◆	$8-$22	509
61 / p. 478		Papa Felipe's	◆◆	$6-$10	515
62 / p. 478		Stuart Anderson's Black Angus Cattle Company	◆◆	$11-$35	517
63 / p. 478	AAA	**Rancher's Club of New Mexico**	◆◆◆◆	$25-$40	516
64 / p. 478		Rudy's Country Store & Bar-B-Q	◆	$7-$10	516
65 / p. 478		Mario's Pizzeria & Ristorante	◆◆	$6-$15	513
66 / p. 478		A Taste of Italy	◆	$4-$7	507
67 / p. 478		Pei Wei	◆	$6-$9	515
68 / p. 478		Paisano's Italian Restaurant	◆◆◆	$8-$17	514
69 / p. 478		Padilla's Mexican Kitchen	◆◆	$5-$8	514
70 / p. 478		Buca di Beppo	◆◆	$9-$11	507
71 / p. 478		Great American Land & Cattle Company	◆◆	$10-$27	511
72 / p. 478		Seasons Rotisserie & Grill	◆◆◆	$15-$39	517
73 / p. 478	AAA	**Church Street Cafe**	◆◆	$6-$9	509
74 / p. 478	AAA	**High Noon Restaurant & Saloon**	◆◆	$13-$27	511
75 / p. 478		Ming Dynasty	◆◆	$7-$10	514
76 / p. 478		La Crepe Michel	◆◆◆	$16-$25	512
77 / p. 478		Eloy's Mexican Restaurant	◆◆	$7-$10	510
78 / p. 478		La Placita on the Plaza	◆◆	$7-$10	512
79 / p. 478		Antiquity Restaurant	◆◆◆	$16-$27	507
80 / p. 478	AAA	**Taj Mahal Cuisine of India**	◆◆	$9-$15	517
81 / p. 478		Cafe Riviera	◆	$4-$7	507
82 / p. 478		Queen of Sushi-Pattaya Thai	◆◆	$8-$15	515

Spotter/Map Page Number	OA	ALBUQUERQUE - Restaurants (continued)	Diamond Rating	Rate Range High Season	Listing Page
83 / p. 478		Capo's Ristorante Italiano	◈◈	$7-$12	508
84 / p. 478		Christy Mae's	◈◈	$6-$10	508
85 / p. 478		La Salita	◈◈	$5-$8	512
86 / p. 478		Paul's Monterey Inn	◈◈	$9-$24	515
87 / p. 478		Plaza Eatery	◈	$3-$6(L)	515
88 / p. 478		Taeja Restaurant	◈◈	$7-$12	517
89 / p. 478		La Esquina Restaurante	◈◈	$6-$9	512
90 / p. 478		Los Cuates del Norte	◈◈	$8-$14	513
91 / p. 478		The Cooperage	◈◈	$12-$32	509
92 / p. 478		Owl Cafe	◈◈	$4-$7	514
93 / p. 478		Monte Carlo Steakhouse	◈◈	$7-$19	514
94 / p. 478		China Star	◈◈	$7-$9	508
95 / p. 478	⬧⬧	**McGrath's Restaurant & Bar**	◈◈◈	$16-$24	513
96 / p. 478		Rallis 4th Street Pub & Grill	◈◈	$6-$10	516
97 / p. 478		Fresh Choices	◈◈	$5-$7	510
98 / p. 478		District Bar & Grill	◈◈	$6-$15	509
99 / p. 478		Nick's Crossroads Cafe	◈◈	$4-$7(L)	514
100 / p. 478		Al's New York Pizza Department	◈	$6-$16	507
101 / p. 478		Tucanos Brazilian Grill	◈◈	$14-$16	518
102 / p. 478		The Artichoke Cafe	◈◈◈	$16-$30	507
103 / p. 478		Gold Street Caffe	◈◈	$5-$16	511
104 / p. 478		Western View Diner and Steakhouse	◈◈	$6-$10	518
105 / p. 478		Weekdays	◈◈	$5-$8(L)	518
106 / p. 478		66 Diner	◈◈	$5-$9	507
107 / p. 478		The Copper Lounge	◈◈	$6-$10	509
108 / p. 478		M & J Restaurant/Sanitary Tortilla Factory	◈◈	$5-$8(L)	513
109 / p. 478		Zinc Wine Bar & Bistro	◈◈◈	$15-$24	519
110 / p. 478	⬧⬧	**Yanni's Mediterranean Bar & Grill**	◈◈◈	$13-$25	518
111 / p. 478		The Gruet Steak House	◈◈◈	$15-$36	511
112 / p. 478		Frontier Restaurant	◈	$4-$10	510
113 / p. 478		Mac's La Sierra Restaurant	◈	$4-$12	513
114 / p. 478		Olympia Cafe	◈	$4-$10	514
115 / p. 478		Gyros Mediterranean	◈	$4-$7	511
116 / p. 478		Mannie's Family Restaurant	◈	$5-$9	513
117 / p. 478		Ragin' Shrimp	◈◈	$7-$13	516
118 / p. 478		Vivace	◈◈	$9-$17	518
119 / p. 478		Graze by Jennifer James	◈◈◈	$12-$16	511
120 / p. 478		El Patio de Albuquerque	◈	$5-$8	510
121 / p. 478		Kelly's Brewery	◈◈	$7-$9	512
122 / p. 478		Gecko's Bar & Tapas	◈◈	$5-$8	510

Spotter/Map Page Number	OA	ALBUQUERQUE - Restaurants (continued)	Diamond Rating	Rate Range High Season	Listing Page
123 / p. 478		Scalo Northern Italian Grill	◆◆◆	$6-$22	517
124 / p. 478		Town House Restaurant & Lounge	◆◆	$9-$25	518
125 / p. 478		Orchid Thai Cuisine	◆◆	$7-$12	514
126 / p. 478		El Taco Tote	◆	$5-$7	510
127 / p. 478		Loyola's Family Restaurant	◆◆	$4-$7	513
128 / p. 478		El Norteno	◆◆	$5-$8	509
129 / p. 478		Powdrell's Barbecue House	◆	$6-$10	515
130 / p. 478		La Fonda del Bosque	◆◆	$6-$8(L)	512
131 / p. 478		La Hacienda Restaurant & Cantina	◆◆	$6-$15	512
132 / p. 478		Pars Cuisine	◆◆	$8-$17	515
133 / p. 478	AAA	**Cervante's**	◆◆	$7-$15	508
134 / p. 478		Copper Canyon Cafe	◆◆	$6-$10	509
		RIO RANCHO - Lodgings			
92 / p. 478	AAA	**Ramada Limited Hotel**	◆◆	$66-$69 SAVE	560
93 / p. 478		Rio Rancho Super 8 Motel	◆◆	$40-$95	560
94 / p. 478	AAA	**Best Western Rio Rancho Inn & Conference Center**	◆◆◆	$59-$119 SAVE	559
95 / p. 478		Hilton Garden Inn	◆◆◆	$150-$160	560
96 / p. 478		Extended StayAmerica Albuquerque-Rio Rancho Blvd	◆◆◆	$110-$115	560
		RIO RANCHO - Restaurants			
137 / p. 478		O'Hare's Grille & Pub	◆◆	$6-$21	560
138 / p. 478		Hot Tamales	◆◆	$7-$8	560
		CORRALES - Lodgings			
99 / p. 478		The Sandhill Crane Bed & Breakfast	◆◆◆	$120-$200	529
100 / p. 478		The Chocolate Turtle Bed & Breakfast	◆◆◆	$60-$120	528
101 / p. 478		Hacienda Manzanal Bed & Breakfast	◆◆◆	$95-$135	529
102 / p. 478		Casa de Koshare	◆◆◆	Failed to provide	528
		CORRALES - Restaurants			
141 / p. 478		Essencia Restaurant	◆◆◆	$12-$22	529
142 / p. 478		Jim White's Casa Vieja	◆◆	$7-$30	529
143 / p. 478		Indigo Crow	◆◆	$13-$25	529
144 / p. 478		Calico Cafe & Bakery	◆◆	$4-$7(L)	529

ALBUQUERQUE pop. 448,607   (See map and index starting on p. 478)—See also BERNALILLO & RIO RANCHO.

—— WHERE TO STAY ——

AIRPORT UNIVERSITY INN   *Book at aaa.com*   Phone: (505)247-0512   **77**

(AAA) (SAVE)   All Year   1P: $59-$105   2P: $59-$105   XP: $7   F18
Location: I-25, exit 228A southbound; exit 222 northbound, just e. 1901 University Blvd SE 87106.
Fax: 505/843-7148. **Facility:** 148 one-bedroom standard units. 2-3 stories, interior corridors. **Parking:** on-site. **Terms:** pets ($50 deposit). **Amenities:** high-speed Internet, voice mail, irons, hair dryers. **Dining:** 6 am-2 & 5-9 pm, cocktails. **Pool(s):** heated outdoor. **Leisure Activities:** whirlpool, exercise room. **Guest Services:** valet laundry. **Business Services:** meeting rooms. **Cards:** AX, CB, DC, DS, JC, MC, VI.
Small-scale Hotel
Special Amenities: free full breakfast and free local telephone calls.

SOME UNITS
(symbols) FEE

ALBUQUERQUE DOUBLETREE HOTEL   *Book at aaa.com*   Phone: 505-247-3344   **55**

(symbols)   Property failed to provide current rates
Location: I-25, exit Central Ave, 0.8 mi w to 2nd St, then 2 blks n; downtown. Located adjacent to the Albuquerque Convention Center. 201 Marquette Ave NW 87102. Fax: 505/247-7025. **Facility:** 295 one-bedroom standard
Large-scale Hotel units. 16 stories, interior corridors. *Bath:* combo or shower only. **Parking:** on-site (fee). **Amenities:** voice mail, irons, hair dryers. *Fee:* video games, high-speed Internet. **Pool(s):** heated outdoor. **Leisure Activities:** exercise room.
Guest Services: gift shop, valet laundry. **Business Services:** meeting rooms, business center.

SOME UNITS
(symbols)

ALBUQUERQUE EMBASSY SUITES HOTEL & CONFERENCE CENTER   *Book at aaa.com*   Phone: 505-245-7100   **53**

(AAA) (SAVE)   All Year [BP]   1P: $99-$750   2P: $99-$750   XP: $10   F18
(symbols)   **Location:** I-25, exit 224B, just w. 1000 Woodward Pl NE 87102. Fax: 505/247-1083. **Facility:** 261 one-bedroom suites. 9 stories, interior corridors. *Bath:* combo or shower only. **Parking:** on-site. **Terms:** package plans.
Amenities: high-speed Internet (fee), dual phone lines, voice mail, safes, irons, hair dryers. **Dining:** 6 am-
Large-scale Hotel 11 pm, cocktails. **Pool(s):** heated indoor. **Leisure Activities:** sauna, whirlpool, exercise room, spa. *Fee:* game room. **Guest Services:** valet and coin laundry. **Business Services:** conference facilities, business center. **Cards:** AX, CB, DC, DS, MC, VI. **Special Amenities: free full breakfast and free newspaper.** *(See color ad p 488)*

SOME UNITS
(symbols)

ALBUQUERQUE INN & SUITES (NOW KNOWN AS EQUUS HOTEL SUITES)   *Book at aaa.com*   Phone: (505)883-8888   **30**

(AAA) (SAVE)   All Year   1P: $69-$109   2P: $69-$109   XP: $5   F12
(symbols)   **Location:** I-40, exit 160, just n to Menaul Blvd, just w, then just s. Located in Northeast Heights. 2401 Wellsley Dr NE
87107. Fax: 505/883-2830. **Facility:** 138 one-bedroom standard units. 2 stories (no elevator), exterior
corridors. *Bath:* combo or shower only. **Parking:** on-site. **Terms:** office hours 6:30 am-10 pm, weekly rates
Motel available, small pets only ($25-$75 fee). **Amenities:** voice mail, irons. **Guest Services:** valet and coin laundry. **Business Services:** PC, fax (fee). **Cards:** AX, CB, DC, DS, JC, MC, VI. **Special Amenities: free local telephone calls and free room upgrade (subject to availability with advance reservations).**

SOME UNITS
(symbols) FEE

THE ALBUQUERQUE MARRIOTT HOTEL   *Book at aaa.com*   Phone: (505)881-6800   **47**

(symbols)   All Year   1P: $94-$175   2P: $94-$174
Location: I-40, exit 162 westbound; exit 162B eastbound, just n. Located in Northeast Heights. 2101 Louisiana Blvd NE
87110. Fax: 505/888-2982. **Facility:** 411 one-bedroom standard units. 17 stories, interior corridors. **Parking:**
Large-scale Hotel on-site. **Terms:** cancellation fee imposed, [AP] meal plan available, package plans. **Amenities:** high-speed
Internet (fee), voice mail, irons, hair dryers. **Pool(s):** heated indoor/outdoor. **Leisure Activities:** saunas, whirlpool, exercise room. **Guest Services:** gift shop, valet and coin laundry. **Business Services:** meeting rooms, business center. **Cards:** AX, CB, DC, DS, JC, MC, VI.

SOME UNITS
(symbols)

(See map and index starting on p. 478)

ALBUQUERQUE MARRIOTT PYRAMID NORTH   *Book at aaa.com*   Phone: (505)821-3333   **6**

(AAA) (SAVE)   All Year   1P: $99-$189
♦♦♦   **Location:** I-25, exit 232, just w, then 1 mi s on Pan American Frwy NE. 5151 San Francisco Rd NE 87109.
Fax: 505/828-0230. **Facility:** 310 one-bedroom standard units. 10 stories, interior corridors. *Bath:* combo or
Large-scale Hotel   shower only. **Parking:** on-site. **Terms:** cancellation fee imposed, package plans. **Amenities:** video games
(fee), high-speed Internet, dual phone lines, voice mail, irons, hair dryers. **Dining:** 6 am-2 & 5-10 pm,
cocktails, nightclub. **Pool(s):** heated indoor/outdoor. **Leisure Activities:** whirlpools, exercise room. *Fee:*
massage. **Guest Services:** gift shop, valet and coin laundry. **Business Services:** conference facilities, business center.
Cards: AX, CB, DC, DS, JC, MC, VI. **Special Amenities: free newspaper.** *(See color ad below)*

SOME UNITS

AMBASSADOR INN   Phone: 505/265-1161   **66**

♦♦   Property failed to provide current rates
Small-scale Hotel   **Location:** Jct Louisiana Blvd and Central Ave, just e. 7407 Central Ave NE 87108. Fax: 505/265-2292. **Facility:** 47
one-bedroom standard units. 2 stories (no elevator), exterior corridors. **Parking:** on-site. **Pool(s):** small
heated indoor. **Leisure Activities:** whirlpool. **Guest Services:** coin laundry. **Business Services:** fax (fee).

SOME UNITS

AMERISUITES (ALBUQUERQUE/AIRPORT)   *Book at aaa.com*   Phone: (505)242-9300   **89**

(AAA) (SAVE)   All Year   1P: $72-$125   2P: $72-$125   XP: $10   F18
♦♦♦   **Location:** I-25, exit 221, 0.3 mi e to University Blvd exit, then just n to Woodward Rd: 1400 Sunport Place Blvd SE
87106. Fax: 505/242-0998. **Facility:** 128 one-bedroom standard units. 6 stories, interior corridors. *Bath:*
Small-scale Hotel   combo or shower only. **Parking:** on-site. **Terms:** cancellation fee imposed, small pets only ($10 extra
charge). **Amenities:** video games (fee), high-speed Internet, dual phone lines, voice mail, irons, hair dryers.
Pool(s): heated outdoor. **Leisure Activities:** exercise room. **Guest Services:** valet and coin laundry, area
transportation-within 3 mi. **Business Services:** meeting rooms. **Cards:** AX, CB, DC, DS, JC, MC, VI. **Special Amenities: free
full breakfast.**

FEE

AMERISUITES (ALBUQUERQUE/MIDTOWN)   *Book at aaa.com*   Phone: (505)881-0544   **25**

(AAA) (SAVE)   All Year [ECP]   1P: $109-$139   2P: $109-$139   XP: $10   F18
♦♦♦   **Location:** I-40, exit 160, just n to Menaul Blvd, then 0.6 mi w. 2500 Menaul Blvd NE 87107. Fax: 505/881-0380.
Facility: 125 one-bedroom standard units. 6 stories, interior corridors. *Bath:* combo or shower only.
Small-scale Hotel   **Parking:** on-site. **Terms:** small pets only ($10 extra charge). **Amenities:** video games (fee), dual phone
lines, voice mail, irons, hair dryers. **Pool(s):** heated outdoor. **Leisure Activities:** exercise room. **Guest
Services:** valet and coin laundry, area transportation-within 5 mi. **Business Services:** meeting rooms, fax.
Cards: AX, DC, DS, MC, VI. **Special Amenities: free expanded continental breakfast.**

SOME UNITS

FEE

(See map and index starting on p. 478)

AMERISUITES (ALBUQUERQUE/UPTOWN) *Book at aaa.com* Phone: (505)872-9000 36

AAA SAVE
▽▽▽▽ SAVE

Small-scale Hotel

All Year [ECP] 1P: $79-$119 2P: $79-$119 XP: $10 F17
Location: I-40, exit 162 westbound; exit 162B eastbound, 0.7 mi n. 6901 Arvada Ave NE 87110. Fax: 505/872-3829. **Facility:** 128 one-bedroom standard units. 6 stories, interior corridors. *Bath:* combo or shower only. **Parking:** on-site. **Terms:** small pets only ($10 extra charge). **Amenities:** video games (fee), voice mail, irons, hair dryers. **Pool(s):** heated outdoor. **Leisure Activities:** exercise room. **Guest Services:** valet and coin laundry. **Business Services:** meeting rooms, business center. **Cards:** AX, DS, MC, VI.
Special Amenities: free full breakfast.

SOME UNITS

🆂⃝ 🛏 &M ⛐ 🛋 VCR 📷 DATA PORT 🖥 🖨 🖳 / ✕ /
FEE

BAYMONT INN & SUITES ALBUQUERQUE NORTH *Book at aaa.com* Phone: (505)345-7500 8

AAA SAVE
▽▽▽▽ SAVE

Small-scale Hotel

All Year [CP] 1P: $63-$73 2P: $70-$80 XP: $7 F18
Location: I-25, exit 231, just w. 7439 Pan American Frwy NE 87109. Fax: 505/345-1616. **Facility:** 98 one-bedroom standard units. 3 stories, interior corridors. **Parking:** on-site. **Amenities:** video games (fee), voice mail, irons, hair dryers. **Pool(s):** heated outdoor. **Leisure Activities:** exercise room. **Guest Services:** valet and coin laundry. **Business Services:** meeting rooms. **Cards:** AX, CB, DC, DS, MC, VI. **Special Amenities:** free expanded continental breakfast and free local telephone calls. *(See color ad below)*

SOME UNITS

🐕 🛋 🛋 📷 DATA PORT 🖳 / ✕ 🖥 🖨 /

BEST WESTERN AMERICAN MOTOR INN *Book at aaa.com* Phone: 505/298-7426 69

AAA SAVE
▽▽ SAVE

Small-scale Hotel

9/29-10/15 [BP] 1P: $99-$149 2P: $109-$169 XP: $10
2/1-9/28 [BP] 1P: $59-$79 2P: $69-$89 XP: $6
10/16-1/31 [BP] 1P: $59-$69 2P: $69-$79 XP: $6
Location: I-40, exit 167 westbound, 0.3 mi w on Central Ave; exit 166 eastbound, right on Juan Tabo, left on Central Ave, then 0.5 mi e. Located in a commercial area. 12999 Central Ave NE 87123. Fax: 505/298-0212. **Facility:** 77 one-bedroom standard units. 2 stories (no elevator), exterior corridors. **Parking:** on-site. **Terms:** cancellation fee imposed, pets ($5-$10 extra charge). **Amenities:** irons, hair dryers. **Dining:** 6 am-9 pm. **Pool(s):** heated outdoor. **Leisure Activities:** whirlpool. **Guest Services:** coin laundry. **Business Services:** meeting rooms. **Cards:** AX, CB, DC, DS, JC, MC, VI. **Special Amenities:** free full breakfast and early check-in/late check-out.

SOME UNITS

🛏 🍴 🛋 📷 DATA PORT 🖥 🖳 / ✕ /
FEE

(See map and index starting on p. 478)

BEST WESTERN EXECUTIVE SUITES   *Book at aaa.com*   Phone: (505)830-0900   **18**

AAA [SAVE]

| | 5/1-10/7 [ECP] | 1P: $74-$139 | 2P: $79-$154 | XP: $10 | F17 |
| | 2/1-4/30 & 10/8-1/31 [ECP] | 1P: $69-$99 | 2P: $74-$104 | XP: $10 | F17 |

▽▽▽▽

Small-scale Hotel

Location: I-25, exit 228, just e. 4630 Pan American Frwy NE 87109 (2616 W Hwy 66, GALLUP, 87301). **Fax:** 505/830-4560. **Facility:** 89 one-bedroom standard units, some with whirlpools. 3 stories, interior corridors. **Bath:** combo or shower only. **Parking:** on-site. **Amenities:** high-speed Internet, voice mail, irons, hair dryers. **Pool(s):** heated indoor. **Leisure Activities:** sauna, whirlpool, exercise room. **Guest Services:** valet and coin laundry. **Business Services:** meeting rooms, business center. **Cards:** AX, CB, DC, DS, JC, MC, VI. **Special Amenities:** free expanded continental breakfast and free local telephone calls.

SOME UNITS

BEST WESTERN INNSUITES HOTEL &
SUITES-AIRPORT ALBUQUERQUE   *Book at aaa.com*   Phone: (505)242-7022   **85**

AAA [SAVE]

| | 10/1-10/15 [BP] | 1P: $119-$159 | 2P: $119-$159 | XP: $10 | F18 |
| | 2/1-9/30 & 10/16-1/31 [BP] | 1P: $69-$109 | 2P: $69-$109 | XP: $10 | F18 |

▽▽▽▽

Small-scale Hotel

Location: I-25, exit 222 northbound; exit 222A southbound, 1 mi e, then just s. 2400 Yale Blvd SE 87106. **Fax:** 505/243-0620. **Facility:** 102 one-bedroom standard units. 2 stories (no elevator), interior corridors. **Parking:** on-site. **Terms:** weekly rates available, pets ($25 fee). **Amenities:** video games (fee), high-speed Internet, voice mail, irons, hair dryers. **Pool(s):** heated outdoor. **Leisure Activities:** whirlpool, basketball. **Guest Services:** valet and coin laundry. **Business Services:** meeting rooms, business center. **Cards:** AX, CB, DC, DS, JC, MC, VI. **Special Amenities:** free full breakfast and free local telephone calls. *(See color ad below)*

SOME UNITS

FEE

(See map and index starting on p. 478)

BEST WESTERN RIO GRANDE INN
Book at aaa.com Phone: (505)843-9500 **38**

AAA SAVE

WWWW

Small-scale Hotel

5/1-10/14 [ECP]	1P: $93-$113	2P: $103-$123	XP: $10	F18
10/15-1/31 [ECP]	1P: $88-$108	2P: $98-$118	XP: $10	F18
2/1-4/30 [ECP]	1P: $83-$103	2P: $93-$113	XP: $10	F18

Location: I-40, exit 157A, just s. 1015 Rio Grande Blvd NW 87104. Fax: 505/843-9238. **Facility:** 173 one-bedroom standard units. 4 stories, interior corridors. **Parking:** on-site. **Terms:** cancellation fee imposed. **Amenities:** high-speed Internet, voice mail, irons, hair dryers. **Dining:** 6 am-10 pm, cocktails. **Pool(s):** heated outdoor. **Leisure Activities:** whirlpool, exercise room. **Guest Services:** valet and coin laundry. **Business Services:** meeting rooms, business center. **Cards:** AX, DC, DS, MC, VI. **Special Amenities:** free continental breakfast and free local telephone calls. *(See color ad below)*

SOME UNITS

BOTTGER MANSION OF OLD TOWN
Phone: (505)243-3639 **51**

AAA SAVE

WWWW

Historic Bed
& Breakfast

4/1-10/31 [BP]	1P: $115-$174	2P: $115-$174	XP: $20
2/1-3/31 & 11/1-1/31 [BP]	1P: $92-$140	2P: $92-$140	XP: $20

Location: I-40, exit Rio Grande Blvd, 1.5 mi s, then just e off Central. Located in the historic Old Town area. 110 San Felipe NW 87104. Fax: 505/243-4378. **Facility:** The classic Victorian home features period furniture and artifacts and is in the historic Old Town area; Thursday afternoons an English tea is served. Smoke free premises. 8 units. 7 one-bedroom standard units. 1 two-bedroom suite. 2 stories (no elevator), interior corridors. *Bath:* combo or shower only. **Parking:** on-site (fee). **Terms:** office hours 8 am-6 pm, 14 day cancellation notice-fee imposed. **Amenities:** hair dryers. **Cards:** AX, DS, MC. **Special Amenities:** free full breakfast and free local telephone calls.

BRITTANIA & W E MAUGER ESTATE BED & BREAKFAST
Book at aaa.com Phone: (505)242-8755 **54**

AAA SAVE

WWWW

Historic Bed
& Breakfast

All Year	1P: $89-$229	2P: $89-$229	XP: $25	F

Location: I-25, exit 225, 1 mi w, then just s on 7th Ave. 701 Roma Ave NW 87102. Fax: 505/842-8835. **Facility:** Centrally located in the downtown area, the restored Queen Anne-style residence features rooms with high ceilings and gorgeous wood work. Smoke free premises. 8 units. 7 one- and 1 two-bedroom standard units. 3 stories (no elevator), interior corridors. *Bath:* shower only. **Parking:** on-site. **Terms:** check-in 4 pm, 10 day cancellation notice-fee imposed, [BP] meal plan available, pets ($30 fee). **Amenities:** high-speed Internet, voice mail, irons, hair dryers. **Cards:** AX, DC, DS, MC, VI. **Special Amenities:** free full breakfast and free local telephone calls.

FEE

(See map and index starting on p. 478)

CANDLEWOOD SUITES Book at aaa.com
▼▼▼▼
Small-scale Hotel
All Year 1P: $59-$109 2P: $59-$109 **Phone:** (505)888-3424 **24**
Location: I-40, exit 160, just n to Menaul Blvd, then 0.5 mi w. 3025 Menaul Blvd NE 87107. Fax: 505/888-3293. **Facility:** 123 one-bedroom standard units with efficiencies. 3 stories, interior corridors. Bath: combo or shower only. **Parking:** on-site. **Terms:** pets ($75-$150 fee). **Amenities:** video library, CD players, voice mail, irons, hair dryers. **Leisure Activities:** exercise room. **Guest Services:** sundries, complimentary laundry. **Cards:** AX, DC, DS, MC, VI.

SOME UNITS
ASK SD 🐾 🍴 ⓰ ⅗M ☎ VCR 📷 DATA PORT 🔌 🖥 🖨 / ✕
FEE

CLUBHOUSE INN & SUITES Book at aaa.com
AAA SAVE
Small-scale Hotel
All Year [BP] 1P: $74-$109 2P: $84-$109 **Phone:** (505)345-0010 **20**
XP: $10 F16
Location: I-25, exit 227A, just e to University Blvd, 0.5 mi s to Menaul Blvd, then 0.5 mi w. 1315 Menaul Blvd NE 87107. Fax: 505/344-3911. **Facility:** 137 one-bedroom standard units. 2 stories (no elevator), interior corridors. Bath: combo or shower only. **Parking:** on-site. **Terms:** pets ($10 extra charge). **Amenities:** voice mail, irons, hair dryers. **Pool(s):** heated outdoor. **Leisure Activities:** whirlpool. **Guest Services:** complimentary evening beverages, valet and coin laundry. **Business Services:** meeting rooms, business center. **Cards:** AX, DC, DS, MC, VI. **Special Amenities:** free full breakfast and free local telephone calls.
(See color ad below)

SOME UNITS
SD 🐾 🍴 ⅗M 🛎 🏊 🍽 🏌 📷 DATA PORT 🔌 / ✕ 🗎 🖨 /
FEE

COMFORT INN-AIRPORT Book at aaa.com
AAA SAVE
▼▼▼
Small-scale Hotel
All Year [CP] 1P: $59-$99 2P: $69-$109 **Phone:** (505)243-2244 **84**
XP: $5 F17
Location: I-25, exit 222A southbound; exit 222 northbound, 1 mi n, then just s. 2300 Yale Blvd SE 87106. Fax: 505/247-2925. **Facility:** 118 one-bedroom standard units. 3 stories, interior/exterior corridors. **Parking:** on-site. **Terms:** pets ($10 fee). **Amenities:** video games (fee). **Pool(s):** small heated outdoor. **Leisure Activities:** whirlpool. **Guest Services:** valet laundry. **Business Services:** PC (fee), fax. **Cards:** AX, CB, DC, DS, JC, MC, VI. **Special Amenities:** early check-in/late check-out. (See color ad p 487)

SOME UNITS
SD ✈ 🐾 🍴 ⅗M ☎ 🏊 🍽 🏌 📷 DATA PORT / ✕ 🗎 🖨 /
FEE

COMFORT INN & SUITES BY CHOICE HOTELS Book at aaa.com
▼▼▼
Small-scale Hotel
All Year 1P: $65-$85 2P: $70-$90 **Phone:** (505)822-1090 **3**
F18
Location: I-25, exit 233, just e via Alameda. 5811 Signal Ave NE 87113. Fax: 505/822-1154. **Facility:** 68 one-bedroom standard units. 3 stories, interior corridors. Bath: combo or shower only. **Parking:** on-site. **Terms:** cancellation fee imposed, pets ($10 extra charge). **Amenities:** high-speed Internet, irons, hair dryers. **Pool(s):** heated indoor. **Leisure Activities:** whirlpool. **Guest Services:** valet and coin laundry. **Business Services:** fax (fee). **Cards:** AX, DC, DS, MC, VI.

SOME UNITS
ASK SD 🐾 ⅗M ☎ 🏊 🍽 📷 DATA PORT 🔌 / ✕ 🗎 🖨 /
FEE

COMFORT INN EAST Book at aaa.com
AAA SAVE
▼▼
Small-scale Hotel
All Year [BP] 1P: $44-$99 2P: $49-$99 **Phone:** (505)294-1800 **70**
XP: $6 F12
Location: I-40, exit 167, just w. Located in a commercial area. 13031 Central Ave NE 87123. Fax: 505/293-1088. **Facility:** 122 one-bedroom standard units. 3 stories (no elevator), exterior corridors. **Parking:** on-site. **Terms:** package plans, small pets only ($3 extra charge). **Amenities:** high-speed Internet, irons, hair dryers. **Dining:** 6 am-1 & 5-8 pm, wine/beer only. **Pool(s):** heated outdoor. **Leisure Activities:** whirlpool. **Guest Services:** valet and coin laundry. **Business Services:** meeting rooms. **Cards:** AX, CB, DC, DS, JC, MC, VI. (See color ad p 493)

SOME UNITS
SD 🐾 🍴 ⅗M ☎ 🏊 🍽 📷 DATA PORT 🔌 / ✕ 🗎 /
FEE FEE

COMFORT INN-MIDTOWN Book at aaa.com
▼▼ ▲▲▲
Small-scale Hotel
All Year 1P: $49-$110 2P: $54-$110 **Phone:** (505)881-3210 **23**
XP: $10 F16
Location: I-25, exit 225 northbound, 1.6 mi n of Frontage Rd to Menaul Blvd, then just e; exit 227 (Commanche Rd) southbound, s on Frontage Rd, 0.8 mi n to Menaul Blvd, then just e. 2015 Menaul Blvd NE 87107. Fax: 505/888-1196. **Facility:** 147 one-bedroom standard units. 3 stories, exterior corridors. **Parking:** on-site. **Terms:** [ECP] meal plan available, pets ($10 fee). **Amenities:** irons, hair dryers. **Pool(s):** small heated outdoor. **Leisure Activities:** whirlpool. **Guest Services:** gift shop, valet and coin laundry. **Business Services:** meeting rooms. **Cards:** AX, CB, DC, DS, JC, MC, VI.

SOME UNITS
ASK SD 🐾 🍴 ⚄ 📷 DATA PORT 🔌 / ✕ 🗎 🖨 /
FEE

(See map and index starting on p. 478)

COMFORT INN WEST *Book at aaa.com* Phone: 505/836-0011 **44**
AAA SAVE
5/1-10/8 [ECP] 1P: $59-$69 2P: $69-$79 XP: $10 F17
2/1-4/30 & 10/9-1/31 [ECP] 1P: $49-$59 2P: $59-$69 XP: $10 F17
Motel **Location:** I-40, exit 155, just s on Coors Rd, then just e. 5712 Iliff Rd NW 87105. Fax: 505/831-8972. **Facility:** 65 one-bedroom standard units. 2 stories (no elevator), exterior corridors. *Bath:* combo or shower only. **Parking:** on-site. **Terms:** package plans. **Amenities:** high-speed Internet, irons, hair dryers. **Pool(s):** heated indoor. **Leisure Activities:** whirlpool. **Cards:** AX, DC, DS, MC, VI. **Special Amenities:** free expanded continental breakfast and free newspaper.
SOME UNITS
[icons]

COUNTRY INN & SUITES *Book at aaa.com* Phone: 505/246-9600 **83**
All Year 1P: $49-$69 2P: $69-$89 XP: $16 F16
Small-scale Hotel **Location:** I-25, exit 222, just e. 2601 Mulberry SE 87106. Fax: 505/243-1749. **Facility:** 80 one-bedroom standard units. 3 stories, interior corridors. *Bath:* combo or shower only. **Parking:** on-site. **Terms:** cancellation fee imposed. **Amenities:** video games (fee), voice mail, irons, hair dryers. **Pool(s):** small heated outdoor. **Leisure Activities:** exercise room. **Guest Services:** valet and coin laundry, area transportation. **Cards:** AX, CB, DC, DS, MC, VI. *(See color ad below)*
SOME UNITS
[icons]

COURTYARD BY MARRIOTT (AIRPORT) *Book at aaa.com* Phone: 505/843-6600 **74**
Property failed to provide current rates
Small-scale Hotel **Location:** I-25, exit 222 northbound; exit 222A southbound, 1 mi e, then just n. 1920 Yale Blvd SE 87106. Fax: 505/843-8740. **Facility:** 150 one-bedroom standard units. 4 stories, interior corridors. *Bath:* combo or shower only. **Parking:** on-site. **Amenities:** high-speed Internet, dual phone lines, voice mail, irons, hair dryers. **Pool(s):** heated indoor. **Leisure Activities:** whirlpool, exercise room. **Guest Services:** valet and coin laundry. **Business Services:** meeting rooms, PC, fax.
SOME UNITS
[icons]

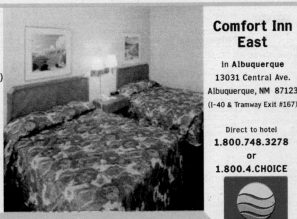

(See map and index starting on p. 478)

COURTYARD BY MARRIOTT JOURNAL CENTER *Book at aaa.com* **Phone:** 505/823-1919 **5**
▽▽▽▽ Property failed to provide current rates
Small-scale Hotel **Location:** I-25, exit 232, just s on Pan American Frwy NE. 5151 Journal Center Blvd NE 87109. **Fax:** 505/823-1918. **Facility:** 150 one-bedroom standard units. 4 stories, interior corridors. *Bath:* combo or shower only. **Parking:** on-site. **Amenities:** high-speed Internet, dual phone lines, voice mail, irons, hair dryers. **Pool(s):** heated indoor. **Leisure Activities:** whirlpool, exercise room. **Guest Services:** gift shop, valet and coin laundry. **Business Services:** meeting rooms.

SOME UNITS
[icons]

DAYS INN-HOTEL CIRCLE *Book at aaa.com* **Phone:** (505)275-3297 **57**
AAA SAVE All Year 1P: $65 2P: $65 XP: $5 F17
▽▽▽▽ **Location:** I-40, exit 165 (Eubank Blvd), just n. 10321 Hotel Cir NE 87123. **Fax:** 505/275-0245. **Facility:** 76 one-bedroom standard units. 2 stories (no elevator), exterior corridors. *Bath:* combo or shower only. **Parking:** on-site. **Terms:** pets ($10 extra charge). **Amenities:** voice mail, safes (fee), hair dryers. **Pool(s):** heated indoor. **Leisure Activities:** sauna, whirlpool. **Guest Services:** coin laundry. **Business Services:** fax (fee). **Cards:** AX, DC, DS, MC, VI. **Special Amenities:** free continental breakfast and free local telephone calls.
Small-scale Hotel

SOME UNITS
[icons] FEE

DAYS INN MIDTOWN **Phone:** (505)884-0250 **26**
▽▽▽▽ All Year 1P: $39-$99 2P: $45-$109 XP: $10 F
Small-scale Hotel **Location:** I-40, exit 160, just n to Menaul Blvd, then 0.8 mi w. 2120 Menaul Blvd NE 87107. **Fax:** 505/883-0594. **Facility:** 199 units. 182 one- and 17 two-bedroom standard units. 2 stories (no elevator), exterior corridors. **Parking:** on-site. **Terms:** 15 day cancellation notice-fee imposed, package plans, pets ($25 fee). **Amenities:** voice mail. *Some:* safes. **Pool(s):** heated outdoor. **Leisure Activities:** exercise room. **Guest Services:** valet and coin laundry. **Business Services:** meeting rooms. **Cards:** AX, CB, DC, DS, JC, MC, VI.

SOME UNITS
[icons] FEE

DAYS INN WEST *Book at aaa.com* **Phone:** (505)836-3297 **40**
▽▽▽▽ All Year 1P: $46-$75 2P: $53-$85 XP: $5 F12
Motel **Location:** I-40, exit 155, just s on Coors Rd, then just w. 6031 Iliff Rd NW 87121. **Fax:** 505/836-1214. **Facility:** 80 one-bedroom standard units. 2 stories (no elevator), exterior corridors. *Bath:* combo or shower only. **Parking:** on-site. **Terms:** pets ($10 extra charge). **Amenities:** high-speed Internet, voice mail, safes (fee), hair dryers. **Pool(s):** heated indoor. **Leisure Activities:** sauna, whirlpool. **Guest Services:** coin laundry. **Business Services:** fax (fee). **Cards:** AX, DC, DS, MC, VI.

SOME UNITS
[icons] FEE

DRURY INN & SUITES-ALBUQUERQUE *Book at aaa.com* **Phone:** (505)341-3600 **16**
▽▽▽▽ All Year [BP] 1P: $86-$138 2P: $96-$148 XP: $10 F18
Small-scale Hotel **Location:** I-25, exit Jefferson St NE, northwest quadrant of exchange. 4310 The 25 Way NE 87109. **Fax:** 505/341-3600. **Facility:** 164 one-bedroom standard units. 6 stories, interior corridors. *Bath:* combo or shower only. **Parking:** on-site. **Amenities:** high-speed Internet, dual phone lines, voice mail, irons, hair dryers. **Pool(s):** heated indoor. **Leisure Activities:** whirlpool, exercise room. **Guest Services:** sundries, complimentary evening beverages, valet and coin laundry. **Business Services:** meeting rooms, business center. **Cards:** AX, CB, DC, DS, MC, VI.

SOME UNITS
[icons]

ECONO LODGE DOWNTOWN/UNIVERSITY *Book at aaa.com* **Phone:** (505)243-1321 **63**
AAA SAVE 3/1-10/7 1P: $39-$55 2P: $49-$69
2/1-2/28 & 10/8-1/31 1P: $32-$42 2P: $39-$49
▽▽▽▽ **Location:** I-25, 224A northbound; exit 224B southbound, just e. 817 Central Ave NE 87102. **Fax:** 505/242-2916. **Facility:** 46 one-bedroom standard units. 2 stories (no elevator), exterior corridors. *Bath:* combo or shower only. **Parking:** on-site. **Terms:** cancellation fee imposed, small pets only ($40 deposit). **Amenities:** hair dryers. **Pool(s):** heated outdoor. **Cards:** AX, DC, DS, MC, VI. **Special Amenities:** free continental breakfast and free local telephone calls.
Small-scale Hotel

SOME UNITS
[icons] FEE

ECONO LODGE MIDTOWN *Book at aaa.com* **Phone:** (505)880-0080 **32**
AAA SAVE 5/1-10/15 [CP] 1P: $50-$55 2P: $55-$60 XP: $5 F18
2/1-4/30 & 10/16-1/31 [CP] 1P: $40-$45 2P: $45-$50 XP: $5 F18
▽▽▽▽ **Location:** I-40, exit 160, just n. 2412 Carlisle Blvd NE 87110. **Fax:** 505/880-0053. **Facility:** 38 one-bedroom standard units. 2 stories (no elevator), exterior corridors. **Parking:** on-site. **Terms:** cancellation fee imposed, package plans. **Cards:** AX, CB, DC, DS, JC, MC, VI. **Special Amenities:** free continental breakfast and free local telephone calls.
Small-scale Hotel

SOME UNITS
[icons]

ECONO LODGE OLD TOWN *Book at aaa.com* **Phone:** (505)243-8475 **49**
AAA SAVE 9/30-10/15 [CP] 1P: $45-$125 2P: $50-$130 XP: $5 F15
4/21-9/29 [CP] 1P: $45-$95 2P: $50-$100 XP: $5 F15
2/1-4/20 [CP] 1P: $40-$65 2P: $45-$70 XP: $5 F15
▽▽▽▽ 10/16-1/31 [CP] 1P: $40-$60 2P: $45-$65 XP: $5 F15
Small-scale Hotel **Location:** I-40, exit 157A, 0.6 mi s on Rio Grande Blvd, then 0.4 mi w. 2321 Central Ave NW 87104. **Fax:** 505/243-4205. **Facility:** 44 one-bedroom standard units. 2 stories (no elevator), exterior corridors. **Parking:** on-site. **Terms:** pets (dogs only, $10 extra charge, in selected units). **Amenities:** high-speed Internet. **Pool(s):** heated indoor. **Leisure Activities:** whirlpool. **Cards:** AX, CB, DC, DS, JC, MC, VI. **Special Amenities:** free continental breakfast and free local telephone calls.

SOME UNITS
[icons] FEE

(See map and index starting on p. 478)

FAIRFIELD INN AIRPORT *Book at aaa.com* Phone: (505)247-1621 **75**

AAA SAVE ▽▽▽▽

Small-scale Hotel

All Year [CP] 1P: $59-$89 2P: $59-$98
Location: I-25, exit 222 northbound; exit 222A southbound, 1 mi e to Yale Blvd; northeast jct of Gibson and Yale blvds. 2300 Centre Ave SE 87106. Fax: 505/247-9719. **Facility:** 118 one-bedroom standard units. 4 stories, interior corridors. **Bath:** combo or shower only. **Parking:** on-site. **Terms:** pets ($75 fee). **Amenities:** high-speed Internet, voice mail, irons, hair dryers. **Pool(s):** heated outdoor. **Leisure Activities:** whirlpool, exercise room. **Guest Services:** valet and coin laundry. **Business Services:** meeting rooms. **Cards:** AX, CB, DC, DS, JC, MC, VI. **Special Amenities:** free expanded continental breakfast and free newspaper.

SOME UNITS

🆂 ⊗ 🐎 🍴 ⅃M ⅌ 🕸 ⇌ 📹 🖳 ⊘ ⊠ 🔋 /
FEE

FAIRFIELD INN BY MARRIOTT *Book at aaa.com* Phone: 505/889-4000 **28**

▽▽▽▽

Small-scale Hotel

Property failed to provide current rates
Location: I-40, exit 160, just n to Menaul Blvd, then 1 mi w. 1760 Menaul Blvd NE 87102. Fax: 505/872-3094. **Facility:** 188 one-bedroom standard units. 3 stories, interior corridors. **Parking:** on-site. **Amenities:** high-speed Internet, irons, hair dryers. **Pool(s):** heated outdoor, heated indoor. **Leisure Activities:** sauna, whirlpool, exercise room. **Guest Services:** valet and coin laundry. **Business Services:** meeting rooms, business center. *(See color ad below)*

SOME UNITS

🍴 ⅃M 🕸 ⇌ ⊠ 📹 🖳 / ⊘ /

GUESTHOUSE INN & SUITES *Book at aaa.com* Phone: (505)271-8500 **58**

▽▽▽▽

Small-scale Hotel

10/1-10/17 1P: $45-$85 2P: $50-$95 XP: $10 F
2/1-9/30 1P: $35-$65 2P: $39-$75 XP: $10 F
10/18-1/31 1P: $35-$45 2P: $35-$50 XP: $5 F
Location: I-40, exit 165, 2 blks n. 10331 Hotel Ave NE 87123. Fax: 505/296-5984. **Facility:** 50 one-bedroom standard units. 2 stories, interior corridors. **Parking:** on-site. **Terms:** 7 day cancellation notice-fee imposed, pets ($10 fee). **Amenities:** irons, hair dryers. **Cards:** AX, CB, DC, DS, JC, MC, VI.

SOME UNITS

ASK 🆂 🐎 🍴 📹 📠 🖳 / ⊠ 🔋 🖥 /
FEE

HACIENDA ANTIGUA INN *Book at aaa.com* Phone: (505)345-5399 **14**

AAA SAVE ▽▽▽▽

Historic Bed & Breakfast

3/1-11/30 [BP] 1P: $149-$189 2P: $149-$189 XP: $25 F12
2/1-2/28 & 12/1-1/31 [BP] 1P: $134-$170 2P: $134-$170 XP: $25 F12
Location: I-25, exit 230 (Osuna Dr), 2 mi w, then just n. 6708 Tierra Dr NW 87107. Fax: 505/345-3855. **Facility:** This adobe hacienda dating to the 1700s features several rooms with a fireplace or a wood-burning stove as well as attractive brick floors. Designated smoking area. 8 one-bedroom standard units. 1 story, interior/exterior corridors. **Bath:** combo or shower only. **Parking:** on-site. **Terms:** check-in 4 pm, 10 day cancellation notice-fee imposed, pets ($30 fee). **Amenities:** voice mail, irons, hair dryers. **Pool(s):** outdoor. **Leisure Activities:** whirlpool. **Cards:** AX, MC, VI. **Special Amenities:** free full breakfast and free local telephone calls.

SOME UNITS

🆂 🐎 ⇌ ⊠ 📠 🔋 🖳 / ⅏ /
FEE

HAMPTON-AIRPORT *Book at aaa.com* Phone: (505)246-2255 **82**

▽▽▽▽

Small-scale Hotel

2/1-10/7 1P: $79-$99 2P: $89-$109 XP: $10 F12
10/8-1/31 1P: $79-$99 2P: $89-$99 XP: $10 F12
Location: I-25, exit 222A southbound; exit 222 northbound, 1 mi e, then just n. 2231 Yale Blvd SE 87106. Fax: 505/246-2288. **Facility:** 62 one-bedroom standard units. 3 stories, exterior corridors. **Parking:** on-site. **Terms:** cancellation fee imposed, [BP] meal plan available. **Amenities:** high-speed Internet, voice mail, irons, hair dryers. **Pool(s):** heated indoor. **Leisure Activities:** sauna, whirlpool. **Guest Services:** valet laundry. **Business Services:** PC, fax (fee). **Cards:** AX, DC, DS, MC, VI.

SOME UNITS

ASK ⊗ 🍴 ⇌ 📹 📠 🖳 / ⊠ /

(See map and index starting on p. 478)

HAMPTON INN-NORTH · *Book at aaa.com*

AAA **SAVE**
6/2-10/15 [BP] · 1P: $84-$89 · 2P: $89-$94
2/1-6/1 & 10/16-1/31 [BP] · 1P: $79-$84 · 2P: $84-$89
Phone: (505)344-1555 **9**

Small-scale Hotel · **Location:** I-25, exit 231, just w. 5101 Ellison NE 87109. Fax: 505/345-2216. **Facility:** 124 one-bedroom standard units. 3 stories, exterior corridors. **Parking:** on-site. **Amenities:** video games (fee), high-speed Internet, dual phone lines, voice mail, irons, hair dryers. **Pool(s):** heated outdoor. **Guest Services:** valet laundry. **Business Services:** meeting rooms. **Cards:** AX, CB, DC, DS, JC, MC, VI. **Special Amenities:** free expanded continental breakfast and free local telephone calls.

SOME UNITS

HAMPTON INN UNIVERSITY-MIDTOWN · *Book at aaa.com*

All Year [ECP] · 1P: $63-$109 · **Phone: (505)837-9300** **34**
XP: $5 · F18

Small-scale Hotel · **Location:** I-40, exit 160. 2300 Carlisle NE 87110. Fax: 505/837-2211. **Facility:** 130 one-bedroom standard units. 4 stories, interior corridors. *Bath:* combo or shower only. **Parking:** on-site. **Amenities:** video games (fee), high-speed Internet, voice mail, irons, hair dryers. **Pool(s):** heated outdoor. **Leisure Activities:** whirlpool. **Guest Services:** valet and coin laundry. **Business Services:** meeting rooms, fax (fee). **Cards:** AX, CB, DC, DS, JC, MC, VI.

SOME UNITS
FEE

HAWTHORN INN & SUITES · *Book at aaa.com*

All Year [BP] · 1P: $69-$149 · 2P: $69-$149 · **Phone: (505)242-1555** **80**

Small-scale Hotel · **Location:** I-25, exit 222 northbound; exit 222A southbound, just e. 1511 Gibson Blvd SE 87106. Fax: 505/242-8801. **Facility:** Designated smoking area. 104 one-bedroom standard units. 4 stories, interior corridors. *Bath:* combo or shower only. **Parking:** on-site. **Terms:** pets ($50 deposit, $5 extra charge). **Amenities:** high-speed Internet, dual phone lines, voice mail, irons, hair dryers. **Pool(s):** heated outdoor. **Leisure Activities:** exercise room. **Guest Services:** gift shop, valet and coin laundry, area transportation. **Business Services:** meeting rooms, PC, fax. **Cards:** AX, DC, DS, MC, VI.

SOME UNITS
FEE

HILTON ALBUQUERQUE · *Book at aaa.com*

All Year · 1P: $69-$175 · 2P: $69-$175 · **Phone: (505)884-2500** **31**
XP: $10 · F18

Large-scale Hotel · **Location:** I-40, exit 160, just n to Menaul Blvd, then 1 mi w. 1901 University Blvd NE 87102. Fax: 505/889-9118. **Facility:** 263 one-bedroom standard units. 2-12 stories, interior corridors. *Bath:* combo or shower only. **Parking:** on-site (fee) and valet. **Terms:** cancellation fee imposed. **Amenities:** high-speed Internet, dual phone lines, voice mail, irons, hair dryers. **Dining:** Rancher's Club of New Mexico, see separate listing. **Pool(s):** heated outdoor, heated indoor. **Leisure Activities:** sauna, whirlpool. **Guest Services:** gift shop, valet and coin laundry. **Business Services:** conference facilities, business center. **Cards:** AX, CB, DC, DS, JC, MC, VI.

SOME UNITS

HILTON GARDEN INN ALBUQUERQUE AIRPORT · *Book at aaa.com*

Phone: 505/765-1000 **86**
Property failed to provide current rates

Small-scale Hotel · **Location:** I-25, exit 222 (Gibson Blvd), 1 mi e, then just s. 2601 Yale Blvd SE 87106. Fax: 505/243-2200. **Facility:** 107 one-bedroom standard units, some with whirlpools. 4 stories, interior corridors. *Bath:* combo or shower only. **Parking:** on-site. **Amenities:** video games (fee), high-speed Internet, dual phone lines, voice mail, irons, hair dryers. **Pool(s):** heated indoor. **Leisure Activities:** whirlpool, exercise room. **Guest Services:** complimentary evening beverages, valet and coin laundry. **Business Services:** meeting rooms, business center.

SOME UNITS

HILTON GARDEN INN ALBUQUERQUE JOURNAL CENTER · *Book at aaa.com*

Phone: 505/314-0800 **12**
Property failed to provide current rates

Small-scale Hotel · **Location:** I-25, exit 231, just e. 5320 San Antonio Dr 87109. Fax: 505/314-0810. **Facility:** 94 one-bedroom standard units. 4 stories, interior corridors. *Bath:* combo or shower only. **Parking:** on-site. **Amenities:** video games (fee), high-speed Internet, dual phone lines, voice mail, safes, irons, hair dryers. **Pool(s):** heated indoor. **Leisure Activities:** whirlpool, exercise room. **Guest Services:** sundries, valet and coin laundry. **Business Services:** meeting rooms, business center.

SOME UNITS

HOLIDAY INN EXPRESS · *Book at aaa.com*

All Year · 1P: $77-$97 · 2P: $82-$102 · **Phone: (505)247-1500** **76**
XP: $5 · F18

Small-scale Hotel · **Location:** I-25, exit 222A, 1 mi e to Yale Blvd, just n, then just e. 2331 Centre Ave SE 87106. Fax: 505/842-8681. **Facility:** 58 one-bedroom standard units. 3 stories, interior corridors. *Bath:* combo or shower only. **Parking:** on-site. **Terms:** cancellation fee imposed. **Amenities:** high-speed Internet, dual phone lines, voice mail, irons, hair dryers. **Pool(s):** heated indoor. **Leisure Activities:** whirlpool. **Guest Services:** valet laundry. **Business Services:** fax. **Cards:** AX, DC, DS, MC, VI.

SOME UNITS

HOLIDAY INN EXPRESS · *Book at aaa.com*

AAA **SAVE**
All Year · 1P: $69 · 2P: $69 · **Phone: (505)275-8900** **59**
XP: $5 · F18

Small-scale Hotel · **Location:** I-40, exit 165 (Eubank Blvd), 2 blks n. 10330 Hotel Ave NE 87123. Fax: 505/275-6000. **Facility:** 104 one-bedroom standard units. 2 stories (no elevator), exterior corridors. *Bath:* combo or shower only. **Parking:** on-site. **Terms:** [ECP] meal plan available, small pets only ($5 extra charge). **Amenities:** dual phone lines, voice mail, safes, irons, hair dryers. **Pool(s):** heated indoor. **Leisure Activities:** sauna, whirlpool, exercise room. **Guest Services:** valet and coin laundry. **Business Services:** meeting rooms, business center. **Cards:** AX, CB, DC, DS, MC, VI. **Special Amenities:** free expanded continental breakfast and free local telephone calls.

SOME UNITS
FEE

(See map and index starting on p. 478)

HOLIDAY INN EXPRESS HOTEL & SUITES — Book at aaa.com
Phone: (505)797-2291 **2**
All Year [CP]   1P: $86   2P: $86   XP: $10   F
Small-scale Hotel   **Location:** I-25, exit 233, just w. 5401 Alameda Blvd NE 87113. Fax: 505/797-2292. **Facility:** 62 one-bedroom standard units. 3 stories, interior corridors. *Bath:* combo or shower only. **Parking:** on-site. **Terms:** cancellation fee imposed. **Amenities:** high-speed Internet, dual phone lines, voice mail, safes, irons, hair dryers. **Pool(s):** heated indoor. **Leisure Activities:** sauna, whirlpool, exercise room. **Guest Services:** valet and coin laundry. **Business Services:** meeting rooms. Cards: AX, DC, DS, MC, VI.
SOME UNITS

HOLIDAY INN EXPRESS-WEST — Book at aaa.com
Phone: (505)836-8600 **42**
All Year   1P: $59-$119   2P: $69-$129
Small-scale Hotel   **Location:** I-40, exit 155, just sw. 6100 Iliff Rd NW 87121. Fax: 505/836-2097. **Facility:** 103 one-bedroom standard units. 3 stories, interior/exterior corridors. **Parking:** on-site. **Terms:** pets ($10 fee). **Amenities:** high-speed Internet, voice mail, irons, hair dryers. **Pool(s):** heated indoor. **Leisure Activities:** sauna, whirlpool, exercise room. **Guest Services:** valet laundry. **Business Services:** meeting rooms, fax. Cards: AX, DC, DS, MC, VI.
FEE   SOME UNITS

HOLIDAY INN SELECT HOTEL
Phone: 505/944-2255 **88**
Property failed to provide current rates
Location: I-25, exit 221, 0.5 mi e to University Blvd, then just n. 1501 Sunport Pl SE 87106. Fax: 505/843-6060. **Facility:** Designated smoking area. 120 units. 100 one-bedroom standard units. 20 one-bedroom suites. 4 stories, interior corridors. *Bath:* combo or shower only. **Parking:** on-site. **Amenities:** high-speed Internet, dual phone lines, voice mail, safes, irons, hair dryers. **Pool(s):** heated indoor. **Leisure Activities:** sauna, whirlpool, exercise room. **Guest Services:** sundries, valet and coin laundry. **Business Services:** conference facilities, business center.

HOMEWOOD SUITES BY HILTON-JOURNAL CENTER — Book at aaa.com
Phone: 505/998-4663 **13**
Property failed to provide current rates
Location: I-25, exit 231 (San Antonio Dr), just e. 5400 San Antonio Dr NE 87109. Fax: 505/998-4667. **Facility:** 63 one-bedroom standard units with efficiencies. 3 stories, interior corridors. *Bath:* combo or shower only. **Parking:** on-site. **Amenities:** DVD players, high-speed Internet, dual phone lines, voice mail, irons, hair dryers. **Pool(s):** small indoor. **Leisure Activities:** whirlpool, exercise room. **Business Services:** meeting rooms, business center.
SOME UNITS

HOMEWOOD SUITES BY HILTON-UPTOWN — Book at aaa.com
Phone: (505)881-7300 **37**
All Year [BP]   1P: $79-$149   2P: $89-$159   XP: $10   F17
Small-scale Hotel   **Location:** I-40, exit 162 westbound; exit 162B eastbound, 0.7 mi n, then just e. 7101 Arvada Ave NE 87110. Fax: 505/881-0041. **Facility:** 151 units. 140 one- and 11 two-bedroom suites with efficiencies. 6 stories, interior corridors. *Bath:* combo or shower only. **Parking:** on-site. **Amenities:** video games (fee), high-speed Internet, dual phone lines, voice mail, irons, hair dryers. **Pool(s):** heated outdoor. **Leisure Activities:** exercise room. **Guest Services:** valet and coin laundry. **Business Services:** meeting rooms, business center. Cards: AX, DC, DS, MC, VI.
SOME UNITS

HOTEL ALBUQUERQUE AT OLD TOWN — Book at aaa.com
Phone: (505)843-6300 **46**
All Year   1P: $89-$254   2P: $89-$254   XP: $15   F18
Large-scale Hotel   **Location:** I-40, exit 157A, 0.4 mi s. 800 Rio Grande Blvd NW 87104. Fax: 505/842-8426. **Facility:** 187 one-bedroom standard units. 11 stories, interior corridors. *Bath:* combo or shower only. **Parking:** on-site. **Terms:** cancellation fee imposed, package plans. **Amenities:** dual phone lines, voice mail, irons, hair dryers. *Fee:* video games, high-speed Internet. **Pool(s):** heated outdoor. **Leisure Activities:** whirlpool, exercise room, spa. **Guest Services:** gift shop, valet laundry. **Business Services:** conference facilities, business center. Cards: AX, CB, DC, DS, JC, MC, VI.
SOME UNITS

THE HOTEL BLUE
Phone: 505/924-2400 **60**
Property failed to provide current rates
Location: 8th and Central Ave; downtown. 717 Central Ave NW 87102. Fax: 505/924-2465. **Facility:** 135 one-bedroom standard units. 6 stories, exterior corridors. *Bath:* combo or shower only. **Parking:** on-site. **Terms:** pets ($25 fee). **Amenities:** high-speed Internet, voice mail, irons, hair dryers. **Pool(s):** outdoor. **Leisure Activities:** exercise room. **Guest Services:** valet laundry, area transportation. **Business Services:** meeting rooms, PC.
FEE   SOME UNITS

HOWARD JOHNSON EXPRESS INN — Book at aaa.com
Phone: 505/828-1600 **7**
4/25-10/10   1P: $60-$70   2P: $65-$75   XP: $5   F17
10/11-1/31   1P: $55-$70   2P: $60-$70   XP: $5   F17
2/1-4/24   1P: $55-$60   2P: $60-$65   XP: $5   F17
Small-scale Hotel   **Location:** I-25, exit 231, 0.8 mi n on frontage road. 7630 Pan American NE 87109 (7630 Pan American Frwy NE). Fax: 505/856-6446. **Facility:** 85 one-bedroom standard units. 3 stories, interior corridors. *Bath:* combo or shower only. **Parking:** on-site. **Terms:** pets ($10 extra charge). **Amenities:** high-speed Internet, irons, hair dryers. **Pool(s):** heated outdoor. **Leisure Activities:** exercise room. **Guest Services:** valet laundry. **Business Services:** meeting rooms, PC, fax. Cards: AX, DS, MC, VI.
FEE   SOME UNITS

(See map and index starting on p. 478)

HYATT REGENCY ALBUQUERQUE *Book at aaa.com* **Phone:** (505)842-1234 **56**

 AAA SAVE All Year 1P: $99-$185 2P: $99-$185 XP: $25 F18
Location: I-25, exit 224B, 0.5 mi w; downtown. 330 Tijeras Ave NW 87102. Fax: 505/766-6710. **Facility:** An impressive lobby with marble pillars and upscale shops is the introduction to this fine downtown hotel, Large-scale Hotel across the street from City Hall. 395 one-bedroom standard units. 20 stories, interior corridors. **Parking:** on-site (fee) and valet. **Terms:** cancellation fee imposed. **Amenities:** dual phone lines, voice mail, irons, hair dryers. *Fee:* video games, high-speed Internet. **Dining:** 2 restaurants, 6:30 am-midnight, cocktails, also, McGrath's Restaurant & Bar, see separate listing, entertainment. **Pool(s):** heated outdoor. **Leisure Activities:** saunas, whirlpools, exercise room. *Fee:* massage. **Guest Services:** gift shop, valet laundry. **Business Services:** conference facilities, business center. **Cards:** AX, CB, DC, DS, JC, MC, VI. *(See color ad below)*

SOME UNITS

🍴 🍸 🕭M 🕭 🖉 🏊 📵 🎥 DATA PORT 📠 / 📡 VCR 📶 /
FEE

SPECTACULAR VIEWS. EXCEPTIONAL ACCOMMODATIONS.

From the heart of Albuquerque to the banks of the Rio Grande, AAA members can enjoy the exceptional amenities and elegant surroundings of the Hyatt Touch at exclusive savings. Simply request the AAA member rate and present your card at check-in. This is not your typical hotel story. This is the Hyatt Touch.™ For reservations, call 800 532 1496 or visit **hyatt.com**.

HYATT
HOTELS & RESORTS ®

Hyatt Regency Albuquerque
At the Albuquerque Convention Center

Hyatt Regency Tamaya Resort & Spa
On the Native American Pueblo of Santa Ana

Show Your Card & Save

Preferred rates are valid now through 1/31/07 at participating Hyatt hotels in the U.S. and Canada. AAA members will receive the special AAA rate based on availability. Hyatt Hotels and Resorts encompasses hotels and resorts managed, franchised or operated by two separate companies—Hyatt Corporation and its affiliates and affiliates of Hyatt International Corporation. ©2006 Hyatt Corp.

LA POSADA DE ALBUQUERQUE... CAPTURING THE ESSENCE OF THE SOUTHWEST

• Historic Boutique Hotel
• Conrad's Downtown Restaurant
• Lobby Bar with Happy Hour

• Meeting & Banquet Space
• Located Downtown
• Walk to Convention Center
• Minutes to University of New Mexico, Kirtland Airforce Base and Airport

La Posada de Albuquerque

$**79-139*** *AAA Rate, Per Room/Per Night, Plus Tax, 1-2 Persons*
*Rates subject to availability. Not applicable to groups.

125 Second Avenue NW • Albuquerque, NM 87102 RESERVATIONS: 1-800-777-5732 or Online: www.LaPosada-Abq.com

(See map and index starting on p. 478)

LA POSADA DE ALBUQUERQUE

Phone: (505)242-9090   [61]

(AAA) (SAVE)

4/1-10/15	1P: $99-$139	2P: $113-$153
2/1-3/31 & 10/16-1/31	1P: $89-$109	2P: $103-$123

[fyi] Under major renovation, scheduled to be completed July 2006. **Last rated:** 🌊🌊🌊 **Location:** Jct Central Ave and 2nd St; downtown. Located in a commercial area. 125 2nd St NW 87102. Fax: 505/242-1945. **Facility:** The property's original lobby, with its warm walnut tones, fine wall mural and hammered-tin light fixtures, has been preserved. 114 units. 111 one-bedroom standard units. 3 one-bedroom suites. 10 stories, interior corridors. *Bath:* combo or shower only. **Parking:** on-site (fee). **Terms:** package plans. **Amenities:** high-speed Internet, voice mail, irons, hair dryers. **Dining:** 6 am-10 pm, Fri & Sat-11 pm, cocktails, entertainment. **Leisure Activities:** *Fee:* massage. **Guest Services:** gift shop. **Business Services:** meeting rooms. **Cards:** AX, CB, DC, DS, MC, VI. *(See color ad p 498)*

Historic
Large-scale Hotel

SOME UNITS

[🅢D] [🍽] [🍸] [📶] [🐾] [DATA PORT] [💻] / [✕] [🔒] /
FEE

LA QUINTA INN ALBUQUERQUE (AIRPORT)   *Book at aaa.com*

Phone: (505)243-5500   [81]

🔷🔷🔷🔷

5/16-8/31 [CP]	1P: $82-$112
9/1-1/31 [CP]	1P: $80-$110
2/1-5/15 [CP]	1P: $78-$108

Small-scale Hotel   **Location:** I-25, exit 222 northbound; exit 222A southbound, 1 mi e. 2116 Yale Blvd SE 87106-4233. Fax: 505/247-8288. **Facility:** 105 one-bedroom standard units. 3 stories, interior/exterior corridors. *Bath:* combo or shower only. **Parking:** on-site. **Terms:** small pets only. **Amenities:** video games (fee), high-speed Internet, voice mail, irons, hair dryers. **Pool(s):** heated outdoor. **Leisure Activities:** exercise room. **Guest Services:** valet and coin laundry. **Cards:** AX, CB, DC, DS, MC, VI. *(See color ad below)*

SOME UNITS

[ASK] [🛬] [🐾] [🍽] [🏋M] [🔒] [🏊] [➰] [🐾] [📶] [📹] [DATA PORT] [💻] / [✕] [🔒] /
FEE

LA QUINTA INN ALBUQUERQUE (I-40 EAST)   *Book at aaa.com*

Phone: (505)884-3591   [33]

(AAA) (SAVE)
🔷🔷🔷

5/1-10/9 [CP]	1P: $65-$95	2P: $70-$100	XP: $5 F18
10/10-1/31 [CP]	1P: $62-$92	2P: $67-$97	XP: $5 F18
2/1-4/30 [CP]	1P: $59-$89	2P: $64-$94	XP: $5 F18

Location: I-40, exit 161 westbound; exit 161B eastbound, just n. 2424 San Mateo Blvd NE 87110-4053. **Small-scale Hotel** Fax: 505/881-3065. **Facility:** 106 units. 99 one- and 7 two-bedroom standard units. 2 stories (no elevator), exterior corridors. *Bath:* combo or shower only. **Parking:** on-site. **Terms:** small pets only. **Amenities:** dual phone lines, voice mail, irons, hair dryers. *Fee:* video games, high-speed Internet. **Pool(s):** heated outdoor. **Guest Services:** valet and coin laundry. **Business Services:** fax. **Cards:** AX, CB, DC, DS, MC, VI. **Special Amenities:** free expanded continental breakfast and free local telephone calls. *(See color ad below)*

SOME UNITS

[🐾] [🍽] [🔒] [➰] [🐾] [📶] [📹] [DATA PORT] [💻] / [✕] [🔒] [📠] /
FEE

LA QUINTA INN ALBUQUERQUE (NORTH)   *Book at aaa.com*

Phone: (505)821-9000   [10]

(AAA) (SAVE)
🔷🔷🔷

4/1-10/31 [CP]	1P: $79-$109
11/1-1/31 [CP]	1P: $75-$105
2/1-3/31 [CP]	1P: $72-$102

Location: I-25, exit 231, just e. 5241 San Antonio Dr NE 87109. Fax: 505/821-2399. **Facility:** 130 one-bedroom **Small-scale Hotel** standard units. 2 stories (no elevator), exterior corridors. *Bath:* combo or shower only. **Parking:** on-site. **Terms:** small pets only. **Amenities:** video games (fee), dual phone lines, voice mail, irons, hair dryers. **Pool(s):** heated outdoor. **Guest Services:** valet and coin laundry. **Business Services:** fax. **Cards:** AX, CB, DC, DS, MC, VI. **Special Amenities:** free expanded continental breakfast and free local telephone calls. *(See color ad below)*

SOME UNITS

[🐾] [🍽] [🏋M] [🔒] [➰] [🐾] [📶] [📹] [DATA PORT] [💻] / [✕] [🔒] [📠] /

(See map and index starting on p. 478)

LA QUINTA INN & SUITES ALBUQUERQUE (WEST) *Book at aaa.com*
Phone: (505)839-1744 **39**
All Year [CP] 1P: $99-$129 XP: $10 F18
Location: I-40, exit 155, just sw. 6101 Iliff Rd NW 87121. Fax: 505/839-1797. **Facility:** 118 one-bedroom
standard units. 5 stories, interior corridors. *Bath:* combo or shower only. **Parking:** on-site. **Amenities:** video
games (fee), high-speed Internet, dual phone lines, voice mail, irons, hair dryers. **Pool(s):** heated outdoor.
Small-scale Hotel
Leisure Activities: whirlpool, exercise room. **Guest Services:** valet and coin laundry. **Business Services:** meeting rooms.
Cards: AX, CB, DC, DS, MC, VI. *(See color ad p 499)*

SOME UNITS
(ASK) [icons] / [icons] /

LA QUINTA SUITES MIDTOWN/UNIVERSITY *Book at aaa.com*
Phone: (505)761-5600 **21**
All Year 1P: $79-$129 2P: $79-$129 XP: $10 F18
Location: Jct University Blvd NE and Menaul Blvd, just e. 2011 Menaul Blvd 87107 (9105 MacAllan Rd NE, 87109).
Fax: 505/761-5601. **Facility:** 72 one-bedroom standard units. 3 stories, interior corridors. *Bath:* combo or
Small-scale Hotel
shower only. **Parking:** on-site. **Amenities:** high-speed Internet, dual phone lines, voice mail. **Pool(s):**
heated indoor. **Leisure Activities:** limited exercise equipment. **Guest Services:** valet and coin laundry. **Business Services:**
meeting rooms, business center. **Cards:** AX, DC, DS, MC, VI. *(See color ad p 499)*

(ASK) [icons]

LUXURY INN
Phone: 505/255-5900 **65**
9/1-10/15 1P: $40-$45 2P: $65-$70 XP: $10 F12
2/1-8/31 1P: $30-$36 2P: $36-$50 XP: $6 F12
10/16-1/31 1P: $30-$36 2P: $36-$45 XP: $6 F12
Location: I-40, exit 162 westbound; exit 162A eastbound, 1.5 mi s, then just w. 6718 Central SE 87108.
Small-scale Hotel Fax: 505/256-4915. **Facility:** 58 one-bedroom standard units. 2 stories (no elevator), exterior corridors.
Parking: on-site. **Terms:** 3 day cancellation notice-fee imposed, package plans. **Pool(s):** heated indoor.
Leisure Activities: whirlpool. **Guest Services:** coin laundry. **Cards:** AX, DC, DS, MC, VI. **Special Amenities:** free continental
breakfast and free local telephone calls. *(See color ad below)*

SOME UNITS
[icons] / [icons] /

MCM ELEGANTE HOTEL *Book at aaa.com*
Phone: (505)884-2511 **27**
All Year 1P: $109-$129 2P: $119-$139 XP: $10 F18
Location: I-40, exit 160, 0.3 mi n to Menaul Blvd, then 1 mi w. 2020 Menaul Blvd NE 87107. Fax: 505/881-4806.
Facility: 342 units. 324 one-bedroom standard units. 18 one-bedroom suites. 2-5 stories, interior corridors.
Small-scale Hotel
Bath: combo or shower only. **Parking:** on-site. **Terms:** cancellation fee imposed, pets ($25 deposit).
Amenities: high-speed Internet, dual phone lines, voice mail, irons, hair dryers. **Pool(s):** heated indoor. **Leisure
Activities:** whirlpool, exercise room. **Guest Services:** gift shop, valet and coin laundry, area transportation. **Business
Services:** meeting rooms, business center. **Cards:** AX, DS, MC, VI.

SOME UNITS
(ASK) [icons] FEE / [icons] /

(See map and index starting on p. 478)

MICROTEL INN & SUITES

Phone: 505/836-1686

◆◆◆
Small-scale Hotel

Property failed to provide current rates
Location: I-40, exit 153, just s; on western edge of city. 9910 Avalon NW 87121. Fax: 505/831-2450. **Facility:** 49 one-bedroom standard units. 3 stories, interior corridors. **Parking:** on-site. **Terms:** pets ($10 extra charge). **Guest Services:** coin laundry. **Business Services:** meeting rooms.

SOME UNITS

🛏 📶 DATA PORT / ✕ 🖥 /
FEE

MONTEREY NON-SMOKERS MOTEL-OLD TOWN   _Book at aaa.com_

Phone: 505/243-3554   **50**

AAA SAVE
◆◆◆
Motel

4/1-10/31	1P: $42-$55	2P: $47-$65	XP: $6 F12
2/1-3/31 & 11/1-1/31	1P: $38-$55	2P: $43-$55	XP: $6 F12

Location: I-40, exit 157A, 0.5 mi s on Rio Grande Blvd, then 0.3 mi w. 2402 Central Ave SW 87104. Fax: 505/243-9701. **Facility:** Smoke free premises. 15 one-bedroom standard units. 1 story, exterior corridors. **Parking:** on-site. **Pool(s):** heated outdoor. **Guest Services:** coin laundry. **Cards:** AX, DS, MC, VI. _(See color ad below)_

SD 🍴 🏊 ✕ 📶 DATA PORT 🖥 🖥

MOTEL 6 #1349   _Book at aaa.com_

Phone: 505/243-8017   **68**

◆
Motel

5/26-10/8	1P: $41-$51	2P: $47-$57	XP: $3 F17
2/1-5/25 & 10/9-1/31	1P: $38-$48	2P: $44-$54	XP: $3 F17

Location: I-25, exit 223, just w. 1000 Avenida Cesar Chavez 87102. Fax: 505/242-5137. **Facility:** 95 one-bedroom standard units. 2 stories (no elevator), exterior corridors. _Bath:_ combo or shower only. **Parking:** on-site. **Terms:** small pets only. **Pool(s):** outdoor. **Guest Services:** coin laundry. **Business Services:** fax. **Cards:** AX, CB, DC, DS, MC, VI.

SOME UNITS

SD 🐕 ♿M ♿ 🏊 📶 DATA PORT / ✕ 🖥 🖥 /

MOTEL 6 ALBUQUERQUE EAST #49   _Book at aaa.com_

Phone: 505/294-4600   **71**

◆
Motel

5/26-1/31	1P: $35-$45	2P: $41-$51	XP: $3 F17
2/1-5/25	1P: $32-$42	2P: $38-$48	XP: $3 F17

Location: I-40, exit 167 (Tramway Blvd), just s, then just w. 13141 Central Ave NE 87123. Fax: 505/294-7564. **Facility:** 122 one-bedroom standard units. 2 stories (no elevator), exterior corridors. _Bath:_ shower only. **Parking:** on-site. **Pool(s):** outdoor. **Business Services:** meeting rooms. **Cards:** AX, CB, DS, MC, VI.

SOME UNITS

SD 🐕 🍴 🏊 📶 / ✕ /

MOTEL 6 ALBUQUERQUE NORTH #1290   _Book at aaa.com_

Phone: 505/821-1472   **4**

◆
Small-scale Hotel

5/1-1/31	1P: $39-$49	2P: $45-$55	XP: $3 F17
2/1-4/30	1P: $37-$47	2P: $43-$53	XP: $3 F17

Location: I-25, exit 232 (Paseo del Norte), just n on Frontage Rd. 8510 Pan American Frwy NE 87113. Fax: 505/821-7344. **Facility:** 125 one-bedroom standard units. 3 stories, interior corridors. _Bath:_ combo or shower only. **Parking:** on-site. **Pool(s):** outdoor. **Guest Services:** coin laundry. **Cards:** AX, CB, DC, DS, MC, VI.

SOME UNITS

SD 🐕 ♿M 🏊 📶 DATA PORT / ✕ /

MOTEL 76

Phone: 505/836-3881   **45**

AAA SAVE
◆◆◆
Small-scale Hotel

All Year   1P: $31-$47   2P: $38-$52   XP: $5   F6

Location: I-40, exit 155 (Coors Blvd), just s. 1521 Coors Blvd NW 87121. Fax: 505/836-2665. **Facility:** 79 one-bedroom standard units. 2 stories (no elevator), exterior corridors. **Parking:** on-site. **Terms:** pets ($25 deposit). **Guest Services:** coin laundry. **Business Services:** fax (fee). **Cards:** AX, DS, MC, VI. **Special Amenities:** free local telephone calls.

SOME UNITS

🐕 🍴 📶 / ✕ /
FEE

(See map and index starting on p. 478)

NATIVO LODGE *Book at aaa.com* Phone: (505)798-4300 **15**
▽▽▽▽

10/1-10/15	1P: $169	2P: $179	XP: $10	F16
2/1-9/30	1P: $89-$119	2P: $99-$129	XP: $10	F16
10/16-1/31	1P: $79-$109	2P: $89-$119	XP: $10	F16

Small-scale Hotel **Location:** I-25, exit 230, just e. 6000 Pan American Frwy NE 87109. Fax: 505/798-4305. **Facility:** 151 one-bedroom standard units. 5 stories, interior corridors. **Parking:** on-site. **Terms:** package plans, pets ($50 extra charge). **Amenities:** high-speed Internet, dual phone lines, voice mail, irons, hair dryers. **Pool(s):** heated indoor/outdoor. **Leisure Activities:** sauna, whirlpool, exercise room. **Guest Services:** valet and coin laundry. **Business Services:** meeting rooms. **Cards:** AX, DC, DS, MC, VI. *(See color ad below)*

SOME UNITS

(ASK) 🛇 🛏️ 🍽️ 🍸 🎇 🌊 ✕ 🐕 DATA PORT 💻 / ✕ 🅱️
FEE   FEE

PLAZA INN ALBUQUERQUE *Book at aaa.com* Phone: (505)243-5693 **52**
(AAA) (SAVE)

9/29-10/8 [CP]	1P: $109-$119	2P: $119-$129	XP: $10	F17
2/1-9/28 & 10/9-1/31 [CP]	1P: $69-$89	2P: $79-$99	XP: $10	F17

▽▽▽▽
Small-scale Hotel **Location:** I-25, exit 225, just e. 900 Medical Arts NE 87102. Fax: 505/843-6229. **Facility:** 120 one-bedroom standard units. 5 stories, interior corridors. **Parking:** on-site. **Terms:** small pets only ($25 fee). **Amenities:** DVD players, video games (fee), high-speed Internet, voice mail, irons, hair dryers. **Dining:** 6 am-11 pm, cocktails. **Pool(s):** heated indoor. **Leisure Activities:** whirlpools, exercise room. **Guest Services:** valet and coin laundry, area transportation-hospitals & Old Town. **Business Services:** meeting rooms, PC, fax (fee). **Cards:** AX, CB, DC, DS, MC, VI. **Special Amenities:** free continental breakfast and free room upgrade (subject to availability with advance reservations). *(See color ad below)*

SOME UNITS

🛇 🛬 🐾 🛏️ 🍽️ 🍸 🏋️ 🎇 🌊 🐕 DATA PORT 💻 / ✕ 🅱️ 🖨️ /
FEE

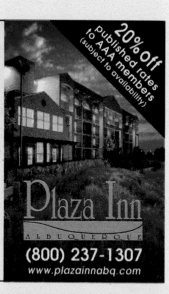

(See map and index starting on p. 478)

QUALITY INN & SUITES ALBUQUERQUE
DOWNTOWN *Book at aaa.com*
Phone: (505)242-5228 35

(AAA) (SAVE)

All Year   1P: $48-$90   2P: $53-$95   XP: $5   F17

Location: I-40, exit 159A, just s via 4th St N. 411 McKnight Ave NW 87102. Fax: 505/766-9218. **Facility:** 92 units. 83 one- and 9 two-bedroom standard units. 4 stories, interior corridors. **Parking:** on-site.

Small-scale Hotel   **Terms:** cancellation fee imposed, weekly rates available, [ECP] meal plan available, small pets only ($10 fee). **Amenities:** high-speed Internet, irons, hair dryers. **Pool(s):** heated outdoor. **Leisure Activities:** whirlpool, exercise room. **Business Services:** meeting rooms, PC, fax (fee). **Cards:** AX, CB, DC, DS, JC, MC, VI. **Special Amenities: free expanded continental breakfast and free local telephone calls.**

SOME UNITS

QUALITY SUITES   *Book at aaa.com*
Phone: (505)797-0850 11

(AAA) (SAVE)

3/3-10/14   1P: $79-$89   2P: $89-$99   XP: $10   F17
2/1-3/2 & 10/15-1/31   1P: $69-$79   2P: $79-$89   XP: $10   F17

Location: I-25, exit 231, just e. 5251 San Antonio Dr NE 87109. Fax: 505/797-7642. **Facility:** 70 one-bedroom standard units. 3 stories, interior corridors. *Bath:* combo or shower only. **Parking:** on-site. **Terms:** [BP] meal

Small-scale Hotel   plan available, pets ($5 extra charge). **Amenities:** high-speed Internet, dual phone lines, safes, irons, hair dryers. **Pool(s):** heated indoor. **Leisure Activities:** whirlpool, exercise room. **Guest Services:** valet and coin laundry. **Business Services:** meeting rooms, business center. **Cards:** AX, CB, DC, DS, JC, MC, VI. **Special Amenities: free full breakfast and free local telephone calls.**

SOME UNITS

QUALITY SUITES-AIRPORT/UNIVERSITY   *Book at aaa.com*
Phone: (505)245-7363 79

(AAA) (SAVE)

All Year   1P: $65-$89   2P: $70-$99   XP: $10   F16

Location: I-25, exit 222 (Gibson Blvd) northbound; exit 222A southbound, just e. 1501 Gibson Blvd SE 87106. Fax: 505/245-8316. **Facility:** 72 one-bedroom standard units. 3 stories, interior corridors. *Bath:* combo or shower only. **Parking:** on-site. **Amenities:** high-speed Internet, dual phone lines, voice mail, safes, irons,

Small-scale Hotel   hair dryers. **Pool(s):** heated indoor. **Leisure Activities:** sauna, whirlpool. **Guest Services:** valet and coin laundry, area transportation-within 3 mi. **Business Services:** meeting rooms, PC, fax (fee). **Cards:** AX, DC, DS, MC, VI. **Special Amenities: free full breakfast and free local telephone calls.**

SOME UNITS

RADISSON HOTEL & CONFERENCE CENTER
Phone: (505)888-3311 29

(AAA) (SAVE)

10/1-10/16   1P: $129-$159   2P: $129-$179   XP: $10   F18
2/1-9/30 & 10/17-1/31   1P: $89-$109   2P: $89-$119   XP: $10   F18

Location: I-40, exit 160, just n. 2500 Carlisle Blvd NE 87110. Fax: 505/888-3999. **Facility:** 366 one-bedroom standard units. 2-4 stories, interior/exterior corridors. *Bath:* combo or shower only. **Parking:** on-site.

Large-scale Hotel   **Terms:** cancellation fee imposed, package plans, pets ($50 fee, in smoking units). **Amenities:** dual phone lines, voice mail, irons, hair dryers. **Dining:** 6 am-11 pm, cocktails. **Pool(s):** heated outdoor, heated indoor. **Leisure Activities:** whirlpool, exercise room. **Guest Services:** gift shop, valet and coin laundry. **Business Services:** conference facilities, PC, fax. **Cards:** AX, DS, JC, MC, VI. **Special Amenities: free full breakfast and free room upgrade (subject to availability with advance reservations).** *(See color ad below)*

SOME UNITS

RAMADA LIMITED   *Book at aaa.com*
Phone: (505)858-3297 1

All Year [ECP]   1P: $69-$79   2P: $69-$79   XP: $6   F14

Location: I-25, exit 233, just w. 5601 Alameda Blvd NE 87113. Fax: 505/858-3298. **Facility:** 80 one-bedroom standard units. 2 stories (no elevator), interior corridors. *Bath:* combo or shower only. **Parking:** on-site.

Small-scale Hotel   **Terms:** pets ($10 extra charge). **Amenities:** voice mail, safes, irons, hair dryers. **Pool(s):** heated indoor. **Leisure Activities:** sauna, whirlpool. **Guest Services:** valet laundry. **Business Services:** meeting rooms. **Cards:** AX, CB, DC, DS, JC, MC, VI.

SOME UNITS

(See map and index starting on p. 478)

RAMADA LIMITED (AIRPORT) *Book at aaa.com*
Phone: 505/242-0036 **72**

(AAA) (SAVE)

2/1-10/10	1P: $45-$65	2P: $50-$70
10/11-1/31	1P: $40-$60	2P: $45-$65

Location: I-25, exit 222 northbound; exit 222A southbound, 1 mi e, then just n. 1801 Yale Blvd SE 87106. Fax: 505/242-0068. **Facility:** 74 one-bedroom standard units. 3 stories, interior corridors. *Bath:* combo or shower only. **Parking:** on-site. **Terms:** pets ($10 extra charge, in smoking units). **Amenities:** voice mail. **Pool(s):** heated indoor. **Leisure Activities:** sauna, whirlpool, exercise room. **Guest Services:** valet and coin laundry. **Business Services:** meeting rooms. **Cards:** AX, DC, DS, MC, VI. **Special Amenities: free continental breakfast and free local telephone calls.**

Small-scale Hotel

SOME UNITS

RED ROOF INN *Book at aaa.com*
Phone: (505)831-3400 **41**

6/25-9/23	1P: $42-$54	2P: $48-$59
1/1-1/31	1P: $38-$52	2P: $43-$57
9/24-12/31	1P: $39-$51	2P: $45-$56
2/1-6/24	1P: $37-$51	2P: $42-$56

Small-scale Hotel

Location: I-40, exit 155 (Coors Blvd), just s, then just w. Located in a commercial area. 6015 Iliff Rd NW 87121. Fax: 505/831-3609. **Facility:** 131 one-bedroom standard units. 2 stories (no elevator), exterior corridors. *Bath:* combo or shower only. **Parking:** on-site. **Terms:** small pets only. **Amenities:** video games (fee), voice mail. **Pool(s):** outdoor. **Guest Services:** coin laundry. **Cards:** AX, CB, DC, DS, MC, VI.

SOME UNITS

RESIDENCE INN NORTH BY MARRIOTT *Book at aaa.com*
Phone: 505/761-0200 **17**

Property failed to provide current rates

Small-scale Hotel

Location: I-25, exit 229 (Jefferson St), just w, just n to The Lane at 25 NE, then just e. 4331 The Lane at 25 NE 87109. Fax: 505/761-0201. **Facility:** 90 units. 33 one-bedroom standard units, some with efficiencies. 45 one- and 12 two-bedroom suites, some with kitchens. 3 stories, interior corridors. *Bath:* combo or shower only. **Parking:** on-site. **Terms:** pets ($50 fee, $7.50 extra charge). **Amenities:** high-speed Internet, dual phone lines, voice mail, irons, hair dryers. **Pool(s):** heated outdoor. **Leisure Activities:** whirlpool, exercise room, sports court. **Guest Services:** valet and coin laundry. **Business Services:** meeting rooms, fax.

SOME UNITS

SANDIA PEAK INN
Phone: 505/831-5036 **62**

(AAA) (SAVE)

2/1-4/30 & 11/1-1/31	1P: $40-$89	2P: $49-$99	XP: $10 D16
5/1-10/31	1P: $49-$79	2P: $59-$89	XP: $10 D16

Small-scale Hotel

Location: I-40, exit 159A (Rio Grande Blvd), just s, then 2 mi w. 4614 Central Ave SW 87105. Fax: 505/831-5040. **Facility:** 22 one-bedroom standard units. 2 stories (no elevator), exterior corridors. **Parking:** on-site. **Terms:** cancellation fee imposed, 10% service charge, small pets only. **Amenities:** high-speed Internet, hair dryers. *Some:* irons. **Pool(s):** small heated indoor. **Business Services:** meeting rooms. **Cards:** AX, CB, DS, MC, VI.

SOME UNITS

SHERATON ALBUQUERQUE UPTOWN *Book at aaa.com*
Phone: (505)881-0000 **19**

(AAA) (SAVE)

All Year	1P: $89-$199	2P: $89-$199 XP: $10 F18

Large-scale Hotel

Location: I-40, exit 162, 0.8 mi n. Located in Northeast Heights. 2600 Louisiana Blvd NE 87110. Fax: 505/881-3736. **Facility:** 294 one-bedroom standard units. 7 stories, interior corridors. *Bath:* combo or shower only. **Parking:** on-site. **Terms:** cancellation fee imposed, pets (dogs only). **Amenities:** dual phone lines, voice mail, irons, hair dryers. *Fee:* video games, high-speed Internet. **Dining:** Classic Grill, see separate listing, entertainment. **Pool(s):** heated indoor. **Leisure Activities:** saunas, whirlpool, exercise room. **Guest Services:** gift shop, valet and coin laundry, area transportation-within 2 mi. **Business Services:** conference facilities, business center. **Cards:** AX, CB, DC, DS, JC, MC, VI. *(See color ad below)*

SOME UNITS

(See map and index starting on p. 478)

SLEEP INN AIRPORT   *Book at aaa.com*   Phone: (505)244-3325   **73**
AAA SAVE   All Year [ECP]   1P: $70   2P: $70   XP: $10   F17
             Location: I-25, exit 222 northbound; exit 222A southbound, 1 mi e to Yale Blvd, then just n. 2300 International Ave SE
▽▽▽▽   87106. Fax: 505/244-3312. Facility: 105 one-bedroom standard units. 1-3 stories, interior corridors. Bath:
             combo or shower only. Parking: on-site. Terms: cancellation fee imposed, package plans, pets ($20
Small-scale Hotel   deposit). Pool(s): heated indoor. Leisure Activities: whirlpool, exercise room. Guest Services: coin
             laundry, area transportation-within 5 mi. Business Services: meeting rooms. Cards: AX, CB, DC, DS, JC,
MC, VI. Special Amenities: free full breakfast and free local telephone calls.

SOME UNITS
[icons] FEE

STARDUST INN   Phone: (505)243-2891   **64**
AAA SAVE   9/6-10/31   1P: $49-$69   2P: $69-$79   XP: $10   F10
             2/1-9/5 & 11/1-1/31   1P: $30-$36   2P: $36-$45   XP: $7   F10
▽   Location: I-25, 224A northbound; exit 224B southbound, just e. 801 Central Ave SE. Fax: 505/242-3915.
             Facility: 30 one-bedroom standard units. 2 stories (no elevator), exterior corridors. Parking: on-site.
Motel   Terms: [ECP] meal plan available, small pets only ($25 deposit, $5 extra charge). Pool(s): outdoor.
             Cards: AX, DS, MC, VI. Special Amenities: free expanded continental breakfast and free local
telephone calls.

SOME UNITS
[icons] FEE

SUN VILLAGE CORPORATE SUITES   Phone: 505/842-6640   **48**
                              Property failed to provide current rates
▽▽▽▽   Location: From University Blvd, just w on Indian School Rd, then just n. 801 Locust NE 87102. Fax: 505/842-6668.
             Facility: Convenient to all four quadrants of the city, the complex is modern and features pleasantly
Condominium   decorated units. 38 units. 19 one-bedroom standard units with kitchens. 10 one- and 9 two-bedroom suites
with kitchens. 2 stories (no elevator), exterior corridors. Parking: on-site. Terms: pets (small cats only, $200 deposit, limit 2).
Amenities: high-speed Internet (fee), irons. Pool(s): heated outdoor. Leisure Activities: sauna, whirlpools, 2 lighted tennis
courts, racquetball court, jogging, playground, exercise room, basketball, shuffleboard, volleyball. Guest Services: coin laundry.
Business Services: meeting rooms, fax.

[icons] FEE

SUPER 8 MOTEL EAST   *Book at aaa.com*   Phone: (505)271-4807   **67**
▽▽   All Year   1P: $45-$60   2P: $50-$125   XP: $5   F12
             Location: I-40, exit 166 (Juan Tabo Blvd), just n to Copper, then just s. 450 Paisano NE 87123. Fax: 505/292-1233.
Small-scale Hotel   Facility: 100 units. 94 one- and 6 two-bedroom standard units. 3 stories, interior corridors. Bath: combo or
             shower only. Parking: on-site. Terms: 5 day cancellation notice, [CP] meal plan available, pets ($5 extra
charge). Amenities: voice mail. Leisure Activities: exercise room. Guest Services: coin laundry. Cards: AX, DC, DS,
MC, VI.

SOME UNITS
ASK [icons] FEE

SUPER 8 MOTEL OF ALBUQUERQUE   *Book at aaa.com*   Phone: (505)888-4884   **22**
▽▽   All Year   1P: $45-$60   2P: $50-$125   XP: $5   F12
             Location: I-25, exit 225 northbound, 1.9 mi n on frontage road to Menaul Blvd, then just e; exit 227 (Comanche Rd)
Small-scale Hotel   southbound, 0.9 mi s to Menaul Blvd, then just e. 2500 University Blvd NE 87107. Fax: 505/883-3831. Facility: 243
             one-bedroom standard units. 3 stories, interior corridors. Bath: combo or shower only. Parking: on-site.
Terms: 5 day cancellation notice, [CP] meal plan available, pets ($5 extra charge). Amenities: voice mail. Guest Services:
coin laundry, area transportation. Business Services: Fee: PC, fax. Cards: AX, DC, DS, MC, VI.

SOME UNITS
ASK [icons] FEE

SUPER 8 MOTEL WEST (ALBUQUERQUE)   Phone: (505)836-5560   **43**
▽▽   All Year   1P: $45-$60   2P: $50-$125   XP: $5   F12
             Location: I-40, exit 155, 0.5 mi s. 6030 Iliff Rd NW. Fax: 505/836-4240. Facility: 98 one-bedroom standard units.
             3 stories, interior corridors. Parking: on-site. Terms: 5 day cancellation notice, [CP] meal plan available,
Small-scale Hotel   small pets only ($5 extra charge). Guest Services: coin laundry. Cards: AX, DC, DS, MC, VI.

SOME UNITS
ASK [icons] FEE

TOWNEPLACE SUITES   Phone: (505)232-5800   **78**
AAA SAVE   All Year   1P: $59-$109   2P: $59-$109
             Location: I-25, exit 222 northbound; exit 222A southbound, 1 mi e to Yale Blvd, at northeast jct of Gibson and Yale
▽▽▽▽   blvds, then just e. 2400 Centre Ave SE 87106. Fax: 505/232-5801. Facility: 108 units. 77 one-bedroom standard
             units with efficiencies. 7 one- and 24 two-bedroom suites with kitchens. 4 stories, interior corridors. Bath:
Small-scale Hotel   combo or shower only. Parking: on-site. Terms: pets ($75 fee). Amenities: high-speed Internet, dual
             phone lines, voice mail, irons, hair dryers. Pool(s): heated outdoor. Leisure Activities: whirlpool, gazebo,
barbecue grill, exercise room. Guest Services: valet and coin laundry. Business Services: meeting rooms, business center.
Cards: AX, CB, DC, DS, JC, MC, VI. Special Amenities: free continental breakfast and free newspaper.

SOME UNITS
[icons] FEE

(See map and index starting on p. 478)

WYNDHAM ALBUQUERQUE AT INTERNATIONAL
SUNPORT *Book at aaa.com*

All Year — 1P: $79-$109 — 2P: $89-$119 — **Phone:** (505)843-7000 — 87 F18

XP: $10

Location: I-25, exit 225 northbound; exit 222A southbound, 1 mi e on Gibson Blvd, then 0.5 mi s. Located adjacent to
Large-scale Hotel — the Albuquerque Sunport. 2910 Yale Blvd SE 87106. Fax: 505/843-6307. **Facility:** 276 one-bedroom standard
units. 15 stories, interior corridors. *Bath:* combo or shower only. **Parking:** on-site. **Terms:** small pets only.
Amenities: video games (fee), high-speed Internet, dual phone lines, voice mail, irons, hair dryers. **Pool(s):** outdoor. **Leisure
Activities:** 2 lighted tennis courts, exercise room, basketball. **Guest Services:** gift shop, valet and coin laundry. **Business
Services:** meeting rooms, business center. **Cards:** AX, CB, DC, DS, JC, MC, VI.

SOME UNITS

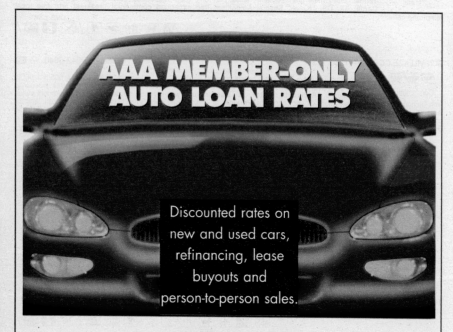

(See map and index starting on p. 478)

──── **WHERE TO DINE** ────

66 DINER
♦♦♦ **Lunch:** $5-$9   **Dinner:** $5-$9   **Phone:** 505/247-1421 `106`
American   **Location:** Jct Central Ave and University Blvd, just w. 1405 Central Ave NE 87106. **Hours:** 11 am-11 pm, Fri-midnight, Sat 8 am-midnight, Sun 8 am-10 pm. **Closed:** 1/1, 11/23, 12/25. **Reservations:** accepted. **Features:** Patrons can return to the 1950s for some of the best burgers and American comfort food in town. Desserts will please, as well. Casual dress. **Parking:** on-site. **Cards:** AX, DS, MC, VI.

AL'S NEW YORK PIZZA DEPARTMENT   **Lunch:** $6-$16   **Dinner:** $6-$16   **Phone:** 505/766-6973 `100`
♦♦   **Location:** Jct 2nd St, just w. 215 Central Ave NW, Suite B 87102. **Hours:** 11 am-11 pm, Fri-midnight, Sat noon-midnight, Sun noon-10 pm. **Closed** major holidays. **Features:** The downtown restaurant's patio affords a good view of busy Central Avenue. A good selection of pizza can be prepared with all the expected topping choices. Also on the menu are salads and pasta dishes, as well as beer and wine. Casual dress; beer & wine only. **Parking:** street. **Cards:** AX, DS, MC, VI.
Italian

ANTIQUITY RESTAURANT   **Dinner:** $16-$27   **Phone:** 505/247-3545 `79`
♦♦♦♦   **Location:** I-40, exit 157A, 0.5 mi s to Romero, then just n of Central Ave; in Old Town. 112 Romero NW 87104. **Hours:** 5 pm-9 pm, Fri & Sat-9:30 pm. **Reservations:** suggested. **Features:** Cozy, intimate restaurant specializing in steak dishes, perfect for that special occasion or a romantic dinner for two. They have a fine selection of wines to suit the most discriminating palate. Very popular with the tourists that frequent Old Town, as well as the local steak connoisseur. Dressy casual; beer & wine only. **Parking:** street. **Cards:** AX, DS, MC, VI.
Continental

THE ARTICHOKE CAFE   **Lunch:** $8-$14   **Dinner:** $16-$30   **Phone:** 505/243-0200 `102`
♦♦♦   **Location:** I-25, exit 224B, s to Central Ave, then w. 424 Central Ave SE 87102. **Hours:** 11 am-2:30 & 5:30-10 pm, Sat from 5:30 pm, Sun 5 pm-9 pm. **Closed:** 11/23, 12/25. **Reservations:** suggested. **Features:** The fine dining establishment features new American cuisine prepared with a Southwestern flair. Creativity marks the appetizers, salads and entrees. Diners will find a sophisticated selection of wines and magical desserts, particularly the luscious creme brulee. Casual dress; beer & wine only. **Parking:** on-site. **Cards:** AX, DC, DS, MC, VI.
American

ASSETS GRILLE & BREWERY CO.   **Lunch:** $6-$15   **Dinner:** $6-$20   **Phone:** 505/889-6400 `38`
♦♦ ♦   **Location:** Jct Louisiana and Montgomery blvds. 6910 Montgomery Blvd NE 87109. **Hours:** 11:30 am-10 pm, Fri & Sat-10:30 pm. **Closed:** 11/23, 12/25; also Sun. **Features:** Be sure to try this restaurant's beer sampler offering several tasty brews made in their on-site microbrewery. The innovative cuisine includes gourmet mini-pizzas and pasta dishes. The setting features a brass rail and dark wood atmosphere. Casual dress; cocktails. **Parking:** on-site. **Cards:** AX, DC, DS, MC, VI.   🍸 🔪
American

A TASTE OF ITALY   **Lunch:** $4-$7   **Dinner:** $4-$7   **Phone:** 505/275-8334 `66`
♦   **Location:** Jct Menaul Blvd, just e. 1945 Juan Tabo Blvd NE 87112. **Hours:** 10 am-9 pm, Fri & Sat-10 pm. **Closed:** 11/23, 12/25; also Sun. **Features:** The modest cafe serves mostly Italian fare: pizza, submarine sandwiches and pasta dishes. Also sharing menu space are some Greek selections, such as gyros, souvlaki and spanakopita. The luncheon buffet is marvelous. Casual dress. **Parking:** on-site. **Cards:** AX, DS, MC, VI.
International

AZUMA   **Lunch:** $7-$11   **Dinner:** $7-$19   **Phone:** 505/880-9800 `30`
♦♦   **Location:** Jct Montgomery and San Mateo blvds, just n. 4701 San Mateo Blvd NE 87109. **Hours:** 11 am-2:30 & 5-10 pm, Fri & Sat-11 pm. **Reservations:** accepted. **Features:** The dragon roll served here has artistic impact and is a tasty meal. The presentation of appetizers and entrees shows careful attention to visual detail. Casual dress; beer & wine only. **Parking:** on-site. **Cards:** AX, DC, DS, MC, VI.   ♿M
Japanese

BREAD AND WINE   **Dinner:** $16-$25   **Phone:** 505/271-2676 `49`
♦♦♦   **Location:** Jct Candelaria Rd; northeast corner. 2740 Wyoming Blvd NE 87111. **Hours:** 5 pm-9 pm. Closed major holidays; also Sun & Mon. **Reservations:** suggested. **Features:** Tender osso buco melts in the mouth, and wine choices are many at the Continental-style eatery. Service shows a European flair. The owner's many years of experience are reflected in the finished product. Dressy casual; beer & wine only. **Parking:** on-site. **Cards:** DS, MC, VI.
Continental

BUCA DI BEPPO   **Lunch:** $9-$11   **Dinner:** $9-$11   **Phone:** 505/872-2822 `70`
♦♦ ♦♦   **Location:** I-40, exit 162, just n. 6520 Americas Pkwy NE 87110. **Hours:** 5 pm-10 pm, Fri & Sat noon-11 pm, Sun noon-10 pm. **Closed:** 11/23, 12/25. **Reservations:** suggested. **Features:** You'll find family sized portions here served in "immigrant Italian" style meant for 2-4 people, including salads, pasta, pizza and other traditional dishes, as well as fine Italian bread baked in-house. Dressy casual; cocktails. **Parking:** on-site. **Cards:** AX, CB, DC, DS, MC, VI.   🍸
Italian

CAFE' O   **Lunch:** $6-$9   **Dinner:** $6-$9   **Phone:** 505/858-0301 `39`
♦   **Location:** Jct Montgomery and Wyoming blvds, southwest corner; in Noble Collectibles Store, Le Morada Plaza Shopping Center. 8216 Montgomery Blvd NE 87109. **Hours:** 10 am-8 pm, Sun 11 am-6 pm. **Closed:** 7/4, 11/23, 12/25. **Reservations:** not accepted. **Features:** The sandwich shop shows a Vietnamese flair in such preparations as the Saigon sub, which has subtle, pleasing flavors. Various spring rolls also are served, as are American sandwich selections. Casual dress. **Parking:** on-site. **Cards:** AX, DS, MC, VI.
International

CAFE RIVIERA   **Lunch:** $4-$7   **Dinner:** $4-$7   **Phone:** 505/255-2800 `81`
♦   **Location:** Jct Carlisle Blvd and Constitution, just w. 3400 Constitution NE 87106. **Hours:** 7 am-9 pm, Fri & Sat-10 pm, Sun 9 am-8 pm. Closed major holidays. **Features:** The cafe has an earthy bookstore setting, with lots of reading material for patrons to peruse while their sandwich is being prepared. Also among choices are nifty salads and soups. Casual dress. **Parking:** on-site. **Cards:** MC, VI.
Mediterranean

(See map and index starting on p. 478)

CAFE' VOILA
French

Lunch: $6-$14   Dinner: $15-$22   Phone: 505/821-2666   (5)
Location: Jct Jefferson St and Paseo del Norte, just s. 7600 Jefferson St 87109. **Hours:** 11 am-2:30 & 5-9 pm; Sunday brunch 9 am-2 pm. Closed major holidays. **Reservations:** accepted. **Features:** Everything French is celebrated here. Quiches are flavorful, soups delightful and salads such as the nicoise are masterfully prepared. The cafe is just the place for lunch or a pleasant dinner. Casual dress; beer & wine only. **Parking:** on-site. **Cards:** AX, DC, DS, MC, VI.
(&M)

CAJUN KITCHEN
Cajun

Lunch: $8-$15   Dinner: $8-$15   Phone: 505-344-5355   (6)
Location: Jct Osuna Rd and Jefferson St, just e. 4500 Osuna Rd NE, Suite 155 87109. **Hours:** 11 am-2:30 & 5-9 pm, Sat from 5 pm. Closed major holidays; also Sun. **Reservations:** accepted. **Features:** The jambalaya is spicy, and these folks sure know how to cook shrimp, crawfish etouffee and catfish. The gumbo and po' boy sandwiches also are great. Casual dress; beer & wine only. **Parking:** on-site. **Cards:** AX, DC, DS, MC, VI.
(&M)

CAPO'S RISTORANTE ITALIANO
Italian

Lunch: $6-$11   Dinner: $7-$12   Phone: 505-242-2007   (83)
Location: Jct Lomas Blvd and 7th St NW, just w. 722 Lomas Blvd NW 87102. **Hours:** 11 am-9 pm, Fri & Sat-9:30 pm. Closed: 1/1, 11/23, 12/25; also Sun. **Reservations:** suggested. **Features:** Established in 1954, this restaurant offers fireside dining in a cozy setting. On the menu of traditional favorites are such dishes as veal, spaghetti, pizza and calzones. Casual dress. **Parking:** on-site. **Cards:** AX, CB, DC, DS, MC, VI.

CASA DE BENAVIDEZ NEW MEXICAN RESTAURANT
Mexican

Lunch: $6-$8   Dinner: $7-$14   Phone: 505/898-3311   (4)
Location: Jct 4th and El Pueblo, just s. 8032 4th St NW 87114. **Hours:** 9 am-8 pm, Thurs & Fri-9 pm, Sat 8 am-9 pm, Sun 8 am-3 pm. Closed major holidays. **Reservations:** accepted. **Features:** The garden patio setting, with a pond and lush foliage, is ideal for relaxing with a margarita and yummy Mexican food. Although the red chile salsa gets most of the buzz, the green chile is also great. Casual dress; cocktails; entertainment. **Parking:** on-site. **Cards:** AX, DS, MC, VI.
(Y) (\)

CERVANTE'S
(AAA)

Regional Mexican

Lunch: $6-$13   Dinner: $7-$15   Phone: 505/262-2253   (133)
Location: Jct San Pedro Blvd. 5801 Gibson Rd SE 87108. **Hours:** 11 am-midnight. Closed major holidays. **Reservations:** accepted. **Features:** Well-prepared New Mexican dishes—including excellent carne adovada, chiles rellenos and homemade tamales are featured at this locally popular restaurant. Served as an appetizer with tortilla chips, salsa commands real authority. Casual dress; cocktails. **Parking:** on-site. **Cards:** AX, DC, DS, MC, VI.
(Y) (\)

CHAMP RIVER BREWING COMPANY
Southwest American

Lunch: $7-$17   Dinner: $8-$17   Phone: 505/342-1800   (26)
Location: I-25, exit 229, just w. 4939 Pan American Frwy NE 87109. **Hours:** 11 am-10 pm, Fri-Sun to 11 pm. Closed: 11/23, 12/25. **Features:** A Santa Fe atmosphere and look, along with Northern New Mexico cuisine, give the impressive new restaurant and brewery its personality. The menu lists a good selection of sandwiches. Casual dress; cocktails. **Parking:** on-site. **Cards:** AX, DC, DS, MC, VI.
(Y)

CHEESE & COFFEE GOURMET DELI
Deli/Subs Sandwiches

Lunch: $6-$8   Phone: 505/883-1226   (55)
Location: Jct Menaul and Louisiana blvds, just n; in Encantada Square. 2679 Louisiana Blvd NE 87110. **Hours:** 11 am-3 pm, Sat 10 am-2 pm. Closed major holidays; also Sun. **Reservations:** accepted. **Features:** Those who visit might think they are in deli heaven. The selection of sandwiches is legion, service is quick and friendly, and they're generous with the coffee. Casual dress. **Parking:** on-site. **Cards:** CB, DC, MC, VI.

CHEZ AXEL
French

Dinner: $11-$21   Phone: 505/881-8104   (34)
Location: Corner of Montgomery and San Pedro, just e. 6209 Montgomery NE 87109. **Hours:** 5 pm-9 pm. Closed: 7/4, 11/23, 12/25; also Sun. **Reservations:** accepted. **Features:** The aromas of France—olive oil, anchovies, warm breads, fresh seafood, tomatoes and herbs—waft through the small, simply decorated dining area. Tempting accompaniments include crunchy French bread and a good selection of desserts and pastries. Casual dress; beer & wine only. **Parking:** on-site. **Cards:** DC, MC, VI.

CHINA STAR
Chinese

Lunch: $7-$9   Dinner: $7-$9   Phone: 505/299-3838   (94)
Location: I-40, exit 166 (Juan Tabo Blvd), 0.7 mi n; jct Lomas Blvd. 880 Juan Tabo Blvd NE 87123. **Hours:** 11 am-9 pm, Fri & Sat-10 pm. Closed: 11/23. **Features:** The eatery serves a full range of Oriental dishes on its humongous buffet: from sushi to Szechuan and everything in between. The dining room is well-decorated. Casual dress. **Parking:** on-site. **Cards:** AX, DC, DS, MC, VI.
(&M)

CHINA STAR SUPER BUFFET
Chinese

Lunch: $6   Dinner: $8   Phone: 505/880-9700   (37)
Location: Jct Montgomery and San Mateo blvds, just w; in Fiesta Crossings Center. 4710 Montgomery Blvd NE 87109. **Hours:** 11 am-9 pm, Fri & Sat-10 pm. Closed: 11/23. **Reservations:** accepted. **Features:** The elegantly decorated buffet restaurant serves a marvelous selection of Chinese dishes and also features colorful sushi. Salads and desserts complement the meal. Casual dress. **Parking:** on-site. **Cards:** AX, DC, DS, MC, VI.

CHRISTY MAE'S
American

Lunch: $5-$8   Dinner: $6-$10   Phone: 505/255-4740   (84)
Location: I-40, exit 162 westbound; exit 162A eastbound, 0.5 mi s on Louisiana Blvd to Lomas Blvd, 0.5 mi w to San Pedro Dr, then just n. 1400 San Pedro Dr NE 87110. **Hours:** 11 am-8 pm. Closed major holidays; also Sun. **Features:** The unpretentious family operation prepares home-style cooking and a good selection of soups, salads, sandwiches and pot pies. Breads and desserts, such as carrot cake, are prepared in house. Casual dress. **Parking:** on-site. **Cards:** AX, DS, MC, VI.

(See map and index starting on p. 478)

CHURCH STREET CAFE   Lunch: $6-$9   Dinner: $6-$9   Phone: 505/247-8522   [73]
AAA
Mexican   **Location:** I-40, exit 157A, 0.5 mi s to Mountain Rd, then just e; in Old Town; near church, just n. 2111 Church St NW 87104. **Hours:** 8 am-4 pm, Thurs-Sat to 8 pm. Closed: 1/1, 12/25. **Reservations:** accepted. **Features:** The 1706 adobe house also contains an art gallery. Tasty Mexican dishes, such as tamales, chiles rellenos and burritos, as well as a selection of sandwiches, are served in the dining room and on the patio. Beer & wine only. **Parking:** street. **Cards:** AX, DS, MC, VI.

CLASSIC GRILL   Lunch: $7-$15   Dinner: $8-$22   Phone: 505/881-0000   [60]
American   **Location:** I-40, exit 162, 0.8 mi w; in Sheraton Albuquerque Uptown. 2600 Louisiana Blvd NE 87110. **Hours:** 6 am-2 & 5-11 pm, Sat & Sun from 6:30 am. **Reservations:** suggested. **Features:** This locally popular restaurant has a warm and inviting atmosphere that's enhanced by rich dark woods and decorative architecture. Creative artwork intensifies its appeal. The varied menu offers sandwiches, pizza, pork, fish and steak. Dressy casual; cocktails. **Parking:** on-site. **Cards:** AX, CB, DS, MC, VI.

THE COOPERAGE   Lunch: $6-$9   Dinner: $12-$32   Phone: 505/255-1657   [91]
American   **Location:** Jct Lomas and Louisiana blvds, just e. 7220 Lomas Blvd NE 87110. **Hours:** 11 am-2:30 & 5-10 pm, Sat noon-2:30 & 5-11 pm, Sun noon-9 pm. Closed: 12/25. **Reservations:** accepted. **Features:** Known for its steaks, prime rib and well-stocked salad bar, the restaurant is a longtime favorite in the Northeast Heights. Its rustic setting and comfortable decor make it a relaxing place in which to enjoy a fine meal. Casual dress; cocktails. **Parking:** on-site. **Cards:** AX, DC, DS, MC, VI.

COPPER CANYON CAFE   Lunch: $6-$10   Dinner: $6-$10   Phone: 505/266-6318   [134]
Southwest American   **Location:** Jct San Mateo and Gibson blvds, just e. 5455 Gibson Blvd SE 87108. **Hours:** 5:30 am-8 pm, Sat from 7 am, Sun 7 am-3 pm. Closed: 1/1, 11/23, 12/25. **Features:** American and Southwestern food is at the heart of the menu at the fast-paced cafe, near Kirtland Air Force Base. Daily luncheon specials are tasty and feature generous portions. Casual dress; beer & wine only. **Parking:** on-site. **Cards:** AX, MC, VI.

THE COPPER LOUNGE   Lunch: $6-$10   Dinner: $6-$10   Phone: 505/242-7490   [107]
American   **Location:** I-25, exit 224B, s to Central Ave, then just e. 1504 Central Ave SE 87106. **Hours:** 11 am-2 am. Closed major holidays; also Sun. **Reservations:** accepted. **Features:** A recent addition between downtown and the University of New Mexico, the popular restaurant serves a grand selection of scrumptious sandwiches and luncheon specials. A lively lounge is on site. Portions are plentiful. Casual dress; cocktails. **Parking:** on-site. **Cards:** AX, DS, MC, VI.

THE COUNTY LINE OF ALBUQUERQUE   Dinner: $8-$20   Phone: 505/856-7477   [2]
Barbecue   **Location:** I-25, exit Tramway Blvd, 5 mi e. 9600 Tramway Blvd NE 87122. **Hours:** 5 pm-9 pm, Sat-4:30 pm-9:30 pm, Sun noon-8:30 pm. Closed: 11/23, 12/25. **Features:** While you sip your aperitif and nibble your hors d'oeuvres, you can enjoy the view of the city from Sandia Peak. Although the specialties are barbecue, you can order steak and seafood. Homemade bread, ice cream and cobbler round out the meal. Casual dress; cocktails. **Parking:** on-site. **Cards:** AX, DC, DS, MC, VI.

DESIGNER'S CAFE   Lunch: $4-$11   Dinner: $8-$15   Phone: 505/856-2233   [3]
American   **Location:** I-25, exit 233, 0.6 mi w. 4801 Alameda Blvd NE 87113. **Hours:** 7 am-8 pm, Sat-2 pm. Closed: 12/25; also Sun. **Features:** The cafe serves a fine roast pork loin with fluffy mashed potatoes, as well as tasty, freshly prepared soups. Casual dress. **Parking:** on-site. **Cards:** MC, VI.

DICKEY'S BARBECUE PIT   Lunch: $7-$12   Dinner: $8-$19   Phone: 505/345-2788   [28]
Barbecue   **Location:** I-25, exit 229, just w, then just s. 4811 Pan American NE 87109. **Hours:** 11 am-8:30 pm, Fri & Sat-9:30 pm. Closed: 11/23, 12/25. **Reservations:** accepted. **Features:** Real Texas-style barbecue is the main meal. Beef brisket is always well-prepared, and guests also will find some fine steaks, a good selection of microbrews and full bar service. Casual dress; beer & wine only. **Parking:** on-site. **Cards:** AX, DC, DS, MC, VI.

DISTRICT BAR & GRILL   Lunch: $6-$15   Dinner: $6-$15   Phone: 505/243-0003   [98]
International   **Location:** Jct 4th St and Central Ave, just n. 115 4th St NW 87102. **Hours:** 11 am-2 am, Sat from 5 pm. Closed: 1/1, 12/25; also Sun & Mon. **Reservations:** accepted. **Features:** The downtown lounge doubles as a busy lunch spot. The eclectic menu includes tapas, sandwiches and salads with an international accent. Dressy casual; cocktails. **Parking:** on-site (fee) and street. **Cards:** AX, DS, MC, VI.

EAST OCEAN CHINESE SEAFOOD RESTAURANT   Lunch: $4-$6   Dinner: $6-$12   Phone: 505/889-9315   [47]
Chinese   **Location:** Jct Candelaria Rd, just n. 3601 Carlisle Blvd NE 87110. **Hours:** 11 am-9:30 pm, Sun from 3 pm. Closed: 7/4, 11/23, 12/25. **Reservations:** accepted. **Features:** A favorite dining spot of the local Asian community, the restaurant prepares delicately flavored seafood dishes, as well as fiery Szechuan selections. This place also is known for its economical luncheon menu. Casual dress; beer & wine only. **Parking:** on-site. **Cards:** DS, MC, VI.

EL NORTENO   Lunch: $5-$8   Dinner: $5-$8   Phone: 505/256-1431   [128]
Mexican   **Location:** Just w of jct Louisiana. 6416 Zuni Rd SE 87108. **Hours:** 10 am-9 pm. Closed major holidays. **Reservations:** suggested. **Features:** This unpretentious eatery, festooned in Mexican beer flags and Juarez banners, serves a Baja cuisine. Its menu includes a savory selection of tacos including tongue and goat, chicken enchiladas, spicy sauteed shrimp, pollo, mole, cerveza and steamers. Casual dress; beer & wine only. **Parking:** on-site. **Cards:** AX, DS, MC, VI.

(See map and index starting on p. 478)

ELOY'S MEXICAN RESTAURANT
Mexican

Lunch: $6-$10   **Dinner:** $7-$10   **Phone:** 505/293-6018   (77)

Location: I-40, exit 164B, just n; in Bellhaven Commercial Center. 1508 Wyoming Blvd NE 87112. **Hours:** 11 am-8 pm, Fri & Sat-9 pm. Closed major holidays; also Sun. **Features:** A friendly, attentive staff greets you at this unpretentious family operation, and the restaurant's good selection of home-style recipes from Mexico and Northern New Mexico will not disappoint your appetite. They also serve a wide choice of beer and wine. Casual dress; beer & wine only. **Parking:** on-site. **Cards:** MC, VI.

EL PATIO DE ALBUQUERQUE
Mexican

Lunch: $5-$8   **Dinner:** $5-$8   **Phone:** 505/268-4245   (120)

Location: I-25, exit 224B, e to Harvard Dr, then just s. 142 Harvard Dr SE 87106. **Hours:** 11 am-9 pm, Fri & Sat-9:30 pm, Sun noon-9 pm. Closed: 11/23, 12/25. **Features:** University students, faculty and staff all dine at this modest restaurant that produces fine chili dishes, like carne adovada and blue corn enchiladas. Casual dress; beer & wine only. **Parking:** on-site.

EL PINTO
Mexican

Lunch: $7-$20   **Dinner:** $7-$20   **Phone:** 505/898-1771   (1)

Location: I-25, exit 234 (Tramway Rd), 3.5 mi w to SR 313 (becomes 4th St), then just s. 10500 4th St NW 87114. **Hours:** 11 am-9 pm, Fri & Sat-10 pm, Sun 10:30 am-9 pm. Closed: 1/1, 11/23, 12/25. **Features:** A Southwestern decor with fireplaces and indoor waterfalls dominates the many rooms of this local favorite established in 1962. They say the 600-seat patio is the state's largest. The menu offers basic New Mexican fare: enchiladas, burritos, chili ribs. Casual dress; cocktails. **Parking:** on-site. **Cards:** AX, DC, DS, MC, VI.

EL TACO TOTE
Mexican

Lunch: $5-$7   **Dinner:** $5-$7   **Phone:** 505/265-5188   (126)

Location: Jct Central Ave and Washington St, just e. 4701 Central Ave NE 87108. **Hours:** 10 am-10 pm. **Features:** The first US location of the famous chain from Mexico is the place to build your tacos the way you like them; a great selection of sauces and toppings are offered to make the basic taco a culinary work of art. Casual dress. **Parking:** on-site. **Cards:** DS, MC, VI.

FLYING STAR CAFE
American

Lunch: $7-$10   **Dinner:** $7-$10   **Phone:** 505/275-8311   (32)

Location: Just n of jct Montgomery. 4501 Juan Tabo Blvd NE 87111. **Hours:** 6 am-11 pm, Fri & Sat-11:30 pm. Closed: 11/23, 12/25. **Features:** This eatery has a trendy coffee-shop setting with an area for reading magazines while enjoying quiche, pizza, salad, stir-fry, sandwiches, baguettes and dessert. They have a good range of coffees and Italian soda, and seating on the outside deck. Casual dress; beer & wine only. **Parking:** on-site. **Cards:** AX, DS, MC, VI.

FOX AND HOUND SMOKEHOUSE & TAVERN
American

Lunch: $7-$15   **Dinner:** $7-$15   **Phone:** 505/344-9430   (14)

Location: I-25, exit 229, just w, then just n. 4301 The Lane @ 25 NE 87109. **Hours:** 11 am-2 am, Sun-midnight. **Reservations:** suggested. **Features:** The combination sports bar and restaurant is popular with the locals who work in the area. Pub food, salads and steaks are specialties of the house. Dressy casual; cocktails. **Parking:** on-site. **Cards:** AX, DS, MC, VI.

FRESH CHOICES
Italian

Lunch: $5-$7   **Dinner:** $5-$7   **Phone:** 505/242-6447   (97)

Location: I-25, exit 224B, 1 mi w; downtown. 402 Central SW 87102. **Hours:** 11 am-9 pm. Closed major holidays. **Reservations:** suggested. **Features:** Fresh Choices has a quaint bistro atmosphere with brick walls and hardwood floors. The buffet offers many items, such as salads, pizza, Italian meatballs, beef stroganoff, herb chicken, muffins, pudding, fresh pies and cakes. Casual dress; beer & wine only. **Parking:** street. **Cards:** AX, MC, VI.

FRONTIER RESTAURANT
Southwest American

Lunch: $4-$10   **Dinner:** $4-$10   **Phone:** 505/266-0550   (112)

Location: Corner of Central and Harvard aves, just e. 2400 Central Ave SW 87106. **Hours:** 24 hours. Closed: 1/1, 12/25. **Features:** Right across the street from the University of New Mexico campus, the well-known dining spot prepares jumbo homemade sweet rolls and a large selection of Southwestern dishes, burgers and sandwiches. Students love this place, which has been in business more than 30 years. Casual dress. **Parking:** on-site. **Cards:** DC, DS, MC, VI.

GARCIA'S KITCHEN
Mexican

Lunch: $4-$9   **Dinner:** $4-$9   **Phone:** 505/275-5812   (46)

Location: Southwest corner of Juan Tabo Blvd and Comanche. 3601 Juan Tabo Blvd NE 87111. **Hours:** 6:30 am-10 pm. Closed: 4/16, 11/23, 12/24, 12/25; also for dinner 12/31. **Reservations:** not accepted. **Features:** Green chili and carne adovada addictions have been born at Garcia's Kitchen. And many tortilla worshipers make pilgrimage here on a regular basis. This bright and flashy restaurant serves breakfast at any time of the day. Casual dress; beer & wine only. **Parking:** on-site. **Cards:** AX, DS, MC, VI.

GARDUNO'S OF MEXICO RESTAURANT & CANTINA
Mexican

Lunch: $8-$12   **Dinner:** $9-$17   **Phone:** 505/821-3030   (9)

Location: I-25, exit 230, just e on San Mateo Blvd, then just n. 5400 Academy Rd NE 87109. **Hours:** 11 am-10 pm, Fri & Sat-10:30 pm, Sun 10:30 am-9:30 pm; Sunday brunch. Closed: 11/23, 12/25. **Reservations:** accepted. **Features:** Garduno's has much to offer: an extensive menu, hearty portions of burritos, nachos, tacos, fajitas and enchiladas, and mariachi music Thursday-Saturday 6 pm-9 pm and Sunday noon-3 pm. This restaurant looks like a Mexican cantina inside and a hacienda outside. Casual dress; cocktails. **Parking:** on-site. **Cards:** AX, DC, DS, MC, VI.

GECKO'S BAR & TAPAS
American

Lunch: $5-$8   **Dinner:** $5-$8   **Phone:** 505/262-1848   (122)

Location: Jct Central Ave and Carlisle Blvd, southwest corner; in Nob Hill Center. 3500 Central Ave SE 87106. **Hours:** 11:30 am-2 am, Sun 11 am-midnight. Closed: 11/23, 12/25. **Features:** The friendly neighborhood lounge serves pub fare, such as hot wings, burgers and nachos, as well as a wide selection of tapas to go along with its spirits. In the Nob Hill area, this place is a favorite with University of New Mexico students. Casual dress; cocktails. **Parking:** on-site. **Cards:** AX, DS, MC, VI.

GEEZAMBONI'S RESTAURANT
Southwest American

Lunch: $5-$9   **Dinner:** $10-$20   **Phone:** 505/345-3354   (29)

Location: I-40, exit 157A, 2.3 mi n, southwest corner of Rio Grande Blvd and Griegos Rd. 3851 Rio Grande Blvd NW 87107. **Hours:** 11 am-2 & 5-9 pm, Sat from 5 pm. Closed major holidays; also Sun. **Reservations:** not accepted. **Features:** In a converted home, the lovely North Valley eatery presents a menu that incorporates such choices as New Mexican-style green chili stew, barbecued brisket, steaks and salads. Casual dress; beer & wine only. **Parking:** on-site. **Cards:** AX, MC, VI.

(See map and index starting on p. 478)

GIN MILL RESTAURANT & TAVERN   **Lunch:** $6-$10   **Dinner:** $6-$16   **Phone:** 505/821-6300   ⑧
American
Location: Jct Academy Rd; in Far North Shopping Center. 6300 San Mateo Blvd NE 87109. **Hours:** 11 am-midnight, Sat & Sun from 9 am. Closed major holidays. **Reservations:** accepted. **Features:** This cozy pub offers several variations of beefy burgers and traditional fiery New Mexican food. Offerings spotlight turkey, huge salads, meatloaf and green chili turkey stew. Their hearty sandwiches include fried egg as well as tuna and red onion. Casual dress; cocktails. **Parking:** on-site. **Cards:** AX, CB, DC, DS, MC, VI.

GOLD STREET CAFFE   **Lunch:** $5-$16   **Dinner:** $5-$16   **Phone:** 505/765-1633   ⑩③
American
Location: I-25, exit 224B, 1 mi w, just s, then just w. 218 Gold Ave SW 87102. **Hours:** 7 am-10 pm, Sun 8 am-2 pm, Mon 7 am-2 pm. Closed: 12/25. **Features:** A popular spot for morning coffee drinkers, the cozy cafe also serves imaginative daily luncheon specials. Delicious pastries are popular with folks from nearby downtown offices and businesses. Casual dress; beer & wine only. **Parking:** on-site (fee). **Cards:** AX, DC, DS, MC, VI.

GRAZE BY JENNIFER JAMES   **Lunch:** $12-$16   **Dinner:** $12-$16   **Phone:** 505/268-4729   ⑪⑨
Nouvelle American
Location: Jct Central Ave and Bryn Mawr. 3128 Central Ave 87106. **Hours:** 11 pm-10 pm, Fri & Sat-11 pm. Closed: 11/23, 12/25; also Sun & Mon. **Reservations:** accepted. **Features:** New in the Nob Hill area, the fine-dining establishment builds its eclectic menu on contemporary American cuisine. Imaginative presentations show refined combinations of tastes. The chef is a rising star in the field. Dressy casual; beer & wine only. **Parking:** street. **Cards:** AX, DS, MC, VI.

GREAT AMERICAN LAND & CATTLE COMPANY   **Lunch:** $5-$13   **Dinner:** $10-$27   **Phone:** 505/292-1510   ⑦①
Steak House
Location: Jct Indian School Rd; in Skyview Center. 1550 Tramway Blvd NE 87112. **Hours:** 11 am-2 & 5-9 pm, Fri-10 pm, Sat 4:30 pm-10 pm, Sun noon-8 pm. Closed: 11/23, 12/25; also Super Bowl Sun. **Features:** This friendly restaurant has beef so tasty and succulent that it vanishes from your plate to a chorus of "mmmms." It's home to a two-pound T-bone. Coleslaw, ranch-style beans, baked potato and a sparkling view of the city will complete your meal. Casual dress; cocktails. **Parking:** on-site. **Cards:** AX, CB, DC, DS, MC, VI.

THE GRUET STEAK HOUSE   **Dinner:** $15-$36   **Phone:** 505/256-9643   ⑪①
Nouvelle Steak House
Location: I-25, exit Central Ave, 2.5 mi e. 3201 Central Ave NE 87106. **Hours:** 5 pm-10 pm, Fri & Sat-11 pm. Closed: 11/23, 12/25. **Reservations:** suggested. **Features:** Built in an old fire station, this fine-dining restaurant is famous for crab cakes with roasted garlic vinaigrette, and grilled filet with red chili and crumbled feta cheese. The trendy upstairs bar has a great view of the mountains. Scrumptious desserts. Dressy casual; cocktails. **Parking:** on-site. **Cards:** AX, DC, DS, MC, VI. **Historic**

GYROS MEDITERRANEAN   **Lunch:** $4-$7   **Dinner:** $4-$7   **Phone:** 505/255-4401   ⑪⑤
Greek
Location: I-25, exit 224B, e to Harvard Ave, then just s. 106 Cornell SE 87106. **Hours:** 11 am-10 pm, Sat from 11:30 am, Sun noon-9 pm. Closed major holidays. **Features:** Across from the university and frequented by students and faculty alike, the restaurant prepares tasty Greek salad and good souvlaki. Don't leave without sampling the baklava. Casual dress; beer & wine only. **Parking:** on-site (fee). **Cards:** AX, DS, MC, VI.

HELLO DELI   **Lunch:** $5-$7   **Phone:** 505/889-3354   ⑤⓪
American
Location: Jct Carlisle Blvd and Candelaria Rd, just w. 3401 Candelaria Rd NE 87107. **Hours:** 7 am-3 pm, Sat & Sun from 8 am. Closed major holidays. **Features:** The popular quick-service eatery specializes in breakfast and lunch. In addition to a fine selection of salads, sandwiches and burgers, guests can order hearty breakfast items anytime. Casual dress. **Parking:** on-site. **Cards:** AX, MC, VI.

HIGH FINANCE   **Lunch:** $7-$10   **Dinner:** $16-$45   **Phone:** 505/243-9742
American
Location: I-25, exit 234, 5.5 mi e to Sandia Peak Tramway base terminal. 40 Tramway Rd 87122. **Hours:** 11 am-3 & 4:30-9 pm. Closed: 11/23. **Reservations:** suggested. **Features:** High Finance offers its cuisine on top of the 10,378-foot Sandia Peak—you'll enjoy a great view of the city. You reach this restaurant only by aerial tramway, with reduced ticket prices when you make reservations. Be prepared for a time-consuming meal. Casual dress; cocktails. **Parking:** on-site (fee). **Cards:** AX, DC, DS, MC, VI.

HIGH NOON RESTAURANT & SALOON   **Lunch:** $6-$10   **Dinner:** $13-$27   **Phone:** 505/765-1455   ⑦④
Regional American
Location: I-40, exit 157A, 0.5 mi s to Mountain Rd, then just e; in Old Town. 425 San Felipe NW 87104. **Hours:** 11 am-9:30 pm, Fri & Sat-10 pm, Sun noon-9 pm. Closed: 1/1, 12/25. **Reservations:** suggested. **Features:** High Noon's eclectic menu offers selections of wild game, certified Angus beef steak, seafood and New Mexican cuisine. Its decor features tri-cultures of northern New Mexico, and part of its structure is the original 250-year-old adobe building. You'll find leisurely paced dining here. Casual dress; cocktails. **Parking:** on-site. **Cards:** AX, DC, DS, MC, VI. **Historic**

HO-LO-MA CHINESE RESTAURANT   **Lunch:** $3-$5   **Dinner:** $5-$11   **Phone:** 505/296-1271   ⑤⑨
Chinese
Location: Jct Wyoming and Menaul Blvds, just e. 8624 Menaul Blvd NE 87112. **Hours:** 11:30 am-9:30 pm, Fri & Sat-10 pm. Closed major holidays. **Reservations:** accepted. **Features:** Generous portions of traditional Chinese fare—such as sweet and sour pork, chow mein and egg foo yong—are the order of the day. Prices are modest. Casual dress; beer & wine only. **Parking:** on-site. **Cards:** AX, DS, MC, VI.

HURRICANE'S CAFE'   **Lunch:** $3-$6   **Dinner:** $4-$8   **Phone:** 505/299-9017   ⑤③
Southwest American
Location: Jct Eubank Blvd and Candelaria Rd, just w; in East Dale Center. 2801 Eubank Blvd NE 87112. **Hours:** 6:30 am-7 pm, Fri & Sat-8 pm, Sun-3 pm. Closed: 4/16, 11/23, 12/25. **Reservations:** accepted. **Features:** Restaurant patrons can expect a disaster in the form of a signature dish called the disaster: a giant burrito filled with ground beef and beans, covered with French fries and smothered with fiery green chili. It's available in four sizes. Also on the menu are modestly priced burgers and sandwiches and great desserts. Casual dress. **Parking:** on-site. **Cards:** MC, VI.

(See map and index starting on p. 478)

IL VICINO
Pizza
Lunch: $7-$9 **Dinner:** $7-$9 **Phone:** 505/271-0882 [35]
Location: Jct Montgomery Blvd and Juan Tabo Rd. 11225 Montgomery Blvd NE 87111. **Hours:** 11 am-10 pm, Fri & Sat-11 pm. Closed: 11/23, 12/25. **Features:** Wood-oven pizza is the signature dish, but great sandwiches and salads also are served. Vino complements the meal. Casual dress; beer & wine only. **Parking:** on-site. **Cards:** DS, MC, VI.

INDIA PALACE
Indian
MC, VI.
Lunch: $8-$9 **Dinner:** $8-$20 **Phone:** 505/271-5009 [42]
Location: Jct Montgomery and Wyoming blvds, just s. 4410 Q Wyoming NE 87111. **Hours:** 11:30 am-2:30 & 5-10 pm. **Reservations:** suggested. **Features:** A daily luncheon buffet features exotic East Indian dishes such as tandoori and makhani chicken, sag paneer, and the lentil soup called dal. Dinner is more formal with elaborate lamb and seafood specialties. Casual dress; beer & wine only. **Parking:** on-site. **Cards:** AX, DS,

JERSEY JACK'S
American
Lunch: $6-$8 **Dinner:** $6-$8 **Phone:** 505/268-1130 [22]
Location: I-25, exit 229 (Jefferson St), just e. 4320 The 25 Way, #650 87109. **Hours:** 7 am-10 pm. Closed: 9/4, 11/23, 12/25. **Reservations:** accepted. **Features:** Popular with the folks who work in nearby offices, the eatery prepares interesting sandwich selections, salads and yummy desserts. Patrons also find a good selection of beer and soft drinks. Service is efficient and friendly. Casual dress. **Parking:** on-site.
Cards: AX, DC, DS, MC, VI.

KELLY'S BREWERY
American
Lunch: $7-$9 **Dinner:** $7-$9 **Phone:** 505/262-2739 [121]
Location: Jct Central and Wellesley aves. 3222 Central Ave SE 87106. **Hours:** 11 am-midnight, Thurs-Sat to 2 am. Closed major holidays. **Features:** A sunny street-side patio area greets guests at this pleasant setting for having drinks or dining with friends. Pub-style food is served with a grand selection of microbrewed beers. Casual dress; cocktails. **Parking:** street. **Cards:** AX, DS, MC, VI.

LA CREPE MICHEL
French
Lunch: $8-$11 **Dinner:** $16-$25 **Phone:** 505/242-1251 [76]
Location: Jct San Felipe and Central Ave, just n; in Old Town. 400 San Felipe NW, #C-2 87104. **Hours:** 11:30 am-2 & 6-9 pm, Sun-2 pm. Closed: 1/1, 11/23, 12/25; also Mon. **Reservations:** accepted. **Features:** Off the beaten path, the well-known Old Town cafe serves fine French cuisine. The crepes are fabulous. Casual dress; beer & wine only. **Parking:** street. **Cards:** MC, VI.

LA ESQUINA RESTAURANTE
Mexican
rise, it has ample garage parking. Casual dress; cocktails. **Parking:** on-site. **Cards:** AX, CB, DC, DS, MC, VI.
Lunch: $6-$8 **Dinner:** $6-$9 **Phone:** 505/242-3432 [89]
Location: 3rd St and Tijeras Ave, lower level. 20 1st Plaza Ctr NW, Galeria 60 87102. **Hours:** 11 am-2:30 pm, Fri 11 am-4 & 5-8:30 pm. Closed major holidays; also Sat & Sun. **Reservations:** suggested, Fri. **Features:** Locals love the Southwestern cuisine served in a comfortable atmosphere. Known best for its blue corn enchiladas, this Mexican restaurant also has a nice dessert selection. Located downtown in the lower level of a high-

LA FONDA DEL BOSQUE
Mexican
biscochitos. Casual dress. **Parking:** on-site. **Cards:** MC, VI.
Lunch: $6-$8 **Phone:** 505/247-9480 [130]
Location: Jct Avenida Cesar Chavez and 4th St, just s. 1701 4th St SW 87102. **Hours:** 7:30 am-3 pm, Sat from 8 am, Sun from 9 am. Closed major holidays; also Mon. **Reservations:** accepted. **Features:** In the Hispanic Cultural Center, the cafeteria-style restaurant makes fine examples of popular New Mexican cuisine. Guests can taste great carne adovada, posole and superior red salsa, as well as desserts such as natillas and

LA HACIENDA RESTAURANT & CANTINA
Mexican
MC, VI.
Lunch: $6-$9 **Dinner:** $6-$15 **Phone:** 505/271-0444 [131]
Location: I-40, exit 167 (Tramway Blvd), just s, then just w. 12935 Central Ave NE 87123. **Hours:** 7 am-9:30 pm, Fri & Sat-10 pm; Sunday brunch. Closed: 11/23, 12/25. **Reservations:** accepted. **Features:** New on the east Central restaurant scene, the eatery prepares recipes proven at the Old Town location. A lively lounge and tasty Mexican fare can be expected. Casual dress; cocktails. **Parking:** on-site. **Cards:** AX, DC, DS,

LANDRY'S SEAFOOD HOUSE
Seafood
Lunch: $9-$12 **Dinner:** $14-$19 **Phone:** 505/875-0101 [27]
Location: I-25, exit 229 (Jefferson St), just e. 5001 Jefferson St NE 87109. **Hours:** 11 am-10 pm, Fri & Sat-11 pm. Closed: 11/23. **Reservations:** accepted. **Features:** An ideal spot for healthy seafood dinners and special occasions, the restaurant produces a wonderful clam chowder. Menu selections come from all the world's oceans. Dressy casual; cocktails. **Parking:** on-site. **Cards:** AX, CB, DC, DS, MC, VI.

LA PLACITA ON THE PLAZA
Mexican
lettuce. Casual dress; cocktails. **Parking:** street. **Cards:** AX, CB, DC, DS, MC, VI.
Lunch: $6-$8 **Dinner:** $7-$10 **Phone:** 505/247-2204 [78]
Location: I-40, exit 157A (Rio Grande Blvd), 0.5 mi s to Romero St, then just e on The Plaza. 206 San Felipe NW 87104. **Hours:** 11 am-8:30 pm. Closed: 1/1, 11/23, 12/25. **Reservations:** accepted. **Features:** New Mexican food is the specialty at this local favorite on the Plaza in Old Town. The Navajo taco is made with Indian fried bread, covered with a wonderful, creamy red chili sauce and topped with melted cheese and shredded

LA SALITA
Mexican
diced tomatoes and melted cheese. The chile salsa is superlative. Casual dress. **Parking:** on-site. **Cards:** MC, VI.
Lunch: $5-$8 **Dinner:** $5-$8 **Phone:** 505/299-9968 [85]
Location: Jct Lomas and Eubank blvds, just n. 1217 Eubank Blvd NE 87112. **Hours:** 11 am-2 & 5-8 pm, Fri-8:30 pm, Mon-2 pm. Closed: 11/23, 12/25; also Sat & Sun. **Features:** A longtime favorite Northeast Heights dining spot, the restaurant serves generous portions of freshly prepared Mexican favorites, including stuffed sopapillas, enchiladas and burritos. Dinners are humongous and colorfully decorated with chopped lettuce,

(See map and index starting on p. 478)

LOS CUATES DEL NORTE
Lunch: $6-$9   **Dinner:** $8-$14   **Phone:** 505/237-2800   (90)
Mexican
Location: Jct Menaul Blvd and Wyoming, just w. 8700 Menaul Blvd NE 87123. **Hours:** 11 am-9 pm. Closed: 12/25. **Features:** This is a large and locally popular restaurant, and you may experience a wait before you can sample its New Mexican cuisine of fajitas, dark red and spicy salsa, hefty burger-filled burritos, chicken enchiladas on corn tortilla or refried beans and rice. Casual dress; beer & wine only. **Parking:** on-site.
Cards: AX, DS, MC, VI.

LOUIE'S PUB & GRILL
Lunch: $5-$8   **Dinner:** $5-$8   **Phone:** 505/881-5333   (57)
Southwest American
Location: I-40, exit 161, just n to Menaul Blvd, then just e. 5603 Menaul Blvd NE 87110. **Hours:** 11 am-midnight, Sun noon-9 pm. Closed major holidays. **Features:** A lively lounge patronized by folks from the surrounding neighborhood, the eatery also serves fine sandwiches, appetizers and salads. Beverages include a large selection of draft beers, wine and liquors. Casual dress; cocktails. **Parking:** on-site. **Cards:** AX, DS, MC, VI.

LOYOLA'S FAMILY RESTAURANT
Lunch: $4-$7   **Dinner:** $4-$7   **Phone:** 505/268-6478   (127)
Mexican
Location: Jct Central and Adams aves. 4500 Central Ave SE 87108. **Hours:** 6 am-2:30 pm, Sat-1:30 pm, Sun 7 am-1:30 pm. Closed: 1/1, 4/16, 12/25; also Mon. **Reservations:** accepted. **Features:** Patrons can dine on both American and New Mexican fare. Reasonable prices, generous portions and exceptional red chili are hallmarks of the neighborhood eatery. Casual dress. **Parking:** on-site. **Cards:** DC, MC, VI.

LUIGI'S ITALIAN RESTAURANT & PIZZERIA
Lunch: $5-$8   **Dinner:** $7-$13   **Phone:** 505/343-0466   (10)
Italian
Location: Jct Solar. 6225 4th St NW 87107. **Hours:** 11 am-9 pm, Fri-10 pm, Sat noon-10 pm, Sun noon-9 pm. Closed major holidays. **Features:** Fare includes pizzas, pasta, shrimp scampi, chicken Florentine and eggplant, plus sandwiches and desserts. Casual dress; beer & wine only. **Parking:** on-site. **Cards:** AX, DC, DS, MC, VI.

MAC'S LA SIERRA RESTAURANT
Lunch: $4-$12   **Dinner:** $4-$12   **Phone:** 505/836-1212   (113)
Southwest American
Location: I-40, exit 155 (Coors Blvd), s to Central Ave, then just e. 6217 Central Ave NW 87105. **Hours:** 5 am-midnight, Sun 6 am-10 pm. Closed: 1/1, 12/25. **Features:** Long a westside landmark, Mac's La Sierra features great steak in the rough, some very tasty Mexican food and a stellar Boston cream pie. Casual dress; beer & wine only. **Parking:** on-site. **Cards:** AX, DC, DS, MC, VI.

M & J RESTAURANT/SANITARY TORTILLA FACTORY
Lunch: $5-$8   **Phone:** 505/243-2444   (108)
Mexican
Location: Just s of jct Central Ave; downtown. 403 2nd St SW 87102. **Hours:** 9 am-4 pm. Closed: Sat & Sun. **Reservations:** accepted. **Features:** Authentic Mexican recipes are used to create this restaurant's homemade flour and corn tortillas, the specialties of the house. The menu offers daily specials. Watercolors and other paintings by various local artists complement the decor. Casual dress. **Parking:** on-site.
Cards: MC, VI.

MANNIE'S FAMILY RESTAURANT
Lunch: $5-$8   **Dinner:** $5-$9   **Phone:** 505/265-1669   (116)
American
Location: Jct Central Ave and Girard. 2900 Central Ave SE 87106. **Hours:** 6 am-9 pm. Closed: 11/23, 12/25. **Reservations:** accepted. **Features:** The longtime campus favorite has been serving folks in the University of New Mexico area for more than 30 years. Moderately priced American and New Mexican food is plated in generous portions. Service is fast. Casual dress; beer & wine only. **Parking:** on-site. **Cards:** AX, DS, MC, VI.

MARIO'S PIZZERIA & RISTORANTE
Lunch: $6-$15   **Dinner:** $6-$15   **Phone:** 505/883-4414   (65)
Italian
Location: I-40, exit 162 (Louisiana Blvd), 0.5 mi n to Indian School Rd, 1 mi w, then just n. 2401 San Pedro Blvd NE 87110. **Hours:** 11 am-9:30 pm, Fri & Sat-10 pm, Sun noon-9:30 pm. Closed major holidays. **Reservations:** accepted. **Features:** The popular neighborhood dining spot has established a loyal following. On the menu are fine pizzas, calzones and pasta dishes. Casual dress; beer & wine only. **Parking:** on-site. **Cards:** AX, CB, DC, DS, MC, VI.

McGRATH'S RESTAURANT & BAR
Lunch: $6-$10   **Dinner:** $16-$24   **Phone:** 505/843-2700   (95)
Continental
Location: I-25, exit 224B, 0.5 mi w; downtown; in Hyatt Regency Albuquerque. 330 Tijeras Ave NW 87102. **Hours:** 6:30 am-10:30 pm. **Reservations:** suggested. **Features:** An upscale downtown eatery, located in one of the city's finest hotels, McGrath's is well known among the many fine restaurants that dot the area. Very popular with the leaders of the business and governmental organizations whose offices are nearby, it's also a favorite of the affluent visitors who are guests at the Hyatt Regency that shares the location. Dressy casual; cocktails. **Parking:** on-site (fee) and valet. **Cards:** AX, CB, DC, DS, JC, MC, VI.

MILLY'S RESTAURANT
Lunch: $5-$7   **Phone:** 505/884-0707   (54)
Southwest American
Location: Jct Candelaria Rd and Princeton Ave. 2100 Candelaria Rd NE 87107. **Hours:** 7 am-2 pm, Fri-3 pm. Closed major holidays. **Reservations:** accepted. **Features:** Hearty breakfasts and lunches are priced moderately. Enticing daily specials such as meatloaf are served with mashed potatoes, gravy and a vegetable. The sandwich selection is substantial. Brownies make a great dessert. Casual dress. **Parking:** on-site. **Cards:** AX, DC, DS, MC, VI.

MIMI'S CAFE
Lunch: $7-$11   **Dinner:** $10-$15   **Phone:** 505/341-0300   (19)
California
Location: I-25, exit 229, just e. 4316 The 25 Way 87109. **Hours:** 7 am-11 pm. Closed: 12/25. **Features:** California cuisine is the specialty. Featured is a large selection of breakfast items, sandwiches, salads and pasta, chicken and meat dishes prepared in a range of styles from American to Italian to Asian. Casual dress; cocktails. **Parking:** on-site. **Cards:** AX, DS, MC, VI.

(See map and index starting on p. 478)

MIMMO'S RISTORANTE & PIZZERIA
Italian
Lunch: $7-$9   **Dinner:** $6-$15   **Phone:** 505/831-4191   48
Location: I-40, exit 155, just n; in Ladera Center. 3301 Coors Blvd NW 87120. **Hours:** 11 am-9 pm, Fri-10 pm, Sat noon-10 pm, Sun noon-9 pm. **Closed:** 1/1, 11/23, 12/25. **Reservations:** accepted. **Features:** A luncheon buffet to die for is served every day at Mimmo's. Try the lasagna, or the pizza, or better yet try a little of everything — it's all tasty. Casual dress; beer & wine only. **Parking:** on-site. **Cards:** AX, CB, DC, DS, MC, VI.

MING DYNASTY
Chinese
Lunch: $6-$7   **Dinner:** $7-$10   **Phone:** 505/296-0298   75
Location: Jct Eubank Blvd and Indian School Rd, just s. 1551 Eubank Blvd NE 87112. **Hours:** 11 am-2 & 4:30-10 pm, Fri & Sat-11 pm, Sun 11 am-11 pm. **Closed:** Tues. **Features:** This traditional US-style Chinese restaurant is complete with a dim sum lunch and a comfortable, ethnically decorated dining room. Casual dress; beer & wine only. **Parking:** on-site. **Cards:** AX, DS, MC, VI.

MONROE'S RESTAURANT
Mexican
Lunch: $5-$9   **Dinner:** $8-$13   **Phone:** 505/881-4224   21
Location: I-25, exit 230 (San Mateo Blvd), 0.4 mi s, then just e. 6051 Osuna Rd NE 87109. **Hours:** 11 am-9 pm, Sat & Sun from 9 am. **Closed:** 7/4, 11/23, 12/25. **Reservations:** accepted. **Features:** Long a popular dining spot for those who enjoy New Mexican food, the restaurant produces local favorites, as well as some seafood dishes popular along the Mexican coast. Casual dress; beer & wine only. **Parking:** on-site. **Cards:** AX, DC, DS, MC, VI.

MONTE CARLO STEAKHOUSE
Steak House
Lunch: $7-$19   **Dinner:** $7-$19   **Phone:** 505/831-2444   93
Location: Jct Central Ave and Tingley Beach Rd, just w of Rio Grande Bridge. 3916 Central Ave SW 87105. **Hours:** 11 am-10 pm, Thurs-Sat to 11 pm. **Closed:** 11/23, 12/25; also Sun. **Reservations:** accepted. **Features:** The neighborhood lounge and grill serves generous cuts of beef, well-prepared New Mexican dishes and a good selection of sandwiches. Patrons can enjoy a favorite drink in the friendly lounge environment. Casual dress; cocktails. **Parking:** on-site. **Cards:** AX, DC, DS, MC, VI.

MYKONOS CAFE & TAVERNA
Greek
Lunch: $7-$13   **Dinner:** $7-$15   **Phone:** 505/291-1116   15
Location: South of convergence of Eubank and Juan Tabo blvds. 5900 Eubank Blvd NE, Suite E-18 87111. **Hours:** 11 am-9 pm, Wed-Sat to 10 pm. **Closed** major holidays. **Reservations:** accepted. **Features:** The popular, family-operated restaurant features traditional Greek dishes, such as moussaka, pastitsio and spanakopita. Deftly prepared from an old family recipe, the avyolemono soup, with its lemony flavor and interesting texture, is particularly pleasing. Dressy casual; cocktails. **Parking:** on-site. **Cards:** AX, DC, MC, VI.

NICK'S CROSSROADS CAFE
Greek
Lunch: $4-$7   **Phone:** 505/242-8369   99
Location: Jct 4th St and Central Ave, just s. 400 Central SW 87102. **Hours:** 7 am-4 pm. **Closed** major holidays; also Sat & Sun. **Features:** The convenient downtown breakfast and lunch eatery prepares a great breakfast burrito with green chile, egg and bacon. A memorable lunch choice is souvlaki supreme. Casual dress. **Parking:** on-site (fee) and street. **Cards:** AX, MC, VI.

OLYMPIA CAFE
Greek
Lunch: $4-$10   **Dinner:** $4-$10   **Phone:** 505/266-5222   114
Location: Corner of Yale Blvd and Central Ave, just e. 2210 Central Ave SE 87106. **Hours:** 11 am-10 pm, Sat from noon. **Closed** major holidays; also Sun. **Features:** This fast-paced cafe produces copious amounts of gyro, mousaka, Greek oven-baked chicken, and all the sides, like browned potatoes, rice and salad to accompany the meal. Casual dress; beer & wine only. **Parking:** street. **Cards:** DS, MC, VI.

ORCHID THAI CUISINE
Thai
Lunch: $5-$10   **Dinner:** $7-$12   **Phone:** 505/265-4047   125
Location: Jct Central Ave and Graceland, southeast corner. 4300 Central Ave SE 87108. **Hours:** 11 am-10 pm, Sun from 5 pm. **Closed:** 7/4, 11/23, 12/25. **Reservations:** accepted. **Features:** Traditional menu offerings range from delicately flavored dishes to fiery hot renditions. Guests can be sure what they order will be flavorful, colorful and exotic. Try the Thai iced tea. Casual dress; beer & wine only. **Parking:** on-site. **Cards:** AX, DC, DS, MC, VI.

ORTEGA'S MEXICAN RESTAURANT & GRILL
Regional Mexican
Lunch: $5-$7   **Dinner:** $6-$9   **Phone:** 505/298-0223   45
Location: Jct Comanche Rd and Wyoming Blvd, just n. 3617 Wyoming Blvd NE 87111. **Hours:** 11 am-9 pm. **Closed** major holidays; also Sun. **Features:** The neighborhood restaurant builds its menu on Mexican favorites, including chiles rellenos, enchiladas, burritos, tamales, tacos and fajitas. The Navajo taco with either red or green chili is especially good. Casual dress; beer & wine only. **Parking:** on-site. **Cards:** AX, MC, VI.

OWL CAFE
American
Lunch: $4-$7   **Dinner:** $4-$7   **Phone:** 505/291-4900   92
Location: I-40, exit 165, just n. 800 Eubank Ave NE 87123. **Hours:** 7 am-10 pm, Fri & Sat-11 pm. **Closed:** 11/23, 12/25. **Features:** The Owl Cafe delivers its unique green-chili cheeseburgers in a 50s diner setting complete with tableside jukeboxes and soda-jerk malts. It also offers a wide-ranging menu of stir-fry veggies, red-chili pork tamales and chicken-fried steak. Casual dress; beer & wine only. **Parking:** on-site. **Cards:** AX, CB, DC, DS, MC, VI.

PADILLA'S MEXICAN KITCHEN
Mexican
Lunch: $5-$8   **Dinner:** $5-$8   **Phone:** 505/262-0115   69
Location: Corner of Indian School Rd and Girard Ave NE, just s. 1510 Girard Ave NE 87106. **Hours:** 11 am-7:45 pm. **Closed** major holidays; also Sun. **Features:** New Mexican favorites—such as carne adovada, tamales and green chili enchiladas stuffed with chicken or beef—are among dishes prepared at the popular eatery, a neighborhood fixture for many years. Casual dress; beer & wine only. **Parking:** on-site.

PAISANO'S ITALIAN RESTAURANT
Italian
Lunch: $7-$9   **Dinner:** $8-$17   **Phone:** 505/298-7541   68
Location: I-40, exit 165 (Eubank Blvd), 1.4 mi n. 1935 Eubank Blvd NE 87112. **Hours:** 11 am-2:30 & 5-10 pm, Sat & Sun from 5 pm. **Closed:** 11/23, 12/25. **Features:** Patrons can unwind on the romantic patio to nosh on colorful traditional dishes, such as green spinach ravioli accented by tasty red marinara sauce. The wine selection is good. Dressy casual; beer & wine only. **Parking:** on-site. **Cards:** DC, MC, VI.

(See map and index starting on p. 478)

PANCHO'S MEXICAN BUFFET Lunch: $4-$6 Dinner: $5-$7 Phone: 505/888-1332   **43**
 Mexican
Location: Jct San Mateo and Montgomery blvds, southwest corner. 4301 San Mateo Blvd NE 87110. **Hours:** 11 am-9 pm, Fri & Sat-9:30 pm. Closed: 11/23, 12/25. **Features:** Included among Mexican specialties are three types of enchiladas to choose from, or better yet, to try. Bring an appetite because it's hard to leave hungry. Casual dress. **Parking:** on-site. **Cards:** AX, DC, DS, MC, VI.

PANZA LLENA CAFE Lunch: $4-$6 Phone: 505/884-1199 **51**
Southwest American
Location: Corner of Candelaria Rd and Girard Ave, just n. 3225 Girard Blvd NE 87107. **Hours:** 6 am-2 pm. Closed major holidays; also Sat & Sun. **Reservations:** accepted. **Features:** Patrons should arrive early for lunch to the popular yet unpretentious eatery, as the daily specials sell out quickly. Fried chicken served on Thursday is worth the wait. Also worthwhile are the scrumptious, freshly prepared desserts. Casual dress. **Parking:** on-site.

PAPA FELIPE'S Lunch: $6-$8 Dinner: $6-$10 Phone: 505/292-8877 **61**
Mexican
Location: Jct Eubank and Menaul blvds, just e. 9800 Menaul Blvd NE 87112. **Hours:** 11 am-9 pm. Closed major holidays. **Reservations:** accepted. **Features:** A welcoming cantina lounge and pleasant, ethnic look are combined with well-prepared food and efficient service at the long-popular dining spot. Try the fresh sopaipillas, and save room for flan. Casual dress; cocktails. **Parking:** on-site. **Cards:** AX, DS, MC, VI.

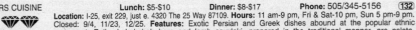

PARS CUISINE Lunch: $5-$10 Dinner: $8-$17 Phone: 505/345-5156 **132**
Mediterranean
Location: I-25, exit 229, just e. 4320 The 25 Way 87109. **Hours:** 11 am-9 pm, Fri & Sat-10 pm, Sun 5 pm-9 pm. Closed: 9/4, 11/23, 12/25. **Features:** Exotic Persian and Greek dishes abound at the popular ethnic restaurant. Both chelo-kebab barg and lamb souvlaki, prepared in the traditional manner, are palate-pleasing. Dressy casual; beer & wine only; entertainment. **Parking:** on-site. **Cards:** AX, DS, MC, VI.

PAUL'S MONTEREY INN Lunch: $6-$10 Dinner: $9-$24 Phone: 505/294-1461 **86**
American
Location: Just n of jct Lomas Blvd. 1000 Juan Tabo NE 87112. **Hours:** 11 am-2:30 & 5-10 pm, Fri & Sat-11 pm. Closed major holidays; also Sun. **Reservations:** suggested. **Features:** Thick and juicy steaks, prime rib, surf and turf, ribs and shrimp—all served in ample portions—make Paul's Monterey Inn a favorite with the locals. The ambience and dark upholstery and wall coverings may remind you of a lounge from the 1960s. Casual dress; cocktails. **Parking:** on-site. **Cards:** AX, CB, DC, DS, MC, VI.

PEI WEI Lunch: $6-$9 Dinner: $6-$9 Phone: 505/883-1570 **67**
Chinese
Location: 0.3 mi n; on west side of street. 2201 Louisiana Blvd NE 87110. **Hours:** 11 am-9 pm, Fri & Sat-10 pm. Closed: 11/23, 12/25. **Features:** The Chinese eatery offers quick service in a pleasant dining room. Included on the imaginative menu are some modern takes on traditional favorites. Casual dress; beer & wine only. **Parking:** on-site. **Cards:** AX, DC, DS, MC, VI.

PERENNIALS RESTAURANT Lunch: $6-$7 Dinner: $6-$15 Phone: 505/888-5800 **18**
American
Location: Jct San Mateo and Osuna blvds, northwest corner; in Fiesta del Norte Center. 6001 San Mateo Blvd NE #B-5 87109. **Hours:** 7 am-2 & 5-9 pm, Sun-2 pm. Closed: 4/16, 12/25; also Mon. **Reservations:** accepted. **Features:** A pleasant, light and bright dining room and diet-conscious menu items are focuses at the eatery. The menu comprises tasty soups, salads and sandwiches, such as the Colonel Chris burger made with Angus beef. There's also a nice selection of wines. Casual dress; beer & wine only. **Parking:** on-site. **Cards:** AX, DS, MC, VI.

P.F. CHANG'S CHINA BISTRO Lunch: $7-$13 Dinner: $9-$18 Phone: 505/344-8282 **16**
Chinese
Location: I-25, exit 230, just w. 4440 The 25 Way NE 87109. **Hours:** 11 am-11 pm, Fri & Sat-midnight. Closed: 11/23, 12/25. **Reservations:** suggested. **Features:** The high-energy bistro's menu reveals a blend of traditional and evolving Chinese fare. The chic dining room is appointed in an Oriental style. Dressy casual; cocktails. **Parking:** on-site. **Cards:** AX, DC, DS, MC, VI.

PLAZA EATERY Lunch: $3-$6 Phone: 505/768-3539 **87**
Southwest American
Location: Jct Marquette Ave and 4th St. One Civic Plaza 87102. **Hours:** 7 am-4 pm. Closed major holidays; also Sat & Sun. **Features:** Breakfast and lunch are served in the cheerful, rapidly paced cafe inside City Hall. Salads, soups and sandwiches, as well as desserts, are produced in house. Casual dress. **Parking:** on-site (fee). **Cards:** MC, VI.

POWDRELL'S BARBECUE HOUSE Lunch: $6-$10 Dinner: $6-$10 Phone: 505/298-6766 **129**
Barbecue
Location: 0.5 mi e of jct Eubank Ave. 11301 Central Ave 87123. **Hours:** 10:30 am-8 pm, Fri & Sat-9 pm. Closed major holidays; also Sun. **Features:** You'll enjoy this popular barbecue house with its deep, smoky, hickory flavors. Sample the pork, ribs, beef, Polish and hot links, or chicken, by the pound or the platter. Meals are served in a casual setting, where napkins are, thankfully, plentiful. Casual dress. **Parking:** on-site. **Cards:** AX, CB, DS, MC, VI.

QUARTERS BAR-B-QUE Lunch: $7-$12 Dinner: $10-$24 Phone: 505/299-9864 **33**
Regional American
Location: I-40, exit 164B eastbound, 3 mi n; exit 164C westbound, 0.5 mi w on Lomas Blvd, then 3.3 mi n. 4516 Wyoming Blvd NE 87111. **Hours:** 11 am-9 pm. Closed: 4/16, 11/23, 12/25; also Sun. **Features:** Quarters is widely known for barbecued spare ribs, beef and hot links, but don't pass up the chance to try the Alaskan King crab legs. Plan to save room for dessert, especially tempting to those with a sweet tooth are their mud pie and cheesecake. Casual dress; cocktails. **Parking:** on-site. **Cards:** AX, DC, DS, MC, VI.

QUEEN OF SUSHI-PATTAYA THAI Lunch: $6-$10 Dinner: $8-$15 Phone: 505/271-4830 **82**
Thai
Location: I-40, exit 165, just n on west side. 1225 Eubank Blvd NE 87112. **Hours:** 11 am-3 & 5-9 pm, Fri-9:30 pm, Sat noon-9:30 pm, Sun noon-9 pm. Closed: 1/1, 11/23, 12/25. **Reservations:** accepted. **Features:** Thai food, as mild or spicy as guests desire, accompanied by fluffy rice is the order of the day at the friendly neighborhood eatery. Curries are colorful and tasty. The Thai iced tea's smooth taste will please. Casual dress; beer & wine only. **Parking:** on-site. **Cards:** AX, DC, DS, MC, VI.

(See map and index starting on p. 478)

RAGIN' SHRIMP
Cajun
Lunch: $7-$9   **Dinner:** $7-$13   **Phone:** 505/254-1544   (117)
Location: I-40, exit 160, 1 mi s on Carlisle Blvd at Copper Ave. 3619 Copper Ave NE 87108. **Hours:** 11 am-2 & 5-9 pm, Fri-10 pm, Sat 4 pm-10 pm, Sun 4 pm-9 pm. Closed major holidays. **Reservations:** accepted. **Features:** The small, chic, Nob Hill eatery specializes in huge gulf shrimp served over rice with Cajun sauce. Also delicious are the jambalaya, chicken breast, pork tenderloin, pasta dishes and French bread. Ragin' dipping sauce complements the entrees. Casual dress; beer & wine only. **Parking:** on-site. **Cards:** AX, DS, MC, VI.

RALLIS 4TH STREET PUB & GRILL
Southwest American
Lunch: $6-$10   **Dinner:** $6-$10   **Phone:** 505/243-1093   (96)
Location: I-25, exit 224B, 0.6 mi w near Civic Plaza; just s of City Hall. 109 4th St NW 87102. **Hours:** 6 am-2 am, Sat & Sun from 9:30 am. Closed: 11/23, 12/25. **Reservations:** accepted. **Features:** Centrally located downtown, this eatery is a favorite of the local business folk, who enjoy the daily luncheon specials, sandwiches and soups produced here. Casual dress; cocktails. **Parking:** street. **Cards:** AX, MC, VI.

RANCHER'S CLUB OF NEW MEXICO
American
Lunch: $10-$26   **Dinner:** $25-$40   **Phone:** 505/884-2500   (63)
Location: I-40, exit 160, just n to Menaul Blvd, then 1 mi w; in Hilton Albuquerque. 1901 University NE 87102. **Hours:** 11:30 am-2 & 5:30-10 pm, Fri-10:30 pm, Sat 5:30 pm-10:30 pm, Sun 5 pm-9 pm. Closed major holidays. **Reservations:** required. **Features:** A fine dining restaurant with an elegant lounge and dining room, that at the same time reflects a ranch motif, yet displays a cultivated, upscale ambience. The house specializes in offering the finest steak and seafood available, grilled over exotic woods and served by a professional staff that is well known for their polish and refinement. Dressy casual; cocktails; entertainment. **Parking:** on-site (fee) and valet. **Cards:** AX, DC, DS, MC, VI.

THE RANGE CAFE
Southwest American
Lunch: $5-$16   **Dinner:** $5-$16   **Phone:** 505/293-2633   (44)
Location: Jct Montgomery and Wyoming blvds, just s. 4200 Wyoming Blvd NE 87111. **Hours:** 7:30 am-9 pm. Closed: 11/23, 12/25. **Features:** The colorful cafe features some of the best dishes of two cultures. In addition to spicy New Mexican food, such as green chili enchiladas, the menu includes good old American food and sandwiches. Casual dress; beer & wine only. **Parking:** on-site. **Cards:** AX, DS, MC, VI.

RICHARD'S MEXICAN RESTAURANT
Mexican
Lunch: $5-$8   **Phone:** 505/881-1039   (56)
Location: Jct Carlisle Blvd, just w; in American Square. 3301 Menaul Blvd NE, Suite 1 87107. **Hours:** 11 am-3:30 pm. Closed major holidays; also Sun. **Features:** Heart-healthy New Mexican cuisine is the specialty, and traditional favorites are prepared to be low in cholesterol and fat but high on flavor and taste. Try the green chili chicken enchiladas. Casual dress; beer & wine only. **Parking:** on-site. **Cards:** AX, DC, DS, MC, VI.

ROBB'S RIBBS
Barbecue
Lunch: $7-$15   **Dinner:** $7-$15   **Phone:** 505/884-7422   (52)
Location: Jct Candelaria. 3000 San Pedro Rd NE 87110. **Hours:** 11 am-8 pm, Fri & Sat-9 pm. Closed major holidays; also Sun & Mon. **Reservations:** accepted, Sat. **Features:** Oak, apple and pecan wood fires help create flavorful meats and sauces at Robb's Ribbs. The fragrant, sweet and spicy sauces are fueled by yellow hots, chili pequin and red chili. Try the homemade spicy beer sausage or tasty smoked chicken. Casual dress; beer & wine only. **Parking:** on-site. **Cards:** AX, DC, DS, MC, VI.

ROCKFISH SEAFOOD GRILL
Seafood
Lunch: $6-$8   **Dinner:** $7-$16   **Phone:** 505/343-8500   (17)
Location: I-25, exit 229, just ne. 4441 The 25 Way NE 87109. **Hours:** 11 am-10 pm, Fri & Sat-11 pm, Sun-9 pm. Closed: 11/23, 12/25. **Features:** The patio is a pleasant evening setting on which to enjoy a drink and perhaps one of the seafood specialties. Among them is the shrimp basket: an ample serving of decadent deep-fried shrimp with waffle fries and apple cider slaw served 1950s style in a plastic basket. Casual dress; cocktails. **Parking:** on-site. **Cards:** AX, DC, DS, MC, VI.

RUDY'S COUNTRY STORE & BAR-B-Q
Barbecue
Lunch: $7-$10   **Dinner:** $7-$10   **Phone:** 505/884-4000   (64)
Location: I-40, exit 160, just n. 2321 Carlisle Blvd NE 87110. **Hours:** 10 am-10 pm. Closed: 11/23, 12/25. **Features:** You'll enjoy a picnic-style, fun-filled visit to Rudy's, where they specialize in slow-smoked, tender, flavorful brisket, and serve meals on butcher paper and bread. The open-air patio offers a great view of the Sandia and Manzano mountains. Casual dress; beer & wine only. **Parking:** on-site. **Cards:** AX, DC, DS, MC, VI.

SADIE'S DINING ROOM
Southwest Mexican
Lunch: $6-$10   **Dinner:** $8-$15   **Phone:** 505/345-5339   (11)
Location: 0.5 mi s of jct Osuna Rd. 6230 4th St NW 87107. **Hours:** 11 am-10 pm, Sun-9 pm. Closed: 11/23, 12/25. **Reservations:** accepted. **Features:** Sadie's is a popular restaurant, with some of the hottest New Mexican food you'll find, so expect a wait to be seated here. The chicken enchilada on corn shell is wonderful. The interior is decorated in the traditional Southwestern pink and turquoise. Casual dress; cocktails. **Parking:** on-site. **Cards:** AX, CB, DC, DS, MC, VI.

SAIGON RESTAURANT
Vietnamese
Lunch: $5-$9   **Dinner:** $5-$9   **Phone:** 505/884-0706   (20)
Location: I-25, exit 230 (San Mateo Blvd), 0.4 mi s; jct San Mateo and Osuna Rd; in Fiesta Norte Center. 6001 San Mateo Blvd NE, #04 87109. **Hours:** 10 am-9 pm. Closed: Tues. **Features:** Preparations served at the ethnic cafe reproduce the subtle, exotic flavors of Vietnam. Casual dress; beer & wine only. **Parking:** on-site. **Cards:** AX, CB, DC, DS, MC, VI.

SANDIAGO'S MEXICAN GRILL
Mexican
Dinner: $8-$18   **Phone:** 505/856-6692
Location: At eastern end of tramway access road; in the same building as tram departure point. 40 Tramway Rd NE 87122. **Hours:** 4:30 pm-9 pm. Closed: 11/23, 12/25. **Reservations:** accepted. **Features:** Dazzling evening city views are available from either the patio or dining room. The fish specialties are prepared in an authentic Mexican style; try the plantain-wrapped halibut for a little bit of Mexico. Save a little room for the heavenly chocolate flan. Casual dress; cocktails. **Parking:** on-site. **Cards:** AX, DS, MC, VI.

(See map and index starting on p. 478)

SANTA FE PEPPERS
▼▼
Mexican

Lunch: $5-$7 **Dinner:** $5-$7 **Phone:** 505/344-7200 ㉓
Location: I-25, exit 229, just e. 4320 The 25 Way NE, Suite 500 87109. **Hours:** 10 am-9 pm, Sun-4 pm. Closed: 11/23, 12/25. **Reservations:** not accepted. **Features:** Diners get to choose the ingredients for their giant burritos. Although the menu says the burritos are "born to be big," gigantic is a far more appropriate adjective. Casual dress. **Parking:** on-site. **Cards:** MC, VI.
&M

SCALO NORTHERN ITALIAN GRILL
▼▼▼
Northern Italian
MC, VI.

Lunch: $6-$13 **Dinner:** $6-$22 **Phone:** 505/255-8782 ⑫③
Location: I-25, exit Central Ave, 2 mi e; in Nob Hill Shopping Center. 3500 Central Ave SE 87106. **Hours:** 11 am-11 pm, Sun 5 pm-9 pm. Closed: 7/4, 11/23, 12/25. **Reservations:** accepted. **Features:** This locally popular restaurant prepares its pasta in-house and offers a good selection of pasta dishes and other entrees. The black-and-white linguine with scallops is especially good. Desserts are tempting too. Patio dining is available. Dressy casual; cocktails. **Parking:** on-site. **Cards:** AX, DC, DS, Ⓨ

SCARPA'S
▼▼ ▼▼
Italian
Parking: on-site. **Cards:** AX, MC, VI.

Lunch: $6-$9 **Dinner:** $6-$9 **Phone:** 505/821-1885 ⑬
Location: Just e of jct San Mateo Blvd. 5500 Academy Rd NE 87109. **Hours:** 11 am-10 pm. Closed: 4/16, 11/23, 12/25. **Features:** Popular with the folks who work in nearby office complexes and stores, the restaurant is known for its imaginative jumbo salad and personal-size pizza. Adventurous pizzas meld exotic ingredients, such as shiitake mushrooms, caramelized onions and Alaskan salmon. Casual dress; beer & wine only.

SEASONS ROTISSERIE & GRILL
▼▼▼
American

Lunch: $6-$9 **Dinner:** $15-$39 **Phone:** 505/766-5100 ㉒
Location: Just n of Old Town; in San Felipe Plaza. 2031 Mountain Rd NW 87104. **Hours:** 11:30 am-2:30 & 5-10 pm, Fri & Sat-10:30 pm, Sun 5 pm-10 pm. Closed: 11/23, 12/25. **Reservations:** suggested. **Features:** Food is creatively prepared, plentiful and earthy at Seasons. The menu offers garlic mashed potatoes, rosemary-roasted chicken, rock shrimp fritters, and clams in a vodka marinara sauce. This two-level bistro has outdoor seating on the second floor. Dressy casual; cocktails. **Parking:** on-site. **Cards:** AX, DC, DS, MC, VI. Ⓨ

SIAM CAFE
▼▼
Thai

Lunch: $6-$8 **Dinner:** $6-$9 **Phone:** 505/883-7334 ㉔
Location: I-25, exit 230, 0.6 mi s; jct Osuna Rd and San Mateo Blvd, just s. 5500 San Mateo Blvd #101 87109. **Hours:** 11 am-9 pm. Closed major holidays; also Sun. **Features:** The speedy lunch buffet appeals to those with limited time. Others might prefer to order from the menu to sample the subtle or spicy flavors of Thai cuisine. In either case, try the Thai iced tea. Casual dress. **Parking:** on-site. **Cards:** DS, MC, VI.

STUART ANDERSON'S BLACK ANGUS CATTLE COMPANY
▼▼ ▼▼
Steak House
Cards: AX, DC, DS, MC, VI.

Lunch: $6-$9 **Dinner:** $11-$35 **Phone:** 505/292-1911 ㉖②
Location: I-40, exit 164B, 0.7 mi n. 2290 Wyoming Blvd NE 87109. **Hours:** 11 am-10 pm, Fri & Sat-11 pm, Sun noon-9 pm. Closed: 12/25. **Reservations:** accepted. **Features:** Dine on chicken, seafood, prime rib and jumbo-size choice steaks, which are prepared the way you like them. The lounge is large and comfortable. Enjoy extravagant desserts, such as the sky-high mud pie. Casual dress; cocktails. **Parking:** on-site. Ⓨ

TACO SAL
▼▼ ▼▼
Mexican

Lunch: $4-$7 **Dinner:** $5-$7 **Phone:** 505/298-2210 ㉘
Location: Jct Eubank and Menaul blvds, northwest corner. 9621 Menaul Blvd NE 87112. **Hours:** 11 am-8 pm. Closed major holidays; also Sun. **Features:** The well-known neighborhood eatery has been on the scene for more than 40 years. Red or green chile tops off the tasty Mexican food. Casual dress; beer & wine only. **Parking:** on-site. **Cards:** MC, VI.

TAEJA RESTAURANT
▼▼ ▼▼
Korean

Lunch: $5-$7 **Dinner:** $7-$12 **Phone:** 505/268-8777 ㉜
Location: At Lomas Blvd and San Pedro; in Fair Plaza Mall. 6001-L Lomas Blvd NE 87110. **Hours:** 11 am-9 pm. Closed: 11/23, 12/25; also Sun. **Reservations:** accepted. **Features:** The Korean barbecue is terrific, and deftly arranged side dishes appeal to the eye as well as the palate. Friendly service and a knowledgeable staff also add to the experience. Casual dress. **Parking:** on-site. **Cards:** DS, MC, VI.

TAJ MAHAL CUISINE OF INDIA
Menu on aaa.com
AAA
▼▼ ▼▼
Indian

Lunch: $8 **Dinner:** $9-$15 **Phone:** 505/255-1994 ㉘⓪
Location: I-40, exit 160, 0.5 mi s. 1430 Carlisle Blvd NE 87110. **Hours:** 11 am-2:30 & 5-9:30 pm, Fri & Sat 5 pm-10 pm. Closed: 11/23, 12/25. **Reservations:** accepted. **Features:** On the menu are such traditional dishes as tandoori, curries, masalas, kormas and saegs. Dressy casual; beer & wine only. **Parking:** on-site. **Cards:** AX, DC, DS, MC, VI.

TASTE OF CHINA
▼▼ ▼▼
Chinese

Lunch: $5-$6 **Dinner:** $7-$8 **Phone:** 505/880-8889 ㉛
Location: Jct San Mateo Blvd and Osuna Rd, just s. 4605 San Mateo Blvd NE 87109. **Hours:** 11 am-9:30 pm, Fri & Sat-10 pm. Closed: 11/23. **Reservations:** accepted. **Features:** The bright, well-furnished restaurant's buffet lines up a wide variety of popular dishes. Many choices keep patrons coming back to try it all. Casual dress. **Parking:** on-site. **Cards:** DS, MC, VI.
&M

TEXAS LAND & CATTLE STEAK HOUSE
▼▼ ▼▼
Steak House

Lunch: $7-$12 **Dinner:** $11-$25 **Phone:** 505/343-9800 ㉕
Location: I-25, exit 229, just s on frontage road. 4949 Pan American Frwy NE 87109. **Hours:** 11 am-10 pm, Fri & Sat-11 pm. Closed: 11/23, 12/25. **Reservations:** accepted. **Features:** A variety of large prime steaks, delicious salads and scrumptious desserts await you at the friendly Texas ranch-style restaurant. Try the signature smoked sirloin, which never fails to please, or the Caesar salad, another favorite. Dessert is an occasion in itself. Casual dress; cocktails. **Parking:** on-site. **Cards:** AX, DC, DS, MC, VI. Ⓨ

(See map and index starting on p. 478)

TOWN HOUSE RESTAURANT & LOUNGE   Lunch: $7-$9   Dinner: $9-$25   Phone: 505/255-0057   [124]
American
Location: Jct Central Ave and Morningside Dr. 3911 Central Ave NE 87108. Hours: 11 am-10 pm. Closed: 1/1, 11/23, 12/25; also Sun. Reservations: accepted. Features: Steaks and Greek food are specialties at the long-popular Central Avenue dining spot and watering hole. Patrons are likely to find this place suitable for unwinding and enjoying a relaxed dinner. Casual dress; cocktails. Parking: on-site. Cards: MC, VI.

TROMBINO'S BISTRO ITALIANO   Lunch: $6-$14   Dinner: $8-$22   Phone: 505/821-5974   [12]
Italian
Location: I-25, exit 230, just s on San Mateo Blvd to Academy Rd, then e. 5415 Academy Rd NE 87109. Hours: 11 am-10 pm, Fri-10:30 pm, Sat 3 pm-10:30 pm, Sun 11 am-9 pm; Sunday brunch. Closed: 11/23, 12/25; also Super Bowl Sun. Features: Well-prepared and delicious entrees—including pasta, veal, poultry, seafood and aged steaks—are served in this locally popular restaurant's Mediterranean atmosphere. Fresh ingredients, tasty homemade breads, sauces, pizza and tempting desserts complete the menu. Casual dress; cocktails. Parking: on-site. Cards: AX, CB, DC, DS, MC, VI.

TUCANOS BRAZILIAN GRILL   Lunch: $9-$10   Dinner: $14-$16   Phone: 505/246-9900   [101]
Brazilian
Location: Jct 1st St. 110 Central Ave SW 87102. Hours: 11 am-9 pm, Thurs-10 pm, Fri & Sat-11 pm, Sun-8 pm. Closed: 12/25. Reservations: accepted. Features: The downtown restaurant caters to meat lovers. Ethnically attired servers bring multiple courses consisting of freshly cooked beef, pork, chicken and sausage to the table on long, swordlike skewers. The salad bar adds to this place's popularity. Casual dress; cocktails. Parking: street. Cards: AX, DC, DS, MC, VI.

VIC'S DAILY CAFE   Lunch: $6-$8   Phone: 505/341-9710   [7]
Southwest American
Location: I-25, exit 230 (Osuna Rd), 0.5 mi w. 3600 Osuna Rd NE, #105 87109. Hours: 6 am-2:30 pm, Sat & Sun 7:30 am-2 pm. Closed major holidays. Features: The cafe is well-known for its green chili sauce, which can be had with breakfast or lunch. It's a nice accompaniment to chicken enchiladas. For those who prefer an American entree, blue ribbon meat loaf is sure to please. Casual dress. Parking: on-site. Cards: AX, MC, VI.

VIVACE   Lunch: $7-$11   Dinner: $9-$17   Phone: 505/268-5965   [118]
Italian
Location: Just e of jct Richmond; in Nob Hill area. 3118 Central Ave SE 87106. Hours: 11:30 am-2 & 5:30-9 pm, Fri-10 pm, Sat 5:30 pm-10 pm, Sun 5:30 pm-9 pm. Closed major holidays. Reservations: suggested. Features: Vivace's is a small, nicely appointed trattoria offering a bounty of pasta, panini and grilled beef and chicken. Or you may want to sample the robust bistecca fiorentina, grilled yellowfin tuna, spaghetti carbonara or mussels steamed in Pernod. Dressy casual; beer & wine only. Parking: street. Cards: AX, DS, MC, VI.

WECK'S   Lunch: $5-$8   Phone: 505/881-0019   [40]
American
Location: Corner of Louisiana and Montgomery blvds, just s of Montgomery Blvd. 3913 Louisiana Blvd NE 87110. Hours: 6:30 am-2 pm. Closed: 1/1, 11/23, 12/25. Features: Although traditional American breakfasts are on the menu, the restaurant's morning specialties are huevos rancheros, carne adovada and burritos served with lots of red or green chili. Portions are generous. Casual dress. Parking: on-site. Cards: AX, DS, MC, VI.

WEEKDAYS   Lunch: $5-$8   Phone: 505/842-8455   [105]
American
Location: Jct 4th St SW and Silver Ave SW, just w; in Alvarado Square-Public Service of NM Building. 415 Silver Ave SW 87102. Hours: 7 am-2 pm. Closed major holidays; also Sat & Sun. Reservations: accepted. Features: If it's Thursday, then it's a popular day to visit the eatery for lunch. It's chicken pot pie day, and patrons love it. Among everyday choices are salads, sandwiches and pastries. Casual dress. Parking: street. Cards: MC, VI.

WESTERN VIEW DINER AND STEAKHOUSE   Lunch: $6-$10   Dinner: $6-$10   Phone: 505/836-2200   [104]
Southwest American
Location: Jct Coors Rd and Central Ave, just e. 6411 Central Ave NW 87105. Hours: 6 am-10 pm, Sun-3 pm. Closed major holidays. Features: Great hand-cut steaks are the signature dish. Other offerings include a fine selection of New Mexican cuisine and delicious pies. Casual dress; beer & wine only. Parking: on-site. Cards: AX, MC, VI.

YANNI'S MEDITERRANEAN BAR & GRILL   Lunch: $6-$10   Dinner: $13-$25   Phone: 505/268-9250   [110]
Mediterranean
Location: I-25, exit 224B, s to Central Ave, then 1.7 mi e. 3109 Central Ave NE 87106. Hours: 11 am-10 pm, Fri & Sat-11 pm, Sun noon-9 pm. Closed: 11/23, 12/25. Reservations: accepted. Features: Convenient to the University of New Mexico and the Nob Hill area, the popular eatery is known for its interesting variety of healthy Mediterranean dishes. Try the delicious pasta entrees or tempting moussaka. The baklava sundae is a sinful dessert. Dressy casual; cocktails. Parking: on-site. Cards: AX, DS, MC, VI.

YEN CHING   Lunch: $5-$7   Dinner: $7-$16   Phone: 505/275-8265   [41]
Chinese
Location: Jct Montgomery and Wyoming blvds, southeast corner. 4410 Wyoming Blvd NE 87111. Hours: 11:30 am-9 pm, Fri & Sat-9:30 pm, Sun 4:30 pm-8:30 pm. Closed: 1/1, 11/23, 12/25. Reservations: accepted. Features: Long the scene of an exceptional luncheon buffet, the restaurant offers guests a bit more formal of a dinner experience. All the traditional Asian favorites are served. Casual dress; beer & wine only. Parking: on-site. Cards: AX, MC, VI.

ZEA ROTISSERIE RESTAURANT   Lunch: $8-$10   Dinner: $8-$19   Phone: 505/878-9327   [36]
International
Location: Jct Montgomery and San Mateo blvd, just w. 4800 Montgomery Blvd NE 87109. Hours: 11 am-10 pm, Fri & Sat-11 pm. Features: Stylish, upscale decor and a varied menu that draws from European, American and Oriental cuisines are the salient features of the popular new restaurant. Dressy casual; cocktails. Parking: on-site. Cards: AX, DS, MC, VI.

(See map and index starting on p. 478)

ZINC WINE BAR & BISTRO   **Lunch:** $8-$12   **Dinner:** $15-$24   **Phone:** 505/254-9462   [109]
▽▽▽   **Location:** Jct Central Ave and Montevista, just e. 3009 Central Ave NE 87106. **Hours:** 11 am-2:30 & 5-10 pm, Fri-11 pm, Sat 5 pm-11 pm; Sunday brunch. Closed major holidays. **Reservations:** suggested. **Features:** A stylish place to be seen, the bistro presents a finer-than-casual menu with French rotisserie meats as a highlight. The wine selection is legend. Dressy casual; cocktails. **Parking:** street. **Cards:** AX, DC, DS,
American
MC, VI.

The following restaurants have not been evaluated by AAA but are listed for your information only.

QUARTERS BBQ RESTAURANT-WEST   **Phone:** 505/897-3341
[fyi]   Not evaluated. **Location:** Jct McMahon Blvd NW and Ellison Dr, just e. 3700 Ellison Dr NW 87114. **Features:** The restaurant's newest location on the west side features a lively lounge scene as well as the barbecue they're
famous for.

ROSA'S ITALIAN KITCHEN   **Phone:** 505/884-7672
[fyi]   Not evaluated. **Location:** Jct Candelaria Rd, just n. 3325 San Mateo Blvd NE 87110. **Features:** Nana was the owner's grandmother, and her recipes are followed carefully to this day. Ravioli is exceptional, and the
chocolate chip cannoli is to die for.

SIG'S   **Phone:** 505/256-0564
[fyi]   Not evaluated. **Location:** Nob Hill; between Wellesley and Bryn Mawr sts. 3211 Central Ave NE 87106. **Features:** The friendly staff at the casual tavern serves innovative appetizers and fresh, homemade desserts, in addition to delicious soups, salads, burgers, vegetarian fare and house specialties. Entertainment options include blues or jazz on Saturday night and Celtic music every Sunday. A wide selection of fine spirits complements sixteen beers on tap.

ALGODONES pop. 688

--- **WHERE TO STAY** ---

HACIENDA VARGAS BED AND BREAKFAST INN   **Phone:** (505)867-9115
(AAA) (SAVE)   All Year [BP]   1P: $79-$139   2P: $89-$149   XP: $15   F12
▽▽▽   **Location:** I-25, exit 248, 0.5 mi w. Train tracks nearby. 1431 SR 313 (El Camino Real) 87001 (PO Box 307).
Historic Bed   Fax: 505/867-0640. **Facility:** Set along the "Royal Road" that once led from Santa Fe to Mexico City, this
& Breakfast   18th-century hacienda features adobe-style architecture. Designated smoking area. 7 one-bedroom standard units. 1 story, interior corridors. **Parking:** on-site. **Terms:** check-in 4 pm, age restrictions may apply, 10 day cancellation notice-fee imposed, weekly rates available, [MAP] meal plan available, package plans, pets (with prior approval). **Leisure Activities:** bicycles, hiking trails, jogging. **Business Services:** meeting rooms. **Cards:** AX, MC, VI. **Special Amenities:** free full breakfast and free local telephone calls.

ALTO

--- **WHERE TO STAY** ---

The following lodging was either not evaluated or did not meet AAA rating requirements but is listed for your information only.

RANCHO RUIDOSO CONDOMINIUMS   **Phone:** 505/336-8103
[fyi]   Not evaluated. **Location:** Jct SR 48, 4.2 mi e on Little Creek Rd (SR 220), just s at sign. 6 Little Creek Rd 88312 (PO Box 62). Facilities, services, and decor characterize a mid-range property.

ARROYO SECO   (See map and index starting on p. 601)—See also TAOS.

--- **WHERE TO STAY** ---

ADOBE AND STARS B & B   **Phone:** (505)776-2776   [24]
▽▽▽   All Year   1P: $110-$185   2P: $110-$185
Location: 1.1 mi ne on SR 150 at Valdez Rd. Located in a rural area. 584 State Hwy 150 87571 (PO Box 2285, TAOS).
Bed & Breakfast   Fax: 505/776-2872. **Facility:** This B&B offers a garden of moving sculptures and a location near the galleries and museums of Taos. Smoke free premises. 8 one-bedroom standard units, some with whirlpools. 1-2 stories, interior/exterior corridors. **Bath:** combo or shower only. **Parking:** on-site. **Terms:** check-in 4 pm, 32 day cancellation notice-fee imposed, small pets only ($20 fee, $50 deposit). **Amenities:** video library, CD players, hair dryers. *Some:* irons. **Leisure Activities:** whirlpool. **Guest Services:** TV in common area. **Business Services:** fax. **Cards:** AX, MC, VI.

SOME UNITS

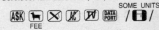
FEE

ALMA DEL MONTE-SPIRIT OF THE MOUNTAIN B&B   **Phone:** (505)776-2721   [23]
▽▽▽   All Year   1P: $150-$240   2P: $170-$260
Location: Jct SR 150, 1.8 mi n on SR 230, 0.6 mi w. 372 Arroyo Seco Rd 87571 (PO Box 617, TAOS).
Bed & Breakfast   Fax: 505/776-8888. **Facility:** The hacienda-style lodging is in a rural setting, away from the noise and traffic of nearby Taos, but close enough to enjoy the museums and dining. Designated smoking area. 5 one-bedroom standard units with whirlpools. 1 story, interior corridors. **Parking:** on-site. **Terms:** check-in 4 pm, age restrictions may apply, 14 day cancellation notice-fee imposed, package plans (dogs only, in kennel). **Amenities:** video library, CD players, irons, hair dryers. **Leisure Activities:** whirlpool. *Fee:* massage. **Guest Services:** complimentary evening beverages, area transportation. **Business Services:** meeting rooms, PC, fax. **Cards:** AX, MC, VI.

(See map and index starting on p. 601)

COTTONWOOD INN BED & BREAKFAST
▼▼▼▼ All Year
Phone: (505)776-5826 ㉕
Location: On SR 150 at SR 230. 02 SR 230 87514 (HCR 74 Box 24609, EL PRADO, 87529). Fax: 505/776-1141.
Bed & Breakfast
1P: $85-$200   2P: $95-$210   XP: $20
Facility: A private balcony is just one place to relax at this inn characterized by patios, gardens with trickling fountains and gathering areas. Smoke free premises. 8 one-bedroom standard units, some with whirlpools. 2 stories (no elevator), interior/exterior corridors. *Bath:* combo or shower only. **Parking:** on-site. **Terms:** check-in 4 pm, 2 night minimum stay - seasonal and/or weekends, 14 day cancellation notice-fee imposed, [BP] meal plan available, package plans, no pets allowed (owner's pet on premises). **Amenities:** hair dryers. **Leisure Activities:** whirlpool, hiking trails, jogging. *Fee:* massage. **Business Services:** fax. **Cards:** AX, DS, MC, VI.

SOME UNITS

(A$K) 🚫 ✕ 🎮 ☎ / 🅦 📷 🖥 📠

─── WHERE TO DINE ───

MOMENTITOS DE LA VIDA
▼▼▼ ▼▼▼ **Dinner:** $19-$39
Location: 4.8 mi ne of jct US 64 and SR 150. 470 SR 150 87514. **Hours:** 5:30 pm-10 pm. Closed: 11/23, 12/25;
Phone: 505/776-3333 ㉑
American
also Mon. **Reservations:** suggested. **Features:** Cross the lantern-lit bridge into an enchanting world of old abode walls, artistic murals, elegant table settings, attentive service and foods on which your eyes and palate will feast. Patio dining under the latilla roof is the favored choice in warm weather. Chris Maher, the talented chef, selects fresh local produce, which he combines with specialty meats and seafood in what he calls creative "new American cuisine". Casual dress; cocktails. **Parking:** on-site. **Cards:** AX, MC, VI. **Historic**

📺 📐

ARTESIA pop. 10,692

─── WHERE TO STAY ───

ARTESIA INN
(AAA) (SAVE) All Year
Phone: 505/746-9801
1P: $38-$48   2P: $45-$55   XP: $7   F12
▼▼▼
Motel
Location: 1.5 mi s on US 285. 1820 S 1st St 88210. Fax: 505/746-9801. **Facility:** 34 one-bedroom standard units. 1 story, exterior corridors. *Bath:* combo or shower only. **Parking:** on-site. **Terms:** pets ($10 fee). **Pool(s):** outdoor. **Business Services:** fax (fee). **Cards:** AX, CB, DC, DS, MC, VI. **Special Amenities:** free local telephone calls and preferred room (subject to availability with advance reservations).

SOME UNITS

(S/D) 🛏 📶 🏊 📷 📶 🖥 🖥 / ✕ /
FEE

BEST WESTERN PECOS INN   *Book at aaa.com*
(AAA) (SAVE) All Year [BP]
Phone: (505)748-3324
1P: $89-$109   2P: $89-$109   XP: $10   F12
▼▼▼ ▼▼▼
Small-scale Hotel
Location: 1.5 mi w on US 82. 2209 W Main 88210. Fax: 505/748-2868. **Facility:** 82 units. 79 one-bedroom standard units. 3 two-bedroom suites, some with kitchens. 2 stories (no elevator), interior corridors. **Parking:** on-site. **Amenities:** high-speed Internet, voice mail, irons, hair dryers. **Dining:** 6 am-9 pm, Sun-8:30 pm, cocktails. **Pool(s):** heated indoor. **Leisure Activities:** sauna, whirlpool, exercise room. **Guest Services:** valet and coin laundry. **Business Services:** meeting rooms, fax (fee). **Cards:** AX, CB, DC, DS, JC, MC, VI. **Special Amenities:** free full breakfast and free local telephone calls.

SOME UNITS

(S/D) 🍴 📐 📷 🚫 📶 (DATA PORT) 📠 🖥 🖥 / ✕ (VCR)
FEE

HOLIDAY INN EXPRESS-ARTESIA   *Book at aaa.com*
(AAA) (SAVE) All Year
Phone: 505/748-3904
2P: $80-$94   XP: $10   F
▼▼▼ ▼▼▼
Small-scale Hotel
Location: 1.6 mi w of jct US 82 and 285. 2210 W Main 88210. Fax: 505/748-3796. **Facility:** 40 one-bedroom standard units. 2 stories (no elevator), interior corridors. *Bath:* combo or shower only. **Parking:** on-site. **Terms:** cancellation fee imposed, pets ($20 fee). **Amenities:** high-speed Internet, voice mail, irons, hair dryers. **Pool(s):** heated outdoor. **Leisure Activities:** exercise room. **Guest Services:** valet and coin laundry. **Business Services:** fax (fee). **Cards:** AX, CB, DC, DS, MC, VI. **Special Amenities:** free expanded continental breakfast and free local telephone calls.

SOME UNITS

🛏 📶 (&M) 🎮 📷 🏊 🐾 (DATA PORT) 🖥 / ✕ 📠 🖥 /
FEE

─── WHERE TO DINE ───

LA FONDA RESTAURANT
▼▼▼ **Lunch:** $5-$12   **Dinner:** $5-$12   **Phone:** 505/746-9411
Mexican
Location: Center. 206 W Main 88210. **Hours:** 11 am-9 pm. Closed major holidays. **Reservations:** accepted. **Features:** The family restaurant combines a Southwestern atmosphere with American fare. Also on the menu are regional and Mexican selections, including flautas, chimichangas and tacos. Portions are large. The luncheon buffet is a popular offering. Casual dress. **Parking:** on-site. **Cards:** AX, DC, DS, MC, VI.

📐

AZTEC pop. 6,378

─── WHERE TO STAY ───

THE STEP BACK INN
(AAA) (SAVE) 5/16-11/15   1P: $82   2P: $98   XP: $8   F12
2/1-5/15 & 11/16-1/31   1P: $70   2P: $74   XP: $8   F12
▼▼▼ ▼▼▼
Motel
Phone: 505/334-1200
Location: Jct US 550 and SR 544. 123 W Aztec Blvd 87410. Fax: 505/334-9858. **Facility:** 39 one-bedroom standard units. 2 stories (no elevator), interior corridors. *Bath:* shower only. **Parking:** on-site. **Amenities:** hair dryers. *Some:* irons. **Cards:** AX, MC, VI. **Special Amenities:** free continental breakfast and free local telephone calls.

SOME UNITS

(S/D) 📶 🎮 📷 / ✕ /

--------- **WHERE TO DINE** ---------

THE MAIN STREET BISTRO　　　　　　　**Lunch:** $5-$8　　　　　　**Phone:** 505/334-0109

American

Location: From US 550, follow sign to Historic downtown; jct US 550 S (Main Ave) and Blanco. 122 N Main Ave 87410. **Hours:** 7 am-4 pm, Sat-noon. Closed: 11/23, 12/25; also Sun. **Reservations:** accepted. **Features:** The cheerful cafe serves a variety of tasty sandwiches, soups and salads in a relaxed atmosphere. Casual dress. **Parking:** on-site. **Cards:** AX, DS, MC, VI.

BELEN pop. 6,901

--------- **WHERE TO STAY** ---------

BEST WESTERN-BELEN　　*Book at aaa.com*　　　　　　　　　　　　　　　　**Phone:** (505)861-3181

(AAA) [SAVE]

Small-scale Hotel

10/1-10/15 [BP]	1P: $80-$90	2P: $85-$95	XP: $5	F
4/1-9/30 [BP]	1P: $70-$80	2P: $75-$85	XP: $5	F
2/1-3/31 & 10/16-1/31 [BP]	1P: $60-$70	2P: $65-$75	XP: $5	F

Location: I-25, exit 191, just w. 2111 Camino del Llano Blvd 87002. Fax: 505/864-7364. **Facility:** 50 one-bedroom standard units. 2 stories (no elevator); interior/exterior corridors. *Bath:* combo or shower only. **Parking:** on-site. **Terms:** weekly rates available, [BP] meal plan available, pets ($20 deposit, $5 extra charge). **Amenities:** high-speed Internet, irons, hair dryers. **Pool(s):** heated outdoor. **Leisure Activities:** exercise room. **Guest Services:** coin laundry. **Business Services:** meeting rooms, fax. **Cards:** AX, CB, DC, DS, MC, VI. **Special Amenities:** early check-in/late check-out and free room upgrade (subject to availability with advance reservations).

SOME UNITS

[icons] FEE

HOLIDAY INN EXPRESS　　*Book at aaa.com*　　　　　　　　　　　　　**Phone:** 505/861-5000

Property failed to provide current rates

Small-scale Hotel

Location: I-25, exit 191, just w. 2110 Camino del Llano 87002. Fax: 505/861-7074. **Facility:** 63 one-bedroom standard units. 2 stories, interior corridors. *Bath:* combo or shower only. **Parking:** on-site. **Terms:** pets ($10 extra charge). **Amenities:** high-speed Internet, dual phone lines, voice mail, irons, hair dryers. **Pool(s):** heated outdoor. **Leisure Activities:** whirlpool, exercise room. **Guest Services:** valet and coin laundry. **Business Services:** conference facilities, fax.

SOME UNITS

[icons] FEE

--------- **WHERE TO DINE** ---------

JAKE & ANDRE'S RESTAURANT　　　**Lunch:** $7-$12　　**Dinner:** $7-$18　　**Phone:** 505/864-2271

Barbecue

Location: I-25, exit 191, just w. 2100 Camino del Llano 87002. **Hours:** 8 am-9 pm, Sun 9 am-1 pm. Closed major holidays. **Features:** While the cafe has a nice selection of sandwiches, burgers and salads, the main attraction is barbecue in the form of tasty ribs, brisket, chicken and pork. Casual dress; beer & wine only. **Parking:** on-site. **Cards:** AX, DS, MC, VI.

BERNALILLO pop. 6,611—See also ALBUQUERQUE.

--------- **WHERE TO STAY** ---------

DAYS INN-BERNALILLO　　*Book at aaa.com*　　　　　　　　　　　　　**Phone:** (505)771-7000

(AAA) [SAVE]

Small-scale Hotel

All Year [CP]　　　　　　　1P: $40-$80　　　　2P: $40-$80

Location: I-25, exit 242, just w. 107 N Camino del Pueblo 87004. Fax: 505/771-7000. **Facility:** 56 one-bedroom standard units. 3 stories, interior corridors. *Bath:* combo or shower only. **Parking:** on-site. **Terms:** pets ($30 deposit, limit 1). **Amenities:** high-speed Internet, safes, hair dryers. **Pool(s):** heated indoor. **Leisure Activities:** whirlpool. **Guest Services:** valet and coin laundry. **Business Services:** meeting rooms, fax (fee). **Cards:** AX, CB, DC, DS, JC, MC, VI. **Special Amenities:** free expanded continental breakfast and free local telephone calls.

SOME UNITS

[icons] FEE

HOLIDAY INN EXPRESS-BERNALILLO　　*Book at aaa.com*　　　　　　　**Phone:** (505)867-1600

(AAA) [SAVE]

Small-scale Hotel

All Year [ECP]　　　　　1P: $65-$90　　　　2P: $65-$90

Location: I-25, exit 242. 119 Bell Ln 87004. Fax: 505/867-0606. **Facility:** 70 one-bedroom standard units. 3 stories, interior corridors. *Bath:* combo or shower only. **Parking:** on-site. **Terms:** package plans. **Amenities:** high-speed Internet, dual phone lines, voice mail, irons, hair dryers. **Pool(s):** heated indoor. **Leisure Activities:** whirlpool, exercise room. **Guest Services:** valet and coin laundry. **Business Services:** meeting rooms, business center. **Cards:** AX, CB, DC, DS, JC, MC, VI. **Special Amenities:** free expanded continental breakfast and free local telephone calls.

SOME UNITS

[icons] FEE

HYATT REGENCY TAMAYA RESORT AND SPA　　*Book at aaa.com*　　　**Phone:** (505)867-1234

(AAA) [SAVE]

Resort
Large-scale Hotel

4/15-11/18	1P: $155-$315	2P: $155-$315	XP: $25	F18
2/1-4/14 & 11/19-1/31	1P: $125-$265	2P: $125-$265	XP: $25	F18

Location: I-25, exit 242, 1 mi w on SR 44 to Tamaya Rd, then 1 mi n, follow signs. 1300 Tuyuna Tr 87004. Fax: 505/867-1400. **Facility:** Horse-drawn-carriage rides along the Rio Grande depart from this newer luxury resort; the guest rooms, restaurants and lobby are well-appointed. 350 one-bedroom standard units. 4 stories, interior corridors. *Bath:* combo or shower only. **Parking:** on-site (fee) and valet. **Terms:** check-in 4 pm, 3 day cancellation notice-fee imposed, $14 service charge, pets (dogs only, $50 fee). **Amenities:** high-speed Internet (fee), dual phone lines, voice mail, safes, irons, hair dryers. **Dining:** 4 restaurants, 6:30 am-11 pm, cocktails, entertainment. **Pool(s):** 3 heated outdoor. **Leisure Activities:** saunas, whirlpools, steamrooms, 2 tennis courts, horseback riding, exercise room, spa, basketball. *Fee:* golf-45 holes. **Guest Services:** gift shop, valet laundry. **Business Services:** conference facilities, business center. **Cards:** AX, CB, DC, DS, JC, MC, VI. *(See color ad p 498)*

SOME UNITS

[icons] FEE

LA HACIENDA GRANDE

Historic Bed & Breakfast

All Year   1P: $109-$149   2P: $109-$149   XP: $25   Phone: (505)867-1887   F

Location: I-25, exit 242, 0.3 mi w to Camino del Pueblo, then 0.5 mi n. 21 Barros Rd 87004. Fax: 505/771-1436. **Facility:** Just a few miles from Albuquerque, this restored 250-year-old hacienda features a central garden and Mexican Colonial ambience. Designated smoking area. 6 one-bedroom standard units. 1 story, interior/exterior corridors. *Bath:* combo or shower only. **Parking:** on-site. **Terms:** check-in 4 pm, 10 day cancellation notice-fee imposed, weekly rates available, pets (in designated units). **Amenities:** irons, hair dryers. **Business Services:** meeting rooms. **Cards:** AX, DS, MC, VI.

SOME UNITS
(ASK) (SD) (dog) (X) (phone) / (TV) (VCR) /

QUALITY INN & SUITES   *Book at aaa.com*

Small-scale Hotel

| 9/30-10/10 | 1P: $85-$125 | 2P: $85-$125 | XP: $5 | F16 |
| 2/1-9/29 & 10/11-1/31 | 1P: $56-$86 | 2P: $56-$86 | XP: $5 | F16 |

Phone: (505)771-9500

Location: I-25, exit 242, just w. 210 N Hill Rd 87004. Fax: 505/771-9400. **Facility:** 57 one-bedroom standard units. 3 stories, interior corridors. *Bath:* combo or shower only. **Parking:** on-site. **Terms:** package plans. **Amenities:** voice mail, irons, hair dryers. **Guest Services:** coin laundry. **Business Services:** meeting rooms. **Cards:** AX, CB, DC, DS, JC, MC, VI.

SOME UNITS
(ASK) (SD) (tel) (LM) (projector) (DATA PORT) (coffee) / (X) (refrig) (microwave) /

------ **WHERE TO DINE** ------

ABUELITA'S NEW MEXICAN RESTAURANT

Mexican

Lunch: $5-$8   Dinner: $5-$8   Phone: 505/867-9988

Location: I-25, exit 242, on US 550, 0.5 mi w, then 0.7 mi s. 621 Camino del Pueblo 87004. **Hours:** 7 am-3 pm, Fri-8:30 pm, Sat 8 am-8:30 pm, Sun 7:30 am-2 pm. Closed major holidays; also Wed. **Reservations:** accepted. **Features:** Abuelita means "grandma" in Spanish, and the unpretentious cafe uses grandma's recipes for its traditional New Mexican dishes. Tamales, enchiladas and carne adovada are good enough to eat every day. Casual dress; beer & wine only. **Parking:** on-site. **Cards:** AX, DS, MC, VI.

PRAIRIE STAR

American

Dinner: $15-$33   Phone: 505/867-3327

Location: I-25, exit 242, 2.2 mi w on US 550 to Tamaya Blvd, then 0.5 mi n. 255 Prairie Star Rd 87004. **Hours:** 5 pm-9 pm, Fri & Sat-10 pm. Closed: 1/1, 7/4, 12/25; also Mon. **Reservations:** suggested. **Features:** The perfect place for that special occasion, a truly romantic setting for a fine dining experience, the Prairie Star restaurant features imaginative, skillfully prepared cuisine, that is a blend of American Nouvelle, Oriental and the flavors and spices used in traditional New Mexican and Mexican cuisine. The result is a colorful and tasty dining experience. Dressy casual; cocktails. **Parking:** on-site. **Cards:** AX, DC, DS, MC, VI.

(cocktail) (refrig)

THE RANGE CAFE

Southwest American

Lunch: $6-$14   Dinner: $6-$14   Phone: 505/867-1700

Location: I-25, exit 240 to Camino del Pueblo, 1 mi n. 925 Camino del Pueblo 87004. **Hours:** 7:30 am-9 pm, Fri & Sat-9:30 pm. Closed: 11/23, 12/25. **Reservations:** accepted. **Features:** The colorful, lively eatery features a mix of New Mexican and good, old American dishes, as well as a fine selection of sandwiches. This spot is a good meeting place for coffee. Casual dress; cocktails. **Parking:** street. **Cards:** AX, DS, MC, VI.

BLOOMFIELD pop. 6,417

------ **WHERE TO STAY** ------

SUPER 8 MOTEL

Motel

Property failed to provide current rates   Phone: 505/632-8886

Location: Jct of US 64 and SR 44. 525 W Broadway Blvd 87413. Fax: 505/632-8886. **Facility:** 42 one-bedroom standard units. 2 stories (no elevator), interior corridors. **Parking:** on-site. **Terms:** pets ($10 fee). **Guest Services:** coin laundry.

SOME UNITS
(tel) (tel+) (refrig) (projector) (DATA PORT) / (X) (refrig) /
FEE

CAPITAN pop. 1,443

------ **WHERE TO DINE** ------

------ *The following restaurant has not been evaluated by AAA* ------
but is listed for your information only.

GREEN HOUSE CAFE

(fyi)

Phone: 505/354-0373

Not evaluated. **Location:** Jct SR 48 and Smokey Bear Blvd. 103 S Lincoln 88316. **Features:** A popular restaurant, whose clientele is willing to drive from the surrounding towns.

CARLSBAD pop. 25,625

──── WHERE TO STAY ────

BEST WESTERN STEVENS INN
Book at aaa.com
Phone: (505)887-2851
AAA SAVE
All Year   1P: $67-$99   2P: $72-$99   XP: $5   F12
Location: 1 mi s on US 62, 180 and 285. 1829 S Canal St 88220 (PO Box 580). Fax: 505/887-6338. **Facility:** 220 one-bedroom standard units, some with kitchens and/or whirlpools. 1-2 stories (no elevator), exterior corridors. *Bath:* combo or shower only. **Parking:** on-site. **Terms:** [BP] meal plan available, small pets only
Small-scale Hotel   ($10 fee). **Amenities:** high-speed Internet, voice mail, irons, hair dryers. **Dining:** The Flume Restaurant, see separate listing, entertainment. **Leisure Activities:** exercise room. **Guest Services:** valet and coin laundry, airport transportation-Carlsbad Airport. **Business Services:** meeting rooms, fax (fee). **Cards:** AX, DC, DS, MC, VI. **Special Amenities: free full breakfast and free room upgrade (subject to availability with advance reservations).**

SOME UNITS
[icons] FEE

CARLSBAD INN
Phone: (505)887-1171
AAA SAVE
6/1-9/15 [CP]	1P: $35-$49	2P: $39-$49	XP: $5 F
3/2-5/31 [CP]	1P: $32-$38	2P: $37-$47	XP: $5 F
2/1-3/1 & 9/16-1/31 [CP]	1P: $30-$35	2P: $36-$46	XP: $5 F

Location: 1.5 mi s on US 62, 180 and 285. 2019 S Canal St 88220. Fax: 505/887-6577. **Facility:** 30 one-bedroom standard units. 2 stories (no elevator), exterior corridors. **Parking:** on-site. **Terms:** cancellation fee imposed,
Motel   small pets only ($20 deposit). **Amenities:** hair dryers. **Pool(s):** heated outdoor. **Leisure Activities:** playground. **Business Services:** fax (fee). **Cards:** AX, DS, MC, VI. **Special Amenities: free continental breakfast and free local telephone calls.**

SOME UNITS
[icons] FEE   VCR FEE

COMFORT INN
Book at aaa.com
Phone: 505/887-1994
Property failed to provide current rates
Location: N on US 285. Located across from the medical center. 2429 W Pierce St 88220. Fax: 505/887-2694.
Small-scale Hotel   **Facility:** 54 one-bedroom standard units, some with whirlpools. 2 stories (no elevator), interior corridors. *Bath:* combo or shower only. **Parking:** on-site. **Terms:** small pets only ($5 extra charge). **Amenities:** high-speed Internet, irons, hair dryers. **Pool(s):** small heated indoor. **Leisure Activities:** whirlpool, limited exercise equipment. **Guest Services:** valet laundry. **Business Services:** fax (fee).

SOME UNITS
[icons] FEE

DAYS INN OF CARLSBAD
Phone: (505)887-7800
AAA SAVE
All Year   1P: $70-$95   2P: $80-$95   XP: $10   F12
Location: 3.5 mi sw on US 62 and 180. 3910 National Parks Hwy 88220. Fax: 505/885-9433. **Facility:** 50 one-bedroom standard units. 2 stories (no elevator), exterior corridors. **Parking:** on-site. **Terms:** 14 day
Small-scale Hotel   cancellation notice, [CP] meal plan available, small pets only ($10 extra charge). **Amenities:** high-speed Internet, irons, hair dryers. **Pool(s):** small heated indoor. **Leisure Activities:** whirlpool. **Guest Services:** valet and coin laundry, airport transportation-Carlsbad Airport. **Business Services:** fax (fee). **Cards:** AX, CB, DC, DS, MC, VI. **Special Amenities: free expanded continental breakfast and free local telephone calls.**

SOME UNITS
[icons] FEE

STAGECOACH INN
Phone: (505)887-1148
AAA SAVE
4/2-9/15	1P: $34-$49	2P: $39-$52	XP: $5 D15
2/1-4/1 & 9/16-1/31	1P: $30-$38	2P: $36-$45	XP: $5 D15

Location: 1 mi s on US 62, 180 and 285. 1819 S Canal St 88220. Fax: 505/887-1148. **Facility:** 55 one-bedroom standard units. 1 story, exterior corridors. *Bath:* combo or shower only. **Parking:** on-site.
Motel   **Terms:** cancellation fee imposed, package plans, pets ($5 fee). **Dining:** 11 am-2 & 5-8 pm; closed Sun & Mon. **Pool(s):** small outdoor, wading. **Leisure Activities:** whirlpool, playground. **Guest Services:** coin laundry. **Business Services:** fax (fee). **Cards:** AX, DC, DS, MC, VI. **Special Amenities: free continental breakfast and free local telephone calls.**

SOME UNITS
[icons] FEE

--------- WHERE TO DINE ---------

BAMBOO GARDEN
Chinese
| | Lunch: $5-$12 | Dinner: $5-$12 | Phone: 505/887-5145 |

Location: 0.7 mi s on US 62, 180 and 285. 1511 S Canal St 88220. **Hours:** 11 am-2 & 5-8:30 pm. Closed major holidays; also Mon. **Reservations:** accepted. **Features:** Patrons can choose from the house specialty duck, volcano shrimp and other Chinese dishes. Casual dress. **Parking:** on-site. **Cards:** MC, VI.

THE FLUME RESTAURANT
American
| | Lunch: $5-$9 | Dinner: $14-$20 | Phone: 505/887-2851 |

Location: 1 mi s on US 62, 180 and 285; in Best Western Stevens Inn. 1829 S Canal St 88220. **Hours:** 6 am-10 pm, Sun-9 pm. **Reservations:** accepted. **Features:** Although prime rib is the specialty, the restaurant also offers a choice of seafood, Mexican and pasta dishes. Vegetable side items accompany the entrees. Casual dress; cocktails; entertainment. **Parking:** on-site. **Cards:** AX, CB, DC, DS, JC, MC, VI.

LUCY'S MEXACALI RESTAURANT
Mexican
| | Lunch: $4-$11 | Dinner: $6-$11 | Phone: 505/887-7714 |

Location: On US 62, 180 and 285, Canal St at Lee St; center. 701 S Canal St 88220. **Hours:** 11 am-9:30 pm. Closed major holidays; also Sun. **Reservations:** accepted. **Features:** Since 1978, the restaurant has specialized in homemade Mexican and American food. Casual dress; cocktails. **Parking:** on-site. **Cards:** AX, DS, MC, VI.

CHAMA pop. 1,199

--------- WHERE TO STAY ---------

BRANDING IRON MOTEL
Motel
| | All Year | 1P: $69-$99 | 2P: $79-$109 | Phone: (505)756-2162 |
| | | | | XP: $10 |

Location: 0.5 mi s. 1511 W Main 87520 (PO Box 557). Fax: 505/756-2162. **Facility:** 41 one-bedroom standard units. 2 stories (no elevator), exterior corridors. *Bath:* combo or shower only. **Parking:** on-site. **Terms:** cancellation fee imposed. **Amenities:** *Some:* irons, hair dryers. **Dining:** 6 am-10 pm; to 8 pm in winter, wine/beer only. **Cards:** AX, DC, DS, JC, MC, VI.

SOME UNITS

THE GANDY DANCER BED & BREAKFAST
Historic Bed & Breakfast
| | All Year [BP] | 1P: $99-$149 | 2P: $99-$149 | Phone: (505)756-2191 |
| | | | | XP: $15   D18 |

Location: Just w of SR 17 via 3rd St. Located in a residential area. 299 Maple Ave 87520 (PO Box 810). Fax: 505/756-2649. **Facility:** Smoke free premises. Within walking distance of a historic train station, this B&B reflects a railroad theme in each room. 7 one-bedroom standard units. 2 stories (no elevator), interior corridors. *Bath:* combo or shower only. **Parking:** on-site. **Terms:** age restrictions may apply, 7 day cancellation notice, package plans. **Amenities:** video library. **Leisure Activities:** whirlpool. **Cards:** AX, DS, MC, VI. **Special Amenities:** free full breakfast and free local telephone calls.

POSADA ENCANTO BED AND BREAKFAST
Bed & Breakfast
| | 5/20-10/31 [ECP] | 1P: $79-$89 | 2P: $89-$110 | Phone: (505)756-1048 |
| | | | | XP: $15   D |

Location: Just w of SR 17 via 3rd St. 277 Maple Ave 87520 (PO Box 536). Fax: 505/756-1843. **Facility:** Pleasant Southwestern flair with decor on rooms. The converted church building is within walking distance of train station and historic town center. Convenient driving to many mountain lake areas. Large TV and VCR with movies in common area. Common phone is available. Smoke free premises. 5 one-bedroom standard units, some with whirlpools. 1 story, interior corridors. *Bath:* combo or shower only. **Parking:** on-site. **Terms:** open 5/20-10/31, check-in 4 pm, age restrictions may apply, 10 day cancellation notice-fee imposed. **Amenities:** video library, hair dryers. *Some:* DVD players. **Leisure Activities:** library, games, picnic table, patio area. **Business Services:** fax. **Cards:** AX, DS, MC, VI. **Special Amenities:** free expanded continental breakfast and free local telephone calls.

SOME UNITS

VISTA DEL RIO LODGE
Motel
	5/1-11/30 [CP]	1P: $75-$85	2P: $80-$90	Phone: (505)756-2138
				XP: $5 F5
	2/1-4/30 & 12/1-1/31 [CP]	1P: $50-$60	2P: $60-$70	XP: $5 F5

Location: 0.5 mi s of SR 17. Located in a quiet area. 2595 US Hwy 84/64 87520 (HCR 75, Box 37). Fax: 505/756-1872. **Facility:** 19 one-bedroom standard units. 1 story, exterior corridors. **Parking:** on-site, winter plug-ins. **Terms:** cancellation fee imposed, pets (in kennel). **Amenities:** hair dryers. *Some:* irons. **Leisure Activities:** whirlpool, fishing, playground. **Guest Services:** valet laundry. **Business Services:** fax. **Cards:** AX, DC, DS, MC, VI.

SOME UNITS

--------- WHERE TO DINE ---------

HIGH COUNTRY RESTAURANT
Southwest American
| | Lunch: $4-$10 | Dinner: $8-$22 | Phone: 505/756-2384 |

Location: SR 17, just n of jct US 64 and 84. 2299 Hwy 17 87520. **Hours:** 11 am-10 pm; Sunday brunch 8 am-noon. Closed: 4/16, 11/23, 12/25. **Reservations:** accepted. **Features:** This eatery close to town center features casual service and dining, a turn-of-the-century saloon and New Mexican favorites such as tamales, steak asada, and red and green chile. The house specialties include garlic shrimp con pequin which may be as hot as you order and Trucha con pinon-mountain trout in a butter and pinon sauce. Casual dress; cocktails. **Parking:** on-site. **Cards:** AX, DS, MC, VI.

CHIMAYO pop. 2,924

———— WHERE TO STAY ————

CASA ESCONDIDA BED & BREAKFAST

Bed & Breakfast

All Year   2P: $89-$149   XP: $18   D11
Phone: (505)351-4805
Location: SR 68, 7.1 mi e on SR 76, 0.5 mi nw on CR 100, follow signs. Located in a rural area. 64 CR 0100 87522 (PO Box 142). Fax: 505/351-2575. **Facility:** Designated smoking area. 8 units. 7 one-bedroom standard units. 1 one-bedroom suite ($149) with efficiency. 2 stories, interior/exterior corridors. *Bath:* combo or shower only. **Parking:** on-site. **Terms:** check-in 4 pm, 14 day cancellation notice, weekly rates available, package plans, pets ($15 extra charge, in limited units). **Amenities:** *Some:* irons, hair dryers. **Leisure Activities:** whirlpool. **Cards:** MC, VI.

SOME UNITS
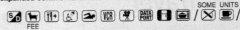
FEE

CIMARRON pop. 917

———— WHERE TO STAY ————

CASA DEL GAVILAN

Historic Bed & Breakfast

5/1-10/31 [BP]	1P: $80-$110	2P: $80-$110	XP: $20 D12
2/1-4/30 [BP]	1P: $75-$105	2P: $75-$105	XP: $20 D12
11/1-1/31 [BP]	1P: $75-$105	2P: $75-$105	XP: $20 D12

Phone: 505-376-2246
Location: SR 21, 5.7 mi s of US 64, follow signs. Located in a secluded area. Hwy 21 S 87714 (PO Box 518). Fax: 505/376-2247. **Facility:** This hacienda-style ranch house dates from 1905 and is in a serene setting with very fine mountain views. Designated smoking area. 5 one-bedroom standard units. 1 story, interior corridors. **Parking:** on-site. **Terms:** 7 day cancellation notice-fee imposed. **Leisure Activities:** hiking trails. **Cards:** DS, MC, VI. **Special Amenities:** free full breakfast and free local telephone calls.

CIMARRON INN & RV PARK

Motel

All Year   1P: $45-$55   2P: $49-$60   XP: $5   F8
Phone: (505)376-2268
Location: On US 64. 212 10th St 87714 (Box 631). Fax: 505/376-4504. **Facility:** 12 one-bedroom standard units. 1 story, exterior corridors. *Bath:* combo or shower only. **Parking:** on-site. **Terms:** cancellation fee imposed, weekly rates available, small pets only. **Business Services:** fax (fee). **Cards:** AX, CB, DC, DS, JC, MC, VI. **Special Amenities:** free local telephone calls and early check-in/late check-out.

SOME UNITS

CLAYTON pop. 2,524

———— WHERE TO STAY ————

BEST WESTERN KOKOPELLI LODGE   *Book at aaa.com*

Small-scale Hotel

All Year [BP]   1P: $71-$165   2P: $71-$165   XP: $8   F17
Phone: (505)374-2589
Location: US 87, 0.5 mi se of jct 56 and 64. 702 S 1st St 88415. Fax: 505/374-2554. **Facility:** 51 units. 50 one-bedroom standard units, some with whirlpools. 1 one-bedroom suite with whirlpool. 2 stories (no elevator), exterior corridors. *Bath:* combo or shower only. **Parking:** on-site. **Terms:** small pets only ($5 extra charge). **Amenities:** irons, hair dryers. **Dining:** Dreamcatcher Dining Room, see separate listing. **Pool(s):** small heated outdoor. **Leisure Activities:** picnic area, playground, shuffleboard. **Guest Services:** gift shop. **Business Services:** fax (fee). **Cards:** AX, CB, DC, DS, MC, VI. **Special Amenities:** free full breakfast and early check-in/late check-out.

SOME UNITS
FEE

DAYS INN & SUITES   *Book at aaa.com*

Small-scale Hotel

All Year   1P: $59-$139   2P: $69-$139   XP: $10   F10
Phone: (505)374-0133
Location: US 87, 1 mi s of jct US 56 and 64. 1120 S 1st St 88415. Fax: 505/374-0285. **Facility:** 41 one-bedroom standard units, some with whirlpools. 2 stories, interior corridors. *Bath:* combo or shower only. **Parking:** on-site. **Terms:** [ECP] meal plan available, small pets only ($5 extra charge, in smoking units). **Amenities:** high-speed Internet, dual phone lines, voice mail, irons, hair dryers. **Pool(s):** heated indoor. **Leisure Activities:** whirlpool, exercise room. **Guest Services:** coin laundry. **Business Services:** fax (fee). **Cards:** AX, DC, DS, MC, VI. **Special Amenities:** free expanded continental breakfast and free local telephone calls.

SOME UNITS
FEE

SUPER 8 MOTEL   *Book at aaa.com*

Motel

5/1-9/10 [CP]	1P: $65-$75	2P: $75-$85	XP: $8 F12
2/1-4/30 & 9/11-1/31 [CP]	1P: $44-$56	2P: $48-$60	XP: $8 F12

Phone: (505)374-8127
Location: US 87, 1 mi se of jct US 56 and 64. 1425 S 1st St 88415. Fax: 505/374-2598. **Facility:** 31 one-bedroom standard units. 2 stories (no elevator), interior corridors. **Parking:** on-site. **Terms:** pets ($7 extra charge). **Cards:** AX, DS, MC, VI.

SOME UNITS
FEE

———— WHERE TO DINE ————

THE EKLUND DINING ROOM & SALOON   **Lunch:** $6-$11   **Dinner:** $8-$32   **Phone:** 505-374-2551

American

Location: On US 56; just s of jct US 64 and 87; center. 15 Main St 88415. **Hours:** 10:30 am-9 pm. Closed: 11/23, 12/25. **Reservations:** accepted. **Features:** Designed in the Victorian style, the restored hotel makes for a nice family restaurant or casual business meeting place. The relaxed, well-lighted environment plays up the site's historical qualities. American dishes are at the heart of the menu. Service is prompt and efficient. Casual dress; cocktails. **Parking:** on-site and street. **Cards:** MC, VI.

CLOUDCROFT pop. 749

―――― WHERE TO STAY ――――

THE LODGE RESORT *Book at aaa.com* Phone: (505)682-2566

| | 4/1-1/31 | 1P: $105-$165 | 2P: $105-$165 |
| | 2/1-3/31 | 1P: $99-$159 | 2P: $99-$159 |

Historic
Small-scale Hotel

Location: US 82, 0.3 mi s. 1 Corona Pl 88317 (PO Box 497). Fax: 505/682-2715. **Facility:** The historic hotel, constructed in 1899, features a fine-dining restaurant, a spa and a nine-hole golf course spread over lush, green hillsides. 60 one-bedroom standard units. 3 stories (no elevator), interior corridors. *Bath:* combo or shower only. **Parking:** on-site. **Terms:** check-in 4 pm, 14 day cancellation notice-fee imposed, weekly rates available, package plans. **Amenities:** irons, hair dryers. **Dining:** Rebecca's, see separate listing. **Pool(s):** heated outdoor. **Leisure Activities:** sauna, whirlpool, winter tubing, croquet, hiking trails, jogging, exercise room, spa, horseshoes, volleyball. *Fee:* golf-18 holes, cross country skiing, snowmobiling, bicycles. **Guest Services:** gift shop, valet laundry. **Business Services:** meeting rooms, PC (fee), fax. **Cards:** AX, DC, DS, MC, VI. *(See color ad below)*

SOME UNITS

―――― WHERE TO DINE ――――

REBECCA'S **Lunch:** $8-$15 **Dinner:** $18-$45 Phone: 505/682-2566

American

Location: US 82, 0.3 mi s; in The Lodge Resort. 1 Corona Pl 88317. **Hours:** 7-10:30 am, 11:30-2 & 5:30-9 pm, Fri & Sat 5:30 pm-10 pm, Sun 7-10 am, 11-2:30 & 5:30-9 pm. **Reservations:** suggested. **Features:** Located in a lovely hotel that dates back to 1899, Rebecca's wonderful stained-glass porch windows enhance the mountain views. Lunch offers sandwiches or pasta. Dinner is formal, with piano music, steak, seafood, and well-known, tasty fruit cobbler. Dressy casual; cocktails. **Parking:** on-site. **Cards:** AX, DC, DS, MC, VI.

CLOVIS pop. 32,667

—— WHERE TO STAY ——

CLOVIS INN & SUITES   *Book at aaa.com*   **Phone:** (505)762-5600
All Year   1P: $49-$55   2P: $52-$58   XP: $8   F12
Location: 1.8 mi e on US 60, 70 and 84. 2912 Mabry Dr 88101. **Fax:** 505/762-6803. **Facility:** 96 units. 95 one-bedroom standard units, some with efficiencies. 1 one-bedroom suite ($69-$74) with efficiency. 2 stories (no elevator), exterior corridors. **Parking:** on-site. **Terms:** [ECP] meal plan available. **Amenities:** high-speed Internet, irons, hair dryers. **Pool(s):** heated outdoor. **Leisure Activities:** whirlpool, exercise room. **Guest Services:** valet and coin laundry, airport transportation-Clovis Airport. **Business Services:** meeting rooms, fax (fee). **Cards:** AX, CB, DC, DS, MC, VI. **Special Amenities:** free expanded continental breakfast and free local telephone calls. *(See color ad below)*

SOME UNITS

COMFORT INN   *Book at aaa.com*   **Phone:** (505)762-4591
All Year   1P: $49   2P: $59   XP: $10   F18
Location: 1 mi e on US 60, 70 and 84. 1616 Mabry Dr 88101. **Fax:** 505/763-6747. **Facility:** 50 one-bedroom standard units. 2 stories (no elevator), exterior corridors. **Parking:** on-site. **Terms:** small pets only ($10 fee). **Amenities:** voice mail, irons, hair dryers. **Pool(s):** heated outdoor. **Guest Services:** valet laundry. **Business Services:** meeting rooms, PC, fax (fee). **Cards:** AX, CB, DC, DS, JC, MC, VI.

SOME UNITS

ECONO LODGE   *Book at aaa.com*   **Phone:** (505)763-3439
All Year   1P: $49-$109   2P: $59-$129   XP: $4   F
Location: 0.5 mi e on US 60, 70 and 84. 1400 E Mabry Dr 88101. **Fax:** 505/769-9022. **Facility:** 46 one-bedroom standard units, some with whirlpools. 1 story, exterior corridors. *Bath:* combo or shower only. **Parking:** on-site. **Terms:** package plans, pets ($10 fee). **Amenities:** high-speed Internet, hair dryers. *Some:* irons. **Pool(s):** heated indoor. **Guest Services:** valet and coin laundry. **Business Services:** fax (fee). **Cards:** AX, DS, MC, VI.

SOME UNITS

HAMPTON INN

Book at aaa.com

All Year [BP]

1P: $79-$99   2P: $89-$109   **Phone: (505)763-3300**

Small-scale Hotel

Location: Jct US 60, 70 and 84, 1.1 mi e. 2212 Mabry Dr 88101. Fax: 505/742-0152. **Facility:** 55 units. 54 one-bedroom standard units. 1 one-bedroom suite ($109-$119). 2 stories, interior corridors. *Bath:* combo or shower only. **Parking:** on-site. **Amenities:** high-speed Internet, dual phone lines, voice mail, irons, hair dryers. *Some:* DVD players (fee). **Pool(s):** heated indoor. **Leisure Activities:** whirlpool, limited exercise equipment. **Guest Services:** valet and coin laundry. **Business Services:** meeting rooms, business center. **Cards:** AX, CB, DC, DS, JC, MC, VI.

SOME UNITS

(ASK) (S☎) (🍴↔) (📖) (🏊) (🎥) (DATA PORT) (📶) (📺) (💻) / (✕) /

HOLIDAY INN CLOVIS

Book at aaa.com

All Year

1P: $59-$109   2P: $59-$109   **Phone: (505)762-4491**

Small-scale Hotel

Location: 1.5 mi e on US 60, 70 and 84. 2700 E Mabry Dr 88101 (PO Box 973). Fax: 505/769-0564. **Facility:** 120 one-bedroom standard units. 2 stories (no elevator), exterior corridors. *Bath:* combo or shower only. **Parking:** on-site. **Terms:** small pets only. **Amenities:** high-speed Internet, voice mail, irons, hair dryers. **Pool(s):** outdoor, heated indoor. **Leisure Activities:** saunas, whirlpool, racquetball court, exercise room. **Guest Services:** valet and coin laundry. **Business Services:** meeting rooms, PC, fax (fee). **Cards:** AX, CB, DC, DS, JC, MC, VI.

SOME UNITS

(ASK) (S☎) (🐕) (🍴) (📺) (&M) (📖) (🖊) (🏊) (✕) (DATA PORT) (💻) / (✕) (📶) (📺) /

HOWARD JOHNSON EXPRESSWAY INN

Book at aaa.com

Property failed to provide current rates

Phone: 505-769-1953

Small-scale Hotel

Location: US 60, 70 and 84, just e. 2920 Mabry Dr 88101. Fax: 505/762-8304. **Facility:** 54 one-bedroom standard units. 2 stories (no elevator), interior corridors. **Parking:** on-site. **Terms:** small pets only ($10 extra charge). **Amenities:** voice mail, honor bars, irons, hair dryers. **Pool(s):** small outdoor. **Leisure Activities:** whirlpool. **Guest Services:** valet and coin laundry. **Business Services:** fax (fee).

SOME UNITS

(🛏) (🍴↔) (🏊) (🎥) (DATA PORT) (📶) (💻) / (✕) /
FEE

LA QUINTA INN & SUITES CLOVIS

(AAA) (SAVE)

Book at aaa.com

All Year [ECP]

1P: $80-$110   2P: $85-$115   XP: $5   **Phone: (505)763-8777**
F17

Small-scale Hotel

Location: Jct US 60/84 and Prince St, 3 mi n. 4521 N Prince St 88101. Fax: 505/763-8778. **Facility:** 66 units. 63 one-bedroom standard units, some with whirlpools. 3 one-bedroom suites with whirlpools. 3 stories, interior corridors. *Bath:* combo or shower only. **Parking:** on-site. **Terms:** small pets only. **Amenities:** high-speed Internet, dual phone lines, voice mail, irons, hair dryers. **Pool(s):** heated indoor. **Leisure Activities:** whirlpool, exercise room. **Guest Services:** sundries, valet and coin laundry. **Business Services:** meeting rooms, business center. **Cards:** AX, DC, DS, MC, VI. **Special Amenities:** free expanded continental breakfast and free local telephone calls. *(See color ad p 527)*

SOME UNITS

(S☎) (🐕) (📺) (🖊) (🏊) (🎥) (DATA PORT) (📶) (📺) (💻) / (✕) /

LA VISTA INN

(AAA) (SAVE)

Motel

All Year

1P: $44-$56   2P: $50-$65   **Phone: 505/762-3808**

Location: 1 mi e on US 60, 70 and 84. Located in a commercial area. 1516 Mabry Dr 88101. Fax: 505/762-1422. **Facility:** 47 one-bedroom standard units. 1 story, exterior corridors. *Bath:* combo or shower only. **Parking:** on-site. **Amenities:** irons, hair dryers. *Some:* high-speed Internet. **Pool(s):** heated outdoor. **Guest Services:** coin laundry. **Business Services:** fax (fee). **Cards:** AX, DS, MC, VI. **Special Amenities:** free continental breakfast and free local telephone calls.

SOME UNITS

(🍴↔) (🏊) (🎥) (DATA PORT) (💻) / (✕) (📶) /
FEE

The following lodging was either not evaluated or did not meet AAA rating requirements but is listed for your information only.

MOTEL 7

(fyi)

Motel

Phone: 505/762-2995

Did not meet all AAA rating requirements for some property operations at time of last evaluation on 01/19/2005. **Location:** Jct US 60,70 and 84. 2620 Mabry Dr 88101. Facilities, services, and decor characterize a basic property.

CORRALES pop. 7,334 (See map and index starting on p. 478)

--- WHERE TO STAY ---

CASA DE KOSHARE

Phone: 505/898-4500   [102]

Property failed to provide current rates

Bed & Breakfast

Location: I-25, exit 233 (Alameda Blvd), 4.5 mi w to Ellison, 0.7 mi n, then just w. 122 Ashley Ln NW 87048. Fax: 505/898-8900. **Facility:** Featuring displays of American Indian artwork, this B&B includes a dining room with adobe walls and an abundance of natural light. Designated smoking area. 4 units. 3 one-bedroom standard units. 1 one-bedroom suite with whirlpool. 1 story, interior corridors. *Bath:* shared or private. **Parking:** on-site. **Terms:** age restrictions may apply. **Amenities:** high-speed Internet, irons, hair dryers. **Leisure Activities:** jogging. **Guest Services:** gift shop, valet laundry.

(✈) (✕) (🎥) (DATA PORT) (📞)

THE CHOCOLATE TURTLE BED & BREAKFAST

Phone: 505/898-1800   [100]

All Year [BP]

1P: $60-$120   2P: $70-$120

Bed & Breakfast

Location: I-25, exit 233 (Alameda Blvd), just w, 4 mi to Corrales Rd, 1 mi n to Meadowlark Ln, then 2 mi w. 1098 W Meadowlark Ln 87048 (PO Box 991). Fax: 505/898-6491. **Facility:** The B&B features a large, colorful, Southwestern-style living room and attractively decorated guest rooms. Smoke free premises. 4 one-bedroom standard units. 1 story, interior corridors. *Bath:* combo or shower only. **Parking:** on-site. **Terms:** check-in 4 pm, age restrictions may apply, cancellation fee imposed. **Amenities:** high-speed Internet. **Cards:** AX, MC, VI.

(ASK) (S☎) (✕) (DATA PORT) (📞)

(See map and index starting on p. 478)

HACIENDA MANZANAL BED & BREAKFAST
Phone: (505)922-1662   101

▼▼▼▼ All Year   2P: $95-$135   XP: $25

Bed & Breakfast **Location:** I-25, exit 233 (Alameda Blvd), 4 mi w to Corrales Rd, 2 mi n to Meadowlark Ln, then just w. 300 W Meadowlark Ln 87048 (PO Box 2667). Fax: 505/922-1909. **Facility:** Spacious guest rooms and baths, Southwestern adobe earth tones and a rural; village setting give this B&B the feel of a retreat. Designated smoking area. 4 one-bedroom standard units, some with whirlpools. 2 stories (no elevator), interior corridors. *Bath:* combo or shower only. **Parking:** on-site. **Terms:** office hours 8 am-10 pm, check-in 5 pm, 3 day cancellation notice, [BP] meal plan available. **Amenities:** hair dryers. **Leisure Activities:** hiking trails, jogging, horseshoes. **Cards:** MC, VI.

ASK ⊆M ⴕ ✕ ✕ DATA PORT ☎

THE SANDHILL CRANE BED & BREAKFAST
Phone: 505-898-2445   99

▼▼▼▼ 10/1-10/15 [BP]   1P: $120-$200   2P: $120-$200   XP: $10   F
2/1-9/30 & 10/16-1/31 [BP]   1P: $90-$190   2P: $90-$190   XP: $10   F

Bed & Breakfast **Location:** I-25, exit 233 (Alameda Blvd), 4 mi w to Corrales Rd, 3 mi n, then 0.5 mi w. 389 Camino Hermosa 87048. **Facility:** A pleasant adobe home with warm, brick floors, this B&B is in Corrales, a small village just a short drive from Albuquerque. Smoke free premises. 4 one-bedroom standard units. 1 story, interior/exterior corridors. *Bath:* some shared or private, combo or shower only. **Parking:** on-site. **Terms:** check-in 4 pm, 3 day cancellation notice-fee imposed, [ECP] meal plan available, package plans. **Business Services:** meeting rooms, fax (fee). **Cards:** AX, MC, VI.

ASK S⊆D ✕ 🎥 DATA PORT 🖥

WHERE TO DINE

CALICO CAFE & BAKERY
Lunch: $4-$7   Phone: 505/890-9150   144

▼▼▼▼ **Location:** Center. 4512 Corrales Rd 87048. **Hours:** 7 am-2 pm. Closed: 11/23, 12/25. **Features:** The cafe celebrates the American cowgirl. In addition to hearty breakfasts, guests can sample from an eclectic selection of sandwiches and delectable cakes, pies and cookies produced in the in-house bakery. Casual dress. **Parking:** on-site. **Cards:** AX, DS, MC, VI.

Southwest American

ESSENCIA RESTAURANT
Lunch: $6-$10   Dinner: $12-$22   Phone: 505/792-4210   141

▼▼▼ **Location:** Center. 4908 Corrales Rd 87048. **Hours:** 11:30 am-1:30 & 5:30-9 pm, Tues-1:30 pm, Sun 11 am-2 pm; Sunday brunch. Closed: 1/1, 12/25. **Reservations:** suggested. **Features:** In the center of the historic town, the fine dining cafe presents an eclectic menu of appetizers, salads and entrees from around the globe. Dressy casual; beer & wine only. **Parking:** on-site. **Cards:** MC, VI.

American

INDIGO CROW
Lunch: $7-$10   Dinner: $13-$25   Phone: 505/898-7000   143

▼▼▼ **Location:** Center. 4515 Corrales Rd 87048. **Hours:** 11:30 am-2 & 5-9 pm. Closed: 11/23, 12/25; also Mon. **Reservations:** accepted. **Features:** A dining room with territorial charm, a patio surrounded by a Mexican-style wall and an imaginative menu are some of the features of this cafe in the center of town. The tasty Cobb salad is gigantic. Casual dress; beer & wine only; entertainment. **Parking:** on-site. **Cards:** AX,

American MC, VI.

🍸

JIM WHITE'S CASA VIEJA
Dinner: $7-$30   Phone: 505/898-7489   142

▼▼▼ **Location:** Center. 4541 Corrales Rd 87048. **Hours:** 5 pm-9 pm. Closed major holidays. **Reservations:** accepted. **Features:** Literally the "old house" in Spanish, this ancient hacienda is now the home of a restaurant that serves New Mexican food, and also features an "Americana grill" comprised of steaks, seafood and pasta dishes, The outdoor patio is a nice dining spot. Dressy casual; cocktails. **Parking:** on-site. **Cards:** AX, DS, MC, VI. **Historic**

Southwest American

🍸 ◹

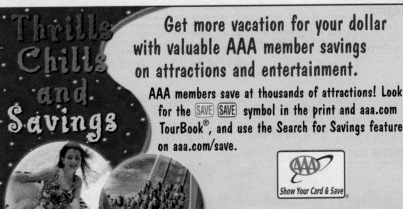

DEMING pop. 14,116

—— **WHERE TO STAY** ——

BEST WESTERN MIMBRES VALLEY INN *Book at aaa.com*

Small-scale Hotel

All Year [CP] 1P: $47-$85 2P: $47-$85 Phone: (505)546-4544
Location: I-10, exit 81, just e. 1500 W Pine 88030. **Fax:** 505/546-9875. **Facility:** 40 one-bedroom standard units. 1 story, exterior corridors. **Parking:** on-site. **Terms:** small pets only. **Amenities:** high-speed Internet, irons, hair dryers. **Pool(s):** heated outdoor. **Business Services:** fax (fee). **Cards:** AX, CB, DC, DS, JC, MC, VI.

SOME UNITS

COMFORT INN & SUITES

[fyi] Small-scale Hotel

Phone: 505/544-3600
All Year 1P: $60-$75 2P: $65-$80 XP: $5 D18
Too new to rate. **Location:** I-10, exit 81, just e. 1010 W Pine St 88030. **Amenities:** 52 units. **Cards:** AX, CB, DC, DS, JC, MC, VI.

DAYS INN *Book at aaa.com*

AAA [SAVE]

Motel

Phone: (505)546-8813
All Year [ECP] 1P: $42-$52 2P: $47-$57 XP: $5 F12
Location: I-10, exit 85 westbound, 2 mi w on business loop; exit 81 eastbound, 1 mi e on business loop. 1601 E Pine St 88030. **Fax:** 505/546-7095. **Facility:** 57 one-bedroom standard units. 2 stories (no elevator), exterior corridors. **Parking:** on-site. **Terms:** small pets only ($5 extra charge). **Amenities:** hair dryers. **Dining:** 11 am-10 pm. **Pool(s):** outdoor. **Cards:** AX, CB, DC, DS, MC, VI. **Special Amenities:** free expanded continental breakfast and free local telephone calls.

SOME UNITS
FEE

GRAND MOTOR INN

AAA [SAVE]

Small-scale Hotel

Phone: (505)546-2632
All Year 1P: $40 2P: $48 XP: $6 F12
Location: I-10, exit 85 westbound, 2 mi w on business loop; exit 82 eastbound, 1 mi e on business loop. 1721 E Pine St 88030 (PO Box 309, 88031). **Fax:** 505/546-4446. **Facility:** 60 one-bedroom standard units, some with whirlpools. 2 stories (no elevator), exterior corridors. **Parking:** on-site. **Terms:** weekly rates available, package plans, small pets only ($5 extra charge). **Dining:** 6 am-9 pm, cocktails, also, Grand Restaurant, see separate listing. **Pool(s):** outdoor. **Guest Services:** valet and coin laundry, area transportation-bus stop & train station. **Business Services:** meeting rooms. **Cards:** AX, CB, DC, DS, MC, VI. *(See color ad below)*

SOME UNITS
FEE

HOLIDAY INN

AAA [SAVE]

Small-scale Hotel

Phone: (505)546-2661
All Year 1P: $50-$60 2P: $50-$60 XP: $6 F17
Location: I-10, exit 85, just w. 4600 E Pine St 88030 (PO Box 1138, 88031). **Fax:** 505/546-6308. **Facility:** 116 one-bedroom standard units, some with whirlpools. 2 stories (no elevator), exterior corridors. *Bath:* combo or shower only. **Parking:** on-site. **Terms:** [BP] meal plan available. **Amenities:** high-speed Internet, hair dryers. **Dining:** Prime Rib Grill, see separate listing. **Pool(s):** outdoor. **Leisure Activities:** exercise room. **Guest Services:** valet and coin laundry. **Business Services:** meeting rooms. **Cards:** AX, CB, DC, DS, MC, VI. **Special Amenities:** free local telephone calls and free newspaper.

SOME UNITS

LA QUINTA INN & SUITES

Small-scale Hotel

Phone: (505)546-0600
All Year 1P: $69-$99 2P: $69-$99 XP: $5 F17
Location: I-10, exit 85, just w. 4300 E Pine St 88030. **Fax:** 505/544-8207. **Facility:** 58 units. 54 one-bedroom standard units. 4 two-bedroom suites ($79-$125). 3 stories, interior corridors. *Bath:* combo or shower only. **Parking:** on-site. **Terms:** small pets only. **Amenities:** high-speed Internet, dual phone lines, voice mail, irons, hair dryers. **Pool(s):** heated outdoor. **Leisure Activities:** whirlpool, exercise room. **Guest Services:** coin laundry. **Business Services:** meeting rooms, business center. **Cards:** AX, CB, DC, DS, JC, MC, VI.

SOME UNITS

———— WHERE TO DINE ————

EL MIRADOR   Lunch: $6-$8   Dinner: $6-$8   Phone: 505/544-7340
Mexican
Location: Center. 510 E Pine St 88030. **Hours:** 6 am-9 pm. **Features:** This modest cafe is very busy at lunch time. You'll find Mexican food here that is prepared in the traditional way, including carefully prepared enchiladas, tacos and burritos. Casual dress. **Parking:** on-site. **Cards:** AX, CB, MC, VI.

GRAND RESTAURANT   Lunch: $5-$17   Dinner: $5-$17   Phone: 505/546-2632
Southwest American
Location: I-10, exit 85 westbound, 2 mi w on business loop; exit 82 eastbound, 1 mi e on business loop; in Grand Motor Inn. 1721 E Pine St 88030. **Hours:** 6 am-9 pm. **Features:** This locally popular restaurant is also attractive to visitors to the area. It features steak, seafood, homemade soup and pie, salad bar, authentic Mexican dishes and daily specials in a casual, family-style setting within the hotel. Casual dress; cocktails. **Parking:** on-site. **Cards:** AX, CB, DC, DS, MC, VI. (See color ad p 530)

PALMA'S ITALIAN GRILL   Lunch: $5-$8   Dinner: $7-$22   Phone: 505/544-3100
Italian
Location: Jct Silver Ave and Pine St; center. 110 S Silver Ave 88030. **Hours:** 11 am-8 pm, Fri & Sat-8:30 pm, Sun-3 pm. Closed: 1/1, 12/25; also Mon. **Reservations:** accepted. **Features:** The menu centers on Italian fare: pasta, including traditional spaghetti with meatballs, and such tempting sandwiches as Italian sausage with fried green peppers and onions on an Italian roll. Casual dress; beer & wine only. **Parking:** street.
Cards: AX, MC, VI.

PRIME RIB GRILL   Lunch: $5-$12   Dinner: $7-$25   Phone: 505/546-2661
American
Location: I-10, exit 85, just w; in Holiday Inn. I-10 & Motel Dr 88030. **Hours:** 6:30 am-1:30 & 5-9:30 pm, Fri-10 pm, Sat 7 am-noon & 5-10 pm, Sun 7 am-1:30 & 5-9 pm. **Features:** The Prime Rib Grill prepares buffets every day and offers home-style cooking as well as Italian and seafood dishes. The dessert selection of cobblers and pie is also good. The casual dining room within the hotel features a Southwestern motif. Casual dress; cocktails; entertainment. **Parking:** on-site. **Cards:** AX, DC, DS, MC, VI.

RANCHER'S GRILL   Lunch: $6-$17   Dinner: $6-$17   Phone: 505/546-8883
Steak House
Location: I-10, exit 82B. 316 E Cedar 88030. **Hours:** 10:30 am-10 pm. Closed: 11/23, 12/25. **Reservations:** not accepted. **Features:** Great steaks and a well-stocked salad bar are hallmarks of the busy eatery. The restaurant is equally popular with travelers and locals who visit frequently. Casual dress; beer & wine only. **Parking:** on-site. **Cards:** AX, DC, DS, MC, VI.

EDGEWOOD pop. 1,893

———— WHERE TO STAY ————

ALTA MAE'S HERITAGE INN   Phone: 505/281-5000
Bed & Breakfast
Property failed to provide current rates
Location: I-40, exit 187, just s to stop sign, then just e. Located in a quiet area. 1950-C Old Route 66 87015. Fax: 505/281-5157. **Facility:** With the ambience of rural New Mexico, this inn offers a dining area and conference room in a tranquil setting. Designated smoking area. 5 one-bedroom standard units, some with whirlpools. 1 story, exterior corridors. **Parking:** on-site. **Terms:** pets (horses only, with prior approval). **Leisure Activities:** whirlpool, hiking trails, horseback riding.

ELEPHANT BUTTE pop. 1,390

———— WHERE TO STAY ————

ELEPHANT BUTTE INN   *Book at aaa.com*   Phone: (505)744-5431
Small-scale Hotel
All Year [CP]   1P: $65-$95   2P: $70-$100   XP: $10   F12
Location: I-25, exit 83, 4 mi e. 401 Hwy 195 87935 (PO Box 996). Fax: 505/744-5044. **Facility:** 47 one-bedroom standard units. 2 stories (no elevator), exterior corridors. *Bath:* combo or shower only. **Parking:** on-site. **Terms:** 3 day cancellation notice-fee imposed, package plans, pets ($15 fee). **Amenities:** irons, hair dryers. **Dining:** 11 am-9 pm; 11 am-2 & 5-9 pm in winter, cocktails. **Pool(s):** heated outdoor. **Leisure Activities:** tennis court, limited exercise equipment. **Guest Services:** valet laundry. **Business Services:** meeting rooms, fax (fee). **Cards:** AX, DC, DS, MC, VI. **Special Amenities: free continental breakfast and free local telephone calls.**
SOME UNITS
FEE

MARINA SUITES MOTEL   *Book at aaa.com*   Phone: 505/744-5269
Motel
Property failed to provide current rates
Location: I-25, exit 83, 4.7 mi e. 200 Country Club Dr 87935 (4717 Elder Ave, SEAL BEACH, CA, 90740). Fax: 505/744-4693. **Facility:** 17 one-bedroom standard units with kitchens. 1 story, exterior corridors. **Parking:** on-site. **Terms:** pets (must be attended). **Amenities:** high-speed Internet.

EL MORRO

———— WHERE TO DINE ————

ANCIENT WAY CAFE   Lunch: $4-$7   Dinner: $9-$15   Phone: 505/783-4612
Southwest American
Location: SR 53, MM 46. HC 61, Box 44 87321. **Hours:** 9 am-7 pm. Closed: 12/25. **Features:** Guests of the associated campground and local folks alike enjoy trying the daily specials produced by the comfortable country-style cafe. Fresh pies are to die for. Casual dress. **Parking:** on-site. **Cards:** AX, DS, MC, VI.

ESPANOLA pop. 9,688

────── **WHERE TO STAY** ──────

BEST WESTERN OHKAY CASINO RESORT   *Book at aaa.com*   Phone: (505)747-1668

🔺🔺🔺 [SAVE]
🔻🔻🔻

6/2-10/5	1P: $89	2P: $139	XP: $10 F
3/31-6/1 & 10/6-1/31	1P: $79	2P: $129	XP: $10 F
2/1-3/30	1P: $69	2P: $119	XP: $10 F

Small-scale Hotel   **Location:** 3.4 mi n of jct US 84 and 285. Hwy 68 1 mi n of Espanola turn right light 87566 (PO Box 1270, SAN JUAN PUEBLO). Fax: 505/747-5695. **Facility:** 101 one-bedroom standard units, some with whirlpools. 3 stories, interior corridors. **Parking:** on-site. **Terms:** cancellation fee imposed, package plans. **Amenities:** voice mail, irons, hair dryers. *Some:* high-speed Internet. **Dining:** 6:30 am-11 pm, Fri & Sat-12:30 am, cocktails, entertainment. **Pool(s):** heated outdoor. **Guest Services:** gift shop. **Business Services:** conference facilities. **Cards:** AX, CB, DC, DS, MC, VI. **Special Amenities:** free local telephone calls and free room upgrade (subject to availability with advance reservations).

SOME UNITS
[S☑] [🐾] [📶] [♨] [🎥] [DATA PORT] [🔌] [💻] / [✕]

COMFORT INN   *Book at aaa.com*   Phone: (505)753-2419

🔺🔺🔺 [SAVE]
🔻🔻

5/15-10/15	1P: $50-$105	2P: $55-$125	XP: $5 F17
3/1-5/14 & 10/16-2/28	1P: $50-$95	2P: $55-$105	XP: $5 F17

Small-scale Hotel   **Location:** US 84 and 285, just s of jct SR 68. 604-B S Riverside Dr 87532. Fax: 505/753-5131. **Facility:** 41 one-bedroom standard units. 2 stories (no elevator), interior corridors. **Parking:** on-site. **Terms:** [ECP] meal plan available. **Amenities:** high-speed Internet, irons, hair dryers. **Pool(s):** heated indoor. **Leisure Activities:** whirlpool. **Cards:** AX, CB, DC, DS, JC, MC, VI. **Special Amenities:** free expanded continental breakfast and free local telephone calls. *(See color ad below)*

SOME UNITS
[S☑] [🐾] [📶] [♨] [🎥] [DATA PORT] [💻] / [✕] [🔌] [🖥] /

ESPANOLA DAYS INN   *Book at aaa.com*   Phone: (505)747-1242

🔻🔻🔻🔻

5/28-10/31 [CP]	1P: $50-$66	2P: $55-$72	XP: $5 F18
2/1-5/27 & 11/1-1/31 [CP]	1P: $40-$54	2P: $45-$59	XP: $5 F18

Small-scale Hotel   **Location:** US 84 and 285, 0.7 mi s of jct SR 68. 807 S Riverside Dr 87532. Fax: 505/753-8089. **Facility:** 40 one-bedroom standard units. 2 stories (no elevator), exterior corridors. **Parking:** on-site. **Terms:** pets ($5 extra charge). **Amenities:** hair dryers. *Some:* irons. **Cards:** AX, CB, DC, DS, MC, VI.

SOME UNITS
[A$K] [S☑] [🐾] [📶] [🎥] / [✕] [🔌] [🖥] /
FEE

INN AT THE DELTA   Phone: 505/753-9466

🔻🔻🔻

     Property failed to provide current rates

Bed & Breakfast   **Location:** US 84 and 285, 1 mi n of jct SR 68, 0.3 mi n of jct SR 30. 243 Paseo de Onate 87532. Fax: 505/753-9446. **Facility:** Hand-carved wooden furniture, original artwork and a kiva fireplace fill each room of this tranquil inn. Smoke free premises. 10 one-bedroom standard units with whirlpools. 1-2 stories (no elevator), exterior corridors. **Parking:** on-site. **Terms:** office hours 7:30 am-10 pm. **Amenities:** high-speed Internet, irons, hair dryers. **Business Services:** meeting rooms.

[📶] [✕]

SUPER 8 MOTEL   Phone: (505)753-5374

🔺🔺🔺 [SAVE]
🔻🔻🔻

5/15-10/14	1P: $45-$100	2P: $50-$105	
2/1-5/14	1P: $38-$85	2P: $45-$100	
10/15-1/31	1P: $38-$90	2P: $40-$100	

Small-scale Hotel   **Location:** US 84 and 285, 0.5 mi s of jct SR 68. 811 S Riverside Dr 87532. Fax: 505/753-5339. **Facility:** 48 one-bedroom standard units. 2 stories (no elevator), interior corridors. **Parking:** on-site, winter plug-ins. **Amenities:** *Some:* irons, hair dryers. **Cards:** AX, CB, DC, DS, JC, MC, VI. **Special Amenities:** free local telephone calls and early check-in/late check-out.

SOME UNITS
[S☑] [🐾] [📶] [🎥] [DATA PORT] / [✕] [🔌] [🖥] [💻] /

FARMINGTON pop. 37,844

—— WHERE TO STAY ——

BEST WESTERN INN & SUITES   *Book at aaa.com*   Phone: (505)327-5221
AAA SAVE   All Year   1P: $79-$99   2P: $89-$109   XP: $10   F12
▽▼◇▼▽   **Location:** 0.8 mi e on US 64 at Bloomfield Blvd and Scott Ave. 700 Scott Ave 87401. Fax: 505/327-1565. **Facility:** 192 one-bedroom standard units. 3 stories, interior corridors. **Parking:** on-site. **Terms:** [BP] meal plan available, package plans, small pets only ($10 fee). **Amenities:** video games, voice mail, irons, hair dryers. *Some:* high-speed Internet. **Dining:** Riverwalk Patio and Grill, see separate listing. **Pool(s):** small heated indoor. **Leisure Activities:** saunas, whirlpool, exercise room. *Fee:* game room. **Guest Services:** valet and coin laundry. **Business Services:** meeting rooms, business center. **Cards:** AX, CB, DC, DS, MC, VI.
Small-scale Hotel
Special Amenities: free full breakfast and free local telephone calls. *(See color ad below)*

SOME UNITS

FEE

CASA BLANCA BED & BREAKFAST INN   Phone: 505/327-6503
Property failed to provide current rates
▽▼◇▼▽   **Location:** 1 blk n of Main Ave; downtown. Located in historic Spanish Hacienda Estate, in a quiet area. 505 E La Plata
Bed & Breakfast   St 87401. Fax: 505/326-5680. **Facility:** Built in the 1950s, this mission-style home is set on a bluff overlooking the community and surrounding cliffs. Several rooms with a fireplace. Smoke free premises. 9 units. 8 one-bedroom standard units, some with kitchens and/or whirlpools. 1 two-bedroom suite with kitchen. 1-2 stories (no elevator), interior/exterior corridors. *Bath:* combo or shower only. **Parking:** on-site. **Terms:** check-in 4 pm. **Amenities:** CD players, high-speed Internet, irons, hair dryers. **Leisure Activities:** whirlpool. **Guest Services:** area transportation. **Business Services:** meeting rooms.

SOME UNITS

COMFORT INN   *Book at aaa.com*   Phone: (505)325-2626
AAA SAVE   4/1-10/31   1P: $69-$109   2P: $79-$119   XP: $10   F19
▽▼◇▼▽   2/1-3/31 & 11/1-1/31   1P: $59-$89   2P: $69-$99   XP: $10   F19
Motel   **Location:** 0.8 mi e on US 64 (Bloomfield Blvd), just n. 555 Scott Ave 87401. Fax: 505/325-7675. **Facility:** 60 one-bedroom standard units, some with whirlpools. 2 stories (no elevator), interior corridors. **Parking:** on-site. **Terms:** [ECP] meal plan available, pets ($10 extra charge). **Amenities:** high-speed Internet, irons, hair dryers. **Pool(s):** small heated outdoor. **Guest Services:** valet laundry. **Business Services:** PC. **Cards:** AX, CB, DC, DS, JC, MC, VI.

SOME UNITS

FEE   FEE

COURTYARD BY MARRIOTT   *Book at aaa.com*   Phone: (505)325-5111
▽▼◇▼▽   All Year   1P: $69-$89   2P: $69-$89
Small-scale Hotel   **Location:** 1 mi e on SR 516 (Main St), just s. 560 Scott Ave 87401. Fax: 505/325-5588. **Facility:** 125 units. 121 one-bedroom standard units, some with whirlpools. 4 one-bedroom suites ($99-$120). 4 stories, interior corridors. *Bath:* combo or shower only. **Parking:** on-site. **Terms:** [BP] meal plan available. **Amenities:** high-speed Internet, dual phone lines, voice mail, irons, hair dryers. **Dining:** The River's Edge Cafe, see separate listing. **Pool(s):** small heated indoor. **Leisure Activities:** whirlpool, exercise room. **Guest Services:** gift shop, valet and coin laundry. **Business Services:** conference facilities, business center. **Cards:** AX, DC, DS, MC, VI.

SOME UNITS

ASK

DAYS INN *Book at aaa.com*   Phone: 505/325-3700

Property failed to provide current rates

▽▽▽
Motel
Location: 1.7 mi e on US 64 (Bloomfield Blvd). 1901 E Broadway 87401. Fax: 505/325-8300. **Facility:** 63 one-bedroom standard units, some with whirlpools. 3 stories, interior corridors. *Bath:* combo or shower only. **Parking:** on-site. **Terms:** pets ($10 extra charge). **Amenities:** high-speed Internet, irons, hair dryers. **Guest Services:** valet and coin laundry. **Business Services:** meeting rooms, PC.

SOME UNITS

FARMINGTON EAST SUPER 8 MOTEL *Book at aaa.com*   Phone: (505)564-8100

AAA SAVE
▽▽▽ ▽▽▽
Small-scale Hotel

4/2-10/31 [CP]	1P: $68-$118	2P: $78-$128	XP: $10	F17
2/1-4/1 & 11/1-1/31 [CP]	1P: $58-$108	2P: $68-$118	XP: $10	F17

Location: On US 550 at Cortez Way. Located in a commercial/shopping area. 4751 Cortez Way 87402. Fax: 505/564-8103. **Facility:** 67 one-bedroom standard units, some with whirlpools. 3 stories, interior corridors. *Bath:* combo or shower only. **Parking:** on-site. **Amenities:** high-speed Internet, safes. **Pool(s):** small heated indoor. **Leisure Activities:** whirlpool. **Guest Services:** coin laundry. **Business Services:** PC. **Cards:** AX, DC, DS, MC, VI. **Special Amenities:** free continental breakfast and free local telephone calls.

SOME UNITS

HOLIDAY INN EXPRESS *Book at aaa.com*   Phone: (505)325-2545

AAA SAVE
▽▽▽
Motel
All Year   1P: $77

Location: 1.6 mi e on US 64 (Bloomfield Blvd), just past jct Broadway, on frontage road. 2110 Bloomfield Blvd 87401. Fax: 505/325-3262. **Facility:** 100 units. 96 one-bedroom standard units. 4 one-bedroom suites. 3 stories, interior corridors. *Bath:* combo or shower only. **Parking:** on-site. **Terms:** pets ($20 fee). **Amenities:** high-speed Internet, dual phone lines, voice mail, irons, hair dryers. **Pool(s):** small heated indoor. **Leisure Activities:** whirlpool, barbecue grill. **Guest Services:** valet and coin laundry. **Business Services:** meeting rooms. **Cards:** AX, DC, DS, MC, VI. **Special Amenities:** free expanded continental breakfast and free local telephone calls.

SOME UNITS

HOLIDAY INN OF FARMINGTON (NOW KNOWN AS BRENTWOOD INN FARMINGTON) *Book at aaa.com*   Phone: (505)325-2288

▽▽▽
Small-scale Hotel
All Year   1P: $79   2P: $84

Location: 1 mi e; at Broadway and Scott Ave. 600 E Broadway 87401. Fax: 505/325-2288. **Facility:** 148 one-bedroom standard units, some with whirlpools. 2 stories (no elevator), interior corridors. **Parking:** on-site. **Terms:** [BP] meal plan available, package plans, pets ($25 fee). **Amenities:** high-speed Internet, dual phone lines, voice mail, irons, hair dryers. **Pool(s):** heated outdoor. **Leisure Activities:** sauna, whirlpool, exercise room. **Guest Services:** valet laundry. **Business Services:** meeting rooms. **Cards:** AX, CB, DC, DS, MC, VI.

SOME UNITS

KNIGHT'S INN *Book at aaa.com*   Phone: (505)325-5061

AAA SAVE
▽
Motel
All Year	1P: $50-$75	2P: $60-$85	XP: $5	F12

Location: From Main St, 0.5 mi n. 701 Airport Dr 87401. Fax: 505/325-5061. **Facility:** 21 one-bedroom standard units. 1 story, exterior corridors. **Parking:** on-site. **Terms:** cancellation fee imposed, weekly rates available. **Amenities:** high-speed Internet, voice mail. *Some:* irons. **Business Services:** PC. **Cards:** AX, DS, MC, VI. **Special Amenities:** free local telephone calls and free room upgrade (subject to availability with advance reservations).

SOME UNITS

LA QUINTA INN FARMINGTON *Book at aaa.com*   Phone: (505)327-4706

▽▽▽
Motel
5/1-8/31 [CP]	1P: $82-$112
9/1-1/31 [CP]	1P: $75-$105
2/1-4/30 [CP]	1P: $72-$102

Location: 1 mi e on SR 516 (Main St), just s. 675 Scott Ave 87401. Fax: 505/325-6583. **Facility:** 106 units. 104 one-bedroom standard units. 2 one-bedroom suites ($112-$152). 2 stories (no elevator), interior/exterior corridors. **Parking:** on-site. **Amenities:** video games, voice mail, irons, hair dryers. **Pool(s):** small heated outdoor. **Guest Services:** valet laundry. **Cards:** AX, CB, DC, DS, MC, VI.

SOME UNITS

THE REGION INN

AAA SAVE

▼▼▼▼

Small-scale Hotel

Phone: (505)325-1191
F

All Year   1P: $45-$67   2P: $45-$67   XP: $10
Location: 0.8 mi e on US 64, just n at jct Scott Ave. 601 E Broadway 87401. Fax: 505/325-1223. **Facility:** 75 units. 73 one-bedroom standard units. 2 one-bedroom suites with whirlpools. 3 stories, interior corridors. *Bath:* combo or shower only. **Parking:** on-site. **Terms:** [ECP] meal plan available, package plans. **Amenities:** high-speed Internet, voice mail, irons, hair dryers. **Dining:** 7 am-10 & 11-10 pm, cocktails. **Pool(s):** heated outdoor. **Leisure Activities:** whirlpool. **Guest Services:** gift shop, valet and coin laundry, area transportation-within 20 mi. **Business Services:** meeting rooms, PC. **Cards:** AX, DC, DS, JC, MC, VI. **Special Amenities:** free expanded continental breakfast and early check-in/late check-out.

SOME UNITS

[icons] FEE

SUPER 8 MOTEL

▼▼▼▼

Motel

Book at aaa.com

Phone: (505)325-1813
F12

All Year   1P: $43-$73   2P: $48-$78   XP: $5
Location: Just n of jct SR 64 (Bloomfield Blvd). 1601 E Broadway 87401. Fax: 505/325-1813. **Facility:** 60 one-bedroom standard units, some with whirlpools. 3 stories (no elevator), interior corridors. *Bath:* combo or shower only. **Parking:** on-site. **Terms:** [ECP] meal plan available, pets ($5 extra charge). **Amenities:** high-speed Internet. *Some:* irons, hair dryers. **Leisure Activities:** *Fee:* game room. **Guest Services:** coin laundry. **Business Services:** PC. **Cards:** AX, CB, DC, DS, JC, MC, VI.

SOME UNITS

[icons] ASK ... FEE ... FEE

TRAVELODGE

AAA SAVE

▼▼▼▼

Motel

Book at aaa.com

Phone: (505)327-0242

5/1-10/31 [CP]   1P: $50-$55   2P: $60-$65   XP: $5   F12
2/1-4/30 & 11/1-1/31 [CP]   1P: $45-$50   2P: $55-$60   XP: $5   F12
Location: 1.1 mi e on SR 516 (Main Ave), just s. 510 Scott Ave 87401. Fax: 505/327-5617. **Facility:** 98 one-bedroom standard units. 3 stories, exterior corridors. **Parking:** on-site. **Amenities:** *Some:* irons, hair dryers. **Pool(s):** small outdoor. **Guest Services:** coin laundry. **Cards:** AX, DC, DS, MC, VI. *(See color ad p 534)*

SOME UNITS

[icons]

WHERE TO DINE

THE BLUFFS

▼▼▼▼

Steak & Seafood

Lunch: $5-$11   **Dinner:** $16-$32   Phone: 505/325-8155
Location: 1.1 mi e on SR 516 (Main St); in Plaza Farmington Shopping Complex. 3450 E Main St 87402. **Hours:** 11 am-2 & 4-9 pm, Fri & Sat-10 pm. Closed major holidays; also Sun. **Reservations:** suggested. **Features:** The sleek new restaurant treats patrons to a fine-dining experience. On the menu are several steak and seafood dishes, including a wonderful filet mignon. Table spacing and lighting allow for privacy. Casual dress; cocktails. **Parking:** on-site. **Cards:** AX, CB, DC, DS, MC, VI.

K B DILLON'S BAR & GRILLE

▼▼▼

American

Lunch: $6-$12   **Dinner:** $14-$25   Phone: 505/325-0222
Location: On US 64 (Bloomfield Blvd); downtown. 101 W Broadway 87401. **Hours:** 11 am-10 pm, Sat from 5 pm. Closed: 7/4, 11/23, 12/25; also Sun. **Reservations:** accepted. **Features:** Appealing to those seeking a hearty meal, the restaurant has rustic surroundings on the outside and a warm, boisterous atmosphere inside. The menu lists steak, poultry, fish and veal choices, as well as several seafood selections. Dressy casual; cocktails. **Parking:** on-site. **Cards:** AX, MC, VI.

THE RIVER'S EDGE CAFE

▼▼▼

American

Lunch: $6-$8   **Dinner:** $10-$19   Phone: 505/325-5111
Location: 1 mi e on SR 516 (Main St), just s; in Courtyard by Marriott. 560 Scott Ave 87401. **Hours:** 6:30-10 am, 11-2 & 5-10 pm. Closed: 11/23, 12/25. **Features:** The menu incorporates breakfast, lunch and dinner items. Beef, seafood, pasta and Mexican foods factor heavily among dinner selections. Pan-seared salmon is especially good. Casual dress; cocktails. **Parking:** on-site. **Cards:** AX, CB, DC, DS, MC, VI.

RIVERWALK PATIO AND GRILL

▼▼▼

American

Lunch: $6-$10   **Dinner:** $8-$18   Phone: 505/327-5221
Location: 0.8 mi e on US 64 at Bloomfield Blvd and Scott Ave; in Best Western Inn & Suites. 700 Scott Ave 87401. **Hours:** 6-10 am, 11:30-2 & 5-10 pm, Fri & Sat-11 pm. Closed: 12/25. **Reservations:** accepted. **Features:** The three-meal hotel restaurant's dinner menu lists a variety of steak and seafood entrees, pasta dishes and sandwiches. The salad and soup bar is well stocked. Varied areas are sectioned off with memorabilia tied to themes of fishing, farm and ranch, sports and the '50s and '60s. Casual dress; cocktails. **Parking:** on-site. **Cards:** AX, CB, DC, DS, MC, VI.

GALISTEO pop. 265

WHERE TO STAY

THE GALISTEO INN

AAA SAVE

▼▼▼▼

Historic
Country Inn

Phone: (505)466-8200

5/1-10/31 [CP]   1P: $85-$205
2/1-4/30 & 11/1-1/31 [CP]   1P: $65-$165
Location: SR 41, exit La Vega. 9 La Vega 87540 (HC 75, Box 4). Fax: 505/466-4008. **Facility:** Horses and llamas graze on the grounds of this 250-year-old country inn with a tree-shaded courtyard and Spanish Colonial design. Smoke free premises. 12 one-bedroom standard units. 1 story, interior/exterior corridors. *Bath:* some shared or private. **Parking:** on-site. **Terms:** office hours 8 am-5 pm, age restrictions may apply, package plans. **Amenities:** *Some:* DVD players. **Dining:** 5 pm-9 pm, Sat & Sun also 11:30 am-2 pm, cocktails. **Pool(s):** heated outdoor. **Leisure Activities:** sauna, whirlpool, pond for picnics. *Fee:* horseback riding, massage. **Business Services:** meeting rooms. **Cards:** AX, DC, MC, VI. **Special Amenities:** free expanded continental breakfast and free local telephone calls.

SOME UNITS

[icons]

GALLUP pop. 20,209

-------- WHERE TO STAY --------

AMERICAS BEST VALUE INN & SUITES *Book at aaa.com* **Phone:** (505)722-0757

AAA SAVE
4/1-10/1 [ECP]　1P: $47-$59　2P: $52-$64　XP: $5　F12
2/1-3/31 & 10/2-1/31 [ECP]　1P: $44-$49　2P: $49-$54　XP: $5　F12
Location: I-40, exit 20, 1 mi w. 2003 US 66 W 87301. Fax: 505/722-0765. **Facility:** 66 units. 44 one-bedroom standard units. 22 one-bedroom suites ($59-$99). 2 stories (no elevator), interior/exterior corridors. *Bath:* Small-scale Hotel combo or shower only. **Parking:** on-site. **Terms:** 3 day cancellation notice, pets (in designated units). **Amenities:** high-speed Internet, voice mail, hair dryers. **Dining:** 7 am-9 pm. **Pool(s):** heated outdoor. **Leisure Activities:** whirlpool, exercise room. **Guest Services:** coin laundry. **Business Services:** meeting rooms, fax. **Cards:** AX, CB, DC, DS, MC, VI. **Special Amenities:** free expanded continental breakfast and early check-in/late checkout. *(See color ad below)*

SOME UNITS
⑤ⓈⒹ 🛏 🍴 ⅏Ⓜ 🍳 📷 DATA PORT 📺 / ✕ 🔒 🖼 /

BEST WESTERN INN & SUITES *Book at aaa.com* **Phone:** (505)722-2221

AAA SAVE
All Year [BP]　1P: $59-$89　2P: $59-$99　XP: $10　F12
Location: I-40, exit 16, 1 mi e. 3009 US 66 W 87301. Fax: 505/722-7442. **Facility:** 126 one-bedroom standard units. 2 stories (no elevator), interior corridors. **Parking:** on-site. **Terms:** weekly rates available, package plans, small pets only ($10 deposit). **Amenities:** irons. **Dining:** 6 am-9 & 5-9:30 pm, Fri & Sat-10 pm, Small-scale Hotel cocktails. **Pool(s):** heated indoor. **Leisure Activities:** sauna, whirlpool, exercise room. *Fee:* game room. **Guest Services:** gift shop, valet and coin laundry. **Business Services:** meeting rooms. **Cards:** AX, CB, DC, DS, MC, VI. **Special Amenities:** free full breakfast and free local telephone calls. *(See color ad below)*

SOME UNITS
⑤ⓈⒹ ✈ 🛏 🍴 🍷 🍳 ✕ 📷 DATA PORT 📺 / ✕ 🔒 🖼 /
FEE

BEST WESTERN RED ROCK INN   *Book at aaa.com*   Phone: 505/722-7600

(AAA) (SAVE)   5/1-10/31 [ECP]   1P: $60-$129   2P: $65-$139   XP: $7
▼▼ ▼▼   2/1-4/30 & 11/1-1/31 [ECP]   1P: $59-$109   2P: $55-$119   XP: $7

Small-scale Hotel   **Location:** I-40, exit 26, 1 mi w. 3010 US 66 E 87301. Fax: 505/722-9770. **Facility:** 77 one-bedroom standard units. 2 stories (no elevator), interior corridors. **Parking:** on-site. **Amenities:** high-speed Internet, irons, hair dryers. **Pool(s):** heated indoor. **Leisure Activities:** sauna, whirlpool, exercise room. **Guest Services:** coin laundry. **Business Services:** meeting rooms, fax (fee). **Cards:** AX, CB, DC, DS, JC, MC, VI.
Special Amenities: free expanded continental breakfast and free local telephone calls.

SOME UNITS

BEST WESTERN ROYAL HOLIDAY MOTEL   *Book at aaa.com*   Phone: (505)722-4900

(AAA) (SAVE)   5/1-10/31 [ECP]   1P: $59-$99   2P: $60-$149   XP: $7
▼▼ ▼▼   11/1-1/31 [ECP]   1P: $59-$89   2P: $59-$99   XP: $7
    2/1-4/30 [ECP]   1P: $54-$89   2P: $59-$99   XP: $7

Small-scale Hotel   **Location:** I-40, exit 20, 0.5 mi s to US 66, then 0.8 mi w. 1903 W Hwy 66 87301. Fax: 505/863-9952. **Facility:** 50 units. 46 one- and 4 two-bedroom standard units. 2 stories (no elevator), interior corridors. **Parking:** on-site. **Terms:** pets ($7 extra charge). **Amenities:** irons, hair dryers. **Pool(s):** heated indoor. **Leisure Activities:** sauna, whirlpool. **Business Services:** fax. **Cards:** AX, DC, DS, MC, VI. **Special Amenities:** free expanded continental breakfast and free local telephone calls.

SOME UNITS

FEE

COMFORT INN   *Book at aaa.com*   Phone: (505)722-0982

(AAA) (SAVE)   5/1-8/31 [BP]   1P: $59-$79   2P: $59-$99   XP: $6   F16
▼▼ ▼▼   2/1-4/30 & 9/1-1/31 [BP]   1P: $49-$69   2P: $59-$79   XP: $6   F16

Motel   **Location:** I-40, exit 16, 0.3 mi e. 3208 US 66 W 87301. Fax: 505/722-2404. **Facility:** 51 one-bedroom standard units. 2 stories (no elevator), interior corridors. **Parking:** on-site. **Terms:** package plans, small pets only ($10 extra charge). **Amenities:** high-speed Internet, irons, hair dryers. **Pool(s):** heated indoor. **Guest Services:** coin laundry. **Cards:** AX, CB, DC, DS, JC, MC, VI. **Special Amenities:** free expanded continental breakfast and free local telephone calls. *(See color ad below)*

SOME UNITS

FEE

DAYS INN-WEST   *Book at aaa.com*   Phone: (505)863-6889

(AAA) (SAVE)   All Year   1P: $40-$70   XP: $10   F
▼▼ ▼▼   **Location:** I-40, exit 16, 0.3 mi e. Adjacent to paved RV/truck parking. 3201 W Hwy 66 87301. Fax: 505/863-6889.

Small-scale Hotel   **Facility:** 74 one-bedroom standard units. 2 stories (no elevator), exterior corridors. **Parking:** on-site. **Amenities:** irons, hair dryers. **Pool(s):** heated indoor. **Leisure Activities:** whirlpool. **Guest Services:** valet and coin laundry. **Cards:** AX, DS, MC, VI. **Special Amenities:** free continental breakfast and early check-in/late check-out.

SOME UNITS

ECONO LODGE — *Book at aaa.com*

◆◆ ◆◆

Small-scale Hotel

5/1-10/31 [ECP]	1P: $40-$80	2P: $45-$85	XP: $5 F16
2/1-4/30 & 11/1-1/31 [ECP]	1P: $30-$58	2P: $35-$60	XP: $5 F16

Phone: (505)722-3800

Location: I-40, exit 16, 0.8 mi e. 3101 US 66 W 87301. Fax: 505/722-3800. **Facility:** 51 one-bedroom standard units. 2 stories (no elevator), interior corridors. **Parking:** on-site. **Terms:** pets ($5 extra charge). **Amenities:** high-speed Internet. **Business Services:** PC, fax (fee). **Cards:** AX, DS, MC, VI.

SOME UNITS
(ASK) (S/D) (🛏) (🍴) (📹) (💻) /(✕)/ FEE

ECONOMY INN

AAA [SAVE]

◆◆

Motel

calls.

5/1-10/31	1P: $27-$30	2P: $35-$39	XP: $5 F10
2/1-4/30 & 11/1-1/31	1P: $24-$27	2P: $31-$35	XP: $5 F10

Phone: (505)863-9301

Location: I-40, exit 20, s to US 66, then 0.5 mi w. 1709 US 66 W 87301. Fax: 505/722-9112. **Facility:** 50 units. 48 one- and 2 two-bedroom standard units. 1-2 stories (no elevator), exterior corridors. *Bath:* combo or shower only. **Parking:** on-site. **Terms:** cancellation fee imposed, weekly rates available, small pets only ($3 extra charge). **Guest Services:** coin laundry. **Cards:** AX, DS, MC, VI. **Special Amenities:** free local telephone calls.

SOME UNITS
(🛏) (🍴) (📹) (🔌) (💻) /(✕)/ FEE

GALLUP TRAVELODGE — *Book at aaa.com*

◆◆ ◆◆

Small-scale Hotel

5/1-9/30 [CP]	1P: $49-$59	2P: $59-$89	XP: $10 F15
2/1-4/30 & 10/1-1/31 [CP]	1P: $39-$49	2P: $44-$54	XP: $10 F15

Phone: 505/722-2100

Location: I-40, exit 16, just e. 3275 US 66 W 87301. Fax: 505/722-2100. **Facility:** 50 one-bedroom standard units. 2 stories (no elevator), interior corridors. **Parking:** on-site. **Terms:** 7 day cancellation notice, pets ($8 extra charge). **Amenities:** irons, hair dryers. **Pool(s):** heated indoor. **Leisure Activities:** whirlpool. **Guest Services:** coin laundry. **Cards:** AX, DS, MC, VI. *(See color ad p 537)*

SOME UNITS
(ASK) (S/D) (🛏) (🍴) (🔌) (🐕) (🏊) (📹) (DATA PORT) (💻) /(✕)/ FEE

HAMPTON INN & SUITES

[fyi]

Small-scale Hotel

Phone: 505/722-4007

Property failed to provide current rates
Too new to rate, opening scheduled for January 2006. **Location:** I-40, exit 20, 1 mi w. 1450 Maloney Ave 87301. Fax: 505/797-9347. **Amenities:** 63 units, coffeemakers, pool.

HOLIDAY INN — *Book at aaa.com*

AAA [SAVE]

◆◆ ◆◆

Small-scale Hotel

All Year [BP]	1P: $59-$99	2P: $64-$104	XP: $5 F18

Phone: (505)722-2201

Location: I-40, exit 16, s to US 66, then 1 mi e. 2915 US 66 W 87301. Fax: 505/722-9616. **Facility:** 212 one-bedroom standard units. 2 stories (no elevator), interior/exterior corridors. **Parking:** on-site. **Terms:** [MAP] meal plan available. **Amenities:** high-speed Internet, dual phone lines, voice mail, irons, hair dryers. **Dining:** 6 am-10 & 6-9 pm, cocktails. **Pool(s):** heated indoor. **Leisure Activities:** sauna, whirlpool, putting green, pool table, table tennis, exercise room. *Fee:* game room. **Guest Services:** valet and coin laundry, area transportation-train & bus station. **Business Services:** conference facilities, PC. **Cards:** AX, CB, DC, DS, JC, MC, VI. **Special Amenities:** free full breakfast and free newspaper. *(See color ad below)*

SOME UNITS
(S/D) (♿) (🍴) (🍷) (🏊) (✕) (📹) (DATA PORT) (💻) /(✕) (🛏)/

LA QUINTA INN & SUITES
Phone: (505)722-2233

WWWW
Small-scale Hotel

5/1-9/30 [CP]   1P: $75-$104
2/1-4/30 & 10/1-1/31 [CP]   1P: $69-$95

Location: I-40, exit 26, just e. 3880 Hwy 66 E 87301. Fax: 505/722-2885. **Facility:** 65 units. 61 one-bedroom standard units. 4 one-bedroom suites, some with whirlpools. 3 stories, interior corridors. *Bath:* combo or shower only. **Parking:** on-site. **Terms:** small pets only. **Amenities:** high-speed Internet, voice mail, irons, hair dryers. **Pool(s):** heated indoor. **Leisure Activities:** sauna, whirlpool, steamroom, exercise room. **Guest Services:** coin laundry. **Business Services:** meeting rooms, business center. **Cards:** AX, CB, DC, DS, MC, VI.

SOME UNITS

MICROTEL INN
Phone: 505-722-2600

AAA SAVE
WWW
Small-scale Hotel

Book at aaa.com

All Year [CP]   1P: $39-$49   2P: $49-$59   D12

Location: I-40, exit 16, just e. 3270 W Hwy 66 87301. Fax: 505/726-2444. **Facility:** 53 one-bedroom standard units. 2 stories (no elevator), interior corridors. *Bath:* combo or shower only. **Parking:** on-site. **Terms:** 5 day cancellation notice. **Cards:** AX, DS, MC, VI. **Special Amenities: free continental breakfast and free local telephone calls.**

SOME UNITS

QUALITY INN & SUITES
Phone: 505/726-1000

AAA SAVE
WWWW
Small-scale Hotel

5/1-10/31 [ECP]   1P: $65-$119   2P: $70-$119   XP: $10   F
2/1-4/30 & 11/1-1/31 [ECP]   1P: $60-$119   2P: $65-$119   XP: $10   F

Location: I-40, exit 20, just n on Munoz Dr, then just w. 1500 W Maloney Ave 87301. Fax: 505/722-4954. **Facility:** 70 one-bedroom standard units. 2 stories (no elevator), interior/exterior corridors. *Bath:* combo or shower only. **Parking:** on-site. **Amenities:** high-speed Internet, voice mail, irons, hair dryers. **Pool(s):** heated indoor. **Leisure Activities:** sauna, whirlpool. **Guest Services:** valet laundry. **Business Services:** meeting rooms. **Cards:** AX, DS, MC, VI. **Special Amenities: free expanded continental breakfast.**

SOME UNITS

RAMADA LIMITED
Phone: (505)726-2700

WWWW
Small-scale Hotel

Book at aaa.com

5/1-10/31   1P: $79-$99   2P: $79-$99   XP: $5   F18
2/1-4/30 & 11/1-1/31   1P: $69-$79   2P: $69-$79   XP: $5   F18

Location: I-40, exit 20, 1 mi w. 1440 W Maloney Ave 87301 (PO Box 91720, ALBUQUERQUE, 87199). Fax: 505/726-2700. **Facility:** 60 one-bedroom standard units. 3 stories, interior corridors. *Bath:* combo or shower only. **Parking:** on-site. **Terms:** 7 day cancellation notice-fee imposed, [ECP] meal plan available, pets ($7 extra charge). **Amenities:** voice mail, irons, hair dryers. **Pool(s):** heated indoor. **Leisure Activities:** whirlpool. **Guest Services:** valet and coin laundry. **Business Services:** meeting rooms. **Cards:** AX, DC, DS, MC, VI.

SOME UNITS

FEE

RED ROOF INN , *Book at aaa.com*
Phone: (505)722-7765

(AAA) (SAVE)

Motel

All Year   1P: $33-$52   2P: $36-$60   XP: $6   F18
Location: I-40, exit 16, just se. Located adjacent to RV/truck parking. 3304 W Hwy 66 87301. Fax: 505/722-4752. **Facility:** 103 one-bedroom standard units. 2 stories (no elevator), exterior corridors. **Parking:** on-site. **Terms:** office hours 5:30 am-8:30 pm, small pets only ($5 extra charge). **Amenities:** *Some:* irons, hair dryers. **Pool(s):** heated outdoor. **Leisure Activities:** whirlpool. **Guest Services:** coin laundry. **Business Services:** meeting rooms. **Cards:** AX, CB, DC, DS, JC, MC, VI. **Special Amenities: free continental breakfast and free local telephone calls.** *(See color ad p 539)*

SLEEP INN   *Book at aaa.com*
Phone: (505)863-3535

(AAA) (SAVE)

Small-scale Hotel

5/1-10/31 [CP]   1P: $60-$70   2P: $70-$80   XP: $5   F12
2/1-4/30 & 11/1-1/31 [CP]   1P: $50-$60   2P: $60-$70   XP: $5   F12
Location: I-40, exit 26, just e. 3820 E US 66 87301. Fax: 505/722-3737. **Facility:** 61 one-bedroom standard units. 2 stories (no elevator), interior corridors. *Bath:* combo or shower only. **Parking:** on-site. **Terms:** 1-2 night minimum stay - seasonal and/or weekends, package plans, pets ($8 extra charge). **Amenities:** high-speed Internet. *Some:* irons, hair dryers. **Pool(s):** heated indoor. **Leisure Activities:** whirlpool. **Guest Services:** coin laundry. **Cards:** AX, DS, MC, VI. **Special Amenities: free continental breakfast and free local telephone calls.** *(See color ad p 539)*

SUPER 8 MOTEL   *Book at aaa.com*
Phone: (505)722-5300

Motel

All Year   1P: $46-$53   2P: $55-$62   XP: $7
Location: I-40, exit 20, s to US 66, then 0.5 mi w. 1715 W US 66 87301. Fax: 505/722-5300. **Facility:** 75 one-bedroom standard units. 2 stories (no elevator), interior corridors. **Parking:** on-site. **Terms:** cancellation fee imposed, [CP] meal plan available, pets ($5 fee). **Pool(s):** heated indoor. **Leisure Activities:** sauna, whirlpool. **Guest Services:** coin laundry. **Business Services:** fax. **Cards:** AX, DS, MC, VI.

The following lodging was either not evaluated or did not meet AAA rating requirements but is listed for your information only.

HAMPTON INN-WEST
Phone: 505/722-7224

(fyi)

Small-scale Hotel

Did not meet all AAA rating requirements for some property operations at time of last evaluation on 07/06/2005. **Location:** I-40, exit 16, just e. 111 Twin Buttes Rd 87301. Facilities, services, and decor characterize a mid-range property.

--- **WHERE TO DINE** ---

CHELLES RESTAURANT
Dinner: $10-$20   Phone: 505/722-7698

American

Location: I-40, exit 16, 1.5 mi e. 2201 W Hwy 66 87301. **Hours:** 4:30 pm-10 pm. Closed major holidays; also Sun. **Reservations:** accepted. **Features:** The place to go for steaks and seafood, the restaurant prepares a good selection of both. Fitting accompaniments include selections from the varied wine list and tempting pastry desserts made in house. Casual dress; beer & wine only. **Parking:** on-site. **Cards:** AX, DS, MC, VI.

EARL'S FAMILY RESTAURANT
Lunch: $5-$12   Dinner: $5-$12   Phone: 505/863-4201

(AAA)

American

Location: I-40, exit 22, just s to US 66, then e. 1400 E Hwy 66 87301. **Hours:** 6 am-9 pm, Sun from 7 am. Closed major holidays. **Reservations:** accepted. **Features:** Since 1947, the landmark family restaurant has served a wide variety of American and Mexican dishes. The favorite steak and enchiladas is a blend of the two cuisines. Casual dress. **Parking:** on-site. **Cards:** AX, MC, VI.

EL SOMBRERO
Lunch: $5-$14   Dinner: $5-$14   Phone: 505/863-4554

Southwest Mexican

Location: I-40, exit 20, just w. 1201 W US 66 87301. **Hours:** 9 am-10:30 pm. Closed: 1/1, 11/23, 12/25. **Features:** Along famous Route 66, the restaurant has a Southwestern feel. Although American dishes are available, Mexican foods reign supreme. The top seller is the sombrero special, with the stuffed sopapilla a close second. Casual dress; beer & wine only. **Parking:** on-site. **Cards:** AX, DS, MC, VI.

KING DRAGON
Lunch: $6-$10   Dinner: $7-$10   Phone: 505/863-6300

Chinese

Location: I-40, exit 20, just n; in American Heritage Shopping Center. 828 N Hwy 491 87301. **Hours:** 11 am-9 pm, Fri & Sat-10 pm. Closed: 11/23, 12/25. **Features:** Specializing in Mandarin, Szechuan and Hunan dishes, the restaurant also lays out a popular buffet at lunch. In addition to beef, pork and chicken entrees, the menu lists a good choice of soups. Portions are generous. Casual dress; cocktails. **Parking:** on-site. **Cards:** AX, DC, DS, MC, VI.

OLYMPIC KITCHEN
Lunch: $5-$8   Dinner: $9-$17   Phone: 505/863-2584

(AAA)

International

Location: I-40, exit 16, just e. 3200 W Route 66 87305. **Hours:** 8 am-10 pm. Closed: 4/16, 11/23, 12/25. **Reservations:** accepted. **Features:** Lunch is informal at this place, which is popular with the local folks who work in town. Dinner is more formal, with a menu focusing on steaks, Greek food and pasta dishes, all accented by fine wines. Casual dress; beer & wine only. **Parking:** on-site. **Cards:** AX, DS, MC, VI.

At 60 mph, if you reach down
to change the radio station
you can travel the length
of a football field.

Stay Focused
Keep your mind on the road.

GRANTS pop. 8,806

―――― **WHERE TO STAY** ――――

BEST WESTERN INN & SUITES   *Book at aaa.com*

Phone: (505)287-7901

AAA SAVE

All Year — 1P: $59-$79 — 2P: $69-$89 — XP: $10 — F12
Location: I-40, exit 85, just w. 1501 E Santa Fe Ave 87020. Fax: 505/285-5751. **Facility:** 126 one-bedroom standard units. 2 stories (no elevator), interior corridors. **Parking:** on-site. **Terms:** small pets only ($10 fee, in smoking units). **Amenities:** irons, hair dryers. **Dining:** 6 am-9 & 5-9 pm, Fri & Sat 5 pm-9:30 pm,
Small-scale Hotel cocktails. **Pool(s):** heated indoor. **Leisure Activities:** sauna, whirlpool, indoor recreation area, exercise room. **Guest Services:** gift shop, valet and coin laundry. **Business Services:** meeting rooms. **Cards:** AX, DC, DS, MC, VI. **Special Amenities:** free full breakfast and free local telephone calls. *(See color ad below)*

SOME UNITS

COMFORT INN   *Book at aaa.com*

Phone: (505)287-8700

5/1-10/31 — 1P: $59-$69 — 2P: $69-$79 — XP: $5 — F18
2/1-4/30 & 11/1-1/31 — 1P: $54-$64 — 2P: $59-$69 — XP: $5 — F18
Small-scale Hotel Fax: 505/287-8700. **Facility:** 52 units. 51 one-bedroom standard units. 1 one-bedroom suite with kitchen. 2 stories (no elevator), interior corridors. *Bath:* combo or shower only. **Parking:** on-site. **Terms:** 7 day cancellation notice-fee imposed, [ECP] meal plan available, package plans, pets ($5 extra charge, in designated units). **Amenities:** irons. **Pool(s):** heated indoor. **Leisure Activities:** whirlpool. **Guest Services:** coin laundry. **Business Services:** meeting rooms, fax (fee). **Cards:** AX, DC, DS, MC, VI.

SOME UNITS

DAYS INN   *Book at aaa.com*

Phone: 505/287-8883

AAA SAVE

5/1-10/31 [CP] — 1P: $50-$70 — 2P: $60-$90 — XP: $10 — F12
11/1-1/31 [CP] — 1P: $40-$60 — 2P: $50-$80 — XP: $10 — F12
2/1-4/30 [CP] — 1P: $40-$60 — 2P: $50-$80 — XP: $10 — F12
Location: I-40, exit 85, 0.3 mi n. Located in a commercial area. 1504 E Santa Fe Ave 87020 (PO Box 29).
Small-scale Hotel Fax: 505/287-7772. **Facility:** 55 one-bedroom standard units. 2 stories (no elevator), exterior corridors. **Parking:** on-site. **Terms:** 3 day cancellation notice, small pets only ($5 extra charge). **Amenities:** voice mail, hair dryers. **Guest Services:** coin laundry. **Cards:** CB, DC, DS, MC, VI. **Special Amenities:** free continental breakfast and free local telephone calls. *(See color ad p 543)*

SOME UNITS

GRANTS TRAVELODGE   *Book at aaa.com*

Phone: (505)287-7800

5/1-10/31 — 1P: $69-$79 — 2P: $69-$79
2/1-4/30 & 11/1-1/31 — 1P: $59-$69 — 2P: $59-$69
Small-scale Hotel Fax: 505/287-7800. **Facility:** 60 one-bedroom standard units. 2 stories (no elevator), exterior corridors. *Bath:* combo or shower only. **Parking:** on-site, winter plug-ins. **Terms:** 7 day cancellation notice-fee imposed, pets ($5 extra charge). **Pool(s):** heated indoor. **Leisure Activities:** whirlpool. **Guest Services:** coin laundry. **Cards:** AX, DC, DS, MC, VI.

SOME UNITS

HOLIDAY INN EXPRESS <u>Book at aaa.com</u>   Phone: 505/285-4676

AAA SAVE
2/1-9/30   1P: $70-$90
10/1-1/31   1P: $60-$80
Small-scale Hotel **Location:** I-40, exit 85, 0.3 mi n. 1496 E Sante Fe Ave 87020 (PO Box 29). Fax: 505/285-6998. **Facility:** 58 one-bedroom standard units. 2 stories (no elevator), interior corridors. **Parking:** on-site. **Terms:** 3 day cancellation notice, small pets only ($10 extra charge, in designated units). **Amenities:** irons, hair dryers. **Pool(s):** heated indoor. **Leisure Activities:** whirlpool. **Guest Services:** coin laundry. **Business Services:** meeting rooms, fax (fee). **Cards:** AX, CB, DC, DS, MC, VI. **Special Amenities:** free continental breakfast and free newspaper.

SOME UNITS
[icons] FEE

SANDS MOTEL   Phone: (505)287-2996

AAA SAVE
All Year   1P: $35   2P: $40-$43   XP: $3   F18
Motel **Location:** I-40, exit 85, 1.5 mi w on Business Loop 40. 112 McArthur St 87020. Fax: 505/287-2107. **Facility:** 24 one-bedroom standard units. 1 story, exterior corridors. **Parking:** on-site, winter plug-ins. **Terms:** [CP] meal plan available, pets ($5 fee). **Business Services:** fax. **Cards:** AX, DS, MC, VI. **Special Amenities:** free continental breakfast and free local telephone calls.

SOME UNITS
[icons] FEE

SUPER 8 GRANTS　*Book at aaa.com*　　　　　　　　　　　　　　　　　**Phone:** 505/287-8811
▽▽▽
　　　　　　　　　　　　　　　　Property failed to provide current rates
Small-scale Hotel　**Location:** I-40, exit 85, just n. 1604 E Santa Fe Ave 87020. Fax: 505/287-8811. **Facility:** 69 one-bedroom standard units. 2 stories (no elevator), interior corridors. **Parking:** on-site, winter plug-ins. **Terms:** pets ($5-$10 fee, in designated units). **Pool(s):** heated indoor. **Leisure Activities:** whirlpool. **Guest Services:** coin laundry.

SOME UNITS

───── *The following lodging was either not evaluated or did not* ─────
meet AAA rating requirements but is listed for your information only.

CIMARRON ROSE B&B　　　　　　　　　　　　　　　　　　　　　　　**Phone:** 505/783-4770
[fyi]　　　Not evaluated. **Location:** Between MM 56 and 57 on SR 53. 689 Oso Ridge Route 87020. Facilities, services, and decor characterize a mid-range property.

───── **WHERE TO DINE** ─────

CANTON CAFE　　　　　　　　**Lunch:** $5-$8　　　　**Dinner:** $5-$8　　　**Phone:** 505/287-8314
▽　　　**Location:** I-40, exit 85, 0.8 mi w on Business Loop 40 (Santa Fe Ave). 1212 E Santa Fe Ave 87020. **Hours:** 11 am-9
Chinese　　pm. Closed: 11/23, 12/25. **Reservations:** accepted. **Features:** Locals keep the eatery busy most days, especially at lunchtime. The luncheon buffet lines up a good selection of traditional items along the lines of sweet and sour pork, Szechuan shrimp and kung pao chicken. Salads and desserts are included on the buffet. Casual dress. **Parking:** on-site. **Cards:** DS, MC, VI.

LA VENTANA RESTAURANT　　　　**Lunch:** $5-$8　　　　**Dinner:** $9-$25　　**Phone:** 505/287-9393
▽▽　**Location:** Just n of Santa Fe Ave; center. 110 1/2 Geis St 87020. **Hours:** 11 am-11 pm. Closed: 1/1, 11/23, 12/25;
American　　also Sun. **Reservations:** suggested. **Features:** The city's business community flocks to the relaxed restaurant's comfortable Southwestern atmosphere. A full-service bar complements tempting selections of great steak, salads and tasty desserts. Try the succulent prime rib or one of a number of well-seasoned
Mexican favorites. Casual dress; cocktails. **Parking:** on-site. **Cards:** AX, CB, DC, DS, MC, VI.

HOBBS pop. 28,657

───── **WHERE TO STAY** ─────

BEST WESTERN EXECUTIVE INN　*Book at aaa.com*　　　　　　　　　　　**Phone:** (505)397-7171
▽▽▽▽　All Year　　　　　　1P: $60-$100　　　2P: $70-$100　　　XP: $10　　　F12
　　　　　Location: US 62/180 and Snyder St. 309 N Marland Blvd 88240. Fax: 505/391-9276. **Facility:** 62 one-bedroom
Small-scale Hotel　standard units. 2 stories (no elevator), exterior corridors. **Parking:** on-site. **Terms:** pets ($10 extra charge). **Amenities:** high-speed Internet, irons, hair dryers. **Pool(s):** small outdoor. **Business Services:** fax (fee). **Cards:** AX, DC, DS, MC, VI.

SOME UNITS

DAYS INN　*Book at aaa.com*　　　　　　　　　　　　　　　　　　　　**Phone:** (505)397-6541
🔺🔺🔺 [SAVE]　All Year [CP]　　　　1P: $49-$59　　　2P: $51-$64　　　XP: $10　　　F
▽▽　　　**Location:** 2 mi e on US 62 and 180. 211 N Marland Blvd 88240. Fax: 505/397-6544. **Facility:** 57 one-bedroom
Motel　　standard units. 2 stories (no elevator), exterior corridors. *Bath:* combo or shower only. **Parking:** on-site. **Terms:** 3 day cancellation notice-fee imposed, small pets only ($10 fee). **Amenities:** high-speed Internet, safes (fee), hair dryers. *Some:* irons. **Pool(s):** small outdoor. **Guest Services:** coin laundry. **Business Services:** fax (fee). **Cards:** AX, DC, DS, MC, VI. **Special Amenities:** free continental breakfast and free local telephone calls.

SOME UNITS

ECONO LODGE　*Book at aaa.com*　　　　　　　　　　　　　　　　　**Phone:** (505)397-3591
🔺🔺🔺 [SAVE]　6/1-1/31　　　　　1P: $45-$55　　　2P: $59-$69　　　XP: $5　　　F18
▽▽　　　2/1-5/31　　　　　1P: $40-$49　　　2P: $49-$59　　　XP: $5　　　F18
　　　　　Location: 2.5 mi e on US 62 and 180. 619 N Marland Blvd 88240. Fax: 505/397-7762. **Facility:** 38 one-bedroom
Small-scale Hotel　standard units. 2 stories (no elevator), exterior corridors. **Parking:** on-site. **Terms:** [CP] meal plan available, package plans, pets ($5 extra charge). **Amenities:** high-speed Internet, irons, hair dryers. **Pool(s):** small heated outdoor. **Guest Services:** coin laundry. **Business Services:** fax (fee). **Cards:** AX, CB, DC, DS, MC, VI. **Special Amenities:** free continental breakfast and free local telephone calls.

SOME UNITS

HAMPTON INN AND SUITES　*Book at aaa.com*　　　　　　　　　　　**Phone:** (505)492-6000
▽▽▽▽　All Year　　　　　　1P: $89-$149　　　2P: $94-$154　　　XP: $5　　　F18
　　　　　Location: Jct SR 18 N and Millen Dr, 1 mi n. 5420 N Lovington Hwy 88242. Fax: 505/492-6001. **Facility:** 67 one-
Small-scale Hotel　bedroom standard units. 3 stories, interior corridors. *Bath:* combo or shower only. **Parking:** on-site. **Terms:** 2-4 night minimum stay - weekends, 5 day cancellation notice. **Amenities:** high-speed Internet, voice mail, irons, hair dryers. **Pool(s):** small heated indoor. **Leisure Activities:** sauna, exercise room. **Business Services:** meeting rooms, business center. **Cards:** AX, CB, DC, DS, JC, MC, VI.

SOME UNITS

HOLIDAY INN EXPRESS   *Book at aaa.com*

(AAA) (SAVE)

▽▽▽▽

Small-scale Hotel

Phone: (505)392-8777

All Year [ECP]   1P: $75-$90   2P: $80-$95   XP: $5   F17
Location: Jct SR 18 and Business 19, 1.2 mi n. 3610 N Lovington Hwy 88240. Fax: 505/392-9321. **Facility:** 65 units. 61 one-bedroom standard units. 4 one-bedroom suites. 3 stories, interior corridors. *Bath:* combo or shower only. **Parking:** on-site. **Amenities:** high-speed Internet, voice mail, irons, hair dryers. **Pool(s):** small heated indoor. **Leisure Activities:** whirlpool, exercise room. **Guest Services:** valet and coin laundry. **Business Services:** meeting rooms, business center. **Cards:** AX, CB, DC, DS, JC, MC, VI.
Special Amenities: free continental breakfast and free local telephone calls.

SOME UNITS

(icons)

HOWARD JOHNSON-HOBBS   *Book at aaa.com*

(AAA) (SAVE)

▽▽▽▽

Small-scale Hotel

Phone: (505)397-3251

All Year [BP]   1P: $65   2P: $75   XP: $7   F15
Location: 2.5 mi e on US 62 and 180. 501 N Marland Blvd 88240. Fax: 505/393-3065. **Facility:** 72 one-bedroom standard units. 2 stories (no elevator), interior/exterior corridors. *Bath:* combo or shower only. **Parking:** on-site. **Terms:** 15% service charge, pets ($7 fee, in smoking units). **Amenities:** high-speed Internet, voice mail, irons, hair dryers. **Dining:** 2 restaurants, 6 am-10 & 5-9 pm, Fri & Sat-10 pm, cocktails, entertainment. **Pool(s):** outdoor. **Guest Services:** valet and coin laundry. **Business Services:** meeting rooms, fax (fee).
Cards: AX, DC, DS, MC, VI. **Special Amenities:** free full breakfast and free local telephone calls.

SOME UNITS

(icons) FEE

RODEWAY INN

(AAA) (SAVE)

▽▽▽▽

Motel

Phone: 505/393-4101

All Year   1P: $47-$55   2P: $50-$55   XP: $5
Location: On US 62 and 180, 2 mi e. 200 N Marland Blvd 88240. Fax: 505/393-4102. **Facility:** 69 one-bedroom standard units. 1 story, exterior corridors. *Bath:* combo or shower only. **Parking:** on-site. **Terms:** [BP] meal plan available, small pets only ($25 deposit). **Pool(s):** outdoor. **Business Services:** fax (fee). **Cards:** AX, DC, DS, MC, VI. **Special Amenities:** free full breakfast and free local telephone calls.

SOME UNITS

(icons) FEE

—————— WHERE TO DINE ——————

CATTLE BARON STEAK AND SEAFOOD
RESTAURANT

▽▽▽▽

Steak House

MC, VI.

Lunch: $6-$23   **Dinner:** $6-$23   Phone: 505/393-2800
Location: Jct Broadway and Grimes, 1.3 mi n; downtown. 1930 N Grimes 88240. **Hours:** 11 am-9:30 pm, Fri & Sat-10 pm, Sun-9 pm. Closed: 11/23, 12/25. **Reservations:** accepted. **Features:** The ranchlike restaurant presents a menu of hand-cut steaks, chicken, seafood and the signature prime rib. Guests can start off the meal with a plate from the huge salad bar. Casual dress; cocktails. **Parking:** on-site. **Cards:** AX, DS,

(icons)

JEMEZ SPRINGS pop. 375

—————— WHERE TO STAY ——————

CANON DEL RIO, A RIVERSIDE INN

▽▽▽▽▽

Bed & Breakfast

Phone: (505)829-4377

4/2-1/31 [BP]   1P: $89-$99   2P: $99-$109   XP: $15
2/1-4/1 [BP]   1P: $89   2P: $99-$109   XP: $10
Location: 1 mi s of center. 16445 Hwy 4 87025 (PO Box 86). Fax: 505/829-4377. **Facility:** Often host to groups, this inn in a remote mountain setting offers massage therapy and other retreatlike luxuries. Designated smoking area. 7 one-bedroom standard units. 1 story, interior/exterior corridors. **Parking:** on-site. **Terms:** age restrictions may apply, 7 day cancellation notice-fee imposed, weekly rates available. **Amenities:** *Some:* hair dryers. **Leisure Activities:** whirlpool, hiking trails. *Fee:* massage. **Business Services:** meeting rooms. **Cards:** AX, DS, MC, VI.

(icons)

LAGUNA

—————— WHERE TO STAY ——————

APACHE CANYON RANCH BED & BREAKFAST
COUNTRY INN

▽▽▽▽

Bed & Breakfast

Phone: 505/836-7220

Property failed to provide current rates
Location: I-40, exit 131, 3 mi n on Tohajiilee Rd. Located in a quiet area. 4 Canyon Dr 87026. Fax: 505/836-2922. **Facility:** Ranch land surrounds this B&B, which also provides a taste of American Indian culture at nearby Native American settlements. Smoke free premises. 4 units. 3 one- and 1 two-bedroom standard units. 1 story, interior/exterior corridors. **Parking:** on-site. **Terms:** office hours 8 am-9 pm. **Amenities:** hair dryers. *Some:* DVD players. **Leisure Activities:** hiking trails, jogging. *Fee:* massage.

SOME UNITS

(icons) / (VCR)

LAS CRUCES pop. 74,267

—————— WHERE TO STAY ——————

BAYMONT INN & SUITES LAS CRUCES   *Book at aaa.com*

(AAA) (SAVE)

▽▽▽▽

Small-scale Hotel

Phone: (505)523-0100

All Year [CP]   1P: $66-$76   2P: $73-$83   XP: $7   F18
Location: I-10, exit 140, just se of jct I-25 and Avenida de Mesilla. 1500 Hickory Dr 88005. Fax: 505/523-0707. **Facility:** 86 one-bedroom standard units. 4 stories, interior corridors. *Bath:* combo or shower only. **Parking:** on-site. **Terms:** pets ($50 deposit). **Amenities:** high-speed Internet, voice mail, irons, hair dryers. **Pool(s):** heated outdoor. **Cards:** AX, CB, DC, DS, MC, VI. **Special Amenities:** free expanded continental breakfast and free local telephone calls. *(See color ad p 489)*

SOME UNITS

FEE

BEST WESTERN MESILLA VALLEY INN *Book at aaa.com* Phone: (505)524-8603
(AAA) (SAVE)   All Year   1P: $59-$79   2P: $62-$89   XP: $8   F17
▼▼ ▼▼   **Location:** I-10, exit 140, just n. 901 Avenida de Mesilla 88005. Fax: 505/526-8437. **Facility:** 160 units. 155 one-
'Small-scale Hotel   and 5 two-bedroom standard units. 2 stories (no elevator), interior/exterior corridors. **Parking:** on-site.
Terms: weekly rates available, package plans. **Amenities:** video games (fee), high-speed Internet, dual
phone lines, voice mail, irons, hair dryers. **Dining:** 6 am-10 pm, Sun-9 pm, cocktails. **Pool(s):** heated
outdoor. **Leisure Activities:** whirlpool. **Guest Services:** valet and coin laundry. **Business Services:**
meeting rooms, PC, fax. **Cards:** AX, CB, DC, DS, JC, MC, VI. **Special Amenities:** free local telephone calls and free room
upgrade (subject to availability with advance reservations).

SOME UNITS
[icons]

BEST WESTERN MISSION INN *Book at aaa.com* Phone: (505)524-8591
(AAA) (SAVE)   All Year [BP]   1P: $49-$69   2P: $59-$79   XP: $8   F12
▼▼ ▼▼   **Location:** I-10, exit 142, 1 mi n. 1765 S Main St 88005. Fax: 505/523-4740. **Facility:** 69 one-bedroom standard
units. 2 stories (no elevator), exterior corridors. **Parking:** on-site. **Terms:** package plans, small pets only
Small-scale Hotel   ($15 fee, in smoking units). **Amenities:** high-speed Internet, voice mail, irons, hair dryers. **Dining:** 6-10 am,
11-2 & 5-9 pm, cocktails. **Pool(s):** heated outdoor. **Leisure Activities:** horseshoes. **Guest Services:** valet
laundry. **Business Services:** meeting rooms, PC, fax. **Cards:** AX, CB, DC, DS, JC, MC, VI.
Special Amenities: free full breakfast and free local telephone calls.

SOME UNITS
[icons] FEE

COMFORT INN OF LAS CRUCES *Book at aaa.com* Phone: (505)527-2000
(AAA) (SAVE)   All Year   1P: $50-$85   2P: $55-$95
▼▼ ▼▼   **Location:** I-10, exit 142, just n. 2585 S Valley Dr 88005. Fax: 505/527-0966. **Facility:** 38 one-bedroom standard
units. 2 stories (no elevator), interior corridors. **Parking:** on-site. **Terms:** [CP] meal plan available.
Amenities: high-speed Internet, hair dryers. **Pool(s):** heated outdoor. **Leisure Activities:** whirlpool.
Small-scale Hotel   **Business Services:** PC, fax (fee). **Cards:** AX, CB, DC, DS, JC, MC, VI.

SOME UNITS
[icons] / [icons] /

COMFORT SUITES BY CHOICE HOTELS *Book at aaa.com* Phone: (505)522-1300
▼▼ ▼▼   All Year   1P: $70-$90   2P: $75-$95   XP: $5   F18
Location: I-25, exit 1. 2101 S Triviz 88001. Fax: 505/522-1313. **Facility:** 61 one-bedroom standard units. 3
Small-scale Hotel   stories, interior corridors. *Bath:* combo or shower only. **Parking:** on-site. **Terms:** cancellation fee imposed,
pets ($15 fee, in smoking units). **Amenities:** high-speed Internet, dual phone lines, irons, hair dryers.
Pool(s): heated indoor. **Leisure Activities:** whirlpool. **Guest Services:** valet laundry. **Business Services:** meeting rooms.
Cards: AX, DC, DS, MC, VI.

SOME UNITS
[icons] FEE

FAIRFIELD INN BY MARRIOTT *Book at aaa.com* Phone: 505/522-6840
▼▼ ▼▼   Property failed to provide current rates
Location: I-25, exit 6 (US 70), 2 blks e to Telshore Blvd, then 0.8 mi s. 2101 Summit Ct 88011. Fax: 505/522-9784.
Small-scale Hotel   **Facility:** 78 one-bedroom standard units. 3 stories, interior corridors. *Bath:* combo or shower only. **Parking:**
on-site. **Amenities:** video games (fee), high-speed Internet, voice mail, irons, hair dryers. **Pool(s):** heated
outdoor. **Leisure Activities:** exercise room. **Guest Services:** valet and coin laundry. **Business Services:** meeting rooms, fax
(fee).

SOME UNITS
[icons] / [icons] /

HAMPTON INN *Book at aaa.com* Phone: (505)526-8311
(AAA) (SAVE)   All Year   1P: $69-$74   2P: $74-$79   XP: $5   F18
▼▼ ▼▼   **Location:** I-10, exit 140. 755 Avenida de Mesilla 88005. Fax: 505/527-2015. **Facility:** 117 one-bedroom standard
units. 2 stories (no elevator), exterior corridors. **Parking:** on-site. **Terms:** 30 day cancellation notice.
Amenities: high-speed Internet, voice mail, irons, hair dryers. **Pool(s):** outdoor. **Leisure**
Small-scale Hotel   **Activities:** exercise room. **Guest Services:** valet laundry. **Business Services:** PC, fax (fee). **Cards:** AX,
CB, DC, DS, MC, VI. **Special Amenities:** free expanded continental breakfast and free newspaper.

SOME UNITS
[icons] / [icons] /

HILLTOP HACIENDA B & B Phone: 505/382-3556
▼▼ ▼   Property failed to provide current rates
Location: I-25, exit 6 (US 70), just e to Del Rey Blvd, 3 mi n, then 1 mi e. 2600 Westmoreland Ave 88012.
Bed & Breakfast   Fax: 505/382-0308. **Facility:** Perched on a hilltop, the Southwestern adobe B&B affords panoramic views of
the valley and mountains from its spacious patios. Designated smoking area. 3 one-bedroom standard units.
2 stories (no elevator), interior corridors. *Bath:* combo or shower only. **Parking:** on-site. **Terms:** age restrictions may apply.
Amenities: video library, irons, hair dryers. **Leisure Activities:** bicycles, hiking trails.

[icon]

HILTON LAS CRUCES *Book at aaa.com* Phone: (505)522-4300
▼▼ ▼▼   All Year   1P: $79-$149   2P: $89-$159   XP: $10   F16
Location: I-25, exit 3 (Lohman Ave), just e. 705 S Telshore Blvd 88011. Fax: 505/522-7657. **Facility:** 203 one-
Large-scale Hotel   bedroom standard units. 7 stories, interior corridors. **Parking:** on-site. **Terms:** package plans, pets ($20
extra charge, in designated units). **Amenities:** video games (fee), high-speed Internet, voice mail, irons, hair
dryers. **Pool(s):** heated outdoor. **Leisure Activities:** whirlpool, exercise room. **Guest Services:** gift shop, valet laundry, area
transportation. **Business Services:** meeting rooms, business center. **Cards:** AX, DC, DS, MC, VI.

SOME UNITS
[icons] FEE   FEE

HOLIDAY INN EXPRESS   **Book at aaa.com**   Phone: (505)527-9947
▼▼▼▼   All Year [ECP]   1P: $59-$189   XP: $7   F18
    Location: I-10, exit 142, 2 blks w. 2200 S Valley Dr 88005. Fax: 505/647-4988. **Facility:** 54 one-bedroom
Small-scale Hotel   standard units, some with whirlpools. 2 stories (no elevator), exterior corridors. **Parking:** on-site.
    Terms: cancellation fee imposed, small pets only ($5-$20 extra charge). **Amenities:** dual phone lines, voice
mail, irons, hair dryers. **Pool(s):** outdoor. **Leisure Activities:** whirlpool, exercise room. **Guest Services:** valet and coin laundry.
Business Services: business center. **Cards:** AX, CB, DC, DS, MC, VI. *(See color ad below)*

SOME UNITS

[ASK] [SD] [🛏] [🖕M] [📶] [🏊] [✈] [DATA PORT] [📠] [🖥] [💻] / [✕] /
FEE

LA QUINTA INN LAS CRUCES   **Book at aaa.com**   Phone: (505)524-0331
▼▼▼▼   All Year [CP]   1P: $73-$83   2P: $80-$90   XP: $7   F18
    Location: I-10, exit 140. 790 Avenida de Mesilla 88005. Fax: 505/525-8360. **Facility:** 139 one-bedroom standard
Small-scale Hotel   units. 2 stories (no elevator), interior corridors. **Parking:** on-site. **Amenities:** video games (fee), dual phone
    lines, voice mail, irons, hair dryers. **Pool(s):** heated outdoor. **Leisure Activities:** exercise room. **Guest**
Services: valet and coin laundry. **Business Services:** meeting rooms, PC, fax (fee). **Cards:** AX, CB, DC, DS, MC, VI.

SOME UNITS

[ASK] [🛏] [🖕M] [📶] [🏊] [✈] [DATA PORT] [💻] / [✕] [📠] [🖥] /

LUNDEEN'S INN OF THE ARTS   Phone: (505)526-3326
▼▼▼▼   All Year   1P: $67   2P: $79   XP: $15
    Location: Center. Located in the historic district. 618 S Alameda Blvd 88005. Fax: 505/647-1334. **Facility:** The
Historic Bed   restored century-old territorial inn also incorporates a gallery that displays an interesting collection of art.
& Breakfast   Smoke free premises. 7 one-bedroom standard units, some with efficiencies or kitchens. 2 stories (no
    elevator), interior corridors. *Bath:* combo or shower only. **Parking:** on-site. **Terms:** cancellation fee imposed,
[BP] meal plan available, small pets only ($15 fee). **Guest Services:** gift shop. **Cards:** AX, CB, DC, DS, MC, VI.

SOME UNITS

[ASK] [🛏] [✕] [✈] / [🖥] /
FEE

RAMADA PALMS DE LAS CRUCES   **Book at aaa.com**   Phone: (505)526-4411
(AAA) [SAVE]   All Year   1P: $65-$175   2P: $65-$195   XP: $10   F12
    Location: I-10, exit 142, just n. 201 E University Ave 88005. Fax: 505/524-0530. **Facility:** 114 one-bedroom
▼▼▼▼   standard units. 2 stories (no elevator), interior corridors. *Bath:* combo or shower only. **Parking:** on-site.
Small-scale Hotel   **Terms:** package plans, small pets only ($25 fee). **Amenities:** voice mail, irons, hair dryers. **Dining:** 6 am-1
    & 5-10 pm, cocktails. **Pool(s):** heated indoor, wading. **Leisure Activities:** exercise room. **Guest Services:**
gift shop, valet and coin laundry. **Business Services:** meeting rooms. **Cards:** AX, CB, DC, DS, MC, VI.

SOME UNITS

[SD] [🛏] [🍴] [🍷] [🖕M] [♿] [📶] [🏊] [✈] [DATA PORT] [💻] / [✕] /
FEE

ROYAL HOST MOTEL   Phone: 505/524-8536
▼▼ ▼▼   All Year   1P: $42-$50   2P: $46-$54   XP: $5
    Location: I-10, exit 139, 1 mi n, then 0.5 mi e on I-10 business route (Picacho St). Located in a commercial area. 2146
~ Motel   W Picacho St 88007 (PO Box 835, FAIRACRES, 88033). Fax: 505/647-1718. **Facility:** 26 one-bedroom standard
    units. 1 story, exterior corridors. *Bath:* combo or shower only. **Parking:** on-site. **Terms:** cancellation fee
imposed, weekly rates available, pets ($10 fee). **Pool(s):** heated outdoor. **Business Services:** fax. **Cards:** AX, DS, MC, VI.

SOME UNITS

[🛏] [🍴] [🏊] [✈] [📠] / [✕] /
FEE

SLEEP INN BY CHOICE HOTELS   **Book at aaa.com**   Phone: (505)522-1700
▼▼▼▼   All Year   1P: $65-$85   2P: $70-$90   XP: $5   F18
    Location: I-25, exit 1. 2121 N Triviz 88001. Fax: 505/522-1515. **Facility:** 63 one-bedroom standard units. 3
Small-scale Hotel   stories, interior corridors. *Bath:* combo or shower only. **Parking:** on-site. **Terms:** cancellation fee imposed,
    pets ($15 fee, in smoking units). **Amenities:** high-speed Internet, hair dryers. **Pool(s):** heated indoor.
Leisure Activities: whirlpool. **Guest Services:** valet laundry. **Business Services:** fax. **Cards:** AX, DC, DS, MC, VI.

SOME UNITS

[ASK] [SD] [🛏] [🖕M] [♿] [📶] [🏊] [♿+] [✈] [DATA PORT] / [✕] [📠] [🖥] [💻] /
FEE

SPRINGHILL SUITES BY MARRIOTT   *Book at aaa.com*

Phone: (505)541-8887

AAA SAVE   All Year   1P: $79-$179   2P: $89-$209   XP: $10   F16
Location: I-10, exit 140. 1611 Hickory Loop 88005. **Fax:** 505/541-8837. **Facility:** 101 one-bedroom standard units. 3 stories, interior corridors. *Bath:* some combo or shower only. **Parking:** on-site. **Terms:** [ECP] meal plan available, package plans. **Amenities:** video games (fee), high-speed Internet, dual phone lines, voice mail, irons, hair dryers. **Pool(s):** heated outdoor. **Leisure Activities:** whirlpool, exercise room. **Guest Services:** valet and coin laundry. **Business Services:** meeting rooms. **Cards:** AX, CB, DC, DS, JC, MC, VI.

Small-scale Hotel

SOME UNITS

The following lodgings were either not evaluated or did not meet AAA rating requirements but are listed for your information only.

SUPER 8 MOTEL

Phone: 505-523-8695

[fyi]   Did not meet all AAA rating requirements for some property operations at time of last evaluation on 06/09/2005. **Location:** I-10, exit 142, 2.8 mi s on US 80, 85 and 180. 245 La Posada Ln 88005. Facilities, services, and decor characterize a mid-range property.

Motel

TOWNEPLACE SUITES LAS CRUCES

Phone: 505-532-6500

[fyi]   Not evaluated. **Location:** I-25, exit 6, just se. 2143 Teleshar Ct 88011. Facilities, services, and decor characterize a mid-range property.

———— WHERE TO DINE ————

ANDELE! RESTAURANTE

Lunch: $2-$8   **Dinner:** $2-$8   **Phone:** 505-526-9631

Mexican
Location: Jct Calle del Norte and Avenida de Mesilla. 2184 Avenida de Mesilla 88005. **Hours:** 8 am-9 pm, Sat & Sun-8 pm, Mon-2:30 pm. Closed major holidays. **Features:** Authentic New Mexican cuisine is served at the popular neighborhood cafe. Carne adovada is excellent, as are the salsas. Leave room for flan. Casual dress; beer & wine only. **Parking:** on-site. **Cards:** AX, DS, MC, VI.

CASA LUNA RISTORANTE ITALIANO

Lunch: $6-$11   **Dinner:** $6-$11   **Phone:** 505-523-0111

Italian
Location: I-25, exit 3 (Lohman Ave), 1 mi w. 1340 E Lohman Dr 88001. **Hours:** 11 am-3 & 5-9 pm, Fri & Sat-10 pm. Closed: 11/23, 12/25. **Reservations:** suggested. **Features:** Casa Luna is a small family-oriented restaurant serving homemade calzones, sausage, pizza, minestrone soup, chicken-fried steak and desserts. They also have lots of finger foods, sandwiches and salads. Casual dress; beer & wine only. **Parking:** on-site. **Cards:** AX, CB, DC, DS, MC, VI.

CATTLE BARON STEAK & SEAFOOD RESTAURANT

Lunch: $6-$12   **Dinner:** $12-$25   **Phone:** 505-522-7533

Steak House
Location: I-25, exit 3 (Lohman Ave), just e, then just s. 790 S Telshor Blvd 88011. **Hours:** 11 am-9:30 pm, Fri & Sat-10 pm. Closed: 11/23, 12/25. **Reservations:** accepted. **Features:** Part of a small chain, the location is usually busy because of its popularity with locals. Guests who try the steak and rock lobster combination aren't sorry. An ample salad bar also is featured. Casual dress; cocktails. **Parking:** on-site. **Cards:** AX, DC, DS, MC, VI.

THE DYNASTY CHINESE CUISINE

Lunch: $5-$7   **Dinner:** $7-$10   **Phone:** 505-525-8116

Chinese
Location: I-10, exit 140, 0.5 mi e; in El Paseo Place. 1210 El Paseo 88005. **Hours:** 11 am-9 pm. Closed: 7/4, 11/23, 12/25. **Reservations:** accepted. **Features:** The Dynasty features a very good buffet of appetizers, soups and a selection of pork, chicken, beef and seafood. They also prepare cooked-to-order meals and four-course family dinners. The fried dumplings and shrimp lo mein are both excellent. Casual dress; beer & wine only. **Parking:** on-site. **Cards:** AX, DS, MC, VI.

FARLEY'S

Lunch: $6-$10   **Dinner:** $6-$10   **Phone:** 505-522-0466

American
Location: I-25, exit 3 (Lohman Ave). 3499 Foothills Rd 88011. **Hours:** 11 am-11 pm, Fri-Sun to midnight. Closed: 11/23, 12/25. **Features:** The menu at the laid-back restaurant includes hot dogs, pizza and grilled cheese for the kids, as well as choices for Mom and Dad, such as ribs, sandwiches, steak, fajitas, soups, salads, beer and fantastic margaritas. Casual dress; cocktails. **Parking:** on-site. **Cards:** AX, DC, DS, MC, VI.

THE GADSDEN PURCHASE

Lunch: $7-$13   **Dinner:** $7-$13   **Phone:** 505-525-3000

American
Location: I-10, exit 142, just s. 1300 Avenida de Mesilla 88005. **Hours:** 7 am-9 pm, Fri & Sat-10 pm, Sun noon-10 pm. **Reservations:** accepted. **Features:** The cheerful, busy neighborhood bar and grill has great sandwiches, appetizers and entrees and a friendly staff and clientele. Casual dress; cocktails. **Parking:** on-site. **Cards:** AX, DS, MC, VI.

GARDUNO'S RESTAURANT

Lunch: $8-$14   **Dinner:** $8-$14   **Phone:** 505/521-7222

Mexican
Location: I-25, exit 3 (Lohman Ave), northeast corner. 500 S Telshor Dr 88011. **Hours:** 11 am-10 pm, Fri & Sat-10:30 pm, Sun 10 am-9:30 pm; Sunday brunch. Closed: 11/23, 12/25. **Reservations:** accepted. **Features:** New on the city's restaurant scene, the eatery features proven recipes from years of development at its sister properties in Albuquerque and points west. A fine selection of tequilas and other liquors is offered. Casual dress; cocktails. **Parking:** on-site. **Cards:** AX, DC, DS, MC, VI.

LORENZO'S

Lunch: $5-$8   **Dinner:** $7-$15   **Phone:** 505/521-3505

Italian
Location: I-25, exit 1S. 1753 E University 88005. **Hours:** 11 am-9 pm, Fri & Sat-9:30 pm, Sun-8:30 pm. Closed major holidays. **Features:** Authentic Sicilian dishes are served at Lorenzo's, which offers imported pasta, varied sauces, hand-tossed pizza with unusual combinations, appetizers, cannelloni, eggplant parmigiana, calamari and seafood. Finish with tiramisu, spumoni or cheesecake. Casual dress; beer & wine only. **Parking:** on-site. **Cards:** AX, DS, MC, VI.

MCMULLAN'S CATTLEMAN'S STEAK HOUSE

Dinner: $11-$22

Phone: 505/382-9051

Steak House

Location: I-25, exit 6, 0.5 mi e. 4401 N Main St (Hwy 70 E) 88012. **Hours:** 5 pm-9 pm, Sun from 3 pm. **Closed:** 1/1, 7/4, 12/25. **Reservations:** accepted. **Features:** The lively lounge has real cowboys and a collection of antique and modern saddles. The selection of beef is hard to beat. Three-layer cake puts a great finishing touch on a meal. Casual dress; cocktails. **Parking:** on-site. **Cards:** AX, DC, MC, VI.

OLD MESILLA PASTRY CAFE-THE SHED RESTAURANT

Lunch: $5-$9   **Dinner:** $5-$9   **Phone:** 505/525-2636

Southwest American

Location: I-10, exit 142, just e, then 1 mi nw. 810 S Valley Dr 88005. **Hours:** 7 am-8 pm. **Closed:** 11/23, 12/25; also Sun. **Features:** This wonderful bakery offers such vegetarian delights as garden burgers and grilled eggplant sandwiches. The wood-burning oven produces pizza, calzone and bread. Breakfast offerings range from huevos rancheros and eggs benedict to pancakes and omelets. Casual dress; beer & wine only. **Parking:** on-site. **Cards:** AX, DS, MC, VI.

PETE'S HACIENDA

Lunch: $7-$18   **Dinner:** $8-$18   **Phone:** 505/532-0790

Southwest American

Location: Jct E University and Espina, just n. 2605 S Espina 88001. **Hours:** 11 am-2 & 4:30-9 pm. Closed major holidays. **Reservations:** accepted. **Features:** Varied fare ranges from Mexican food to steak, seafood and chicken dishes. Guests can expect a bright, spacious dining room, friendly service and a good value for the money. Casual dress; beer & wine only. **Parking:** on-site. **Cards:** AX, CB, DC, DS, MC, VI.

RANCHWAY BBQ & MEXICAN FOOD

Lunch: $5-$9   **Dinner:** $5-$9   **Phone:** 505/523-7361

Southwest Barbecue

Location: I-10, exit 142, 2.7 mi nw. 604 N Valley Dr 88005. **Hours:** 8 am-8 pm, Sat-3 pm. Closed major holidays; also Sun. **Features:** Limited barbecue selections share menu space with attractive Mexican offerings. This place is popular with the folks who work in the area. Casual dress. **Parking:** on-site. **Cards:** MC, VI.

LAS VEGAS pop. 14,565

—— WHERE TO STAY ——

COMFORT INN   *Book at aaa.com*

Phone: (505)425-1100

5/1-10/31	1P: $65-$125	2P: $65-$125	XP: $5 F16
2/1-4/30 & 11/1-1/31	1P: $60-$110	2P: $60-$110	XP: $5 F16

Small-scale Hotel

Location: I-25, exit 347, just sw, US 85 and I-25 business route. 2500 N Grand Ave 87701. Fax: 505/454-8404. **Facility:** 101 one-bedroom standard units. 2 stories (no elevator), interior corridors. *Bath:* combo or shower only. **Parking:** on-site. **Terms:** small pets only (in smoking units). **Amenities:** voice mail, irons, hair dryers. *Some:* high-speed Internet. **Pool(s):** small heated indoor. **Leisure Activities:** whirlpool, exercise room. **Guest Services:** coin laundry. **Business Services:** fax (fee). **Cards:** AX, DC, DS, MC, VI. **Special Amenities:** free full breakfast and free local telephone calls.

SOME UNITS

DAYS INN-LAS VEGAS   *Book at aaa.com*

Phone: (505)425-1967

All Year	1P: $62-$69	2P: $67-$72	XP: $6 F12

Small-scale Hotel

Location: I-25, exit 347, 0.8 mi sw, US 85 and I-25 business route. 2000 N Grand Ave 87701. Fax: 505/425-3837. **Facility:** 36 one-bedroom standard units. 2 stories (no elevator), interior corridors. **Parking:** on-site. **Terms:** [CP] meal plan available. **Amenities:** hair dryers. **Pool(s):** small heated indoor. **Leisure Activities:** whirlpool. **Business Services:** fax (fee). **Cards:** AX, DC, DS, MC, VI. **Special Amenities:** free continental breakfast.

SOME UNITS

EL CAMINO MOTEL

Phone: 505/425-5994

5/1-9/30	1P: $45-$55	2P: $55-$65	XP: $6 F12
2/1-4/30 & 10/1-1/31	1P: $40-$50	2P: $50-$60	XP: $6 F12

Motel

Location: I-25, exit 345, 0.3 mi w, US 85 and I-25 business route. 1152 N Grand Ave 87701. Fax: 505/425-5447. **Facility:** 23 one-bedroom standard units. 1-2 stories, exterior corridors. **Parking:** on-site, winter plug-ins. **Terms:** 1-2 night minimum stay, package plans, small pets only ($6 extra charge). **Dining:** 6 am-9 pm. **Business Services:** fax (fee). **Cards:** AX, CB, DC, DS, MC, VI. **Special Amenities:** free local telephone calls and early check-in/late check-out.

SOME UNITS

FEE

INN ON THE SANTA FE TRAIL   *Book at aaa.com*

Phone: 505/425-6791

4/15-10/31	1P: $69-$79	2P: $74-$84	XP: $5
2/1-4/14	1P: $59-$69	2P: $64-$74	XP: $5
11/1-1/31	1P: $59-$64	2P: $64-$74	XP: $5

Motel

Location: I-25, exit 345, 0.5 mi n; I-25 business route and US 84, 0.3 mi w. 1133 N Grand Ave 87701. Fax: 505/425-0417. **Facility:** 31 units. 29 one-bedroom standard units. 1 one- and 1 two-bedroom suites ($95-$155) with kitchens. 1-2 stories, exterior corridors. **Parking:** on-site. **Terms:** pets ($5 extra charge). **Dining:** Blackjack's Grill, see separate listing. **Pool(s):** heated outdoor. **Leisure Activities:** whirlpool. **Guest Services:** coin laundry. **Business Services:** fax (fee). **Cards:** AX, DS, MC, VI. **Special Amenities:** free continental breakfast and free local telephone calls.

SOME UNITS

FEE

PLAZA HOTEL

AAA **SAVE**

▼▼▼▼▼

Historic
Small-scale Hotel

				Phone: (505)425-3591
5/1-9/30 [BP]	1P: $79-$139	2P: $79-$139	XP: $8	F17
2/1-4/30 & 10/1-1/31 [BP]	1P: $69-$129	2P: $69-$129	XP: $8	F17

Location: I-25, exit 343W, just w, follow signs to Old Town Plaza. 230 Plaza 87701. Fax: 505/425-9659. **Facility:** This 1882 Western Victorian hotel on the main square of town offers nicely appointed rooms and common areas. 36 units. 32 one-bedroom standard units. 4 one-bedroom suites. 3 stories, interior corridors. **Parking:** street. **Terms:** package plans, pets ($10 fee). **Amenities:** high-speed Internet, irons. **Dining:** Landmark Grill, see separate listing. **Leisure Activities:** Fee: massage. **Business Services:** meeting rooms, business center. **Cards:** AX, DC, DS, MC, VI. **Special Amenities:** free full breakfast and preferred room (subject to availability with advance reservations).

SOME UNITS

SUPER 8 MOTEL-LAS VEGAS   *Book at aaa.com*

▼▼▼▼

Motel

			Phone: (505)425-5288
All Year	1P: $49-$61	2P: $53-$73	XP: $3 F16

Location: I-25, exit 347, 0.8 mi sw, US 85 and I-25 business route. 2029 N Grand Ave 87701. Fax: 505/454-8481. **Facility:** 36 one-bedroom standard units. 2 stories (no elevator), interior corridors. **Parking:** on-site. **Terms:** [CP] meal plan available, package plans. **Amenities:** safes (fee). Some: irons, hair dryers. **Guest Services:** coin laundry. **Business Services:** fax (fee). **Cards:** AX, DC, DS, MC, VI.

SOME UNITS

——— **WHERE TO DINE** ———

BLACKJACK'S GRILL

AAA

▼▼▼▼

Steak & Seafood

Dinner: $12-$25   Phone: 505/425-6791

Location: I-25, exit 345, 0.5 mi n; I-25 business route and US 84, 0.3 mi w; in Inn on the Santa Fe Trail. 1133 N Grand Ave 87701. **Hours:** 5 pm-8:30 pm, Fri & Sat-9 pm. Closed: 12/25. **Reservations:** suggested. **Features:** Steaks, shrimp, scallops, trout and a wide selection of contemporary Italian dishes tempt the patron in an intimate setting with more relaxed outdoor dining available as well. Casual dress; beer & wine only. **Parking:** on-site. **Cards:** AX, DS, MC, VI.

LANDMARK GRILL

▼▼▼▼

American

Lunch: $6-$9   **Dinner:** $6-$22   Phone: 505/425-3591

Location: I-25, exit 343W, just w, follow signs to Old Town Plaza; in Plaza Hotel. 230 Plaza 87701. **Hours:** 7 am-2 & 5-9 pm. **Reservations:** suggested. **Features:** The menu offers new Mexican specialties, steaks, pasta and desserts in a comfortable Victorian dining room. Casual dress; cocktails. **Parking:** street. **Cards:** AX, CB, DC, DS, MC, VI. **Historic**

LINCOLN

——— **WHERE TO STAY** ———

CASA DE PATRON BED & BREAKFAST INN

▼▼▼▼

Historic Bed
& Breakfast

Property failed to provide current rates   Phone: 505/653-4676

Location: Center. Hwy 380 E, MM 98 88338 (PO Box 27). Fax: 505/653-4671. **Facility:** At an elevation of 5,700 feet, the single-story adobe home, built circa 1860, keeps cool naturally during the summer. Designated smoking area. 7 units. 5 one-bedroom standard units, some with whirlpools. 2 cottages. 1 story, interior/exterior corridors. Bath: combo or shower only. **Parking:** on-site. **Terms:** open 5/1-10/31. **Amenities:** Some: irons, hair dryers. **Business Services:** meeting rooms, fax.

SOME UNITS

LORDSBURG pop. 3,379

——— **WHERE TO STAY** ———

BEST WESTERN-WESTERN SKIES INN   *Book at aaa.com*

AAA **SAVE**

▼▼▼▼

Small-scale Hotel

			Phone: (505)542-8807
All Year	1P: $59-$99	2P: $69-$109	XP: $10 F17

Location: I-10, exit 22, just s. 1303 S Main St 88045. Fax: 505/542-8895. **Facility:** 40 one-bedroom standard units. 1 story, exterior corridors. **Parking:** on-site. **Terms:** [BP] meal plan available, pets ($5-$10 extra charge). **Amenities:** high-speed Internet, irons, hair dryers. **Dining:** 6 am-9:30 pm. **Pool(s):** heated outdoor. **Leisure Activities:** horseshoes. **Guest Services:** coin laundry. **Business Services:** fax. **Cards:** AX, DS, MC, VI. **Special Amenities:** free local telephone calls and free newspaper.

SOME UNITS

DAYS INN & SUITES   *Book at aaa.com*

AAA **SAVE**

▼▼▼▼

Small-scale Hotel

			Phone: (505)542-3600
All Year [BP]	1P: $69-$79	2P: $79-$89	XP: $10 F

Location: I-10, exit 20, just n. 1426 W Motel Dr 88045. Fax: 505/542-3601. **Facility:** 56 one-bedroom standard units. 2 stories (no elevator), interior corridors. **Parking:** on-site. **Amenities:** safes, hair dryers. Some: irons. **Pool(s):** heated indoor. **Leisure Activities:** whirlpool, exercise room. **Business Services:** fax. **Cards:** AX, CB, DC, DS, MC, VI. **Special Amenities:** free continental breakfast and free local telephone calls.

SOME UNITS

HOLIDAY INN EXPRESS   *Book at aaa.com*

▼▼▼▼

Small-scale Hotel

			Phone: (505)542-3666
All Year	1P: $85-$99	2P: $85-$99	

Location: I-10, exit 22, just s. 1408 S Main St 88045. Fax: 505/542-3665. **Facility:** 40 one-bedroom standard units. 2 stories (no elevator), exterior corridors. Bath: combo or shower only. **Parking:** on-site. **Terms:** small pets only ($50 fee). **Amenities:** high-speed Internet, dual phone lines, irons, hair dryers. **Pool(s):** heated outdoor. **Cards:** AX, CB, DC, DS, JC, MC, VI.

SOME UNITS

SUPER 8 MOTEL   *Book at aaa.com*   Phone: (505)542-8882

AAA SAVE

2/1-12/15   1P: $50-$60   2P: $60-$70   XP: $10   F
12/16-1/31   1P: $60-$70   2P: $70   XP: $10   F

Location: I-10, exit 22, just s. 110 E Maple 88045. **Fax:** 505/542-8882. **Facility:** 41 one-bedroom standard units. 2 stories (no elevator), interior corridors. **Parking:** on-site. **Terms:** package plans, pets ($5 extra charge).

Small-scale Hotel   **Cards:** AX, DC, DS, MC, VI. **Special Amenities:** free local telephone calls and free newspaper.

SOME UNITS

FEE

--------- **WHERE TO DINE** ---------

KRANBERRY'S FAMILY RESTAURANT   **Lunch:** $5-$8   **Dinner:** $7-$11   Phone: 505/542-9400

Location: I-10, exit 22, just s. 1405 S Main St 88045. **Hours:** 6 am-9:30 pm. Closed: 12/25. **Reservations:** accepted. **Features:** In an atmosphere much like that found at well-known pancake house chains, the restaurant serves generous breakfasts, lunches and dinners. The menu lists a good selection of good old American food, including burgers, sandwiches and cooked-to-order dinners. Just off the interstate, the clean, bright setting appeals to motorists and locals alike. Casual dress. **Parking:** on-site. **Cards:** AX, DS, MC, VI.

American

LOS ALAMOS pop. 11,909

---------- WHERE TO STAY ----------

BEST WESTERN HILLTOP HOUSE HOTEL   *Book at aaa.com*

Phone: (505)662-2441

(AAA) (SAVE)

All Year [ECP]   1P: $79-$254   2P: $89-$264   XP: $10   F13
▽▽ ▽▽

Location: Center. Located in the business district. 400 Trinity Dr 87544. Fax: 505/662-5913. **Facility:** 92 units. 91 one- and 1 two-bedroom standard units. 3 stories, interior corridors. *Bath:* combo or shower only. **Parking:** on-site. **Terms:** check-in 4 pm. **Amenities:** high-speed Internet, dual phone lines, voice mail, irons, hair dryers. **Pool(s):** heated indoor. **Leisure Activities:** sauna, exercise room. **Guest Services:** valet and coin laundry. **Business Services:** meeting rooms. **Cards:** AX, CB, DC, DS, JC, MC, VI. **Special Amenities:** free expanded continental breakfast and free local telephone calls. *(See color ad below)*

Small-scale Hotel

SOME UNITS

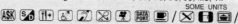

HOLIDAY INN EXPRESS   *Book at aaa.com*

Phone: (505)661-1110

▽▽ ▽▽ ▽▽

All Year   1P: $90-$100   2P: $90-$100   XP: $10   F16

Small-scale Hotel

Location: Center. 2455 Trinity Dr 87544. Fax: 505/661-2657. **Facility:** 55 one-bedroom standard units. 3 stories, interior corridors. *Bath:* combo or shower only. **Parking:** on-site. **Terms:** [CP] meal plan available. **Amenities:** high-speed Internet, voice mail, safes, irons, hair dryers. **Leisure Activities:** sauna, whirlpool, exercise room. **Guest Services:** valet laundry. **Business Services:** meeting rooms. **Cards:** AX, CB, DC, DS, JC, MC, VI.

SOME UNITS

QUALITY INN & SUITES

Phone: 505/662-7211

(fyi)

Property failed to provide current rates

Small-scale Hotel

Under major renovation, scheduled to be completed May 2006. **Last rated:** ▽▽ **Location:** Center. 2175 Trinity Dr 87544. Fax: 505/661-7714. **Facility:** 74 one-bedroom standard units. 3 stories (no elevator), interior corridors. **Parking:** on-site. **Amenities:** high-speed Internet, voice mail, irons, hair dryers. **Pool(s):** heated outdoor. **Guest Services:** valet laundry. **Business Services:** conference facilities.

SOME UNITS

---------- WHERE TO DINE ----------

THE BLUE WINDOW BISTRO   *Menu on aaa.com*   **Lunch:** $6-$9   **Dinner:** $9-$22   Phone: 505/662-6305

(AAA)

▽▽ ▽▽

International

Location: 0.5 mi w of jct SR 502 and Central Ave. 813 Central Ave 87544. **Hours:** 11 am-2:30 & 5-9 pm, Sat from 8:30 am; Saturday brunch. Closed major holidays; also Sun. **Reservations:** accepted. **Features:** This busy eatery has a pleasant, cheerful atmosphere that appeals to business people, tourists and staffers at the Los Alamos National Laboratory. On the menu are a good selection of popular New Mexican dishes, sandwiches, salads and desserts. Casual dress; beer & wine only. **Parking:** on-site. **Cards:** AX, DC, DS, MC, VI.

LOS LUNAS pop. 10,034

—— WHERE TO STAY ——

DAYS INN   *Book at aaa.com*   **Phone:** (505)865-5995

10/1-10/31	1P: $60-$65	2P: $75-$80	XP: $5	F12
5/1-9/30 & 11/1-1/31	1P: $46-$50	2P: $54-$59	XP: $5	F12
2/1-4/30	1P: $42-$46	2P: $50-$54	XP: $5	F12

Location: I-25, exit 203, just s to entrance at southeast corner. 1919 Main St SW 87031. **Fax:** 505/865-9490.
Small-scale Hotel **Facility:** 46 one-bedroom standard units. 2 stories (no elevator), interior corridors. **Parking:** on-site. **Terms:** small pets only ($15 fee). **Amenities:** hair dryers. **Pool(s):** heated indoor. **Leisure Activities:** whirlpool. **Cards:** AX, DC, DS, MC, VI. **Special Amenities:** free continental breakfast and free local telephone calls.

SOME UNITS

WESTERN SKIES INN & SUITES   **Phone:** (505)865-0001

All Year [CP]   1P: $49-$79   2P: $59-$89   XP: $10   F16
Location: I-25, exit 203, just n. 2258 Sun Ranch Village Loop 87031. **Fax:** 505/865-3348. **Facility:** 57 one-
Small-scale Hotel bedroom standard units. 3 stories, interior corridors. **Bath:** combo or shower only. **Parking:** on-site. **Terms:** pets ($10 extra charge, in smoking units, no birds or snakes). **Pool(s):** heated outdoor. **Guest Services:** coin laundry. **Business Services:** meeting rooms. **Cards:** AX, CB, DC, DS, MC, VI.

SOME UNITS

—— WHERE TO DINE ——

HENRIETTA'S RESTAURANT   **Lunch:** $5-$7   **Dinner:** $6-$8   **Phone:** 505/865-5284
Location: Center. 740 Main St 87031. **Hours:** 7 am-9 pm, Sun-8 pm. Closed: 1/1, 11/23, 12/25.
Reservations: accepted. **Features:** Right in the center of town, the restaurant serves breakfast anytime
Southwest during the day. A good selection of burgers, sandwiches, soups and salads also is offered. Chicken-fried
American steak satisfies. Casual dress; beer & wine only. **Parking:** on-site. **Cards:** AX, DS, MC, VI.

LOVINGTON pop. 9,471

—— WHERE TO STAY ——

LOVINGTON INN   **Phone:** (505)396-5346

All Year   1P: $49   2P: $54
Location: Jct US 82 and SR 18, 1 mi w. 1600 W Ave D 88260. **Fax:** 505/396-1492. **Facility:** 61 units. 59 one-
bedroom standard units. 2 two-bedroom suites ($65-$75). 2 stories (no elevator), exterior corridors. **Bath:**
combo or shower only. **Parking:** on-site. **Terms:** pets ($10 deposit). **Amenities:** irons, hair dryers. **Dining:** 5 am-11 & 5-9 pm, Sun-11 am, cocktails. **Guest Services:** coin laundry. **Business Services:**
Small-scale Hotel meeting rooms, fax (fee). **Cards:** AX, DS, MC, VI. **Special Amenities:** free continental breakfast and free
local telephone calls.

SOME UNITS

MADRID

—— WHERE TO DINE ——

—— The following restaurant has not been evaluated by AAA ——
but is listed for your information only.

THE MINE SHAFT TAVERN   **Phone:** 505/473-0743
[fyi]   Not evaluated. **Location:** Center. 2846 SR 14 87010. **Features:** Originally built for coal miners' entertainment,
the rustic watering hole serves a good selection of sandwiches, lunch and dinner specials and spirits to
please its jovial clientele.

MESILLA pop. 2,180

—— WHERE TO STAY ——

MESON DE MESILLA   **Phone:** 505/525-9212
Property failed to provide current rates
Location: I-10, exit 140, 0.4 mi s. 1803 Avenida de Mesilla 88046 (PO Box 1212). **Fax:** 505/527-4196.
Facility: Designated smoking area. 16 units. 15 one-bedroom standard units. 1 one-bedroom suite with
Country Inn kitchen. 2 stories (no elevator), interior/exterior corridors. **Parking:** on-site. **Terms:** small pets only ($10
extra charge). **Dining:** restaurant, see separate listing. **Pool(s):** outdoor.

SOME UNITS

———— WHERE TO DINE ————

DOUBLE EAGLE RESTAURANT **Lunch:** $6-$11 **Dinner:** $11-$30 **Phone:** 505/523-6700

Steak & Seafood

Location: In historic plaza in Old Mesilla. **Hours:** 11 am-10 pm, Sun-9 pm. **Reservations:** suggested. **Features:** On the National Register of Historic Places, the restaurant is decorated with baccarat crystal and 19th-century art. A cafe inside the restaurant prepares regional cuisine, including delicious grilled chicken Mesilla and banana enchiladas. The formal dining room is a fine dining restaurant in its own right. Dressy casual; cocktails. **Parking:** on-site. **Cards:** AX, DC, DS, MC, VI. **Historic**

LA POSTA DE MESILLA *Menu on aaa.com* **Lunch:** $7-$14 **Dinner:** $7-$14 **Phone:** 505/524-3524

AAA

Mexican

Location: I-10, exit 142, on the eastern edge of the plaza. 2410 Calle de San Albino 88046. **Hours:** 11 am-9 pm, Fri & Sat-9:30 pm. Closed: 11/23, 12/25; also Mon. **Reservations:** accepted. **Features:** Once a stagecoach stop, the 1840s adobe structure now houses an atrium of shops and Southwestern gourmet foods. The restaurant serves traditional New Mexican meals, all cooked to order. Enchilada plates are especially tasty. Casual dress; cocktails. **Parking:** on-site. **Cards:** AX, DC, DS, MC, VI. **Historic**

MESON DE MESILLA RESTAURANT **Dinner:** $22-$30 **Phone:** 505/525-9212

Regional Continental

Location: I-10, exit 140, 0.4 mi s; in Meson de Mesilla. 1803 Ave de Mesilla 88046. **Hours:** 5:30 pm-9:30 pm, Fri & Sat-10:30 pm. Closed: 12/25; also Mon. **Reservations:** suggested. **Features:** This adobe restaurant has the warmth and hospitality of traditional European styling. The menu changes to reflect the freshest ingredients available. The chef, working on the cutting edge of preparation methods, creates the desserts, dressings and sauces. Dressy casual; cocktails. **Parking:** on-site. **Cards:** AX, DC, DS, MC, VI.

MORIARTY pop. 1,765

─── WHERE TO STAY ───

COMFORT INN
AAA SAVE

Book at aaa.com

Phone: (505)832-6666

| | | | XP: $10 | F17 |
5/2-10/31 [ECP] — 1P: $69-$109 — 2P: $69-$109 — XP: $10 — F17
2/1-5/1 & 11/1-1/31 [ECP] — 1P: $59-$79 — 2P: $59-$79 — XP: $10 — F17

Location: I-40, exit 194, just s, then 1 mi e. 119 Route 66 E 87035 (PO Box 280). Fax: 505/832-1282. **Facility:** 61 units. 54 one-bedroom standard units. 7 one-bedroom suites ($89-$129). 2 stories (no elevator), interior corridors. *Bath:* combo or shower only. **Parking:** on-site. **Terms:** cancellation fee imposed.
Small-scale Hotel **Amenities:** irons, hair dryers. **Pool(s):** heated indoor. **Cards:** AX, CB, DC, DS, JC, MC, VI.
Special Amenities: free expanded continental breakfast and free local telephone calls.

SOME UNITS

DAYS INN
AAA SAVE

Book at aaa.com

Phone: (505)832-4451

5/1-7/31 — 1P: $49-$69 — 2P: $55-$79
2/1-4/30 & 8/1-10/31 — 1P: $49-$59 — 2P: $59-$69
11/1-1/31 — 1P: $49-$59 — 2P: $55-$59

Location: I-40, exit 194. Located in a commercial area. 1809 Route 66 W 87035 (PO Box 367). Fax: 505/832-6464.
Small-scale Hotel **Facility:** 41 one-bedroom standard units. 2 stories (no elevator), interior corridors. **Parking:** on-site.
Terms: [CP] meal plan available, package plans, pets ($5 extra charge). **Amenities:** hair dryers.
Cards: AX, DC, DS, MC, VI. **Special Amenities:** free expanded continental breakfast and free newspaper.

SOME UNITS
FEE

ECONO LODGE
AAA SAVE

Book at aaa.com

Phone: (505)832-4457

10/1-10/16 — 1P: $50-$65 — 2P: $55-$69
2/1-9/30 & 10/17-1/31 — 1P: $39-$59 — 2P: $44-$65

Location: I-40, exit 194, 0.5 mi se on US 66 and I-40 business loop. Located in a commercial area. 1316 Route 66 W 87035 (PO Box 1610). Fax: 505/832-9323. **Facility:** 29 one-bedroom standard units. 2 stories (no elevator), interior corridors. **Parking:** on-site. **Terms:** cancellation fee imposed, pets ($5 extra charge).
Small-scale Hotel **Amenities:** *Some:* hair dryers. **Business Services:** fax (fee). **Cards:** AX, DS, MC, VI. **Special Amenities:**
free expanded continental breakfast and free local telephone calls.

SOME UNITS
FEE

HOLIDAY INN EXPRESS
AAA SAVE

Book at aaa.com

Phone: (505)832-5000

All Year [ECP] — 1P: $93 — 2P: $93

Location: I-40, exit 194, 0.4 mi e. 1507 Route 66 87035 (PO Box 2295). Fax: 505/832-5005. **Facility:** 70 one-bedroom standard units. 2 stories (no elevator), interior corridors. *Bath:* combo or shower only. **Parking:** on-site. **Terms:** cancellation fee imposed, pets ($10 extra charge). **Amenities:** high-speed Internet, dual phone lines, voice mail, irons, hair dryers. **Pool(s):** heated indoor. **Leisure Activities:** whirlpool. *Fee:* game room.
Small-scale Hotel **Guest Services:** valet and coin laundry. **Business Services:** meeting rooms. **Cards:** AX, CB, DC, DS, JC, MC, VI. **Special Amenities:** free expanded continental breakfast and free newspaper.

SOME UNITS
FEE

SUNSET MOTEL
AAA SAVE

Phone: (505)832-4234

All Year [CP] — 1P: $39-$44 — 2P: $47-$54 — XP: $4 — F12

Location: I-40, exit 197, 1 mi w, then 0.5 mi e. 501 E Route 66 87035 (PO Box 36). **Facility:** Classic property located along historic Route 66, built by owner in 1949. 18 one-bedroom standard units. 1 story, exterior corridors. **Parking:** on-site. **Guest Services:** airport transportation-Moriarty Airport. **Cards:** DS, MC, VI.
Classic Motel **Special Amenities:** free continental breakfast and free local telephone calls. *(See color ad below)*

SOME UNITS

SUPER 8 MOTEL   *Book at aaa.com*   Phone: (505)832-6730

(AAA) (SAVE)

6/1-9/30 [ECP]	1P: $50-$65	2P: $65-$70	XP: $4 F12
2/1-5/31 & 10/1-1/31 [ECP]	1P: $49-$60	2P: $60-$65	XP: $4 F12

Small-scale Hotel

Location: I-40, exit 194, 0.5 mi e on Central Ave. 1611 W Old Route 66 87035 (PO Box 1127). Fax: 505/832-6730. **Facility:** 68 one-bedroom standard units. 2 stories (no elevator), interior corridors. *Bath:* combo or shower only. **Parking:** on-site. **Terms:** pets ($20 deposit). **Guest Services:** coin laundry. **Business Services:** meeting rooms. **Cards:** AX, CB, DC, DS, MC, VI. **Special Amenities:** free expanded continental breakfast and free local telephone calls.

SOME UNITS

——— WHERE TO DINE ———

THE BUFORD STEAKHOUSE   **Lunch:** $6-$9   **Dinner:** $6-$20   Phone: 505/832-6525

— American

Location: I-40, exit 196, just n. Hwy 41 N 87035. **Hours:** 9 am-9 pm, Fri & Sat-10 pm, Sun 11 am-8 pm. Closed: 11/23, 12/25. **Features:** Although the town for which it's named is long gone, the busy, inviting steak house is for real. Tasty beef cuts are prepared to guests' likings. Portions are generous. Splurge on one of the tempting desserts. Casual dress; cocktails. **Parking:** on-site. **Cards:** AX, DS, MC, VI.

EL COMEDOR DE ANAYAS   **Lunch:** $6-$12   **Dinner:** $6-$12   Phone: 505/832-4442

Southwest American

Location: I-40, exit 194, just e. 1005 Old Route 66 87035. **Hours:** 6:30 am-9 pm. Closed: 4/16, 11/23, 12/25. **Reservations:** accepted. **Features:** The friendly, Western-style eatery has served the town's residents for many years. Southwestern dishes, sandwiches and steaks are offered at reasonable prices. Casual dress; beer & wine only. **Parking:** on-site. **Cards:** AX, DS, MC, VI.

JENK'S CAFE'   **Lunch:** $5-$8   **Dinner:** $5-$16   Phone: 505/832-1905

American

Location: I-40, exit 194, just e. 1805 Old Route 66 87035. **Hours:** 6 am-9 pm, Sun 7 am-3 pm. Closed: 4/16, 11/23, 12/25. **Reservations:** accepted. **Features:** The modest, small-town cafe prepares American heartland food along the lines of chicken-fried steak with mashed potatoes and mixed vegetables. Follow the meal with a slice of carrot cake for dessert. Casual dress. **Parking:** on-site. **Cards:** AX, DS, MC, VI.

SHORTY'S BAR BE CUE   **Lunch:** $4-$6   **Dinner:** $7-$10   Phone: 505/832-0400

Barbecue

Location: Center. 1202 Main St 87035. **Hours:** 11 am-9 pm; to 8 pm in winter. Closed major holidays; also Sun & Mon. **Features:** The modest eatery is a favorite of locals and travelers. Barbecued beef is particularly special. Casual dress. **Parking:** on-site. **Cards:** AX, DS, MC, VI.

OJO CALIENTE

——— WHERE TO STAY ———

RANCHO DE SAN JUAN COUNTRY INN & RESTAURANT   Phone: 505/753-6818

(AAA) (SAVE)

5/1-10/31	2P: $225-$525	XP: $25	D15
2/1-4/30 & 11/1-12/31	2P: $200-$500	XP: $25	D15

Country Inn

Location: On US 285, 11 mi nw at MM 340; right on Rancho de San Juan Dr. Located in a rural area. RR 34020 US Hwy 285 87533 (PO Box 4140, ESPANOLA). Fax: 505/753-6818. **Facility:** These luxury accommodations are in a serene rural setting, with four casitas remotely located a short distance from the main lodge. Smoke free premises. 15 units. 11 one-bedroom standard units, some with kitchens and/or whirlpools. 4 one-bedroom suites with kitchens and whirlpools. 1 story, exterior corridors. *Bath:* combo or shower only. **Parking:** on-site. **Terms:** open 2/1-12/31, office hours 7 am-11 pm, age restrictions may apply, 30 day cancellation notice-fee imposed, [MAP] meal plan available, package plans. **Amenities:** CD players, voice mail, irons, hair dryers. *Some:* DVD players. **Dining:** Rancho de San Juan Restaurant, see separate listing. **Leisure Activities:** hiking trails. *Fee:* massage. **Guest Services:** gift shop, valet laundry. **Business Services:** meeting rooms. **Cards:** AX, DS, MC, VI. **Special Amenities:** free local telephone calls and free room upgrade (subject to availability with advance reservations).

SOME UNITS

——— WHERE TO DINE ———

RANCHO DE SAN JUAN RESTAURANT   **Dinner:** $55-$100   Phone: 505/753-6818

Continental

Location: On US 285, 11 mi nw at MM 340; right on Rancho San Juan Dr; in Rancho De San Juan Country Inn & Restaurant. RR 34020, US Hwy 285 87549. **Hours:** Open 2/1-12/31; 5:30 pm-9 pm. Closed: Sun & Mon. **Reservations:** suggested. **Features:** You'll find an excellent fine dining restaurant that features gourmet cuisine, truly fine wines, svelte service and an eclectic art collection, all in a rural New Mexico setting. Dressy casual; cocktails. **Parking:** on-site. **Cards:** AX, DS, MC, VI.

PENASCO pop. 572

——— WHERE TO DINE ———

SUGAR NYMPHS BISTRO   **Lunch:** $6-$9   **Dinner:** $11-$16   Phone: 505/587-0311

American

Location: Center of village on SR 75. 15046 Hwy 75 87553. **Hours:** 11:30 am-2:30 & 5:30-8 pm, Sun 11 am-2 pm; hours vary in summer. Closed major holidays; also Mon-Wed. **Features:** If you have time for a scenic drive between Santa Fe and Taos be sure to stop into this charming little restaurant located off the beaten track. Fresh salads and sandwiches are served in an old adobe house in the center of a village that feels like you've just stepped back in time. Casual dress. **Parking:** on-site. **Cards:** MC, VI.

PINOS ALTOS

──────── WHERE TO STAY ────────

BEAR CREEK MOTEL & CABINS
Phone: 505/388-4501
❤❤ ❤❤
All Year   1P: $99-$159   2P: $99-$159   XP: $10   D3
Cabin
Location: 1 mi n on SR 15. 88 Main St 88053 (PO Box 53082). Fax: 505/538-5583. **Facility:** 15 cabins. 2 stories, exterior corridors. **Parking:** on-site. **Terms:** office hours 9 am-7 pm, 2 night minimum stay - weekends, 10 day cancellation notice, weekly rates available, package plans, pets ($10-$15 fee). **Leisure Activities:** hiking trails. **Business Services:** fax. **Cards:** AX, CB, DC, DS, MC, VI.

SOME UNITS
(ASK) (S✆) (🐾) (AC) (DATA PORT) (💻) / (🛏) (📷) /
FEE

──────── WHERE TO DINE ────────

THE BUCKHORN SALOON   **Dinner: $14-$20**   **Phone: 505/538-9911**
❤❤ ❤❤
Steak House
Location: Center. 25 Main St 88053. **Hours:** 6 pm-10 pm. Closed: 1/1, 11/23, 12/25; also Sun. **Reservations:** suggested. **Features:** The original 1870s saloon makes diners feel as though they have stepped back in time. The specialty is cooked-to-order steaks. Portions are healthy, and the bar is lively. Casual dress; cocktails. **Parking:** on-site. **Cards:** DS, MC, VI.

(🍽) (🚬)

PLACITAS pop. 3,452

──────── WHERE TO STAY ────────

──────── *The following lodging was either not evaluated or did not* ────────
meet AAA rating requirements but is listed for your information only.

HACIENDA DE PLACITAS INN OF THE ARTS   **Phone: 505/867-0082**
(fyi)
Not evaluated. **Location:** I-25, exit 242, 4.9 mi e. 491 Hwy 165 87043. Facilities, services, and decor characterize a mid-range property.

POJOAQUE PUEBLO

──────── WHERE TO STAY ────────

CITIES OF GOLD HOTEL   *Book at aaa.com*   **Phone: (505)455-0515**
(AAA) (SAVE)   1P: $86-$119   2P: $86-$119   XP: $10   F15
❤❤ ❤❤
Small-scale Hotel
Location: On US 84/265, just n. Located adjacent to a casino. 10A Cities of Gold Rd 87506. Fax: 505/455-3060. **Facility:** 121 one-bedroom standard units. 2 stories, interior corridors. *Bath:* combo or shower only. **Parking:** on-site. **Terms:** cancellation fee imposed, [AP] & [MAP] meal plans available, package plans, 18% service charge, pets ($25 deposit). **Amenities:** video games (fee), voice mail, irons, hair dryers. *Some:* DVD players. **Dining:** 6:30 am-11:30 & 4:30-10 pm, cocktails. **Guest Services:** coin laundry. **Business Services:** meeting rooms, business center. **Cards:** AX, DS, MC, VI.

SOME UNITS
(S✆) (🐾) (🍽) (⚅M) (♿) (🏊) (📺) (DATA PORT) (💻) / (✕) (VCR) (🛏) (📷) /
FEE

RANCHOS DE TAOS pop. 2,390   (See map and index starting on p. 601)—See also TAOS.

──────── WHERE TO STAY ────────

BUDGET HOST INN   **Phone: (505)758-2524**   (28)
(AAA) (SAVE)
All Year   1P: $43-$55   2P: $48-$70   XP: $5   F8
❤
Motel
Location: On SR 68; center. 1798 Paseo Del Pueblo Sur 87557 (PO Box 729). Fax: 505/758-1989. **Facility:** 27 one-bedroom standard units. 2 stories (no elevator), exterior corridors. **Parking:** on-site. **Terms:** 3 day cancellation notice-fee imposed, [CP] meal plan available, pets ($7.50 fee). **Amenities:** *Some:* irons. **Business Services:** fax (fee). **Cards:** AX, DS, MC, VI.

SOME UNITS
(🛏) (🍽+) (💻) / (✕) (DATA PORT) (🛏) (📷) /
FEE   FEE   FEE

──────── WHERE TO DINE ────────

THE STAKEOUT GRILL & BAR   **Dinner: $19-$30**   **Phone: 505/758-2042**   (28)
(AAA)
Location: 4 mi sw on SR 68, 1.3 mi e on gravel road at sign. 101 Stakeout Dr 87557. **Hours:** Open 2/1-11/10 & 12/10-1/31; 5 pm-close. **Reservations:** accepted. **Features:** Overlooking the valley from Outlaw Hill, the
❤❤ ❤❤
Continental
restaurant affords views of fabulous desert sunsets and the mountains in the distance. Seating on the seasonal patio offers the best vantage points. Friendly, yet expert, staff members serve attractively presented dishes, such as grilled shrimp scampi, lobster, duck, steaks cooked to order and crab legs. Among palate-tempting desserts are chocolate ganache cake and coconut creme brulee. Casual dress; cocktails. **Parking:** on-site. **Cards:** AX, CB, DC, DS, MC, VI.

(🍽) (🚬)

TRADING POST CAFE   **Lunch: $7-$9**   **Dinner: $10-$19**   **Phone: 505/758-5089**   (24)
❤❤ ❤❤
Continental
Location: On SR 68, jct SR 518. 4179 Hwy 68 87557. **Hours:** 11:30 am-9:30 pm, Sun from 5 pm. Closed: 11/23, 12/25; also Mon. **Features:** Italian dishes—such as bistecca Fiorentina, pasta bolognese and piccata Milanese—are prepared with the freshest ingredients and served in the cozy dining room or on the breezy patio. The wine list includes many good-value choices. Accomplished servers are prompt and friendly. Homemade desserts are simply a must, so be sure to save room. Casual dress; beer & wine only. **Parking:** on-site. **Cards:** AX, DC, DS, MC, VI.

(🍽) (🚬)

RATON pop. 7,282

——— WHERE TO STAY ———

BEST WESTERN SANDS   *Book at aaa.com*   **Phone:** (505)445-2737

	1P: $77-$99	2P: $77-$99	XP: $3	F17
6/9-9/4	1P: $77-$99	2P: $77-$99	XP: $3	F17
9/5-1/31	1P: $55-$89	2P: $55-$89	XP: $3	F17
2/1-5/11	1P: $55-$79	2P: $55-$79	XP: $3	F17
5/12-6/8	1P: $66-$77	2P: $66-$77	XP: $3	F17

Motel **Location:** I-25, exit 451, just w. 300 Clayton Rd 87740. Fax: 505/445-4053. **Facility:** 50 one-bedroom standard units. 1 story, interior/exterior corridors. *Bath:* combo or shower only. **Parking:** on-site. **Amenities:** high-speed Internet, irons, hair dryers. **Dining:** 6 am-9 pm. **Pool(s):** heated outdoor. **Leisure Activities:** whirlpool, playground. **Guest Services:** valet laundry. **Business Services:** fax (fee). **Cards:** AX, CB, DC, DS, MC, VI. **Special Amenities:** free local telephone calls.

SOME UNITS — FEE FEE FEE

BUDGET HOST RATON   **Phone:** (505)445-3655

5/16-9/15 [CP]	1P: $50	2P: $55	XP: $5	F8
3/1-5/15 & 9/16-1/31 [CP]	1P: $39	2P: $44	XP: $5	F8

Motel **Location:** I-25, exit 454, 0.8 mi s on I-25 business loop. 136 Canyon Dr 87740. Fax: 505/445-3461. **Facility:** 27 units. 26 one- and 1 two-bedroom standard units. 1 story, exterior corridors. *Bath:* combo or shower only. **Parking:** on-site. **Terms:** open 3/1-1/31, small pets only ($2 extra charge). **Amenities:** *Some:* hair dryers. **Business Services:** fax (fee). **Cards:** AX, CB, DC, DS, MC, VI. **Special Amenities:** free continental breakfast and free local telephone calls.

SOME UNITS — FEE

COMFORT INN   *Book at aaa.com*   **Phone:** 505/445-4200

5/20-9/30	1P: $77-$107	2P: $87-$112	XP: $5	F12
2/1-5/19	1P: $66-$96	2P: $76-$101	XP: $5	F12
10/1-1/31	1P: $62-$92	2P: $72-$97	XP: $5	F12

Small-scale Hotel **Location:** I-25, exit 451, just w. US 64 and 87. 533 Clayton Rd 87740. Fax: 505/445-7144. **Facility:** 63 units. 62 one-bedroom standard units. 1 one-bedroom suite. 2 stories (no elevator), interior corridors. **Parking:** on-site. **Terms:** [CP] meal plan available. **Amenities:** irons, hair dryers. **Pool(s):** small heated indoor. **Leisure Activities:** whirlpool, exercise room. **Guest Services:** coin laundry. **Business Services:** fax (fee). **Cards:** AX, DC, DS, MC, VI.

SOME UNITS

HOLIDAY INN EXPRESS HOTEL & SUITES   *Book at aaa.com*   **Phone:** (505)445-1500

All Year [ECP]	1P: $110-$220	2P: $120-$230	XP: $10	F18

Small-scale Hotel **Location:** I-25, exit 450, just w. 101 Card Ave 87740. Fax: 505/445-7650. **Facility:** 80 units. 78 one-bedroom standard units, some with whirlpools. 2 one-bedroom suites. 2 stories, interior corridors. *Bath:* combo or shower only. **Parking:** on-site. **Amenities:** video library, high-speed Internet, dual phone lines, voice mail, irons, hair dryers. *Some:* DVD players, video games (fee). **Pool(s):** small heated indoor. **Leisure Activities:** whirlpool, exercise room. **Guest Services:** valet and coin laundry. **Business Services:** meeting rooms, business center. **Cards:** AX, DC, DS, MC, VI. **Special Amenities:** free expanded continental breakfast and free local telephone calls.

SOME UNITS

MOTEL 6 RATON #279   *Book at aaa.com*   **Phone:** 505/445-2777

6/25-8/6	1P: $45-$55	2P: $51-$61	XP: $3	F17
8/7-10/1	1P: $39-$49	2P: $45-$55	XP: $3	F17
2/1-6/24 & 10/2-1/31	1P: $33-$43	2P: $39-$49	XP: $3	F17

Motel **Location:** I-25, exit 451, just w. 1600 Cedar St 87740. Fax: 505/445-5359. **Facility:** 102 one-bedroom standard units. 2 stories (no elevator), exterior corridors. *Bath:* shower only. **Parking:** on-site. **Terms:** small pets only. **Pool(s):** outdoor. **Guest Services:** coin laundry. **Business Services:** fax (fee). **Cards:** AX, CB, DC, DS, MC, VI.

SOME UNITS

THE RATON PASS INN   **Phone:** (505)445-3641

5/15-9/30 [CP]	1P: $46	2P: $52	XP: $5	F8
2/1-5/14 & 10/1-1/31 [CP]	1P: $36	2P: $42	XP: $5	F8

Motel **Location:** I-25, exit 454, 0.8 mi s. 308 Canyon Dr 87740. **Facility:** 14 one-bedroom standard units. 1 story, exterior corridors. **Parking:** on-site. **Terms:** pets ($2 extra charge). **Cards:** MC, VI. **Special Amenities:** free continental breakfast and free local telephone calls.

SOME UNITS — FEE

SUPER 8 RATON   *Book at aaa.com*   **Phone:** 505/445-2355

Property failed to provide current rates

Motel **Location:** I-25, exit 451, just nw. 1610 Cedar 87740. Fax: 505/445-7653. **Facility:** 48 one-bedroom standard units. 3 stories (no elevator), interior corridors. **Parking:** on-site. **Amenities:** safes (fee). **Business Services:** fax (fee).

SOME UNITS

——— WHERE TO DINE ———

PAPPAS SWEET SHOP RESTAURANT   *Menu on aaa.com*   **Lunch:** $6-$10 **Dinner:** $9-$25 **Phone:** 505/445-9811

American **Location:** I-25, exit 451, 0.5 mi w on US 64 and 87, then just s on US 64. 1201 S 2nd St 87740. **Hours:** 11 am-2 & 5-9 pm. Closed major holidays; also Sun. **Reservations:** suggested, in season. **Features:** This restaurant's well-rounded menu offers spaghetti, steak, seafood and sandwiches. You'll also find displays of antiques, collectibles and items related to the family-owned restaurant and its early years of candy and ice cream making. Casual dress; cocktails. **Parking:** on-site. **Cards:** AX, DS, MC, VI.

SHANG HAI II RESTAURANT   *Menu on aaa.com*   **Lunch:** $4-$6   **Dinner:** $6-$14   **Phone:** 505/445-2933

(AAA)
▽▽
Chinese

Location: I-25, exit 451, 0.5 mi w. 1156 S 2nd St 87740. **Hours:** 11 am-9:30 pm. **Reservations:** accepted. **Features:** A nice family restaurant or casual business meeting place, serving a broad variety of Chinese dishes or a buffet. Well lighted. Very relaxed environment and the service is prompt and efficient. Casual dress; beer & wine only. **Parking:** on-site. **Cards:** AX, DS, MC, VI.

RED RIVER pop. 484

—— WHERE TO STAY ——

ALPINE LODGE   **Phone:** (505)754-2952

(AAA) [SAVE]
▽▽
Motel

All Year   1P: $58-$120   2P: $58-$120
Location: Just nw of center on SR 38. 417 W Main St 87558 (PO Box 67). Fax: 505/754-6421. **Facility:** Smoke free premises. 46 units. 28 one-bedroom standard units. 9 one-, 7 two- and 2 three-bedroom suites, some with kitchens. 1-3 stories (no elevator), interior/exterior corridors. *Bath:* combo or shower only. **Parking:** on-site, winter plug-ins. **Terms:** office hours 8 am-9 pm, 30 day cancellation notice-fee imposed, package plans. **Amenities:** *Some:* irons, hair dryers. **Leisure Activities:** whirlpools, fishing, ski in & ski out lodge, picnic areas, barbecue pits, outdoor pavillion, playground. *Fee:* downhill & cross country skiing, snowmobiling. **Guest Services:** coin laundry. **Business Services:** meeting rooms, fax (fee). **Cards:** AX, DS, MC, VI. **Special Amenities:** free local telephone calls and early check-in/late check-out.

SOME UNITS

LAZY MINER LODGE   **Phone:** (505)754-6444

▽
Motel

2/1-3/31   1P: $54-$69   2P: $54-$109   XP: $10
6/1-9/30   1P: $49-$80   2P: $49-$80   XP: $10
4/1-5/31 & 10/1-1/31   1P: $25-$55   2P: $30-$55   XP: $5
Location: SR 38, just w of jct SR 578. 505 E Main St 87558 (PO Box 836). **Facility:** 12 units. 6 one-, 5 two- and 1 three-bedroom suites, some with kitchens. 2 stories (no elevator), exterior corridors. **Parking:** on-site. **Terms:** 30 day cancellation notice-fee imposed. **Amenities:** *Some:* irons, hair dryers. **Leisure Activities:** whirlpool, fishing, playground. *Fee:* downhill & cross country skiing. **Cards:** AX, DS, MC, VI.

SOME UNITS

THE RIVERSIDE LODGE & CABINS   **Phone:** 505/754-2252

(AAA) [SAVE]
▽▽
Historic Motel

12/19-1/3   1P: $82-$121   2P: $82-$121
6/1-12/18 & 1/4-1/31   1P: $65-$97   2P: $65-$97
2/1-5/31   1P: $63-$95   2P: $63-$95
Location: On SR 38; center. 201 E Main St 87558 (PO Box 249). Fax: 505/754-2495. **Facility:** Individual, duplex housekeeping cabins and apartments; some lodge rooms, many fireplaces. On grounds along the Red River. Smoke free premises. 60 units. 4 one- and 13 two-bedroom standard units. 11 one- and 32 two-bedroom suites, some with kitchens. 1-2 stories (no elevator), exterior corridors. *Bath:* combo or shower only. **Parking:** on-site. **Terms:** office hours 8 am-7 pm, 2-3 night minimum stay - seasonal, cancellation fee imposed, [AP] meal plan available, package plans. **Amenities:** video library (fee). *Some:* voice mail, hair dryers. **Leisure Activities:** whirlpool, fishing, ski in & ski out, pavillion, playground, horseshoes, shuffleboard. **Business Services:** meeting rooms. **Cards:** DS, MC, VI. **Special Amenities:** free local telephone calls.

SOME UNITS

—— WHERE TO DINE ——

TEXAS REDS STEAKHOUSE   **Dinner:** $7-$41   **Phone:** 505/754-2964

▽▽
West American

Location: On SR 38; center. 111 E Main 87558. **Hours:** 5 pm-9:30 pm. Closed: Mon-Thurs 4/1-5/15. **Features:** The old wooden building in the heart of Red River houses a fun saloon downstairs and hearty Western style meals served upstairs. Steaks are the house specialty, although chicken, buffalo, lamb, fish and pork dishes are offered. Start with the complimentary roasted peanuts in the shell and progress to dessert drinks that are called "ice cream afters." Fast and friendly service are the order of the day in this popular Old West style eatery. Casual dress; cocktails. **Parking:** on-site. **Cards:** AX, DC, DS, MC, VI.

RIO RANCHO pop. 51,765   (See map and index starting on p. 478)—See also ALBUQUERQUE.

—— WHERE TO STAY ——

BEST WESTERN RIO RANCHO INN &
CONFERENCE CENTER   *Book at aaa.com*   **Phone:** (505)892-1700   94

(AAA) [SAVE]
▽▽▽
Small-scale Hotel

6/1-1/31   1P: $59-$109   2P: $59-$119
2/1-5/31   1P: $59-$99   2P: $59-$109
Location: I-25, exit 233 (Alameda Blvd), 6.5 mi w; I-40, exit 155, 10 mi n on Coors Rd/Coors Bypass to SR 528, then 1 mi n. 1465 Rio Rancho Blvd 87124. Fax: 505/892-4628. **Facility:** 118 one-bedroom standard units. 1-2 stories (no elevator), exterior corridors. **Parking:** on-site. **Terms:** 30 day cancellation notice-fee imposed, [BP] meal plan available, pets ($25 fee). **Amenities:** voice mail, irons, hair dryers. **Pool(s):** heated outdoor. **Leisure Activities:** whirlpool, exercise room. **Guest Services:** valet and coin laundry. **Business Services:** conference facilities. **Cards:** AX, CB, DC, DS, JC, MC, VI. **Special Amenities:** free expanded continental breakfast and free local telephone calls.

SOME UNITS

FEE

(See map and index starting on p. 478)

DAYS INN   Book at aaa.com

AAA SAVE

10/1-10/15 [CP]	1P: $85-$105	2P: $85-$105	XP: $8	F16
4/1-9/30 [CP]	1P: $49-$65	2P: $55-$75	XP: $8	F16
2/1-3/31 & 10/16-1/31 [CP]	1P: $45-$65	2P: $45-$65	XP: $8	F16

Small-scale Hotel   **Location:** I-25, exit 233 (Alameda Blvd), 8 mi w on SR 528; I-40, exit 155, 8 mi on Coors Rd (SR 448). 4200 Crestview Dr 87124. Fax: 505/896-3321. **Facility:** 46 one-bedroom standard units. 2 stories (no elevator), exterior corridors. **Parking:** on-site. **Terms:** small pets only ($10 fee). **Amenities:** high-speed Internet, hair dryers. **Pool(s):** heated indoor. **Leisure Activities:** whirlpool. **Business Services:** fax (fee). **Cards:** AX, DS, MC, VI. **Special Amenities:** free continental breakfast and free local telephone calls.

SOME UNITS

EXTENDED STAYAMERICA ALBUQUERQUE-RIO RANCHO BLVD   Book at aaa.com   **Phone:** (505)892-7900   96

4/30-10/16	1P: $110	2P: $115	XP: $5	F17
2/1-4/29 & 10/17-1/31	1P: $50	2P: $55	XP: $5	F17

Small-scale Hotel   **Location:** I-25, exit 233 (Alameda Blvd), 6 mi w (becomes SR 528/Rio Rancho Blvd). 2221 Rio Rancho Blvd 87124. Fax: 505/892-7999. **Facility:** 109 one-bedroom standard units with kitchens. 3 stories, interior corridors. *Bath:* combo or shower only. **Parking:** on-site. **Terms:** cancellation fee imposed, small pets only ($25 extra charge). **Amenities:** dual phone lines, voice mail, irons, hair dryers. **Fee:** video games, high-speed Internet. **Pool(s):** heated outdoor. **Leisure Activities:** exercise room, basketball. **Guest Services:** valet and coin laundry. **Business Services:** meeting rooms. **Cards:** AX, DC, DS, MC, VI.

SOME UNITS

HILTON GARDEN INN   Book at aaa.com   **Phone:** (505)896-1111   95

10/2-10/31	1P: $150	2P: $160	XP: $10	F18
2/1-10/1 & 11/1-1/31	1P: $110	2P: $120	XP: $10	F18

Small-scale Hotel   **Location:** I-25, exit 233 (Alameda Blvd), then n (becomes SR 528/Rio Rancho Blvd). Located across from Intel, convenient to retail area. 1771 Rio Rancho Blvd 87124. Fax: 505/896-2100. **Facility:** 129 one-bedroom standard units. 4 stories, interior corridors. *Bath:* combo or shower only. **Parking:** on-site. **Terms:** cancellation fee imposed. **Amenities:** video games (fee), high-speed Internet, dual phone lines, voice mail, irons, hair dryers. **Pool(s):** heated indoor. **Leisure Activities:** whirlpool, exercise room. **Guest Services:** valet and coin laundry. **Business Services:** meeting rooms, business center. **Cards:** AX, CB, DC, DS, JC, MC, VI.

SOME UNITS

RAMADA LIMITED HOTEL   Book at aaa.com   **Phone:** (505)892-5998   92

AAA SAVE

11/22-1/31 [ECP]	1P: $66	2P: $69	XP: $5	F12
2/1-11/21 [ECP]	1P: $61	2P: $63	XP: $5	F12

Small-scale Hotel   **Location:** I-25, exit 233 (Alameda Blvd), 8 mi w; I-40, exit 155, 8 mi n on Coors Rd (SR 448). 4081 High Resort Blvd 87124. Fax: 505/892-9131. **Facility:** 58 one-bedroom standard units. 2 stories (no elevator), interior corridors. **Parking:** on-site. **Terms:** pets ($25 deposit, $10 extra charge, in designated units). **Amenities:** voice mail, irons, hair dryers. **Pool(s):** heated indoor. **Leisure Activities:** whirlpool. **Guest Services:** valet laundry. **Business Services:** meeting rooms. **Cards:** AX, CB, DC, DS, JC, MC, VI. **Special Amenities:** free expanded continental breakfast and free local telephone calls.

SOME UNITS

RIO RANCHO SUPER 8 MOTEL   Book at aaa.com   **Phone:** 505/896-8888   93

All Year	1P: $40-$90	2P: $45-$95	XP: $5 F12

Small-scale Hotel   **Location:** I-25, exit 233 (Alameda Blvd), 0.5 mi w, 3.8 mi nw on SR 528, then just e. 4100 Barbara Loop 87124. Fax: 505/896-2665. **Facility:** 48 one-bedroom standard units. 2 stories (no elevator), interior corridors. **Parking:** on-site. **Terms:** [CP] meal plan available, pets ($6 extra charge). **Business Services:** fax. **Cards:** AX, DS, MC, VI.

SOME UNITS

─────── **WHERE TO DINE** ───────

HOT TAMALES

Lunch: $7-$8	**Dinner:** $7-$8	**Phone:** 505/962-0123	138

Mexican   **Location:** Jct Barbara Loop and Rio Rancho Blvd. 1520 Rio Rancho Blvd 87124. **Hours:** 11 am-8 pm. Closed major holidays. **Features:** Quick service, great spicy tamales, burritos, enchiladas and tacos are served here. The chile packs a punch with great New Mexico flavor. Casual dress. **Parking:** on-site. **Cards:** MC, VI.

O'HARE'S GRILLE & PUB

Lunch: $6-$8	**Dinner:** $6-$21	**Phone:** 505/896-0123	137

American   **Location:** Jct SR 528 and Southern Blvd; in Rio Rancho Shopping Center. 4100 Southern Blvd SE 87124. **Hours:** 11 am-10 pm. Closed major holidays; also Sun. **Features:** Guests unwind in the busy, cheerful place with a meal complemented by a choice from the large selection of beers and spirits. The friendly pub attracts folks who work in the neighborhood. A short lunchtime wait is typical. Casual dress; cocktails. **Parking:** on-site. **Cards:** AX, DC, DS, MC, VI.

─────── *The following restaurants have not been evaluated by AAA* ───────
but are listed for your information only.

FEDERICO'S MEXICAN FOOD   **Phone:** 505/891-7218

fyi   Not evaluated. **Location:** Jct SR 528 and Barbara Loop SE, just e. 1590 Deborah Rd SE 87124. **Features:** This quick-serve restaurant is new on the town's restaurant scene; the enchilalda plate is scrumptious.

SMOKEHOUSE BBQ   **Phone:** 505/892-1914

fyi   Not evaluated. **Location:** Jct SR 528 and Barbara Loop, just e. Hwy 528 & Barbara Loop 87124. **Features:** Near the Intel plant in Rio Rancho, the neighborhood restaurant sells great barbecue brisket by the pound, as well as great meals with side dishes. Breakfast is served daily.

ROSWELL pop. 45,293

——— WHERE TO STAY ———

BEST WESTERN EL RANCHO PALACIO *Book at aaa.com*   **Phone:** (505)622-2721

AAA [SAVE] All Year   1P: $55-$75   2P: $65-$85   XP: $5   F
Location: 1.8 mi n on US 70 and 285. 2205 N Main St 88201. **Fax:** 505/622-2725. **Facility:** 45 one-bedroom standard units. 2 stories (no elevator), exterior corridors. **Parking:** on-site. **Terms:** 7 day cancellation notice, weekly rates available. **Amenities:** high-speed Internet, irons, hair dryers. **Pool(s):** small heated outdoor.
Small-scale Hotel **Leisure Activities:** whirlpool. **Business Services:** business center. **Cards:** AX, CB, DC, DS, MC, VI.
Special Amenities: free expanded continental breakfast and free local telephone calls.
SOME UNITS

BEST WESTERN SALLY PORT INN & SUITES *Book at aaa.com*   **Phone:** (505)622-6430
AAA [SAVE] All Year   1P: $69-$89   2P: $79-$99   XP: $10   F12
Location: 1.5 mi n on US 70 and 285. 2000 N Main St 88201. **Fax:** 505/623-7631. **Facility:** 124 one-bedroom standard units. 2 stories (no elevator), interior corridors. **Parking:** on-site. **Terms:** [BP] meal plan available, package plans, small pets only ($10 extra charge, in smoking units). **Amenities:** high-speed Internet, voice
Small-scale Hotel mail, irons, hair dryers. **Dining:** 6 am-10 & 5-9 pm, Fri & Sat-10 pm, cocktails. **Pool(s):** heated indoor.
Leisure Activities: saunas, whirlpool, indoor recreation area, exercise room. **Guest Services:** valet and coin laundry, airport transportation-Roswell Airport, beauty salon. **Business Services:** meeting rooms, fax (fee). **Cards:** AX, CB, DC, DS, MC, VI. **Special Amenities:** free full breakfast and free local telephone calls. *(See color ad below)*
SOME UNITS

BUDGET INN-NORTH   **Phone:** (505)623-6050
AAA [SAVE] All Year   1P: $30-$38   2P: $35-$50   XP: $5   F
Location: 1.8 mi n on US 70 and 285. 2101 N Main St 88201. **Fax:** 505/623-8546. **Facility:** 42 one-bedroom standard units. 1 story, exterior corridors. **Parking:** on-site. **Terms:** small pets only ($5 extra charge). **Pool(s):** small outdoor. **Leisure Activities:** whirlpool. **Business Services:** fax (fee). **Cards:** AX, DS,
Motel MC, VI. **Special Amenities:** free continental breakfast and free local telephone calls.   SOME UNITS

BUDGET INN WEST   **Phone:** (505)623-3811
All Year   1P: $32-$40   2P: $35-$55   XP: $5   F14
Location: 2 mi w on US 70 and 380. 2200 W 2nd St 88201. **Fax:** 505/623-7030. **Facility:** 29 one-bedroom standard units, some with efficiencies. 2 stories (no elevator), exterior corridors. **Parking:** on-site.
Small-scale Hotel **Terms:** small pets only ($2 extra charge). **Pool(s):** small outdoor. **Leisure Activities:** whirlpool. **Business Services:** fax (fee). **Cards:** AX, DS, MC, VI.   SOME UNITS

COMFORT INN *Book at aaa.com*   **Phone:** 505/623-4567
AAA [SAVE] All Year   1P: $59-$99   2P: $69-$129   XP: $10   F12
Location: On US 70 and 285, 3 mi n. 3595 N Main St 88201. **Fax:** 505/623-4848. **Facility:** 55 one-bedroom standard units, some with whirlpools. 2 stories (no elevator), interior corridors. **Bath:** combo or shower only.
Parking: on-site. **Terms:** small pets only. **Amenities:** high-speed Internet, voice mail, irons, hair dryers.
Small-scale Hotel **Pool(s):** heated indoor. **Leisure Activities:** whirlpool, exercise room. **Guest Services:** valet and coin laundry. **Business Services:** PC, fax. **Cards:** AX, DC, DS, MC, VI. **Special Amenities:** free continental breakfast and free local telephone calls.   SOME UNITS

COUNTRY CLUB BED & BREAKFAST

Bed & Breakfast

Phone: 505/317-0845
F10

All Year [BP] 1P: $79-$109 2P: $99-$139 XP: $30
Location: US 285 to Country Club Rd, 4 blks e. 400 E Country Club Rd 88201. Fax: 505/625-1013. **Facility:** Designated smoking area. 4 units. 3 one- and 1 two-bedroom standard units. 2 stories (no elevator), interior corridors. *Bath:* combo or shower only. **Parking:** on-site. **Terms:** weekly rates available, package plans. **Amenities:** *Some:* high-speed Internet. **Guest Services:** complimentary laundry. **Cards:** AX, DS, MC, VI.

(ASK) (S𝐃) (✕) (☎)

DAYS INN *Book at aaa.com*

(AAA) (SAVE)

Small-scale Hotel

Phone: (505)623-4021
F12

All Year 1P: $55-$85 2P: $60-$90 XP: $7
Location: 0.8 mi n on US 70 and 285. 1310 N Main St 88201. Fax: 505/623-0079. **Facility:** 62 one-bedroom standard units. 2 stories (no elevator), exterior corridors. **Parking:** on-site. **Terms:** 7 day cancellation notice. **Amenities:** high-speed Internet, irons, hair dryers. **Pool(s):** small outdoor. **Leisure Activities:** whirlpool. **Business Services:** meeting rooms, fax (fee). **Cards:** AX, CB, DC, DS, MC, VI. **Special Amenities:** free expanded continental breakfast and free local telephone calls.

SOME UNITS
(S𝐃) (🛏) (🍴) (🅿) (🏊) (📹) (DATA PORT) (▣) / (✕) (🛢) (🖥) /

FAIRFIELD INN & SUITES *Book at aaa.com*

Small-scale Hotel

Phone: 505/624-1300

All Year [ECP] 1P: $89-$169 2P: $89-$169
Location: Jct US 380 and 285, 0.7 mi n. 1201 N Main St 88201. Fax: 505/624-1305. **Facility:** 67 one-bedroom standard units. 3 stories, interior corridors. *Bath:* combo or shower only. **Parking:** on-site. **Amenities:** high-speed Internet, voice mail, irons, hair dryers. *Some:* CD players. **Pool(s):** small heated outdoor. **Leisure Activities:** whirlpool, exercise room. **Guest Services:** valet and coin laundry. **Business Services:** meeting rooms, business center. **Cards:** AX, CB, DC, DS, JC, MC, VI.

SOME UNITS
(ASK) (S𝐃) (🍴) (🖥) (🔧) (📞) (📹) (DATA PORT) (▣) / (✕) (🛢) (🖥) /

FRONTIER MOTEL *Book at aaa.com*

(AAA) (SAVE)

Motel

Phone: (505)622-1400
F12

All Year 1P: $32-$40 2P: $36-$44 XP: $4
Location: 2.5 mi n on US 70 and 285. 3010 N Main St 88201. Fax: 505/622-1405. **Facility:** 38 one-bedroom standard units. 1 story, exterior corridors. *Bath:* combo or shower only. **Parking:** on-site. **Terms:** 30 day cancellation notice, [CP] meal plan available. **Amenities:** high-speed Internet. **Pool(s):** small outdoor. **Business Services:** PC, fax (fee). **Cards:** AX, DS, MC, VI. *(See color ad below)*

SOME UNITS
(S𝐃) (🛏) (🍴) (🏊) (📹) (🛢) (🖥) / (✕) /

HAMPTON INN AND SUITES *Book at aaa.com*

Small-scale Hotel

Phone: (505)623-5151

All Year [BP] 1P: $85 2P: $90
Location: Jct US 70 and 285 N, 1 mi s. 3607 N Main St 88201. Fax: 505/623-8969. **Facility:** 70 one-bedroom standard units. 3 stories, interior corridors. *Bath:* combo or shower only. **Parking:** on-site. **Terms:** 2 night minimum stay, cancellation fee imposed. **Amenities:** video games (fee), high-speed Internet, dual phone lines, voice mail, irons, hair dryers. **Pool(s):** small indoor. **Leisure Activities:** sauna, whirlpool, exercise room. **Guest Services:** sundries, valet and coin laundry. **Business Services:** meeting rooms, business center. **Cards:** AX, DC, DS, MC, VI.

SOME UNITS
(ASK) (S𝐃) (🍴) (🏊) (✕) (🔧) (DATA PORT) (🛢) (🖥) (▣) / (✕) /

HOLIDAY INN EXPRESS *Book at aaa.com*

Small-scale Hotel

Phone: (505)627-9900
F18

All Year 1P: $85-$130 2P: $85-$130 XP: $10
Location: US 70. 2300 N Main St 88201. Fax: 505/627-9963. **Facility:** 80 one-bedroom standard units, some with efficiencies. 3 stories, interior corridors. *Bath:* combo or shower only. **Parking:** on-site. **Terms:** [ECP] meal plan available, small pets only. **Amenities:** high-speed Internet, voice mail, irons, hair dryers. *Some:* dual phone lines. **Pool(s):** small heated indoor. **Leisure Activities:** sauna, whirlpool, exercise room. **Guest Services:** valet and coin laundry. **Business Services:** meeting rooms, PC, fax (fee). **Cards:** AX, CB, DC, DS, MC, VI.

SOME UNITS
(ASK) (S𝐃) (♿) (🛏) (🍴) (🔧) (📞) (🏊) (✕) (📹) (DATA PORT) (▣) / (✕) (🛢) (🖥) /

LEISURE INN

All Year [CP]   1P: $32-$38   2P: $42-$48   XP: $6

Phone: (505)622-2575   D12

Small-scale Hotel

Location: 2.5 mi w on US 70 and 380. 2700 W 2nd St 88201. Fax: 505/622-2575. **Facility:** 90 one-bedroom standard units. 1-2 stories (no elevator), exterior corridors. **Parking:** on-site, winter plug-ins. **Terms:** small pets only ($5 extra charge, in designated units). **Pool(s):** heated outdoor. **Leisure Activities:** exercise room, sports court, basketball. **Guest Services:** coin laundry, airport transportation-Roswell Airport. **Business Services:** meeting rooms, fax (fee). **Cards:** AX, DS, MC, VI. **Special Amenities:** free continental breakfast and free local telephone calls.

SOME UNITS

RAMADA LIMITED

Book at aaa.com

Phone: 505/623-9440

Small-scale Hotel

Property failed to provide current rates

Location: 2.5 mi w on US 70 and 380. 2803 W 2nd St 88201. Fax: 505/622-9708. **Facility:** 58 one-bedroom standard units. 2 stories (no elevator), interior/exterior corridors. **Parking:** on-site. **Terms:** pets ($50 deposit). **Amenities:** voice mail, irons, hair dryers. **Pool(s):** heated outdoor. **Leisure Activities:** exercise room. *Fee:* game room. **Guest Services:** coin laundry. **Business Services:** meeting rooms, fax (fee).

SOME UNITS

WESTERN INN

Phone: 505/623-9425

Motel

Property failed to provide current rates

Location: Jct US 70/285/380, 2.2 mi n. 2331 N Main St 88201. Fax: 505/623-7285. **Facility:** 29 one-bedroom standard units. 1 story, exterior corridors. *Bath:* combo or shower only. **Parking:** on-site. **Terms:** small pets only ($5 extra charge). **Pool(s):** outdoor. **Business Services:** fax.

SOME UNITS

——— WHERE TO DINE ———

CATTLE BARON STEAK & SEAFOOD

Lunch: $7-$10   **Dinner:** $10-$21   **Phone:** 505/622-2465

Steak & Seafood

Location: US 380 and 285, 0.7 mi n. 1113 N Main St 88201. **Hours:** 11 am-9:30 pm, Fri & Sat-10 pm, Sun-9 pm. Closed: 11/23, 12/25. **Reservations:** accepted. **Features:** The ranchlike restaurant presents a menu of hand-cut steaks, chicken, seafood and the signature prime rib. Guests can start off the meal with a plate from the huge salad bar. Casual dress; cocktails. **Parking:** on-site. **Cards:** AX, CB, DC, DS, MC, VI.

KWAN DEN

Lunch: $6-$8   **Dinner:** $7-$10   **Phone:** 505/622-4192

Chinese

Location: 0.8 mi w on US 70 and 285; corner of 2nd St and Union Ave. 1000 W 2nd St 88201. **Hours:** 11 am-9 pm. Closed: 11/23, 12/25. **Reservations:** accepted. **Features:** Lunch and dinner buffets—which line up traditional preparations of beef, shrimp, chicken and pork—offer the best value at the comfortable restaurant. The menu also lists a limited number of American chicken and seafood dishes. Service is prompt and friendly. Casual dress. **Parking:** on-site. **Cards:** AX, DS, MC, VI.

PEPPERS GRILL & BAR

Lunch: $5-$8   **Dinner:** $7-$16   **Phone:** 505/623-1700

American

Location: US 70 and 285; corner of Main and 6th sts. 500 N Main St 88201. **Hours:** 11 am-10 pm. Closed major holidays; also Sun. **Reservations:** accepted. **Features:** The restaurant prepares a good variety of appetizers, burgers, salads, pasta, sandwiches and traditional Mexican dishes, as well as steak and seafood entrees, for lunch and dinner. Entertainers perform on the patio Friday and Saturday in summer. Casual dress; cocktails. **Parking:** on-site. **Cards:** AX, CB, DC, DS, MC, VI.

RUIDOSO pop. 7,698

──────── **WHERE TO STAY** ────────

BEST WESTERN PINE SPRINGS INN
Phone: 505/378-8100

◆◆ ◆◆

Small-scale Hotel

Property failed to provide current rates

Location: Just n; center. Located across from the racetrack. 1420 W Hwy 70 88346 (PO Box 2100, RUIDOSO DOWNS). Fax: 505/378-8215. **Facility:** 100 one-bedroom standard units. 2 stories (no elevator); exterior corridors. *Bath:* combo or shower only. **Parking:** on-site. **Terms:** check-in 4 pm. **Amenities:** irons, hair dryers. **Pool(s):** heated outdoor. **Leisure Activities:** whirlpool, exercise room. **Guest Services:** coin laundry. **Business Services:** meeting rooms.

SOME UNITS

BEST WESTERN RUIDOSO INN   *Book at aaa.com*
Phone: (505)257-3600

◆◆◆◆

Small-scale Hotel

All Year   1P: $79-$139   2P: $89-$149   XP: $5   F13

Location: US 70, just w of jct Sudderth Dr, just n. 97 Camelot Dr 88345 (PO Box 7460, 88355). Fax: 505/257-3900. **Facility:** 57 units. 48 one-bedroom standard units. 9 two-bedroom suites ($119-$225). 3 stories, interior corridors. *Bath:* combo or shower only. **Parking:** on-site. **Terms:** [ECP] meal plan available, package plans. **Amenities:** dual phone lines, irons, hair dryers. **Pool(s):** heated indoor. **Leisure Activities:** whirlpool, exercise room. **Guest Services:** coin laundry. **Business Services:** meeting rooms, business center. **Cards:** AX, DC, DS, MC, VI.

SOME UNITS

BLACK BEAR LODGE
Phone: (505)257-1459

AAA SAVE

◆◆◆◆

Bed & Breakfast

All Year [ECP]   1P: $109-$149   2P: $119-$159

Location: 0.9 mi w of jct SR 48 and Sudderth Dr. 428 Main Rd 88345. Fax: 505/630-8310. **Facility:** Exceptionally well decorated, this B&B in the Upper Canyon area combines luxury with serene simplicity. Smoke free premises. 4 one-bedroom standard units with whirlpools. 1 story, interior corridors. **Parking:** on-site. **Terms:** office hours 8 am-10 pm, 14 day cancellation notice-fee imposed. **Amenities:** hair dryers. **Cards:** AX, DS, MC, VI. **Special Amenities:** free expanded continental breakfast and preferred room (subject to availability with advance reservations).

COMFORT INN-RUIDOSO   *Book at aaa.com*
Phone: (505)257-2770

AAA SAVE

◆◆◆◆

Small-scale Hotel

12/16-1/31 [ECP]	1P: $109-$149	2P: $109-$149	XP: $10	F17
2/1-9/24 & 11/25-12/15 [ECP]	1P: $79-$149	2P: $79-$149	XP: $10	F17
9/25-11/24 [ECP]	1P: $59-$119	2P: $59-$119	XP: $10	F17

Location: On SR 48 S, then e. 2709 Sudderth Dr 88345. Fax: 505/257-2760. **Facility:** 54 one-bedroom standard units. 3 stories, interior corridors. *Bath:* combo or shower only. **Parking:** on-site. **Terms:** package plans. **Amenities:** high-speed Internet, safes, irons, hair dryers. **Pool(s):** heated indoor. **Leisure Activities:** sauna, whirlpool, exercise room. **Guest Services:** valet and coin laundry. **Business Services:** meeting rooms, business center. **Cards:** AX, DC, DS, MC, VI. **Special Amenities:** free expanded continental breakfast and free newspaper.

SOME UNITS

CROWN POINT CONDOMINIUMS
Phone: 505/257-7641

◆◆ ◆◆

Condominium

Property failed to provide current rates

Location: US 70 W; at entrance to Camelot Subdivision, follow Crown Dr. 220 Crown Dr 88355 (PO Box 7159). Fax: 505/257-9183. **Facility:** Perched on a high mountain ridge, the attractive vacation condos offer spectacular views of the town below as well as the pine-covered mountains. 60 units. 36 two- and 24 three-bedroom suites with kitchens. 1 story, exterior corridors. **Parking:** on-site. **Terms:** office hours 8 am-9 pm, check-in 4 pm. **Amenities:** dual phone lines, voice mail, irons, hair dryers. **Pool(s):** heated outdoor. **Leisure Activities:** 2 lighted tennis courts, exercise room, sports court, basketball. **Guest Services:** coin laundry. **Business Services:** meeting rooms, PC.

DAN DEE CABINS
Phone: 505/257-2165

AAA SAVE

◆◆◆◆ ◆◆

Cabin

6/15-9/4	1P: $109-$179	2P: $109-$179	XP: $10
12/15-1/31	1P: $94-$167	2P: $94-$167	XP: $10
2/1-6/14 & 9/5-12/14	1P: $84-$149	2P: $84-$149	XP: $10

Location: 0.8 mi w on Upper Canyon Rd. 310 Main Rd 88345 (PO Box 844, 88355). Fax: 505/257-0094. **Facility:** 13 cabins. 1 story, exterior corridors. *Bath:* combo or shower only. **Parking:** on-site. **Terms:** office hours 9 am-9 pm, 2 night minimum stay - weekends, 14 day cancellation notice, package plans, pets ($10 fee). **Amenities:** high-speed Internet. **Leisure Activities:** whirlpool, playground. **Cards:** DS, MC, VI. **Special Amenities:** free newspaper.

FEE

FOREST HOME CABINS
Phone: 505/257-4504

Cabin

Property failed to provide current rates
Location: 1 mi w of jct SR 48 and Sudderth Dr. 436 Main Ave 88355 (PO Box 2068, 88345). Fax: 505/257-4488. **Facility:** 14 cabins, some with whirlpools. 1 story, exterior corridors. *Bath:* combo or shower only. **Parking:** on-site. **Terms:** office hours 9 am-8 pm. **Leisure Activities:** horseshoes, volleyball.

SOME UNITS

HAWTHORN SUITES CONFERENCE & GOLF RESORT *Book at aaa.com*
Phone: (505)258-5500

Small-scale Hotel

All Year [BP]   1P: $195-$215   2P: $195-$215
Location: 2.5 mi n on SR 48. 107 Sierra Blanca Dr 88345. Fax: 505/258-2419. **Facility:** 120 units. 90 one-bedroom standard units, some with efficiencies. 27 one- and 3 two-bedroom suites ($226-$349). 3 stories. interior corridors. *Bath:* combo or shower only. **Parking:** on-site. **Terms:** small pets only. **Amenities:** high-speed Internet, dual phone lines, voice mail, irons, hair dryers. **Pool(s):** heated indoor. **Leisure Activities:** whirlpool, lighted tennis court, playground, exercise room. **Fee:** golf-18 holes, massage. **Guest Services:** gift shop, complimentary evening beverages: Wed, valet and coin laundry. **Business Services:** conference facilities, fax. **Cards:** AX, CB, DC, DS, MC, VI.

SOME UNITS

HOLIDAY INN EXPRESS
Phone: (505)257-3736

AAA SAVE

Small-scale Hotel

All Year   1P: $89-$179   2P: $89-$179
Location: US 70, just w of jct Hwy 70 88345. Fax: 505/257-5202. **Facility:** 104 one-bedroom standard units. 3 stories, interior corridors. *Bath:* combo or shower only. **Parking:** on-site. **Amenities:** high-speed Internet, voice mail, irons, hair dryers. **Pool(s):** heated outdoor. **Leisure Activities:** whirlpool. **Guest Services:** coin laundry. **Business Services:** meeting rooms, fax. **Cards:** AX, CB, DC, DS, JC, MC, VI. **Special Amenities:** free continental breakfast and free newspaper.

SOME UNITS

INN OF THE MOUNTAIN GODS RESORT & CASINO *Book at aaa.com*
Phone: (505)464-7777

AAA SAVE

Resort
Large-scale Hotel

All Year   1P: $99-$500   2P: $99-$500   XP: $10   F12
Location: 1.5 mi w; on the Mescalero Apache Reservation. 287 Carrizo Canyon Rd (Rt 4) (PO Box 157, MESCALERO, 88340). Fax: 505/464-7005. **Facility:** The combination resort and casino on the Mescalero Apache Reservation features a breathtaking view of the nearby lake and the pristine natural setting; luxurious, upscale accomodations, magnificent architecture, and superior service can be found here as well. 246 one-bedroom standard units, some with whirlpools. 8 stories, interior corridors. **Parking:** on-site. **Terms:** 3 day cancellation notice-fee imposed, package plans, pets ($25 fee). **Dining:** 3 restaurants, 6 am-11 pm, Fri & Sat-midnight, cocktails, also, Wendell's Steak & Seafood Restaurant, see separate listing, entertainment. **Pool(s):** heated indoor. **Leisure Activities:** saunas, whirlpool, skiing, snowboarding, sporting clays, exercise room. **Fee:** boats, canoes, paddleboats, fishing, golf-18 holes, massage, horseshoes. **Guest Services:** gift shop, valet and coin laundry, area transportation (fee). **Business Services:** conference facilities, business center. **Cards:** AX, DS, MC, VI. *(See color ad below)*

SOME UNITS

FEE   FEE

A VIEW WITH A ROOM.

Presenting luxurious accommodations at the all-new Inn of the Mountain Gods Resort & Casino. Rooms here are sanctuaries, providing guests with spectacular mountain views and all the modern conveniences anyone could ever need. A well-appointed room is just another one of the many things to experience at the Inn of the Mountain Gods Resort & Casino. **One Mountain. Many Sides.**

Mescalero, NM, near Ruidoso. For reservations, call
1-800-545-9011 or visit www.innofthemountaingods.com.

Four Diamond Award

Inn of the MOUNTAIN GODS RESORT & CASINO

World-class Resort   Casino Apache   Ski Apache   Championship Golf   A Mescalero Apache Enterprise®

INNSBROOK VILLAGE COUNTRY CLUB & RESORT

Phone: 505/258-3589

Property failed to provide current rates

Vacation Home

Location: 2 mi n on SR 48. 146 Geneva Dr 88345. Fax: 505/258-4500. **Facility:** The well-decorated and maintained, 1- to 3-bedroom units are suitable for a family vacation, and all units have a kitchen. 79 vacation homes, some with pools. 1-3 stories (no elevator), exterior corridors. **Parking:** on-site. **Terms:** office hours 8 am-5 pm, check-in 4 pm. **Amenities:** irons. **Leisure Activities:** fishing, 2 tennis courts, playground, exercise room, horseshoes, shuffleboard, volleyball. *Fee:* golf-9 holes.

QUALITY INN

Phone: (505)378-4051

| | | | XP: $10 | F |

Small-scale Hotel

All Year   1P: $60-$170   2P: $60-$170   XP: $10   F
Location: Jct US 70 and SR 48. 307 Hwy 70 W 88355. Fax: 505/378-5427. **Facility:** 52 one-bedroom standard units. 2 stories (no elevator), interior corridors. **Terms:** 1-5 night minimum stay - seasonal, cancellation fee imposed, [ECP] meal plan available. **Amenities:** high-speed Internet, dual phone lines, voice mail, irons, hair dryers. **Pool(s):** heated indoor. **Guest Services:** coin laundry. **Business Services:** meeting rooms, fax (fee). **Cards:** AX, CB, DC, DS, JC, MC, VI. **Special Amenities: free continental breakfast and free local telephone calls.**

SOME UNITS

RUIDOSO LODGE CABINS

Phone: (505)257-2510

5/27-9/4	1P: $129-$149	2P: $139-$159	XP: $20
9/5-1/31	1P: $99-$129	2P: $109-$139	XP: $20
2/1-5/26	1P: $89-$129	2P: $99-$129	XP: $20

Cabin

Location: 0.7 mi w on Upper Canyon Rd. 300 Main Rd 88345. Fax: 505/257-2248. **Facility:** These modern yet rustic-looking wood cabins, located in the Upper Canyon area, are very well maintained and comfortable. 9 cabins, some with whirlpools. 1 story, exterior corridors. **Parking:** on-site. **Terms:** office hours 9 am-8 pm, 14 day cancellation notice-fee imposed. **Amenities:** irons, hair dryers. **Leisure Activities:** fishing. **Cards:** DS, MC, VI.

SOME UNITS

STORY BOOK CABINS

Phone: 505/257-2115

| | | | XP: $10 |

Cabin

All Year   1P: $99-$119   2P: $99-$189   XP: $10
Location: 1 mi w on Upper Canyon Rd. 410 Main Rd 88345. Fax: 505/257-7512. **Facility:** Rustic but comfortable cabins located in Ruidoso's Upper Canyon area are surrounded by tall pine trees. 15 cabins, some with whirlpools. 1 story, exterior corridors. **Parking:** on-site. **Terms:** office hours 8:30 am-8:30 pm, 2 night minimum stay, 14 day cancellation notice, package plans. **Amenities:** high-speed Internet. *Some:* DVD players, irons, hair dryers. **Leisure Activities:** fishing, barbecue grills, hiking trails. **Business Services:** fax. **Cards:** AX, CB, DC, DS, JC, MC, VI.

SOME UNITS

TRAVELODGE

Book at aaa.com

Phone: (505)378-4471

5/16-9/30 & 12/16-1/31 [CP]	1P: $45-$150	2P: $45-$150	XP: $5	F17
2/1-5/15 & 10/1-12/15 [CP]	1P: $45-$110	2P: $45-$110	XP: $5	F17

Small-scale Hotel

Location: Jct of US 70 and SR 48. 159 W Hwy 70 88345. Fax: 505/378-4409. **Facility:** 59 one-bedroom standard units. 1 story, exterior corridors. *Bath:* combo or shower only. **Parking:** on-site. **Terms:** small pets only ($10 extra charge). **Amenities:** hair dryers. **Pool(s):** heated outdoor. **Leisure Activities:** whirlpool. **Business Services:** fax. **Cards:** AX, DC, DS, MC, VI.

SOME UNITS

FEE

THE VILLAGE LODGE

Book at aaa.com

Phone: (505)258-5442

All Year   1P: $129   2P: $129

Condominium

Location: 2 mi n on SR 48. 1000 Mechem Dr 88345. Fax: 505/258-3127. **Facility:** The facility consists of well-maintained, apartment-style suites with living rooms, refrigerators and microwaves. Designated smoking area. 28 units. 27 one- and 1 two-bedroom suites, some with kitchens. 2 stories (no elevator), exterior corridors. **Parking:** on-site. **Terms:** office hours 9 am-9 pm, check-in 4 pm, 14 day cancellation notice, package plans, pets (small dogs only, $10 fee). **Amenities:** high-speed Internet, dual phone lines, irons, hair dryers. **Leisure Activities:** whirlpool. **Business Services:** fax. **Cards:** DS, MC, VI. **Special Amenities: free local telephone calls and early check-in/late check-out.**

FEE

WHISPERING PINE CABINS

Phone: 505/257-4311

All Year   1P: $89-$265   2P: $89-$265

Cabin

Location: 0.9 mi w of jct SR 48 and Suddenth Dr. 422 Main Rd 88345. Fax: 505/257-4548. **Facility:** Designated smoking area. 10 cabins, some with whirlpools. 1 story, exterior corridors. *Bath:* combo or shower only. **Parking:** on-site. **Terms:** office hours 9 am-9 pm, 2 night minimum stay - weekends, 14 day cancellation notice-fee imposed, weekly rates available, package plans, pets ($10 fee). **Amenities:** DVD players, high-speed Internet, irons, hair dryers. **Leisure Activities:** whirlpool, fishing. **Cards:** DS, MC, VI. **Special Amenities: free local telephone calls and early check-in/late check-out.**

SOME UNITS

FEE

The following lodgings were either not evaluated or did not meet AAA rating requirements but are listed for your information only.

DCR RESORTS

[fyi]

Phone: 505/258-3283

Not evaluated. **Location:** Center. 200 Granite St 88345. Facilities, services, and decor characterize a mid-range property.

PINECLIFF VILLAGE

[fyi]

Phone: 505/378-4427

Not evaluated. **Location:** US 70, just w of jct Sudderth Dr. 401 Hwy 70 W 88345. Facilities, services, and decor characterize a mid-range property.

---------- **WHERE TO DINE** ----------

CAFE RIO

▼▼

Italian

Lunch: $5-$8   **Dinner:** $5-$8   **Phone:** 505/257-7746
Location: Center. 2547 Sudderth Dr 88345. **Hours:** 11:20 am-7:50 pm. Closed: 11/23, 12/25; also 3 weeks in April & Nov. **Features:** The main-street cafe serves pizza, salads, jambalaya and a fine selection of sandwiches. There's a great selection of ice cream and desserts, including cakes baked on site. Casual dress; beer & wine only. **Parking:** street.

CATTLE BARON STEAK & SEAFOOD

▼▼▼▼

Steak & Seafood

Lunch: $5-$8   **Dinner:** $9-$23   **Phone:** 505/257-9355
Location: 1.3 mi s. 657 Sudderth Dr 88345. **Hours:** 11 am-10 pm, Fri & Sat-10:30 pm, Sun-9:30 pm. **Reservations:** accepted. **Features:** The bustling, casual, Western-style atmosphere at Cattle Baron's proves the popularity of its menu, which offers steak, seafood, prime rib, filet mignon and shrimp scampi in satisfying portions. It also has one of the most extensive salad bars imaginable. Casual dress; cocktails.
Parking: on-site. **Cards:** AX, DC, DS, MC, VI.   〔🍸〕〔🚭〕

CORNERSTONE BAKERY CAFE

▼▼▼▼

Bakery/Desserts

Lunch: $6-$8   **Phone:** 505/257-1842
Location: 1 mi n of jct US 70 and Sudderth Dr. 359 Sudderth Dr 88345. **Hours:** 7:30 am-3:30 pm. **Features:** The bakery and cafe has a bright, clean look. Sandwiches, soups and desserts are perfect for a casual lunch. Bakery items, such as the strawberry-filled croissant, are exceptional. Casual dress. **Parking:** on-site. **Cards:** AX, DS, MC, VI.

EL CAMINO NUEVO

▼▼▼▼

Mexican

Lunch: $6-$15   **Dinner:** $6-$15   **Phone:** 505/258-4312
Location: On SR 48, 1 mi n of jct Sudderth Dr. 1025 Mechem Dr 88345. **Hours:** 11 am-9 pm. Closed: 4/16, 11/23, 12/25. **Reservations:** suggested. **Features:** Adobe-style architecture and terra-cotta tile floors provide the backdrop for a "New Mex" meal. Proudly displayed throughout the restaurant, Southwestern prints from local artists add to the festive atmosphere. The wide variety of selections are marked by good presentation, sizeable portions and reasonable prices. Dressy casual; beer & wine only. **Parking:** on-site. **Cards:** AX, DS, MC, VI.

LE BISTRO

▼▼▼▼

French

Lunch: $6-$7   **Dinner:** $12-$16   **Phone:** 505/257-0132
Location: Center. 2800 Sudderth Dr 88345. **Hours:** 11:30 am-2 & 5:30-9 pm. Closed: Sun. **Reservations:** accepted. **Features:** Along the main road winding through town, you will find French country cuisine that is very flavorful and easy to appreciate. The seafood casserole in white wine shallot cream sauce has a slightly sweet flavor that pleases the palate. Dessert crepes are very light and add the perfect finale to a good meal. The single red column near the center of the building seems to support the dark wood beams that spiral outward with impressive ease. Casual dress; beer & wine only. **Parking:** on-site. **Cards:** AX, MC, VI.   〔🍸〕

PASTA CAFE'

▼▼▼▼

Italian

Lunch: $6-$10   **Dinner:** $10-$16   **Phone:** 505/257-6666
Location: Center; midtown area. 2331 Sudderth Dr 88345. **Hours:** 11 am-9:30 pm, Fri & Sat-10:30 pm. **Features:** Casual, informal dining and traditional Italian fare are what patrons find here. Chicken Marsala is a classic. Casual dress; cocktails. **Parking:** on-site. **Cards:** AX, DS, MC, VI.   〔🍸〕〔🚭〕

RESTAURANT JEZEBEL

▼▼▼▼ ▼▼▼▼

International

Dinner: $19-$31   **Phone:** 505/257-5883
Location: Center; in Gazebo Shopping Center. 2117 Sudderth Dr #7 88345. **Hours:** 5:30 pm-10 pm. Closed: Wed. **Reservations:** accepted. **Features:** A superior fine dining experience awaits you at this relatively new Ruidoso restaurant. Accomplished service, an eclectic menu that is expertly executed and a fine selection of wines can be expected. The Banannas Foster is to die for. Dressy casual; beer & wine only. **Parking:** on-site. **Cards:** AX, DC, MC, VI.

SANTINO'S ITALIAN

▼▼▼▼

Italian

Lunch: $12-$20   **Dinner:** $12-$20   **Phone:** 505/257-7540
Location: Jct SR 48 and Sudderth Dr; center. 2823 Sudderth Dr 88345. **Hours:** 5 pm-9 pm, Fri-Sun also 11:30 am-2:30 pm. Closed: 11/23, 12/25. **Reservations:** accepted. **Features:** The classy setting displays photographic art from years gone by. Service is efficient and friendly, and such traditional dishes as lasagna are expertly prepared. Clams Santino are extraordinary. Casual dress; cocktails. **Parking:** on-site.
Cards: AX, DC, DS, MC, VI.   〔🍸〕

TEXAS CLUB

▼▼▼▼

Steak House

Dinner: $12-$30   **Phone:** 505/258-3325
Location: Jct SR 48 and Sudderth Dr, 2 mi n, just e. 212 Metz Dr 88345. **Hours:** 5 pm-9:30 pm, Fri & Sat-10 pm. Closed: 1/1, 12/25; also Mon & Tues. **Features:** Diners interested in meeting real Texans and noshing on great steaks will find the lively, fun restaurant just the ticket. On the menu is a good selection of pasta, chicken and fish dishes. Casual dress; cocktails. **Parking:** on-site. **Cards:** AX, DS, MC, VI.   〔🍸〕〔🚭〕

WENDELL'S STEAK & SEAFOOD RESTAURANT

▼▼▼▼

Steak House

Lunch: $8-$14   **Dinner:** $26-$41   **Phone:** 505/464-7777
Location: 1.5 mi w; on the Mescalero Apache Reservation; in Inn of the Mountain Gods Resort & Casino. 287 Carrizo Canyon Rd 88340. **Hours:** 8 am-10 pm. **Reservations:** suggested. **Features:** This is a fine dining restaurant that offers locally grown and harvested elk as well a fine beef cuts, fowl and seafood dishes. The professional staff will make your meal a memorable occasion. Dressy casual; cocktails. **Parking:** on-site.
Cards: AX, CB, DC, DS, MC, VI.   〔♿M〕〔🍸〕

RUIDOSO DOWNS pop. 1,894

---------- **WHERE TO STAY** ----------

AMERIHOST INN & SUITES   *Book at aaa.com*

▼▼▼▼

Small-scale Hotel

          All Year   **Phone:** (505)378-1199
          1P: $69-$119   2P: $79-$139   XP: $10   F17
Location: Center. 2191 Hwy 70 W 88346. Fax: 505/378-1234. **Facility:** 61 one-bedroom standard units, some with whirlpools. 3 stories, interior corridors. *Bath:* combo or shower only. **Parking:** on-site. **Terms:** 3 night minimum stay - seasonal and/or weekends, 4 day cancellation notice-fee imposed, [CP] meal plan available, package plans. **Amenities:** high-speed Internet, irons, hair dryers. **Pool(s):** heated indoor. **Leisure Activities:** whirlpool, limited exercise equipment. **Guest Services:** coin laundry. **Business Services:** meeting rooms, business center. **Cards:** AX, DS, MC, VI.

SOME UNITS

〔ASK〕〔♿M〕〔♿〕〔🏊〕〔🐾〕〔DATA PORT〕〔🖥〕〔🍽〕〔🖨〕 / 〔✕〕 /

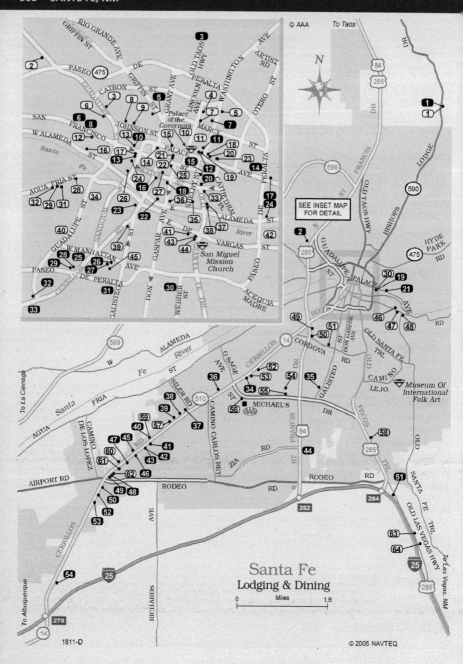

Sante Fe
Lodging & Dining

Santa Fe Accommodations

This index helps you "spot" where approved accommodations and restaurants are located on the corresponding detailed maps. Lodging rate ranges are for comparison only and show the property's high season; rates are per night, unless only weekly (W) rates are available. Restaurant rate range is for dinner, unless only lunch (L) is served. Turn to the listing page for more detailed rate information and consult display ads for special promotions.

Spotter/Map Page Number	OA	SANTA FE - Lodgings	Diamond Rating	Rate Range High Season	Listing Page
1 / p. 568		Bishop's Lodge Resort & Spa - see color ad p 574	◇◇◇	Failed to provide	573
2 / p. 568		The Lodge at Santa Fe - see color ad p 585	◇◇◇	$116-$242	585
3 / p. 568	AAA	Casa de la Cuma B & B	◇◇◇	$125-$170 SAVE	575
4 / p. 568		Adobe Abode	◇◇◇	$135-$185	573
5 / p. 568	AAA	Spencer House Bed & Breakfast Inn	◇◇◇	$135-$175 SAVE	589
6 / p. 568		Casapueblo Inn	◇◇◇	Failed to provide	575
7 / p. 568		Territorial Inn	◇◇◇	Failed to provide	589
8 / p. 568	AAA	Las Palomas	◇◇◇	$149-$279 SAVE	585
9 / p. 568		Grant Corner Inn	◇◇◇	Failed to provide	577
10 / p. 568	AAA	Eldorado Hotel - see color ad p 576	◇◇◇◇	$219-$1500 SAVE	576
11 / p. 568		Hotel Plaza Real	◇◇◇	$109-$199	580
12 / p. 568	AAA	Inn of the Anasazi	◇◇◇◇	$209-$489 SAVE	582
13 / p. 568		Hilton of Santa Fe	◇◇◇	Failed to provide	579
14 / p. 568	AAA	Hacienda Nicholas	◇◇◇	$120-$190 SAVE	578
15 / p. 568	AAA	La Fonda Hotel - see color ad p 583	◇◇◇	$219-$389 SAVE	583
16 / p. 568		Otra Vez en Santa Fe	◇◇◇	$200-$225	586
17 / p. 568		The Madeleine	◇◇	$135-$210	586
18 / p. 568		Hotel St Francis - see color ad p 581	◇◇◇	$129-$259	581
19 / p. 568	AAA	La Posada de Santa Fe - see color ad p 584	◇◇◇	$188-$287 SAVE	584
20 / p. 568		The Inn & Spa at Loretto	◇◇◇	$365-$470	582
21 / p. 568		Alexander's Inn	◇◇◇	$185-$220	573
22 / p. 568		Inn of the Governors - see color ad p 582	◇◇◇	$179-$314	582
23 / p. 568		The Old Santa Fe Inn	◇◇◇	$109-$309	586
24 / p. 568	AAA	Inn On The Alameda - see color ad p 583	◇◇◇	$195-$295 SAVE	583
25 / p. 568	AAA	Santa Fe Motel & Inn	◇◇	$109-$169 SAVE	588
26 / p. 568		El Farolito Bed & Breakfast Inn	◇◇◇	$190-$235	576
27 / p. 568	AAA	El Paradero Bed & Breakfast	◇◇	$85-$170 SAVE	576
28 / p. 568	AAA	The Hacienda at Hotel Santa Fe - see color ad p 578	◇◇◇◇	$318 SAVE	578
29 / p. 568	AAA	Hotel Santa Fe - see color ad p 581	◇◇◇	$197-$376 SAVE	582
30 / p. 568		Four Kachinas Inn	◇◇◇	$175-$205	577
31 / p. 568	AAA	Las Brisas de Santa Fe	◇◇◇	$200-$300 SAVE	585
32 / p. 568	AAA	Santa Fe Plaza Travelodge	◇◇	$79-$199 SAVE	588
33 / p. 568	AAA	Sage Inn - see color ad p 587	◇◇	$98-$134 SAVE	587
34 / p. 568	AAA	El Rey Inn - see color ad p 577	◇◇◇	$99-$225 SAVE	577
35 / p. 568		Residence Inn by Marriott	◇◇◇	$189-$269	587

Spotter/Map Page Number	OA	SANTA FE - Lodgings (continued)	Diamond Rating	Rate Range High Season	Listing Page
36 / p. 568	AAA	Best Western Lamplighter Inn - see color ad p 574	◇◇	$59-$129 SAVE	573
37 / p. 568		Park Inn - see color ad p 586	◇◇	$79-$114	586
38 / p. 568		Motel 6 - 150	◇	$45-$65	586
39 / p. 568	AAA	Quality Inn - see color ad p 587	◇◇	$55-$160 SAVE	587
40 / p. 568		Santa Fe Courtyard by Marriott - see color ad p 588	◇◇◇	$59-$169	588
41 / p. 568	AAA	Comfort Suites by Choice Hotels	◇◇◇	$60-$190 SAVE	576
42 / p. 568	AAA	Holiday Inn Express - see color ad p 580	◇◇	$99-$119 SAVE	580
43 / p. 568	AAA	Econo Lodge	◇◇	$69-$150 SAVE	576
44 / p. 568	AAA	Camel Rock Suites	◇◇	$79-$99 SAVE	575
45 / p. 568	AAA	Hampton Inn Santa Fe - see color ad p 579	◇◇	$79-$189 SAVE	579
46 / p. 568	AAA	Best Western Inn of Santa Fe - see color ad p 573	◇◇	$55-$125 SAVE	573
47 / p. 568	AAA	Luxury Inn	◇◇	$50-$199 SAVE	585
48 / p. 568	AAA	Budget Host Inn	◇◇	$52-$95 SAVE	574
49 / p. 568	AAA	Holiday Inn	◇◇◇	$119-$159 SAVE	579
50 / p. 568		Fairfield Inn by Marriott	◇◇	$79-$119	577
51 / p. 568	AAA	The Bobcat Inn	◇◇	$85-$150 SAVE	574
52 / p. 568	AAA	La Quinta Inn Santa Fe - see color ad p 584	◇◇	$102-$147 SAVE	585
53 / p. 568	AAA	Comfort Inn - see color ad p 575	◇◇◇	$59-$169 SAVE	575
54 / p. 568		Sleep Inn - see color ad p 588	◇◇	$59-$189	589
		SANTA FE - Restaurants			
1 / p. 568		Las Fuentes	◇◇◇	$18-$35	593
2 / p. 568		Jinja Asia Cafe	◇◇◇	$6-$17	593
3 / p. 568		El Encanto	◇◇◇	$16-$25	592
4 / p. 568	AAA	Osteria d'Assisi	◇◇	$27-$34	594
5 / p. 568	AAA	Santacafe	◇◇◇	$17-$27	595
6 / p. 568		Tulips	◇◇◇	$22-$31	596
7 / p. 568		Il Piatto	◇◇	$15-$18	593
8 / p. 568		Shohko Cafe	◇◇	$10-$26	595
9 / p. 568	AAA	O'Keeffe Cafe	◇◇◇	$16-$25	594
10 / p. 568		Paul's Restaurant of Santa Fe	◇◇	$15-$25	594
11 / p. 568		The Bull Ring	◇◇◇	$20-$40	590
12 / p. 568		Vanessie	◇◇◇	$16-$30	596
13 / p. 568	AAA	The Old House - see color ad p 576	◇◇◇◇	$20-$32	594
14 / p. 568		Cafe Paris	◇◇	$10-$18	590
15 / p. 568		Swig	◇◇◇	$6-$18	596
16 / p. 568		Los Mayas	◇◇◇	$14-$19	594
17 / p. 568	AAA	Pinon Grill	◇◇◇	$19-$40	595
18 / p. 568		Anasazi Restaurant	◇◇◇	$25-$30	589
19 / p. 568		The Burrito Company	◇	$4-$8	590

Spotter/Map Page Number	OA	SANTA FE - Restaurants (continued)	Diamond Rating	Rate Range High Season	Listing Page
20 / p. 568		The Shed	◈◈	$9-$20	595
21 / p. 568		Plaza Restaurant	◈	$8-$12	595
22 / p. 568		Ore House on the Plaza	◈◈	$13-$27	594
23 / p. 568	AAA	La Casa Sena Restaurant	◈◈◈	$19-$36	593
24 / p. 568		Blue Corn Cafe and Brewery	◈◈	$8-$16	590
25 / p. 568		Longevity Cafe' & Emporium	◈◈	$4-$7	593
26 / p. 568		Coyote Cafe	◈◈◈	$20-$38	592
27 / p. 568		Cafe Pasqual's	◈◈	$18-$30	590
28 / p. 568		Cafe San Estevan	◈◈◈	$12-$27	590
29 / p. 568		Kasasoba	◈◈◈	$8-$20	593
30 / p. 568	AAA	Fuego - see color ad p 584	◈◈◈◈	$30-$38	592
31 / p. 568		Pranzo Italian Grill	◈◈	$8-$20	595
32 / p. 568		Ristra	◈◈◈	$18-$34	595
33 / p. 568		Baleen Sante Fe	◈◈◈	$17-$37	589
34 / p. 568		Cowgirl BBQ & Western Grill	◈◈	$8-$15	592
35 / p. 568		Julian's	◈◈◈	$22-$36	593
36 / p. 568		India Palace	◈◈	$10-$20	593
37 / p. 568		315 Restaurant & Wine Bar	◈◈◈	$17-$29	589
38 / p. 568	AAA	Upper Crust Pizza	◈	$7-$25	596
39 / p. 568	AAA	Saveur	◈◈	$6-$12(L)	595
40 / p. 568		Tomasita's Santa Fe Station	◈◈	$8-$14	596
41 / p. 568		The Pink Adobe	◈◈	$12-$28	594
42 / p. 568		Cafe de Artistes	◈	$8-$18	590
43 / p. 568		Rio Chama Steakhouse	◈◈◈	$14-$35	595
44 / p. 568		Guadalupe Café	◈	$8-$15	593
45 / p. 568	AAA	Cafe' Oasis	◈◈	$11-$17	590
46 / p. 568		The Compound Restaurant	◈◈◈	$20-$32	592
47 / p. 568		Geronimo	◈◈◈◈	$20-$50	592
48 / p. 568		El Farol Restaurant	◈◈◈	$25-$30	592
49 / p. 568		Asado Brazilian Grill	◈◈	$13-$19	589
50 / p. 568		Maria's New Mexican Kitchen	◈◈	$9-$20	594
51 / p. 568		Whole Body Cafe	◈◈	$4-$8	596
52 / p. 568		Dara Thai Restaurant	◈◈	$8-$15	592
53 / p. 568		The Pantry	◈◈	$6-$13	594
54 / p. 568		Chocolate Maven Bakery & Cafe	◈◈	$8-$13(L)	592
55 / p. 568	AAA	Hidden Chicken Cafe	◈	$5-$15	593
56 / p. 568		Bert's La Taqueria	◈◈	$10-$30	589
57 / p. 568	AAA	Tortilla Flats	◈◈	$6-$11	596
58 / p. 568		Chilacas Restaurant & Cantina	◈◈	$7-$15	590
59 / p. 568		Cafe Santa Fe - see color ad p 588	◈◈	$12-$25	590

Spotter/Map Page Number	OA	SANTA FE - Restaurants (continued)	Diamond Rating	Rate Range High Season	Listing Page
60 / p. 568		Guadalajara Grill	▽▽	$7-$15	592
61 / p. 568		Osaka Bistro Sushi & Sake Bar	▽▽	$10-$20	594
62 / p. 568		Blue Corn Cafe II	▽▽	$8-$16	590
63 / p. 568		Harry's Road House	▽▽	$8-$12	593
64 / p. 568		Steaksmith at El Gancho	▽▽	$9-$30	595

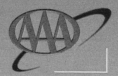

SANTA FE pop. 62,203   (See map and index starting on p. 568)

—————— WHERE TO STAY ——————

ADOBE ABODE
▼▼▼▼

Historic Bed & Breakfast

Phone: (505)983-3133   **④**

All Year [BP]   1P: $135-$185   2P: $135-$185   XP: $20   D12
Location: Jct McKenzie St and 3 1/2 blks e of the historic plaza. 202 Chappelle St 87501. Fax: 505/983-3132. **Facility:** Rooms in the adobe home, circa 1907, vary in size from cozy to spacious and are appointed in eclectic themes, such as "English garden" and "bronco". Designated smoking area. 6 units. 5 one-bedroom standard units. 1 one-bedroom suite. 1 story, interior/exterior corridors. *Bath:* combo or shower only. **Parking:** on-site and street. **Terms:** 2 night minimum stay - seasonal, 14 day cancellation notice-fee imposed, package plans. **Amenities:** voice mail, irons, hair dryers. **Guest Services:** valet laundry. **Cards:** MC, VI.

SOME UNITS

(A$K) (S☐) (¶¶⁺) (🏃) (✕) (🐾) (DATA PORT) (💻) / (🍴) (🔒) /

ALEXANDER'S INN
▼▼▼▼

Bed & Breakfast

Phone: (505)986-1431   **㉑**

5/1-10/31 [BP]   1P: $185-$220   2P: $185-$220   XP: $25   F5
2/1-4/30 [BP]   1P: $170-$200   2P: $170-$200   XP: $25   F5
11/1-1/31 [BP]   1P: $185-$195   2P: $185-$195   XP: $25   F5
Location: Just e of jct Paseo De Peralta; 6 blks e of historic plaza. 529 E Palace Ave 87501. Fax: 505/989-9839. **Facility:** Fireplaces add to the ambience of some guest rooms in the Victorian bungalow home, which was built in 1903. Designated smoking area. 10 units. 5 one-bedroom standard units. 5 one-bedroom suites, some with kitchens and/or whirlpools. 1-2 stories, interior/exterior corridors. *Bath:* some shared or private, combo or shower only. **Parking:** on-site. **Terms:** 2 night minimum stay - weekends, age restrictions may apply, 14 day cancellation notice-fee imposed, pets ($20 fee). **Amenities:** high-speed Internet, voice mail, hair dryers. *Some:* irons. **Leisure Activities:** whirlpool. *Fee:* massage. **Guest Services:** gift shop, valet laundry. **Cards:** AX, MC, VI.

SOME UNITS

(A$K) (🛏) (¶¶⁺) (✕) (DATA PORT) / (📺) (VCR) (🔒) (🍴) (💻) /
FEE   FEE

BEST WESTERN INN OF SANTA FE   *Book at aaa.com*
(AAA) (SAVE)
▼▼▼▼

Small-scale Hotel

Phone: (505)438-3822   **㊻**

5/26-10/28 [ECP]   1P: $55-$125   2P: $65-$125
2/1-5/25 & 10/29-1/31 [ECP]   1P: $40-$75   2P: $45-$85
Location: I-25, exit 278, 2.8 mi n. 3650 Cerrillos Rd 87507. Fax: 505/438-3795. **Facility:** 97 units. 83 one-bedroom standard units, some with whirlpools. 14 one-bedroom suites ($75-$205). 3 stories, interior corridors. **Parking:** on-site. **Terms:** package plans, small pets only. **Amenities:** voice mail, safes, irons, hair dryers. *Some:* high-speed Internet. **Pool(s):** heated indoor. **Leisure Activities:** whirlpool. **Guest Services:** valet and coin laundry. **Cards:** AX, CB, DC, DS, MC, VI. **Special Amenities:** free expanded continental breakfast and free local telephone calls. *(See color ad below)*

SOME UNITS

(S☐) (🛏) (¶¶⁺) (🍳) (🐎) (🎬) (DATA PORT) (💻) / (✕) (🔒) (🍴) /

BEST WESTERN LAMPLIGHTER INN   *Book at aaa.com*
(AAA) (SAVE)
▼▼▼▼

Small-scale Hotel

Phone: (505)471-8000   **㊱**

5/19-10/14   1P: $59-$109   2P: $69-$129
2/1-5/18 & 10/15-1/31   1P: $45-$75   2P: $55-$99
Location: I-25, exit 278, 7.7 mi n. 2405 Cerrillos Rd 87505. Fax: 505/471-1397. **Facility:** 79 units. 76 one- and 3 two-bedroom standard units, some with kitchens. 2 stories, exterior corridors. **Parking:** on-site. **Terms:** [ECP] meal plan available. **Amenities:** irons, hair dryers. *Some:* high-speed Internet. **Pool(s):** heated indoor. **Leisure Activities:** whirlpool, recreation room with table tennis, limited exercise equipment. **Guest Services:** valet and coin laundry. **Cards:** AX, CB, DC, DS, JC, MC, VI. **Special Amenities:** free expanded continental breakfast and free local telephone calls. *(See color ad p 574)*

SOME UNITS

(S☐) (¶¶⁺) (🐎) (✕) (🎬) (DATA PORT) (🔒) (💻) / (✕) (VCR) (🍴) /

BISHOP'S LODGE RESORT & SPA   *Book at aaa.com*
▼▼▼▼

Resort
Large-scale Hotel

Phone: 505/983-6377   **①**

Property failed to provide current rates
Location: 3.5 mi n of jct Paseo De Peralta. Located in a quiet area. 1297 N Bishop's Lodge Rd 87501 (PO Box 2367, 87504). Fax: 505/989-8739. **Facility:** Expansive landscaped grounds surround the 1800s ranch-style resort, situated in the foothills of the Sangre de Cristo Mountains. 111 units. 107 one- and 4 two-bedroom standard units. 1-3 stories (no elevator), interior/exterior corridors. *Bath:* combo or shower only. **Parking:** on-site. **Terms:** check-in 4 pm, pets ($150 deposit, $20 extra charge). **Amenities:** high-speed Internet, voice mail, safes, honor bars, irons, hair dryers. **Dining:** Las Fuentes, see separate listing. **Pool(s):** heated outdoor. **Leisure Activities:** whirlpools, 2 tennis courts, recreation programs, hiking trails, playground, exercise room, spa. *Fee:* horseback riding. **Guest Services:** gift shop, valet laundry, area transportation. **Business Services:** conference facilities, business center. *(See color ad p 574)*

SOME UNITS

(🛏) (🍴) (🍷) (🍳) (🐎) (✕) (DATA PORT) (🔒) (💻) / (✕) (VCR)
FEE

(See map and index starting on p. 568)

THE BOBCAT INN

Phone: (505)988-9239   **51**

All Year [BP]   1P: $85-$150   2P: $85-$150   XP: $20   F5
Location: I-25, exit 284, just n on Old Pecos Trail, then 4.3 mi ne. Located in a rural area. 442A Old Las Vegas Hwy 87505. Fax: 505/988-2680. **Facility:** This secluded property was originally an old hacienda that has been authentically renovated and is surrounded by pinon and juniper trees. Designated smoking area. 5 one-bedroom standard units, some with whirlpools. 1 story, interior/exterior corridors. *Bath:* combo or shower only. **Parking:** on-site. **Terms:** check-in 4 pm, age restrictions may apply, 14 day cancellation notice-fee imposed. **Amenities:** hair dryers. *Some:* CD players. **Leisure Activities:** bird-watching, hiking trails. *Fee:* massage. **Business Services:** meeting rooms, PC, fax. **Cards:** DS, MC, VI. **Special Amenities:** free full breakfast and free local telephone calls.

Bed & Breakfast

SOME UNITS

BUDGET HOST INN   *Book at aaa.com*

Phone: (505)438-8950   **48**

5/16-8/20	1P: $52-$85	2P: $55-$95	XP: $5	F12
8/21-11/20	1P: $50-$75	2P: $52-$85	XP: $5	F12
2/1-5/15	1P: $43-$65	2P: $46-$75	XP: $5	F12
11/21-1/31	1P: $43-$65	2P: $45-$75	XP: $5	F12

Small-scale Hotel **Location:** I-25, exit 278, 1.5 mi n. 4044 Cerrillos Rd 87507. Fax: 505/471-9129. **Facility:** 47 one-bedroom standard units. 2 stories (no elevator), interior corridors. **Parking:** on-site. **Amenities:** high-speed Internet, voice mail, irons, hair dryers. **Pool(s):** small heated outdoor. **Leisure Activities:** whirlpool. **Business Services:** PC (fee). **Cards:** AX, CB, DC, DS, MC, VI. **Special Amenities:** free expanded continental breakfast and free local telephone calls.

SOME UNITS

(See map and index starting on p. 568)

CAMEL ROCK SUITES   *Book at aaa.com*   Phone: (505)989-3600   **44**

AAA SAVE

Motel

All Year 1P: $79-$89 2P: $89-$99 XP: $10 F16
Location: 0.8 mi n on S St. Francis Dr, just e on Zia via access drive. 3007 S St. Frances Dr 87505.
Fax: 505/989-1058. **Facility:** 123 units. 122 one-bedroom standard units with kitchens. 1 one-bedroom suite with kitchen. 2 stories (no elevator), exterior corridors. *Bath:* combo or shower only. **Parking:** on-site. **Terms:** 3 day cancellation notice, pets ($25 fee, $100 deposit, in limited units). **Amenities:** *Some:* dual phone lines, voice mail, irons, hair dryers. **Guest Services:** valet and coin laundry, airport transportation-Santa Fe Airport, area transportation-casino & plaza. **Business Services:** meeting rooms, fax (fee). **Cards:** AX, CB, DC, DS, JC, MC, VI. **Special Amenities:** free continental breakfast and free local telephone calls.

SOME UNITS

CASA DE LA CUMA B & B   Phone: (505)983-1717   **3**

AAA SAVE

Bed & Breakfast

5/1-10/31 [ECP] 2P: $125-$170 XP: $20
3/1-4/30 [ECP] 2P: $110-$150 XP: $20
2/1-2/28 & 11/1-1/31 [ECP] 2P: $95-$135 XP: $20
Location: Just w off Old Taos Hwy. 105 Paseo de la Cuma 87501. Fax: 505/983-2241. **Facility:** Near Cross of the Martyrs, the 1950s adobe-style B&B offers a patio with a fire pit, a unit with a wood-burning fireplace and evaporative coolers. Designated smoking area. 4 units. 3 one-bedroom standard units, some with whirlpools. 1 one-bedroom suite ($135-$170). 1 story, interior/exterior corridors. *Bath:* combo or shower only. **Parking:** on-site. **Terms:** 2-3 night minimum stay - weekends, 14 day cancellation notice-fee imposed, package plans, no pets allowed (owner's pet on premises). **Amenities:** video library, irons, hair dryers. *Some:* DVD players, CD players. **Leisure Activities:** whirlpool. *Fee:* massage. **Guest Services:** valet laundry. **Business Services:** PC, fax. **Cards:** AX, DS, MC, VI. **Special Amenities:** free expanded continental breakfast and free local telephone calls.

SOME UNITS

CASAPUEBLO INN   *Book at aaa.com*   Phone: 505/988-4455   **6**

Small-scale Hotel

Property failed to provide current rates
Location: Jct Guadalupe St. 138 Park Ave 87501. Fax: 505/983-6003. **Facility:** Designated smoking area. 32 units. 12 one-bedroom standard units. 20 one-bedroom suites with kitchens. 1-2 stories (no elevator), exterior corridors. *Bath:* combo or shower only. **Parking:** on-site. **Terms:** office hours 7 am-5 pm, check-in 4 pm, pets ($50 fee). **Amenities:** CD players, voice mail, safes, honor bars, irons, hair dryers. **Guest Services:** valet laundry. **Business Services:** meeting rooms, fax (fee).

COMFORT INN   *Book at aaa.com*   Phone: (505)474-7330   **53**

AAA SAVE

Small-scale Hotel

All Year [ECP] 1P: $59-$169 2P: $59-$169 XP: $10 F18
Location: I-25, exit 278, 1.6 mi n. 4312 Cerrillos Rd 87507. Fax: 505/474-7330. **Facility:** 83 one-bedroom standard units, some with whirlpools. 3 stories, interior corridors. *Bath:* combo or shower only. **Parking:** on-site. **Amenities:** voice mail, irons, hair dryers. **Pool(s):** heated indoor. **Leisure Activities:** whirlpool. **Guest Services:** valet and coin laundry. **Business Services:** fax (fee). **Cards:** AX, CB, DC, DS, JC, MC, VI. **Special Amenities:** free expanded continental breakfast and free local telephone calls.

(See color ad below)

SOME UNITS

(See map and index starting on p. 568)

COMFORT SUITES BY CHOICE HOTELS

AAA SAVE

Small-scale Hotel

Book at aaa.com

All Year 1P: $60-$190 2P: $60-$190 XP: $6

Phone: 505/473-9004 41 F

Location: I-25, exit 278, 2 mi n, then just e. 1435 Avenida de las Americas 87505. **Fax:** 505/438-4627. **Facility:** 60 one-bedroom standard units. 3 stories, interior corridors. **Bath:** combo or shower only. **Parking:** on-site. **Amenities:** high-speed Internet, irons, hair dryers. **Pool(s):** heated indoor. **Leisure Activities:** whirlpools. **Guest Services:** valet laundry. **Cards:** AX, CB, DC, DS, JC, MC, VI. **Special Amenities:** free continental breakfast and free local telephone calls.

SOME UNITS

ECONO LODGE

AAA SAVE

Small-scale Hotel

Book at aaa.com

7/1-8/31	1P: $69-$99	2P: $79-$150	XP: $10 D17
5/1-6/30	1P: $59-$69	2P: $69-$79	XP: $10 D17
9/1-1/31	1P: $45-$59	2P: $49-$79	XP: $10 D17
2/1-4/30	1P: $45-$59	2P: $49-$65	XP: $5 D17

Phone: (505)471-4000 43

Location: I-25, exit 278, 3 mi n. 3470 Cerrillos Rd 87507. **Fax:** 505/474-4394. **Facility:** 76 one-bedroom standard units. 3 stories, interior corridors. **Bath:** combo or shower only. **Parking:** on-site. **Terms:** package plans. **Amenities:** irons, hair dryers. **Pool(s):** small heated outdoor. **Guest Services:** valet laundry. **Cards:** AX, DC, DS, MC, VI. **Special Amenities:** free continental breakfast and free newspaper.

SOME UNITS

ELDORADO HOTEL

AAA SAVE

Large-scale Hotel

Book at aaa.com

All Year 1P: $219-$1500 2P: $219-$1500 XP: $20

Phone: (505)988-4455 10 F16

Location: Just w of The Plaza at Sandoval St. 309 W San Francisco 87501. **Fax:** 505/995-4543. **Facility:** Custom decor marks the hotel's public facilities and large rooms, which have bathrooms with granite vanities, thick robes and magnifying mirrors. 219 one-bedroom standard units. 5 stories, interior corridors. **Parking:** on-site (fee). **Terms:** check-in 4 pm, 1-4 night minimum stay - seasonal, 3 day cancellation notice, pets ($50 fee). **Amenities:** CD players, high-speed Internet, dual phone lines, voice mail, safes, honor bars, irons, hair dryers. **Dining:** 6:30 am-11 pm, cocktails, also, The Old House, see separate listing, entertainment. **Pool(s):** heated outdoor. **Leisure Activities:** saunas, whirlpool, exercise room. *Fee:* massage. **Guest Services:** gift shop, valet laundry, beauty salon. **Business Services:** conference facilities, business center. **Cards:** AX, CB, DC, DS, JC, MC, VI. *(See color ad below)*

SOME UNITS

FEE

EL FAROLITO BED & BREAKFAST INN

Historic Bed & Breakfast

5/1-10/31 [ECP]	1P: $190-$235	2P: $190-$235	XP: $15
2/1-4/30 [ECP]	1P: $160-$190	2P: $160-$190	XP: $15
11/1-1/31 [ECP]	1P: $160-$185	2P: $160-$185	XP: $15

Phone: (505)988-1631 26

Location: Cerrillos Rd, just e on Paseo de Peralta. 514 Galisteo St 87501 (512 Webber St, 87505). **Fax:** 505/989-1323. **Facility:** The conveniently located B&B's individual casitas feature kiva fireplaces, Southwestern-style furnishings, elegant bed coverings and modern baths. Smoke free premises. 8 one-bedroom standard units. 1 story, exterior corridors. **Parking:** on-site. **Terms:** 2 night minimum stay - weekends, 15 day cancellation notice-fee imposed. **Amenities:** irons, hair dryers. *Some:* CD players. **Guest Services:** valet laundry. **Cards:** AX, DS, MC, VI.

SOME UNITS

EL PARADERO BED & BREAKFAST

AAA SAVE

Bed & Breakfast

5/1-10/31	1P: $85-$160	2P: $95-$170	XP: $15
3/1-4/30 & 11/1-1/31	1P: $80-$145	2P: $90-$155	XP: $15
2/1-2/28	1P: $70-$125	2P: $80-$135	XP: $15

Phone: 505/988-1177 27

Location: 0.3 mi s on Cerrillos Rd, 1/2 blk e. 220 W Manhattan Ave 87501. **Fax:** 505/988-3577. **Facility:** At this early 1800s farmhouse, an easy walk to the Guadalupe Street district, tea can be taken under a cherry tree or in the bright breakfast room. Smoke free premises. 14 units. 11 one- and 1 two-bedroom standard units. 2 one-bedroom suites with efficiencies. 1-2 stories (no elevator), interior/exterior corridors. **Bath:** combo or shower only. **Parking:** on-site. **Terms:** office hours 8 am-8:30 pm, 2-3 night minimum stay - weekends, age restrictions may apply, 14 day cancellation notice, pets (dogs only, $15 extra charge, in limited units). **Amenities:** hair dryers. **Guest Services:** valet laundry. **Business Services:** fax. **Cards:** AX, MC, VI. **Special Amenities:** free full breakfast and free local telephone calls.

SOME UNITS

FEE

(See map and index starting on p. 568)

EL REY INN *Book at aaa.com* Phone: (505)982-1931 **34**

AAA SAVE

◊◊◊◊

	1P: $99-$225	2P: $99-$225
5/16-10/31	1P: $99-$225	2P: $99-$225
3/1-5/15	1P: $89-$199	2P: $89-$199
2/1-2/28 & 11/1-1/31	1P: $79-$199	2P: $79-$199

Location: I-25, exit 278, 6 mi nw. 1862 Cerrillos Rd 87505. Fax: 505/989-9249. **Facility:** Smoke free premises. 86
Small-scale Hotel units. 78 one-bedroom standard units, some with efficiencies. 8 two-bedroom suites, some with kitchens. 1-
2 stories (no elevator), exterior corridors. *Bath:* combo or shower only. **Parking:** on-site. **Amenities:** voice
mail, safes, irons, hair dryers. *Some:* DVD players. **Pool(s):** heated outdoor. **Leisure Activities:** sauna, whirlpools, playground,
exercise room. **Guest Services:** coin laundry. **Business Services:** PC. **Cards:** AX, CB, DC, DS, MC, VI. **Special Amenities:**
free continental breakfast. *(See color ad below)*

SOME UNITS

⊞ ⌖M ⊘ ⇴ ⊠ ✕ 🎥 DATA PORT ▣ / VCR 🖭 🖳 /

FAIRFIELD INN BY MARRIOTT *Book at aaa.com* Phone: 505/474-4442 **50**

◊◊◊◊ ◊◊

	1P: $79-$119	2P: $79-$119
5/2-10/15	1P: $79-$119	2P: $79-$119
10/16-1/31	1P: $49-$89	2P: $49-$89
2/1-5/1	1P: $49-$79	2P: $49-$79

Small-scale Hotel **Location:** I-25, exit 278, 2 mi n. 4150 Cerrillos Rd 87507. Fax: 505/474-7569. **Facility:** 56 one-bedroom standard
units. 2 stories (no elevator), interior corridors. **Parking:** on-site. **Terms:** cancellation fee imposed, pets ($15 extra charge).
Amenities: video library, high-speed Internet, dual phone lines, voice mail, irons, hair dryers. *Some:* DVD players. **Pool(s):**
small heated indoor. **Leisure Activities:** limited exercise equipment. **Guest Services:** valet laundry. **Business Services:** PC.
Cards: AX, DC, DS, MC, VI.

SOME UNITS

A$K 🐾 ⊞ ⌖ ⊘ ⇴ 🎥 DATA PORT 🖳 🖭 ▣ / ✕ /
FEE

FOUR KACHINAS INN Phone: (505)988-1631 **30**

◊◊◊

	1P: $175-$205	2P: $175-$205	XP: $15
5/1-10/31 [ECP]	1P: $175-$205	2P: $175-$205	XP: $15
2/1-4/30 [ECP]	1P: $140-$175	2P: $140-$175	XP: $15
11/1-1/31 [ECP]	1P: $120-$160	2P: $120-$160	XP: $15

Bed & Breakfast **Location:** Jct Cerrillos Rd and Paseo de Peralta, 4 blks e, then just s. 512 Webber St 87505. Fax: 505/989-1323.
Facility: Rooms appointed with Spanish Colonial reproductions and breakfast served in a room that opens onto a sunlit patio
enhance the inn's appeal. Smoke free premises. 5 one-bedroom standard units. 1-2 stories (no elevator), interior/exterior
corridors. **Parking:** on-site. **Terms:** 2 night minimum stay - weekends, 15 day cancellation notice-fee imposed, no pets allowed
(owner's pet on premises). **Amenities:** irons, hair dryers. *Some:* DVD players, CD players. **Leisure Activities:** whirlpool. **Guest
Services:** valet laundry. **Cards:** AX, DS, MC, VI.

SOME UNITS

✕ / 🖭 ▣ /

GRANT CORNER INN Phone: 505/983-6678 **9**

◊◊◊

Property failed to provide current rates
Location: 1 blk e of historic plaza. 122 Grant Ave 87501. Fax: 505/983-1526. **Facility:** A comfortable Victorian
style home near the plaza, this property gives the visitor a feel for what Santa Fe was like in the late 19th
Bed & Breakfast Century. Designated smoking area. 8 one-bedroom standard units. 3 stories (no elevator), interior corridors.
Bath: combo or shower only. **Parking:** on-site. **Terms:** office hours 8 am-7 pm. **Amenities:** irons, hair dryers. **Leisure
Activities:** *Fee:* massage. **Guest Services:** gift shop, valet laundry. **Business Services:** meeting rooms, fax.

SOME UNITS

⊞ ⌖M ⌖ ✕ 🎥 / VCR 🖭 🖳 /

(See map and index starting on p. 568)

THE HACIENDA AT HOTEL SANTA FE

(AAA) (SAVE)
▽▽▽ ▽▽▽

4/13-8/26 [CP]	1P: $318	2P: $318	XP: $20	**Phone: (505)982-1200** 28
8/27-12/20 [CP]	1P: $252	2P: $252	XP: $20	F17
2/1-4/12 & 12/21-1/31 [CP]	1P: $219	2P: $219	XP: $20	F17

Small-scale Hotel
Location: At Cerrillos Rd, 0.6 mi s of The Plaza. 1501 Paseo de Peralta 87501. Fax: 505/984-2211. **Facility:** This newly built, adobe-style property has richly appointed rooms, some with fireplaces and private balconies. 35 units. 23 one-bedroom standard units. 12 one-bedroom suites ($239-$699), some with whirlpools. 3 stories, interior corridors. *Bath:* combo or shower only. **Parking:** on-site. **Terms:** check-in 4 pm, 3 day cancellation notice-fee imposed, pets ($20 fee). **Amenities:** video games (fee), CD players, high-speed Internet, dual phone lines, voice mail, safes, honor bars, hair dryers. *Some:* DVD players, fax. **Dining:** 7 am-10 pm, cocktails. **Pool(s):** heated outdoor. **Leisure Activities:** whirlpool. *Fee:* massage. **Guest Services:** valet laundry, airport transportation (fee)-Albuquerque International Airport, area transportation-within 1 mi. **Business Services:** conference facilities, PC. **Cards:** AX, CB, DC, DS, JC, MC, VI. **Special Amenities: free expanded continental breakfast and free newspaper.** *(See color ad below)*

SOME UNITS

[icons] S/D ⊞ ☎ FEE ☎ FEE ⊞ ⊞ 24 ▼ ♿ ➔ ⊞ ✕ ⚐ DATA PORT ⊞ / VCR ⊞ ⊟

HACIENDA NICHOLAS

(AAA) (SAVE)
▽▽▽ ▽▽▽

5/1-10/31 [BP]	1P: $120-$190	2P: $120-$190	XP: $25	**Phone: (505)986-1431** 14
2/1-4/30 [BP]	1P: $110-$175	2P: $110-$175	XP: $25	F5
11/1-1/31 [BP]	1P: $100-$160	2P: $100-$160	XP: $25	F5

Bed & Breakfast
Location: Just e of jct Paseo de Peralta; 4 blks e of historic plaza. 320 E Marcy St 87501. Fax: 505/982-8572. **Facility:** A Southwestern flair—including vigas, high ceilings and thick adobe walls—gives this property a "Santa Fe" feeling. Designated smoking area. 7 one-bedroom standard units. 1 story, interior/exterior corridors. *Bath:* combo or shower only. **Parking:** on-site. **Terms:** office hours 7 am-8 pm, 2 night minimum stay - weekends, 14 day cancellation notice-fee imposed, pets ($20 fee). **Amenities:** voice mail, hair dryers. *Some:* CD players. **Leisure Activities:** *Fee:* massage. **Guest Services:** gift shop, valet laundry. **Business Services:** fax. **Cards:** AX, MC, VI.

SOME UNITS

[icons] 🛏 ⊞ FEE ➔ FEE ✕ DATA PORT / VCR /

(See map and index starting on p. 568)

HAMPTON INN SANTA FE *Book at aaa.com* Phone: (505)474-3900 **45**

AAA SAVE

▼▼▼▼ Small-scale Hotel

5/26-10/31	1P: $79-$189	2P: $79-$189
11/1-1/31	1P: $69-$139	2P: $69-$139
2/1-5/25	1P: $69-$109	2P: $69-$109

Location: I-25, exit 278, 2.5 mi n. 3625 Cerrillos Rd 87505. Fax: 505/474-4440. **Facility:** 81 one-bedroom standard units. 2 stories (no elevator), interior corridors. *Bath:* combo or shower only. **Parking:** on-site. **Terms:** 14% service charge, pets (must be attended). **Amenities:** high-speed Internet, dual phone lines, voice mail, irons, hair dryers. **Pool(s):** heated indoor. **Leisure Activities:** sauna, whirlpool, exercise room. **Guest Services:** valet laundry. **Cards:** AX, DC, DS, MC, VI. **Special Amenities:** free expanded continental breakfast and free local telephone calls. *(See color ad below)*

SOME UNITS

🆂🔽 🐾 🔩M ⬆️ 🍴 🏊 ✖️ 📷 📶 💻 / ✖️ 🛢️ 🖥️ /

HILTON OF SANTA FE *Book at aaa.com* Phone: 505-988-2811 **13**

▼▼▼▼ Small-scale Hotel

Property failed to provide current rates

Location: Just sw of The Plaza; between San Francisco and W Alameda sts. 100 Sandoval St 87501 (PO Box 25104, 87504). Fax: 505/986-6435. **Facility:** 157 units. 153 one-bedroom standard units. 3 one- and 1 two-bedroom suites. 3 stories, interior/exterior corridors. **Parking:** on-site (fee). **Terms:** check-in 4 pm. **Amenities:** high-speed Internet, voice mail, safes, irons, hair dryers. **Dining:** Pinon Grill, see separate listing. **Pool(s):** heated outdoor. **Leisure Activities:** whirlpool, exercise room. **Guest Services:** gift shop, valet laundry, area transportation. **Business Services:** conference facilities, business center.

SOME UNITS

✈️ 🍴 🍸 🔩 🏊 💻 / ✖️ 🛢️ 🖥️ /

HOLIDAY INN *Book at aaa.com* Phone: (505)473-4646 **49**

AAA SAVE

▼▼▼▼ Small-scale Hotel

5/21-8/30	1P: $119-$129	2P: $129-$159
9/1-1/31	1P: $109-$129	2P: $119-$139
2/1-5/20	1P: $99-$109	2P: $109-$129

Location: I-25, exit 278, 2.3 mi n just n of Rodeo Dr. 4048 Cerrillos Rd 87507. Fax: 505/473-2186. **Facility:** 130 one-bedroom standard units. 4 stories, interior corridors. *Bath:* combo or shower only. **Parking:** on-site. **Terms:** cancellation fee imposed, package plans. **Amenities:** high-speed Internet, voice mail, irons, hair dryers. **Dining:** 6:30 am-10 & 5-9 pm, cocktails. **Pool(s):** heated indoor/outdoor. **Leisure Activities:** saunas, whirlpool. **Guest Services:** gift shop, valet laundry, airport transportation-Santa Fe Airport. **Business Services:** meeting rooms. **Cards:** AX, DC, DS, JC, MC, VI.

SOME UNITS

🆂🔽 ✈️ 🍴 🍸 🔩M 🐾 🏊 👪 📷 📶 💻 / ✖️ 🛢️ 🖥️ /
FEE

(See map and index starting on p. 568)

HOLIDAY INN EXPRESS

AAA SAVE
VVV VVV

7/1-9/30 [ECP]	1P: $99-$119	2P: $99-$119
5/1-6/30 [ECP]	1P: $79-$99	2P: $79-$99
2/1-4/30 & 10/1-1/31 [ECP]	1P: $79-$89	2P: $79-$89

Phone: (505)474-7570 42

Small-scale Hotel

Location: I-25, exit 278, 3 mi n. 3450 Cerrillos Rd 87507. Fax: 505/474-6342. **Facility:** 76 one-bedroom standard units. 2 stories (no elevator), interior corridors. *Bath:* combo or shower only. **Parking:** on-site. **Terms:** cancellation fee imposed, package plans. **Amenities:** safes (fee), irons, hair dryers. **Pool(s):** small heated indoor. **Leisure Activities:** sauna, whirlpool. **Guest Services:** valet laundry. **Cards:** AX, DS, MC, VI. **Special Amenities:** free expanded continental breakfast and free local telephone calls. *(See color ad below)*

SOME UNITS

HOTEL PLAZA REAL   *Book at aaa.com*

VVVV VVVV

5/2-8/21	1P: $109-$199
8/22-1/31	1P: $99-$149
2/1-5/1	1P: $89-$149

Phone: (505)988-4900 11

XP: $20	F12
XP: $20	F12
XP: $20	F12

Small-scale Hotel

Location: Just ne of The Plaza; center. 125 Washington Ave 87501. Fax: 505/983-9322. **Facility:** 56 units. 55 one-bedroom standard units, some with efficiencies and/or whirlpools. 1 one-bedroom suite ($109-$419) with kitchen (no utensils). 2-3 stories, interior/exterior corridors. **Parking:** on-site (fee). **Terms:** 3 day cancellation notice-fee imposed, package plans, small pets only ($50 fee). **Amenities:** voice mail, irons, hair dryers. **Guest Services:** valet laundry. **Business Services:** meeting rooms. **Cards:** AX, DC, DS, MC, VI.

SOME UNITS

FEE

(See map and index starting on p. 568)

HOTEL ST FRANCIS   *Book at aaa.com*

▼▼▼▼▼
Historic
Small-scale Hotel

All Year   1P: $129-$249   2P: $139-$259   XP: $15   Phone: (505)983-5700   **18**

Location: Just s of The Plaza. 210 Don Gaspar Ave 87501. Fax: 505/989-7690. **Facility:** A "Grand Dame" of a hotel, the St Francis sits in the heart of Santa Fe. Re-built in 1920 and listed on the National Registry of Historic Places, the west-facing front porch is a favored place to sit in the late afternoon, have a cool beverage and watch passersby. An outdoor shaded patio is one option to choose for breakfast. The units have an eclectic blend of comfortable furnishings, each with its own "guardian" angel and baths have all the modern conveniences. 82 one-bedroom standard units, some with kitchens. 3 stories, interior corridors. *Bath:* combo or shower only. **Parking:** on-site (fee). **Terms:** 3 day cancellation notice-fee imposed. **Amenities:** voice mail, safes, irons, hair dryers. **Guest Services:** valet laundry. **Business Services:** meeting rooms, PC. **Cards:** AX, CB, DC, DS, MC, VI. *(See color ad below)*

SOME UNITS

(ASK) (S/D) (YI) (Y) (🌿) (👥) FEE (🐾) (DATA PORT) (🔒) / (✕) (💻) /

What would it be like to have your own place in Santa Fe?

(See map and index starting on p. 568)

HOTEL SANTA FE   *Book at aaa.com*   Phone: (505)982-1200   [29]

AAA SAVE	4/13-8/26	1P: $197-$376	2P: $197-$376	XP: $20	F17
▽▽▽◇▽▽▽	8/27-12/20	1P: $147-$338	2P: $147-$338	XP: $20	F17
	12/21-1/31	1P: $120-$291	2P: $120-$291	XP: $20	F17
	2/1-4/12	1P: $120-$253	2P: $120-$253	XP: $20	F17

Small-scale Hotel **Location:** At Cerrillos Rd, 0.6 mi s of The Plaza. 1501 Paseo de Peralta 87501. Fax: 505/955-7878. **Facility:** 128 one-bedroom standard units. 3 stories, interior corridors. **Parking:** on-site. **Terms:** check-in 4 pm, [BP] meal plan available, package plans, pets ($20 extra charge, with prior approval). **Amenities:** video games (fee), high-speed Internet, dual phone lines, voice mail, honor bars, irons. *Some:* safes, hair dryers. **Dining:** 7 am-10 pm, cocktails. **Pool(s):** heated outdoor. **Leisure Activities:** whirlpool, Native American dance demonstrations, weekends in season. *Fee:* massage. **Guest Services:** gift shop, valet and coin laundry, airport transportation (fee)-Albuquerque Airport, area transportation-within 1 mi. **Business Services:** meeting rooms, PC. **Cards:** AX, CB, DC, DS, JC, MC, VI. *(See color ad p 581)*

SOME UNITS
[icons] FEE FEE

THE INN & SPA AT LORETTO   *Book at aaa.com*   Phone: (505)988-5531   [20]

▽▽▽◇▽▽▽	5/26-10/21	1P: $365-$470	2P: $365-$470	XP: $25	F18
	4/1-5/25 & 10/22-1/31	1P: $279-$335	2P: $279-$335	XP: $25	F18
Small-scale Hotel	2/1-3/31	1P: $240-$299	2P: $240-$299	XP: $25	F18

Location: Just s of The Plaza. Located in the historic district. 211 Old Santa Fe Tr 87501. Fax: 505/984-7968. **Facility:** 134 units. 129 one-bedroom standard units. 4 one- and 1 two-bedroom suites, some with kitchens. 5 stories, interior corridors. *Bath:* combo or shower only. **Parking:** on-site (fee) and valet. **Terms:** check-in 4 pm, 3 day cancellation notice-fee imposed, package plans. **Amenities:** CD players, dual phone lines, voice mail, honor bars, irons, hair dryers. *Fee:* video games, high-speed Internet. *Some:* DVD players. **Pool(s):** heated outdoor. **Leisure Activities:** exercise room, spa. **Guest Services:** valet laundry. *Fee:* beauty salon. **Business Services:** conference facilities, business center. **Cards:** AX, CB, DC, DS, MC, VI.

SOME UNITS
[icons]

INN OF THE ANASAZI   *Book at aaa.com*   Phone: (505)988-3030   [12]

AAA SAVE   All Year   1P: $209-$489

▽▽▽◇▽▽▽   **Location:** Just ne of The Plaza. 113 Washington Ave 87501. Fax: 505/988-3277. **Facility:** Guest rooms all have fireplaces, poster beds, welcoming bowls of fruit, live orchids and traditional ceilings of vigas and latillas. Designated smoking area. 56 one-bedroom standard units. 3 stories, interior corridors. **Parking:** valet. Small-scale Hotel **Terms:** check-in 4 pm, 2-4 night minimum stay - weekends, 14 day cancellation notice-fee imposed, package plans. **Amenities:** dual phone lines, voice mail, safes, honor bars, irons, hair dryers. *Some:* DVD players, CD players. **Dining:** Anasazi Restaurant, see separate listing. **Leisure Activities:** *Fee:* massage. **Guest Services:** valet laundry. **Business Services:** meeting rooms, administrative services. **Cards:** AX, CB, DC, DS, MC, VI. **Special Amenities:** free local telephone calls and free newspaper.

[icons]

INN OF THE GOVERNORS   *Book at aaa.com*   Phone: (505)982-4333   [22]

▽▽▽◇▽▽▽	6/29-10/21 [BP]	1P: $179-$314	2P: $179-$314	XP: $15	F
	10/22-1/31 [BP]	1P: $143-$314	2P: $143-$314	XP: $15	F
Small-scale Hotel	3/2-6/28 [BP]	1P: $152-$269	2P: $152-$269	XP: $15	F
	2/1-3/1 [BP]	1P: $143-$251	2P: $143-$251	XP: $15	F

Location: Center. Located in the historic district. 101 W Alameda Ave 87501. Fax: 505/989-9149. **Facility:** 100 one-bedroom standard units. 2-3 stories, interior/exterior corridors. **Parking:** on-site. **Terms:** check-in 4 pm, package plans. **Amenities:** high-speed Internet, voice mail, safes, irons, hair dryers. *Some:* honor bars. **Pool(s):** heated outdoor. **Guest Services:** valet laundry. **Business Services:** meeting rooms, PC. **Cards:** AX, CB, DC, DS, JC, MC, VI. *(See color ad below)*

SOME UNITS
[icons]

(See map and index starting on p. 568)

INN ON THE ALAMEDA   *Book at aaa.com*   Phone: (505)984-2121   **24**

5/1-10/31 [ECP]	1P: $195-$295	2P: $195-$295	XP: $15 F16
11/1-1/31 [ECP]	1P: $130-$295	2P: $130-$295	XP: $15 F16
2/1-4/30 [ECP]	1P: $130-$275	2P: $130-$275	XP: $15 F16

Small-scale Hotel **Location:** 4 blks e of The Plaza; at Paseo de Peralta. 303 E Alameda Ave 87501. Fax: 505/986-8325. **Facility:** 71 units. 61 one-bedroom standard units. 10 one-bedroom suites ($255-$375). 1-3 stories (no elevator), interior/exterior corridors. *Bath:* combo or shower only. **Parking:** on-site. **Terms:** check-in 4 pm, 2 night minimum stay - seasonal, 3 day cancellation notice-fee imposed, package plans, small pets only ($20 extra charge, limit 1, in designated units). **Amenities:** voice mail, irons, hair dryers. *Some:* CD players, safes. **Leisure Activities:** whirlpools, exercise room. *Fee:* massage. **Guest Services:** complimentary evening beverages, valet and coin laundry. **Business Services:** meeting rooms, PC. **Cards:** AX, DC, DS, MC, VI. **Special Amenities: free expanded continental breakfast and free local telephone calls.** *(See color ad below)*

SOME UNITS

LA FONDA HOTEL   *Book at aaa.com*   Phone: (505)982-5511   **15**

All Year   1P: $219-$389   2P: $219-$389   XP: $15   F12

Historic Large-scale Hotel **Location:** On Santa Fe Plaza. 100 E San Francisco St 87501. Fax: 505/988-2952. **Facility:** The current building dates to the 1920s, but there has been an inn on this site since 1620; whimsically hand-painted furnishings accent the decor. 167 units. 147 one-bedroom standard units. 18 one- and 2 two-bedroom suites. 5 stories, interior corridors. **Parking:** on-site (fee). **Terms:** cancellation fee imposed, package plans. **Amenities:** high-speed Internet, voice mail, safes, irons, hair dryers. *Some:* CD players, dual phone lines. **Dining:** 7 am-10 pm, cocktails, entertainment. **Pool(s):** heated outdoor. **Leisure Activities:** whirlpools, exercise room. *Fee:* massage. **Guest Services:** gift shop, valet laundry. **Business Services:** conference facilities, business center. **Cards:** AX, CB, DC, DS, JC, MC, VI. *(See color ad below)*

SOME UNITS

(See map and index starting on p. 568)

LA POSADA DE SANTA FE   *Book at aaa.com*   Phone: (505)986-0000   **19**

AAA SAVE

| | 6/12-10/29 & 12/23-1/31 | 1P: $188-$287 | 2P: $188-$287 | XP: $20 | F12 |
| | 2/1-6/11 & 10/30-12/22 | 1P: $134-$260 | 2P: $134-$260 | XP: $20 | F12 |

Small-scale Hotel   **Location:** Jct Paseo de Peracta and E Palace Ave. 330 E Palace Ave 87501. Fax: 505/982-5474. **Facility:** 157 units. 153 one-bedroom standard units. 2 one- and 2 two-bedroom suites ($377-$1800). 1-2 stories (no elevator), exterior corridors. *Bath:* combo or shower only. **Parking:** on-site (fee) and valet. **Terms:** check-in 4 pm, 3 day cancellation notice-fee imposed, $13 service charge. **Amenities:** dual phone lines, voice mail, honor bars, irons, hair dryers. **Dining:** 7-10:30 am, 11-3 & 5:30-9 pm, cocktails, also, Fuego, see separate listing. **Pool(s):** heated outdoor. **Leisure Activities:** whirlpool, exercise room, spa. **Guest Services:** gift shop, valet laundry. **Business Services:** conference facilities, business center. **Cards:** AX, DC, DS, MC, VI. *(See color ad below)*

SOME UNITS

(See map and index starting on p. 568)

LA QUINTA INN SANTA FE   *Book at aaa.com*   **Phone: (505)471-1142**   52

AAA (SAVE)

6/1-10/8 [CP]	1P: $102-$140	2P: $107-$147	XP: $5	F18
10/9-10/31 [CP]	1P: $79-$112	2P: $84-$117	XP: $5	F18
11/1-1/31 [CP]	1P: $68-$98	2P: $74-$104	XP: $5	F18
2/1-5/31 [CP]	1P: $62-$92	2P: $67-$97	XP: $5	F18

Small-scale Hotel **Location:** I-25, exit 278, 1.8 mi n. 4298 Cerrillos Rd 87507. Fax: 505/438-7219. **Facility:** 130 one-bedroom standard units. 3 stories, interior/exterior corridors. **Bath:** combo or shower only. **Parking:** on-site. **Terms:** small pets only. **Amenities:** video games (fee), voice mail, irons, hair dryers. **Pool(s):** heated outdoor. **Guest Services:** valet and coin laundry. **Cards:** AX, CB, DC, DS, MC, VI. **Special Amenities:** free expanded continental breakfast and free local telephone calls. *(See color ad p 584)*

SOME UNITS / FEE FEE

LAS BRISAS DE SANTA FE   **Phone: (505)982-5795**   31

AAA (SAVE)

6/1-10/31	1P: $200-$300	2P: $200-$300	
4/1-10/31	1P: $185-$285	2P: $185-$285	
2/1-3/31 & 11/1-1/31	1P: $155-$255	2P: $155-$255	

Condominium **Location:** Just e of jct Paseo de Peralta. 624 Galisteo St 87501. Fax: 505/982-7900. **Facility:** Nestled within a quiet neighborhood, yet just a short distance from the historic downtown Santa Fe district, these fully equipped units await. 12 units. 2 one-, 9 two- and 1 three-bedroom suites with kitchens, some with whirlpools. 1-2 stories (no elevator), exterior corridors. **Parking:** on-site. **Terms:** office hours 9 am-5 pm, 30 day cancellation notice-fee imposed, weekly rates available. **Amenities:** irons, hair dryers. *Some:* DVD players, high-speed Internet. **Business Services:** fax. **Cards:** MC, VI. **Special Amenities:** free newspaper.

SOME UNITS

LAS PALOMAS   *Book at aaa.com*   **Phone: (505)982-5560**   8

AAA (SAVE)

All Year   1P: $149-$279   XP: $20   F18

Motel **Location:** Just w of jct Guadalupe St. 460 W San Francisco St 87501. Fax: 505/982-5562. **Facility:** 39 units. 8 one-bedroom standard units with efficiencies. 31 one-bedroom suites, some with efficiencies or kitchens. 1 story, exterior corridors. **Bath:** combo or shower only. **Parking:** on-site. **Terms:** check-in 4 pm, 2-4 night minimum stay - weekends, 14 day cancellation notice-fee imposed, package plans, pets ($50 fee). **Amenities:** video library, DVD players, CD players, high-speed Internet, voice mail, honor bars, irons, hair dryers. *Some:* safes. **Leisure Activities:** sauna, whirlpool, library, exercise room. **Guest Services:** valet and coin laundry. **Business Services:** meeting rooms, PC. **Cards:** AX, CB, DC, DS, MC, VI. **Special Amenities:** free expanded continental breakfast and free newspaper.

SOME UNITS / FEE

THE LODGE AT SANTA FE   **Phone: (505)992-5800**   2

7/1-8/31	1P: $116-$242	XP: $10	F17
2/1-6/30 & 9/1-1/31	1P: $80-$134	XP: $10	F17

Small-scale Hotel **Location:** Jct of Cerrillos Rd and St Francis Dr (US 84/285), 1.1 mi nw to Alamo Dr, just w, then just n. 750 N St. Francis Dr 87501. Fax: 505/992-5865. **Facility:** 146 units. 129 one-bedroom standard units. 9 one- and 8 two-bedroom suites ($100-$262). 1-2 stories, interior/exterior corridors. **Bath:** combo or shower only. **Parking:** on-site. **Terms:** check-in 4 pm, 3 day cancellation notice-fee imposed, [BP], [CP] & [ECP] meal plans available, package plans. **Amenities:** high-speed Internet, voice mail, irons, hair dryers. **Pool(s):** heated outdoor. **Leisure Activities:** whirlpool, exercise room. **Guest Services:** valet and coin laundry, area transportation. **Business Services:** conference facilities. **Cards:** AX, DC, DS, JC, MC, VI. *(See color ad below)*

SOME UNITS

LUXURY INN   *Book at aaa.com*   **Phone: (505)473-0567**   47

AAA (SAVE)

All Year [CP]   1P: $50-$199   2P: $50-$199   XP: $10   F12

Motel **Location:** I-25, exit 278, 1.8 mi n. 3752 Cerrillos Rd 87507. Fax: 505/471-9139. **Facility:** 51 one-bedroom standard units. 2 stories (no elevator), interior corridors. **Parking:** on-site. **Terms:** [CP] meal plan available. **Amenities:** high-speed Internet, irons, hair dryers. **Pool(s):** heated outdoor. **Leisure Activities:** whirlpool. **Cards:** AX, DC, DS, MC, VI. **Special Amenities:** free continental breakfast and free local telephone calls.

SOME UNITS

(See map and index starting on p. 568)

THE MADELEINE Phone: (505)986-1431 **17**

	5/1-10/31 [BP]	1P: $135-$210	2P: $135-$210	XP: $25	F5
Historic Bed & Breakfast	2/1-4/30 [BP]	1P: $115-$175	2P: $115-$175	XP: $25	F5
	11/1-1/31 [BP]	1P: $110-$160	2P: $110-$160	XP: $25	F5

Location: Just e of jct Paseo De Peralta and 3 blks e of the historic plaza. 106 Faithway St 87501. Fax: 505/982-8572. **Facility:** This cozy B&B offers individually decorated rooms and is conveniently located near the Historic Plaza. Designated smoking area. 8 one-bedroom standard units. 3 stories (no elevator), interior/exterior corridors. *Bath:* some shared or private, combo or shower only. **Parking:** on-site. **Terms:** 2 night minimum stay - weekends, age restrictions may apply, 14 day cancellation notice-fee imposed. **Amenities:** high-speed Internet, voice mail, hair dryers. *Some:* CD players, irons. **Guest Services:** gift shop, valet laundry. **Cards:** AX, MC, VI.

SOME UNITS
(ASK) (TI+) (⌘) (✕) (DATA PORT) / (⚹) (🔌) (🖥) /
  FEE

MOTEL 6 - 150 *Book at aaa.com* Phone: 505/473-1380 **38**

	5/26-9/4	1P: $45-$59	2P: $51-$65	XP: $3	F17
Motel	2/1-5/25	1P: $39-$49	2P: $45-$55	XP: $3	F17
	9/5-1/31	1P: $39-$45	2P: $45-$51	XP: $3	F17

Location: I-25, exit 278, 3.8 mi n. 3007 Cerrillos Rd 87505. Fax: 505/473-7784. **Facility:** 104 one-bedroom standard units. 2 stories (no elevator), exterior corridors. *Bath:* shower only. **Parking:** on-site. **Terms:** small pets only. **Pool(s):** heated outdoor. **Cards:** AX, CB, DC, DS, MC, VI.

SOME UNITS
(S🔊) (🛏) (TI+) (🖥) (🛋) (✻) (DATA PORT) / (✕) (🔌) (🖥) /
  FEE FEE

THE OLD SANTA FE INN *Book at aaa.com* Phone: (505)995-0800 **23**

| | 5/1-10/31 | 1P: $109-$309 | 2P: $109-$309 | XP: $20 | F |
| Motel | 2/1-4/30 & 11/1-1/31 | 1P: $79-$129 | 2P: $79-$129 | XP: $20 | F |

Location: Just sw of Historic Santa Fee Plaza; center. 320 Galisteo St 87501. Fax: 505/995-0400. **Facility:** Smoke free premises. 43 units. 40 one-bedroom standard units, some with whirlpools. 3 one-bedroom suites ($129-$309) with whirlpools. 1-2 stories (no elevator), interior/exterior corridors. **Parking:** on-site. **Terms:** check-in 4 pm, 3-4 night minimum stay - seasonal and/or weekends, 3 day cancellation notice-fee imposed. **Amenities:** CD players, high-speed Internet, voice mail, irons, hair dryers. **Leisure Activities:** exercise room. **Guest Services:** gift shop, valet laundry, area transportation. **Business Services:** meeting rooms, business center. **Cards:** AX, DC, DS, MC, VI.

SOME UNITS
(ASK) (S🔊) (TI+) (🛋) (📷) (✕) (VCR) (✻) (DATA PORT) (🖥) / (🔌) (🖥) /

OTRA VEZ EN SANTA FE Phone: (505)988-2244 **16**

	12/16-1/31	1P: $200	2P: $200-$225	XP: $25
	6/1-10/31	1P: $160	2P: $160-$190	XP: $25
Condominium	2/1-5/31 & 11/1-12/15	1P: $140	2P: $140-$165	XP: $25

Location: Just s of The Plaza; center. 202 Galisteo St 87501 (PO Box 2927, 87504). Fax: 505/989-5094. **Facility:** Well-appointed units in Santa Fe style. Some with fireplace. Smoke free premises. 18 units. 10 one- and 8 two-bedroom suites with kitchens. 3 stories, interior/exterior corridors. **Parking:** on-site. **Terms:** office hours 8 am-1 am, 3 night minimum stay - weekends, 3 day cancellation notice. **Amenities:** irons, hair dryers. *Some:* DVD players. **Leisure Activities:** whirlpool. **Guest Services:** complimentary laundry. **Cards:** AX, MC, VI.

(ASK) (TI+) (✕) (VCR) (✻) (🔌) (🖥) (🖥)

PARK INN *Book at aaa.com* Phone: (505)471-3000 **37**

	7/1-8/31	1P: $79-$114	2P: $79-$114	XP: $5	F
Small-scale Hotel	9/1-1/31	1P: $49-$79	2P: $49-$79	XP: $5	F
	5/1-6/30	1P: $52-$69	2P: $52-$69	XP: $5	F
	2/1-4/30	1P: $49-$59	2P: $49-$59	XP: $5	F

Location: I-25, exit 278, 7 mi n. 2907 Cerrillos Rd 87507. Fax: 505/424-7561. **Facility:** 100 one-bedroom standard units, some with whirlpools. 2 stories (no elevator), exterior corridors. **Parking:** on-site. **Terms:** cancellation fee imposed, weekly rates available, package plans, pets ($50 deposit, $10 extra charge). **Amenities:** voice mail, safes, irons, hair dryers. **Pool(s):** heated outdoor. **Leisure Activities:** whirlpool, exercise room. **Guest Services:** valet and coin laundry, area transportation. **Business Services:** meeting rooms, PC. **Cards:** AX, DS, MC, VI. *(See color ad below)*

SOME UNITS
(ASK) (S🔊) (📶) (🛏) (TI+) (🛋) (✻) (DATA PORT) (🖥) / (✕) (🔌) (🖥) /
  FEE

(See map and index starting on p. 568)

QUALITY INN   *Book at aaa.com*   Phone: 505/471-1211   **39**
[AAA] [SAVE]
5/16-8/31   1P: $55-$150   2P: $65-$160   XP: $5   F18
[diamond diamond][diamond diamond]   2/1-5/15 & 9/1-1/31   1P: $49-$99   2P: $49-$99   XP: $3   F18
Small-scale Hotel   **Location:** I-25, exit 278B, 3.8 mi n. 3011 Cerrillos Rd 87507. Fax: 505/438-9535. **Facility:** 99 one-bedroom standard units. 2 stories (no elevator), interior corridors. **Parking:** on-site. **Terms:** [BP] meal plan available, package plans, pets ($10 extra charge). **Amenities:** irons, hair dryers. **Dining:** 7 am-10 pm; hours vary in winter, cocktails. **Pool(s):** heated outdoor. **Guest Services:** valet laundry, airport transportation-Santa Fe Airport. **Business Services:** meeting rooms. **Cards:** AX, CB, DC, DS, MC, VI. **Special Amenities:** free full breakfast and free newspaper. *(See color ad below)*

SOME UNITS
[✈] [🛏] [🍴] [🏊] [❄] [📶] / [✕] [DATA PORT] [🛗] [📷] /
FEE

RESIDENCE INN BY MARRIOTT   *Book at aaa.com*   Phone: (505)988-7300   **35**
[diamond diamond][diamond diamond]
5/15-10/15 & 12/31-1/31   1P: $189-$269
Small-scale Hotel   2/1-5/14 & 10/16-12/14   1P: $129-$249
Location: I-25, exit 282, 1.7 mi n on St Francis Dr to St Michaels Dr, just e, then just n. 1698 Galisteo St 87505. Fax: 505/988-3243. **Facility:** 120 one-bedroom standard units with kitchens. 2 stories (no elevator), exterior corridors. **Parking:** on-site. **Terms:** cancellation fee imposed, pets ($75 fee, limit 2). **Amenities:** high-speed Internet, voice mail, irons, hair dryers. **Pool(s):** heated outdoor. **Leisure Activities:** whirlpools, sports court. **Guest Services:** valet and coin laundry. **Business Services:** meeting rooms. **Cards:** AX, CB, DC, DS, JC, MC, VI.

SOME UNITS
[ASK] [Sb] [✈] [🏊] [🏃] [❄] [DATA PORT] [🛗] [📷] [📶] / [✕] /
FEE

SAGE INN   *Book at aaa.com*   Phone: (505)982-5952   **33**
[AAA] [SAVE]
5/14-9/2   1P: $98-$134   XP: $10   F16
[diamond diamond][diamond diamond]   9/3-10/14   1P: $98-$125   XP: $10   F16
Motel   2/1-5/13   1P: $89-$109   XP: $10   F16
10/15-1/31   1P: $89-$107   XP: $10   F16
Location: 0.4 mi ne of St. Francis Dr (US 84). 725 Cerrillos Rd 87505. Fax: 505/984-8879. **Facility:** 154 one-bedroom standard units. 2 stories, exterior corridors. **Parking:** on-site. **Terms:** cancellation fee imposed, pets ($25 fee). **Amenities:** voice mail, irons, hair dryers. **Pool(s):** small heated outdoor. **Guest Services:** valet laundry. **Cards:** AX, DC, DS, JC, MC, VI. **Special Amenities:** free continental breakfast and free local telephone calls. *(See color ad below)*

SOME UNITS
[Sb] [🛏] [🍴] [🌀] [🏊] [❄] [DATA PORT] [📶] / [✕] [🛗] /
FEE   FEE

(See map and index starting on p. 568)

SANTA FE COURTYARD BY MARRIOTT   *Book at aaa.com*   **Phone:** (505)473-2800   **40**
All Year   1P: $59-$169   2P: $59-$169   XP: $10   F
Small-scale Hotel   **Location:** I-25, exit 278, 3.2 mi n. 3347 Cerrillos Rd 87507. Fax: 505/473-4905. **Facility:** 213 units. 182 one-bedroom standard units. 31 one-bedroom suites. 3 stories, interior/exterior corridors. *Bath:* combo or shower only. **Parking:** on-site. **Terms:** cancellation fee imposed. **Amenities:** high-speed Internet, dual phone lines, voice mail, irons, hair dryers. **Dining:** Cafe Santa Fe, see separate listing. **Pool(s):** heated indoor. **Leisure Activities:** whirlpools, exercise room. *Fee:* massage. **Guest Services:** gift shop, valet and coin laundry, area transportation. **Business Services:** conference facilities. **Cards:** AX, DC, DS, MC, VI. *(See color ad below)*

SOME UNITS

(ASK) (SD) (✈) (†↑) (&M) (⊠) (∅) (🐎) (✕) (🎥) (DATA PORT) (🔒) (🖥) / (✕) (📷)

SANTA FE MOTEL & INN   *Book at aaa.com*   **Phone:** (505)982-1039   **25**
(AAA) (SAVE)   5/1-10/31   1P: $109-$169   2P: $109-$169   XP: $10   F12
    3/1-4/30   1P: $89-$135   2P: $89-$135   XP: $10   F12
    11/1-1/31   1P: $69-$135   2P: $69-$135   XP: $10   F12
Motel   2/1-2/28   1P: $69-$129   2P: $69-$129   XP: $10   F12
Location: 4 blks sw of The Plaza. 510 Cerrillos Rd 87501. Fax: 505/986-1275. **Facility:** 23 one-bedroom standard units, some with efficiencies. 1-2 stories (no elevator), exterior corridors. *Bath:* combo or shower only. **Parking:** on-site. **Terms:** 3 day cancellation notice-fee imposed, pets ($15 extra charge, in limited units). **Amenities:** high-speed Internet, voice mail, honor bars, irons, hair dryers. *Some:* DVD players. **Business Services:** PC. **Cards:** AX, DC, DS, MC, VI. **Special Amenities:** free expanded continental breakfast and free newspaper.

SOME UNITS

(SD) (🐂) (🎥) (DATA PORT) / (✕) (VCR) (🔒) (🖥) (📷) /
FEE

SANTA FE PLAZA TRAVELODGE   *Book at aaa.com*   **Phone:** (505)982-3551   **32**
(AAA) (SAVE)   7/1-8/31   1P: $79-$150   2P: $79-$199   XP: $10   F17
    5/1-6/30   1P: $69-$79   2P: $79-$89   XP: $10   F17
    2/1-4/30 & 9/1-1/31   1P: $59-$69   2P: $69-$79   XP: $10   F17
Small-scale Hotel   **Location:** 0.8 mi sw of The Plaza. 646 Cerrillos Rd 87505. Fax: 505/983-8624. **Facility:** 49 one-bedroom standard units. 2 stories (no elevator), interior/exterior corridors. *Bath:* combo or shower only. **Parking:** on-site. **Terms:** package plans, small pets only ($10 extra charge). **Amenities:** safes (fee), hair dryers. *Some:* irons. **Pool(s):** outdoor. **Cards:** AX, DC, DS, MC, VI. **Special Amenities:** free continental breakfast.

SOME UNITS

(SD) (🐂) (†↑+) (∅) (🐎) (🎥) (DATA PORT) (🔒) (🖥) / (✕) (📷)
FEE

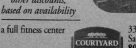

(See map and index starting on p. 568)

SLEEP INN   *Book at aaa.com*   Phone: (505)474-9500   **54**
▼▼ ▼▼   All Year [CP]   1P: $59-$189   2P: $59-$189   XP: $10   F18
    Location: I-25, exit 278, 0.3 mi n. Located adjacent to the Santa Fe Premium Outlet stores. 8376 Cerrillos Rd 87507.
Small-scale Hotel   Fax: 505/474-9535. **Facility:** 99 one-bedroom standard units. 3 stories, interior corridors. *Bath:* combo or
    shower only. **Parking:** on-site. **Terms:** package plans, $1 service charge, pets ($10 extra charge, with prior
approval). **Amenities:** high-speed Internet, voice mail. *Some:* irons, hair dryers. **Pool(s):** small heated outdoor. **Leisure
Activities:** whirlpool, exercise room. **Guest Services:** coin laundry. **Business Services:** meeting rooms. **Cards:** AX, CB, DC,
DS, JC, MC, VI. *(See color ad p 588)*

SOME UNITS

(ASK) (S🅓) (🛏) (🔥M) (🔒) (🚭) (📷) (🕯) (DATA PORT) / (✕) (🏧) (🍽) (☕) /
            FEE

SPENCER HOUSE BED & BREAKFAST INN   Phone: (505)988-3024   **5**
(AAA) (SAVE)   All Year [BP]   1P: $135-$175   2P: $135-$175   XP: $20   D15
▼▼ ▼▼   **Location:** Jct Chappelle St; 3 1/2 blks e of the historic plaza. 222 McKenzie St 87501. Fax: 505/988-3024.
    Facility: Built in 1923, the Mediterranean-style adobe home has comfortable and homey rooms with a
Bed & Breakfast   mixture of Hispanic and 20th-century artifacts. Smoke free premises. 6 one-bedroom standard units, some
    with kitchens and/or whirlpools. 1 story, interior/exterior corridors. **Parking:** street. **Terms:** age restrictions
    may apply, 14 day cancellation notice-fee imposed, package plans, no pets allowed (owner's pet on
premises). **Amenities:** high-speed Internet, hair dryers. *Some:* irons. **Guest Services:** valet laundry. **Cards:** DS, MC, VI.
Special Amenities: free full breakfast and free newspaper.

SOME UNITS

(S🅓) (🍴) (✕) / (📺) (🌀) (🏧) (🍽) (☕) /

TERRITORIAL INN   *Book at aaa.com*   Phone: 505/989-7737   **7**
▼▼ ▼▼   Property failed to provide current rates
    Location: 3 blks from Santa Fe Plaza. 215 Washington Ave 87501. Fax: 505/986-9212. **Facility:** Period
Bed & Breakfast   reproductions, modern baths, shirred fabric ceiling treatments and a brick-paved rose garden add to the
    elegance of the 1890s shaded home. Smoke free premises. 14 one-bedroom standard units. 1 story, interior
corridors. **Parking:** on-site. **Terms:** office hours 7 am-7 pm, age restrictions may apply. **Amenities:** voice mail, irons, hair
dryers. **Leisure Activities:** spa. **Guest Services:** gift shop, complimentary evening beverages.

SOME UNITS

(🍴) (✕) (VCR) (🕯) (DATA PORT) / (🏧) /

─────── *The following lodging was either not evaluated or did not* ───────
meet AAA rating requirements but is listed for your information only.

DANCING GROUND OF THE SUN BED AND
    BREAKFAST   Phone: 505/986-9797
(fyi)   Did not meet all AAA rating requirements for some property operations at time of last evaluation on
    10/08/2004. **Location:** 5 blks e of The Plaza. 711 Paseo de Peralta 87501. Facilities, services, and decor characterize
Bed & Breakfast   a mid-range property.

─────── **WHERE TO DINE** ───────

315 RESTAURANT & WINE BAR   **Lunch:** $8-$12   **Dinner:** $17-$29   Phone: 505/986-9190   **37**
▼▼ ▼▼   **Location:** 0.5 mi s of The Plaza at De Vargas. 315 Old Santa Fe Tr 87501. **Hours:** 11:30 am-2 & 5:30-9:30 pm,
    Sun & Mon from 5:30 pm; to 9 pm in winter. **Reservations:** suggested. **Features:** Excellent French and
French   American preparations and a seasonal menu greet diners at the intimate restaurant. Pate, steak and
    seafood are the focus of the menu, which also includes such splendid desserts as warm tarte tatin with
creme fraise. Dressy casual; beer & wine only. **Parking:** street. **Cards:** AX, CB, DC, DS, MC, VI.

ANASAZI RESTAURANT   **Lunch:** $15-$20   **Dinner:** $25-$30   Phone: 505/988-3236   **18**
▼▼ ▼▼   **Location:** Just ne of The Plaza; in Inn of the Anasazi. 113 Washington Ave 87501. **Hours:** 7-10:30 am, 11:30-2:30 &
    5:30-10 pm, Sun 11 am-2:30 pm. **Reservations:** suggested. **Features:** You'll be treated to superior food
Regional American   preparation and presentation and an upscale-casual dining experience at Anasazi's. The chef offers
    innovative preparation methods of stylish Western cuisine, featuring organic produce, free-range meats and
fresh fish. Casual dress; cocktails. **Parking:** valet. **Cards:** AX, CB, DC, DS, JC, MC, VI.   (🍸)

ASADO BRAZILIAN GRILL   **Lunch:** $10-$12   **Dinner:** $13-$19   Phone: 505/986-9963   **49**
▼▼ ▼▼   **Location:** Just e of jct Cerrillos Rd. 1007 St. Francis Dr 87505. **Hours:** 11 am-2:30 & 4:30-9 pm, Fri & Sat-10 pm,
    Sun 11:30 am-9 pm. Closed: 1/1, 11/23, 12/25. **Reservations:** accepted. **Features:** Food continues to
Brazilian   come until patrons say "no mas" at the popular restaurant. Friendly servers keep bringing the day's
    offerings of grilled steak, chicken, pork, lamb and sausage, along with grilled vegetables, until diners turn
over a green wooden block to show red. Casual dress. **Parking:** on-site. **Cards:** AX, MC, VI.

BALEEN SANTE FE   **Lunch:** $8-$14   **Dinner:** $17-$37   Phone: 505/984-7915   **33**
▼▼ ▼▼   **Location:** Just se of The Plaza; in The Inn & Spa at Loretto. 211 Old Santa Fe Tr 87501. **Hours:** 7:30 am-3 & 5:30-
    10 pm. **Reservations:** suggested, for dinner. **Features:** A cheerful monkey holding a lantern sits on the
Regional American   table, inviting guests to find a bit of joy in their dining experience. This should not be difficult at Baleen,
    where the staff is friendly and the food creative. Among dinner offerings are lobster paella, seared sushi-
grade tuna, Roquefort-crusted filet mignon and goat cheese- and herb-crusted rack of lamb. Casual dress; cocktails. **Parking:**
valet. **Cards:** AX, CB, DC, DS, MC, VI.   (🍸)

BERT'S LA TAQUERIA   **Lunch:** $5-$15   **Dinner:** $10-$30   Phone: 505/474-0791   **56**
▼▼ ▼▼   **Location:** Just se of jct Cerrillos Rd; in St. Michael's Village West Shopping Center. 1620 St. Michael's Dr 87505.
    Hours: 11 am-9:30 pm. Closed: 1/1, 12/25; also Sun. **Reservations:** accepted. **Features:** Along with the
Mexican   basics—tortillas and salsas—the restaurant prepares dishes that take a first step toward the more
    innovative cuisine of central Mexico. Beef, pork and seafood dishes show influences from the Aztecs, Spain
and France. Weekday lunch specials are served family-style. Casual dress; beer & wine only. **Parking:** on-site. **Cards:** AX, DC,
DS, MC, VI.

(See map and index starting on p. 568)

BLUE CORN CAFE AND BREWERY   Lunch: $7-$12   Dinner: $8-$16   Phone: 505/984-1800   (24)
Location: Center. 133 Water St 87501. **Hours:** 11 am-9 pm, Fri-Sun to 10 pm. Closed: 11/23, 12/25.
Reservations: not accepted. **Features:** Upstairs just off The Plaza, the restaurant beckons diners to feast
Southwestern   on ample servings of New Mexican cuisine with an American twist. Watch passersby on Water and Galisteo
streets as you sip a cool libation—perhaps one of the daily margarita specials or a selection from an
extensive list of brewery choices—and indulge your appetite. The staff is friendly and attentive. Casual dress; cocktails.
Parking: street. **Cards:** AX, CB, DC, DS, MC, VI.

BLUE CORN CAFE II   Lunch: $7-$12   Dinner: $8-$16   Phone: 505/438-1800   (62)
Location: I-25, exit 278, 2 mi n. 4056 Cerrillos Rd 87505. **Hours:** 11 am-10 pm, Fri & Sat-11 pm. Closed: 11/23,
12/25. **Reservations:** not accepted. **Features:** Across the street from Villa Linda Mall on the southern
Southwestern   outskirts of town, the cafe provides the same menu and tastes of its sister restaurant downtown. Northern
New Mexican cuisine, great margaritas and handcrafted microbrews are served. Casual dress; cocktails.
Parking: on-site. **Cards:** AX, CB, DC, DS, MC, VI.

THE BULL RING   Lunch: $10-$20   Dinner: $20-$40   Phone: 505/982-3328   (11)
Location: Just n of The Plaza; in Wells Fargo Bldg. 150 Washington Ave 87501. **Hours:** 11:30 am-3 & 5-10 pm, Sat
& Sun from 5 pm. Closed: 1/1, 12/25. **Reservations:** suggested. **Features:** Renowned for its USDA prime
Steak & Seafood   steaks, the restaurant also prepares good seafood entrees. Side dishes are served family style, and the
porterhouse is large enough for two. Casual dress; cocktails. **Parking:** street. **Cards:** MC, VI.

THE BURRITO COMPANY   Lunch: $4-$8   Dinner: $4-$8   Phone: 505/982-4453   (19)
Location: Between Marcy St and Palace Ave; downtown. 111 Washington Ave 87501. **Hours:** 7:30 am-3 pm, Fri 7
am-5 pm, Sat 8 am-5 pm. Closed: 12/25. **Features:** Just off The Plaza, the laid-back restaurant is open for
Regional American   breakfast, lunch and dinner. It is especially convenient for those wanting a quick meal. Casual dress.
Parking: street. **Cards:** MC, VI.

CAFE DE ARTISTES   Lunch: $5-$8   Dinner: $8-$18   Phone: 505/820-2535   (42)
Location: Paseo de Peralta, just e. 223 B Canyon 87501. **Hours:** 8:30 am-5 pm; to 10 pm in summer. Closed
major holidays. **Reservations:** accepted. **Features:** The cafe is the perfect place to stop for a quick bite
Deli/Subs   after visiting the galleries along Canyon Road. Representative of French bistro fare are quality sandwiches,
Sandwiches   coffee drinks and baked goods. Casual dress; wine only. **Parking:** street. **Cards:** MC, VI.

CAFE' OASIS   Lunch: $7-$12   Dinner: $11-$17   Phone: 505/983-9599   (45)
Location: From Cerrillos Rd, just e on Paseo de Peralta, then just ne. 526 Galisteo St 87501. **Hours:** 9:30 am-
midnight, Fri & Sat-2 am. **Reservations:** accepted. **Features:** The people of Cafe Oasis cherish the art of
healthy eating and encourage others to join them in their appreciation. Distinctively designed rooms invite
International   patrons to get comfortable and dig in. The friendly staff serves a variety of international and American
dishes. Casual dress; wine only. **Parking:** on-site. **Cards:** MC, VI.

CAFE PARIS   Lunch: $9-$15   Dinner: $10-$18   Phone: 505/986-9162   (14)
Location: Town Center via San Francisco; just w of the plaza. 31 Burro Alley 87501. **Hours:** 11:30 am-9 pm; Sat &
Sun from 8 am. Closed: Mon. **Reservations:** accepted. **Features:** In historic Burro Alley, the cozy
French   restaurant brings French cuisine to the city. Chicken cordon bleu, filet mignon with green pepper sauce,
shrimp Provencal and beef bourguignon stand out on the menu. Patrons love this place for coffee and
dessert, as the French pastries are a decadent treat. Casual dress; wine only. **Parking:** street. **Cards:** AX, DC, DS, MC, VI.

CAFE PASQUAL'S   Lunch: $8-$16   Dinner: $18-$30   Phone: 505/983-9340   (27)
Location: Center; just sw of The Plaza. 121 Don Gaspar Ave 87501. **Hours:** 7 am-3 & 5:30-10 pm, Sun 8 am-2
pm. Closed: 11/23, 12/24, 12/25. **Reservations:** required, for dinner. **Features:** Hand-painted murals adorn
Regional American   the walls of the restaurant, known for regional American dishes. Casual dress; beer & wine only. **Parking:**
street. **Cards:** AX, MC, VI.

CAFE SAN ESTEVAN   Dinner: $12-$27   Phone: 505/995-1996   (28)
Location: From jct Guadalupe St, just w; in Sanbusco shopping area. 428 Agua Fria St 87501. **Hours:** 5:30 pm-9
pm, Fri & Sat-9:30 pm, Sun 10 am-2 pm; call for holiday hours. Closed: Zozobra Festival.
Reservations: accepted. **Features:** For a true Santa Fe dining experience, chef-owner Estevan Garcia
Southwest   creates delicious Southwestern dishes with a modern twist. Candles, religious icons and "santos" accent the
American   warm, rustic decor. Dressy casual; wine only. **Parking:** on-site. **Cards:** AX, MC, VI.

CAFE SANTA FE   Dinner: $12-$25   Phone: 505/473-2800   (59)
Location: I-25, exit 278 (Cerrillos Rd), 3.2 mi n; in Santa Fe Courtyard by Marriott. 3347 Cerrillos Rd 87507.
Hours: 6:30 am-10 & 5-10 pm, Sun 6:30 am-noon & 5-10 pm. **Reservations:** accepted. **Features:** The
Regional American   menu centers on Southwestern favorites, such as enchiladas and fajitas, as well as steak and seafood.
and other lodgings.   Corn chowder with green chiles is delicious. In the Courtyard by Marriott, the restaurant is near shopping
Casual dress; cocktails. **Parking:** on-site. **Cards:** AX, CB, DC, DS, MC, VI. *(See color ad p 588)*

CHILACAS RESTAURANT & CANTINA   Lunch: $7-$15   Dinner: $7-$15   Phone: 505/984-2272   (58)
Location: I-25, exit 284, 0.8 mi n or CR 466 (Old Pecos Tr). 2239 Old Pecos Tr 87505. **Hours:** 11:30 am-9 pm; to 8
pm in winter. Closed: Sun & Mon in winter. **Reservations:** accepted. **Features:** The cantina's menu lists
Regional Mexican   traditional regional favorites, such as enchiladas and rellenos, as well as smokehouse specialties, including
baby back ribs, smoked sausage and mesquite-hickory-smoked brisket. Casual dress; cocktails. **Parking:**
on-site. **Cards:** AX, DC, DS, MC, VI.

Approved

The Symbols of Quality

Only properties that meet the strict quality criteria to become AAA Approved receive a AAA Diamond rating. This means that every AAA Approved lodging and restaurant, regardless of its Diamond rating, delivers the basic qualities members require.

Diamond ratings provide an easy way to select quality lodgings and restaurants with the amenities and degree of sophistication you desire.

Each Approved and Diamond rated establishment is visited and thoroughly reviewed by AAA's professional evaluators.

One Diamond lodgings are basic, no-frills accommodations appealing to the budget-minded. Restaurants offer simple, affordable dining in a casual or self-service style.

Two Diamond lodgings show modest enhancements in décor and amenities. Restaurants are informal yet rise above the ordinary, often well-suited to family dining.

Three Diamond lodgings offer a higher level of physical appeal, comfort and amenities. Restaurants provide a more creative, upscale, adult-oriented experience.

Four Diamond lodgings feature a high level of service amid upscale surroundings. Restaurants offer fine distinctive dining with complex menu offerings and a highly skilled staff.

Five Diamond lodgings offer extraordinary luxury, personalized services, and extensive amenities. Restaurants are world-class, providing innovative cuisine and impeccable service.

For quality assurance, choose only AAA Approved lodgings and restaurants. Then for a perfect match, select the Diamond rating that best meets your needs.

(See map and index starting on p. 568)

CHOCOLATE MAVEN BAKERY & CAFE
Lunch: $8-$13   Phone: 505/984-1980   [54]

American

Location: From jct St. Michael's and Cerrillos Rd, just n on Cerrillos Rd to 2nd St, then 0.6 mi e; in industrial building. 821 W San Mateo Rd 87505. **Hours:** 7:30 am-10:30 & 11-3 pm; Sat & Sun 9 am-3 pm. Closed: 1/1, 11/23, 12/25. **Reservations:** not accepted. **Features:** Those looking for an escape from the hustle and bustle of downtown should seek out this cozy and distinctive cafe. Soups, salads, sandwiches, pizza and baked goods are made from the freshest ingredients. The friendly and attentive staff enhances the dining experience. Casual dress. **Parking:** on-site. **Cards:** AX, DC, DS, MC, VI.

THE COMPOUND RESTAURANT
Lunch: $10-$20   Dinner: $20-$32   Phone: 505/982-4353   [46]

American

Location: From Paseo de Peralta, 0.4 mi e. 653 Canyon Rd 87501. **Hours:** noon-2 & 6-9 pm, Sat & Sun from 6 pm. **Reservations:** suggested. **Features:** In an adobe-style hacienda, the restaurant prepares a variety of contemporary American cuisine. The menu includes classic sweetbreads and foie gras starters. Entrees include a variety of seafood, steaks, lamb and chicken. Grilled beef tenderloin with Italian Cepe O'Brian potatoes and foie gras hollandaise is a must for beef lovers. Casual dress; cocktails. **Parking:** on-site. **Cards:** AX, MC, VI.

COWGIRL BBQ & WESTERN GRILL
Lunch: $5-$12   Dinner: $8-$15   Phone: 505/982-2565   [34]

Regional American

Location: Just sw of The Plaza. 319 S Guadalupe St 87501. **Hours:** 11 am-midnight, Sat & Sun from 8:30 am. Closed: 11/23, 12/25. **Reservations:** accepted. **Features:** Cowgirl memorabilia is abundant in the locally favorite eatery. The menu includes Southwest regional, Cajun and barbecue dishes. Casual dress; cocktails; entertainment. **Parking:** street. **Cards:** AX, DS, MC, VI.

COYOTE CAFE
Dinner: $20-$38   Phone: 505/983-1615   [26]

Southwestern

Location: Just sw of The Plaza; between Ortiz and Galisteo sts. 132 W Water St 87501. **Hours:** 6 pm-9 pm, Fri & Sat from 5:30 pm. **Reservations:** suggested. **Features:** Located on the second floor of a variety of shops and just a short walk from the historic Plaza, one will find this attractive restaurant. The innovative menu specializes in New American-Southwestern cuisine prepared by a professional chef. The ambience is very trendy with an exhibition kitchen and an interesting Southwestern touch with horsehair upholstery. The well trained service staff is very professional and attentive. A must have is the chocolate mousse for dessert. Dressy casual; cocktails. **Parking:** street. **Cards:** AX, DS, MC, VI.

DARA THAI RESTAURANT
Lunch: $8-$15   Dinner: $8-$15   Phone: 505/995-0887   [52]

Thai

Location: Jct Cerrillos Rd and Second St. 1710 Cerrillos Rd 87505. **Hours:** 11 am-2:30 & 4:30-9 pm, Fri & Sat-10 pm. Closed: 11/23, 12/25; also Sun. **Reservations:** accepted. **Features:** Patrons walk into another culture by eating at the ethnic restaurant. Brightly painted murals and decor help create an authentically Thai atmosphere. Delicious vegetarian and meat dishes will please the whole family. Casual dress; wine only. **Parking:** on-site. **Cards:** AX, DS, MC, VI.

EL ENCANTO
Lunch: $8-$14   Dinner: $16-$25   Phone: 505/988-5991   [3]

Mexican

Location: Sw of The Plaza, just w; corner of Guadalupe and Agua Fria. 235 N Guadalupe St 87501. **Hours:** 11:30 am-2:30 & 5-close. Closed major holidays; also Sun. **Reservations:** suggested. **Features:** Chef Olea infuses innovative and traditional Mexican dishes with unique flavors and ingredients reflective of Mexico City. In the historic Guadalupe district, the restaurant occupies a 19th-century former convent. The slate-tiled ante room opens onto a network of adobe-walled galleries and dining rooms. Casual dress; cocktails. **Parking:** on-site. **Cards:** AX, DS, MC, VI.

EL FAROL RESTAURANT
Lunch: $8-$10   Dinner: $25-$30   Phone: 505/983-9912   [48]

Spanish

Location: From Paseo de Peralta, 0.5 mi e. 808 Canyon Rd 87501. **Hours:** 11:30 am-2 & 5-10 pm; from 11 am 5/15-9/15. **Reservations:** suggested. **Features:** In the fashionable Canyon Road area, the restaurant occupies an old, adobe-style building with a rustic interior. The menu contains a variety of Spanish beef, lamb, veal and seafood preparations. On the wine list is a good variety of Spanish and New World wines, several available by the glass. Dressy casual; cocktails. **Parking:** on-site (fee). **Cards:** AX, DC, DS, MC, VI.

FUEGO
Lunch: $12-$18   Dinner: $30-$38   Phone: 505/954-9670   [30]

International

Location: Jct Paseo de Peracta and E Palace Ave; in La Posada de Santa Fe; downtown. 330 E Palace Ave 87501. **Hours:** 7 am-10:30 & 11:30-9:30 pm. **Reservations:** suggested. **Features:** Dinner is served in a traditonal Santa Fe dining room, with formal charm and ambiance. Decorative, imaginatively arranged menu selections contain the finest fowl, meat and game available and, of course, a seasonal menu is featured. Service is very polished and meal presentation is raised to an art form. Dressy casual; cocktails. **Parking:** valet. **Cards:** AX, MC, VI. *(See color ad p 584)*

GERONIMO
Lunch: $8-$15   Dinner: $20-$50   Phone: 505/982-1500   [47]

Regional International

Location: 0.5 mi e of jct Paseo de Peralta. 724 Canyon Rd 87501. **Hours:** 11:30 am-2 & 6-9:30 pm, Mon from 6 pm. **Reservations:** suggested. **Features:** Whether you choose to dine on the porch and watch the art gallery aficionados or gift shoppers pass by, or inside in the quietly elegant surroundings, the polished and attentive service will smooth your dining experience. The Southwestern cuisine style brings you fresh seafood dishes such as pan broiled Alaskan Halibut or the signature grilled black pepper elk tenderloin. Don't plan to skip dessert - ginger creme brulee or angelica soaked flourless chocolate torte are not to be missed. Dressy casual; cocktails. **Parking:** on-site and valet. **Cards:** AX, MC, VI.

GUADALAJARA GRILL
Lunch: $6-$15   Dinner: $7-$15   Phone: 505/424-3544   [60]

Mexican

Location: Jct Zafarano Dr; in Plaza del Norte. 3877 Cerrillos Rd 87501. **Hours:** 10:30 am-9 pm, Fri & Sat-10 pm, Sun 10 am-9 pm. **Features:** Patrons can nosh on fresh Mexican cuisine while enjoying a sporting event on a strategically placed TV set. The extensive menu lists typical fare, including enchiladas, burritos, chimichangas, chiles rellenos, tamales and tacos. For heartier appetites, the rib-eye steak and shrimp plate or fresh tilapia served with vegetables and rice hits the spot. The restaurant is known for its many grilled shrimp variations. Casual dress; beer & wine only. **Parking:** on-site. **Cards:** AX, MC, VI.

(See map and index starting on p. 568)

GUADALUPE CAFE

Southwestern

Lunch: $6-$9   **Dinner:** $8-$15   **Phone:** 505/982-9762   (44)

Location: From Cerrillos Rd, se on E Alameda, then just n. 422 Old Santa Fe Tr 87501. **Hours:** 7 am-2 & 5-9 pm, Sat from 8 am, Sun 8 am-2 pm. **Closed:** 11/23, 12/25. **Reservations:** not accepted. **Features:** The bustling cafe serves Mexican-style comfort food. Those who stop in during traditional meal times should be prepared to wait at this local favorite. Diners should take up the wait staff on their offer to reserve a slice of not-to-be-missed homemade pie. Casual dress; beer & wine only. **Parking:** on-site. **Cards:** DC, MC, VI.

HARRY'S ROAD HOUSE

Southwest American

Lunch: $5-$8   **Dinner:** $8-$12   **Phone:** 505/989-4629   (63)

Location: I-25, exit 284 (Old Pecos Tr), 0.8 mi se on Frontage Rd (Old Las Vegas Hwy). Rt 19 87505. **Hours:** 7 am-9:30 pm. **Closed:** 11/23, 12/25. **Features:** The friendly, casual staff give attentive service. You may dine inside, on the porch, or in the garden surrounded by flowers. Next comes menu choices—grilled fish tacos, blue corn turkey enchiladas or grilled pork chops. The homemade desserts are mouthwatering—bread and rice pudding, ice cream sandwiches or lemon meringue pie. Casual dress; cocktails. **Parking:** on-site. **Cards:** MC, VI.

HIDDEN CHICKEN CAFE

American

Menu on aaa.com   **Lunch:** $5-$15   **Dinner:** $5-$15   **Phone:** 505/474-4424   (55)

Location: I-25, exit 282, 1.2 mi n on St Francis Dr, then just w; in Plaza Del Sol. 730 St Michaels Dr, Suite 3RW 87505. **Hours:** 11 am-8 pm. **Closed:** 5/29; also Sun. **Features:** The popular eatery nurtures a cheerful, pleasant atmosphere. On the menu are rotisserie chicken, roasted ribs, salads and sandwiches, including some with Southwestern and Oriental flavors. Casual dress; beer & wine only. **Parking:** on-site. **Cards:** AX, DS, MC, VI.

IL PIATTO

Italian

Lunch: $6-$12   **Dinner:** $15-$18   **Phone:** 505/984-1091   (7)

Location: Between Lincoln Ave and Washington St; just n of The Plaza. 95 W Marcy St 87501. **Hours:** 11:30 am-2 & 5:30-9:30 pm, Sat & Sun from 5:30 pm. **Closed:** 1/1; also 12/24. **Reservations:** suggested, for dinner. **Features:** In the heart of the downtown historic district and only one block from the Plaza, the restaurant tempts patrons with such specialties as grilled calamari, pancetta-wrapped trout, roasted chicken peperonata and roasted garlic- and basil-stuffed duck breast. Pasta is made fresh daily. Casual dress; beer & wine only. **Parking:** street. **Cards:** AX, DS, MC, VI.

INDIA PALACE

Indian

Lunch: $9-$14   **Dinner:** $10-$20   **Phone:** 505/986-5859   (36)

Location: At rear of Water St parking lot. 227 Don Gaspar 87501. **Hours:** 11:30 am-2:30 & 5-10 pm. **Closed:** Super Bowl Sun. **Reservations:** accepted. **Features:** Authentic northern Indian cuisine is offered here. Tourist, and local business people frequent this restaurant. A lunch buffet is available and is an excellent way for first-time diners to experience the flavor of India. Patio dining is available. Casual dress; cocktails. **Parking:** on-site. **Cards:** DC, DS, MC, VI.

JINJA ASIA CAFE

Asian

Lunch: $6-$17   **Dinner:** $6-$17   **Phone:** 505/982-4321   (2)

Location: Just nw of Paseo de Peralta; in DeVargas Center Mall. 510 N Guadalupe 87501. **Hours:** 11 am-10 pm. Closed major holidays. **Reservations:** not accepted. **Features:** The cafe appeals to diners who do not want to limit themselves to one style of cuisine. Thai, Japanese, Chinese and Vietnamese dishes are served in an elegant but relaxed atmosphere. Casual dress; cocktails. **Parking:** on-site. **Cards:** AX, DC, DS, MC, VI.

JULIAN'S

Italian

Lunch: $6-$20   **Dinner:** $22-$36   **Phone:** 505/988-2355   (35)

Location: Just se of The Plaza; corner of Alameda and Shelby sts. 221 Shelby St 87501. **Hours:** 11:30 am-2:30 & 5:30-10 pm, Sun & Mon from 5:30 pm. **Closed:** 11/23. **Reservations:** suggested. **Features:** Representative of classic Northern Italian dishes are piccata di vitello and pollo al agrodolce. The appetizer combining several salamis, olives and sliced Parmesan cheese is delightful. The decor is decidedly Southwestern, but artwork depicts the Old World. Casual dress; cocktails. **Parking:** street. **Cards:** AX, DC, DS, MC, VI.

KASASOBA

Japanese

Lunch: $7-$13   **Dinner:** $8-$20   **Phone:** 505/984-1969   (29)

Location: Jct Guadalupe, just s; near Sanbusco shopping area. 544B Agua Fria 87501. **Hours:** 11:30 am-2 & 5:30-9 pm, Fri-9:30 pm, Sat 5:30 pm-9:30 pm, Sun 5:30 pm-9 pm. **Closed:** 11/23, 12/25. **Reservations:** accepted. **Features:** The intimate and hip Japanese restaurant prepares a variety of dishes with a contemporary flair. Noodle soups—ramen, udon and soba—are the specialty, but flavorful tempura and sushi dishes also are on the menu. For a memorable treat, try the fried freshwater crab appetizer or something from the extensive sake menu. Parking is limited. Casual dress; wine only. **Parking:** on-site. **Cards:** MC, VI.

LA CASA SENA RESTAURANT

Regional American

Lunch: $8-$13   **Dinner:** $19-$36   **Phone:** 505/988-9232   (23)

Location: Just e of The Plaza. 125 E Palace Ave 87501. **Hours:** 11:30 am-3 & 5:30-10 pm, Sun from 11 am. **Closed:** 12/25. **Reservations:** suggested. **Features:** La Casa Sena features excellent regional preparation of traditional menu selections. You'll find that the servers are attentive and knowledgeable, and a large outdoor dining area is available. They also have an extensive wine list. Dressy casual; cocktails; entertainment. **Parking:** street. **Cards:** AX, CB, DC, DS, MC, VI. **Historic**

LAS FUENTES

Regional American

Lunch: $9-$14   **Dinner:** $18-$35   **Phone:** 505/983-6377   (1)

Location: 3.5 mi n of Paseo De Peralta; in Bishop's Lodge Resort & Spa. 1297 Bishops Lodge Rd 87504. **Hours:** 7-10 am, 11-2 & 6-10 pm, Sun 7:30-10 am, 11-2 & 6-9 pm. **Reservations:** suggested. **Features:** This restaurant features upscale dining in a relaxed Southwestern atmosphere. Specialties include very good New American and Southwestern cuisine selections. The outdoor patio/lounge has a fireplace and overlooks the Sangre de Christo Mountains. Casual dress; cocktails. **Parking:** on-site. **Cards:** AX, DC, DS, MC, VI.

LONGEVITY CAFE' & EMPORIUM

Vegetarian

Lunch: $4-$7   **Dinner:** $4-$7   **Phone:** 505/986-0403   (25)

Location: Center; in Plaza Mercado. 112 W San Francisco St 87501. **Hours:** 11 am-midnight, Sun-7 pm. **Closed:** 11/23, 12/25. **Reservations:** not accepted. **Features:** Patrons can rejuvenate their body, mind and spirit at the distinctive vegetarian cafe. If the nutritious raw and vegetarian food does not entice, the specialty tea, "elixir" beverages and organic pies certainly will. Casual dress. **Parking:** street. **Cards:** AX, MC, VI.

(See map and index starting on p. 568)

LOS MAYAS   **Dinner:** $14-$19   **Phone:** 505/986-9930   [16]
▼▼▼   **Location:** Jct Guadalupe and Water St; center. 409 W Water St 87501. **Hours:** 5 pm-10 pm.
Mexican   **Reservations:** accepted. **Features:** Diners can take a break from the typical Mexican-American fare and try seafood preparations at the distinctive Mexican restaurant. The adventurous might taste nopal asado, a grilled cactus and vegetables dish, to start the meal. Ordering flan, which is made in house and one of the best found anywhere, is a must for dessert. Dressy casual; wine only. **Parking:** street. **Cards:** AX, DS, MC, VI.

MARIA'S NEW MEXICAN KITCHEN   **Lunch:** $8-$15   **Dinner:** $9-$20   **Phone:** 505/983-7929   [50]
▼▼▼ ▼   **Location:** Just e of jct St. Francis Dr. 555 W Cordova Rd 87501. **Hours:** 11 am-4 & 5-10 pm, Sun noon-10 pm.
Mexican   Closed: 11/23, 12/25. **Reservations:** accepted. **Features:** A local favorite, this kitchen has been cooking and serving traditional Mexican fare for generations; a casual atmosphere and friendly service make it a great place to kick back, have a margarita and enjoy some spicy chile. Casual dress; cocktails. **Parking:** on-site. **Cards:** AX, DC, DS, MC, VI.

O'KEEFFE CAFE   *Menu on aaa.com*   **Lunch:** $8-$21   **Dinner:** $16-$25   **Phone:** 505/946-1065   [9]
(AAA)   **Location:** Just w of The Plaza at Sandoval St; next to Georgia O'Keeffe Museum. 217 Johnson St 87501. **Hours:** 11
▼▼▼ ▼   am-3 & 5:30-10 pm. Closed: 1/1, 11/23, 12/25. **Reservations:** accepted. **Features:** The quaint cafe is ideal
American   for diners seeking a distinctive dining experience. Chefs create dishes so artistic that patrons can't help but "ooh" and "ahh" at everything that exits the kitchen. The extensive wine list all but guarantees a perfect glass or bottle for any meal. The attractive decor enhances the overall experience, and guests may be tempted to sit in the comfortable chairs for hours. Dressy casual; beer & wine only. **Parking:** street.
Cards: AX, DS, MC, VI.

THE OLD HOUSE   **Dinner:** $20-$32   **Phone:** 505/988-4455   [13]
(AAA)   **Location:** Just w of The Plaza at Sandoval St; in Eldorado Hotel. 309 W San Francisco St 87501. **Hours:** 5:30 pm-10
pm. **Reservations:** suggested. **Features:** This dining gem is just a short walk from many wonderful shops
▼▼▼ ▼   in historic downtown Santa Fe. A cozy and intimate dining spot with its' Southwestern flair offers a very
Southwestern   welcoming and professional waitstaff. The menu is ever-changing with a variety of dishes created by their reknown on-site chef. Dressy casual; cocktails. **Parking:** valet. **Cards:** AX, CB, DC, DS, MC, VI.
(See color ad p 576)   ⅄

ORE HOUSE ON THE PLAZA   **Lunch:** $6-$13   **Dinner:** $13-$27   **Phone:** 505/983-8687   [22]
▼▼▼ ▼▼▼   **Location:** On The Plaza, at San Francisco St. 50 Lincoln Ave 87501. **Hours:** 11:30 am-10 pm, Sun from noon.
Closed: 11/23, 12/25. **Reservations:** suggested, for dinner. **Features:** You'll find this jewel set on the
Southwestern   second floor directly on The Plaza. Enjoy indoor dining or the sights of The Plaza green from the balcony which overlooks the many shops and sights of old Santa Fe. The Southwestern themed atmosphere is relaxing and service staff is professional. The menu offers many favorites such as the rack of lamb, grilled shrimp, chimayo chile chicken, blackened prime rib or how about a classic burger. The restaurant specializes in over 100 varieties of margaritas. Casual dress; cocktails; entertainment. **Parking:** street. **Cards:** AX, MC, VI.   ⅄

OSAKA BISTRO SUSHI & SAKE BAR   **Lunch:** $10-$20   **Dinner:** $10-$20   **Phone:** 505/471-6691   [61]
▼▼▼ ▼▼▼   **Location:** Corner of Cerrillos Rd and Zafarano St. 3501 A Zafarano Dr 87501. **Hours:** noon-2 & 4:30-10 pm, Sun
4:30 pm-9 pm, Mon 4:30 pm-10 pm. Closed: 1/1, 12/25. **Reservations:** accepted. **Features:** The trendy
Sushi   bistro is a showcase for the freshest sushi outside of Japan. Distinctive bar lights and custom tables help create a memorable ambience. Casual dress; beer & wine only. **Parking:** on-site. **Cards:** AX, DS, MC, VI.   ⅄

OSTERIA D'ASSISI   *Menu on aaa.com*   **Lunch:** $10-$12   **Dinner:** $27-$34   **Phone:** 505/986-5858   [4]
(AAA)   **Location:** 1 blk n of The Plaza. 58 S Federal Place 87501. **Hours:** 11 am-3 & 5-10 pm. Closed: 12/25.
Reservations: suggested. **Features:** A convenient, busy restaurant near both the business and cultural
▼▼▼ ▼▼▼   centers of the city of Santa Fe. Frequented by tourists, business people and the professionals who work in
Northern   the nearby Federal Courthouse. All enjoy the comfortable surroundings and the delicious Northern Italian
Italian   cuisine offered here. Casual dress; cocktails. **Parking:** street. **Cards:** AX, DC, DS, MC, VI.   ⅄

THE PANTRY   **Lunch:** $5-$8   **Dinner:** $6-$13   **Phone:** 505/986-0022   [53]
▼▼▼ ▼▼▼   **Location:** I-25, exit 278, 6 mi nw. 1820 Cerrillos 87505. **Hours:** 6:30 am-9 pm, Sun from 7 am. Closed: 11/23,
Southwest   12/25. **Reservations:** not accepted. **Features:** Genuine New Mexican cuisine draws locals and tourists to
American   this laid-back restaurant. The menu consists of traditional favorites: burritos, enchiladas, green chile stew and much more. Casual dress; beer & wine only. **Parking:** on-site. **Cards:** DS, MC, VI.

PAUL'S RESTAURANT OF SANTA FE   **Lunch:** $7-$10   **Dinner:** $15-$25   **Phone:** 505/982-8738   [10]
▼▼▼ ▼▼▼   **Location:** Just n of The Plaza; between Lincoln Ave and Washington St. 72 W Marcy St 87501. **Hours:** 11:30 am-2 &
5:30-9 pm. Closed: 12/25. **Reservations:** suggested, for dinner. **Features:** Paul's Restaurant is a simple,
Nouvelle American   cheerful bistro with an imaginative cuisine that reflects a variety of influences, including French Provincial and Southwestern tastes. Paul's will appeal to those looking for a great meal in a relaxed environment. Casual dress; beer & wine only. **Parking:** street. **Cards:** AX, DC, DS, MC, VI.

THE PINK ADOBE   **Lunch:** $6-$9   **Dinner:** $12-$28   **Phone:** 505/983-7712   [41]
▼▼▼ ▼▼▼   **Location:** 2 blks s of The Plaza. 406 Old Santa Fe Tr 87501. **Hours:** 11:30 am-2 & 5:30-9:30 pm. Closed major
holidays. **Reservations:** suggested. **Features:** Established in 1944 and known for its "pink" adobe look, this
Continental   restaurant is located in what was previously an approximately 350-year-old home. It is located just a short
walk from the Plaza and its many popular shops. The restaurant is popular with locals and visitors alike and frequented by famous actors and politicians. Several intimate dining rooms, each with a fireplace enhances your dining experience. Casual dress; cocktails; entertainment. **Parking:** street. **Cards:** AX, CB, DC, DS, MC, VI.   ⅄

(See map and index starting on p. 568)

PINON GRILL   Dinner: $19-$40   Phone: 505/986-6400   [17]
American
Location: Just sw of The Plaza; between San Francisco and W Alameda sts; in Hilton of Santa Fe. 100 Sandoval St 87505. **Hours:** 5 pm-10 pm; to 9 pm in winter. **Reservations:** suggested. **Features:** In the Hilton Inn on the site of a 300-year-old hacienda, the restaurant is only a few blocks from Historic Plaza. Mesquite, sassafras and pecan hardwoods are used to prepare grilled dishes, including preparations of beef, pork, seafood and game. The duck chimichanga appetizer with mango salsa is a must. Casual dress; cocktails. **Parking:** on-site. **Cards:** AX, CB, DC, DS, JC, MC, VI.

PLAZA RESTAURANT   Lunch: $6-$12   Dinner: $8-$12   Phone: 505/982-1664   [21]
American
Location: West side of The Plaza. 54 Lincoln Ave 87501. **Hours:** 7 am-10 pm. **Closed:** 11/23, 12/25. **Features:** You'll receive a good basic meal for not very much money at the Plaza, which has provided continuous service since 1918. It's a cozy diner with a variety of classic favorites. They also have New Mexican specialties and a few Greek dishes. Casual dress; beer & wine only. **Parking:** street. **Cards:** AX, DS, MC, VI. **Historic**

PRANZO ITALIAN GRILL   Lunch: $8-$11   Dinner: $8-$20   Phone: 505/984-2645   [31]
Italian
Location: 3 blks s of The Plaza; in Sanbusco Center. 540 Montezuma St 87501. **Hours:** 11:30 am-3 & 5-10 pm, Fri & Sat-midnight. **Closed:** 11/23, 12/25. **Reservations:** accepted. **Features:** Located in a renovated warehouse and dressed in a contemporary art deco theme, Pranzo is popular with locals who recommend its grilled favorites of chicken, steak and seafood dishes. The pasta and thin-crust pizza are also a hit. Casual dress; cocktails. **Parking:** on-site. **Cards:** AX, DS, MC, VI.

RIO CHAMA STEAKHOUSE   Lunch: $8-$14   Dinner: $14-$35   Phone: 505/955-0765   [43]
Steak & Seafood
Location: 2 blks s of The Plaza; center. 414 Old Santa Fe Tr 87501. **Hours:** 11 am-3 & 5-10 pm. **Closed:** 11/23, 12/25. **Reservations:** suggested. **Features:** In the heart of the downtown historic district and only a few blocks from the Plaza, the restaurant presents a menu of prime and choice dry-aged steaks, prime rib, chops and seafood. The atmosphere is casual yet dignified in the intimate dining rooms. Casual dress; cocktails. **Parking:** on-site. **Cards:** AX, DC, DS, MC, VI.

RISTRA   Dinner: $18-$34   Phone: 505/982-8608   [32]
Regional Continental
Location: Just w of Guadalupe Rd. 548 Agua Fria St 87501. **Hours:** 6 pm-9:30 pm, Fri & Sat from 5:30 pm; from 5:30 pm 6/1-8/31. **Reservations:** suggested. **Features:** A short distance from the historic Guadalupe Road, this cozy house boasts friendly, accomplished staff members who expertly serve delectable dishes. Appetizers range from black Mediterranean mussels with chipotle and mint to fire-roasted poblano stuffed with brandade of salt cod. Seasonally changing entrees might include such good choices as seared Alaskan halibut, elk tenderloin or duck leg confit. Patio dining under tall evergreens is refreshing. Casual dress; cocktails. **Parking:** on-site. **Cards:** AX, MC, VI.

SANTACAFE   *Menu on aaa.com*   Lunch: $8-$10   Dinner: $17-$27   Phone: 505/984-1788   [5]
Nouvelle American
Location: Just ne of The Plaza; between Marcy St and Paseo de Peralta. 231 Washington Ave 87501. **Hours:** 11:30 am-2 & 6-close. **Reservations:** suggested. **Features:** This trendy, upscale, fine dining restaurant near The Plaza in Santa Fe, caters to affluent tourist and local business/professional clientele. Crisp linens, knowledgeable waitstaff, fine wines and American Nouvelle cuisine are the order of the day here. A refined ambience is blended with classic Santa Fe architecture inside a grand old hacienda that was constructed in 1854. Casual dress; cocktails. **Parking:** on-site. **Cards:** AX, MC, VI. **Historic**

SAVEUR   Lunch: $6-$12   Phone: 505/989-4200   [39]
French
Location: Jct Galisteo, Cerrillos and Montezuma St; downtown. 204 Montezuma St 87501. **Hours:** 8 am-3:45 pm. Closed major holidays; also Sat & Sun. **Reservations:** accepted. **Features:** The casual restaurant is set up much like a traditional cafeteria, but the food is healthier and of considerably higher quality. Diners can choose from an impressive salad bar, gourmet sandwiches and even fresh French entrees. Casual dress. **Parking:** on-site. **Cards:** AX, CB, DC, DS, MC, VI.

THE SHED   Lunch: $5-$10   Dinner: $9-$20   Phone: 505/982-9030   [20]
Regional American
Location: Just e of The Plaza. 113 1/2 E Palace 87501. **Hours:** 11 am-2:30 & 5:30-9 pm. **Closed:** 1/1, 11/23, 12/25; also Sun. **Reservations:** accepted, for dinner. **Features:** Red and green chili enchiladas and mocha cake are the specialties at The Shed, located in a 17th-century fortified hacienda. Its casual dining features northern New Mexican dishes. It has been owned/operated by three generations of the Carswell family. Casual dress; cocktails. **Parking:** street. **Cards:** AX, DC, DS, MC, VI. **Historic**

SHOHKO CAFE   Lunch: $5-$18   Dinner: $10-$26   Phone: 505/982-9708   [8]
Japanese
Location: Just e of jct W San Francisco St. 321 Johnson St 87501. **Hours:** 11:30 am-2 & 5:30-close, Fri & Sat from 5:30 pm. **Closed:** Sun. **Reservations:** accepted. **Features:** Diners are in for a relaxing meal with friendly service in a quaint adobe-style setting. Established in 1976, the restaurant is known for its fresh sushi, sashimi, bento box specials, rice bowls and noodle dishes. Ingredients such as eel, soft-shell crab, tuna, mackerel, salmon, shrimp, yellowtail and albacore are used to create the various sushi rolls. Casual dress; beer & wine only. **Parking:** on-site. **Cards:** AX, DS, MC, VI.

STEAKSMITH AT EL GANCHO   Dinner: $9-$30   Phone: 505/988-3333   [64]
Steak & Seafood
Location: I-25, exit 284 (Old Pecos Tr), 1 mi se on Frontage Rd (Old Las Vegas Hwy). 104B Old Las Vegas Hwy 87501. **Hours:** 5 pm-9:30 pm. Closed major holidays. **Reservations:** suggested. **Features:** A locally popular steak house, on the outskirts of Santa Fe, the Steaksmith lives up to its name, preparing fine beef in a way that has pleased steak lovers for many years. Tender, juicy cuts are grilled to perfection, complimented by homemade bread, tasty salads and the traditional dishes that complete the picture of a real meal for real people. Casual dress; cocktails. **Parking:** on-site. **Cards:** AX, CB, DC, DS, MC, VI.

(See map and index starting on p. 568)

SWIG
Asian

Dinner: $6-$18   Phone: 505/995-0400 15

Location: Just w of The Plaza at Grant. 135 W Palace Ave, Level 3 87501. **Hours:** 5 pm-2 am. Closed: 11/23, 12/25; also Sun & Mon. **Reservations:** not accepted. **Features:** A haven of hipness in this casual Southwestern city, the outrageous, contemporary restaurant must be experienced at least once. The Bamboo room is the perfect place to enjoy an elegant meal. The menu consists of artistically presented Asian tapas, a highly sophisticated take on "bar food." For a pre- or post-dinner drink, head to the Blue (non-smoking) or Orange (smoking) room. Dressy casual; cocktails. **Parking:** street. **Cards:** AX, JC, MC.

TOMASITA'S SANTA FE STATION
Regional American

Lunch: $7-$12   Dinner: $8-$14   Phone: 505/983-5721 40

Location: From The Plaza, just w on Alameda St, then just s. 500 S Guadalupe St 87501. **Hours:** 11 am-10 pm. Closed: 1/1, 11/23, 12/25; also Sun. **Reservations:** not accepted. **Features:** A restored train station is the setting for this busy, bustling restaurant, which serves large portions of traditional New Mexican cuisine including its specialty burritos, blue corn enchiladas and rellenos. Locals and visitors alike dine here. Casual dress; cocktails. **Parking:** on-site. **Cards:** AX, DS, MC, VI.

TORTILLA FLATS
Southwestern

Lunch: $5-$10   Dinner: $6-$11   Phone: 505/471-8685 57

Location: I-25, exit 278B, 3.5 mi ne. 3139 Cerrillos Rd 87505. **Hours:** 7 am-9 pm, Fri & Sat-10 pm; to 10 pm 5/31-9/4. Closed: 11/23, 12/25. **Features:** The Southwestern theme here is inviting with an adobe style look to the interior. The waitstaff is casual and welcoming offering friendly service. The menu specializes in New Mexican themed treats such as chili rellenos, enchiladas, carne adovada and quesadillas. Try the chicken enchilada served on a blue corn shell and even the mild sauce used will set your taste buds dancing. Casual dress; cocktails. **Parking:** on-site. **Cards:** DS, MC, VI.

TULIPS
Continental

Dinner: $22-$31   Phone: 505/989-7340 6

Location: Jct McKenzie St. 222 N Guadalupe St 87501. **Hours:** 6 pm-10 pm. Closed: Sun & Mon. **Features:** The fine-dining experience is cozy at the chef-owner-run restaurant. A husband-and-wife team does nothing short of pampering guests while preparing such fabulous a la minute meals as New Zealand elk tenderloin prepared with three-cheese risotto, green beans, roasted carrots and red chile raspberry sauce. It's a must try. Dressy casual; cocktails. **Parking:** on-site. **Cards:** MC, VI.

UPPER CRUST PIZZA
American

Lunch: $5-$12   Dinner: $7-$25   Phone: 505/982-0000 38

Location: 0.5 mi s of The Plaza at De Vargas. 329 Old Santa Fe Tr 87501. **Hours:** 11 am-11 pm; to 10 pm in winter. Closed: 11/23, 12/25. **Reservations:** not accepted. **Features:** A short distance from The Plaza, this eatery provides fresh, made-to-order meals for light appetites or lean budgets. Try the Build-A-Pizza, calzones or sandwiches with your choice of bread. Porch, back patio or inside dining available. Casual dress; beer & wine only. **Parking:** on-site. **Cards:** DS, MC, VI.

VANESSIE
American

Dinner: $16-$30   Phone: 505/982-9966 12

Location: Just w of Guadalupe St; parking entrance just w on Water St. 434 W San Francisco 87501. **Hours:** 5:30 pm-9:30 pm. Closed: 11/23, 12/25. **Reservations:** suggested. **Features:** Serving the best of beef and lamb dishes for many years, the restaurant upholds the tradition of attentive service, pleasing flavors and hearty portions. Casual dress; cocktails; entertainment. **Parking:** on-site. **Cards:** AX, DS, MC, VI.

WHOLE BODY CAFE
Deli/Subs
Sandwiches

Lunch: $4-$8   Dinner: $4-$8   Phone: 505/986-0362 51

Location: I-25, exit 282, 2.3 mi n on St. Francis Dr, just w on Cordova; in The Source Designer's Marketplace. 333 Cordova Rd 87505. **Hours:** 7 am-9 pm. Closed: 11/23, 12/25. **Reservations:** accepted. **Features:** The eatery focuses on organic and healthy food choices. Vegetarian and raw foods dominate, but turkey and tuna sandwiches also are available. Visitors also enjoy specialty coffees, fruit smoothies, fresh juices and elixirs. Casual dress. **Parking:** on-site. **Cards:** DS, MC, VI.

———— *The following restaurants have not been evaluated by AAA* ————
but are listed for your information only.

BACK ROAD PIZZA
fyi

Phone: 505/955-9055

Not evaluated. **Location:** From jct St. Michael's and Cerrillos, just n on Cerrillos, then just e; in Second Stree Studios complex. 1807 2nd St 87505. **Features:** Guests can experience the creativity of Santa Fe by dining in the bohemian pizza joint, which lines its walls with paintings by local artists.

BUMBLE BEE'S BAJA GRILL
fyi

Phone: 505/988-3278

Not evaluated. **Location:** Jct Cerrillos Rd and Vegas Verdes; downtown. 3701 Cerrillos Rd. **Features:** A quick alternative to fast food, the restaurant serves freshly prepared tacos, burritos and other Mexican fare both for drive-through guests and those dining in.

YIN YANG
fyi

Phone: 505/986-9279

Not evaluated. **Location:** Just sw of the Plaza, near jct of Montezuma and Galisteo/Cerrillos; in the Design Center. 418 Cerrillos Rd 87501. **Features:** The Chinese restaurant specializes in Hunan- and Peking-style comfort food, including many seafood, beef, chicken and vegetarian options.

SANTA ROSA pop. 2,744

———— **WHERE TO STAY** ————

BEST WESTERN ADOBE INN   *Book at aaa.com*   Phone: (505)472-3446

Small-scale Hotel

5/1-9/30	1P: $56-$65	2P: $69-$79	XP: $5	F18
10/1-1/31	1P: $56-$60	2P: $69-$79	XP: $5	F18
2/1-4/30	1P: $56-$60	2P: $56-$60	XP: $5	F18

Location: I-40, exit 275. 1501 Historic Route 66 88435. **Fax:** 505/472-5759. **Facility:** 56 one-bedroom standard units. 1-2 stories (no elevator), exterior corridors. **Parking:** on-site. **Terms:** 3 day cancellation notice, [CP] meal plan available, small pets only. **Amenities:** high-speed Internet, irons, hair dryers. **Pool(s):** heated outdoor. **Business Services:** fax (fee). **Cards:** AX, CB, DC, DS, JC, MC, VI. **Special Amenities:** free continental breakfast and free local telephone calls.

SOME UNITS

BEST WESTERN SANTA ROSA INN
Book at aaa.com
Phone: 505/472-5877

(AAA) (SAVE)

Motel

11/1-1/31	1P: $60-$70	2P: $67-$82	XP: $8	F12
3/1-10/31	1P: $60-$69	2P: $67-$80	XP: $8	F12
2/1-2/28	1P: $60-$69	2P: $67-$75	XP: $8	F12

Location: I-40, exit 277, 0.5 mi w. 3022 Historic Route 66 88435 (PO Box 501). Fax: 505/472-5880. **Facility:** 44 one-bedroom standard units. 1 story, exterior corridors. **Parking:** on-site. **Terms:** small pets only. **Amenities:** high-speed Internet, irons, hair dryers. **Pool(s):** heated outdoor. **Guest Services:** coin laundry. **Business Services:** PC, fax (fee). **Cards:** AX, CB, DC, DS, JC, MC, VI. **Special Amenities:** free continental breakfast and free local telephone calls.

SOME UNITS

CHECK INN EXPRESS
Phone: 505/472-5412

(AAA) (SAVE)

Small-scale Hotel

11/1-1/31	1P: $67-$74	2P: $77-$80	XP: $10
7/1-10/31	1P: $67-$70	2P: $75-$80	XP: $10
3/2-6/30	1P: $65-$70	2P: $70-$80	XP: $10
2/1-3/1	1P: $57-$67	2P: $67-$77	XP: $10

Location: I-40, exit 277, 0.3 mi w. 3300 Historic Route 66 88435 (PO Box 304). Fax: 505/472-5556. **Facility:** 78 one-bedroom standard units. 2 stories (no elevator), interior corridors. **Parking:** on-site. **Terms:** pets (in smoking units). **Amenities:** irons, hair dryers. **Pool(s):** heated indoor. **Leisure Activities:** whirlpool. **Guest Services:** coin laundry. **Business Services:** meeting rooms, fax. **Cards:** AX, CB, DC, DS, JC, MC, VI. **Special Amenities:** free continental breakfast and free local telephone calls.

SOME UNITS

COMFORT INN
Book at aaa.com
Phone: (505)472-5570

(AAA) (SAVE)

Small-scale Hotel

4/1-8/1	1P: $79-$89	2P: $84-$94	XP: $5	F17
8/2-10/1	1P: $62-$72	2P: $67-$77	XP: $5	F17
2/1-3/31 & 10/2-1/31	1P: $59-$69	2P: $64-$74	XP: $5	F17

Location: I-40, exit 277, 0.3 mi w. 3343 Historic Route 66 88435. Fax: 505/472-5575. **Facility:** 45 one-bedroom standard units. 2 stories (no elevator), exterior corridors. **Parking:** on-site. **Terms:** 15 day cancellation notice, pets ($10-$15 fee). **Amenities:** high-speed Internet, irons, hair dryers. **Pool(s):** heated indoor. **Leisure Activities:** whirlpool. **Guest Services:** coin laundry. **Business Services:** fax. **Cards:** AX, DC, DS, MC, VI. **Special Amenities:** free expanded continental breakfast and free room upgrade (subject to availability with advance reservations).

SOME UNITS

FEE

DAYS INN OF SANTA ROSA
Book at aaa.com
Phone: (505)472-5985

(AAA) (SAVE)

Small-scale Hotel

3/1-10/31	1P: $60-$90	2P: $60-$90	XP: $5	F12
2/1-2/28 & 11/1-1/31	1P: $55-$75	2P: $55-$85	XP: $5	F12

Location: I-40, exit 275. 1830 Historic Route 66 88435. Fax: 505/472-5989. **Facility:** 50 one-bedroom standard units. 2 stories (no elevator), exterior corridors. **Parking:** on-site. **Terms:** [ECP] meal plan available, pets ($5 fee). **Amenities:** high-speed Internet, irons, hair dryers. **Guest Services:** coin laundry, airport transportation-Santa Rosa Municipal Airport. **Business Services:** PC, fax (fee). **Cards:** AX, DS, MC, VI. **Special Amenities:** free expanded continental breakfast and free newspaper.

SOME UNITS

FEE

HOLIDAY INN EXPRESS
Book at aaa.com
Phone: (505)472-5411

(AAA) (SAVE)

Small-scale Hotel

2/1-1/12	1P: $89	2P: $99	XP: $10	F18
1/13-1/31	1P: $79	2P: $89	XP: $10	F18

Location: I-40, exit 277, 0.4 mi w. 3202 Will Rogers Dr 88435. Fax: 505/472-3537. **Facility:** 69 one-bedroom standard units. 3 stories, interior corridors. **Bath:** combo or shower only. **Parking:** on-site. **Amenities:** high-speed Internet, voice mail, irons, hair dryers. **Guest Services:** coin laundry. **Business Services:** business center. **Cards:** AX, CB, DC, DS, JC, MC, VI. **Special Amenities:** free expanded continental breakfast and free local telephone calls.

LA QUINTA INN-SANTA ROSA
Book at aaa.com
Phone: 505/472-4800

(AAA) (SAVE)

Small-scale Hotel

All Year	1P: $60-$64	2P: $73-$77	XP: $10	F17

Location: I-40, exit 275, just e. 1701 Historic Route 66 88435. Fax: 505/472-4809. **Facility:** 60 one-bedroom standard units. 2 stories (no elevator), interior corridors. **Bath:** combo or shower only. **Parking:** on-site. **Terms:** [ECP] meal plan available, small pets only. **Amenities:** video library (fee), high-speed Internet, dual phone lines, voice mail, safes, irons, hair dryers. **Pool(s):** small heated indoor. **Leisure Activities:** whirlpool. **Guest Services:** coin laundry. **Business Services:** meeting rooms, PC, fax (fee). **Cards:** AX, CB, DC, DS, MC, VI. **Special Amenities:** free expanded continental breakfast and free local telephone calls.

SOME UNITS

FEE

MOTEL 6 - 273
Book at aaa.com
Phone: 505/472-3045

Motel

5/26-9/4	1P: $42-$52	2P: $48-$58	XP: $3	F17
2/1-5/25 & 9/5-1/31	1P: $37-$47	2P: $43-$53	XP: $3	F17

Location: I-40, exit 277, 0.3 mi w. 3400 Historic Route 66 88435. Fax: 505/472-5923. **Facility:** 89 one-bedroom standard units. 2 stories (no elevator), exterior corridors. **Bath:** shower only. **Parking:** on-site. **Terms:** small pets only. **Pool(s):** small outdoor. **Guest Services:** coin laundry. **Business Services:** fax (fee). **Cards:** AX, CB, DC, DS, MC, VI.

SOME UNITS

SUPER 8 MOTEL-SANTA ROSA
Book at aaa.com
Phone: 505/472-5388

Motel

Property failed to provide current rates
Location: I-40, exit 275, just w. 1201 Historic Route 66 88435. Fax: 505/472-5388. **Facility:** 88 one-bedroom standard units. 2 stories (no elevator), interior corridors. **Bath:** combo or shower only. **Parking:** on-site. **Terms:** small pets only ($10 fee). **Amenities:** *Some:* irons, hair dryers. **Guest Services:** coin laundry. **Business Services:** *Fee:* PC, fax.

SOME UNITS

FEE

TRAVELODGE

(AAA) [SAVE]

Small-scale Hotel

Book at aaa.com

3/1-10/31	1P: $50-$65	2P: $50-$75	XP: $5 F12
2/1-2/28 & 11/1-1/31	1P: $45-$55	2P: $45-$75	XP: $5 F12

Phone: (505)472-3494

Location: I-40, exit 275, just n. 1819 Will Rogers Dr 88435. **Fax:** 505/472-3294. **Facility:** 36 one-bedroom standard units. 1 story, exterior corridors. **Parking:** on-site. **Terms:** [CP] meal plan available, small pets only (in selected units). **Amenities:** high-speed Internet, hair dryers. *Some:* irons. **Pool(s):** small outdoor. **Guest Services:** coin laundry. **Cards:** AX, DS, MC, VI. **Special Amenities:** free continental breakfast and free local telephone calls.

SOME UNITS

[S/D] [🐕] [♨] [🏊] [📷] [DATA PORT] [💻] / [✕] [🔌] [📺] /

——— WHERE TO DINE ———

SILVER MOON RESTAURANT

(AAA)

American

Lunch: $7-$17   **Dinner:** $7-$17   **Phone:** 505/472-3162

Location: I-40, exit 277, just n. 3525 Historic Route 66 88435. **Hours:** 6 am-9:30 pm. Closed: 11/23, 12/25. **Reservations:** accepted. **Features:** Established in 1959, the restaurant fits into the Route 66 nostalgia. The relaxed atmosphere is suitable for families and travelers. The menu blends a nice variety of both American and traditional Mexican fare. Casual dress. **Parking:** on-site. **Cards:** MC, VI.

[�]

SANTA TERESA

——— WHERE TO DINE ———

BILLY CREWS

Southwest American

Lunch: $6-$10   **Dinner:** $20-$30   **Phone:** 505/589-2071

Location: Jct SR 273 (McNutt Rd) and SR 184 (Country Club Dr), just e. 1200 Country Club Rd 88008. **Hours:** 11:30 am-3 & 5:30-10 pm, Fri & Sat-11 pm, Sun noon-midnight, Mon 11:30 am-3 pm. Closed: 1/1, 11/23, 12/25. **Features:** Semiformal in the evenings, the setting is less formal during lunch, which is served in the lounge. Great, generously sized steaks are cooked to order. Casual dress; cocktails. **Parking:** on-site. **Cards:** AX, DC, DS, MC, VI.

[🍸] [🍴] [◻]

SILVER CITY pop. 10,545

——— WHERE TO STAY ———

BEAR MOUNTAIN LODGE

Bed & Breakfast

All Year [BP]	1P: $105-$190	2P: $115-$200	XP: $15

Phone: 505-538-2538

Location: US 180, n on Alabama St to Cottage Sans Rd, 3 mi n. 2251 Cottage San Rd 88062 (PO Box 1163). **Fax:** 505/534-1827. **Facility:** The lodge offers spacious rooms and public areas as well as upscale decor and a secluded rural setting. Designated smoking area. 11 one-bedroom standard units, some with kitchens and/or whirlpools. 2 stories (no elevator), interior corridors. *Bath:* combo or shower only. **Parking:** on-site. **Terms:** 2 night minimum stay, 14 day cancellation notice, [AP] meal plan available, package plans. **Amenities:** hair dryers. **Leisure Activities:** recreation programs, bicycles, hiking trails. **Guest Services:** gift shop. **Cards:** AX, MC, VI.

SOME UNITS

[♿] [✕] [✕] [DATA PORT] / [🍴] [🔌] /

COMFORT INN

Small-scale Hotel

Book at aaa.com

5/15-10/15	1P: $50-$150	2P: $55-$175	XP: $5 F17
2/1-5/14 & 10/16-1/31	1P: $45-$125	2P: $50-$150	XP: $5 F17

Phone: (505)534-1883

Location: 1.5 mi e on US 180 and SR 90. 1060 E Hwy 180 88061. **Fax:** 505/534-0778. **Facility:** 52 one-bedroom standard units, some with whirlpools. 2 stories (no elevator), interior corridors. **Parking:** on-site. **Terms:** [ECP] meal plan available, pets ($10 fee). **Amenities:** high-speed Internet, irons, hair dryers. **Pool(s):** heated indoor. **Leisure Activities:** whirlpool. **Guest Services:** valet and coin laundry. **Business Services:** meeting rooms, fax. **Cards:** AX, CB, DC, DS, JC, MC, VI. *(See color ad below)*

SOME UNITS

[ASK] [S/D] [🐕] [♨] [🏊] [📷] [DATA PORT] [💻] / [✕] [🔌] [📺] /
FEE

ECONO LODGE SILVER CITY   *Book at aaa.com*   Phone: (505)534-1111

(AAA) (SAVE)
| 5/1-9/30 [ECP] | 1P: $40-$89 | 2P: $45-$99 | XP: $7 | F17 |
| 2/1-4/30 & 10/1-1/31 [ECP] | 1P: $40-$69 | 2P: $45-$79 | XP: $7 | F17 |

Location: 1.5 mi ne on US 180 and SR 90. 1120 Hwy 180 E 88061. **Fax:** 505/534-2222. **Facility:** 62 one-bedroom
standard units. 3 stories, interior corridors. *Bath:* combo or shower only. **Parking:** on-site. **Terms:** pets ($25
Small-scale Hotel   deposit, $7 extra charge, cash customers). **Amenities:** high-speed Internet, safes, hair dryers. **Pool(s):**
heated indoor. **Leisure Activities:** whirlpool, exercise room. **Guest Services:** valet and coin laundry.
Business Services: meeting rooms, PC, fax. **Cards:** AX, DC, DS, MC, VI. **Special Amenities:** free expanded continental
breakfast and free local telephone calls.

SOME UNITS

HOLIDAY INN EXPRESS   *Book at aaa.com*   Phone: (505)538-2525

(AAA) (SAVE)
| 4/23-1/31 [ECP] | 1P: $99-$119 |
| 2/1-4/22 [ECP] | 1P: $89-$109 |

Location: 3 mi ne on US 180 and SR 90. 1103 Superior St 88061. **Fax:** 505/538-2525. **Facility:** 60 one-bedroom
standard units, some with whirlpools. 3 stories, interior corridors. *Bath:* combo or shower only. **Parking:** on-
Small-scale Hotel   site. **Terms:** small pets only (in limited units). **Amenities:** high-speed Internet, dual phone lines, voice mail,
irons, hair dryers. **Leisure Activities:** whirlpool, exercise room. **Guest Services:** valet and coin laundry.
Business Services: meeting rooms, business center. **Cards:** AX, CB, DC, DS, MC, VI. **Special Amenities:** free expanded
continental breakfast and free local telephone calls.

SOME UNITS

MOTEL 6   Phone: 505-538-3711

(fyi)   Property failed to provide current rates
Under major renovation, scheduled to be completed August 2005. **Last rated:** Location: 3 mi ne on jct
Small-scale Hotel   US 180 and SR 90. 3420 Hwy 180 E 88061. **Fax:** 505/538-3711. **Facility:** 76 one-bedroom standard units. 2
stories (no elevator), exterior corridors. **Parking:** on-site. **Terms:** small pets only. **Guest Services:** coin
laundry. **Business Services:** meeting rooms.

SOME UNITS

SUPER 8 MOTEL   *Book at aaa.com*   Phone: (505)388-1983

| 5/15-10/15 | 1P: $38-$98 | 2P: $48-$100 | XP: $5 | F17 |
| 2/1-5/14 & 10/16-1/31 | 1P: $28-$78 | 2P: $34-$88 | XP: $5 | F17 |

Small-scale Hotel   **Location:** 1.5 mi ne on US 180 and SR 90. 1040 E Hwy 180 88061. **Fax:** 505/388-1983. **Facility:** 68 one-bedroom
standard units. 2 stories (no elevator), interior corridors. **Parking:** on-site. **Terms:** [CP] meal plan available,
pets ($10 fee). **Amenities:** video library (fee). **Cards:** AX, CB, DC, DS, JC, MC, VI.

SOME UNITS

——— WHERE TO DINE ———

DIANE'S RESTAURANT AND BAKERY   **Lunch:** $8-$10   **Dinner:** $14-$22   Phone: 505-538-8722

Location: Center; in historic downtown. 510 N Bullard St 88061. **Hours:** 11 am-2 & 5:30-9 pm; Saturday &
Sunday brunch 9 am-2 pm. **Closed:** 1/1, 12/25; also Mon. **Reservations:** accepted. **Features:** What looks
International   like an unassuming cafe and bakery turns out to be a fine-dining establishment. In the evenings, the eatery
presents an upscale menu that lists a good selection of appetizers, such as spanakopita; tasty soups; and
fish, poultry and beef entrees. Casual dress; beer & wine only. **Parking:** street. **Cards:** MC, VI.

RED BARN FAMILY STEAK HOUSE   **Lunch:** $5-$8   **Dinner:** $7-$20   Phone: 505-538-5666

Location: Center. 708 Silver Heights Blvd 88061. **Hours:** 11 am-9 pm, Fri & Sat-10 pm. **Closed:** 11/23.
Reservations: accepted. **Features:** A longtime favorite of the local folks, the traditional steak house
Steak House   features a well-stocked salad bar, generous steaks and a good selection of desserts. Also on site is a lively
lounge. Casual dress; cocktails. **Parking:** on-site. **Cards:** AX, DS, MC, VI.

SHEVEK & MI   *Menu on aaa.com*   **Lunch:** $6-$8   **Dinner:** $10-$20   Phone: 505-534-9168

(AAA)   **Location:** Center. 602 N Bullard St 88061. **Hours:** 10:30 am-9 pm, Fri-11 pm, Sat & Sun 8:30 am-9 pm. **Closed:**
1/1, 12/25. **Features:** Part of the cafe used to be a bookstore, and it still has a wall of books that guests can
browse while dining. New York-style delicatessen sandwiches are served, as are daily specials and fine
Mediterranean   baked goods. Try the chocolate brownies with pinons. Casual dress; beer & wine only. **Parking:** street.
Cards: MC, VI.

SOCORRO pop. 8,877

——— WHERE TO STAY ———

ECONO LODGE   *Book at aaa.com*   Phone: (505)835-1500

(AAA) (SAVE)
| All Year | 1P: $35-$60 | 2P: $35-$60 | XP: $5 | F |

Location: I-25, exit 150, 1 mi s. 713 California Ave 87801 (PO Box 977). **Fax:** 505/835-1500. **Facility:** 66 one-
bedroom standard units. 1-2 stories (no elevator), exterior corridors. **Parking:** on-site. **Terms:** weekly rates
available, [ECP] meal plan available, small pets only ($5 extra charge). **Amenities:** *Some:* hair dryers.
Small-scale Hotel   **Pool(s):** heated outdoor. **Leisure Activities:** sauna, whirlpool, exercise room. **Cards:** AX, CB, DC, DS, JC,
MC, VI. **Special Amenities:** free expanded continental breakfast and free local telephone calls.

SOME UNITS

HOLIDAY INN EXPRESS *Book at aaa.com* **Phone:** (505)838-0556
All Year 1P: $90
Small-scale Hotel **Location:** Center. 1100 California Ave NE 87801. Fax: 505/838-0598. **Facility:** 120 one-bedroom standard units. 2 stories (no elevator), interior/exterior corridors. **Parking:** on-site. **Terms:** cancellation fee imposed, [ECP] meal plan available, package plans, small pets only ($10 extra charge). **Amenities:** video games (fee), high-speed Internet, dual phone lines, voice mail, irons, hair dryers. **Pool(s):** heated indoor. **Leisure Activities:** whirlpools, exercise room. **Guest Services:** valet and coin laundry. **Business Services:** conference facilities, PC, fax (fee). **Cards:** AX, CB, DC, DS, JC, MC, VI.

SOME UNITS

MOTEL 6 #392 *Book at aaa.com* **Phone:** 505/835-4300
5/26-1/31 1P: $35-$45 2P: $41-$51 XP: $3 F17
2/1-5/25 1P: $33-$43 2P: $39-$49 XP: $3 F17
Small-scale Hotel **Location:** I-25, exit 147. 807 S US 85 87801. Fax: 505/835-3108. **Facility:** 95 one-bedroom standard units. 2 stories (no elevator), exterior corridors. *Bath:* shower only. **Parking:** on-site. **Pool(s):** outdoor. **Guest Services:** coin laundry. **Cards:** AX, CB, DC, DS, MC, VI.

SOME UNITS

———— **WHERE TO DINE** ————

EL CAMINO FAMILY RESTAURANT **Lunch:** $5-$8 **Dinner:** $5-$16 **Phone:** 505/835-1180
American **Location:** I-25, exit 150, 1 mi s. 707 California Ave 87801. **Hours:** 24 hours. **Features:** The family-oriented restaurant caters to hungry diners. New Mexican and American food are served in generous quantities. Casual dress; cocktails. **Parking:** on-site. **Cards:** AX, DS, MC, VI.

EL SOMBRERO **Lunch:** $5-$11 **Dinner:** $5-$11 **Phone:** 505/835-3945
Mexican **Location:** I-25, exit 150, just e. 210 Mesquite 87801. **Hours:** 11 am-9 pm. Closed major holidays; also Super Bowl Sun. **Reservations:** accepted. **Features:** Diners can order their favorite New Mexican dish at this locally popular cafe. Chili, in red or green varieties, has authority, and the enchilada plate is a treat. Casual dress; beer & wine only. **Parking:** on-site. **Cards:** AX, DC, DS, MC, VI.

RANCHER'S STEAK HOUSE **Lunch:** $7-$12 **Dinner:** $9-$18 **Phone:** 505/835-2678
Steak House **Location:** On Main St; center. 606 N California St 87801. **Hours:** 11 am-2 & 5-9 pm, Sat & Sun noon-9 pm. Closed: 12/25. **Reservations:** accepted. **Features:** Although this place is all about great steaks prepared to order, patrons also will find a lounge, a well-decorated dining room and professional service. Casual dress; cocktails. **Parking:** on-site. **Cards:** AX, CB, DC, DS, MC, VI.

SOCORRO SPRINGS BREWING COMPANY **Lunch:** $5-$10 **Dinner:** $5-$10 **Phone:** 505/838-0650
American **Location:** I-25, exit 150, center; on Main St through town. 1012 California St 87801. **Hours:** 11 am-10 pm. Closed: 11/23, 12/25. **Features:** Near the central plaza, the brew pub satisfies patrons with well-made suds in several varieties, as well as pizza and sandwiches. Also tempting are a number of good desserts. A Southwestern look complements the location. Casual dress; beer & wine only. **Parking:** on-site. **Cards:** AX, DS, MC, VI.

VAL VERDE STEAK HOUSE **Lunch:** $6-$13 **Dinner:** $10-$40 **Phone:** 505/835-3380
Regional American **Location:** I-25, exit 150, just e of California; center. 203 Manzanares Ave 87801. **Hours:** 11 am-2 & 5:30-9 pm, Fri-9:30 pm, Sat 5 pm-9:30 pm, Sun 5:30 pm-9 pm. Closed: 7/4, 12/25. **Reservations:** accepted. **Features:** In a hotel that dates back to the days of the Old West, the dining establishment serves fine beef and some spicy New Mexican cuisine. The food is well-prepared and the setting genuine. Casual dress; cocktails. **Parking:** on-site. **Cards:** AX, DC, DS, MC, VI.

———— *The following restaurant has not been evaluated by AAA* ————
but is listed for your information only.

TINA'S RESTAURANT **Phone:** 505/835-3340
[fyi] Not evaluated. **Location:** Center; on Main St through town. 1006 N California St 87801. **Features:** Original New Mexican cuisine is popular with both travelers and locals. The setting is modest.

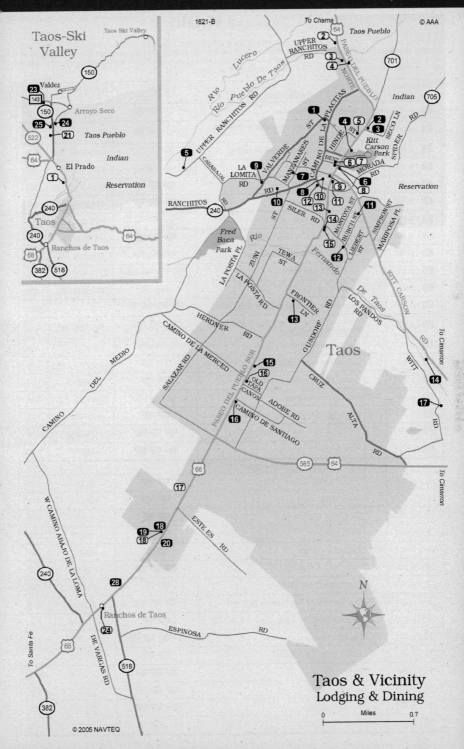

Taos-Ski Valley

Taos Ski Valley

150

Valdez
23
143
150
25   24
21   Taos Pueblo

Indian

El Prado
1

Reservation

Taos
240

240

Ranchos de Taos
64

240
68
382   518

1621-B

To Chama
84   Taos Pueblo

2
UPPER RANCHITOS RD
3
4

701

Indian
705

1

5

UPPER RANCHITOS RD

RANCHITOS
240

Fred Baca Park

Rio

LA POSTA PL

ZUNI ST

LA POSTA RD

TEWA ST

HERDNER RD

CAMINO DE LA MERCED

SALAZAR RD

PASEO DEL PUEBLO SUR

CAMINO DEL MEDIO

CAMINO

W CAMINO ABAJO DE LA LOMA

240

To Santa Fe
68

DE VARGAS RD

382

© 2005 NAVTEQ

LA LOMITA RD

VALVERDE

RD

4   5
ST

6   7

7

8

9
11

12   10
13

14

15

MONTOYA ST

BURCH ST

LIEBERT ST

12

1

9

8

10

SILER RD

Fernando

FRONTIER LN
13

GUSDORF RD

Taos

CRUZ

ALTA RD

585   64

17

18
19
18
20

ESTE ES RD

28

Ranchos de Taos
24

ESPINOSA   RD

518

CAMINO DE LA PLACITAS

HINDE ST

Camino de la

BENT

MORADA

6

SIMPSON ST

MARIPOSA PL

SECO LN

SPIDER RD

Kitt Carson Park

Reservation

De   Taos

LOS PANDOS RD

KIT CARSON

WITT

RD

14

17

To Cimarron

To Cimarron

OLD TAPA

CANON

ADOBE RD

CAMINO DE SANTIAGO

15

16

16

Taos & Vicinity
Lodging & Dining

0   Miles   0.7

N

© AAA

Taos and Vicinity

This index helps you "spot" where approved accommodations and restaurants are located on the corresponding detailed maps. Lodging rate ranges are for comparison only and show the property's high season; rates are per night, unless only weekly (W) rates are available. Restaurant rate range is for dinner, unless only lunch (L) is served. Turn to the listing page for more detailed rate information and consult display ads for special promotions.

Spotter/Map Page Number	OA	TAOS - Lodgings	Diamond Rating	Rate Range High Season	Listing Page
1 / p. 601	AAA	Orinda Bed & Breakfast	◈◈◈	$89-$130 SAVE	607
2 / p. 601	AAA	Best Western Kachina Lodge & Meetings Center	◈◈◈	$99-$155 SAVE	604
3 / p. 601	AAA	Brooks Street Inn Bed and Breakfast	◈◈◈	$119-$189 SAVE	604
4 / p. 601	AAA	Fechin Inn	◈◈◈	$127-$359 SAVE	606
5 / p. 601		Casa Europa Inn & Gallery	◈◈◈	Failed to provide	605
6 / p. 601	AAA	The Historic Taos Inn	◈◈◈	$60-$190 SAVE	606
7 / p. 601	AAA	La Posada de Taos - see color ad p 607	◈◈◈	$125-$225 SAVE	607
8 / p. 601		Hotel La Fonda De Taos	◈◈◈	$119-$699	606
9 / p. 601	AAA	Dreamcatcher Bed & Breakfast	◈◈◈	$89-$124 SAVE	605
10 / p. 601	AAA	Inn on La Loma Plaza	◈◈◈	$120-$325 SAVE	606
11 / p. 601	AAA	Burch Street Casitas	◈◈	$89-$135 SAVE	605
12 / p. 601	AAA	Casa de las Chimeneas Inn & Spa	◈◈◈◈	$150-$325 SAVE	605
13 / p. 601	AAA	American Artists Gallery House Bed & Breakfast - see color ad p 604	◈◈◈	$95-$195 SAVE	604
14 / p. 601	AAA	Inn On The Rio - see color ad p 607	◈◈◈	$79-$129 SAVE	606
15 / p. 601	AAA	Adobe Sun God Lodge	◈◈	$60-$110 SAVE	604
16 / p. 601		Quality Inn - see color ad p 607	◈◈	$59-$109	607
17 / p. 601	AAA	San Geronimo Lodge	◈◈◈	$95-$150 SAVE	608
18 / p. 601		Comfort Suites - see color ad p 605	◈◈	$69-$159	605
19 / p. 601		Sagebrush Inn - see color ad p 608	◈◈◈	$59-$110	608
20 / p. 601		Hampton Inn	◈◈◈	$89-$99	606
		TAOS - Restaurants			
1 / p. 601		Orlando's New Mexican Cafe	◈◈	$7-$12	610
2 / p. 601		Sheva Cafe	◈◈	$5-$16	610
3 / p. 601		Taos Pizza Outback	◈◈	$6-$15	610
4 / p. 601		Fiesta Mexicana	◈◈	$9-$12	609
5 / p. 601	AAA	Michael's Kitchen	◈	$6-$13	610
6 / p. 601		Apple Tree Restaurant	◈◈◈	$14-$26	609
7 / p. 601		Bent Street Deli & Cafe	◈◈	$12-$19	609
8 / p. 601	AAA	Doc Martin's At The Historic Taos Inn	◈◈◈	$17-$32	609
9 / p. 601		Ogelvies Taos Grill & Bar	◈◈	$10-$26	610
10 / p. 601		Joseph's Table	◈◈◈◈	$19-$36	610
11 / p. 601		Eske's Brew Pub & Eatery	◈◈	$7-$14	609
12 / p. 601		Byzantium	◈◈◈	$13-$38	609
13 / p. 601		Downtown Bistro	◈◈◈	$11-$18	609
14 / p. 601		Lambert's of Taos	◈◈◈	$15-$30	610
15 / p. 601		Ginza Restaurant	◈	$9-$16	609

Spotter/Map Page Number	OA	TAOS - Restaurants (continued)	Diamond Rating	Rate Range High Season	Listing Page
16 / p. 601		Don Fernando De Taos	◆◆	$14-$20	609
17 / p. 601		Guadalajara Grill	◆	$4-$13	610
18 / p. 601	AAA	**Los Vaqueros**	◆◆	$12-$30	610
		ARROYO SECO - Lodgings			
23 / p. 601		Alma del Monte-Spirit of the Mountain B&B	◆◆◆◆	$150-$260	519
24 / p. 601		Adobe and Stars B & B	◆◆◆	$110-$185	519
25 / p. 601		Cottonwood Inn Bed & Breakfast	◆◆◆	$85-$210	520
		ARROYO SECO - Restaurant			
21 / p. 601		Momentitos de la Vida	◆◆◆◆	$19-$39	520
		RANCHOS DE TAOS - Lodgings			
28 / p. 601	AAA	**Budget Host Inn**	◆	$43-$70 [SAVE]	557
		RANCHOS DE TAOS - Restaurant			
24 / p. 601		Trading Post Cafe	◆◆	$10-$19	557

TAOS pop. 4,700 (See map and index starting on p. 601)—*See also ARROYO SECO & RANCHOS DE TAOS.*

—————— **WHERE TO STAY** ——————

ADOBE SUN GOD LODGE   *Book at aaa.com*

AAA SAVE Motel

All Year   1P: $60-$110   2P: $60-$110   **Phone: (505)758-3162** [15]

Location: SR 68, 1.8 mi sw of jct US 64 and Taos Plaza. 919 Paseo del Pueblo Sur 87571 (PO Box 1713). Fax: 505/758-1716. **Facility:** 53 units. 47 one-bedroom standard units. 6 one-bedroom suites. 1-2 stories (no elevator), exterior corridors. **Parking:** on-site. **Terms:** weekly rates available, small pets only ($10 fee). **Amenities:** *Some:* irons, hair dryers. **Leisure Activities:** whirlpool, picnic pavillion. **Guest Services:** coin laundry. **Business Services:** PC, fax. **Cards:** AX, DS, MC, VI. **Special Amenities:** free continental breakfast and free local telephone calls.

SOME UNITS

AMERICAN ARTISTS GALLERY HOUSE BED & BREAKFAST

AAA SAVE Bed & Breakfast

All Year   1P: $95-$195   2P: $95-$195   **Phone: (505)758-4446** [13]
                                                                        XP: $25

Location: 1 mi s of jct US 64 and Taos Plaza. 0.3 mi e. 132 Frontier Ln 87571 (PO Box 584). Fax: 505/758-0497. **Facility:** Local artwork, which decorates the gallery and the walls of every room, represents the three diverse cultures that meet in Taos. Smoke free premises. 10 units. 8 one-bedroom standard units, some with kitchens and/or whirlpools. 2 one-bedroom suites. 1 story, interior/exterior corridors. *Bath:* combo or shower only. **Parking:** on-site. **Terms:** 2 night minimum stay - weekends, 14 day cancellation notice-fee imposed, package plans, pets ($25 fee, in limited units, with prior approval, owner's pet on premises). **Amenities:** CD players, hair dryers. *Some:* irons. **Leisure Activities:** whirlpool, swamp coolers available. *Fee:* massage. **Business Services:** PC. **Cards:** AX, DS, MC, VI. **Special Amenities:** free full breakfast and free local telephone calls. *(See color ad below)*

SOME UNITS

BEST WESTERN KACHINA LODGE & MEETINGS CENTER   *Book at aaa.com*

AAA SAVE Motel

12/21-1/31   1P: $99-$155   2P: $99-$155   **Phone: (505)758-2275** [2]
5/25-10/25   1P: $89-$139   2P: $99-$149   XP: $10   F12
2/1-5/24 & 10/26-12/20   1P: $79-$99   2P: $79-$99   XP: $10   F12
                                                                        XP: $10   F12

Location: US 64, 0.5 mi n of jct SR 68 and Taos Plaza. 413 Paseo del Pueblo Norte 87571 (PO Box NN). Fax: 505/758-9207. **Facility:** 118 one-bedroom standard units, some with kitchens. 1-2 stories, interior/exterior corridors. **Parking:** on-site. **Terms:** weekly rates available, package plans. **Amenities:** voice mail, irons, hair dryers. **Dining:** 2 restaurants, 5 am-9 pm, cocktails, entertainment. **Pool(s):** heated outdoor. **Leisure Activities:** whirlpool, Native American dance performances daily 5/7-10/31, art gallery. **Guest Services:** gift shop, valet and coin laundry, airport transportation-Taos Municipal Airport, area transportation-within 5 mi. **Business Services:** meeting rooms. **Cards:** AX, DC, DS, MC, VI. **Special Amenities:** free full breakfast and free local telephone calls.

SOME UNITS

BROOKS STREET INN BED AND BREAKFAST

AAA SAVE Bed & Breakfast

12/15-12/31 [BP]   1P: $119-$189   2P: $119-$189   **Phone: (505)758-1489** [3]
2/1-12/14 & 1/1-1/31 [BP]   1P: $89-$149   2P: $89-$149   XP: $20   D12
                                                                        XP: $20   D12

Location: 0.3 mi n on US 64 from jct SR 68 and Taos Plaza, just e. 119 Brooks St 87571 (4954 NDCBU). Fax: 505/758-7525. **Facility:** Wind sculptures, "yard art" and patios decorate the gardens of the comfortable inn, which features wine openers and baskets of "kisses" in its rooms. Designated smoking area. 6 one-bedroom standard units. 1 story, interior/exterior corridors. *Bath:* combo or shower only. **Parking:** on-site. **Terms:** check-in 4 pm, 2-3 night minimum stay - seasonal and/or weekends, age restrictions may apply, 14 day cancellation notice-fee imposed, package plans, small pets only ($10 fee, with prior approval). **Amenities:** video library, CD players, hair dryers. *Some:* irons. **Leisure Activities:** barbecue grill, hammocks & swing, library. **Guest Services:** gift shop, airport transportation-Taos Airport. **Cards:** DS, MC, VI. **Special Amenities:** free full breakfast and free room upgrade (subject to availability with advance reservations).

(See map and index starting on p. 601)

BURCH STREET CASITAS   Phone: (505)737-9038   **11**
AAA SAVE   All Year   1P: $89-$125   2P: $99-$135   XP: $10   F12
▼▼ ▼▼   **Location:** US 64, just e of jct SR 68, just s. 310 Burch St 87571 (6416 NDCBU). Fax: 505/737-9038. **Facility:** 4
Motel   one-bedroom suites with kitchens. 1 story, exterior corridors. **Parking:** on-site. **Terms:** check-in 4 pm, 3
night minimum stay - seasonal and/or weekends, 21 day cancellation notice-fee imposed, weekly rates
available, pets (dogs only, $10 fee). **Amenities:** CD players, irons, hair dryers. **Guest Services:**
complimentary laundry. **Business Services:** fax (fee). **Cards:** MC, VI. **Special Amenities:** free local
telephone calls and preferred room (subject to availability with advance reservations).

[S/D] [X] [AC] [VCR] [DATA PORT] [icons]
FEE

CASA DE LAS CHIMENEAS INN & SPA   _Book at aaa.com_   Phone: (505)758-4777   **12**
AAA SAVE   All Year [MAP]   1P: $150-$325   2P: $175-$325   XP: $15
▼▼▼▼ ▼▼▼▼   **Location:** S from jct US 64 and SR 68, 0.3 mi on US 68, e on Los Pandos, then just s, follow signs; center. 405
Bed & Breakfast   Cordoba Rd 87571 (Box 5303 NDCBU). Fax: 505/758-3976. **Facility:** The luxurious B&B—incorporating private
patios, baths with hand-painted tiles and welcoming gardens—offers a retreat from the bustle of The Plaza.
Designated smoking area. 8 units. 6 one-bedroom standard units, some with whirlpools. 2 one-bedroom
suites ($325) with whirlpools. 1 story, exterior corridors. _Bath:_ combo or shower only. **Parking:** on-site.
Terms: office hours 7 am-10 pm, 14 day cancellation notice, package plans. **Amenities:** video library, CD players, irons, hair
dryers. **Leisure Activities:** sauna, whirlpool, exercise room. _Fee:_ yoga instruction, custom picnic packs, massage. **Guest
Services:** gift shop, coin laundry. **Business Services:** PC, fax (fee). **Cards:** AX, DC, DS, MC, VI. **Special Amenities:** free full
breakfast and free local telephone calls.

[S/D] [icons] [X] [X] [AC] [VCR] [icons] [DATA PORT] [icons]

CASA EUROPA INN & GALLERY   Phone: 505/758-9798   **5**
▼▼▼▼   Property failed to provide current rates
Historic Bed   **Location:** 1.7 mi s from jct US 64. 840 Upper Ranchitos Rd 87571 (HC 68, Box 3F). Fax: 505/758-9798.
& Breakfast   **Facility:** Nestled in a heavily treed valley, the inn—boasting elegant rooms appointed with French and
English furnishings—serves pastries in the summer. Designated smoking area. 7 units. 6 one-bedroom
standard units, some with whirlpools. 1 one-bedroom suite with kitchen. 2 stories, interior/exterior corridors.
Bath: combo or shower only. **Parking:** on-site. **Terms:** small pets only ($10 fee, in designated unit). **Amenities:** CD players,
hair dryers. _Some:_ DVD players, irons. **Leisure Activities:** sauna, whirlpool. **Guest Services:** gift shop, valet laundry, area
transportation. **Business Services:** meeting rooms, fax.

SOME UNITS
[icons] [icons] [X] [AC] [icons] / [TV] [VCR] [icons] [icons] /
FEE

COMFORT SUITES   _Book at aaa.com_   Phone: (505)751-1555   **18**
▼▼ ▼▼   All Year [ECP]   1P: $69-$149   2P: $69-$159   XP: $10   F18
Small-scale Hotel   **Location:** SR 68, 3 mi sw of jct US 64 and Taos Plaza. 1500 Paseo del Pueblo Sur 87571 (PO Box 1268).
Fax: 505/751-1991. **Facility:** 60 one-bedroom standard units. 2 stories (no elevator), interior corridors. _Bath:_
combo or shower only. **Parking:** on-site. **Terms:** package plans. **Amenities:** high-speed Internet, irons, hair
dryers. **Pool(s):** small heated outdoor. **Leisure Activities:** whirlpool. **Guest Services:** valet laundry. **Business Services:**
conference facilities, business center. **Cards:** AX, CB, DC, DS, JC, MC, VI. _(See color ad below)_

SOME UNITS
[ASK] [S/D] [icons] [icons] [icons] [icons] [icons] [icons] [icons] [DATA PORT] [icons] / [X] /
FEE

DREAMCATCHER BED & BREAKFAST   Phone: (505)758-0613   **9**
AAA SAVE   All Year [BP]   1P: $89-$124   2P: $89-$124   XP: $25
▼▼ ▼▼   **Location:** 0.4 mi wsw of Taos Plaza; center. 416 La Lomita Rd 87571 (PO Box 2069). Fax: 505/751-0115.
Bed & Breakfast   **Facility:** Relaxing is encouraged at the B&B, which offers hammocks in the large garden, a selection of
board games and comfortable beds. Smoke free premises. 7 units. 6 one- and 1 two-bedroom standard
units. 1 story, exterior corridors. _Bath:_ combo or shower only. **Parking:** on-site. **Terms:** office hours 8 am-10
pm, check-in 4 pm, 2 night minimum stay - seasonal, 15 day cancellation notice-fee imposed, no pets
allowed (owner's pets on premises). **Amenities:** CD players, irons, hair dryers. **Leisure Activities:** whirlpool, hammocks, picnic
areas with tables. **Business Services:** fax. **Cards:** AX, DS, MC, VI. **Special Amenities:** free full breakfast and free local
telephone calls.

[icons] [X] [AC] [icons] [icons] [icons] [icons]

(See map and index starting on p. 601)

FECHIN INN — *Book at aaa.com*

AAA SAVE
◊◊◊◊◊

Small-scale Hotel

All Year [CP]   1P: $127-S359   2P: $127-$359   XP: $15   **Phone: (505)751-1000**   **4**   F
Location: Just n on US 64 of jct SR 68 and Taos Plaza. Located adjacent to Kit Carson Park. 227 Paseo del Pueblo Norte 87571. Fax: 505/751-7338. **Facility:** 84 units. 70 one-bedroom standard units. 14 one-bedroom suites. 2 stories, interior corridors. *Bath:* combo or shower only. **Parking:** on-site. **Terms:** check-in 4 pm, 3 day cancellation notice, pets ($50 fee). **Amenities:** voice mail, hair dryers. *Some:* irons. **Leisure Activities:** whirlpool, library, exercise room. *Fee:* massage. **Guest Services:** valet and coin laundry. **Business Services:** meeting rooms, PC. **Cards:** AX, DC, DS, MC, VI. **Special Amenities:** free continental breakfast.

SOME UNITS

HAMPTON INN — *Book at aaa.com*

◊◊◊◊

Small-scale Hotel

All Year   1P: $89-$99   **Phone: (505)737-5700**   **20**
Location: SR 68, 3 mi s of Taos Plaza. 1515 Paseo del Pueblo Sur 87571. Fax: 505/737-5701. **Facility:** 71 one-bedroom standard units, some with whirlpools. 2 stories, interior corridors. *Bath:* combo or shower only. **Parking:** on-site. **Terms:** package plans. **Amenities:** video games, high-speed Internet, dual phone lines, voice mail, irons, hair dryers. **Pool(s):** heated indoor. **Leisure Activities:** whirlpool. **Guest Services:** coin laundry. **Cards:** AX, DC, DS, MC, VI.

SOME UNITS

THE HISTORIC TAOS INN

AAA SAVE
◊◊◊◊

Classic Motel

All Year   1P: $60-$190   2P: $60-$190   **Phone: (505)758-2233**   **6**
Location: On US 64, just n of jct SR 68 and Taos Plaza; center. 125 Paseo del Pueblo Norte 87571. Fax: 505/758-5776. **Facility:** Sitting on the outdoor patio to watch passersby on the Old Taos Highway is local tradition in this inn which dates from the late 1800s. Intimate in size but with all the modern conveniences, you are just a step from the historic Plaza with many museums, galleries and shops. Relax in the shady interior courtyard or in the redwood-walled, plant-filled "garden spa" whirlpool room. Most guestrooms have fireplaces, hand-painted tile baths and attractive southwestern decor. 36 units. 33 one-bedroom standard units. 3 one-bedroom suites ($175-$225). 1-2 stories (no elevator), interior/exterior corridors. **Parking:** on-site. **Terms:** office hours 6 am-midnight, 14 day cancellation notice-fee imposed, package plans. **Amenities:** voice mail, irons, hair dryers. **Dining:** Doc Martin's At The Historic Taos Inn, see separate listing, entertainment. **Leisure Activities:** whirlpool. **Cards:** AX, DS, MC, VI. **Special Amenities:** free local telephone calls and free newspaper.

SOME UNITS

HOTEL LA FONDA DE TAOS — *Book at aaa.com*

◊◊◊◊

Historic Small-scale Hotel

All Year   2P: $119-$699   **Phone: (505)758-2211**   **8**
Location: Center; on Taos Plaza. 108 S Plaza 87571. Fax: 505/758-8508. **Facility:** A circa 1820s hotel expanded in 1937 and completely renovated in 2002, this long-standing property is on the Historic Taos Plaza. Smoke free premises. 25 units. 19 one-bedroom standard units. 6 one-bedroom suites ($179-$199), some with kitchens. 3 stories, interior corridors. **Parking:** on-site. **Terms:** 7 day cancellation notice, package plans. **Amenities:** high-speed Internet, voice mail, irons, hair dryers. *Some:* DVD players, CD players. **Dining:** Joseph's Table, see separate listing. **Leisure Activities:** *Fee:* massage. **Business Services:** conference facilities, fax (fee). **Cards:** AX, CB, DC, DS, MC, VI.

SOME UNITS

INN ON LA LOMA PLAZA

AAA SAVE
◊◊◊◊

Historic Bed & Breakfast

All Year [BP]   1P: $120-S310   2P: $135-$325   XP: $25   **Phone: (505)758-1717**   **10**   F12
Location: 0.3 mi sw on Ranchitos Rd, just w of Taos Plaza. 315 Ranchitos Rd 87571 (PO Box 4159). Fax: 505/751-0155. **Facility:** This hitoric Inn just off the Plaza, has a lovely view of the Sangre de Cristo Mountains. Individually decorated rooms include fireplaces. Smoke free premises. 7 one-bedroom standard units, some with efficiencies. 2 stories (no elevator), interior/exterior corridors. *Bath:* combo or shower only. **Parking:** on-site. **Terms:** office hours 6 am-10 pm, 15 day cancellation notice-fee imposed, package plans. **Amenities:** video library, CD players, irons, hair dryers. *Some:* DVD players. **Leisure Activities:** whirlpool, playground. *Fee:* massage. **Guest Services:** valet laundry. **Business Services:** meeting rooms, PC. **Cards:** AX, DS, MC, VI. **Special Amenities:** free full breakfast and free local telephone calls.

SOME UNITS

INN ON THE RIO

AAA SAVE
◊◊◊◊

Bed & Breakfast

All Year [BP]   1P: $79-$109   2P: $99-$129   XP: $20   **Phone: (505)758-7199**   **14**
Location: US 64, 1.5 mi e of jct SR 68 and Taos Plaza. Located in a residential area. 910 Kit Carson Rd 87571. Fax: 505/751-1816. **Facility:** The exterior and interior murals and hand-painted furniture were done by two renowned, local folk artists. You'll find the inn just a short drive down Kit Carson Road from the historic Plaza. A patio beside the pool has picnic tables and a barbecue grill, as well as unusual garden "art". 12 one-bedroom standard units. 1 story, exterior corridors. *Bath:* combo or shower only. **Parking:** on-site. **Terms:** office hours 8 am-8 pm, 15 day cancellation notice-fee imposed, package plans, pets ($20 extra charge). **Amenities:** *Some:* irons, hair dryers. **Pool(s):** heated outdoor. **Leisure Activities:** whirlpool, barbecue grills & picnic area. **Guest Services:** gift shop. **Cards:** AX, DS, MC, VI. **Special Amenities:** free full breakfast and preferred room (subject to availability with advance reservations). (See color ad p 607)

SOME UNITS

(See map and index starting on p. 601)

LA POSADA DE TAOS　　　　　　　　　　　　　　　　　　　　　　　　　　Phone: 505/758-8164　**7**

AAA SAVE

	6/13-10/31	1P: $125-$225	2P: $125-$225	XP: $15	F16
	2/1-6/12	1P: $120-$199	2P: $120-$199	XP: $15	F16
	11/1-1/31	1P: $104-$174	2P: $104-$174	XP: $15	F16

Historic Bed & Breakfast

Location: From plaza, just w on Don Fernando, just s on Manzanares, just w. 309 Juanita Ln 87571 (PO Box 1118). **Fax:** 505/751-4696. **Facility:** The B&B has a shady courtyard garden, a bright sunroom and many historic architectural elements that enhance the decor. Smoke free premises. 6 one-bedroom standard units. 1 story, interior/exterior corridors. *Bath:* combo or shower only. **Parking:** on-site. **Terms:** check-in 4 pm, 10 day cancellation notice-fee imposed, package plans, no pets allowed (owner's pet on premises). **Amenities:** hair dryers. *Some:* irons. **Leisure Activities:** *Fee:* massage. **Business Services:** meeting rooms, fax. **Cards:** AX, DC, DS, MC, VI. **Special Amenities:** free full breakfast and free local telephone calls. *(See color ad below)*

SOME UNITS

🆂🅳 ✖ 🄺 📶 🅩 💻 /

ORINDA BED & BREAKFAST　　　　　　　　　　　　　　　　　　　　　Phone: (505)758-8581　**1**

AAA SAVE　All Year [BP]　　　　　　　　　　　2P: $89-$130　　　　XP: $20　　　D10

Bed & Breakfast

Location: Just w from jct Don Fernando and Camino de la Placita, then just s; look for Orinda sign. 461 Valverde St 87571 (4451 NDCBU). **Fax:** 505/751-4895. **Facility:** Large trees shade the grounds of the pueblo-style B&B, which features rooms decorated in the Southwestern style. Smoke free premises. 5 units. 4 one-bedroom standard units, some with whirlpools. 1 one-bedroom suite ($105-$240). 2 stories (no elevator), interior/exterior corridors. **Terms:** check-in 4 pm, 14 day cancellation notice-fee imposed, small pets only ($10 extra charge, owner's pet on premises). **Amenities:** video library, CD players, irons, hair dryers. *Some:* DVD players. **Guest Services:** area transportation-within 5 mi. **Business Services:** PC, fax. **Cards:** AX, DS, MC, VI.

SOME UNITS

🛏 🛢 ✖ 🍴 💻 / 🄺 VCR 🄳🄰🅃🄰 🅩 /
FEE

QUALITY INN　*Book at aaa.com*　　　　　　　　　　　　　　Phone: (505)758-2200　**16**

All Year [BP]　　1P: $59-$99　　2P: $59-$109　　XP: $10　　F18

Small-scale Hotel

Location: SR 68, 2 mi sw of jct US 64 and Taos Plaza. 1043 Paseo del Pueblo Sur 87571 (PO Box 2319). **Fax:** 505/758-9009. **Facility:** 99 units. 97 one-bedroom standard units. 2 one-bedroom suites, some with kitchens. 2 stories (no elevator), interior/exterior corridors. **Parking:** on-site. **Terms:** package plans, pets ($7 extra charge). **Amenities:** high-speed Internet, irons, hair dryers. *Some: Fee:* safes. **Pool(s):** heated outdoor. **Leisure Activities:** whirlpool. **Guest Services:** valet laundry. **Business Services:** meeting rooms. **Cards:** AX, CB, DC, DS, JC, MC, VI. *(See color ad below)*

SOME UNITS

ASK 🆂🅳 🛏 🍴 🍽 🐾 🏊 🐾 😊 🄳🄰🅃🄰 💻 / ✖ 🍴 /
　　　　FEE　　　　　　　　　FEE　　　　　PORT　　　　　FEE FEE

(See map and index starting on p. 601)

SAGEBRUSH INN   *Book at aaa.com*

▽▽▽▽
All Year   **Phone: (505)758-2254**   **19**
Location: SR 68, 3 mi sw of jct US 64 and Taos Plaza.   1P: $59-$110   2P: $59-$110   XP: $10   F18
Historic   1508 Paseo del Pueblo Sur 87571 (PO Box 557).
Small-scale Hotel   Fax: 505/758-5077. **Facility:** Pueblo-style exterior; main building circa 1929, once frequented by Georgia
O'Keefe. Public areas and rooms with a strong Southwestern atmosphere; some units with kiva fireplace.
100 units. 68 one-bedroom standard units. 32 one-bedroom suites ($79-$185). 1-2 stories (no elevator),
exterior corridors. **Parking:** on-site. **Terms:** 3 day cancellation notice, package plans, pets ($7 extra charge). **Amenities:** irons,
hair dryers. **Dining:** Los Vaqueros, see separate listing. **Pool(s):** heated outdoor. **Leisure Activities:** whirlpools. **Guest**
Services: valet laundry. **Business Services:** conference facilities, business center. **Cards:** AX, CB, DC, DS, JC, MC, VI.
(See color ad below)

SOME UNITS

SAN GERONIMO LODGE

🔺🔺🔺 SAVE
▽▽▽▽
All Year [BP]   **Phone: (505)751-3776**   **17**
Location: 1.3 mi e of jct SR 68 and Taos Plaza on US 64 (Kit Carson Rd), 0.6 mi s. Located in a quiet country area.   1P: $95-$150   2P: $95-$150   XP: $10   F6
Historic Bed   1101 Witt Rd 87571. Fax: 505/751-1493. **Facility:** 1925 adobe lodge. Large units nicely appointed with locally-
& Breakfast   made furnishings and art; some with gas or wood burning fireplace. Designated smoking area. 18 one-
bedroom standard units. 2 stories (no elevator), interior/exterior corridors. **Bath:** combo or shower only.
Parking: on-site. **Terms:** office hours 6 am-8 pm, 10 day cancellation notice-fee imposed, small pets only
($10 fee, in designated units). **Amenities:** hair dryers. *Some:* high-speed Internet, irons. **Pool(s):** heated
outdoor. **Leisure Activities:** whirlpool, yoga workshops, poetry, knitting workshops, library, gas barbecue grills. *Fee:* massage.
Guest Services: gift shop. **Business Services:** meeting rooms, PC, fax (fee). **Cards:** AX, DS, MC, VI. **Special Amenities:**
free full breakfast and free local telephone calls.

(See map and index starting on p. 601)

——————— The following lodging was either not evaluated or did not ———————
meet AAA rating requirements but is listed for your information only.

DON FERNANDO DE TAOS HOTEL & SUITES   Phone: 505/758-4444
[fyi]   Did not meet all AAA rating requirements for some property operations at time of last evaluation on
10/13/2004. **Location:** SR 68, 1.8 mi sw of jct US 64 and Taos Plaza. 1005 Paseo del Pueblo Sur 87571 (PO Drawer
Small-scale Hotel   V). Facilities, services, and decor characterize a mid-range property.

——————— WHERE TO DINE ———————

APPLE TREE RESTAURANT   **Lunch:** $7-$13   **Dinner:** $14-$26   **Phone:** 505/758-1900   ⑥
▼▼▼▼   **Location:** Just n of Taos Plaza, just w of US 64. 123 Bent St 87571. **Hours:** 11:30 am-3 & 5-close, Sun from 11
am. **Reservations:** suggested. **Features:** Dining under the unusual 50-year-old apple tree on the patio is a
Southwest   unique experience in Taos. Accomplished service in this relaxed, yet romantic atmosphere serves up
American   specialties such as grilled filet mignon, mango beef enchiladas, or sesame crusted salmon salad. Dessert
from the on-site bakery may be chosen from a tempting tray brought tableside. Cozy dining inside or watch
small sparrows alight to pick up fallen crumbs on the gravel patio. Casual dress; beer & wine only. **Parking:** street. **Cards:** AX,
CB, DC, DS, MC, VI.

BENT STREET DELI & CAFE   **Lunch:** $6-$10   **Dinner:** $12-$19   **Phone:** 505/758-5787   ⑦
▼▼▼▼   **Location:** Just n of Taos Plaza, just w of US 64. 120 Bent St 87571. **Hours:** 8 am-9 pm. **Closed:** 11/23, 12/25; also
Sun. **Reservations:** accepted. **Features:** A block off The Plaza, the restaurant serves breakfast, lunch and
American   dinner. Patio seating is a nice good-weather option. Casual dress; beer & wine only. **Parking:** street.
Cards: MC, VI.   [K]

BYZANTIUM   **Dinner:** $13-$38   **Phone:** 505/751-0805   ⑫
▼▼▼▼   **Location:** Just s of Taos Plaza; in Courtyard at Ledoux and La Placita. 112 La Placita 87571. **Hours:** 5 pm-close.
Closed: 11/23, 12/25; also Tues & Wed. **Reservations:** accepted. **Features:** A visit to Taos is not complete
American   without a meal at the distinctive restaurant. All of the dishes are creative, attractively presented and taste
wonderful. Friendly staff take good care of patrons. Casual dress; wine only. **Parking:** on-site. **Cards:** AX,
MC, VI.   [K]

DOC MARTIN'S AT THE HISTORIC
TAOS INN   *Menu on aaa.com*   **Lunch:** $6-$11   **Dinner:** $17-$32   **Phone:** 505/758-1977   ⑧
(AAA)   **Location:** On US 64, just n of jct SR 68 and Taos Plaza; center; in The Historic Taos Inn. 125 Paseo del Pueblo Norte
87571. **Hours:** 7-11 am, 11:30-2:30 & 5:30-close. **Reservations:** suggested, for dinner and brunch.
▼▼▼▼   **Features:** In historic Doc Martin's Restaurant, it is easy to imagine that the Taos artist group might be sitting
nearby swapping yarns. The outside patio bar is a favorite local meeting place even today. The
Regional   accomplished service highlights dishes combining New American style with New Mexican influences. Pinon
American   crusted salmon, or Southwestern lacquered duck are two choices. Tempting desserts are too luscious to
miss - citrus cheesecake or chocolate mousse with roasted banana sauce. Dressy casual; cocktails.
Parking: on-site. **Cards:** AX, DS, MC, VI. **Historic**   [Y]

DON FERNANDO DE TAOS   **Lunch:** $6-$10   **Dinner:** $14-$20   **Phone:** 505/758-4444   ⑯
▼▼▼   **Location:** SR 68, 1.8 mi sw of jct US 64 and Taos Plaza; in Don Fernando de Taos Hotel & Suites. 1005 Paseo de
Pueblo Sur 87571. **Hours:** 6:30 am-2 & 5-10 pm. **Reservations:** accepted. **Features:** Serving breakfast,
American   lunch and dinner, the hotel restaurant prepares a good selection of steaks and seafood along with several
Mexican dishes. A prime rib buffet is offered every Friday except the third one of each month, when a
seafood buffet is the norm. In the Holiday Inn, this place is close to shopping and Taos Plaza. Casual dress; cocktails. **Parking:**
on-site. **Cards:** AX, MC, VI.   [Y]

DOWNTOWN BISTRO   **Lunch:** $6-$12   **Dinner:** $11-$18   **Phone:** 505/737-5060   ⑬
▼▼▼▼   **Location:** SR 68, 0.3 mi sw of jct US 64 and Taos Plaza; at Pueblo Alegre Mall. 223 Paseo del Pueblo Sur 87571.
Hours: 11:30 am-2:30 & 5-9 pm. **Closed:** Tues. **Reservations:** not accepted. **Features:** The bistro takes
American   pride in transforming food into art. The menu changes frequently but always lists something to tantalize the
taste buds. Dressy casual; cocktails. **Parking:** on-site. **Cards:** MC, VI.   [Y]

ESKE'S BREW PUB & EATERY   **Lunch:** $7-$10   **Dinner:** $7-$14   **Phone:** 505/758-1517   ⑪
▼▼▼   **Location:** Just w of Taos Plaza. 106 Des Georges Ln 87571. **Hours:** 11:30 am-10:30 pm; from 4 pm in winter; to
10 pm 5/27-10/31. **Closed:** 12/25; also first 2 weeks of Nov. **Reservations:** not accepted. **Features:** First-
American   timers should erase from their mind the dark, smoke-filled pub they've come to expect. Instead, this place is
a bright, cheery and smoke-free place to dine. Try the club sandwich: a hearty stack of meat between two
slices of beer-battered oat bread. Both beer and root beer are made on site. Casual dress; beer & wine only. **Parking:** on-site.
Cards: MC, VI.   [K]

FIESTA MEXICANA   **Lunch:** $6-$12   **Dinner:** $9-$12   **Phone:** 505/758-4015   ④
▼▼▼   **Location:** Jct La Posta. 703 Paseo Del Pueblo Sur 87571. **Hours:** 11 am-9 pm. **Features:** The restaurant is a
relaxing spot for good Mexican fare. The service staff is casual and friendly. Dishes range from enchiladas,
Mexican   burritos, chimichangas and chiles rellenos to tacos, tostadas, taquitos and fajitas. Also available are
breakfast foods: omelets, huevos rancheros, tacos de chorizo, fiesta eggs and more. Casual dress; beer &
wine only. **Parking:** on-site. **Cards:** MC, VI.

GINZA RESTAURANT   **Lunch:** $9-$16   **Dinner:** $9-$16   **Phone:** 505/758-7645   ⑮
▼   **Location:** SR 68, 0.4 mi sw of jct US 64 and Taos Plaza. 321-C Paseo del Pueblo Sur 87571. **Hours:** 11:30 am-2 &
5-9:30 pm, Sat from 5 pm. Closed major holidays; also Sun. **Reservations:** accepted. **Features:** The
Asian   restaurant offers an extensive variety of Japanese, Chinese and Korean food at reasonable prices. Entrees
are large enough for two people to share. Casual dress; wine only. **Parking:** on-site. **Cards:** AX, DC, DS,
JC, MC, VI.

(See map and index starting on p. 601)

GUADALAJARA GRILL
Mexican

Lunch: $4-$13 **Dinner:** $4-$13 **Phone:** 505/751-0063 [17]
Location: SR 68, 2.7 mi s of Taos Plaza. 1384 Paseo Del Pueblo Sur 87571. **Hours:** 10:30 am-9:30 pm, Sun from 11 am; hours may vary in winter. Closed major holidays; also 6/3. **Reservations:** not accepted. **Features:** The Mexican restaurant puts all the staples on its menu: tacos, burritos and seafood enchiladas. Orders are taken at the counter, and cordial servers deliver them to the table. Casual dress; beer & wine only. **Parking:** on-site. **Cards:** MC, VI.

JOSEPH'S TABLE
Continental

Lunch: $15-$25 **Dinner:** $19-$36 **Phone:** 505/751-4512 [10]
Location: Center; on Taos Plaza; in Hotel La Fonda De Taos. 108 A S Taos Plaza 87571. **Hours:** 11:30 am-2:30 & 5:30-10 pm; hours may vary in winter. **Features:** Directly on the historic Plaza, the creative and artistically decorated restaurant is a fabulous fine-dining spot. A treat for the palate awaits in such Chef Joseph creations as seven-way lucky duck breast with foie gras, confit chicharrones, aspic and mousse with corn creme brulee. Another creation is Alaskan halibut with tarragon compound butter and fresh strawberries. Dressy casual; cocktails. **Parking:** street. **Cards:** AX, DS, MC, VI.

LAMBERT'S OF TAOS
American

Dinner: $15-$30 **Phone:** 505/758-1009 [14]
Location: SR 68, 0.4 mi sw of jct US 64 and Taos Plaza. 309 Paseo del Pueblo Sur 87571. **Hours:** 5:30 pm-9 pm, Fri & Sat-9:30 pm. Closed: 11/23; also Super Bowl Sun. **Reservations:** suggested. **Features:** A short walk from the historic Plaza, the restaurant is surrounded by trees and a small garden. Casual, friendly servers provide expert assistance to diners. After a complimentary aperitif, dinner choices include such dishes as the specialty pepper-crusted lamb loin with red wine demi-glace. The decadent chocolate mousse with raspberry sauce is enough to share. Casual dress; cocktails. **Parking:** on-site. **Cards:** AX, DC, DS, MC, VI.

LOS VAQUEROS
American

Menu on aaa.com
Dinner: $12-$30 **Phone:** 505/758-2254 [18]
Location: SR 68, 3 mi sw of jct US 64 and Taos Plaza; in Sagebrush Inn. 1508 Paseo del Pueblo Sur 87571. **Hours:** 5:30 pm-10 pm. **Reservations:** accepted. **Features:** In the Historic Sagebrush Inn, the menu lists a variety of steaks, seafood and Mexican offerings. The salad bar is a good meal accompaniment. Casual dress; cocktails. **Parking:** on-site. **Cards:** AX, CB, DC, DS, JC, MC, VI.

MICHAEL'S KITCHEN
Southwest American

Lunch: $6-$9 **Dinner:** $6-$13 **Phone:** 505/758-4178 [5]
Location: US 64, 0.3 mi n of jct SR 68 and Taos Plaza. 304C Paseo del Pueblo Norte 87571. **Hours:** Open 2/1-10/31 & 12/7-1/31; 7 am-8:30 pm. Closed major holidays. **Reservations:** not accepted. **Features:** Michael's Kitchen, just north of The Plaza and a short distance to the pueblo, is a bustling eatery with a rustic atmosphere. Casual and friendly service serves up choices such as nachos, tamales, burgers, chicken tacos, salads, green chili and enchiladas. Breakfast can be ordered any time of day. Bakery on premises. Casual dress. **Parking:** on-site. **Cards:** AX, DS, MC, VI.

OGELVIES TAOS GRILL & BAR
American

Lunch: $7-$12 **Dinner:** $10-$26 **Phone:** 505/758-8866 [9]
Location: Center; on east side of Taos Plaza. 103 E Plaza, Suite I 87571. **Hours:** 11 am-close. Closed: call for closing dates 11/1-12/15. **Reservations:** not accepted. **Features:** The menu includes examples of Mexican, Italian and American cuisine. Top off a delicious meal with a slice of homemade pie. Casual dress; cocktails. **Parking:** street. **Cards:** AX, DC, DS, MC, VI.

ORLANDO'S NEW MEXICAN CAFE
Mexican

Lunch: $7-$12 **Dinner:** $7-$12 **Phone:** 505/751-1450 [1]
Location: 1.8 mi n on SR 64. 1114 Don Juan Valdez Ln 87571. **Hours:** 10:30 am-9 pm. **Features:** The busy spot offers cozy inside seating or popular umbrella tables outdoors. Fresh Mexican eats include burritos, enchiladas, tamales, chiles rellenos, chimichangas, tacos and yummy nacho dishes. Casual dress; beer & wine only. **Parking:** on-site.

SHEVA CAFE
Middle Eastern

Lunch: $5-$16 **Dinner:** $5-$16 **Phone:** 505/737-9290 [2]
Location: 1.2 mi nnw of Taos Plaza. 812 B Paseo del Pueblo Norte 87571. **Hours:** 8 am-10 pm, Sat 5 pm-midnight. Closed: Yom Kippor. **Features:** Colorful murals decorate the interior and exterior of the cafe, which presents a menu dominated by Middle Eastern and Israeli dishes. This is the place to go for hummus, spanakopita, falafel, baklava and coffee. Casual dress; wine only. **Parking:** on-site. **Cards:** DS, MC, VI.

TAOS PIZZA OUTBACK
Italian

Lunch: $6-$15 **Dinner:** $6-$15 **Phone:** 505/758-3112 [3]
Location: Just nw of jct Camino de la Placita. 712 Paseo de Pueblo Norte 87571. **Hours:** 11 am-9 pm, Fri & Sat-10 pm; to 10 pm in summer. Closed: 11/23, 12/25. **Reservations:** accepted. **Features:** At the heart of the menu are freshly made pizzas, calzones and pasta dishes. The quaint restaurant proudly serves local and organic produce, which means the salads are mighty tasty. Desserts are displayed near the entrance so diners can plan ahead. Casual dress; wine only. **Parking:** on-site. **Cards:** AX, DS, MC, VI.

THOREAU pop. 1,863

——— WHERE TO STAY ———

ZUNI MOUNTAIN LODGE
Bed & Breakfast

All Year **1P:** $60 **2P:** $95 **Phone:** 505/862-7769
XP: $20 D12
Location: I-40, exit 53, 13 mi s on SR 612, then w. Located in a secluded area. 40 W Perch Dr 87323 (PO Box 5114). **Fax:** 505/862-7616. **Facility:** Designated smoking area. 7 units. 6 one- and 1 two-bedroom standard units. 1-3 stories (no elevator), interior/exterior corridors. **Bath:** combo or shower only. **Parking:** on-site. **Terms:** 14 day cancellation notice-fee imposed, weekly rates available, pets (with prior approval). **Leisure Activities:** basketball, volleyball.

TRUTH OR CONSEQUENCES pop. 7,289

―――――― WHERE TO STAY ――――――

BEST WESTERN HOT SPRINGS MOTOR INN   *Book at aaa.com*   Phone: (505)894-6665

(AAA) [SAVE]
WWW
Motel

4/1-10/31	1P: $59-$69	2P: $59-$69
2/1-3/31 & 11/1-1/31	1P: $57-$62	2P: $57-$62

Location: I-25, exit 79. 2270 N Date St 87901. Fax: 505/894-6665. **Facility:** 41 units. 40 one-bedroom standard units. 1 one-bedroom suite. 1 story, exterior corridors. **Parking:** on-site. **Amenities:** voice mail, irons, hair dryers. **Dining:** 7 am-8 pm, Fri & Sat-9 pm, wine/beer only. **Pool(s):** heated outdoor. **Guest Services:** valet and coin laundry. **Business Services:** meeting rooms, fax (fee). **Cards:** AX, DC, DS, MC, VI.
Special Amenities: free continental breakfast and free local telephone calls.

SOME UNITS

COMFORT INN & SUITES   Phone: (505)894-1660

WWWW
Small-scale Hotel

All Year	1P: $49-$85	2P: $55-$120	XP: $6	F18

Location: I-25, exit 79, just e. 2250 N Date St 87901 (PO Box 3489). Fax: 505/894-1580. **Facility:** 50 units. 49 one-bedroom standard units. 1 two-bedroom suite ($75-$120) with whirlpool. 2 stories (no elevator), interior corridors. *Bath:* combo or shower only. **Terms:** [CP] meal plan available, package plans. **Amenities:** high-speed Internet, dual phone lines, voice mail, irons, hair dryers. **Pool(s):** heated indoor. **Leisure Activities:** whirlpool, exercise room. **Guest Services:** valet and coin laundry. **Business Services:** meeting rooms. **Cards:** AX, CB, DC, DS, MC, VI.

SOME UNITS

SUPER 8 MOTEL   *Book at aaa.com*   Phone: (505)894-7888

(AAA) [SAVE]
WW WW
Motel

5/15-10/15	1P: $38-$88	2P: $48-$98
2/1-5/14 & 10/16-1/31	1P: $38-$78	2P: $43-$85

Location: I-25, exit 79, just s. 2151 N Date St 87901 (PO Box 3039). Fax: 505/894-7883. **Facility:** 40 one-bedroom standard units. 2 stories (no elevator), interior corridors. **Parking:** on-site. **Business Services:** fax. **Cards:** AX, CB, DC, DS, JC, MC, VI. **Special Amenities:** free continental breakfast and preferred room (subject to availability with advance reservations).

SOME UNITS

―――――― WHERE TO DINE ――――――

BAR-B-QUE ON BROADWAY   Lunch: $5-$8   Phone: 505/894-7047

WWW
Barbecue

Location: I-25, exit 79, 1.9 mi se thru center of town. 308 Broadway 87901. **Hours:** 7 am-4 pm. Closed: 11/23, 12/25. **Features:** The barbecue brisket tastes great and the portions are generous at this busy cafe. The combination of fast service, a good selection of sandwiches and daily specials have made this cafe a local favorite. Casual dress. **Parking:** on-site. **Cards:** MC, VI.

LA COCINA RESTAURANT   Lunch: $6-$9   Dinner: $8-$16   Phone: 505/894-6499

WWW
Mexican

Location: I-25, exit 79, just s. #1 Lakeway Dr 87935. **Hours:** 10:30 am-9 pm, Fri-Sun to 10 pm. Closed major holidays. **Reservations:** accepted. **Features:** The sign out front says "hot stuff," and sure enough the New Mexican cuisine has real authority in the chili department. Red and green varieties make dishes here a chili-lover's delight. Casual dress; beer & wine only. **Parking:** on-site. **Cards:** DS, MC, VI.

LOS ARCOS   Dinner: $10-$23   Phone: 505/894-6200

WWWW
American

Location: I-25, exit 83, 0.5 mi e. 1400 N Date St 87901. **Hours:** 5 pm-9:30 pm, Fri & Sat-10:30 pm. Closed: 11/23, 12/25. **Reservations:** suggested. **Features:** The restaurant brought fine dining to town many years ago. One of the steak and seafood combinations is just the ticket for a special occasion. Also good are the salads and desserts. Dressy casual; cocktails. **Parking:** on-site. **Cards:** AX, DS, MC, VI.

PACIFIC GRILL   Lunch: $6-$12   Dinner: $8-$20   Phone: 505/894-7687

WW
Seafood

Location: Center. 304 S Pershing St 87901. **Hours:** 11 am-2 & 5-9 pm. Closed major holidays; also Sun. **Reservations:** accepted. **Features:** Fine Pacific Rim recipes are used to produce some mighty tasty seafood dishes, including several really interesting shrimp and fish choices. Casual dress. **Parking:** on-site. **Cards:** AX, CB, DS, MC, VI.

TUCUMCARI pop. 5,989

―――――― WHERE TO STAY ――――――

AMERICANA MOTEL   Phone: (505)461-0431

(AAA) [SAVE]
WW
Motel

2/1-10/31	1P: $21-$28	2P: $32-$40	XP: $3	D12
11/1-1/31	1P: $21-$28	2P: $30-$40	XP: $2	D12

Location: I-40, exit 332, 1.5 mi n on SR 18, then 0.5 mi e on US 66. 406 E Tucumcari Blvd 88401. **Facility:** 14 one-bedroom standard units. 1 story, exterior corridors. *Bath:* combo or shower only. **Parking:** on-site. **Terms:** small pets only ($5 fee). **Cards:** AX, DS, MC, VI.

SOME UNITS
FEE

AMERICAS BEST VALUE INN   Phone: (505)461-4484

(AAA) [SAVE]
WWWW
Motel

All Year	1P: $29-$48	2P: $35-$48	XP: $6	F12

Location: I-40, exit 333, n to Tucumcari Blvd, then 0.6 mi w. 1023 E Tucumcari Blvd 88401. Fax: 505/461-4484. **Facility:** 46 one-bedroom standard units. 1-2 stories, exterior corridors. *Bath:* combo or shower only. **Parking:** on-site. **Terms:** small pets only ($5 extra charge, in designated units). **Pool(s):** heated outdoor. **Guest Services:** coin laundry. **Business Services:** fax (fee). **Cards:** AX, DS, MC, VI. **Special Amenities:** free expanded continental breakfast and free room upgrade (subject to availability with advance reservations).

SOME UNITS
FEE

BEST WESTERN DISCOVERY INN   *Book at aaa.com*   Phone: (505)461-4884

AAA [SAVE]

5/1-10/31	1P: $79-$95	2P: $79-$95	XP: $5 F17
2/1-4/30 & 11/1-1/31	1P: $63-$78	2P: $63-$78	XP: $5 F17

Small-scale Hotel

Location: I-40, exit 332. 200 E Estrella 88401. **Fax:** 505/461-2463. **Facility:** 107 one-bedroom standard units. 2 stories (no elevator), exterior corridors. **Parking:** on-site. **Terms:** small pets only ($5 extra charge, in designated units). **Amenities:** irons, hair dryers. *Some:* high-speed Internet. **Dining:** 6 am-9 pm, Fri & Sat-10 pm, wine/beer only. **Pool(s):** heated outdoor. **Leisure Activities:** whirlpool, exercise room. **Guest Services:** gift shop, coin laundry. **Business Services:** meeting rooms, fax (fee). **Cards:** AX, CB, DC, DS, MC, VI. **Special Amenities:** free expanded continental breakfast and free local telephone calls. *(See color ad below)*

SOME UNITS

BUDGET INN   Phone: (505)461-4139

AAA [SAVE]

All Year	1P: $25-$30	2P: $30-$45	XP: $5 F12

Motel

Location: I-40, exit 332, 1 mi n to Tucumari Blvd, then 1 mi w. 824 W Tucumari Blvd 88401 (PO Box 666). **Fax:** 505/461-4320. **Facility:** 24 one-bedroom standard units. 1 story, exterior corridors. **Parking:** on-site. **Terms:** pets ($5 fee). **Amenities:** high-speed Internet. **Cards:** AX, DS, MC, VI. **Special Amenities:** free continental breakfast and early check-in/late check-out.

SOME UNITS

COMFORT INN   *Book at aaa.com*   Phone: (505)461-4094

5/1-8/31	1P: $61	2P: $69	XP: $6 F16
9/1-1/31	1P: $55	2P: $65	XP: $6 F16
2/1-4/30	1P: $55	2P: $61	XP: $6 F16

Small-scale Hotel

Location: I-40, exit 335, 0.5 mi w. 2800 E Tucumcari Blvd 88401. **Fax:** 505/461-4099. **Facility:** 59 one-bedroom standard units. 2 stories (no elevator), exterior corridors. **Parking:** on-site. **Terms:** 7 day cancellation notice, pets ($6 extra charge). **Amenities:** irons, hair dryers. **Pool(s):** small outdoor. **Business Services:** PC, fax (fee). **Cards:** AX, CB, DC, DS, MC, VI.

SOME UNITS

DAYS INN   *Book at aaa.com*   Phone: 505/461-3158

AAA [SAVE]

5/1-10/15	1P: $55-$65	2P: $60-$70	XP: $5
2/1-4/30 & 10/16-1/31	1P: $50-$60	2P: $55-$65	XP: $5

Small-scale Hotel

Location: I-40, exit 332, just n. 2623 S First St 88401. **Fax:** 505/461-4871. **Facility:** 40 one-bedroom standard units. 2 stories (no elevator), interior/exterior corridors. **Parking:** on-site. **Terms:** [ECP] meal plan available, small pets only ($5 fee). **Amenities:** high-speed Internet, hair dryers. **Business Services:** fax (fee). **Cards:** AX, DC, DS, MC, VI. **Special Amenities:** free continental breakfast and free local telephone calls.

SOME UNITS

HAMPTON INN
◇◇◇
Small-scale Hotel

<u>Book at aaa.com</u>
5/25-10/31 [BP]
3/15-5/24 & 11/1-1/31 [BP]
2/1-3/14 [BP]

1P: $85-$129   2P: $89-$129
1P: $75-$109   2P: $79-$109
1P: $65-$99   2P: $69-$99

Phone: (505)461-1111

Location: I-40, exit 335, 0.7 mi w. 3409 E Route 66 88401 (PO Box 1045). Fax: 505/461-0000. **Facility:** 58 one-bedroom standard units. 3 stories, interior corridors. *Bath:* combo or shower only. **Parking:** on-site. **Terms:** package plans. **Amenities:** video games (fee), high-speed Internet, voice mail, irons, hair dryers. **Pool(s):** small heated indoor. **Leisure Activities:** sauna, whirlpool. **Guest Services:** coin laundry. **Business Services:** fax. **Cards:** AX, DC, DS, MC, VI.
(See color ad below)

SOME UNITS

(ASK) (S🕭) (🛉+) (🔊M) (🖪) (🏊) (🏄) (DATA PORT) (🖥) / (✕) (🛢) (📺) /

HOLIDAY INN
AAA (SAVE)
◇◇◇
Small-scale Hotel

<u>Book at aaa.com</u>
5/16-11/7 [BP]
2/1-5/15 & 11/8-1/31 [BP]

1P: $84-$99   2P: $84-$99
1P: $79-$92   2P: $79-$92

Phone: (505)461-3780

Location: I-40, exit 335, 0.3 mi w on US 66. 3716 E Tucumcari Blvd 88401 (PO Box 808). Fax: 505/461-3931. **Facility:** 100 one-bedroom standard units. 2 stories (no elevator), exterior corridors. **Parking:** on-site. **Terms:** pets ($6 fee). **Amenities:** high-speed Internet, irons, hair dryers. **Dining:** Branding Iron Restaurant, see separate listing. **Pool(s):** heated outdoor. **Leisure Activities:** whirlpool, playground, exercise room. **Guest Services:** gift shop, coin laundry. **Business Services:** meeting rooms, fax. **Cards:** AX, CB, DC, DS, JC, MC, VI. **Special Amenities:** free full breakfast and free local telephone calls. *(See color ad below)*

SOME UNITS

(S🕭) (🛉) (🍽) (Y) (🔊M) (🚭) (🏊) (✕) (🏄) (DATA PORT) (🖥) / (✕) (🛢) /
FEE

MICROTEL INN-TUCUMCARI   *Book at aaa.com*

AAA [SAVE]

Small-scale Hotel

All Year [BP]   1P: $56-$70   2P: $66-$90   XP: $6   F16

Phone: (505)461-0600

Location: I-40, exit 332, just n. 2420 S 1st St 88401. Fax: 505/461-0800. **Facility:** 54 one-bedroom standard units. 2 stories (no elevator), interior corridors. *Bath:* combo or shower only. **Parking:** on-site. **Terms:** small pets only ($6 extra charge). **Amenities:** high-speed Internet, hair dryers. **Pool(s):** heated indoor. **Leisure Activities:** whirlpool, exercise room. **Guest Services:** coin laundry. **Business Services:** fax (fee). **Cards:** AX, DC, DS, MC, VI. **Special Amenities:** free expanded continental breakfast and free local telephone calls.

SOME UNITS

SUPER 8 MOTEL   *Book at aaa.com*

AAA [SAVE]

Motel

All Year   1P: $48-$58   2P: $50-$75   XP: $4   F12

Phone: (505)461-4444

Location: I-40, exit 335, just w. 4001 E Tucumcari Blvd 88401 (PO Box 806). Fax: 505/461-4320. **Facility:** 62 one-bedroom standard units. 2 stories (no elevator), interior corridors. **Parking:** on-site, winter plug-ins. **Terms:** small pets only ($5 extra charge). **Amenities:** high-speed Internet. **Pool(s):** heated indoor. **Business Services:** fax (fee). **Cards:** AX, CB, DC, DS, MC, VI. **Special Amenities:** free expanded continental breakfast and early check-in/late check-out.

SOME UNITS

TUCUMCARI INN

Small-scale Hotel

All Year [ECP]   1P: $34-$39   2P: $39-$45   XP: $5   D12

Phone: (505)461-7800

Location: I-40, exit 333, 0.5 mi n to Tucumcari Blvd, then just w. 1700 E Tucumcari Blvd 88401. Fax: 505/461-7800. **Facility:** 38 one-bedroom standard units, some with kitchens. 1 story, exterior corridors. **Parking:** on-site. **Terms:** cancellation fee imposed, pets ($5 fee). **Pool(s):** small heated outdoor. **Guest Services:** coin laundry. **Cards:** DS, MC, VI.

SOME UNITS

——— WHERE TO DINE ———

BRANDING IRON RESTAURANT   **Dinner:** $8-$20

American

Phone: 505/461-3780

Location: I-40, exit 335, 0.3 mi w on US 66; in Holiday Inn. 3716 E Tucumcari Blvd 88401. **Hours:** 6 am-10 & 5-9 pm, Fri & Sat-10 pm. Closed: 12/25. **Reservations:** accepted. **Features:** Pleasing service awaits patrons of the restaurant, which offers a nice cross-section of American fare. Dinner specials are prepared daily. Casual dress; cocktails. **Parking:** on-site. **Cards:** AX, CB, DC, DS, JC, MC, VI.

DEL'S RESTAURANT   **Lunch:** $5-$13   **Dinner:** $5-$13

American

Phone: 505/461-1740

Location: I-40, exit 333, 1.5 n on Mountain Rd, then 0.5 mi w. 1202 E Route 66 88401. **Hours:** 7 am-9 pm. Closed: 12/25; also Sun. **Reservations:** accepted. **Features:** Colorful Southwestern decor punctuates the dining room at the casual, family restaurant. Among offerings of American and Mexican cuisine are several health-conscious dishes. Casual dress. **Parking:** on-site. **Cards:** MC, VI.

VAUGHN pop. 539

——— WHERE TO STAY ———

BEL-AIR MOTEL

AAA [SAVE]

Motel

All Year   1P: $40-$48   2P: $48-$55   XP: $3

Phone: 505/584-2241

Location: 1 mi e on US 54, 60 and 285. 1004 US 54/60/285 88353 (PO Box 68). **Facility:** 21 one-bedroom standard units. 1 story, exterior corridors. *Bath:* combo or shower only. **Parking:** on-site, winter plug-ins. **Terms:** office hours 8 am-10 pm. **Amenities:** hair dryers. **Cards:** AX, CB, DC, MC, VI. **Special Amenities:** free local telephone calls.

OAK TREE INN   *Book at aaa.com*

AAA [SAVE]

Small-scale Hotel

All Year   1P: $60-$90   2P: $65-$95   XP: $5   F18

Phone: (505)584-8733

Location: 1.5 mi e on US 54, 60 and 285. Jct State Hwy 54/60 & 285 88353 (PO Box 559). Fax: 505/584-9601. **Facility:** Smoke free premises. 60 one-bedroom standard units. 2 stories (no elevator), interior/exterior corridors. *Bath:* combo or shower only. **Parking:** on-site. **Terms:** 7 day cancellation notice, weekly rates available, pets ($5 extra charge). **Amenities:** *Some:* irons, hair dryers. **Dining:** 24 hours. **Leisure Activities:** whirlpool, exercise room. **Guest Services:** coin laundry. **Business Services:** meeting rooms. **Cards:** AX, CB, DC, DS, MC, VI. **Special Amenities:** free continental breakfast and free local telephone calls.

SOME UNITS

WHITE ROCK pop. 6,045

——— WHERE TO STAY ———

HAMPTON INN & SUITES   *Book at aaa.com*

Small-scale Hotel

Property failed to provide current rates

Phone: 505/672-3838

Location: Center. 124 State Hwy 4 87544. Fax: 505/672-0111. **Facility:** 72 units. 71 one-bedroom standard units. 1 one-bedroom suite with kitchen. 3 stories, interior corridors. *Bath:* combo or shower only. **Parking:** on-site. **Terms:** check-in 4 pm. **Amenities:** high-speed Internet, voice mail, irons, hair dryers. **Leisure Activities:** sauna, exercise room. **Guest Services:** valet and coin laundry. **Business Services:** meeting rooms, business center. *(See color ad p 552)*

SOME UNITS

WHITES CITY

─── WHERE TO STAY ───

BEST WESTERN CAVERN INN
Phone: (505)785-2291

AAA SAVE

5/15-9/14 [BP]	1P: $80-$110	2P: $80-$110	XP: $6	F17
2/1-5/14 & 9/15-1/31 [BP]	1P: $70-$100	2P: $70-$100	XP: $6	F17

Location: US 62 and 180 at SR 7. 17 Carlsbad Caverns Hwy 88268 (PO Box 128). Fax: 505/785-2283. **Facility:** 63 one-bedroom standard units. 2 stories (no elevator), exterior corridors. **Parking:** on-site. Small-scale Hotel **Terms:** cancellation fee imposed, package plans, small pets only ($10 extra charge). **Amenities:** irons, hair dryers. *Some:* high-speed Internet. **Pool(s):** heated outdoor. **Leisure Activities:** whirlpool, waterslide, hiking trails. **Guest Services:** gift shop. **Business Services:** meeting rooms, fax (fee). **Cards:** AX, DC, DS, MC, VI. **Special Amenities:** free full breakfast and free local telephone calls. *(See color ad p 523)*

SOME UNITS

[icons] FEE

BEST WESTERN GUADALUPE INN   *Book at aaa.com*
Phone: (505)785-2291

AAA SAVE

5/15-9/14 [BP]	1P: $80-$110	2P: $80-$110	XP: $6	F17
9/15-1/31 [BP]	1P: $70-$110	2P: $70-$110	XP: $6	F17
2/1-5/14 [BP]	1P: $70-$100	2P: $70-$100	XP: $6	F17

Motel **Location:** US 62 and 180 at SR 7. 17 Carlsbad Caverns Hwy 88268 (PO Box 128). Fax: 505/785-2283. **Facility:** 42 one-bedroom standard units. 1 story, exterior corridors. **Parking:** on-site. **Terms:** cancellation fee imposed, package plans. **Amenities:** irons, hair dryers. *Some:* high-speed Internet. **Guest Services:** gift shop. **Business Services:** meeting rooms, fax (fee). **Cards:** AX, DC, DS, MC, VI. **Special Amenities:** free full breakfast and free local telephone calls. *(See color ad p 523)*

SOME UNITS

[icons]

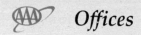

Offices

Cities with main offices are listed in **BOLD TYPE** and toll-free member service numbers in *ITALIC TYPE*.
All are closed Saturdays, Sundays and holidays unless otherwise indicated.
The type of service provided is designated below the name of the city where the office is located:

✦ Auto travel services, including books/maps, marked maps and on-demand Triptik maps
● Auto travel services, including books/maps, marked maps, but no on-demand Triptik maps
■ Provides books/maps only. No marked maps or on-demand Triptik maps available
▲ Travel agency services

NATIONAL OFFICE: 1000 AAA DRIVE, HEATHROW, FLORIDA 32746-5063, (407) 444-7000

ARIZONA

CHANDLER—AAA ARIZONA, 4040 W RAY RD STE 2, 85226. MON-FRI 8:30-5:30, SAT 9-1. (602) 274-1116.✦▲

MESA—AAA ARIZONA, 262 E UNIVERSITY DR, 85201. MON-FRI 8-5, SAT 9-1. (602) 274-1116.✦▲

PEORIA—AAA ARIZONA, 7422 W THUNDERBIRD RD, 85381. MON-FRI 9-6, SAT 9-1. (602) 274-1116.✦▲

PHOENIX—**AAA ARIZONA,** 3144 N 7TH AVE, 85013. MON-FRI 8-5. (602) 274-1116.✦▲

PHOENIX—AAA ARIZONA, 4046 E GREENWAY RD, 85032. MON-FRI 8-5, SAT 9-1. (602) 274-1116.✦▲

PRESCOTT—AAA ARIZONA, 3767 KARICIO LN #1-C, 86303. MON-FRI 8-5. (928) 776-5122.✦▲

SCOTTSDALE—AAA ARIZONA, 701 N SCOTTSDALE RD, 85257. MON-FRI 8-5. (602) 274-1116.✦▲

SUN CITY WEST—AAA ARIZONA, 19802 R H JOHNSON BLVD, 85375. MON-FRI 8-5. (602) 274-1116.✦▲

TUCSON—AAA ARIZONA, 6950 N ORACLE RD, 85704. MON-FRI 8-5, SAT 9-1. (520) 885-0694.✦▲

TUCSON—AAA ARIZONA, 8204 E BROADWAY, 85710. MON-FRI 8-5. (520) 296-7461.✦▲

NEW MEXICO

ALBUQUERQUE—**AAA NEW MEXICO,** 10501 MONTGOMERY NE, 87111. MON-FRI 8:30-5, SAT 9-1. (505) 291-6611.✦▲

ALBUQUERQUE—AAA NEW MEXICO, 9231 COORS RD NW STE 5&6, 87114. MON-FRI 8:30-5, SAT 9-1. (505) 792-1938.✦▲

LAS CRUCES—AAA NEW MEXICO, 3991 E LOHMAN AVE STE #A, 88011. MON-FRI 8:30-5. (505) 523-5681.✦▲

SANTA FE—AAA NEW MEXICO, 1644 ST MICHAELS DR, 87505. MON-FRI 8:30-5, SAT 9-1. (505) 471-6620.✦▲

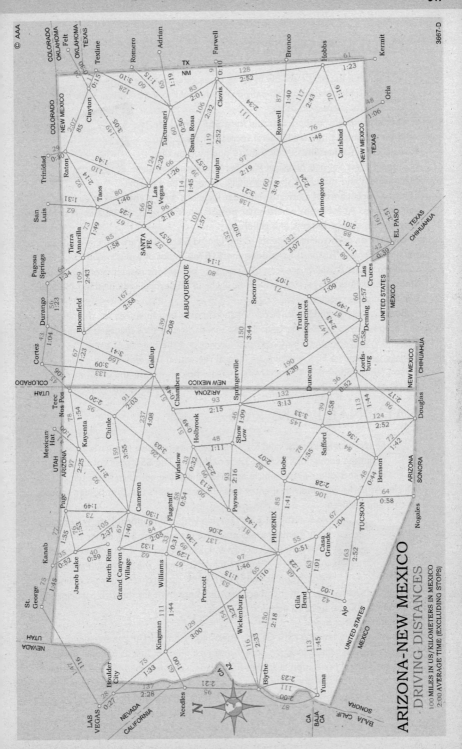

ARIZONA–NEW MEXICO
DRIVING DISTANCES

100 MILES IN US/KILOMETERS IN MEXICO
2:00 AVERAGE TIME (EXCLUDING STOPS)

© AAA

3667-D

GOLDEN PASSPORTS

Golden Passports, available in three types, offer benefits and significant savings to individuals who plan to visit federal recreation sites.

The *Golden Eagle Passport*, available for a **$65** annual fee, is valid for entrance only to all federal recreation areas that have an entrance fee. Sites include those operated by the National Forest Service, National Park Service, Bureau of Land Management and the U.S. Fish and Wildlife Service. The passport admits all occupants of a private vehicle at locations where entrance is on a per vehicle basis. At locations where a per person fee is charged, the pass covers the pass holder, spouse, parents and children.

Citizens or permanent residents of the United States who are 62 and older can obtain *Golden Age Passports* for a one-time **$10** fee. Proof of age is required.

Golden Access Passports are free to citizens or permanent residents of the United States (regardless of age) who are medically blind or permanently disabled. Medical documention is required.

Both *Golden Age* and *Golden Access Passports* cover entrance fees for the holder and accompanying private party to all national parks and sites managed by the U.S. Fish and Wildlife Service, the U.S. Forest Service and the Bureau of Land Management, plus a 50% discount on federal recreation use fees. When a per person fee is imposed, the pass covers the pass holder, spouse and children. Apply in person at a federally operated area where an entrance fee is charged.

NATIONAL PARKS PASS

The *National Parks Pass*, valid for 1 year from its first use in a park, allows unlimited admissions to all U.S. national parks. The **$50** pass covers all occupants of a private vehicle at parks where the entrance fee is per vehicle. At parks with individual entry fees, the pass covers the pass holder, spouse, parents and children.

As a result of a partnership with the National Park Foundation, AAA members may purchase the pass for **$48**, either through AAA's internet site (www.aaa.com) or by visiting a participating AAA office. Members may also phone the National Park Foundation at **(888) 467-2757** or purchase the pass online at www.nationalparks.org. Non-members may purchase the pass through participating AAA offices for the full **$50** price or online at www.nationalparks.org.

For an upgrade fee of **$15**, a Golden Eagle Hologram sticker can be added to a *National Parks Pass*. The hologram covers entrance fees not just at national parks, but at any federal recreation area that has an admission fee. Valid for the duration of the *National Parks Pass* to which it is affixed, the Golden Eagle hologram is available at National Park Service, Fish and Wildlife Service and Bureau of Land Management fee stations.

Points of Interest Index

Index Legend

⬥ GEM: Points of Interest Offering a *Great Experience for Members*®

MUSIC HALLS & OPERA HOUSES

NATIONALITIES & ETHNIC AREAS

NATURAL BRIDGES

NATURAL PHENOMENA

NATURE CENTERS

NATURE TRAILS

OBSERVATORIES

PAINTINGS

PARKS, CITY; STATE; PROVINCIAL

SAVE *Attraction Admission Discount Index*

Bed & Breakfast Lodgings Index

Some bed and breakfasts listed below might have historical significance. Those properties are also referenced in the Historical index. The indication that continental [CP] or full breakfast [BP] is included in the room rate reflects whether a property is a Bed-and-Breakfast facility.

Country Inns Index

Some of the following country inns can also be considered as bed-and-breakfast operations. The indication that continental [CP] or full breakfast [BP] is included in the room rate reflects whether a property is a Bed-and-Breakfast facility.

Historical Lodgings & Restaurants Index

Some of the following historical lodgings can also be considered as bed-and-breakfast operations. The indication that continental [CP] or full breakfast [BP] is included in the room rate reflects whether a property is a Bed-and-Breakfast facility.

632

Historical Lodgings & Restaurants (cont'd)

Resorts Index

Many establishments are located in resort areas; however, the following places have extensive on-premises recreational facilities:

Comprehensive City Index

Here is an alphabetical list of all cities appearing in this TourBook® guide. Cities are presented by state/province. Page numbers under the POI column indicate where points of interest text begins. Page numbers under the L&R column indicate where lodging and restaurant listings begin.

Comprehensive City Index (cont'd)

Precautions Can Save A Vacation!

Travelers are faced with the task of protecting themselves while in a strange environment. Although there is no way to guarantee absolute protection from crime, the experts—law enforcement officials—advise travelers to take a proactive approach to securing their property and ensuring their safety.

- Make sure the hotel desk clerk does not announce your room number; if he/she does, quietly request a new room assignment.

- Ask front desk personnel which areas of town to avoid and what, if any, special precautions should be taken when driving a rental car (some criminals target tourists driving rental cars).

- Never open the door to a stranger; use the peephole and request identification. If you are still unsure, call the front desk to verify the identity of the person and the purpose of his/her visit.

- Carry money separately from credit cards or use a "fanny pack." Carry your purse close to your body and your wallet in an inside coat or front trouser pocket. Never leave luggage unattended, and use your business address, if possible, on luggage tags.

- Beware of distractions staged by would-be scam artists, especially groups of children that surround you, or a stranger who accidentally spills something on you. They may be lifting your wallet.

- If using an automatic teller machine (ATM), choose one in a well-lit area with plenty of foot traffic, such as one at a grocery store. Law enforcement officials suggest that machines inside establishments are generally safer to use.

- Use room safes or safety deposit boxes provided by the hotel. Store all valuables out of sight, even when you are in the room.

- Law enforcement agencies consider card-key (electronic) door locks the most secure.

Protect Precious Cargo

Today, all 50 states have laws requiring children of a certain age or size to be restrained while riding in a passenger vehicle. Set the standard as a safety role model! Buckle up every time, and ensure passengers stay securely fastened for the entire trip.

Use these tips from AAA's award-winning **Seated, Safe & Secure** campaign:

Choose Age and Size Appropriate Seats. From rear-facing infant seats to convertible and forward-facing car seats to belt-positioning boosters, stay apprised of state requirements, manufacturer's instructions, and safety ratings for the wide scope of safety restraint options.

Plan Seating Positions. Seat all passengers age 12 and under in the back. The safest spot for a car seat is <u>usually</u> the center position of the back seat (in SUVs and vans, use the center position in the second row of seats). Always check the manufacturer's instructions!

Do Your Homework. Read your car seat and vehicle owner's manuals carefully to ensure proper installation based on your vehicle's seat design. When renting a car, bring your own child safety seats or reserve them with your rental. AAA helped Hertz develop its current **Buckle Up Baby** program. Hertz has trained many employees to install car seats it makes available to its customers.

Install Seats Correctly. Insert the vehicle seat belt or LATCH straps through the car seat's designated belt paths, and secure using the vehicle's seat belt buckle or LATCH anchor points. Never use more than one seat belt to secure the car seat. Ensure that the seat moves no more than one inch — from side-to-side or up-and-down — at the points of installation.

Secure Your Child. Make sure the car seat harness or seat belt is properly positioned and fits your child snugly and securely, lying flat and untwisted against the body.

For more information about child passenger safety and related topics, contact your local club office or visit **aaa.com/publicaffairs.**

aaa.com